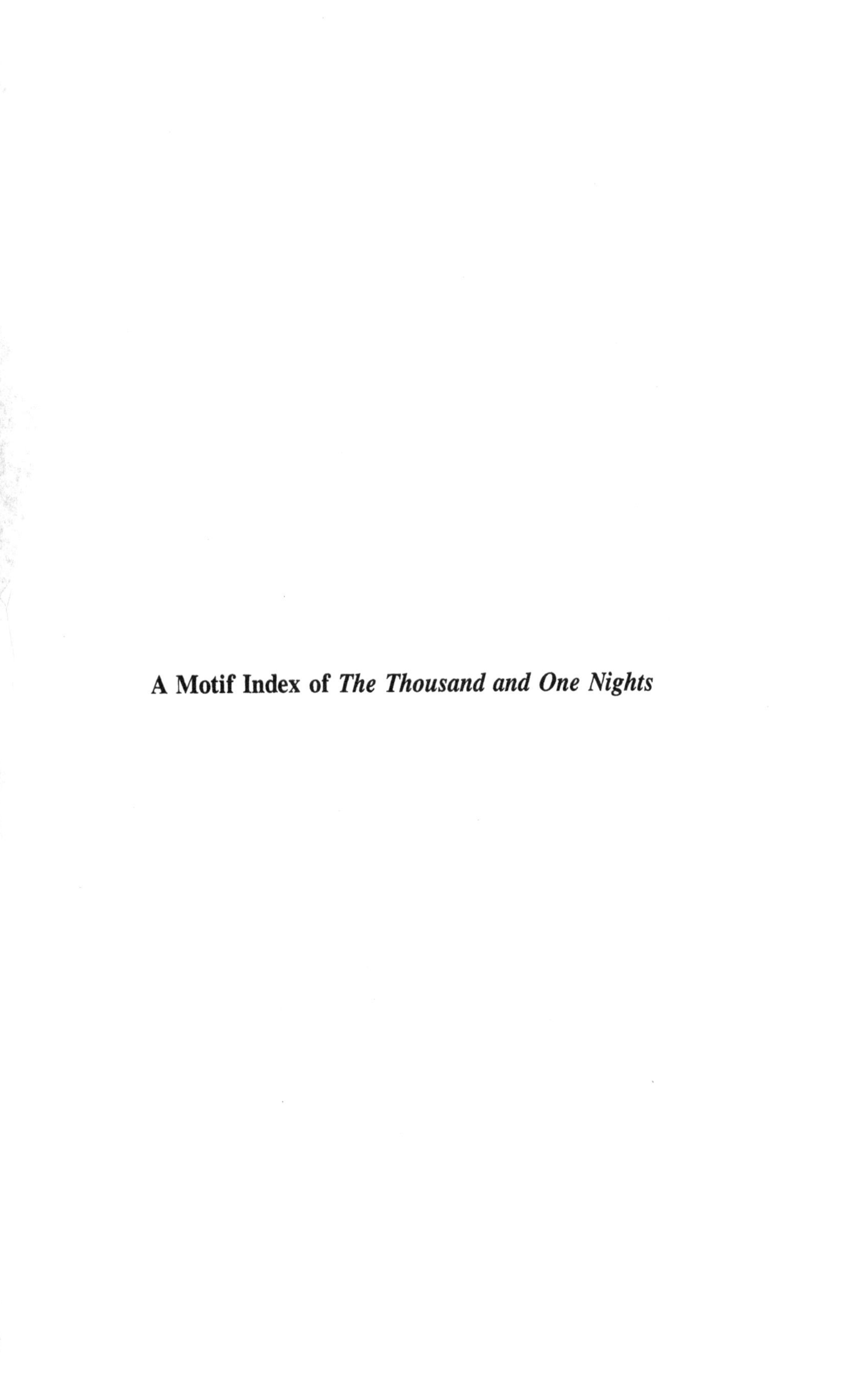

A Motif Index of *The Thousand and One Nights*

Cover of Volume 1

(Also see p. 16)

'Alfu laylah wa laylah

dhât al-ḥawâdith al-¿ajîbah wa al-qiṣaṣ al-muṭribah al-gharîbah: layâlihâ gharâmun fî gharam wa tafâṣîlu ḥubbin wa ¿ishqin wa hayâm! wa nawâdir fukâhiyyah wa laṭâ'if wa ṭarâ'if 'adabiyyah, bi al-ṣuwari al-mudhishati al-badî¿ah—min abda¿î mâ kân wa manâẓir 'u¿jûbah min ¿ajâ'ib al-zamân.

al-mujallad al-'awwal

Thousand Nights and a Night

which has wondrous events and thrilling strange stories: its nights are infatuation through and through, and details of amour, erotic love, and passionate adoration! [In addition to] humorous anecdotes, and literary witticism and rarities. [Presented] with exquisite and amazing illustrations: of the most exquisite in existence, and scenes that are a wonder of the wonders of the ages.

First Volume

A Motif Index of *The Thousand and One Nights*

HASAN M. EL-SHAMY

INDIANA UNIVERSITY PRESS

BLOOMINGTON AND INDIANAPOLIS

This book is a publication of

Indiana University Press
601 North Morton Street
Bloomington, Indiana 47404-3797 USA

http://iupress.indiana.edu

Telephone orders	800-842-6796
Fax orders	812-855-7931
Orders by e-mail	iuporder@indiana.edu

The paper used in this publication meets the minimum requirements of American National Standard for Information Sciences—Permanence of Paper for Printed Library Materials, ANSI Z39.48-1984.

Cataloging information is available from the Library of Congress.

ISBN-13 978-0-253-34834-0 (cl.)
ISBN-10 0-253-34834-X (cl.)

1 2 3 4 5 11 10 09 08 07 06

Table of Contents

ACKNOWLEDGMENTS

I wish to express my thanks and gratitude to the National Museum of Ethnology (MINPAKU), Osaka, Japan for the support so generously given to the project of "A Motif Index of *Alf laylah wa laylah*." During my tenure as a Visiting Professor at the National Museum of Ethnology, and Fellow of its Institute of Advanced Studies in Anthropology (May 1-August 31, 2002), the basic foundation for the present work was formulated and an electronic (digital) first draft completed and presented as seminar materials to members of the Museum and the Institute.

I am especially indebted to Dr. Naomichi Ishige, the Museum's Director General then, and to professors Tetsuo Nishio and Yuriko Yamanaka of the National Museum of Ethnology for the courtesy and hospitality they and every member of the Museum's staff showed me and my family during our stay in Japan. I am also grateful to Professor Jun'ichi Oda, of the Institute for the Study of Languages and Cultures of Asia, Tokyo University of Foreign Languages for his support and hospitality.

Special thanks to Professor Dr. Ulrich Marzolph, Georg-August University, and senior member of the editorial committee, *Enzyklopädie des Märchens*, Göttingen, Germany. The encouragement and endorsements he accorded the present index as well as other works are greatly appreciated.

The support given this research project by Michael W. Lundell, Sponsoring Editor, Indiana University Press, has been indispensable. His backing of a broad spectrum of folklore studies has been critical for maintaining the vitality of folklore scholarship.

Special thanks are due Indiana University Press. The publication of the present volume in commemoration of the passing of three centuries since *The Thousand and One Nights* was introduced to Europe is part of the Press' long and distinguished history in providing pioneering works in folklore and related disciplines. In this respect, the Press has maintained the torch so brightly lit by Stith Thompson's monumental *Motif-Index of Folk Literature*.

I am also grateful to many friends and colleagues at Indiana University and elsewhere, especially Professors William F. Hansen, Salih J. Altoma, and members of Indiana University's Department of Folklore and Ethnomusicology.

A Note on Transliteration

The transliteration system adopted in this work is as follows:

'/a	ا/ء
b	ب
t	ت
th	ث
g/j	ج
ḥ	ح
kh	خ
d	د
dh	ذ
r	ر
z	ز
s	س
sh	ش
ṣ	ص
ḍ	ض
ṭ	ط
ẓ	ظ
¿[1]	ع
gh	غ
f	ف
q	ق
k	ك
l	ل
m	م
n	ن
h	ه
w	و
y	ي

Short vowels:

a	*fatḥah*
i/e	*kasrah*
o/u	*ḍammah*

Long vowels:

â	aa
î	ee/ii
û	oo/ou/ô
ai/ä	*'imâlah*

---

[1]For the rationale for using ¿ in lieu of the letter c/superscript (e.g., ᶜAlî) or the open single quote ('), see H. El-Shamy, "A Response [to H. Jason's Review of *Folk Traditions of the Arab World: A Guide to Motif Classification]*," *Asian Folklore Studies*, Vol. 57, No. 2 (Nagoya, Japan: 1998), pp. 345-55, p. 352 ("*Issue six*").

See also "Remarks on Burton's transliterations," p. 441, below.

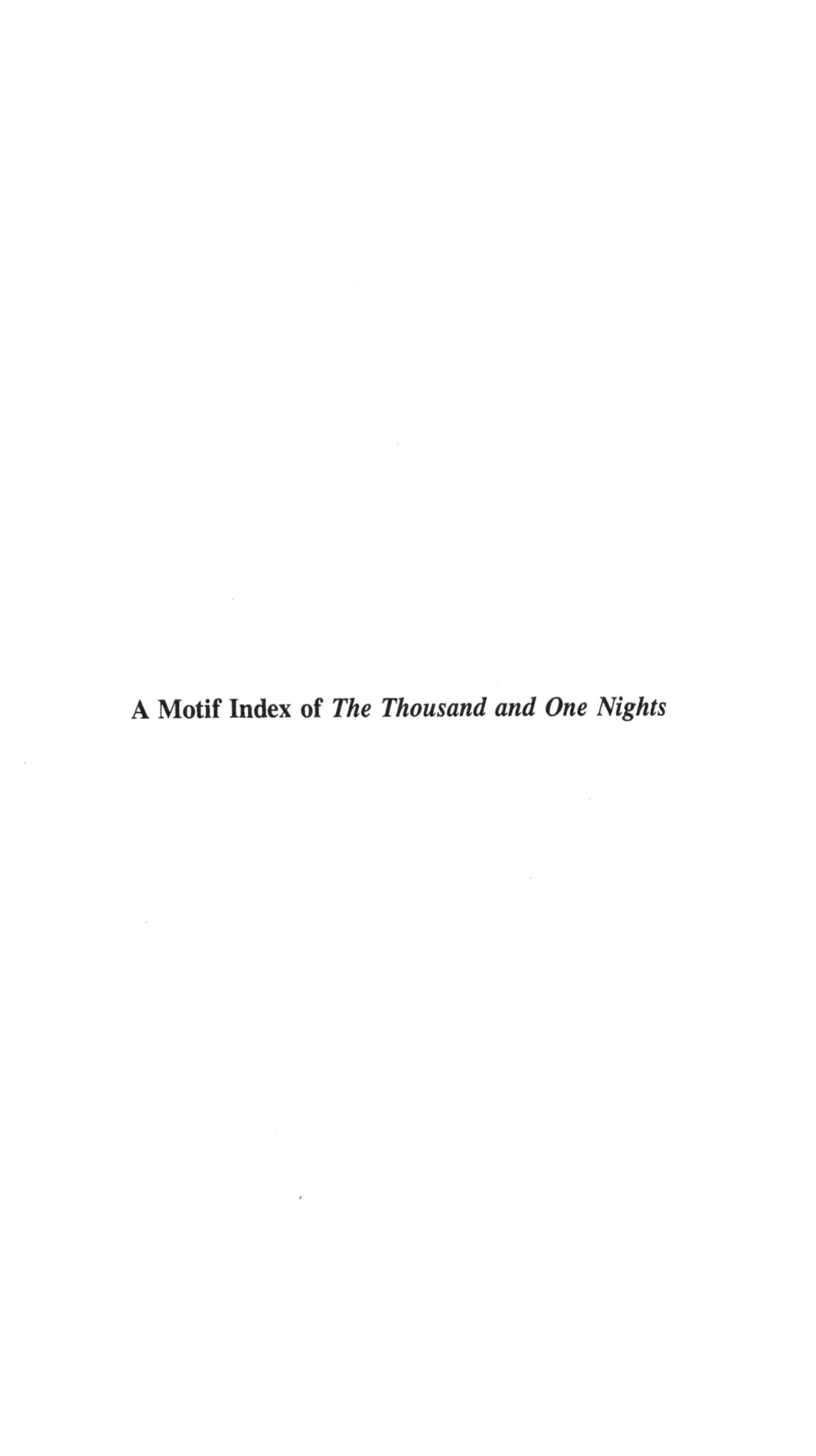

A Motif Index of *The Thousand and One Nights*

INTRODUCTION[1]

Theoretical Orientation.

This index complements Hasan El-Shamy's *Folk Traditions of the Arab World: A Guide to Motif Classification* (or *GMC*); and *Types of the Folktale in the Arab World: a Demographically Oriented Approach* (or *DOTTI*).[2] Like its two predecessors, it is based on three verifiable theoretical principles developed and documented within the context of treating folklore as cognitive behavior and labeled "Folkloric Behavior."[3]

First: Most of the narratives constituting *Alf laylah wa laylah* in the Arabic language are literary representations of traditional folktales. These tales may be assumed to have been in oral circulation at the time(s) the book was being cumulatively formulated, and may represent older versions of contemporary folktales.[4] The rendering of the orally transmitted and aurally perceived communications into the written down and visually perceived format was the work of scribes or clerics schooled in the various branches of the Arabic language. They recast the anthology's contents into the literary style known as "*'inshâ*" (see below) and colored them with their own male-oriented and clerical worldviews.

Second: Folklore, like the rest of the culture to which it belongs, must be learned by its bearers. The occurrence in daily life of any item of lore such as a tale, or a proverb, involves the entire learning process (motivation, intervening stimuli (context), responses, effect--rewards and punishments, retention, recall, remembering, etc.). Similarly, the affective components of lore must be examined first as learned "sentiments" before seeking explanations in biologically based "emotions" (e.g., psychoanalytic interpretations).[5]

Third: The existence of lore is not dependent on the presence of a folk group. Lore is also born by individuals and social groups who, from a sociological perspective, may or may not be characterized as a "folk" community. *No one is lore-free*. Thus, an item of lore (e.g., the tale titled "The Taming of the Shrew") may be born by Shakespeare (or another member of the culture elite), by a Hollywood scriptwriter or popular-song speculator, or by an African hunter, horticulturist, or university professor. The difference among the various renditions of such an item would be in the degree of its traditionality and formularization, regardless of whether its bearer is "folksy" or not.[6]

---

[1]A more detailed version of this Introduction was published under the title: "A Motif Index of *Alf Laylah wa Laylah*: Its Relevance to the Study of Culture, Society, the Individual, and Character Transmutation," in *Journal of Arabic Literature*. (Brill, Leiden). Vol. 36, No. 3, pp. 235-68; (henceforth *JAL*).

[2]2 vols., Bloomington: Indiana University Press, 1995; and 2004, respectively.

[3]A term coined by the present writer. See: Hasan El-Shamy, "Folkloric Behavior: A Theory for the Study of the Dynamics of Traditional Culture." [A case study of the stability and change in the lore of the Egyptian community in Brooklyn, N.Y.]. Doctoral dissertation, Indian University, Bloomington, 1967.
This work provided the theoretical foundations for contextual and performance folkloristic approaches.

[4]For example, "Jûdar" (or Jawdar) shows strong typological similarities to AT 561, *Aladdin*, in association with AT 563, *The Table, the Ass, and the Stick*. Also, "Nûr al-Dîn and Shams al-Dîn" belongs to Tale-type 871B§, *Spirits Transport Young Man to Sleeping Girl*; while Abû Qîr and Abû Ṣîr identified by the present writer as AT 980*, *The Painter and the Architect*. [The vile dyer and the noble barber (Abû-Qîr and Abû-Ṣîr)], is likely to be an earlier variant of AT 613, *The Two Travelers (Truth and Falsehood)*. [Evil person blinds and mutilates his good-hearted companion (brother)]. For details, see Type 561, text No. 4, and Type 871B§, text No. 2, and 980* text No. 1 in Hasan El-Shamy, *Types of the Folktale in the Arab World*. Also see: Hasan El-Shamy, "Mythological Constituents of *Alf Laylah wa Laylah wa Laylah*," in *The Arabian Nights and Orientalism: Perspectives from East and West*, Yuriko Yamanaka and Tetsuo Nishio, eds. (London: I.B. Tauris, 2006) pp. 25-46.

[5]See the "*homo volens*" model, in Hasan El-Shamy, "Behaviorism and the Text," *Folklore Today: A Festschrift for Richard M. Dorson*, Linda Dégh, Henry Glassie and Felix Oinas, eds. (Bloomington, 1976), pp. 145-160, pp. 147-49; and "Emotionskomponente," *Enzyklopädie des Märchens* (Göttingen) Vol. 3, nos. 4-5 (1981), pp. 1391-95; (heceforth: *EM*).
For applications of the Freudian and Jungian approaches to AT 326, *The Youth Who Wanted to Learn What Fear Is*, see: H. El-Shamy, "¿ilm al-nafs al-taḥlîlî wa al-folklore (Psychoanalysis and Folklore [1])." *Al-Majallah*, no. 117, (Cairo, September, 1966), pp. 33-41; and "al-lâshu¿ûr al-jamâ¿î wa al-folklore (Collective Unconsciousness and Folklore) [2]." *Al-Majallah*, no. 126, (Cairo June 1967), pp. 21-29.
On the concepts of "Motivation and Folkloric Behavior," "Informant's Motivation," and "Operant's Motivation," see. El-Shamy, "Folkloric Behavior," pp. 54-59; and "Behaviorism and the Text," pp. 155-56.

[6]See: Hasan El-Shamy, "Psychologically-based Criteria for Classification by Motif and Tale-Type," *Journal of Folklore Research*, Vol. 34, No. 3, pp. 233-43. p. 233. Also see: El-Shamy, "Folk Group," *Folklore: An Encyclopedia of Forms, Methods, and History*, T. A. Green, ed. (ABC-CLIO, Santa Barbara: 1997), and H. El-Shamy, *Folktales of Egypt: Collected, Translated and Annotated with Middle Eastern and African Parallels* (University of Chicago Press, 1980), p. li.

The scribes presumed to have written down *Alf laylah*'s tales acted in their capacity as learned men or clerics as well as bearers of oral folk traditions, including full folk narratives. Unlike their counterparts who wrote down religious stories under their names, such as Aḥmad ibn Muḥammad al-Tha¿labî (d. 1035 or 37) or Muḥammad ibn ¿Abdu-Allâh al-Kisâ'î (fl. 11 century),[7] recorders of *Alf laylah*'s tales chose to remain anonymous arguably due to the negative views religious circles held about the non-religious folktale. (See notes no. 56-60, below).

Unlike *GMC* which gives "samples of references to occurrences [of motifs] in the Arab World,"[8] the present index seeks to be as exhaustive as practically possible, under economic and technical limitations, in designating the contents of a single anthology of tales. The total number of motifs identified is more than 5,500. The majority of these motifs are newly generated and culture-specific. The total number of narratives identified and treated is 207 (divided in the original into 1001 portions each designated as a "Night/*laylah*"). Many of these narratives are composite texts incorporating *serially* multiple tale-types and hundreds of motifs. Presently, the manuscript for the updated *GMC* contains some 27,000 motifs. Many motifs cited here are subsidiaries of general entries that are not listed (e.g., Mot. A102.13, "Loving kindness of God" is a detail of Mot. A102, "Characteristics of deity"; only the first is listed).

A Tale of Two '*Nights*'

Before Antoine Galland introduced to Europe in 1704 his translation of *'Alf laylah wa laylah* under the title *Mille et une Nuits* multiple manuscripts (editions) of the anthology existed for centuries side by side in countries stretching from India to Morocco. These more or less separate works share a core of narratives linked together loosely by a frame story in which the heroine, Shahrzâd, is also the raconteuress. These manuscripts also diverge; numerous tales are found only in one edition and are absent from the others.[9]

European editions based on a particular 'original manuscript,' sought to augment the *Nights*' contents by adding narratives to the original—a practice begun by Galland. Many of the added tales came from oral traditions.[10] Thus, a secondary cycle of the *Nights* was introduced to Europe and, subsequently, to readers throughout the world, and to scholars of the Arab-Moslem worlds in the East. However, these European edition had no circulation among Arab folk groups.

The facts that there are two distinct "One Thousand Nights and a Night" narrative cycles and that these cycles need to be viewed separately was pointed out in 1988. Addressing the 13th Annual Symposium on "The Telling of Stories: Approach to a traditional Craft" (held at The Centre of Vernacular Literature of the Middle Ages, Odense University) the present writer stated:

> Although each native edition seems to have had a domain of wider circulation, it would be useful to differentiate between two categories of this anthology: native, typically referred to as *'Alf laylah wa laylah* (*Thousand Nights and a Night*), and European, often labelled "*The Arabian Nights.*" The European being a composite of a number of native editions and other narratives not found in the native ones, thus, being more inclusive but less representative of the actual edition(s) circulating in one country (or area of domain).[11]

Subsequently, this viewpoint was also expressed in 1995 by Robert L. Mack in his introduction to an English translation of Galland's edition of the anthology:

---

[7]Aḥmad Ibn Muḥammad al-Tha¿labî, *Kitâb qiṣaṣ al-'anbiyâ'* (*The Book of Prophets' Stories*). Cairo, n.d., and Muḥammad ibn ¿Abdullah Al-Kisâ'î, *Qiṣaṣ al-'anbiyâ' (Vita Prophitorum)*, Isaac Eisenberg, ed. Brill: Leiden 1922.

[8]See: Hasan El-Shamy, *Folk Traditions of the Arab World*, Vol. 1, p. xvii).

[9]See: Burton, "Comparative Table of the Tales in the Principal Editions of the Thousand and One Nights," Vol. 10, pp.514-31; Chauvin's "Tables des éditions du texte," *Bibliographie*, Vol. 4, pp. 187-93; and Elisséeff's Table des "concordances," *Thèmes*, pp. 185-205; See: *The Arabian Nights Encyclopedia*, Ulrich Marzolph, Richard van Leeuwen et al., eds. (Santa Barbara, 2004), "Concordance of Quoted Texts," pp. 743-82. See also note 94, p. 671, below.
Compare Muḥsin Mahdî, ed., *'Alf laylah wa laylah min 'uṣûlih al-¿arabiyyah al-'ûlâ ("The Thousand and One Nights From the Earliest Known Sources: Arabic Text Edited with Introduction by [...]")*. Leiden, 1984, esp. pp. 14-52.

The edition treated here seems to have once included "*ḥikâyat al-ṣa¿îdî wa zawjatihi al-'ifrinjiyyah* (The Tale of the Man of Upper Egypt and His Frankish Wife)". It is listed in the table of contents of Vol. 4, as given on p. 161 (which corresponds to Burton, Vol. 9, pp. 19-24). However, no Arabic text of the story is found in our edition. Consequently, the story is included in the present work; the motifs given are based on Burton's English text.

[10]See notes 13, 16, 17 and related data below. Also see Burton's list of tales and remarks, p. 671, below.

[11]Hasan El-Shamy, "Oral Traditional Tales and the Thousand Nights and a Night: The Demographic Factor," in *The Telling of Stories: Approaches to a Traditional Craft*. Morton Nøjgaard et. al, eds. (Odense, Denmark: Odense University Press, 1990), pp. 63-117, p. 84.

> [...], some of the most popular stories in the Nights (the so-called 'orphan stories', including 'Aladdin; or, the Wonderful Lamp') appear never to have been part of the 'real' Eastern collection at all, and were for a long time thought to have been the intrusive products of the Western imagination.[12]

Burton seems to have sensed the qualitative differences between the original tales in *Alf laylah*'s manuscripts and the additions derived from oral traditions. Thus he, as did many of his contemporaries, prematurely concluded that "[t]he Fairy Tale in The Nights is wholly and purely Persian."[13]

The narrative materials European editors implanted into *Alf laylah* tend to eclipse, at least numerically, the anthology's authentic contents; they also radically alter, and even distort, the overall nature of native anthologies. Currently, reference works dealing with *The Arabian Nights* list 551 independent tales as constituting the global full range of the anthology.[14] Meanwhile, it may be assumed that the number of tales the edition under consideration contains (i.e., 207 units, of which a few are sub-stories; e.g., stories by Spies 1-6 within the *sîrah* of ¿Umar al-Nu¿mân: *Alf*, Vol. 1, pp. 219-25; Burton, Vol. 2, pp. 196-210) is more or less typical of native editions. Thus, a significant number of some 340 additional units may be suspected as probably intrusive.

Description of the Index

This motif-index treats an authentic folk edition of *Alf laylah wa laylah*.[15] The folk traditional quality of this edition applies to its contents, printing techniques, raw materials, drawings, commercial outlets and readership (usually read to a throng of people). A critical aspect of this edition is that it is free of drastic alterations and intrusive texts inserted by European editors. Interesting as these augmentations may be, they represent the editor's own taste and worldview, but they drastically alter the overall character of the original anthology. The majority of the annexed texts were taken from field collections of oral traditional tales, and included genres not present in any of the original manuscripts.[16] One such genre is the "Zaubermärchen," typically narrated by females.[17]

As stated elsewhere, al-Jâḥiẓ ('Abû-¿Uthmân ¿Amr ibn Baḥr, d. 868 or 9 A.D.) was the first Arab scholar to offer a classification of folk traditions by gender based on his own fieldwork and interviews with informants.[18] He proceeded from a boldly proclaimed intellectual premise that "A woman is of sound religion, sexual-honor, and heart, unless ... [motivated by scruples or lust]," thus discrediting the popular assertion that "Women are lacking in mind and religion."[19] Al-Jâḥiẓ's associated *al-khurâfât* (the irrational, or the mythical) with "*qawl al-nisâ' wa 'ashbâh al-nisâ'* (the say of women and the

---

[12]*Arabian Nights' Entertainment*. Edited with an Introduction by Robert L. Mack (Oxford University Press, 1995) pp. xii-xiii.

[13]Burton, X: 127.

[14]See: *The Arabian Nights Encyclopedia*, U. Marzolph, et al., eds, pp. 745-82.

[15]4 vols., Maktabat al-Jumhûriyyh: Cairo, n.d. (See p. ii).

[16]It was pointed out that "The *Type Index* identifies 64 tale-types in *The Arabian Nights* (Chauvin, *Bibliographie*, Vols. 5-7)." However, the majority of these texts are from collections of orally circulating folktale; only a handful of these tale-types designate a text from *Alf laylah*.
See: Hasan El-Shamy, "Oral Traditional Tales and the Thousand Nights and a Night: The Demographic Factor," p. 85, n. 109. Also compare the chart titled "Locations of Tale-types in the Arab World," in El-Shamy, *Folk Traditions of the Arab World*, pp. 414-41. The chart reports 199 tale-types in the Aarne-Thompson's *The Types of the Folktale* (Helsinki, 1961), and identifies 240 tale-types in Chauvin's *Bibliographie*.

[17]These tale-types include: 123, *The Wolf and the Kids*; 310, *The Maiden in the Tower: [Louliyyah]*; 327, *The Children and the Ogre*; 403, *The Black and the White Bride*; 408, *The Three Oranges*; 432, *The Prince as Bird*; 450, *Little Brother and Little Sister*; 451, *The Maiden Who Seeks her Brothers*; 480, *The Spinning Women by the Spring. The Kind and Unkind Girls* (Mot.: S24.1.1§, Widow induces girl to kill her mother and persuade father to marry the widow); 510, *Cinderella and Cap o' Rushes*; 510B, *The Dress of Gold, of Silver, and of Stars*; 511, *One-Eye, Two-Eyes, Three-Eyes*; 511A, *The Little Red Ox*; 707, *The Three Golden Sons*; 720, *My Mother Slew Me; My Father Ate Me; The Juniper Tree*; 872*, *Brother and Sister*; 879, *The Basil Maidens (The Sugar Puppet, Viola)*; 894, *The Ghoulish Schoolmaster and the Stone of Pity*; 898, *The Daughter of the Sun. (The Speechless Maiden; the Puppet Bride)*; 923C§, *Girl Wins against Boy (usually, her Eldest Paternal-cousin) in a Contest of Worth*; 1387*, *Woman must do Everything like her Neighbors*.
Also see: "The Gender Difference," El-Shamy, "Demographic Factor," p. 83. With reference to AT 707, *The Three Golden Sons*. [Cast away infant sister and brother(s) reunited ...], see H. El-Shamy, *Folktales of Egypt*, pp. 255-56.

[18]See: Hasan El-Shamy, "Emergence of Classification of Folk Traditions," in *Tales Arab Women Tell and the Behavioral Patterns they Portray*, (Bloomington: Indiana University Press, 1999), pp. 10-13.

[19]Motif: W256.6.1§, "'Women are lacking in mind and religion'". For occurrences of this theme in the *Nights*, see Section: "Motifs of The Thousand and One Nights," below.

womenlike [i.e., womanlike, the effeminate]." Women-bound tales are virtually non-existent in *Alf laylah*. In the rare cases where such a folktale seems to have been included, presumably in the format the adult male writer was able to recall it, the written rendition proves to be radically different from its presumed oral counterparts.[20]

The goal of the present work is to identify the variety of cultural, social, psychological and literary themes described in *Alf laylah* and to correlate these themes to their counterparts in international indexes of folk literature and related fields,[21] as well as to other relevant Arab-Islamic literatures such as proverbs, riddles, ethnographic reports, elite literary works, and the like. In this respect a folk narrative is perceived as a description of life and living, real or—as is the case with *Alf laylah*—fictitious. As will be demonstrated, currently available indexes do not address the majority of issues that give *Alf laylah* its distinctiveness and render it representative of an important phase of the development of Arab-Islamic civilization and regional cultures.

Typology and Classification

A variety of quantitative and qualitative devices (terms) are employed to designate various aspects of sociocultural phenomena. In addition to anthropological terms such as culture element/trait, culture complex, culture institution, etc.,[22] a host of folkloristic concepts were devised by scholars to allow for more precise identification and treatment of the materials under investigation. The "tale-type" and the "motif" (applied in the present work) are two of these analytical-classificatory devices.

The Tale-type and the Motif[23]

The current situation with reference to the discovery by Arab literary scholars of the literary significance of *Alf laylah* is comparable to the interest shown in Finland toward the *Kalevala* epic. Elias Lönnrot constituted this literary work that became Finland's national heritage from folklore elements he collected from the field in the nineteenth century. Theories and hypotheses about the age, place of origin, travel routes, and meaning of its components were advanced with little regard to objective research measures. In reaction to these speculative approaches, Finish folklorists developed a research method for answering these questions which came to be known as the "Historical-Geographical" method. The concept of 'tale-type' was introduced as a research tool for this new approach; meanwhile the concept of 'motif' became active on the analytical scene some two decades later. Students of the *Arabian Nights* seem to have made no use of these useful folkloristic devices or the theoretical

[20]Hasan El-Shamy: "The Oral Connections of *the Arabian Nights*," in *The Arabian Nights Encyclopedia*, Marzolph et al. eds., pp. 9-13.

One of the examples given is AT 327, *The Children and the Ogre*, which is well known among all the populations of the Arab World. In *Alf laylah*, the tale assumes uncharacteristic political overtones, e.g., "Prince and Ghoulah (Treacherous Minister)" (*Alf*, Vol. 1, p. 19; Chauvin 6: 26 No. 197; *EAN* no. 12, p. 329), and "King's Son and Ogress (Careless Minister)" (*Alf*, Vol. 3, p. 144; Chauvin Vol. 8, pp. 40-41 No. 8B; King's Favorite Son and Ogress *EAN*, no. 188, p. 264). Interestingly enough, a parallel situation is found in modern times concerning a female-oriented tale revolving around intense rivalry among sisters (titled "Pearls-on-Vines," AT 432, *The Prince as Bird*). In a vaguely remembered idiosyncratic rendition submitted in writing by an adult male member of the elite (superior court Justice) [...], the rivalry among sisters is dissipated, and transformed into a political conflict (war). The attitude expressed toward an "ugly" slave-girl is devoid of the hostility characteristic of females' attitudes toward slave-girls (Motif: P187§, "Inherent rivalry between mistress and young female slave"), and is replaced by legal or ethical considerations (keeping a promise).

See: Hasan El-Shamy, *Tales Arab Women Tell*, no. 33-1, pp. 270-72; and *DOTTI*, Type 432, variant no. 21 from Egypt.

[21]Reference here is made primarily to Antti Aarne, and Stith Thompson, *The Types of the Folktale*, and Stith Thompson, *Motif-Index of Folk Literature*, 6 vols. (Bloomington, 1955-58). (Recently expertly expanded and updated with over 2,000 citations from a prepublication copy of El-Shamy's *DOTTI*; see: Hans-Jörg Uther, p. 19, below).

In their treatment of *The Arabian Nights*, both works rely almost totally on Chauvin's *Bibliographie*. The translation by Richard F. Burton, *Arabian Nights: The Book of the Thousand Nights and a Night* (London, 1894) is cited 61 times in the Motif-Index but only once (p. 459) in the Type-Index.

[22]For Arabic explanations of anthropological terms, see: *Qâmûs mustalhât al-'ithnoloajyâ wa al-folklore* (A. Hultkranz, *General Ethnological Concepts*), Mohammad El-Gohary/[Jawharî] and Hasan El-Shamy, tr. eds., (El-Marif, Cairo, 1972).

[23]These concepts were introduced in the late 1960s to readers of Arabic. See: Ḥasan El-Shamy: "nuẓum fahrasat al-qaṣaṣ al-sha¿bî: fihrist al-motîf (Systems of Classification of Folk Narratives: The Motif-Index)," *al-Funûn al-Shâbia [Sha¿biyyah]*, Cairo, Vol. 2, no. 9 (June, 1969), pp. 81-91; and "nuẓum fahrasat al-qaṣaṣ al-sha¿bî: fihrist al-ṭirâz (Systems of Classification of Folk Narratives: The Type-Index)" *al-Funûn al-Shâbia* Vol. 2, no. 8 (March, 1969), pp. 29-40. A more comprehensive presentation offered evaluation of the misuse of the concepts of "tale-type" and "motif" as applied in Arabic folklore studies, and sample applications based on arabized tale-type and motif numerical systems; see: Ḥasan El-Shamy, "nuẓum wa 'ansâq fahrasat al-ma'thûr al-sha¿bî (Methods and Systems for the Classification of Folk Traditions)," *al-Ma'thûrât al-Sha¿biyyah*, Vol. 3, no. 12, (Doha, October, 1988), pp. 77-109.

arguments on which they were based.[24] Collateral aspects of the quest for origins germane to attempts to reconstruct *Alf laylah* from "the earliest known sources" which Muhsin Mahdi seeks, are the concepts of "*Urform*"/"Archetype" (oldest or original form), "normal form" (the typical or most recurrent form) and "Oikotype" (natural form that is totally dependent on the environment, "*al-ṭirâz al-ṭabî¿î*").[25]

The term tale-type stands for a recurrent full folk story usually found crossculturally; the term does not indicate a tale's literary genre as the word 'type' may suggest (hence, the present writer's Arabic translation: "*ṭirâz*," rather than the literal: "*naw¿*". The concept was developed and applied by the Finn Antti Aarne in his *Verzeichnis der Märchentypen* (1910). The eminent American folklorist Stith Thompson adopted the concept and expanded Aarne's work under the title *The Types of the Folktale* (in 1928, and 1961). Though arising from the views of the "Finnish School" and shackled by problems of linkage to search for a tale's origins, the usefulness of the concept of tale-type as a tool of identification and analysis transcends these limitations.

A tale-type is designated by an Arabic number, extending from 1 to 2411, followed by a statement describing its contents (e.g., AT 1, "*The Theft of Fish* [Playing dead so as to be placed with food]"; AT 551, "*The Sons on a Quest for a Wonderful Remedy for their Father.* [Jealous brothers as rivals (adversaries)]"; AT 1426, "*The Wife Kept in a Box*"). The number may end with a letter or an asterisk indicating that it is a subtype or a standard variation on a cardinal tale-type (e.g., the new Tale-types 551A§, "*Only One Brother is Successful in Seeking Riches (Wealth).* Other brothers are jealous," and 551B§, "*Only One Sister is Successful on Quest (Seeking Riches).* Other sisters are jealous");[26] or AT 1426*, "*Man with Unfaithful Wife Comforted* when he sees jealous husband who carefully guards wife cuckolded." The frame story for *Alf laylah,* within which all constituent narratives are subsumed has been designated as a variation on Tale-types AT 1426 and 1426* under 1426A§, "*Cuckolded Husband Kills a New Bride Each Night* so as to avenge self on women. (Shahryâr)."[27] Assigning the same tale-type number to two texts separated from each other by time or distance presupposes that each is likely to be related to the other especially concerning origin (as in the case of AT 1426* in *Alf laylah* and in an Indian source. Cf. note no. 4, above). The rationale here is that due to the fact that a full tale is multiplex (composed of numerous components), an independent origin (polygenesis) for separate occurrences is not very likely.

Meanwhile, the term "motif" (which is to be differentiated from the psychological concepts of "motive" and "motivation") denotes a smaller cultural component recurrent in "oral literature," a wider field of lore which includes narrative as well as non-narrative materials such as proverbs, riddles, lyric chants, beliefs, customs, formulas, etc. The term also has greater potential for application to a broader spectrum of social, cultural and psychological phenomena expressed by folk groups in their lore as a matter of empirical observation on their environment.[28]

---

[24]A notable exception that may be mentioned here is Nikita Elesséeff's *Thèmes et motifs de mille et une nuits: essai de classification* (Beirut, 1949), where Elesséeff registers his awareness of the existence of both the tale-type and the motif classificatory schemas. However, this awareness is limited to the mere citing of the titles of the indexes in his "Bibliographie des ouvrages consulté" under A. Aarne (p. 213), and S. Thompson (p. 221). The contents of the registers of motifs Elesséeff calls "Thèmes et motifs" (pp. 89-170), and "Accessoires èpique" (pp. 173-183) are simply alphabetical arrangements of themes similar to those given by Chauvin, and Burton--among others--in their general indexes. No attempt was made classify a story by "tale-type," nor to implement Thompson's motif system for the classification of any topic in the *Nights* as folk-literature.

[25]The method and its underlying theoretical arguments were introduced to readers of Arabic in 1972. See: *naẓariyyât al-folklore al-mu¿âṣirah* ("Theories of Folklore and Folklife Studies,") in Richard M. Dorson, ed., *Folklore and Folklife: an Introduction),* M. El-Gohary and H. El-Shamy, trs. eds., Dâr al-Kutub al-Jâmi¿iyyah, Cairo, 1972, pp. 43-61.
For explanations of the "Archetype" and "Oikotype" in Arabic contexts, see pp. 47, 49. Also cf. Hasan El-Shamy, *Brother and Sister. Type 872*: A Cognitive Behavioristic Text Analysis of a Middle Eastern Oikotype* (Folklore Monograph Series, Vol. 8, Folklore Publications Group, Bloomington, 1979).

[26]These are, 551A§: "Second Shaykh/Treacherous Brothers" (*A* 1: 11-13; Chauvin 7: 129 No. 397); "¿Abdallah ibn Fâḍel and His Brothers" (*A* 4: 266-88; Chauvin 5: 2 No. 2). 551B§ "First Lady/Zubaydah's Treacherous Sisters" (*A* 1: 53-57; Chauvin 5: 4 No. 443).

[27]In spite of the fact that both stories are included in Chauvin's treatment of the *Arabian Nights* (Vol. 5 188 No. 111, and Vol. 8 59 No. 24), the Type Index cites no Arabic occurrences of either tale-type.

[28]On the concordance of theoretical comments based on empirical observation made in folklore, see: El-Shamy, *Folk Traditions of the Arab World,* Vol. 1 p. xiv.

Constituents of a Motif

Whatever the definition of the term "motif" may be, it is to be perceived as merely a classificatory device. As such, the motif is a research tool for identifying and artificially isolating smaller, more manageable, components of traditional cultural expressions for the purpose of studying them with specificity and systemic meaningfulness.[29] A motif is designated by a letter indicating its general nature within Thompson's motif schema, followed by a Arabic number (e.g., A1.1, "Sun-god as creator"; B11, "Dragon"; C46, "Tabu: offending fairy"; J1185, "Execution escaped by story telling," and J1185.1, "Sheherezade: story with indefinite sequel told to stave off execution"). Thompson classified the contents of his *Motif-Index* into twenty-three chapters, each dealing with a distinct cultural or social field and assigned an alphabetical letter ranging from A to Z (e.g., A: Mythology, B: Animals, C: Tabu, D: Magic, E: The Dead, etc., with the letters I, O, and Y excluded).[30] Thus, the central theme of the new Tale-type 1426A§ (cited above) would be depicted by the following motif in the "J" section titled "The Wise and the Foolish": J1185.1, "Sheherezade: ...." Additional, more specific identification is provided by a new motif in the "S" section titled "Unnatural Cruelty": S62.1.1§, "Shahryâr (Sheheryar) kills a new wife (bride) every night so as to avenge self on women"; and the new motifs in the "W" section titled "Traits of Character": W28.5.1§, ‡"Maiden offers to sacrifice herself for womankind. (Sheherezade)"; W256.6§, "Stereotyping: gender (sex) traits;" W256.6.0.1§, ‡"Females stereotyped--general".

Since a motif is typically simplex (composed of few components) a connection is *not* assumed to exist between its occurrence in expressions separated by time or space. However, there are exceptions where motifs, like tale-types, are multiplex.[31]

Islam and the Narrative

Little is known about the narrative lore in the lands that became the Arab World after the advent of Islam in the seventh century A.D. Available tale-type and motif indexes virtually ignored the narrative lore of ancient Middle Eastern civilizations. For example, the rich and readily available literature from ancient Egypt is barely mentioned in either index. Even the renowned ancient text of the "*The Faithless Wife*. Batu: the Egyptian 'Two Brothers' Tale" (AT 318) received no bibliographic reference in the Aarne-Thompson *The Types of the Folktale* that would link it to an ancient Egyptian source; it also received no mention at all in Thompson's *Motif-Index*.[32]

Islam, like its two monotheistic predecessors, Judaism and Christianity, has been strongly averse to the narrative and other artistic expressions (e.g., poetry, painting, sculpture, song, dances) associated with polytheism. Islamic teachers, who assumed the responsibility for telling the best and most truthful narratives, considered narrating for entertainment an idle activity that bordered on violation of religious doctrine.[33] From the viewpoint of formal Islamic dogma, narrating for purposes other than expressing religious and historical truth should be negatively valued and judged inadvisable. These teachings specify the guidelines for *ideal* patterns of behavior: according to the Koran (12:3, 18:13), narration should follow the ultimate truth of God. The religious authority Imam al-Ghazzâlî (A.D. 1058-1111) stated that narratives constituted a *bid¿ah* ("a heretic fad") strictly prohibited by the Pious Predecessors. He permitted only one exception: "if a story deals with prophets ... concerning their religions and [if] the narrator is truthful, and with correct attributions [along the chain of transmission], I see no harm

[29]See: El-Shamy, *Folk Traditions of the Arab World*, Vol. 1, p. 16.

[30]These chapters are as follows: **A**. MYTHOLOGICAL MOTIFS; **B**. ANIMALS; **C**. TABU; **D**. MAGIC; **E**. THE DEAD; **F**. MARVELS; **G**. OGRES; **H**. TESTS; **J**. THE WISE AND THE FOOLISH; **K**. DECEPTIONS; **L**. REVERSAL OF FORTUNE; **M**. ORDAINING THE FUTURE; **N**. CHANCE AND FATE; **P**. SOCIETY; **Q**. REWARDS AND PUNISHMENTS; **R**. CAPTIVES AND FUGITIVES; **S**. UNNATURAL CRUELTY; **T**. SEX; **U**. THE NATURE OF LIFE; **V**. RELIGION; **W**. TRAITS OF CHARACTER; **X**. HUMOR; **Z**. MISCELLANEOUS GROUPS OF MOTIFS.
There are 1730 original subdivisions of these cardinal themes.

[31]For examples of exceptions that constitute multiplex systems, see: El-Shamy, "A Motif Index of *Alf Laylah wa Laylah*," *JAL*, Vol. 36, pp. 243-44 notes no. 23-25.

[32]See: H. El-Shamy, "Maspero's *Contes populaires* in Folklore Indexes," in Gaston C. Maspero, *Popular Stories of Ancient Egypt*, Hasan El-Shamy, ed. (Santa Barbara, 2002, and Oxford, 2004), pp. 14-15.
For other studies based on insufficient data representing the Arab World, see: Hasan El-Shamy, "Towards A Demographically Oriented Type Index for Tales of the Arab World," *Cahiers de Littérature Orale*, n°. 23: *La tradition au présent (Monde arabe)*, Praline Gay-Para, ed. (Paris, 1988), pp. 15-40. pp. 21-23.

[33]See: "Attitudes toward Narration," in Hasan El-Shamy, *Folktales of Egypt*, p. xlvii.

in him."[34] This attitude, starting with ¿Umar Ibn al-Khaṭṭâb (d. 644) expelling *al-quṣṣâṣ* (narrators) from mosques, prevailed until modern times especially among the elite and the pious. Ibn al-Nadîm (d. 995), in his *Fihrist*, indicated his knowledge of the *Alf laylah* manuscript and, in congruence with this religious attitude, judged the contents as frivolous.[35] Registering the Registering the general attitude of 'good men' of his time toward folk stories, Burton wrote that

> ... the taint still lingers in Al-Islam: it will be said of a pious man, "He always studies the Koran, the Traditions and other books of Law and Religion; and *he never reads poems nor listens to music or to stories.*"[36]

Written and Oral Traditions[37]

Among folk groups two categories of narratives are thought of as separate from each other: those that come from books and those that come from oral folk tradition. "Book stories," typically referred to as *qiṣaṣ*, usually deal with religious and historical themes. Tales from *Alf laylah*, a work generally viewed as a "folk book," are normally not narrated; but read by oneself or to listeners. Inclusive data recently made available in El-Shamy's *DOTTI* amply substantiates this finding. AT 1426*, "*Man with Unfaithful Wife Comforted*" was reported only once in Arab oral traditions. Likewise, new Tale-type 1426A§, "*Cuckolded Husband Kills a New Bride Each Night* [...]." has not been reported from oral traditions except three times; yet in all three instances the concordance of the oral text with the specifics of Tale-type 1426A§ is either superficial or fragmentary (thus, they are reported in *DOTTI* as merely comparable). In numerous cases where an *Alf laylah* tale seems to be in agreement with and oral traditional counterpart, it is more likely that the oral traditional account provided the basis for the written one.[38] This viewpoint is amply demonstrated by recent additions to the anthology at the hands of European editors.

Cases where full texts from *Alf laylah* were reported to be "performed" in oral traditions by non-professional tale tellers are extremely rare and should be viewed as exceptions generated under atypical data-collecting circumstances.

Alf laylah's Texts and Oral Traditional Tales

Apart from the near total absence of women-bound tales, there are three main areas where differences can be readily observed between *Alf laylah's* written stories and orally communicated folktales: 1) use of "*'inshâ*"-style, 2) blatant Eroticism, and 3) narrative plots and details. Of these, nos. 1 and 2 are especially associated with the worldview of a cleric, a character typically linked to religious dogma, language rules and grammar. In older Arab-Moslem society the two skills were interdependent aspects of a cleric's image.[39]

1). Use of "*'inshâ*"-style

As pointed above, narrating *truthful* stories is the only sort of narrative behavior endorsed by formal Islam (constituting 'ideal culture,' or presumed culture: things as they are supposed to be--good or bad). Within the realm of what is perceived to be 'truthful,' fantasy, exaggerations, and hyperbole are usually labeled *balâghah* (rhetoric) or *faṣâḥah* (eloquence), a cornerstone of classical Arabic literary expression. With reference to poetry, 'lying' is taken as a necessary evil--or normal abnormality)--and is not only tolerated but appreciated.[40] For a person 'enculturated'/'socialized' (i.e., raised since infancy) in an Arab community, the style of the Arabic language that permeates *Alf laylah* is radically different from how that person communicates with others on a daily basis. The style is a reminder of certain classroom

---

[34]Quoted in ¿Abd al-Jalîl ¿Îsâ Abû al-Naṣr, *Ṣafwat ṣaḥîḥ al-Bukhârî* (*The Choicest from Bukhari's Authenticated [Utterances of Prophet Muhammad]*), Cairo, 1953, Vol. 4, pp. 216-19. Also see "God's Language, Man's Parlance," in El-Shamy, "Demographic Factor," pp. 66-67.

[35]Hasan El-Shamy, "Demographic Factor" p. 66. Also see Heinz Grotzfeld, "The Manuscript Tradition of the *Arabian Nights*," in *The Arabian Nights Encyclopedia*, Marzolph et al. eds., p. 18.

[36]Burton, Vol. 10, p. 128 (emphasis added).

[37]See: Hasan El-Shamy, *Folktales of Egypt*, lxviii-li.

[38]See: El-Shamy, *Folktales of Egypt*, pp. lxviii-l.

[39]For a concise description of worldview, see Hasan El-Shamy, "African World View and Religion," *Introduction to Africa*, P. Martin and P. O'Meara, eds., (Bloomington: Indiana University Press, 1977, pp. 208-20. Also see "Lore and Life Space," in El-Shamy, *Tales Arab Women Tell*, pp. 7-8.

[40]A literary cliché states, "*'a¿dhabu al-shi¿ri 'akdhabuh*" (The sweetest of poetry is that with the most lies). On the viability of poetry despite Islamic prohibitions, see El-Shamy, *Folktales of Egypt*, p. xlvii. Also see "God's Language and Man's Parlance," in El-Shamy, "The Demographic Factor," pp. 65-67.

experiences during elementary and secondary education, and of listening to preachers at mosques or other places of worship during one's lifetime.

Putting rhetoric to work in school curricula is termed "*'inshâ*,"[41] a word that literally designates a construction or something built of separate constituents. The word signifies a literary composition in classical, academic Arabic, not in the vernacular. A salient form of such a style is *saj¿* (rhymed-prose) which does not normally appear in the oral narration of prose folktales.[42] Writing aids meant to assist pupils in developing the skill of "*'inshâ*" abound in the form of books offering lists of topics accompanied by impressive short formulas constituting famous quotations, poetic passages, literary clichés, and the like, with which an essay is to be adorned (or 'inlaid') and thus aesthetically constructed. Usually, an ascription, such as 'And in this respect The Lord states in His Noble Book,' 'As a poet has said,' 'A saying by the wise comes to mind in this connection,' etc. accompanies the quotation. Imposing this *'inshâ* style on orally transmitted folktales is the literary writer's idea of salvaging the folk's verbal lore from its ungarnished vernacular language and then upgrading it to a level thought to be worthy of being viewed as literature (*'adab*).

Introducing his monumental annotated translation of the *Nights*, Richard F. Burton describes *saj¿* as absolutely indispensable. Thus he writes:

> This rhymed prose may be "un-English" and unpleasant, even irritating to the British ear; still I look upon it as a *sine quâ non* for a complete reproduction of the original.[43]

In the "Terminal Essay," Burton reaffirms his stand:

> Thus universally used the assonance has necessarily been abused, and its excess has given rise to the saying "Al-Saj'a faj'a [(i.e., *al-saj¿ah faj¿ha*)]"--prose rhyme's a pest. English translators have, unwisely I think, agreed in rejecting it, while Germans have not.[44]

This literary style harkens back to the early stages of the emergence of written records in Middle Eastern civilizations. Examples from ancient Egyptian literature (e.g., "The Lamentations of the Fellah") rendered in writing by professional scribes give ample evidence of the dominance of the highly valued *'inshâ*-like style applied at the expense of the message's clarity and accuracy.[45] Certain topics, dramatic situations and stages for action seem to constitute "formula-serviceable environment" and thus invite *'inshâ*-style.[46] These include beauty, love and sex, nature, predestination and fate, women's wiles, tragedy and the inevitability of death. This is the case with *Alf lylah*, and similar once orally transmitted folktales that were taken out of oral circulation and augmented with 'literary' characteristics and other rhetorical devices.[47] Typical folk narration is free of these mental shackles added as a matter of course to literary renditions of true, orally recurrent folktales.

2). **Blatant Eroticism**

Among the majority of Arabs and Muslims, especially the elite and the pious, *Alf laylah* represents not only the frivolous but also the sinfully obscene (*al-fâḥish*). Gratuitous sexual scenes, lyrics and vocabulary recur throughout the book. An event that occurred in Egypt in the 1980's placed additional pressure on the study of folklore in general and the collecting and publishing of folk narratives in particular. A vehement reaction by "fundamentalist" Moslems to the "immorality" expressed in the

---

[41]I.e., *'inshâ'un*--typically appears in the idiom "*'inshâ talk*" and is pronounced "*'inshâ*." It is differentiated from the classical Arabic "*'inshâ'*" which is applied in formal usage to designate constructing out of physical matter or substance such as brick or metal (e.g., Ministry of *'inshâ'* and *ta¿mîr*). Motif: Z1.0.1§, "*'inshâ*-style literary composition: constituted mainly from copied (memorized) famous quotations". Similar expressions are: "‡Mastabahs-talk (relaxed, informal, careless, not binding, etc.--like that uttered while sitting on a mastabah-porch)" (Motif: Z70.5.1§); and "‡'*masâṭîl*-talk'/'*ghuraz*-talk': irresponsible, bizarre, 'crazy'--like that uttered by 'the stoned' at one of the hashish-'stands' (lit., 'hashish-stitches')" (Z70.5.2§); see: El-Shamy, *Tales Arab Women Tell*, p. 56 n. 77.

Also compare Burton's view on "rhymed prose" in notes 42-43, below.

[42]On the use of rhymed prose and other devices of tropes, see: El-Shamy, "Demographic Factor," pp. 77-79.

[43]Burton, Vol. 1, p. xiv.

[44]Burton, Vol. 10, pp. 255-56.

[45]See: El-Shamy, "Written and Oral Traditions," in Maspero, *Popular Stories of Ancient Egypt*, pp. xxvi-xxxviii.

[46]See: El-Shamy, *Tales Arab Women Tell*, p. 23, n. 35.

[47]See: "The Language and other Stylistic Features," in El-Shamy, "The Demographic Factor," pp. 77-83. Concerning the use of poetry in the "Arabian Nights," Enno Littmann observed that the poems can be omitted with no adverse consequences to the prose text. Also see: Littmann, "Alf layla wa-layla," in the *Encyclopaedia of Islam*, 2nd ed., (Leiden, 1960), Vol. 1, p. 364.

story of "The Porter and the Three Ladies of Baghdad,"[48] in which erotic descriptions of provocative sexual displays are graphically presented, without any intercourse actually taking place, led to the temporary banning of sale of *Alf laylah* in Egypt. In folk narration, glaring erotic scenes--á la the introductory episode in the story of "The Porter and the Three Ladies of Baghdad" do not occur (except for the genres of the erotic joke and the jest). Yet, references to sexual encounters, incest, overt and latent homosexuality, potential anal intercourse, and sex organs do occur; their appearance, however, is infrequent, mostly by inference or allusion, and as required by the narrative course of action and context.[49] In the overwhelming majority of these folk expressions, the "obscene" word is merely *the* instrument for referring to an object or an act as it occurs in the normal course of living.

A facet of a male cleric's worldview is revealed in how certain images of human physical postures invite comparisons with other grammatical rules, images of Arabic script, and postures associated with religious rituals. Only a language specialist or grammarian would see his world in these grammatical terms, and only a person of a like training and mind set would be able to comprehend the nature of the intricate images and scholastic concepts these similes generate. None of the themes cited here has so far been encountered in orally communicated folktales.[50]

3). Plots and Narrative Details (Tale-types and Motifs)

For centuries, students of the folktale have observed the strong similarities among certain stories narrated across the globe. Numerous theories and hypothesis were developed to explain how these seemingly unvarying features came about. Some argued that the similarities were due to borrowing from a common source, such as India, which they saw as the birthplace for all "fairy tales." Others advanced the view that the similarities were due to the psychic unity of mankind. Whatever the assumption might have been, these "theories" tended to be too general and lacked precision as to what constituted the unit of analysis (i.e., the whole tale or tale-type, the tale's famous title, a salient theme or motif, etc.). This lax attitude still persists, and the impressionistic viewpoints still dominate. (See below)

As might be expected in works that seek global coverage (without sufficient primary data for certain areas), neither the *Types of the Folktale* by Aarne and Thompson, nor the *Motif-Index* by Thompson adequately addresses Arab-Islamic materials in general or *Alf laylah* (*The Arabian Nights*) in particular. Furthermore, data from the Arab World were only sketchily addressed and numerous motifs were imprecisely identified. Critical facets of Arab-Islamic cultures and societies are totally absent in both sorts of indexes; these facets recur in the region's lore and are pivotal for an accurate understanding of its folk traditions.

The present index offers a scores of innovative additions to the available motifs system; it also presents new fields of inquiry such as laws, kinship, markets (in Section P) and symbolism (in Section Z).[51] When applied in a systemic manner, the new data opens new research vistas for students of traditional cultures, communities and patterns of thinking.

Why an Arabic Original as Bases for Analysis

The reasons for opting to rely primarily on an indigenous edition of *Alf laylah* are multiple. However, beside being free from non-representative augmentations and omissions (see notes 9 and 15, above), two areas seem to stand out in this regard: I) the accuracy of the translation and precision in conveyance of connotative meanings and sentiments not readily observable in a written text, and II) the theoretical implications constituted by the manner in which texts are presented and interpreted (i.e., systemic representativeness).

I. **Issues of Translation and Symbolic Significance**

Along with the inaccuracies and generalities in presenting kinship ties in translation (e.g., uncle, sister-in-law, etc.),[52] the exact meaning of some Arabic words and expressions seem to evade even the most competent translators.

[48]For details see: El-Shamy, "Demographic Factor," pp. 69-71. The episode dealing with the erotic exchanges is designated as new Tale-type: 1425B§, "*Seduction: Putting the Bird (or Animal) in its Natural Habitat.*" Chauvin characterizes this episode as "obscéne plaisanteries." See: Chauvin 5: 251, no. 148.

[49]For cases expressed in tales constituting tale-types see: El-Shamy, "Demographic Factor," pp. 79-83.

[50]For details, see: El-Shamy, "A Motif Index of *Alf Laylah wa Laylah*," *JAL*, Vol. 36, pp. 247-49, 258-59.

[51]See list in El-Shamy, "A Motif Index of *Alf Laylah wa Laylah*," *JAL*, Vol. 36, pp. 250-59.

[52]For details, see El-Shamy, "A Motif Index of *Alf Laylah wa Laylah*," *JAL*, Vol. 36, pp. 254-58.

Certain words may be perceived differently, but within the bounds of the correct, according to the perceiver's worldview and past experiences. For example, Burton perceived the Arabic word *qibṭ* as denoting a "Nazarene" (i.e., a *naṣrânî*, or Christian or a person from the city of al-Nâṣirah). However, though described as "*naṣranî*/Christian" the character concerned presents himself as "*kâna mawlidî bi-Miṣr wa 'anâ min qibṭihâ*/my birth was in Egypt and I am of her Copts". Thus, the present work uses the title "Copt Broker's Story" in lieu of "Nazarene Broker's Story".[53] Similarly, Burton perceives the name "Ṣafiyyah," the Frankish concubine of King ¿Umar al-Nu¿mân, as denoting "Sofiyah or Sophia," and equates it with the "Aya Sophia" mosque/church in "Stumbl" (Constantinople).[54] However, the name—which is derived from the root *ṣfw* (pronounced *ṣa-fa-wa*), meaning to be clear, crystalline, pure, or the like—is very common among Arab and Moslem groups and occurs in a variety of forms such as Ṣâfî, Ṣafâ', Ṣafwat.[55] It is also the name of Prophet Mohammad's Jewish wife, who would also be characterized and addressed as "*'Umm al-mu'minîn*/Mother of the Believers". Consequently, the present work uses Ṣafiyyah in lieu of Sophia.

However, some translations are inaccurate or erroneous. An example of such an inaccuracy is the translation of the Arabic word "*ṭalqah*"—a single contraction associated with childbirth or labor pains (pl.: *ṭalq*)— as "divorce".[56] In his eleventh century account of the life histories of prophets, ¿Abd-Allâh al-Kisâ'î writes about an imagined exchange between Eve and God in which Eve complains of the severity of punishments He imposed on her and 'her daughters' to-be (i.e., future female offspring). Eve complains to God:

> ... *ḍarabtanî bi-al-najâsah, wa ḥarramtanî al-jum¿ah wa al-jamâ¿ah, fa* [*sic. i.e., *wa*] *ghayri dhâlika mina al-ḥabal wa al-ṭalq fa 'as'aluka yâ rabb 'an tu¿ṭînî mithlamâ 'a¿ṭaytahum .... fa qâla lahâ ....*[57]

In his translation of al-Kisâ'î's *Qiṣaṣ al-'anbiyâ'*, W. M. Thackston renders this passage addressed to God as follows:

> You have afflicted me with ritual-impurity and denied me the right to assemble at the Friday congregational prayer-service and further burdened me with pregnancy and *divorce*. I implore You, O Lord, to grant me something as You have granted these others.
> "Verily," said God, ...[58]

Clearly, divorce is not an element in the situation Eve describes. Moreover, divorce is not one of the "fifteen additional afflictions" God is said to have inflicted on Eve and her daughters (womankind),[59] nor had divorce taken place at that early stage (scene) of this parareligious mythical account describing man's fall or "Paradise lost". The ensuing text places the issue within definite childbirth context, which Thackston translates correctly: "Furthermore, if a woman die during childbirth, her place shall be among the ranks of the martyrs."

Yet, he perceives the phrase "... *ya'khudhuhâ al-ṭalq* (she is taken away [i.e., dies] by labor contractions)" as repudiation or divorce of a woman; consequently, he translates the expression as:

> ... There is no woman *repudiated* but God gives her the wages of a martyr for each *repudiation*. If she gives birth and is sound, she shall be told, "God has forgiven you your past sins, be they as vast as the ocean." If a woman dies in childbirth, she dies a martyr ....

---

[53] *Alf*, Vol. 1, pp. 88-96; Burton, Vol. 1, 262-278.

[54] ¿Umar al-Nu¿mân and Sons: *Alf*, Vol. 1, p. 163; Burton, Vol. 2, p. 79 n. 1.

[55] Motif: Z183.0.1§, "Meaning of a name".

[56] The root of the word is "ṭalaqa". Its basic meaning is 'to release' or 'to set free'. Thus, in various forms it may mean 'to divorce' or 'to eject'. In the context of parturition, the word *ṭalqah* designates a single bodily movement that 'pushes'/'expels' a fetus out of the womb.

[57] al-Kisâ'î, *Qiṣaṣ al-'anbiyâ'*, p. 50; (*fa- in the original, which is clearly a copying error). p. 50.
The motifs here are: A1650.5.2§, God's (fifteen) additional afflictions on women ('Eve and her daughters'); A1650.5.2.3§, ‡Punishment of Eve: labor pains and childbirth pains; A1650.5.2.4§, ‡Punishment of Eve: deficiency in religion (faith); A1650.5.2.4.1§, ‡Menstruous women may not perform certain required religious services (e.g., fasting, prayers), and thus deficient in religion; A1650.5.2.5§, ‡Punishment of Eve: deficiency in reason (mind); A1650.5.2.14§, ‡Punishment of Eve: Friday Prayer-service (at mosque) may not be held with only women (*lâ tan¿aqid bihinna*—i.e., they would not constitute a legitimate congregation).

[58] *The Tales of the Prophets of al-Kisa'i*. (Boston: Twayne, 1978), p. 54 (emphasis added).

[59] Motif: A1650.5.2§, "God's (fifteen) additional afflictions on women ('Eve and her daughters')".

Here, God's reward to a woman is promised not for being subjected to *ṭalâq* (divorce) initiated by her husband, but for the pains and sufferings associated with her *ṭalq* (childbirth).[60]

Similarly, Wilhelm Spitta translated the vernacular Arabic truism "*yâ wâkhdu kullu, yâ târku kullu!*" (an esoteric Sufi-mystical cliché meaning: You who owns/takes all, are you who loses/leaves all [at death]) as "I *either* take it all, *or* leave it all."[61] In the motif classificatory schema based on the sociocultural and psychological nature of themes and actions, the meaning of the expression falls within the newly introduced category of "merits and demerits" of wealth and futility of life (Chapter U). Meanwhile the meaning of Spitta's translation comes under "Choices" (Chapter J). However, no choice is implied in the mystical expression.[62]

Another situation where inaccuracy seems to recur deals with perceiving members of the category of reptiles labelled "snakes". These may appear as *thu¿bân* (snake), *ḥayyah/'af¿â* (viper), or serpent (*'uf¿uwân*). Neither the word *tinnîn/tannîn* (dragon) nor the supernatural creature designated by the word is mentioned in *Alf laylah* under consideration here. Yet, in Burton's translation, rightly providing the foundation for many reference works, the words snake, serpent, viper, and dragon seem to have been cast in the same imprecise language and used synonymously.[63]

Due to the importance of the symbolic significance of such creatures, real or fictitious, a reconsideration of how they are re-presented in translation is needed. This fact was pointed by the present writer in 1980 in reference to the exact nature of "viper" and "dragon" in J. Contineau's translation of an Arab legend:[64]

---

[60]Motif: T583.0.1.2§, ‡Labor-pains (pangs of labor, 'ṭalq'/makhâḍ); V463.7.5.2§, ‡"Martyrdom: dying during childbirth".

To his credit, Burton translates the word *ṭalq* correctly as "pangs of labour".

[61]*Grammatik des arabischen Vulgärdialektes von Ägypten* (Leipzig, 1880), no. 3, pp. 444-48, esp. p. 444. (emphasis added). Following Spitta, A. O. Green, in his *Modern Arabic Stories* (Cairo, 1886), no. 10, pp. 44-49 (Eng. tr. p. 55), adopted the same erroneous translation. It is worth mentioning here that many of Spitta's texts were appropriated by J. C. Mardrus and given as components of his European Edition of *Le Livre des Mille Nuits et Une Nuit; trad. litterale et complete du texte Arabe* (Paris, 1900-4).

An recent field text from Egypt is given by H. El-Shamy in *Tales Told Around the World*, R.M. Dorson gen. ed. (Chicago, 1975)—(the sketchy types and motifs were selected by the Folklore Institute's editorial staff from El-Shamy's original annotation of the tale, which was part of his *Folktales of Egypt*, MS, 1971). Also see El-Shamy, "Oral Traditional Tales and the Thousand Nights and a Night: The Demographic Factor," p. 74, n. 56.

[62]Motifs U292§, ‡Merits and demerits of wealth and poverty; U292.1§, ‡Demerits of wealth (being rich); U292.1.1§, ‡'He who owns much loses much'.

[63]The following are examples: (1) A salient case of this situation is "The Queen of the Serpents" where the Arabic text speaks of "*malikat al-ḥayyât*" (*Alf*, Vol. 3, p. 20ff.), but Burton translates the word as "serpents" (Burton, Vol. 5, pp. 303ff.), (Motif: B225.1, Kingdom of serpents"). Thus, a new more representative motif was introduced: B225.3§, "‡Kingdom of vipers: all females".

(2) In the story "The Eldest Lady's Tale," the phrase "*ḥayyah* (viper)" pursued by "*thu¿bân* (snake)" (*Alf*, Vol. 1, p. 57) is given as "serpent" pursued by "dragon" (Burton, Vol. 1, p. 172).

(3) In the story of "The serpent which fled from the charmer," although the Arabic text speaks of "*ḥayyah* (viper)" (*Alf*, Vol. 2, p. 3[illegible], the translation gives it as "serpent" (Burton, Vol. 3, p. 145). Yet Burton speaks of this serpent in feminine terms: "A man saw her affrighted and said to her...". Consequently, the story is given here as "Escaped Viper Ungrateful". Also see: El-Shamy, *Folktales of Egypt*, p. lv n. 40.

(4) Similarly, in Sindbâd's Second Voyage "*ḥayyah*" (*Alf*, Vol. 3, p. 89) is given as "serpent" (Burton, Vol. 6 p. 17); and in Seventh Voyage "*ḥayyât* (vipers)" (*Alf*, Vol. 3 pp. 117, 121) is given as "serpents" (Burton, Vol. 6, p. 69).

(5) Meanwhile, in "Judar and his Brethren" the text speaks of "*thu¿bânayn*" (two snakes) (*Alf*, Vol. 3, p. 186), but the translation gives it as "two dragons" (Burton, Vol. 6, p. 229).

(6) Similarly, in the "Rogueries of Dalilah the Crafty and her Daughter Zaynab the Coney-catcher," the Arabic "*thu¿bân* (snake)" (*Alf*, Vol. 3, p. 213) is given as "dragon" (Burton, Vol. 7, p. 145).

(7) Also, in "Abdullah bin Fazil and His Brothers," the Arabic text speaks of "white *ḥayyah* [(viper)] and black snake" (*Alf*, Vol. 4, p. 272), translated as "snake" and "dragon," respectively (Burton, Vol. 9, p. 315).

(8) In "King Sindibad and his Falcon," the word "*ḥayyah*" (*Alf*, Vol. 1, p. 19) is given correctly as "vipers" (Burton, Vol. 1, p. 52).

For additional discussion on this issue, see El-Shamy, "A Motif Index of *Alf Laylah wa Laylah*," *JAL*, Vol. 36, pp. 259-60, esp. notes 89-92.

[64]*Le dialecte arabe de Palmyre*, 2 vols. (Beirut, 1934), p. 112.

Contineau translated *ḥayyi*, which signifies viper and is invariably perceived as female, as "dragon," which is perceived as male. Obviously his substitution of one creature for the other, though understandable, is erroneous.[65]

The *ḥayyah* (viper), more than any other reptile, occupies a central position in Arabic and Islamic beliefs; this idea is conveyed in the new motif B3§, ‡"Viper (*ḥayyah*, female serpent) as animal central to supernatural beliefs (religious records)," especially in belief cycles related to motif A2585.1.1§, ‡"Enmity between viper and man began with her role in the fall of Adam (and Eve)".[66] However, it may be stated that all vipers are snakes, but not all snakes are vipers.

Another sort of inaccuracy in data derived from texts in translation may be viewed as contextual in nature. Not only is the meaning of a word dependent on the context but also the extent to which a translator may clarify an ambiguity. An example from *Alf laylah* involves implicit expression of the brother-sister tie or bond in the story of Ghânim ibn Ayyûb. The Arabic text speaks of a rich merchant named Ayyûb who

> ... *lahu mâl wa lahu walad ..., yusammîhi Ghânim ibn Ayyûb ...; wa lahu 'ukht 'ismuhâ Fitnah min farti husnihâ wa jamâlihâ. fa-tuwuffiya wâliduhumâ ....*[67]

The exact translation of this passage is that Ayyûb, the merchant,

> ... has wealth and has a son ..., whom he names Ghânim ibn Ayyûb ...; and *he [the son] has a sister named Fitnah* [so named] due to the excess of her comeliness and beauty. The father of the two of them died ....

In the Arabic passage, the writer/narrator perceives Ghânim (the son) in association with the father, while associating Fitnah (the daughter) only with her brother.[68] Burton presents this cluster of kinship ties as that of the merchant Ayyûb

> had a son ... named Ghánim .... *He had also a daughter, own sister to Ghánim*, who was called Fitnah, a damsel unique in beauty and loveliness. Their father died ....[69]

Although Burton's English translation is more specific, it is less accurate for it injects a link between Fitnah and her father Ayyûb not present in the Arabic text. Consequently, the primacy of the brother-sister association and its psychological significance are dissipated in the English text. In a parallel cultural sphere, a study of kinship ties among possessing *zar*-spirits (labeled *'asyâd ez-zâr*) concluded that in a situation where a triad of father-daughter-son are involved "the brother and sister relationship ... overrides that of the daughter and father."[70]

Another secondary aspect of this *Alf laylah* text is that the reporting of the girl's beauty occurs in association with her brother as a "cognitive cluster". The same phenomenon was reported in a parallel folk narrative situation dealing with brother and sister. Analyzing thirty-nine variants of Type 872*, *Brother and Sister* it was observed that

> The narrator of variant 20 was reminded of the sister's virginity only when the brother and sister are alone in a forbidden chamber. The tomb of the dead parents generates fear in the sister. Similarly, the narrator of variant 28 thought of the sister's beauty *only* while she and her brother were in a cave.[71]

---

[65]El-Shamy, *Folktales of Egypt*, notes to tale no. 34 "*Mari Girgis and the Beast*," p. 280.

[66]Other examples are: A2145.6.1§, ‡Vipers from ebb-tide (breathing) of Hell; A2145.7.1§, ‡Hell's vipers (and scorpions) are the offspring of Khalît and Malît (mythical hybrids's first pregnancy); A2579.1.1§, ‡Why the viper (snake, serpent) is immortal; B17.9.1.1§, ‡Viper, by nature, practices deception (camouflage) and injustice (*ẓulm*); D1375.7.1§, ‡Devil's touch (kiss) causes viper(s) to grow on person; F337.3§, Fairy (in viper form) saved from pursuer (unwanted suitor): grateful; Z192.2.1§, Symbolism: viper--treacherous female.

[67]*Alf*, Vol. 1, p. 146.

[68]Motif: P798.1.0.5§, "Triads revolving around brother and sister as unbalanced (Sethian syndrome)".

[69]Burton, Vol. 2, p. 45 (emphasis added).

[70]Hasan El-Shamy, "Belief Characters as Anthropomorphic Psychosocial Realities," in *al-kitâb al-sanawî li-ᶜilm al-'igtimâᶜ* (*Annual Review of Sociology*), Department of Sociology, Cairo University, Vol. 3, (1982), pp. 7-36 (Arabic Abstract, pp. 389-393), p. 27; cf. Enno Littmann, *Arabische Geisterbeschwörungen aus Ägypten*, Leipzig, 1950, pp. 35-36).

[71]El-Shamy, *Brother and Sister. Type 872**, pp. 41-42. (Emphasis is in the original).

From the examples cited above, it may be concluded that reliance on an original Arabic text, rather than translations thereof, lessens the possibility of the occurrence of such inaccuracies.

II. Theoretical Speculations

Areas where this index offers assistance to students of literature, communal studies and the individual are numerous. Providing accurate data for comparison and verification, and curbing unfounded theoretical speculations leading to impressionistic conclusions are two such areas.

A dilemma faced in folklore scholarship is that there are powerful theories that seem to make sense from an abstract perspective but fail when applied to real living lore. Many 'theories' are based on inaccurate translations of texts; others are founded on résumés provided in indexes or academic studies.

Theories with racial overtones, such as C.W. Von Sydow's on the origin of the *Märchen* as a genre and its presumed absence among certain peoples who--according to von Sydow--lacked imagination and creativity (including ancient Egyptians, Semites and other Middle Eastern groups), were based on the erroneous premise that there were no such tales circulating among members of these nations. Von Sydow was unaware of the fact that among Arabs and Muslims, for example, the *Zaubermärchen* (fairytale) is a woman's 'cultural specialty' and that men refrain from telling this sort (genre) of tale.[72] Since most field collectors were adult European males, they had no access to women tale-tellers. Thus, early tale collections reflected this fact, which collectors mistook as representative of the entire population. It is in this respect that women engage in more creative and imaginative narrative activities than do adult males. But, as pointed out (see notes 32-35, above), it is the kind of creativity that formal Islam frowns upon.

Another case of western theory imposed on Arab traditions is the application of the Freudian Oedipal theory to Arab-Islamic materials by Allen Johnson, and Douglas Price-Williams.[73] Not only that the data on which the study was based is deficient and unrepresentative, it was also altered to comply with the predetermined hypothesis.[74]

A similar situation is found in an attempt by Peter Gilet[75] to apply a Proppian morphological pattern to Middle Eastern/Berber texts. With specific reference to a tale that can be shown to date back to Egyptian antiquity, the pattern failed to materialize ("does not happen") despite the liberties Gilet took with the redefining of the specifics of the field text and its persona. Gilet explained, "That this does not happen is perhaps because in fact the story has been *told in reverse order*, [...]."[76]

In other words, Gilet sees actual Middle Eastern life as wrong and has been going in the reverse direction for 3,200 years. But the theory is right, even though, by Gilet's own admission, it fails repeatedly to produce the anticipated results.

With specific reference to *Alf laylah*, an all-inclusive claim about the nature of female-male relationships and the role of Shahrzad's tale-telling proves to be another case of a theory not supported by textual or sociocultural realities. In her *Woman's Body, Woman's Word: Gender and Discourse in Arabo-Islamic Writing*, Fedwa Malti-Douglas argues that through narrating to her husband, Shahrzad's

> ... body has been transmuted into word and back into body. Corporeality is the final word, as Shahrazad relinquishes her role of narrator for that of perfect woman: mother and *lover*.[77]

---

[72]For a brief outline of the hypothesis see El-Shamy, "The *Märchen* Among Non-Aryans," in Maspero, *Popular Stories of Ancient Egypt*, p. 23. Also see C.W. Von Sydow, "Das Märchen als indogermanische Tradition (Auszug) übertragen von Lily Weiser," *Niederdeutsche Zeitschrift für Volkskunde*, Vol. 4 (1926), pp. 207-15.

[73]*Oedipus Ubiquitous: The Family Complex in World Folk Literature*. Stanford, Cal., 1996.

[74]For the details of this case see "The Systemic Qualities of Meaning, and the Role of Folkloristic Annotations," in El-Shamy, *Tales Arab Women Tell*, pp. 13-16.
Compare the psychoanalytic interpretation Ibrahim Muhawi and Sharif Kanaana cultivate concerning the story of "The Golden Rod in the Valley of Vermilion" (in their *Speak, Bird, Speak Again: Palestinian Arab Folktales*, (Berkeley, 1989). Notably, their interpretation makes no mention of El-Shamy's "Brother-Sister Syndrome Theory," but duplicates its findings especially with reference to the affective patterns within the kinship group. See El-Shamy, *Tales Arab Women Tell*, pp. 16-18.

[75]*Vladimir Propp and the Universal Folktale: Recommissioning an Old Paradigm--Story as Initiation*, New York: P. Lang, 1998.

[76](Emphasis added). For details see Hasan El-Shamy's review of the book in *Asian Folklore Studies* (Nazan University: Nagoya, Japan) Vol. 61, (2001) No. 1, pp. 153-57, p. 157.

[77]Princeton: Princeton UP, 1992. p. 28; emphasis added.

Embracing Malti-Douglas' thesis, Susanne Enderwitz concludes that

> ... at the end of the storytelling cycle, the readers and/or listeners--together with the king--discover that Shahrazâd has given birth to three sons. The king spares her life, not only because she has given birth to his children who would otherwise lose their mother, but because *he has fallen in love* with her for her purity, virtue, and piety. The city is lavishly decorated, marriage takes place, and they live happily together until they die. ....[78]

This impressive argument would be factual and a welcome psychosocial development in Arab-Islamic character if *Alf laylah* was actually concluded as postulated by Malti-Douglas and Enderwitz. An examination of the *Arabic* text should provide the necessary evidence for the presence or absence of '*love*' as a component of the scene. The word "*hubb*" (love) does not appear in the Arabic text in the edition under investigation nor in Burton's translation.[79]

A primary criterion for ascertaining the traditionality of an aspect of culture is its continuity in time and space.[80] Continuity in space requires that the item concerned be known to a majority of the members of a community, and that it also appears in a variety of pertinent situations. Before seeking interpretations in individualistic sources, meaning should be sought first in relevant traditions in the system to which a folkloric item belongs.[81]

Regrettably, no where is there any mention of the word "love" or even an allusion to an emotion or a sentiment[82] that may be perceived as the type of love on the basis of which Malti-Douglas and Enderwitz build their 'theory' and elicit their conclusions. Perhaps the only situation where *hubb* ("love") between a married couple is presented as such occurs in the story of ¿Alâ' al-Dîn Abû al-Shâmât. The Arabic text states that a merchant "*ma¿ahu zawjah yuhibbuhâ wa tuhibbuh* (with him is a wife whom he loved and she loved him)".[83] However, this marital love is inconsequential for it plays no actual role in the developing of the narrative plot. Moreover, the 'loving' husband blames and curses his 'beloved' wife for the immoral conduct of men in the marketplace vis-à-vis their handsome son (an act with which she had absolutely no connection).[84] This absence of 'love' is a feature that can also be inferred from the motif-spectrum that I developed for this concluding scene of *Alf laylah*, and made available to researchers in the present index.[85]

As already documented, Shahrzâd escapes her husband's wrath in the same manners other persecuted heroines in Arab folktales do: by total submission and appeasement.[86] A case that can further illustrate this tradition in Arabic lore, is the female-bound tale titled "Pomegranate Kernels on Gold Trays."[87] According to the fifty-three (53) renditions cited in *DOTTI*, the tale may be summarized as follows:

---

[78]"Shahrazâd Is One of Us: Practical Narrative, Theoretical Discussion, and Feminist Discourse."In *Marvels & Tales: Journal of Fairy-Tale Studies*, Vol. 18, No. 2 (Detroit: Wayne State University Press, 2004), pp. 187-200. p. 190, (emphasis added). The same assertion is repeated on p. 196.

[79]*Alf*, Vol. 4, pp. 317-18; and Burton, Vol. 10, p. 54. For details, see: El-Shamy, "*A Motif Index of* Alf Laylah wa Laylah," *JAL*, Vol. 36, pp. 263-64.

[80]See: El-Shamy, "Psychologically-Based Criteria for Classification by Motif and Tale Type," in *Journal of Folklore Research*, Vol. 34, No. 3, (1997), p. 233.

[81]H. El-Shamy, "Sentiment, Genre, and Tale Typology: Meaning in Middle Eastern and African Tales," in *Papers III*. The 8th Congress for the International Society for Folk Narrative Research, R. Kvideland and T. Selberg, eds., pp. 255-283 (Bergen, Norway, 1985). Also (revised and expanded) in *al-Ma'thûrât al-Sha*^{c}*biyyah*, Vol. 1 (Doha, Qatar, 1986), no. 3, pp. 41-51.

[82]On the difference between 'emotion' and 'sentiment,' see El-Shamy, *Folktales of Egypt*, p. xlvi, n. 12; also see El-Shamy, "Emotionskomponente," in *EM*, Vol. 3, nos. 4-5, pp. 1391-95.

[83]*Alf*, Vol. 2, p. 147. (Burton, Vol. 4, p. 29) translates this phrase as: [a merchant] "*owned* a wife whom he loved and who loved him" (emphasis added). See Motif T202.3§, "Affectionate couple", p. 337-38, below.

[84]Motifs Z43.7.1§, ‡Pecking order: chain of aggressive actions and displaced reactions, started against the weak and ending with the weakest; P210.0.1.1§, ‡Husband blames his wife for strangers's misconduct (life's common problems).

[85]Shahryâr-Shahrzâd: Conclusion. (Tale-type: 1426A§), *Alf*, Vol. 4, p. 317. See *DOTTI*. For the motif spectrum, see El-Shamy, "*A Motif Index of* Alf Laylah wa Laylah," *JAL*, Vol. 36, pp. 263-64, n. 102.

[86]E.g., Types: 756D§, *The Most Devout will Enter Paradise First: Obedient Wife*; 901, Taming of the Shrew; 909§, *Taming the Disgruntled (Shrewish) Husband is Like Taming a Lion: with Patience and Tenderness (Appeasement)*. See details in "*A Motif Index of* Alf Laylah wa Laylah," *JAL*, Vol. 36, pp. 263-68.

[87]AT 894, *The ogre Schoolmaster and the Stone of Pity*. El-Shamy, *Tales Arab Women Tell*, No. 13, pp. 143-51, 425-26.

A young girl inadvertently witnesses her cleric-instructor (¿arrîf) 'eating' a child (or a corpse). She flees, lives in poverty but due to her good looks ends up marrying a prince. Upon delivering her first child, the demon teacher bursts out of the wall of the room where she and her infant are placed. He asks her about what she had seen. She appeases him by claiming that she saw him teaching children knowledge and good manners. None the less, he takes the infant away and smears her mouth with blood. Her in-laws accuse her of cannibalism and treat her accordingly. The demon teacher puts her to the same test with her following newborns (usually two); in every case she keeps the teacher's secret and appeases him with lies and flattery.

Privately, the heroine tells her story and enumerates the injustices she has suffered to a rock ('Stone of Pity'): the stone ruptures in sympathy. Yet, her ordeal continues.

Finally, her husband is resolved to remarry. On his wedding day, the ogre teacher returns the children back to her "well disciplined, educated, ready [to go]" as reward for keeping his secret.

The children spoil their father's wedding; their mother's innocence is established, and she is reunited with her husband and children.

True to the dominant pattern in Arab World lore, the ogre teacher is *never* punished for his murderous cannibalism (or, perhaps—symbolically, sodomy),[88] just as King Shahryâr received no punishment for the serial killing of his young 'one-night stand' brides. As concluded in the introductory statement to an oral rendition (performance) by an adult woman of "Pomegranate Kernels on Gold Trays":

Curiously enough, the tale's "normal form" does not include punishment for the ogre schoolmaster, a fact that perhaps is reflective of its scarcity in real life, especially in law courts.[89]

Concluding Statement

If progress and development are to be made in any sphere of life--whether women's rights, systems of government, religious laws or the arts--an accurate, objective and ethically neutral assessment of the social and cultural facts as they are actually practiced must *first* be achieved. Impressions and impressionistic studies, regardless of well-meaning underlying motivation, lead only to the creation of fallacies which in turn generate harmful social, cultural and psychological constructs. Folk culture and its literatures play an enormous role in the shaping of worldviews and psychological attitudes toward central aspects of life such as the proper roles assigned to males and females, the limits of governmental power, and the nature of good and evil.

In 2004, numerous cultural and academic institutions celebrated the passage of three centuries since the momentous cultural event initiated by Antoine Galland's work. This "*Motif Index of* Alf laylah wa laylah" is part of the celebration.[90] It is hoped that the original data this work offers will provide a first step to scholars in both the humanities and the social sciences toward addressing *Alf laylah wa laylah*—and eventually *The Arabian Nights*, its European offspring, in a more objective manner. Both descriptive-comparative methods and theoretical-applied approaches alike will find its contents relevant to their pursuits. As current drastic political events amply demonstrate, understanding folk traditions of the Arab World is of critical importance to scholars, policy-makers and laymen, especially in the new global setting created by modern technology and instant dissemination of diverse information.

---

[88]Motifs: Z170.0.1§, ‡Symbolism: eating (swallowing, chewing)—sexual activity; T472.0.1§, Pedophilia. An adult's abnormal sexual desire for children; P423.0.3.1§, ‡Children's teacher as pedophile.

[89]*Tales Arab Women Tell*, p. 144 (original is italicized). The recurrence and female-orientedness of the tale are reported as follows:

"**Occurrences**: 52 additional texts are available. The ratio of f[emale]:m[ale] narrators is 31:4--mostly under age 20". (p. 425).

The significance of the age of the male narrators of this tale-type is that they are still under the influence of childhood experiences (enculturation by women) and have not been yet completely resocialized into male roles according to which adult males are expected not to tell such "women's stuff". On the concepts of "role" and "resocialization" in this context, both developed and introduced by the present writer, see El-Shamy, *"Folkloric Behavior," p. 65, and 83; Folktales of Egypt*, p. lii, lxviii; *Brother and Sister: Type 872**, p. 51; and *Tales Arab Women Tell*, p. 9, 22 n. 28.

[90]These include (**A**) Symposia: "Symposium on The *Arabian Nights* and Orientalism in Resonance," at the National Museum of Ethnology, Osaka, Japan, December 12-13, 2002; and "The 57th Wolfenbütteler Symposion on Forschungs- und Studienstätte für europäische Kulturgeschichte: 'The Arabian Nights: Past and Present: (1704-2004),' September 4-8," 2004, at Herzog August Bibliothek Wulfenbüttel, Wulfenbüttel, Germany. (**B**) Publications: *The Arabian Nights Encyclopedia*, U. Marzolph et al., eds. (2004); *The Thousand and One Nights*, *JAL*, Vol. 36 No. 3, Special Issue (2005); *The Arabian Nights and Orientalism: Perspectives from East and West*, Y. Yamanaka and T. Nishio, eds. (2005); *The Arabian Nights: Past and Present*, *Marvels & Tales: Journal of Fairy-Tale Studies*, Special Issue, U. Marzolph, guest ed. (2004); Margaret Sironval, *Album Mille et Une Nuits*: Iconographie choisie et commentée (Gallimard: 2005).

بسم الله الرحمن الرحيم

الحمد لله رب العالمين والصلاة والسلام على سيد المرسلين سيدنا ومولانا محمد وعلى آله وصحبه صلاة وسلاما دائمين متلازمين إلى يوم الدين (وبعد) فان سير الأولين صارت عبرة للآخرين لكي يرى الانسان العبر التي حصلت لغيره فيعتبر ويطالع حديث الامم السالفة وما جرى لهم فينزجر فسبحان من جعل حديث الأولين عبرة لقوم آخرين «فمن» تلك العبر الحكايات التي تسمى ألف ليلة وليلة وما فيها من الغرائب والامثال

(حكايات الملك شهريار وأخيه الملك شاه زمان)

(حكى) والله أعلم انه كان فيما مضى من قديم الزمان وسالف العصر والأوان ملك من ملوك ساسان بجزائر الهند والصين صاحب جند وأعوان وخدم وحشم له ولدان أحدهما كبير والآخر صغير وكانا فارسين بطلين وكان الكبير أفرس من الصغير وقد ملك البلاد وحكم بالعدل بين العباد وأحبه أهل بلاده ومملكته وكان اسمه الملك شهريار وكان أخوه الصغير اسمه الملك شاه زمان وكان ملك سمرقند العجم ولم يزل الامر مستقيما في بلادهما وكل واحد منهما في مملكته حاكم عادل في رعيته مدة عشرين سنة وهم في غاية البسط والانشراح ولم يزالا على هذه الحالة الى ان اشتاق الكبير إلى أخيه الصغير فأمر وزيره أن يسافر اليه ويحضر به فأجابه بالسمع والطاعة وسافر حتى وصل بالسلامة ودخل على أخيه وبلغه السلام واعلمه ان أخاه مشتاق اليه وقصده أن يزوره فأجابه بالسمع والطاعة وتجهز للسفر وأخرج خيامه وجماله وبغاله وخدمه وأعوانه وأقام وزيره حاكما في بلاده وخرج طالبا بلاد أخيه فلما كان في نصف الليل تذكر حاجة نسيها في قصره فرجع ودخل قصره فوجد زوجته راقدة في فراشه معانقة عبدا اسود من العبيد فلما رأى هذا اسودت الدنيا في وجهه وقال في نفسه اذا كان هذا الامر قد وقع وأنا ما فارقت المدينة فكيف حال هذه العاهرة اذا غبت عند أخي مدة ثم انه سل سيفه وضرب الاثنين فقتلهما في الفراش ورجع من وقته وساعته وأمر بالرحيل وسار الى أن وصل الى مدينة أخيه ففرح أخيه بقدومه ثم خرج اليه ولاقاه وسلم عليه ففرح به غاية الفرح وزين له المدينة وجلس معه يتحدث بانشراح فتذكر الملك شاه زمان ما كان من أمر زوجته فحصل عنده غم زائد واصفر لونه وضعف جسمه فلما رآه أخوه على هذه الحالة ظن في نفسه أن ذلك بسبب مفارقته بلاده ومملكته فترك سبيله ولم يسأل عن ذلك ثم انه قال له في بعض الايام يا أخي اني أنا في باطني جرح ولم يخبره بما رأى من زوجته فقال اني اريد ان تسافر معي الى الصيد والقنص لعله ينشرح صدرك فأبى ذلك فسافر أخوه وحده الى الصيد وكان في قصر الملك شبابيك تطل على بستان أخيه فنظر واذا بباب القصر قد فتح وخرج منه عشرون جارية وعشرون عبدا وامرأة أخيه تمشي بينهم وهي في غاية الحسن والجمال حتى وصلوا الى فسقية وخلعوا ثيابهم وجلسوا مع بعضهم واذا بامرأة الملك قالت يا مسعود

'Alf laylah wa laylah, first page (p. 2), Vol. 1. Also see p. ii, above.

Bismi Allâhi al-Rahamân al-Rahîm*

Al-hamdu li-Allâhi rabbi al-¿âlamîn, wa al-ṣalâtu wa al-salâmu ¿alâ sayyidi al-mursalîn, sayyidinâ wa mawlânâ Muhammad, wa ¿alâ 'âlihi wa ṣahbihi: ṣalatan wa salâman dâ'imayni mutalâzimayni 'ilâ yawmi al-dîn. (wa ba¿d) fa'inna siyara al-'awwalîn ṣârat ¿ibratan li-'al-'âkharîn li-kayy yarâ al-'insânu al-¿ibara 'allatî hasalt li-ghayrihi fa-ya¿tabir, wa yutâli¿u hadîtha al-'umami al-sâlifati wa mâ jarâ lahum fa-yanzajir. fa subhâna man ja¿ala hadîtha al-'awwalîn ¿ibratan li-qawmin 'âkharîn. "fa-min" tilka al-¿ibar al-hikâyât allatî tusammâ 'Alf laylah wa laylah wamâ fîhâ nina al-gharâ'bi wa al-'amthâl

In The name of God the Merciful the Compassionate*

Praise be to God the Lord of the Universe; and prayer-blessing and graces be upon our lord Mohammed: Lord of Apostolic Men, and upon his family and companion train: Prayer and blessings enduring and grace which unto the Doomsday shall remain. (And afterwards): verily the *siyar* (life histories) of those gone before us have become instances and examples to men of our modern day; so that folk may view what admonishing chances befell other folk and may therefrom be admonished, and that they may peruse the annals of antique peoples and all that has betided them, and be thereby ruled and restrained. Praise, therefore, be to Him who hath made the histories of the past an admonition unto the present! "[Now]" of such instances are the tales called: A Thousand Nights and a Night, together with what it contains of eccentricities and parables

———————————

*Opening '*basmalh*' ("In the name of God ...") and inaugural first paragraph. There are some variations between the present Arabic text and Burton's translation (Vol. 1, pp. 1-2). The translation is partly based on Burton's.

References Cited and Bibliography

Aarne, Antti, and Stith Thompson, *The Types of the Folktale: A Classification and Bibliography*. Folklore Fellows Communications, No. 184 (Helsinki, 1964).

Abû al-Naṣr, ¿Abd al-Jalîl ¿Îsâ, *Ṣafwat ṣaḥîḥ al-Bukhârî* (*The Choicest from Bukhari's Authenticated [Utterances of Prophet Muhammad]*). Vol. 4 (Cairo, 1953).

Alf laylah wa laylah. 4 vols. (Maktabat al-Jumhûriyyh: Cairo, n.d.).

The Arabian Nights Encyclopedia. Ulrich Marzolph, and Richard van Leeuwen, eds., with the collaboration of Hassan Wassouf. (Santa Barbara, 2004).

Burton, Richard F., *Arabian Nights: The Book of the Thousand Nights and a Night*. Vls. 1-10, (London, 1894).

Chauvin, Victor, *Bibliographie des ouvrages arabes ou relatifs aux Arabes: publiés dans l'Europe chrétienne de 1810 à 1885*. 12 vols. (Liége, 1892-1922).

Chraïbi, Aboubakr, ed., *Contes nouveaux des 1001 Nuits: Étude du manuscrit Reinhardt*. (Paris: Maisonneuve, 1996).

Contineau, J., *Le dialecte arabe de Palmyre*. 2 vols. (Beirut, 1934).

Dorson, R.M., gen. ed., *Tales Told Around the World*. (Chicago, 1975).

__________, *naẓariyyât al-folklore al-mu¿âṣirah* ("Concepts [i.e., Theories] of Folklore and Folklife Studies,") in R.M. Dorson, ed., *Folklore and Folklife: an Introduction)*, Mohammad El-Gohary and Hasan El-Shamy, trs. eds. (Dâr al-Kutub al-Jâmi¿iyyah: Cairo, 1972).

Elisséeff, Nikita, *Thèmes et motifs de mille et une nuits: essai de classification*. (Beirut, 1949).

Enderwitz, Susanne, "Shahrazâd Is One of Us: Practical Narrative, Theoretical Discussion, and Feminist Discourse."In *Marvels & Tales: Journal of Fairy-Tale Studies*. Vol. 18, No. 2. (Detroit: Wayne State University Press, 2004).

Folklore: An Encyclopedia of Forms, Methods, and History, T. A. Green, ed. (ABC-CLIO, Santa Barbara: 1997).

Gilet, Peter, *Vladimir Propp and the Universal Folktale: Recommissioning an Old Paradigm--Story as Initiation*. (New York: P. Lang, 1998).

Green, Arthur Octavious, *Modern Arabic Stories* (Cairo, 1886).

Grotzfeld, Heinz, "The Manuscript Tradition of the *Arabian Nights*," in *The Arabian Nights Encyclopedia*, Ulrich Marzolph et al. eds., pp. 17-21.

Hultkranz, Åke, *Qâmûs muṣṭalḥât al-'ithnoloajyâ wa al-folklore* (*General Ethnological Concepts, International Dictionary of Regional European Ethnology and Folklore*, Vol. 1, Copenhagen, 1960), Mohammad El-Gohary/[Jawharî] and Hasan El-Shamy, tr. eds. (El-Marif: Cairo, 1972).

Johnson, Allen, and Douglas Price-Williams, *Oedipus Ubiquitous: The Family Complex in World Folk Literature*. (Stanford: Stanford University Press, 1996).

Kisâ'î (al-), Muhammad ibn ¿Abdullah, *Qiṣaṣ al-'anbiyâ' (Vita Prophitorum)*. Isaac Eisenberg, ed. (Leiden: Brill, 1922).

Littmann, Enno, "Alf layla wa-layla" in *Encyclopaedia of Islam*. 2nd ed. (Brill: Leiden, 1960), Vol. 1, pp. 358-64.

__________, *Arabische Geisterbeschwörungen aus Ägypten*. (Otto Harrassowitz: Leipzig, 1950).

Mack, L. Robert, ed., *Arabian Nights' Entertainment*. Edited with an Introduction by Robert L. Mack (Oxford, New York: Oxford Uunversity Press, 1995).

Mahdî, Muḥsin, ed., *'Alf laylah wa laylah min 'uṣûlih al-¿arabiyyah al-'ûlâ ("The Thousand and One Nights From the Earliest Known Sources: Arabic Text Edited with Introduction by [...]"). 3 vols.* (Leiden: Brill, 1984).

Malti-Douglas, Fedwa. *Woman's Body, Woman's Word: Gender and Discourse in Arabo-Islamic Writing*. (Princeton: Princeton University Press, 1992).

Mardrus, J. C., *Le Livre des Mille Nuits et Une Nuit; trad. litterale et complete du texte Arabe*. (Paris, 1900-4).

Maspero, Gaston C., *Popular Stories of Ancient Egypt*. Edited and with an Introduction [and Tale-type and Motif identifications] by Hasan El-Shamy (ABC-CLIO, Santa Barbara, Oxford, England, 2002).

Mrzolph, Ulrich, et. al, eds. (see: *The Arabian Nights Encyclopedia*, above).

Muhawi, Ibrahim, and Sharif Kanaana, *Speak, Bird, Speak Again: Palestinian Arab Folktales*. (Berkeley: University of California Press, 1989).

Shamy (el-), Hasan, "¿ilm al-nafs al-taḥlîlî wa al-folklore (Psychoanalysis and Folklore [1])." *Al-Majallah*, no. 117 (Cairo, September, 1966), pp. 33-41; and al-lâshu¿ûr al-jamâ¿î wa al-folklore (Collective Unconsciousness and Folklore) [2]." *Al-Majallah*, no. 126 (Cairo June 1967), pp. 21-29.

__________, "African World View and Religion," *Introduction to Africa*, P. Martin and P. O'Meara, eds. (Bloomington, Indiana University Press, 1977), pp. 208-20.

__________, "Behaviorism and the Text," *Folklore Today: A Festschrift for Richard M. Dorson*, Linda Dégh, Henry Glassie and Felix Oinas, eds. (Bloomington, 1976), pp. 145-60.

__________, "Belief Characters as Anthropomorphic Psychosocial Realities," in *al-kitâb al-sanawî li-ᶜilm al-'igtimâᶜ* (*Annual Review of Sociology*), Department of Sociology, Cairo University, Vol. 3, (1982), pp. 7-36 (Arabic Abstract, pp. 389-93).

__________, *Brother and Sister. Type 872*: A Cognitive Behavioristic Text Analysis of a Middle Eastern Oikotype*. (Folklore Monograph Series, Vol. 8, Folklore Publications Group, Bloomington, 1979).

__________, "Emotionskomponente," *Enzyklopädie des Märchens*, (Göttingen) Vol. 3, nos. 4-5 (1981), pp. 1391-95.

__________, *Folk Traditions of the Arab World: A Guide to Motif Classification*. 2 vols. (Bloomington: Indiana University Press, 1995).

__________, "Folk Group," *Folklore: An Encyclopedia of Forms, Methods, and History*, T. A. Green, ed. (ABC-CLIO, Santa Barbara: 1997), pp. 318-22.

__________, "Folkloric Behavior: A Theory for the Study of the Dynamics of Traditional Culture." [A case study of the stability and change in the lore of the Egyptian community in Brooklyn, N.Y.]. Doctoral dissertation. (Indian University, Bloomington, 1967).

__________, *Folktales of Egypt: Collected, Translated and Annotated with Middle Eastern and African Parallels*. (Chicago: University of Chicago Press, 1980).

__________, "A Motif Index for *Alf Laylah wa-laylah* (The Thousand Nights and a Night)"," in *Minpaku Anthropology Newsletter*, No. 15 (Osaka, Japan, 2002), pp. 5-7.

__________, "A Motif Index of *Alf Laylah wa Laylah*: Its Relevance to the Study of Culture, Society, the Individual, and Character Transmutation," in *Journal of Arabic Literature*. (Brill, Leiden). Vol. 36 No. 3, pp. 235-68.

__________, "Mythological Constituents of *Alf Laylah wa Laylah wa Laylah*," in *The Arabian Nights and Orientalism: Perspectives from East and West*, Yuriko Yamanaka and Tetsuo Nishio, eds. (London, I.B. Tauris, 2006) pp. 25-46.

__________, "nuẓum fahrasat al-qaṣaṣ al-sha¿bî: fihrist al-motîf (Systems of Classification of Folk Narratives: The Motif-Index)," *al-Funûn al-Shâbia [Sha¿biyyah]*, Vol. 2, no. 9 (Cairo, June, 1969), pp. 81-91.

__________, "nuẓum fahrasat al-qaṣaṣ al-sha¿bî: fihrist al-ṭirâz (Systems of Classification of Folk Narratives: The Type-Index)," *al-Funûn al-Shâbia*, Vol. 2, no. 8 (Cairo, March, 1969), pp. 29-40.

__________, "nuẓum wa 'ansâq fahrasat al-ma'thûr al-sha¿bî (Methods and Systems for the Classification of Folk Traditions)," *al-Ma'thûrât al-Sha¿biyyah*, Vol. 3, no. 12, (Doha, October, 1988), pp. 77-109.

__________, "The Oral Connections of *the Arabian Nights*," in *The Arabian Nights Encyclopedia*, Marzolph et al. eds. (2004), pp. 9-13.

__________, "Oral Traditional Tales and the Thousand Nights and a Night: The Demographic Factor," in *The Telling of Stories: Approaches to a Traditional Craft*. Morton Nøjgaard et. al, eds. (Odense, Denmark: Odense University Press, 1990), pp. 63-117.

__________, "Psychologically-Based Criteria for Classification by Motif and Tale Type," in *Journal of Folklore Research*, Vol. 34, No. 3, (Bloomington, 1997), pp. 233-243.

__________, Review of the Peter Gilet's *Vladimir Propp and the Universal Folktale: recommissioning an old paradigm--story as initiation*. (New York: 1998). *Asian Folklore Studies* (Nazan University, Nagoya, Japan), Vol. 61, (2001) No. 1: pp. 153-57.

________, "A Response [to H. Jason's Review of *Folk Traditions of the Arab World: A Guide to Motif Classification*," *Asian Folklore Studies*, Vol. 57, No. 2 (Nagoya, Japan: 1998), pp. 345-55.

__________, "Sentiment, Genre, and Tale Typology: Meaning in Middle Eastern and African Tales," in *Papers III*. The 8th Congress for the International Society for Folk Narrative Research, R. Kvideland and T. Selberg, eds., pp. 255-283 (Bergen, Norway, 1985). Also (revised and expanded) in *al-Ma'thûrât al-Sha*[c]*biyyah*, Vol. 1 (Doha, Qatar, 1986), no. 3, pp. 41-51.

__________, *Tales Arab Women Tell and the Behavioral Patterns they Portray*. (Bloomington: Indiana University Press, 1999).

__________, "Towards A Demographically Oriented Type Index for Tales of the Arab World," *Cahiers de Littérature Orale*, n°. 23: *La tradition au présent (Monde arabe)*, Praline Gay-Para, ed. (Paris, 1988).

Spitta, Wilhelm, *Grammatik des arabischen Vulgärdialektes von Ägypten*. (Leipzig, 1880).

Thackston, W. M., tr. ed., *The Tales of the Prophets of al-Kisa'i* (Boston: Twayne, 1978).

Tha¿labî (al-), Aḥmad Ibn Muḥammad, *Kitâb qiṣaṣ al-'anbiyâ' (The Book of Prophets' Stories)*. (Cairo, Ben Shaqrûn, n.d.).

Thompson, Stith., *Motif Index of Folk-Literature*, 6 vols. (Bloomington: Indiana University Press, 1955-58).

Uther, Hans-Jörg, *The Types of International Folktales: A Classification and Bibliography. Folklore Fellows Communications* No. 284. Helsinki, 2004.

Von Sydow, C.W., "Das Märchen als indogermanische Tradition (Auszug) übertragen von Lily Weiser," *Niederdeutsche Zeitschrift für Volkskunde*, Vol. 4 (Leipzig, 1926).

Abbreviations and Signs: A Note on Data Presentation

Primary Sources

Alf:	*Alf Laylah wa Laylah*. 4 vols., Maktabat al-Jumhûriyyh: Cairo, n.d.
Burton:	*Arabian Nights: The Book of the Thousand Nights and a Night*, Richard F. Burton, tr. ed., Vols. 1-10, London, 1894.

Secondary References

AT/AaTh:	Antti Aarne and Stith Thompson's *The Types of the Folktale*: A Classification and Bibliography, *Folklore Fellows Communications* No. 184. Helsinki, 1961, 1964.
ATU:	Hans-Jörg Uther, *The Types of International Folktales: A Classification and Bibliography*. *Folklore Fellows Communications* No. 284. Helsinki, 2004.
ANE:*[91]	*The Arabian Nights Encyclopedia*, Ulrich Marzolph, Richard van Leeuwen, et al. eds. Santa Barbara, 2004.
Chauvin:*	Victor Chauvin, *Bibliographie des ouvrages arabes ou relatifs aux arabes: publiés dans l'Europe chrétienne de 1810 à 1885*. 12 vols. Liège, 1892-1922.
DOTTI:	Hasan El-Shamy, *Types of the Folktale in the Arab World: a Demographically Oriented Approach*. Bloomington, 2004.
GMC:	Hasan El-Shamy, *Folk Traditions of the Arab World: A Guide to Motif Classification*, 2 vols., Bloomington, 1995.
Motif:	Stith Thompson, *Motif-Index of Folk Literature*, 6 vols., Bloomington, 1955-58, first published between 1932-36; or Hasan M. El-Shamy, *Folk Traditions of the Arab World: A Guide to Motif Classification*, 2 vols., Bloomington, 1995.
PSAE:	Gaston C. Maspero, *Popular Stories of Ancient Egypt*, Hasan El-Shamy, ed. ABC-CLIO, Santa Barbara, 2002, and Oxford, 2004.

Editorial

§:	(Section sign) at the end of a number indicates a new motif added by Hasan El-Shamy to the Thompson motif system or a new tale-type added to the Aarne-Thompson tale-type system. (This replaces the dysfunctional practice of indicating an addition by an asterisk to the left of the number).
‡:	(Double dagger)indicates a newer motif developed or added after the publication of El-Shamy, *Folk Traditions of the Arab World* (1995).
(xxx):	Item (theme) is not included.
[??]/[!!]:	Doubtful or ambiguous.
,-():	Comparative or explanatory data associated with the reference cited; such comments are placed after the reference to which the note pertains. This innovation facilitates digital classification.

. [91]*Both Chauvin and *ANE* are encyclopedic works that provide resumés of the stories (in French and English, respectively). They are cited chronologically.

Motifs of *The Thousand and One Nights*

A. MYTHOLOGICAL AND RELATED BELIEF MOTIFS

A5.5§, ‡Creation of the universe for the sake of a certain (sacred) person—(e.g., Abraham, Mohammed, Zoroaster/Zardusht). (Cf. A6.3.0.1§).
Bulûqiya: *Alf* III 23-24; Burton V 306. Chauvin VII 54 No. 77; *ANE* 130-32 No. 177.□

A5.5.1§, ‡Creation of the universe for the sake of Prophet Mohammed. (Cf. V215§).
Bulûqiya: *Alf* III 23-24; Burton V 306. Chauvin VII 54 No. 77; *ANE* 130-32 No. 177.□

A5.5.1.1§, ‡'Had it not been for Prophet Mohammed there would have been no universe' (paradise, hell, sky, earth, sun, moon, etc.).
Bulûqiya: *Alf* III 23-24; Burton V 306. Chauvin VII 54 No. 77; *ANE* 130-32 No. 177.□

A6.1§, ‡Humans (*'ince*), like jinn, were created solely to worship God. (Cf. V248.2§).
Tawaddud: Slavegirl Sold and Regained: *Alf* II 312; Burton V 212,-("serve me [God]"). Chauvin VII 117-19 No. 387; *ANE* 408-10 No. 157.□

A6.2§, ‡Purpose of life is to worship God.
Spy, First Maiden/¿Umar al-Nu¿mân: *Alf* I 219; Burton II 196. *ANE* 432 No. 39/passim.□

A6.3.0.1§, ‡Women were created solely for men. (Cf. A5.5§, C160.0.1§).
Hasan of Basrah: *Alf* IV 3, 50; Burton VIII 42. Chauvin VII 29-35 No. 212A; *ANE* 207-10 No. 230.□

A54.3§, Eblis (Lucifer) as rebel angel. See: *GMC*.
Bulûqiya: *Alf* III 33; Burton V 320. Chauvin VII 54 No. 77; *ANE* 130-32 No. 177.□

A54.3.1.1§, Eblis refuses to prostrate himself before Adam. See: *GMC*. (Cf. A1213.2§, C62.5.1.1§).
Bulûqiya: *Alf* III 33; Burton V 320. Chauvin VII 54 No. 77; *ANE* 130-32 No. 177.□

A54.3.3§, ‡Arrogance (conceit) caused angel Eblis to become Satan. (Cf. A604.3.1.0.1§).
King Jalî¿âd and Shimâs: *Alf* IV 157; Burton IX 81. Chauvin VI 9-11 No. 184; *ANE* 237-38 No. 236.□

A63.5.1, Satan seduces Adam to sin because he is jealous of him. See: *GMC*.
King Jalî¿âd and Shimâs: *Alf* IV 157,-(*hasad*); Burton IX 81,-(envy). Chauvin VI 9-11 No. 184; *ANE* 237-38 No. 236.□

A64§, ‡Spying satan(s): devil attempt(s) to learn heavenly secrets by eavesdropping on sky-worlds. See: *DOTTI*. (Cf. A157.8.1§, F69§, K1164§).
Qamar al-Zamân and Budûr: *Alf* II 71,-(jinni-woman/passim); Burton III 223,-(listen by stealth to the converse of the angels). Chauvin V 204-12 No. 120; *ANE* 341-45 No. 61.□

A65§, ‡Satan's *waswasah* (instigation) causes sinning. (Cf. G303.9.4).
King ¿Umar al-Nu¿mân and Sons: *Alf* I 182; Burton II 123. Chauvin VI 112-24 No. 277; *ANE* 430-34 No. 39;
Hammâd: Treacherous Bedouin: *Alf* II 21-022,-(Iblis); Burton III 111. Chauvin VI 124 n. 1 No. 277; *ANE* 200 No. 43;
Ma¿rûf the Cobbler: *Alf* IV 315; Burton X 51,-(Iblis's prompting). Chauvin VI 81-82 No. 250; *ANE* 291-93 No. 262.□

A102.0.1.1§, ‡Opposite attributes of God (e.g., forgiver-vengeful, honorer-abaser, etc.). (Cf. Z183.0.1§).
Crow and Viper: *Alf* IV 141; Burton IX 47. Chauvin II 219 No. 152/5; *ANE* 162 No. 240.□

A102.0.2.1§, ‡Mankind created to be dependent on (needy for) God.
King Jalî¿âd and Shimâs: *Alf* IV 157; Burton IX 80. Chauvin VI 9-11 No. 184; *ANE* 237-38 No. 236.□

A102.1.2§, ‡Certain things only God knows. (Cf. H502.1).
King ¿Umar al-Nu¿mân and Sons: *Alf* I 208,-cf./(why God willed an incest); Burton II 175. Chauvin VI 112-24 No. 277; *ANE* 430-34 No. 39;
Tawaddud: Slavegirl Sold and Regained: *Alf* II 310,-(number of heavens's gates); Burton V 207 Chauvin VII 117-19 No. 387; *ANE* 408-10 No. 157;
Tawaddud: Slavegirl Sold and Regained: *Alf* III 2,-(five); Burton V 230-31. Chauvin VII 117-19 No. 387; *ANE* 408-10 No. 157.□

A102.1.2.1§, ‡Five things known only to God: Time of End of World (*al-sâ¿ah*), when and where rain will occur, [gender of] what is in wombs, one's future earnings, place of one's death. (Cf. A630.2.1§, H830§).
Tawaddud: Slavegirl Sold and Regained: *Alf* III 2; Burton V 230. Chauvin VII 117-19 No. 387; *ANE* 408-10 No. 157.□

A102.4.0.1§, ‡The Hand of Omnipotence (*yad al-Qudrah*). (Cf. A611.0.2§).
Tawaddud: Slavegirl Sold and Regained: *Alf* III 5; Burton V 237. Chauvin VII 117-19 No. 387; *ANE* 408-10 No. 157.□

A102.4.2§, ‡God: 'King of kings,' 'Lord of lords,' (or the like).
Ma¿rûf the Cobbler: *Alf* IV 308-9,-(poem); Burton X 35. Chauvin VI 81-82 No. 250; *ANE* 291-93 No. 262.□

A102.6.0.1§, ‡The One whose existence has no beginning and no end (*al-Sarmadiyy*, i.e., God).
City of Brass: *Alf* III 135,-(formulaic); Burton VI 115. Chauvin V 32-35 No. 16; *ANE* 146-50 No. 180;
Sayf al-Mulûk: *Alf* III 302,-cf.; Burton VIII 6,-(the First, without beginning, and the Last, without end). Chauvin VII 64-73 No. 348; *ANE* 362-64 No. 229.□

A102.6.1§, ‡'The [eternally] Living-One' (*al-Ḥayy*).
Hasan of Basrah: *Alf* IV 55,-(Ever-lasting/formulaic); Burton VIII 155. Chauvin VII 29-35 No. 212A; *ANE* 207-10 No. 230;
Shahriyâr and Shahrzâd: *Alf* IV 318,-(formulaic); Burton X 55. Chauvin V 190-91 No. 111/pt.; *ANE* 371 No. 1.□

A102.6.1.1§, ‡"'*Dahr* (Time)' is 'God'" (i.e., they are one and the same: euphemistically). (Cf. C494.1§, Z122.7§).
Tawaddud: Slavegirl Sold and Regained: *Alf* III 4; Burton V 230. Chauvin VII 117-19 No. 387; *ANE* 408-10 No. 157.□

A102.13, ‡Loving kindness of God. (Cf. T1.3.1§).
King Jalî¿âd and Shimâs: *Alf* IV 157, 59,-(toward man); Burton IX 80,-(Allah loveth mankind). Chauvin VI 9-11 No. 184; *ANE* 237-38 No. 236.□

A102.13.2§, ‡Equanimity (*ḥilm*) of God.
Jullanâr of the Sea: *Alf* III 265,-(at unbelievers); Burton VII 298,-(long suffering). Chauvin V 147-51 No. 73; *ANE* 248-51 No. 227.□

A102.14.1§, ‡Mercy of God.
King Jalî¿âd and Shimâs: *Alf* IV 158; Burton IX 81. Chauvin VI 9-11 No. 184; *ANE* 237-38 No. 236.□

A102.14.3§, ‡Forgiveness of God. See: *DOTTI*. (Cf. V21, V315.3§, V441).
Wolf and Fox: *Alf* II 30; Burton III 132,-("Verily, the Lord pardoneth his erring servant ..."). Chauvin II 227 No. 6; *ANE* 450 No. 47;
Qamar al-Zamân and Budûr: *Alf* II 110,-(*niṭâq 'aflâk al-maghfirah*/'the sphere of the constellations of forgiveness'); Burton III 305,-(heaven's forgiveness). Chauvin V 204-12 No. 120; *ANE* 341-45 No. 61;
Mock Caliph/¿Alî al-Jawharî: *Alf* II 200; Burton IV 148,-(forgiveness of Almighty Allah). Chauvin V 99-100 No. 174; *ANE* 304-5 No. 73;
¿Alî Shâr and Zumurrud: *Alf* II 232; Burton IV 220,-(forgiveness of Allah). Chauvin V 89-91 No. 28; *ANE* 100-1 No. 82;
Water-carrier and Goldsmith's Wife: *Alf* II 286,-cf.; Burton V 90,-(forgiveness of the Lord). Chauvin VI 192 No. 361; *ANE* 444 No. 122;
Angel of Death and Proud King: *Alf* III 9,-(place for *maghfirah*); Burton V 248. Chauvin VI 183-84 No. 349/[pt. 1]; *ANE* 104 No. 158.□

A102.14.3.1.1§, ‡Angels with forms of terrestrial creatures plead with God to forgive sins of living beings in their forms (e.g., human's, animal's, bird's, etc.). (Cf. A494.0.1.1§, V231.1, V231.7.1§).
Bulûqiya: *Alf* III 35; Burton V 323. Chauvin VII 54 No. 77; *ANE* 130-32 No. 177.□

A102.16, Justice of god. (Cf. M400.2§).
Lover Who Feigned Himself a Thief: *Alf* II 205; Burton IV 156,-('God is not unjust towards mankind'). Chauvin VII 134-35 No. 403; *ANE* 272 No. 76.□

A102.17.0.1§, ‡Natural disasters (catastrophes) as expression of God's wrath. See: *DOTTI*.
Hasan of Basrah: *Alf* III 307,-(storm due to injustice); Burton VIII 17. Chauvin VII 29-35 No. 212A; *ANE* 207-10 No. 230.□

A157.8.1§, ‡Shooting star destroys satan (devil, demon) flying near (spying on) heavens. See: *DOTTI*. (Cf. Q552.1.0.1§).
Nûr al-Dîn ¿Alî and Son: *Alf* I 73,-(afrit); Burton I 224. Chauvin VI 102-6 No. 270; *ANE* 317-19 No. 22;
King's Favorite Son and Ogress: *Alf* III 144,-cf./(claim); Burton VI 141. Chauvin VIII 40-41 No. 8B; *ANE* 264 No. 188.□

A171.4§, ‡God answers questions. (Dialogue between God and a creature, usually a sacred person). See: *DOTTI*.
Bulûqiya: *Alf* III 36; Burton V 324. Chauvin VII 54 No. 77; *ANE* 130-32 No. 177.□

A182.3.0.1.2§, ‡God speaks from heaven to Moses (at the bush).
Tawaddud: Slavegirl Sold and Regained: *Alf* III 5,-cf.; Burton V 239. Chauvin VII 117-19 No. 387; *ANE* 408-10 No. 157.□

A182.3.9.1§, ‡God causes knowledge to evade mortal—(*tams*).
Anîs al-Jalîs: *Alf* I 129; Burton II 9. Chauvin V 120-24 No. 58; *ANE* 316-17 No. 35.□

A182.3.9.2§, ‡God erases knowledge from mortal's mind—(*naskh*: abrogation).
Tawaddud: Slavegirl Sold and Regained: *Alf* II 305, 311,-cf.,/(*naskh*); Burton V 194, 209,-cf./(abrogation). Chauvin VII 117-19 No. 387; *ANE* 408-10 No. 157.□

A185.9.1§, ‡Adam violated his covenant with God. (Cf. W154.29.0.1§).
Bulûqiya: *Alf* III 34-35; Burton V 322. Chauvin VII 54 No. 77; *ANE* 130-32 No. 177.□

A185.13, ‡God puts mortal to test. See: *DOTTI*.
Hermit Tempted by Angel: *Alf* II 27; Burton III 126. Chauvin II 226 No. 3; *ANE* 221 No. 45/pt. 2.□

A189.7.1§, ‡'God forgets no one': every creature gets a predestined livelihood. See: *DOTTI*. (Cf. A604.5.2§, J1014.0.2.1§, J2068.3§).
King Jalî¿âd and Shimâs: *Alf* IV 155,-(man-beast); Burton IX 32-34. Chauvin VI 9-11 No. 184; *ANE* 237-38 No. 236.□

A189.7.3§, New life comes with its livelihood. See: *DOTTI*; *GMC*. (Cf. A661.0.1.1.4§, N100.1.2.1§).
Landsman ¿Abdallah and Merman ¿Abdallah: *Alf* IV 198; Burton IX 165,-(xxx). Chauvin V 6-7 No. 3; *ANE* 65-66 No. 256.□

A194.2.1§, 'God may give respite, but never neglect'. See: *DOTTI*; *GMC*. (Cf. Q550.0.1§, Q550.0.3§).
Fisherman and Afrit: Ingratitude: *Alf* I 23; Burton I 62. Chauvin VI 26 No. 197; *ANE* 183-84 No. 8.□

A418.2.1§, ‡Angel of Qâf mountain chain. (He has control of the Mountain in his grip). (Cf. A1145.5§, F709.5.2.1§).
Bulûqiya: *Alf* III 35; Burton V 323. Chauvin VII 54 No. 77; *ANE* 130-32 No. 177.□

A462.3§, ‡'God is beautiful and likes beauty'. (Cf. J2203.1§).
Jeweler's Wife and Qamar al-Zamân: *Alf* IV 238,-(poem); Burton IX 249. Chauvin V 212-14 No. 121; *ANE* 345-47 No. 260.□

A494.0.1.1§, ‡Angel of livelihoods intercedes with God on behalf of living beings whose form(s) he assumes (e.g., human's, animal's, bird's, etc.). (Cf. A102.14.3.1.1§, V232).
Bulûqiya: *Alf* III 35,-cf.; Burton V 323. Chauvin VII 54 No. 77; *ANE* 130-32 No. 177.□

A498, ‡Deity of stone.
Ḥâtim's Hospitality: *Alf* II 181; Burton IV 95-96. Chauvin VI 49 No. 215; *ANE* 216 No. 64.□

A512.3.1§, Christ as son of God. See: *GMC*.
Nûr al-Dîn and Maryam: *Alf* IV 128; Burton IX 15. Chauvin V 52-54 No. 271; *ANE* 98-99 No. 233.□

A517§, ‡Culture-hero as ruler of the entire world (cosmocrator)—(Alexander, Solomon, etc.). See: *PSAE*. (Cf. D1335.5.2.0.1§).
Bulûqiya: *Alf* III 24,-(Solomon); Burton V 308. Chauvin VII 54 No. 77; *ANE* 130-32 No. 177.□

A573.1§, ‡'Men of the unknown' (*rijâl al-ghayb*): clique (community) of deceased deified humans believed to be living in Paradise. (Cf. V1.1.2.2§).
King ¿Umar al-Nu¿mân and Sons: *Alf* I 226; Burton II 212,-(the Invisible Controuls). Chauvin VI 112-24 No. 277; *ANE* 430-34 No. 39.□

A583§, ‡Culture-hero as demon slayer. (He kills devil, dragon, evil spirit, and the like).
Abû Muḥammad Lazybones: *Alf* II 215,-(al-Khiḍr/presumably); Burton IV 175 n. 1. Chauvin VI 64-67 No. 233; *ANE* 71-73 No. 78.□

A604.3§, *maktûb, muqaddar, qismah* (written, predestined, kismet)—one's fated lot. See: *DOTTI*; *GMC*; *PSAE*. (Cf. N101.0.1.1§, U169.3§).
Ḥammâd: Treacherous Bedouin: *Alf* II 20,-(poem/*qaḍâ*); Burton III 111,-(flight from doom). Chauvin VI 124 n. 1 No. 277; *ANE* 200 No. 43;
Mock Caliph/¿Alî al-Jawharî: *Alf* II 200,-(sinning,/is "*mastûr*"); Burton IV 148,-(written in the Book of Destiny). Chauvin V 99-100 No. 174; *ANE* 304-5 No. 73;
Sayf al-Mulûk: *Alf* III 282; Burton VII 337,-(written from all eternity). Chauvin VII 64-73 No. 348; *ANE* 362-64 No. 229.□

A604.3.1§, ‡Origin of sinning (depravity). (Cf. U230.0.3§, V315.0.1§).
King Jalî¿âd and Shimâs: *Alf* IV 157; Burton IX 80-81. Chauvin VI 9-11 No. 184; *ANE* 237-38 No. 236.□

A604.3.1.0.1§, ‡Iblis (Satan) as the first sinner. (Cf. A54.3.3§).
King Jalî¿âd and Shimâs: *Alf* IV 157; Burton IX 81. Chauvin VI 9-11 No. 184; *ANE* 237-38 No. 236.□

A604.5.2§, ‡Creation of livelihoods. (Cf. A189.7.1§).
Fish and Crab: *Alf* IV 140; Burton IX 44. Chauvin II 219 No. 152/4; *ANE* 185-86 No. 239.□

A604.5.2.1§, ‡Livelihoods created before 'things' (creatures). (Cf. J2068.3§).
King Jalî¿âd and Shimâs: *Alf* IV 139; Burton IX 44. Chauvin VI 9 No. 184; *ANE* 237-38 No. 236;
Fish and Crab: *Alf* IV 140; Burton IX 44. Chauvin II 219 No. 152/4; *ANE* 185-86 No. 239.□

A604.5.2.2§, ‡Lifespan tied to predestined livelihood: creature dies when preordained livelihood has been exhausted. See: *DOTTI*. (Cf. A661.0.1.1.4§).
Birds, Beasts, and Carpenter: *Alf* II 26,-(*'istîfâ' al-rizq*); Burton III 124,-(accomplishing predestined livelihood). Chauvin II 225-26 No. 1; *ANE* 126 No. 44;
Poisoning from Flying Kite: *Alf* III 173-74,-(*ḥayyah*/viper); Burton VI 201-2,-("serpent"). Chauvin 8: 33-34 No. 1; *ANE* 160-61 No. 181/passim.□

A608§, ‡Determination of *al-ḥalâl* (the licit, legitimate) and of *al-ḥarâm* (the illicit, sinful) for man. (Cf. C1.1§).
King Jalî¿âd and Shimâs: *Alf* IV 159; Burton IX 85. Chauvin VI 9-11 No. 184; *ANE* 237-38 No. 236.□

A611.0.1.1§, Creator's command: "Be!"—it becomes. (Cf. Z119.0.2§, Z183.2.1.1§).
Anîs al-Jalîs: *Alf* I 126-27,-(poem: creation of beautiful eyes); Burton II 3. Chauvin V 120-24 No. 58; *ANE* 316-17 No. 35;
¿Alî ibn Bakkâr: *Alf* II 42,-(poem: creation of beautiful eyes); Burton III 163. Chauvin V 153 No. 76; *ANE* 92-93 No. 60;
Tawaddud: Slavegirl Sold and Regained: *Alf* III 5; Burton V 237, 240. Chauvin VII 117-19 No. 387; *ANE* 408-10 No. 157;
Conversion of Princess by Khawwâṣ: *Alf* III 15; Burton V 286. Chauvin V 239 No. 139; *ANE* 145 No. 171.□

A611.0.2§, ‡Creation by 'The Hand of Omnipotence (*yad al-Qudrah*)'. (God created certain things via this divine entity). (Cf. A102.4.0.1§).
Tawaddud: Slavegirl Sold and Regained: *Alf* III 5; Burton V 237. Chauvin VII 117-19 No. 387; *ANE* 408-10 No. 157.□

A611.0.4§, ‡God—though omnipotent—creates one thing from another. (Cf. A1440.5.1§).
King Jalî¿âd and Shimâs: *Alf* IV 156,-(He does not create a thing except from another [thing]); Burton IX 77,-("He shall create naught but from something"). Chauvin VI 9-11 No. 184; *ANE* 237-38 No. 236.□

A630.1.1§, ‡Adam created from clay (mud), mud from foam (*zabad*), foam from sea, sea from darkness, darkness from bull, bull from whale, whale from rock, rock from ruby (gem), ruby from water, water from [God's] Omnipotence (*al-Qudrah*). (Cf. A2810.1§).
Tawaddud: Slavegirl Sold and Regained: *Alf* III 5; Burton V 240. Chauvin VII 117-19 No. 387; *ANE* 408-10 No. 157.□

A630.2§, ‡Things God created prior to creating man (creatures, *al-khalq*). (Cf. H502.1).
Tawaddud: Slavegirl Sold and Regained: *Alf* III 5; Burton V 237. Chauvin VII 117-19 No. 387; *ANE* 408-10 No. 157.□

A630.2.1§, ‡Five things created before Creation: (water, dust/dirt, sleep, darkness, fruits). (Cf. A102.1.2.1§).
Tawaddud: Slavegirl Sold and Regained: *Alf* III 5; Burton V 237. Chauvin VII 117-19 No. 387; *ANE* 408-10 No. 157.□

A650.1.2§, ‡The world is suspended within the universe by a celestial viper (named Falaq). (Cf. A671.0.1.1.4§).
Bulûqiya: *Alf* III 36-37,-cf.; Burton V 325. Chauvin VII 54 No. 77; *ANE* 130-32 No. 177.□

A651.1.4, Seven heavens. See: *GMC*.
Tawaddud: Slavegirl Sold and Regained: *Alf* III 5; Burton V 239. Chauvin VII 117-19 No. 387; *ANE* 408-10 No. 157.□

A651.3, ‡Worlds above and below.
Bulûqiya: *Alf* III 35-36; Burton V 324. Chauvin VII 54 No. 77; *ANE* 130-32 No. 177.□

A652.3.1§, *Sidrat-al-Muntahâ*: the Lote-tree of the Extremity of the universe. (Zizyphus lotus). See: *GMC*.
Bulûqiya: *Alf* III 79; Burton V 393 n. 2,-(Zizyphus lotus). Chauvin VII 54 No. 77; *ANE* 130-32 No. 177.□

A661.0.1.0.1§, ‡Doors (gates) of the sky.
Tawaddud: Slavegirl Sold and Regained: *Alf* II 310,-(doors); Burton V 207. Chauvin VII 117-19 No. 387; *ANE* 408-10 No. 157;
Three Wishes: *Alf* III 162; Burton VI 181. Chauvin VIII 51-52 No. 19; *ANE* 419-20 No. 199;
Ibrâhîm and Jamîlah: *Alf* IV 225,-(passim); Burton IX 221. Chauvin VI 52-53 No. 218; *ANE* 227-29 No. 258.□

A661.0.1.0.2§, ‡Paradise has several gates. (Usually seven).
Tâj al-Mulûk: *Alf* I 292,-(passim/rhetorical); Burton III 15. Chauvin V 126-28 No. 60; *ANE* 406-8 No. 40;
Tawaddud: Slavegirl Sold and Regained: *Alf* II 307,-(eight); Burton V 198. Chauvin VII 117-19 No. 387; *ANE* 408-10 No. 157.□

A661.0.1.1.4§, ‡'Door of Livelihood': from heavens to Earth. A creature's preordained sustenance is sent down from heaven via that door; it is shut when that creature's lifetime expires. (Cf. A189.7.3§, A604.5.2.2§, N100.1.1§).
Tawaddud: Slavegirl Sold and Regained: *Alf* II 310; Burton V 207. Chauvin VII 117-19 No. 387; *ANE* 408-10 No. 157.□

A661.0.1.1.5§, ‡'Door of Deeds': from Earth to heaven. A person's deeds ascend to heaven and enter via that door; it is shut when that person dies.
Tawaddud: Slavegirl Sold and Regained: *Alf* II 310; Burton V 207. Chauvin VII 117-19 No. 387; *ANE* 408-10 No. 157.□

A661.0.1.3.1§, Archangel Ruḍwân as porter of heaven. See: *DOTTI*; *GMC*. (Cf. A671.1.1§, V247.0.1§).
Tâj al-Mulûk: *Alf* I 292,-(passim/simile), 295,-(passim/simile); Burton III 15, 23,-(Rizwan). Chauvin V 126-28 No. 60; *ANE* 406-8 No. 40;
¿Alî Shâr and Zumurrud: *Alf* II 220,-(poem/passim); Burton IV 195. Chauvin V 89-91 No. 28; *ANE* 100-1 No. 82;
Nûr al-Dîn and Maryam: *Alf* IV 80, 81,-(passim/simile); Burton VIII 265. Chauvin V 52-54 No. 271; *ANE* 98-99 No. 233.□

A661.0.5.2§, Soul-path (*aṣ-ṣirâṭ al-mustaqîm*): sharper than razor's edge, thinner than a hair. See: *GMC*.

Tawaddud: Slavegirl Sold and Regained: *Alf* III 6; Burton V 241. Chauvin VII 117-19 No. 387; *ANE* 408-10 No. 157.□

A661.0.5.2.2§, ‡Traversing the Soul-path (*ṣirâṭ*) requires 3000 years descending, 1000 years ascending, and 1000 years of leveled travel.
Tawaddud: Slavegirl Sold and Regained: *Alf* III 6; Burton V 241. Chauvin VII 117-19 No. 387; *ANE* 408-10 No. 157.□

A661.1.1.1§, ‡Inhabitants of Paradise divided into strata. See: *DOTTI*; *GMC*.
Jewish Tray-maker and Temptress: *Alf* III 14,-cf./(degrees); Burton V 268. Chauvin VI 187-88 No. 354; *ANE* 169 No. 166.□

A665.0.2§, God's omnipotence supports the sky 'without columns'. See: *GMC*.
¿Abdallah ibn Fâḍil: Treacherous Brothers: *Alf* IV 276; Burton IX 324. Chauvin V 2-4 No. 2; *ANE* 63-65 No. 261.□

A671.0.1.1.4§, ‡Hell is presently located inside the belly of celestial viper (Midgard Serpent, or the like). (Cf. A650.1.2§, B3§).
Bulûqiya: *Alf* III 37; Burton V 325. Chauvin VII 54 No. 77; *ANE* 130-32 No. 177.□

A671.0.5.1§, Hell has seven doors (gates). See: *GMC*. (Cf. A661.0.1.0.2§).
Tawaddud: Slavegirl Sold and Regained: *Alf* III 6,-(poem); Burton V 240. Chauvin VII 117-19 No. 387; *ANE* 408-10 No. 157.□

A671.1.1§, Archangel Mâlik: porter (guardian) of hell. (Cf. A661.0.1.3.1§, V247.0.1§).
Tâj al-Mulûk: *Alf* I 293,-(xxx); Burton III 20,-(poem). Chauvin V 126-28 No. 60; *ANE* 406-8 No. 40.□

A671.2.4.14§, Seven strata of hell's fires. See: *DOTTI*; *GMC*.
Bulûqiya: *Alf* III 32-33; Burton V 318,-(stages). Chauvin VII 54 No. 77; *ANE* 130-32 No. 177.□

A671.2.9, ‡Scorpions in hell. (Cf. A2145.7.1§).
Bulûqiya: *Alf* III 33; Burton V 319. Chauvin VII 54 No. 77; *ANE* 130-32 No. 177.□

A679§, Interrogative angels (Nâkir and Nakîr, Munkir and Nakrân, etc.) question the dead at time of burial. See: *DOTTI*; *GMC*.
Abû Qîr and Abû Ṣîr: *Alf* IV 197,-(passim/simile); Burton IX 163. Chauvin V 15-17 No. 10; *ANE* 75-77 No. 255;
Ma¿rûf the Cobbler: *Alf* IV 313-14,—(passim/Munkir and Nakîr); Burton X 47. Chauvin VI 81-82 No. 250; *ANE* 291-93 No. 262.□

A684.1.1§, ‡Devilish fruit (*zaqqûm*) as food in hell.
King ¿Umar al-Nu¿mân and Sons: *Alf* I 214,-cf./(poem/simile, *zaqqûm*/*ghislîn*); Burton II 186,/(xxx). Chauvin VI 112-24 No. 277; *ANE* 430-34 No. 39;
Man from Yaman and Six Salve-girls: Flyting: *Alf* II 249,-(simile, *zaqqûm*); Burton IV 259. Chauvin VI 151 No. 313; *ANE* 289-90 No. 84.□

A684.2.1§, ‡Pus and boiling water as drinks in hell (ghassâq/ghislîn, *ḥamîm*/*ghislîn*).
King ¿Umar al-Nu¿mân and Sons: *Alf* I 214,-cf./(poem: *zaqqûm*/*ghislîn*); Burton II 186,-(xxx). Chauvin VI 112-24 No. 277; *ANE* 430-34 No. 39.□

A694.0.2§, Paradise in Islam.
Tâj al-Mulûk: *Alf* I 293-94; Burton III 19 n. 1. Chauvin V 126-28 No. 60; *ANE* 111-13 No. 40.□

A694.3§, ‡Paradise as garden (Garden of Eden). (Cf. A671.0.5.1§, F818).
Anîs al-Jalîs: *Alf* I 135-37,-cf.; Burton II 24. Chauvin V 120-24 No. 58; *ANE* 316-17 No. 35;
Budûr and Jubayr ibn ¿Umayr: *Alf* II 236,-(xxx); Burton IV 232. Chauvin VII 93-94 No. 374; *ANE* 243-44 No. 83;
Tawaddud: Slavegirl Sold and Regained: *Alf* III 5,-(creation of Paradise); Burton V 237,-(creation of garden of Eden). Chauvin VII 117-19 No. 387; *ANE* 408-10 No. 157;
Bulûqiya: *Alf* III 28,-(simile); Burton V 313. Chauvin VII 54 No. 77; *ANE* 130-32 No. 177;
Nûr al-Dîn and Maryam: *Alf* IV 80-82,-cf./(garden as paradise); Burton VIII 266-73. Chauvin V 52-54 No. 271; *ANE* 98-99 No. 233.□

A704.0.1§, ‡First sky is 'lowest': closest to Earth.
Qamar al-Zamân and Budûr: *Alf* II 71,-(passim); Burton III 224,-(lowest of the heavens). Chauvin V 204-12 No. 120; *ANE* 341-45 No. 61.□

A768.4§, ‡Types and functions of the stars.
Tawaddud: Slavegirl Sold and Regained: *Alf* III 3; Burton V 233. Chauvin VII 117-19 No. 387; *ANE* 408-10 No. 157.□

A768.4.1§, ‡Stars anchored to the lowest sky like lanterns—they illuminate Earth.
Tawaddud: Slavegirl Sold and Regained: *Alf* III 3; Burton V 233. Chauvin VII 117-19 No. 387; *ANE* 408-10 No. 157.□

A768.4.2§, ‡Stars with which satans (devils) are shot if they eavesdrop on heavens. (Cf. A157.8.1§, F1021.2.4§).
Tawaddud: Slavegirl Sold and Regained: *Alf* III 3; Burton V 233. Chauvin VII 117-19 No. 387; *ANE* 408-10 No. 157.□

A768.4.3§, ‡Stars suspended in the air (space)—they illuminate the seas and their contents.
Tawaddud: Slavegirl Sold and Regained: *Alf* III 3; Burton V 233. Chauvin VII 117-19 No. 387; *ANE* 408-10 No. 157.□

A785§, ‡'Residence' (location) of major planets within the seven skies.
Tawaddud: Slavegirl Sold and Regained: *Alf* III 3; Burton V 233. Chauvin VII 117-19 No. 387; *ANE* 408-10 No. 157.□

A785.1§, ‡Saturn (Zuḥal) resides in the Seventh Sky.
Tawaddud: Slavegirl Sold and Regained: *Alf* III 3; Burton V 233. Chauvin VII 117-19 No. 387; *ANE* 408-10 No. 157.□

A785.2§, ‡Jupiter (al-Mushtarî/Mushturâ) resides in the Sixth Sky.
Tawaddud: Slavegirl Sold and Regained: *Alf* III 3; Burton V 233. Chauvin VII 117-19 No. 387; *ANE* 408-10 No. 157.□

A785.3§, ‡Mars (al-Marrîkh/Mirrîkh) resides in the Fifth Sky.
Tawaddud: Slavegirl Sold and Regained: *Alf* III 3; Burton V 233. Chauvin VII 117-19 No. 387; *ANE* 408-10 No. 157.□

A785.4§, ‡Sun (al-Shams) resides in the Fourth Sky.
Tawaddud: Slavegirl Sold and Regained: *Alf* III 3; Burton V 233. Chauvin VII 117-19 No. 387; *ANE* 408-10 No. 157.□

A785.5§, ‡Venus (al-Zahrah) resides in the Third Sky.
Tawaddud: Slavegirl Sold and Regained: *Alf* III 3; Burton V 233. Chauvin VII 117-19 No. 387; *ANE* 408-10 No. 157.□

A785.6§, ‡Mercury (¿Uṭârid) resides in the Second Sky.
Tawaddud: Slavegirl Sold and Regained: *Alf* III 3; Burton V 233. Chauvin VII 117-19 No. 387; *ANE* 408-10 No. 157.□

A785.7§, ‡Moon (al-Qamar) resides in the First Sky.
Tawaddud: Slavegirl Sold and Regained: *Alf* III 3; Burton V 233. Chauvin VII 117-19 No. 387; *ANE* 408-10 No. 157.□

A787, Relation of planets to human life.
Tawaddud: Slavegirl Sold and Regained: *Alf* III 2-4; Burton V 229-30. Chauvin VII 117-19 No. 387; *ANE* 408-10 No. 157.□

A787.5§, ‡Character (nature) of the twelve signs of the Zodiac.
Tawaddud: Slavegirl Sold and Regained: *Alf* III 3; Burton V 229. Chauvin VII 117-19 No. 387; *ANE* 408-10 No. 157.□

A787.5.1§, ‡Three signs correspond to (four) personality types. (Cf. M302.4.3§).
Tawaddud: Slavegirl Sold and Regained: *Alf* III 3-4; Burton V 234. Chauvin VII 117-19 No. 387; *ANE* 408-10 No. 157.□

A789.2§, ‡Relations of planets (stars) to times (days, hours, etc.).
Tawaddud: Slavegirl Sold and Regained: *Alf* III 2-3; Burton V 230-31. Chauvin VII 117-19 No. 387; *ANE* 408-10 No. 157.□

A789.2.1§, ‡Certain day controls certain planet.
Tawaddud: Slavegirl Sold and Regained: *Alf* III 2-4; Burton V 231-32. Chauvin VII 117-19 No. 387; *ANE* 408-10 No. 157.□

A789.2.1.1§, ‡Sun controlled ("owned") by Sunday.
Tawaddud: Slavegirl Sold and Regained: *Alf* III 2; Burton V 231. Chauvin VII 117-19 No. 387; *ANE* 408-10 No. 157.□

A789.2.1.2§, ‡Moon controlled ("owned") by Monday.
Tawaddud: Slavegirl Sold and Regained: *Alf* III 2; Burton V 231,(belongs to). Chauvin VII 117-19 No. 387; *ANE* 408-10 No. 157.□

A789.2.1.3§, ‡ Mars (al-Marrîkh) controlled ("owned") by Tuesday.
Tawaddud: Slavegirl Sold and Regained: *Alf* III 3; Burton V 232. Chauvin VII 117-19 No. 387; *ANE* 408-10 No. 157.□

A789.2.1.4§, ‡Mercury (¿Uṭârid) controlled ("owned") by Wednesday.
Tawaddud: Slavegirl Sold and Regained: *Alf* III 3; Burton V 232. Chauvin VII 117-19 No. 387; *ANE* 408-10 No. 157.□

A789.2.1.5§, ‡Jupiter (Mushtarî/Mushturâ) controlled ("owned") by Thursday.
Tawaddud: Slavegirl Sold and Regained: *Alf* III 3; Burton V 232. Chauvin VII 117-19 No. 387; *ANE* 408-10 No. 157.□

A789.2.1.6§, ‡Venus (al-Zahrah) controlled ("owned") by Friday.
Tawaddud: Slavegirl Sold and Regained: *Alf* III 3; Burton V 232. Chauvin VII 117-19 No. 387; *ANE* 408-10 No. 157.□

A789.2.1.7§, ‡Saturn (Zuḥal) controlled ("owned") by Saturday.
Tawaddud: Slavegirl Sold and Regained: *Alf* III 3; Burton V 232. Chauvin VII 117-19 No. 387; *ANE* 408-10 No. 157.□

A844.2, Earth supported by bull. See: *GMC*.
Bulûqiya: *Alf* III 36; Burton V 324. Chauvin VII 54 No. 77; *ANE* 130-32 No. 177.□

A844.2.1§, ‡Astronomical measurements of bull supporting Earth. (Named al-Rayyân).
Bulûqiya: *Alf* III 36; Burton V 324. Chauvin VII 54 No. 77; *ANE* 130-32 No. 177.□

A844.3.1§, ‡Earth supported by whale. (His name is Lûtiyyâ).
Bulûqiya: *Alf* III 36,-cf./(*ḥût*/whale/masc.); Burton V 324,-(huge fish / [fem.]). Chauvin VII 54 No. 77; *ANE* 130-32 No. 177.□

A872.1, Seven seas encircle the world. See: *GMC*. (Cf. Z71.5.2.0.1§).
Bulûqiya: *Alf* III 26-31,-cf.; Burton V 307-11. Chauvin VII 54 No. 77; *ANE* 130-32 No. 177.□

A872.1.0.1§, ‡Tour (crossing) of the seven seas.
Bulûqiya: *Alf* III 26-31; Burton V 307-11. Chauvin VII 54 No. 77; *ANE* 130-32 No. 177.□

A874§, Seven strata of earth. See: *GMC*. (Cf. Z71.5.2.5§).
Tawaddud: Slavegirl Sold and Regained: *Alf* III 5; Burton V 239. Chauvin VII 117-19 No. 387; *ANE* 408-10 No. 157;
Bulûqiya: *Alf* III 36; Burton V 324,-(seven stages). Chauvin VII 54 No. 77; *ANE* 130-32 No. 177.□

A876, Midgard Serpent. A serpent surrounds the earth. See: *GMC*; *PSAE*. (Cf. A671.0.1.1.4§).
Bulûqiya: *Alf* III 36,-(viper); Burton V 325. Chauvin VII 54 No. 77; *ANE* 130-32 No. 177.□

A965.5.1§, ‡Mountain of ice shields earth from heat of hell's fire. (Cf. F810.1.1§).
Bulûqiya: *Alf* III 36; Burton V 324. Chauvin VII 54 No. 77; *ANE* 130-32 No. 177.□

A1002.2.0.1§, ‡Latter Days (*'Âkhir al-Zamân*).
Bulûqiya: *Alf* III 22,-(*'Âkhir al-Zamân*/passim); Burton V 304,-(latter days). Chauvin VII 54 No. 77; *ANE* 130-32 No. 177.□

A1093.1§, ‡Archangel Isrâfîl will blow the trumpet, announcing commencement of End of World. See: *DOTTI*. (Cf. D1346.5.1.1§, V247.0.1§).
Bulûqiya: *Alf* III 26,-(first blowing); Burton V 310. Chauvin VII 54 No. 77; *ANE* 130-32 No. 177.□

A1100.2§, ‡Creation of opposites (*'aḍdâd*). (Cf. U20§, U103§).
Tawaddud: Slavegirl Sold and Regained: *Alf* III 3; Burton V 234. Chauvin VII 117-19 No. 387; *ANE* 408-10 No. 157.□

A1105§, Peace established among the animals. See: *GMC*.

Nuzhat al-Zamân Tested/¿Umar al-Nu¿mân: *Alf* I 205; Burton II 168. Chauvin VI 116, n.1/passim No. 277; *ANE* 432,/passim No. 39.□

A1114§, ‡Origin (source) of world waters.
Bulûqiya: *Alf* III 37; Burton V 326. Chauvin VII 54 No. 77; *ANE* 130-32 No. 177.□

A1114.1§, ‡All waters of the world (salt and sweet) spring from water reservoir located under God's Throne.
Bulûqiya: *Alf* III 37; Burton V 326. Chauvin VII 54 No. 77; *ANE* 130-32 No. 177.□

A1145.5§, Earthquakes from movements of Qâf mountains. See: *GMC*. (Cf. A418.2.1§).
Bulûqiya: *Alf* III 35; Burton V 323. Chauvin VII 54 No. 77; *ANE* 130-32 No. 177.□

A1170, Origin of night and day. See: *GMC*.
Tawaddud: Slavegirl Sold and Regained: *Alf* II 319,-cf.; Burton V 228. Chauvin VII 117-19 No. 387; *ANE* 408-10 No. 157.□

A1174.7§, ‡Angel of night and day.
Bulûqiya: *Alf* III 35,-(Mîkhâ'îl); Burton V 323. Chauvin VII 54 No. 77; *ANE* 130-32 No. 177.□

A1179.3§, ‡A day is created of a nighttime followed by daylight time. (Night labeled: "Eve of ....").
Copt Broker's Story: Lover's Sacrifices Repaid: *Alf* I 92,-("*laylat al-Jum¿ah*"/i.e, Thursday night); Burton I 269,-("Friday night"[??]). Chauvin VI 80 No. 249; *ANE* 313-14 No. 24;
Birds, Beasts, and Carpenter: *Alf* II 25,-cf./(xxx); Burton III 121. Chauvin II 225-26 No. 1; *ANE* 126 No. 44.□

A1213.1§, ‡Adamites given preference (superiority) over all of God's creatures (e.g., angels, jinn, etc.).
¿Abdallah ibn Fâḍil: Treacherous Brothers: *Alf* IV 283; Burton IX 339. Chauvin V 2-4 No. 2; *ANE* 63-65 No. 261.□

A1213.2§, ‡God orders angels to prostrate themselves before Adam (as acknowledgment of his privileged status). (Cf. A54.3.1.1§).
Bulûqiya: *Alf* III 34; Burton V 322. Chauvin VII 54 No. 77; *ANE* 130-32 No. 177.□

A1241.0.1§, ‡Adam made from clay brought from earth crust (*'adîm al-'arḍ*). (Cf. A1260.1.1.1§).
Tawaddud: Slavegirl Sold and Regained: *Alf* II 314, III 5,-(*turâb*/earth/dirt); Burton V 218, 240. Chauvin 7: 117-19 No. 387; *ANE* 408 No. 157.□

A1241.3.1§, ‡Clay ("*ṭînah*") with which God created Adam was fermented for forty days.
Bulûqiya: *Alf* III 34; Burton V 322. Chauvin VII 54 No. 77; *ANE* 130-32 No. 177.□

A1260.1.1.1§, ‡Adam made from water, mud (dirt), fire, and air. (Cf. A1241.0.1§).
Tawaddud: Slavegirl Sold and Regained: *Alf* II 314; Burton V 218. Chauvin VII 117-19 No. 387; *ANE* 408-10 No. 157.□

A1274.4.1§, ‡Fourteen brothers and sisters born to first hybrid demons (Khalît and Malît). (Cf. A1552.5§).
Bulûqiya: *Alf* III 33; Burton V 319. Chauvin VII 54 No. 77; *ANE* 130-32 No. 177.□

A1300.0.1§, ‡God made a reason (cause) for everything.
Anîs al-Jalîs: *Alf* I 138; Burton II 27,-("appointeth a cause"). Chauvin V 120-24 No. 58; *ANE* 316-17 No. 35.□

A1331.3§, ‡Paradise lost because of temptation by woman (Eve). (Cf. W256.6.3.2.1§).
Shahriyâr and Shâhzamân: *Alf* I 5,-(poem); Burton I 13. Chauvin V 188-89 No. 111; *ANE* 370-71 No. 1.□

A1371.5§, Deviant women from Adam's 'crooked rib'. See: *GMC*. (Cf. W256.6.3.1§).
Nuzhat al-Zamân Tested/¿Umar al-Nu¿mân: *Alf* I 202; Burton II 161. Chauvin VI 116, n.1/passim No. 277; *ANE* 432,/passim No. 39.□

A1383.3.2§, ‡Origin of first [garment] tail dragged on earth: Hajar's due to bashfulness (*ḥayâ'*) toward Sarah.
Tawaddud: Slavegirl Sold and Regained: *Alf* III 4; Burton V 236. Chauvin VII 117-19 No. 387; *ANE* 408-10 No. 157.□

A1384.3§, ‡Being sin-prone is part of human nature (being an Adamite). (Cf. U102.1§).

King Jalî¿âd and Shimâs: *Alf* IV 157-58; Burton IX 80-82. Chauvin VI 9-11 No. 184; *ANE* 237-38 No. 236.□

A1396§, ‡Why a limb (body organs) acts in a certain manner. (Cf. V318.1.2.2§).
King Jalî¿âd and Shimâs: *Alf* IV 158-59; Burton IX 85. Chauvin VI 9-11 No. 184; *ANE* 237-38 No. 236.□

A1396.1§, ‡Limb (organs) acts in obedience to God's Will (Command).
King Jalî¿âd and Shimâs: *Alf* IV 159; Burton IX 85,-(member). Chauvin VI 9-11 No. 184; *ANE* 237-38 No. 236.□

A1413.6§, ‡Harnessing (channeling) of water power.
Bulûqiya: *Alf* III 37; Burton V 326,-(between mountain ranges). Chauvin VII 54 No. 77; *ANE* 130-32 No. 177.□

A1413.6.1§, ‡Celestial dam harnesses all waters of universe. (Located in sky, under God's Throne). (Cf. A1114.1§).
Bulûqiya: *Alf* III 37; Burton V 326. Chauvin VII 54 No. 77; *ANE* 130-32 No. 177.□

A1413.6.1.1§, ‡Celestial dam with mountains (of precious stone) as flood-gates.
Bulûqiya: *Alf* III 37; Burton V 326. Chauvin VII 54 No. 77; *ANE* 130-32 No. 177.□

A1413.7§, ‡Control of flow of waters from (celestial) sources.
Bulûqiya: *Alf* III 37; Burton V 326. Chauvin VII 54 No. 77; *ANE* 130-32 No. 177.□

A1413.7.1§, ‡Confluence (convergence) spot of two seas. Strait (*Majma¿ al-Bahrayn*).
Bulûqiya: *Alf* III 37; Burton V 326. Chauvin VII 54 No. 77; *ANE* 130-32 No. 177.□

A1413.7.2§, ‡Doorkeeper of Cape of '*Majma¿ al-Bahrayn*'. (Cf. C611.1.0.1§).
Bulûqiya: *Alf* III 37; Burton V 326. Chauvin VII 54 No. 77; *ANE* 130-32 No. 177.□

A1432.2.3§, ‡Gold comes from elixir constituted of sun-dried flowers.
Bulûqiya: *Alf* III 29; Burton V 315. Chauvin VII 54 No. 77; *ANE* 130-32 No. 177.□

A1440.5.1§, ‡Craftsman's (artist's) creativity is no innovation (creation). See: *DOTTI*. (Cf. A611.0.4§, F888.0.1§).
King Jalî¿âd and Shimâs: *Alf* IV 156; Burton IX 77,-(originating). Chauvin VI 9-11 No. 184; *ANE* 237-38 No. 236;
Jeweler's Wife and Qamar al-Zamân: *Alf* IV 254,-cf.; Burton IX 278. Chauvin V 212-14 No. 121; *ANE* 345-47 No. 260.□

A1471.8§, ‡Why commerce is preferred as profession. (Cf. P431, P431.0.4§).
¿Alâ' al-Dîn Abû al-Shâmât: *Alf* II 172; Burton IV 77,-("Allah blesseth trade"). Chauvin V 43-49 No. 18; *ANE* 85-87 No. 63.□

A1471.8.1§, ‡Being a merchant (buying and selling): an occupation blessed by God. (Cf. P770§).
¿Alâ' al-Dîn Abû al-Shâmât: *Alf* II 172; Burton IV 77. Chauvin V 43-49 No. 18; *ANE* 85-87 No. 63.□

A1552.5§, ‡Scores of twin brothers and sisters children of first demonic parents marry each other. (Cf. A1274.4.1§).
Bulûqiya: *Alf* III 33; Burton V 319. Chauvin VII 54 No. 77; *ANE* 130-32 No. 177.□

A1557.3.1§, ‡Men walk ahead of women so as to not violate their modesty. (Cf. T5.1.4§, T380.6.1§).
Spy, Fifth Maiden/¿Umar al-Nu¿mân: *Alf* I 223; Burton II 206. *ANE* 432 No. 39/passim.□

A1613.1.2§, ‡Blacks as sons of Ham.
City of Brass: *Alf* III 137,-(*'awlâd Ḥâm*); Burton VI 119,-(lineage of Ham). Chauvin V 32-35 No. 16; *ANE* 146-50 No. 180;
Nûr al-Dîn and Maryam: *Alf* IV 122; Burton IX 4. Chauvin V 52-54 No. 271; *ANE* 98-99 No. 233.□

A1617, ‡Origin of place-name. See: *DOTTI*. (Cf. Z183.0.1§).
Butcher Wardân and Bear Lover: *Alf* II 252,-("Wardân-Market"); Burton IV 297. Chauvin V 177-78 No. 101; *ANE* 442-43 No. 101;
Uns al-Wujûd and al-Ward: *Alf* II 271,-(*Jabal al-Thaklâ*/passim); Burton V 37,-(Mount of the Bereaved Mother). Chauvin VI 127-29 No. 282; *ANE* 438 No. 104;
City of Brass: *Alf* III 132,-(City); Burton VI 101. Chauvin V 32-35 No. 16; *ANE* 146-50 No. 180;

Jawdar and His Treacherous Brethren: *Alf* III 200,-(al-Jawdariyyah); Burton VI 254 n. 2. Chauvin V 257-60 No. 154; *ANE* 244-45 No. 209;
Abû Qîr and Abû Ṣîr: *Alf* IV 197,-(Abû-Qîr); Burton IX 134-65. Chauvin V 15-17 No. 10; *ANE* 75-77 No. 255.□

A1617.1.1§, ‡Why mountain is called "*Thaklâ* Mountain" (Mother bereft of children).
Uns al-Wujûd and al-Ward: *Alf* II 280; Burton V 56. Chauvin VI 127-29 No. 282; *ANE* 438 No. 104.□

A1650.2.1§, ‡Custom of differentiating religious groups by color of dress introduced. (Cf. D692, P722.3§, V131.3§).
Ensorcelled Prince/Husband: *Alf* I 29; Burton I 77. Chauvin VI 56-58 No. 222; *ANE* 176 No. 13.□

A1650.5.2.0.1§, ‡Eve blamed for Adamites's troubles on earth—(due to eviction from paradise). Usually blame extended to 'her daughters'.
Shahriyâr and Shâhzamân: *Alf* I 5,-(poem/passim)‡ Burton I 13. Chauvin V 188-89 No. 111; *ANE* 370-71 No. 1.□

A1689.11.3§, Disbelievers more powerful (rich) than believers since former have the here-and-now, but not the hereafter. See: *DOTTI*.
Water-fowl and Tortoise: *Alf* II 28,-cf./('*dunyâ* is home for the homeless'); Burton III 130,-(The world is the dwelling of ...). Chauvin II 226-27 No. 5; *ANE* 444 No. 46.□

A1895.1§, Bat created by Jesus.
Tawaddud: Slavegirl Sold and Regained: *Alf* II 311,-(passim); Burton V 211. Chauvin VII 117-19 No. 387; *ANE* 408-10 No. 157.□

A2145.6§, ‡Origin of vipers. (Cf. B3§)
Bulûqiya: *Alf* III 23,-ff.; Burton V 306. Chauvin VII 54 No. 77; *ANE* 130-32 No. 177.□

A2145.6.1§, ‡Vipers from ebb-tide (breathing) of Hell.
Bulûqiya: *Alf* III 23; Burton V 306. Chauvin VII 54 No. 77; *ANE* 130-32 No. 177.□

A2145.7.1§, ‡Hell's vipers (and scorpions) are the offspring of Khalît and Malît (mythical hybrids's first pregnancy). (Cf. A671.2.9, B14.6§, B14.7§).
Bulûqiya: *Alf* III 33; Burton V 319. Chauvin VII 54 No. 77; *ANE* 130-32 No. 177.□

A2810§, ‡Earthly goods from residuals of plant from Paradise.
Bulûqiya: *Alf* III 74; Burton V 384. Chauvin VII 54 No. 77; *ANE* 130-32 No. 177.□

A2810.1§, ‡Plant from paradise eaten by animal on Earth: animal's excreta become beneficial goods (products). (Cf. A630.1.1§).
Bulûqiya: *Alf* III 74; Burton V 384. Chauvin VII 54 No. 77; *ANE* 130-32 No. 177.□

A2811, Origin of silk. See: *GMC*.
Bulûqiya: *Alf* III 74; Burton V 384. Chauvin VII 54 No. 77; *ANE* 130-32 No. 177.□

A2812, Origin of musk.
Bulûqiya: *Alf* III 74; Burton V 384. Chauvin VII 54 No. 77; *ANE* 130-32 No. 177.□

A2813, Origin of honey. See: *GMC*.
Bulûqiya: *Alf* III 74; Burton V 384. Chauvin VII 54 No. 77; *ANE* 130-32 No. 177.□

A2814, Origin of spices. See: *GMC*.
Bulûqiya: *Alf* III 74; Burton V 384. Chauvin VII 54 No. 77; *ANE* 130-32 No. 177.□

A2921§, ‡Origins of Iblis.
Bulûqiya: *Alf* III 33; Burton V 319. Chauvin VII 54 No. 77; *ANE* 130-32 No. 177.□

A2921.1§, ‡Eblis: born as one of the fourteen children of Khalît and Malît. He disobeyed his father by refusing to marry one of his seven twin-sisters, and was transformed into a worm (which became Eblis). (Cf. A1552.5§, Q325.2§, Q551.3.0.1.2§).
Bulûqiya: *Alf* III 33; Burton V 319. Chauvin VII 54 No. 77; *ANE* 130-32 No. 177.□

B. ANIMALS

B3§, ‡Viper (*ḥayyah*, female serpent)—as animal central to supernatural beliefs (religious records). (Cf. A650.1.2§, A2145.6§, M205.9.7.1§, Z192.2.1§).
Eldest Lady's Story: Treacherous Sisters: *Alf* I 57; Burton I 172. Chauvin V 4 No. 443; *ANE* 174-75 No. 19;
King ¿Umar al-Nu¿mân and Sons: *Alf* I 257-58,-cf./(poem/passim); Burton II 275,-(scald she bear, speckled snake). Chauvin VI 112-24 No. 277; *ANE* 430-34 No. 39;
Escaped Viper Ungrateful: *Alf* II 35; Burton III 145. Chauvin II 227 No. 9; *ANE* 450,/passim No. 47;
Abû Muḥammad Lazybones: *Alf* II 212-13; Burton IV 173. Chauvin VI 64-67 No. 233; *ANE* 71-73 No. 78;
Tawaddud: Slavegirl Sold and Regained: *Alf* III 5,-(Moses's Staff), 7,-(viper's tail); Burton V 238,-("serpent"), 242. Chauvin VII 117-19 No. 387; *ANE* 408-10 No. 157;
Bulûqiya/Ḥâsib/Queen of Vipers: *Alf* III 20, 22, 23, 26-27, 33, 36-37, 80; Burton V 302ff. Chauvin VII 54 No. 77; *ANE* 130-32 No. 177;
Sindbâd's Second Voyage: *Alf* III 89; Burton VI 18. Chauvin VII 9-14 No. 373B; *ANE* 385 No. 179;
Sindbâd's Seventh Voyage: *Alf* III 117, 121; Burton VI 69-70. Chauvin VII 26-29 No. 373G; *ANE* 386-87 No. 179;
Hasan of Basrah: *Alf* IV 25; Burton VIII 86,-(pied snake [??]). Chauvin VII 29-35 No. 212A; *ANE* 207-10 No. 230;
¿Abdallah ibn Fâḍil: Treacherous Brothers: *Alf* IV 272; Burton IX 315. Chauvin V 2-4 No. 2; *ANE* 63-65 No. 261.□

B3.1§, ‡Viper with human face.
Bulûqiya/Ḥâsib/Queen of Vipers: *Alf* III 21; Burton V 302. Chauvin VII 54 No. 77; *ANE* 130-32 No. 177.□

B3.2§, ‡Fire-breathing viper. (Cf. N582.1§).
Bulûqiya: *Alf* III 27; Burton V 312. Chauvin VII 54 No. 77; *ANE* 130-32 No. 177.□

B3.3.1§, ‡Winged viper.
Eldest Lady's Story: Treacherous Sisters: *Alf* I 57,-(jinni-maiden in viper form); Burton I 172. Chauvin V 4 No. 443; *ANE* 174-75 No. 19.

B14.6§, ‡Khalît: mythical animal created in the image (form) of lion with tail of viper. Its length is worth twenty years of travel.
Bulûqiya: *Alf* III 33; Burton V 319. Chauvin VII 54 No. 77; *ANE* 130-32 No. 177.□

B14.7§, ‡Malît: mythical animal created in the image (form) of wolf, with tail of female-tortoise.
Bulûqiya: *Alf* III 33; Burton V 319. Chauvin VII 54 No. 77; *ANE* 130-32 No. 177.□

B15.7.18§, ‡Locust as hybrid of many (mighty) animals: horse's face, elephant's eyes, ox's neck, stag's antlers, lion's chest, scorpion's belly, eagle's wings, camel's thigh, ostrich's leg, viper's tale. (Cf. Z71.5.6.17§).
Tawaddud: Slavegirl Sold and Regained: *Alf* III 7,-(variation); Burton V 242. Chauvin VII 117-19 No. 387; *ANE* 408-10 No. 157.□

B16.5.1, ‡Giant devastating serpent.
Bulûqiya: *Alf* III 38,-(snake/*thu¿bân*); Burton V 327. Chauvin VII 54 No. 77; *ANE* 130-32 No. 177.□

B31.1, Roc. A giant bird which carries off men in its claws. See: *ANE*; *DOTTI*; *GMC*.
Sindbâd's Second Voyage: *Alf* III 89; Burton VI 16. Chauvin VII 9-14 No. 373B; *ANE* 385 No. 179;
Abû Qîr and Abû Ṣîr: *Alf* IV 185,-(passim/simile); Burton IX 141,-(Rukh). Chauvin V 15-17 No. 10; *ANE* 75-77 No. 255.□

B31.1.1, Roc's egg. See: *ANE*; *DOTTI*; *GMC*.
Sindbâd's Fifth Voyage: *Alf* III 107; Burton VI 48. Chauvin 7: 21 No. 373E; *ANE* 386 No. 179.□

B31.1.2, ‡Roc drops rock on ship. Rock is so large that it destroys ship. See: *ANE*; *GMC*.
Sindbâd's Fifth Voyage: *Alf* III 107; Burton VI 49. Chauvin 7: 21 No. 373E; *ANE* 386 No. 179.□

B31.1.3§, ‡Roc's chick: fed elephants whole.
Sindbâd's Second Voyage: *Alf* III 89; Burton VI 16. Chauvin 7: 9 No. 373B; *ANE* 385 No. 179.□

B39.5§, Bird from hell (*'abâbîl*). See: *GMC*.

Tawaddud: Slavegirl Sold and Regained: *Alf* II 311,-(passim); Burton V 211,-(swallow). Chauvin VII 117-19 No. 387; *ANE* 408-10 No. 157.□

B41.2, Flying horse. See: *ANE*; *DOTTI*; *GMC*. (Cf. D1626.1).
Third Qalandar: Magnetic Mountain: *Alf* I 53; Burton I 161. Chauvin V 200-3 No. 117; *ANE* 340-41 No. 18.□

B71, Sea horse. See: *ANE*.
Sindbâd's First Voyage: *Alf* III 85; Burton VI 8. Chauvin VII 7-9 No. 373A; *ANE* 385 No. 179.□

B80.9.1§, ‡Fire-breathing mermen (when angry). (Cf. F1041.16.1.2§).
Jullanâr of the Sea: *Alf* III 251; Burton VII 273. Chauvin V 147-51 No. 73; *ANE* 248-51 No. 227.□

B81, Mermaid. See: *GMC*.
City of Brass: *Alf* III 138; Burton VI 121,-("daughters of the deep"). Chauvin V 32-35 No. 16; *ANE* 146-50 No. 180.□

B81.0.1.1§, ‡Mermaid dies when taken out of water. See: *DOTTI*.
City of Brass: *Alf* III 138; Burton VI 121. Chauvin V 32-35 No. 16; *ANE* 146-50 No. 180.□

B81.0.2, Woman from water world. See: *DOTTI*; *GMC*. (Cf. F725.5).
Bulûqiya: *Alf* III 30-31; Burton V 315. Chauvin VII 54 No. 77; *ANE* 130-32 No. 177;
Jullanâr of the Sea: *Alf* III 249; Burton VII 275. Chauvin V 147-51 No. 73; *ANE* 248-51 No. 227.□

B81.13.11, ‡Mermaid captured. (Cf. F387.1.1§).
Jullanâr of the Sea: *Alf* III 249; Burton VII 269. Chauvin V 147-51 No. 73; *ANE* 248-51 No. 227.□

B81.2, ‡Mermaid marries man.
Jullanâr of the Sea: *Alf* III 247-48; Burton VII 266. Chauvin V 147-51 No. 73; *ANE* 248-51 No. 227.□

B82, Merman. See: *ANE*; *DOTTI*; *GMC*.
Landsman ¿Abdallah and Merman ¿Abdallah: *Alf* IV 199; Burton IX 170. Chauvin V 6-7 No. 3; *ANE* 65-66 No. 256.□

B82.6, ‡Merman caught by fisherman (released). See: *DOTTI*.
Landsman ¿Abdallah and Merman ¿Abdallah: *Alf* IV 199; Burton IX 169. Chauvin V 6-7 No. 3; *ANE* 65-66 No. 256.□

B101.1.3§, ‡Bird with members of jewels and precious metals.
Bulûqiya: *Alf* III 74; Burton V 383. Chauvin VII 54 No. 77; *ANE* 130-32 No. 177.□

B121.7§, ‡Wise tortoise. See: *DOTTI*.
Water-fowl and Tortoise: *Alf* II 29; Burton III 130. Chauvin II 226-27 No. 5; *ANE* 444 No. 46.□

B128.1§, ‡Animal uses strategy. See: *DOTTI*. (Cf. K830§).
Flea and She-mouse: *Alf* II 38; Burton III 152-54. Chauvin II 228 No. 12; *ANE* 186 No. 52.□

B131.3, ‡Bird betrays woman's infidelity. (Cf. J134.5§).
Masrûr and Zayn al-Mawâsif: *Alf* IV 65; Burton VIII 232. Chauvin VI 82-84 No. 251; *ANE* 294-95 No. 232.□

B143.1.3, ‡Warning parrot. See: *DOTTI*.
Husband and Parrot: *Alf* III 140-41,-cf.; Burton I 53. Chauvin VI 139 No. 294; *ANE* 226 No. 11.□

B143.1.4, ‡Falcon saves master from drinking poisoned water. See: *DOTTI*.
King Sindbâd and Falcon: *Alf* I 19; Burton I 51-52. Chauvin V 289 No. 173; *ANE* 383 No. 10.□

B147.2.2.1, [= B147.2.2.3], Crow/[(raven)] as bird of ill-omen. See: *DOTTI*; *GMC*.
¿Alâ' al-Dîn Abû al-Shâmât: *Alf* II 157,/implicit (*'akhadhahâ al-ghurâb wa târ*/crow/raven took [joy] and flew away); Burton IV 52,-(raven taketh it and flieth away). Chauvin V 43-49 No. 18; *ANE* 85-87 No. 63;
Man from Yaman and Six Salve-girls: Flyting: *Alf* II 246,-cf./(simile); Burton IV 250. Chauvin VI 151 No. 313; *ANE* 289-90 No. 84;
Uns al-Wujûd and al-Ward: *Alf* II 281; Burton V 58. Chauvin VI 127-29 No. 282; *ANE* 438 No. 104;
City of Brass: *Alf* III 130; Burton VI 102. Chauvin 5: 32-35 No. 16; *ANE* 146-50 No. 180.□

B147.2.2.4, Owl as bird of ill-omen.

Man from Yaman and Six Salve-girls: Flyting: *Alf* II 249,-cf./(simile/owl-faced); Burton IV 259,-(face of owl in gloom). Chauvin VI 151 No. 313; *ANE* 289-90 No. 84;
Uns al-Wujûd and al-Ward: *Alf* II 281; Burton V 58. Chauvin VI 127-29 No. 282; *ANE* 438 No. 104.□

B161.3, Wisdom from eating serpent. See: *GMC*. (Cf. D1017.3§, F950.0.4.4.1§).
Bulûqiya: *Alf* III 79,-(drinking liquified viper flesh); Burton V 393. Chauvin VII 54 No. 77; *ANE* 130-32 No. 177.□

B163.1, ‡Wisdom from fox.
Wolf and Fox: *Alf* II 31-35,-cf./(fox's sayings); Burton III 132-46. Chauvin II 227 No. 6; *ANE* 450 No. 47.□

B184.1.1, Horse (mule) with magic speed. See: *ANE*.
Jawdar and His Treacherous Brethren: *Alf* III 184,-cf./(she-mule/jinni); Burton VI 225. Chauvin V 257-60 No. 154; *ANE* 244-45 No. 209.□

B184.1.3.1§, ‡Magic horse from water world mates with ordinary mare: hybrid offspring with marvelous qualities. (Cf. B754.9.5§, P774.2.5.2.2§).
Sindbâd's First Voyage: *Alf* III 85; Burton VI 8. Chauvin VII 7-9 No. 373A; *ANE* 385 No. 179.□

B211, Animal uses human speech. See: *GMC*; *PSAE*.
Bulûqiya/Ḥâsib/Queen of Vipers: *Alf* III 21; Burton V 302. Chauvin VII 54 No. 77; *ANE* 130-32 No. 177.□

B211.6.1, Speaking snake (serpent). See: *PSAE*.
Bulûqiya/Ḥâsib/Queen of Vipers: *Alf* III 21; Burton V 302. Chauvin VII 54 No. 77; *ANE* 130-32 No. 177.□

B215.5, ‡Serpent language.
Bulûqiya/Ḥâsib/Queen of Vipers: *Alf* III 21; Burton V 302. Chauvin VII 54 No. 77; *ANE* 130-32 No. 177.□

B215.9.1.1§, ‡Human transformed to animal communicates by gesture (nodding). See: *DOTTI*.
First Shaykh: Sorceress Wife: *Alf* I 10; Burton I 28. Chauvin VII 129-30 No. 396; *ANE* 376-77 No. 5;
Third Shaykh: Transformation by Wife: *Alf* I 13; Burton I 37. Chauvin VII 130 No. 398; *ANE* 378 No. 7;
¿Abdallah ibn Fâḍil: Treacherous Brothers: *Alf* IV 270; Burton IX 310. Chauvin V 2-4 No. 2; *ANE* 63-65 No. 261.□

B216.1§, ‡Knowledge of animal language as gift from deity. See: *DOTTI*. (Cf. V223.5.0.1§).
Bull and Ass: *Alf* I 5; Burton I 16. Chauvin V 179-80 No. 104; *ANE* 129-30 No. 2;
Merchant's Curious Wife: *Alf* I 6; Burton I 16. Chauvin V 179-80 No. 104; *ANE* 298-99 No. 3.□

B217, Animal language learned. See: *GMC*. (Cf. K1969.5.1§).
Page Feigns Knowing Bird Language: *Alf* III 156,-cf./(claim); Burton VI 170. Chauvin VIII 49-50 No. 17; *ANE* 321-22 No. 197.□

B220.1§, ‡Social meeting of animals—(as *majlis*). See: *DOTTI*.
Bulûqiya: *Alf* III 28-29; Burton V 313-14. Chauvin VII 54 No. 77; *ANE* 130-32 No. 177.□

B221.1, Kingdom of monkeys. See: *ANE*; *DOTTI*; *GMC*.
Jânshâh: *Alf* III 43; Burton V 334-35,-(apes). Chauvin VII 39-44 No. 153; *ANE* 238-41 No. 178;
Sindbâd's Third Voyage: *Alf* III 93,-(monkeys' mountain/an island); Burton VI 24. Chauvin VII 15-18 No. 373C; *ANE* 385-86 No. 179.□

B221.1.1§, ‡Community of monkeys (apes, etc.).
Sindbâd's Fifth Voyage: *Alf* III 110,-(city); Burton VI 53. Chauvin VII 21-24 No. 373E; *ANE* 386 No. 179;
Sayf al-Mulûk: *Alf* III 285-86; Burton VII 343-45. Chauvin VII 64-73 No. 348; *ANE* 362-64 No. 229.□

B225.1, Kingdom of serpents. See: *ANE*.
Bulûqiya/Ḥâsib/Queen of Vipers: *Alf* III 21,-cf./(vipers); Burton V 302. Chauvin VII 54 No. 77; *ANE* 130-32 No. 177.□

B225.3§, ‡Kingdom of vipers: all females. (Cf. F112, F127.1, P722.1§).

Bulûqiya/Ḥâsib/Queen of Vipers: *Alf* III 20; Burton V 303. Chauvin VII 54 No. 77; *ANE* 130-32 No. 177.□

B237, ‡Drinking-bout assembly of animals.
Bulûqiya: *Alf* III 28-29; Burton V 313. Chauvin VII 54 No. 77; *ANE* 130-32 No. 177.□

B236.0.2§, ‡Animal ruler appointed as result of selection. See: *DOTTI*. (Cf. P11.7§).
Crows and Hawk: *Alf* IV 144; Burton IX 54. Chauvin II 220 No. 152/8; *ANE* 162 No. 243.□

B236.0.3.1§, ‡Man selected ruler of animals (birds).
Jânshâh: *Alf* III 44,-(sultan of monkeys); Burton V 335. Chauvin VII 39-44 No. 153; *ANE* 238-41 No. 178.□

B240.4, Lion as king of animals. See: *DOTTI*. (Cf. J814, Z194.2.1.2§).
Jackals and Wolf as Umpire: *Alf* IV 167; Burton IX 104-5. Chauvin II 223 No. 152/21; *ANE* 235 No. 252.□

B241.2.2, King of monkeys. See: *DOTTI*; *GMC*.
Jânshâh: *Alf* III 44,-(sultan); Burton V 335. Chauvin VII 39-44 No. 153; *ANE* 238-41 No. 178.□

B242, King of birds. See: *GMC*.
Jânshâh: *Alf* III 49,-(sheik Naṣr); Burton V 343. Chauvin VII 39-44 No. 153; *ANE* 238-41 No. 178.□

B242.1.7, ‡Peacock king of birds.
Sparrow as Peacock's Vizier: *Alf* II 40; Burton III 161-62. Chauvin II 230 No. 20; *ANE* 398 No. 59.□

B242.2.1, ‡King of crows. See: *DOTTI*.
Crows and Hawk: *Alf* IV 144; Burton IX 54. Chauvin II 220 No. 152/8; *ANE* 162 No. 243.□

B244.1.1.1§, ‡Queen of vipers.
Bulûqiya/Ḥâsib/Queen of Vipers: *Alf* III 22,-("*malikat al-ḥayyât*, ... /Queen of vipers); Burton V 303,-("Queen of the Serpents and their Sultanah"). Chauvin VII 54 No. 77; *ANE* 130-32 No. 177.□

B250.2§, ‡Animal's (bird's, insect's) faith in god tested. (Cf. H258§).
Spider Upbraids Wind: *Alf* IV 146-47,-(spider's); Burton IX 59-60. Chauvin II 220 No. 152/10; *ANE* 398 No. 245.□

B251.4.2§, ‡What animal (bird) says when it prays.
Hermit and Pigeons: *Alf* II 27,-(when leader dies followers disperse); Burton III 126. Chauvin II 226 No. 2; *ANE* 221 No. 45/pt. 1.□

B252.1.1§, ‡Animal (bird) as hermit (aesthetic, anchorite).
Hedgehog and Wood-pigeons: *Alf* II 39,-(porcupine); Burton III 156. Chauvin II 229 No. 15; *ANE* 220 No. 55.□

B256.4, Domesticated wolves.
Nuzhat al-Zamân Tested/¿Umar al-Nu¿mân: *Alf* I 205; Burton II 168. Chauvin VI 116, n.1/passim No. 277; *ANE* 432,/passim No. 39.□

B256.4.0.1§, Wolf as honest shepherd. See: *GMC*.
Nuzhat al-Zamân Tested/¿Umar al-Nu¿mân: *Alf* I 205,-(wolves and dogs); Burton II 168. Chauvin VI 116, n.1/passim No. 277; *ANE* 432,/passim No. 39.□

B256.5, ‡Obedience of the feathered creatures to the commands of saint.
Devotee Prince: Ascetic's Death: *Alf* II 290; Burton V 111-12. Chauvin VI 193-94 No. 363; *ANE* 167-68 No. 134.□

B263.6.1§, ‡War between monkeys (apes) and ants. (Cf. B873.4).
Jânshâh: *Alf* III 45-46; Burton V 338. Chauvin VII 39-44 No. 153; *ANE* 238-41 No. 178.□

B263.6.2§, ‡War between monkeys and ogres.
Jânshâh: *Alf* III 44-45; Burton V 336. Chauvin VII 39-44 No. 153; *ANE* 238-41 No. 178.□

B266.2§, ‡Animals fight with men over land. (Cf. U86§).
Sindbâd's Fifth Voyage: *Alf* III 110; Burton VI 53-54. Chauvin VII 21-24 No. 373E; *ANE* 386 No. 179.□

B266.2.1§, ‡War (battles) of men and monkeys over city. (Cf. F766.2.1§).

Sindbâd's Fifth Voyage: *Alf* III 110; Burton VI 53-54. Chauvin VII 21-24 No. 373E; *ANE* 386 No. 179.□

B275.1.4§, ‡Animal (bird) executed for murdering another (of its kind).
Qamar al-Zamân and Budûr: *Alf* II 105; Burton III 293. Chauvin V 204-12 No. 120; *ANE* 341-45 No. 61.□

B275.4.1§, ‡Lion executed for devouring person. See: *DOTTI*.
Lovers of Banû ¿Udhrah and Lion: *Alf* III 209; Burton VII 123. Chauvin V 106-7 No. 37, V 116 No. 52; *ANE* 274 No. 218/[2].□

B279.2.1§, ‡Animal (bird, fish) true to covenant in spite of great difficulties. (Cf. E168.2§, M202).
Ensorcelled Prince/Husband: *Alf* I 24; Burton I 63, 64. Chauvin VI 56-58 No. 222; *ANE* 176 No. 13.□

B291.1.0.1.1§, ‡Pigeon as letter carrier. See: *DOTTI*. (Cf. P14.22.3§).
King ¿Umar al-Nu¿mân and Sons: *Alf* I 243; Burton II 248. Chauvin VI 112-24 No. 277; *ANE* 430-34 No. 39;
Dalîla the Swindler: *Alf* III 213; Burton VII 146. Chauvin V 245-50 No. 147; *ANE* 163-64 No. 224.□

B299.0.1.1§, ‡Animal (bird) takes revenge on another animal (bird). See: *DOTTI*. (Cf. K811.8§).
Wolf and Fox: *Alf* II 35; Burton III 132-46. Chauvin II 227 No. 6; *ANE* 450 No. 47.□

B299.1.3.1§, ‡Magic (flying) horse ridden: damages rider's eye. See: *DOTTI*. (Cf. B41.2, F889.3.1§).
Third Qalandar: Magnetic Mountain: *Alf* I 53; Burton I 161,-(steed). Chauvin V 200-3 No. 117; *ANE* 340-41 No. 18.□

B299.8.0.1.1§, ‡Fish build (dig out) dwellings.
Landsman ¿Abdallah and Merman ¿Abdallah: *Alf* IV 206; Burton IX 184. Chauvin V 6-7 No. 3; *ANE* 65-66 No. 256.□

B299.9.2.1§, ‡Self-herding sheep.
Hermit Tempted by Angel: *Alf* II 27; Burton III 126. Chauvin II 226 No. 3; *ANE* 221 No. 45/pt. 2.□

B302§, ‡Animal (bird) spies for man (master, mistress): conveys useful information. See: *DOTTI*.
Husband and Parrot: *Alf* III 140-41; Burton I 53. Chauvin VI 139 No. 294; *ANE* 226 No. 11.□

B304.1§, ‡Wild animal tamed (appeased, domesticated) by food.
Hunter Rides Lion: Devoured: *Alf* IV 153; Burton IX 72. Chauvin II 222 No. 152/15.□

B312.4, Helpful animal purchased. See: *DOTTI*.
Abû Muhammad Lazybones: *Alf* II 208; Burton IV 167. Chauvin VI 64-67 No. 233; *ANE* 71-73 No. 78.□

B313.5.1§, ‡Helpful animal(s) bewitched former paramour(s) of sorceress. (Cf. B772, N349.6§).
Jullanâr of the Sea: *Alf* III 266; Burton VII 296. Chauvin V 147-51 No. 73; *ANE* 248-51 No. 227.□

B325.1, Animal bribed with food. See: *DOTTI*; *GMC*. (Cf. K318.1§).
King ¿Umar al-Nu¿mân and Sons: *Alf* II 8,-(dog); Burton III 88. Chauvin VI 112-24 No. 277; *ANE* 430-34 No. 39.□

B331.1, Faithful falcon killed through misunderstanding. See: *ANE*; *DOTTI*; *GMC*.
King Sindbâd and Falcon: *Alf* I 18; Burton I 52. Chauvin V 289 No. 173; *ANE* 383 No. 10.□

B331.3.1§, Truth-speaking parrot hastily killed. See: *DOTTI*.
Husband and Parrot: *Alf* III 141; Burton I 53. Chauvin VI 139 No. 294; *ANE* 226 No. 11.□

B335.4.1§, ‡Wife demands life of parrot who has accused her (as price for reconciliation). See: *DOTTI*.
Husband and Parrot: *Alf* III 141; Burton I 53. Chauvin VI 139 No. 294; *ANE* 226 No. 11.□

B431.2, Helpful lion. See: *DOTTI*; *GMC*.
Uns al-Wujûd and al-Ward: *Alf* II 273; Burton V 41-42. Chauvin VI 127-29 No. 282; *ANE* 438 No. 104.□

B441.1, Helpful monkey. See: *DOTTI*; *GMC*. (Cf. B544.1.1§).
Abû Muhammad Lazybones: *Alf* II 208; Burton IV 167-68. Chauvin VI 64-67 No. 233; *ANE* 71-73 No. 78.□

B441.1.1, Helpful ape. See: *DOTTI*; *GMC*.

Abû Muhammad Lazybones: *Alf* II 208,-cf.; Burton IV 167. Chauvin VI 64-67 No. 233; *ANE* 71-73 No. 78.□

B450.1§, ‡Bird guides person to town.
Qamar al-Zamân and Budûr: *Alf* II 97,-cf.; Burton III 279. Chauvin V 204-12 No. 120; *ANE* 341-45 No. 61.□

B455.2, ‡Helpful falcon. See: *DOTTI*. (Cf. B331.1, P806.7.1§).
King Sindbâd and Falcon: *Alf* I 19; Burton I 51-52. Chauvin V 289 No. 173; *ANE* 383 No. 10.□

B455.5, ‡Helpful kite (bird, [vulture]). See: *DOTTI*.
Crow and Viper: *Alf* IV 141; Burton IX 46. Chauvin II 219 No. 152/5; *ANE* 162 No. 240.□

B473, Helpful dolphin. See: *ANE*.
¿Abdallah ibn Fâdil: Treacherous Brothers: *Alf* IV 287; Burton IX 346. Chauvin V 2-4 No. 2; *ANE* 63-65 No. 261.□

B473.1§, ‡Dolphin saves drowning person. (Cf. N887§).
¿Abdallah ibn Fâdil: Treacherous Brothers: *Alf* IV 287; Burton IX 346. Chauvin V 2-4 No. 2; *ANE* 63-65 No. 261.□

B542.1.1.1§, ‡Roc carries marooned man to safety. See: *DOTTI*.
Sindbâd's Second Voyage: *Alf* III 89; Burton VI 17. Chauvin VII 9-14 No. 373B; *ANE* 385 No. 179.□

B542.2, Escape on flying horse. See: *ANE*; *DOTTI*; *GMC*. (Cf. B552.1.2§, F889.3.1§).
Ebony Horse: *Alf* II 258; Burton V 15. Chauvin V 221-31 No. 130; *ANE* 172-74 No. 103□

B544.1.1§, ‡Monkey releases imprisoned master. See: *DOTTI*. (Cf. B441.1).
Abû Muhammad Lazybones: *Alf* II 209; Burton IV 168. Chauvin VI 64-67 No. 233; *ANE* 71-73 No. 78.□

B552, Man carried by bird. See: *ANE*; *DOTTI*; *GMC*. (Cf. D2135, F174.2§).
Jânshâh: *Alf* III 66, 72; Burton V 369, 372. Chauvin VII 39-44 No. 153; *ANE* 238-41 No. 178; **Sindbâd's Second Voyage**: *Alf* III 89; Burton VI 17. Chauvin VII 9-14 No. 373B; *ANE* 385 No. 179; **Man Who Never Laughs**: *Alf* III 153,-(*¿Uqâb*/Phoenix-like eagle—usually female); Burton VI 163,-(great eagle). Chauvin VIII 47-48 No. 15; *ANE* 285-86 No. 195.□

B552.1.2§, ‡Man (Sindbad) fastens himself to giant bird (roc) and is carried by it. See: *DOTTI*. (Cf. B542.2).
Sindbâd's Second Voyage: *Alf* III 89; Burton VI 17. Chauvin VII 9-14 No. 373B; *ANE* 385 No. 179.□

B562.1.0.1, Helpful animal discovers jewel. See: *DOTTI*.
Abû Muhammad Lazybones: *Alf* II 209,-cf.; Burton IV 168. Chauvin VI 64-67 No. 233; *ANE* 71-73 No. 78.□

B563.1.0.1§, ‡Lion shows lover road taken by beloved. See: *DOTTI*.
Uns al-Wujûd and al-Ward: *Alf* II 273; Burton V 39. Chauvin VI 127-29 No. 282; *ANE* 438 No. 104.□

B566.2§, ‡Cock (husband of fifty hens) advises man as to how to control wife—(by force, beating). (Cf. T205.1§, Z194.3.1.1§).
Merchant's Curious Wife: *Alf* I 6; Burton I 22. Chauvin V 179-80 No. 104; *ANE* 298-99 No. 3.□

B595.1§, ‡Flea as mouse's confederate: bites man thus diverting his attention. (Cf. K641.0.1§).
Flea and She-mouse: *Alf* II 38; Burton III 153. Chauvin II 228 No. 12; *ANE* 186 No. 52.□

B599.5§, ‡One animal (bird) helps another. See: *DOTTI*.
Flea and She-mouse: *Alf* II 38; Burton III 153. Chauvin II 228 No. 12; *ANE* 186 No. 52.□

B611.1, ‡Bear paramour.
Butcher Wardân and Bear Lover: *Alf* II 250; Burton IV 294. Chauvin V 177-78 No. 101; *ANE* 442-43 No. 101.□

B611.6, Monkey [(ape)] paramour. See: *DOTTI*; *GMC*.
King's Daughter and Ape: *Alf* II 253; Burton IV 297-99. Chauvin V 178 No. 102; *ANE* 262-63 No. 102.□

B652.1, ‡Marriage to swan-maiden. See: *DOTTI*. (Cf. D361.1).
Hasan of Basrah: *Alf* IV 5; Burton VIII 46. Chauvin VII 29-35 No. 212A; *ANE* 207-10 No. 230.□

B727§, ‡Animal with luminous body or face.
Bulûqiya/Ḥâsib/Queen of Vipers: *Alf* III 21; Burton V 302. Chauvin VII 54 No. 77; *ANE* 130-32 No. 177.□

B731.11.1§, White viper.
Abû Muḥammad Lazybones: *Alf* II 212-13; Burton IV 173. Chauvin VI 64-67 No. 233; *ANE* 71-73 No. 78.□

B749.1.1§, ‡Marvelous (thoroughbred) horse. See: *DOTTI*; (Cf. F989.17).
King ¿Umar al-Nu¿mân and Sons: *Alf* I 256,-(like Antar's/simile); Burton II 273,-("stallion like Abjar, which was Antar's charger"). Chauvin VI 112-24 No. 277; *ANE* 430-34 No. 39.□

B749.1.2§, ‡Marvelous (thoroughbred) camel. (Cf. F989.17).
Omar and Young Badawî: Returning to be Executed: *Alf* II 288; Burton V 101. Chauvin V 216 No. 125; *ANE* 429-30 No. 130.□

B754, ‡Sexual habits of animals.
Sindbâd's First Voyage: *Alf* III 85; Burton VI 8. Chauvin VII 7-9 No. 373A; *ANE* 385 No. 179.□

B754.9.2§, ‡Animal(s) with unusual sexual appetite. (Cf. T468§, T469§).
Butcher Wardân and Bear Lover: *Alf* II 252,-(bear); Burton IV 294. Chauvin V 177-78 No. 101; *ANE* 442-43 No. 101.□

B754.9.5§, ‡Sexual intercourse between different species (of animals). (Cf. B184.1.3.1§).
Sindbâd's First Voyage: *Alf* III 85; Burton VI 8. Chauvin VII 7-9 No. 373A; *ANE* 385 No. 179.□

B759.3.1§, ‡Whales (sharks) circle around prey.
Sindbâd's Seventh Voyage: *Alf* III 117; Burton VI 70. Chauvin VII 26-29 No. 373G; *ANE* 386-87 No. 179.□

B762, Monkeys attack by throwing coconuts. See: *ANE*; *DOTTI*; *GMC*. (Cf. B786, J60.1.1§).
Sindbâd's Fifth Voyage: *Alf* III 110,-(city); Burton VI 54. Chauvin VII 21-24 No. 373E; *ANE* 386 No. 179.□

B763.1.1§, ‡Snake attracted to milk. See: *PSAE*.
Bulûqiya: *Alf* III 25; Burton V 309. Chauvin VII 54 No. 77; *ANE* 130-32 No. 177.□

B772, Shipwrecked man repulsed by animals. As he floats to shore animals push him back into water. See: *ANE*; *GMC*.
Jullanâr of the Sea: *Alf* III 264; Burton VII 295. Chauvin V 147-51 No. 73; *ANE* 248-51 No. 227.□

B778.1.1§, ‡Ichneumon (weasel, mongoose) as thief.
She-mouse and Ichneumon: *Alf* II 35-6; Burton III 147. Chauvin II 228 No. 10; *ANE* 306 No. 49.□

B778.1.2§, ‡Mouse (rat) as thief. See: *DOTTI*.
Flea and She-mouse: *Alf* II 35,-(mouse); Burton III 153. Chauvin II 228 No. 12; *ANE* 186 No. 52.□

B778.5§, ‡Thieving bird. See: *DOTTI*.
Stolen Necklace/Hasty Accusation: *Alf* III 163-64; Burton VI 182. Chauvin VIII 53 No. 20; *ANE* 398 No. 200.□

B784.2.1.4.1§, ‡Worms driven out of woman's vagina by fumigation. (Cf. F950.0.5.0.1§).
King's Daughter and Ape: *Alf* II 253; Burton IV 298. Chauvin V 178 No. 102; *ANE* 262-63 No. 102.□

B786, Monkeys always copy men. See: *DOTTI*; *GMC*. (Cf. B762).
Sindbâd's Fifth Voyage: *Alf* III 110,-(city); Burton VI 54. Chauvin VII 21-24 No. 373E; *ANE* 386 No. 179.□

B790.1§, ‡Animal dies upon hearing human voice. (Cf. F688.5.3§).
Landsman ¿Abdallah and Merman ¿Abdallah: *Alf* IV 204-5; Burton IX 181. Chauvin V 6-7 No. 3; *ANE* 65-66 No. 256.□

B811.3.5.1§, Sacred she-camel (*nâqah*). See: *GMC*.
Tawaddud: Slavegirl Sold and Regained: *Alf* III 4; Burton V 235. Chauvin VII 117-19 No. 387; *ANE* 408-10 No. 157.□

B811.7§, ‡ Sacred wolf.
Tawaddud: Slavegirl Sold and Regained: *Alf* III 4; Burton V 235. Chauvin VII 117-19 No. 387; *ANE* 408-10 No. 157.□

B811.8§, ‡ Sacred dog.
Tawaddud: Slavegirl Sold and Regained: *Alf* III 4; Burton V 235. Chauvin VII 117-19 No. 387; *ANE* 408-10 No. 157.□

B811.9§, ‡ Sacred donkey (ass).
Tawaddud: Slavegirl Sold and Regained: *Alf* III 4; Burton V 235. Chauvin VII 117-19 No. 387; *ANE* 408-10 No. 157.□

B811.10§, ‡ Sacred mule.
Tawaddud: Slavegirl Sold and Regained: *Alf* III 4; Burton V 235. Chauvin VII 117-19 No. 387; *ANE* 408-10 No. 157.□

B811.10.1§, ‡ Sacred she-mule.
Tawaddud: Slavegirl Sold and Regained: *Alf* III 4; Burton V 235. Chauvin VII 117-19 No. 387; *ANE* 408-10 No. 157.□

B873.2.10§, ‡Giant rhinoceros.
Sindbâd's Second Voyage: *Alf* III 91; Burton VI 21. Chauvin VII 9-14 No. 373B; *ANE* 385 No. 179.□

B873.2.10.1§, ‡Giant rhinoceros carries (impales) elephant on its horn.
Sindbâd's Second Voyage: *Alf* III 91; Burton VI 21. Chauvin VII 9-14 No. 373B; *ANE* 385 No. 179.□

B873.4, ‡Giant ant. See: *ANE*. (Cf. B263.6.1§).
Jânshâh: *Alf* III 46; Burton V 338. Chauvin VII 39-44 No. 153; *ANE* 238-41 No. 178.□

B874.3, ‡Giant whale. See: *DOTTI*.
Sindbâd's Seventh Voyage: *Alf* III 117; Burton VI 70. Chauvin VII 26-29 No. 373G; *ANE* 386-87 No. 179.□

B875.1.0.1§, ‡Giant viper—(female). See: *DOTTI*.
Bulûqiya/Ḥâsib/Queen of Vipers: *Alf* III 20; Burton V 302. Chauvin VII 54 No. 77; *ANE* 130-32 No. 177;
Sindbâd's Second Voyage: *Alf* III 89; Burton VI 18. Chauvin VII 9-14 No. 373B; *ANE* 385 No. 179;
Sindbâd's Seventh Voyage: *Alf* III 121; Burton VI 75. Chauvin VII 26-29 No. 373G; *ANE* 386-87 No. 179.□

B875.2, Giant crocodile. See: *GMC*.
Sayf al-Mulûk: *Alf* III 285,-(*hâ'il*); Burton VII 343,-(frightful). Chauvin VII 64-73 No. 348; *ANE* 362-64 No. 229.□

C. TABU

C1.1§, ‡*al-ḥarâm*: sacred (religious) tabu. 'The illegitimate' (illicit, 'not permitted')—opposite of: *al-ḥalâl* (the licit or legitimate, permitted by God). See: *DOTTI*. (Cf. A608§, C59§, C60§).
King Jalî¿âd and Shimâs: *Alf* IV 155; Burton IX 32-34. Chauvin VI 9-11 No. 184; *ANE* 237-38 No. 236.□

C1.1.1§, ‡The profane (*najis/najas/'nagâsah'*): the opposite of the pure/immaculate (*ṭâhir/ṭuhr*). (Cf. V96.3.1§).
al-'Amjad and al-'As¿ad: *Alf* II 114; Burton III 311,-(vile [??]). Chauvin V 208-10 No. 120[.1]; *ANE* 341-42 No. 61/pt. 2;
Lady and Five Suitors Deceived: *Alf* III 160-61; Burton VI 178. Chauvin VIII 50-51 No. 18; *ANE* 266 No. 198;
¿Abdallah ibn Fâḍil: Treacherous Brothers: *Alf* IV 282,-(food touched by dogs); Burton IX 337. Chauvin V 2-4 No. 2; *ANE* 63-65 No. 261.□

C3.1§, ‡Near-tabu: failure to thank God (for His boon: food, healing, marriage, etc.). See: *DOTTI*. (Cf. Q223.2.1§, T160.1§).
Nuzhat al-Zamân Tested/¿Umar al-Nu¿mân: *Alf* I 202,-cf.; Burton II 162. Chauvin VI 116, n.1/passim No. 277; *ANE* 432,/passim No. 39.□

C47§, ‡Tabu: failing to submit to supernatural being (phantom). See: *DOTTI*.
Jawdar and His Treacherous Brethren: *Alf* III 186; Burton VI 228. Chauvin V 257-60 No. 154; *ANE* 244-45 No. 209.□

C51.1.0.1§, ‡Violating holy sanctuary (shrine) tabu. (Cf. P760.2.2.1§).
Sindbâd's Seventh Voyage: *Alf* III 117,-cf.; Burton VI 69. Chauvin VII 26-29 No. 373G; *ANE* 386-87 No. 179.□

C51.1.0.2§, ‡Tabu: praying at shrine for aid with an act that constitutes a sin.
Sweep and Noble Lady: Infidelity Repaid: *Alf* II 188; Burton IV 125. Chauvin VI 148 No. 306; *ANE* 403-4 No. 72.□

C51.3.1.1§, ‡Tabu: mention of God's name during magic ritual (sorcery).
Abû Muḥammad Lazybones: *Alf* II 215; Burton IV 175. Chauvin VI 64-67 No. 233; *ANE* 71-73 No. 78.□

C51.5.1§, ‡Tabu: imitating God's creation. By painting or sculpting an 'image' (picture, statue) of creature with soul (life).
Tawaddud: Slavegirl Sold and Regained: *Alf* II 317,-cf.; Burton V 223, n. 2. Chauvin VII 117-19 No. 387; *ANE* 408-10 No. 157.□

C59§, ‡Tabu: ritual uncleanliness while before God (performing religious duties: prayers, etc.). See: *DOTTI*. (Cf. C1.1§, V58.4.1§).
House with the Belvedere: *Alf* III 169; Burton VI 194. Chauvin VIII 57-58 No. 23; *ANE* 223 No. 203.□

C60§, ‡Tabu: violators of ablution-state (*wuḍû'*: being ritually clean)—ritual contaminants (*nagâsah*): acts and objects that defile, or cause ritual uncleanliness and becoming unfit to perform certain religious rituals. See: *DOTTI*. (Cf. C1.1§, V58.4.1§).
al-'Amjad and al-'As¿ad: *Alf* II 114,-(passim); Burton III 311. Chauvin V 208-10 No. 120[.1]; *ANE* 341-42 No. 61/pt. 2.□

C60.1§, ‡Ritual polluter: erotic touch (e.g., physical contact with member of opposite sex, or the like). See: *DOTTI*.
Dalîla the Swindler: *Alf* III 214; Burton VII 148,-(ablution made null and void). Chauvin V 245-50 No. 147; *ANE* 163-64 No. 224;
Jeweler's Wife and Qamar al-Zamân: *Alf* IV 241,-(homosexual); Burton IX 253. Chauvin V 212-14 No. 121; *ANE* 345-47 No. 260.□

C60.1.1§, ‡Ritual polluter: sexual intercourse (being *junub*, in a state of *janâbah*). See: *PSAE*. (Cf. V96.3§).
Jeweler's Wife and Qamar al-Zamân: *Alf* IV 241; Burton IX 253. Chauvin V 212-14 No. 121; *ANE* 345-47 No. 260.□

C60.1.2§, ‡Ritual polluter: involuntary emission (autoerotic ejaculation, 'wet dream'). (Cf. T474.0.1§).

Mercury ¿Alî: *Alf* III 233; Burton VII 183. Chauvin V 248-50 No. 147; *ANE* 301-3 No. 225.□

C60.2.1§, ‡Ritual polluter: touching unclean animal (dog, pig). See: *DOTTI*.
Hind bint al-Nu¿mân and al-Ḥajjâj: *Alf* III 202-3; Burton VII 98. Chauvin V 1-15-4 No. 50; *ANE* 221-22 No. 212.□

C61.5§, ‡Tabu: not accepting fate (destiny: God's preordained judgment). (Cf. A604.3.1§, V318.1§, V318.4§).
Ma¿rûf the Cobbler: *Alf* IV 308-9,-(poem); Burton X 35. Chauvin VI 81-82 No. 250; *ANE* 291-93 No. 262.□

C62.5.1.1§, ‡Tabu: kneeling or prostrating self before a being other than The One-God. (Cf. A54.3.1.1§, P20.5.2§).
Wolf and Fox: *Alf* II 30,-(fox prostrates himself before wolf); Burton III 133. Chauvin II 227 No. 6; *ANE* 450 No. 47;
Man from Yaman and Six Salve-girls: Flyting: *Alf* II 245,-(poem/last line); Burton IV 248. Chauvin 6: 151 No. 313; *ANE* 289 No. 84;
Rake's Trick Against Chaste Wife: *Alf* III 142,-(xxx); Burton VI 136,-(prostration must be made to Allah only). Chauvin 8: 37 No. 5; *ANE* 350 No. 185;
Man Who Never Laughs: *Alf* III 154,-cf./(mere forbidding); Burton VI 165. Chauvin VIII 47-48 No. 15; *ANE* 285-86 No. 195;
Sayf al-Mulûk: *Alf* III 275,-(Solomon forbids it); Burton VII 319,-(It befitteth not a man prostrate himself to earth save before Allah). Chauvin VII 64-73 No. 348; *ANE* 362-64 No. 229.□

C105.1§, ‡Tabu: exposing private parts of body (*¿awrah*). See: *DOTTI*. (Cf. C106§, P783.2.3.1§, T55.6.3§).
Hasan of Basrah: *Alf* IV 3; Burton VIII 41,-(cover my shame). Chauvin VII 29-35 No. 212A; *ANE* 207-10 No. 230.□

C105.3.1§, ‡Tabu: looking at privates of corpse of member of opposite sex. See: *DOTTI*.
Ghânim ibn Ayyûb: *Alf* I 156; Burton II 65,-("unlawful"). Chauvin VI 14 No. 188; *ANE* 192-93 No. 36.□

C106§, ‡Tabu: woman going (seen) unveiled in public—(*sufûr*). See: *DOTTI*. (Cf. C105.1§, F565.5.1§, P783.3§, T380.7§).
Pretty Gray-haired Woman Retorts: *Alf* II 302,-cf.; Burton V 163. Chauvin VI 153 No. 318; *ANE* 77-78 No. 152.□

C106.1§, ‡Tabu: woman going (seen) with 'naked' head in public: hair (uncovered). See: *DOTTI*. (Cf. P681.1.1.2.1§, P780§, X52).
Pretty Gray-haired Woman Retorts: *Alf* II 302-3; Burton V 163. Chauvin VI 153 No. 318; *ANE* 77-78 No. 152;
Qamar al-Zamân and Budûr: *Alf* II 95,-(implicit/daughter before father); Burton III 275. Chauvin V 204-12 No. 120; *ANE* 341-45 No. 61.□

C113, Tabu: sodomy.
Dispute Concerning Males and Females: *Alf* II 302,-(xxx); Burton V 160. Chauvin VI 153 No. 317; *ANE* 291 No. 151.□

C116.1§, ‡Tabu: sexual intercourse while wearing sacred object (writing).
Ma¿rûf the Cobbler: *Alf* IV 315-16; Burton X 51. Chauvin VI 81-82 No. 250; *ANE* 291-93 No. 262.□

C119.4§, ‡Tabu: conjugal intercourse without mentioning (thanking) God. (Cf. C3.1§, V57.4§).
Nuzhat al-Zamân Tested/¿Umar al-Nu¿mân: *Alf* I 202-3,-cf.; Burton II 162. Chauvin VI 116, n.1/passim No. 277; *ANE* 432,/passim No. 39.□

C119.5§, ‡Tabu: exposed sexual intercourse. (Or, intercourse in public place). (Cf. T160.0.2.3§, T189.3§).
Man [Gardener] and His Wife: *Alf* IV 165; Burton IX 98. Chauvin II 223 No. 152/19; *ANE* 289 No. 250.□

C135§, ‡Tabu: neglecting religious duties (services) after reaching puberty. (Cf. P548.1§, T380.2§).
Qamar al-Zamân and Budûr: *Alf* II 108; Burton III 301,-(age of "canonical responsibility"). Chauvin V 204-12 No. 120; *ANE* 341-45 No. 61.□

C160.0.1§, ‡Celibacy (*rahbanah*, monk-like, nun-like): *makrûh* ('disliked', almost-tabu, merely tolerated)—not the way for Moslems. See: *DOTTI*. (Cf. T100.0.2§, T316§).
Hasan of Basrah: *Alf* IV 50,-(judge's belief); Burton VIII 137. Chauvin VII 29-35 No. 212A; *ANE* 207-10 No. 230.□

C166.1§, ‡Tabu: polyandry (multiple husbands). See: *DOTTI*.
¿Alâ' al-Dîn Abû al-Shâmât: *Alf* II 169; Burton IV 74. Chauvin V 43-49 No. 18; *ANE* 85-87 No. 63.□

C240, Tabu: eating food of certain person. See: *GMC*. (Cf. M151.4.1§).
King ¿Umar al-Nu¿mân and Sons: *Alf* II 7; Burton II 87. Chauvin VI 112-24 No. 277; *ANE* 430-34 No. 39.□

C272.0.1§, ‡Tabu: having to do with wine (as to its production, distribution, consumption).
Anîs al-Jalîs: *Alf* I 137; Burton II 25. Chauvin V 120-24 No. 58; *ANE* 316-17 No. 35.□

C289§, Tabu: eating with left hand. See: *GMC*. (Cf. C548.1§).
Copt Broker's Story: Lover's Sacrifices Repaid: *Alf* I 89; Burton I 264. Chauvin VI 80 No. 249; *ANE* 313-14 No. 24.□

C312.2.1, Tabu: looking at princess on public appearance [NOT TABU]. See: *DOTTI*; *GMC*. (Cf. P96§).
Sweep and Noble Lady: Infidelity Repaid: *Alf* II 188,-cf./(not as tabu/ruler's order); Burton IV 126. Chauvin VI 148 No. 306; *ANE* 403-4 No. 72.□

C401, ‡Tabu: speaking during certain time.
Jânshâh: *Alf* III 46; Burton V 339. Chauvin VII 39-44 No. 153; *ANE* 238-41 No. 178.□

C401.2, Tabu: speaking during seven days of danger. See: *ANE*; *DOTTI*; *GMC*.
Craft and Malice of Women/Frame: *Alf* III 139; Burton VI 114. Chauvin VIII 33-34 No. 1; *ANE* 160-61 No. 181;
King's Son and Afrit's Mistress: *Alf* III 173,-cf.; Burton VI 201. Chauvin VIII 59 No. 24; *ANE* 263-64 No. 204.□

C401.3, Tabu: speaking while searching for treasure. See: *GMC*.
Jawdar and His Treacherous Brethren: *Alf* III 185-86; Burton VI 228. Chauvin V 257-60 No. 154; *ANE* 244-45 No. 209.□

C411, Tabu: asking about marvels which one sees. See: *GMC*.
Man Who Never Laughs: *Alf* III 152,-cf./(mere prohibition); Burton VI 161. Chauvin VIII 47-48 No. 15; *ANE* 285-86 No. 195.□

C411.1, Tabu: asking for reason of an unusual action. See: *DOTTI*; *GMC*. (Cf. Q340.1§).
Man Who Never Laughs: *Alf* III 152; Burton VI 161. Chauvin VIII 47-8 No. 15; *ANE* 285-86 No. 195.□

C411.1.1§, ‡Tabu: asking for reason of inexplicable self-punishment (face-slapping, weeping, wailing).
Man Who Never Laughs: *Alf* III 152; Burton VI 161. Chauvin VIII 47-48 No. 15; *ANE* 285-86 No. 195.□

C414.1.1§, ‡Tabu: asking God for (about) something of unknown consequence.
Serpent-charmer and Wife: *Alf* IV 145; Burton IX 56. Chauvin II 220 No. 152/9; *ANE* 368 No. 244.□

C431, Tabu: uttering the name of god (or gods). See: *ANE*; *DOTTI*; *GMC*.
Third Qalandar: Magnetic Mountain: *Alf* I 52; Burton I 143. Chauvin V 200-3 No. 117; *ANE* 340-41 No. 18;
Abû Muḥammad Lazybones: *Alf* II 215; Burton IV 175. Chauvin VI 64-67 No. 233; *ANE* 71-73 No. 78;
Sindbâd's Seventh Voyage: *Alf* III 120-21; Burton VI 75. Chauvin VII 26-29 No. 373G; *ANE* 386-87 No. 179.□

C431.1§, ‡Tabu: uttering the name of god while trafficking with demons (jinn, devils, etc.).
Third Qalandar: Magnetic Mountain: *Alf* I 52; Burton I 143. Chauvin V 200-3 No. 117; *ANE* 340-41 No. 18;
Sindbâd's Seventh Voyage: *Alf* III 120-21; Burton VI 75. Chauvin VII 26-29 No. 373G; *ANE* 386-87 No. 179.□

C433.1, Person obnoxious for his sins spoken of as "the other" [("distant-one")].
¿Alî Shâr and Zumurrud: *Alf* II 229,-(*"'anâ al-'ab¿ad", "al-ba¿îd"*); Burton IV 215,-("far one"). Chauvin V 89-91 No. 28; *ANE* 100-1 No. 82.□

C434§, Names of dangerous things (animal, disease, murder, etc.) are not to be uttered at a person without use of precautionary measures (e.g., "Distant one," "Away from you"). See: *DOTTI*; *GMC*.
Fisherman and Afrit: Ingratitude: *Alf* I 15,-(*yâ ba¿îd*); Burton I 41,-(distant one). Chauvin VI 23-25 No. 195; *ANE* 183-84 No. 8;
King ¿Umar al-Nu¿mân and Sons: *Alf* II 16,-(incest); Burton III 102 n. 1,-(use of euphemism). Chauvin VI 112-24 No. 277; *ANE* 430-34 No. 39;
¿Alî Shâr and Zumurrud: *Alf* II 229,-(*al-'ab¿ad*); Burton IV 215. Chauvin V 89-91 No. 28; *ANE* 100-1 No. 82;
Ma¿rûf the Cobbler: *Alf* IV 290,-(*al-ba¿îd*); Burton X 4,-(the far one). Chauvin VI 81-82 No. 250; *ANE* 291-93 No. 262.□

C434.2§, ‡Tabu: mention of evil entity or thing lest it materializes.
King ¿Umar al-Nu¿mân and Sons: *Alf* I 214,-(separation/poem-3); Burton II 187,-('Severance'). Chauvin VI 112-24 No. 277; *ANE* 430-34 No. 39;
Budûr and Jubayr ibn ¿Umayr: *Alf* II 240,-(reprimand for mention of separation); Burton IV 239. Chauvin VII 93-94 No. 374; *ANE* 243-44 No. 83;
Sindbâd's Fourth Voyage: *Alf* III 103,-(death); Burton VI 41. Chauvin VII 18-20 No. 373D; *ANE* 386 No. 179.□

C486§, ‡Tabu: backbiting (evil-speaking).
King ¿Umar al-Nu¿mân and Sons: *Alf* I 252; Burton II 264,-(backbiting is blameable). Chauvin VI 112-24 No. 277; *ANE* 430-34 No. 39.□

C494.1§, ‡Tabu: cursing 'Time' (*Dahr*, fate). (Cf. A102.6.1.1§, Z122.7§).
Tawaddud: Slavegirl Sold and Regained: *Alf* III 4; Burton V 230. Chauvin VII 117-19 No. 387; *ANE* 408-10 No. 157.□

C521, ‡Tabu: dismounting from horse.
Bulûqiya: *Alf* III 34,-(mare); Burton V 320. Chauvin VII 54 No. 77; *ANE* 130-32 No. 177.□

C548.1§, ‡Tabus associated with use of left hand (in greeting, cooking, etc.): it is the instrument for wiping one's own excreta and urine. (Cf. C289§, U284.2.1§).
Copt Broker's Story: Lover's Sacrifices Repaid: *Alf* I 89; Burton I 264. Chauvin VI 80 No. 249; *ANE* 313-14 No. 24;
Jewish Doctor's Story: Sororicide: *Alf* I 99; Burton I 288. Chauvin VI 89 No. 253; *ANE* 242 No. 26;
Sweep and Noble Lady: Infidelity Repaid: *Alf* II 190,-(poem); Burton IV 129. Chauvin VI 148 No. 306; *ANE* 403-4 No. 72.□

C549§, ‡Tabu: ostentatious display (publication) of assets—miscellaneous. (Cf. H502.0.1.1§, W166.2§).
Nuzhat al-Zamân Tested/¿Umar al-Nu¿mân: *Alf* I 201; Burton II 158. Chauvin VI 116, n.1/passim No. 277; *ANE* 432,/passim No. 39.□

C611, Forbidden chamber. Person allowed to enter all chambers of house except one. See: *ANE*; *DOTTI*; *GMC*.
Third Qalandar: Magnetic Mountain: *Alf* I 53; Burton I 159. Chauvin V 200-3 No. 117; *ANE* 340-41 No. 18;
Jânshâh: *Alf* III 50; Burton V 344. Chauvin VII 39-44 No. 153; *ANE* 238-41 No. 178.□

C611.1, Forbidden door. All doors may be entered [(opened)] except one. See: *ANE*; *DOTTI*; *GMC*. (Cf. N794§).
Man Who Never Laughs: *Alf* III 153-55; Burton VI 162, 165. Chauvin VIII 47-48 No. 15; *ANE* 285-86 No. 195;
Hasan of Basrah: *Alf* III 314; Burton VIII 28. Chauvin VII 29-35 No. 212A; *ANE* 207-10 No. 230.□

C611.1.0.1§, ‡Tabu: all persons forbidden to open door (gate) except one designated (supernatural) agent. See: *DOTTI*. (Cf. A1413.7.2§).
Bulûqiya: *Alf* III 37,-(Gabriel); Burton V 326. Chauvin VII 54 No. 77; *ANE* 130-32 No. 177.□

C611.1.2§, ‡Forbidden building (castle, palace, house, temple, etc.).
City of Labtayt/Treasure of Toléde: *Alf* II 183; Burton IV 99. Chauvin VI 90-91 No. 254; *ANE* 265-66 No. 67.□

C711, Tabu: going into bath on return from serpent kingdom. See: *ANE*.
Bulûqiya: *Alf* III 34; Burton V 322. Chauvin VII 54 No. 77; *ANE* 130-32 No. 177.□

C721, ‡Tabu: bathing. (Cf. E765.4.8.1§).
Bulûqiya: *Alf* III 34; Burton V 322. Chauvin VII 54 No. 77; *ANE* 130-32 No. 177.□

C745§, ‡Tabu: heeding a relative's plea for mercy or courtesy. (Cf. D1767.1.1.1.1§).
Jawdar and His Treacherous Brethren: *Alf* III 186; Burton VI 229-30. Chauvin V 257-60 No. 154; *ANE* 244-45 No. 209.□

C770.0.1§, ‡Tabu: arrogance (conceit, display of pride). (Cf. W166§).
King ¿Umar al-Nu¿mân and Sons: *Alf* I 242,-(displeases God); Burton II 245. Chauvin VI 112-24 No. 277; *ANE* 430-34 No. 39.□

C770.1, Tabu: overweening pride in good fortune forbidden. [Arrogant man swallowed by earth].
Tawaddud: Slavegirl Sold and Regained: *Alf* II 316; Burton V 221. Chauvin VII 117-19 No. 387; *ANE* 408-10 No. 157;
Angel of Death and Proud King: *Alf* III 8; Burton V 247. Chauvin VI 183-84 No. 349/[pt. 1]; *ANE* 104 No. 158.□

C770.2§, ‡Tabu: arrogant public display (walk). (Cf. W166§).
Tawaddud: Slavegirl Sold and Regained: *Alf* II 316; Burton V 221. Chauvin VII 117-19 No. 387; *ANE* 408-10 No. 157;
Angel of Death and Proud King: *Alf* III 8; Burton V 247. Chauvin VI 183-84 No. 349/[pt. 1]; *ANE* 104 No. 158.□

C787.3§, ‡Tabu: making too much profit (price-gouging). See: *DOTTI*. (Cf. P774.2.0.2§).
Nûr al-Dîn and Maryam: *Alf* IV 101,-cf.; Burton VIII 312. Chauvin V 89-91 No. 28; *ANE* 98-99 No. 233.□

C792§, ‡Tabu: use of others's possessions without permission. (Cf. P174.2.1§).
Ghânim ibn Ayyûb: *Alf* I 155; Burton II 63. Chauvin VI 14 No. 188; *ANE* 192-93 No. 36.□

C827§, ‡Tabu: thinking accusatory (evil) thoughts about others—unfounded (undeserved) suspicion. (Cf. K2059.9.2§, T481.0.1§, V301.1§).
Qamar al-Zamân and Budûr: *Alf* II 110,-(poem); Burton III 305. Chauvin V 204-12 No. 120; *ANE* 341-45 No. 61.□

C837, Tabu: losing bridle in selling man transformed to a horse. Disenchantment follows. See: *DOTTI*; *GMC*.
Jullanâr of the Sea: *Alf* III 268,-(she-mule); Burton VII 305. Chauvin V 147-51 No. 73; *ANE* 248-51 No. 227.□

C845.5.1§, ‡Tabu: dodging supernatural being's strike (blow, attack).
Jawdar and His Treacherous Brethren: *Alf* III 186; Burton VI 228. Chauvin V 257-60 No. 154; *ANE* 244-45 No. 209.□

C867.2§, ‡Tabu: cruelty to a human being.
Jânshâh: *Alf* III 68,-(*yaḥillu*/to be legitimate, to lover); Burton V 374,-(deal righteously, as Allah would have one deal). Chauvin VII 39-44 No. 153; *ANE* 238-41 No. 178.□

C867.2.3§, ‡Tabu: ridiculing physical deformity (ugliness). (Cf. X144§).
Hunchback's Tale: Resuscitated: *Alf* I 85; Burton I 255. Chauvin V 180-82 No. 105,-cf./(implicit); *ANE* 224-25 No. 23.□

C867.2.4.1§, ‡Dragging man by rope is tabu (sinful). (Cf. S186.1.2§).
Sweep and Noble Lady: Infidelity Repaid: *Alf* II 189; Burton IV 126. Chauvin VI 148 No. 306; *ANE* 403-4 No. 72.□

C868.1§, ‡Tabu: spoiling earth (i.e., damaging environment: land, natural resources, atmosphere, etc.).
Landsman ¿Abdallah and Merman ¿Abdallah: *Alf* IV 200,-(fisher's net); Burton IX 170. Chauvin V 6-7 No. 3; *ANE* 65-66 No. 256.□

C869.1§, ‡Tabu: suicide.
Ruined Baghdadi and His Slave-girl: *Alf* IV 130; Burton IX 25. Chauvin V 152-53 No. 75; *ANE* 353 No. 235.□

C869.3§, ‡Tabu: mercy killing. (Cf. J227.9.1§, P528§).

King Jalî¿âd and Shimâs: *Alf* IV 161,-(xxx); Burton IX 90, n. 1,-(comparative comment). Chauvin VI 9-11 No. 184; *ANE* 237-38 No. 236.□

C878.0.1§, ‡Tabu: luxurious (ostentatious) clothing. (Cf. P72§).
Ruined Baghdadi and His Slave-girl: *Alf* IV 130; Burton IX 26. Chauvin V 152-53 No. 75; *ANE* 353 No. 235.□

C898.1.1§, Tabu: wailing for the dead. See: *DOTTI*. (Cf. Z111.9.4§).
Landsman ¿Abdallah and Merman ¿Abdallah: *Alf* IV 207; Burton IX 187. Chauvin V 6-7 No. 3; *ANE* 65-66 No. 256.□

C901.0.1§, Tabu: feigning disability (sickness, blindness, etc.).
Barber's Third Brother: Exposes Blind Robbers: *Alf* I 115,-cf.; Burton I 331,-(abuse the gracious gifts of Allah). Chauvin V 159-60 No. 83; *ANE* 118 No. 31.□

C901.1.3.0.1§, ‡Tabu imposed by spouse (wife, husband).
Man Who Never Laughs: *Alf* III 155,-(by wife); Burton VI 165. Chauvin VIII 47-48 No. 15; *ANE* 285-86 No. 195.□

C910.1§, ‡Physical (bodily) changes as a result of breaking tabu.
Bulûqiya: *Alf* III 77,-(stomach blackened); Burton V 389. Chauvin VII 54 No. 77; *ANE* 130-32 No. 177.□

C936, ‡War lost because of breaking tabu.
City of Labtayt/Treasure of Tolêde: *Alf* II 183; Burton IV 100. Chauvin VI 90-91 No. 254; *ANE* 265-66 No. 67.□

C936.1§, ‡Nation conquered because of breaking tabu.
City of Labtayt/Treasure of Tolêde: *Alf* II 183; Burton IV 100. Chauvin VI 90-91 No. 254; *ANE* 265-66 No. 67.□

C952, Immediate return to other world because of broken tabu. See: *DOTTI*.
Man Who Never Laughs: *Alf* III 155; Burton VI 166. Chauvin VIII 47-48 No. 15; *ANE* 285-86 No. 195.□

C981§, ‡Rue (regret, sorrow) because of breaking tabu. (Cf. F956.7.7.2§).
Man Who Never Laughs: *Alf* III 155,-(opening forbidden door); Burton VI 166. Chauvin VIII 47-48 No. 15; *ANE* 285-86 No. 195.□

D. MAGIC AND SIMILAR SUPERNATURAL OCCURRENCES

D1§, ‡sihr (magic, sorcery): controlling (coercing, harnessing) the supernatural and the natural by means of supernatural agents other than God and His powers. (Cf. D1420.0.1§, G583).
Jânshâh: *Alf* III 66-67,-(*'aqsâm*/incantations); Burton V 371,-(conjuring). Chauvin VII 39-44 No. 153; *ANE* 238-41 No. 178.□

D5.4.1§, ‡Rape (attempted rape) by enchanted (bewitched) person.
Mercury ¿Alî: *Alf* III 241; Burton VII 200. Chauvin V 248-50 No. 147; *ANE* 301-3 No. 225.□

D8§, ‡Enchanted kingdom (cities, mountains, people, etc.). See: *DOTTI*. (Cf. F768.1).
Ensorcelled Prince/Husband: *Alf* I 23; Burton I 77. Chauvin VI 56-58 No. 222; *ANE* 176 No. 13.□

D10, Transformation to person of different sex. See: *ANE*; *DOTTI*; *GMC*.
Enchanted Spring: Change of Sex: *Alf* III 146-47; Burton VI 146. Chauvin VIII 43 No. 11; *ANE* 175-76 No. 191.□

D12, Transformation: man to woman. See: *DOTTI*; *GMC*; *PSAE*.
Enchanted Spring: Change of Sex: *Alf* III 146-47; Burton VI 146. Chauvin VIII 43 No. 11; *ANE* 175-76 No. 191.□

D113.2, ‡Transformation: man to bear.
Mercury ¿Alî: *Alf* III 242; Burton VII 201. Chauvin V 248-50 No. 147; *ANE* 301-3 No. 225.□

D118.2, ‡Transformation: man (woman) to monkey. See: *DOTTI*.
Second Qalandar: Afrit's Wife: *Alf* I 47; Burton I 122. Chauvin V 197-200 No. 116; *ANE* 338-39 No. 16.□

D132, Transformation: man to ass (mule, jennet, etc.). See: *DOTTI*; *GMC*.
Jullanâr of the Sea: *Alf* III 268; Burton VII 296. Chauvin V 147-51 No. 73; *ANE* 248-51 No. 227.□

D132.1, Transformation: man to ass. See: *DOTTI*; *GMC*.
Mercury ¿Alî: *Alf* III 241; Burton VII 199. Chauvin V 248-50 No. 147; *ANE* 301-3 No. 225.□

D132.2.1§, Transformation: woman to she-mule. See: *DOTTI*; *GMC*.
Jullanâr of the Sea: *Alf* III 268; Burton VII 304. Chauvin V 147-51 No. 73; *ANE* 248-51 No. 227.□

D133, ‡Transformation[: man] to cow (bull, calf, etc.). See: *DOTTI*.
First Shaykh: Sorceress Wife: *Alf* I 10,-(heifer); Burton I 28. Chauvin VII 129-30 No. 396; *ANE* 376-77 No. 5.□

D141, Transformation: man to dog. See: *ANE*; *DOTTI*; *GMC*.
Mercury ¿Alî: *Alf* III 242; Burton VII 202. Chauvin V 248-50 No. 147; *ANE* 301-3 No. 225;
¿Abdallah ibn Fâḍil: Treacherous Brothers: *Alf* IV 280; Burton IX 333. Chauvin V 2-4 No. 2; *ANE* 63-65 No. 261.□

D141.1, Transformation: woman to bitch. See: *DOTTI*; *GMC*.
Eldest Lady's Story: Treacherous Sisters: *Alf* I 57,-cf.; Burton I 172. Chauvin V 4 No. 443; *ANE* 174-75 No. 19;
Wife's device to cheat: (Weeping Bitch as Bluff): *Alf* III 149,-(claim); Burton VI 153. Chauvin VIII 45-46 No. 13; *ANE* 447-49 No. 193.□

D150, Transformation: man to bird. See: *ANE*.
Jullanâr of the Sea: *Alf* III 260; Burton VII 289. Chauvin V 147-51 No. 73; *ANE* 248-51 No. 227.□

D150.0.1§, ‡Transformation: man to colorful (beautiful) bird.
Jullanâr of the Sea: *Alf* III 260; Burton VII 289. Chauvin V 147-51 No. 73; *ANE* 248-51 No. 227.□

D157, ‡Transformation: man to parrot.
Jullanâr of the Sea: *Alf* III 260,-cf.; Burton VII 289. Chauvin V 147-51 No. 73; *ANE* 248-51 No. 227.□

D170.1§, ‡Transformation: man to colored fish. See: *DOTTI*. (Cf. D692, V131.3§).
Ensorcelled Prince/Husband: *Alf* I 29; Burton I 77. Chauvin VI 56-58 No. 222; *ANE* 176 No. 13.□

D231, Transformation: man to stone. See: *ANE*. (Cf. F768.1, Q551.3.4).
Ensorcelled Prince/Husband: *Alf* I 29,-cf.; Burton I 76-77. Chauvin VI 56-58 No. 222; *ANE* 176 No. 13.□

D361.1, Swan Maiden. See: *DOTTI*.
Jânshâh: *Alf* III 50,-(dove); Burton V 345. Chauvin VII 39-44 No. 153; *ANE* 238-41 No. 178;
Hasan of Basrah: *Alf* III 315,-ff.; Burton VIII 31. Chauvin VII 29-35 No. 212A; *ANE* 207-10 No. 230.□

D361.1.1, Swan Maiden finds her wings and resumes her form. See: *DOTTI*.
Jânshâh: *Alf* III 58; Burton V 357. Chauvin VII 39-44 No. 153; *ANE* 238-41 No. 178;
Hasan of Basrah: *Alf* IV 11-12; Burton VIII 59. Chauvin VII 29-35 No. 212A; *ANE* 207-10 No. 230.□

D361.1.2§, ‡Swan maiden recovers her feather dress (coat) and resumes her form. See: *DOTTI*.
Jânshâh: *Alf* III 52, III 55,-(pigeons); Burton V 346. Chauvin VII 39-44 No. 153; *ANE* 238-41 No. 178.□

D452.1.2.1§, ‡Transformation: island to mountain.
Ensorcelled Prince/Husband: *Alf* I 29; Burton I 77. Chauvin VI 56-58 No. 222; *ANE* 176 No. 13.□

D475.1.9, ‡Transformation: copper to gold. (Cf. D1242.0.1.1§, K1966).
Hasan of Basrah: *Alf* III 303,-cf./(alchemist's claim); Burton VIII 9. Chauvin VII 29-35 No. 212A; *ANE* 207-10 No. 230.□

D475.1.9.1§, ‡Transformation: silver to gold.
City of Labtayt/Treasure of Tolède: *Alf* II 184; Burton IV 101. Chauvin VI 90-91 No. 254; *ANE* 265-66 No. 67.□

D555, Transformation by drinking. See: *ANE*.
Enchanted Spring: Change of Sex: *Alf* III 146; Burton VI 146; . Chauvin 8: 43 No. 11; *ANE* 175 No. 191.□

D591.1§, ‡Transformation by bathing in magic well (spring). See: *DOTTI*.
Enchanted Spring: Change of Sex: *Alf* III 146-47; Burton VI 146. Chauvin VIII 43 No. 11; *ANE* 175-76 No. 191.□

D615, ‡Transformation combat. Fight between contestants who strive to outdo each other in successive transformations. See: *ANE*; *DOTTI*; *GMC*.
Second Qalandar: Afrit's Wife: *Alf* I 49; Burton I 134. Chauvin V 197-200 No. 116; *ANE* 338-39 No. 16.□

D615.7§, ‡Transformation combat between person (magician, saint, sorceress, etc.) and demon.
Second Qalandar: Afrit's Wife: *Alf* I 49; Burton I 134. Chauvin V 197-200 No. 116; *ANE* 338-39 No. 16.□

D625§, ‡Monthly transformation.
Sindbâd's Seventh Voyage: *Alf* III 120; Burton VI 74-75. Chauvin VII 26-29 No. 373G; *ANE* 386-87 No. 179.□

D625.1§, ‡Ordinary person becomes winged demon monthly. (Cf. F402.3.1§).
Sindbâd's Seventh Voyage: *Alf* III 120; Burton VI 74-75. Chauvin VII 26-29 No. 373G; *ANE* 386-87 No. 179.□

D658.3.4§, ‡Woman (queen) transforms self to bird (animal) in order to copulate with men she had bewitched into birds (animals). (Cf. T33.1§).
Jullanâr of the Sea: *Alf* III 266; Burton VII 301. Chauvin V 147-51 No. 73; *ANE* 248-51 No. 227.□

D659.15.1§, ‡Maiden (woman) transforms self to bird and flies away from suitor. See: *DOTTI*.
Jânshâh: *Alf* III 52,-(pigeon/dove); Burton V 346. Chauvin VII 39-44 No. 153; *ANE* 238-41 No. 178.□

D661, ‡Transformation as punishment. See: *DOTTI*. (Cf. D691).
First Shaykh: Sorceress Wife: *Alf* I 11; Burton I 31. Chauvin VII 129-30 No. 396; *ANE* 376-77 No. 5;
Third Shaykh: Transformation by Wife: *Alf* I 13,-ff.; Burton I 36. Chauvin VII 130 No. 398; *ANE* 378 No. 7.□

D661.6.1§, ‡Woman transforms lover (husband) to animal for desiring another (slave-girl). (Cf. P187.1§, Q241.1).
Jullanâr of the Sea: *Alf* III 266; Burton VII 298. Chauvin V 147-51 No. 73; *ANE* 248-51 No. 227.□

D665.2, ‡Transformation of stepchild to be rid of him. See: *DOTTI*.

First Shaykh: Sorceress Wife: *Alf* I 10; Burton I 28. Chauvin VII 129-30 No. 396; *ANE* 376-77 No. 5.□

D665.3, ‡Jealous co-wife transforms the other. See: *DOTTI*. (Cf. K2222).
First Shaykh: Sorceress Wife: *Alf* I 10; Burton I 28. Chauvin VII 129-30 No. 396; *ANE* 376-77 No. 5.□

D661.5§, ‡Transformation as sort of imprisonment (abduction): the enchanted is unrecognized by relatives. (Cf. F1035.6.2.1§).
Mercury ¿Alî: *Alf* III 242,-(hero bewitched into bear); Burton VII 202. Chauvin V 248-50 No. 147; *ANE* 301-3 No. 225.□

D671, Transformation flight. Fugitives transform themselves in order to escape detection by pursuer. See: *DOTTI*; *GMC*.
Jullanâr of the Sea: *Alf* III 269; Burton VII 306. Chauvin V 147-51 No. 73; *ANE* 248-51 No. 227.□

D671.0.3§, ‡Fugitive transforms self to different animals. See: *DOTTI*.
¿Abdallah ibn Fâḍil: Treacherous Brothers: *Alf* IV 279; Burton IX 331. Chauvin V 2-4 No. 2; *ANE* 63-65 No. 261.□

D682.5.1§, ‡Partial transformation to stone (petrification). See: *DOTTI*.
Ensorcelled Prince/Husband: *Alf* I 23; Burton I 76-77. Chauvin VI 56-58 No. 222; *ANE* 176 No. 13.□

D682.5.1.1§, ‡Transformation: lower half of body turned into stone. See: *DOTTI*. (Cf. K1535.1).
Ensorcelled Prince/Husband: *Alf* I 23; Burton I 76-77. Chauvin VI 56-58 No. 222; *ANE* 176 No. 13.□

D691, Daily beating of men transformed to dogs [as preventive measure]. Necessary unless hero himself is to be transformed. See: *ANE*; *DOTTI*; *GMC*. (Cf. Q458.1, T232.3.1§).
Eldest Lady's Story: Treacherous Sisters: *Alf* I 57,-(transformed women); Burton I 172. Chauvin V 4 No. 443; *ANE* 174-75 No. 19;
¿Abdallah ibn Fâḍil: Treacherous Brothers: *Alf* IV 268, 280; Burton IX 306, 333. Chauvin V 2-4 No. 2; *ANE* 63-65 No. 261.□

D692, City's Inhabitants transformed to fish. Different classes [(religious denominations)] to different colored fish. See: *ANE*; *DOTTI*; *GMC*. (Cf. D170.1§, F401.3.15.1§, V131.3§).
Ensorcelled Prince/Husband: *Alf* I 29; Burton I 77. Chauvin VI 56-58 No. 222; *ANE* 176 No. 13.□

D721.2, ‡Disenchantment by hiding skin (covering).
Hasan of Basrah: *Alf* IV 2-3,-cf.; Burton VIII 41. Chauvin VII 29-35 No. 212A; *ANE* 207-10 No. 230.□

D731, Disenchantment by obedience and kindness. See: *DOTTI*. (Cf. N543.4§).
Jawdar and His Treacherous Brethren: *Alf* III 186,-cf./(*rasad* by *'imtithâl*); Burton VI 228,-(undoing enchantment by obedience). Chauvin V 257-60 No. 154; *ANE* 244-45 No. 209.□

D746.1§, ‡Phantom (ghost) defeated by submission. See: *DOTTI*. (Cf. C47§, E11.1).
Jawdar and His Treacherous Brethren: *Alf* III 186; Burton VI 228. Chauvin V 257-60 No. 154; *ANE* 244-45 No. 209.□

D765.1, ‡Disenchantment by removing cause of enchantment. (Cf. D1380.0.2.1§, K979§).
Ensorcelled Prince/Husband: *Alf* I 30,-cf.; Burton I 80. Chauvin VI 56-58 No. 222; *ANE* 176 No. 13.□

D766.1.1, Disenchantment by water and command. See: *DOTTI*; *GMC*.
Eldest Lady's Story: Treacherous Sisters: *Alf* I 61; Burton I 185. Chauvin VI 144-45 No. 302; *ANE* 174-75 No. 19;
Jullanâr of the Sea: *Alf* III 269, 370; Burton VII 306. Chauvin V 147-51 No. 73; *ANE* 248-51 No. 227.□

D766.1.1.1§, ‡Disenchantment by sprinkling water (on the bewitched) and command. (Cf. D2075§).
First Shaykh: Sorceress Wife: *Alf* I 11; Burton I 31. Chauvin VII 129-30 No. 396; *ANE* 376-77 No. 5;
Third Shaykh: Transformation by Wife: *Alf* I 13; Burton I 36. Chauvin VII 130 No. 398; *ANE* 378 No. 7;
Ensorcelled Prince/Husband: *Alf* I 30; Burton I 80. Chauvin VI 56-58 No. 222; *ANE* 176 No. 13;

Eldest Lady's Story: Treacherous Sisters: *Alf* I 60; Burton I 185. Chauvin V 98 No. 33; *ANE* 174-75 No. 19;
Jullanâr of the Sea: *Alf* III 263,-(bird); Burton VII 294. Chauvin V 147-51 No. 73; *ANE* 248-51 No. 227.□

D791.1, Disenchantment after end of specified time.
Second Shaykh: Treacherous Brothers: *Alf* I 13; Burton I 35. Chauvin V 6 No. 397; *ANE* 377-78 No. 6.□

D791.1.2§, ‡Disenchantment at end of ten years.
Second Shaykh: Treacherous Brothers: *Alf* I 13; Burton I 35. Chauvin V 6 No. 397; *ANE* 377-78 No. 6.□

D791.2.0.1§, ‡Disenchantment by only the enchanter. (Cf. H1398.1§).
Second Shaykh: Treacherous Brothers: *Alf* I 13; Burton I 35. Chauvin V 6 No. 397; *ANE* 377-78 No. 6.□

D791.2.2.1.1§, ‡Maiden will disenchant man only if she may marry him and transform his enchanter.
First Shaykh: Sorceress Wife: *Alf* I 10; Burton I 31. Chauvin VII 129-30 No. 396; *ANE* 376-77 No. 5.□

D818.1, ‡Magic object received from magician. See: *DOTTI*.
Jawdar and His Treacherous Brethren: *Alf* III 189, 194; Burton VI 234, 243. Chauvin V 257-60 No. 154; *ANE* 244-45 No. 209.□

D832, Magic object acquired by acting as umpire for fighting heirs. See: *ANE*; *DOTTI*; *GMC*.
Hasan of Basrah: *Alf* IV 42-43; Burton VIII 121-22. Chauvin VII 29-35 No. 212A; *ANE* 207-10 No. 230.□

D862, ‡Magic object taken away by force.
Jawdar and His Treacherous Brethren: *Alf* III 193; Burton VI 241. Chauvin V 257-60 No. 154; *ANE* 244-45 No. 209.□

D865, Magic jewel carried off by bird. See: *ANE*.
Qamar al-Zamân and Budûr: *Alf* II 97; Burton III 279. Chauvin 5: 204 No. 120; *ANE* 341-345 No. 61;
Hasan of Basrah: *Alf* IV 39; Burton VIII 113; . Chauvin 7: 29 No. 212A; *ANE* 207 No. 230.□

D866, ‡Magic object destroyed. See: *DOTTI*. (Cf. F889.3.1§, J328.1§).
Ebony Horse: *Alf* II 267,-cf.; Burton V 31. Chauvin V 221-31 No. 130; *ANE* 172-74 No. 103;
Jawdar and His Treacherous Brethren: *Alf* III 201,-(ring, bag); Burton VI 256. Chauvin V 257-60 No. 154; *ANE* 244-45 No. 209.□

D866.0.1§, ‡Magic automatic object destroyed (rendered ineffective).
Ebony Horse: *Alf* II 267; Burton V 31. Chauvin V 221-31 No. 130; *ANE* 172-74 No. 103.□

D866.3§, ‡Magic object destroyed because of its evil social consequences. (Cf. J328.1§).
Jawdar and His Treacherous Brethren: *Alf* III 201,-(ring, bag); Burton VI 256. Chauvin V 257-60 No. 154; *ANE* 244-45 No. 209.□

D871.2§, ‡Magic object given away to kind helper.
Hasan of Basrah: *Alf* IV 52; Burton VIII 141. Chauvin VII 29-35 No. 212A; *ANE* 207-10 No. 230.□

D881.3§, ‡Magic object recovered by use of magic ring. See: *DOTTI*.
Jawdar and His Treacherous Brethren: *Alf* III 195; Burton VI 245. Chauvin V 257-60 No. 154; *ANE* 244-45 No. 209;
Sayf al-Mulûk: *Alf* III 289,-(box containing soul); Burton VII 351. Chauvin VII 64-73 No. 348; *ANE* 362-64 No. 229.□

D882.5§, ‡Stolen magic object stolen back by hero's wife. See: *DOTTI*.
Ma¿rûf the Cobbler: *Alf* IV 312,-(second wife); Burton X 45. Chauvin VI 81-82 No. 250; *ANE* 291-93 No. 262.□

D896§, ‡Magic object lost and voluntarily returned to owner by finder.
Abû Qîr and Abû Ṣîr: *Alf* IV 196; Burton IX 159. Chauvin V 15-17 No. 10; *ANE* 75-77 No. 255.□

D905, ‡Magic storm. See: *DOTTI*.
Third Qalandar: Magnetic Mountain: *Alf* I 52; Burton I 140-41. Chauvin V 200-3 No. 117; *ANE* 340-41 No. 18.□

D915.4.1, ‡Sabbatical river. Dry on Sabbath. See: *ANE*.
Jânshâh: *Alf* III 46; Burton V 337. Chauvin VII 39-44 No. 153; *ANE* 238-41 No. 178.□

D921.3.3.1§, ‡Lake Qârûn (Korah): treasure lake. See: *DOTTI*.
Jawdar and His Treacherous Brethren: *Alf* III 180, 183; Burton VI 217, 218,/219,/222. Chauvin V 257-60 No. 154; *ANE* 244-45 No. 209.□

D927, ‡Magic spring. See: *DOTTI*.
Enchanted Spring: Change of Sex: *Alf* III 146-47; Burton VI 146. Chauvin VIII 43 No. 11; *ANE* 175-76 No. 191.□

D961.1, ‡Garden produced by magic.
¿Alâ' al-Dîn Abû al-Shâmât: *Alf* II 180,-cf.; Burton IV 92. Chauvin V 43-49 No. 18; *ANE* 85-87 No. 63.□

D963§, ‡Field conjured up—with land, river, crop, etc. See: *DOTTI*. (Cf. D1607§, D2157.6).
Jullanâr of the Sea: *Alf* III 267; Burton VII 302-3. Chauvin V 147-51 No. 73; *ANE* 248-51 No. 227.□

D1002.0.1§, ‡Excrements of 'holy man' works wonders ('holy shit').
King ¿Umar al-Nu¿mân and Sons: *Alf* I 232, 234; Burton II 222, 223. Chauvin VI 112-24 No. 277; *ANE* 430-34 No. 39.□

D1016.1.1§, ‡Magic ritual requires slaughtering of white cock.
Abû Muḥammad Lazybones: *Alf* II 212-13; Burton IV 172. Chauvin VI 64-67 No. 233; *ANE* 71-73 No. 78.□

D1017.3§, ‡Magic flesh of snake (viper). (Cf. B161.3, F950.0.4.4.1§).
Bulûqiya: *Alf* III 79-80; Burton V 391-94. Chauvin VII 54 No. 77; *ANE* 130-32 No. 177.□

D1030.1, Food supplied by magic. See: *DOTTI*; *GMC*. (Cf. F849.0.1.1§).
Jawdar and His Treacherous Brethren: *Alf* III 184; Burton VI 224. Chauvin V 257-60 No. 154; *ANE* 244-45 No. 209.□

D1071, Magic jewel (jewels). See: *GMC*. (Cf. D1380.11).
King ¿Umar al-Nu¿mân and Sons: *Alf* I 164,-(report of); Burton II 82. Chauvin VI 112-24 No. 277; *ANE* 430-34 No. 39.□

D1132.1, Palace produced by magic. See: *DOTTI*; *GMC*.
Jawdar and His Treacherous Brethren: *Alf* III 195; Burton VI 245-46. Chauvin V 257-60 No. 154; *ANE* 244-45 No. 209.□

D1211.1§, ‡Magic drum supplies riding-animals (transportation).
Hasan of Basrah: *Alf* III 308, 313,-cf./(calls supernatural animals), IV 8; Burton VIII 18, 27, 49. Chauvin VII 29-35 No. 212A; *ANE* 207-10 No. 230.□

D1242.0.1§, ‡Magic elixir (nectar).
Hasan of Basrah: *Alf* III 307; Burton VIII 18,-(Elixir). Chauvin VII 29-35 No. 212A; *ANE* 207-10 No. 230.□

D1242.0.1.1§, ‡Magic elixir transforms one metal to another. (Cf. D475.1.9).
City of Labtayt/Treasure of Tolède: *Alf* II 184; Burton IV 101. Chauvin VI 90 No. 254; *ANE* 265-66 No. 67.□

D1254, Magic staff. (Cf. D1472.2.12§).
Jânshâh: *Alf* III 67; Burton V 371. Chauvin VII 39-44 No. 153; *ANE* 238-41 No. 178.□

D1254.2, ‡Magic rod. (Cf. D1470.1.25).
¿Alâ' al-Dîn Abû al-Shâmât: *Alf* II 176,-(locates lost objects); Burton IV 87. Chauvin V 43-49 No. 18; *ANE* 85-87 No. 63.□

D1266, Magic book. See: *DOTTI*; *GMC*; *PSAE*.
Jawdar and His Treacherous Brethren: *Alf* III 182; Burton VI 221. Chauvin V 257-60 No. 154; *ANE* 244-45 No. 209.□

D1266.1, Magic writings (gramerye [gramarye], runes). See: *GMC*; *PSAE*. (Cf. D1421.1.3.1§, D1500.1.34, F883.6§, M116.4§).
Ma¿rûf the Cobbler: *Alf* IV 304; Burton X 28. Chauvin VI 81-82 No. 250; *ANE* 291-93 No. 262.□

D1272, Magic circle. See: *DOTTI*; *GMC*.

Second Qalandar: Afrit's Wife: *Alf* I 49; Burton I 133-34. Chauvin V 197-200 No. 116; *ANE* 338-39 No. 16.□

D1273.0.6§, *'raqwah'/ruqwah*: charm containing sacred words renders invulnerable (protects). See: *GMC*; *PSAE*.
¿Alâ' al-Dîn Abû al-Shâmât: *Alf* II 148; Burton IV 32-33. Chauvin V 43-49 No. 18; *ANE* 85-87 No. 63.□

D1273.3, Bible [(holy)] text as magic spell. See: *GMC*. (Cf. D1766, V90§).
Jânshâh: *Alf* III 66,-(use of *'aqsâm*/oaths); Burton V 369. Chauvin VII 39-44 No. 153; *ANE* 238-41 No. 178.□

D1273.6.1§, ‡'Supernatural power (right) of a letter (of the alphabet).
¿Alâ' al-Dîn Abû al-Shâmât: *Alf* II 180,-cf.; Burton IV 93. Chauvin V 43-49 No. 18; *ANE* 85-87 No. 63.□

D1273.8§, ‡Magic formula (incantation) summons demon (afrit, jinni, etc.)—usually by coercion. (Cf. G583, N813).
Second Qalandar: Afrit's Wife: *Alf* I 49; Burton I 134. Chauvin V 197-200 No. 116; *ANE* 338-39 No. 16;
Jânshâh: *Alf* III 66-67,-(controls); Burton V 370. Chauvin VII 39-44 No. 153; *ANE* 238-41 No. 178.□

D1288.1§, ‡Vanishing magic coin: disappears or turns to worthless object after it has been spent.
Barber's Fourth Brother: Illusionary Experiences: *Alf* I 116; Burton I 331–34. Chauvin V 160-61 No. 84; *ANE* 119 No. 32.□

D1311.6.5§, ‡Magic incantation ('fix') linked to star(s).
al-Rashîd and Omani Merchant: *Alf* IV 217; Burton IX 203. Chauvin VI 111-12 No. 276; *ANE* 201-2 No. 257.□

D1311.6.6§, ‡Medical recipe linked to stars. (Treatment that is mixture of the scientific and the magical).
Ni¿mah and Nu¿m: Stolen Wife Regained: *Alf* II 139; Burton IV 12. Chauvin VI 96-97 No. 263; *ANE* 314 No. 62.□

D1311.15, ‡Magic rod used for divination.
¿Alâ' al-Dîn Abû al-Shâmât: *Alf* II 169,-(*qaḍîb*); Burton IV 73. Chauvin V 43-49 No. 18; *ANE* 85-87 No. 63.□

D1313.3, Copper horseman indicates road. See: *ANE*.
Jinn Imprisoned in Flasks: *Alf* III 127; Burton VI 95. Chauvin VII 113 No. 380=no/text; *ANE* 146 No. 180.□

D1314.2.3, ‡Divining rod points to house of thief.
¿Alâ' al-Dîn Abû al-Shâmât: *Alf* II 169,-(points to location of stolen goods); Burton IV 73. Chauvin V 43-49 No. 18; *ANE* 85-87 No. 63.□

D1323.1, Magic clairvoyant mirror. See: *DOTTI*; *GMC*.
City of Labtayt/Treasure of Tolède: *Alf* II 184,-(shows *al-'aqâlîm al-sab¿ah*); Burton IV 101,-(seven climates of the world). Chauvin VI 90-91 No. 254; *ANE* 265-66 No. 67.□

D1323.4, Magic clairvoyant sphere [(part of ball)]. Shows all that passes on earth by looking at that part of globe. See: *ANE*; *GMC*.
Jawdar and His Treacherous Brethren: *Alf* III 182; Burton VI 220. Chauvin V 257-60 No. 154; *ANE* 244-45 No. 209.□

D1323.5.1§, ‡Kohl (powder) when worn gives clairvoyance of buried treasures. (Cf. D1331.3.2, D1388.0.7.2§, J166.4.1§).
Jawdar and His Treacherous Brethren: *Alf* III 183; Burton VI 222. Chauvin V 257-60 No. 154; *ANE* 244-45 No. 209.□

D1331.3.2, Powder [(kohl)] causes supernatural sight and blindness. See: *DOTTI*; *GMC*.
Jawdar and His Treacherous Brethren: *Alf* III 183,-cf.; Burton VI 222. Chauvin V 257-60 No. 154; *ANE* 244-45 No. 209.□

D1335.5.2.0.1§, ‡Magic ring gives power to rule ('ring of kingship'). (Cf. A517§, D1470.1.15).
Bulûqiya: *Alf* III 24,-(Solomon's Ring); Burton V 307. Chauvin VII 54 No. 77; *ANE* 130-32 No. 177.□

D1344, Magic object gives invulnerability. See: *GMC*. (Cf. D1380.0.2.1§).
King ¿Umar al-Nu¿mân and Sons: *Alf* I 232; Burton II 222. Chauvin VI 112-24 No. 277; *ANE* 430-34 No. 39.□

D1346.5.1§, ‡Herb of immortality.
Bulûqiya: *Alf* III 26; Burton V 312. Chauvin VII 54 No. 77; *ANE* 130-32 No. 177.□

D1346.5.1.1§, ‡Herb extends life till End of World (blowing of trumpet). (Cf. A1093.1§).
Bulûqiya: *Alf* III 26; Burton V 310. Chauvin VII 54 No. 77; *ANE* 130-32 No. 177.□

D1346.10.1§, ‡Water of immortality: makes one immortal when drunk. See: *DOTTI*.
Bulûqiya: *Alf* III 28; Burton V 312. Chauvin VII 54 No. 77; *ANE* 130-32 No. 177.□

D1347.3, ‡Magic medicine makes sterile fertile.
¿Alâ' al-Dîn Abû al-Shâmât: *Alf* II 148,-cf./(*mu¿akkir al-bayḍ*/"egg-clouder [i.e., like fertilized chicken egg]"); Burton IV 31-32,-(seed-thickener). Chauvin V 43-49 No. 18; *ANE* 85-87 No. 63.□

D1347.7§, ‡Magic serpent (eaten) causes fecundity. (Cf. T188.1§).
Sayf al-Mulûk: *Alf* III 275; Burton VII 321. Chauvin VII 64-73 No. 348; *ANE* 362-64 No. 229.□

D1361.15, Magic cap renders invisible: tarnkappe [(cap of invisibility)]. See: *ANE*; *DOTTI*; *GMC*.
Hasan of Basrah: *Alf* IV 42-43; Burton VIII 120. Chauvin VII 29-35 No. 212A; *ANE* 207-10 No. 230.□

D1361.18, Magic sword renders invisible. See: *GMC*. (Cf. D1561.2.4).
Abû Muhammad Lazybones: *Alf* II 215; Burton IV 176. Chauvin VI 64-67 No. 233; *ANE* 71-73 No. 78.□

D1367.1, Magic plant causes insanity. See: *ANE*.
Sindbâd's Fourth Voyage: *Alf* III 101,-cf./(food/oil); Burton VI 36,-("food"/"cocoa-nut oil"). Chauvin VII 18-20 No. 373D; *ANE* 386 No. 179□

D1380.0.1, Magic object protects a city. See: *GMC*.
City of Brass: *Alf* III 132,-cf.; Burton VI 109. Chauvin V 32-35 No. 16; *ANE* 146-50 No. 180.□

D1380.0.2§, ‡Protection as long as magic protecting agent remains.
Abû Muḥammad Lazybones: *Alf* II 212-13; Burton IV 172. Chauvin VI 64-67 No. 233; *ANE* 71-73 No. 78.□

D1380.0.2.1§, ‡Removal of magic protecting agent renders vulnerable. (Cf. D765.1).
Abû Muḥammad Lazybones: *Alf* II 212-13; Burton IV 172. Chauvin VI 64-67 No. 233; *ANE* 71-73 No. 78.□

D1380.0.2.1.1§, ‡Destruction of magic protecting agent allows evil spirit to gain access to previously protected person (or site).
Abû Muḥammad Lazybones: *Alf* II 212-13; Burton IV 172. Chauvin VI 64-67 No. 233; *ANE* 71-73 No. 78.□

D1380.0.2.2§, ‡Site (mountain, city) impenetrable as long as magic statue of horseman remains mounted on horse.
Third Qalandar: Magnetic Mountain: *Alf* I 51; Burton I 141. Chauvin V 200-3 No. 117; *ANE* 340-41 No. 18.□

D1381.2.1§, ‡Cleric's (holy man's) excrements (urine) protect from attack.
King ¿Umar al-Nu¿mân and Sons: *Alf* I 232, 234; Burton II 222,-(excrement of the Chief Patriarch), 223. Chauvin VI 112-24 No. 277; *ANE* 430-34 No. 39.□

D1380.11, ‡Magic jewel protects. (Cf. D1071).
King ¿Umar al-Nu¿mân and Sons: *Alf* I 164,-(report of); Burton II 82. Chauvin VI 112-24 No. 277; *ANE* 430-34 No. 39.□

D1381.20, ‡Sacred relics protect against attack.
King ¿Umar al-Nu¿mân and Sons: *Alf* I 232; Burton II 222. Chauvin VI 112-24 No. 277; *ANE* 430-34 No. 39.□

D1380.20.1§, ‡Magic runes protect against evil spirit (jinni, afrit, etc.).
Abû Muḥammad Lazybones: *Alf* II 212-13; Burton IV 172. Chauvin VI 64-67 No. 233; *ANE* 71-73 No. 78.□

D1388.0.7.2§, ‡Kohl when applied to eyes protects from drowning. (Cf. D1323.5.1§).

Jullanâr of the Sea: *Alf* III 252; Burton VII 275,-(eye powder). Chauvin V 147-51 No. 73; *ANE* 248-51 No. 227.□

D1400.1.4.2, Magic saber conquers enemy. See: *ANE*.
Jawdar and His Treacherous Brethren: *Alf* III 182,-(sword); Burton VI 222. Chauvin V 257-60 No. 154; *ANE* 244-45 No. 209□

D1408.1, Magic sphere burns up country. By turning that part of the globe to the sun, one can make any place on earth burn up. See: *ANE*; *GMC*. (Cf. D1402.12.1§).
Jawdar and His Treacherous Brethren: *Alf* III 182; Burton VI 221. Chauvin V 257-60 No. 154; *ANE* 244-45 No. 209.□

D1402.12.1§, ‡Magic ring emits killer laser-like beam. (Cf. D1408.1).
Abû Qîr and Abû Ṣîr: *Alf* IV 195; Burton IX 159,-(flash of lightening). Chauvin V 15-17 No. 10; *ANE* 75-77 No. 255.□

D1419.1, ‡Magic object compels person to laugh (shriek). See: *ANE*.
City of Brass: *Alf* III 132,-cf./(scene); Burton VI 108. Chauvin V 32-35 No. 16; *ANE* 146-50 No. 180□

D1420.0.1§, ‡Supernatural being (spirit, genie, angel, etc.) assigned as 'servant' of magic object—('servant' controlled by object's owner). See: *DOTTI*. (Cf. F403.2.2.5).
Jawdar and His Treacherous Brethren: *Alf* III 182, 201,-cf./(new owner); Burton VI 221, 256. Chauvin V 257-60 No. 154; *ANE* 244-45 No. 209;
Hasan of Basrah: *Alf* IV 43; Burton VIII 121. Chauvin VII 29-35 No. 212A; *ANE* 207-10 No. 230.□

D1421.0.3, Magic hair when thrown in fire summons supernatural helper. See: *DOTTI*; *GMC*. (Cf. D1421.1.9).
Portress Amînah: Bitten Cheek: *Alf* I 60,-(genie); Burton I 185. Chauvin V 98-99 No. 33; *ANE* 326-27 No. 20.□

D1421.1.3.1§, ‡Magic writings summon genie (when touched). (Cf. D1266.1).
Second Qalandar: Afrit's Wife: *Alf* I 44,-(summons afrit); Burton I 118,-(graven talisman). Chauvin V 197-200 No. 116; *ANE* 338-39 No. 16.□

D1421.1.6, ‡Magic ring summons genie. See: *ANE*; *DOTTI*. (Cf. D1470.1.15).
Ma¿rûf the Cobbler: *Alf* IV 304; Burton X 28. Chauvin VI 81-82 No. 250; *ANE* 291-93 No. 262.□

D1421.1.7, ‡Magic incense (when burned) summons genie.
Abû Muḥammad Lazybones: *Alf* II 216,-(musk); Burton IV 177. Chauvin VI 64-67 No. 233; *ANE* 71-73 No. 78.□

D1421.1.9, ‡Magic hair summons demon. (Cf. D1421.0.3).
Eldest Lady's Story: Treacherous Sisters: *Alf* I 60,-(female jinni); Burton I 184. Chauvin V 98 No. 33; *ANE* 174-75 No. 19.□

D1427.6§, ‡Magic rod compels people to follow orders.
¿Alâ' al-Dîn Abû al-Shâmât: *Alf* II 176; Burton IV 87. Chauvin V 43-49 No. 18; *ANE* 85-87 No. 63.□

D1470.1.15, Magic wishing-ring. [Solomon's Ring]. See: *DOTTI*; *GMC*. (Cf. D1335.5.2.0.1§, D1662.1).
Bulûqiya: *Alf* III 24; Burton V 307. Chauvin VII 54 No. 77; *ANE* 130-32 No. 177;
Jawdar and His Treacherous Brethren: *Alf* III 194; Burton VI 243. Chauvin V 257-60 No. 154; *ANE* 244-45 No. 209.□

D1470.1.25, ‡Magic wishing-rod. (Cf. D1254.2).
Hasan of Basrah: *Alf* IV 42-43,-cf.; Burton VIII 120. Chauvin VII 29-35 No. 212A; *ANE* 207-10 No. 230.□

D1470.1.42, ‡Magic wishing-jewel.
¿Alâ' al-Dîn Abû al-Shâmât: *Alf* II 180,-(bead); Burton IV 92. Chauvin V 43-49 No. 18; *ANE* 85-87 No. 63.□

D1470.2.10§, ‡Magic saddlebags supply food and treasure. See: *DOTTI*. (Cf. D1472.1.22).
Jawdar and His Treacherous Brethren: *Alf* III 189, 193; Burton VI 224, 235, 239-40. Chauvin V 257-60 No. 154; *ANE* 244-45 No. 209.□

D1472.2.12§, ‡Magic staff (cane, rod) supplies food. (Cf. D1254.2, D1254).
Jânshâh: *Alf* III 67; Burton V 371. Chauvin VII 39-44 No. 153; *ANE* 238-41 No. 178.□

D1472.1.22, Magic bag (sack) supplies food. See: *ANE*. (Cf. D1470.2.10§).
Jawdar and His Treacherous Brethren: *Alf* III 184; Burton VI 224ff. Chauvin V 257-60 No. 154; *ANE* 244-45 No. 209.□

D1475, Magic object furnishes soldiers. See: *DOTTI*. (Cf. F252.3).
¿Alâ' al-Dîn Abû al-Shâmât: *Alf* II 180; Burton IV 93. Chauvin V 43-49 No. 18; *ANE* 85-87 No. 63.□

D1475.8§, ‡Magic engraving (drawing) of horse and man furnishes horseman (warrior). (Cf. D1620.1.2).
¿Alâ' al-Dîn Abû al-Shâmât: *Alf* II 180; Burton IV 93. Chauvin V 43-49 No. 18; *ANE* 85-87 No. 63.□

D1476.5§, ‡Demon-servant (genie, afrit, etc.) of magic object furnishes slaves. See: *DOTTI*. (Cf. N813).
Jawdar and His Treacherous Brethren: *Alf* III 196; Burton VI 245. Chauvin V 257-60 No. 154; *ANE* 244-45 No. 209.□

D1500.1.2.1§, ‡Magic healing precious stone (gem).
al-Rashîd and Omani Merchant: *Alf* IV 217; Burton IX 202-3. Chauvin VI 111-12 No. 276; *ANE* 201-2 No. 257.□

D1500.1.34, ‡Magic writings heal. (Cf. D1266.1).
al-Rashîd and Omani Merchant: *Alf* IV 217; Burton IX 203. Chauvin VI 111-12 No. 276; *ANE* 201-2 No. 257.□

D1520.17, Magic transportation by sofa. See: *ANE*; *GMC*.
¿Alâ' al-Dîn Abû al-Shâmât: *Alf* II 180; Burton IV 93. Chauvin V 43-49 No. 18; *ANE* 85-87 No. 63; **Jânshâh**: *Alf* III 71; Burton V 376. Chauvin VII 39-44 No. 153; *ANE* 238-41 No. 178.□

D1524.1, ‡Magic object permits man to walk on water.
Bulûqiya: *Alf* III 37; Burton V 327. Chauvin VII 54 No. 77; *ANE* 130-32 No. 177.□

D1524.1.1, ‡Medicine on feet permits man to walk on water.
Bulûqiya: *Alf* III 24, 37,-(water); Burton V 308, 326-27. Chauvin VII 54 No. 77; *ANE* 130-32 No. 177.□

D1532.6.1§, ‡Magic feather-dress bears person aloft. (Cf. D721.2).
Hasan of Basrah: *Alf* IV 2; Burton VIII 40. Chauvin VII 29-35 No. 212A; *ANE* 207-10 No. 230.□

D1551.9.1§, ‡Magic formula causes waters to divide (part). See: *DOTTI*; *PSAE*.
Jawdar and His Treacherous Brethren: *Alf* III 185-86; Burton VI 228. Chauvin V 257-60 No. 154; *ANE* 244-45 No. 209.□

D1561.2.4, Charm gives invisibility and power of moving everywhere. See: *DOTTI*. (Cf. D1361.18).
Abû Muḥammad Lazybones: *Alf* II 215,-(on sword); Burton IV 176. Chauvin VI 64-67 No. 233; *ANE* 71-73 No. 78.□

D1607§, Self-performing chore: (cooking, cleaning, etc.) gets itself done.
Devotee Prince: Ascetic's Death: *Alf* II 290,-cf./(wall builds itself/bricks lay themselves); Burton V 111-12. Chauvin VI 193-94 No. 363; *ANE* 167-68 No. 134.□

D1610.3.0.1§, ‡Plant (herb) speaks of its attributes. (Cf. Z175.1).
Bulûqiya: *Alf* III 25; Burton V 308. Chauvin VII 54 No. 77; *ANE* 130-32 No. 177.□

D1610.5, ‡Speaking head.
Dûban and King Yûnân: *Alf* I 23,-(deceptive claim); Burton I 58. Chauvin V 275-76 No. 156; *ANE* 459 No. 9.□

D1620.0.1, ‡Automatic doll.
City of Brass: *Alf* III 137,-cf.; Burton VI 118. Chauvin V 32-35 No. 16; *ANE* 146-50 No. 180.□

D1620.1.2, Automatic statue of a horseman. See: *ANE*; *GMC*.
Third Qalandar: Magnetic Mountain: *Alf* I 51,-(brass); Burton I 141. Chauvin V 200-3 No. 117; *ANE* 340-41 No. 18.□

D1620.2.1, Automatic statue of horse. See: *DOTTI*; *GMC*. (Cf. F889.3.1§).
Third Qalandar: Magnetic Mountain: *Alf* I 51,-(brass); Burton I 141. Chauvin V 200-3 No. 117; *ANE* 340-41 No. 18;
Ebony Horse: *Alf* II 254,-cf.; Burton V 2. Chauvin V 221-31 No. 130; *ANE* 172-74 No. 103.□

D1626.1, Artificial flying horse. See: *DOTTI*; *GMC*.
Ebony Horse: *Alf* II 254,-cf.; Burton V 2-3. Chauvin V 221-31 No. 130; *ANE* 172-74 No. 103.□

D1629§, ‡Entertainment automata: musicians, dancers, and singers come out of magic object (box) and perform. See: *DOTTI*.
Ma¿rûf the Cobbler: *Alf* IV 306-7,-cf./(*¿arâyis al-kunûz*); Burton X 31,-("Brides of the Treasure"). Chauvin VI 81-82 No. 250; *ANE* 291-93 No. 262.□

D1654.9.1, Corpse cannot be moved. See: *DOTTI*; *GMC*.
Prior Becomes Moslem: al-Anbârî: *Alf* II 299; Burton V 144. Chauvin V 237-38 No. 137; *ANE* 330-31 No. 147.□

D1662.1, Magic ring works by being stroked [(rubbed)]. See: *DOTTI*; *GMC*. (Cf. D1470.1.15).
Ma¿rûf the Cobbler: *Alf* IV 304; Burton X 28. Chauvin VI 81-82 No. 250; *ANE* 291-93 No. 262.□

D1693.3§, Moses's staff becomes serpent [(viper)] and swallows magicians' rods (snakes). See: *DOTTI*.
King ¿Umar al-Nu¿mân and Sons: *Alf* I 240,-(poem/passim); Burton II 242. Chauvin VI 112-24 No. 277; *ANE* 430-34 No. 39;
Tawaddud: Slavegirl Sold and Regained: *Alf* III 5,-cf.; Burton V 238. Chauvin VII 117-19 No. 387; *ANE* 408-10 No. 157.□

D1705§, *barakah* (blessedness): supernatural [positive] power residing in object, act, or person. See: *DOTTI*; *GMC*; *PSAE*. (Cf. M440.1§).
Ghânim ibn Ayyûb: *Alf* I 157,-(blessedness of intent); Burton II 76. Chauvin VI 14 No. 188; *ANE* 192-93 No. 36;
King ¿Umar al-Nu¿mân and Sons: *Alf* I 226; Burton II 213. Chauvin VI 112-24 No. 277; *ANE* 430-34 No. 39;
Anûshirawân and Village Damsel: *Alf* II 285; Burton V 88. Chauvin VI 26-27 No. 198; *ANE* 106 No. 121;
Tawaddud: Slavegirl Sold and Regained: *Alf* III 3,-(in crops/passim); Burton V 232. Chauvin VII 117-19 No. 387; *ANE* 408-10 No. 157;
Dalîla the Swindler: *Alf* III 217; Burton VII 150. Chauvin V 245-50 No. 147; *ANE* 163-64 No. 224;
Jullanâr of the Sea: *Alf* III 249,-(inscription on Solomon's Seal); Burton VII 275. Chauvin V 147-51 No. 73; *ANE* 248-51 No. 227;
Abû al-Ḥasan al-Khorâsânî (and Caliph's Favorite): *Alf* IV 236; Burton IX 243. Chauvin V 218-20 No. 129; *ANE* 68-69 No. 259.□

D1706§, ‡A person's *barakah* (*mabrûk*-person). (Cf. V210).
¿Alâ' al-Dîn Abû al-Shâmât: *Alf* II 154,-(*sayyidah* Nafîsah); Burton IV 46. Chauvin V 43-49 No. 18; *ANE* 85-87 No. 63;
Island King/Pious Jewish Merchant: *Alf* III 17,-(counsels); Burton V 292. Chauvin VI 161 No. 325; *ANE* 234 No. 174.□

D1707§, ‡Blessed objects. See: *DOTTI*; *PSAE*.
King ¿Umar al-Nu¿mân and Sons: *Alf* I 175,-(beads/precious stones *kathîrat al-barakât*); Burton II 110,-(givers of good fortune). Chauvin VI 112-24 No. 277; *ANE* 430-34 No. 39;
Jullanâr of the Sea: *Alf* III 249,-(Solomon's ring); Burton VII 275. Chauvin V 147-51 No. 73; *ANE* 248-51 No. 227;
Nûr al-Dîn and Maryam: *Alf* IV 103,-(monastery); Burton VIII 316. Chauvin V 52-54 No. 271; *ANE* 98-99 No. 233.□

D1707.1.3§, ‡Blessed thought (intent). (Cf. D1708§).
Ghânim ibn Ayyûb: *Alf* I 157; Burton II 76. Chauvin VI 14 No. 188; *ANE* 192-93 No. 36.□

D1707.1.5.1§, ‡Sacred words (from holy book) blessed.
Tawaddud: Slavegirl Sold and Regained: *Alf* II 312-13; Burton V 213,-("Basmalah"). Chauvin VII 117-19 No. 387; *ANE* 408-10 No. 157.□

D1707.2§, ‡Blessed bodily organ (limb).

Qamar al-Zamân and Budûr: *Alf* II 72,-cf.; Burton III 227. Chauvin V 204-12 No. 120; *ANE* 341-45 No. 61.□

D1707.3§, ‡Blessed animals.
Bulûqiya: *Alf* III 23,-cf./(vipers/*sharîfah*); Burton V 306,-(noble creatures). Chauvin VII 54 No. 77; *ANE* 130-32 No. 177.□

D1707.8§, ‡Blessed places.
¿Alâ' al-Dîn Abû al-Shâmât: *Alf* II 172,-(Alexandria); Burton IV 76. Chauvin V 43-49 No. 18; *ANE* 85-87 No. 63.□

D1708§, ‡Blessed acts (deeds). (Cf. A1471.8.1§, D1707.1.3§).
Sindbâd's Seventh Voyage: *Alf* III 119,-(*barakah*/blessedness); Burton VI 73,-(Allah's blessing). Chauvin VII 26-29 No. 373G; *ANE* 386-87 No. 179;
Abû al-Ḥasan al-Khorâsânî (and Caliph's Favorite): *Alf* IV 236,-("his coming"); Burton IX 243. Chauvin V 218-20 No. 129; *ANE* 68-69 No. 259.□

D1708.1§, ‡Use of right side blessed. (Cf. C289§).
Tawaddud: Slavegirl Sold and Regained: *Alf* II 307; Burton V 196. Chauvin VII 117-19 No. 387; *ANE* 408-10 No. 157.□

D1708.4§, ‡Certain happening (occurrence) blessed (e.g., arrival or departure of someone, or the like).
Abû al-Ḥasan al-Khorâsânî (and Caliph's Favorite): *Alf* IV 236-37,-("his coming"); Burton IX 243. Chauvin V 218-20 No. 129; *ANE* 68-69 No. 259.□

D1710.1§, ‡Requirements for performance of magic rituals. Success depends on using person or object with specific qualities. (Cf. D1714.1.2§, N543).
Jawdar and His Treacherous Brethren: *Alf* III 186,-(speaking is tabu); Burton VI 228. Chauvin V 257-60 No. 154; *ANE* 244-45 No. 209;
Hasan of Basrah: *Alf* III 308,-(certain person's name); Burton VIII 18-19. Chauvin VII 29-35 No. 212A; *ANE* 207-10 No. 230.□

D1711.1.4§, ‡Jew as magician.
Mercury ¿Alî: *Alf* III 240; Burton VII 197. Chauvin V 248-50 No. 147; *ANE* 301-3 No. 225.□

D1711.4, ‡Druid as magician.
Jânshâh: *Alf* III 67,-('monk'/Yaghmûs); Burton V 371. Chauvin VII 39-44 No. 153; *ANE* 238-41 No. 178.□

D1711.10.7§, ‡People from North Africa (*maghrabîs*, "maghrebians") as magicians. See: *DOTTI*.
Jawdar and His Treacherous Brethren: *Alf* III 180; Burton VI 217,-(Moor). Chauvin V 257-60 No. 154; *ANE* 244-45 No. 209.□

D1712.0.2§, ‡King (caliph) as augurer (oracle, soothsayer).
Butcher Wardân and Bear Lover: *Alf* II 252; Burton IV 296. Chauvin V 177-78 No. 101; *ANE* 442-43 No. 101.□

D1713, ‡Magic power of hermit (saint, yogi). See: *DOTTI*. (Cf. D1705§, V220.0.6§).
King ¿Umar al-Nu¿mân and Sons: *Alf* I 256; Burton II 272. Chauvin VI 112-24 No. 277; *ANE* 430-34 No. 39.□

D1714.1.2§, ‡Magic healing by chaste virgin (woman). See: *DOTTI*; *PSAE*. (Cf. H413.7§).
¿Abdallah ibn Fâḍil: Treacherous Brothers: *Alf* IV 287; Burton IX 348. Chauvin V 2-4 No. 2; *ANE* 63-65 No. 261.□

D1716.1, Magic power of the idiot. See: *DOTTI*; *GMC*.
Dalîla the Swindler: *Alf* III 217,-cf./(claim); Burton VII 152. Chauvin V 245-50 No. 147; *ANE* 163-64 No. 224.□

D1752§, *barakah* (blessedness) passes from body to body. See: *DOTTI*. (Cf. D1705§, M440.1§, V220.0.6.1§).
King ¿Umar al-Nu¿mân and Sons: *Alf* I 256; Burton II 272,-(blessing takes effect on him ...). Chauvin VI 112-24 No. 277; *ANE* 430-34 No. 39.□

D1761, Magic results produced by wishing. See: *DOTTI*; *GMC*.
Three Wishes: *Alf* III 162; Burton VI 181. Chauvin VIII 51-52 No. 19; *ANE* 419-20 No. 199.□

D1761.0.2, Limited number of wishes granted. See: *DOTTI*.

Three Wishes: *Alf* III 162; Burton VI 181. Chauvin VIII 51-52 No. 19; *ANE* 419-20 No. 199.□

D1761.3.1§, Wishing by *ṭâqat al-qadr* ('[Light-]Halo of Power'). See: *DOTTI*; *GMC*. (Cf. V59.0.1§).
Three Wishes: *Alf* III 162; Burton VI 180. Chauvin VIII 51-52 No. 19; *ANE* 419-20 No. 199.□

D1766, Magic results produced by religious ceremony. [*siḥr nûrânî, ¿ulwî* (upper magic)]. See: *DOTTI*; *GMC*. (Cf. D1273.3).
Bulûqiya: *Alf* III 24,-(passim/*al-rûḥânî*/spiritualism); Burton V 308,-(white magic). Chauvin VII 54 No. 77; *ANE* 130-32 No. 177.□

D1766.2, Magic results produced by sacrifice.
Hasan of Basrah: *Alf* III 306; Burton VIII 15. Chauvin VII 29-35 No. 212A; *ANE* 207-10 No. 230.□

D1767.1.1.1.1§, ‡Disrobing parent (mother) as magic ritual. See: *DOTTI*. (Cf. C745§, T405.2§).
Jawdar and His Treacherous Brethren: *Alf* III 187; Burton VI 229. Chauvin V 257-60 No. 154; *ANE* 244-45 No. 209.□

D1778.1§, ‡Magic results from striking earth with magic rod.
Hasan of Basrah: *Alf* IV 42-43; Burton VIII 121. Chauvin VII 29-35 No. 212A; *ANE* 207-10 No. 230.□

D1812.3.2, Fortune told by cutting sand. [*raml/rammâl*]. See: *DOTTI*; *GMC*.
¿Alâ' al-Dîn Abû al-Shâmât: *Alf* II 178; Burton IV 90,-(tablets of geomancy). Chauvin V 43-49 No. 18; *ANE* 85-87 No. 63;
¿Alî Shâr and Zumurrud: *Alf* II 229; Burton IV 214ff. Chauvin V 89-91 No. 28; *ANE* 100-1 No. 82;
Jawdar and His Treacherous Brethren: *Alf* III 194,-(*takht raml*); Burton VI 243,-(geomantic figure). Chauvin V 257-60 No. 154; *ANE* 244-45 No. 209;
Mercury ¿Alî: *Alf* III 231, 240; Burton VII 181. Chauvin V 248-50 No. 147; *ANE* 301-3 No. 225.□

D1812.3.3, Future revealed in dream. [Divination through interpretation of dreams]. See: *DOTTI*. (Cf. J157, V517§).
Wolf and Fox: *Alf* II 34; Burton III 143. Chauvin II 227 No. 6; *ANE* 450 No. 47.□

D1812.3.3.1, ‡Truest dreams at daybreak.
Qamar al-Zamân and Budûr: *Alf* II 87,-(last third of night/implicit); Burton III 258. Chauvin V 204-12 No. 120; *ANE* 341-45 No. 61.□

D1812.3.3.10, Dream interpreted by opposites. See: *DOTTI*.
Wolf and Fox: *Alf* II 34; Burton III 144,-(dancing in=wedding=falling in imminent deadly danger). Chauvin II 227 No. 8; *ANE* 450 No. 47.□

D1812.4.2§, ‡The unknown revealed by presentiment: "knowledge within". (Cf. F657§).
¿Alî Shâr and Zumurrud: *Alf* II 221,-(my heart senses separation); Burton IV 199,-(my heart presageth a parting). Chauvin V 89-91 No. 28; *ANE* 100-1 No. 82;
Nûr al-Dîn and Maryam: *Alf* IV 98; Burton VIII 308-9. Chauvin V 52-54 No. 271; *ANE* 98-99 No. 233.□

D1812.5.1.7, Meeting certain persons (animals) a bad omen.
Ma¿n Rewards a Bedouin for Gift: *Alf* II 183; Burton IV 99. Chauvin VI 78 No. 248; *ANE* 291 No. 66.□

D1812.5.1.27, Croaking of raven as bad omen.
City of Brass: *Alf* III 130; Burton VI 102. Chauvin 5: 32-35 No. 16; *ANE* 146-50 No. 180;
Masrûr and Zayn al-Mawâṣif: *Alf* IV 68,-(poem); Burton VIII 242. Chauvin VI 82-84 No. 251; *ANE* 294-95 No. 232.□

D1812.5.1.27.1, Hooting of owl a bad omen.
City of Brass: *Alf* III 130; Burton VI 102. Chauvin 5: 32-35 No. 16; *ANE* 146-50 No. 180.□

D1814.4§, ‡Advice from supernatural spirit or being (e.g., al-Khiḍr, St. George, etc.).
¿Abdallah ibn Fâḍil: Treacherous Brothers: *Alf* IV 277; Burton IX 327. Chauvin V 2-4 No. 2; *ANE* 63-65 No. 261.□

D1814.5§, ‡Advice from ogress (or ogre).
Prince and Ogress: *Alf* I 20; Burton I 55. Chauvin VI 26 No. 197; *ANE* 329 No. 12;
King's Favorite Son and Ogress: *Alf* III 144; Burton VI 141. Chauvin VIII 40-41 No. 8B; *ANE* 264 No. 188.□

D1825.1, Second sight. Power to see future happenings. See: *ANE*. (Cf. F657§).
¿Alî Shâr and Zumurrud: *Alf* II 221; Burton IV 199,-(presaging). Chauvin V 89-91 No. 28; *ANE* 100-1 No. 82.□

D1846.5, ‡Invulnerability bestowed by saint.
King ¿Umar al-Nu¿mân and Sons: *Alf* I 245,-cf./(invisibility); Burton II 251. Chauvin VI 112-24 No. 277; *ANE* 430-34 No. 39.□

D1846.5.3§, ‡Invulnerability through saint's excreta (urine). (Cf. D1381.2.1§, D1381.20).
King ¿Umar al-Nu¿mân and Sons: *Alf* I 232, 234; Burton II 222, 223. Chauvin VI 112-24 No. 277; *ANE* 430-34 No. 39.□

D1905.3, Love by curse. See: *DOTTI*.
Budûr and Jubayr ibn ¿Umayr: *Alf* II 239; Burton IV 238. Chauvin VII 93-94 No. 374; *ANE* 243-44 No. 83.□

D1925.1, Barrenness removed by eating or drinking. See: *DOTTI*.
Sayf al-Mulûk: *Alf* III 275; Burton VII 321. Chauvin VII 64-73 No. 348; *ANE* 362-64 No. 229.□

D1932.1§, ‡Wall opens to let in a being with supernatural power (afrit, ogre, magician, etc.) and then closes after he exits. See: *DOTTI*.
Ensorcelled Prince/Husband: *Alf* I 24-25; Burton I 63. Chauvin VI 56-58 No. 222; *ANE* 176 No. 13;
Ma¿rûf the Cobbler: *Alf* IV 292; Burton X 6. Chauvin VI 81-82 No. 250; *ANE* 291-93 No. 262.□

D1934§, ‡Earth diver: supernatural being with the ability to dive into earth.
Second Qalandar: Afrit's Wife: *Alf* I 46; Burton I 120. Chauvin V 197-200 No. 116; *ANE* 338-39 No. 16.□

D1960, Magic sleep. See: *DOTTI*; *GMC*. (Cf. K331.2.1.3§, N396.1§).
King ¿Umar al-Nu¿mân and Sons: *Alf* I 247,-cf./(miraculous); Burton II 256. Chauvin VI 112-24 No. 277; *ANE* 430-34 No. 39.□

D1972, Lover's magic sleep at rendezvous. (Cf. T35.0.2.1§).
¿Azîz and ¿Azîzah: *Alf* I 275-78,-cf./(non-magic); Burton II 312-15. Chauvin V 144-45 No. 71; *ANE* 111-13 No. 41.□

D1981.2, Magic invisibility of saints. (Cf. V229.8.3§).
Conversion of Princess by Khawwâṣ: *Alf* III 15,-(miraculous); Burton V 285. Chauvin V 239 No. 139; *ANE* 145 No. 171.□

D1982, ‡Certain objects invisible.
Mercury ¿Alî: *Alf* III 240,-(*qaṣr*/palace); Burton VII 198,-(castle). Chauvin V 248-50 No. 147; *ANE* 301-3 No. 225.□

D1982.6§, ‡Building (palace, castle) rendered invisible-visible by magic.
Mercury ¿Alî: *Alf* III 240; Burton VII 197-98. Chauvin V 248-50 No. 147; *ANE* 301-3 No. 225.□

D1982.6.1§, ‡Building (palace, castle) visible only when owner is inside.
Mercury ¿Alî: *Alf* III 240; Burton VII 197-98. Chauvin V 245-50 No. 147; *ANE* 301-3 No. 225.□

D1983.3§, ‡Invisibility conferred by holy man (prophet, saint, aesthetic, etc.). (Cf. D1981.2).
King ¿Umar al-Nu¿mân and Sons: *Alf* I 245,-(invisibility); Burton II 251. Chauvin VI 112-24 No. 277; *ANE* 430-34 No. 39.□

D1983.3.1§, ‡Saint's shadow renders person (object) invisible. (Cf. V229.8.3§).
King ¿Umar al-Nu¿mân and Sons: *Alf* I 245; Burton II 251. Chauvin VI 112-24 No. 277; *ANE* 430-34 No. 39.□

D1983.3.1.1§, ‡Only two persons may be concealed simultaneously by saint's shadow.
King ¿Umar al-Nu¿mân and Sons: *Alf* I 245; Burton II 251. Chauvin VI 112-24 No. 277; *ANE* 430-34 No. 39.□

D2031, Magic illusion.
Barber's Fourth Brother: Illusionary Experiences: *Alf* I 116; Burton I 332. Chauvin V 160-61 No. 84; *ANE* 119 No. 32.□

D2031.20.1§, ‡Meat hanging in butcher shop made to look as if human corpse. See: *DOTTI*.
Barber's Fourth Brother: Illusionary Experiences: *Alf* I 116; Burton I 332–33. Chauvin V 159-60 No. 83; *ANE* 119 No. 32.□

D2065.1.1§, Epilepsy from possession by jinn. See: *DOTTI*; *GMC*. (Cf. D2176.3.4).
Ebony Horse: *Alf* II 264,-(*ṣar¿ah*); Burton V 38. Chauvin V 221-31 No. 130; *ANE* 172-74 No. 103.□

D2070, Bewitching. See: *DOTTI*; *GMC*.
Enchanted Spring: Change of Sex: *Alf* III 146,-cf.; Burton VI 146. Chauvin VIII 43 No. 11; *ANE* 175-76 No. 191;
Jullanâr of the Sea: *Alf* III 260; Burton VII 289. Chauvin V 147-51 No. 73; *ANE* 248-51 No. 227.□

D2071, Evil Eye. Bewitching by means of a glance. See: *GMC*. (Cf. W199.3.3.1§).
Tawaddud: Slavegirl Sold and Regained: *Alf* III 6,-(riddle); Burton V 242. Chauvin VII 117-19 No. 387; *ANE* 408-10 No. 157;
Nûr al-Dîn and Maryam: *Alf* IV 99,-(poem); Burton VIII 308,-(jealousy). Chauvin V 52-54 No. 271; *ANE* 98-99 No. 233.□

D2071.1.3.1.2§, ‡Child hidden so as to avert Evil Eye. (Cf. J147, J674.4§).
¿Alâ' al-Dîn Abû al-Shâmât: *Alf* II 149; Burton IV 33. Chauvin V 43-49 No. 18; *ANE* 85-87 No. 63;
Jeweler's Wife and Qamar al-Zamân: *Alf* IV 238; Burton IX 247. Chauvin V 212-14 No. 121; *ANE* 345-47 No. 260.□

D2071.1.3.1.3§, ‡Ugly person (object) presented with handsome one to avert Evil Eye.
Nûr al-Dîn ¿Alî and Son: *Alf* I 72; Burton I 222. Chauvin VI 102-6 No. 270; *ANE* 317-19 No. 22.□

D2071.1.4.0.2§, ‡Holy verse (text) guards against Evil Eye. (Cf. V90§).
Tâj al-Mulûk: *Alf* I 293,-cf./(God's name); Burton III 19. Chauvin V 126-28 No. 60; *ANE* 406-8 No. 40;
Ebony Horse: *Alf* II 256,-(Koranic,/poem); Burton V 4,-(xxx/poem not included). Chauvin V 221-31 No. 130; *ANE* 172-74 No. 103.□

D2071.1.4.3§, Salt as guard against Evil Eye. See: *GMC*.
¿Alâ' al-Dîn Abû al-Shâmât: *Alf* II 148; Burton IV 33. Chauvin V 43-49 No. 18; *ANE* 85-87 No. 63.□

D2071.3.1§, ‡Most of the dead ('inhabitants of graves') [are there] because of '*al-¿ayn*' (the Evil Eye).
¿Alâ' al-Dîn Abû al-Shâmât: *Alf* II 148; Burton IV 36,-(those in their long homes). Chauvin V 43-49 No. 18; *ANE* 85-87 No. 63.□

D2072.3.2§, ‡Magic paralysis caused by magician (sorcerer).
Mercury ¿Alî: *Alf* III 240; Burton VII 198. Chauvin V 248-50 No. 147; *ANE* 301-3 No. 225.□

D2074.2.2, Summoning by burning of hair. See: *GMC*.
Eldest Lady's Story: Treacherous Sisters: *Alf* I 60; Burton I 184. Chauvin V 98 No. 33; *ANE* 174-75 No. 19.□

D2075§, ‡Bewitching by means of magic formula and sprinkling enchanting substance (e.g., water, dust, or the like). (Cf. D766.1.1.1§).
Second Qalandar: Afrit's Wife: *Alf* I 49,-(enchanting into ape); Burton I 126. Chauvin V 197-200 No. 116; *ANE* 338-39 No. 16;
Ensorcelled Prince/Husband: *Alf* I 29,-cf./(formula); Burton I 76-77. Chauvin VI 56-58 No. 222; *ANE* 176 No. 13.□

D2121.2, Magic journey with [(i.e., requiring)] closed eyes. See: *GMC*.
Bulûqiya: *Alf* III 74; Burton V 384-85. Chauvin VII 54 No. 77; *ANE* 130-32 No. 177.□

D2121.5, Magic journey: man carried by spirit or devil. See: *DOTTI*; *GMC*.
Nûr al-Dîn ¿Alî and Son: *Alf* I 72; Burton I 214. Chauvin VI 102-6 No. 270; *ANE* 317-19 No. 22;
Enchanted Spring: Change of Sex: *Alf* III 146; Burton VI 147. Chauvin VIII 43 No. 11; *ANE* 175-76 No. 191;
Sayf al-Mulûk: *Alf* III 299,-(female jinni); Burton VII 372. Chauvin VII 64-73 No. 348; *ANE* 362-64 No. 229.□

D2121.5.1§, ‡Demon (afrit, jinni, magician, etc.) flies man to destination—usually by carrying him on his back. See: *DOTTI*. (Cf. D2135, F414.1).
Sindbâd's Seventh Voyage: *Alf* III 120; Burton VI 75. Chauvin VII 26-29 No. 373G; *ANE* 386-87 No. 179;
Jawdar and His Treacherous Brethren: *Alf* III 194; Burton VI 244. Chauvin V 257-60 No. 154; *ANE* 244-45 No. 209;
Jullanâr of the Sea: *Alf* III 269; Burton VII 306. Chauvin V 147-51 No. 73; *ANE* 248-51 No. 227;

Hasan of Basrah: *Alf* IV 23; Burton VIII 81. Chauvin VII 29-35 No. 212A; *ANE* 207-10 No. 230;
¿Abdallah ibn Fâḍil: Treacherous Brothers: *Alf* IV 287,-(al-Khiḍr); Burton IX 348. Chauvin V 2-4 No. 2; *ANE* 63-65 No. 261;
Ma¿rûf the Cobbler: *Alf* IV 293; Burton X 6. Chauvin VI 81-82 No. 250; *ANE* 291-93 No. 262.□

D2121.5.1.1§, ‡Jinn woman (female-jinni) carries man on her back and flies him to destination. See: *DOTTI*.
Qamar al-Zamân and Budûr: *Alf* II 71; Burton III 224. Chauvin V 204-12 No. 120; *ANE* 341-45 No. 61;
Jânshâh: *Alf* III 55,-cf.; Burton V 352. Chauvin VII 39-44 No. 153; *ANE* 238-41 No. 178.□

D2122.5, Journey with magic speed by saint. See: *GMC*. (Cf. V225).
Bulûqiya: *Alf* III 74,-(al-Khiḍr); Burton V 384-85. Chauvin VII 54 No. 77; *ANE* 130-32 No. 177.□

D2135, Magic air journey. See: *DOTTI*; *GMC*. (Cf. B552, F174.2§).
Enchanted Spring: Change of Sex: *Alf* III 146; Burton VI 148. Chauvin VIII 43 No. 11; *ANE* 175-76 No. 191.□

D2144.4.2§, ‡Person attempting to steal magic object (ring, book) burned up (by magic or curse).
Bulûqiya: *Alf* III 26-27; Burton V 312. Chauvin VII 54 No. 77; *ANE* 130-32 No. 177.□

D2157.6, ‡Field cultivated and sowed by magic. See: *DOTTI*. (Cf. D963§).
Jullanâr of the Sea: *Alf* III 267; Burton VII 302-3. Chauvin V 147-51 No. 73; *ANE* 248-51 No. 227.□

D2161.0.5§, Power of healing a gift.
¿Abdallah ibn Fâḍil: Treacherous Brothers: *Alf* IV 287; Burton IX 348. Chauvin V 2-4 No. 2; *ANE* 63-65 No. 261.□

D2161.3.8, Insanity magically cured.
al-Rashîd and Omani Merchant: *Alf* IV 217; Burton IX 203. Chauvin VI 111-12 No. 276; *ANE* 201-2 No. 257.□

D2176.3.4, Devil cast out of possessed man's body. (Cf. D2065.1.1§, F381.0.1§).
Ebony Horse: *Alf* II 267,cf./("*¿âriḍ*"/[usually, of the jinni]); Burton V 30,-("*devil*" [!!]). Chauvin V 221-31 No. 130; *ANE* 172-74 No. 103.□

D2176.3.6.1§, ‡Evil spirit exorcised by imprisonment (threat of imprisonment).
Ebony Horse: *Alf* II 267,-(claim, *'asjinu al-¿âriḍ*); Burton V 30,-(possessed by *devil* to be exorcised [??]). Chauvin V 221-31 No. 130; *ANE* 172-74 No. 103.□

D2177.1, Demon enclosed in bottle. See: *ANE*; *DOTTI*. (Cf. R181).
Abû Muḥammad Lazybones: *Alf* II 216; Burton IV 178. Chauvin VI 64-67 No. 233; *ANE* 71-73 No. 78;
Jinn Imprisoned in Flasks: *Alf* III 122; Burton VI 84. Chauvin VII 113 No. 380; *ANE* 146 No. 180.□

D2177.1.2§, ‡Demon (jinni, afrit) imprisoned by his own kind.
Abû Muḥammad Lazybones: *Alf* II 216; Burton IV 178. Chauvin VI 64-67 No. 233; *ANE* 71-73 No. 78.□

D2177.3.1§, ‡Afrit (jinni) imprisoned in stone column.
Jinn Imprisoned in Flasks: *Alf* III 127; Burton VI 96. Chauvin VII 113 No. 380=no/text; *ANE* 146 No. 180.□

D2198.1§, ‡Spirits (*'a¿wân/khuddâm*) put to do a human's bidding—(saint's, magician's). (Cf. D1420.0.1§, G583, N813).
Jawdar and His Treacherous Brethren: *Alf* III 195; Burton VI 245-46. Chauvin V 257-60 No. 154; *ANE* 244-45 No. 209;
Ma¿rûf the Cobbler: *Alf* IV 306; Burton X 30. Chauvin VI 81-82 No. 250; *ANE* 291-93 No. 262.□

D2198.5§, ‡Spirits (jinn) give man a beating. (Cf. Q458.1).
Jawdar and His Treacherous Brethren: *Alf* III 187; Burton VI 231. Chauvin V 257-60 No. 154; *ANE* 244-45 No. 209.□

E. THE DEAD

E11.1, Second blow resuscitates. First kills. See: *ANE*; *DOTTI*; *GMC*.
Sayf al-Mulûk: *Alf* III 293-94; Burton VII 361. Chauvin VII 64-73 No. 348; *ANE* 362-64 No. 229.□

E68, Apparently dead persons revived when certain thing happens. Proper prince appears, or the like. See: *ANE*; *DOTTI*; *GMC*. (Cf. F668.9.2.1§).
Hunchback's Tale: Resuscitated: *Alf* I 125,-(extraction of choking object); Burton I 351. Chauvin V 180-82 No. 105; *ANE* 224-25 No. 23.□

E125.2.2§, ‡Sister(s) nurse(s) back to health seemingly dead brother. See: *DOTTI*.
King ¿Umar al-Nu¿mân and Sons: *Alf* I 188,-cf.; Burton II 133. Chauvin VI 112-24 No. 277; *ANE* 430-34 No. 39.□

E168.2§, ‡Fishes in frying pan come to life (speak). See: *DOTTI*.
Ensorcelled Prince/Husband: *Alf* I 23-24; Burton I 63, 64. Chauvin VI 56-58 No. 222; *ANE* 176 No. 13.□

E178.1.1§, ‡Certain animals will be resurrected at Judgment Day (exceptional cases: e.g., dog, ass). See: *DOTTI*. (Cf. Q172.0.4§).
Tawaddud: Slavegirl Sold and Regained: *Alf* III 4; Burton V 235. Chauvin VII 117-19 No. 387; *ANE* 408-10 No. 157.□

E178.3§, ‡Reunion of families (chaste lovers, friends, etc.) on Resurrection Day. (Cf. T334.3§).
Prior Becomes Moslem: al-Anbârî: *Alf* II 298,-cf.; Burton V 143. Chauvin V 237-38 No. 137; *ANE* 330-31 No. 147;
Abû al-Hasan al-Khorâsânî (and Caliph's Favorite): *Alf* IV 235,-(poem); Burton IX 242. Chauvin V 218-20 No. 129; *ANE* 68-69 No. 259.□

E178.4§, ‡Victim of injustice (cruelty) faces his (her) unjust persecutor on Judgment (Resurrection) Day.
Ghânim ibn Ayyûb: *Alf* I 159; Burton II 71. Chauvin VI 14 No. 188; *ANE* 192-93 No. 36.□

E180§, Life-like mummy.
City of Brass: *Alf* III 135; Burton VI 114. Chauvin V 32-35 No. 16; *ANE* 146-50 No. 180;
Ma¿rûf the Cobbler: *Alf* IV 307,-cf./(*¿arâyis al-kunûz*); Burton X 31,-("Brides of the Treasure"). Chauvin VI 81-82 No. 250; *ANE* 291-93 No. 262.□

E180.1§, Mummy thought to be living person. See: *DOTTI*; *GMC*.
City of Brass: *Alf* III 135; Burton VI 114. Chauvin V 32-35 No. 16; *ANE* 146-50 No. 180.□

E180.2§, ‡Mummy with moving eyes (mounted on mercury).
City of Brass: *Alf* III 135; Burton VI 114,-(quicksilver). Chauvin V 32-35 No. 16; *ANE* 146-50 No. 180.□

E192.6.1§, ‡Corpse thrown into sea (river) drifts to its home.
Abû Qîr and Abû Ṣîr: *Alf* IV 197; Burton IX 164. Chauvin V 15-17 No. 10; *ANE* 75-77 No. 255.□

E291.2.1.1§, ‡Ghost of dead treasure owner protects contents of own tomb (treasure).
Jawdar and His Treacherous Brethren: *Alf* III 186; Burton VI 228. Chauvin V 257-60 No. 154; *ANE* 244-45 No. 209.□

E291.2.2, ‡Ghost animal guards treasure. (Cf. E422.9.1.1§).
Jawdar and His Treacherous Brethren: *Alf* III 186,-(lion); Burton VI 228. Chauvin V 257-60 No. 154; *ANE* 244-45 No. 209.□

E341, The grateful dead. See: *DOTTI*; *GMC*.
Jewish qâḍî and His Devout Wife: *Alf* III 10-11,-cf./(near-dead); Burton V 258. Chauvin VI 154-55 No. 321; *ANE* 242 No. 163.□

E350§, ‡Dead returns to ensure that guests receive hospitality. See: *DOTTI*. (Cf. E508§, E780.4.1§, P230.15§).
Ḥâtim's Hospitality: *Alf* II 181-82; Burton IV 95-96. Chauvin VI 49 No. 215; *ANE* 216 No. 64.□

E350.1§, ‡Dead hospitable person causes guest's animal to be slaughtered for food and then compensates guest for slaughtered animal (usually by providing a substitute).
Ḥâtim's Hospitality: *Alf* II 181; Burton IV 94-96. Chauvin VI 49 No. 215; *ANE* 216 No. 64.□

E406§, Immovable corpse. See: *GMC*. (Cf. D1654.9.1).
Prior Becomes Moslem: al-Anbârî: *Alf* II 299,-("*waliyyah*"); Burton V 144,-("waliyah"/"saintess"). Chauvin V 237-38 No. 137; *ANE* 330-31 No. 147.□

E406.1§, ‡Corpse can be moved only when certain thing happens (condition met). (Cf. E68).
Prior Becomes Moslem: al-Anbârî: *Alf* II 299,-(to be buried as Moslem); Burton V 144. Chauvin V 237-38 No. 137; *ANE* 330-31 No. 147.□

E422.9.1.1§, ‡Living corpse guards treasure (tomb). See: *DOTTI*. (Cf. N581.3.1§).
Jawdar and His Treacherous Brethren: *Alf* III 186; Burton VI 229. Chauvin V 257-60 No. 154; *ANE* 244-45 No. 209.□

E422.9.2§, ‡Series of living corpses as phantom guards.
Jawdar and His Treacherous Brethren: *Alf* III 186; Burton VI 229-30. Chauvin V 257-60 No. 154; *ANE* 244-45 No. 209.□

E422.9.2.1§, ‡Treasure (tomb) protected by series of phantom guards. See: *DOTTI*. (Cf. H1423, Z71.5.13§).
Jawdar and His Treacherous Brethren: *Alf* III 186; Burton VI 229. Chauvin V 257-60 No. 154; *ANE* 244-45 No. 209.□

E451.9.1§, ‡*hâmah* ceases to appear when revenge is accomplished. (Cf. E473.2§).
Qamar al-Zamân and Budûr: *Alf* II 105,-cf./(murdered bird's/implicit); Burton III 293 n. 1. Chauvin V 204-12 No. 120; *ANE* 341-45 No. 61.□

E473.2§, ‡*hâmah*: ghost of murdered person in owl-form that cries for revenge. (Cf. E451.9.1§).
Qamar al-Zamân and Budûr: *Alf* II 105,-(murdered bird's/implicit); Burton III 293 n. 1. Chauvin V 204-12 No. 120; *ANE* 341-45 No. 61.□

E721.1.0.1§, The dead 'come to' (communicate with) the living in dreams (visions). (Cf. P233.10.1§)
Qamar al-Zamân and Budûr: *Alf* II 96,-(son sees his father in a *manâm*/vision); Burton III 277,-(son saw his father in a "dream"). Chauvin V 204-12 No. 120; *ANE* 341-45 No. 61.□

E508§, ‡Hospitable phantom (ghost). See: *DOTTI*. (Cf. E350§).
Ḥâtim's Hospitality: *Alf* II 181-82; Burton IV 95-96. Chauvin VI 49 No. 215; *ANE* 216 No. 64.□

E710, External soul. See: *ANE*; *DOTTI*; *GMC*; *PSAE*.
Sayf al-Mulûk: *Alf* III 288; Burton VII 350. Chauvin VII 64-73 No. 348; *ANE* 362-64 No. 229.□

E713, Soul hidden in a series of coverings. See: *DOTTI*.
Sayf al-Mulûk: *Alf* III 288; Burton VII 350,-(in crop of a sparrow ...). Chauvin VII 64-73 No. 348; *ANE* 362-64 No. 229.□

E722.0.1§, ‡Gasping (*shahqah*) accompanies soul's departure from body at death.
Anîs al-Jalîs: *Alf* I 129; Burton II 10. Chauvin V 120-24 No. 58; *ANE* 316-17 No. 35;
King ¿Umar al-Nu¿mân and Sons: *Alf* I 319; Burton III 74. Chauvin VI 112-24 No. 277; *ANE* 430-34 No. 39;
¿Alî ibn Bakkâr: *Alf* II 64; Burton III 209,-(sobbed). Chauvin V 153 No. 76; *ANE* 92-93 No. 60;
Bulûqiya/Ḥâsib/Queen of Vipers: *Alf* III 19, 22; Burton V 299, 304,-(sigh). Chauvin VII 54 No. 77; *ANE* 130-32 No. 177;
Masrûr and Zayn al-Mawâṣif: *Alf* IV 77; Burton VIII 257. Chauvin VI 82-84 No. 251; *ANE* 294-95 No. 232.□

E722.0.2.1§, ‡Soul being extracted out of body emits scraping sound of excruciating pain—(*hashrajah*/*sakarât al-mawt*).
King Jalî¿âd and Shimâs: *Alf* IV 161,-(*sakrât al-mawt*); Burton IX 90,-(death agony). Chauvin VI 9-11 No. 184; *ANE* 237-38 No. 236.□

E732, Soul in form of bird. See: *DOTTI*; *GMC*.
Sayf al-Mulûk: *Alf* III 290,-(jinni's/sparrow); Burton VII 351. Chauvin VII 64-73 No. 348; *ANE* 362-64 No. 229.□

E755.0.4.1§, *al-barzakh* (Isthmus) as the abode of humans' souls. See: *GMC*.
¿Azîz and ¿Azîzah: *Alf* I 282,-(poem); Burton II 325,-(Hades-tombed). Chauvin V 144-45 No. 71; *ANE* 111-13 No. 41.□

E755.2.8.[1], Series of hells. (Cf. A671.2.4.14§).
Bulûqiya: *Alf* III 32-33; Burton V 318. Chauvin VII 54 No. 77; *ANE* 130-32 No. 177.□

E765.4.8.1§, ‡Queen of vipers will die when man (hero) bathes.
Bulûqiya: *Alf* III 34; Burton V 322. Chauvin VII 54 No. 77; *ANE* 130-32 No. 177.□

E780.4.1§, ‡Bone in grave would express owner's feeling when alive. (Cf. E350§).
Ensorcelled Prince/Husband: *Alf* I 29,-cf./(poem); Burton I 75,/("... my bones responsive to your cry"). Chauvin VI 56-58 No. 222; *ANE* 176 No. 13;
Reeve's Story: Why Maimed by Bride: *Alf* I 97,-cf./(poem); Burton I 280. Chauvin V 220-21 No. 305; *ANE* 351 No. 25;
Anîs al-Jalîs: *Alf* I 141,-(poem); Burton II 32. Chauvin V 120-24 No. 58; *ANE* 316-17 No. 35.□

E783.5.1§, ‡Severed head speaks. (Cf. D1610.5).
Dûban and King Yûnân: *Alf* I 23,-(deceptive claim); Burton I 58. Chauvin V 275-76 No. 156; *ANE* 459 No. 9.□

F. MARVELS

F55.3§, ‡Mountain so high that no clouds can reach its peak.
Hasan of Basrah: *Alf* III 308; Burton VIII 19. Chauvin VII 29-35 No. 212A; *ANE* 207-10 No. 230.□

F69§, Tour of sky-worlds. See: *DOTTI*.
Bulûqiya: *Alf* III 79-80,-(passim); Burton V 393. Chauvin VII 54 No. 77; *ANE* 130-32 No. 177.□

F110.3§, Perilous sea-voyage. See: *DOTTI*; *GMC*; *PSAE*.
¿Abdallah ibn Fâḍil: Treacherous Brothers: *Alf* IV 271; Burton IX 314. Chauvin V 2-4 No. 2; *ANE* 63-65 No. 261.□

F110.3.1§, Sindbad's sea-voyages. See: *DOTTI*; *GMC*.
Sindbâd's First Voyage: *Alf* III 83-122; Burton VI 4ff. Chauvin VII 7-9 No. 373A; *ANE* 385 No. 179.□

F111, Journey to earthly paradise. See: *DOTTI*; *GMC*.
Bulûqiya: *Alf* III 28; Burton V 313. Chauvin VII 54 No. 77; *ANE* 130-32 No. 177.□

F112, ‡Journey to Land of Women. Island of women, land of maidens, country of the Amazons, etc. See: *DOTTI*. (Cf. B225.3§).
Man Who Never Laughs: *Alf* III 153-54; Burton VI 165. Chauvin VIII 47-48 No. 15; *ANE* 285-86 No. 195.□

F112.0.1.1, ‡Journey to island inhabited by only one (beautiful) woman.
Ibrâhîm and Jamîlah: *Alf* IV 224-26; Burton IX 207-29. Chauvin VI 52-53 No. 218; *ANE* 227-29 No. 258.□

F112.0.3§, ‡Community of mermaidens (water spirits): all females. (Cf. F499.3.5§).
Landsman ¿Abdallah and Merman ¿Abdallah: *Alf* IV 205; Burton IX 182. Chauvin V 6-7 No. 3; *ANE* 65-66 No. 256.□

F112.1, ‡Man on Island of Fair Women overcome by loving women.
Man Who Never Laughs: *Alf* III 154,-cf.; Burton VI 165. Chauvin VIII 47-48 No. 15; *ANE* 285-86 No. 195;
Ibrâhîm and Jamîlah: *Alf* IV 224-25; Burton IX 207-29. Chauvin VI 52-53 No. 218; *ANE* 227-29 No. 258.□

F112.2, ‡City of women. (Cf. P722.1.1§).
Landsman ¿Abdallah and Merman ¿Abdallah: *Alf* IV 205; Burton IX 183. Chauvin V 6-7 No. 3; *ANE* 65-66 No. 256.□

F112.4§, ‡In land of women females govern (rule) the state, males perform domestic and menial chores. (Cf. P20.5§, P722.1§).
Man Who Never Laughs: *Alf* III 154; Burton VI 165. Chauvin VIII 47-48 No. 15; *ANE* 285-86 No. 195.□

F127.1, ‡Journey to serpent kingdom. (Cf. B225.3§).
Bulûqiya/Ḥâsib/Queen of Vipers: *Alf* III 21,-cf./(vipers); Burton V 302. Chauvin VII 54 No. 77; *ANE* 130-32 No. 177.□

F129.4.2, ‡Voyage to Isle [(City, Land)] of Truth. People cannot lie. See: *DOTTI*.
Jullanâr of the Sea: *Alf* III 269,-cf./(city); Burton VII 305. Chauvin V 147-51 No. 73; *ANE* 248-51 No. 227;
Ma¿rûf the Cobbler: *Alf* IV 294-95; Burton X 9-10. Chauvin VI 81-82 No. 250; *ANE* 291-93 No. 262.□

F129.4.9.1§, ‡Journey to uninhabited island.
Island King/Pious Jewish Merchant: *Alf* III 16,-cf.; Burton V 291. Chauvin VI 161 No. 325; *ANE* 234 No. 174;
Sindbâd's Second Voyage: *Alf* III 88; Burton VI 15. Chauvin VII 9-14 No. 373B; *ANE* 385 No. 179.□

F129.4.9.2§, ‡Journey to island (land) of cannibals. See: *DOTTI*. (Cf. G19.1§, G407§).
Abû Muḥammad Lazybones: *Alf* II 209; Burton IV 168,-(Isle of the Zunuj). Chauvin VI 64-67 No. 233; *ANE* 71-73 No. 78;
Jânshâh: *Alf* III 42,-cf.; Burton V 332. Chauvin VII 39-44 No. 153; *ANE* 238-41 No. 178;

Sayf al-Mulûk: *Alf* III 282,-cf./(involuntary); Burton VII 339. Chauvin VII 64-73 No. 348; *ANE* 362-64 No. 229.□

F129.5.2§, ‡Land from which no traveler has ever returned. (Cf. F130.5.1§).
Hasan of Basrah: *Alf* IV 51,-(Wâq Islands); Burton VIII 139. Chauvin VII 29-35 No. 212A; *ANE* 207-10 No. 230.□

F130.5.1§, ‡'Wâq-el-Wâq': (Indonesia, Japan, etc.). (Cf. F129.5.2§).
Hasan of Basrah: *Alf* IV 51; Burton VIII 139. Chauvin VII 29-35 No. 212A; *ANE* 207-10 No. 230.□

F129.7, ‡Journey to land of naked people.
Sindbâd's Fourth Voyage: *Alf* III 101,-cf./(island,/refuge); Burton VI 35-36. Chauvin VII 18-20 No. 373D; *ANE* 386 No. 179.□

F132.1, ‡Earthly paradise on mountain. (Cf. F111).
Hasan of Basrah: *Alf* III 311; Burton VIII 23-24. Chauvin VII 29-35 No. 212A; *ANE* 207-10 No. 230.□

F133, Submarine otherworld. See: *DOTTI*; *GMC*.
Jullanâr of the Sea: *Alf* III 247, 249,-(=F0725); Burton VII 268-69, 275. Chauvin V 147-51 No. 73; *ANE* 248-51 No. 227;
Landsman ¿Abdallah and Merman ¿Abdallah: *Alf* IV 200; Burton IX 165-88. Chauvin V 6-7 No. 3; *ANE* 65-66 No. 256.□

F133.1, Marine counterpart to land. See: *DOTTI*; *GMC*. (Cf. F724§).
Landsman ¿Abdallah and Merman ¿Abdallah: *Alf* IV 200; Burton IX 165-88. Chauvin V 6-7 No. 3; *ANE* 65-66 No. 256.□

F173.4§, No wailing or sorrow over the dead in utopian otherworld. See: *DOTTI*.
Landsman ¿Abdallah and Merman ¿Abdallah: *Alf* IV 207; Burton IX 187. Chauvin V 6-7 No. 3; *ANE* 65-66 No. 256.□

F174.2§, Hero (prayer-crier) carried off to otherworld by bird. (Cf. B552, D2135).
Man Who Never Laughs: *Alf* III 153,-cf.; Burton VI 163. Chauvin VIII 47-48 No. 15; *ANE* 285-86 No. 195.□

F174.3§, ‡Person carried back from otherworld by bird. See: *DOTTI*. (Cf. N794§).
Man Who Never Laughs: *Alf* III 155; Burton VI 166. Chauvin VIII 47-48 No. 15; *ANE* 285-86 No. 195.□

F179§, Piety (religious exercise) as a system of earnings (economic) in utopian otherworld. See: *DOTTI*. (Cf. P170.0.1.1).
King ¿Umar al-Nu¿mân and Sons: *Alf* I 225,-cf./(damsels for performing extra religious duties); Burton II 196. Chauvin VI 112-24 No. 277; *ANE* 430-34 No. 39.□

F200.0.1§, ‡Solomon as supreme ruler of all jinn and similar beings (afrits, dwarfs, elves, etc.).
Fisherman and Afrit: Ingratitude: *Alf* I 15; Burton I 40-41. Chauvin VI 23-25 No. 195; *ANE* 183-84 No. 8;
Sayf al-Mulûk: *Alf* III 274; Burton VII 316. Chauvin VII 64-73 No. 348; *ANE* 362-64 No. 229;
Landsman ¿Abdallah and Merman ¿Abdallah: *Alf* IV 199,-(afrits/passim); Burton IX 169. Chauvin V 6-7 No. 3; *ANE* 65-66 No. 256.□

F200.7.2§, ‡Social stratification in jinn societies.
Qamar al-Zamân and Budûr: *Alf* II 71,-(implicit); Burton III 224. Chauvin V 204-12 No. 120; *ANE* 341-45 No. 61.□

F200.7.2.1§, ‡Hierarchy in jinn societies: military-like.
Hasan of Basrah: *Alf* IV 47; Burton VIII 132. Chauvin VII 29-35 No. 212A; *ANE* 207-10 No. 230;
Ma¿rûf the Cobbler: *Alf* IV 304; Burton X 28. Chauvin VI 81-82 No. 250; *ANE* 291-93 No. 262.□

F200.9.1§, ‡Powerful jinni labeled: "afrit" (usually "afrit from the jinn"). (Cf. F480.6§, Z94.5.2.1§).
Ma¿rûf the Cobbler: *Alf* IV 293,-(*¿âmir al-makân*); Burton X 9. Chauvin VI 81-82 No. 250; *ANE* 291-93 No. 262.□

F200.9.2§, ‡Evil jinni labeled: "satan" (*shayṭân*, "devil," "Eblis"). See: *DOTTI*. (Cf. J1786).
Ebony Horse: *Alf* II 256,-(*shayṭan min al-jinn*/a satan of the jinn); Burton V 10,-("a devil of the jinn"). Chauvin V 221-31 No. 130; *ANE* 172-74 No. 103;
Mercury ¿Alî: *Alf* III 233; Burton VII 183. Chauvin V 248-50 No. 147; *ANE* 301-3 No. 225;

Ma¿rûf the Cobbler: *Alf* IV 304; Burton X 28. Chauvin VI 81-82 No. 250; *ANE* 291-93 No. 262.□

F230, Appearance of fairies.
Fisherman and Afrit: Ingratitude: *Alf* I 14-15; Burton I 41. Chauvin VI 23-25 No. 195; *ANE* 183-84 No. 8;
Qamar al-Zamân and Budûr: *Alf* II 76; Burton III 235. Chauvin V 204-12 No. 120; *ANE* 341-45 No. 61.□

F231.3.1§, ‡Flying jinn have bird's wings and plumage. ("Flyers"). (Cf. F458§, V229.29§).
Qamar al-Zamân and Budûr: *Alf* II 70,-('flyer'/drawing); Burton III 222/223.-(drawing). Chauvin V 204-12 No. 120; *ANE* 341-45 No. 61;
Jullanâr of the Sea: *Alf* III 269,-(¿ifrît); Burton VII 306,-(Ifrit). Chauvin V 147-51 No. 73; *ANE* 248-51 No. 227;
Hasan of Basrah: *Alf* IV 12,-cf.; Burton VIII 61. Chauvin VII 29-35 No. 212A; *ANE* 207-10 No. 230.□

F233.0.1§, Color of jinni (fairy) is one of its racial (ethnic) attributes.
Sayf al-Mulûk: *Alf* III 300-1; Burton VIII 1-2. Chauvin VII 64-73 No. 348; *ANE* 362-64 No. 229;
¿Abdallah ibn Fâḍil: Treacherous Brothers: *Alf* IV 279; Burton IX 330-31. Chauvin V 2-4 No. 2; *ANE* 63-65 No. 261.□

F233.1.1§, Blue fairy.
Sayf al-Mulûk: *Alf* III 287,-(son of king of Blue Jinn); Burton VII 348. Chauvin VII 64-73 No. 348; *ANE* 362-64 No. 229.□

F234.0.2, Fairy as shape-shifter. See: *DOTTI*; *GMC*. (Cf. F401.0.1.1.1§, G640.1§).
Nûr al-Dîn ¿Alî and Son: *Alf* I 72; Burton I 220. Chauvin VI 102-6 No. 270; *ANE* 317-19 No. 22.□

F234.0.4.1§, ‡Jinni (fairy) assumes the form of person so as to enable that person to escape.
¿Alâ' al-Dîn Abû al-Shâmât: *Alf* II 177; Burton IV 89. Chauvin V 43-49 No. 18; *ANE* 85-87 No. 63.□

F234.1.9.8§, ‡Fairy in form of mouse.
Nûr al-Dîn ¿Alî and Son: *Alf* I 71,-(afrit); Burton I 220. Chauvin VI 102-6 No. 270; *ANE* 317-19 No. 22.□

F234.1.16.4§, ‡Fairy in form of flea.
Qamar al-Zamân and Budûr: *Alf* II 76; Burton III 236. Chauvin V 204-12 No. 120; *ANE* 341-45 No. 61.□

F252.1.0.1.1§—(formerly-F0252.1.0.1§), ‡King of the jinn. See: *GMC*. (Cf. Z100.2§).
Bulûqiya: *Alf* III 32; Burton V 316. Chauvin VII 54 No. 77; *ANE* 130-32 No. 177;
Jawdar and His Treacherous Brethren: *Alf* III 183,-(Red-Jinn); Burton VI 222. Chauvin V 257-60 No. 154; *ANE* 244-45 No. 209;
Sayf al-Mulûk: *Alf* III 287,-(son of); Burton VII 348,-(Sovran of the Jann). Chauvin VII 64-73 No. 348; *ANE* 362-64 No. 229;
Hasan of Basrah: *Alf* III 311; Burton VIII 24. Chauvin VII 29-35 No. 212A; *ANE* 207-10 No. 230.□

F252.1.0.1.2§, ‡Jinn prince.
Enchanted Spring: Change of Sex: *Alf* III 147,-(royal prince); Burton VI 147. Chauvin VIII 43 No. 11; *ANE* 175-76 No. 191.□

F252.1.0.1.3§, ‡Jinn princess.
Hasan of Basrah: *Alf* III 319; Burton VIII 39. Chauvin VII 29-35 No. 212A; *ANE* 207-10 No. 230.□

F252.1.0.2, ‡King of Land under Water.
Jullanâr of the Sea: *Alf* III 249; Burton VII 268-69. Chauvin V 147-51 No. 73; *ANE* 248-51 No. 227.□

F252.3, Fairy army. (Cf. D1475, D1778.1§, G302.9.10.1§).
Jinn Imprisoned in Flasks: *Alf* III 128; Burton VI 99-100. Chauvin VII 113 No. 380=no/text; *ANE* 146 No. 180;
Jawdar and His Treacherous Brethren: *Alf* III 199,-(afrits); Burton VI 252. Chauvin V 257-60 No. 154; *ANE* 244-45 No. 209;
Hasan of Basrah: *Alf* IV 48; Burton VIII 135. Chauvin VII 29-35 No. 212A; *ANE* 207-10 No. 230.□

F252.3.2§, ‡Jinn armies clash (in battle).

Jinn Imprisoned in Flasks: *Alf* III 128; Burton VI 98. Chauvin VII 113 No. 380=no/text; *ANE* 146 No. 180;
Hasan of Basrah: *Alf* IV 48, 49; Burton VIII 135. Chauvin VII 29-35 No. 212A; *ANE* 207-10 No. 230. □

F271.1.2.2§, ‡Magic feather-dress that gives power of flying manufactured by magician of the jinn. (Cf. D1532.6.1§).
Hasan of Basrah: *Alf* IV 2; Burton VIII 40. Chauvin VII 29-35 No. 212A; *ANE* 207-10 No. 230. □

F269.1§—(formerly-F251.0.8§), Jinn profess faith in certain religions. (Cf. V333§).
Abû Muḥammad Lazybones: *Alf* II 213-14; Burton IV 173,-(true-believing Jinn). Chauvin VI 64-67 No. 233; *ANE* 71-73 No. 78. □

F300, Marriage or liaison with fairy. See: *DOTTI*; *GMC*.
Sayf al-Mulûk: *Alf* III 280,-(falling in love); Burton VII 331. Chauvin VII 64-73 No. 348; *ANE* 362-64 No. 229;
Hasan of Basrah: *Alf* IV 5,-(marriage); Burton VIII 45. Chauvin VII 29-35 No. 212A; *ANE* 207-10 No. 230. □

F301.6, Fairy lover abducts fairy wife of mortal. (Cf. F324).
Abû Muḥammad Lazybones: *Alf* II 212-13; Burton IV 172. Chauvin VI 64-67 No. 233; *ANE* 71-73 No. 78. □

F302, Fairy mistress. Mortal man marries or lives with fairy woman. See: *DOTTI*; *GMC*. (Cf. T111.5.1§).
Jânshâh: *Alf* III 71; Burton V 376. Chauvin VII 39-44 No. 153; *ANE* 238-41 No. 178. □

F302.0.3§, Jinn-'*mikhawiyyah*' ('bebrothering'): jinniyyah (fairy, jinn-woman) as a man's foster-sister. See: *DOTTI*; *GMC*. (Cf. P274.1, P311.0.2§, T42.2.1§).
Hasan of Basrah: *Alf* III 310; Burton VIII 22-23. Chauvin VII 29-35 No. 212A; *ANE* 207-10 No. 230;

¿Abdallah ibn Fâḍil: Treacherous Brothers: *Alf* IV 280, 286; Burton IX 333,344 . Chauvin V 2-4 No. 2; *ANE* 63-65 No. 261. □

F302.0.3.3§, ‡Jinni foster sister helps her human foster brother. (Cf. N815.1.1§).
Second Shaykh: Treacherous Brothers: *Alf* I 11,-cf./(consort/wife); Burton I 34. Chauvin VII 130 No. 397; *ANE* 377-78 No. 6;
Hasan of Basrah: *Alf* IV 16-17,-(reaching beloved); Burton VIII 66. Chauvin VII 29-35 No. 212A; *ANE* 207-10 No. 230. □

F302.7.1.1§, ‡Jinni foster-sister kind to human brother's family.
Hasan of Basrah: *Alf* IV 54; Burton VIII 143. Chauvin VII 29-35 No. 212A; *ANE* 207-10 No. 230. □

F305.2, ‡Offspring of fairy and mortal extraordinarily beautiful.
Jullanâr of the Sea: *Alf* III 252,-(mermaid's/like full moon); Burton VII 274. Chauvin V 147-51 No. 73; *ANE* 248-51 No. 227. □

F307.1§, ‡Amicable relations between fairy wife and her human husband's mother and sister. See: *DOTTI*.
Jullanâr of the Sea: *Alf* III 252; Burton VII 274-75. Chauvin V 147-51 No. 73; *ANE* 248-51 No. 227;
Hasan of Basrah: *Alf* IV 54; Burton VIII 154-55. Chauvin VII 29-35 No. 212A; *ANE* 207-10 No. 230. □

F324, ‡Girl abducted by fairy. See: *DOTTI*. (Cf. F301.6, R16.3).
Abû Muḥammad Lazybones: *Alf* II 212-13; Burton IV 172. Chauvin VI 64-67 No. 233; *ANE* 71-73 No. 78. □

F324.5§, ‡Man abducted by fairies (jinn).
Uns al-Wujûd and al-Ward: *Alf* II 280,-(she-jinni); Burton V 56. Chauvin VI 127-29 No. 282; *ANE* 438 No. 104. □

F330.0.1§, ‡Fairy (jinni) repays a kindness.
Abû Muḥammad Lazybones: *Alf* II 214; Burton IV 174. Chauvin VI 64-67 No. 233; *ANE* 71-73 No. 78. □

F337.2§, ‡Fairy grateful to mortal (person) for saving a relative from danger.

Abû Muḥammad Lazybones: *Alf* II 214,-(sister); Burton IV 174. Chauvin VI 64-67 No. 233; *ANE* 71-73 No. 78.□

F337.3§, Fairy (in viper form) saved from pursuer (unwanted suitor): grateful. See: *DOTTI*; *GMC*.
Eldest Lady's Story: Treacherous Sisters: *Alf* I 57; Burton I 172,-(serpent/dragon). Chauvin V 4 No. 443; *ANE* 174-75 No. 19;
Abû Muḥammad Lazybones: *Alf* II 212-13; Burton IV 173. Chauvin VI 64-67 No. 233; *ANE* 71-73 No. 78;
¿Abdallah ibn Fâḍil: Treacherous Brothers: *Alf* IV 272; Burton IX 315,-("snake" fleeing black dragon [!!]). Chauvin V 2-4 No. 2; *ANE* 63-65 No. 261.□

F337.3.1§, ‡Jinni-maiden (woman) grateful for protection from sexual assault (recusing her sexual honor or modesty).
¿Abdallah ibn Fâḍil: Treacherous Brothers: *Alf* IV 279; Burton IX 330-31. Chauvin V 2-4 No. 2; *ANE* 63-65 No. 261.□

F337.3.1.1§, ‡White viper (actually jinni-maiden in viper form) grateful for rescue from black one (who is usually unwanted male). (Cf. B731.11.1§).
Abû Muḥammad Lazybones: *Alf* II 212-13; Burton IV 173. Chauvin VI 64-67 No. 233; *ANE* 71-73 No. 78.□

F341.2, ‡Fairy ransoms self with wish. (Cf. R114.1§).
Fisherman and Afrit: Ingratitude: *Alf* I 15, 16,-cf.; Burton I 42,-cf./(Ifrit). Chauvin VI 26 No. 197; *ANE* 183-84 No. 8.□

F359.3.1§, ‡Theft of cap (of invisibility) from jinn children. See: *DOTTI*. (Cf. D832).
Hasan of Basrah: *Alf* IV 43; Burton VIII 122. Chauvin VII 29-35 No. 212A; *ANE* 207-10 No. 230.□

F372.1.1§, ‡Woman from water world living in human world requires midwife of her own kind (species). (Cf. B81.0.2, F569.9§).
Jullanâr of the Sea: *Alf* III 249; Burton VII 269-70. Chauvin V 147-51 No. 73; *ANE* 248-51 No. 227.□

F374, ‡Longing in fairyland to visit home.
Hasan of Basrah: *Alf* IV 53-54; Burton VIII 140ff. Chauvin VII 29-35 No. 212A; *ANE* 207-10 No. 230.□

F381.0.1§, ‡Fairy (jinni, spirit) possesses man. See: *DOTTI*; *GMC*. (Cf. D2176.3.4).
Qamar al-Zamân and Budûr: *Alf* II 73,-cf./(passim); Burton III 228. Chauvin V 204-12 No. 120; *ANE* 341-45 No. 61.□

F381.0.5§, ‡Fairy (jinni, spirit) possesses by 'riding' ('mounting,' 'wearing') victim.
Qamar al-Zamân and Budûr: *Alf* II 73,/(passim/*by "rukûb"* the afflicted); Burton III 228,-(by mounting victim). Chauvin V 204-12 No. 120; *ANE* 341-45 No. 61.□

F382.3.2§, ‡Certain prayer-ritual renders one immune to jinn's power.
¿Abdallah ibn Fâḍil: Treacherous Brothers: *Alf* IV 283; Burton IX 339. Chauvin V 2-4 No. 2; *ANE* 63-65 No. 261.□

F382.3.4§, ‡Mention of God's name causes demon (jinni/fairy, devil, etc.) to burn up (be reduced to ashes).
Abû Muḥammad Lazybones: *Alf* II 215; Burton IV 175. Chauvin VI 64-67 No. 233; *ANE* 71-73 No. 78.□

F384.0.1§, ‡Objects that have (magic) power against fairies.
Fisherman and Afrit: Ingratitude: *Alf* I 15; Burton I 40. Chauvin VI 23-25 No. 195; *ANE* 183-84 No. 8.□

F384.5§, ‡Lead powerful against fairies.
Fisherman and Afrit: Ingratitude: *Alf* I 15; Burton I 40. Chauvin VI 23-25 No. 195; *ANE* 183-84 No. 8.□

F369.9.1§, ‡ Jinni (afrit) offers help to wailing person so as to get him to be quiet. (Cf. N813).
Ma¿rûf the Cobbler: *Alf* IV 293; Burton X 60. Chauvin VI 81-82 No. 250; *ANE* 291-93 No. 262.□

F387.1.1§, ‡Girl from water world captured by a human and sold as slave. (Cf. B81.13.11).
Jullanâr of the Sea: *Alf* III 247; Burton VII 268-69. Chauvin V 147-51 No. 73; *ANE* 248-51 No. 227.□

F389.4, ‡Fairy killed by mortal. See: *DOTTI*. (Cf. F451.4.5.4§, N331.1.5§).
Trader and Afrit: Accidental Fairy-cide: *Alf* I 8; Burton I 24. Chauvin VI 22-23 No. 194; *ANE* 419-20 No. 4;
Sayf al-Mulûk: *Alf* III 290; Burton VII 352,-(son of Blue King, the jinni). Chauvin VII 64-73 No. 348; *ANE* 362-64 No. 229.□

F401.0.1.1.1§, ‡Afrit (jinni) assumes form of wind or smoke. (Cf. F234.0.2).
Fisherman and Afrit: Ingratitude: *Alf* I 14, 23; Burton I 40, 61. Chauvin VI 23-25 No. 195; *ANE* 183-84 No. 8;
Jinn Imprisoned in Flasks: *Alf* III 122-23; Burton VI 84. Chauvin VII 113 No. 380=no/text; *ANE* 146 No. 180.□

F401.3.1.1§, Spirit in form of mule. See: *DOTTI*; *GMC*.
Jawdar and His Treacherous Brethren: *Alf* III 184-85,-(she-mule); Burton VI 225. Chauvin V 257-60 No. 154; *ANE* 244-45 No. 209;
Ma¿rûf the Cobbler: *Alf* IV 306,-(jinn as beasts of burden); Burton X 30. Chauvin VI 81-82 No. 250; *ANE* 291-93 No. 262.□

F401.3.8.1§, ‡Spirit (jinni) in form of viper. See: *DOTTI*.
Abû Muhammad Lazybones: *Alf* II 212-13; Burton IV 173. Chauvin VI 64-67 No. 233; *ANE* 71-73 No. 78.□

F401.3.9§, Spirit in form of monkey. See: *DOTTI*; *GMC*.
Abû Muhammad Lazybones: *Alf* II 212,-(jinni-*mârid*); Burton IV 170. Chauvin VI 64-67 No. 233; *ANE* 71-73 No. 78.□

F401.3.15.1§, ‡Jinni (afrit) in form of fish. See: *DOTTI*. (Cf. B81, B82, D692, G303.3.3.5).
Jawdar and His Treacherous Brethren: *Alf* III 183; Burton VI 223. Chauvin V 257-60 No. 154; *ANE* 244-45 No. 209.□

F401.6, Spirit in human form. See: *DOTTI*; *GMC*. (Cf. V231.9.1§).
Prince and Ogress: *Alf* I 19; Burton I 54. Chauvin VI 26 No. 197; *ANE* 329 No. 12;
King's Favorite Son and Ogress: *Alf* III 143-44,-(treacherous intent/fin); Burton VI 140-42. Chauvin VIII 40-41 No. 8B; *ANE* 264 No. 188;
Jawdar and His Treacherous Brethren: *Alf* III 198,-(eunuch) 199; Burton VI 250. Chauvin V 257-60 No. 154; *ANE* 244-45 No. 209.□

F402.3.1§, ‡City where men grow wings and fly periodically. (Cf. D625.1§).
Sindbâd's Seventh Voyage: *Alf* III 120; Burton VI 74-75. Chauvin VII 26-29 No. 373G; *ANE* 386-87 No. 179.□

F403.2.3.4, ‡Familiar spirit brings news with magic speed.
Portress Amînah: Bitten Cheek: *Alf* I 61,-cf./(jinni-woman reveals culprit); Burton I 186. Chauvin V 98-99 No. 33; *ANE* 326-27 No. 20.□

F403.2.3.4.1§, ‡Jinn carry news (message). (Cf. F403.2.3.4).
¿Abdallah ibn Fâdil: Treacherous Brothers: *Alf* IV 288; Burton IX 349. Chauvin V 2-4 No. 2; *ANE* 63-65 No. 261.□

F403.2.2.5, Demon as familiar spirit. [*khâdim-suflî* (nether servant)]. See: *GMC*. (Cf. D1420.0.1§).
Jawdar and His Treacherous Brethren: *Alf* III 184,-(*khâdim marsûd*); Burton VI 225,-(servant). Chauvin V 257-60 No. 154; *ANE* 244-45 No. 209.□

F414.1, Lover transported to girl's apartment in fortress by spirit. See: *DOTTI*. (Cf. N722§).
Nûr al-Dîn ¿Alî and Son: *Alf* I 72; Burton I 214. Chauvin VI 102-6 No. 270; *ANE* 317-19 No. 22.□

F415, Demon occupies oracular artificial head and gives responses to questions. (Cf. V1.2.5§).
Jinn Imprisoned in Flasks: *Alf* III 127,-cf.; Burton VI 98. Chauvin VII 113 No. 380=no/text; *ANE* 146 No. 180.□

F420, Water-spirits. See: *GMC*.
Qamar al-Zamân and Budûr: *Alf* II 71,-('diver'); Burton III 225. Chauvin V 204-12 No. 120; *ANE* 341-45 No. 61.□

F420.6.1, Marriage or liaison of mortals and water-spirits. See: *DOTTI*; *GMC*. (Cf. F300).
Second Shaykh: Treacherous Brothers: *Alf* I 11,-cf.; Burton I 34. Chauvin V 6 No. 397; *ANE* 377-78 No. 6;

Jullanâr of the Sea: *Alf* III 247-48; Burton VII 266. Chauvin V 147-51 No. 73; *ANE* 248-51 No. 227;

Sayf al-Mulûk: *Alf* III 298; Burton VIII 5. Chauvin VII 64-73 No. 348; *ANE* 362-64 No. 229.□

F420.6.1.5, Water-maidens make conditions for lovers. See: *PSAE*.
Sayf al-Mulûk: *Alf* III 298,-cf./(jinni-princess); Burton VII 369. Chauvin VII 64-73 No. 348; *ANE* 362-64 No. 229.□

F451.4.5.2.1§, ‡Jinni (fairy, etc.) testifies.
¿Abdallah ibn Fâḍil: Treacherous Brothers: *Alf* IV 288,-(tribes); Burton IX 349. Chauvin V 2-4 No. 2; *ANE* 63-65 No. 261.□

F451.4.5.4§, ‡The killing of a jinni or afrit by a human ('fairy-cide') taken to court. See: *DOTTI*. (Cf. F389.4, N331.1.5§).
Trader and Afrit: Accidental Fairy-cide: *Alf* I 8; Burton I 24. Chauvin VI 22-23 No. 194; *ANE* 419-20 No. 4;
Sayf al-Mulûk: *Alf* III 300,-(killing of jinni); Burton VIII 2. Chauvin VII 64-73 No. 348; *ANE* 362-64 No. 229.□

F458§, Air spirits. See: *GMC*. (Cf. F231.3.1§).
Qamar al-Zamân and Budûr: *Alf* II 71,-('flyer'); Burton III 222. Chauvin V 204-12 No. 120; *ANE* 341-45 No. 61.□

F480, House-spirits. ['Dwellers' (¿ummâr)]. See: *GMC*.
Hasan of Basrah: *Alf* IV 48,-cf.; Burton VIII 134. Chauvin VII 29-35 No. 212A; *ANE* 207-10 No. 230.□

F480.6§, ‡Jinni as house-spirit (a place's *¿âmir*). See: *DOTTI*.
Ma¿rûf the Cobbler: *Alf* IV 293,-(*¿âmir al-makân*); Burton X 6,-(Haunter of a place). Chauvin VI 81-82 No. 250; *ANE* 291-93 No. 262.□

F499.3.5§, Habitat of the jinn. (Cf. F112.0.3§, G135§).
Bulûqiya: *Alf* III 32; Burton V 317,-(abiding-place). Chauvin VII 54 No. 77; *ANE* 130-32 No. 177;
Hasan of Basrah: *Alf* III 308,-(palace inhabited by jinn ogres an satans/*jânn, ghîlân, wa shayâṭîn*); Burton VIII 20. Chauvin VII 29-35 No. 212A; *ANE* 207-10 No. 230;
Sayf al-Mulûk: *Alf* III 279,-(garden of Iram, son of ¿Âd); Burton VII 331. Chauvin VII 64-73 No. 348; *ANE* 362-64 No. 229.□

F499.3.5.3§, ‡Jinn dwell in old ruins (temples, monuments). See: *PSAE*.
Qamar al-Zamân and Budûr: *Alf* II 69,-(in Roman well); Burton III 223. Chauvin V 204-12 No. 120; *ANE* 341-45 No. 61.□

F499.3.5.3.1§, ‡Jinn dwell in cemeteries.
Nûr al-Dîn ¿Alî and Son: *Alf* I 69,-(*¿âmirah*/populated); Burton I 211,-(haunted). Chauvin VI 102-6 No. 270; *ANE* 317-19 No. 22.□

F499.9.1§, ‡Serving-boys of Paradise (*wildân*). (Cf. V232, V384.1.3§).
Dispute Concerning Males and Females: *Alf* II 301; Burton V 162. Chauvin VI 153 No. 317; *ANE* 291 No. 151.□

F499.9.1.1§, ‡Beardless waiters of Paradise are for serving foods and drinks only. (Cf. J1288.3.1§).
Dispute Concerning Males and Females: *Alf* II 302,-(*wildân*); Burton V 160. Chauvin VI 153 No. 317; *ANE* 291 No. 151.□

F511.0.1.1, Headless person with eyes (eye) and mouth on breast. See: *GMC*. (Cf. F512.6§).
Abû Muḥammad Lazybones: *Alf* II 215,-cf./(jinni/eyes in chest); Burton IV 176. Chauvin VI 64-67 No. 233; *ANE* 71-73 No. 78.□

F511.1, ‡Person unusual as to his face.
¿Alî Shâr and Zumurrud: *Alf* II 226,-(Robber); Burton IV 208. Chauvin V 89-91 No. 28; *ANE* 100-1 No. 82.□

F512.6§, ‡People with eyes in their chests (breasts). (Cf. F511.0.1.1).
Abû Muḥammad Lazybones: *Alf* II 215,-(*fî ṣudûrihim*); Burton IV 176,-(in their breasts). Chauvin VI 64-67 No. 233; *ANE* 71-73 No. 78.□

F515.1.2§, ‡Person with thumbs cut off (on hand and foot). See: *DOTTI*. (Cf. S161).

Reeve's Story: Why Maimed by Bride: *Alf* I 96; Burton I 279. Chauvin V 220-21 No. 305; *ANE* 351 No. 25.□

F519.1§, ‡Hunchback person. See: *DOTTI*. (Cf. F576.2§, K2271).
Hunchback's Tale: Resuscitated: *Alf* I 85; Burton I 255. Chauvin V 180-82 No. 105; *ANE* 224-25 No. 23.□

F519.1.1§, ‡Hunchback as helper. (Cf. N887§).
Ibrâhîm and Jamîlah: *Alf* IV 222-23; Burton IX 214-15, 217. Chauvin VI 52-53 No. 218; *ANE* 227-29 No. 258.□

F525, Person with half a body. [(*shiq*)].
Jânshâh: *Alf* III 42,-cf.; Burton V 333. Chauvin VII 39-44 No. 153; *ANE* 238-41 No. 178.□

F525.2, Man splits into two parts. See: *ANE*; *DOTTI*.
Jânshâh: *Alf* III 42; Burton V 333. Chauvin VII 39-44 No. 153; *ANE* 238-41 No. 178.□

F527.5, ‡Black man.
Barber's Fifth Brother: Daydreams/Defeats Robbers: *Alf* I 120; Burton I 340. Chauvin V 161 No. 85; *ANE* 119-20 No. 33.□

F531, Giant. A person of enormous size. See: *DOTTI*; *GMC*; *PSAE*.
Bulûqiya: *Alf* III 31,-cf.; Burton V 316. Chauvin VII 54 No. 77; *ANE* 130-32 No. 177.□

F531.1, ‡Appearance of giant.
Hasan of Basrah: *Alf* IV 48,-(Afrit); Burton VIII 134. Chauvin VII 29-35 No. 212A; *ANE* 207-10 No. 230.□

F531.1.7.2, ‡Black giant.
Barber's Fifth Brother: Daydreams/Defeats Robbers: *Alf* I 120,-cf.; Burton I 340. Chauvin V 161 No. 85; *ANE* 119-20 No. 33.□

F531.2.1, ‡Extremely tall giant. (Cf. F533).
Bulûqiya: *Alf* III 31,-(forty cubits high); Burton V 316. Chauvin VII 54 No. 77; *ANE* 130-32 No. 177.□

F531.2.1.2.1§, ‡Giant (jinni) so tall that his head is touching clouds (sky).
Fisherman and Afrit: Ingratitude: *Alf* I 14; Burton I 41. Chauvin VI 23-25 No. 195; *ANE* 183-84 No. 8.□

F531.2.1.2.2§, ‡Giant forty cubits tall.
Bulûqiya: *Alf* III 31; Burton V 316. Chauvin VII 54 No. 77; *ANE* 130-32 No. 177.□

F533, ‡Remarkably tall man. (Cf. F531.2.1).
Sayf al-Mulûk: *Alf* III 285; Burton VII 344. Chauvin VII 64-73 No. 348; *ANE* 362-64 No. 229.□

F541.9, ‡Eyes shed tears of blood. [(Formulaic)].
¿Alî ibn Bakkâr: *Alf* II 48,-cf./(poem); Burton III 177. Chauvin V 153 No. 76; *ANE* 92-93 No. 60.□

F541.12§, ‡Remarkably beautiful eyes: size, color, etc.
Masrûr and Zayn al-Mawâṣif: *Alf* IV 55; Burton VIII 205. Chauvin VI 82-84 No. 251; *ANE* 294-95 No. 232.□

F541.12.1§, ‡Gazelle's eyes.
Porter and Ladies of Baghdad: *Alf* I 32; Burton I 84. Chauvin V 251-52 No. 148; *ANE* 324-26 No. 14.□

F541.13§, ‡Remarkably beautiful eyebrows.
Porter and Ladies of Baghdad: *Alf* I 32; Burton I 84. Chauvin V 251-52 No. 148; *ANE* 324-26 No. 14.□

F541.13.2§, ‡Joined eyebrows.
¿Alî ibn Bakkâr: *Alf* II 41; Burton III 163. Chauvin V 153 No. 76; *ANE* 92-93 No. 60;
Qamar al-Zamân and Budûr: *Alf* II 86; Burton III 255. Chauvin V 204-12 No. 120; *ANE* 341-45 No. 61;
Lovers of Basra/Ḍamrah: *Alf* III 210; Burton VII 130. Chauvin V 118 No. 54; *ANE* 273 No. 220;
Masrûr and Zayn al-Mawâṣif: *Alf* IV 55; Burton VIII 205. Chauvin VI 82-84 No. 251; *ANE* 294-95 No. 232.□

F543.5.1.2§, ‡Remarkably narrow (straight) nose.

Qamar al-Zamân and Budûr: *Alf* II 72; Burton III 226. Chauvin V 204-12 No. 120; *ANE* 341-45 No. 61.□

F543.5.1.2.1§, ‡Nose as narrow as sword's edge.
Qamar al-Zamân and Budûr: *Alf* II 72; Burton III 226. Chauvin V 204-12 No. 120; *ANE* 341-45 No. 61;
Tawaddud: Slavegirl Sold and Regained: *Alf* II 304; Burton V 191. Chauvin VII 117-19 No. 387; *ANE* 408-10 No. 157.□

F544.0.7.1§, ‡Mouth the size of ring (jewelry). (Cf. Z186.9.1§).
Masrûr and Zayn al-Mawâṣif: *Alf* IV 55; Burton VIII 206. Chauvin VI 82-84 No. 251; *ANE* 294-95 No. 232.□

F545, ‡Other facial features.
¿Alî Shâr and Zumurrud: *Alf* II 226,-(Robber); Burton IV 208-9. Chauvin V 89-91 No. 28; *ANE* 100-1 No. 82.□

F545.1, ‡Remarkable beard. See: *DOTTI*.
al-'Amjad and al-'As¿ad: *Alf* II 121, 146; Burton III 325, IV 27,-(flowing over breast). Chauvin V 208-10 No. 120[.1]; *ANE* 341-42 No. 61/pt. 2;
¿Alî Shâr and Zumurrud: *Alf* II 226,-(ugly/robber's); Burton IV 208. Chauvin V 89-91 No. 28; *ANE* 100-1 No. 82;
Jinn Imprisoned in Flasks: *Alf* III 123,-(drawing); Burton VI 84,-(xxx). Chauvin VII 113 No. 380=no/text; *ANE* 146 No. 180;
Hasan of Basrah: *Alf* IV 19; Burton VIII 74,-(flowing down to navel). Chauvin VII 29-35 No. 212A; *ANE* 207-10 No. 230;
Jeweler's Wife and Qamar al-Zamân: *Alf* IV 239, 241,-(drawing); Burton IX 250,-(gray hairs). Chauvin V 212-14 No. 121; *ANE* 345-47 No. 260.□

F545.1.7.1§, ‡Beard with whiskers like porcupine quills. (Cf. J484.2§).
¿Alî Shâr and Zumurrud: *Alf* II 226,-(robber's); Burton IV 208,-(feathers/variant). Chauvin V 89-91 No. 28; *ANE* 100-1 No. 82.□

F545.1.9.1§, ‡Forked beard.
al-'Amjad and al-'As¿ad: *Alf* II 121; Burton III 325. Chauvin V 208-10 No. 120[.1]; *ANE* 341-42 No. 61/pt. 2;
al-Rashîd and Omani Merchant: *Alf* IV 211; Burton IX 194. Chauvin VI 111-12 No. 276; *ANE* 201-2 No. 257.□

F545.3.3§, ‡Mole (*khâl, ḥasanah, shâmah*) on cheek. (Cf. F511.1).
Ensorcelled Prince/Husband: *Alf* I 27; Burton I 68. Chauvin VI 56-58 No. 222; *ANE* 176 No. 13;
¿Alî ibn Bakkâr: *Alf* II 50,-(poem/musk); Burton III 179. Chauvin V 153 No. 76; *ANE* 92-93 No. 60;

¿Alâ' al-Dîn Abû al-Shâmât: *Alf* II 149; Burton IV 33. Chauvin V 43-49 No. 18; *ANE* 85-87 No. 63;
Nûr al-Dîn and Maryam: *Alf* IV 95,-(poem); Burton VIII 299. Chauvin V 52-54 No. 271; *ANE* 98-99 No. 233.□

F547.0.1§, ‡Remarkable vagina.
¿Alî Shâr and Zumurrud: *Alf* II 234,-(simile); Burton IV 227. Chauvin V 89-91 No. 28; *ANE* 100-1 No. 82.□

F547.3.0.1§, Donkey's penis. See: *DOTTI*; *GMC*. (Cf. Z194.1.3.2.1§).
Mercury ¿Alî: *Alf* III 241; Burton VII 200,-(that which his begetter left him). Chauvin V 248-50 No. 147; *ANE* 301-3 No. 225.□

F547.3.1.2.1§, ‡Man with penis so large that he cannot stand up straight. See: *DOTTI*. (Cf. T271.3§).
Three Wishes: *Alf* III 162; Burton VI 181. Chauvin VIII 51-52 No. 19; *ANE* 419-20 No. 199.□

F547.3.7§, ‡Limp (droopy) penis—like dough or wax or the like. (Cf. P220§, T367.2.1.1§).
Nûr al-Dîn and Maryam: *Alf* IV 92,-(poem/wax); Burton VIII 293. Chauvin V 52-54 No. 271; *ANE* 98-99 No. 233.□

F547.5.2, Enormous vagina. See: *DOTTI*. (Cf. X704§).
Hârûn and Zubaydah in Bath: *Alf* II 284,-cf.; Burton V 76. Chauvin VI 142 No. 298; *ANE* 203-4 No. 111.□

F547.5.2.1§, Wide vagina: man's organs fall in it. See: *GMC*. (Cf. J1542.2.2§).

Qamar al-Zamân and Budûr: *Alf* II 109,-cf./(poem: wider than king's conquered lands); Burton III 304,-(Showest me fairest victory [??]). Chauvin V 204-12 No. 120; *ANE* 341-45 No. 61.□

F555.0.3.4§, ‡Remarkable grey (white) hair.
Pretty Gray-haired Woman Retorts: *Alf* II 303; Burton V 163. Chauvin VI 153 No. 318; *ANE* 77-78 No. 152.□

F555.0.3.4.1§, ‡Grey (white) hair gives dignified appearance. (Cf. F580§).
Sindbâd and Porter: *Alf* III 82; Burton VI 3. Chauvin VII 1 No. 373; *ANE* 383-85 No. 179/pt.□

F559.9.1.1§, ‡Mighty broken wind.
King ¿Umar al-Nu¿mân and Sons: *Alf* I 167; Burton II 88. Chauvin VI 112-24 No. 277; *ANE* 430-34 No. 39.□

F559.9.1.1.1§, ‡'Broken wind causes whirlwind on earth and smoke-trail in sky'.
King ¿Umar al-Nu¿mân and Sons: *Alf* I 167; Burton II 88. Chauvin VI 112-24 No. 277; *ANE* 430-34 No. 39.□

F560.1§, ‡Nation of remarkable ways of life.
Sindbâd's First Voyage: *Alf* III 86,-(India); Burton VI 10-11. Chauvin VII 7-9 No. 373A; *ANE* 385 No. 179.□

F561.1.1§, ‡People who live on meats only.
Jinn Imprisoned in Flasks: *Alf* III 122; Burton VI 84. Chauvin VII 113 No. 380=no/text; *ANE* 146 No. 180.□

F561.2, Ichthyophages [(Ichthyophagous)]. People who live on fish. See: *GMC*.
Landsman ¿Abdallah and Merman ¿Abdallah: *Alf* IV 206,-cf.; Burton IX 183, 185. Chauvin V 6-7 No. 3; *ANE* 65-66 No. 256.□

F562.6.1§, ‡People who reside in caves.
Jinn Imprisoned in Flasks: *Alf* III 123; Burton VI 84. Chauvin VII 113 No. 380=no/text; *ANE* 146 No. 180;
City of Brass: *Alf* III 137; Burton VI 119. Chauvin V 32-35 No. 16; *ANE* 146-50 No. 180.□

F565.2.1§, Amazons-like maiden. See: *DOTTI*; *GMC*. (Cf. K1322.2§).
King ¿Umar al-Nu¿mân and Sons: *Alf* I 179, II 5,-(Fâtin); Burton II 118, III 82. Chauvin VI 112-24 No. 277; *ANE* 430-34 No. 39;
Bahrâm and Datmâ: *Alf* III 164; Burton VI 184. Chauvin VIII 54-57 No. 22; *ANE* 114-15 No. 202.□

F565.5.1§, ‡Band of strong unveiled women. (Cf. C106§, T55.6.3§).
Jeweler's Wife and Qamar al-Zamân: *Alf* IV 241-42,-(homosexual); Burton IX 256. Chauvin V 212-14 No. 121; *ANE* 345-47 No. 260.□

F566.3§, Celibate groups (monks, clerics, saints, etc.). See: *DOTTI*; *GMC*.
Masrûr and Zayn al-Mawâṣif: *Alf* IV 77; Burton VIII 256-57. Chauvin VI 82-84 No. 251; *ANE* 294-95 No. 232.□

F567.4§, ‡The desert-loner: self-banished man lives alone in the desert. (Sometimes accompanied by only one favorite person). (Cf. H1586.4.1§, N764.1§, T93.1).
Hammâd: Treacherous Bedouin: *Alf* II 16; Burton III 106. Chauvin VI 124 n. 1 No. 277; *ANE* 200 No. 43;
Lovers of Banû ¿Udhrah and Lion: *Alf* III 207; Burton VII 118. Chauvin V 106-7 No. 37, 116 No. 52; *ANE* 274 No. 218/[2].□

F569.3, Silent person. See: *DOTTI*; *GMC*.
Barber's Tale of Himself: Joins Doomed Party: *Alf* I 110; Burton I 317–19. Chauvin V 156-57 No. 80; *ANE* 115-17 No. 28.□

F569.3.1§, ‡Silent melancholy woman (girl). (Cf. P191.1.5§).
Jullanâr of the Sea: *Alf* III 247-48,-(Jullanâr); Burton VII 267. Chauvin V 147-51 No. 73; *ANE* 248-51 No. 227;
Hasan of Basrah: *Alf* IV 4; Burton VIII 43. Chauvin VII 29-35 No. 212A; *ANE* 207-10 No. 230.□

F569.9§, ‡Lifestyles in conflict (rural-urban, nomadic-settler, modern-conventional/traditional, etc.)—each is unusual for the other(s). See: *DOTTI*; *PSAE*. (Cf. F770.0.1§, T103§, U135).
Sweep and Noble Lady: Infidelity Repaid: *Alf* II 189-90,-(rich/poor); Burton IV 126-30. Chauvin VI 148 No. 306; *ANE* 403-4 No. 72;

Jullanâr of the Sea: *Alf* III 249,-(water-world/childbearing); Burton VII 270. Chauvin V 147-51 No. 73; *ANE* 248-51 No. 227;
Landsman ¿Abdallah and Merman ¿Abdallah: *Alf* IV 207,-(mermen's-Men of land); Burton IX 187. Chauvin V 6-7 No. 3; *ANE* 65-66 No. 256.□

F571, ‡Extremely old person. See: *PSAE*.
Merchant's Curious Wife: *Alf* I 6,-(one hundred and twenty years of marriage); Burton I 21. Chauvin V 179-80 No. 104; *ANE* 298-99 No. 3;
al-'Amjad and al-'As¿ad: *Alf* II 121; Burton III 325. Chauvin V 208-10 No. 120[.1]; *ANE* 341-42 No. 61/pt. 2.□

F571.0.1§, ‡Physical attributes of being very old.
Portress Amînah: Bitten Cheek: *Alf* I 57,-(woman/described); Burton I 174. Chauvin V 98-99 No. 33; *ANE* 326-27 No. 20;
Ebony Horse: *Alf* II 254,-(xxx); Burton V 3-4,-(man/described). Chauvin V 221-31 No. 130; *ANE* 172-74 No. 103;
Nûr al-Dîn and Maryam: *Alf* IV 93, 94; Burton VIII 292-93. Chauvin V 52-54 No. 271; *ANE* 98-99 No. 233.□

F571.7, Person hundreds of years old. See: *PSAE*.
Jânshâh: *Alf* III 67,-(millennia/since Noah's time); Burton V 372. Chauvin VII 39-44 No. 153; *ANE* 238-41 No. 178.□

F571.9.1§, ‡Senility (*zamânah*): madness (diminished mental capacity) from old age. See: *DOTTI*. (Cf. F571.9.1§, P220§).
Qamar al-Zamân and Budûr: *Alf* II 68,-cf./(accusation); Burton III 218-19,-(great in age and small of wit). Chauvin V 204-12 No. 120; *ANE* 341-45 No. 61.□

F574, Luminous person. (Cf. Z62.5.1§, Z159.2.4§).
Jinni Keeps Mistress in Box: *Alf* I 3,-(poem); Burton I 11. Chauvin V 188-89 No. 111; *ANE* 370 No. 1/pt.;
Dûban and King Yûnân: *Alf* I 17,-(face/poem); Burton I 47. Chauvin V 275-76 No. 156; *ANE* 459 No. 9.□

F574.1, Resplendent beauty. Woman's face lights up the dark. See: *DOTTI*; *GMC*.
Qamar al-Zamân and Budûr: *Alf* II 72; Burton III 227. Chauvin V 204-12 No. 120; *ANE* 341-45 No. 61;
Lovers of Basra/Ḍamrah: *Alf* III 210; Burton VII 130. Chauvin V 118 No. 54; *ANE* 273 No. 220;
Jullanâr of the Sea: *Alf* III 247; Burton VII 267. Chauvin V 147-51 No. 73; *ANE* 248-51 No. 227;
Abû al-Ḥasan al-Khorâsânî (and Caliph's Favorite): *Alf* IV 231; Burton IX 234. Chauvin V 218-20 No. 129; *ANE* 68-69 No. 259.□

F574.3, Holy man ([prophet], hero) emits light.
¿Abdallah ibn Fâḍil: Treacherous Brothers: *Alf* IV 276; Burton IX 327. Chauvin V 2-4 No. 2; *ANE* 63-65 No. 261.□

F574.9.2.1§, ‡Glowing (healthy) skin: silver-like (gold-like).
Dûban and King Yûnân: *Alf* I 17; Burton I 48. Chauvin V 275-76 No. 156; *ANE* 459 No. 9.□

F575, Remarkable beauty. See: *DOTTI*; *GMC*. (Cf. F1041.8.1, T474.0.2§).
Anîs al-Jalîs: *Alf* I 126; Burton II 3. Chauvin V 120-24 No. 58; *ANE* 316-17 No. 35;
Mock Caliph/¿Alî al-Jawharî: *Alf* II 195-96,-(poem); Burton IV 139. Chauvin V 99-100 No. 174; *ANE* 304-5 No. 73;
Dispute Concerning Males and Females: *Alf* II 301,-(female's/described); Burton V 156, 159-60. Chauvin VI 153 No. 317; *ANE* 291 No. 151;
Hasan of Basrah: *Alf* III 316, IV 5, 28-29; Burton VIII 32, 93. Chauvin 7: 29 No. 212A; *ANE* 207 No. 230;
Nûr al-Dîn and Maryam: *Alf* IV 91; Burton VIII 290-91. Chauvin V 52-54 No. 271; *ANE* 98-99 No. 233.□

F575.0.2§, ‡Intelligence (wit) as trait of beauty. (Cf. F605.1§).
Qamar al-Zamân and Budûr: *Alf* II 72; Burton III 226. Chauvin V 204-12 No. 120; *ANE* 341-45 No. 61.□

F575.1, ‡Remarkably beautiful woman. See: *DOTTI*.
¿Alî ibn Bakkâr: *Alf* II 41-42; Burton III 163. Chauvin V 153 No. 76; *ANE* 92-93 No. 60;

Qamar al-Zamân and Budûr: *Alf* II 72; Burton III 226. Chauvin V 204-12 No. 120; *ANE* 341-45 No. 61;
Budûr and Jubayr ibn ¿Umayr: *Alf* II 236; Burton IV 231. Chauvin VII 93-94 No. 374; *ANE* 243-44 No. 83;
Masrûr and Zayn al-Mawâṣif: *Alf* IV 55; Burton VIII 205. Chauvin VI 82-84 No. 251; *ANE* 294-95 No. 232.□

F575.1.0.1§, ‡Plump (full-bodied) woman—beautiful (pleasing). (Cf. F575.1.5.6.1.1§, J1413§).
Hârûn and Zubaydah in Bath: *Alf* II 284,-cf.; Burton V 76. Chauvin VI 142 No. 298; *ANE* 203-4 No. 111.□

F575.1.0.1.1§, ‡ 'Silent (mute) bracelets': (euphemism) for woman's plump wrist or ankle. (Cf. J1413§).
Qamar al-Zamân and Budûr: *Alf* II 109,-(poem/ankle bracelet); Burton III 302,-(anklet rings)/. Chauvin V 204-12 No. 120; *ANE* 341-45 No. 61;
Lovers of Basra/Ḍamrah: *Alf* III 210,-cf.; Burton VII 131. Chauvin V 118 No. 54; *ANE* 273 No. 220.□

F575.1.0.1.1.1§, ‡Bracelet (anklet) prevents woman's flesh from flowing down her wrist (ankle).
Qamar al-Zamân and Budûr: *Alf* II 72; Burton III 226. Chauvin V 204-12 No. 120; *ANE* 341-45 No. 61.□

F575.1.2.1§, ‡Old woman more beautiful than when youthful, except for gray hair. (Cf. K1872.9.6.1§).
Pretty Gray-haired Woman Retorts: *Alf* II 303; Burton V 163. Chauvin VI 153 No. 318; *ANE* 77-78 No. 152.□

F575.1.5.1§, Beautiful ('broad,' 'high') buttocks. See: *GMC*. (Cf. Z186.6§).
King ¿Umar al-Nu¿mân and Sons: *Alf* I 169, 170,-(like sea waves/like mound of crystal); Burton II 96, 98,-(back and hinder cheeks). Chauvin VI 112-24 No. 277; *ANE* 430-34 No. 39;
Tâj al-Mulûk: *Alf* I 293,-(boy's); Burton III 17-18. Chauvin V 126-28 No. 60; *ANE* 406-8 No. 40;
Qamar al-Zamân and Budûr: *Alf* II 67,-(poem/male's); Burton III 217-18. Chauvin V 204-12 No. 120; *ANE* 341-45 No. 61;
Hasan of Basrah: *Alf* IV 5; Burton VIII 46. Chauvin VII 29-35 No. 212A; *ANE* 207-10 No. 230.□

F575.1.5.1.2§, ‡Remarkable beauty: woman with buttocks so heavy that she cannot stand up (she is pulled down by their weight). (Cf. Z186.6.2§).
Qamar al-Zamân and Budûr: *Alf* II 72,-(poem); Burton III 226. Chauvin V 204-12 No. 120; *ANE* 341-45 No. 61.□

F575.1.5.5.1§, ‡Pomegranate-like breast. See: *DOTTI*. (Cf. Z166.1§).
King ¿Umar al-Nu¿mân and Sons: *Alf* I 167; Burton II 88. Chauvin VI 112-24 No. 277; *ANE* 430-34 No. 39;
Hasan of Basrah: *Alf* III 316,-(poem), IV 5; Burton VIII 32, 46. Chauvin VII 29-35 No. 212A; *ANE* 207-10 No. 230.□

F575.1.5.6§, ‡Remarkably beautiful abdomen.
King ¿Umar al-Nu¿mân and Sons: *Alf* I 167; Burton II 88. Chauvin VI 112-24 No. 277; *ANE* 430-34 No. 39;
Qamar al-Zamân and Budûr: *Alf* II 97; Burton III 278-79. Chauvin V 204-12 No. 120; *ANE* 341-45 No. 61.□

F575.1.5.6.1.1§, ‡Fleshy abdomen (with folds of fat)—pleasing. (Cf. F575.1.0.1§).
Porter and Ladies of Baghdad: *Alf* I 32; Burton I 84. Chauvin V 251-52 No. 148; *ANE* 324-26 No. 14;
Qamar al-Zamân and Budûr: *Alf* II 97; Burton III 278. Chauvin V 204-12 No. 120; *ANE* 341-45 No. 61;
Hasan of Basrah: *Alf* III 316,-(poem); Burton VIII 32. Chauvin VII 29-35 No. 212A; *ANE* 207-10 No. 230.□

F575.1.5.6.4§, ‡Remarkably beautiful waist.
King ¿Umar al-Nu¿mân and Sons: *Alf* I 170,-(slender, like a rod); Burton II 99. Chauvin VI 112-24 No. 277; *ANE* 430-34 No. 39.□

F575.1.5.6.2§, ‡Beautiful deep navel ('inny'—"cup's-seat"). See: *DOTTI*. (Cf. Z105§).

Porter and Ladies of Baghdad: *Alf* I 32; Burton I 84-85. Chauvin V 251-52 No. 148; *ANE* 324-26 No. 14;
Nûr al-Dîn ¿Alî and Son: *Alf* I 73,-(*muḥaqqaqah*/cupped); Burton I 224,-(xxx/"with something below it" [??]). Chauvin VI 102-6 No. 270; *ANE* 317-19 No. 22;
Qamar al-Zamân and Budûr: *Alf* II 97; Burton III 278. Chauvin V 204-12 No. 120; *ANE* 341-45 No. 61;
Tawaddud: Slavegirl Sold and Regained: *Alf* II 304; Burton V 191. Chauvin VII 117-19 No. 387; *ANE* 408-10 No. 157;
Hasan of Basrah: *Alf* III 316, IV 5; Burton VIII 33, 46. Chauvin VII 29-35 No. 212A; *ANE* 207-10 No. 230.□

F575.1.5.7§, ‡Remarkably beautiful thigh(s).
Nûr al-Dîn ¿Alî and Son: *Alf* I 73,-(male's/crystal-like); Burton I 224. Chauvin VI 102-6 No. 270; *ANE* 317-19 No. 22;
Qamar al-Zamân and Budûr: *Alf* II 111; Burton III 306. Chauvin V 204-12 No. 120; *ANE* 341-45 No. 61;
Dispute Concerning Males and Females: *Alf* II 302,-(like columns of pearl); Burton V 160. Chauvin VI 153 No. 317; *ANE* 291 No. 151;
Hasan of Basrah: *Alf* III 316,-(poem/like columns), IV 5, 46; Burton VIII 33. Chauvin VII 29-35 No. 212A; *ANE* 207-10 No. 230.□

F575.1.5.8§, ‡Remarkably beautiful leg(s).
Nûr al-Dîn ¿Alî and Son: *Alf* I 73; Burton I 224. Chauvin VI 102-6 No. 270; *ANE* 317-19 No. 22;
King ¿Umar al-Nu¿mân and Sons: *Alf* I 167,-(*marmar*); Burton II 88,-(calves of alabaster). Chauvin VI 112-24 No. 277; *ANE* 430-34 No. 39.□

F575.1.5.12.1§, ‡Remarkably soft fingers. (Cf. Z62.6.4§, Z65.4§).
Masrûr and Zayn al-Mawâṣif: *Alf* IV 57; Burton VIII 217. Chauvin VI 82-84 No. 251; *ANE* 294-95 No. 232.□

F575.1.6§, ‡Beauty that disorients (dazzles) the beholder. See: *DOTTI*; *PSAE*.
Reeve's Story: Why Maimed by Bride: *Alf* I 96-97; Burton I 280. Chauvin V 220-21 No. 305; *ANE* 351 No. 25;
King ¿Umar al-Nu¿mân and Sons: *Alf* I 199,-(people *buhitû*); Burton II 153,-(wondered [??]). Chauvin VI 112-24 No. 277; *ANE* 430-34 No. 39;
Budûr and Jubayr ibn ¿Umayr: *Alf* II 237,-cf./(young man's); Burton IV 234,-(confounded by his beauty). Chauvin VII 93-94 No. 374; *ANE* 243-44 No. 83;
Masrûr and Zayn al-Mawâṣif: *Alf* IV 75; Burton VIII 245. Chauvin VI 82-84 No. 251; *ANE* 294-95 No. 232;
al-Rashîd and Omani Merchant: *Alf* IV 213,-(poem/East-West); Burton IX 196,-("dazed and dazzled"). Chauvin VI 111-12 No. 276; *ANE* 201-2 No. 257;
Abû al-Ḥasan al-Khorâsânî (and Caliph's Favorite): *Alf* IV 231; Burton IX 234. Chauvin V 218-20 No. 129; *ANE* 68-69 No. 259;
Jeweler's Wife and Qamar al-Zamân: *Alf* IV 248,-cf./(young man's); Burton IX 268. Chauvin V 212-14 No. 121; *ANE* 345-47 No. 260.□

F575.1.6.1§, ‡Woman so beautiful whoever sees her desires her (falls in love). See: *DOTTI*. (Cf. T81.2, T474.0.2§).
Masrûr and Zayn al-Mawâṣif: *Alf* IV 56,-(violator reprimanded); Burton VIII 206. Chauvin VI 82-84 No. 251; *ANE* 294-95 No. 232.□

F575.1.6.2§, ‡Woman's beauty causes pious man to neglect worship. (Cf. F566.3§, T428§).
Hasan of Basrah: *Alf* IV 10,-cf./(Caliph may commit sin); Burton VIII 54,-(Caliph would barter his soul's good for worldly lust). Chauvin VII 29-35 No. 212A; *ANE* 207-10 No. 230.□

F575.1.6.2.1§, ‡Woman's beauty causes celibate person (monk) to become lustful. See: *DOTTI*.
Masrûr and Zayn al-Mawâṣif: *Alf* IV 77; Burton VIII 256. Chauvin VI 82-84 No. 251; *ANE* 294-95 No. 232.□

F575.1.6.2.2§, ‡Person cannot resist sex drive: must have intercourse without delay. (Cf. T469§).
Hârûn, Slave-girl and Judge Abû-Yûsuf: *Alf* II 202; Burton IV 154. Chauvin VII 114 No. 383; *ANE* 204 No. 75.□

F575.1.6.3§, ‡Woman's beauty compels beholder to perform prayer ritual (prostrate self, kneel, etc.). (Cf. T187.0.2§).

Second Qalandar: Afrit's Wife: *Alf* I 43,-(prostrate self); Burton I 116. Chauvin V 197-200 No. 116; *ANE* 338-39 No. 16;
Jullanâr of the Sea: *Alf* III 247,-(glorify The Creator); Burton VII 267. Chauvin V 147-51 No. 73; *ANE* 248-51 No. 227;
Hasan of Basrah: *Alf* IV 5,-cf./(kiss ground), 9; Burton VIII 46, 56. Chauvin VII 29-35 No. 212A; *ANE* 207-10 No. 230.□

F575.1.6.4§, ‡Woman's beauty reported to queen causes demand that she visit palace.
Hasan of Basrah: *Alf* IV 10; Burton VIII 54. Chauvin VII 29-35 No. 212A; *ANE* 207-10 No. 230.□

F575.1.6.5§, ‡Woman's beauty makes her faultless (mistakes seem less serious).
King ¿Umar al-Nu¿mân and Sons: *Alf* I 169; Burton II 96. Chauvin VI 112-24 No. 277; *ANE* 430-34 No. 39;
Masrûr and Zayn al-Mawâṣif: *Alf* IV 76ff.; Burton VIII 250ff. Chauvin VI 82-84 No. 251; *ANE* 294-95 No. 232.□

F575.1.6.5.1§, ‡Beauty as intercessor. (Cf. P776.1.2.1§).
Anîs al-Jalîs: *Alf* I 136,-(for two lovers); Burton II 24. Chauvin V 120-24 No. 58; *ANE* 316-17 No. 35;
King ¿Umar al-Nu¿mân and Sons: *Alf* I 169,-(poem); Burton II 96. Chauvin VI 112-24 No. 277; *ANE* 430-34 No. 39;
Ni¿mah and Nu¿m: Stolen Wife Regained: *Alf* II 141; Burton IV 17. Chauvin VI 96-97 No. 263; *ANE* 314 No. 62;
Jullanâr of the Sea: *Alf* III 248; Burton VII 266,-(saves from royal wrath). Chauvin V 147-51 No. 73; *ANE* 248-51 No. 227;
Masrûr and Zayn al-Mawâṣif: *Alf* IV 73,-(admired); Burton VIII 245-46. Chauvin VI 82-84 No. 251; *ANE* 294-95 No. 232;
Ibrâhîm and Jamîlah: *Alf* IV 226,-(man's); Burton IX 222. Chauvin VI 52-53 No. 218; *ANE* 227-29 No. 258.□

F575.1.7§, ‡Awe-evoking beauty (intimidates beholder).
King ¿Umar al-Nu¿mân and Sons: *Alf* I 170; Burton II 96. Chauvin VI 112-24 No. 277; *ANE* 430-34 No. 39;
Lovers of Basra/Ḍamrah: *Alf* III 210; Burton VII 130. Chauvin V 118 No. 54; *ANE* 273 No. 220.□

F575.2, Handsome man. See: *DOTTI*.
¿Alî ibn Bakkâr: *Alf* II 41; Burton III 163. Chauvin V 153 No. 76; *ANE* 92-93 No. 60;
Sweep and Noble Lady: Infidelity Repaid: *Alf* II 190; Burton IV 128. Chauvin VI 148 No. 306; *ANE* 403-4 No. 72;
Mock Caliph/¿Alî al-Jawharî: *Alf* II 191; Burton IV 131. Chauvin V 99-100 No. 174; *ANE* 304-5 No. 73;
Lover Who Feigned Himself a Thief: *Alf* II 204; Burton IV 155. Chauvin VII 134-35 No. 403; *ANE* 272 No. 76;
Craft and Malice of Women/Frame: *Alf* III 139; Burton VI 124. Chauvin VIII 33-34 No. 1; *ANE* 160-61 No. 181;
Lovers of Basra/Ḍamrah: *Alf* III 212; Burton VII 134. Chauvin V 118 No. 54; *ANE* 273 No. 220;
Nûr al-Dîn and Maryam: *Alf* IV 80; Burton VIII 265. Chauvin V 52-54 No. 271; *ANE* 98-99 No. 233.□

F575.3, Remarkably beautiful child. See: *DOTTI*.
Jeweler's Wife and Qamar al-Zamân: *Alf* IV 238; Burton IX 247. Chauvin V 212-14 No. 121; *ANE* 345-47 No. 260.□

F575.4§, ‡Remarkably beautiful youth (boy).
Eldest Lady's Story: Treacherous Sisters: *Alf* I 55; Burton I 167. Chauvin V 4 No. 443; *ANE* 174-75 No. 19;
Portress Amînah: Bitten Cheek: *Alf* I 58-59; Burton I 180. Chauvin V 98-99 No. 33; *ANE* 326-27 No. 20;
Nûr al-Dîn ¿Alî and Son: *Alf* I 64, 77; Burton I 195, 214. Chauvin VI 102-6 No. 270; *ANE* 317-19 No. 22;
Anîs al-Jalîs: *Alf* I 126-27,-(poem: creation of beautiful eyes); Burton II 4-5. Chauvin V 120-24 No. 58; *ANE* 316-17 No. 35;
Tâj al-Mulûk: *Alf* I 266, 2927; Burton II 292, III 16. Chauvin V 126-28 No. 60; *ANE* 406-8 No. 40;

Qamar al-Zamân and Budûr: *Alf* II 67; Burton III 213. Chauvin V 204-12 No. 120; *ANE* 341-45 No. 61;
¿Alâ' al-Dîn Abû al-Shâmât: *Alf* II 149; Burton IV 34. Chauvin V 43-49 No. 18; *ANE* 85-87 No. 63;
Mock Caliph/¿Alî al-Jawharî: *Alf* II 191; Burton IV 131. Chauvin V 99-100 No. 174; *ANE* 304-5 No. 73;
Tawaddud: Slavegirl Sold and Regained: *Alf* II 304,-(infant); Burton V 189-90. Chauvin VII 117-19 No. 387; *ANE* 408-10 No. 157;
Ibrâhîm and Jamîlah: *Alf* IV 221; Burton IX 212. Chauvin VI 52-53 No. 218; *ANE* 227-29 No. 258.□

F575.5§, 'Joseph's beauty'. See: *GMC*.
Tâj al-Mulûk: *Alf* I 294,-(implicit); Burton III 21. Chauvin V 126-28 No. 60; *ANE* 406-8 No. 40.□

F576, Extraordinary ugliness. See: *DOTTI*.
King ¿Umar al-Nu¿mân and Sons: *Alf* I 236; Burton II 234. Chauvin VI 112-24 No. 277; *ANE* 430-34 No. 39;
¿Alâ' al-Dîn Abû al-Shâmât: *Alf* II 165; Burton IV 66. Chauvin V 43-49 No. 18; *ANE* 85-87 No. 63;
¿Alî Shâr and Zumurrud: *Alf* II 219,-(blue eyes); Burton IV 192. Chauvin V 89-91 No. 28; *ANE* 100-1 No. 82.□

F576.1§, ‡Extraordinarily ugly face (features).
Dûban and King Yûnân: *Alf* I 18; Burton I 49,-(vizier's, unsightly). Chauvin V 275-76 No. 156; *ANE* 459 No. 9;
¿Alî Shâr and Zumurrud: *Alf* II 226,-(robber's); Burton IV 208. Chauvin V 89-91 No. 28; *ANE* 100-1 No. 82.□

F576.1.1§, ‡Extraordinarily ugliness: 'blue eyes on black face'.
¿Alî Shâr and Zumurrud: *Alf* II 219,-(blue eyes),-cf.; Burton IV 192. Chauvin V 89-91 No. 28; *ANE* 100-1 No. 82;
Hasan of Basrah: *Alf* IV 25,-(blue eyes only); Burton VIII 86. Chauvin VII 29-35 No. 212A; *ANE* 207-10 No. 230.□

F576.2§, ‡Extraordinarily ugly physical posture (hunchback, very short neck, or the like). See: *DOTTI*. (Cf. F519.1§, K2271, X144§).
Nûr al-Dîn ¿Alî and Son: *Alf* I 70; Burton I 213. Chauvin VI 102-6 No. 270; *ANE* 317-19 No. 22;
Hunchback's Tale: Resuscitated: *Alf* I 85; Burton I 255. Chauvin V 180-82 No. 105; *ANE* 224-25 No. 23;
King ¿Umar al-Nu¿mân and Sons: *Alf* I 236,-(of Rûmî old woman); Burton II 234. Chauvin VI 112-24 No. 277; *ANE* 430-34 No. 39.□

F577.4.1§, ‡Husband and wife (groom and bride) identical in appearance (they look alike). (Cf. P253.15§).
Qamar al-Zamân and Budûr: *Alf* II 100; Burton III 283. Chauvin V 204-12 No. 120; *ANE* 341-45 No. 61;
Ni¿mah and Nu¿m: Stolen Wife Regained: *Alf* II 139; Burton IV 12. Chauvin VI 96-97 No. 263; *ANE* 314 No. 62.□

F579.1.1§, ‡Social group of dissimilar members. See: *DOTTI*.
King ¿Umar al-Nu¿mân and Sons: *Alf* I 168,-(*tawâ'if*); Burton II 95,-(rabble of tribesmen gathered together). Chauvin VI 112-24 No. 277; *ANE* 430-34 No. 39.□

F579.2§, ‡Association of different species (foul and fish, bird and land animal, carnivore and herbivore, etc.).
Francolin and Tortoises: *Alf* IV 172; Burton IX 113. Chauvin II 224 No. 152/23; *ANE* 188 No. 254.□

F580§, Person of awe-inspiring appearance. See: *DOTTI*; *GMC*. (Cf. F555.0.3.4.1§, P427, W17§).
Third Qalandar: Magnetic Mountain: *Alf* I 52; Burton I 144. Chauvin V 200-3 No. 117; *ANE* 340-41 No. 18;
¿Alî ibn Bakkâr: *Alf* II 59,-(woman singer-concubine); Burton III 198. Chauvin V 153 No. 76; *ANE* 92-93 No. 60;
al-'Amjad and al-'As¿ad: *Alf* II 121,-(old man); Burton III 325. Chauvin V 208-10 No. 120[.1]; *ANE* 341-42 No. 61/pt. 2;
Ma¿n Rewards a Bedouin for Gift: *Alf* II 183; Burton IV 98. Chauvin VI 78 No. 248; *ANE* 291 No. 66;

Sindbâd and Porter: *Alf* III 82,-cf.; Burton VI 3. Chauvin VII 1 No. 373; *ANE* 383-85 No. 179/pt.;
Mercury ¿Alî: *Alf* III 227,-(*haybah*); Burton VII 172,-("fear"/[*khawf*]). Chauvin V 248-50 No. 147; *ANE* 301-3 No. 225.□

F580.1§, ‡Man's (dervish's) awe-inspiring appearance splits crowd of people.
Jeweler's Wife and Qamar al-Zamân: *Alf* IV 239; Burton IX 250. Chauvin V 212-14 No. 121; *ANE* 345-47 No. 260.□

F585.1, Fatal enticement of phantom women. See: *DOTTI*; *GMC*.
City of Brass: *Alf* III 132,-cf.; Burton VI 109. Chauvin V 32-35 No. 16; *ANE* 146-50 No. 180.□

F585.5§, ‡Magic phantoms as guardians of treasure. See: *DOTTI*.
Jawdar and His Treacherous Brethren: *Alf* III 186,-(corpse without soul); Burton VI 229ff. Chauvin V 257-60 No. 154; *ANE* 244-45 No. 209.□

F605.1§, Remarkably intelligent person.
Qamar al-Zamân and Budûr: *Alf* II 72; Burton III 226. Chauvin V 204-12 No. 120; *ANE* 341-45 No. 61.□

F610.0.1, ‡Remarkably strong woman.
King ¿Umar al-Nu¿mân and Sons: *Alf* I 166-67,-(maiden/athlete); Burton II 87. Chauvin VI 112-24 No. 277; *ANE* 430-34 No. 39.□

F610.0.7§, ‡Remarkably handsome community (nation). (Cf. W256.1§).
¿Alî Shâr and Zumurrud: *Alf* II 227,-(Turks); Burton IV 210-11. Chauvin V 89-91 No. 28; *ANE* 100-1 No. 82.□

F614.10, Strong man fights whole army alone.
Ebony Horse: *Alf* II 257; Burton V 12-13. Chauvin V 221-31 No. 130; *ANE* 172-74 No. 103.□

F628.1.1.1.1§, ‡Strong man kills lion single-handed with one blow of sword. (Cf. F628.4.3§)
Mercury ¿Alî: *Alf* III 230; Burton VII 178. Chauvin V 248-50 No. 147; *ANE* 301-3 No. 225.□

F628.4.0.1§, ‡Strong woman's mighty spear-cast (sword blow).
Nûr al-Dîn and Maryam: *Alf* IV 125,-(woman's); Burton IX 4-5. Chauvin V 52-54 No. 271; *ANE* 98-99 No. 233.□

F628.4.3§, ‡Strong man's mighty sword blow splits person (ferocious beast) in two. (Cf. F628.1.1.1.1§).
Mercury ¿Alî: *Alf* III 230; Burton VII 178. Chauvin V 248-50 No. 147; *ANE* 301-3 No. 225.□

F628.4.3.1§, ‡Mighty sword blow splits man 'from shoulder to dangling privates'. See: *DOTTI*.
King ¿Umar al-Nu¿mân and Sons: *Alf* I 174,-(... *min 'am¿â'ihi*/out of his bowels); Burton II 108,-(came out glittering from his vitals). Chauvin VI 112-24 No. 277; *ANE* 430-34 No. 39;
Ḥammâd: Treacherous Bedouin: *Alf* II 20,-(his *¿alâ'iq*); Burton III 112,-("apple of his throat"). Chauvin VI 124 n. 1 No. 277; *ANE* 200 No. 43;
¿Alâ' al-Dîn Abû al-Shâmât: *Alf* II 154; Burton IV 44. Chauvin V 43-49 No. 18; *ANE* 85-87 No. 63;
Hasan of Basrah: *Alf* III 313; Burton VIII 27. Chauvin VII 29-35 No. 212A; *ANE* 207-10 No. 230;
Nûr al-Dîn and Maryam: *Alf* IV 123, 125; Burton IX 4-5, 10. Chauvin V 52-54 No. 271; *ANE* 98-99 No. 233.□

F632.0.1§, ‡Ways of mighty eaters: gluttonous eating. See: *DOTTI*. (Cf. W125).
¿Alî Shâr and Zumurrud: *Alf* II 230,-(Kurd's); Burton IV 217. Chauvin V 89-91 No. 28; *ANE* 100-1 No. 82.□

F632.0.1.1§, ‡'Eating like an ogre eats': gluttonous eating.
Jawdar and His Treacherous Brethren: *Alf* III 180; Burton VI 218,-("cannibals"). Chauvin V 257-60 No. 154; *ANE* 244-45 No. 209;
Abû Qîr and Abû Ṣîr: *Alf* IV 185; Burton IX 140. Chauvin V 15-17 No. 10; *ANE* 75-77 No. 255.□

F646.1§, ‡Erogenous zone: under left armpit (woman's).
Ma¿rûf the Cobbler: *Alf* IV 300; Burton X 21. Chauvin VI 81-82 No. 250; *ANE* 291-93 No. 262.□

F649.1§, ‡Sincerity (purity of soul) gives telepathic powers of knowledge.
Conversion of Princess by Khawwâṣ: *Alf* III 15,-(*ṣafat al-khawâṭir*); Burton V 285,-(heart and soul are whole). Chauvin V 239 No. 139; *ANE* 145 No. 171.□

F657§, Mystical knowledge (intuition, presentiment). See: *DOTTI*. (Cf. D1812.4.2§, D1825.1, H175.7§).
¿Alî Shâr and Zumurrud: *Alf* II 221,-(my heart senses); Burton IV 199,-(my heart presageth a parting). Chauvin V 89-91 No. 28; *ANE* 100-1 No. 82;
Nûr al-Dîn and Maryam: *Alf* IV 98,-(my heart senses); Burton VIII 308-9,-(my heart presageth me). Chauvin V 52-54 No. 271; *ANE* 98-99 No. 233.□

F657.2§, ‡'Lovers's mystical knowledge (*mukâshafah*).
Budûr and Jubayr ibn ¿Umayr: *Alf* II 239; Burton IV 238. Chauvin VII 93-94 No. 374; *ANE* 243-44 No. 83.□

F657.2.1§, ‡'Lovers's hearts have eyes (vision) that see what cannot be seen by the gaze of onlookers'.
Budûr and Jubayr ibn ¿Umayr: *Alf* II 239; Burton IV 238. Chauvin VII 93-94 No. 374; *ANE* 243-44 No. 83.□

F663.1§, ‡Skilful smith produces unknown article (saddle hardware) from mere description. See: *DOTTI*.
Sindbâd's Fourth Voyage: *Alf* III 102; Burton VI 39. Chauvin VII 18-20 No. 373D; *ANE* 386 No. 179.□

F668.9.2.1§, ‡Patient healed (revived) by extracting object blocking throat. See: *DOTTI*. (Cf. E68).
Hunchback's Tale: Resuscitated: *Alf* I 125,-(with tweezers); Burton I 351. Chauvin V 163-64 No. 86; *ANE* 224-25 No. 23.□

F669.1.1§, ‡Person so skilled in administration (managing others) that he can use a spider web as harness for unruly group. (Cf. J1110.1.4§, K300.0.2§).
Portress Amînah: Bitten Cheek: *Alf* I 57,-(poem,/old woman); Burton I 174. Chauvin V 98-99 No. 33; *ANE* 326-27 No. 20;
Dalîla the Swindler: *Alf* III 213,-cf./(old woman can wile [male] snake out of his den); Burton VII 145,-("could wile the very dragon out of his den"). Chauvin V 248-50 No. 147; *ANE* 163-64 No. 224.□

F671.3§, ‡Resourceful person makes sea worthy raft (boat). (Cf. R217.1§).
Uns al-Wujûd and al-Ward: *Alf* II 275; Burton V 45. Chauvin VI 127-29 No. 282; *ANE* 438 No. 104;
Sindbâd's Sixth Voyage: *Alf* III 114; Burton VI 62. Chauvin VII 24-27 No. 373F; *ANE* 386 No. 179;
Sindbâd's Seventh Voyage: *Alf* III 119; Burton VI 71. Chauvin VII 26-29 No. 373G; *ANE* 386-87 No. 179;
Sayf al-Mulûk: *Alf* III 285; Burton VII 342-43. Chauvin VII 64-73 No. 348; *ANE* 362-64 No. 229.□

F671.3.1§, ‡Raft (boat) made of furniture.
Sayf al-Mulûk: *Alf* III 290; Burton VII 352. Chauvin VII 64-73 No. 348; *ANE* 362-64 No. 229.□

F674, ‡Skillful painter. Can paint from description of a dream. See: *DOTTI*.
Tâj al-Mulûk: *Alf* I 300; Burton III 33. Chauvin V 126-28 No. 60; *ANE* 406-8 No. 40.□

F674.1§, ‡Lifelike painting from model. See: *DOTTI*. (Cf. A1440.5.1§, T11.2).
Goldsmith and Cashmere Singer: *Alf* III 150; Burton VI 156. Chauvin VIII 46-47 No. 14; *ANE* 196 No. 194;
Ibrâhîm and Jamîlah: *Alf* IV 219; Burton IX 207. Chauvin VI 52-53 No. 218; *ANE* 227-29 No. 258.□

F675.5§, ‡Skilful carpenter produces unknown article (saddle frame) from mere description. See: *DOTTI*.
Sindbâd's Fourth Voyage: *Alf* III 102; Burton VI 39. Chauvin VII 18-20 No. 373D; *ANE* 386 No. 179.□

F676.3§, ‡Thief so clever that 'he (she) can lift (steal) kohl off one's eye-(lashes)'. See: *DOTTI*.
¿Alâ' al-Dîn Abû al-Shâmât: *Alf* II 166; Burton IV 68. Chauvin V 43-49 No. 18; *ANE* 85-87 No. 63;
Mercury ¿Alî: *Alf* III 236; Burton VII 189. Chauvin V 248-50 No. 147; *ANE* 301-3 No. 225.□

F679.8, ‡Skill at chess-playing. (Cf. K92.4.1§, Z178.9.1§).
King ¿Umar al-Nu¿mân and Sons: *Alf* I 172; Burton II 104. Chauvin VI 112-24 No. 277; *ANE* 430-34 No. 39;

Tawaddud: Slavegirl Sold and Regained: *Alf* III 7; Burton V 243. Chauvin VII 117-19 No. 387; *ANE* 408-10 No. 157;
Masrûr and Zayn al-Mawâṣif: *Alf* IV 57-59; Burton VIII 216-18. Chauvin VI 82-84 No. 251; *ANE* 294-95 No. 232.□

F679.9.1§, ‡Skillful singer-musician plays in various styles. (Cf. H35.1.0.1§, Z117.6.2§).
¿Alî ibn Bakkâr: *Alf* II 57; Burton III 195. Chauvin V 153 No. 76; *ANE* 92-93 No. 60;
Mock Caliph/¿Alî al-Jawharî: *Alf* II 194,-(twenty-four); Burton IV 135,-(four-and-twenty modes). Chauvin V 99-100 No. 174; *ANE* 304-5 No. 73;
Budûr and Jubayr ibn ¿Umayr: *Alf* II 243,-(eleven modes); Burton IV 245. Chauvin VII 93-94 No. 374; *ANE* 243-44 No. 83;
Isḥâq al-Mûṣilî and Merchant's Singer: *Alf* II 296; Burton V 130. Chauvin VI 59 No. 225; *ANE* 233 No. 142;
Tawaddud: Slavegirl Sold and Regained: *Alf* III 7; Burton V 245,-(modes). Chauvin VII 117-19 No. 387; *ANE* 408-10 No. 157.□

F679.9.2§, ‡Skillful singer-musician sings in various languages.
King ¿Umar al-Nu¿mân and Sons: *Alf* I 171; Burton II 102. Chauvin VI 112-24 No. 277; *ANE* 430-34 No. 39.□

F679.12.1§, ‡Precious stones (diamonds, emeralds, etc.) retrieved from bottom of inaccessible valley with the help of vultures. (Meat thrown from great heights into valley, stones adhere to meat, vultures carry meat along with stones to valley ridge where miners can collect them). See: *DOTTI*. (Cf. F756.8.1§, P806.7.1§).
Sindbâd's Second Voyage: *Alf* III 90; Burton VI 19. Chauvin VII 9-14 No. 373B; *ANE* 385 No. 179.□

F688.5§, Strong-man's mighty shout: kills. See: *DOTTI*.
Jinn Imprisoned in Flasks: *Alf* III 129,-(jinni's); Burton VI 100. Chauvin VII 113 No. 380=no/text; *ANE* 146 No. 180.□

F688.5.1§, ‡Person dazed from strong-man's mighty shout.
Jinn Imprisoned in Flasks: *Alf* III 128; Burton VI 100. Chauvin VII 113 No. 380=no/text; *ANE* 146 No. 180.□

F688.5.3§, ‡Man's shout kills predator (animal). (Cf. B790.1§).
Landsman ¿Abdallah and Merman ¿Abdallah: *Alf* IV 205,-cf.; Burton IX 181,-(scream). Chauvin V 6-7 No. 3; *ANE* 65-66 No. 256.□

F688.6§, ‡Supernatural being's (jinni's, demon's, or the like) mighty shriek causes death (fainting).
Hasan of Basrah: *Alf* IV 37,-(jinni-queen's); Burton VIII 111,-([variant: scream and kick]). Chauvin VII 29-35 No. 212A; *ANE* 207-10 No. 230.□

F689.0.1§, ‡Music (melody) so moving that it can energize the lifeless (melt solid rock or iron).
Anîs al-Jalîs: *Alf* I 140; Burton II 30,-("made all hearts yearn to her"). Chauvin V 120-24 No. 58; *ANE* 316-17 No. 35;
¿Alâ' al-Dîn Abû al-Shâmât: *Alf* II 158, 162, 177; Burton IV 54, 60, 88. Chauvin V 43-49 No. 18; *ANE* 85-87 No. 63;
Isḥâq al-Mûṣilî and Merchant's Singer: *Alf* II 296,-(gives death to the living and life to the dead); Burton V 131,-("deaden"/"quicken"). Chauvin VI 59 No. 225; *ANE* 233 No. 142.□

F689.0.2§, ‡David's marvelous music (psalms)—(*mazâmîr* Dâwûd/*'Âl* Dâwûd).
¿Alâ' al-Dîn Abû al-Shâmât: *Alf* II 156, 162; Burton IV 50, 60. Chauvin V 43-49 No. 18; *ANE* 85-87 No. 63.□

F689.1§, ‡Ecstacy from immersion in music (song). (Cf. P196.8.2§).
Porter and Ladies of Baghdad: *Alf* I 37-038,-cf.; Burton I 99. Chauvin V 251-52 No. 148; *ANE* 324-26 No. 14;
King ¿Umar al-Nu¿mân and Sons: *Alf* I 171; Burton II 100-1. Chauvin VI 112-24 No. 277; *ANE* 430-34 No. 39;
¿Alâ' al-Dîn Abû al-Shâmât: *Alf* II 177; Burton IV 88. Chauvin V 43-49 No. 18; *ANE* 85-87 No. 63;
Mock Caliph/¿Alî al-Jawharî: *Alf* II 194-95,-cf.; Burton IV 135. Chauvin V 99-100 No. 174; *ANE* 304-5 No. 73;
Budûr and Jubayr ibn ¿Umayr: *Alf* II 239,-(avoided); Burton IV 237. Chauvin VII 93-94 No. 374; *ANE* 243-44 No. 83;

Isḥâq al-Mûṣilî and Merchant's Singer: *Alf* II 296; Burton V 132,-(excess of delight). Chauvin VI 59 No. 225; *ANE* 233 No. 142.□

F689.1.1§, ‡Madness from listening to marvelous music or song (violent reactions: ecstatic convulsions, clothes slit, self-injury, etc.).
Porter and Ladies of Baghdad: *Alf* I 37; Burton I 99. Chauvin V 251-52 No. 148; *ANE* 324-26 No. 14;
Mock Caliph/¿Alî al-Jawharî: *Alf* II 194-95,-cf.; Burton IV 135. Chauvin V 99-100 No. 174; *ANE* 304-5 No. 73.□

F690§, ‡Person of remarkable swiftness with weapons (firearms, swords, etc.).
Ebony Horse: *Alf* II 257; Burton V 11,-("doughtier"). Chauvin V 221-31 No. 130; *ANE* 172-74 No. 103.□

F690.1§, ‡'Quick-draw' (of weapon, firearm).
Ebony Horse: *Alf* II 257; Burton V 11. Chauvin V 221-31 No. 130; *ANE* 172-74 No. 103.□

F690.1.1§, ‡Swiftness-of-draw of weapon overawes opponent: declines challenge (duel). (Cf. P556.7§, P677.4§).
Ebony Horse: *Alf* II 257; Burton V 11. Chauvin V 221-31 No. 130; *ANE* 172-74 No. 103.□

F699.1, Marvelous dancers. See: *DOTTI*; *GMC*. (Cf. P483.4§).
Ibrâhîm and Jamîlah: *Alf* IV 225-26,-(poem); Burton IX 221-22. Chauvin VI 52-53 No. 218; *ANE* 227-29 No. 258.□

F699.2§, ‡Marvelous singer(s). (Cf. P428.0.1§).
Mock Caliph/¿Alî al-Jawharî: *Alf* II 198,-(test); Burton IV 144. Chauvin V 99-100 No. 174; *ANE* 304-5 No. 73.□

F701.4§, ‡Land of Truth (Justice): no one lies, no one distrusts, no one refuses to help. (Cf. F129.4.2).
Ma¿rûf the Cobbler: *Alf* IV 294,-(Ikhtiyân al-Khatan/Khitn); Burton X 9-10. Chauvin VI 81-82 No. 250; *ANE* 291-93 No. 262.□

F706.1§, ‡City (land) where the sun never rises.
Abû Muḥammad Lazybones: *Alf* II 215; Burton IV 175. Chauvin VI 64-67 No. 233; *ANE* 71-73 No. 78.□

F708.4§, Country without baths (bathhouses). See: *DOTTI*.
Abû Qîr and Abû Ṣîr: *Alf* IV 189; Burton IX 148. Chauvin V 15-17 No. 10; *ANE* 75-77 No. 255.□

F708.5§, Country without dyers (colored clothes). See: *DOTTI*.
Abû Qîr and Abû Ṣîr: *Alf* IV 186; Burton IX 142-43. Chauvin V 15-17 No. 10; *ANE* 75-77 No. 255.□

F708.9.1§, ‡Country without fire. See: *DOTTI*.
Landsman ¿Abdallah and Merman ¿Abdallah: *Alf* IV 206; Burton IX 184. Chauvin V 6-7 No. 3; *ANE* 65-66 No. 256.□

F708.9.1.1§, ‡Country where cooking is unknown. See: *DOTTI*.
Landsman ¿Abdallah and Merman ¿Abdallah: *Alf* IV 206; Burton IX 184. Chauvin V 6-7 No. 3; *ANE* 65-66 No. 256.□

F709.1.1§, ‡Nation of the naked in otherworld (e.g., mermen). See: *DOTTI*.
Landsman ¿Abdallah and Merman ¿Abdallah: *Alf* IV 206; Burton IX 182-83. Chauvin V 6-7 No. 3; *ANE* 65-66 No. 256.□

F709.5.1.1§, ‡Wâq-el-Wâq: country at end of earth. See: *DOTTI*.
Hasan of Basrah: *Alf* IV 14, 18,31 ; Burton VIII 65, 72-73, 88. Chauvin VII 29-35 No. 212A; *ANE* 207-10 No. 230.□

F709.5.2.1§, ‡Qâf Mountains: faraway.
Jânshâh: *Alf* III 49; Burton V 344. Chauvin VII 39-44 No. 153; *ANE* 238-41 No. 178.□

F709.5.2.2§, ‡White Land, beyond Qâf Mountains: faraway.
Bulûqiya: *Alf* III 32; Burton V 317. Chauvin VII 54 No. 77; *ANE* 130-32 No. 177;
Jânshâh: *Alf* III 68,-cf./(Crystal Mountain); Burton V 371. Chauvin VII 39-44 No. 153; *ANE* 238-41 No. 178.□

F709.5.2.2.0.1§, ‡White Land, beyond Qâf Mountains, is "Land of Shaddâd ibn ¿Âd".

Bulûqiya: *Alf* III 32; Burton V 317. Chauvin VII 54 No. 77; *ANE* 130-32 No. 177.□

F709.5.2.2.1§, ‡White Land, beyond Qâf Mountains, inhabited by jinn. (Cf. F499.3.5§).
Bulûqiya: *Alf* III 32; Burton V 317. Chauvin VII 54 No. 77; *ANE* 130-32 No. 177.□

F709.5.2.2.2§, ‡White Land, beyond Qâf Mountains, is meeting-place for angels (with certain mission).
Bulûqiya: *Alf* III 36; Burton V 324. Chauvin VII 54 No. 77; *ANE* 130-32 No. 177.□

F709.5.3.1§, ‡The Ruined Quarter of earth: faraway. See: *DOTTI*.
Ma¿rûf the Cobbler: *Alf* IV 311; Burton X 42. Chauvin VI 81-82 No. 250; *ANE* 291-93 No. 262.□

F709.6.1§, ‡Nation (kingdom) of scattered islands (archipelago).
Qamar al-Zamân and Budûr: *Alf* II 96,-(inner and outer islands); Burton III 276,-(Islands of the Inner and Outer Seas). Chauvin V 204-12 No. 120; *ANE* 341-45 No. 61.□

F709.8.1§, ‡Deadly site: "To enter is to die ('perish'), to exit is to live ('be reborn')".
¿Abdallah ibn Fâḍil: Treacherous Brothers: *Alf* IV 272,-(turbulent sea); Burton IX 314,-(xxx). Chauvin V 2-4 No. 2; *ANE* 63-65 No. 261.□

F708.9.2§, ‡Country where saddles are unknown.
Sindbâd's Fourth Voyage: *Alf* III 101; Burton VI 39. Chauvin VII 18-20 No. 373D; *ANE* 386 No. 179.□

F711.7§, ‡Sea of treasures. (Cf. Z183.0.1§).
Uns al-Wujûd and al-Ward: *Alf* II 271-72,-(*baḥr ak-kunûz*/"Sea of Treasures"); Burton V 37. Chauvin VI 127-29 No. 282; *ANE* 438 No. 104.□

F713, ‡Extraordinary pond (lake).
Ensorcelled Prince/Husband: *Alf* I 23; Burton I 77, 80. Chauvin VI 56-58 No. 222; *ANE* 176 No. 13.□

F713.7§, ‡Extraordinary artificial lake (pool). (Cf. F780§).
Hârûn and Zubaydah in Bath: *Alf* II 284; Burton V 75. Chauvin VI 142 No. 298; *ANE* 203-4 No. 111.□

F716.6§, ‡Marvelous decorative fountain (in palace, garden) with extraordinary accessories (birds, sounds, gems, etc.). (Cf. F770.1§, F888§).
Jânshâh: *Alf* III 50-51; Burton V 345. Chauvin VII 39-44 No. 153; *ANE* 238-41 No. 178.□

F713.8§, ‡Extraordinary inhabitants of pond (lake).
Ensorcelled Prince/Husband: *Alf* I 23,-(fish); Burton I 80. Chauvin VI 56-58 No. 222; *ANE* 176 No. 13;
Jawdar and His Treacherous Brethren: *Alf* III 183,-(afrits in form of fish); Burton VI 223. Chauvin V 257-60 No. 154; *ANE* 244-45 No. 209.□

F721.5.3§, ‡Underground palace as living quarters. (Maiden, woman, etc. found in it). See: *DOTTI*. (Cf. J674.4§, R45, T381.0.2.1§).
Second Qalandar: Afrit's Wife: *Alf* I 43,-cf.; Burton I 116. Chauvin V 197-200 No. 116; *ANE* 338-39 No. 16;
Third Qalandar: Magnetic Mountain: *Alf* I 53,-(for flying horse); Burton I 159. Chauvin V 200-3 No. 117; *ANE* 340-41 No. 18.□

F721.6§, ‡Subterranean town hall (public square). Public meeting hall built underground. (Cf. F780§).
¿Alî Shâr and Zumurrud: *Alf* II 228,-(*maydân/taḥta al-qaṣr*); Burton IV 212,-("*in front of* the palace a horse-course"). Chauvin V 89-91 No. 28; *ANE* 100-1 No. 82.□

F724.1§, ‡Wonders of sea world are more numerous (greater) than wonders of the land.
Landsman ¿Abdallah and Merman ¿Abdallah: *Alf* IV 205; Burton IX 183-64. Chauvin V 6-7 No. 3; *ANE* 65-66 No. 256.□

F724§, ‡Wonders of the sea world. (Cf. F133.1).
Sindbâd's Third Voyage: *Alf* III 99,-(described); Burton VI 33. Chauvin VII 15-18 No. 373C; *ANE* 385-86 No. 179;
City of Brass: *Alf* III 138; Burton VI 121. Chauvin V 32-35 No. 16; *ANE* 146-50 No. 180;
Jullanâr of the Sea: *Alf* III 249; Burton VII 275. Chauvin V 147-51 No. 73; *ANE* 248-51 No. 227.□

F725, Submarine world. See: *DOTTI*.
Bulûqiya: *Alf* III 30-31; Burton V 315. Chauvin VII 54 No. 77; *ANE* 130-32 No. 177;

Jullanâr of the Sea: *Alf* III 247, 249; Burton VII 268-69. Chauvin V 147-51 No. 73; *ANE* 248-51 No. 227;
Landsman ¿Abdallah and Merman ¿Abdallah: *Alf* IV 200; Burton IX 165-88. Chauvin V 6-7 No. 3; *ANE* 65-66 No. 256.□

F725.5, ‡People live under sea. (Cf. B81.0.2).
Bulûqiya: *Alf* III 30-31; Burton V 315. Chauvin VII 54 No. 77; *ANE* 130-32 No. 177.□

F731, ‡Island covered with treasure.
Sindbâd's Sixth Voyage: *Alf* III 113; Burton VI 59-61. Chauvin VII 24-27 No. 373F; *ANE* 386 No. 179.□

F731.4, ‡Stones of island are jewels.
Sindbâd's Sixth Voyage: *Alf* III 113; Burton VI 60. Chauvin VII 24-27 No. 373F; *ANE* 386 No. 179.□

F731.5, ‡Island of amber (glass).
Sindbâd's Sixth Voyage: *Alf* III 113,-(valley); Burton VI 61. Chauvin VII 24-27 No. 373F; *ANE* 386 No. 179.□

F731.9.1§, ‡Uninhabited island becomes populated and center of commerce upon discovery of treasure on it.
Island King/Pious Jewish Merchant: *Alf* III 16; Burton V 291. Chauvin VI 161 No. 325; *ANE* 234 No. 174.□

F732.3, Island of camphor. See: *GMC*.
Sindbâd's Second Voyage: *Alf* III 91,-cf./(extracted); Burton VI 20. Chauvin VII 9-14 No. 373B; *ANE* 385 No. 179.□

F732.5§, ‡Island of sandal wood.
Sindbâd's Seventh Voyage: *Alf* III 118-19; Burton VI 71, 73. Chauvin VII 26-29 No. 373G; *ANE* 386-87 No. 179.□

F732.8§, ‡Island of musk.
Sindbâd's Sixth Voyage: *Alf* III 113,-(valley); Burton VI 60. Chauvin VII 24-27 No. 373F; *ANE* 386 No. 179.□

F754, Magnetic mountain. Pulls nails out of ships that approach it. See: *DOTTI*; *GMC*.
Third Qalandar: Magnetic Mountain: *Alf* I 51; Burton I 140. Chauvin V 200-3 No. 117; *ANE* 340-41 No. 18.□

F756.8§, ‡Valley of precious metals and stones. See: *DOTTI*.
Jânshâh: *Alf* III 49,-(gems); Burton V 342. Chauvin VII 39-44 No. 153; *ANE* 238-41 No. 178.□

F756.8.1§, ‡Valley of diamonds. See: *DOTTI*. (Cf. F679.12.1§, F840.0.2.1.1§).
Sindbâd's Second Voyage: *Alf* III 90-91; Burton VI 18-19. Chauvin VII 9-14 No. 373B; *ANE* 385 No. 179;
Sindbâd's Third Voyage: *Alf* III 98; Burton VI 31. Chauvin VII 15-18 No. 373C; *ANE* 385-86 No. 179.□

F761.2, City of brass. See: *ANE*; *DOTTI*; *GMC*.
Abû Muḥammad Lazybones: *Alf* II 215-16,-(passim); Burton IV 175. Chauvin VI 64-67 No. 233; *ANE* 71-73 No. 78;
City of Brass: *Alf* III 129-38; Burton VI 101. Chauvin V 32-35 No. 16; *ANE* 146-50 No. 180.□

F761.3.1§, ‡City of crystal (and marble).
Jânshâh: *Alf* III 42; Burton V 334. Chauvin VII 39-44 No. 153; *ANE* 238-41 No. 178.□

F766.1§, ‡Deserted (abandoned) city repopulated (when danger has passed). See: *DOTTI*.
Ensorcelled Prince/Husband: *Alf* I 31,-cf.; Burton I 80. Chauvin VI 56-58 No. 222; *ANE* 176 No. 13.□

F766.2.1§, ‡City occupied by people during daytime, and by monkeys during tight. (Cf. B266.2.1§).
Sindbâd's Fifth Voyage: *Alf* III 110; Burton VI 54. Chauvin VII 21-24 No. 373E; *ANE* 386 No. 179.□

F766.3§, ‡Still (empty) city. City with no person in its public domains (streets, shops, marketplaces, etc.) during certain period. See: *DOTTI*.

Eldest Lady's Story: Treacherous Sisters: *Alf* I 54; Burton I 164. Chauvin V 4 No. 443; *ANE* 174-75 No. 19;
Jeweler's Wife and Qamar al-Zamân: *Alf* IV 242-43; Burton IX 256. Chauvin V 212-14 No. 121; *ANE* 345-47 No. 260.□

F766.3.1§, ‡Still (empty) city suddenly comes to life. See: *DOTTI*.
Ensorcelled Prince/Husband: *Alf* I 31,-cf.; Burton I 80. Chauvin VI 56-58 No. 222; *ANE* 176 No. 13;
Jeweler's Wife and Qamar al-Zamân: *Alf* IV 242; Burton IX 254-56. Chauvin V 212-14 No. 121; *ANE* 345-47 No. 260.□

F767, Inaccessible city. See: *DOTTI*; *GMC*. (Cf. P570§).
City of Brass: *Alf* III 129-30; Burton VI 101-2. Chauvin V 32-35 No. 16; *ANE* 146-50 No. 180.□

F768.1, City of petrified people. See: *ANE*; *DOTTI*; *GMC*. (Cf. D231, F766.3§, Q551.3.4).
Eldest Lady's Story: Treacherous Sisters: *Alf* I 54; Burton I 164-65. Chauvin V 4 No. 443; *ANE* 174-75 No. 19;
Abû Muḥammad Lazybones: *Alf* II 215,-(passim); Burton IV 175. Chauvin VI 64-67 No. 233; *ANE* 71-73 No. 78;
¿Abdallah ibn Fâḍil: Treacherous Brothers: *Alf* IV 273; Burton IX 318ff. Chauvin V 2-4 No. 2; *ANE* 63-65 No. 261.□

F768.2.1§, City of the mummified (the dead). See: *DOTTI*; *GMC*. (Cf. V61.0.3.1§).
City of Brass: *Alf* III 132-33; Burton VI 110=11. Chauvin V 32-35 No. 16; *ANE* 146-50 No. 180.□

F769.5§, ‡City of remarkably good living: 'fair-city'. See: *DOTTI*. (Cf. J1077.2.1§, W256.1§).
Jewish Doctor's Story: Sororicide: *Alf* I 100,-(Damascus); Burton I 289. Chauvin VI 89 No. 253; *ANE* 242 No. 26;
¿Alî Shâr and Zumurrud: *Alf* II 227; Burton IV 210. Chauvin V 89-91 No. 28; *ANE* 100-1 No. 82;
Nûr al-Dîn and Maryam: *Alf* IV 90,-(Alexandria); Burton VIII 288-89. Chauvin V 52-54 No. 271; *ANE* 98-99 No. 233;
al-Rashîd and Omani Merchant: *Alf* IV 211,-(al-Baṣrah); Burton IX 193. Chauvin VI 111-12 No. 276; *ANE* 201-2 No. 257.□

F769.7§, ‡City of fabulous wealth (wealthy inhabitants).
City of Labtayt/Treasure of Tolède: *Alf* II 183-4; Burton IV 100. Chauvin VI 90-91 No. 254; *ANE* 265-66 No. 67.□

F769.8.1.1§, ‡Iram—city of columns (City of "Shaddâd Son-of-¿Âd"). See: *DOTTI*. (Cf. F771.14§).
Ma¿rûf the Cobbler: *Alf* IV 305,-(passim); Burton X 29. Chauvin 6: 81-82 No. 250; *ANE* 291 No. 262.□

F770.1§, ‡Marvelous building technique (architecture). See: *DOTTI*. (Cf. F716.6§, F888§).
City of Brass: *Alf* III 130,-(impenetrable city wall); Burton VI 102. Chauvin 5: 32-35 No. 16; *ANE* 146-50 No. 180□

F770.0.1§, ‡Extraordinary architecture and furnishings betray owner's lifestyle (and taste). (Cf. F569.9§, U60.2§).
Abû al-Ḥasan al-Khorâsânî (and Caliph's Favorite): *Alf* IV 229; Burton IX 229-30. Chauvin V 218-20 No. 129; *ANE* 68-69 No. 259.□

F771, ‡Extraordinary castle (house, palace).
Qamar al-Zamân and Budûr: *Alf* II 72; Burton III 227. Chauvin V 204-12 No. 120; *ANE* 341-45 No. 61;
Mock Caliph/¿Alî al-Jawharî: *Alf* II 193; Burton IV 133-34. Chauvin V 99-100 No. 174; *ANE* 304-5 No. 73.□

F771.1.1, ‡Golden castle (palace, house).
Qamar al-Zamân and Budûr: *Alf* II 72; Burton III 227. Chauvin V 204-12 No. 120; *ANE* 341-45 No. 61.□

F771.1.1.2, Palace of gold and silver bricks. See: *DOTTI*; *GMC*.
Jânshâh: *Alf* III 42,-cf.; Burton V 334. Chauvin VII 39-44 No. 153; *ANE* 238-41 No. 178.□

F771.1.2, ‡Silver castle.
Qamar al-Zamân and Budûr: *Alf* II 72; Burton III 227. Chauvin V 204-12 No. 120; *ANE* 341-45 No. 61.□

F771.1.4, ‡Steel [(iron)] castle (house). See: *DOTTI*.
Qamar al-Zamân and Budûr: *Alf* II 72; Burton III 227. Chauvin V 204-12 No. 120; *ANE* 341-45 No. 61.□

F771.1.5, ‡Palace of jewels.
Qamar al-Zamân and Budûr: *Alf* II 72; Burton III 228. Chauvin V 204-12 No. 120; *ANE* 341-45 No. 61.□

F771.1.5.2, ‡House of [(palace)] sapphire.
Qamar al-Zamân and Budûr: *Alf* II 72; Burton III 228. Chauvin V 204-12 No. 120; *ANE* 341-45 No. 61.□

F771.1.6, Crystal castle [(palace)]. See: *DOTTI*.
Qamar al-Zamân and Budûr: *Alf* II 72; Burton III 227. Chauvin V 204-12 No. 120; *ANE* 341-45 No. 61;
Jânshâh: *Alf* III 42, 43; Burton V 334. Chauvin VII 39-44 No. 153; *ANE* 238-41 No. 178.□

F771.2.1, ‡Castle in the air. See: *DOTTI*.
Hasan of Basrah: *Alf* III 310; Burton VIII 22. Chauvin VII 29-35 No. 212A; *ANE* 207-10 No. 230.□

F771.5.3, ‡Serpent-hall.
Bulûqiya/Ḥâsib/Queen of Vipers: *Alf* III 20-21; Burton V 302. Chauvin VII 54 No. 77; *ANE* 130-32 No. 177.□

F771.14§, ‡Palace (castle) built by extraordinary personage (or being). (Cf. F769.8.1.1§).
Sayf al-Mulûk: *Alf* III 286,-(Yâfeth *ibn* Nûḥ); Burton VII 346,-(Japhet son of Noah). Chauvin VII 64-73 No. 348; *ANE* 362-64 No. 229.□

F771.15.1§, ‡Seven palaces.
Qamar al-Zamân and Budûr: *Alf* II 72; Burton III 227. Chauvin V 204-12 No. 120; *ANE* 341-45 No. 61.□

F771.15.2§, ‡Twelve palaces. (Cf. Z71.8, Z72.8§).
King ¿Umar al-Nu¿mân and Sons: *Alf* I 168,-(*quṣûr*); Burton II 78,-(pavilions). Chauvin VI 112-24 No. 277; *ANE* 430-34 No. 39.□

F776, ‡Extraordinary gate.
City of Brass: *Alf* III 133; Burton VI 110. Chauvin V 32-35 No. 16; *ANE* 146-50 No. 180.□

F777.5.1§, ‡Wall with paint so glossy that one can see own image in it.
Copt Broker's Story: Lover's Sacrifices Repaid: *Alf* I 92; Burton I 270,-(gypsum). Chauvin VI 80 No. 249; *ANE* 313-14 No. 24.□

F778.1§, ‡Extraordinary human furnishings (e.g., gate-keepers, pages, slaves, etc.). (Cf. R12.6§).
Jawdar and His Treacherous Brethren: *Alf* III 195-96,-(slaves); Burton VI 246. Chauvin V 257-60 No. 154; *ANE* 244-45 No. 209.□

F779§, ‡Extraordinary bathhouse (or steam bath: 'sauna'/'*nûrah*'). See: *DOTTI*.
Nûr al-Dîn ¿Alî and Son: *Alf* I 66,-cf.; Burton I 201. Chauvin VI 102-6 No. 270; *ANE* 317-19 No. 22;
¿Alî Shâr and Zumurrud: *Alf* II 234,-(simile); Burton IV 227. Chauvin V 89-91 No. 28; *ANE* 100-1 No. 82;
Tawaddud: Slavegirl Sold and Regained: *Alf* III 6,-cf./(*noarah*/most pleasant for women); Burton V 242,-(depilatory for women). Chauvin VII 117-19 No. 387; *ANE* 408-10 No. 157;
Abû Qîr and Abû Ṣîr: *Alf* IV 189; Burton IX 149-50. Chauvin V 15-17 No. 10; *ANE* 75-77 No. 255.□

F779.1§, ‡Extraordinary experiences while bathing (usually illusory, hallucinatory). See: *DOTTI*. (Cf. N793.1§, T16.0.3§, Z186.8.3§).
Tâj al-Mulûk: *Alf* I 293-94,-cf.; Burton III 18-19. Chauvin V 126-28 No. 60; *ANE* 111-13 No. 40;
Hashish Eater's Dream: *Alf* II 9; Burton III 91-93. Chauvin VI 124 No. 278; *ANE* 216 No. 42;
¿Alî Shâr and Zumurrud: *Alf* II 234,-cf.; Burton IV 227. Chauvin V 89-91 No. 28; *ANE* 100-1 No. 82.□

F779.1.1§, ‡Steam-bathing compared to experiences in paradise and hell.
Tâj al-Mulûk: *Alf* I 293-94,-cf.; Burton III 19 n. 1. Chauvin V 126-28 No. 60; *ANE* 111-13 No. 40.□

F779.2§, ‡Bathing as cure. (Cf. F950).

Bulûqiya: *Alf* III 80; Burton V 394. Chauvin VII 54 No. 77; *ANE* 130-32 No. 177;
al-Rashîd and Omani Merchant: *Alf* IV 208; Burton IX 189. Chauvin VI 111-12 No. 276; *ANE* 201-2 No. 257.□

F779.2.1§, ‡Steam-bathing as cure (promoter of good health). (Cf. F950).
Abû Qîr and Abû Ṣîr: *Alf* IV 190; Burton IX 150. Chauvin V 15-17 No. 10; *ANE* 75-77 No. 255.□

F779.2.2§, ‡Sweating as treatment (cure).
Dûban and King Yûnân: *Alf* I 17; Burton I 47. Chauvin V 275-76 No. 156; *ANE* 459 No. 9;
Bulûqiya: *Alf* III 80; Burton V 394. Chauvin VII 54 No. 77; *ANE* 130-32 No. 177;
Abû Qîr and Abû Ṣîr: *Alf* IV 188; Burton IX 146. Chauvin V 15-17 No. 10; *ANE* 75-77 No. 255.□

F780§, ‡Extraordinary industrial constructs (structures). (Cf. F721.6§).
¿Alî Shâr and Zumurrud: *Alf* II 228; Burton IV 212,-("horse-course"). Chauvin V 89-91 No. 28; *ANE* 100-1 No. 82.□

F781.2.2§, ‡As many rooms in palace as days in a year (i.e., 360, 365, etc.). (Cf. T380.0.1.1§, T469.2§, Z72.6).
King ¿Umar al-Nu¿mân and Sons: *Alf* I 162-63, 163,-cf./(in twelve places), 168; Burton II 78,-(in pavilions), 95. Chauvin VI 112-24 No. 277; *ANE* 430-34 No. 39.□

F781.2.2.1§, ‡Three hundred and sixty-six rooms (in palace).
King ¿Umar al-Nu¿mân and Sons: *Alf* I 168; Burton II 95. Chauvin VI 112-24 No. 277; *ANE* 430-34 No. 39.□

F782.2.1§, ‡Door of precious metals (gold, silver, etc.).
Sayf al-Mulûk: *Alf* III 290; Burton VII 352. Chauvin VII 64-73 No. 348; *ANE* 362-64 No. 229.□

F782.9.1§, ‡Mechanical door (gate) opens with remote device (*lawlab*).
Abû Muḥammad Lazybones: *Alf* II 207,-cf.; Burton IV 165. Chauvin VI 64-67 No. 233; *ANE* 71-73 No. 78;
City of Brass: *Alf* III 133; Burton VI 109. Chauvin V 32-35 No. 16; *ANE* 146-50 No. 180.□

F782.9.2§, ‡Door (gate) so heavy that it opens with thunderous sound.
City of Brass: *Alf* III 133; Burton VI 110. Chauvin V 32-35 No. 16; *ANE* 146-50 No. 180.□

F789, ‡Extraordinary buildings and furnishings—miscellaneous.
Mock Caliph/¿Alî al-Jawharî: *Alf* II 193; Burton IV 133-34. Chauvin V 99-100 No. 174; *ANE* 304-5 No. 73;
Abû Muḥammad Lazybones: *Alf* II 206-7; Burton IV 163. Chauvin VI 64-67 No. 233; *ANE* 71-73 No. 78.□

F789.4§, ‡Remarkable portrait (painting). (Cf. M369.5.3§).
Tâj al-Mulûk: *Alf* I 300; Burton III 33. Chauvin V 126-28 No. 60; *ANE* 406-8 No. 40;
City of Labtayt/Treasure of Tolède: *Alf* II 183; Burton IV 100. Chauvin VI 90-91 No. 254; *ANE* 265-66 No. 67.□

F789.4.1§, ‡Painting evokes personal feelings in viewer (beholder). (Cf. U245§).
Tâj al-Mulûk: *Alf* I 290, 300; Burton 3, 3III: 8. Chauvin V 126-28 No. 60; *ANE* 406-8 No. 40.□

F789.5.1§, ‡Marvelous shiny-coating of base metal.
Sindbâd's Fourth Voyage: *Alf* III 102,-(with *qasdîr*/solder); Burton VI 39,("tinned"). Chauvin VII 18-20 No. 373D; *ANE* 386 No. 179.□

F810.1§, ‡Plant of extraordinary colors.
Nûr al-Dîn and Maryam: *Alf* IV 80-83; Burton VIII 266-73. Chauvin V 52-54 No. 271; *ANE* 98-99 No. 233.□

F810.1.1§, ‡Plant with colors of fire and ice. (Cf. A965.5.1§, U20§).
Nûr al-Dîn and Maryam: *Alf* IV 80-83; Burton VIII 266-73. Chauvin V 52-54 No. 271; *ANE* 98-99 No. 233.□

F811.8, Tree with fruits like human heads. Attached by hair. See: *ANE*; *GMC*.
Bulûqiya: *Alf* III 29; Burton V 315. Chauvin VII 54 No. 77; *ANE* 130-32 No. 177.□

F814, ‡Extraordinary flowers.
Nûr al-Dîn and Maryam: *Alf* IV 80-82; Burton VIII 266-73. Chauvin V 52-54 No. 271; *ANE* 98-99 No. 233.□

F818, ‡Extraordinary garden. (Cf. A694.3§).
Nûr al-Dîn and Maryam: *Alf* IV 80-82,-(described); Burton VIII 266-73. Chauvin V 52-54 No. 271; *ANE* 98-99 No. 233.□

F818.3§, ‡Series of extraordinary gardens. See: *DOTTI*.
Third Qalandar: Magnetic Mountain: *Alf* I 53; Burton I 159. Chauvin V 200-3 No. 117; *ANE* 340-41 No. 18.□

F818.4§, ‡Marvelous garden with talking birds.
Copt Broker's Story: Lover's Sacrifices Repaid: *Alf* I 92; Burton I 270. Chauvin VI 80 No. 249; *ANE* 313-14 No. 24.□

F821, ‡Extraordinary dress (clothes, robe, etc.).
Abû Muḥammad Lazybones: *Alf* II 207; Burton IV 164. Chauvin VI 64-67 No. 233; *ANE* 71-73 No. 78.□

F821.12§, ‡Extremely fragile textile—(like spider-web).
¿Abdallah ibn Fâḍil: Treacherous Brothers: *Alf* IV 273; Burton IX 318. Chauvin V 2-4 No. 2; *ANE* 63-65 No. 261.□

F821.12.1§, ‡Cloth (textile) so old that it turns into dust when touched.
¿Abdallah ibn Fâḍil: Treacherous Brothers: *Alf* IV 273; Burton IX 318. Chauvin V 2-4 No. 2; *ANE* 63-65 No. 261.□

F826.5§, ‡Marvelous jewelry (unique pieces of precious stones, e.g., individual gem, diamond ring, pearl necklace, ruby bracelets, etc.). (Cf. P447.7.0.1§).
King ¿Umar al-Nu¿mân and Sons: *Alf* I 164,-(enormous size); Burton II 82. Chauvin VI 112-24 No. 277; *ANE* 430-34 No. 39;
Mock Caliph/¿Alî al-Jawharî: *Alf* II 196; Burton IV 140. Chauvin V 99-100 No. 174; *ANE* 304-5 No. 73;
Abû Muḥammad Lazybones: *Alf* II 206-7; Burton IV 161-62. Chauvin VI 64-67 No. 233; *ANE* 71-73 No. 78;
Devotee Prince: Ascetic's Death: *Alf* II 291,-(ruby); Burton V 114. Chauvin VI 193-94 No. 363; *ANE* 167-68 No. 134;
Hasan of Basrah: *Alf* IV 11,-(necklace); Burton VIII 58. Chauvin VII 29-35 No. 212A; *ANE* 207-10 No. 230.□

F826.6§, ‡Luminous jewel.
Bulûqiya: *Alf* III 29; Burton V 315. Chauvin VII 54 No. 77; *ANE* 130-32 No. 177;
City of Brass: *Alf* III 135,(like sun); Burton VI 114. Chauvin V 32-35 No. 16; *ANE* 146-50 No. 180.□

F827.9.4§, ‡Woman unusual as to her ornaments (jewelry).
King ¿Umar al-Nu¿mân and Sons: *Alf* I 199,-(style/size/quality); Burton II 153. Chauvin VI 112-24 No. 277; *ANE* 430-34 No. 39;
City of Brass: *Alf* III 135,-cf./(female mummy); Burton VI 114. Chauvin V 32-35 No. 16; *ANE* 146-50 No. 180;
Dalîla the Swindler: *Alf* III 213; Burton VII 147. Chauvin V 245-50 No. 147; *ANE* 163-64 No. 224.□

F827.9.4.1§, ‡Person with much jewelry (ornaments) likened to mummy adorned with jewels ("treasure-doll"). (Cf. V67.3.1.2§, Z62).
Dalîla the Swindler: *Alf* III 213,-(*¿arûsat kanz*); Burton VII 147,-(Bride of the Hoards/"fairy damsel"). Chauvin V 245-50 No. 147; *ANE* 163-64 No. 224.□

F838, ‡Extraordinary knife.
Jeweler's Wife and Qamar al-Zamân: *Alf* IV 252; Burton IX 275. Chauvin V 212-14 No. 121; *ANE* 345-47 No. 260.□

F839.1.1§, ‡Human bone as weapon.
Sindbâd's Fourth Voyage: *Alf* III 105; Burton VI 44. Chauvin VII 18-20 No. 373D; *ANE* 386 No. 179.□

F840.0.2.1§, ‡Diamond as hardest substance.
Sindbâd's Second Voyage: *Alf* III 90; Burton VI 19. Chauvin VII 9-14 No. 373B; *ANE* 385 No. 179.□

F840.0.2.1.1§, ‡Only diamond can cut (bore hole) in other hard substances (e.g., jewels, metals, etc.). See: *DOTTI*. (Cf. F756.8.1§).

Sindbâd's Second Voyage: *Alf* III 90; Burton VI 19. Chauvin VII 9-14 No. 373B; *ANE* 385 No. 179.□

F844.1§, ‡Nail(s) of precious stone (metal)—usually in wooden objects (chest, door) or in base metal (iron). (Cf. F782.2.1§).
Sayf al-Mulûk: *Alf* III 290; Burton VII 352. Chauvin VII 64-73 No. 348; *ANE* 362-64 No. 229.□

F849§, ‡Remarkably delicious (liked) dishes—(ordinary foods). (Cf. H35.2, J1343).
Hunchback's Tale: Resuscitated: *Alf* I 85,-(fried fish, lemon, etc.); Burton I 255. Chauvin V 180-82 No. 105; *ANE* 224-25 No. 23;
Copt Broker's Story: Lover's Sacrifices Repaid: *Alf* I 93,-(fried colocasia, peppered rice, ...); Burton I 272. Chauvin VI 80 No. 249; *ANE* 313-14 No. 24;
¿Alî Shâr and Zumurrud: *Alf* II 222,-(fried cheese, honey, bananas); Burton IV 201. Chauvin V 89-91 No. 28; *ANE* 100-1 No. 82;
Jawdar and His Treacherous Brethren: *Alf* III 184; Burton VI 224. Chauvin V 257-60 No. 154; *ANE* 244-45 No. 209.□

F849.0.1.1§, ‡Food (drink) so delicious, as if from otherworld. (Cf. D1030.1).
Jawdar and His Treacherous Brethren: *Alf* III 184,-cf.; Burton VI 224. Chauvin V 257-60 No. 154; *ANE* 244-45 No. 209.□

F849.1.1§, ‡The basic meat delicacy. (Meat on top of rice, broth-soaked bread, stuffing, or a similar starchy food; labeled: *fattah*, "meat and potatoes," or the like). (Cf. W125).
Second Qalandar: Afrit's Wife: *Alf* I 48,-(poem); Burton I 131,-(variant/poems). Chauvin V 197-200 No. 116; *ANE* 338-39 No. 16;
Reeve's Story: Why Maimed by Bride: *Alf* I 98,-("zirbâjah"/garlic sauce); Burton I 278, 286,-(marinated ragout). Chauvin V 220-21 No. 305; *ANE* 351 No. 25.□

F849.1.3§, ‡Loved fowl dishes. See: *DOTTI*.
Barber's Sixth Brother: Emasculated by Abductor: *Alf* I 122,-(*qatâyif*); Burton I 344-45. Chauvin V 163-64 No. 86; *ANE* 120 No. 34.□

F849.1.4§, ‡Loved fish dishes. See: *DOTTI*.
Anîs al-Jalîs: *Alf* I 142; Burton II 33. Chauvin V 120-24 No. 58; *ANE* 316-17 No. 35.□

F849.2.2§, ‡Loved fruit dish: pomegranate kernels stew.
Nûr al-Dîn ¿Alî and Son: *Alf* I 80, 81-83; Burton I 234, 235. Chauvin VI 102-6 No. 270; *ANE* 317-19 No. 22.□

F849.2.3§, ‡Loved starchy (root) dish: taro (*qulqâs*/Colocasia esclenta/ 'malanga').
Copt Broker's Story: Lover's Sacrifices Repaid: *Alf* I 93; Burton I 272. Chauvin VI 80 No. 249; *ANE* 313-14 No. 24.□

F849.3.2.1§, ‡Loved dish: sour-milk-gravy (*kishk*)—with chicken (broth).
¿Alî Shâr and Zumurrud: *Alf* II 229,-("*kishk*"); Burton IV 214,-(porridge). Chauvin V 89-91 No. 28; *ANE* 100-1 No. 82.□

F849.3.1.2§, ‡Loved rice pudding ('rice-with-milk').
¿Alî Shâr and Zumurrud: *Alf* II 228-33,-(sweet rice); Burton IV 215-22. Chauvin V 89-91 No. 28; *ANE* 100-1 No. 82□

F849.3.3.1§, ‡Loved dish: fried cheese.
¿Alî Shâr and Zumurrud: *Alf* II 222,-(cheese/honey); Burton IV 201. Chauvin V 89-91 No. 28; *ANE* 100-1 No. 82.□

F849.3.6§, ‡Loved sweet food (pastry, sweets). (Cf. J1732.5§).
Barber's Sixth Brother: Emasculated by Abductor: *Alf* I 122,-(*qatâyif*); Burton I 344. Chauvin V 163-64 No. 86; *ANE* 120 No. 34.□

F849.9§, ‡Other loved foods and drinks (alcoholic and non-alcoholic)—miscellaneous.
Barber's Sixth Brother: Emasculated by Abductor: *Alf* I 122; Burton I 345-46. Chauvin V 163-64 No. 86; *ANE* 120 No. 34.□

F849.9.1§, ‡Brewed cereal (barley, bread)—labeled: *bûẓah* (native Egyptian beer). See: *PSAE*. (Cf. P610.1.2.1.1§).
Ensorcelled Prince/Husband: *Alf* I 28; Burton I 71,-(wine). Chauvin VI 56-58 No. 222; *ANE* 176 No. 13.□

F855.2, ‡Statue animated by water or wind. See: *GMC*.
King ¿Umar al-Nu¿mân and Sons: *Alf* I 171,-("air"); Burton II 101. Chauvin VI 112-24 No. 277; *ANE* 430-34 No. 39.□

F855.2.1§, ‡Statues animated by mercury.
City of Brass: *Alf* III 135; Burton VI 114. Chauvin V 32-35 No. 16; *ANE* 146-50 No. 180.□

F879.2§, ‡Poison so potent that it causes body to disintegrate. (Cf. S111.10.1§).
King ¿Umar al-Nu¿mân and Sons: *Alf* I 227; Burton II 214. Chauvin VI 112-24 No. 277; *ANE* 430-34 No. 39.□

F880.4.1§, ‡Gold manufactured from plant (sun-dried flowers). (In certain land).
Bulûqiya: *Alf* III 29; Burton V 315. Chauvin VII 54 No. 77; *ANE* 130-32 No. 177.□

F883.1.6, ‡Heavenly books. (Cf. Z1.1.1§).
¿Alâ' al-Dîn Abû al-Shâmât: *Alf* II 178; Burton IV 90. Chauvin V 43-49 No. 18; *ANE* 85-87 No. 63.□

F883.1.7§, ‡Encyclopedic book: contains definitive information on a host of fields.
City of Labtayt/Treasure of Tolède: *Alf* II 183-4; Burton IV 100-101. Chauvin VI 90-91 No. 254; *ANE* 265-66 No. 67.□

F883.1.9.1.1§, ‡Story (tale) written in gold. (Cf. J163.5§, Z67.7.1§).
Ibn Sabâ'ik/Sayf al-Mulûk: *Alf* III 273; Burton VII 312. Chauvin VII 65 No. 348/pt.; *ANE* 309-10 No. 228.□

F883.3.1§, ‡Letter delivered by shooting it attached to arrow (spear, or the like).
King's Son and Merchant's Wife: *Alf* III 156; Burton VI 168. Chauvin VIII 48-49 No. 16; *ANE* 263 No. 196.□

F883.4§, ‡Writing in golden (silvery) letters—("with gold-water", "with silver-water").
Qamar al-Zamân and Budûr: *Alf* II 112; Burton III 307. Chauvin V 204-12 No. 120; *ANE* 341-45 No. 61.□

F883.5§, ‡Calligraphy: extraordinary writing style. See: *DOTTI*. (Cf. P425.2§).
Second Qalandar: Afrit's Wife: *Alf* I 47; Burton I 128-29. Chauvin V 197-200 No. 116; *ANE* 338-39 No. 16;
Basra Girls in Poetry Contest: *Alf* III 205,-cf.; Burton VII 112,-(characters of the utmost beauty). Chauvin VI 144 No. 301; *ANE* 107-8 No. 216.□

F883.5.1§, ‡Arabic script (writing) styles: *riq¿ah, mashq, thuluth*, etc.
Second Qalandar: Afrit's Wife: *Alf* I 47; Burton I 128. Chauvin V 197-200 No. 116; *ANE* 338-39 No. 16.□

F883.6§, ‡Mysterious writing. (Cf. D1266.1).
Qamar al-Zamân and Budûr: *Alf* II 97; Burton III 279. Chauvin V 204-12 No. 120; *ANE* 341-45 No. 61.□

F883.6.1§, ‡Script (writing) that looks like ants (ants' scratching).
¿Alâ' al-Dîn Abû al-Shâmât: *Alf* II 175; Burton IV 84,-(ant-tracks). Chauvin V 43-49 No. 18; *ANE* 85-87 No. 63;
al-Rashîd and Omani Merchant: *Alf* IV 216; Burton IX 201. Chauvin VI 111-12 No. 276; *ANE* 201-2 No. 257;
Ma¿rûf the Cobbler: *Alf* IV 304; Burton X 28. Chauvin VI 81-82 No. 250; *ANE* 291-93 No. 262.□

F888§, ‡Extraordinary (marvelous) craftsmanship (non-magical). See: *DOTTI*; *PSAE*. (Cf. F716.6§, F770.1§, J2411.0.1§).
Abû Muḥammad Lazybones: *Alf* II 207,-cf.; Burton IV 163. Chauvin VI 64-67 No. 233; *ANE* 71-73 No. 78;
City of Brass: *Alf* III 131,-(ladder); Burton VI 107. Chauvin V 32-35 No. 16; *ANE* 146-50 No. 180.□

F888.0.1§, ‡Innovation ('from own brains,' following no model or pattern, etc.). (Cf. A1440.5.1§).
Goldsmith and Cashmere Singer: *Alf* III 150; Burton VI 157. Chauvin VIII 46-47 No. 14; *ANE* 196 No. 194;
Jeweler's Wife and Qamar al-Zamân: *Alf* IV 254; Burton IX 278,-("my own wit"). Chauvin V 212-14 No. 121; *ANE* 345-47 No. 260.□

F888.1§, ‡Inimitable handiwork.

¿Azîz and ¿Azîzah: *Alf* I 289,-(portrait); Burton III 5-6. Chauvin V 144-45 No. 71; *ANE* 111-13 No. 41;
Jeweler's Wife and Qamar al-Zamân: *Alf* IV 252; Burton IX 275. Chauvin V 212-14 No. 121; *ANE* 345-47 No. 260.□

F888.1.1§, ‡Inimitable jewelry. See: *DOTTI*. (Cf. K1874.2.1.2§).
Jeweler's Wife and Qamar al-Zamân: *Alf* IV 252-55,-(knife); Burton IX 275. Chauvin V 2f2-14 No. 121; *ANE* 345-47 No. 260.□

F889.1.1.1.1§, ‡ Compressible lute.
Nûr al-Dîn and Maryam: *Alf* IV 84-85,-(lute: poem); Burton VIII 281. Chauvin V 52-54 No. 271; *ANE* 98-99 No. 233.□

F888.1.3§, ‡Marvelous glassware (crystal, china).
Barber's Sixth Brother: Emasculated by Abductor: *Alf* I 123,-(poem); Burton I 349. Chauvin V 163-64 No. 86; *ANE* 120 No. 34.□

F888.1.4§, ‡Marvelous textile (embroidery).
¿Alî Shâr and Zumurrud: *Alf* II 221; Burton IV 198. Chauvin V 89-91 No. 28; *ANE* 100-1 No. 82;
Nûr al-Dîn and Maryam: *Alf* IV 97-98; Burton VIII 306. Chauvin V 52-54 No. 271; *ANE* 98-99 No. 233.□

F889.3.1§, ‡Flying mechanical horse. (Controlled by *lawlab*/mechanical device). See: *DOTTI*. (Cf. B41.2, B542.2, D1620.2.1, D1626.1).
Ebony Horse: *Alf* II 254; Burton V 2ff. Chauvin V 221-31 No. 130; *ANE* 172-74 No. 103.□

F891.1§, ‡Marvelous machine detects intruders (enemies) and sounds alarm. ("Early warning system").
Ebony Horse: *Alf* II 254,-(trumpet/horn); Burton V 2. Chauvin V 221-31 No. 130; *ANE* 172-74 No. 103.□

F897.1.2§, ‡Navigation at sea by star(s). See: *DOTTI*.
Nûr al-Dîn and Maryam: *Alf* IV 112,-cf.; Burton VIII 333. Chauvin V 52-54 No. 271; *ANE* 98-99 No. 233.□

F897.3§, ‡Following landmarks (travel signs) to destination. (Cf. P418.7§).
Jânshâh: *Alf* III 55-56,-cf.; Burton V 352-53. Chauvin VII 39-44 No. 153; *ANE* 238-41 No. 178.□

F897.3.1§, ‡Travel route (directions, map, chart) from one place to another. See: *DOTTI*.
Nûr al-Dîn ¿Alî and Son: *Alf* I 65-66,-(N. E. Egypt to S. Iraq), 79,-(N. Iraq); Burton I 198-99, 239-40. Chauvin VI 102-6 No. 270; *ANE* 317-19 No. 22;
Nûr al-Dîn and Maryam: *Alf* IV 90,-(N. Egypt); Burton VIII 288. Chauvin V 52-54 No. 271; *ANE* 98-99 No. 233.□

F898.0.2.0.1§, ‡"Coptic year": three hundred and sixty days.
King ¿Umar al-Nu¿mân and Sons: *Alf* I 162-63; Burton II 78. Chauvin VI 112-24 No. 277; *ANE* 430-34 No. 39.□

F898.2.1.1§, ‡At the yellowing of the sun (i.e., late afternoon).
¿Azîz and ¿Azîzah: *Alf* I 272; Burton II 306. Chauvin V 144-45 No. 71; *ANE* 111-13 No. 41;
Bulûqiya: *Alf* III 75; Burton V 385. Chauvin VII 54 No. 77; *ANE* 130-32 No. 177.□

F898.2.2§, ‡Time reckoned in relation to required daily prayers.
Tailor's Story/Barber of Baghdad: *Alf* I 106,-cf.; Burton I 309. Chauvin V 154-56 No. 78; *ANE* 405-6 No. 27;
Jeweler's Wife and Qamar al-Zamân: *Alf* IV 261,-cf.; Burton IX 293. Chauvin V 212-14 No. 121; *ANE* 345-47 No. 260;
Ma¿rûf the Cobbler: *Alf* IV 292,-(xxx),-(*¿aṣr*/mid-afternoon); Burton X 6-7,-("hour of mid-afternoon prayer"). Chauvin VI 81-82 No. 250; *ANE* 291-93 No. 262.□

F898.3§, ‡Mechanical device indicates time (watch, clock, sun-dial, etc.).
Ebony Horse: *Alf* II 254,-(peacock); Burton V 2. Chauvin V 221-31 No. 130; *ANE* 172-74 No. 103.□

F899.3, ‡Enormous cage. (Cf. G114.4.1§).
Sayf al-Mulûk: *Alf* III 283; Burton VII 339. Chauvin VII 64-73 No. 348; *ANE* 362-64 No. 229.□

F901.2, Extraordinary twofold death: burning, drowning. See: *DOTTI*.
Abû Qîr and Abû Ṣîr: *Alf* IV 194; Burton IX 155-56. Chauvin V 15-17 No. 10; *ANE* 75-77 No. 255.□

F911.4.2§, ‡Whale swallows ship. See: *DOTTI*. (Cf. B874.3).
Sindbâd's Seventh Voyage: *Alf* III 117; Burton VI 70,-("fish"). Chauvin VII 26-29 No. 373G; *ANE* 386-87 No. 179.□

F912.6§, ‡Fatal swallowing: food swallowed kills swallower. See: *DOTTI*.
Hunchback's Tale: Resuscitated: *Alf* I 87,-cf.; Burton I 255. Chauvin V 180-82 No. 105; *ANE* 224-25 No. 23;
Wild Ass and Jackal: *Alf* IV 142; Burton IX 49. Chauvin II 219 No. 152/6; *ANE* 449 No. 241.□

F931.4.4§, ‡Waves that look like mountains. See: *DOTTI*. (Cf. F962.1.1§).
Third Qalandar: Magnetic Mountain: *Alf* I 52; Burton I 144,-(billow like a hillock). Chauvin V 200-3 No. 117; *ANE* 340-41 No. 18;
Hasan of Basrah: *Alf* III 310; Burton VIII 22. Chauvin VII 29-35 No. 212A; *ANE* 207-10 No. 230.□

F931.4.5§, ‡Wave so high that the bottom of the deep sea (ocean) can be seen. See: *DOTTI*.
Sindbâd's Fifth Voyage: *Alf* III 107; Burton VI 49. Chauvin VII 21-24 No. 373E; *ANE* 386 No. 179.□

F942.3.2§, ‡Ground opens when spirit (jinni, afrit) strikes it. He enters and disappears underground.
Ensorcelled Prince/Husband: *Alf* I 24; Burton I 62. Chauvin VI 56-58 No. 222; *ANE* 176 No. 13.□

F944.3, ‡Island sinks into sea. See: *PSAE*. (Cf. J1761.1).
Sindbâd's First Voyage: *Alf* III 84,-cf./ (whale/fish); Burton VI 5. Chauvin VII 7-9 No. 373A; *ANE* 385 No. 179.□

F946§, ‡Underwater abode (hiding place). See: *DOTTI*. (Cf. R319§).
Jawdar and His Treacherous Brethren: *Alf* III 180, 183,-cf.; Burton VI 218. Chauvin V 257-60 No. 154; *ANE* 244-45 No. 209.□

F946.1.1§, ‡Casket (box, coffin, flask, etc.) hidden underwater. See: *DOTTI*.
Bulûqiya: *Alf* III 24; Burton V 307. Chauvin VII 54 No. 77; *ANE* 130-32 No. 177.□

F950, Marvelous cures. See: *DOTTI*; *GMC*. (Cf. V9§).
King ¿Umar al-Nu¿mân and Sons: *Alf* I 189-90,-cf./(nourishing foods); Burton II 136-37. Chauvin VI 112-24 No. 277; *ANE* 430-34 No. 39;
Ridiculous Eye Salve: *Alf* II 287,-cf.; Burton V 98-99. Chauvin V 281 No. 165; *ANE* 236 No. 129.□

F950.0.1.4§, ‡Liquor (wine) used to treat pain (distress). (Cf. U283.1.1.1§).
Copt Broker's Story: Lover's Sacrifices Repaid: *Alf* I 94-95; Burton I 274, 275. Chauvin VI 80 No. 249; *ANE* 313-14 No. 24.□

F950.0.2.1§, ‡Drug-induced illusion (hallucination). See: *DOTTI*. (Cf. K776.4§, W210§).
Nûr al-Dîn ¿Alî and Son: *Alf* I 73,-(accusation); Burton I 225. Chauvin VI 102-6 No. 270; *ANE* 317-19 No. 22;
Hashish Eater's Dream: *Alf* II 9; Burton III 91. Chauvin VI 124 No. 278; *ANE* 216 No. 42.□

F950.0.2.1.1.1§, ‡Hashish recommended as remedy (treatment) for lack of success.
Wolf and Fox: *Alf* II 33,-(poem,/grass/pun ??); Burton III 140,-(grass). Chauvin II 227 No. 6; *ANE* 450 No. 47.□

F950.0.4.4.1§, ‡Viper flesh improves health (cures). (Cf. B161.3, D1017.3§).
Bulûqiya: *Alf* III 79-80,-(viper); Burton V 3 391. Chauvin VII 54 No. 77; *ANE* 130-32 No. 177.□

F950.0.5.0.1§, ‡Marvelous cure from fumigation (burning herb, incense). (Cf. B784.2.1.4.1§).
King's Daughter and Ape: *Alf* II 253; Burton IV 298. Chauvin V 178 No. 102; *ANE* 262-63 No. 102.□

F950.0.5.1.1§, ‡Marvelous herb: "blood of the two brothers" (dragon's blood).
King ¿Umar al-Nu¿mân and Sons: *Alf* I 237; Burton II 236. Chauvin VI 112-24 No. 277; *ANE* 430-34 No. 39.□

F950.0.5.1.3.1§, ‡Aloe as medicine (cure).
Merchant and Robbers: *Alf* IV 166; Burton IX 100. Chauvin II 223 No. 152/20; *ANE* 297 No. 251.□

F950.4, Sickness (madness) cured by coition. See: *DOTTI*. (Cf. F956.7.5§, T82.9.1§).
King's Daughter and Ape: *Alf* II 253; Burton IV 298. Chauvin V 178 No. 102; *ANE* 262-63 No. 102;

Tawaddud: Slavegirl Sold and Regained: *Alf* II 317; Burton V 225. Chauvin VII 117-19 No. 387; *ANE* 408-10 No. 157.□

F950.10.1§, ‡Branding with hot iron as cure. See: *DOTTI*. (Cf. F959.8.1.2§).
King ¿Umar al-Nu¿mân and Sons: *Alf* I 313,-(poem); Burton III 59. Chauvin VI 112-24 No. 277; *ANE* 430-34 No. 39;
Dalîla the Swindler: *Alf* III 221; Burton VII 161. Chauvin V 245-50 No. 147; *ANE* 163-64 No. 224.□

F950.10.1.1§, ‡Bleeding stopped by branding with hot iron.
¿Azîz and ¿Azîzah: *Alf* I 287,-cf.; Burton III 2. Chauvin V 144-45 No. 71; *ANE* 111-13 No. 41.□

F950.10.1.2§, ‡Bleeding stopped with ashes (burnt wood or the like).
¿Azîz and ¿Azîzah: *Alf* I 273; Burton II 307,-(tinder of rags). Chauvin V 144-45 No. 71; *ANE* 111-13 No. 41.□

F950.10.1.3§, ‡Bleeding stopped with boiling oil (tar).
Jewish Doctor's Story: Sororicide: *Alf* I 101,-(oil); Burton I 297. Chauvin VI 89 No. 253; *ANE* 242 No. 26.□

F950.10.2§, ‡*fasd* (blood-letting) as cure.
Tailor's Story/Barber of Baghdad: *Alf* I 105; Burton I 306. Chauvin V 154-56 No. 78; *ANE* 405-6 No. 27.□

F950.10.6.1§, ‡Tooth pulled as cure. (Cf. F959.8.1.3§).
Dalîla the Swindler: *Alf* III 221; Burton VII 161. Chauvin V 245-50 No. 147; *ANE* 163-64 No. 224.□

F951.1.1.1§, ‡Saffron as aphrodisiac in lesbian intercourse.
King ¿Umar al-Nu¿mân and Sons: *Alf* I 236; Burton II 234. Chauvin VI 112-24 No. 277; *ANE* 430-34 No. 39.□

F956.7§, ‡Preventive diagnoses (and practices) that reduce potential for illness (promoters of good health). (Cf. T187.0.1§).
al-Rashîd and Omani Merchant: *Alf* IV 208; Burton IX 189. Chauvin VI 111-12 No. 276; *ANE* 201-2 No. 257.□

F956.7.3§, ‡Hunger (austere diet, fasting) promotes good health. (Cf. F1041.9.8§).
Tawaddud: Slavegirl Sold and Regained: *Alf* II 316; Burton V 222. Chauvin VII 117-19 No. 387; *ANE* 408-10 No. 157;
Merchant and Robbers: *Alf* IV 166; Burton IX 100. Chauvin II 223 No. 152/20; *ANE* 297 No. 251.□

F956.7.5§, ‡Coition promotes good health (preventive medication). (Cf. F950.4).
Tawaddud: Slavegirl Sold and Regained: *Alf* II 317-18; Burton V 225. Chauvin VII 117-19 No. 387; *ANE* 408-10 No. 157.□

F956.7.5.1.1§, ‡Sexual intercourse with (healthy) young woman rejuvenates older man.
Tawaddud: Slavegirl Sold and Regained: *Alf* II 318; Burton V 226. Chauvin VII 117-19 No. 387; *ANE* 408-10 No. 157.□

F956.7.5.1.2§, ‡Sexual intercourse with old woman causes sickness.
Tawaddud: Slavegirl Sold and Regained: *Alf* II 318; Burton V 225. Chauvin VII 117-19 No. 387; *ANE* 408-10 No. 157.□

F956.7.6.2§, ‡Narrating (tale-telling, giving descriptions of life and living) sets mind at ease. See: *DOTTI*. (Cf. P470§, U245§).
Budûr and Jubayr ibn ¿Umayr: *Alf* II 243,-(*'insharah ṣadr al-khalîfah, and* ...); Burton IV 245,-(heart lightened, restlessness and oppression forsook listener). Chauvin VII 93-94 No. 374; *ANE* 243-44 No. 83;
Ibn Sabâ'ik/Sayf al-Mulûk: *Alf* III 273,-(read to listener from a book); Burton VII 312. Chauvin VII 65 No. 348/pt.; *ANE* 309-10 No. 228.□

F956.7.6.2.1§, ‡Narrating (tale-telling) animates the sluggish.
Porter and Ladies of Baghdad: *Alf* I 35; Burton I 95. Chauvin V 251-52 No. 148; *ANE* 324-26 No. 14.□

F956.7.6.3§, ‡Listening to stories (or watching enactments of life and living) sets mind at ease. See: *DOTTI*. (Cf. J1080§, P470.0.1§, P807§).
King ¿Umar al-Nu¿mân and Sons: *Alf* I 260; Burton II 282. Chauvin VI 112-24 No. 277; *ANE* 430-34 No. 39.□

F956.7.7.1.1.2§, ‡Mother places self between her child (son, daughter) and father's (her husband's) wrath.
Anîs al-Jalîs: *Alf* I 129; Burton II 32. Chauvin V 120-24 No. 58; *ANE* 316-17 No. 35.□

F956.7.7.2§, ‡Venting frustration (expressing sorrow) by causing pain to oneself (hitting own head, slapping own face, biting own finger, or the like). See: *DOTTI*. (Cf. P681.1.1.2.2.1§, T24.9.2.1.1§).
Anîs al-Jalîs: *Alf* I 128,-(rent own garment/pull out beard); Burton II 7. Chauvin V 120-24 No. 58; *ANE* 316-17 No. 35;
Qamar al-Zamân and Budûr: *Alf* II 104,-(slap own face/pull out beard); Burton III 290. Chauvin V 204-12 No. 120; *ANE* 341-45 No. 61;
Tawaddud: Slavegirl Sold and Regained: *Alf* II 304,-(*suqiṭa fî yadayhi*/lit.); Burton V 191,-(bit his hands in bitter penitence). Chauvin VII 117-19 No. 387; *ANE* 408-10 No. 157;
Hasan of Basrah: *Alf* IV 2; Burton VIII 41. Chauvin VII 29-35 No. 212A; *ANE* 207-10 No. 230.□

F956.7.7.6.1§, ‡Frustration: person plucks out own beard (hair).
Anîs al-Jalîs: *Alf* I 128; Burton II 7. Chauvin V 120-24 No. 58; *ANE* 316-17 No. 35;
Second Eunuch/Kâfûr's Half-lie: *Alf* I 149; Burton II 53. Chauvin V 278 No. 161; *ANE* 178-79 No. 38;
Qamar al-Zamân and Budûr: *Alf* II 104; Burton III 290. Chauvin V 204-12 No. 120; *ANE* 341-45 No. 61;
¿Alî Shâr and Zumurrud: *Alf* II 231; Burton IV 219. Chauvin V 89-91 No. 28; *ANE* 100-1 No. 82;
Sindbâd's Third Voyage: *Alf* III 92; Burton VI 23. Chauvin VII 15-18 No. 373C; *ANE* 385-86 No. 179;
Sindbâd's Sixth Voyage: *Alf* III 112; Burton VI 59. Chauvin VII 24-27 No. 373F; *ANE* 386 No. 179;
Sindbâd's Seventh Voyage: *Alf* III 116-17; Burton VI 69. Chauvin VII 24 No. 373F; *ANE* 386-87 No. 179.□

F959.8.1.2§, ‡Insanity (idiocy) treated by branding with hot iron (usually of head or temples). See: *DOTTI*. (Cf. F950.10.1§).
Dalîla the Swindler: *Alf* III 221; Burton VII 161. Chauvin V 245-50 No. 147; *ANE* 163-64 No. 224.□

F959.8.1.3§, ‡Insanity (idiocy) treated by pulling out teeth (usually wisdom-teeth). See: *DOTTI*. (Cf. F950.10.6.1§).
Dalîla the Swindler: *Alf* III 221; Burton VII 161. Chauvin V 245-50 No. 147; *ANE* 163-64 No. 224.□

F959.8.4§, ‡Insane person chained (imprisoned).
Qamar al-Zamân and Budûr: *Alf* II 86; Burton III 255-56. Chauvin V 204-12 No. 120; *ANE* 341-45 No. 61.□

F959.9.0.1§, ‡Beauty-aid containing harmful element (poison or the like). See: *DOTTI*. (Cf. N649.2§).
Abû Qîr and Abû Ṣîr: *Alf* IV 193; Burton IX 155. Chauvin V 15-17 No. 10; *ANE* 75-77 No. 255.□

F959.9.1§, ‡Marvelous hair removing potion (drug). See: *DOTTI*.
Nuzhat al-Zamân Tested/¿Umar al-Nu¿mân: *Alf* I 202,-cf./(practice/plucking armpit hair); Burton II 160. Chauvin VI 112-124 No. 277; *ANE* 432,/passim No. 39;
Abû Qîr and Abû Ṣîr: *Alf* IV 193; Burton IX 155. Chauvin V 15-17 No. 10; *ANE* 75-77 No. 255.□

F962.1.1§, ‡Storm wrecks (sinks) ship. See: *DOTTI*; *PSAE*. (Cf. F931.4.4§, N301.2.1§).
Third Qalandar: Magnetic Mountain: *Alf* I 52,-cf.; Burton I 141,-(Loadstone Mountain). Chauvin V 200-3 No. 117; *ANE* 340-41 No. 18;
Sindbâd's Fourth Voyage: *Alf* III 100; Burton VI 35. Chauvin VII 18-20 No. 373D; *ANE* 386 No. 179;
Jawdar and His Treacherous Brethren: *Alf* III 193; Burton VI 242. Chauvin V 257-60 No. 154; *ANE* 244-45 No. 209;
Jullanâr of the Sea: *Alf* III 263; Burton VII 295. Chauvin V 147-51 No. 73; *ANE* 248-51 No. 227;
Sayf al-Mulûk: *Alf* III 282; Burton VII 336-37. Chauvin VII 64-73 No. 348; *ANE* 362-64 No. 229;
¿Abdallah ibn Fâḍil: Treacherous Brothers: *Alf* IV 271; Burton IX 314. Chauvin V 2-4 No. 2; *ANE* 63-65 No. 261.□

F962.1.1.1§, ‡Storm lifts ship out of sea and casts it on land (mountain).
Sindbâd's Seventh Voyage: *Alf* III 117; Burton VI 70. Chauvin VII 26-29 No. 373G; *ANE* 386-87 No. 179.□

F962.1.2§, ‡Storm throws ship off course—sailors lost. See: *PSAE*. (Cf. N390§).

al-'Amjad and al-'As¿ad: *Alf* II 127,-cf.; Burton III 340. Chauvin V 208-10 No. 120[.1]; *ANE* 341-42 No. 61/pt. 2;
Uns al-Wujûd and al-Ward: *Alf* II 278; Burton V 53. Chauvin VI 127-29 No. 282; *ANE* 438 No. 104;
Jânshâh: *Alf* III 41; Burton V 332. Chauvin VII 39-44 No. 153; *ANE* 238-41 No. 178;
Sindbâd's Sixth Voyage: *Alf* III 112; Burton VI 59. Chauvin VII 24-27 No. 373F; *ANE* 386 No. 179;

¿Abdallah ibn Fâḍil: Treacherous Brothers: *Alf* IV 271; Burton IX 314. Chauvin V 2-4 No. 2; *ANE* 63-65 No. 261.□

F962.12.6§, ‡Food (on dining table) descends from heaven.
Bulûqiya: *Alf* III 74; Burton V 384. Chauvin VII 54 No. 77; *ANE* 130-32 No. 177.□

F963.7§, ‡Wind blowing against stone images (idols) causes them to howl. (Cf. F966.2.1§).
Ḥâtim's Hospitality: *Alf* II 181; Burton IV 95. Chauvin VI 49 No. 215; *ANE* 216 No. 64.□

F966, Voices from heaven (or from the air). [*hâtif*/'*munâdî*']. See: *DOTTI*; *GMC*; *PSAE*.
Third Qalandar: Magnetic Mountain: *Alf* I 52; Burton I 142. Chauvin V 200-3 No. 117; *ANE* 340-41 No. 18;
Birds, Beasts, and Carpenter: *Alf* II 25,-(warns); Burton III 123,-(mysterious voice). Chauvin II 225-26 No. 1; *ANE* 126 No. 44;
Ḥâtim's Hospitality: *Alf* II 181, 213; Burton IV 94-95, 173. Chauvin VI 49 No. 215; *ANE* 216 No. 64;
Conversion of Princess by Khawwâṣ: *Alf* III 15,-(*nûdîtu min zawâyâ baytî*); Burton V 285,-("it was cried to me from the dark places of my house"). Chauvin V 239 No. 139; *ANE* 145 No. 171;
Island King/Pious Jewish Merchant: *Alf* III 16; Burton V 291. Chauvin VI 161 No. 325; *ANE* 234 No. 174;
Man Who Never Laughs: *Alf* III 154; Burton VI 166. Chauvin VIII 47-48 No. 15; *ANE* 285-86 No. 195.□

F966.2.1§, ‡Mysterious wailing (weeping) voices heard from mountain. (Cf. F963.7§).
Uns al-Wujûd and al-Ward: *Alf* II 280; Burton V 56. Chauvin VI 127-29 No. 282; *ANE* 438 No. 104.□

F967.0.1§, ‡Drought (lack of rain, dry river, etc.).
Ma¿n Rewards a Bedouin for Gift: *Alf* II 183; Burton IV 98. Chauvin VI 78 No. 248; *ANE* 291 No. 66;
City of Brass: *Alf* III 136; Burton VI 116. Chauvin V 32-35 No. 16; *ANE* 146-50 No. 180;
King Jalî¿âd and Shimâs: *Alf* IV 139; Burton IX 45. Chauvin VI 9 No. 184; *ANE* 237-38 No. 236.□

F969.7, Famine. See: *DOTTI*; *GMC*. (Cf. Z71.5.9§).
City of Brass: *Alf* III 136,-cf./(drought); Burton VI 116. Chauvin V 32-35 No. 16; *ANE* 146-50 No. 180;
King Jalî¿âd and Shimâs: *Alf* IV 139,-cf.; Burton IX 44-45. Chauvin VI 9 No. 184; *ANE* 237-38 No. 236.□

F969.7.1§, ‡Extraordinary measures taken during famine.
City of Brass: *Alf* III 136,-cf./(drought); Burton VI 116. Chauvin V 32-35 No. 16; *ANE* 146-50 No. 180.□

F971.1.1§, ‡Dry staff (rod) becomes tree and bears fruit (instantly, or overnight).
Tawaddud: Slavegirl Sold and Regained: *Alf* III 5,-cf.; Burton V 238. Chauvin VII 117-19 No. 387; *ANE* 408-10 No. 157;
¿Abdallah ibn Fâḍil: Treacherous Brothers: *Alf* IV 277; Burton IX 327. Chauvin V 2-4 No. 2; *ANE* 63-65 No. 261.□

F971.1.2§, ‡Seed becomes tree and bears fruit instantly (overnight). (Cf. V222.12.3§).
¿Abdallah ibn Fâḍil: Treacherous Brothers: *Alf* IV 277; Burton IX 327. Chauvin V 2-4 No. 2; *ANE* 63-65 No. 261.□

F971.5.0.1§, Plants (fruits, flowers) produced out of season. See: *DOTTI*.
Ma¿n Rewards a Bedouin for Gift: *Alf* II 182,-(*qaththâ'*/curly cucumbers); Burton IV 98. Chauvin VI 78 No. 248; *ANE* 291 No. 66;
al-Rashîd and Omani Merchant: *Alf* IV 211,-(al-Baṣrah); Burton IX 193. Chauvin VI 111-12 No. 276; *ANE* 201-2 No. 257.□

F979.25.1.1§, ‡Branch (switch) from certain tree so durable that it is used as whip (for punishment). (Cf. Q458.3§).
Merchant's Curious Wife: *Alf* I 6,-(berry-tree); Burton I 21. Chauvin V 179-80 No. 104; *ANE* 298-99 No. 3;
Portress Amînah: Bitten Cheek: *Alf* I 60,-(quince/*safarjal*); Burton I 183. Chauvin V 98-99 No. 33; *ANE* 326-27 No. 20;
King ¿Umar al-Nu¿mân and Sons: *Alf* I 211; Burton II 181,-(almond tree wood). Chauvin VI 112-24 No. 277; *ANE* 430-34 No. 39.□

F980.1§, ‡Extraordinary size of animal.
Sindbâd's First Voyage: *Alf* III 86, 89; Burton VI 11, 16. Chauvin VII 7-9 No. 373A; *ANE* 385 No. 179;
Sindbâd's Second Voyage: *Alf* III 91; Burton VI 21. Chauvin VII 9-14 No. 373B; *ANE* 385 No. 179.□

F980.3.1§, ‡Fish with animal's (owl's, cow's, donkey's) face.
Sindbâd's First Voyage: *Alf* III 86; Burton VI 11. Chauvin VII 7-9 No. 373A; *ANE* 385 No. 179;
Sindbâd's Third Voyage: *Alf* III 99; Burton VI 23. Chauvin VII 15-18 No. 373C; *ANE* 385-86 No. 179.□

F988, ‡Extraordinary limbs of animals. (Cf. F980.1§).
Sindbâd's Second Voyage: *Alf* III 91; Burton VI 21. Chauvin VII 9-14 No. 373B; *ANE* 385 No. 179.□

F988.4§, ‡Rhinoceros with extraordinarily long horn.
Sindbâd's Second Voyage: *Alf* III 91; Burton VI 21. Chauvin VII 9-14 No. 373B; *ANE* 385 No. 179.□

F989.16.3§, ‡Swarms of birds block the sun so as to provide shade for person—(they act as umbrella). See: *DOTTI*.
Sayf al-Mulûk: *Alf* III 274; Burton VII 318. Chauvin VII 64-73 No. 348; *ANE* 362-64 No. 229.□

F989.17, Marvelously swift horse. See: *DOTTI*; *GMC* (Cf. B749.1.1§).
King ¿Umar al-Nu¿mân and Sons: *Alf* I 318-19; Burton III 76. Chauvin VI 112-24 No. 277; *ANE* 430-34 No. 39.□

F989.25.2§, Dog dominates over lion.
¿Alâ' al-Dîn Abû al-Shâmât: *Alf* II 169,-cf.; Burton IV 74. Chauvin V 43-49 No. 18; *ANE* 85-87 No. 63.□

F1012.1.5§, ‡Long search for filthiest (most disgusting) person. (Cf. T480.2§).
Sweep and Noble Lady: Infidelity Repaid: *Alf* II 190,-(four days); Burton IV 128. Chauvin VI 148 No. 306; *ANE* 403-4 No. 72.□

F1012.5.1§, ‡Celebration lasts for forty days and forty nights. (Cf. P681.0.1§, P965§, T136.0.1§).
Ma¿rûf the Cobbler: *Alf* IV 300; Burton X 19. Chauvin VI 81-82 No. 250; *ANE* 291-93 No. 262.□

F1013.1.1§, ‡Cloud of dust indicates arrival or departure of weighty character (creature, force, etc.). See: *DOTTI*.
Trader and Afrit: Accidental Fairy-cide: *Alf* I 8,-(jinni); Burton I 27. Chauvin VI 22-23 No. 194; *ANE* 419-20 No. 4;
King ¿Umar al-Nu¿mân and Sons: *Alf* I 216; Burton II 190. Chauvin VI 112-24 No. 277; *ANE* 430-34 No. 39;
¿Alâ' al-Dîn Abû al-Shâmât: *Alf* II 180; Burton IV 92-93. Chauvin V 43-49 No. 18; *ANE* 85-87 No. 63;
Hasan of Basrah: *Alf* III 318; Burton VIII 37. Chauvin VII 29-35 No. 212A; *ANE* 207-10 No. 230.□

F1013.1.2§, ‡Cloud of dust indicates arrival of horsemen (army).
First Qalandar: Brother-Sister Incest: *Alf* I 42; Burton I 111. Chauvin V 196-97 No. 115; *ANE* 337-38 No. 15;
Anîs al-Jalîs: *Alf* I 144; Burton II 42. Chauvin V 120-24 No. 58; *ANE* 316-17 No. 35;
King ¿Umar al-Nu¿mân and Sons: *Alf* I 177, 185, 218; Burton II 114, 128, 194. Chauvin VI 112-24 No. 277; *ANE* 430-34 No. 39;
Tâj al-Mulûk: *Alf* I 305,-cf./(army like turbulent sea); Burton III 42. Chauvin V 126-28 No. 60; *ANE* 406-8 No. 40;

al-'Amjad and al-'As¿ad: *Alf* II 146; Burton IV 27. Chauvin V 208-10 No. 120[.1]; *ANE* 341-42 No. 61/pt. 2;
Bulûqiya: *Alf* III 31; Burton V 316. Chauvin VII 54 No. 77; *ANE* 130-32 No. 177;
Hasan of Basrah: *Alf* IV 49; Burton VIII 135. Chauvin VII 29-35 No. 212A; *ANE* 207-10 No. 230.□

F1021.2.3§, Bird's eye view: flight so high that earth is seen as small object (ball, nut, etc.). See: *DOTTI*; *GMC*.
Second Qalandar: Afrit's Wife: *Alf* I 47; Burton I 127. Chauvin V 197-200 No. 116; *ANE* 338-39 No. 16.□

F1021.2.4§, ‡Flight so high that voices of angels in heavens are heard. (Cf. A768.4.2§).
Abû Muhammad Lazybones: *Alf* II 215; Burton IV 174. Chauvin VI 64-67 No. 233; *ANE* 71-73 No. 78;
Sindbâd's Seventh Voyage: *Alf* III 120; Burton VI 75. Chauvin VII 26-29 No. 373G; *ANE* 386-87 No. 179;
Hasan of Basrah: *Alf* IV 23; Burton VIII 81. Chauvin VII 29-35 No. 212A; *ANE* 207-10 No. 230.□

F1034.2, Magician carries mistress in his body. She in turn has paramour in hers. See: *DOTTI*.
Jinni Keeps Mistress in Box: *Alf* I 4-05,-cf./(demon); Burton I 11. Chauvin V 188-91 No. 111; *ANE* 370-71 No. 1.□

F1035.6.2.1§, Girl would conceal her sweetheart in her 'own eye (under eyelid)' and cover him with kohl (formulaic). (Cf. Z66.1§).
Budûr and Jubayr ibn ¿Umayr: *Alf* II 242,-(poem); Burton IV 242,-(between "eyes and eyelids"). Chauvin VII 93-94 No. 374; *ANE* 243-44 No. 83.□

F1035.7§, ‡Object concealed in hair.
Tâj al-Mulûk: *Alf* I 299,-(birds); Burton III 31. Chauvin V 126-28 No. 60; *ANE* 406-8 No. 40.□

F1035.9.1§, ‡Object concealed in underwear. (Cf. K1872.8.3§).
Ghânim ibn Ayyûb: *Alf* I 153,-cf./(pledge of chastity); Burton II 60. Chauvin VI 14 No. 188; *ANE* 192-93 No. 36;
Qamar al-Zamân and Budûr: *Alf* II 96,-(jewel); Burton III 279. Chauvin V 204-12 No. 120; *ANE* 341-45 No. 61.□

F1039§, ‡Frightful event(s) or experience(s). See: *DOTTI*.
Spy, Second Maiden/¿Umar al-Nu¿mân: *Alf* I 221,-(*'akhwaf*/most frightful); Burton II 201,-(most perilous). *ANE* 432,/passim No. 39.□

F1039.1§, ‡Fright from sight of death (corpse). See: *DOTTI*.
Water-fowl and Tortoise: *Alf* II 28,-(corpse of slain man); Burton III 129,-(human carcass). Chauvin II 226-27 No. 5; *ANE* 444 No. 46.□

F1040§, ‡Aversion: dislike with impulse to turn away. See: *DOTTI*. (Cf. T160.0.4§, T311, W22.3.1§).
Lovers of Basra/Damrah: *Alf* III 211; Burton VII 133. Chauvin V 118 No. 54; *ANE* 273 No. 220;
Ibrâhîm and Jamîlah: *Alf* IV 220-21; Burton IX 211. Chauvin VI 52-53 No. 218; *ANE* 227-29 No. 258.□

F1040.7.1§, ‡Aversion to sexual intercourse. See: *DOTTI*. (Cf. T311, T463.8§).
Ibrâhîm and Jamîlah: *Alf* IV 220-21,-(maiden averse to men); Burton IX 211. Chauvin VI 52-53 No. 218; *ANE* 227-29 No. 258;
Nûr al-Dîn and Maryam: *Alf* IV 121,-cf./(*mustahin*/timid); Burton IX 2,-(ashamed). Chauvin V 52-54 No. 271; *ANE* 98-99 No. 233.□

F1041.1.1, Death from a broken heart. See: *DOTTI*; *GMC*.
¿Azîz and ¿Azîzah: *Alf* I 280; Burton II 322. Chauvin V 144-45 No. 71; *ANE* 111-13 No. 41;
¿Alâ' al-Dîn Abû al-Shâmât: *Alf* II 161,-cf., 172; Burton IV 58, 80. Chauvin V 43-49 No. 18; *ANE* 85-87 No. 63;
¿Alî ibn Bakkâr: *Alf* II 64, 65; Burton III 209, 211. Chauvin V 153 No. 76; *ANE* 92-93 No. 60.□

F1041.1.10, ‡Death (illness) from envy. (Cf. W195).
King ¿Umar al-Nu¿mân and Sons: *Alf* I 186-87,-(illness); Burton II 130. Chauvin VI 112-24 No. 277; *ANE* 430-34 No. 39.□

F1041.1.2, ‡Death from grief for death of lover or relative. See: *DOTTI*. (Cf. T81.7).
¿Alî ibn Bakkâr: *Alf* II 65; Burton III 211. Chauvin V 153 No. 76; *ANE* 92-93 No. 60.□

F1041.1.2.1, Lover dies beside dying sweetheart. See: *DOTTI*; *GMC*. (Cf. T81.1.1§).
Lovers of Banû Ṭay'/Death from Love: *Alf* II 297; Burton V 137. Chauvin V 111 No. 45; *ANE* 273 No. 145;
Lovers of Banû ¿Udhrah and Lion: *Alf* III 209; Burton VII 123. Chauvin V 106-7 No. 37, 116 No. 52; *ANE* 274/[2] No. 218.□

F1041.1.3, Death from sorrow or chagrin. See: *DOTTI*. (Cf. P234.2.1§, T81).
Lazy Sower (Farmer): *Alf* II 39,-(*zâri¿*); Burton III 157,-("husbandman"). Chauvin II 229 No. 16;
Man Who Never Laughs: *Alf* III 155; Burton VI 166. Chauvin VIII 47-48 No. 15; *ANE* 285-86 No. 195;
Hârûn and Arab Girl: *Alf* III 204; Burton VII 110. Chauvin VI 143 No. 300; *ANE* 202 No. 215;
Lovers of Banû ¿Udhrah and Lion: *Alf* III 209; Burton VII 123. Chauvin V 106-7 No. 37, 116 No. 52; *ANE* 274 No. 218/[2].□

F1041.1.9, Death from jealousy. See: *DOTTI*.
Enchanted Spring: Change of Sex: *Alf* III 148; Burton VI 149,-(father orders son's execution). Chauvin VIII 43 No. 11; *ANE* 175-76 No. 191.□

F1041.2, Horripilation. Hair rises on end in extraordinary fashion from joy, anger, or love. See: *PSAE*. (Cf. F1041.11.5§).
King ¿Umar al-Nu¿mân and Sons: *Alf* I 167,-(woman's body hair, like porcupine's); Burton II 88. Chauvin VI 112-24 No. 277; *ANE* 430-34 No. 39.□

F1041.8.1, Madness from seeing beautiful woman. See: *DOTTI*; *GMC*. (Cf. F1041.8.2.1§).
King ¿Umar al-Nu¿mân and Sons: *Alf* I 180,-(*khubila bynahu wa bayn ¿aqlih*/became crazed); Burton II 119,-(reason fled his head). Chauvin VI 112-24 No. 277; *ANE* 430-34 No. 39;
House with the Belvedere: *Alf* III 168; Burton VI 191. Chauvin VIII 57-58 No. 23; *ANE* 223 No. 203.□

F1041.8.1.0.1§, War waged to procure beautiful woman. See: *DOTTI*.
Jullanâr of the Sea: *Alf* III 260,-(battle); Burton VII 287. Chauvin V 147-51 No. 73; *ANE* 248-51 No. 227.□

F1041.8.1.2§, ‡Woman so beautiful that whoever sees her becomes sick from love (or dies). See: *DOTTI*. (Cf. F1041.8.2.1§).
House with the Belvedere: *Alf* III 168; Burton VI 191. Chauvin VIII 57-58 No. 23; *ANE* 223 No. 203.□

F1041.8.2.1§, ‡Grief (chagrin, obsession) from seeing an unattainable beauty (woman). See: *DOTTI*. (Cf. F1041.8.1).
Jeweler's Wife and Qamar al-Zamân: *Alf* IV 241; Burton IX 256. Chauvin V 212-14 No. 121; *ANE* 345-47 No. 260.□

F1041.8.4, ‡Madness from thirst.
City of Brass: *Alf* III 132,-cf./(hallucination); Burton VI 109. Chauvin V 32-35 No. 16; *ANE* 146-50 No. 180.□

F1041.9.1.4§, ‡Man (husband, king) becomes ill from wife's infidelity. See: *DOTTI*.
Shahriyâr and Shâhzamân: *Alf* I 2-3; Burton I 4. Chauvin V 188-91 No. 111; *ANE* 370-71 No. 1.□

F1041.9.2.2§, ‡Loss of appetite and skin-color from keeping secret (person becomes thin, pale, yellow, etc.). See: *DOTTI*.
Shahriyâr and Shâhzamân: *Alf* I 2-3; Burton I 4. Chauvin V 188-91 No. 111; *ANE* 370-71 No. 1.□

F1041.9.4.1.1§, ‡Yellowness of skin from illness. (Cf. K1996.2§).
Shahriyâr and Shâhzamân: *Alf* I 2; Burton I 4. Chauvin V 188-91 No. 111; *ANE* 370-71 No. 1;
Tâj al-Mulûk: *Alf* I 267; Burton II 295. Chauvin V 126-28 No. 60; *ANE* 406-8 No. 40;
Man from Yaman and Six Salve-girls: Flyting: *Alf* II 249,-(poem); Burton IV 259. Chauvin VI 151 No. 313; *ANE* 289-90 No. 84;
Tawaddud: Slavegirl Sold and Regained: *Alf* II 315,-(indicates *yaraqân*); Burton V 220,-(of white of eyes). Chauvin VII 117-19 No. 387; *ANE* 408-10 No. 157.□

F1041.9.4.4.1§, ‡Fainting away from shock, fright or sudden realization (usually at hearing bad news).
Ni¿mah and Nu¿m: Stolen Wife Regained: *Alf* II 139,-(reunion with sweetheart is near); Burton IV 14. Chauvin VI 96-97 No. 263; *ANE* 314 No. 62;

¿Alî Shâr and Zumurrud: *Alf* II 232,-(responsibility for losing sweetheart); Burton IV 225. Chauvin V 89-91 No. 28; *ANE* 100-1 No. 82;
Hasan of Basrah: *Alf* IV 15, 16; Burton VIII 66, 67. Chauvin VII 29-35 No. 212A; *ANE* 207-10 No. 230.□

F1041.9.7.1§, ‡Retired person becomes ill (unhealthy) from lack of activity. (Cf. P16.1.5§).
King ¿Umar al-Nu¿mân and Sons: *Alf* I 308; Burton III 49. Chauvin VI 112-24 No. 277; *ANE* 430-34 No. 39.□

F1041.9.8§, ‡Illness (dulness) from fullness (of stomach). (Cf. F956.7.3§, W155.0.2§).
Spy, Old Woman/¿Umar al-Nu¿mân: *Alf* I 224; Burton II 205-07. *ANE* 432 No. 39/passim;
Merchant and Robbers: *Alf* IV 166; Burton IX 100. Chauvin II 223 No. 152/20; *ANE* 297 No. 251.□

F1041.9.8.1.2§, ‡Immobility (sluggishness) from obesity (fatness).
Man from Yaman and Six Salve-girls: Flyting: *Alf* II 248; Burton IV 252. Chauvin VI 151 No. 313; *ANE* 289-90 No. 84.□

F1041.9.9.2§, ‡Paralysis from shock (chagrin, sorrow). (Cf. S123.1.1§).
Second Eunuch/Kâfûr's Half-lie: *Alf* I 149; Burton II 53,-(sudden palsy). Chauvin V 278 No. 161; *ANE* 178-79 No. 38.□

F1041.11, Laughing and crying at the same time ([...]).
King ¿Umar al-Nu¿mân and Sons: *Alf* I 214,-(at reunion w/sister/poem-3); Burton II 187. Chauvin VI 112-24 No. 277; *ANE* 430-34 No. 39;
¿Azîz and ¿Azîzah: *Alf* I 276,-cf.; Burton II 312. Chauvin V 144-45 No. 71; *ANE* 111-13 No. 41.□

F1041.11.1, Laughter from chagrin.
¿Azîz and ¿Azîzah: *Alf* I 276; Burton II 312,-(smile of reproach). Chauvin V 144-45 No. 71; *ANE* 111-13 No. 41.□

F1041.11.3§, ‡Weeping from happiness ('tears of joy').
King ¿Umar al-Nu¿mân and Sons: *Alf* I 214,-(poem-3); Burton II 187. Chauvin VI 112-24 No. 277; *ANE* 430-34 No. 39;
Wolf and Fox: *Alf* II 31,-(fox's); Burton III 135. Chauvin II 227 No. 6; *ANE* 450 No. 47;
Jânshâh: *Alf* III 57,-(poem); Burton V 355. Chauvin VII 39-44 No. 153; *ANE* 238-41 No. 178.□

F1041.11.5§, ‡Fainting away from joy (happiness). (Cf. F1041.2).
Nûr al-Dîn ¿Alî and Son: *Alf* I 81-83; Burton I 244. Chauvin VI 102-6 No. 270; *ANE* 317-19 No. 22;
Qamar al-Zamân and Budûr: *Alf* II 107; Burton III 298. Chauvin V 204-12 No. 120; *ANE* 341-45 No. 61;
¿Alâ' al-Dîn Abû al-Shâmât: *Alf* II 177,-(reunion); Burton IV 88. Chauvin V 43-49 No. 18; *ANE* 85-87 No. 63;
Jânshâh: *Alf* III 56; Burton V 354. Chauvin VII 39-44 No. 153; *ANE* 238-41 No. 178;
Bulûqiya: *Alf* III 74-75; Burton V 385,-(swoon away). Chauvin VII 54 No. 77; *ANE* 130-32 No. 177;
Hasan of Basrah: *Alf* IV 55,-cf.; Burton VIII 155. Chauvin VII 29-35 No. 212A; *ANE* 207-10 No. 230.□

F1041.15.1§, ‡Addiction as an illness. Adverse effects of excessive consumption of commodity or service (e.g., food, drink, drug, or sex, entertainment, etc.). (Cf. T468§, P195.0.4.1§, P196.1§, T450.0.2.1§).
Copt Broker's Story: Lover's Sacrifices Repaid: *Alf* I 93; Burton I 272. Chauvin VI 80 No. 249; *ANE* 313-14 No. 24.□

F1041.16.0.1§, ‡'Anger-vein' (in temple or between eyes) throbs when man is angered.
Anîs al-Jalîs: *Alf* I 134, 139; Burton II 19, 29,-(vein-of-rage). Chauvin V 120-24 No. 58; *ANE* 316-17 No. 35.□

F1041.16.1.2§, ‡Man's nostrils flash sparks when enraged. (Cf. B80.9.1§).
King ¿Umar al-Nu¿mân and Sons: *Alf* I 162; Burton II 77. Chauvin VI 112-24 No. 277; *ANE* 430-34 No. 39.□

F1041.16.2§, ‡Man's nostrils drip blood due to anger.
al-'Amjad and al-'As¿ad: *Alf* II 116; Burton III 315. Chauvin V 208-10 No. 120[.1]; *ANE* 341-42 No. 61/pt. 2.□

F1041.17.3§, ‡Fainting away from fear (horror). See: *DOTTI*; *PSAE*. (Cf. V462.2.3.1§).

Jawdar and His Treacherous Brethren: *Alf* III 195; Burton VI 244. Chauvin V 257-60 No. 154; *ANE* 244-45 No. 209.□

F1041.17.4§, ‡Involuntary defecation (urination) from fear. See: *DOTTI.*
Fisherman and Afrit: Ingratitude: *Alf* I 23; Burton I 61. Chauvin VI 26 No. 197; *ANE* 183-84 No. 8.□

F1041.21.9.1§, Death from shame (humiliation). See: *DOTTI.*
¿Azîz and ¿Azîzah: *Alf* I 281,-cf./(*qahr*); Burton II 322. Chauvin V 144-45 No. 71; *ANE* 111-13 No. 41.□

F1042.1§, ‡Compulsion to steal. See: *DOTTI.* (Cf. W157).
Copt Broker's Story: Lover's Sacrifices Repaid: *Alf* I 93,-cf.; Burton I 273. Chauvin VI 80 No. 249; *ANE* 313-14 No. 24.□

F1042.2§, ‡Compulsion to lie. (Cf. W166.2§, X901).
Second Eunuch/Kâfûr's Half-lie: *Alf* I 148; Burton II 51. Chauvin V 278 No. 161; *ANE* 178-79 No. 38.□

F1042.3§, ‡Compulsion to cleanse oneself (certain limb or body part). (Cf. J567.1.1§).
Reeve's Story: Why Maimed by Bride: *Alf* I 96,-(forty times); Burton I 279. Chauvin V 220-21 No. 305; *ANE* 351 No. 25.□

F1043.1§, Hallucinatory experiences from sensory deprivation. (Cf. F1046§).
King ¿Umar al-Nu¿mân and Sons: *Alf* I 308,-(*tâ'ish al-¿aql*); Burton III 49,-(dull of wit [??]). Chauvin V 126-28 No. 60; *ANE* 430-34 No. 39.□

F1045, Night spent in tree. See: *DOTTI*; *GMC.*
Ghânim ibn Ayyûb: *Alf* I 147,-(palm-tree); Burton II 47. Chauvin VI 14-16 No. 188; *ANE* 192-93 No. 36.□

F1046§, ‡Hallucination: false perception without adequate stimuli. (Cf. F1043.1§, W210§).
City of Brass: *Alf* III 132,-(maidens like houris); Burton VI 108. Chauvin V 32-35 No. 16; *ANE* 146-50 No. 180.□

F1051, Prodigious weeping. Usually by saint. (Cf. U245.0.1.1.1§).
Devotee Prince: Ascetic's Death: *Alf* II 290; Burton V 111. Chauvin VI 193-94 No. 363; *ANE* 167-68 No. 134.□

F1053.1§, ‡Laughing so hard till falling backwards on floor (or the like). (Cf. F1041.11.1).
Merchant's Curious Wife: *Alf* I 6; Burton I 20. Chauvin V 179-80 No. 104; *ANE* 298-99 No. 3;
Porter and Ladies of Baghdad: *Alf* I 35; Burton I 91. Chauvin V 251-52 No. 148; *ANE* 324-26 No. 14;
Hunchback's Tale: Resuscitated: *Alf* I 124; Burton I 350. Chauvin V 180-82 No. 105; *ANE* 224-25 No. 23;
Anîs al-Jalîs: *Alf* I 141; Burton II 32,-(xxx). Chauvin V 120-24 No. 58; *ANE* 316-17 No. 35;
¿Azîz and ¿Azîzah: *Alf* I 285; Burton II 330,-(over on back for excess of merriment). Chauvin V 144-45 No. 71; *ANE* 111-13 No. 41;
Tâj al-Mulûk: *Alf* I 295; Burton III 22. Chauvin V 126-28 No. 60; *ANE* 406-8 No. 40;
King ¿Umar al-Nu¿mân and Sons: *Alf* I 309; Burton III 50. Chauvin VI 112-24 No. 277; *ANE* 430-34 No. 39;
Qamar al-Zamân and Budûr: *Alf* II 110-11; Burton III 306. Chauvin V 204-12 No. 120; *ANE* 341-45 No. 61;
Kurd's Sack/¿Alî the Persian: *Alf* II 202; Burton IV 152. Chauvin V 279 No. 162; *ANE* 99-100 No. 74;
Jullanâr of the Sea: *Alf* III 258,-(sarcasm); Burton VII 285. Chauvin V 147-51 No. 73; *ANE* 248-51 No. 227.□

F1068.1, Tokens from a dream. Man brings objects received during a dream. See: *GMC.* (Cf. N660.1§).
Prior Becomes Moslem: al-Anbârî: *Alf* II 299,-(apple); Burton V 143. Chauvin V 237-38 No. 137; *ANE* 330-31 No. 147.□

F1068.2, Wound received in dream. Still there when person wakes. See: *GMC.*
Nûr al-Dîn ¿Alî and Son: *Alf* I 83,-cf./(deception); Burton I 248. Chauvin VI 102-6 No. 270; *ANE* 317-19 No. 22.□

F1068.2.3§, ‡Taste of food eaten in dream still in mouth next day.
Prior Becomes Moslem: al-Anbârî: *Alf* II 299; Burton V 143. Chauvin V 237-38 No. 137; *ANE* 330-31 No. 147.□

F1068.3§, ‡Erotic dreams. See: *DOTTI*.
Hashish Eater's Dream: *Alf* II 10; Burton III 92-93. Chauvin VI 124 No. 278; *ANE* 216 No. 42.□

F1068.3.1§, ‡Erotic experience in dream with tangible results. See: *DOTTI*.
Hashish Eater's Dream: *Alf* II 10; Burton III 92. Chauvin VI 124 No. 278; *ANE* 216 No. 42.□

F1083.3§, ‡Seat (sofa, couch) suspended in air.
Jânshâh: *Alf* III 72; Burton V 378,-(litter). Chauvin VII 39-44 No. 153; *ANE* 238-41 No. 178.□

F1084.4.1§, ‡Heaps of flesh (corpses, organs) mark (litter) battle field—*malḥamah*.
King ¿Umar al-Nu¿mân and Sons: *Alf* I 231, 257; Burton II 222. Chauvin VI 112-24 No. 277; *ANE* 430-34 No. 39.□

G. OGRES AND SATAN[92]

G2§, ‡Appearance of ogre (ogress).
Sindbâd's Third Voyage: *Alf* III 94; Burton VI 24. Chauvin VII 15-18 No. 373C; *ANE* 385-86 No. 179.□

G2.1§, ‡Hideous ogre (ogress).
Sindbâd's Third Voyage: *Alf* III 94; Burton VI 24-25. Chauvin VII 15-18 No. 373C; *ANE* 385-86 No. 179.□

G11.11, ‡Cannibal with extraordinary features. See: *DOTTI*.
Sindbâd's Fourth Voyage: *Alf* III 100; Burton VI 36-37. Chauvin VII 18-20 No. 373D; *ANE* 386 No. 179.□

G11.4, ‡Negro cannibal.
Ghânim ibn Ayyûb: *Alf* I 147; Burton II 48. Chauvin VI 14-16 No. 188; *ANE* 192-93 No. 36;
Sayf al-Mulûk: *Alf* III 282; Burton VII 336-37. Chauvin VII 64-73 No. 348; *ANE* 362-64 No. 229.□

G11.18, Cannibal tribe. See: *DOTTI*; *GMC*.
Sindbâd's Third Voyage: *Alf* III 92; Burton VI 23-24. Chauvin VII 15-18 No. 373C; *ANE* 385-86 No. 179;
Sayf al-Mulûk: *Alf* III 283; Burton VII 339. Chauvin VII 64-73 No. 348; *ANE* 362-64 No. 229.□

G19.1§, ‡Cannibals live on island (island of cannibals). (Cf. F129.4.9.2§).
Sayf al-Mulûk: *Alf* III 284; Burton VII 339. Chauvin VII 64-73 No. 348; *ANE* 362-64 No. 229.□

G78.1, Cannibalism in times of famine. See: *DOTTI*; *GMC*.
Fox and Crow: *Alf* II 37,-(starved fox eats own young); Burton III 150. Chauvin II 228 No. 154.11; *ANE* 188 No. 51.□

G82.0.1§, ‡Cannibal tests captive's fatness (readiness to be eaten).
Sindbâd's Third Voyage: *Alf* III 94; Burton VI 25. Chauvin VII 15-18 No. 373C; *ANE* 385-86 No. 179.□

G82.2§, ‡Cannibals raise (shepherd) own herd of humans.
Sindbâd's Fourth Voyage: *Alf* III 101; Burton VI 35-36. Chauvin VII 18-20 No. 373D; *ANE* 386 No. 179;
Sayf al-Mulûk: *Alf* III 292; Burton VII 359. Chauvin VII 64-73 No. 348; *ANE* 362-64 No. 229.□

G82.3§, Cannibal's fodder (fattening). Fodder causes gluttony and insanity: victim fattened. See: *DOTTI*.
Sindbâd's Fourth Voyage: *Alf* III 101; Burton VI 36. Chauvin VII 18-20 No. 373D; *ANE* 386 No. 179.□

G82.3.2§, ‡Cannibal's drink (milk) causes blindness.
Sayf al-Mulûk: *Alf* III 292,-(milk); Burton VII 360. Chauvin VII 64-73 No. 348; *ANE* 362-64 No. 229.□

G99§, ‡Cannibalism among animals (eating flesh of own kind). (Cf. U44.1§).
Fox and Crow: *Alf* II 37; Burton III 150. Chauvin II 228 No. 11; *ANE* 188 No. 51.□

G100.1, Giant ogre (Fomorian).
Sindbâd's Third Voyage: *Alf* III 94; Burton VI 24-25. Chauvin VII 15-18 No. 373C; *ANE* 385-86 No. 179.□

G114.4§, ‡Ogre (cannibal) keeps humans as pets.
Sayf al-Mulûk: *Alf* III 283-84,-(as singing birds); Burton VII 339. Chauvin VII 64-73 No. 348; *ANE* 362-64 No. 229.□

---

[92]With reference to the idiosyncratic grouping of "Satan" with "Ogres", it has been stated that such a perception constitutes the effect of "The Personal Factor in Indexing". Thus,

> [...], a person with an Arab culture orientation (cognitive system, worldview) would not be apt to seek information on "[...] The Devil, Satan, The Bad Man, Old Nick, etc." (Motif: G303) in the Chapter titled: "OGRES" (Motif: G0), nor under the subcategory: "Other ogres" (Motif: G300); for such a person, an ogre is a man-eating supernatural being, while "The Devil, Satan, ..." is *never* perceived in that role of predatory *carnivora*. (See: El-Shamy, *Folk Traditions of the Arab World*, Vol. 1, pp. xxi-xxii).

G114.4.1§, ‡Caged humans as 'singing' pets: kept by cannibal. (Cf. F899.3).
Sayf al-Mulûk: *Alf* III 283; Burton VII 339-40. Chauvin VII 64-73 No. 348; *ANE* 362-64 No. 229.□

G121.3§, ‡Ogre's (ogress's) eyes emit sparks. See: *DOTTI*.
Trader and Afrit: Accidental Fairy-cide: *Alf* I 8,-(Afrit's); Burton I 27. Chauvin VI 22-23 No. 194; *ANE* 419-20 No. 4.□

G128§, ‡Size of giant (Fomorian).
Trader and Afrit: Accidental Fairy-cide: *Alf* I 8,-("*¿ifrît*"), 9,-(drawing/"jinni"); Burton I 24. Chauvin VI 22-23 No. 194; *ANE* 419-20 No. 4;
Sindbâd's Third Voyage: *Alf* III 94; Burton VI 24. Chauvin VII 15-18 No. 373C; *ANE* 385-86 No. 179.□

G135§, Habitat of giant ogres. (Cf. F499.3.5§).
Hasan of Basrah: *Alf* III 308,-(palace inhabited by jinn ogres an satans/*jânn, ghîlân, wa shayâṭîn*); Burton VIII 20. Chauvin VII 29-35 No. 212A; *ANE* 207-10 No. 230.□

G242.5.1§, ‡Witches flies through the air on pottery water-tank (*zîr*).
Hasan of Basrah: *Alf* IV 46; Burton VIII 131. Chauvin VII 29-35 No. 212A; *ANE* 207-10 No. 230.□

G242.7, ‡Person flying with witches makes mistake and falls.
Abû Muḥammad Lazybones: *Alf* II 215,-cf.; Burton IV 175. Chauvin VI 64-67 No. 233; *ANE* 71-73 No. 78.□

G264, La Belle Dame San Merci. Witch entices men with offers of love and then deserts or destroys them. See: *DOTTI*; *GMC*. (Cf. T33.1§).
Jullanâr of the Sea: *Alf* III 266,-(Queen Lâb); Burton VII 298. Chauvin V 147-51 No. 73; *ANE* 248-51 No. 227;
Sayf al-Mulûk: *Alf* III 284,-cf./(implicit); Burton VII 341. Chauvin VII 64-73 No. 348; *ANE* 362-64 No. 229.□

G275, ‡Witch defeated. See: *DOTTI*. (Cf. K618.1§).
Ensorcelled Prince/Husband: *Alf* I 30,-cf./(killed); Burton I 81. Chauvin VI 56-58 No. 222; *ANE* 176 No. 13.□

G284, ‡Witch as helper.
Hasan of Basrah: *Alf* IV 46; Burton VIII 131. Chauvin VII 29-35 No. 212A; *ANE* 207-10 No. 230.□

G291, Witch executed for engaging in witchcraft. See: *DOTTI*; *GMC*.
Goldsmith and Cashmere Singer: *Alf* III 150,-cf.; Burton VI 157. Chauvin VIII 46-47 No. 14; *ANE* 196 No. 194.□

G302.3, Form of demon.
Jinn Imprisoned in Flasks: *Alf* III 127,-(Afrit); Burton VI 96. Chauvin VII 113 No. 380=no/text; *ANE* 146 No. 180.□

G302.4.6.1.1§, ‡Demon with predator's (lion's) paws.
Jinn Imprisoned in Flasks: *Alf* III 127; Burton VI 97. Chauvin VII 113 No. 380=no/text; *ANE* 146 No. 180.□

G302.4.7.1.1§, ‡Three-eyed demon.
Jinn Imprisoned in Flasks: *Alf* III 127; Burton VI 96. Chauvin VII 113 No. 380=no/text; *ANE* 146 No. 180.□

G302.4.9.1.1§, ‡Demons with long hair (like tail of horse).
Jinn Imprisoned in Flasks: *Alf* III 127; Burton VI 96. Chauvin VII 113 No. 380=no/text; *ANE* 146 No. 180.□

G302.7.1.1§, Sexual relationship between woman and demon (ogre, afrit, etc.). See: *DOTTI*; *GMC*.
Jinni Keeps Mistress in Box: *Alf* I 4; Burton I 11-13. Chauvin V 188-89 No. 111; *ANE* 370 No. 1/pt.□

G302.7.2§, ‡Princess (woman, maiden) ravished by demon (ogre, afrit, etc.).
Jinni Keeps Mistress in Box: *Alf* I 4; Burton I 12. Chauvin V 188-89 No. 111; *ANE* 370 No. 1/pt.;
Second Qalandar: Afrit's Wife: *Alf* I 44; Burton I 116. Chauvin V 197-200 No. 116; *ANE* 338-39 No. 16;
King's Son and Afrit's Mistress: *Alf* III 172; Burton VI 200. Chauvin VIII 59 No. 24; *ANE* 263-64 No. 204.□

G303.0.1§, ‡Other entities labeled 'satan'.
Jawdar and His Treacherous Brethren: *Alf* III 198,-(jinni/"shyṭân"); Burton VI 249,-(devil). Chauvin V 257-60 No. 154; *ANE* 244-45 No. 209.□

G302.9.6, ‡Demons fool men in their dreams. (Cf. J157.8.1§, V517§).
Qamar al-Zamân and Budûr: *Alf* II 82,-cf.; Burton III 246. Chauvin V 204-12 No. 120; *ANE* 341-45 No. 61.□

G302.9.10.1§, ‡Demon army. (Cf. F252.3).
Jinn Imprisoned in Flasks: *Alf* III 127; Burton VI 93. Chauvin VII 113 No. 380=no/text; *ANE* 146 No. 180.□

G303.3.1, The devil in human form. See: *DOTTI*; *GMC*. (Cf. V231.9.1§).
Sindbâd's Fifth Voyage: *Alf* III 108; Burton VI 51. Chauvin VII 21-24 No. 373E; *ANE* 386 No. 179.□

G303.3.3.5, ‡Devil in form of fish. (Cf. F401.3.15.1§).
Jawdar and His Treacherous Brethren: *Alf* III 183,-cf./(afrits); Burton VI 223. Chauvin V 257-60 No. 154; *ANE* 244-45 No. 209.□

G303.9.0.1§, ‡Satan's wiles (cleverness). (Cf. G303.9.4).
Craft and Malice of Women/Frame: *Alf* III 145; Burton VI 144. Chauvin VIII 43 No. 11; *ANE* 175-76 No. 181.□

G303.9.0.1.1§, ‡'Truly the wiles of Satan are weak' (when compared to women's powers)—[Male's interpretation of scripture].
Craft and Malice of Women/Frame: *Alf* III 145; Burton VI 144. Chauvin VIII 43 No. 11; *ANE* 175-76 No. 181.□

G303.9.4, The devil as a tempter. See: *DOTTI*; *GMC*.
Water-carrier and Goldsmith's Wife: *Alf* II 285,-cf.; Burton V 90. Chauvin VI 192 No. 361; *ANE* 444 No. 122;
Jawdar and His Treacherous Brethren: *Alf* III 195; Burton VI 244. Chauvin V 257-60 No. 154; *ANE* 244-45 No. 209.□

G303.9.4.0.5.1.1§, ‡Eblis blows into a man's nostrils: the man becomes arrogant.
Angel of Death and Proud King: *Alf* III 8; Burton V 247. Chauvin VI 183-84 No. 349/[pt. 1]; *ANE* 104 No. 158.□

G303.9.4.5.4§, ‡Satan causes forgetfulness. See: *DOTTI*. (Cf. U64.2§).
Hasan of Basrah: *Alf* IV 17; Burton VIII 70. Chauvin VII 29-35 No. 212A; *ANE* 207-10 No. 230.□

G303.16.2.1§, ‡Devil's power countervailed by reciting holy scripture. See: *DOTTI*.
Lady and Five Suitors Deceived: *Alf* III 162,-cf.; Burton VI 179. Chauvin VIII 50-51 No. 18; *ANE* 266 No. 198;
Mercury ¿Alî: *Alf* III 233; Burton VII 193. Chauvin V 248-50 No. 147; *ANE* 301-3 No. 225.□

G303.22.0.1§, ‡Devil (demon) serves man so that man may serve him. See: *DOTTI*.
Abû Muḥammad Lazybones: *Alf* II 211-12,-(monkey); Burton IV 171. Chauvin VI 64-67 No. 233; *ANE* 71-73 No. 78.□

G311, Old man of the sea. Burr-woman. Ogre who jumps on one's back and sticks there magically. See: *ANE*; *GMC*.
Sindbâd's Fifth Voyage: *Alf* III 110,-cf./(*shaykh al-baḥr*); Burton VI 53. Chauvin VII 21-24 No. 373E; *ANE* 386 No. 179;
Sayf al-Mulûk: *Alf* III 292,-cf.; Burton VII 358. Chauvin VII 64-73 No. 348; *ANE* 362-64 No. 229.□

G360, Ogres with monstrous features. See: *GMC*.
Second Qalandar: Afrit's Wife: *Alf* I 49; Burton I 134. Chauvin V 197-200 No. 116; *ANE* 338-39 No. 16.□

G376.0.3§, ‡Ogress in form of woman (girl). See: *DOTTI*.
Prince and Ogress: *Alf* I 19; Burton I 54-55. Chauvin VI 26 No. 197; *ANE* 329 No. 12;
King's Favorite Son and Ogress: *Alf* III 144; Burton VI 140. Chauvin VIII 40-41 No. 8B; *ANE* 264 No. 188.□

G406, Lost (marooned) person falls into ogre's power. See: *DOTTI*.

King's Favorite Son and Ogress: *Alf* III 144; Burton VI 140-42. Chauvin VIII 40-41 No. 8B; *ANE* 264 No. 188.□

G407§, ‡Lost ship (boat) lands on shores of land of ogres (cannibals). See: *DOTTI*. (Cf. F129.4.9.2§).
Abû Muhammad Lazybones: *Alf* II 209; Burton IV 167-68. Chauvin VI 64-67 No. 233; *ANE* 71-73 No. 78;
Jânshâh: *Alf* III 42; Burton V 333. Chauvin VII 39-44 No. 153; *ANE* 238-41 No. 178;
Sindbâd's Fourth Voyage: *Alf* III 100; Burton VI 35. Chauvin VII 18-20 No. 373D; *ANE* 386 No. 179.□

G417.1§, ‡Ogress poses as stranded (lost) woman and asks for a ride.
Prince and Ogress: *Alf* I 20; Burton I 54-55. Chauvin VI 26 No. 197; *ANE* 329 No. 12;
King's Favorite Son and Ogress: *Alf* III 143-44,-(treacherous intent/fin); Burton VI 140-42. Chauvin VIII 40-41 No. 8B; *ANE* 264 No. 188.□

G511, ‡Ogre blinded.
Sindbâd's Third Voyage: *Alf* III 96; Burton VI 27. Chauvin VII 15-18 No. 373C; *ANE* 385-86 No. 179.□

G511.1.1§, ‡Ogre blinded by driving the skewer he uses to roast victims into his eye(s).
Sindbâd's Third Voyage: *Alf* III 96; Burton VI 27. Chauvin VII 15-18 No. 373C; *ANE* 385-86 No. 179.□

G565§, Escape from ogre (ogress, witch, etc.). See: *DOTTI*; *GMC*.
Sindbâd's Fourth Voyage: *Alf* III 100; Burton VI 37-38. Chauvin VII 18-20 No. 373D; *ANE* 386 No. 179.□

G583, ‡Demons coerced by tabus of druid. (Cf. D1§, D1273.8§).
Jânshâh: *Alf* III 66-67,-cf./(*'aqsâm*/incantations); Burton V 370. Chauvin VII 39-44 No. 153; *ANE* 238-41 No. 178.□

G640.1§, ‡Ogre (ogress, demon) as shape-shifter. See: *DOTTI*. (Cf. F234.0.2, G264).
Second Qalandar: Afrit's Wife: *Alf* I 49,-(afrit); Burton I 134. Chauvin V 197-200 No. 116; *ANE* 338-39 No. 16.□

H. TESTS

H10, Recognition through common knowledge. See: *DOTTI*.
Ma¿rûf the Cobbler: *Alf* IV 294; Burton X 8-9. Chauvin VI 81-82 No. 250; *ANE* 291-93 No. 262.□

H11.1, ‡Recognition by telling life history. See: *DOTTI*. (Cf. J169.0.1§, N747§, Z201.1§).
King ¿Umar al-Nu¿mân and Sons: *Alf* I 213, II 11-13; Burton II 185-86. Chauvin VI 112-24 No. 277; *ANE* 430-34 No. 39;
Island King/Pious Jewish Merchant: *Alf* III 16-18; Burton V 293. Chauvin VI 161 No. 325; *ANE* 234 No. 174.□

H11.1.4, ‡Recognition by tracing ancestry. (Cf. N731.4).
King ¿Umar al-Nu¿mân and Sons: *Alf* II 11; Burton III 95. Chauvin VI 112-24 No. 277; *ANE* 430-34 No. 39.□

H11.5§, ‡Recognition through shared childhood experiences in same neighborhood (district).
Ma¿rûf the Cobbler: *Alf* IV 294; Burton X 8-9. Chauvin VI 81-82 No. 250; *ANE* 291-93 No. 262.□

H15.2.1§, ‡Identity proven by recalling experience shared with tester.
Sindbâd's First Voyage: *Alf* III 87; Burton VI 12. Chauvin VII 7-9 No. 373A; *ANE* 385 No. 179;
Sindbâd's Third Voyage: *Alf* III 98-99; Burton VI 31-32. Chauvin VII 15-18 No. 373C; *ANE* 385-86 No. 179.□

H34§, ‡Recognition by personal literary style (of writing, composition, etc.).
Masrûr and Zayn al-Mawâṣif: *Alf* IV 72; Burton VIII 243. Chauvin VI 82-84 No. 251; *ANE* 294-95 No. 232.□

H34.0.1§, ‡Recognition by characteristic handwriting.
King ¿Umar al-Nu¿mân and Sons: *Alf* II 15,-ff.; Burton III 101-2. Chauvin VI 112-24 No. 277; *ANE* 430-34 No. 39;
Ni¿mah and Nu¿m: Stolen Wife Regained: *Alf* II 139; Burton IV 14. Chauvin VI 96-97 No. 263; *ANE* 314 No. 62.□

H35.1, Recognition by unique manner of playing lute. See: *ANE*; *GMC*.
Ruined Baghdadi and His Slave-girl: *Alf* IV 131; Burton IX 27. Chauvin V 152-53 No. 75; *ANE* 353 No. 235.□

H35.1.0.1§, ‡Recognition by unique musical style. (Cf. F679.9.1§).
¿Alâ' al-Dîn Abû al-Shâmât: *Alf* II 177; Burton IV 88. Chauvin V 43-49 No. 18; *ANE* 85-87 No. 63;
Ruined Baghdadi and His Slave-girl: *Alf* IV 131,-cf.; Burton IX 24-32. Chauvin V 152-53 No. 75; *ANE* 353 No. 235.□

H35.1.0.2§, ‡Recognition by unique ability to set (tune) musical instrument.
Isḥâq al-Mûṣilî and Merchant's Singer: *Alf* II 296; Burton V 131. Chauvin VI 59 No. 225; *ANE* 233 No. 142;
Ruined Baghdadi and His Slave-girl: *Alf* IV 131; Burton IX 27. Chauvin V 152-53 No. 75; *ANE* 353 No. 235.□

H35.2, Recognition by unique cookery. See: *ANE*; *DOTTI*; *GMC*.
Nûr al-Dîn ¿Alî and Son: *Alf* I 81-83; Burton I 244. Chauvin VI 102-6 No. 270; *ANE* 317-19 No. 22.□

H35.3.2, ‡Recognition by embroidery.
Nûr al-Dîn and Maryam: *Alf* IV 102-3,-(poem); Burton VIII 314. Chauvin V 52-54 No. 271; *ANE* 98-99 No. 233.□

H35.3.3§, ‡Recognition by unique manner of weaving (carpet-making, basket-making, etc.). See: *DOTTI*.
Nûr al-Dîn and Maryam: *Alf* IV 104; Burton VIII 318. Chauvin V 52-54 No. 271; *ANE* 98-99 No. 233.□

H35.7§, ‡Identification by manner of knocking on door (for admission).
Mercury ¿Alî: *Alf* III 230, 235; Burton VII 179, 188. Chauvin V 248-50 No. 147; *ANE* 301-3 No. 225.□

H43.1§, ‡Recognition by tinkling ('whispering') of jewelry—(usually, bracelets).
Lovers of Basra/Ḍamrah: *Alf* III 210; Burton VII 131. Chauvin V 118 No. 54; *ANE* 273 No. 220;

Budûr and Jubayr ibn ¿Umayr: *Alf* II 242; Burton IV 243. Chauvin VII 93-94 No. 374; *ANE* 243-44 No. 83.□

H49.2.1§, ‡Fool recognized by his long beard. (Cf. W256.8.3.1§, X1727.2§).
Nûr al-Dîn and Maryam: *Alf* IV 94; Burton VIII 298. Chauvin V 52-54 No. 271; *ANE* 98-99 No. 233.□

H49.3§, ‡Poor person recognized as impoverished rich by 'traces of gracious living' still showing on him.
Man Who Never Laughs: *Alf* III 152; Burton VI 160,-("trace of gentle breeding"). Chauvin VIII 47-48 No. 15; *ANE* 285-86 No. 195.□

H62.1.5.1§, ‡Person bewitched into male animal (donkey, dog, monkey, bird, etc.) recognized by daughter (wife) of new owner: she is bashful and veils her face from the male stranger. See: *DOTTI*. (Cf. T380.2.1§).
First Shaykh: Sorceress Wife: *Alf* I 10,-(calf); Burton I 28. Chauvin VII 129-30 No. 396; *ANE* 376-77 No. 5;
Third Shaykh: Transformation by Wife: *Alf* I 13,-(dog); Burton I 36. Chauvin VII 130 No. 398; *ANE* 378 No. 7;
Second Qalandar: Afrit's Wife: *Alf* I 48,-(monkey); Burton I 126. Chauvin V 197-200 No. 116; *ANE* 338-39 No. 16;
Mercury ¿Alî: *Alf* III 243; Burton VII 201. Chauvin V 248-50 No. 147; *ANE* 301-3 No. 225;
Jullanâr of the Sea: *Alf* III 262,-(colorful bird); Burton VII 293. Chauvin V 147-51 No. 73; *ANE* 248-51 No. 227.□

H65.3§, ‡Tell-tale facial expression as indicator of mood-change.
Nûr al-Dîn ¿Alî and Son: *Alf* I 74,-(happiness due to a night of lovemaking); Burton I 227. Chauvin VI 102-6 No. 270; *ANE* 317-19 No. 22;
King ¿Umar al-Nu¿mân and Sons: *Alf* I 85,-(complexion grows dusty-grey); Burton II 127. Chauvin VI 112-24 No. 277; *ANE* 430-34 No. 39;
Hârûn and Arab Girl: *Alf* III 204; Burton VII 110. Chauvin VI 143 No. 300; *ANE* 202 No. 215.□

H69§, Marks of worship (piety, religiosity): physical indicators. (Cf. W4§).
Spy, Third Maiden/¿Umar al-Nu¿mân: *Alf* I 222,-(mark at Resurrection Day); Burton II 203,-(increase of honour). *ANE* 432 No. 39/passim;
King ¿Umar al-Nu¿mân and Sons: *Alf* I 238; Burton II 237-38. Chauvin VI 112-24 No. 277; *ANE* 430-34 No. 39.□

H69.0.1§, ‡Excessive display of one's religiosity (piety) distrusted. See: *DOTTI*. (Cf. J564.0.1§, K2058).
King ¿Umar al-Nu¿mân and Sons: *Alf* I 251,-(*mafâsid al-mutnatti¿în bi al-dîn*), 259; Burton II 264,-(show of devotion to religion that bred not bane), 276. Chauvin VI 112-24 No. 277; *ANE* 430-34 No. 39.□

H70§, Marks of worship (piety, religiosity): character indicators. See: *DOTTI*. (Cf. P617.1§).
King ¿Umar al-Nu¿mân and Sons: *Alf* I 238; Burton II 237-38. Chauvin VI 112-24 No. 277; *ANE* 430-34 No. 39;
House with the Belvedere: *Alf* III 167,-cf.; Burton VI 190. Chauvin VIII 57-58 No. 23; *ANE* 223 No. 203;
Dalîla the Swindler: *Alf* III 213; Burton VII 146. Chauvin V 245-50 No. 147; *ANE* 163-64 No. 224;
Hasan of Basrah: *Alf* III 303,-(general); Burton VIII 9,-(manifest signs of virtue). Chauvin VII 29-35 No. 212A; *ANE* 207-10 No. 230.□

H70.1§, ‡Signs of piety: attire (cleric's vestments and apparel: turban, rosary, etc.). See: *DOTTI*. (Cf. K2058).
Jawdar and His Treacherous Brethren: *Alf* III 198; Burton VI 250. Chauvin V 257-60 No. 154; *ANE* 244-45 No. 209.□

H70.2§, ‡Sign of piety: mildness of manners (frailty).
Jawdar and His Treacherous Brethren: *Alf* III 198; Burton VI 250. Chauvin V 257-60 No. 154; *ANE* 244-45 No. 209.□

H70.2.1§, ‡Sign of piety: improving the environment.
House with the Belvedere: *Alf* III 167,-(clearing the road); Burton VI 190. Chauvin VIII 57-58 No. 23; *ANE* 223 No. 203.□

H70.3.1§, ‡Sign of piety: citing sacred texts.
Birds, Beasts, and Carpenter: *Alf* II 26; Burton III 1. Chauvin II 225-26 No. 1; *ANE* 126 No. 44;
House with the Belvedere: *Alf* III 167,-(*tasbîḥ*); Burton VI 190. Chauvin VIII 57-58 No. 23; *ANE* 223 No. 203.□

H81.2, Clandestine visit of princess to hero betrayed by token. See: *DOTTI*; *GMC*.
Jeweler's Wife and Qamar al-Zamân: *Alf* IV 250; Burton IX 269-70. Chauvin V 212-14 No. 121; *ANE* 345-47 No. 260.□

H82, Identifying token sent with messenger. [(" *'amârah*")].
Devotee Prince: Ascetic's Death: *Alf* II 290,-(ruby); Burton V 113. Chauvin VI 193-94 No. 363; *ANE* 167-68 No. 134.□

H92, Identification by necklace. See: *DOTTI*; *GMC*.
Goldsmith and Cashmere Singer: *Alf* III 150; Burton VI 159. Chauvin VIII 46-47 No. 14; *ANE* 196 No. 194.□

H93, ‡Identification by jewel. See: *DOTTI*.
King ¿Umar al-Nu¿mân and Sons: *Alf* I 208; Burton II 174. Chauvin VI 112-24 No. 277; *ANE* 430-34 No. 39;
Qamar al-Zamân and Budûr: *Alf* II 107; Burton III 298. Chauvin V 204-12 No. 120; *ANE* 341-45 No. 61;
Devotee Prince: Ascetic's Death: *Alf* II 291,-(ruby/*yâqûtah*); Burton V 115. Chauvin VI 193-94 No. 363; *ANE* 167-68 No. 134.□

H94.9.1§, ‡Identification through ring concealed in book.
Qamar al-Zamân and Budûr: *Alf* II 95; Burton III 274. Chauvin V 204-12 No. 120; *ANE* 341-45 No. 61.□

H96, Identification by amulet. See: *DOTTI*; *GMC*.
Nûr al-Dîn ¿Alî and Son: *Alf* I 75; Burton I 229. Chauvin VI 102-6 No. 270; *ANE* 317-19 No. 22.□

H157.6§, ‡Wife (girl) mystically attracted to husband's (beloved's) property.
Qamar al-Zamân and Budûr: *Alf* II 107; Burton III 297,-(by decree of destiny). Chauvin V 204-12 No. 120; *ANE* 341-45 No. 61.□

H151.8, Husband attracted by wife's power of healing: recognition follows. See: *DOTTI*.
¿Abdallah ibn Fâḍil: Treacherous Brothers: *Alf* IV 287; Burton IX 348. Chauvin V 2-4 No. 2; *ANE* 63-65 No. 261.□

H175.7§, Blood-relative mystically recognized: 'Blood's yearning,' 'Blood's howling'. See: *DOTTI*; *GMC*. (Cf. T160.0.4§).
King ¿Umar al-Nu¿mân and Sons: *Alf* II 8,-(*al-'arwâḥ/al-'ashbâḥ*); Burton III 88,-("soul yearned to soul and body longed for body"). Chauvin VI 112-24 No. 277; *ANE* 430-34 No. 39;
Nûr al-Dîn ¿Alî and Son: *Alf* I 77, 80,-(son-father); Burton I 234,-("blood drew to blood"). Chauvin VI 102-6 No. 270; *ANE* 317-19 No. 22;
King ¿Umar al-Nu¿mân and Sons: *Alf* I 199,-(*ḥanna al-dam*), II 12; Burton II 154,-(blood yearned to blood), III 97. Chauvin VI 112-24 No. 277; *ANE* 430-34 No. 39.□

H213.1§, ‡Person suspected of amorous intrigue asked to kill or maim partner in infidelity as proof of innocence. Refusal would indicate guilt.
Second Qalandar: Afrit's Wife: *Alf* I 46; Burton I 121. Chauvin V 197-200 No. 116; *ANE* 338-39 No. 16.□

H249§, ‡Oath by the sacred as test of truth. (Cf. M119.0.1§, M119.9§).
Craft and Malice of Women/Frame: *Alf* III 177; Burton VI 212. Chauvin VIII 33-34 No. 1; *ANE* 160-61 No. 181.□

H257, Holiness of saint tested: asked to perform miracles. See: *DOTTI*. (Cf. V220.0.6§).
King ¿Umar al-Nu¿mân and Sons: *Alf* I 238,-(ruse); Burton II 237. Chauvin VI 112-24 No. 277; *ANE* 430-34 No. 39.□

H258§, Strength of faith (belief) in God tested. See: *DOTTI*; *GMC*. (Cf. B250.2§).
Spider Upbraids Wind: *Alf* IV 146-47,-(spider's); Burton IX 59-60. Chauvin II 220 No. 152/10; *ANE* 398 No. 245.□

... demands to prevent marriage. See: *ANE*; *DOTTI*; *GMC*.

Nûr al-Dîn ¿Alî and Son: *Alf* I 65; Burton I 196. Chauvin VI 102-6 No. 270; *ANE* 317-19 No. 22.□

H332.1.1.1§, ‡Maiden will marry only the man who can defeat her in combat (duel). See: *DOTTI*.
King ¿Umar al-Nu¿mân and Sons: *Alf* II 5; Burton III 82. Chauvin VI 112-24 No. 277; *ANE* 430-34 No. 39;
Bahrâm and Datmâ: *Alf* III 164; Burton VI 184. Chauvin VIII 54-57 No. 22; *ANE* 114-15 No. 202.□

H332.3, ‡Suitor test: duel with father-in-law.
Ebony Horse: *Alf* II 257; Burton V 12. Chauvin V 221-31 No. 130; *ANE* 172-74 No. 103.□

H337.1§, ‡Suitor task: to steal from magician (ogre). See: *DOTTI*. (Cf. T52.0.2§).
Mercury ¿Alî: *Alf* III 240; Burton VII 197. Chauvin V 248-50 No. 147; *ANE* 301-3 No. 225.□

H413.7§, ‡Special powers of chaste woman: healing the sick. See: *DOTTI*. (Cf. D1714.1.2§, V221).
Jewish qâḍî and His Devout Wife: *Alf* III 10; Burton V 256. Chauvin VI 154-55 No. 321; *ANE* 242 No. 163.□

H420.1§, ‡Tests of love: wife (fiancee) departs and asks to be followed to her own parental home. (Cf. R134.1§, T198.3.1§, T298.0.1.1§).
Jânshâh: *Alf* III 58,-(Jawhar's fortress); Burton V 357,-(at "Castle of Jewels"). Chauvin VII 39-44 No. 153; *ANE* 238-41 No. 178.□

H466.1, Feigned absence to test wife's faithfulness. See: *DOTTI*.
Shahriyâr and Shâhzamân: *Alf* I 3; Burton I 9. Chauvin V 188-91 No. 111; *ANE* 370-71 No. 1.□

H486.6.1§, ‡Host's failure to eat with guest indicates that host is a bastard. See: *DOTTI*. (Cf. P335.1§, W103§, W251§).
¿Alî Shâr and Zumurrud: *Alf* II 222; Burton IV 201. Chauvin V 89-91 No. 28; *ANE* 100-1 No. 82.□

H502, ‡Test of learning. See: *DOTTI*.
King ¿Umar al-Nu¿mân and Sons: *Alf* I 171-72,-(poem about lovers); Burton II 102. Chauvin VI 112-24 No. 277; *ANE* 430-34 No. 39;
Tâj al-Mulûk: *Alf* I 293,-(poem about bathhouse); Burton III 19. Chauvin V 126-28 No. 60; *ANE* 406-8 No. 40.□

H502.0.1§, ‡Comprehensive examination: all fields of knowledge tested. See: *DOTTI*.
Tawaddud: Slavegirl Sold and Regained: *Alf* II 305-19, III 7; Burton V 193-245. Chauvin VII 117-19 No. 387; *ANE* 408-10 No. 157.□

H502.0.1.1§, ‡Display of comprehensive knowledge. (Cf. C549§).
Nuzhat al-Zamân Tested/¿Umar al-Nu¿mân: *Alf* I 200-206; Burton II 154. Chauvin VI 116, n.1/passim No. 277; *ANE* 432,/passim No. 39;
Tawaddud: Slavegirl Sold and Regained: *Alf* II 306-19, III 7; Burton V 193-245. Chauvin VII 117-19 No. 387; *ANE* 408-10 No. 157.□

H502.1, ‡Test of religious learning. See: *DOTTI*. (Cf. A102.1.2.1§, A630.2§, H1573.4.3§).
Tawaddud: Slavegirl Sold and Regained: *Alf* II 306-10; Burton V 195-206. Chauvin VII 117-19 No. 387; *ANE* 408-10 No. 157.□

H503, ‡Test of musical ability. See: *DOTTI*. (Cf. H509.4).
Mock Caliph/¿Alî al-Jawharî: *Alf* II 198; Burton IV 144. Chauvin V 99-100 No. 174; *ANE* 304-5 No. 73;
Ishâq al-Mûṣilî and Merchant's Singer: *Alf* II 296,-cf.; Burton V 131. Chauvin VI 59 No. 225; *ANE* 233 No. 142;
Tawaddud: Slavegirl Sold and Regained: *Alf* II 305,-cf.; Burton V 244. Chauvin VII 117-19 No. 387; *ANE* 408-10 No. 157.□

H504.4§, ‡Contest in cooking (baking). See: *DOTTI*.
Nûr al-Dîn ¿Alî and Son: *Alf* I 81; Burton I 242-43. Chauvin VI 102-6 No. 270; *ANE* 317-19 No. 22.□

H507, Wit combat [(duel)]. Test in repartee. See: *GMC*. (Cf. W47§).
¿Alî bin Ṭâhir and Mu'nis: *Alf* II 303; Burton V 164. Chauvin VI 154 No. 319; *ANE* 101 No. 153.□

H509.3, ‡Chess game as test.
Tawaddud: Slavegirl Sold and Regained: *Alf* III 7; Burton V 243. Chauvin VII 117-19 No. 387; *ANE* 408-10 No. 157;

Ibrâhîm and Jamîlah: *Alf* IV 220; Burton IX 210. Chauvin VI 52-53 No. 218; *ANE* 227-29 No. 258.□

H509.4, Test of poetic ability. See: *DOTTI*.
King ¿Umar al-Nu¿mân and Sons: *Alf* I 171-72; Burton II 102-3. Chauvin VI 112-24 No. 277; *ANE* 430-34 No. 39;
Tâj al-Mulûk: *Alf* I 293,-cf./(memory/poem about bathhouse); Burton III 19. Chauvin V 126-28 No. 60; *ANE* 406-8 No. 40;
Hârûn and Arab Girl: *Alf* III 203; Burton VII 108. Chauvin VI 143 No. 300; *ANE* 202 No. 215.□

H509.4.0.1§, ‡Poetry contest: prize to be awarded for best verse (ode). (Cf. P807.1.3§, P427.7.1).
Basra Girls in Poetry Contest: *Alf* III 205-6; Burton VII 111-13. Chauvin VI 144 No. 301; *ANE* 107-8 No. 216.□

H509.4.4.1§, ‡Ability to alter one aspect of poem while maintaining rest as test. (E.g., change end rhyme, keep meaning).
Hârûn and Arab Girl: *Alf* III 203-4; Burton VII 108. Chauvin VI 143 No. 300; *ANE* 202 No. 215.□

H530, Riddles. See: *DOTTI*; *GMC*.
Tawaddud: Slavegirl Sold and Regained: *Alf* II 318-19; Burton V 226. Chauvin VII 117-19 No. 387; *ANE* 408-10 No. 157.□

H548, Riddle [(riddling)] contest. See: *DOTTI*; *GMC*.
Tawaddud: Slavegirl Sold and Regained: *Alf* III 4-7,-(riddling questions); Burton V 227-42. Chauvin VII 117-19 No. 387; *ANE* 408-10 No. 157.□

H561.5, ‡King and clever minister. King propounds riddles and questions to his clever minister. See: *DOTTI*.
King Jalî¿âd and Shimâs: *Alf* IV 134,-cf./(dream); Burton IX 33. Chauvin VI 9-11 No. 184; *ANE* 237-38 No. 236.□

H580, Enigmatic statements. Apparently senseless remarks (or acts) interpreted figuratively prove wise. (Cf. V384.0.1§, Z95.0.1§). See: *GMC*.
Mercury ¿Alî: *Alf* III 227; Burton VII 172. Chauvin V 248-50 No. 147; *ANE* 301-3 No. 225.□

H591, Extraordinary actions explained. See: *DOTTI*; *PSAE*.
¿Abdallah ibn Fâḍil: Treacherous Brothers: *Alf* IV 268; Burton IX 310. Chauvin V 2-4 No. 2; *ANE* 63-65 No. 261.□

H591.4§, ‡Eccentric treatment of animal explained.
¿Abdallah ibn Fâḍil: Treacherous Brothers: *Alf* IV 268; Burton IX 310. Chauvin V 2-4 No. 2; *ANE* 63-65 No. 261.□

H591.4.1§, ‡Simultaneous cruel and kind treatments of dog(s) explained. See: *DOTTI*.
Porter and Ladies of Baghdad: *Alf* I 38; Burton I 97-98. Chauvin V 251-52 No. 148; *ANE* 324-26 No. 14;
¿Abdallah ibn Fâḍil: Treacherous Brothers: *Alf* IV 268; Burton IX 306. Chauvin V 2-4 No. 2; *ANE* 63-65 No. 261.□

H591.4.4.1§, ‡Wearing costume designated for specific social order (class, profession) by non-member explained. (Cf. P13.9.3.3.1§).
Abû al-Ḥasan al-Khorâsânî (and Caliph's Favorite): *Alf* IV 230-37; Burton IX 232ff. Chauvin V 218-20 No. 129; *ANE* 68-69 No. 259.□

H591.5§, ‡Failure to observe rules of courtesy (greeting, welcoming) explained. See: *DOTTI*.
Hishâm and Arab Youth: *Alf* II 184; Burton IV 101. Chauvin V 288 No. 172; *ANE* 222-23 No. 68.□

H592.7§, ‡Predator (lion, wolf, etc.) in another man's garden (field): chieftain (king) who seeks to seduce man's wife. See: *DOTTI*.
King Dissuaded by Virtuous Wife: *Alf* II 294; Burton V 122. Chauvin VII 120-21 No. 391; *ANE* 260-61 No. 138.□

H597§, ‡Enigmatic statement about a female (woman, girl). See: *DOTTI*.
King Dissuaded by Virtuous Wife: *Alf* II 294; Burton V 122. Chauvin VII 120-21 No. 391; *ANE* 260-61 No. 138.□

H597.1§, ‡Enigmatic statement: the unplowed (uncultivated) field or garden. (Female deprived of conjugal relations). See: *DOTTI*. (Cf. T185.3§, Z168.1§, Z197.3.4§).

King Dissuaded by Virtuous Wife: *Alf* II 294; Burton V 122. Chauvin VII 120-21 No. 391; *ANE* 260-61 No. 138.□

H607.3, Princess declares her love through sign language, not understood. See: *ANE*; *DOTTI*; *GMC*.
¿Azîz and ¿Azîzah: *Alf* I 270; Burton II 300. Chauvin V 144-45 No. 71; *ANE* 111-13 No. 41.□

H659.13.1, What is the most pleasant? Love [(sexual intercourse)]. See: *DOTTI*; *GMC*. (Cf. T1.3.1§).
Tawaddud: Slavegirl Sold and Regained: *Alf* III 6,-cf./(temporary pleasure); Burton V 242. Chauvin VII 117-19 No. 387; *ANE* 408-10 No. 157.□

H607.3.1§, ‡Girl declares her intentions by means of objects she leaves with beloved: not understood. See: *DOTTI*. (Cf. T55.14§).
¿Azîz and ¿Azîzah: *Alf* I 275,-(salt, coal), 277,-(cube of bone, tip-cat stick, stone of green date, carob pod), 278,-(sharp razor, iron coin); Burton II 312-15. Chauvin V 144-45 No. 71; *ANE* 111-13 No. 41;
Jeweler's Wife and Qamar al-Zamân: *Alf* IV 250,-(knife/kill); Burton IX 269-70. Chauvin V 212-14 No. 121; *ANE* 345-47 No. 260.□

H611.2, Sign message sent by girl to enamored prince. Interpreted by prince's friend. See: *DOTTI*.
Jeweler's Wife and Qamar al-Zamân: *Alf* IV 248; Burton IX 269-70. Chauvin V 212-14 No. 121; *ANE* 345-47 No. 260.□

H614.5§, ‡Explanation of enigmatic phenomenon: peculiar personal appearance. See: *DOTTI*. (Cf. S186.9.1§).
First Qalandar: Brother-Sister Incest: *Alf* I 39; Burton I 104. Chauvin V 196-97 No. 115; *ANE* 337-38 No. 15;
Second Qalandar: Afrit's Wife: *Alf* I 42; Burton I 113-39. Chauvin V 197-200 No. 116; *ANE* 338-39 No. 16;
Third Qalandar: Magnetic Mountain: *Alf* I 51; Burton I 139-61. Chauvin V 200-3 No. 117; *ANE* 340-41 No. 18;
Mock Caliph/¿Alî al-Jawharî: *Alf* II 195ff.; Burton IV 139-48. Chauvin V 99-100 No. 174; *ANE* 304-5 No. 73;
Man of Upper Egypt and Frankish Wife: Alf IV 16?,-(text missing); Burton IX 19. Chauvin V 240 No. 140; *ANE*: No. 234.□

H614.6§, ‡Explanation of enigmatic phenomenon: peculiar behavior in public (e.g., laughing, weeping, waiting, or the like).
Jeweler's Wife and Qamar al-Zamân: *Alf* IV 241; Burton IX 255. Chauvin V 212-14 No. 121; *ANE* 345-47 No. 260.□

H639§, ‡What is the most frightful?. See: *DOTTI*.
Spy, Second Maiden/¿Umar al-Nu¿mân: *Alf* I 221,-cf.; Burton II 201. *ANE* 432 No. 39/passim.□

H640.1§, ‡Most noble trait of character: *al-ḥayâ'* (proper bashfulness—may also be labeled "*¿iffah, sharaf*" (chastity, honor). See: *DOTTI*. (Cf. Ẉ170.1§).
Nuzhat al-Zamân Tested/¿Umar al-Nu¿mân: *Alf* I 201; Burton II 159,-(modesty). Chauvin VI 116, n.1/passim No. 277; *ANE* 432,/passim No. 39.□

H648.4§, ‡What is the best lie? A lie that wards off harm and brings about benefit.
King Jalî¿âd and Shimâs: *Alf* IV 160; Burton IX 87. Chauvin VI 9-11 No. 184; *ANE* 237-38 No. 236.□

H649.1§, ‡What is the worst truth? Conceit due to power or property. (Cf. W166§).
King Jalî¿âd and Shimâs: *Alf* IV 160; Burton IX 87. Chauvin VI 9-11 No. 184; *ANE* 237-38 No. 236.□

H679.7.1§, ‡What is faster than an arrow? (Evil Eye).
Tawaddud: Slavegirl Sold and Regained: *Alf* III 6; Burton V 242-("swifter than poison"). Chauvin VII 117-19 No. 387; *ANE* 408-10 No. 157.□

H679.8.1§, ‡What is sharper than cutting blade (sword, knife, etc.)? (Tongue). (Cf. W47.1.3§).
Tawaddud: Slavegirl Sold and Regained: *Alf* III 6; Burton V 241-42. Chauvin VII 117-19 No. 387; *ANE* 408-10 No. 157.□

H709.1§, ‡Puzzles requiring arithmetic ability (adding, subtracting, multiplying, etc.).
Tawaddud: Slavegirl Sold and Regained: *Alf* III 4; Burton V 236. Chauvin VII 117-19 No. 387; *ANE* 408-10 No. 157.□

H709.1.1§, ‡Puzzle: part of a flock of pigeons alighted on tree while another alighted on ground. The ones on the tree said to the ones on the ground "If one of you joined us on top your number becomes one third of all of us, but if one of us joined you on the ground your number becomes one half of all of us." How many pigeons were in the flock? (12: 7 on tree, 5 on ground).
Tawaddud: Slavegirl Sold and Regained: *Alf* III 4; Burton V 237. Chauvin VII 117-19 No. 387; *ANE* 408-10 No. 157.□

H724§, ‡Riddle: when given to eat (fed), she lives; when given to drink, she dies. (Fire).
Tawaddud: Slavegirl Sold and Regained: *Alf* III 5; Burton V 240. Chauvin VII 117-19 No. 387; *ANE* 408-10 No. 157.□

H766§, ‡Riddle: two lovers denied pleasure of intercourse (union) despite embracing each other by night while standing guard, but separating in morning to stay apart. (A door's two panels).
Tawaddud: Slavegirl Sold and Regained: *Alf* III 5-6,-(poem); Burton V 240. Chauvin VII 117-19 No. 387; *ANE* 408-10 No. 157.□

H767.4§, ‡Riddle: what is death while still alive? Answer: poverty. (Cf. U69.3§).
Tawaddud: Slavegirl Sold and Regained: *Alf* III 7; Burton V 242. Chauvin VII 117-19 No. 387; *ANE* 408-10 No. 157.□

H776§, ‡Why was water with impurities given to the thirsty king to drink? (So as to drink slowly: more safe).
Anûshirawân and Village Damsel: *Alf* II 285; Burton V 88. Chauvin VI 26-27 No. 198; *ANE* 106 No. 121.□

H808§, ‡Riddles (puzzles) based on legal principles—(usually religious laws, *sharî¿ah*). (Cf. H810).
Tawaddud: Slavegirl Sold and Regained: *Alf* III 4,-(sinful-legitimate regard); Burton V 235-36. Chauvin VII 117-19 No. 387; *ANE* 408-10 No. 157.□

H808.1§, ‡The cycle of the sinful-legitimate amorous regard (glance). A man looked at someone else's slave-girl in the morning (sinful), at noon he purchased her for himself (became legitimate), in the afternoon he freed her (became sinful), at sunset he married her (became legitimate), in late evening he divorced her (became sinful), in the morning he restored her (became legitimate). (Cf. T481.0.2§).
Tawaddud: Slavegirl Sold and Regained: *Alf* III 4; Burton V 235-36. Chauvin VII 117-19 No. 387; *ANE* 408-10 No. 157.□

H810, ‡Riddles based on the Bible or legend. See: *GMC*. (Cf. H808§).
Tawaddud: Slavegirl Sold and Regained: *Alf* III 4; Burton V 236. Chauvin VII 117-19 No. 387; *ANE* 408-10 No. 157.□

H812.1§, ‡Riddle: with what did Adam and Eve cover their genitals on Earth? (Fig leaves).
Bulûqiya: *Alf* III 74,-cf./(non-riddle); Burton V 384. Chauvin VII 54 No. 77; *ANE* 130-32 No. 177.□

H816.1§, ‡Who is the female created from male? (Eve from Adam).
Tawaddud: Slavegirl Sold and Regained: *Alf* III 5; Burton V 238. Chauvin VII 117-19 No. 387; *ANE* 408-10 No. 157.□

H816.2§, ‡Who is the male created from female? (Christ from Mary).
Tawaddud: Slavegirl Sold and Regained: *Alf* III 5; Burton V 238. Chauvin VII 117-19 No. 387; *ANE* 408-10 No. 157.□

H821, ‡Riddle: what was the walking tomb with the living tenant? (Jonah and the whale). See: *GMC*.
Tawaddud: Slavegirl Sold and Regained: *Alf* III 4; Burton V 236. Chauvin VII 117-19 No. 387; *ANE* 408-10 No. 157.□

H830§, ‡Riddles (riddling questions) about things known only to God. (Cf. A102.1.2.1§, H502.1).
Tawaddud: Slavegirl Sold and Regained: *Alf* III 2; Burton V 230. Chauvin VII 117-19 No. 387; *ANE* 408-10 No. 157.□

H845.1.1§, ‡Riddling question: what male lays eggs. Answer: [Male] "snake"/*shujâ¿* (lit.: 'valiant'). (Cf. Z95.0.1§).
Tawaddud: Slavegirl Sold and Regained: *Alf* II 318,-(*shujâ¿*/male snake); Burton V 226,-("What serpent layeth eggs?" "The Su'ban [i.e., *thu¿bân*] or dragon"). Chauvin VII 117-19 No. 387; *ANE* 408-10 No. 157.□

H887.2§, ‡Riddle: what does a bird say?. See: *DOTTI*. (Cf. W4.2§).
Hermit and Pigeons: *Alf* II 27,-(pigeon); Burton III 126. Chauvin II 226 No. 2; *ANE* 221 No. 45/pt.1.□

H887.2.5§, ‡Riddle: what does a dove (pigeon) say?.
Hermit and Pigeons: *Alf* II 27,-cf.; Burton III 126. Chauvin II 226 No. 2; *ANE* 221 No. 45/pt. 1.□

H887.3§, ‡Riddle: what does an animal say?.
Birds, Beasts, and Carpenter: *Alf* II 26,-(deer); Burton III 125. Chauvin II 225-26 No. 1; *ANE* 126 No. 44.□

H901.1, Heads placed on stakes for failure in performance of task. See: *DOTTI*; *GMC*. (Cf. Q421.1).
Qamar al-Zamân and Budûr: *Alf* II 94; Burton III 256. Chauvin V 204-12 No. 120; *ANE* 341-45 No. 61.□

H911, Tasks assigned at the suggestion of jealous rivals. See: *DOTTI*.
Abû Qîr and Abû Ṣîr: *Alf* IV 193; Burton IX 155. Chauvin V 15-17 No. 10; *ANE* 75-77 No. 255.□

H950.1§, Task evaded by subterfuge: procrastination. See: *DOTTI*.
Abû Qîr and Abû Ṣîr: *Alf* IV 183; Burton IX 134-37. Chauvin V 15-17 No. 10; *ANE* 75-77 No. 255.□

H1078§, ‡Task: bringing large number of insects (fleas, lice) in male-and-female pairs. (Cf. K199.2.1§).
Sandal-wood Merchant and Sharpers: *Alf* III 175; Burton VI 205. Chauvin VIII 60-62 No. 26; *ANE* 359-60 No. 205.□

H1133.3, ‡Task: building castle in sea. (Cf. F771.2.1).
King Jalî¿âd and Shimâs: *Alf* IV 171; Burton IX 111. Chauvin VI 9 No. 184; *ANE* 237-38 No. 236.□

H1142.3, ‡Task: drinking the sea dry: countertask: stop all the rivers.
Sandal-wood Merchant and Sharpers: *Alf* III 174,-cf.; Burton VI 204. Chauvin VIII 60-62 No. 26; *ANE* 359-60 No. 205.□

H1142.4§, ‡Task: drinking the sea dry; countertask: holding the sea mouth [as if a water skin].
Sandal-wood Merchant and Sharpers: *Alf* III 175; Burton VI 206. Chauvin VIII 60-62 No. 26; *ANE* 359-60 No. 205.□

H1151.27.1§, ‡Task: stealing purse of gold protected by alarm system.
Mercury ¿Alî: *Alf* III 237; Burton VII 190. Chauvin V 248-50 No. 147; *ANE* 301-3 No. 225.□

H1151.27.2§, ‡Task: stealing valuable garment.
Mercury ¿Alî: *Alf* III 240; Burton VII 197. Chauvin V 248-50 No. 147; *ANE* 301-3 No. 225.□

H1171§, ‡Task: fetch bottle(s) containing imprisoned demon(s). See: *DOTTI*. (Cf. D2177.1).
Jinn Imprisoned in Flasks: *Alf* III 122; Burton VI 83-101. Chauvin VII 113 No. 380=no/text; *ANE* 146 No. 180;
City of Brass: *Alf* III 138; Burton VI 119. Chauvin V 32-35 No. 16; *ANE* 146-50 No. 180.□

H1181, Task: raising hidden treasure. See: *DOTTI*; *GMC*.
City of Brass: *Alf* III 132,-cf./(general); Burton VI 109. Chauvin V 32-35 No. 16; *ANE* 146-50 No. 180;
Jawdar and His Treacherous Brethren: *Alf* III 183; Burton VI 223. Chauvin V 257-60 No. 154; *ANE* 244-45 No. 209.□

H1182, Task: letting king hear something that neither he nor his subjects have ever heard. [A loan]. See: *DOTTI*; *GMC*. (Cf. P775.2.2.1§).
Budûr and Jubayr ibn ¿Umayr: *Alf* II 235,-cf./(strange/unique occurrence); Burton IV 230. Chauvin VII 93-94 No. 374; *ANE* 243-44 No. 83;
Man from Yaman and Six Salve-girls: Flyting: *Alf* II 244,-cf.; Burton IV 245. Chauvin VI 151 No. 313; *ANE* 289-90 No. 84;
Ibn Sabâ'ik/Sayf al-Mulûk: *Alf* III 271,-(story); Burton VII 309-10. Chauvin VII 65 No. 348/pt.; *ANE* 309-10 No. 228.□

H1199.2, Task: healing sick person. See: *DOTTI*. (Cf. Q382.1§).
Conversion of Princess by Khawwâṣ: *Alf* III 15; Burton V 284. Chauvin V 239 No. 139; *ANE* 145 No. 171.□

H1219.9§, ‡Quest assigned by umpire (judge).
Jawdar and His Treacherous Brethren: *Alf* III 183; Burton VI 222. Chauvin V 257-60 No. 154; *ANE* 244-45 No. 209.□

H1219.9.1§, ‡Article of dispute is to be awarded to the party who can bring certain object(s).
Jawdar and His Treacherous Brethren: *Alf* III 183; Burton VI 222. Chauvin V 257-60 No. 154; *ANE* 244-45 No. 209.□

H1229.5§, ‡Quest undertaken: acquiring bride wealth (*mahr*). See: *DOTTI*. (Cf. P475.0.2§, T52.0.2.3.4§).
King ¿Umar al-Nu¿mân and Sons: *Alf* II 3,-(robbery); Burton III 78. Chauvin VI 112-24 No. 277; *ANE* 430-34 No. 39.□

H1258§, ‡Quest for ultimate (sacred) truth.
Bulûqiya: *Alf* III 23; Burton V 305ff. Chauvin VII 54 No. 77; *ANE* 130-32 No. 177.□

H1258.1§, ‡Quest for future sacred deliverer of humanity. (Cf. M363.5§, V215§, V515.1).
Bulûqiya: *Alf* III 23; Burton V 304. Chauvin VII 54 No. 77; *ANE* 130-32 No. 177.□

H1292.21§, ‡(Question on quest): Why has the man been sitting (residing) between two graves? Answer: He is awaiting his own death, his beloved is buried in one and he wants to be buried in the other. See: *DOTTI*.
Jânshâh: *Alf* III 38; Burton V 327-28. Chauvin VII 39-44 No. 153; *ANE* 238-41 No. 178.□

H1311.1, King seeks one richer (more magnificent) than himself. See: *DOTTI*; *GMC*.
Nuzhat al-Zamân Tested/¿Umar al-Nu¿mân: *Alf* I 206; Burton II 171. Chauvin VI 116, n.1/passim No. 277; *ANE* 432,/passim No. 39.□

H1311.1.2§, Chieftain seeks one who is more chivalrous than himself. See: *GMC*.
Mercury ¿Alî: *Alf* III 227; Burton VII 173. Chauvin V 248-50 No. 147; *ANE* 301-3 No. 225.□

H1314§, Quest for greater grief. See: *DOTTI*; *GMC*. (Cf. J886§, W30.5§).
Shahriyâr and Shâhzamân: *Alf* I 2-3,-(same grief/calamity); Burton I 10. Chauvin V 188-91 No. 111; *ANE* 370-71 No. 1.□

H1319, ‡Quest for the unique—miscellaneous.
Abû Muḥammad Lazybones: *Alf* II 206-7,-(jewel); Burton IV 162. Chauvin VI 64-67 No. 233; *ANE* 71-73 No. 78.□

H1319.7§, Quest for the strangest (most bizarre) life experience (story). See: *DOTTI*. (Cf. H1314§, H1382.2).
Ensorcelled Prince/Husband: *Alf* I 26; Burton I 69-82. Chauvin VI 56-58 No. 222; *ANE* 176 No. 13; **Man from Yaman and Six Salve-girls: Flyting**: *Alf* II 244,-(never heard); Burton IV 245. Chauvin VI 151 No. 313; *ANE* 289-90 No. 84.□

H1319.8.1§, ‡Quest for the largest jewel. (Cf. P13.9.3.1.1§).
Abû Muḥammad Lazybones: *Alf* II 206-7; Burton IV 162. Chauvin VI 64-67 No. 233; *ANE* 71-73 No. 78.□

H1321.1, Quest for Water of Life (which will resuscitate). See: *DOTTI*; *GMC*.
Bulûqiya: *Alf* III 28,-cf.; Burton V 309. Chauvin VII 54 No. 77; *ANE* 130-32 No. 177.□

H1333.2.1, ‡Quest for plant of immortality.
Bulûqiya: *Alf* III 28; Burton V 310. Chauvin VII 54 No. 77; *ANE* 130-32 No. 177.□

H1373.1§, ‡Quest for bottled jinni or demon. (Cf. R181).
City of Brass: *Alf* III 132,-(City of Brass); Burton VI 101. Chauvin V 32-35 No. 16; *ANE* 146-50 No. 180.□

H1376.6, Quest for happiness. See: *DOTTI*; *GMC*.
Bulûqiya: *Alf* III 22-23,-cf./(truth); Burton V 304-5. Chauvin VII 54 No. 77; *ANE* 130-32 No. 177.□

H1376.7.1§, ‡Failure on quest to gain immortality—(e.g., Gilgamesh, Alexander, etc.). See: *DOTTI*.
Bulûqiya: *Alf* III 27-28; Burton V 312. Chauvin VII 54 No. 77; *ANE* 130-32 No. 177.□

H1376.10§, Quest: learning women's wiles. See: *DOTTI*; *GMC*.
Craft and Malice of Women/Frame: *Alf* III 139,-cf./(task/proving); Burton VI 139ff. Chauvin VIII 33-34 No. 1; *ANE* 160-61 No. 181.□

H1381.2.2.1.1, Boy twitted with illegitimacy seeks unknown father. See: *ANE*; *DOTTI*; *GMC*.
Nûr al-Dîn ¿Alî and Son: *Alf* I 76; Burton I 231-32. Chauvin VI 102-6 No. 270; *ANE* 317-19 No. 22.□

H1381.3.1.2.1, ‡Quest for unknown woman whose picture has aroused man's love. See: *DOTTI*. (Cf. T11.2).

Goldsmith and Cashmere Singer: *Alf* III 150; Burton VI 156. Chauvin VIII 46-47 No. 14; *ANE* 196 No. 194;
Sayf al-Mulûk: *Alf* III 279; Burton VII 330ff. Chauvin VII 64-73 No. 348; *ANE* 362-64 No. 229;
Ibrâhîm and Jamîlah: *Alf* IV 219; Burton IX 208. Chauvin VI 52-53 No. 218; *ANE* 227-29 No. 258.□

H1381.3.1.5§, ‡Quest for bride of honorable (noble) descent (*'aṣîlah*, of *ḥasab* and *nasab*). See: *DOTTI*. (Cf. P208.9.1§, U135.0.1§).

Jullanâr of the Sea: *Alf* III 255,-(to match groom's); Burton VII 279. Chauvin V 147-51 No. 73; *ANE* 248-51 No. 227.□

H1382.2, Quest for unknown story (epic). (Cf. H1319.7§, P470.0.1§).

Ibn Sabâ'ik/Sayf al-Mulûk: *Alf* III 271; Burton VII 3309-10. Chauvin VII 65 No. 348/pt.; *ANE* 309-10 No. 228.□

H1385.3, ‡Quest for vanished wife (mistress). See: *DOTTI*.

¿Alî ibn Bakkâr: *Alf* II 58,-cf./(stolen); Burton III 198. Chauvin V 153 No. 76; *ANE* 92-93 No. 60;
Jânshâh: *Alf* III 58; Burton V 357. Chauvin VII 39-44 No. 153; *ANE* 238-41 No. 178;
Hasan of Basrah: *Alf* IV 12ff.; Burton VIII 61. Chauvin VII 29-35 No. 212A; *ANE* 207-10 No. 230;
Nûr al-Dîn and Maryam: *Alf* IV 107; Burton VIII 323. Chauvin V 52-54 No. 271; *ANE* 98-99 No. 233.□

H1385.3.13§, ‡Quest for vanished son.

Qamar al-Zamân and Budûr: *Alf* II 103-4; Burton III 290. Chauvin V 204-12 No. 120; *ANE* 341-45 No. 61.□

H1385.4, Quest for vanished husband. See: *DOTTI*. (Cf. N349.4§).

Qamar al-Zamân and Budûr: *Alf* II 99; Burton III 282. Chauvin V 204-12 No. 120; *ANE* 341-45 No. 61.□

H1385.5, Quest for vanished lover. See: *DOTTI*; *GMC*.

Qamar al-Zamân and Budûr: *Alf* II 88-90; Burton III 259-62. Chauvin V 204-12 No. 120; *ANE* 341-45 No. 61.□

H1385.5.1§, ‡Quest for vanished beloved (maiden). See: *DOTTI*. (Cf. T44§).

Uns al-Wujûd and al-Ward: *Alf* II 272; Burton V 39. Chauvin VI 127-29 No. 282; *ANE* 438 No. 104.□

H1385.6, Quest for lost sister. See: *DOTTI*.

King ¿Umar al-Nu¿mân and Sons: *Alf* I 191,-(poem); Burton II 137. Chauvin VI 112-24 No. 277; *ANE* 430-34 No. 39.□

H1387§, Quest for explanations of eccentric (enigmatic) occurrences observed by chieftain reveals tragic life experiences. See: *DOTTI*; *GMC*. (Cf. P14.19.1§, U115).

Jânshâh: *Alf* III 38, 73,-cf./(explanation given); Burton V 327-28, 381. Chauvin VII 39-44 No. 153; *ANE* 238-41 No. 178;
Abû al-Ḥasan al-Khorâsânî (and Caliph's Favorite): *Alf* IV 230,-cf.; Burton IX 231ff. Chauvin V 218-20 No. 129; *ANE* 68-69 No. 259;
¿Abdallah ibn Fâḍil: Treacherous Brothers: *Alf* IV 267; Burton IX 306. Chauvin V 2-4 No. 2; *ANE* 63-65 No. 261.□

H1398.1§, ‡Quest for the enchanter (bewitcher, deliverer of magic spell). (Cf. D791.2.0.1§).

Second Shaykh: Treacherous Brothers: *Alf* I 13; Burton I 35. Chauvin V 6 No. 397; *ANE* 377-78 No. 6.□

H1423, ‡Fear test: fighting with spirits [(demons)]. (Cf. E422.9.2.1§).

Jawdar and His Treacherous Brethren: *Alf* III 186,-cf.; Burton VI 229. Chauvin V 257-60 No. 154; *ANE* 244-45 No. 209.□

H1553, Test of patience. See: *DOTTI*. (Cf. H1573.9.1§).

Spider Upbraids Wind: *Alf* IV 147,-(spider's); Burton IX 59. Chauvin II 220 No. 152/10; *ANE* 398 No. 245.□

H1558.7, Test of friendship: the power of money. Spendthrift loses his friends in poverty. See: *DOTTI*; *GMC*.

Anîs al-Jalîs: *Alf* I 130,-cf./(poem); Burton II 14. Chauvin V 120-24 No. 58; *ANE* 316-17 No. 35;
¿Alî Shâr and Zumurrud: *Alf* II 218; Burton IV 191. Chauvin V 89-91 No. 28; *ANE* 100-1 No. 82.□

H1561.7.1§, ‡Test of valor: warrior maiden masks as man and attacks adversary (whom she admires).
King ¿Umar al-Nu¿mân and Sons: *Alf* I 179-80; Burton II 118. Chauvin VI 112-24 No. 277; *ANE* 430-34 No. 39.□

H1562.9, ‡Test of strength: wrestling.
King ¿Umar al-Nu¿mân and Sons: *Alf* I 166; Burton II 87. Chauvin VI 112-24 No. 277; *ANE* 430-34 No. 39.□

H1565, Test of gratitude. See: *DOTTI*; *GMC*.
Spider Upbraids Wind: *Alf* IV 147,-(spider's); Burton IX 59. Chauvin II 220 No. 152/10; *ANE* 398 No. 245.□

H1573.2.1, Magic [(supernatural)] manifestation required as proof in test of saintliness. (Cf. V220.0.6§).
Devotee Prince: Ascetic's Death: *Alf* II 290,-cf./(bird obeys saintly youth); Burton V 111-12. Chauvin VI 193-94 No. 363; *ANE* 167-68 No. 134.□

H1573.4.3§, Power of Islam tested. See: *DOTTI*. (Cf. H502.1).
Prior Becomes Moslem: al-Anbârî: *Alf* II 299,-(lifting body of deceased); Burton V 144. Chauvin V 237-38 No. 137; *ANE* 330-31 No. 147.□

H1573.9.1§, ‡God puts non-human forms of life (animal, bird, insect, etc.) to test. See: *DOTTI*. (Cf. H1553)
Spider Upbraids Wind: *Alf* IV 147,-(faith of she-spider tested); Burton IX 59-60. Chauvin II 220 No. 152/10; *ANE* 398 No. 245.□

H1574, Test of social position. See: *DOTTI*.
Ma¿rûf the Cobbler: *Alf* IV 298; Burton X 16. Chauvin VI 81-82 No. 250; *ANE* 291-93 No. 262.□

H1574.4§, ‡Test of the newly rich (the formerly poor). See: *DOTTI*.
Ma¿rûf the Cobbler: *Alf* IV 298; Burton X 16-17. Chauvin VI 81-82 No. 250; *ANE* 291-93 No. 262.□

H1574.5§, ‡Test of vocation: person posing as professional tested for skills. See: *DOTTI*.
Mercury ¿Alî: *Alf* III 234-36,-(cook); Burton VII 185. Chauvin V 248-50 No. 147; *ANE* 301-3 No. 225;
Abû al-Ḥasan al-Khorâsânî (and Caliph's Favorite): *Alf* IV 233; Burton IX 237. Chauvin V 218-20 No. 129; *ANE* 68-69 No. 259;
Ma¿rûf the Cobbler: *Alf* IV 298; Burton X 16. Chauvin VI 81-82 No. 250; *ANE* 291-93 No. 262.□

H1574.5.1§, ‡Merchant recognized by precision in bookkeeping (money matters: "By the penny!"). (Non-merchant recognized by loose or haphazard handling of money). (Cf. P144.2.1§).
Abû al-Ḥasan al-Khorâsânî (and Caliph's Favorite): *Alf* IV 233; Burton IX 237. Chauvin V 218-20 No. 129; *ANE* 68-69 No. 259.□

H1579.1§, ‡Test to detect a pedophile (homoerotic sodomite). (Cf. T472.0.1§).
Jeweler's Wife and Qamar al-Zamân: *Alf* IV 240; Burton IX 252. Chauvin V 212-14 No. 121; *ANE* 345-47 No. 260.□

H1579.1.1§, ‡Man's virtue tested by having him tempted by 'pretty boy'. (Cf. T330.1§).
Jeweler's Wife and Qamar al-Zamân: *Alf* IV 240; Burton IX 252. Chauvin V 212-14 No. 121; *ANE* 345-47 No. 260.□

H1580.1§, Sex organ (orifice) examined: tight or wide.
Hasan of Basrah: *Alf* III 315-16,-(poem); Burton VIII 32. Chauvin VII 29-35 No. 212A; *ANE* 207-10 No. 230.□

H1580.1.3§, ‡Examining a woman's 'abstinence' (lack of use, 'fidelity').
¿Azîz and ¿Azîzah: *Alf* I 286,-(tight); Burton II 331,-(strait). Chauvin V 144-45 No. 71; *ANE* 111-13 No. 41;
Hasan of Basrah: *Alf* III 315-16,-(tight/poem); Burton VIII 32. Chauvin VII 29-35 No. 212A; *ANE* 207-10 No. 230.□

H1580.1.3.1§, ‡Examining vagina to find out whether it is tight or loose ('wide'). (Cf. Z189§).

¿Azîz and ¿Azîzah: *Alf* I 286,-cf./(poem); Burton II 331. Chauvin V 144-45 No. 71; *ANE* 111-13 No. 41.□

H1582.0.1§, ‡Person too sick to be recognized by close relatives.
Ghânim ibn Ayyûb: *Alf* I 158, 161; Burton II 70. Chauvin VI 14 No. 188; *ANE* 192-93 No. 36.□

H1582.6.1§, ‡ Fatness (being plump) indicates good health. (Cf. J1413§).
King ¿Umar al-Nu¿mân and Sons: *Alf* I 308; Burton III 49. Chauvin VI 112-24 No. 277; *ANE* 430-34 No. 39;
Hasan of Basrah: *Alf* III 312; Burton VIII 25. Chauvin VII 29-35 No. 212A; *ANE* 207-10 No. 230.□

H1582.7.3.2§, ‡Proof of gender: genitals shown (examined).
Qamar al-Zamân and Budûr: *Alf* II 103,-(*'arathâ nafsahâ*/showed her herself); Burton III 288,-(showed her person). Chauvin V 204-12 No. 120; *ANE* 341-45 No. 61.□

H1586.3§, ‡Test of species: ability to perform task.
Second Qalandar: Afrit's Wife: *Alf* I 47; Burton I 127-28. Chauvin V 197-200 No. 116; *ANE* 338-39 No. 16.□

H1586.3.1§, ‡Test: monkey (transformed man) can write (in different styles).
Second Qalandar: Afrit's Wife: *Alf* I 47; Burton I 128. Chauvin V 197-200 No. 116; *ANE* 338-39 No. 16.□

H1586.3.3§, ‡Test: man thought to be demon (afrit, jinni) can recite passage from holy book (scripture).
Lady and Five Suitors Deceived: *Alf* III 162; Burton VI 179. Chauvin VII 50-51 No. 18; *ANE* 266 No. 198.□

H1586.4§, ‡Test of species: sociality.
City of Brass: *Alf* III 137; Burton VI 119. Chauvin V 32-35 No. 16; *ANE* 146-50 No. 180.□

H1586.4.1§, ‡Demons (jinn) recognized by living in isolation (in remote regions). (Cf. F567.4§).
City of Brass: *Alf* III 137; Burton VI 119,-("cut off from mankind"). Chauvin V 32-35 No. 16; *ANE* 146-50 No. 180.□

H1587.2§, ‡Test of race: color of skin examined for permanence. See: *DOTTI*. (Cf. K1816.13).
Mercury ¿Alî: *Alf* III 234; Burton VII 186. Chauvin V 248-50 No. 147; *ANE* 301-3 No. 225.□

H1596.0.2§, ‡Who is more beautiful (handsome): mine or yours?. (Cf. N74§).
Nûr al-Dîn ¿Alî and Son: *Alf* I 70,-cf.; Burton I 213-14. Chauvin VI 102-6 No. 270; *ANE* 317-19 No. 22;
Qamar al-Zamân and Budûr: *Alf* II 73-76; Burton III 225. Chauvin V 204-12 No. 120; *ANE* 341-45 No. 61.□

H1597.1§, ‡Debate as to whether men's or women's wiles are more potent. (Cf. J571.5).
Craft and Malice of Women/Frame: *Alf* III 139,-cf.; Burton VI 128. Chauvin VIII 33-34 No. 1; *ANE* 160-61 No. 181.□

J. THE WISE AND THE FOOLISH

J0, Acquisition and possession of wisdom.
Spy, First Maiden/¿Umar al-Nu¿mân: *Alf* I 219; Burton II 196. *ANE* 432 No. 39/passim.□

J1.0.1§, ‡Types of brain (capacity to know): given and acquired (*mawhûb-maksûb/muktasab*).
Tawaddud: Slavegirl Sold and Regained: *Alf* II 306; Burton V 195-96. Chauvin VII 117-19 No. 387; *ANE* 408-10 No. 157.□

J2§, ‡Mind (reason) must curb desires (urges of the body). (Cf. J1.0.1§, J751.0.1§, J1077.0.1.1§).
Hungry Eagle Snared: *Alf* IV 152,-(*¿Uqâb kâsir*); Burton IX 70,-("Ossifrage"/bone-breaking). Chauvin II 127-128 No. 133,-cf.□

J3.1.2§, ‡Upon seeing dishonesty (theft) rewarded honest person becomes dishonest. See: *DOTTI*.
Dalîla the Swindler: *Alf* III 212; Burton VII 145. Chauvin V 245-50 No. 147; *ANE* 163-64 No. 224.□

J3.2.3§, ‡Punishment for mistakes breeds goodness, lack of punishment breeds evil.
Wolf and Fox: *Alf* II 30; Burton III 134. Chauvin II 227 No. 6; *ANE* 450 No. 47;
Fakir and Jar of Butter: *Alf* IV 138,-cf.; Burton IX 41. Chauvin II 218-19 No. 152/3; *ANE* 179-80 No. 238.□

J3.2.4§, ‡Thought of hereafter (fear of God, paradise, hell) causes person to change sinful intent (plan). See: *DOTTI*. (Cf. T72, W4.3§).
King Dissuaded by Virtuous Wife: *Alf* II 294; Burton V 121. Chauvin VII 120-21 No. 391; *ANE* 260-61 No. 138;
Man of Upper Egypt and Frankish Wife: Alf IV 16?,-(text missing); Burton IX 20. Chauvin V 240 No. 140; *ANE*: No. 234;
Ruined Baghdadi and His Slave-girl: *Alf* IV 130; Burton IX 25. Chauvin V 152-53 No. 75; *ANE* 353 No. 235;
Jeweler's Wife and Qamar al-Zamân: *Alf* IV 266; Burton IX 303. Chauvin V 212-14 No. 121; *ANE* 345-47 No. 260.□

J10.1.1.2§, ‡Unforgettable first sexual intercourse (marriage, husband, wife). See: *DOTTI*. (Cf. T163§).
King's Daughter and Ape: *Alf* II 253,-cf.; Burton IV 297. Chauvin V 178 No. 102; *ANE* 262-63 No. 102.□

J10.3§, ‡A social group's first impression of a person (thing) sets the tone for its attitude toward him (it). (Cf. J170.3§).
Ma¿rûf the Cobbler: *Alf* IV 295; Burton X 12. Chauvin VI 81-82 No. 250; *ANE* 291-93 No. 262.□

J10.3.1§, ‡How a person (thing) is first introduced to a group sets the tone for group's attitude toward him (it).
Ma¿rûf the Cobbler: *Alf* IV 295; Burton X 10-11. Chauvin VI 81-82 No. 250; *ANE* 291-93 No. 262.□

J12.1§, ‡Guests at banquet avoid food eaten by persons at the time they are punished (captured).
¿Alî Shâr and Zumurrud: *Alf* II 229,-(sweet rice-eaters punished/rice avoided); Burton IV 215. Chauvin V 89-91 No. 28; *ANE* 100-1 No. 82.□

J17.0.1§, ‡Animal's advice: "Beware of man". See: *DOTTI*. (Cf. Z42.1.1§).
Birds, Beasts, and Carpenter: *Alf* II 23; Burton III 115. Chauvin II 225-26 No. 1; *ANE* 126 No. 44.□

J17.2§, ‡Animals (wild) avoid man.
Hermit Tempted by Angel: *Alf* II 27; Burton III 128. Chauvin II 226 No. 3; *ANE* 221 No. 45/pt. 2.□

J20§, Conditioning: effects associated with past experience cause man (animal) to respond accordingly (conditioned response). See: *DOTTI*; *GMC*. (Cf. K830.1§, M209.5§).
Reeve's Story: Why Maimed by Bride: *Alf* I 96-99,-(eating); Burton I 279, 287. Chauvin V 220-21 No. 305; *ANE* 351 No. 25;
¿Alî Shâr and Zumurrud: *Alf* II 229-33,-(sweet rice-punishment/rice avoided); Burton IV 215-22. Chauvin V 89-91 No. 28; *ANE* 100-1 No. 82;
King's Daughter and Ape: *Alf* II 253,-cf./(first intercourse); Burton IV 297. Chauvin V 178 No. 102; *ANE* 262-63 No. 102;
Dalîla the Swindler: *Alf* III 226,-(Bedouin-city); Burton VII 169,-(eating honey-fritters). Chauvin V 245-50 No. 147; *ANE* 163-64 No. 224;

Merchant and Robbers: *Alf* IV 166; Burton IX 100. Chauvin II 223 No. 152/20; *ANE* 297 No. 251.□

J20.5§, Traumatic experience. See: *DOTTI*; *GMC*.
Reeve's Story: Why Maimed by Bride: *Alf* I 98; Burton I 278-79. Chauvin V 220-21 No. 305; *ANE* 351 No. 25.□

J21.1, "Consider the end". See: *DOTTI*; *GMC*. (Cf. J751.0.1§).
She-mouse and Ichneumon: *Alf* II 36; Burton III 148. Chauvin II 227 No. 6; *ANE* 306 No. 49;
al-'Amjad and al-'As¿ad: *Alf* II 116,-cf./; Burton III 315. Chauvin V 208-10 No. 120[.1]; *ANE* 341-42 No. 61/pt. 2.□

J21.2.4.2§, ‡"Use your weapon only for a deserved punishment". (Cf. U10).
Ma¿rûf the Cobbler: *Alf* IV 316; Burton X 52. Chauvin VI 81-82 No. 250; *ANE* 291-93 No. 262.□

J21.2.6, "Control your anger at the beginning": counsel proved wise by experience. See: *DOTTI*.
King Jalî¿âd and Shimâs: *Alf* IV 161,-cf.; Burton IX 89. Chauvin VI 9-11 No. 184; *ANE* 237-38 No. 236.□

J21.8.2§, "Do not take an oath". See: *DOTTI*; *GMC*.
Island King/Pious Jewish Merchant: *Alf* III 16; Burton V 290. Chauvin VI 161 No. 325; *ANE* 234 No. 174.□

J21.13, "Never believe what is beyond belief". See: *DOTTI*.
King ¿Umar al-Nu¿mân and Sons: *Alf* I 242,-cf./(miraculous feats); Burton II 246. Chauvin VI 112-24 No. 277; *ANE* 430-34 No. 39.□

J21.25, "Do not keep bad company". See: *DOTTI*.
¿Alî Shâr and Zumurrud: *Alf* II 217; Burton IV 189. Chauvin V 89-91 No. 28; *ANE* 100-1 No. 82.□

J21.25.1§, ‡"Do not keep close company with anyone". (Cf. P302.0.1§).
¿Alî Shâr and Zumurrud: *Alf* II 217; Burton IV 187,-(over-familiar). Chauvin V 89-91 No. 28; *ANE* 100-1 No. 82.□

J21.30, "Never have to do with a woman unless wed to her".
¿Alî Shâr and Zumurrud: *Alf* II 218,-cf./(implicit/*al-nisâ' al-zawânî*/fornicating women/whores); Burton IV 190,-(whoreson fellows [??]). Chauvin V 89-91 No. 28; *ANE* 100-1 No. 82.□

J21.30.1§, "Betray not a trust even if you happened to be a betrayer". See: *DOTTI*; *GMC*. (Cf. U138.3.1§).
¿Alâ' al-Dîn Abû al-Shâmât: *Alf* II 171; Burton IV 74. Chauvin V 43-49 No. 18; *ANE* 85-87 No. 63.□

J21.32, ‡"Do not marry more than one woman". (Cf. M144.1§, M255.2§, T144.0.1.1§).
Anîs al-Jalîs: *Alf* I 129; Burton II 9. Chauvin V 120-24 No. 58; *ANE* 316-17 No. 35;
Qamar al-Zamân and Budûr: *Alf* II 76,-(poem); Burton III 225. Chauvin V 204-12 No. 120; *ANE* 341-45 No. 61.□

J21.37, "Do not take a woman's advice": counsel proved wise by experience. See: *DOTTI*; *GMC*. (Cf. W256.6.1§).
Nuzhat al-Zamân Tested/¿Umar al-Nu¿mân: *Alf* I 201,-cf./(evil ones/*'ashrâr al-nâs*[!!]); Burton II 159. Chauvin VI 116, n.1/passim No. 277; *ANE* 432,/passim No. 39;
Lady's Lovers as Pursuer and Fugitive: *Alf* III 143; Burton VI 139. Chauvin VIII 38-39 No. 7; *ANE* 267 No. 187;
Jeweler's Wife and Qamar al-Zamân: *Alf* IV 256,-cf./(poem); Burton IX 282. Chauvin V 212-14 No. 121; *ANE* 345-47 No. 260.□

J21.37.1§, ‡'Seek their [(women's)] advice and act contrary-wise'. (Cf. W256.6.3.2.2§).
Man [Gardener] and His Wife: *Alf* IV 165,-(passim); Burton IX 98. Chauvin II 223 No. 152/19; *ANE* 289 No. 250.□

J21.55.0.1§, ‡"If you keep company with God, God will keep company with you". See: *DOTTI*.
¿Alî Shâr and Zumurrud: *Alf* II 217; Burton IV 187. Chauvin V 89-91 No. 28; *ANE* 100-1 No. 82.□

J21.55.1§, ‡"Don't drink liquor.". See: *DOTTI*. (Cf. C272.0.1§).
¿Alî Shâr and Zumurrud: *Alf* II 217; Burton IV 189. Chauvin V 89-91 No. 28; *ANE* 100-1 No. 82.□

J21.55.2§, ‡"Don't commit fornication.". See: *DOTTI*. (Cf. J21.25).

¿Alî Shâr and Zumurrud: *Alf* II 217,-cf.; Burton IV 190. Chauvin V 89-91 No. 28; *ANE* 100-1 No. 82.□

J21.55.2.1§, ‡"Never have to do with prostitutes". (Cf. J21.30).
¿Alî Shâr and Zumurrud: *Alf* II 218,-cf./(*al-nisâ' al-zawânî*/implicit); Burton IV 190. Chauvin V 89-91 No. 28; *ANE* 100-1 No. 82.□

J21.55.5§, ‡"Don't commit an injustice.". See: *DOTTI*. (Cf. U210.0.1§).
King Jalî¿âd and Shimâs: *Alf* IV 161,-cf.,/(be just); Burton IX 89,-(do equal justice). Chauvin VI 9-11 No. 184; *ANE* 237-38 No. 236.□

J21.57§, ‡"Seek the advice of elders (the wise).". See: *DOTTI*. (Cf. J21.37, W250.6.2§).
¿Alî Shâr and Zumurrud: *Alf* II 217; Burton IV 189. Chauvin V 89-91 No. 28; *ANE* 100-1 No. 82;
King Jalî¿âd and Shimâs: *Alf* IV 161; Burton IX 89. Chauvin VI 9-11 No. 184; *ANE* 237-38 No. 236.□

J21.57.1§, ‡"Do not ignore the opinion (wishes) of the majority.". (Cf. P500.2§).
King Jalî¿âd and Shimâs: *Alf* IV 161; Burton IX 89. Chauvin VI 9-11 No. 184; *ANE* 237-38 No. 236.□

J21.58.1§, ‡"'Be merciful to those who are on Earth, He who is (or those who are) in heavens will be merciful to you'".
¿Alî Shâr and Zumurrud: *Alf* II 217; Burton IV 189. Chauvin V 89-91 No. 28; *ANE* 100-1 No. 82.□

J21.58.1.1§, ‡"[If you] are merciful to the weaker, the stronger will be merciful to you". See: *DOTTI*.
¿Alî Shâr and Zumurrud: *Alf* II 217; Burton IV 187. Chauvin V 89-91 No. 28; *ANE* 100-1 No. 82.□

J26, Enemies can be won more by kindness than cruelty. See: *DOTTI*. (Cf. J1514§, W11.5).
Mouse and Cat: *Alf* IV 135-36; Burton IX 36. Chauvin II 218 No. 152/2; *ANE* 305-6 No. 237;
King Jalî¿âd and Shimâs: *Alf* IV 161,-(*ma¿rûf*); Burton IX 89. Chauvin VI 9-11 No. 184; *ANE* 237-38 No. 236.□

J26.0.1§, ‡Kindness, even to the undeserving, is recommended.
Wolf and Fox: *Alf* II 30,-(poem); Burton III 132. Chauvin II 227 No. 6; *ANE* 450 No. 47.□

J26.1§, ‡Predator (lion, ogre, etc.) won over by kindness. See: *DOTTI*.
Uns al-Wujûd and al-Ward: *Alf* II 272-3,-(flattery); Burton V 40-41. Chauvin VI 127-29 No. 282; *ANE* 438 No. 104.□

J60§, ‡Imitative (social) learning—other aspects of learning from observation.
King ¿Umar al-Nu¿mân and Sons: *Alf* II 8,-(praising); Burton III 89,-(folk ape one another). Chauvin VI 112-24 No. 277; *ANE* 430-34 No. 39.□

J60.1.1§, ‡Goods acquired or retrieved by inducing animal (monkey) to imitate (copy) man. (Cf. B762, B786).
Sindbâd's Fifth Voyage: *Alf* III 111; Burton VI 55. Chauvin VII 21-24 No. 373E; *ANE* 386 No. 179.□

J80, Wisdom (knowledge) taught by parable. See: *DOTTI*; *GMC*; *PSAE*. (Cf. J170§).
Shahriyâr and Shâhzamân: *Alf* I 5; Burton I 13. Chauvin V 188-89 No. 111; *ANE* 370-71 No. 1.□

J80.1.2§, ‡Father illustrates the necessity of resisting woman's demands. See: *DOTTI*.
Shahriyâr and Shâhzamân: *Alf* I 5; Burton I 15. Chauvin V 188-89 No. 111; *ANE* 370-71 No. 1.□

J81, The dishes of the same flavor. See: *ANE*; *DOTTI*.
King Dissuaded by Virtuous Wife: *Alf* II 294; Burton V 121. Chauvin VII 120-21 No. 391; *ANE* 260-61 No. 138.□

J120, Wisdom learned from children. See: *ANE*; *DOTTI*; *GMC*.
King Jalî¿âd and Shimâs: *Alf* IV 173-74; Burton IX 115. Chauvin VI 9 No. 184; *ANE* 237-38 No. 236.□

J123.2§, ‡Clever child dismisses seemingly just decision by judge. (Provides overlooked legal premise). See: *DOTTI*.
Stolen Purse/Joint Depositors: *Alf* III 177; Burton VI 209-11. Chauvin VIII 63-64 No. 25; *ANE* 399 No. 207.□

J126§, ‡Child rebukes an adult for misconduct (indiscretion). See: *DOTTI*. (Cf. C119.5§, P753.0.1.1§, T189.3§).

Debauchee and Three Years Old Child: *Alf* III 176; Burton VI 208. Chauvin VIII 62-63 No. 147; *ANE* 166-67 No. 206.□

J129§, ‡Children as spreaders (source) of news (information)—miscellaneous. (Cf. P431.1).
Mercury ¿Alî: *Alf* III 230; Burton VII 179. Chauvin V 248-50 No. 147; *ANE* 301-3 No. 225.□

J133.0.1§, ‡Animal behavior copied (imitated) by man. See: *DOTTI*.
Anîs al-Jalîs: *Alf* I 139,-(poem,/horses drink to whistle's sound); Burton II 29. Chauvin V 120-24 No. 58; *ANE* 316-17 No. 35.□

J134.5§, ‡Behavior of household animals (birds) reveals family secret. (Cf. B131.3).
Masrûr and Zayn al-Mawâṣif: *Alf* IV 65; Burton VIII 232. Chauvin VI 82-84 No. 251; *ANE* 294-95 No. 232.□

J134.5.1§, ‡Host's pet bird (animal) too friendly to guest: guest posing as new friend is a frequent visitor during host's absence. (Cf. B131.3).
Masrûr and Zayn al-Mawâṣif: *Alf* IV 65; Burton VIII 232. Chauvin VI 82-84 No. 251; *ANE* 294-95 No. 232.□

J134.5.2§, ‡Pet's (cat's, dog's) behavior indicates where various activities (cooking, storing, etc.) are undertaken within house.
Mercury ¿Alî: *Alf* III 235,-(cat's); Burton VII 186-87. Chauvin V 248-50 No. 147; *ANE* 301-3 No. 225.□

J141.0.1§, ‡Schooling at home: teacher(s) instruct(s) pupil at pupil's home.
Nûr al-Dîn ¿Alî and Son: *Alf* I 68; Burton I 205. Chauvin VI 102-6 No. 270; *ANE* 317-19 No. 22;
Tâj al-Mulûk: *Alf* I 265-66; Burton II 291. Chauvin V 126-28 No. 60; *ANE* 406-8 No. 40;
¿Alâ' al-Dîn Abû al-Shâmât: *Alf* II 149, 173; Burton IV 33, 79. Chauvin V 43-49 No. 18; *ANE* 85-87 No. 63;
Jeweler's Wife and Qamar al-Zamân: *Alf* IV 238,-(mother instructs daughter, father instructs son); Burton IX 247. Chauvin V 212-14 No. 121; *ANE* 345-47 No. 260.□

J141.1§, ‡Adroit instructors (masters) as teachers for a youth. (Cf. J149§).
Tâj al-Mulûk: *Alf* I 265-66; Burton II 291. Chauvin V 126-28 No. 60; *ANE* 406-8 No. 40.□

J142.0.1§, ‡The uneducated (ignorant) is always unfairly treated.
King ¿Umar al-Nu¿mân and Sons: *Alf* I 260,-(poem/*'akhû-al-jahâlah ... maghbûn*); Burton II 279,-(folly's brother ... forlorn and glum). Chauvin VI 112-24 No. 277; *ANE* 430-34 No. 39.□

J147, Child confined to keep him in ignorance of life. Useless. See: *DOTTI*; *GMC*.
Ibrâhîm and Jamîlah: *Alf* IV 219; Burton IX 207. Chauvin VI 52-53 No. 218; *ANE* 227-29 No. 258.□

J148.0.3§, ‡'No [new] admonition in repetition'.
Sayf al-Mulûk: *Alf* III 302; Burton VIII 5,-(in repetition is no fruition). Chauvin VII 64-73 No. 348; *ANE* 362-64 No. 229.□

J148.1§, ‡Completion of basic religious schooling: 'He read, repeated, and concluded [by reciting from memory]'.
¿Alâ' al-Dîn Abû al-Shâmât: *Alf* II 173; Burton IV 79. Chauvin V 43-49 No. 18; *ANE* 85-87 No. 63.□

J149§, ‡The value of education (schooling). See: *PSAE*. (Cf. J141.1§, P774.2.3.1§, P775.2.2§).
Hârûn, Slave-girl and Judge Abû-Yûsuf: *Alf* II 204; Burton IV 155,-(religious learning). Chauvin VII 114 No. 383; *ANE* 204 No. 75;
Bulûqiya: *Alf* III 80-81,-cf.; Burton V 35-96. Chauvin VII 54 No. 77; *ANE* 130-32 No. 177;
Fakir and Jar of Butter: *Alf* IV 137; Burton IX 41. Chauvin II 218-19 No. 152/3; *ANE* 179-80 No. 238.□

J149.1§, ‡Educated person earns much money and esteem (respect). See: *DOTTI*.
Hârûn, Slave-girl and Judge Abû-Yûsuf: *Alf* II 204; Burton IV 155. Chauvin VII 114 No. 383; *ANE* 204 No. 75;
Tawaddud: Slavegirl Sold and Regained: *Alf* II 305,-ff.; Burton V 194. Chauvin VII 117-19 No. 387; *ANE* 408-10 No. 157.□

J149.2.1§, ‡Captive (slave) freed because of his literacy (can read and write).

al-'Amjad and al-'As¿ad: *Alf* II 127,-cf.; Burton III 341. Chauvin V 208-10 No. 120[.1]; *ANE* 341-42 No. 61/pt. 2.□

J149.3§, ‡Animal thought to be educated (intelligent) honored. (Proves to be enchanted person).
Second Qalandar: Afrit's Wife: *Alf* I 47; Burton I 127-28. Chauvin V 197-200 No. 116; *ANE* 338-39 No. 16.□

J149.4.1§, ‡Learning ways of adversaries (enemies) gives power over them.
King ¿Umar al-Nu¿mân and Sons: *Alf* I 184; Burton II 128. Chauvin VI 112-24 No. 277; *ANE* 430-34 No. 39.□

J150.1§, ‡"Literature of advice [giving]": wisdom (knowledge) in form of counsel given by the wise (father, sage, vizier, philosopher, or the like). (Cf. P319.0.1§).
Spy, Old Woman/¿Umar al-Nu¿mân: *Alf* I 225; Burton II 208-10. *ANE* 432 No. 39/passim;
Wolf and Fox: *Alf* II 29-35; Burton III 132-46. Chauvin II 227 No. 6; *ANE* 450 No. 47;
¿Alî Shâr and Zumurrud: *Alf* II 217-18; Burton IV 189-90. Chauvin V 89-91 No. 28; *ANE* 100-1 No. 82;
King Jalî¿âd and Shimâs: *Alf* IV 161; Burton IX 89-90. Chauvin VI 9-11 No. 184; *ANE* 237-38 No. 236.□

J152, ‡Wisdom (knowledge) from sage (teacher).
King Jalî¿âd and Shimâs: *Alf* IV 134; Burton IX 34. Chauvin VI 9-11 No. 184; *ANE* 237-38 No. 236.□

J154, Wise words of dying father. See: *DOTTI*; *GMC*. (Cf. M250.1§).
¿Alî Shâr and Zumurrud: *Alf* II 217; Burton IV 187. Chauvin V 89-91 No. 28; *ANE* 100-1 No. 82;
Tawaddud: Slavegirl Sold and Regained: *Alf* II 304,-cf./(creation of); Burton V 237. Chauvin VII 117-19 No. 387; *ANE* 408-10 No. 157;
King Jalî¿âd and Shimâs: *Alf* IV 161,-(king); Burton IX 89. Chauvin VI 9-11 No. 184; *ANE* 237-38 No. 236.□

J155.0.1§, ‡Women savant (wise woman or wise girl). See: *DOTTI*. (Cf. P179.1.1§).
King ¿Umar al-Nu¿mân and Sons: *Alf* I 310,-cf./(young girl); Burton III 52-53. Chauvin VI 112-24 No. 277; *ANE* 430-34 No. 39;
Dispute Concerning Males and Females: *Alf* II 300; Burton V 154-63. Chauvin VI 153 No. 317; *ANE* 291 No. 151.□

J155.3.1§, ‡Husband ignores his wife's advice: disastrous results. See: *DOTTI*. (Cf. J1701.0.1§).
Nûr al-Dîn and Maryam: *Alf* IV 100,-(mistress' advice); Burton VIII 310-11. Chauvin V 52-54 No. 271; *ANE* 98-99 No. 233;
Landsman ¿Abdallah and Merman ¿Abdallah: *Alf* IV 201,-(*'iktim sirrak*); Burton IX 172,-(keep thy secret). Chauvin V 6-7 No. 3; *ANE* 65-66 No. 256.□

J155.4, ‡Wife as [wise] adviser. See: *DOTTI*. (Cf. J21.37, J1701.0.1§, T210.1.1§).
Ma¿rûf the Cobbler: *Alf* IV 303-4; Burton X 24. Chauvin VI 81-82 No. 250; *ANE* 291-93 No. 262.□

J155.9.1§, ‡Daughter as adviser.
Shahriyâr and Shâhzamân: *Alf* I 5,-(poem); Burton I 15. Chauvin V 188-89 No. 111; *ANE* 370-71 No. 1.□

J155.9.2§, ‡Sister as adviser. See: *DOTTI*. (Cf. P253.6.1§, P742.1§).
Ni¿mah and Nu¿m: Stolen Wife Regained: *Alf* II 143,-(to her brother); Burton IV 20-23. Chauvin VI 96-97 No. 263; *ANE* 314 No. 62.□

J157, Wisdom (knowledge) from dream. [Instructive dream]. See: *DOTTI*; *GMC*; *PSAE*. (Cf. D1812.3.3).
Tâj al-Mulûk: *Alf* I 299; Burton III 31. Chauvin V 126-28 No. 60; *ANE* 406-8 No. 40;
Uns al-Wujûd and al-Ward: *Alf* II 270,-(nurse's deception/*manâm*); Burton V 34-35,-(saw in my sleep). Chauvin VI 127-29 No. 282; *ANE* 438 No. 104;
King Jalî¿âd and Shimâs: *Alf* IV 134; Burton IX 35. Chauvin VI 9-11 No. 184; *ANE* 237-38 No. 236.□

J157.8.1§, ‡Satan misleads in dreams (and similar experiences, such as communication with the dead). (Cf. G302.9.6).
Qamar al-Zamân and Budûr: *Alf* II 82,-(divers foods,/satan's instigation); Burton III 246. Chauvin V 204-12 No. 120; *ANE* 341-45 No. 61.□

J157.8.2§, ‡Physiological state of sleeper as cause of misleading dream (e.g., full stomach, being cold, or the like).
¿Azîz and ¿Azîzah: *Alf* I 276,-cf./(full stomach causes sleep); Burton II 312. Chauvin V 144-45 No. 71; *ANE* 111-13 No. 41;
Qamar al-Zamân and Budûr: *Alf* II 82,-(divers foods,/satan's instigation); Burton III 246. Chauvin V 204-12 No. 120; *ANE* 341-45 No. 61.□

J163.5§, ‡The value of ownership of a story. See: *DOTTI*. (Cf. F883.1.9.1.1§, J170.3§).
Ibn Sabâ'ik/Sayf al-Mulûk: *Alf* III 271-72; Burton VII 312. Chauvin VII 65 No. 348/pt.; *ANE* 309-10 No. 228.□

J163.5.1§, ‡Story purchased from owner. (Cf. Q92§).
Ibn Sabâ'ik/Sayf al-Mulûk: *Alf* III 271-72; Burton VII 312. Chauvin VII 65 No. 348/pt.; *ANE* 309-10 No. 228.□

J163.5.2§, ‡Story purchased for gold (high price). See: *DOTTI*.
Ibn Sabâ'ik/Sayf al-Mulûk: *Alf* III 271-73; Burton VII 312. Chauvin VII 65 No. 348/pt.; *ANE* 309-10 No. 228.□

J163.5.2.1§, ‡Neck-narrative (neck-tale): condemned person pardoned for a story. See: *DOTTI*. (Cf. P535.5§, Q92§).
Trader and Afrit: Accidental Fairy-cide: *Alf* I 8; Burton I 24-37. Chauvin VI 22-23 No. 194; *ANE* 419-20 No. 4;
Three Apples: Hasty Uxoricide: *Alf* I 64,-(told by vizier); Burton I 194. Chauvin VI 144-45 No. 302; *ANE* 414-15 No. 21;
King ¿Umar al-Nu¿mân and Sons: *Alf* II 16; Burton III 102ff. Chauvin VI 112-24 No. 277; *ANE* 430-34 No. 39.□

J163.5.2.2§, ‡Story told as an act of benevolence (charity, almsgiving). See: *DOTTI*.
Ibn Sabâ'ik/Sayf al-Mulûk: *Alf* III 272; Burton VII 313. Chauvin VII 65 No. 348/pt.; *ANE* 309-10 No. 228.□

J163.5.3.1§, ‡Owner of story sets tale-telling conditions for buyer (teller-to-be). See: *DOTTI*. (Cf. P470§).
Ibn Sabâ'ik/Sayf al-Mulûk: *Alf* III 272-73; Burton VII 313. Chauvin VII 65 No. 348/pt.; *ANE* 309-10 No. 228.□

J163.5.3.2§, ‡Story must not be told casually, or to the unworthy. (Story not to be told on sidewalks, to women, slave-girls, slaves, idiots, juveniles, etc.). See: *DOTTI*.
Ibn Sabâ'ik/Sayf al-Mulûk: *Alf* III 271-73; Burton VII 313. Chauvin VII 65 No. 348/pt.; *ANE* 309-10 No. 228.□

J164, Wisdom from God. [(*'ilhâm*)]. (Cf. V318.3§).
Bulûqiya: *Alf* III 80,-cf.; Burton V 393, 395. Chauvin VII 54 No. 77; *ANE* 130-32 No. 177.□

J166, ‡Wisdom from books. (Cf. M302.8).
Shahriyâr and Shâhzamân: *Alf* I 5; Burton I 15. Chauvin V 188-89 No. 111; *ANE* 370-71 No. 1;
Ni¿mah and Nu¿m: Stolen Wife Regained: *Alf* II 143,-(story); Burton IV 21. Chauvin VI 96-97 No. 263; *ANE* 314 No. 62;
Bulûqiya: *Alf* III 22; Burton V 304-5. Chauvin VII 54 No. 77; *ANE* 130-32 No. 177.□

J166.0.1§, ‡Book (written scroll) as sole inheritance.
Bulûqiya/Ḥâsib/Queen of Vipers: *Alf* III 19; Burton V 299. Chauvin VII 54 No. 77; *ANE* 130-32 No. 177.□

J166.4.1§, ‡Book gives accounts of all hidden treasures. (Cf. D1323.5.1§).
Jawdar and His Treacherous Brethren: *Alf* III 182; Burton VI 221. Chauvin V 257-60 No. 154; *ANE* 244-45 No. 209.□

J167.1.1§, ‡Story (history) recorded to be read for generations: one generation after another.
Qamar al-Zamân and Budûr: *Alf* II 96; Burton III 279. Chauvin V 204-12 No. 120; *ANE* 341-45 No. 61.□

J167.3§, Wisdom from repentant sinner. (Cf. V229.12).
King ¿Umar al-Nu¿mân and Sons: *Alf* I 319; Burton III 74. Chauvin VI 112-24 No. 277; *ANE* 430-34 No. 39;

Pretty Gray-haired Woman Retorts: *Alf* II 302-3,-cf.; Burton V 164. Chauvin VI 153 No. 318; *ANE* 77-78 No. 152.□

J167.7§, ‡Token of harsher punishment: physical reminder of the harsher punishment that should have been received. (Cf. M209§).
Portress Amînah: Bitten Cheek: *Alf* I 60; Burton I 182. Chauvin V 98-99 No. 33; *ANE* 326-27 No. 20;
Reeve's Story: Why Maimed by Bride: *Alf* I 99,-(implicit); Burton I 287. Chauvin V 220-21 No. 305; *ANE* 351 No. 25;
Mock Caliph/¿Alî al-Jawharî: *Alf* II 199,-(severe beating); Burton IV 146. Chauvin V 99-100 No. 174; *ANE* 304-5 No. 73.□

J169§, *sîrah/siyar*: personal life-history (biography, vita). See: *DOTTI*; *GMC*; *PSAE*. (Cf. P12.15.5.1§, P470.0.1§, Z203§).
King ¿Umar al-Nu¿mân and Sons: *Alf* II 21; Burton III 114,-(wonderful events that had betided ...). Chauvin VI 112-24 No. 277; *ANE* 430-34 No. 39;
Jinn Imprisoned in Flasks: *Alf* III 127-29,-(Dâhish ibn al-'A¿mash's); Burton VI 96-101. Chauvin VII 113 No. 380=no/text; *ANE* 146 No. 180;
Mercury ¿Alî: *Alf* III 246; Burton VII 209,-(histories). Chauvin V 248-50 No. 147; *ANE* 301-3 No. 225.□

J169.0.1§, ‡Personal experience narrative by story's character; (e.g., Ahura's, Lost Sailor's, Sinuhe's, Sindbad's, etc.). See: *DOTTI*; *PSAE*. (Cf. Z201.1§).
King ¿Umar al-Nu¿mân and Sons: *Alf* II 16; Burton III 102ff. Chauvin VI 112-24 No. 277; *ANE* 430-34 No. 39.□

J169.0.2§, ‡Truth revealed through personal experience account (eye witness). (Cf. J1150.1§).
King ¿Umar al-Nu¿mân and Sons: *Alf* II 11-13; Burton III 97-98. Chauvin VI 112-24 No. 277; *ANE* 430-34 No. 39.□

J169.5§, Epitaph: inscription on grave sums up owner's accomplishments in life. See: *DOTTI*; *GMC*; *PSAE*. (Cf. L413).
¿Azîz and ¿Azîzah: *Alf* I 282,-cf.; Burton II 324-25. Chauvin V 144-45 No. 71; *ANE* 111-13 No. 41.□

J170§, ‡Wisdom acquired from story (personal life history, parable, exemplum, or the like). (Cf. J80, J571.5).
Shahriyâr and Shâhzamân: *Alf* I 2,-(foreword/non-tale); Burton I 1. Chauvin V 188-91 No. 111; *ANE* 370-71 No. 1;
Ensorcelled Prince/Husband: *Alf* I 27,-cf.; Burton I 69-82. Chauvin VI 56-58 No. 222; *ANE* 176 No. 13;
Nuzhat al-Zamân Tested/¿Umar al-Nu¿mân: *Alf* I 206,-(of piety); Burton II 169. Chauvin VI 116, n.1/passim No. 277; *ANE* 432,/passim No. 39.□

J170.2§, ‡King orders story recorded as history (and parable). See: *PSAE*. (Cf. Z67.7.1§).
Portress Amînah: Bitten Cheek: *Alf* I 60; Burton I 183. Chauvin V 98-99 No. 33; *ANE* 326-27 No. 20;
Three Apples: Hasty Uxoricide: *Alf* I 64; Burton I 194. Chauvin VI 144-45 No. 302; *ANE* 414-15 No. 21;
Nûr al-Dîn ¿Alî and Son: *Alf* I 84; Burton I 254. Chauvin VI 102-6 No. 270; *ANE* 317-19 No. 22;
Hunchback's Tale: Resuscitated: *Alf* I 88,-(governor), 124-25; Burton I 262, 351. Chauvin V 180-82 No. 105; *ANE* 224-25 No. 23;
Ghânim ibn Ayyûb: *Alf* I 162; Burton II 76. Chauvin VI 14 No. 188; *ANE* 192-93 No. 36;
King ¿Umar al-Nu¿mân and Sons: *Alf* II 21; Burton III 114. Chauvin VI 112-24 No. 277; *ANE* 430-34 No. 39;
Qamar al-Zamân and Budûr: *Alf* II 96, 112,-(*bi mâ' al-dhahab*/in gold-water); Burton III 276, 307,-(in letters of gold). Chauvin V 204-12 No. 120; *ANE* 341-45 No. 61;
Sindbâd's Sixth Voyage: *Alf* III 116; Burton VI 68. Chauvin VII 24-27 No. 373F; *ANE* 386 No. 179;

Mercury ¿Alî: *Alf* III 246; Burton VII 209. Chauvin V 248-50 No. 147; *ANE* 301-3 No. 225.□

J170.3§, ‡'People are reports' (i.e., a person's worth is what is told about his life). See: *DOTTI*. (Cf. J10.3§, J163.5§, K2107.3§).

Ma¿rûf the Cobbler: *Alf* IV 294-95,-cf.; Burton X 10-11. Chauvin VI 81-82 No. 250; *ANE* 291-93 No. 262.□

J170.5§, ‡Tyrannical person (king, ruler, etc.) repents upon hearing story. See: *DOTTI*. (Cf. U245§).
Hermit Tempted by Angel: *Alf* II 27; Burton III 126. Chauvin II 226 No. 3; *ANE* 221 No. 45/pt. 2.□

J171, Proverbial wisdom: counsels.
King Jalî¿âd and Shimâs: *Alf* IV 161; Burton IX 89. Chauvin VI 9-11 No. 184; *ANE* 237-38 No. 236.□

J175.1§, ‡Wisdom from young boy (juvenile). (Cf. P110.1.3§).
Hishâm and Arab Youth: *Alf* II 184-85; Burton IV 101-3. Chauvin V 288 No. 172; *ANE* 222-23 No. 68;
King Jalî¿âd and Shimâs: *Alf* IV 175; Burton IX 116-17. Chauvin VI 9 No. 184; *ANE* 237-38 No. 236.□

J189.1.1§, ‡Marvelous knowledge of anatomy (organ functions).
Tawaddud: Slavegirl Sold and Regained: *Alf* II 315; Burton V 218-19. Chauvin VII 117-19 No. 387; *ANE* 408-10 No. 157.□

J191.1, Solomon as wise man. See: *DOTTI*; *GMC*.
Sayf al-Mulûk: *Alf* III 275; Burton VII 318. Chauvin VII 64-73 No. 348; *ANE* 362-64 No. 229.□

J191.3§, Luqmân as wise man. See: *DOTTI*; *GMC*.
Spy, Second Maiden/¿Umar al-Nu¿mân: *Alf* I 220; Burton II 199. *ANE* 432 No. 39/passim.□

J191.5§, Alexander as wise man. See: *DOTTI*; *GMC*.
Spy, First Maiden/¿Umar al-Nu¿mân: *Alf* I 220; Burton II 199. *ANE* 432 No. 39/passim.□

J191.9.1.1§, ‡Wise men don't talk about outcome of operations that are still in progress (E.g., trip, battle, pregnancy, etc.).
Mouse and Cat: *Alf* IV 137; Burton IX 39. Chauvin II 218 No. 152/2; *ANE* 305-6 No. 237.□

J192.3, Wisdom from the Greeks.
Bulûqiya/Ḥâsib/Queen of Vipers: *Alf* III 18; Burton V 298. Chauvin VII 54 No. 77; *ANE* 130-32 No. 177;
City of Brass: *Alf* III 130,-cf.; Burton VI 103. Chauvin V 32-35 No. 16; *ANE* 146-50 No. 180.□

J195.1§, ‡Wisdom (knowledge) from the nomads (Bedouins). See: *DOTTI*.
Nuzhat al-Zamân Tested/¿Umar al-Nu¿mân: *Alf* I 201,-(*'A¿râbiyy*); Burton II 158. Chauvin VI 116, n.1/passim No. 277; *ANE* 432,/passim No. 39.□

J211.4§, ‡Flight from humiliation (enslavement) recommended. (Cf. U310.0.1§).
First Qalandar: Brother-Sister Incest: *Alf* I 41,-(poem); Burton I 109. Chauvin V 196-97 No. 115; *ANE* 337-38 No. 15;
Anîs al-Jalîs: *Alf* I 135,-(poem); Burton II 19. Chauvin V 120-24 No. 58; *ANE* 316-17 No. 35;
Sindbâd's Sixth Voyage: *Alf* III 114,-(poem); Burton VI 62. Chauvin VII 24-27 No. 373F; *ANE* 386 No. 179.□

J215.1.1, Do not set a hungry guard over food. See: *GMC*. (Cf. J754.1§, J2756.3§).
Mouse and Cat: *Alf* IV 135,-cf.; Burton IX 36. Chauvin II 218 No. 152/2; *ANE* 305-6 No. 237.□

J223, ‡Choice between evils: pay tribute or lose both money and life.
Two Kings, Just and Unjust: *Alf* IV 149; Burton IX 65-67. Chauvin II 221 No. 152/12; *ANE* 422 No. 246.□

J224§, ‡Choice between evils: confessing to lesser crime or being accused of more serious one (murder, adultery, etc.).
Jewish Doctor's Story: Sororicide: *Alf* I 101; Burton I 296-97. Chauvin VI 89 No. 253; *ANE* 242 No. 26;
Lover Who Feigned Himself a Thief: *Alf* II 204; Burton IV 158. Chauvin VII 134-35 No. 403; *ANE* 272 No. 76.□

J224.1§, ‡Innocent person falsely confesses to stealing a valuable item (necklace) rather than reveal murder of owner at his home. See: *DOTTI*. (Cf. J1141.4, N616§).
Jewish Doctor's Story: Sororicide: *Alf* I 101; Burton I 296-97. Chauvin VI 89 No. 253; *ANE* 242 No. 26.□

J224.2§, ‡Lover trapped while on clandestine visit to his beloved confesses to theft in order to spare his lady from public disgrace. (Cf. W14.6.1§).
Lover Who Feigned Himself a Thief: *Alf* II 204; Burton IV 158. Chauvin VII 134-35 No. 403; *ANE* 272 No. 76.□

J226.5.1§, ‡Choice: former husband or new (current) husband.
Man of Upper Egypt and Frankish Wife: Alf IV 16?,-(text missing); Burton IX 19,-(new chosen). Chauvin V 240 No. 140; *ANE*: No. 234.□

J227.9.1§, ‡Death-wish: person in misery wishes to die. See: *DOTTI*; *PSAE*. (Cf. C869.3§, P528§, S110.0.2§, W172.5§).
Three Apples: Hasty Uxoricide: *Alf* I 61,-(old fisherman); Burton I 187. Chauvin VI 144-45 No. 302; *ANE* 414-15 No. 21;
King ¿Umar al-Nu¿mân and Sons: *Alf* I 183, 192; Burton II 124. Chauvin VI 112-24 No. 277; *ANE* 430-34 No. 39;
Tâj al-Mulûk: *Alf* I 306; Burton III 44. Chauvin V 126-28 No. 60; *ANE* 406-8 No. 40;
Jawdar and His Treacherous Brethren: *Alf* III 195; Burton VI 244. Chauvin V 257-60 No. 154; *ANE* 244-45 No. 209.□

J228.1§, ‡Poverty with higher standing with God preferred to wealth with lower standing with God.
Jewish Tray-maker and Temptress: *Alf* III 14; Burton V 267-68. Chauvin VI 187-88 No. 354; *ANE* 169 No. 166.□

J229, ‡Choice between evils—miscellaneous.
Sandal-wood Merchant and Sharpers: *Alf* III 174,-cf./(lose all od drinks sea water); Burton VI 203. Chauvin VIII 60-62 No. 26; *ANE* 359-60 No. 205.□

J229.16.5§, Choice: how to be killed by ogre (devoured, dismembered, etc.). See: *DOTTI*; *GMC*.
Fisherman and Afrit: Ingratitude: *Alf* I 15; Burton I 41. Chauvin VI 23-25 No. 195; *ANE* 183-84 No. 8;
Escaped Viper Ungrateful: *Alf* II 35,-(viper); Burton III 145. Chauvin II 227 No. 9; *ANE* 450,/passim No. 47.□

J229.16.6§, ‡Afrit (jinni), about to transform captive, gives choice of form into which to be transformed.
Second Qalandar: Afrit's Wife: *Alf* I 47,-(afrit); Burton I 127. Chauvin V 197-200 No. 116; *ANE* 338-39 No. 16.□

J229.17.1§, ‡Choice: breaking one's own oath (pledge) or friend's. (Cf. T39.1.4§).
Bulûqiya: *Alf* III 76; Burton V 387. Chauvin VII 54 No. 77; *ANE* 130-32 No. 177.□

J234.2§, ‡Health chosen above all else. (Cf. U253.1.2§).
Hind bint al-Nu¿mân and al-Ḥajjâj: *Alf* III 202-3; Burton VII 99. Chauvin V 115-4 No. 50; *ANE* 221-22 No. 212.□

J237.1§, ‡Spouse chosen rather than material gain (wealth).
Eldest Lady's Story: Treacherous Sisters: *Alf* I 56; Burton I 171. Chauvin V 4 No. 443; *ANE* 174-75 No. 19.□

J242.4, ‡Peacock proved to be bad king. Chosen because of beauty; too weak to defend his flock.
Sparrow as Peacock's Vizier: *Alf* II 41,-cf.; Burton III 162. Chauvin II 230 No. 20; *ANE* 398 No. 59.□

J248§, Luck preferred to cleverness.
Sparrow as Peacock's Vizier: *Alf* II 41,-cf.; Burton III 162. Chauvin II 230 No. 20; *ANE* 398 No. 59.□

J265§, ‡Consider the merits of the advice (counsel) before the appearance of the advisor. See: *DOTTI*.
Stolen Purse/Joint Depositors: *Alf* III 177,-cf.; Burton VI 210. Chauvin VIII 63-64 No. 25; *ANE* 399 No. 207.□

J267.3§, ‡Choice between believable lie or unbelievable (fantastic) truth. See: *DOTTI*. (Cf. J751.1).
Ma¿rûf the Cobbler: *Alf* IV 294; Burton X 10. Chauvin VI 81-82 No. 250; *ANE* 291-93 No. 262.□

J267.3.1§, ‡Believable lies chosen. See: *DOTTI*.
Ma¿rûf the Cobbler: *Alf* IV 294-95; Burton X 10-11. Chauvin VI 81-82 No. 250; *ANE* 291-93 No. 262.□

J285.0.1.1§, ‡"He who seeks high honors without hard work, wastes his life seeking the impossible". (Cf. W113.2§).
Sindbâd's First Voyage: *Alf* III 83,-(poem); Burton VI 5. Chauvin VII 7-9 No. 373A; *ANE* 385 No. 179.□

J285.1.1§, ‡'A favor (good deed) begun must be carried to its completion [before it is considered a favor]'.
King ¿Umar al-Nu¿mân and Sons: *Alf* I 192,-(*ḥasanah*); Burton II 139,-(kindly service). Chauvin VI 112-24 No. 277; *ANE* 430-34 No. 39.□

J291.1.1§, ‡'The numerous would overcome the courageous (few)'. See: *DOTTI*. (Cf. L313§).
Sindbâd's Third Voyage: *Alf* III 93; Burton VI 24. Chauvin VII 15-18 No. 373C; *ANE* 385-86 No. 179.□

J324§, ‡Present pleasure (play) preferred to future benefits from work (learning). (Cf. J149§, J1067§).
Francolin and Tortoises: *Alf* IV 172; Burton IX 114,-(transient pleasure). Chauvin II 224 No. 152/23; *ANE* 188 No. 254.□

J328.1§, ‡New invention (machine, medicine, etc.) destroyed (suppressed) for fear of its consequences. See: *DOTTI*. (Cf. D866.3§, F889.3.1§).
Ebony Horse: *Alf* II 267,-(mechanical horse); Burton V 31. Chauvin V 221-31 No. 130; *ANE* 172-74 No. 103.□

J340, Choices: little gain, big loss.
Francolin and Tortoises: *Alf* IV 172; Burton IX 114-15. Chauvin II 224 No. 152/23; *ANE* 188 No. 254.□

J355.1, Widow's meal. King upbraids wind for blowing away a poor widow's last cup of meal. [God's justice vindicated]. See: *DOTTI*.
Spider Upbraids Wind: *Alf* IV 147,-cf./(spider's web); Burton IX 59-60. Chauvin II 220 No. 152/10; *ANE* 398 No. 245.□

J373§, ‡Foolishness of ignoring major matters (problems) and dwelling on minor ones (comforts, pleasures). (Cf. P500.0.3§).
Man Who Had a Milk-camel: Loses Both: *Alf* IV 164; Burton IX 97. Chauvin VI 9 No. 184.□

J393.1§, ‡Merchant finds safety among enemy (disbelievers), but not among own people (believers).
King ¿Umar al-Nu¿mân and Sons: *Alf* I 239; Burton II 240. Chauvin VI 112-24 No. 277; *ANE* 430-34 No. 39.□

J401.0.1, "A friend is known in need". See: *DOTTI*.
Cat and Crow: *Alf* II 36; Burton III 149. Chauvin II 226 No. 4; *ANE* 142 No. 50.□

J405.1.1§, ‡'Keep your dog hungry: it will follow you'. (Cf. W40§).
Nuzhat al-Zamân Tested/¿Umar al-Nu¿mân: *Alf* I 201; Burton II 159. Chauvin VI 116, n.1/passim No. 277; *ANE* 432,/passim No. 39.□

J410, Association of equals and of unequals.
Nuzhat al-Zamân Tested/¿Umar al-Nu¿mân: *Alf* I 202; Burton II 161. Chauvin VI 116, n.1/passim No. 277; *ANE* 432,/passim No. 39.□

J410.1§, ‡Rules of interaction with those of higher, equal, and lower social rank—(body posture, greeting, speaking, sitting, etc.).
Nuzhat al-Zamân Tested/¿Umar al-Nu¿mân: *Alf* I 202,-(commoners, emirs); Burton II 161. Chauvin VI 116, n.1/passim No. 277; *ANE* 432,/passim No. 39.□

J445.2.1.1.1§, ‡Slave-girl ridicules old buyer (owner-to-be). (Cf. T367.2.1.1§).
Nûr al-Dîn and Maryam: *Alf* IV 92-96; Burton VIII 292-93. Chauvin V 52-54 No. 271; *ANE* 98-99 No. 233.□

J451, Contagiousness of bad company. (Cf. U245.0.1.1§).
¿Alî Shâr and Zumurrud: *Alf* II 217,-(-gen.); Burton IV 187. Chauvin V 89-91 No. 28; *ANE* 100-1 No. 82.□

J456§, ‡Twice a liar: flattering (the undeserving), and then telling the unflattering truth.
Ma¿rûf the Cobbler: *Alf* IV 297; Burton X 15. Chauvin VI 81-82 No. 250; *ANE* 291-93 No. 262.□

J482.4§, Young man advised to choose as wife a girl who would profess to be with him against 'Time'. See: *DOTTI*; *GMC*. (Cf. W250.5.1§, Z122.7§).

Nuzhat al-Zamân Tested/¿Umar al-Nu¿mân: *Alf* I 201-2,-(*¿alâ al-Dahr*); Burton II 159,-(against fate). Chauvin VI 116, n.1/passim No. 277; *ANE* 432,/passim No. 39.□

J484.2§, ‡Beardless (young) lover preferred to bearded: latter prickly. (Cf. F545.1.7.1§, U281.3.1§).
Barber's Second Brother: Humiliated by Playgirl: *Alf* I 113; Burton I 327,-(no hair to scratch and prick). Chauvin V 158 No. 82; *ANE* 117-18 No. 30;
Bearded and Beardless Men as Lovers: *Alf* II 303; Burton V 165. Chauvin V 112 No. 48; *ANE* 450 No. 154;
Lovers of Basra/Ḍamrah: *Alf* III 210-12,-cf./(handsome); Burton VII 130. Chauvin V 118 No. 54; *ANE* 273 No. 220.□

J484.3§, ‡Bearded (mature) lover preferred to beardless: former satisfies (delivers, experienced).
Barber's Second Brother: Humiliated by Playgirl: *Alf* I 113; Burton I 326–27. Chauvin V 158 No. 82; *ANE* 117-18 No. 30;
Bearded and Beardless Men as Lovers: *Alf* II 303; Burton V 165. Chauvin V 112 No. 48; *ANE* 450 No. 154.□

J514, One should not be greedy. See: *DOTTI*; *GMC*. (Cf. W151.0.3§).
City of Brass: *Alf* III 137; Burton VI 118. Chauvin V 32-35 No. 16; *ANE* 146-50 No. 180.□

J514.7§, ‡Greedy treasure-finder dissatisfied with fabulous riches he has seized seeks one more gem (on corpse). He is killed in the process.
City of Brass: *Alf* III 137; Burton VI 118. Chauvin V 32-35 No. 16; *ANE* 146-50 No. 180.□

J532§, ‡Unambitious person instructed to name a (large) grant commensurate with own worth (or giver's rank). (Cf. W113§).
Jawdar and His Treacherous Brethren: *Alf* III 190,-(mother/modest food); Burton VI 235. Chauvin V 257-60 No. 154; *ANE* 244-45 No. 209.□

J532.1§, ‡King instructs unambitious man to name a (large) grant commensurate with king's rank (not a small one).
King ¿Umar al-Nu¿mân and Sons: *Alf* I 309; Burton III 50. Chauvin VI 112-24 No. 277; *ANE* 430-34 No. 39.□

J535§, 'To be obeyed, demand [only] the possible'.
Fox and Crow: *Alf* II 37,-cf.; Burton III 151. Chauvin II 228 No. 11; *ANE* 188 No. 51.□

J551, Intemperate zeal in truth-telling.
Barber's Sixth Brother: Emasculated by Abductor: *Alf* I 123,-cf./(joker slapped); Burton I 346-47. Chauvin V 163-64 No. 86; *ANE* 120 No. 34.□

J559§, ‡Intemperance in opposition (disapproval, discontent). (Cf. J2519.5§).
Barber's Sixth Brother: Emasculated by Abductor: *Alf* I 123,-(practical joker slapped); Burton I 346-47. Chauvin V 163-64 No. 86; *ANE* 120 No. 34.□

J564.0.1§, ‡Intemperance in (display of) piety. See: *DOTTI*. (Cf. H69.0.1§).
Nuzhat al-Zamân Tested/¿Umar al-Nu¿mân: *Alf* I 206; Burton II 162, 170. Chauvin VI 116, n.1/passim No. 277; *ANE* 432,/passim No. 39.□

J567.1.1§, ‡Person needs to wash hands with three different cleansers, forty-times each. See: *DOTTI*. (Cf. J20§).
Reeve's Story: Why Maimed by Bride: *Alf* I 96; Burton I 278. Chauvin V 220-21 No. 305; *ANE* 351 No. 25.□

J570.1§, ‡'Rue is in haste' ('Haste makes waste)'.
King Sindbâd and Falcon: *Alf* I 19; Burton I 52. Chauvin V 289 No. 173; *ANE* 383 No. 10;
Husband and Parrot: *Alf* III 141; Burton I 54. Chauvin VI 139 No. 294; *ANE* 226 No. 11;
Craft and Malice of Women/Frame: *Alf* III 155,-([illogical parable]); Burton VI 166. Chauvin VIII 47-48 No. 15; *ANE* 285-86 No. 181.□

J570.1.1§, ‡'Haste is from Satan'. (Cf. J851§).
Tailor's Story/Barber of Baghdad: *Alf* I 106; Burton I 308. Chauvin V 154-56 No. 78; *ANE* 405-6 No. 27.□

J571, Avoid hasty judgment. See: *DOTTI*.
Ni¿mah and Nu¿m: Stolen Wife Regained: *Alf* II 143,-(by king/caliph); Burton IV 21. Chauvin VI 96-97 No. 263; *ANE* 314 No. 62.□

J571.0.1§, ‡Don't get angry (control your anger).
King Jalî¿âd and Shimâs: *Alf* IV 161; Burton IX 89. Chauvin VI 9-11 No. 184; *ANE* 237-38 No. 236.□

J571.4.4§, ‡Avoid excessive punishment.
King Jalî¿âd and Shimâs: *Alf* IV 161; Burton IX 89. Chauvin VI 9-11 No. 184; *ANE* 237-38 No. 236.□

J571.5, King restrained from hasty judgment by being told story. See: *DOTTI*.
Craft and Malice of Women/Frame: *Alf* III 139; Burton VI 128ff. Chauvin VIII 33-34 No. 1; *ANE* 160-61 No. 181.□

J571.9.1§, ‡Ruler (father) restrained from hasty action by counselor (courtier, vizier, etc.). See: *DOTTI*. (Cf. P14.15.1).
King's Son and Afrit's Mistress: *Alf* III 173; Burton VI 199-202. Chauvin VIII 59 No. 24; *ANE* 263-64 No. 204.□

J583§, ‡Wisdom of keeping secret from others. See: *DOTTI*.
Merchant's Curious Wife: *Alf* I 6; Burton I 16, 216. Chauvin V 179-80 No. 104; *ANE* 298-99 No. 3;
Porter and Ladies of Baghdad: *Alf* I 33,-(poem); Burton I 87. Chauvin V 251-52 No. 148; *ANE* 324-26 No. 14;
King ¿Umar al-Nu¿mân and Sons: *Alf* I 314,-(poem/of love recommended); Burton III 61. Chauvin VI 112-24 No. 277; *ANE* 430-34 No. 39.□

J583.1§, ‡Person blindfolded and then led to secret site (of crime, treasure, etc.). See: *DOTTI*. (Cf. J1158).
Butcher Wardân and Bear Lover: *Alf* II 250; Burton IV 293. Chauvin V 177-78 No. 101; *ANE* 442-43 No. 101.□

J584.1§, ‡'Not every time will the jar be [dropped and turn] safe (whole)'.
Three Apples: Hasty Uxoricide: *Alf* I 63,-(*wa-lâ kull marrah tislam al-jarrah*); Burton I 193,-("nor shall the crock come of safe from every shock"). Chauvin VI 144-45 No. 302; *ANE* 414-15 No. 21;
Sindbâd's Second Voyage: *Alf* III 88,-(xxx); Burton VI 15. Chauvin VII 9-14 No. 373B; *ANE* 385 No. 179;
Dalîla the Swindler: *Alf* III 222; Burton VII 162,-(the crock shall not always escape the shock). Chauvin V 245-50 No. 147; *ANE* 163-64 No. 224;
Nûr al-Dîn and Maryam: *Alf* IV 115; Burton VIII 339,-(crock). Chauvin V 52-54 No. 271; *ANE* 98-99 No. 233.□

J634, ‡King takes measures against assassination. See: *DOTTI*.
Abû Qîr and Abû Ṣîr: *Alf* IV 193; Burton IX 156. Chauvin V 15-17 No. 10; *ANE* 75-77 No. 255.□

J634.4§, ‡King orders execution of person for mere suspicion of intending to assassinate him. See: *DOTTI*.
Abû Qîr and Abû Ṣîr: *Alf* IV 193; Burton IX 157. Chauvin V 15-17 No. 10; *ANE* 75-77 No. 255.□

J637§, ‡Distrust (suspicion) is a commendable insight (*fiṭnah*).
Wolf and Fox: *Alf* II 34,-(poem); Burton III 140. Chauvin II 227 No. 6; *ANE* 450 No. 47.□

J637.1§, ‡Blind trust (benevolence, good intentions) leads to disaster. (Cf. Z122.7.1§).
Wolf and Fox: *Alf* II 34,-(poem); Burton III 140. Chauvin II 227 No. 6; *ANE* 450 No. 47;
Nûr al-Dîn and Maryam: *Alf* IV 99,-(trusting Time); Burton VIII 309. Chauvin V 52-54 No. 271; *ANE* 98-99 No. 233.□

J640.1§, ‡Foolishness of placing one's safety in enemy's hands. See: *DOTTI*.
Mouse and Cat: *Alf* IV 135-26; Burton IX 36. Chauvin II 218 No. 152/2; *ANE* 305-6 No. 237.□

J652.4.4§, ‡Warning against foreigners (Europeans/Franks, Arabs, orientals).
Nûr al-Dîn and Maryam: *Alf* IV 99-100; Burton VIII 309,-(xxx). Chauvin V 52-54 No. 271; *ANE* 98-99 No. 233.□

J652.5.1§, ‡Warnings against person with certain characteristics.
Nûr al-Dîn and Maryam: *Alf* IV 99-100; Burton VIII 309. Chauvin V 52-54 No. 271; *ANE* 98-99 No. 233.□

J670.1§, ‡Children taught defensive arts (riding, dueling, etc.).

Tâj al-Mulûk: *Alf* I 266; Burton II 291,-(cavalarice and knightly exercises). Chauvin V 126-28 No. 60; *ANE* 406-8 No. 40;
¿Alâ' al-Dîn Abû al-Shâmât: *Alf* II 173; Burton IV 79. Chauvin V 43-49 No. 18; *ANE* 85-87 No. 63.□

J674.4§, ‡Child raised in sealed (windowless, underground, etc.) quarters to protect him from danger. See: *DOTTI*. (Cf. D2071.1.3.1.2§, J147, T257.9.0.1§).
¿Alâ' al-Dîn Abû al-Shâmât: *Alf* II 149; Burton IV 33. Chauvin V 43-49 No. 18; *ANE* 85-87 No. 63.□

J675.0.1§, Preemptive actions: anticipatory treachery countervailed by treacherous acts. See: *DOTTI*. (Cf. K2173§, P794.2§, P550.5§).
Dûban and King Yûnân: *Alf* I 20,-(kill before getting killed); Burton I 56,-(deceive). Chauvin V 275-76 No. 156; *ANE* 459 No. 9;
Wife's device to cheat: (Weeping Bitch as Bluff): *Alf* III 149-50,-cf.; Burton VI 155. Chauvin VIII 45-46 No. 13; *ANE* 447-49 No. 193;
King Jalî¿âd and Shimâs: *Alf* IV 170-71; Burton IX 107-8. Chauvin VI 9 No. 184; *ANE* 237-38 No. 236.□

J679.1§, ‡'He who intrudes into what is not his business, will hear what will not please him'. (Cf. Q340.1§).
Porter and Ladies of Baghdad: *Alf* I 35; Burton I 93. Chauvin V 251-52 No. 148; *ANE* 324-26 No. 14.□

J679.5§, ‡Truth-speaking meddler fails to prove his report (claim): punished for 'slander'. See: *DOTTI*. (Cf. J551, J2143, K2107.3§, K2150, N680.3§, P526.0.2§).
Husband and Parrot: *Alf* III 141,-cf.; Burton I 53. Chauvin VI 139 No. 294; *ANE* 226 No. 11.□

J682, Foolishness of alliance with the weak.
Francolin and Tortoises: *Alf* IV 172; Burton IX 114. Chauvin II 224 No. 152/23; *ANE* 188 No. 254.□

J684.6§, ‡Being owned (as slave) by the powerful (rich) guarantees comfortable living. (Cf. P178.5.1§).
Ruined Baghdadi and His Slave-girl: *Alf* IV 130; Burton IX 24. Chauvin V 152-53 No. 75; *ANE* 353 No. 235.□

J700.1§, ‡Wisdom of choosing that which is compatible with one's own attributes (limitations). (Cf. P530§, T91).
Ebony Horse: *Alf* II 263-64,-(villain's ruse); Burton V 27. Chauvin V 221-31 No. 130; *ANE* 172-74 No. 103.□

J702.0.1§, ‡Learning a trade (craft) is a necessity.
Tâj al-Mulûk: *Alf* I 292,-(being a merchant/business); Burton III 16. Chauvin V 126-28 No. 60; *ANE* 406-8 No. 40.□

J702.0.1.1§, ‡'A craft (trade) in hand shields from poverty'.
Jawdar and His Treacherous Brethren: *Alf* III 178,-cf./(implicit/fisherman); Burton VI 214. Chauvin V 257-60 No. 154; *ANE* 244-45 No. 209.□

J708.5§, Gift-giving (exchange of presents) as farsighted economy. See: *DOTTI*; *GMC*. (Cf. P771.1§, W11).
Ma¿n Rewards a Bedouin for Gift: *Alf* II 182-83,-cf.; Burton IV 98-99. Chauvin VI 78 No. 248; *ANE* 291 No. 66.□

J708.5.2§, ‡'Harvesting [a gift]': gift received in reciprocity to one given. See: *DOTTI*.
Sindbâd's First Voyage: *Alf* III 87; Burton VI 13. Chauvin VII 7-9 No. 373A; *ANE* 385 No. 179;
Abû Qîr and Abû Ṣîr: *Alf* IV 194,-(repaying a kindness); Burton IX 158. Chauvin V 15-17 No. 10; *ANE* 75-77 No. 255.□

J708.8§, ‡'Planting a kindness (*jamîl/'gimîl,' ma¿rûf*): harvesting a kindness. See: *DOTTI*; *PSAE*. (Cf. F179§, J26, P320.0.5.1§, P327, Q40, W14.0.2§).
Portress Amînah: Bitten Cheek: *Alf* I 60; Burton I 184,-(sowed the seed of kindness). Chauvin V 98-99 No. 33; *ANE* 326-27 No. 20;
Wolf and Fox: *Alf* II 31,-(poem); Burton III 136. Chauvin II 227 No. 6; *ANE* 450 No. 47;
Abû Qîr and Abû Ṣîr: *Alf* IV 191,-(with king's steward); Burton IX 153,-(with king's sea-captain). Chauvin V 15-17 No. 10; *ANE* 75-77 No. 255.□

J711, In time of plenty provide for want. See: *DOTTI*; *GMC*. (Cf. P603.1§).
Lazy Sower (Farmer): *Alf* II 39,-cf.; Burton III 156-57,-("husbandman"). Chauvin II 229 No. 16□

J712.1, City without provisions but with much money starves. See: *ANE*; *DOTTI*; *GMC*.
City of Brass: *Alf* III 133; Burton VI 111. Chauvin V 32-35 No. 16; *ANE* 146-50 No. 180.□

J716§, Hunger drives to risk-taking. See: *DOTTI*. (Cf. U248.1§).
Crow and Viper: *Alf* IV 141,-cf./(implicit); Burton IX 46. Chauvin II 219 No. 152/5; *ANE* 162 No. 240;
Hungry Eagle Snared: *Alf* IV 152,-(*¿Uqâb kâsir*); Burton IX 70,-("Ossifrage"/bone-breaking). Chauvin II 127-128 No. 133,-cf.;
Hunter Rides Lion: Devoured: *Alf* IV 153; Burton IX 72. Chauvin II 222 No. 152/15.□

J716.1§, ‡Fisher (hunter) disregards danger in pursuit of catch (game): painful results. (Cf. W151.9.3§).
Foolish Fisher: *Alf* IV 162; Burton IX 93-95. Chauvin II 222 No. 152/16; *ANE* 187 No. 248.□

J751.1, Truth the best policy. (Cf. U192.0.1§).
Fox and Crow: *Alf* II 37,-cf.; Burton III 151. Chauvin II 228 No. 11; *ANE* 188 No. 51.□

J754.1§, ‡Do not set hay (dry grass) next to fire. (Cf. J215.1.1).
King ¿Umar al-Nu¿mân and Sons: *Alf* I 313-14,-(figurative); Burton III 59,-(to join Halfah [dry] grass and fire is risky). Chauvin VI 112-24 No. 277; *ANE* 430-34 No. 39.□

J751.0.1§, ‡Look before you leap. See: *DOTTI*. (Cf. J2§, J21.1).
Wolf and Fox: *Alf* II 32,-cf./(consider the consequences); Burton III 135,-(variant). Chauvin II 227 No. 6; *ANE* 450 No. 47;
Flea and She-mouse: *Alf* II 36,-cf./(consider the consequences); Burton III 148. Chauvin II 228 No. 12; *ANE* 186 No. 52;
Hungry Eagle Snared: *Alf* IV 152,-(*¿Uqâb kâsir*); Burton IX 70,-("Ossifrage"/bone-breaking). Chauvin II 127-128 No. 133,-cf.;
Foolish Fisher: *Alf* IV 163; Burton IX 93-94. Chauvin II 222 No. 152/16; *ANE* 187 No. 248.□

J751.2§, ‡Fulfill your promise(s).
King Jalî¿âd and Shimâs: *Alf* IV 161; Burton IX 89. Chauvin VI 9-11 No. 184; *ANE* 237-38 No. 236.□

J758.8§, ‡Adviser's counsel rejected.
Wolf and Fox: *Alf* II 29; Burton III 132. Chauvin II 227 No. 6; *ANE* 450 No. 47.□

J759§, ‡Repartee concerning age (the old and the young). See: *DOTTI*.
Pretty Gray-haired Woman Retorts: *Alf* II 302-3; Burton V 163. Chauvin VI 153 No. 318; *ANE* 77-78 No. 152.□

J760.0.1§, ‡Living person prepares for own burial. See: *PSAE*.
Jânshâh: *Alf* III 73; Burton V 381. Chauvin VII 39-44 No. 153; *ANE* 238-41 No. 178.□

J760.1§, ‡Burial plot (grave) prepared (along with other accompaniments—coffin, shrouds, prayers, etc.). See: *DOTTI*; *PSAE*.
¿Azîz and ¿Azîzah: *Alf* I 307,-(by mother for absent son); Burton III 46. Chauvin V 144-45 No. 71; *ANE* 111-13 No. 41;
Jânshâh: *Alf* III 38, 73,-cf.; Burton V 327-28, 380,-(tombs). Chauvin VII 39-44 No. 153; *ANE* 238-41 No. 178;
Hasan of Basrah: *Alf* III 305,-(by mother for absent son); Burton VIII 15. Chauvin VII 29-35 No. 212A; *ANE* 207-10 No. 230.□

J760.2§, ‡Shroud (undertaker) taken along when visiting person doomed to death. See: *DOTTI*.
First Shaykh: Sorceress Wife: *Alf* I 10; Burton I 29. Chauvin VII 129-30 No. 396; *ANE* 376-77 No. 5;
Shahriyâr and Shahrzâd: *Alf* IV 315; Burton X 50. Chauvin VI 81-82 No. 250; *ANE* 291-93 No. 1.□

J761.0.1§, ‡Appearance of gray hair (whiskers) causes concern.
¿Alâ' al-Dîn Abû al-Shâmât: *Alf* II 147; Burton IV 29. Chauvin V 43-49 No. 18; *ANE* 85-87 No. 63;
City of Brass: *Alf* III 136; Burton VI 117,-(hoary hairs). Chauvin V 32-35 No. 16; *ANE* 146-50 No. 180;
Dalîla the Swindler: *Alf* III 213; Burton VII 147. Chauvin V 245-50 No. 147; *ANE* 163-64 No. 224.□

J761.5§, ‡The aged (weak) need to rely on strategy, not on physical strength. See: *DOTTI*. (Cf. L458.1§).
Saker and Birds: *Alf* II 38; Burton III 155. Chauvin II 228 No. 13; *ANE* 357-58 No. 53.□

J811, Wisdom of concessions to power.
Water-fowl and Tortoise: *Alf* II 28,-cf./(general); Burton III 130. Chauvin II 226-27 No. 5; *ANE* 444 No. 46;
Mock Caliph/¿Alî al-Jawharî: *Alf* II 198,-(Zubaydah's power); Burton IV 144. Chauvin V 99-100 No. 174; *ANE* 304-5 No. 73.□

J813§, ‡Enemy whose friendship is a must. (Cf. N101, P795§).
King ¿Umar al-Nu¿mân and Sons: *Alf* II 8,-(poem,/implicit); Burton III 89. Chauvin VI 112-24 No. 277; *ANE* 430-34 No. 39.□

J814, Flattery of the great. (Cf. Z194.2.1.2§) .
Uns al-Wujûd and al-Ward: *Alf* II 272,-(lion); Burton V 40. Chauvin VI 127-29 No. 282; *ANE* 438 No. 104.□

J815.5.5§, ‡Tactful (kind) reply.
¿Alî bin Ṭâhir and Mu'nis: *Alf* II 303; Burton V 164. Chauvin VI 154 No. 319; *ANE* 101 No. 153.□

J816.5§, ‡Unjust act of ruler brought to his attention by reminding him of exemplary justice of his predecessor.
Nuzhat al-Zamân Tested/¿Umar al-Nu¿mân: *Alf* I 203; Burton II 163. Chauvin VI 116, n.1/passim No. 277; *ANE* 432,/passim No. 39.□

J818.2§, ‡Caution in advising wayward (despotic) king.
King Jalî¿âd and Shimâs: *Alf* IV 162; Burton IX 91. Chauvin VI 9-11 No. 184; *ANE* 237-38 No. 236.□

J837.2.1§, ‡When the threats fail try soft-talk (promise reward). (Cf. J26).
Fisherman and Afrit: Ingratitude: *Alf* I 16; Burton I 44. Chauvin VI 23-25 No. 195; *ANE* 183-84 No. 8;
Jawdar and His Treacherous Brethren: *Alf* III 198; Burton VI 249. Chauvin V 257-60 No. 154; *ANE* 244-45 No. 209.□

J837.2.2§, ‡One gets by ruse what cannot be gotten by the sword.
Ma¿rûf the Cobbler: *Alf* IV 312,-(poem); Burton X 44. Chauvin VI 81-82 No. 250; *ANE* 291-93 No. 262.□

J838.1§, ‡Moving away from own home to avoid abusive (unwelcome) neighbor. (Cf. R213.3§).
Birds, Beasts, and Carpenter: *Alf* II 24,-(*thaqîl*/unbearable); Burton III 120,-(tyrant). Chauvin II 225-26 No. 1; *ANE* 126 No. 44;
Crow and Viper: *Alf* IV 141; Burton IX 46. Chauvin II 219 No. 152/5; *ANE* 162 No. 240.□

J838.1.1§, ‡Person moves away from town (country) to escape meddler.
Tailor's Story/Barber of Baghdad: *Alf* I 103; Burton I 301. Chauvin V 154-56 No. 78; *ANE* 405-6 No. 27.□

J850§, ‡Consolation in misfortune by patience. See: *DOTTI*. (Cf. U262, W26, W26.0.1.2§, Z95.1§).
¿Alâ' al-Dîn Abû al-Shâmât: *Alf* II 158,-(poem); Burton IV 54. Chauvin V 43-49 No. 18; *ANE* 85-87 No. 63;
Masrûr and Zayn al-Mawâṣif: *Alf* IV 72; Burton VIII 243. Chauvin VI 82-84 No. 251; *ANE* 294-95 No. 232.□

J851§, ‡Patience is the best remedy (medicine) for suffering. See: *DOTTI*. (Cf. J570.1§).
¿Alî ibn Bakkâr: *Alf* II 53,-(poems); Burton III 186. Chauvin V 153 No. 76; *ANE* 92-93 No. 60;
Sayf al-Mulûk: *Alf* III 283,-(poem); Burton VII 337. Chauvin VII 64-73 No. 348; *ANE* 362-64 No. 229;
King Jalî¿âd and Shimâs: *Alf* IV 139; Burton IX 45. Chauvin VI 9 No. 184; *ANE* 237-38 No. 236;
Fish and Crab: *Alf* IV 140; Burton IX 45. Chauvin II 219 No. 152/4; *ANE* 185-86 No. 239;
King Jalî¿âd and Shimâs: *Alf* IV 161; Burton IX 89. Chauvin VI 9-11 No. 184; *ANE* 237-38 No. 236.□

J857§, ‡Proud person keeps news of his misfortune secret so as to avoid enemy's *shamâtah* (pleasure in his suffering).

Jeweler's Wife and Qamar al-Zamân: *Alf* IV 261; Burton IX 292. Chauvin V 212-14 No. 121; *ANE* 345-47 No. 260.□

J882.2, Man with unfaithful wife comforted when he sees jealous husband who carefully guards wife cuckolded. See: *ANE*; *DOTTI*.
Shahriyâr and Shâhzamân: *Alf* I 2-3,-cf./(brother's wife); Burton I 4. Chauvin V 188-91 No. 111; *ANE* 370-71 No. 1;
Jinni Keeps Mistress in Box: *Alf* I 4-5,-(jinni's/afrit's mistress); Burton I 11. Chauvin V 188-91 No. 111; *ANE* 370-71 No. 1.□

J886§, Greater grief: person seeks consolation in adversity. See: *DOTTI*; *GMC*. (Cf. H1314§, W30.5§).
Shahriyâr and Shâhzamân: *Alf* I 2-3,-(same grief/calamity); Burton I 10,-(like calamity). Chauvin V 188-91 No. 111; *ANE* 370-71 No. 1;
Jawdar and His Treacherous Brethren: *Alf* III 195,-(Joseph's, 'proverbial usage'); Burton VI 244. Chauvin V 257-60 No. 154; *ANE* 244-45 No. 209.□

J910.0.1§, ‡Exemplary humility of a ruler (caliph, king, etc.).
Nuzhat al-Zamân Tested/¿Umar al-Nu¿mân: *Alf* I 203-4,-(Omar's); Burton II 163-64. Chauvin VI 116, n.1/passim No. 277; *ANE* 432,/passim No. 39.□

J910.2§, ‡Humility of great savant(s).
Spy, Old Woman/¿Umar al-Nu¿mân: *Alf* I 224-25,-(Imam al-Shâfi¿î); Burton II 207-8. *ANE* 432 No. 39/passim.□

J950.1§, ‡Lowly presuming to be great (powerful) becomes abusive and insufferable. See: *DOTTI*. (Cf. W166§).
Barber's Fifth Brother: Daydreams/Defeats Robbers: *Alf* I 118,-(in day-dream); Burton I 335-38. Chauvin V 161 No. 85; *ANE* 119-20 No. 33.□

J951.7.1§, ‡Poor cobbler claims to be rich merchant. See: *DOTTI*.
Ma¿rûf the Cobbler: *Alf* IV 295; Burton X 10-11. Chauvin VI 81-82 No. 250; *ANE* 291-93 No. 262.□

J953, Self-deception of the lowly. (Cf. W199.9.1§).
Barber's Fifth Brother: Daydreams/Defeats Robbers: *Alf* I 118; Burton I 335-37. Chauvin V 161 No. 85; *ANE* 119-20 No. 33;
Foolish Weaver: *Alf* II 40,-cf.; Burton III 160. Chauvin II 229 No. 19; *ANE* 187 No. 58.□

J1014§, ‡Making a living (by earning wages). See: *DOTTI*. (Cf. P771.3.5§, P775.4§).
al-Rashîd and Omani Merchant: *Alf* IV 216; Burton IX 200. Chauvin VI 111-12 No. 276; *ANE* 201-2 No. 257;
Abû al-Ḥasan al-Khorâsânî (and Caliph's Favorite): *Alf* IV 231,-cf./(follow father's trade); Burton IX 233. Chauvin V 218-20 No. 129; *ANE* 68-69 No. 259.□

J1014.0.2§, ‡Work (industry) is a blessing (from God).
Spy, Fourth Maiden/¿Umar al-Nu¿mân: *Alf* I 222,-(*bâb al-¿amal*); Burton II 204,-("gate of action"). *ANE* 432 No. 39/passim.□

J1014.0.2.1§, ‡It is fortunate for a person to make a living ('receive livelihood') in own country (town). (Cf. A189.7.1§, J2068.3§, J2068.3§).
¿Alâ' al-Dîn Abû al-Shâmât: *Alf* II 152; Burton IV 40. Chauvin V 43-49 No. 18; *ANE* 85-87 No. 63.□

J1014.1§, ‡"Wages are claimed by the clever (hireling), and paid by the clever (employer)". (Cf. P431.0.4§).
Mercury ¿Alî: *Alf* III 230; Burton VII 179. Chauvin V 248-50 No. 147; *ANE* 301-3 No. 225.□

J1015§, Wealth gained by risk-taking and hard work. See: *DOTTI*; *GMC*.
Sindbâd's First Voyage: *Alf* III 83; Burton VI 5. Chauvin VII 7-9 No. 373A; *ANE* 385 No. 179.□

J1016§, ‡Glory (success) is achieved in proportion to hard work. (Cf. N190§, N100.1.1.1§).
Nûr al-Dîn ¿Alî and Son: *Alf* I 65,-cf./(poem/moving away); Burton I 196. Chauvin VI 102-6 No. 270; *ANE* 317-19 No. 22;
Sindbâd's First Voyage: *Alf* III 83,-(poem); Burton VI 5. Chauvin VII 7-9 No. 373A; *ANE* 385 No. 179.□

J1016.0.1§, ‡Idleness ("comfort") is valueless.

¿Abdallah ibn Fâḍil: Treacherous Brothers: *Alf* IV 270; Burton IX 312,-("peace is priceless"). Chauvin V 2-4 No. 2; *ANE* 63-65 No. 261.□

J1016.0.1.1§, ‡Life's enjoyment is in hard work (laboring oneself).
Nûr al-Dîn ¿Alî and Son: *Alf* I 65,-(poem); Burton I 196. Chauvin VI 102-6 No. 270; *ANE* 317-19 No. 22.□

J1016.0.1.1.1§, ‡'No comfort except after hard work'.
¿Alî ibn Bakkâr: *Alf* II 55; Burton III 191-92. Chauvin V 153 No. 76; *ANE* 92-93 No. 60.□

J1028.1§, ‡Mutually complementary differences. See: *DOTTI*.
Blind and Cripple Corporate: *Alf* IV 150,-cf.; Burton IX 70. Chauvin II 221 No. 152/13; *ANE* 127 No. 247.□

J1030.1§, ‡Maturity (growing up, independence, 'individuation') gained by leaving home. See: *DOTTI*. (Cf. J1077§, J2068§).
Nûr al-Dîn ¿Alî and Son: *Alf* I 65,-(poem); Burton I 198. Chauvin VI 102-6 No. 270; *ANE* 317-19 No. 22;
King ¿Umar al-Nu¿mân and Sons: *Alf* I 187,-cf./(twin brother and sister); Burton II 132. Chauvin VI 112-24 No. 277; *ANE* 430-34 No. 39.□

J1056§, ‡Youth disregards elder's warning and suffers consequences. (Cf. P253.6.2§).
¿Alâ' al-Dîn Abû al-Shâmât: *Alf* II 153; Burton IV 42. Chauvin V 43-49 No. 18; *ANE* 85-87 No. 63.□

J1062, Cure yourself before doctoring others. (Cf. U275§).
Sick Man Tries to Heal Another: *Alf* II 32; Burton III 140. Chauvin II 227 No. 8.□

J1062.2, Doctor unable to cure himself scorned. See: *GMC*.
Sick Man Tries to Heal Another: *Alf* II 32; Burton III 140. Chauvin II 227 No. 8.□

J1063.0.1§, Projection: attributing to others one's own shortcomings (defects). See: *DOTTI*.
Reeve's Story: Why Maimed by Bride: *Alf* I 98-99,-(sane groom called crazy); Burton I 287,-(beaten severely). Chauvin V 220-21 No. 305; *ANE* 351 No. 25;
Tailor's Story/Barber of Baghdad: *Alf* I 108,-(by barber); Burton I 317. Chauvin V 154-56 No. 78; *ANE* 405-6 No. 27.□

J1067§, ‡The stupid pupil (apprentice) fails to learn. See: *DOTTI*.
Bulûqiya/Ḥâsib/Queen of Vipers: *Alf* III 19; Burton V 299. Chauvin VII 54 No. 77; *ANE* 130-32 No. 177.□

J1071, Results of labor lost in a moment of procrastination. See: *DOTTI*. (Cf. W123.2§).
Lazy Sower (Farmer): *Alf* II 39,-(*zâri¿*); Burton III 156-57,-("husbandman"). Chauvin II 229 No. 16.□

J1076.0.1§, ‡'Avoid traveling, even a one mile trip'.
¿Alâ' al-Dîn Abû al-Shâmât: *Alf* II 152; Burton IV 40. Chauvin V 43-49 No. 18; *ANE* 85-87 No. 63.□

J1077§, ‡Merits of distant travel. See: *DOTTI*; *PSAE*. (Cf. J1030.1§, J2068§, U290§).
Nûr al-Dîn ¿Alî and Son: *Alf* I 65,-(poem); Burton I 197–98. Chauvin VI 102-6 No. 270; *ANE* 317-19 No. 22;
Abû Qîr and Abû Ṣîr: *Alf* IV 184,-(poem); Burton IX 138. Chauvin V 15-17 No. 10; *ANE* 75-77 No. 255.□

J1077.0.1§, ‡Love of distant travel.
King ¿Umar al-Nu¿mân and Sons: *Alf* I 241; Burton II 244. Chauvin VI 112-24 No. 277; *ANE* 430-34 No. 39;
Nûr al-Dîn and Maryam: *Alf* IV 80; Burton VIII 264. Chauvin V 52-54 No. 271; *ANE* 98-99 No. 233.□

J1077.0.1.1§, ‡Irresistible urge (compulsion) to travel. (Cf. P426.2.3§).
Conversion of Princess by Khawwâṣ: *Alf* III 14; Burton V 283. Chauvin V 239 No. 139; *ANE* 145 No. 171.□

J1077.1§, ‡Traveling allows interaction with (knowledge of) different peoples (races, nations, ethnic groups). See: *DOTTI*. (Cf. P426.2.3§).
Sindbâd's Second Voyage: *Alf* III 88; Burton VI 14. Chauvin VII 7 No. 373; *ANE* 385 No. 179;

Sindbâd's Fifth Voyage: *Alf* III 108; Burton VI 48. Chauvin VII 21-24 No. 373E; *ANE* 386 No. 179;

Sindbâd's Seventh Voyage: *Alf* III 116; Burton VI 69. Chauvin VII 24 No. 373F; *ANE* 386-87 No. 179;
Abû Qîr and Abû Şîr: *Alf* IV 184; Burton IX 138. Chauvin V 15-17 No. 10; *ANE* 75-77 No. 255.□

J1077.2§, ‡Traveling allows enjoyment of different landscapes, ('wonders of the world', scenes, etc.). (Tourism).
Jewish Doctor's Story: Sororicide: *Alf* I 100; Burton I 289. Chauvin VI 89 No. 253; *ANE* 242 No. 26;
Sindbâd's Second Voyage: *Alf* III 88; Burton VI 14. Chauvin VII 7 No. 373; *ANE* 385 No. 179;
Abû Qîr and Abû Şîr: *Alf* IV 184; Burton IX 138. Chauvin V 15-17 No. 10; *ANE* 75-77 No. 255.□

J1077.2.1§, ‡Falling in love with a country (city). (Cf. F769.5§).
al-Rashîd and Omani Merchant: *Alf* IV 211,-(al-Başrah); Burton IX 193. Chauvin VI 111-12 No. 276; *ANE* 201-2 No. 257.□

J1077.2.1.1§, ‡Falling in love with a country (city) from mere mention of its merits.
Copt Broker's Story: Lover's Sacrifices Repaid: *Alf* I 89,-cf./(Egypt); Burton I 264. Chauvin VI 80 No. 249; *ANE* 313-14 No. 24;
Jewish Doctor's Story: Sororicide: *Alf* I 100,-(Egypt); Burton I 290. Chauvin VI 89 No. 253; *ANE* 242 No. 26;
House with the Belvedere: *Alf* III 166,-(*bilâd Baghdâd*); Burton VI 189,-(city of Baghdad). Chauvin VIII 57-58 No. 23; *ANE* 223 No. 203.□

J1077.3§, ‡Traveling as source of pride. (Cf. P772.1.2§).
¿Alâ' al-Dîn Abû al-Shâmât: *Alf* II 151,-(for men only); Burton IV 39. Chauvin V 43-49 No. 18; *ANE* 85-87 No. 63.□

J1077.4§, ‡Traveling as remedy for emotional troubles (e.g., depression, failure, or the like). (Cf. F950).
¿Azîz and ¿Azîzah: *Alf* I 289,-(sadness); Burton III 6. Chauvin V 144-45 No. 71; *ANE* 111-13 No. 41.□

J1080§, ‡Sleeplessness: person unable to fall (stay) asleep due to worries. See: *DOTTI*. (Cf. F956.7.6.3§, T24.9.1§).
Shahriyâr and Shahrzâd: *Alf* I 7,-(*qalaq*); Burton I 23. Chauvin V 188-89 No. 111; *ANE* 370-71 No. 1;
Ghânim ibn Ayyûb: *Alf* I 147; Burton II 47. Chauvin VI 14-16 No. 188; *ANE* 192-93 No. 36;
Qamar al-Zamân and Budûr: *Alf* II 69,-(king *mutashawwish al-khâţir*); Burton III 220. Chauvin V 204-12 No. 120; *ANE* 341-45 No. 61;
Mock Caliph/¿Alî al-Jawharî: *Alf* II 191; Burton IV 130. Chauvin V 99-100 No. 174; *ANE* 304-5 No. 73;
Kurd's Sack/¿Alî the Persian: *Alf* II 200; Burton IV 149, 150. Chauvin V 279 No. 162; *ANE* 99-100 No. 74;
Budûr and Jubayr ibn ¿Umayr: *Alf* II 235; Burton IV 228. Chauvin VII 93-94 No. 374; *ANE* 243-44 No. 83;
Basra Girls in Poetry Contest: *Alf* III 204; Burton VII 110. Chauvin VI 144 No. 301; *ANE* 107-8 No. 216;
al-Rashîd and Omani Merchant: *Alf* IV 208; Burton IX 188. Chauvin VI 111-12 No. 276; *ANE* 201-2 No. 257.□

J1101§, ‡'Caution is [the better] half of cleverness (intelligence)'.
Wolf and Fox: *Alf* II 30; Burton III 134. Chauvin II 227 No. 6; *ANE* 450 No. 47.□

J1110.1§, ‡Remarkable deeds by person clever at debate (argument, persuasion). See: *DOTTI*. (Cf. F676.3§).
King ¿Umar al-Nu¿mân and Sons: *Alf* I 236; Burton II 234. Chauvin VI 112-24 No. 277; *ANE* 430-34 No. 39.□

J1110.1.4§, ‡Person so clever that 'he (she) can wile the snake out of own den (hole)'. (Cf. F669.1.1§).
Dalîla the Swindler: *Alf* III 213,-(*al-thu¿bân*/male snake); Burton VII 145,-("dragon"). Chauvin V 248-50 No. 147; *ANE* 163-64 No. 224.□

J1111.4.1§, Clever Bedouin's daughter. See: *DOTTI*.

Hârûn and Arab Girl: *Alf* III 204; Burton VII 108-10. Chauvin VI 143 No. 300; *ANE* 202 No. 215.□

J1112, Clever wife. See: *DOTTI*. (Cf. R152).
Shahriyâr and Shahrzâd: *Alf* I 7; Burton I 29ff. Chauvin V 188-89 No. 111; *ANE* 370-71 No. 1.□

J1112.1.0.3§, Wife reforms (tames) wayward (disgruntled, shrewish) husband—as she would a lion: by appeasement. See: *DOTTI*.
Shahriyâr and Shahrzâd: *Alf* IV 317,-cf.; Burton X 54-55. Chauvin V 190-91 No. 111/pt.; *ANE* 371 No. 1.□

J1113, Clever boy. See: *DOTTI*; *GMC*.
Hishâm and Arab Youth: *Alf* II 184,-cf.; Burton IV 101-3. Chauvin V 288 No. 172; *ANE* 222-23 No. 68;
Devout Jewess and Wicked Elders: *Alf* II 286,-(Dânyâl/Daniel); Burton V 97. Chauvin VI 193-93 No. 362; *ANE* 169 No. 128;
Debauchee and Three Years Old Child: *Alf* III 176; Burton VI 208. Chauvin VIII 62-63 No. 147; *ANE* 166-67 No. 206;
Mercury ¿Alî: *Alf* III 230; Burton VII 179. Chauvin V 248-50 No. 147; *ANE* 301-3 No. 225.□

J1117.1.1§, Fox as trickster. See: *DOTTI*; *GMC*.
Wolf and Fox: *Alf* II 30-35; Burton III 132-46. Chauvin II 227 No. 6; *ANE* 450 No. 47.□

J1117.4§, Hedgehog (porcupine) as trickster. See: *DOTTI*; *GMC*.
Hedgehog and Wood-pigeons: *Alf* II 39,-(porcupine); Burton III 156-58. Chauvin II 229 No. 15; *ANE* 220 No. 55.□

J1129§, Female trickster. See: *DOTTI*; *GMC*. (Cf. P431.2§).
Dalîla the Swindler: *Alf* III 212-27; Burton VII 144ff. Chauvin V 245-50 No. 147; *ANE* 163-64 No. 224.□

J1129.1§, Dalîlah as trickster. See: *DOTTI*.
Dalîla the Swindler: *Alf* III 212-27; Burton VII 144ff. Chauvin V 245-50 No. 147; *ANE* 163-64 No. 224.□

J1140.3§, Mysterious murder solved: murderer detected. See: *DOTTI*; *GMC*. (Cf. S118.5§).
Three Apples: Hasty Uxoricide: *Alf* I 61; Burton I 186–94. Chauvin VI 144-45 No. 302; *ANE* 414-15 No. 21.□

J1141.1.9.1§, ‡Culprit led to believe detective knows truth by supernatural means (e.g., cutting sand, familiar spirit, or the like): confesses. (Cf. D1812.3.2).
¿Alî Shâr and Zumurrud: *Alf* II 229-31; Burton IV 215. Chauvin V 89-91 No. 28; *ANE* 100-1 No. 82.□

J1141.1.19.1§, ‡Confession sought or obtained by torture. See: *DOTTI*. (Cf. N482).
¿Alâ' al-Dîn Abû al-Shâmât: *Alf* II 175; Burton IV 83. Chauvin V 43-49 No. 18; *ANE* 85-87 No. 63;
Stolen Necklace/Hasty Accusation: *Alf* III 164; Burton VI 182-83. Chauvin VIII 53 No. 20; *ANE* 398 No. 200;
Jawdar and His Treacherous Brethren: *Alf* III 193; Burton VI 241. Chauvin V 257-60 No. 154; *ANE* 244-45 No. 209;
¿Abdallah ibn Fâḍil: Treacherous Brothers: *Alf* IV 288; Burton IX 349. Chauvin V 2-4 No. 2; *ANE* 63-65 No. 261.□

J1141.1.19.1.1§, ‡Confession obtained by threatening with torture (execution). (Cf. N482.3§).
Masrûr and Zayn al-Mawâṣif: *Alf* IV 76; Burton VIII 257. Chauvin VI 82-84 No. 251; *ANE* 294-95 No. 232.□

J1141.1.19.1.2§, ‡Confession obtained by torture valueless: made to escape pain (torment).
Jewish Doctor's Story: Sororicide: *Alf* I 101; Burton I 296. Chauvin VI 89 No. 253; *ANE* 242 No. 26;
Qamar al-Zamân and Budûr: *Alf* II 81, 82,-cf.; Burton III 243, 246. Chauvin V 204-12 No. 120; *ANE* 341-45 No. 61;
Masrûr and Zayn al-Mawâṣif: *Alf* IV 76,-cf.; Burton VIII 257. Chauvin VI 82-84 No. 251; *ANE* 294-95 No. 232.□

J1141.4, ‡Confession induced by bringing an unjust action against accused. False message to thief's wife to send the stolen jewel case as bribe to the judge. She does. See: *DOTTI*; *GMC*. (Cf. J224.1§).

Three Apples: Hasty Uxoricide: *Alf* I 61; Burton I 190. Chauvin VI 144-45 No. 302; *ANE* 414-15 No. 21.□

J1141.4.1§, ‡Confession induced by threatening collective (extreme) punishment against the entire community of the accused. (Cf. S101§).
Portress Amînah: Bitten Cheek: *Alf* I 59; Burton I 180,-(kill every donkey boy). Chauvin V 98-99 No. 33; *ANE* 326-27 No. 20.□

J1142.7.1§, ‡Examination of semen as method of detecting sexual crime. (Cf. K2112.2.5§).
Rake's Trick Against Chaste Wife: *Alf* III 142; Burton VI 136. Chauvin VIII 37 No. 5; *ANE* 350-1 No. 185.□

J1148§, Self-incrimination due to tongue-slip (projection, compulsion to confess). See: *DOTTI*. (Cf. J1149.10.1§, K1067.1§, N474.1§, N616§).
Isḥâq al-Mûṣilî and Khadîjah bint al-Ḥasan: *Alf* II 188,-cf.; Burton IV 124. Chauvin V 241-42 No. 142; *ANE* 232 No. 71;
Masrûr and Zayn al-Mawâṣif: *Alf* IV 65; Burton VIII 232. Chauvin VI 82-84 No. 251; *ANE* 294-95 No. 232.□

J1149.10.1§, ‡Sleeper talks in his sleep: secret (crime) is thus revealed (detected). (Cf. J1148§).
Masrûr and Zayn al-Mawâṣif: *Alf* IV 65; Burton VIII 232. Chauvin VI 82-84 No. 251; *ANE* 294-95 No. 232.□

J1149.14§, ‡Evidence acquired through ruse (trick). (Cf. K2153.2§).
Goldsmith and Cashmere Singer: *Alf* III 151; Burton VI 157-58. Chauvin VIII 46-47 No. 14; *ANE* 196 No. 194.□

J1150.1§, ‡Eyewitness account (testimony) more reliable than hearsay. (Cf. J169.0.2§).
King ¿Umar al-Nu¿mân and Sons: *Alf* II 8,-(formulaic); Burton III 89. Chauvin VI 112-24 No. 277; *ANE* 430-34 No. 39;
Kurd's Sack/¿Alî the Persian: *Alf* II 200,-cf./(formulaic); Burton IV 149. Chauvin V 279 No. 162; *ANE* 99-100 No. 74;
Budûr and Jubayr ibn ¿Umayr: *Alf* II 235; Burton IV 230. Chauvin VII 93-94 No. 374; *ANE* 243-44 No. 83;
Man from Yaman and Six Salve-girls: Flyting: *Alf* II 244,-(never heard/formulaic); Burton IV 245. Chauvin VI 151 No. 313; *ANE* 289-90 No. 84.□

J1150.1.1§, ‡Eyewitness account more reliable than visions or divinations. (Cf. J1990.0.1§).
Lovers of Banû ¿Udhrah and Lion: *Alf* III 206; Burton VII 117. Chauvin V 116-17 No. 52; *ANE* 274 No. 218/[2];
Nûr al-Dîn and Maryam: *Alf* IV 109; Burton VIII 326-27. Chauvin V 52-54 No. 271; *ANE* 98-99 No. 233.□

J1151.2§, ‡Awe-evoking surroundings compel witnesses to be truthful. See: *DOTTI*.
Abû al-Ḥasan al-Khorâsânî (and Caliph's Favorite): *Alf* IV 230,-cf./(caliph's); Burton IX 232. Chauvin V 218-20 No. 129; *ANE* 68-69 No. 259.□

J1153, Separate examination of witnesses discredits testimony. See: *DOTTI*.
Devout Jewess and Wicked Elders: *Alf* II 286; Burton V 98. Chauvin VI 193-93 No. 362; *ANE* 169 No. 128.□

J1153.1, Susanna and the elders: separate examination of witnesses [discredits accusation]. See: *ANE*; *DOTTI*; *GMC*. (Cf. K2112).
Devout Jewess and Wicked Elders: *Alf* II 286; Burton V 98. Chauvin VI 193-93 No. 362; *ANE* 169 No. 128.□

J1154.1, Parrot [(caused to be)] unable to tell husband details as to wife's infidelity. See: *ANE*; *DOTTI*; *GMC*.
Husband and Parrot: *Alf* III 141; Burton I 53. Chauvin VI 139 No. 294; *ANE* 226 No. 11.□

J1158, ‡Witness claims not to have seen crime. See: *DOTTI*. (Cf. P520.1§).
Jawdar and His Treacherous Brethren: *Alf* III 180; Burton VI 219. Chauvin V 257-60 No. 154; *ANE* 244-45 No. 209.□

J1159.1§, Ghoulish evidence of murder: (human limbs, organs). See: *DOTTI*.
Lovers of Banû ¿Udhrah and Lion: *Alf* III 209; Burton VII 123. Chauvin V 106-7 No. 37, 116 No. 52; *ANE* 274 No. 218/[2].□

J1161, Literal pleading: letter of law has been met. See: *DOTTI*.
Stolen Purse/Joint Depositors: *Alf* III 177,-cf.; Burton VI 210. Chauvin VIII 63-64 No. 25; *ANE* 399 No. 207.□

J1161.1, ‡The three joint depositors may have their money back when all demand it. [...]. See: *DOTTI*.
Stolen Purse/Joint Depositors: *Alf* III 176,-(four depositors); Burton VI 209. Chauvin VIII 63-64 No. 25; *ANE* 399 No. 207.□

J1163, Pleading for accused by means of parable. See: *DOTTI*; *GMC*.
Hishâm and Arab Youth: *Alf* II 184-85,-cf.; Burton IV 103. Chauvin V 288 No. 172; *ANE* 222-23 No. 68.□

J1170, Clever judicial decisions. See: *DOTTI*.
Hârûn, Slave-girl and Judge Abû-Yûsuf: *Alf* II 202; Burton IV 153-55. Chauvin VII 114 No. 383; *ANE* 204 No. 75.□

J1172.3.1.1§, ‡Ungrateful demon (jinni, afrit) returned to captivity. (Cf. D2177.1, K717, R181).
Fisherman and Afrit: Ingratitude: *Alf* I 15; Burton I 44. Chauvin VI 23-25 No. 195; *ANE* 183-84 No. 8.□

J1174.2, Complaint about the stolen kiss. Woman is allowed to take one in return. See: *GMC*. (Cf. T42.4.1§).
¿Alî ibn Bakkâr: *Alf* II 43,-cf./(poem); Burton III 166. Chauvin V 153 No. 76; *ANE* 92-93 No. 60.□

J1181, ‡Execution escaped by use of special permissions granted the condemned. See: *DOTTI*. (Cf. K2020§)
Shahriyâr and Shahrzâd: *Alf* IV 317; Burton X 54-55. Chauvin V 190-91 No. 111/pt.; *ANE* 371 No. 1.□

J1185.1, Sheherezade: story with indefinite sequel told to stave off execution. See: *ANE*; *DOTTI*; *GMC*. (Cf. J1675.1.3§, K551.28§, S62.1.1§).
Shahriyâr and Shâhzamân: *Alf* I 1,-(entire work); Burton I 1-24. Chauvin V 188-89 No. 111; *ANE* 370-71 No. 1.□

J1192, The bribed judge. See: *DOTTI*; *GMC*. (Cf. P426.0.8§, P520§).
¿Alâ' al-Dîn Abû al-Shâmât: *Alf* II 157,-(given gratuity/*'iḥsân*); Burton IV 53. Chauvin VI 14 No. 188; *ANE* 192-93 No. 63.□

J1192.5§, ‡Biased judge: with personal interest in litigant (accused).
Masrûr and Zayn al-Mawâṣif: *Alf* IV 75-76; Burton VIII 248. Chauvin VI 82-84 No. 251; *ANE* 294-95 No. 232.□

J1192.5.1§, ‡Judge (cleric) falls in love with litigant. (Cf. P421.0.3.1§).
Masrûr and Zayn al-Mawâṣif: *Alf* IV 75-76; Burton VIII 250. Chauvin VI 82-84 No. 251; *ANE* 294-95 No. 232.□

J1199.1§, ‡Judgment on impersonal case secured before personal case is presented. See: *DOTTI*. (Cf. P526.0.3§).
Ni¿mah and Nu¿m: Stolen Wife Regained: *Alf* II 143; Burton IV 21. Chauvin VI 96-97 No. 263; *ANE* 314 No. 62.□

J1215§, ‡Know-all person (*"'Abu-el-¿Urraif"*): a talkative fool. See: *DOTTI*. (Cf. K1969.0.1§, X252.3.3§).
Tailor's Story/Barber of Baghdad: *Alf* I 103-9; Burton I 301-17. Chauvin V 154-56 No. 78; *ANE* 405-6 No. 27.□

J1241, Clever dividing which favors the divider. See: *DOTTI*. (Cf. P760.9.1.3§).
Jackals and Wolf as Umpire: *Alf* IV 167,-cf.; Burton IX 103-6. Chauvin II 223 No. 152/21; *ANE* 235 No. 252.□

J1251.1, Humiliated lover in repartee with disdainful [(scornful)] mistress. See: *DOTTI*; *GMC*.
Hind bint al-Nu¿mân and al-Ḥajjâj: *Alf* III 202-3,-(suitor); Burton VII 98. Chauvin V 115-4 No. 50; *ANE* 221-22 No. 212.□

J1256.2.1§, ‡Woman declares her acquired privilege as mother (usually over childless rival). See: *DOTTI*.
Shahriyâr and Shahrzâd: *Alf* IV 317,-cf./(implied, three sons); Burton X 54. Chauvin V 190-91 No. 111/pt.; *ANE* 371 No. 1.□

J1277.1§, ‡Color (race) of child is not that of parents.
Man of Upper Egypt and Frankish Wife: Alf IV 16?,-(text missing); Burton IX 19. Chauvin V 240 No. 140; *ANE*: No. 234.□

J1280, Repartee with ruler (judge, etc.). See: *DOTTI*; *GMC*.
Hishâm and Arab Youth: *Alf* II 184; Burton IV 101-3. Chauvin V 288 No. 172; *ANE* 222-23 No. 68.□

J1288§, ‡Repartee concerning (sinful) sexual misdeeds (deviance). See: *DOTTI*.
Pretty Gray-haired Woman Retorts: *Alf* II 303,-(poem); Burton V 164. Chauvin VI 153 No. 318; *ANE* 77-78 No. 152.□

J1288.3§, ‡Repartee concerning anal intercourse. See: *DOTTI*. (Cf. U284.3§, T463.8§).
Qamar al-Zamân and Budûr: *Alf* II 109,-(poem); Burton III 304. Chauvin V 204-12 No. 120; *ANE* 341-45 No. 61;
Dispute Concerning Males and Females: *Alf* II 300-2; Burton V 156-57. Chauvin VI 153 No. 317; *ANE* 291 No. 151;
Pretty Gray-haired Woman Retorts: *Alf* II 303,-(poem); Burton V 164. Chauvin VI 153 No. 318; *ANE* 77-78 No. 152.□

J1288.3.1§, ‡Homosexuality (sodomy) is a pleasure not found in the eternal life (hereafter); it is available only in the here-and-now. (Cf. F499.9.1.1§).
Dispute Concerning Males and Females: *Alf* II 301,-(poem); Burton V 157. Chauvin VI 153 No. 317; *ANE* 291 No. 151.□

J1288.3.2§, ‡Male subject for sodomy doesn't menstruate, get pregnant, nor financial support (alimony).
Dispute Concerning Males and Females: *Alf* II 301; Burton V 156. Chauvin VI 153 No. 317; *ANE* 291 No. 151.□

J1289.21§, Is ill-omen induced by ruler's cruelty or a man's ugliness (being one-eyed)?. See: *DOTTI*; *GMC*. (Cf. N134.2.1§).
Barber's Fourth Brother: Illusionary Experiences: *Alf* I 116,-(implicit); Burton I 332–34. Chauvin V 160-61 No. 84; *ANE* 119 No. 32.□

J1291.6§, ‡"Did she (he) write the letter with her (his) hand?" "Do people write with their feet!".
Budûr and Jubayr ibn ¿Umayr: *Alf* II 242; Burton IV 243. Chauvin VII 93-94 No. 374; *ANE* 243-44 No. 83.□

J1326§, ‡Drunkard's excuse ("I was drunk", "The liquor made me do it!", or the like). (Cf. P196.1§).
Barber's Sixth Brother: Emasculated by Abductor: *Alf* I 123; Burton I 347. Chauvin V 163-64 No. 86; *ANE* 120 No. 34.□

J1331, Persistent beggar invited upstairs. [Only to be denied alms]. See: *DOTTI*; *GMC*.
Barber's Third Brother: Exposes Blind Robbers: *Alf* I 114-5; Burton I 329. Chauvin V 159-60 No. 83; *ANE* 118 No. 31.□

J1343, The liking of food and drink. See: *GMC*.
Second Qalandar: Afrit's Wife: *Alf* I 48,-(poem); Burton I 131,-(variant/poems). Chauvin V 197-200 No. 116; *ANE* 338-39 No. 16.□

J1343.0.2§, ‡The longing for a certain delicacy (food, sweets, etc.). See: *DOTTI*. (Cf. T570.1§, U135).
Ma¿rûf the Cobbler: *Alf* IV 289,-(*kunâfah*); Burton X 1,-(vermicelli-cake). Chauvin VI 81-82 No. 250; *ANE* 291-93 No. 262.□

J1347.2.2§, ‡Religious occasions (Bairam festivities, Ramadan, Prophet's Birthday, ¿Âshûrâ, Christmas, Epiphany, etc.): foods provided. See: *DOTTI*. (Cf. V76§).
Mercury ¿Alî: *Alf* III 239,-cf./(*kaḥk el-¿îd*,/during Big Bairam); Burton VII 196 n.,-(sweet buns). Chauvin V 248-50 No. 147; *ANE* 301-3 No. 225.□

J1347.1§, ‡Personal occasions furnish opportunity to get delicious foods.
¿Alâ' al-Dîn Abû al-Shâmât: *Alf* II 148,-(birth); Burton IV 33. Chauvin V 43-49 No. 18; *ANE* 85-87 No. 63.□

J1347.2.1.3§, ‡Circumcision procession (celebration): foods provided to guests. See: *DOTTI*.
Mercury ¿Alî: *Alf* III 238,-cf.; Burton VII 194. Chauvin V 248-50 No. 147; *ANE* 301-3 No. 225.□

J1347.2.4§, ‡An eve for God's sake, or for God's people (Sufi occasion, '*khatmah*'): food provided. See: *DOTTI*.
Reeve's Story: Why Maimed by Bride: *Alf* I 96; Burton I 278. Chauvin V 220-21 No. 305; *ANE* 351 No. 25.□

J1347.2.5§, ‡Funeral feast: meat provided to condolers (guests, mourners). (Cf. V65.6§).
Ghânim ibn Ayyûb: *Alf* I 146; Burton II 47. Chauvin VI 14-16 No. 188; *ANE* 192-93 No. 36.□

J1350, Rude retorts. See: *DOTTI*.
Three Apples: Hasty Uxoricide: *Alf* I 62,-(vizier's,/not know the *ghayb*); Burton I 188,-(not inspector of murdered folk). Chauvin VI 144-45 No. 302; *ANE* 414-15 No. 21.□

J1360.0.1§, ‡The envious accusers should be ignored; a jealous person is never helpful.
Nûr al-Dîn ¿Alî and Son: *Alf* I 73,-(poem); Burton I 223. Chauvin VI 102-6 No. 270; *ANE* 317-19 No. 22;
Qamar al-Zamân and Budûr: *Alf* II 76,-(poem); Burton III 235. Chauvin V 204-12 No. 120; *ANE* 341-45 No. 61;
¿Alî Shâr and Zumurrud: *Alf* II 221,-(poem); Burton IV 198. Chauvin V 89-91 No. 28; *ANE* 100-1 No. 82.□

J1352, Person calls another an ass. See: *DOTTI*.
Hishâm and Arab Youth: *Alf* II 184; Burton IV 101. Chauvin V 288 No. 172; *ANE* 222-23 No. 68.□

J1381.1§, ‡Repayment of debt makes further borrowing (lending) possible. (Cf. P776§).
Nûr al-Dîn and Maryam: *Alf* IV 96-97; Burton VIII 302. Chauvin V 52-54 No. 271; *ANE* 98-99 No. 233.□

J1385§, 'Debt is grief by night, humiliation by day'. See: *DOTTI*; *GMC*.
Landsman ¿Abdallah and Merman ¿Abdallah: *Alf* IV 199,-cf.; Burton IX 168. Chauvin V 6-7 No. 3; *ANE* 65-66 No. 256.□

J1391.12§, ‡Thief's (criminal's) excuse: crime predestined. (Cf. N101.5.1§, V318§, U230.0.3§).
¿Alâ' al-Dîn Abû al-Shâmât: *Alf* II 166; Burton IV 69,-(decreed). Chauvin V 43-49 No. 18; *ANE* 85-87 No. 63;
Bulûqiya: *Alf* III 75, 78,-(attempted murder/theft by partners); Burton V 386, 391,-(fore-ordained from all eternity). Chauvin VII 54 No. 77; *ANE* 130-32 No. 177.□

J1391.13§, ‡Thief's (criminal's) excuse: "It was only a game (contest)". (Cf. K305).
Dalîla the Swindler: *Alf* III 225; Burton VII 170. Chauvin V 245-50 No. 147; *ANE* 163-64 No. 224.□

J1400, Repartee concerning false reform.
Pretty Gray-haired Woman Retorts: *Alf* II 302-3; Burton V 164. Chauvin VI 153 No. 318; *ANE* 77-78 No. 152.□

J1410, Repartee concerning fatness. See: *DOTTI*. (Cf. X151, Z84.2.2.2§).
Man from Yaman and Six Salve-girls: Flyting: *Alf* II 247-48; Burton IV 252-48. Chauvin VI 151 No. 313; *ANE* 289-90 No. 84.□

J1413§, Fat is beautiful. (Cf. F575.1.0.1§, U101.0.2§, U281§).
Man from Yaman and Six Salve-girls: Flyting: *Alf* II 247; Burton IV 254. Chauvin VI 151 No. 313; *ANE* 289-90 No. 84;
Hârûn and Zubaydah in Bath: *Alf* II 284,-cf.; Burton V 76. Chauvin VI 142 No. 298; *ANE* 203-4 No. 111.□

J1430, Repartee concerning doctors and patients. See: *DOTTI*.
Ridiculous Eye Salve: *Alf* II 287,-cf.; Burton V 99. Chauvin V 281 No. 165; *ANE* 236 No. 129.□

J1435§, ‡Repartee concerning medicine (treatment, cure, etc.). See: *DOTTI*.
Ridiculous Eye Salve: *Alf* II 287; Burton V 98-99. Chauvin V 281 No. 165; *ANE* 236 No. 129.□

J1449§, ‡Person calls another 'worthless'. See: *DOTTI*. (Cf. J1352).
Hind bint al-Nu¿mân and al-Ḥajjâj: *Alf* III 202,-(*dirham*—as compared to *dinar*); Burton VII 99. Chauvin V 115-4 No. 50; *ANE* 221-22 No. 212.□

J1450.1.1§, ‡Callowness of youth: man calls youth (son) inexperienced ('green', immature, etc.). (Cf. P248.0.2§, W256.7.2§).
Qamar al-Zamân and Budûr: *Alf* II 68; Burton III 218,-(youthful folly and boyish ignorance). Chauvin V 204-12 No. 120; *ANE* 341-45 No. 61;

Bearded and Beardless Men as Lovers: *Alf* II 303; Burton V 165. Chauvin V 112 No. 48; *ANE* 450 No. 154.□

J1450.1.2§, ‡Feeblemindedness of old age: youth calls mature man (father) senile. (Cf. F571.9.1§).
Qamar al-Zamân and Budûr: *Alf* II 68; Burton III 218-19. Chauvin V 204-12 No. 120; *ANE* 341-45 No. 61.□

J1512.2, ‡To return the eye to the one-eyed man. "Let me have your other so that I can see whether the one I bring you matches.". See: *ANE*; *DOTTI*. (Cf. K251.7.1§).
Sandal-wood Merchant and Sharpers: *Alf* III 175-76; Burton VI 206. Chauvin VIII 60-62 No. 26; *ANE* 359-60 No. 205.□

J1514§, ‡Wisdom of benevolence (exercising goodwill), and foolishness of malevolence (harboring ill-will). See: *DOTTI*. (Cf. J26, P775.2§, V301.1§, W10).
Thief and His Monkey: *Alf* II 40; Burton III 159. Chauvin II 229 No. 18; *ANE* 413 No. 57.□

J1514.2§, ‡Benevolence may be met only with benevolence. (Cf. W154.0.1§).
Jullanâr of the Sea: *Alf* III 251; Burton VII 273,-(kindness). Chauvin V 147-51 No. 73; *ANE* 248-51 No. 227.□

J1514.5§, ‡'He who would dig a pit for another will [himself] fall in it'. See: *PSAE*. (Cf. J1514§).
Wolf and Fox: *Alf* II 32; Burton III 136. Chauvin II 227 No. 6; *ANE* 450 No. 47;
Bulûqiya: *Alf* III 79; Burton V 393. Chauvin VII 54 No. 77; *ANE* 130-32 No. 177;
King Jalî¿âd and Shimâs: *Alf* IV 182; Burton IX 133. Chauvin VI 9 No. 184; *ANE* 237-38 No. 236.□

J1520§, ‡Swindler-to-be swindled by intended victim. (Cf. L406§).
Mercury ¿Alî: *Alf* III 235; Burton VII 187. Chauvin V 248-50 No. 147; *ANE* 301-3 No. 225.□

J1524.2.1§, ‡Jinni-servant of magic object rebukes former master for carelessness. See: *DOTTI*.
Ma¿rûf the Cobbler: *Alf* IV 311; Burton X 42. Chauvin VI 81-82 No. 250; *ANE* 291-93 No. 262.□

J1532.5.1§, ‡Man committing adultery with woman rebuked by her child. (Cf. J1847.4.1§).
Debauchee and Three Years Old Child: *Alf* III 176; Burton VI 208. Chauvin VIII 62-63 No. 147; *ANE* 166-67 No. 206.□

J1551.12.1§, ‡Host serves make-believe food, guest repays with actual punishment (slaps, insults or the like).
Barber's Sixth Brother: Emasculated by Abductor: *Alf* I 122; Burton I 344. Chauvin V 163-64 No. 86; *ANE* 120 No. 34.□

J1549.2.1§, ‡Woman will heal love-sick man as an act of 'benevolence' (for being in love with her).
¿Alî bin Ṭâhir and Mu'nis: *Alf* II 303; Burton V 164. Chauvin VI 154 No. 319; *ANE* 101 No. 153.□

J1655.3, Coins concealed in jar of oil (pickles [olives]). See: *DOTTI*. (Cf. K1872.8§).
Qamar al-Zamân and Budûr: *Alf* II 106-7,-(olives); Burton III 295. Chauvin V 204-12 No. 120; *ANE* 341-45 No. 61.□

J1661.2.1§, ‡Keys to rooms of various functions (cooking, storing, etc.) detected by residuals left on them.
Mercury ¿Alî: *Alf* III 235; Burton VII 187. Chauvin V 248-50 No. 147; *ANE* 301-3 No. 225.□

J1675.1.3§, ‡King's (husband's) attention attracted by story-telling. See: *DOTTI*.
Shahriyâr and Shahrzâd: *Alf* I 7, 13; Burton I 29. Chauvin V 188-89 No. 111; *ANE* 370-71 No. 1.□

J1675.1.4§, ‡Ruler's attention attracted by making false accusation (claim).
Island King/Pious Jewish Merchant: *Alf* III 17,-(by mother/wife); Burton V 293. Chauvin VI 161 No. 325; *ANE* 234 No. 174.□

J1675.9§, King's promise of safety secured before breaking news to him. See: *DOTTI*; *GMC*.
Sayf al-Mulûk: *Alf* III 280,-(*'amân*); Burton VII 333,-(immunity). Chauvin VII 64-73 No. 348; *ANE* 362-64 No. 229.□

J1701.0.1§, ‡Wife's (foolish) advice proves disastrous. See: *DOTTI*. (Cf. J675.0.1§).
Man [Gardener] and His Wife: *Alf* IV 165; Burton IX 98. Chauvin II 223 No. 152/19; *ANE* 289 No. 250;
King Jalî¿âd and Shimâs: *Alf* IV 169; Burton IX 107. Chauvin VI 9 No. 184; *ANE* 237-38 No. 236;
Francolin and Tortoises: *Alf* IV 172-73,-cf./(implicit/female tortoises counsel male bird); Burton IX 114. Chauvin VI 9 No. 184; *ANE* 237-38 No. 254.□

J1701.0.1.1§, ‡Lover's (friend's) advice proves disastrous.
Francolin and Tortoises: *Alf* IV 172; Burton IX 114. Chauvin II 224 No. 152/23; *ANE* 188 No. 254.□

J1732.5§, ‡Countryman (Bedouin) unacquainted with city pastry (sweets). See: *DOTTI*. (Cf. P110.1.3§).
Dalîla the Swindler: *Alf* III 223-24; Burton VII 164-65. Chauvin V 245-50 No. 147; *ANE* 163-64 No. 224.□

J1742, The countryman in the great world [(city)]. See: *DOTTI*; *GMC*. (Cf. J1016.0.1§).
Dalîla the Swindler: *Alf* III 223,-(Bedouin); Burton VII 164. Chauvin V 245-50 No. 147; *ANE* 163-64 No. 224.□

J1742.6.1.3§, ‡Mystic's acts (prayers) mistaken for signs of insanity (madness). (Cf. V220.0.6§).
Conversion of Princess by Khawwâṣ: *Alf* III 15; Burton V 285. Chauvin V 239 No. 139; *ANE* 145 No. 171.□

J1745.0.1§, ‡Absurd ignorance of genitals. (Cf. J1919.5.4§).
Porter and Ladies of Baghdad: *Alf* I 33,-(pretended); Burton I 91. Chauvin V 251-52 No. 148; *ANE* 324-26 No. 14.□

J1746, Absurd ignorance of reading. See: *DOTTI*.
Illiterate Schoolmaster: *Alf* II 293; Burton V 119-21. Chauvin VI 137 No. 289; *ANE* 231 No. 137.□

J1761.1, Whale thought to be island. See: *ANE*; *DOTTI*; *GMC*.
Sindbâd's First Voyage: *Alf* III 84; Burton VI 5-6. Chauvin VII 7-9 No. 373A; *ANE* 385 No. 179.□

J1766.3§, ‡Disguised ruler (caliph, king, etc.) mistaken for poor laborer.
Anîs al-Jalîs: *Alf* I 141; Burton II 32. Chauvin V 120-24 No. 58; *ANE* 316-17 No. 35.□

J1766.4.1§, ‡Woman mistaken for man.
King ¿Umar al-Nu¿mân and Sons: *Alf* I 240,-(old woman); Burton II 242. Chauvin VI 112-24 No. 277; *ANE* 430-34 No. 39.□

J1769.2.2§, ‡Corpse thought to be burglar.
Hunchback's Tale: Resuscitated: *Alf* I 86-87; Burton I 258. Chauvin V 180-82 No. 105; *ANE* 224-25 No. 23.□

J1768.2.1.1§, ‡Youth thought to be a man's lover (actually his son).
¿Alâ' al-Dîn Abû al-Shâmât: *Alf* II 150; Burton IV 36. Chauvin V 43-49 No. 18; *ANE* 85-87 No. 63.□

J1768.2.3.1§, ‡Maiden thinks handsome stranger, who appears in her quarters unexpectedly, is actually her rejected suitor.
Ebony Horse: *Alf* II 256; Burton V 9. Chauvin V 221-31 No. 130; *ANE* 172-74 No. 103.□

J1768.2.4.1§, ‡Maiden thinks the stranger appearing unexpectedly in her chamber is spy on her conduct. (Cf. J567.1.1§).
Qamar al-Zamân and Budûr: *Alf* II 87-88; Burton III 258. Chauvin V 204-12 No. 120; *ANE* 341-45 No. 61.□

J1786, ‡Man thought to be a devil or ghost.
Lady and Five Suitors Deceived: *Alf* III 162; Burton VI 179. Chauvin VIII 50-51 No. 18; *ANE* 266 No. 198;
Mercury ¿Alî: *Alf* III 233; Burton VII 183. Chauvin V 248-50 No. 147; *ANE* 301-3 No. 225.□

J1798§, ‡Which is real and which is illusory? (The actual is mistaken for imaginary (dream-like)—or the imaginary is mistaken for actual.
Nûr al-Dîn ¿Alî and Son: *Alf* I 82-84,-cf./(deception); Burton I 246-47. Chauvin VI 102-6 No. 270; *ANE* 317-19 No. 22;
Qamar al-Zamân and Budûr: *Alf* II 86-87; Burton III 256. Chauvin V 204-12 No. 120; *ANE* 341-45 No. 61.□

J1808§, Name of object (or month, season, etc.) mistaken for person's name (or vice versa). See: *DOTTI*.
¿Alâ' al-Dîn Abû al-Shâmât: *Alf* II 166,-(girl-flower); Burton IV 68. Chauvin V 43-49 No. 18; *ANE* 85-87 No. 63.□

J1809.3§, ‡Mildness (patience, kindness, etc.) mistaken for weakness.

Hunter Rides Lion: Devoured: *Alf* IV 153,-(lion's); Burton IX 72. Chauvin II 222 No. 152/15.□

J1809.3.1.1§, ‡Hunter thinks lion, who is grateful for food, can be ridden: hunter killed by lion. (Cf. F575.5§).
Hunter Rides Lion: Devoured: *Alf* IV 153; Burton IX 72. Chauvin II 222 No. 152/15.□

J1809.3.2§, ‡Ruler's (king's) mildness should not be mistaken for weakness.
King Jalî¿âd and Shimâs: *Alf* IV 153,-ff.; Burton IX 72. Chauvin VI 9-11 No. 184; *ANE* 237-38 No. 236;
Hunter Rides Lion: Devoured: *Alf* IV 153,-(simile); Burton IX 72. Chauvin II 222 No. 152/15.□

J1809.5§, ‡Sage (saint) mistaken for sorcerer (magician). (Cf. K2123).
King ¿Umar al-Nu¿mân and Sons: *Alf* I 241; Burton II 245. Chauvin VI 112-24 No. 277; *ANE* 430-34 No. 39.□

J1810.1.1§, ‡Human cries of pain (wailing) thought to be singing.
Sayf al-Mulûk: *Alf* III 283; Burton VII 340. Chauvin VII 64-73 No. 348; *ANE* 362-64 No. 229.□

J1811, Animal cries misunderstood.
Third Shaykh: Transformation by Wife: *Alf* I 13,-cf.; Burton I 36-37. Chauvin VII 130 No. 398; *ANE* 378 No. 7.□

J1820, Inappropriate action from misunderstanding. See: *DOTTI*.
Schoolmaster Who Fell in Love by Report: Mourns: *Alf* II 292[]; Burton V 117-18. Chauvin VI 136 No. 287; *ANE* 367 No. 135.□

J1847.2§, ‡Victim of crime condemned due to pity-evoking appearance of criminal. See: *DOTTI*.
Copt Broker's Story: Lover's Sacrifices Repaid: *Alf* I 93; Burton I 273. Chauvin VI 80 No. 249; *ANE* 313-14 No. 24.□

J1847.4.1§, ‡Whose shame (sin, 'ill-omen,' etc.) is greater: that of the one with a legitimate need (hunger) easily fulfilled, or that of the one with illicit desire (fornication) that cannot be satisfied? (Hungry boy's retort at his mother's seducer). See: *DOTTI*.
Debauchee and Three Years Old Child: *Alf* III 176; Burton VI 208. Chauvin VIII 62-63 No. 147; *ANE* 166-67 No. 206.□

J1847.5§, ‡Inappropriate (foolish) interpretation of chivalry (courtliness, graciousness).
Barber's Tale of Himself: Joins Doomed Party: *Alf* I 110; Burton I 317–18. Chauvin V 156-57 No. 80; *ANE* 115-17 No. 28.□

J1848§, Acts intended to be kind (humorous) produce opposite result. See: *DOTTI*.
House with the Belvedere: *Alf* III 169,-(kindness); Burton VI 194. Chauvin VIII 57-58 No. 23; *ANE* 223 No. 203.□

J1848.2§, ‡Good counsel (advice) proves harmful.
Nuzhat al-Zamân Tested/¿Umar al-Nu¿mân: *Alf* I 206,-(austerity/piety spoils king's life); Burton II 171. Chauvin VI 116, n.1/passim No. 277; *ANE* 432,/passim No. 39.□

J1848.3§, Old person acts too youthful (childish): rebuked. See: *DOTTI*.
¿Alî Shâr and Zumurrud: *Alf* II 219,-(man with dyed beard); Burton IV 192-93. Chauvin V 89-91 No. 28; *ANE* 100-1 No. 82;
Budûr and Jubayr ibn ¿Umayr: *Alf* II 236; Burton IV 232. Chauvin VII 93-94 No. 374; *ANE* 243-44 No. 83.□

J1849.5.1§, ‡Parent (mother) mistakes seductive acts his (her) child is receiving (from an adult) for innocent ones: no action. See: *DOTTI*.
al-'Amjad and al-'As¿ad: *Alf* II 112-13; Burton III 311-12. Chauvin V 208-10 No. 120[.1]; *ANE* 341-42 No. 61/pt. 2.□

J1849.6.2§, ‡Look of puzzlement (confusion, stupidity) thought to be of graveness (severity). See: *DOTTI*.
Illiterate Schoolmaster: *Alf* II 293; Burton V 120. Chauvin VI 137 No. 289; *ANE* 231 No. 137.□

J1913.4§, ‡Dying (gravely sick) person thought to be 'stoned' (drug addict).
King ¿Umar al-Nu¿mân and Sons: *Alf* I 188; Burton II 134. Chauvin VI 112-24 No. 277; *ANE* 430-34 No. 39.□

J1913.6§, ‡Price of an 'inexpensive' article (service) raised through mutually misunderstood gesture (murmur). Owner thinks buyer is ridiculing him by offering too high a price and makes gestures to that effect, but buyer thinks owner thinks offer is too low and raises his offer—(this happens repeatedly).
al-Rashîd and Omani Merchant: *Alf* IV 216-17; Burton IX 202. Chauvin VI 111-12 No. 276; *ANE* 201-2 No. 257.□

J1919.5.4§, ‡Fool undergoes castration to rid self of seemingly useless organ (or to test function of testicles). See: *DOTTI.*
Schoolmaster (Dominie) Castrates Self: *Alf* II 293; Burton V 119. Chauvin VI 137 No. 288; *ANE* 186 No. 136.□

J1990.0.1§, ‡Seemingly absurd claim (wisdom) verified (proven) by application. See: *DOTTI.*
Nuzhat al-Zamân Tested/¿Umar al-Nu¿mân: *Alf* I 201,-cf./(dog's hunger); Burton II 158. Chauvin VI 116, n.1/passim No. 277; *ANE* 432,/passim No. 39.□

J2055.1.1§, ‡Predator selected king: preys on subjects. See: *DOTTI.*
Crows and Hawk: *Alf* IV 144; Burton IX 54. Chauvin II 220 No. 152/8; *ANE* 162 No. 243.□

J2060, Absurd plans. Air-castles. See: *DOTTI*; *GMC.*
Barber's Fifth Brother: Daydreams/Defeats Robbers: *Alf* I 117; Burton I 335–37. Chauvin V 161 No. 85; *ANE* 119-20 No. 33.□

J2061, Air-castle shattered by lack of forethought. See: *DOTTI.*
Barber's Fifth Brother: Daydreams/Defeats Robbers: *Alf* I 118; Burton I 338. Chauvin V 161 No. 85; *ANE* 119-20 No. 33;
Fakir and Jar of Butter: *Alf* IV 137-38; Burton IX 41. Chauvin II 218-19 No. 152/3; *ANE* 179-80 No. 238.□

J2061.1, Air-castle: the jar of honey to be sold. [Broken]. See: *DOTTI*; *GMC.*
Fakir and Jar of Butter: *Alf* IV 137,-(clarified-butter); Burton IX 40-41. Chauvin II 218-19 No. 152/3; *ANE* 179-80 No. 238.□

J2061.1.1, ‡Air-castle: basket of glassware to be sold. In his excitement he breaks the glassware. See: *ANE*; *DOTTI.*
Barber's Fifth Brother: Daydreams/Defeats Robbers: *Alf* I 118; Burton I 335–37. Chauvin V 161 No. 85; *ANE* 119-20 No. 33.□

J2061.5§, ‡Imagined dispute over how to receive with pretended disinterest the imagined beautiful bride. See: *DOTTI.*
Barber's Fifth Brother: Daydreams/Defeats Robbers: *Alf* I 118; Burton I 337-38. Chauvin V 161 No. 85; *ANE* 119-20 No. 33.□

J2063, Distress over imagined troubles of unborn child. See: *DOTTI.*
Nûr al-Dîn ¿Alî and Son: *Alf* I 65-66; Burton I 196-97. Chauvin VI 102-6 No. 270; *ANE* 317-19 No. 22.□

J2063.2§, ‡Quarrel over imagined disagreement (dispute) over unborn child(ren). See: *DOTTI.* (Cf. T137.5).
Nûr al-Dîn ¿Alî and Son: *Alf* I 65; Burton I 196-97. Chauvin VI 102-6 No. 270; *ANE* 317-19 No. 22.□

J2068§, ‡Inaction is harmful, action is useful,.
Nûr al-Dîn ¿Alî and Son: *Alf* I 65,-(poem); Burton I 196. Chauvin VI 102-6 No. 270; *ANE* 317-19 No. 22.□

J2068.1.1§, ‡Still water becomes stagnant. (Cf. A189.7.1§).
Nûr al-Dîn ¿Alî and Son: *Alf* I 65,-(poem); Burton I 198. Chauvin VI 102-6 No. 270; *ANE* 317-19 No. 22.□

J2068.2§, ‡Unmarried girl (boy), like stored commodity, will 'rot'.
Sayf al-Mulûk: *Alf* III 299,-cf.; Burton VII 372. Chauvin VII 64-73 No. 348; *ANE* 362-64 No. 229.□

J2068.3§, ‡Acquiring livelihood (making a living) requires action.
Nûr al-Dîn ¿Alî and Son: *Alf* I 65,-cf./(poem); Burton I 196. Chauvin VI 102-6 No. 270; *ANE* 317-19 No. 22.□

J2068.3.1§, ‡Hunter needs to seek prey in its own natural environment.

Nûr al-Dîn ¿Alî and Son: *Alf* I 65,-(poem/arrow); Burton I 198. Chauvin VI 102-6 No. 270; *ANE* 317-19 No. 22.□

J2068.3.2§, ‡Lions must leave jungle to hunt in open land.
Nûr al-Dîn ¿Alî and Son: *Alf* I 65,-(poem); Burton I 198. Chauvin VI 102-6 No. 270; *ANE* 317-19 No. 22.□

J2071, Three foolish wishes. See: *DOTTI*.
Three Wishes: *Alf* III 162; Burton VI 181. Chauvin VIII 51-52 No. 19; *ANE* 419-20 No. 199.□

J2075, The transferred wish. [Wasted on a trifle]. See: *DOTTI*.
Three Wishes: *Alf* III 162; Burton VI 181. Chauvin VIII 51-52 No. 19; *ANE* 419-20 No. 199.□

J2118.1§, ‡Meddler tries to save friend from presumed peril: causes him much harm. (The barber of Baghdad). See: *DOTTI*.
Tailor's Story/Barber of Baghdad: *Alf* I 108; Burton I 315. Chauvin V 154-56 No. 78; *ANE* 405-6 No. 27.□

J2143, Foolish interference in quarrel of the strong fatal to the weak.
Anîs al-Jalîs: *Alf* I 134,-cf.; Burton II 18. Chauvin V 120-24 No. 58; *ANE* 316-17 No. 35;
Sparrow as Peacock's Vizier: *Alf* II 41,-cf.; Burton III 162. Chauvin II 230 No. 20; *ANE* 398 No. 59.□

J2143.4§, ‡Followers (servants) advised not to interfere in fight between their masters: unwise if masters are reconciled.
Anîs al-Jalîs: *Alf* I 134; Burton II 17-18. Chauvin V 120-24 No. 58; *ANE* 316-17 No. 35.□

J2146.3§, ‡Man leaps into river and drowns in effort to hold on to a fish.
Foolish Fisher: *Alf* IV 163,-(drowning fisher); Burton IX 93-94. Chauvin II 222 No. 152/16; *ANE* 187 No. 248.□

J2175.4, ‡Man lets his infant son play in river. Son drowns.
Fuller and His Son: Drowned: *Alf* III 141; Burton VI 134. Chauvin VIII 36 No. 4; *ANE* 189 No. 184.□

J2198.0.1§, ‡Anticipatory calamity: person expects it and reacts accordingly (e.g., cries, wails, etc.).
Nûr al-Dîn ¿Alî and Son: *Alf* I 65-66; Burton I 196. Chauvin VI 144-45 No. 302; *ANE* 317-19 No. 22.□

J2198.3.1§, ‡Parents quarrel over their plans for arranged marriage of their unborn children.
Nûr al-Dîn ¿Alî and Son: *Alf* I 65; Burton I 196-97. Chauvin VI 102-6 No. 270; *ANE* 317-19 No. 22.□

J2199.4.7.1§, ‡Gold (money) as sole product (possession) leads to starvation: production of food (agriculture, etc.) neglected. See: *DOTTI*.
Second Qalandar: Afrit's Wife: *Alf* I 43,-cf./(money making as only craft); Burton I 115. Chauvin V 197-200 No. 116; *ANE* 338-39 No. 16;
City of Brass: *Alf* III 133; Burton VI 111. Chauvin V 32-35 No. 16; *ANE* 146-50 No. 180.□

J2202.1§, ‡Man prays that God grant him sexual liaison with married woman.
Sweep and Noble Lady: Infidelity Repaid: *Alf* II 188; Burton IV 125. Chauvin VI 148 No. 306; *ANE* 403-4 No. 72.□

J2203§, ‡Sinning in compliance with God's fashion.
Jeweler's Wife and Qamar al-Zamân: *Alf* IV 238,-(poem); Burton IX 249. Chauvin V 212-14 No. 121; *ANE* 345-47 No. 260.□

J2203.1§, ‡Sinful interest in a beautiful person rationalized: 'God is beautiful and loves beauty'.
Jeweler's Wife and Qamar al-Zamân: *Alf* IV 238,-(poem); Burton IX 249. Chauvin V 212-14 No. 121; *ANE* 345-47 No. 260.□

J2214.16.1§, ‡Folly of thinking that all women are wicked ('Not all of them!'). See: *DOTTI*.
Hasan of Basrah: *Alf* IV 9; Burton VIII 54. Chauvin VII 29-35 No. 212A; *ANE* 207-10 No. 230;
Jeweler's Wife and Qamar al-Zamân: *Alf* IV 266; Burton IX 304,-(disease of insanity). Chauvin V 212-14 No. 121; *ANE* 345-47 No. 260;
Shahriyâr and Shahrzâd: *Alf* IV 317,-(implicit); Burton X 54. Chauvin V 190-91 No. 111/pt.; *ANE* 371 No. 1.□

J2215.7§, Religious services (or God) blamed. See: *GMC*.

Jeweler's Wife and Qamar al-Zamân: *Alf* IV 238,-(poem); Burton IX 249. Chauvin V 212-14 No. 121; *ANE* 345-47 No. 260.□

J2215.7.1§, ‡God created temptation but ordered worshippers not to give in.
Jeweler's Wife and Qamar al-Zamân: *Alf* IV 238,-(poem); Burton IX 249. Chauvin V 212-14 No. 121; *ANE* 345-47 No. 260.□

J2218.9.1§, ‡One approving (disapproving) voice lends credence to seemingly absurd claim. See: *DOTTI*.
Portress Amînah: Bitten Cheek: *Alf* I 58-59,-(old woman's); Burton I 179. Chauvin V 98-99 No. 33; *ANE* 326-27 No. 20;
Nuzhat al-Zamân Tested/¿Umar al-Nu¿mân: *Alf* I 201,-(dog treatment); Burton II 158. Chauvin VI 116, n.1/passim No. 277; *ANE* 432,/passim No. 39.□

J2218.9.2§, ‡Happy (well-adjusted) person coaxed by peers to change to their life-style.
¿Alâ' al-Dîn Abû al-Shâmât: *Alf* II 151,-(travel); Burton IV 39. Chauvin V 43-49 No. 18; *ANE* 85-87 No. 63.□

J2311.13§, ‡Proverbial report on "So-and-so" (i.e., John Doe) taken literally. See: *DOTTI*.
Schoolmaster Who Fell in Love by Report: Mourns: *Alf* II 292; Burton V 117-18. Chauvin VI 136 No. 287; *ANE* 367 No. 135.□

J2311.13.1§, ‡Fool hears (proverbial) report on death of 'So-and-so': he mourns the death. See: *DOTTI*.
Schoolmaster Who Fell in Love by Report: Mourns: *Alf* II 292; Burton V 117-18. Chauvin VI 136 No. 287; *ANE* 367 No. 135.□

J2392§, ‡Curiosity (inquisitiveness) proves disastrous (fatal). See: *DOTTI*.
Serpent-charmer and Wife: *Alf* IV 146; Burton IX 57-58. Chauvin II 220 No. 152/9; *ANE* 368 No. 244.□

J2392.2§, ‡Ignoring instructions and opening closed container: snakes (wasps, scorpions, etc.) come out and attack (kill) opener. See: *DOTTI*.
Serpent-charmer and Wife: *Alf* IV 146; Burton IX 57. Chauvin II 220 No. 152/9; *ANE* 368 No. 244.□

J2401, Fatal imitation. See: *DOTTI*; *GMC*.
Foolish Weaver: *Alf* II 40,-(of acrobat); Burton III 160. Chauvin II 229 No. 154.19; *ANE* 187 No. 58;
Wild Ass and Jackal: *Alf* IV 142; Burton IX 48-50. Chauvin II 219 No. 152/6; *ANE* 449 No. 241.□

J2411.0.1§, ‡Foolish imitation of the unique (non-magical). Painful results for imitator. See: *DOTTI*.
Foolish Weaver: *Alf* II 40; Burton III 160. Chauvin II 229 No. 19; *ANE* 187 No. 58.□

J2415, Foolish imitation of lucky man. [Jealous imitator disappointed]. See: *DOTTI*; *GMC*.
Thief and His Monkey: *Alf* II 40,-cf.; Burton III 159. Chauvin II 229 No. 18; *ANE* 413 No. 57.□

J2501.2§, ‡Excesses (immoderation) reprimanded.
Ma¿rûf the Cobbler: *Alf* IV 296; Burton X 14,-(to brown, not to burn bread). Chauvin VI 81-82 No. 250; *ANE* 291-93 No. 262.□

J2519.2§, ‡Death of an unknown absurdly mourned. See: *DOTTI*.
Schoolmaster Who Fell in Love by Report: Mourns: *Alf* II 292[]; Burton V 118. Chauvin VI 136 No. 287; *ANE* 367 No. 135.□

J2519.5§, ‡Intemperance in mourning. See: *DOTTI*.
Ensorcelled Prince/Husband: *Alf* I 29; Burton I 74-77. Chauvin VI 56-58 No. 222; *ANE* 176 No. 13.□

J2520.1§, ‡Man thinking of himself as 'silent' (possessing the wisdom of silence) is unwilling to speak up to save own life.
Barber's Tale of Himself: Joins Doomed Party: *Alf* I 110; Burton I 318. Chauvin V 156-57 No. 80; *ANE* 115-17 No. 28.□

J2756§, ‡Foolish placing of trust.
Mouse and Cat: *Alf* IV 135-36,-(mouse trusts cat); Burton IX 36. Chauvin II 218 No. 152/2; *ANE* 305-6 No. 237.□

J2756.3§, ‡Shortsightedness in assignment of tasks. (Cf. J215.1.1).
Mouse and Cat: *Alf* IV 135,-cf.; Burton IX 36. Chauvin II 218 No. 152/2; *ANE* 305-6 No. 237.□

J2631, Boastful coward frightened when he sees strong adversaries. See: *DOTTI*.
King ¿Umar al-Nu¿mân and Sons: *Alf* II 4; Burton III 80. Chauvin VI 112-24 No. 277; *ANE* 430-34 No. 39.□

J2631.1§, ‡Braggart of horsemanship (fighting prowess) abandons companion at time of battle.
King ¿Umar al-Nu¿mân and Sons: *Alf* II 4; Burton III 80. Chauvin VI 112-24 No. 277; *ANE* 430-34 No. 39.□

K. DECEPTIONS

K92.4.1§, ‡Chess game won by distracting opponent's attention: girl makes seductive gestures (motions) that disorient her male opponent.
King ¿Umar al-Nu¿mân and Sons: *Alf* I 172; Burton II 104. Chauvin VI 112-24 No. 277; *ANE* 430-34 No. 39;
Masrûr and Zayn al-Mawâṣif: *Alf* IV 57-59; Burton VIII 216-18. Chauvin VI 82-84 No. 251; *ANE* 294-95 No. 232.□

K92.4.2§, ‡Chess game won by distracting opponent's attention: opponent's property hidden.
Ibrâhîm and Jamîlah: *Alf* IV 220,-(*jirâb*/purse); Burton IX 210. Chauvin VI 52-53 No. 218; *ANE* 227-29 No. 258.□

K94§, ‡Seduction (sex-appeal) as means of attracting king's (judge's) attention. See: *DOTTI*.
King ¿Umar al-Nu¿mân and Sons: *Alf* I 225,-(offering five damsels); Burton II 196. Chauvin VI 112-24 No. 277; *ANE* 430-34 No. 39.□

K196, Selling by trick: literal bargain. See: *DOTTI*.
Sandal-wood Merchant and Sharpers: *Alf* III 174; Burton VI 203-3. Chauvin VIII 60-62 No. 26; *ANE* 359-60 No. 205.□

K199.2.1§, ‡Buying an item for "Whatever [price] you may say." Trickster names impossible price (e.g., bushel of fleas of which half are males and half females—or the like). See: *DOTTI*.
Sandal-wood Merchant and Sharpers: *Alf* III 176; Burton VI 206-7. Chauvin VIII 60-62 No. 26; *ANE* 359-60 No. 205.□

K199.2.2§, ‡Payment with "Whatever should be satisfactory to you." Trickster pays with: "May God bless our king" (or the like). See: *DOTTI*.
Sandal-wood Merchant and Sharpers: *Alf* III 176,-cf.; Burton VI 206-7. Chauvin VIII 60-62 No. 26; *ANE* 359-60 No. 205.□

K2151.2§, ‡The seemingly dead is abandoned in street and made to look as if leaning against wall: one unsuspecting passer-by after another tries to awaken him and thinks that he caused his death.
Hunchback's Tale: Resuscitated: *Alf* I 87; Burton I 259. Chauvin V 180-82 No. 105; *ANE* 224-25 No. 23.□

K231.2, Reward for accomplishment of task deceptively withheld. See: *DOTTI*.
Barber's First Brother: Free Labor for Coquette: *Alf* I 112; Burton I 324. Chauvin V 157-58 No. 81; *ANE* 117 No. 29.□

K231.2.3§, ‡Nonsexual service rendered (usually involving labor), promised sexual reward deceptively withheld.
Barber's First Brother: Free Labor for Coquette: *Alf* I 112,-(sewing); Burton I 324. Chauvin V 157-58 No. 81; *ANE* 117 No. 29.□

K231.2.2.1§, ‡Sexual service rendered, server robbed by receiver (client). See: *DOTTI*.
Woman Who Made Husband Sift Dust: *Alf* III 145; Burton VI 143. Chauvin VIII 42 No. 10; *ANE* 452-53 No. 190.□

K231.2.5.1§, ‡Ground animal (porcupine) refuses to share fruit which bird (pigeon) felled from tree for the two of them.
Hedgehog and Wood-pigeons: *Alf* II 39; Burton III 156-57. Chauvin II 229 No. 15; *ANE* 220 No. 55.□

K249.5§, ‡Debtor flees to avoid creditors (repayment of debt). See: *DOTTI*.
Mercury ¿Alî: *Alf* III 228; Burton VII 175. Chauvin V 248-50 No. 147; *ANE* 301-3 No. 225;
Ma¿rûf the Cobbler: *Alf* IV 302; Burton X 24. Chauvin VI 81-82 No. 250; *ANE* 291-93 No. 262.□

K249.6.1§, ‡Payment with broken wind (or the like).
Ridiculous Eye Salve: *Alf* II 287; Burton V 99. Chauvin V 281 No. 165; *ANE* 236 No. 129.□

K251.7§, ‡Terms of payment for damages preclude acceptance of compensation.
Sandal-wood Merchant and Sharpers: *Alf* III 175-76; Burton VI 203-4. Chauvin VIII 60-62 No. 26; *ANE* 359-60 No. 205.□

K251.7.1§, ‡Weighing eyes to see whether they are equal in value: "An eye for an eye." The one-eyed accuser declines the test: he will be blinded while the accused would be left with one eye.

Sandal-wood Merchant and Sharpers: *Alf* III 175-76; Burton VI 206. Chauvin VIII 60-62 No. 26; *ANE* 359-60 No. 205.□

K252.5§, ‡Free person attired like slave (mameluke) sold as slave. See: *DOTTI*.
Dalîla the Swindler: *Alf* III 222; Burton VII 162. Chauvin V 245-50 No. 147; *ANE* 163-64 No. 224.□

K289.9.3.1§, ‡Religious prohibition of having to do with liquor deceptively evaded.
Anîs al-Jalîs: *Alf* I 137; Burton II 24-25. Chauvin V 120-24 No. 58; *ANE* 316-17 No. 35.□

K300.0.2§, ‡'Trickstery' as a necessary means of survival. (Cf. F669.1.1§).
Wolf and Fox: *Alf* II 33,-(poem: "Live by deception ...."); Burton III 140. Chauvin II 227 No. 6; *ANE* 450 No. 47.□

K301.2.1§, ‡Several brothers as robbers.
¿Alî ibn Bakkâr: *Alf* II 59; Burton III 198. Chauvin V 153 No. 76; *ANE* 92-93 No. 60.□

K302, Female master thief. See: *ANE*.
Barber's Fifth Brother: Daydreams/Defeats Robbers: *Alf* I 118ff.,-cf.; Burton I 339ff. Chauvin V 161 No. 85; *ANE* 119-20 No. 33;
Dalîla the Swindler: *Alf* III 213-226,-(mother and daughter); Burton VII 145-67. Chauvin V 245-50 No. 147; *ANE* 163-64 No. 224.□

K303.2.3.1§, ‡Corpse (cadaver) stolen or borrowed. See: *DOTTI*; *PSAE*.
Goldsmith and Cashmere Singer: *Alf* III 152,-cf./(person sentenced to die); Burton VI 153-54. Chauvin VIII 46-47 No. 14; *ANE* 196 No. 194.□

K305, Contest in stealing. See: *DOTTI*; *GMC*.
Dalîla the Swindler: *Alf* III 225; Burton VII 170. Chauvin V 245-50 No. 147; *ANE* 163-64 No. 224.□

K305.1.1§, ‡Thieving contest between mother and daughter.
Dalîla the Swindler: *Alf* III 225,-cf./(implicit); Burton VII 167. Chauvin V 245-50 No. 147; *ANE* 163-64 No. 224.□

K305.4§, ‡Mother and daughter execute a series of clever thefts by fraud.
Dalîla the Swindler: *Alf* III 213-26; Burton VII 145-67. Chauvin V 245-50 No. 147; *ANE* 163-64 No. 224.□

K306, Thieves steal from each other. See: *DOTTI*.
Merchant from Sindah and Sharpers: *Alf* II 39; Burton III 158. Chauvin II 229 No. 154/17; *ANE* 297-98 No. 56.□

K308.1§, ‡Daughter surpasses mother as thief (trickster). See: *DOTTI*.
Dalîla the Swindler: *Alf* III 225; Burton VII 168. Chauvin V 245-50 No. 147; *ANE* 163-64 No. 224.□

K311, Thief in disguise. See: *DOTTI*.
Merchant and Robbers: *Alf* IV 166; Burton IX 100. Chauvin II 223 No. 152/20; *ANE* 297 No. 251.□

K311.16.4§, ‡Thief disguised as pregnant woman.
Mercury ¿Alî: *Alf* III 237; Burton VII 190-91. Chauvin V 248-50 No. 147; *ANE* 301-3 No. 225.□

K318.1§, ‡Watchdog bribed with food (meat, bone).
King ¿Umar al-Nu¿mân and Sons: *Alf* II 8; Burton III 88. Chauvin VI 112-24 No. 277; *ANE* 430-34 No. 39.□

K318.5§, ‡Watchdog(s) killed with poisoned food.
Mercury ¿Alî: *Alf* III 235; Burton VII 187. Chauvin V 248-50 No. 147; *ANE* 301-3 No. 225.□

K330.1, ‡Man gulled into giving up his clothes. See: *DOTTI*.
Dalîla the Swindler: *Alf* III 217; Burton VII 152-53. Chauvin V 245-50 No. 147; *ANE* 163-64 No. 224.□

K331.2.1.1, ‡Theft after putting owner to sleep by lousing her.
¿Alî Shâr and Zumurrud: *Alf* II 226; Burton IV 209. Chauvin V 89-91 No. 28; *ANE* 100-1 No. 82.□

K331.2.1.3§, ‡Thief induces guard to sleep by yawning (hypnotic suggestion). See: *DOTTI*. (Cf. D1960).
Dalîla the Swindler: *Alf* III 222,-cf.; Burton VII 161. Chauvin V 245-50 No. 147; *ANE* 163-64 No. 224.□

K332.1, ‡Theft by giving narcotic to guardian of goods. See: *DOTTI*; *PSAE*.

Dalîla the Swindler: *Alf* III 225; Burton VII 168. Chauvin V 245-50 No. 147; *ANE* 163-64 No. 224.□

K332.3§, ‡Consent (promise) secured from person when he is drunk.
First Qalandar: Brother-Sister Incest: *Alf* I 39; Burton I 105. Chauvin V 196-97 No. 115; *ANE* 337-38 No. 15.□

K334.4§, ‡Sparrow in hawk's mouth escapes when hawk smiles at sparrow's flattery. See: *DOTTI*.
Hishâm and Arab Youth: *Alf* II 184-85,-(poem); Burton IV 103. Chauvin V 288 No. 172; *ANE* 222-23 No. 68.□

K335.0.4, ‡Owner frightened away from goods by a bluff. See: *DOTTI*.
Shepherd and Rogue's Bluff: *Alf* IV 168-69; Burton IX 106. Chauvin II 223-24 No. 152/22; *ANE* 378 No. 253.□

K336.3§, ‡Trickster sends partner(s) on errand, meantime he escapes with the goods.
Barber's Fifth Brother: Daydreams/Defeats Robbers: *Alf* I 121,-(*Rûmî*-girl); Burton I 342. Chauvin V 161 No. 85; *ANE* 119-20 No. 33.□

K338.1§, ‡Thief ties owner's foot while he escapes with goods.
Ruined Baghdadi and His Slave-girl: *Alf* IV 130; Burton IX 25. Chauvin V 152-53 No. 75; *ANE* 353 No. 235.□

K339§, ‡Thief pretends to help owner: steals goods. See: *DOTTI*.
Dalîla the Swindler: *Alf* III 217-18; Burton VII 153-54. Chauvin V 245-50 No. 147; *ANE* 163-64 No. 224.□

K339.3.1§, ‡Thief pretends to treat barren woman (sterile man): steals goods. See: *DOTTI*.
Dalîla the Swindler: *Alf* III 217; Burton VII 153. Chauvin V 245-50 No. 147; *ANE* 163-64 No. 224.□

K340.1§, ‡Sexual attraction used to distract owner's (guard's) attention: sex-appeal used as lure. See: *DOTTI*.
Dalîla the Swindler: *Alf* III 216; Burton VII 152. Chauvin V 245-50 No. 147; *ANE* 163-64 No. 224; **Mercury ¿Alî**: *Alf* III 231; Burton VII 181. Chauvin V 248-50 No. 147; *ANE* 301-3 No. 225; **Masrûr and Zayn al-Mawâṣif**: *Alf* IV 57-59,-cf.; Burton VIII 216-18. Chauvin VI 82-84 No. 251; *ANE* 294-95 No. 232.□

K340.2§, ‡Owner separated from goods by giving him hope of economic gain. See: *DOTTI*.
Hasan of Basrah: *Alf* IV 43; Burton VIII 122. Chauvin VII 29-35 No. 212A; *ANE* 207-10 No. 230.□

K340.2.4§, ‡Dishonest umpire sets deceptive race between owners of object(s): steals the goods when contestants are away.
Hasan of Basrah: *Alf* IV 43; Burton VIII 122. Chauvin VII 29-35 No. 212A; *ANE* 207-10 No. 230.□

K341.3.1§, ‡Thief distracts attention by staging sham birth or miscarriage (abortion). See: *DOTTI*.
Mercury ¿Alî: *Alf* III 237,-(miscarriage); Burton VII 191. Chauvin V 248-50 No. 147; *ANE* 301-3 No. 225.□

K341.18.1§, ‡Owner's attention distracted by performing animal (monkey). Meanwhile goods are stolen.
Thief and His Monkey: *Alf* II 40; Burton III 159. Chauvin II 229 No. 18; *ANE* 413 No. 57.□

K345.2, Thief sent into well by trickster. See: *DOTTI*.
Mercury ¿Alî: *Alf* III 232-33,-cf.; Burton VII 183. Chauvin V 248-50 No. 147; *ANE* 301-3 No. 225.□

K345.2.1§, ‡Man volunteers to help woman by going into well to retrieve golden ornament. She steals his clothes and leaves him naked. See: *DOTTI*.
Mercury ¿Alî: *Alf* III 232-33; Burton VII 182. Chauvin V 248-50 No. 147; *ANE* 301-3 No. 225.□

K362, Theft by presenting false order to guardian. See: *DOTTI*.
Stolen Purse/Joint Depositors: *Alf* III 176-77; Burton VI 209. Chauvin VIII 63-64 No. 25; *ANE* 399 No. 207.□

K362.10, Give him what he wants. [Theft by message with double-meaning]. See: *DOTTI*.
Stolen Purse/Joint Depositors: *Alf* III 177; Burton VI 209. Chauvin VIII 63-64 No. 25; *ANE* 399 No. 207.□

K365.5§, ‡Theft by bribing the guard.
Goldsmith and Cashmere Singer: *Alf* III 151-2,-cf.; Burton VI 157-58. Chauvin VIII 46-47 No. 14; *ANE* 196 No. 194.□

K366.1.5§, ‡Theft by trained monkey.
Thief and His Monkey: *Alf* II 40; Burton III 159. Chauvin II 229 No. 154.18; *ANE* 413 No. 57.□

K367.1§, ‡Abduction by spirit(s) 'controlled' by magician.
Jawdar and His Treacherous Brethren: *Alf* III 195-96; Burton VI 244. Chauvin V 257-60 No. 154; *ANE* 244-45 No. 209;
Mercury ¿Alî: *Alf* III 243,-(jinni-'*¿oan*'); Burton VII 20. Chauvin V 248-50 No. 147; *ANE* 301-3 No. 225.□

K368.1§, ‡Old woman sees person receive large sum of money: she coaxes him to a place where he is attacked and robbed (by her confederates).
Barber's Fifth Brother: Daydreams/Defeats Robbers: *Alf* I 118; Burton I 339. Chauvin V 161 No. 85; *ANE* 119-20 No. 33.□

K419.11.1§, ‡Blame for missing person (child) fastened on wolf (or the like).
Bulûqiya/Ḥâsib/Queen of Vipers: *Alf* III 20; Burton V 301. Chauvin VII 54 No. 77; *ANE* 130-32 No. 177.□

K419.12.1§, ‡Blame for missing person fastened on jinn (fairies).
¿Abdallah ibn Fâḍil: Treacherous Brothers: *Alf* IV 288; Burton IX 348. Chauvin V 2-4 No. 2; *ANE* 63-65 No. 261.□

K430§, ‡Groom induced to take off magic ring because bride thinks its genie is spying on her.
Ma¿rûf the Cobbler: *Alf* IV 312; Burton X 45. Chauvin VI 81-82 No. 250; *ANE* 291-93 No. 262.□

K437.6§, ‡One victim survives robbers's murderous assault; he kills them by luring each away from the others and then attacking him (her). See: *DOTTI*.
Barber's Fifth Brother: Daydreams/Defeats Robbers: *Alf* I 120; Burton I 341–43. Chauvin V 161 No. 85; *ANE* 119-20 No. 33.□

K452, Unjust umpire misappropriates disputed goods. See: *DOTTI*; *GMC*.
Jackals and Wolf as Umpire: *Alf* IV 167,-(wolf); Burton IX 103-4. Chauvin II 223 No. 152/21; *ANE* 235 No. 252.□

K452.2§, ‡Unjust umpire usurps disputed goods for himself.
Hasan of Basrah: *Alf* IV 43; Burton VIII 122. Chauvin VII 29-35 No. 212A; *ANE* 207-10 No. 230;
Jackals and Wolf as Umpire: *Alf* IV 167; Burton IX 103. Chauvin II 223 No. 152/21; *ANE* 235 No. 252.□

K454§, *ṭufaylî* (uninvited guest, parasite, sponger). See: *DOTTI*; *GMC*.
Barber's Tale of Himself: Joins Doomed Party: *Alf* I 110; Burton I 317–19. Chauvin V 156-57 No. 80; *ANE* 115-17 No. 28;
Isḥâq al-Mûṣilî and Merchant's Singer: *Alf* II 296; Burton V 130. Chauvin VI 59 No. 225; *ANE* 233 No. 142.□

K455.5.2§, ‡Trickster leaves hired infant (maiden, old man) with merchant as surety and escapes with merchandise. See: *DOTTI*.
Dalîla the Swindler: *Alf* III 220,-(stolen infant); Burton VII 157. Chauvin V 245-50 No. 147; *ANE* 163-64 No. 224.□

K476.1.1.1§, ‡Rocks substituted for food (rice, sugar). See: *DOTTI*.
Woman Who Made Husband Sift Dust: *Alf* III 145; Burton VI 143. Chauvin VIII 42 No. 10; *ANE* 452-53 No. 190.□

K477.4.1§, ‡Woman (widow) poses as beautiful young girl and secures judge's (umpire's) attention; he rules conscientiously (in her favor). See: *DOTTI*.
Dalîla the Swindler: *Alf* III 225,-cf.; Burton VII 168. Chauvin V 245-50 No. 147; *ANE* 163-64 No. 224.□

K490.2§, ‡Performing prayers as excuse.
Qamar al-Zamân and Budûr: *Alf* II 101-2; Burton III 285-87. Chauvin V 204-12 No. 120; *ANE* 341-45 No. 61;
Jewish Tray-maker and Temptress: *Alf* III 13; Burton V 266. Chauvin VI 187-88 No. 354; *ANE* 169 No. 166.□

K490.2.2§, ‡Praying as excuse for procrastination: wait till after prayers time.

Qamar al-Zamân and Budûr: *Alf* II 101-2; Burton III 285. Chauvin V 204-12 No. 120; *ANE* 341-45 No. 61.□

K490.9.1§, ‡Visiting shrines (religious festivals, the pious, saints, etc.) as excuse to leave house.
Ni¿mah and Nu¿m: Stolen Wife Regained: *Alf* II 134; Burton IV 4, 6. Chauvin VI 96-97 No. 263; *ANE* 314 No. 62.□

K499.11§, ‡Unjust partner: dodges work (by feigning illness or pretending to work), and then demands a share. See: *DOTTI*.
Abû Qîr and Abû Ṣîr: *Alf* IV 185; Burton IX 140. Chauvin V 15-17 No. 10; *ANE* 75-77 No. 255.□

K501.3.1§, ‡Document chewed (swallowed) so as to destroy evidence of crime.
Anîs al-Jalîs: *Alf* I 143; Burton II 39. Chauvin V 120-24 No. 58; *ANE* 316-17 No. 35;
House with the Belvedere: *Alf* III 168; Burton VI 192. Chauvin VIII 57-58 No. 23; *ANE* 223 No. 203.□

K512, Compassionate executioner. A servant charged with killing the hero (heroine) arranges the escape of the latter. See: *ANE*; *DOTTI*; *GMC*.
First Qalandar: Brother-Sister Incest: *Alf* I 41; Burton I 108. Chauvin V 196-97 No. 115; *ANE* 337-38 No. 15.□

K512.1.2§, Compassionate executioner: animal's (bird's) blood in bottle as proof. See: *DOTTI*; *GMC*.
al-'Amjad and al-'As¿ad: *Alf* II 119,-(lion's); Burton III 321. Chauvin V 208-10 No. 120[.1]; *ANE* 341-42 No. 61/pt. 2.□

K512.2.2.2§, ‡Compassionate executioner: substituted convict (sentenced to death). See: *DOTTI*.
¿Alâ' al-Dîn Abû al-Shâmât: *Alf* II 171,-cf./(deception); Burton IV 75. Chauvin V 43-49 No. 18; *ANE* 85-87 No. 63.□

K512.6§, ‡Compassionate executioner: finds excuses to delay carrying out order. See: *DOTTI*.
Anîs al-Jalîs: *Alf* I 144,-cf.; Burton II 42. Chauvin V 120-24 No. 58; *ANE* 316-17 No. 35;
Tâj al-Mulûk: *Alf* I 305; Burton III 42. Chauvin V 126-28 No. 60; *ANE* 406-8 No. 40;
Hishâm and Arab Youth: *Alf* II 184; Burton IV 102-3. Chauvin V 288 No. 172; *ANE* 222-23 No. 68;
Nûr al-Dîn and Maryam: *Alf* IV 116; Burton VIII 339. Chauvin V 52-54 No. 271; *ANE* 98-99 No. 233;
Abû Qîr and Abû Ṣîr: *Alf* IV 194; Burton IX 158. Chauvin V 15-17 No. 10; *ANE* 75-77 No. 255.□

K521.1.1, ‡Man sewed in animal's hide carried off by birds. (Cf. F671.3§, W217§). See: *ANE*.
Jânshâh: *Alf* III 48,-cf., 65; Burton V 341, 367. Chauvin VII 39-44 No. 153; *ANE* 238-41 No. 178;
Sindbâd's Second Voyage: *Alf* III 90-cf.; Burton VI 19. Chauvin VII 9-14 No. 373B; *ANE* 385 No. 179;
Hasan of Basrah: *Alf* III 309-cf.; Burton VIII 20. Chauvin VII 29-35 No. 212A; *ANE* 207-10 No. 230.□

K522, Escape by shamming death. See: *DOTTI*; *GMC*.
Barber's Fifth Brother: Daydreams/Defeats Robbers: *Alf* I 120; Burton I 340. Chauvin V 161 No. 85; *ANE* 119-20 No. 33.□

K522.1.2§, ‡Attackers deceived when victim-to-be shams death (and lies among the slain). He is left for dead.
Jeweler's Wife and Qamar al-Zamân: *Alf* IV 244, 261; Burton IX 258, 293. Chauvin V 212-14 No. 121; *ANE* 345-47 No. 260.□

K523.0.1, Illness (madness, dumbness, etc.) feigned to escape unwelcome marriage. See: *DOTTI*; *GMC*.
Ebony Horse: *Alf* II 264,-(madness); Burton V 28. Chauvin V 221-31 No. 130; *ANE* 172-74 No. 103.□

K523.1, Escape by shamming madness [(idiocy)]. See: *DOTTI*; *GMC*.
Nûr al-Dîn and Maryam: *Alf* IV 109; Burton VIII 326. Chauvin V 52-54 No. 271; *ANE* 98-99 No. 233.□

K550.3§, ‡Captor busied with performing task while captive escapes. See: *DOTTI*.
Barber's Fifth Brother: Daydreams/Defeats Robbers: *Alf* I 121,-cf.; Burton I 340-41. Chauvin V 161 No. 85; *ANE* 119-20 No. 33.□

K551.28§, ‡Respite from death until story is told [permits escape]. (Cf. J1185.1); See: *DOTTI*.
Shahriyâr and Shâhzamân: *Alf* I 1,-(entire work); Burton I 1-24. Chauvin V 188-89 No. 111; *ANE* 370-71 No. 1.□

K618.1§, ‡Sorceress deceived into restoring transformed person(s) to original form. See: *DOTTI*.
Ensorcelled Prince/Husband: *Alf* I 23; Burton I 80. Chauvin VI 56-58 No. 222; *ANE* 176 No. 13.□

K625, ‡Escape by giving narcotic to guard.
Nûr al-Dîn and Maryam: *Alf* IV 122,-(hated husband); Burton IX 3. Chauvin V 52-54 No. 271; *ANE* 98-99 No. 233.□

K626, ‡Escape by bribing the guard. See: *DOTTI*.
Goldsmith and Cashmere Singer: *Alf* III 151-2,-cf.; Burton VI 157-58. Chauvin VIII 46-47 No. 14; *ANE* 196 No. 194.□

K626.1, Escape by throwing money (treasure) so that guards [(pursuers)] fight over it. See: *DOTTI*; *GMC*.
Tailor's Story/Barber of Baghdad: *Alf* I 108; Burton I 315-16. Chauvin V 154-56 No. 78; *ANE* 405-6 No. 27.□

K638.9.2§, ‡Escape from swallower by making self swallow-proof.
Sindbâd's Third Voyage: *Alf* III 97; Burton VI 29. Chauvin VII 15-18 No. 373C; *ANE* 385-86 No. 179.□

K641.0.1§, ‡One animal (bird) saves another by luring attacking enemy away. See: *DOTTI*.
Flea and She-mouse: *Alf* II 38; Burton III 151-54. Chauvin II 228 No. 12; *ANE* 186 No. 52.□

K641.0.2§, ‡One animal (bird) saves another by luring help in the direction of victim-to-be: attacker flees or is killed. See: *DOTTI*.
Cat and Crow: *Alf* II 36; Burton III 149-50. Chauvin II 226 No. 4; *ANE* 142 No. 50.□

K642.2.1§, ‡Female pigeon pecks net and frees her snared mate.
Tâj al-Mulûk: *Alf* I 299; Burton III 31. Chauvin V 126-28 No. 60; *ANE* 406-8 No. 40.□

K652, Fox climbs from the pit on wolf's back. See: *DOTTI*.
Wolf and Fox: *Alf* II 34; Burton III 143-44. Chauvin II 227 No. 6; *ANE* 450 No. 47.□

K712§, ‡Prey lured into predator's power by flattery or promise of reward. See: *DOTTI*.
Barber's Fifth Brother: Daydreams/Defeats Robbers: *Alf* I 118,-(promise of love); Burton I 339. Chauvin V 161 No. 85; *ANE* 119-20 No. 33;
Hasan of Basrah: *Alf* III 303; Burton VIII 8. Chauvin VII 29-35 No. 212A; *ANE* 207-10 No. 230;
Nûr al-Dîn and Maryam: *Alf* IV 101,-cf./(selling); Burton VIII 312. Chauvin V 52-54 No. 271; *ANE* 98-99 No. 233;
¿Abdallah ibn Fâdil: Treacherous Brothers: *Alf* IV 285,-(banquet); Burton IX 342. Chauvin V 2-4 No. 2; *ANE* 63-65 No. 261.□

K712.0.1§, ‡Victim captured by a promise: "Come here and receive!".
Merchant's Curious Wife: *Alf* I 6,-(tell secret); Burton I 22. Chauvin V 179-80 No. 104; *ANE* 298-99 No. 3;
Falcon and Partridge: *Alf* II 32; Burton III 138. Chauvin II 227 No. 7; *ANE* 180 No. 48;
Escaped Viper Ungrateful: *Alf* II 35,-(promise of reward); Burton III 145. Chauvin II 227 No. 9; *ANE* 450,/passim No. 47;
¿Alâ' al-Dîn Abû al-Shâmât: *Alf* II 176,-cf./(abduction); Burton IV 84-85. Chauvin V 43-49 No. 18; *ANE* 85-87 No. 63.□

K712.0.2.2§, ‡Victim invited to learn wonderful skill (magical craft) and thus falls into deceiver's power.
Hasan of Basrah: *Alf* III 303; Burton VIII 8. Chauvin VII 29-35 No. 212A; *ANE* 207-10 No. 230.□

K712.1§, ‡Victim captured by offer of marriage (or sexual liaison).
Barber's Fifth Brother: Daydreams/Defeats Robbers: *Alf* I 120; Burton I 339. Chauvin V 161 No. 85; *ANE* 119-20 No. 33;
King ¿Umar al-Nu¿mân and Sons: *Alf* I 225,-(acquiring five damsels); Burton II 196. Chauvin VI 112-24 No. 277; *ANE* 430-34 No. 39;
Hasan of Basrah: *Alf* III 305; Burton VIII 13. Chauvin VII 29-35 No. 212A; *ANE* 207-10 No. 230.□

K712.3.2§, ‡Person invited to attend religious ritual (visit saint, magic healing, etc.) but is taken to an isolated place where he is attacked (robbed, raped, or the like).
Ni¿mah and Nu¿m: Stolen Wife Regained: *Alf* II 134; Burton IV 4. Chauvin VI 96-97 No. 263; *ANE* 314 No. 62;
Dalîla the Swindler: *Alf* III 217; Burton VII 149. Chauvin V 245-50 No. 147; *ANE* 163-64 No. 224.□

K712.3.3§, ‡Falling into 'host's' power by accepting plea to perform social duty (e.g., attend wedding, funeral, visit the sick, or the like). See: *DOTTI*.
Portress Amînah: Bitten Cheek: *Alf* I 57,-(wedding); Burton I 174. Chauvin V 98-99 No. 33; *ANE* 326-27 No. 20.□

K712.7.1§, ‡Fox sees another fox inside orchard feasting on fruits and enters to join him; feaster proves to be a dummy set as trap by gardener to capture fox. See: *DOTTI*.
Wolf and Fox: *Alf* II 30,-(report); Burton III 134. Chauvin II 227 No. 6; *ANE* 450 No. 47.□

K713, Deception into allowing oneself to be fettered. See: *DOTTI*.
Birds, Beasts, and Carpenter: *Alf* II 25,-(young lion); Burton III 122. Chauvin II 225-26 No. 1; *ANE* 126 No. 44.□

K713.1.3, ‡Animal persuaded to be tied by promise of food.
Falcon and Partridge: *Alf* II 32,-(partridge); Burton III 138. Chauvin II 227 No. 7; *ANE* 180 No. 48.□

K714, Deception into entering box (or prison). See: *DOTTI*.
King ¿Umar al-Nu¿mân and Sons: *Alf* I 241; Burton II 244,-(dark room in hermitage). Chauvin VI 112-24 No. 277; *ANE* 430-34 No. 39.□

K714.9.2§, ‡Fox persuades bear (wolf) to jump into pit by promise of food. See: *DOTTI*.
Wolf and Fox: *Alf* II 30; Burton III 135. Chauvin II 227 No. 6; *ANE* 450 No. 47.□

K717, Deception into bottle (vessel). See: *ANE*; *DOTTI*.
Fisherman and Afrit: Ingratitude: *Alf* I 15; Burton I 43-44. Chauvin VI 23-25 No. 195; *ANE* 183-84 No. 8.□

K730, Victim trapped. See: *DOTTI*.
Wolf and Fox: *Alf* II 31,-(in pit); Burton III 135,-(in cleft). Chauvin II 227 No. 6; *ANE* 450 No. 47.□

K749.14§, ‡Smith cuts fetters and helps captives escape.
Masrûr and Zayn al-Mawâṣif: *Alf* IV 74; Burton VIII 247. Chauvin VI 82-84 No. 251; *ANE* 294-95 No. 232.□

K760§, ‡Capture by impersonating slain enemy. See: *DOTTI*.
Ensorcelled Prince/Husband: *Alf* I 30,-(wife's paramour); Burton I 78-79. Chauvin VI 56-58 No. 222; *ANE* 176 No. 13.□

K774.3§, ‡Capture by sight of face of woman masking as man.
Bahrâm and Datmâ: *Alf* III 164,-(defeat in combat); Burton VI 185. Chauvin VIII 54-57 No. 22; *ANE* 114-15 No. 202.□

K775.1, ‡Capture by taking aboard ship to inspect wares. See: *DOTTI*.
Hasan of Basrah: *Alf* III 305,-cf.; Burton VIII 14. Chauvin VII 29-35 No. 212A; *ANE* 207-10 No. 230.□

K776, Capture by intoxication (or narcotic). See: *DOTTI*; *PSAE*.
¿Alî Shâr and Zumurrud: *Alf* II 222,-(opium in food); Burton IV 201. Chauvin V 89-91 No. 28; *ANE* 100-1 No. 82.□

K776.4§, ‡Drug-induced hypnotic suggestion. See: *DOTTI*.
First Qalandar: Brother-Sister Incest: *Alf* I 39,-cf./(liquor influence); Burton I 105. Chauvin V 196-97 No. 115; *ANE* 337-38 No. 15.□

K781, ‡Castle captured with assistance of owner's daughter. She loves the attacker.
Mercury ¿Alî: *Alf* III 243,-cf.; Burton VII 204. Chauvin V 248-50 No. 147; *ANE* 301-3 No. 225.□

K811.1, Enemies invited to banquet and killed. See: *GMC*.
Jawdar and His Treacherous Brethren: *Alf* III 200-1,-(brother)/-cf.; Burton VI 255. Chauvin V 257-60 No. 154; *ANE* 244-45 No. 209;

King Jalî¿âd and Shimâs: *Alf* IV 170-71,-cf.; Burton IX 108. Chauvin VI 9 No. 184; *ANE* 237-38 No. 236.□

K811.8§, ‡Victim trapped and his enemies led to him.
Wolf and Fox: *Alf* II 35; Burton III 146. Chauvin II 227 No. 6; *ANE* 450 No. 47.□

K811.8.1§, ‡Fox traps wolf in vineyard (garden) and leads owners to him (wolf killed and fox has the vineyard to himself).
Wolf and Fox: *Alf* II 35; Burton III 146. Chauvin II 227 No. 6; *ANE* 450 No. 47.□

K815.8, ‡Hawk persuades doves to elect him their king. Kills them. See: *DOTTI*.
Crows and Hawk: *Alf* IV 144,-cf./(crows); Burton IX 54. Chauvin II 220 No. 152/8; *ANE* 162 No. 243.□

K830§, ‡Gradual reinforcement of behavior in order to deceive. Series of rewards conditions (lulls) intended victim into a predictable behavior pattern used to attack him.
King ¿Umar al-Nu¿mân and Sons: *Alf* I 225; Burton II 212. Chauvin VI 112-24 No. 277; *ANE* 430-34 No. 39;
Merchant and Robbers: *Alf* IV 166; Burton IX 100. Chauvin II 223 No. 152/20; *ANE* 297 No. 251;
Jeweler's Wife and Qamar al-Zamân: *Alf* IV 247-48,-(gold jewelry given away); Burton IX 254-55. Chauvin V 212-14 No. 121; *ANE* 345-47 No. 260.□

K830.1§, ‡Victim induced to develop a pattern of behavior (through rewards), and then attacked. See: *DOTTI*.
Page Feigns Knowing Bird Language: *Alf* III 157; Burton VI 170-71. Chauvin VIII 49-50 No. 17; *ANE* 321-22 No. 197.□

K830.1.1§, ‡Seduction by offering gradual (nonsexual) rewards: seducer's credibility thus established.
Page Feigns Knowing Bird Language: *Alf* III 157,-(seduction); Burton VI 170-71. Chauvin VIII 49-50 No. 17; *ANE* 321-22 No. 197;
Bahrâm and Datmâ: *Alf* III 166; Burton VI 186. Chauvin VIII 54-57 No. 22; *ANE* 114-15 No. 202.□

K842, Dupe persuaded to take prisoner's place in sack: killed [(drowned)]. See: *DOTTI*.
Dalîla the Swindler: *Alf* III 224; Burton VII 164. Chauvin V 245-50 No. 147; *ANE* 163-64 No. 224.□

K841.3§, ‡Man sentenced to be executed substituted for innocent wrongly condemned to death. See: *DOTTI*.
¿Alâ' al-Dîn Abû al-Shâmât: *Alf* II 171; Burton IV 75. Chauvin V 43-49 No. 18; *ANE* 85-87 No. 63.□

K871.1, ‡Army intoxicated and overcome.
King ¿Umar al-Nu¿mân and Sons: *Alf* I 247,-cf.; Burton II 256. Chauvin VI 112-24 No. 277; *ANE* 430-34 No. 39.□

K871.3§, ‡Person (enemy) intoxicated and overcome (killed).
¿Alâ' al-Dîn Abû al-Shâmât: *Alf* II 179; Burton IV 91. Chauvin V 43-49 No. 18; *ANE* 85-87 No. 63;
Sindbâd's Fifth Voyage: *Alf* III 108,-(demon); Burton VI 52. Chauvin VII 21-24 No. 373E; *ANE* 386 No. 179;
Sayf al-Mulûk: *Alf* III 292,-(demon); Burton VII 358. Chauvin VII 64-73 No. 348; *ANE* 362-64 No. 229.□

K871.3.2§, ‡Person intoxicated (drugged, etc.) and then disfigured (mutilated). See: *DOTTI*; *PSAE*.
¿Azîz and ¿Azîzah: *Alf* I 287,-cf.; Burton III 2. Chauvin V 144-45 No. 71; *ANE* 111-13 No. 41.□

K920.2.1§, ‡Posthumous killing: mechanical device left by grave-owner kills intruder.
City of Brass: *Alf* III 137; Burton VI 118. Chauvin V 32-35 No. 16; *ANE* 146-50 No. 180.□

K951, Murder by choking.
Jeweler's Wife and Qamar al-Zamân: *Alf* IV 265; Burton IX 300. Chauvin V 212-14 No. 121; *ANE* 345-47 No. 260;
¿Abdallah ibn Fâḍil: Treacherous Brothers: *Alf* IV 286-87; Burton IX 344,-(throttle). Chauvin V 2-4 No. 2; *ANE* 63-65 No. 261.□

K959.2, ‡Murder in one's sleep [i.e., of sleeping person].
King ¿Umar al-Nu¿mân and Sons: *Alf* I 257-58; Burton II 275. Chauvin VI 112-24 No. 277; *ANE* 430-34 No. 39.□

K979§, ‡Cause of invulnerability treacherously nullified.

Abû Muhammad Lazybones: *Alf* II 212-13; Burton IV 172. Chauvin VI 64-67 No. 233; *ANE* 71-73 No. 78.□

K979.1§, ‡Man deceived into destroying protective agent: becomes vulnerable.
Abû Muhammad Lazybones: *Alf* II 212-13; Burton IV 172. Chauvin VI 64-67 No. 233; *ANE* 71-73 No. 78.□

K992§, ‡Misleading advice. See: *DOTTI*.
Abû Qîr and Abû Sîr: *Alf* IV 193; Burton IX 155. Chauvin V 15-17 No. 10; *ANE* 75-77 No. 255.□

K992.1§, ‡Trickster seeking revenge on blind men feigns blindness and claims that a beating by the police has 'cured' (reformed) him; he recommends the same 'cure' for his blind adversaries. See: *DOTTI*; *GMC*.
Barber's Third Brother: Exposes Blind Robbers: *Alf* I 115; Burton I 329-30. Chauvin V 159-60 No. 83; *ANE* 118 No. 31.□

K1020, Deception into disastrous attempt to procure food. See: *DOTTI*.
Wild Ass and Jackal: *Alf* IV 142,-cf.; Burton IX 49. Chauvin II 219 No. 152/6; *ANE* 449 No. 241.□

K1020.1.1§, ‡Trickster persuades dupe to surrender all his provisions; dupe goes hungry.
Hedgehog and Wood-pigeons: *Alf* II 39,-(porcupine tricks bird); Burton III 156. Chauvin II 229 No. 15; *ANE* 220 No. 55.□

K1027.1§, ‡Animal caught by coaxing it into cage containing food.
Bulûqiya: *Alf* III 25,-(viper); Burton V 309. Chauvin VII 54 No. 77; *ANE* 130-32 No. 177.□

K1022.8§, ‡Thieves persuade naive boy to steal for them but he is caught by owner: they absolve themselves while he is punished.
Boy and thieves: Guilty Accomplice: *Alf* IV 163-64; Burton IX 96. Chauvin II 222-23 No. 152/17; *ANE* 128 No. 249.□

K1039§, Cooking pebbles (stones) in pot so as to induce hungry children to wait for food. See: *DOTTI*; *GMC*.
Nuzhat al-Zamân Tested/¿Umar al-Nu¿mân: *Alf* I 203; Burton II 164. Chauvin VI 116, n.1/passim No. 277; *ANE* 432,/passim No. 39.□

K1065.1§, ‡Tortoises persuade bird to pluck off his feathers: attacked by weasel. See: *DOTTI*.
Francolin and Tortoises: *Alf* IV 172-73; Burton IX 114. Chauvin II 224 No. 152/23; *ANE* 188 No. 254.□

K1067.1§, ‡Trap question: posed in order to place adversary in trouble if answered properly. (Cf. J1148§).
Tawaddud: Slavegirl Sold and Regained: *Alf* III 6,-(Ali or al-¿Abbâs); Burton V 241. Chauvin VII 117-19 No. 387; *ANE* 408-10 No. 157.□

K1073§, ‡Useless surgical operation induced by trickster (thief). See: *DOTTI*.
Dalîla the Swindler: *Alf* III 221; Burton VII 161. Chauvin V 245-50 No. 147; *ANE* 163-64 No. 224.□

K1073.1§, ‡Doctor duped into performing surgery on healthy unsuspecting victim. Victim reported to be in critical need of cure (e.g., branding, circumcision, teeth-pulling, etc.) but reluctant to undergo treatment. See: *DOTTI*.
Dalîla the Swindler: *Alf* III 221; Burton VII 161. Chauvin V 245-50 No. 147; *ANE* 163-64 No. 224.□

K1082.0.1, ‡Enemies duped into fighting each other.
King ¿Umar al-Nu¿mân and Sons: *Alf* I 248; Burton II 256. Chauvin VI 112-24 No. 277; *ANE* 430-34 No. 39.□

K1164§, ‡Secret learned by spying (eavesdropping). See: *DOTTI*.
Butcher Wardân and Bear Lover: *Alf* II 251; Burton IV 294. Chauvin V 177-78 No. 101; *ANE* 442-43 No. 101;
Uns al-Wujûd and al-Ward: *Alf* II 270,-(by reading love letter); Burton V 34. Chauvin VI 127-29 No. 282; *ANE* 438 No. 104.□

K1164.1.4§, ‡Husband learns wife's secret by spying on her. See: *DOTTI*.
Shahriyâr and Shâhzamân: *Alf* I 3; Burton I 9. Chauvin V 188-91 No. 111; *ANE* 370-71 No. 1;
Masrûr and Zayn al-Mawâsif: *Alf* IV 66; Burton VIII 232-33. Chauvin VI 82-84 No. 251; *ANE* 294-95 No. 232.□

K1165, ‡Secret learned by intoxicating dupe.
Mercury ¿Alî: *Alf* III 234; Burton VII 185. Chauvin V 248-50 No. 147; *ANE* 301-3 No. 225.□

K1210, Humiliated or baffled lovers. See: *DOTTI*.
Bahrâm and Datmâ: *Alf* III 165; Burton VI 185. Chauvin VIII 54-57 No. 22; *ANE* 114-15 No. 202.□

K1210.0.1§, ‡Hidden paramour discovered (accidentally). See: *DOTTI*.
Tailor's Story/Barber of Baghdad: *Alf* I 107; Burton I 315. Chauvin V 154-56 No. 78; *ANE* 405-6 No. 27.□

K1214.1.1, Importunate lover is induced to undergo a series of humiliations. See: *DOTTI*; *GMC*; *PSAE*.
Barber's First Brother: Free Labor for Coquette: *Alf* I 111-12,-(turns mill); Burton I 322. Chauvin V 156-57 No. 80; *ANE* 117, No. 29.□

K1218.1.4.1, Four importunate lovers are forced to hide in four-compartmented chest which is sold. See: *DOTTI*.
Lady and Five Suitors Deceived: *Alf* III 158-59; Burton VI 175. Chauvin VIII 50-51 No. 18; *ANE* 266 No. 198.□

K1218.1.9.1§, ‡The entrapped suitor is forced to substitute for labor animal (by turning mill, pulling plough or the like). He is driven with a whip.
Barber's First Brother: Free Labor for Coquette: *Alf* I 111-12,-(harnessed to mill); Burton I 322. Chauvin V 156-57 No. 80; *ANE* 117, No. 29.□

K1218.9.9.1§, ‡Lecher given a rendezvous: message sent by taunting trickster. See: *DOTTI*.
Lady and Five Suitors Deceived: *Alf* III 158-59; Burton VI 172-79. Chauvin VIII 50-51 No. 18; *ANE* 266 No. 198.□

K1236.2.1§, ‡Woman disguises as her husband (fiance) to escape abuse in his absence (death).
Qamar al-Zamân and Budûr: *Alf* II 100; Burton III 284. Chauvin V 204-12 No. 120; *ANE* 341-45 No. 61.□

K1226§, ‡Promise of sexual liaison with beautiful woman induces man to undergo series of spiraling (ascending) humiliations (slapping, shaving of beard and eyebrows, nakedness, etc.). See: *DOTTI*; *PSAE*.
Barber's First Brother: Free Labor for Coquette: *Alf* I 111; Burton I 322. Chauvin V 157-58 No. 81; *ANE* 117 No. 29.□

K1227.1.2§, ‡Seducer put off by promise of better surroundings: "Better at my house", "Better at night", or the like.
Lady and Five Suitors Deceived: *Alf* III 158-59; Burton VI 174,-(better in my place). Chauvin VIII 50-51 No. 18; *ANE* 266 No. 198;
Mercury ¿Alî: *Alf* III 232,-(at night); Burton VII 182. Chauvin V 248-50 No. 147; *ANE* 301-3 No. 225.□

K1227.12§, ‡Escape from undesired suitor by demanding that he wait till required waiting period (*¿iddah*) of formerly married bride-to-be is over.
Jawdar and His Treacherous Brethren: *Alf* III 201; Burton VI 256,-(days of widowhood). Chauvin V 257-60 No. 154; *ANE* 244-45 No. 209;
Ma¿rûf the Cobbler: *Alf* IV 311; Burton X 43,(period of widowhood). Chauvin VI 81-82 No. 250; *ANE* 291-93 No. 262.□

K1241, Trickster rides dupe horseback. See: *DOTTI*; *GMC*.
Sindbâd's Fifth Voyage: *Alf* III 108; Burton VI 51. Chauvin VII 21-24 No. 373E; *ANE* 386 No. 179.□

K1245§, ‡Humiliating nakedness through deception: person tricked into nudity. See: *DOTTI*.
Jânshâh: *Alf* III 55; Burton V 350. Chauvin VII 39-44 No. 153; *ANE* 238-41 No. 178;
Hasan of Basrah: *Alf* IV 3; Burton VIII 41. Chauvin VII 29-35 No. 212A; *ANE* 207-10 No. 230.□

K1266.1§, ‡Victim's mouth shut (gagged) to prevent him from calling for help (speaking).
Jawdar and His Treacherous Brethren: *Alf* III 193; Burton VI 240,-("pinioning"). Chauvin V 257-60 No. 154; *ANE* 244-45 No. 209.□

K1271.1, Threat to tell of amorous intrigue used as blackmail. See: *DOTTI*.
Devout Jewess and Wicked Elders: *Alf* II 286; Burton V 97. Chauvin VI 193-93 No. 362; *ANE* 169 No. 128.□

K1289.1§, King induced by girl to kneel before her. See: *DOTTI*.
Hind bint al-Nu¿mân and al-Ḥajjâj: *Alf* III 203,-(viceroy); Burton VII 99. Chauvin V 115-4 No. 50; *ANE* 221-22 No. 212.□

K1304§, ‡Arranging for maiden's (woman's) beauty to be 'accidentally' displayed so as to coax suitor-to-be.
Jawdar and His Treacherous Brethren: *Alf* III 199-200; Burton VI 253. Chauvin V 257-60 No. 154; *ANE* 244-45 No. 209.□

K1305§, Deceptive marriage arrangements: the man is tricked. See: *DOTTI*; *GMC*.
Barber's First Brother: Free Labor for Coquette: *Alf* I 111; Burton I 322. Chauvin V 156-57 No. 80; *ANE* 117, No. 29.□

K1305.3§, ‡Man deceived into marrying a non-virgin.
King ¿Umar al-Nu¿mân and Sons: *Alf* I 208; Burton II 175. Chauvin VI 112-24 No. 277; *ANE* 430-34 No. 39.□

K1315.1.3§, ‡Seduction under pretense of fulfilling the predestined (enacting God's Will, or the like).
Qamar al-Zamân and Budûr: *Alf* II 110,-cf.; Burton III 305. Chauvin V 204-12 No. 120; *ANE* 341-45 No. 61.□

K1315.5, Seduction by posing as nobleman. See: *DOTTI*.
Mock Caliph/¿Alî al-Jawharî: *Alf* II 199,-cf./(attract attention); Burton IV 146. Chauvin V 99-100 No. 174; *ANE* 304-5 No. 73.□

K1307§, Deceptive marriage arrangements: the girl (woman) is tricked.
Bahrâm and Datmâ: *Alf* III 166; Burton VI 187. Chauvin VIII 54-57 No. 22; *ANE* 114-15 No. 202.□

K1321, Seduction by man disguised as woman. See: *DOTTI*; *GMC*.
Tâj al-Mulûk: *Alf* I 303; Burton III 37. Chauvin V 126-28 No. 60; *ANE* 406-8 No. 40.□

K1322.2§, The lovely warrior-maiden (masking as man) is at last defeated and her identity revealed. See: *DOTTI*; *GMC*.
King ¿Umar al-Nu¿mân and Sons: *Alf* I 179; Burton II 118. Chauvin VI 112-24 No. 277; *ANE* 430-34 No. 39.□

K1325.1.1§, ‡Seduction by feigned involuntary (unintentional) contact during sleep.
Mercury ¿Alî: *Alf* III 229,-(male); Burton VII 177. Chauvin V 248-50 No. 147; *ANE* 301-3 No. 225.□

K1327.1§, ‡Seduction by pretended ignorance of sex: person of opposite sex explains (instructs). See: *DOTTI*.
Porter and Ladies of Baghdad: *Alf* I 35; Burton I 90-92. Chauvin V 251-52 No. 148; *ANE* 324-26 No. 14.□

K1332, Seduction by taking aboard ship to inspect wares. See: *DOTTI*.
¿Alâ' al-Dîn Abû al-Shâmât: *Alf* II 176,-cf./(abduction); Burton IV 85. Chauvin V 43-49 No. 18; *ANE* 85-87 No. 63.□

K1335, Seduction (or wooing) by stealing clothes [(feathers)] of bathing girl (swan maiden). See: *DOTTI*.
Hasan of Basrah: *Alf* IV 5; Burton VIII 45. Chauvin VII 29-35 No. 212A; *ANE* 207-10 No. 230.□

K1337§, ‡Seduction by frightening into submission. (Usually through supernatural affliction: enchantment, illness, or the like).
Wife's device to cheat: (Weeping Bitch as Bluff): *Alf* III 149; Burton VI 153. Chauvin VIII 45-46 No. 13; *ANE* 447-49 No. 193.□

K1339, Girl tricked into man's room (power)—miscellaneous. See: *DOTTI*.
Ni¿mah and Nu¿m: Stolen Wife Regained: *Alf* II 135; Burton IV 6-7. Chauvin VI 96-97 No. 263; *ANE* 314 No. 62.□

K1342, Entrance into woman's (man's) room by hiding in chest. See: *DOTTI*; *GMC*.
Reeve's Story: Why Maimed by Bride: *Alf* I 98; Burton I 283. Chauvin V 220-21 No. 305; *ANE* 351 No. 25;
King's Son and Merchant's Wife: *Alf* III 155-56; Burton VI 168. Chauvin VIII 48-49 No. 16; *ANE* 263 No. 196;
Abû al-Hasan al-Khorâsânî (and Caliph's Favorite): *Alf* IV 233; Burton IX 239. Chauvin V 218-20 No. 129; *ANE* 68-69 No. 259.□

K1342.0.1, Man carried into woman's room hidden in basket. See: *DOTTI*.
Isḥâq al-Mûṣilî and Khadîjah bint al-Ḥasan: *Alf* II 185,-cf.; Burton IV 119. Chauvin V 241-42 No. 142; *ANE* 232 No. 71.□

K1343.1, ‡Man drawn up into female apartments in basket.
Isḥâq al-Mûṣilî and Khadîjah bint al-Ḥasan: *Alf* II 185,-cf.; Burton IV 119. Chauvin V 241-42 No. 142; *ANE* 232 No. 71.□

K1344, Tunnel entrance to guarded maiden's chamber. [Underground passage]. See: *DOTTI*; *GMC*.
Abû Muḥammad Lazybones: *Alf* II 216; Burton IV 176. Chauvin VI 64-67 No. 233; *ANE* 71-73 No. 78;
Jeweler's Wife and Qamar al-Zamân: *Alf* IV 252,-(*sirdâb*); Burton IX 274,-(underground-way). Chauvin V 212-14 No. 121; *ANE* 345-47 No. 260.□

K1349.1.0.1§, ‡Disguise as woman (girl) to enter women's quarters.
Qamar al-Zamân and Budûr: *Alf* II 87; Burton III 257. Chauvin V 204-12 No. 120; *ANE* 341-45 No. 61.□

K1350, Woman persuaded (or wooed) by trick. See: *DOTTI*.
Portress Amînah: Bitten Cheek: *Alf* I 57; Burton I 179. Chauvin V 98-99 No. 33; *ANE* 326-27 No. 20.□

K1351, The weeping bitch. [Procuress throws pepper in animal's eyes and claims that it is transformed woman who did not respond to wooer. Virtuous woman persuaded]. See: *DOTTI*; *GMC*.
Wife's device to cheat: (Weeping Bitch as Bluff): *Alf* III 148; Burton VI 152-54. Chauvin VIII 45-46 No. 13; *ANE* 447-49 No. 193.□

K1351.3§, Seduction by claiming to be a transformed animal. See: *DOTTI*; *GMC*.
Wife's device to cheat: (Weeping Bitch as Bluff): *Alf* III 149,-cf.; Burton VI 153. Chauvin VIII 45-46 No. 13; *ANE* 447-49 No. 193.□

K1351.4§, ‡ ‡Seduction by promise of nonsexual marriage.
Bahrâm and Datmâ: *Alf* III 165,-(kiss then divorce); Burton VI 186. Chauvin VIII 54-57 No. 22; *ANE* 114-15 No. 202.□

K1363.1.3§, Seduction: putting the animal (mule) in his natural habitat. See: *DOTTI*.
Porter and Ladies of Baghdad: *Alf* I 35; Burton I 92. Chauvin V 251-52 No. 148; *ANE* 324-26 No. 14.□

K1370.3.1§, ‡Feigning blindness so as to spy on woman.
Barber's Third Brother: Exposes Blind Robbers: *Alf* I 115; Burton I 330. Chauvin V 159-60 No. 83; *ANE* 118 No. 31.□

K1381.1§, Person drugged (made drunk) and then raped. See: *DOTTI*.
King ¿Umar al-Nu¿mân and Sons: *Alf* I 182; Burton II 122-23. Chauvin VI 112-24 No. 277; *ANE* 430-34 No. 39.□

K1381.3§, ‡Female takes sexual advantage of (rapes) drugged man. See: *DOTTI*.
Qamar al-Zamân and Budûr: *Alf* II 79,-cf.; Burton III 241. Chauvin V 204-12 No. 120; *ANE* 341-45 No. 61;
Jeweler's Wife and Qamar al-Zamân: *Alf* IV 249; Burton IX 268. Chauvin V 212-14 No. 121; *ANE* 345-47 No. 260.□

K1386.1§, ‡Lecherous official won over by a woman's promise of sexual liaison: she reneges on her promise after he has kept his.
Lady and Five Suitors Deceived: *Alf* III 158-59; Burton VI 172-79. Chauvin VIII 50-51 No. 18; *ANE* 266 No. 198.□

K1397.1§, Seduction (rape) by threatening woman with defamation and causing scandal: woman fears for her reputation and surrenders. See: *DOTTI*; *GMC*.
Man [Gardener] and His Wife: *Alf* IV 165,-cf.; Burton IX 98. Chauvin II 223 No. 152/19; *ANE* 289 No. 250.□

K1397.2§, ‡Male (man, boy) seduced by threatening him. See: *DOTTI*.
Jinni Keeps Mistress in Box: *Alf* I 4; Burton I 12. Chauvin V 188-89 No. 111; *ANE* 370 No. 1/pt.;
King's Son and Afrit's Mistress: *Alf* III 172; Burton VI 200. Chauvin VIII 59 No. 24; *ANE* 263-64 No. 204.□

K1397.3§, ‡Trickster causes unattainable woman to be cast-off (imprisoned) so that he may gain control over her. See: *DOTTI*.
Goldsmith and Cashmere Singer: *Alf* III 150-51; Burton VI 158. Chauvin VIII 46-47 No. 14; *ANE* 196 No. 194.□

K1397.6.1§, ‡Lesbian blackmail: 'dike' threatens girl with defamation if she does not succumb to her seduction.
King ¿Umar al-Nu¿mân and Sons: *Alf* I 236; Burton II 234. Chauvin VI 112-24 No. 277; *ANE* 430-34 No. 39.□

K1501, Cuckold. Husband deceived by adulterous wife. See: *DOTTI*.
Page Feigns Knowing Bird Language: *Alf* III 157; Burton VI 171. Chauvin VIII 49-50 No. 17; *ANE* 321-22 No. 197;
House with the Belvedere: *Alf* III 172; Burton VI 199. Chauvin VIII 57-58 No. 23; *ANE* 223 No. 203.□

K1510.2, Wife of philanderer gets revenge by having an affair herself. See: *DOTTI*.
Sweep and Noble Lady: Infidelity Repaid: *Alf* II 188; Burton IV 129. Chauvin VI 148 No. 306; *ANE* 403-4 No. 72.□

K1511.1, Adulteress refuses to admit husband under pretence that he is a stranger. [Husband forgot password]. See: *DOTTI*; *GMC*.
Masrûr and Zayn al-Mawâṣif: *Alf* IV 66-67,-cf.; Burton VIII 233-34. Chauvin VI 82-84 No. 251; *ANE* 294-95 No. 232.□

K1514.4.1.1§, ‡Would-be adulterer husband beaten by his would-be adulteress wife. Procuress brings man to woman, he proves to be her husband: wife beats him pretending that she was testing his fidelity. See: *DOTTI*.
Wife's device to cheat: (Weeping Bitch as Bluff): *Alf* III 149-50; Burton VI 155. Chauvin VIII 45-46 No. 13; *ANE* 447-49 No. 193.□

K1514.17, Adulteress together with lover while husband sleeps. See: *GMC*.
Jeweler's Wife and Qamar al-Zamân: *Alf* IV 249,-cf.; Burton IX 268. Chauvin V 212-14 No. 121; *ANE* 345-47 No. 260.□

K1514.20§, ‡Man persuaded to arrange for wife's lover to live next door as neighbor. See: *DOTTI*.
Jeweler's Wife and Qamar al-Zamân: *Alf* IV 251; Burton IX 273. Chauvin V 212-14 No. 121; *ANE* 345-47 No. 260.□

K1517, Paramour escapes by disguise. See: *DOTTI*.
Lady's Lovers as Pursuer and Fugitive: *Alf* III 143; Burton VI 138-39. Chauvin VIII 38-39 No. 7; *ANE* 267 No. 187.□

K1517.1, The lovers as pursuer and fugitive. [Husband deceived]. See: *ANE*; *DOTTI*; *GMC*.
Lady's Lovers as Pursuer and Fugitive: *Alf* III 143; Burton VI 138-39. Chauvin VIII 38-39 No. 7; *ANE* 267 No. 187.□

K1519.1§, ‡Woman feigns illness (falling) in order to explain why she is lying on her back before a youth (seducer).
Page Feigns Knowing Bird Language: *Alf* III 157; Burton VI 171. Chauvin VIII 49-50 No. 17; *ANE* 321-22 No. 197.□

K1521.2, ‡Paramour successfully hidden in chest.
Tailor's Story/Barber of Baghdad: *Alf* I 107; Burton I 315. Chauvin V 154-56 No. 78; *ANE* 405-6 No. 27.□

K1523, Underground passage to paramour's house. See: *ANE*.
Jeweler's Wife and Qamar al-Zamân: *Alf* IV 252,-(*sirdâb*); Burton IX 274,-(underground-way). Chauvin V 212-14 No. 121; *ANE* 345-47 No. 260.□

K1534.1§, ‡Husband made to sift dirt. Wife, whose food purchase was replaced with dirt and rocks during her sexual liaison with merchant, claims that she dropped the money on ground and that she brought the dirt home to search for it. See: *DOTTI*.
Woman Who Made Husband Sift Dust: *Alf* III 145; Burton VI 144. Chauvin VIII 42 No. 10; *ANE* 452-53 No. 190.□

K1535.1, ‡Adulteress transforms man to stone up to the waist. See: *DOTTI*.

Ensorcelled Prince/Husband: *Alf* I 29; Burton I 76-77. Chauvin VI 56-58 No. 222; *ANE* 176 No. 13.□

K1543, The marked coat in the wife's room. See: *DOTTI*.
House with the Belvedere: *Alf* III 169,-(veil); Burton VI 194. Chauvin VIII 57-58 No. 23; *ANE* 223 No. 203.□

K1551, ‡Husband returns home secretly and spies on adulteress and lovers. See: *DOTTI*.
Shahriyâr and Shâhzamân: *Alf* I 3; Burton I 4. Chauvin V 188-91 No. 111; *ANE* 370-71 No. 1;
Masrûr and Zayn al-Mawâṣif: *Alf* IV 66; Burton VIII 232-33. Chauvin VI 82-84 No. 251; *ANE* 294-95 No. 232.□

K1553.1.1§, ‡Lover hidden in chest (closet) discovered by husband.
King's Son and Merchant's Wife: *Alf* III 156; Burton VI 169. Chauvin VIII 48-49 No. 16; *ANE* 263 No. 196.□

K1561, The husband meets the paramour in the wife's place.
Barber's First Brother: Free Labor for Coquette: *Alf* I 112; Burton I 324. Chauvin V 157-58 No. 81; *ANE* 117 No. 29.□

K1586.0.1§, ‡Paramour gains access to mistress by gaining husband's (father's, etc.) confidence.
Jeweler's Wife and Qamar al-Zamân: *Alf* IV 248; Burton IX 266. Chauvin V 212-14 No. 121; *ANE* 345-47 No. 260.□

K1590.1.1§, ‡Mark from a kiss said to be insect bite (mosquito, flea, etc.). See: *DOTTI*.
Jeweler's Wife and Qamar al-Zamân: *Alf* IV 249; Burton IX 269. Chauvin V 212-14 No. 121; *ANE* 345-47 No. 260.□

K1590.1.1.1§, ‡Why beardless youth has bite-marks on face while bearded man does not? 'Mosquitos' (actually woman) prefer the tender-tasting.
Jeweler's Wife and Qamar al-Zamân: *Alf* IV 249; Burton IX 269. Chauvin V 212-14 No. 121; *ANE* 345-47 No. 260.□

K1590.4§, ‡Lover's bite said to be caused by animal (camel horse, etc.).
Portress Amînah: Bitten Cheek: *Alf* I 58-59; Burton I 180. Chauvin V 98-99 No. 33; *ANE* 326-27 No. 20.□

K1591.0.1, ‡Faithless wife kills magic parrot which has betrayed her. See: *DOTTI*.
Husband and Parrot: *Alf* III 141; Burton I 52-54. Chauvin VI 139 No. 294; *ANE* 226 No. 11.□

K1613, Poisoner poisoned with his own poison. See: *DOTTI*.
Merchant from Sindah and Sharpers: *Alf* II 39-40; Burton III 158. Chauvin II 229 No. 154/17; *ANE* 297-98 No. 56;
Bulûqiya: *Alf* III 79; Burton V 392-93. Chauvin VII 54 No. 77; *ANE* 130-32 No. 177.□

K1626, Would-be killer killed. See: *DOTTI*; *GMC*.
al-'Amjad and al-'As¿ad: *Alf* II 126; Burton III 337. Chauvin V 208-10 No. 120[.1]; *ANE* 341-42 No. 61/pt. 2;
Ma¿rûf the Cobbler: *Alf* IV 316; Burton X 52. Chauvin VI 81-82 No. 250; *ANE* 291-93 No. 262.□

K1626.4§, ‡Drunken person about to commit murder is himself killed.
al-'Amjad and al-'As¿ad: *Alf* II 126; Burton III 337. Chauvin V 208-10 No. 120[.1]; *ANE* 341-42 No. 61/pt. 2.□

K1627.1§, ‡Murder (assassination) plot foiled when conspirator(s) betray(s) plan.
¿Alâ' al-Dîn Abû al-Shâmât: *Alf* II 174; Burton IV 81. Chauvin V 43-49 No. 18; *ANE* 85-87 No. 63.□

K1633.1.1§, The evil counsel: death by burning and drowning; applied to counselor. See: *DOTTI*.
Abû Qîr and Abû Ṣîr: *Alf* IV 194; Burton IX 155. Chauvin V 15-17 No. 10; *ANE* 75-77 No. 255.□

K1634.2§, ‡Advice about how to dodge responsibility (avoid work) proves disastrous to adviser.
Bull and Ass: *Alf* I 6; Burton I 17-18. Chauvin V 179-80 No. 104; *ANE* 129-30 No. 2.□

K1667.3§, Poor man cheated: his daughters get revenge. See: *DOTTI*; *GMC*.
Dalîla the Swindler: *Alf* III 213,-cf./(wife and daughter); Burton VII 146. Chauvin V 245-50 No. 147; *ANE* 163-64 No. 224.□

K1667.4§, ‡Poor man cheated: his wife recovers his loss (gets revenge). See: *DOTTI*.

Dalîla the Swindler: *Alf* III 213,-cf.; Burton VII 146. Chauvin V 248-50 No. 147; *ANE* 163-64 No. 224.□

K1678§, Ass induces overworked bullock to feign sickness. See: *DOTTI*.
Bull and Ass: *Alf* I 6; Burton I 17-18. Chauvin V 179-80 No. 104; *ANE* 129-30 No. 2.□

K1683.1§, ‡Chaste woman punishes procuress—(has servants beat her till unconscious, thrown out).
Tâj al-Mulûk: *Alf* I 299; Burton III 30. Chauvin V 126-28 No. 60; *ANE* 406-8 No. 40.□

K1683.3§, ‡Chaste man punishes messenger delivering message of illicit love.
al-'Amjad and al-'As¿ad: *Alf* II 113, 115; Burton III 311, 313. Chauvin V 208-10 No. 120[.1]; *ANE* 341-42 No. 61/pt. 2.□

K1771, Bluffing threat. See: *DOTTI*; *GMC*.
Shepherd and Rogue's Bluff: *Alf* IV 168-69; Burton IX 106. Chauvin II 223-24 No. 152/22; *ANE* 378 No. 253;
King Jalî¿âd and Shimâs: *Alf* IV 177; Burton IX 123. Chauvin VI 9 No. 184; *ANE* 237-38 No. 236.□

K1772.1§, ‡ Sham indignation. Guilty pretends to be deeply offended by mere inquiry (suspicion). See: *DOTTI*.
Jeweler's Wife and Qamar al-Zamân: *Alf* IV 254; Burton IX 279. Chauvin V 212-14 No. 121; *ANE* 345-47 No. 260.□

K1812, King in disguise. See: *GMC*.
Anîs al-Jalîs: *Alf* I 139; Burton II 29. Chauvin V 120-24 No. 58; *ANE* 316-17 No. 35;
Abû al-Hasan al-Khorâsânî (and Caliph's Favorite): *Alf* IV 229; Burton IX 229. Chauvin V 218-20 No. 129; *ANE* 68-69 No. 259.□

K1812.17, King in disguise to spy out his kingdom. See: *ANE*; *DOTTI*; *GMC*.
Porter and Ladies of Baghdad: *Alf* I 35-36; Burton I 96. Chauvin V 251-52 No. 148; *ANE* 324-26 No. 14;
King Jalî¿âd and Shimâs: *Alf* IV 173; Burton IX 115. Chauvin VI 9 No. 184; *ANE* 237-38 No. 236.□

K1814.5§, Woman disguised as man is visited by her unsuspecting husband. See: *DOTTI*.
Qamar al-Zamân and Budûr: *Alf* II 108; Burton III 299-300. Chauvin V 204-12 No. 120; *ANE* 341-45 No. 61.□

K1816.1, ‡Gardener disguise. See: *DOTTI*.
Bahrâm and Datmâ: *Alf* III 165; Burton VI 185. Chauvin VIII 54-57 No. 22; *ANE* 114-15 No. 202.□

K1816.13, Disguise as salve. See: *DOTTI*.
al-'Amjad and al-'As¿ad: *Alf* II 124,-cf./(owner of house plays role of slave to intruder); Burton III 335. Chauvin V 208-10 No. 120[.1]; *ANE* 2 341-42 No. 61/pt.;
Ghânim ibn Ayyûb: *Alf* I 157,-cf./(servant/slave/??); Burton II 67. Chauvin VI 14 No. 188; *ANE* 192-93 No. 36;
Mercury ¿Alî: *Alf* III 234; Burton VII 184. Chauvin V 248-50 No. 147; *ANE* 301-3 No. 225.□

K1816.13.1§, Disguise as salve-woman. See: *DOTTI*; *GMC*.
Jeweler's Wife and Qamar al-Zamân: *Alf* IV 254-55,-(wife visits husband's shop); Burton IX 280. Chauvin V 212-14 No. 121; *ANE* 345-47 No. 260.□

K1816.14§, ‡Disguise as fisher.
Anîs al-Jalîs: *Alf* I 141,- (caliph's); Burton II 32. Chauvin V 120-24 No. 58; *ANE* 316-17 No. 35.□

K1816.14.1§, ‡Caliph (king, prince, etc.) exchanges clothes with fisher (and masks as fisher).
Anîs al-Jalîs: *Alf* I 141; Burton II 32. Chauvin V 120-24 No. 58; *ANE* 316-17 No. 35.□

K1817.1, Disguise as beggar (pauper). See: *DOTTI*; *GMC*.
Barber's Third Brother: Exposes Blind Robbers: *Alf* I 115; Burton I 330. Chauvin V 159-60 No. 83; *ANE* 118 No. 31.□

K1817.1.1, ‡Disguise as fakir [(hermit)].
Uns al-Wujûd and al-Ward: *Alf* II 272,-(unspecified); Burton V 39-(as fakir). Chauvin VI 127-29 No. 282; *ANE* 438 No. 104.□

K1817.4, ‡Disguise as merchant. See: *DOTTI*; *PSAE*.
King ¿Umar al-Nu¿mân and Sons: *Alf* I 237; Burton II 235. Chauvin VI 112-24 No. 277; *ANE* 430-34 No. 39;

Merchant from Sindah and Sharpers: *Alf* II 39; Burton III 158. Chauvin II 229 No. 154/17; *ANE* 297-98 No. 56;
Ishâq al-Mûṣilî and Khadîjah bint al-Ḥasan: *Alf* II 188; Burton IV 124. Chauvin V 241-42 No. 142; *ANE* 232 No. 71;
Mock Caliph/¿Alî al-Jawharî: *Alf* II 191; Burton IV 130. Chauvin V 99-100 No. 174; *ANE* 304-5 No. 73;
al-Rashîd and Omani Merchant: *Alf* IV 208; Burton IX 189. Chauvin VI 111-12 No. 276; *ANE* 201-2 No. 257;
Abû al-Ḥasan al-Khorâsânî (and Caliph's Favorite): *Alf* IV 229,-(house/tongue of praise); Burton IX 230. Chauvin V 218-20 No. 129; *ANE* 68-69 No. 259.□

K1817.4.0.1§, ‡Disguise as slaver (merchant in slaves).
al-'Amjad and al-'As¿ad: *Alf* II 127,-(*jallâb*/'fetcher/bringer'); Burton III 340,-(slave-dealer). Chauvin V 208-10 No. 120[.1]; *ANE* 341-42 No. 61/pt. 2.□

K1817.4.1.2§, ‡Disguise as peddler so as to gather news (usually of escaped or missing person). See: *DOTTI*.
¿Alî Shâr and Zumurrud: *Alf* II 225; Burton IV 205-6. Chauvin V 89-91 No. 28; *ANE* 100-1 No. 82.□

K1818, Disguise as sick man. See: *DOTTI*; *GMC*.
Sindbâd's Fifth Voyage: *Alf* III 108; Burton VI 50-51. Chauvin VII 21-24 No. 373E; *ANE* 386 No. 179.□

K1818.3.5§, ‡Disguise as performer of amusing marvels (acrobat, juggler, snake-charmer, etc.).
Mercury ¿Alî: *Alf* III 238,-(snake charmer); Burton VII 193. Chauvin V 248-50 No. 147; *ANE* 301-3 No. 225.□

K1820§, ‡Disguise by masking as member of a community (tribe, nation, ethnic group, family, etc.) other than one's own. See: *DOTTI*.
King ¿Umar al-Nu¿mân and Sons: *Alf* II 21,-(*al-'afrang*); Burton III 113,-(Franks). Chauvin VI 112-24 No. 277; *ANE* 430-34 No. 39.□

K1820.1§, ‡Disguise as member of a different religion or sect (e.g., Christian, Jew, Moslem, etc. masks as of the other faith).
King ¿Umar al-Nu¿mân and Sons: *Alf* I 184, II 21; Burton II 128, III 113,-(Franks). Chauvin VI 112-24 No. 277; *ANE* 430-34 No. 39;
Jawdar and His Treacherous Brethren: *Alf* III 183,-(as Jewish merchant); Burton VI 223. Chauvin V 257-60 No. 154; *ANE* 244-45 No. 209.□

K1821.2, ‡Disguise by painting body.
Mercury ¿Alî: *Alf* III 233; Burton VII 183. Chauvin V 248-50 No. 147; *ANE* 301-3 No. 225.□

K1821.3, Disguise by veiling face.
Anîs al-Jalîs: *Alf* I 141; Burton II 31. Chauvin V 120-24 No. 58; *ANE* 316-17 No. 35.□

K1821.5.1§, ‡Person disguises as slave by dyeing self black. See: *DOTTI*.
Mercury ¿Alî: *Alf* III 233; Burton VII 183-84. Chauvin V 248-50 No. 147; *ANE* 301-3 No. 225.□

K1821.8, ‡Disguise as old man. See: *DOTTI*.
Bahrâm and Datmâ: *Alf* III 165; Burton VI 185. Chauvin VIII 54-57 No. 22; *ANE* 114-15 No. 202.□

K1825.1.1, Lover masks as doctor to reach sweetheart. See: *ANE*; *DOTTI*; *GMC*.
Ebony Horse: *Alf* II 264; Burton V 27. Chauvin V 221-31 No. 130; *ANE* 172-74 No. 103.□

K1825.1.7§, ‡Robber masks as physician (doctor) so as to steal (murder).
Merchant and Robbers: *Alf* IV 166; Burton IX 100. Chauvin II 223 No. 152/20; *ANE* 297 No. 251.□

K1825.5, ‡Disguise as soldier. See: *DOTTI*.
¿Alî Shâr and Zumurrud: *Alf* II 227,-(heroine); Burton IV 210. Chauvin V 89-91 No. 28; *ANE* 100-1 No. 82;
Ma¿rûf the Cobbler: *Alf* IV 302,-(*mamlûk*); Burton X 24. Chauvin VI 81-82 No. 250; *ANE* 291-93 No. 262.□

K1825.8, ‡Disguise as astrologer. See: *DOTTI*.
Qamar al-Zamân and Budûr: *Alf* II 93,-cf.; Burton III 270. Chauvin V 204-12 No. 120; *ANE* 341-45 No. 61;

Ni¿mah and Nu¿m: Stolen Wife Regained: *Alf* II 137; Burton IV 10. Chauvin VI 96-97 No. 263; *ANE* 314 No. 62.□

K1825.10§, ‡Disguise as sailor (seaman).
Ruined Baghdadi and His Slave-girl: *Alf* IV 130; Burton IX 24-32. Chauvin V 152-53 No. 75; *ANE* 353 No. 235.□

K1826.2, Disguise as ascetic. See: *GMC*.
Goldsmith and Cashmere Singer: *Alf* III 151; Burton VI 158. Chauvin VIII 46-47 No. 14; *ANE* 196 No. 194.□

K1826.2.1§, ‡Disguise as dervish.
¿Alâ' al-Dîn Abû al-Shâmât: *Alf* II 158; Burton IV 54. Chauvin V 43-49 No. 18; *ANE* 85-87 No. 63.□

K1827.1.1§, ‡Woman disguises as *shaikhah* ('saintess', anchorite, etc.). See: *DOTTI*.
King ¿Umar al-Nu¿mân and Sons: *Alf* I 219,-cf.; Burton II 196. Chauvin VI 112-24 No. 277; *ANE* 430-34 No. 39;
Ni¿mah and Nu¿m: Stolen Wife Regained: *Alf* II 133; Burton IV 4. Chauvin VI 96-97 No. 263; *ANE* 314 No. 62;
Dalîla the Swindler: *Alf* III 213; Burton VII 146. Chauvin V 245-50 No. 147; *ANE* 163-64 No. 224.□

K1827.1.1.1§, ‡Woman disguises as anchorite to poison enemies.
King ¿Umar al-Nu¿mân and Sons: *Alf* I 227; Burton II 212-14. Chauvin VI 112-24 No. 277; *ANE* 430-34 No. 39.□

K1831.2.3.1§, ‡Adulteress claims that paramour is her brother.
Lady and Five Suitors Deceived: *Alf* III 158; Burton VI 173. Chauvin VIII 50-51 No. 18; *ANE* 266 No. 198.□

K1832, Disguise by changing voice. See: *DOTTI*; *GMC*.
Mouse and Cat: *Alf* IV 135; Burton IX 35. Chauvin II 218 No. 152/2; *ANE* 305-6 No. 237.□

K1836.6§, ‡Husband (lover) disguises as woman so as to gain access to women's quarters and search for his wife (sweetheart).
Ni¿mah and Nu¿m: Stolen Wife Regained: *Alf* II 140-41; Burton IV 15. Chauvin VI 96-97 No. 263; *ANE* 314 No. 62.□

K1837, Disguise of woman in man's clothes. See: *ANE*; *DOTTI*; *GMC*.
King ¿Umar al-Nu¿mân and Sons: *Alf* I 187; Burton II 132. Chauvin VI 112-24 No. 277; *ANE* 430-34 No. 39;
Man Who Never Laughs: *Alf* III 154; Burton VI 163. Chauvin VIII 47-48 No. 15; *ANE* 285-86 No. 195.□

K1837.6.2§, ‡Disguise of woman as sailor (ship's captain).
Nûr al-Dîn and Maryam: *Alf* IV 112; Burton VIII 332. Chauvin V 52-54 No. 271; *ANE* 98-99 No. 233.□

K1837.8, Woman in male disguise made king. See: *DOTTI*.
¿Alî Shâr and Zumurrud: *Alf* II 227; Burton IV 210,-(sultan). Chauvin V 89-91 No. 28; *ANE* 100-1 No. 82.□

K1839.12.1§, ‡Midget (pygmy) poses as infant (child). See: *DOTTI*.
Hunchback's Tale: Resuscitated: *Alf* I 87,-cf.; Burton I 256. Chauvin V 180-82 No. 105; *ANE* 224-25 No. 23.□

K1839.7.1§, Disguise as European (foreigner). See: *GMC*.
King ¿Umar al-Nu¿mân and Sons: *Alf* II 21; Burton III 114. Chauvin VI 112-24 No. 277; *ANE* 430-34 No. 39.□

K1861.1, Hero sewed up in animal hide so as to be carried to height by bird. See: *ANE*; *DOTTI*; *GMC*.
Jânshâh: *Alf* III 48, 65; Burton V 341, 367. Chauvin VII 39-44 No. 153; *ANE* 238-41 No. 178;
Sindbâd's Second Voyage: *Alf* III 90; Burton VI 19. Chauvin VII 9-14 No. 373B; *ANE* 385 No. 179;
Hasan of Basrah: *Alf* III 309; Burton VIII 20. Chauvin VII 29-35 No. 212A; *ANE* 207-10 No. 230.□

K1868, Deception by pretending sleep.
Dalîla the Swindler: *Alf* III 222; Burton VII 161. Chauvin V 245-50 No. 147; *ANE* 163-64 No. 224.□

K1869.0.2§, ‡Dead said to be sick (fainted). See: *DOTTI*.
Hunchback's Tale: Resuscitated: *Alf* I 87; Burton I 256. Chauvin V 180-82 No. 105; *ANE* 224-25 No. 23.□

K1872.3.2§, ‡Secret letter (message) hidden in goods sent to intended recipient. (Concealed in medicine, clothes, or the like).
Ni¿mah and Nu¿m: Stolen Wife Regained: *Alf* II 139; Burton IV 13. Chauvin VI 96-97 No. 263; *ANE* 314 No. 62.□

K1872.6§, ‡Secret identity (religious, sectarian, national, etc.) of person (spy) tattooed on invisible part of body.
¿Alâ' al-Dîn Abû al-Shâmât: *Alf* II 172,-(sectarianism); Burton IV 78. Chauvin V 43-49 No. 18; *ANE* 85-87 No. 63.□

K1872.8§, ‡Money (jewels, treasure) camouflaged so as to escape detection.
Qamar al-Zamân and Budûr: *Alf* II 106,-(treasure/gold); Burton III 295. Chauvin V 204-12 No. 120; *ANE* 341-45 No. 61.□

K1872.8.3§, ‡Valuables (jewels, money, document) hidden in underwear worn—(e.g., underpants, brazier, trousers' belt, or the like).
Qamar al-Zamân and Budûr: *Alf* II 97,-(jewel); Burton III 279. Chauvin V 204-12 No. 120; *ANE* 341-45 No. 61.□

K1872.9.5.1§, ‡Mouth of deep pit (well) camouflaged with thin cover (of grass, straw, rug, or the like).
Wolf and Fox: *Alf* II 30; Burton III 134. Chauvin II 227 No. 6; *ANE* 450 No. 47.□

K1872.9.6.1§, ‡Dyeing of gray hair as means of hiding indicators (signs) of aging.
¿Alî Shâr and Zumurrud: *Alf* II 219; Burton IV 193. Chauvin V 89-91 No. 28; *ANE* 100-1 No. 82;
Nûr al-Dîn and Maryam: *Alf* IV 93; Burton VIII 294-95. Chauvin V 52-54 No. 271; *ANE* 98-99 No. 233.□

K1873§, The sinful (that which is tabu) made to seem legitimate. See: *DOTTI*.
Anîs al-Jalîs: *Alf* I 137,-(liquor); Burton II 26. Chauvin V 120-24 No. 58; *ANE* 316-17 No. 35.□

K1874.2.1§, ‡Husband driven insane with pseudo-doubles. His private possessions exhibited before him at his workplace, then quickly returned to his home before his arrival (usually via tunnel): he thinks he has seen a double and regrets having suspected his wife. See: *DOTTI*.
Jeweler's Wife and Qamar al-Zamân: *Alf* IV 253; Burton IX 276-77. Chauvin V 212-14 No. 121; *ANE* 345-47 No. 260.□

K1874.2.1.1§, ‡Man's own wife as pseudo-double: wife persuades her husband that she is someone else.
Jeweler's Wife and Qamar al-Zamân: *Alf* IV 253; Burton IX 276. Chauvin V 212-14 No. 121; *ANE* 345-47 No. 260.□

K1874.2.1.2§, ‡Craftsman's prized works as pseudo-double. See: *DOTTI*.
Jeweler's Wife and Qamar al-Zamân: *Alf* IV 253; Burton IX 275-76. Chauvin V 212-14 No. 121; *ANE* 345-47 No. 260.□

K1875, Deception by sham blood. [By stabbing bag of blood, trickster makes dupe think that he is bleeding]. See: *DOTTI*.
Qamar al-Zamân and Budûr: *Alf* II 103,-cf./(defloration); Burton III 289. Chauvin V 204-12 No. 120; *ANE* 341-45 No. 61;
Mercury ¿Alî: *Alf* III 237,-cf.; Burton VII 191. Chauvin V 248-50 No. 147; *ANE* 301-3 No. 225.□

K1877.2§, ‡Deception: egg white as sham semen. See: *DOTTI*.
Rake's Trick Against Chaste Wife: *Alf* III 1472; Burton VI 135. Chauvin VIII 37 No. 5; *ANE* 350-1 No. 185.□

K1881.1.1.1§, ‡Illusion: beautiful maidens surrounded by water inviting men to join them: men leap to their death on solid dry rock.
City of Brass: *Alf* III 132; Burton VI 109. Chauvin V 32-35 No. 16; *ANE* 146-50 No. 180.□

K1883, Illusory enemies.
King Jalî¿âd and Shimâs: *Alf* IV 177; Burton IX 123. Chauvin VI 9 No. 184; *ANE* 237-38 No. 236.□

K1886.1, Mirage. Illusory water and land. See: *GMC*.

City of Brass: *Alf* III 132,-(lake); Burton VI 109. Chauvin V 32-35 No. 16; *ANE* 146-50 No. 180.□

K1887.1, ‡Echo answers.
King ¿Umar al-Nu¿mân and Sons: *Alf* I 248; Burton II 256,-(rewording the shout). Chauvin VI 112-24 No. 277; *ANE* 430-34 No. 39.□

K1893.1§, Mock storm. See: *DOTTI*.
Husband and Parrot: *Alf* III 141; Burton I 53. Chauvin VI 139 No. 294; *ANE* 226 No. 11.□

K1895§, False proof (of death): grave containing buried animal (sheep) as evidence of someone's death. See: *DOTTI*; *GMC*.
Ghânim ibn Ayyûb: *Alf* I 156; Burton II 65,-("unlawful"). Chauvin VI 14 No. 188; *ANE* 192-93 No. 36;
Hasan of Basrah: *Alf* IV 14; Burton VIII 61. Chauvin VII 29-35 No. 212A; *ANE* 207-10 No. 230;
Masrûr and Zayn al-Mawâṣif: *Alf* IV 79; Burton VIII 262. Chauvin VI 82-84 No. 251; *ANE* 294-95 No. 232.□

K1896§, ‡False proof (of slaying): parts (head, limb, organ) of the already slain presented by imposter as own accomplishment.
King ¿Umar al-Nu¿mân and Sons: *Alf* I 244,-(head of slain enemy); Burton II 250-51. Chauvin VI 112-24 No. 277; *ANE* 430-34 No. 39.□

K1912, False virgin. Various deceptive practices to mask bride as virgin. See: *DOTTI*.
King ¿Umar al-Nu¿mân and Sons: *Alf* I 208,-cf./(implicit); Burton II 175. Chauvin VI 112-24 No. 277; *ANE* 430-34 No. 39.□

K1912.1§, False virgin's pseudo-bleeding: pouch of bird (animal) blood—will rupture at defloration (intercourse). See: *DOTTI*; *GMC*.
First Eunuch: Bukhayt Deflowers Mistress: *Alf* I 148; Burton II 50. Chauvin V 277 No. 160; *ANE* 178 No. 37.□

K1913.1§, ‡False defloration: pseudo bleeding. See: *DOTTI*.
Qamar al-Zamân and Budûr: *Alf* II 103,-(chicken's blood); Burton III 289. Chauvin V 204-12 No. 120; *ANE* 341-45 No. 61.□

K1915, The false bridegroom (substitute bridegroom). See: *DOTTI*; *GMC*.
Ebony Horse: *Alf* II 261,-cf.; Burton V 20-21. Chauvin V 221-31 No. 130; *ANE* 172-74 No. 103.□

K1915.3, Handsome man substitutes for ugly as bridegroom: wins bride.
Nûr al-Dîn ¿Alî and Son: *Alf* I 71-72; Burton I 220-21. Chauvin VI 102-6 No. 270; *ANE* 317-19 No. 22.□

K1917.5.1§, ‡Penniless wooer. "My caravans are coming soon", "My ships, carrying my merchandize, are about to arrive", (or the like). See: *DOTTI*.
Ma¿rûf the Cobbler: *Alf* IV 294-95; Burton X 10-11. Chauvin VI 81-82 No. 250; *ANE* 291-93 No. 262.□

K1931.1.0.1§, ‡Impostor(s) throw(s) brother overboard into sea. See: *DOTTI*.
Second Shaykh: Treacherous Brothers: *Alf* I 11; Burton I 34. Chauvin V 6 No. 397; *ANE* 377-78 No. 6;
¿Abdallah ibn Fâḍil: Treacherous Brothers: *Alf* IV 278,-cf./(brothers); Burton IX 330. Chauvin V 2-4 No. 2; *ANE* 63-65 No. 261.□

K1931.2, Impostors abandon hero in lower world. See: *DOTTI*.
Bulûqiya/Ḥâsib/Queen of Vipers: *Alf* III 20,-cf.; Burton V 300. Chauvin VII 54 No. 77; *ANE* 130-32 No. 177.□

K1952.1.2§, ‡Youth said by helpful notable person to be a relative of his (nephew or the like).
Nûr al-Dîn ¿Alî and Son: *Alf* I 66; Burton I 200. Chauvin VI 102-6 No. 270; *ANE* 317-19 No. 22.□

K1952.8.1§, ‡Sham servants (slaves).
al-'Amjad and al-'As¿ad: *Alf* II 124; Burton III 333. Chauvin V 208-10 No. 120[.1]; *ANE* 341-42 No. 61./pt. 2□

K1952.9§, ‡Impersonating the ruler (king, emperor, etc.). See: *DOTTI*.
Abû al-Ḥasan al-Khorâsânî (and Caliph's Favorite): *Alf* IV 233; Burton IX 238. Chauvin V 218-20 No. 129; *ANE* 68-69 No. 259.□

K1952.9.1§, ‡Rich man poses as caliph or king (sham-caliph). See: *DOTTI*.
Mock Caliph/¿Alî al-Jawharî: *Alf* II 191-93, 199; Burton IV 130-34, 146. Chauvin V 99-100 No. 174; *ANE* 304-5 No. 73.□

K1952.9.2§, ‡Fugitive in king's palace (women's quarters) masks as the king (caliph).
Abû al-Ḥasan al-Khorâsânî (and Caliph's Favorite): *Alf* IV 233,-(as caliph); Burton IX 238. Chauvin V 218-20 No. 129; *ANE* 68-69 No. 259.□

K1955, Sham physician. See: *DOTTI*; *GMC*.
Merchant and Robbers: *Alf* IV 166; Burton IX 100. Chauvin II 223 No. 152/20; *ANE* 297 No. 251.□

K1958, Sham teacher. [An illiterate] pretends to read a document brought him as a letter. It is a tax receipt. See: *DOTTI*; *GMC*.
Illiterate Schoolmaster: *Alf* II 293; Burton V 120. Chauvin VI 137 No. 289; *ANE* 231 No. 137.□

K1966, Alchemist. See: *DOTTI*; *GMC*.
Hasan of Basrah: *Alf* III 303; Burton VIII 9. Chauvin VII 29-35 No. 212A; *ANE* 207-10 No. 230.□

K1969.0.1§, ‡Pretended knowledge: ignorant poses as knowledgeable. See: *DOTTI*.
Illiterate Schoolmaster: *Alf* II 293,-cf.; Burton V 120. Chauvin VI 137 No. 289; *ANE* 231 No. 137.□

K1969.5.1§, ‡Person pretends to know language of animals (birds, insects, etc.). See: *DOTTI*.
Page Feigns Knowing Bird Language: *Alf* III 156; Burton VI 170. Chauvin VIII 49-50 No. 17; *ANE* 321-22 No. 197.□

K1979§, ‡Sham miraculous manifestations—miscellaneous.
King ¿Umar al-Nu¿mân and Sons: *Alf* I 238; Burton II 238. Chauvin VI 112-24 No. 277; *ANE* 430-34 No. 39.□

K1979.1.1§, ‡Money made to appear mysteriously—as if from 'heaven' (from air).
Dalîla the Swindler: *Alf* III 214; Burton VII 149. Chauvin V 245-50 No. 147; *ANE* 163-64 No. 224.□

K1979.2§, ‡Sham miracle-like manifestations: knowledge of a person's private matters. See: *DOTTI*.
Dalîla the Swindler: *Alf* III 214; Burton VII 149. Chauvin V 245-50 No. 147; *ANE* 163-64 No. 224.□

K1996§, Means of feigning illness by shamming physical symptoms.
Bull and Ass: *Alf* I 6; Burton I 17-18. Chauvin V 179-80 No. 104; *ANE* 129-30 No. 2;
King ¿Umar al-Nu¿mân and Sons: *Alf* I 237; Burton II 236. Chauvin VI 112-24 No. 277; *ANE* 430-34 No. 39;
Mouse and Cat: *Alf* IV 135,-(voice); Burton IX 35. Chauvin II 218 No. 152/2; *ANE* 305-6 No. 237;
King Jalî¿âd and Shimâs: *Alf* IV 169,-(bandage head); Burton IX 107. Chauvin VI 9 No. 184; *ANE* 237-38 No. 236.□

K1996.2§, Feigning illness by shamming physical symptoms: saffron dye on face to simulate 'yellowness' (paleness) of death. See: *DOTTI*; *GMC*.
Masrûr and Zayn al-Mawâsif: *Alf* IV 64; Burton VIII 230. Chauvin VI 82-84 No. 251; *ANE* 294-95 No. 232.□

K1996.4.2§, ‡Beggar's feigned disability (e.g., blindness, lameness, etc.). See: *DOTTI*.
Barber's Third Brother: Exposes Blind Robbers: *Alf* I 115; Burton I 328–31. Chauvin V 159-60 No. 83; *ANE* 118 No. 31.□

K1997.1§—(formerly-K1997§), Shamming spirit possession by feigning behavior of the possessed (insane). See: *GMC*.
Qamar al-Zamân and Budûr: *Alf* II 86; Burton III 286. Chauvin V 204-12 No. 120; *ANE* 341-45 No. 61;
Ebony Horse: *Alf* II 264; Burton V 28. Chauvin V 221-31 No. 130; *ANE* 172-74 No. 103.□

K2010, Hypocrite pretends friendship but attacks.
King ¿Umar al-Nu¿mân and Sons: *Alf* II 8; Burton III 88. Chauvin VI 112-24 No. 277; *ANE* 430-34 No. 39;
Wolf and Fox: *Alf* II 30,-(wolf); Burton III 133-34. Chauvin II 227 No. 6; *ANE* 450 No. 47;
Jullanâr of the Sea: *Alf* III 260,-(daughter of defeated king); Burton VII 289. Chauvin V 147-51 No. 73; *ANE* 248-51 No. 227;
Abû Qîr and Abû Ṣîr: *Alf* IV 192-93; Burton IX 154. Chauvin V 15-17 No. 10; *ANE* 75-77 No. 255.□

K2010.0.1§, ‡'Feign weakness till you are in control' (i.e., 'Stoop to conquer'). See: *DOTTI*.

¿Alî Shâr and Zumurrud: *Alf* II 222,-(implicit); Burton IV 198-99. Chauvin V 89-91 No. 28; *ANE* 100-1 No. 82.□

K2020§, Deception through secured promise of a granted wish. See: *DOTTI*; *GMC*. (Cf. J1181)
Tawaddud: Slavegirl Sold and Regained: *Alf* III 8,-cf./(to be restored to original master/owner); Burton V 245. Chauvin VII 117-19 No. 387; *ANE* 408-10 No. 157;
Shahriyâr and Shahrzâd: *Alf* IV 317,-cf.; Burton X 54. Chauvin V 190-91 No. 111/pt.; *ANE* 371 No. 1.□

K2020.1§, ‡Eblis secures God's promise of longevity (till Resurrection-Day) and then vows to corrupt Adam's offspring.
King Jalî¿âd and Shimâs: *Alf* IV 157; Burton IX 82. Chauvin VI 9-11 No. 184; *ANE* 237-38 No. 236.□

K2021.1, The bitten cheek. [In reconciliation man allowed to kiss woman's cheek: he scars it]. See: *ANE*; *DOTTI*; *GMC*.
Portress Amînah: Bitten Cheek: *Alf* I 58-59,-cf.; Burton I 179. Chauvin V 98-99 No. 33; *ANE* 326-27 No. 20.□

K2024§, ‡Treacherous guest.
¿Alî Shâr and Zumurrud: *Alf* II 222; Burton IV 201. Chauvin V 89-91 No. 28; *ANE* 100-1 No. 82.□

K2024.1.1§, ‡Treacherous guest murders sleeping host. See: *DOTTI*.
Hammâd: Treacherous Bedouin: *Alf* II 20; Burton III 111. Chauvin VI 124 n. 1 No. 277; *ANE* 200 No. 43.□

K2025§, Deceitful exploitation of rules of hospitality. See: *DOTTI*.
Dalîla the Swindler: *Alf* III 216-17; Burton VII 152. Chauvin V 245-50 No. 147; *ANE* 163-64 No. 224.□

K2025.2§, ‡Trickster appeals for protection with intent to implicate helper. See: *DOTTI*.
Dalîla the Swindler: *Alf* III 223; Burton VII 165. Chauvin V 245-50 No. 147; *ANE* 163-64 No. 224.□

K2042.0.1§, ‡Self-mutilation so as to persuade enemy that one has been mistreated (cast out) by own people.
King ¿Umar al-Nu¿mân and Sons: *Alf* I 237,-cf.; Burton II 236. Chauvin VI 112-24 No. 277; *ANE* 430-34 No. 39.□

K2051.7§, ‡Lover wants to kiss "chaste" girl, she advises him to wait till she is drunk (unconscious).
Ghânim ibn Ayyûb: *Alf* I 153; Burton II 60. Chauvin VI 14 No. 188; *ANE* 192-93 No. 36.□

K2052.1.1§, ‡Bride pretends shame before invisible spirits (jinn).
Ma¿rûf the Cobbler: *Alf* IV 312; Burton X 44. Chauvin VI 81-82 No. 250; *ANE* 291-93 No. 262.□

K2054.5§, ‡Feigned dispute (quarrel) to mulct victim.
Wife's device to cheat: (Weeping Bitch as Bluff): *Alf* III 149; Burton VI 155. Chauvin VIII 45-46 No. 13; *ANE* 447-49 No. 193;
House with the Belvedere: *Alf* III 171; Burton VI 197-98. Chauvin VIII 57-58 No. 23; *ANE* 223 No. 203.□

K2056.1§, 'A stepmother can neither love nor be loved'. See: *GMC*.
Ma¿rûf the Cobbler: *Alf* IV 315,-cf./(implicit); Burton X 49. Chauvin VI 81-82 No. 250; *ANE* 291-93 No. 262.□

K2058, Pretended piety. See: *DOTTI*.
King ¿Umar al-Nu¿mân and Sons: *Alf* I 238; Burton II 237. Chauvin VI 112-24 No. 277; *ANE* 430-34 No. 39;
Hedgehog and Wood-pigeons: *Alf* II 39; Burton III 156. Chauvin II 229 No. 15; *ANE* 220 No. 55;
Jawdar and His Treacherous Brethren: *Alf* III 198; Burton VI 250. Chauvin V 257-60 No. 154; *ANE* 244-45 No. 209.□

K2058.2§, ‡Feigned piety (religiosity) to mulct victim. See: *DOTTI*.
Hedgehog and Wood-pigeons: *Alf* II 39; Burton III 156. Chauvin II 229 No. 15; *ANE* 220 No. 55.□

K2058.2.1§, ‡Trickster masks as saintly and induces victims to entrust their goods to him. He steals the goods. See: *DOTTI*.
King ¿Umar al-Nu¿mân and Sons: *Alf* I 227; Burton II 212-14. Chauvin VI 112-24 No. 277; *ANE* 430-34 No. 39;

Dalîla the Swindler: *Alf* III 217; Burton VII 153. Chauvin V 245-50 No. 147; *ANE* 163-64 No. 224.□

K2058.2.3§, ‡Abduction under pretence of performing religious duty or bestowing supernatural power.
King ¿Umar al-Nu¿mân and Sons: *Alf* I 227; Burton II 213. Chauvin VI 112-24 No. 277; *ANE* 430-34 No. 39.□

K2058.3§, ‡Entering intended victim's home under pretence of need to perform prayers (ablution). See: *DOTTI*.
Barber's Fifth Brother: Daydreams/Defeats Robbers: *Alf* I 118; Burton I 339. Chauvin V 161 No. 85; *ANE* 119-20 No. 33;
Ni¿mah and Nu¿m: Stolen Wife Regained: *Alf* II 133; Burton IV 4. Chauvin VI 96-97 No. 263; *ANE* 314 No. 62;
House with the Belvedere: *Alf* III 168; Burton VI 193. Chauvin VIII 57-58 No. 23; *ANE* 223 No. 203.□

K2059.9.1.1§, ‡Fornicating now, and then repenting immediately after.
Qamar al-Zamân and Budûr: *Alf* II 110; Burton III 305. Chauvin V 204-12 No. 120; *ANE* 341-45 No. 61.□

K2059.9.2§, ‡Excuse: sinning merely to justify undeserved condemnation (by adversaries, censurers, etc.).
Qamar al-Zamân and Budûr: *Alf* II 110,-(poem); Burton III 305. Chauvin V 204-12 No. 120; *ANE* 341-45 No. 61.□

K2059.9.3.1§, ‡Excuse: sinning so as to absolve slanderer of the sin of thinking evil thoughts.
Qamar al-Zamân and Budûr: *Alf* II 110,-(poem); Burton III 305,-(let's justify and free their souls). Chauvin V 204-12 No. 120; *ANE* 341-45 No. 61.□

K2096.6§, ‡Bribe claimed to be a gift (charity). See: *DOTTI*.
¿Alâ' al-Dîn Abû al-Shâmât: *Alf* II 157; Burton IV 53. Chauvin V 43-49 No. 18; *ANE* 85-87 No. 63;
Jeweler's Wife and Qamar al-Zamân: *Alf* IV 246; Burton IX 259. Chauvin V 212-14 No. 121; *ANE* 345-47 No. 260.□

K2099.5.1§, ‡Hypocritical brother(s).
¿Abdallah ibn Fâḍil: Treacherous Brothers: *Alf* IV 280; Burton IX 329-30. Chauvin V 2-4 No. 2; *ANE* 63-65 No. 261.□

K2107.3§, ‡Rumor mongering. False report concocted and spread (so as to slander). See: *DOTTI*.
Ma¿rûf the Cobbler: *Alf* IV 299,-(suspected); Burton X 18. Chauvin VI 81-82 No. 250; *ANE* 291-93 No. 262.□

K2107.3.2.1§, ‡Rumor that girl is engaged (promised to relative) causes would-be suitor to refrain from proposing to her.
Ma¿rûf the Cobbler: *Alf* IV 299,-(accusation that girl *tabûr*); Burton X 18,-(so that girl would "lie fallow"). Chauvin VI 81-82 No. 250; *ANE* 291-93 No. 262.□

K2108.1§, ‡Healthy said (alleged) to be sick. See: *DOTTI*.
¿Alâ' al-Dîn Abû al-Shâmât: *Alf* II 156,-(leper); Burton IV 49. Chauvin V 43-49 No. 18; *ANE* 85-87 No. 63;
Dalîla the Swindler: *Alf* III 217; Burton VII 153. Chauvin V 245-50 No. 147; *ANE* 163-64 No. 224.□

K2108.2.1§, ‡Medicine (cosmetic aid) reported to intended user as 'poison'. See: *DOTTI*.
Abû Qîr and Abû Ṣîr: *Alf* IV 193; Burton IX 156. Chauvin V 15-17 No. 10; *ANE* 75-77 No. 255.□

K2108.6.1§, ‡Person falsely accused of forging a document.
Anîs al-Jalîs: *Alf* I 143; Burton II 39. Chauvin V 120-24 No. 58; *ANE* 316-17 No. 35.□

K2111, Potiphar's wife [and Joseph]. See: *ANE*; *DOTTI*; *GMC*; *PSAE*.
Craft and Malice of Women/Frame: *Alf* III 139; Burton VI 128. Chauvin VIII 33-34 No. 1; *ANE* 160-61 No. 181.□

K2111.5.1§, ‡Stepmother falsely accuses stepson of sexual misconduct. (Also made by a father's other sex partners (e.g., concubine, slavegirl, girlfriend).
al-'Amjad and al-'As¿ad: *Alf* II 116; Burton III 314. Chauvin V 208-10 No. 120[.1]; *ANE* 341-42 No. 61/pt. 2;
Craft and Malice of Women/Frame: *Alf* III 139,-(father' favorite consort); Burton VI 139. Chauvin VIII 33-34 No. 1; *ANE* 160-61 No. 181.□

K2112, Woman slandered as adulteress (prostitute). (Usually by unsuccessful suitor). (Crescentia, Genoveva, Susanna),. See: *ANE*; *DOTTI*; *GMC*.
Three Apples: Hasty Uxoricide: *Alf* I 63,-(unintentionally); Burton I 191. Chauvin VI 144-45 No. 302; *ANE* 414-15 No. 21;
Devout Jewess and Wicked Elders: *Alf* II 286; Burton V 97. Chauvin VI 193-93 No. 362; *ANE* 169 No. 128.□

K2112.1, False tokens of woman's unfaithfulness. See: *DOTTI*; *GMC*.
Three Apples: Hasty Uxoricide: *Alf* I 63,-(apple); Burton I 191. Chauvin VI 144-45 No. 302; *ANE* 414-15 No. 21;
House with the Belvedere: *Alf* III 169; Burton VI 194. Chauvin VIII 57-58 No. 23; *ANE* 223 No. 203.□

K2112.2.5§, ‡Egg white placed on innocent woman's bed (as if man's emission, semen). See: *DOTTI*.
Rake's Trick Against Chaste Wife: *Alf* III 142; Burton VI 135. Chauvin VIII 37 No. 5; *ANE* 350-1 No. 185.□

K2113.5§, Female slandered as lesbian.
King ¿Umar al-Nu¿mân and Sons: *Alf* I 236,-cf.; Burton II 234. Chauvin VI 112-24 No. 277; *ANE* 430-34 No. 39.□

K2116.1.1, Innocent woman accused of killing her new-born children. See: *DOTTI*.
Jewish qâḍî and His Devout Wife: *Alf* III 10; Burton V 256. Chauvin VI 154-55 No. 321; *ANE* 242 No. 163.□

K2120§, ‡Innocent (chaste) man slandered as seducer. (Bata, Joseph, etc.). See: *DOTTI*.
al-'Amjad and al-'As¿ad: *Alf* II 116; Burton III 314. Chauvin V 208-10 No. 120[.1]; *ANE* 2 341-42 No. 61/pt.;
Craft and Malice of Women/Frame: *Alf* III 139; Burton VI 127-28. Chauvin VIII 33-34 No. 1; *ANE* 160-61 No. 181.□

K2122§, ‡Merchant (vendor) falsely accused of cheating. See: *DOTTI*.
Barber's Fourth Brother: Illusionary Experiences: *Alf* I 116; Burton I 332-33. Chauvin V 160-61 No. 84; *ANE* 119 No. 32.□

K2123, Innocent woman accused of using witchcraft. See: *DOTTI*; *GMC*. (Cf. J1809.5§).
Goldsmith and Cashmere Singer: *Alf* III 150-51; Burton VI 158. Chauvin VIII 46-47 No. 14; *ANE* 196 No. 194.□

K2127, ‡False accusation of theft. See: *DOTTI*.
¿Alâ' al-Dîn Abû al-Shâmât: *Alf* II 169,-(by thief acting as diviner); Burton IV 73. Chauvin V 43-49 No. 18; *ANE* 85-87 No. 63;
Stolen Necklace/Hasty Accusation: *Alf* III 164; Burton VI 182-83. Chauvin VIII 53 No. 20; *ANE* 398 No. 200;
Abû Qîr and Abû Ṣîr: *Alf* IV 189,-(being a thief); Burton IX 147-48. Chauvin V 15-17 No. 10; *ANE* 75-77 No. 255;
Landsman ¿Abdallah and Merman ¿Abdallah: *Alf* IV 201; Burton IX 173. Chauvin V 6-7 No. 3; *ANE* 65-66 No. 256.□

K2130.1§, ‡'Wedge-driver' (*'isfingî, mahmûz*-person): trouble-maker who drives wedges or spurs trouble between persons (usually by poison-pen, praising one to adversary, or the like). See: *DOTTI*.
Dûban and King Yûnân: *Alf* I 18; Burton I 40. Chauvin V 289 No. 173; *ANE* 383 No. 9;
House with the Belvedere: *Alf* III 168; Burton VI 192. Chauvin VIII 57-58 No. 23; *ANE* 223 No. 203;
Abû Qîr and Abû Ṣîr: *Alf* IV 193; Burton IX 156. Chauvin V 15-17 No. 10; *ANE* 75-77 No. 255.□

K2131.6§, ‡Old woman destroys (seeks to destroy) couple's marriage. See: *DOTTI*.
¿Alâ' al-Dîn Abû al-Shâmât: *Alf* II 156,-(fails); Burton IV 49. Chauvin V 43-49 No. 18; *ANE* 85-87 No. 63;
Wife's device to cheat: (Weeping Bitch as Bluff): *Alf* III 148; Burton VI 154. Chauvin VIII 45-46 No. 13; *ANE* 447-49 No. 193.□

K2139§, ‡Poisonous medicine for king: envious man gives king's barber (doctor, etc.) a supposedly healing substance (actually poison), then he reports to the king that the barber plans to assassinate him with that 'medicine'. See: *DOTTI*.
Abû Qîr and Abû Ṣîr: *Alf* IV 193; Burton IX 156. Chauvin V 15-17 No. 10; *ANE* 75-77 No. 255.□

K2141.1§, ‡Jealous courtier shakes king's confidence in his physician (councillor). (Cf. K2130.1§).
Dûban and King Yûnân: *Alf* I 18; Burton I 50-52. Chauvin V 289 No. 173; *ANE* 383 No. 9.□

K2142, ‡Two persons informed separately about each other's death.
Second Eunuch/Kâfûr's Half-lie: *Alf* I 148; Burton II 51-52. Chauvin V 278 No. 161; *ANE* 178-79 No. 38.□

K2142.1§, ‡Husband and wife informed separately about each other's death in collapse of building (or the like): communal crisis follows. See: *DOTTI*.
Second Eunuch/Kâfûr's Half-lie: *Alf* I 148; Burton II 51-52. Chauvin V 278 No. 161; *ANE* 178-79 No. 38.□

K2150, Innocent made to appear guilty. See: *DOTTI*; *GMC*.
House with the Belvedere: *Alf* III 169; Burton VI 194. Chauvin VIII 57-58 No. 23; *ANE* 223 No. 203.□

K2150.1.2§, Marked coat left in room of chaste woman brings about accusation of infidelity. See: *DOTTI*; *GMC*.
House with the Belvedere: *Alf* III 169,-(veil); Burton VI 194. Chauvin VIII 57-58 No. 23; *ANE* 223 No. 203.□

K2152, Unresponsive corpse. See: *DOTTI*; *GMC*.
Hunchback's Tale: Resuscitated: *Alf* I 87; Burton I 258. Chauvin V 180-82 No. 105; *ANE* 224-25 No. 23.□

K2153.2§, ‡Woman wounds self (or smears self with blood) and accuses husband (lover). See: *DOTTI*.
Ma¿rûf the Cobbler: *Alf* IV 290; Burton X 4. Chauvin VI 81-82 No. 250; *ANE* 291-93 No. 262.□

K2155, Evidence of crime left so that dupe is blamed. See: *GMC*.
She-mouse and Ichneumon: *Alf* II 36; Burton III 148. Chauvin II 227 No. 6; *ANE* 306 No. 49;
¿Alâ' al-Dîn Abû al-Shâmât: *Alf* II 167,-(stolen goods); Burton IV 72. Chauvin V 43-49 No. 18; *ANE* 85-87 No. 63.□

K2155.3§, ‡Slanderer wounds person and then accuses him (her) of receiving injury during illicit activity. See: *DOTTI*.
Goldsmith and Cashmere Singer: *Alf* III 151; Burton VI 158. Chauvin VIII 46-47 No. 14; *ANE* 196 No. 194.□

K2165, Sham blind man throws suspicion on real blind. See: *ANE*.
Barber's Third Brother: Exposes Blind Robbers: *Alf* I 114-5; Burton I 329. Chauvin V 159-60 No. 83; *ANE* 118 No. 31.□

K2171.1§, ‡The ichneumon steals the grain (sesame) and makes mouse look guilty of the crime.
She-mouse and Ichneumon: *Alf* II 35-6; Burton III 147. Chauvin II 228 No. 10; *ANE* 306 No. 49.□

K2173§, ‡Guilty party makes innocent accuser look guilty (by means of stronger, louder accusations).
Wife's device to cheat: (Weeping Bitch as Bluff): *Alf* III 149-50; Burton VI 155. Chauvin VIII 45-46 No. 13; *ANE* 447-49 No. 193.□

K2211, Treacherous brother. See: *DOTTI*; *GMC*.
Second Shaykh: Treacherous Brothers: *Alf* I 11; Burton I 32-35. Chauvin V 6 No. 397; *ANE* 377-78 No. 6.□

K2211.0.1, Treacherous elder brother(s). See: *DOTTI*; *GMC*.
Jawdar and His Treacherous Brethren: *Alf* III 178,-ff.; Burton VI 213ff. Chauvin V 257-60 No. 154; *ANE* 244-45 No. 209;
¿Abdallah ibn Fâḍil: Treacherous Brothers: *Alf* IV 269; Burton IX 310ff. Chauvin V 2-4 No. 2; *ANE* 63-65 No. 261.□

K2211.1, Treacherous brother-in-law. See: *DOTTI*; *GMC*.
Jewish qâḍî and His Devout Wife: *Alf* III 10,-(wife's); Burton V 256. Chauvin VI 154-55 No. 321; *ANE* 242 No. 163.□

K2211.4§, Treacherous paternal-cousin(s). See: *DOTTI*; *GMC*.
Enchanted Spring: Change of Sex: *Alf* III 146; Burton VI 145. Chauvin VIII 43 No. 11; *ANE* 175-76 No. 191;
Ibrâhîm and Jamîlah: *Alf* IV 227; Burton IX 226. Chauvin VI 52-53 No. 218; *ANE* 227-29 No. 258.□

K2213, ‡ Treacherous wife. See: *DOTTI*; *GMC*.
First Shaykh: Sorceress Wife: *Alf* I 9,-(father's); Burton I 28. Chauvin VII 129-30 No. 396; *ANE* 376-77 No. 5.□

K2213.3, Faithless wife plots with paramour against husband's life. See: *DOTTI*.
Third Shaykh: Transformation by Wife: *Alf* I 13; Burton I 36-37. Chauvin VII 130 No. 398; *ANE* 378 No. 7.□

K2213.4.4§, ‡Demon's secret of vulnerability disclosed by his wife (mistress, captive-woman, etc.). See: *DOTTI*.
Abû Muḥammad Lazybones: *Alf* II 216; Burton IV 177. Chauvin VI 64-67 No. 233; *ANE* 71-73 No. 78.□

K2201§, ‡Treacherous betrayal of (friend's or relative's) secret.
King ¿Umar al-Nu¿mân and Sons: *Alf* II 3,-(mistress'); Burton III 78. Chauvin VI 112-24 No. 277; *ANE* 430-34 No. 39.□

K2213.6, Faithless wife transforms husband. See: *DOTTI*.
Jullanâr of the Sea: *Alf* III 266; Burton VII 301. Chauvin V 147-51 No. 73; *ANE* 248-51 No. 227.□

K2214.1.3§, ‡Daughter assists her beloved in killing her father.
¿Alâ' al-Dîn Abû al-Shâmât: *Alf* II 179-80; Burton IV 92. Chauvin V 43-49 No. 18; *ANE* 85-87 No. 63.□

K2214.3, Treacherous son: leads revolt against his father to whom he owes all.
Abû al-Ḥasan al-Khorâsânî (and Caliph's Favorite): *Alf* IV 237; Burton IX 245. Chauvin V 218-20 No. 129; *ANE* 68-69 No. 259.□

K2214.3.0.1§, ‡Treacherous son(s): abuse(s) mother.
Jawdar and His Treacherous Brethren: *Alf* III 189; Burton VI 234. Chauvin V 257-60 No. 154; *ANE* 244-45 No. 209.□

K2218.2, ‡Treacherous father-in-law. (Cf. T92.9.3.1§); See: *DOTTI*.
King ¿Umar al-Nu¿mân and Sons: *Alf* I 182,-cf./(rapes son's wife-to-be); Burton II 123. Chauvin VI 112-24 No. 277; *ANE* 430-34 No. 39.□

K2218.3§, Treacherous stepmother. See: *DOTTI*; *GMC*; *PSAE*.
First Shaykh: Sorceress Wife: *Alf* I 9; Burton I 28. Chauvin VII 129-30 No. 396; *ANE* 376-77 No. 5.□

K2222, Treacherous co-wife (concubine). See: *DOTTI*; *GMC*.
Craft and Malice of Women/Frame: *Alf* III 139; Burton VI 123-24. Chauvin VIII 33-34 No. 1; *ANE* 160-61 No. 181.□

K2222.1§, ‡Treacherous deserted wife (old neglected co-wife).
Ma¿rûf the Cobbler: *Alf* IV 315-16; Burton X 51. Chauvin VI 81-82 No. 250; *ANE* 291-93 No. 262.□

K2234§, ‡Treacherous (cruel) seducer. See: *DOTTI*.
Devout Jewess and Wicked Elders: *Alf* II 286; Burton V 97. Chauvin VI 193-93 No. 362; *ANE* 169 No. 128;
Jewish qâḍî and His Devout Wife: *Alf* III 10; Burton V 256. Chauvin VI 154-55 No. 321; *ANE* 242 No. 163;
Shipwrecked Woman and Her Child: *Alf* III 12; Burton V 260. Chauvin VI 160 No. 324; *ANE* 379 No. 164.□

K2234.2§, ‡Seducer kills (threatens to kill) woman's child(ren) if she does not surrender. See: *DOTTI*.
Jewish qâḍî and His Devout Wife: *Alf* III 10; Burton V 256. Chauvin VI 154-55 No. 321; *ANE* 242 No. 163;
Shipwrecked Woman and Her Child: *Alf* III 11; Burton V 260. Chauvin VI 160 No. 324; *ANE* 379 No. 164.□

K2246.3.1§, ‡Treacherous lawman steals (destroys) evidence in his care.
Barber's Fifth Brother: Daydreams/Defeats Robbers: *Alf* I 121; Burton I 343. Chauvin V 161 No. 85; *ANE* 119-20 No. 33.□

K2248, Treacherous minister [(vizier)]. See: *DOTTI*; *GMC*.
Dûban and King Yûnân: *Alf* I 18; Burton I 49. Chauvin V 275-76 No. 156; *ANE* 459 No. 9;

Prince and Ogress: *Alf* I 19; Burton I 55. Chauvin VI 26 No. 197; *ANE* 329 No. 12;
First Qalandar: Brother-Sister Incest: *Alf* I 40; Burton I 107. Chauvin V 196-97 No. 115; *ANE* 337-38 No. 15;
Anîs al-Jalîs: *Alf* I 125; Burton II 2. Chauvin V 120-24 No. 58; *ANE* 316-17 No. 35;
Ni¿mah and Nu¿m: Stolen Wife Regained: *Alf* II 133,-cf.; Burton IV 3. Chauvin VI 96-97 No. 263; *ANE* 314 No. 62;
Enchanted Spring: Change of Sex: *Alf* III 146,-(bribed with gifts); Burton VI 145. Chauvin VIII 43 No. 11; *ANE* 175-76 No. 191;
Ibn Sabâ'ik/Sayf al-Mulûk: *Alf* III 271; Burton VII 309. Chauvin VII 65 No. 348/pt.; *ANE* 309-10 No. 228;
Ma¿rûf the Cobbler: *Alf* IV 307, 311; Burton X 32. Chauvin VI 81-82 No. 250; *ANE* 291-93 No. 262.□

K2249.4, ‡Treacherous merchant. See: *DOTTI*.
Jânshâh: *Alf* III 47; Burton V 340. Chauvin VII 39-44 No. 153; *ANE* 238-41 No. 178;
Woman Who Made Husband Sift Dust: *Alf* III 145,-cf.; Burton VI 143-44. Chauvin VIII 42 No. 10; *ANE* 452-53 No. 190.□

K2251.1, Treacherous slave-girl. See: *DOTTI*.
King ¿Umar al-Nu¿mân and Sons: *Alf* II 3,-(betrays secret); Burton III 78. Chauvin VI 112-24 No. 277; *ANE* 430-34 No. 39;
al-Rashîd and Omani Merchant: *Alf* IV 215,-(vengeful/betrays secret); Burton IX 199. Chauvin VI 111-12 No. 276; *ANE* 201-2 No. 257.□

K2250.2§, ‡Treacherous (dishonest) workman (hireling). See: *DOTTI*.
King ¿Umar al-Nu¿mân and Sons: *Alf* I 188; Burton II 134. Chauvin VI 112-24 No. 277; *ANE* 430-34 No. 39;
Abû Qîr and Abû Ṣîr: *Alf* IV 183; Burton IX 134-35. Chauvin V 15-17 No. 10; *ANE* 75-77 No. 255.□

K2251, Treacherous slave. See: *DOTTI*; *GMC*.
Three Apples: Hasty Uxoricide: *Alf* I 63,-cf.; Burton I 191. Chauvin VI 144-45 No. 302; *ANE* 414-15 No. 21;
King ¿Umar al-Nu¿mân and Sons: *Alf* I 184,-(murders mistress); Burton II 129. Chauvin VI 112-24 No. 277; *ANE* 430-34 No. 39.□

K2259.8§, ‡Scientist (inventor, discoverer) as villain.
Ebony Horse: *Alf* II 261; Burton V 20-21. Chauvin V 221-31 No. 130; *ANE* 172-74 No. 103.□

K2261, Treacherous negro (Moor).
Three Apples: Hasty Uxoricide: *Alf* I 63,-cf.; Burton I 191. Chauvin VI 144-45 No. 302; *ANE* 414-15 No. 21;
Barber's Fifth Brother: Daydreams/Defeats Robbers: *Alf* I 120,-(robber); Burton I 340. Chauvin V 161 No. 85; *ANE* 119-20 No. 33;
King ¿Umar al-Nu¿mân and Sons: *Alf* I 184-85,-(murders mistress), II 12; Burton II 129, III 96,-(lustful villain). Chauvin VI 112-24 No. 277; *ANE* 430-34 No. 39.□

K2266.1§, Treacherous blue-eyed man. See: *DOTTI*; *GMC*.
Sandal-wood Merchant and Sharpers: *Alf* III 174; Burton VI 203. Chauvin VIII 60-62 No. 26; *ANE* 359-60 No. 205.□

K2267.1§, Jinni helper turns against human friend. See: *DOTTI*.
Abû Muḥammad Lazybones: *Alf* II 212; Burton IV 173. Chauvin VI 64-67 No. 233; *ANE* 71-73 No. 78.□

K2271, ‡Hunchback villain.
King ¿Umar al-Nu¿mân and Sons: *Alf* I 236,-(old woman); Burton II 233,-(back humped). Chauvin VI 112-24 No. 277; *ANE* 430-34 No. 39.□

K2285.1.1§, Dervish as villain. See: *DOTTI*; *GMC*.
Jeweler's Wife and Qamar al-Zamân: *Alf* IV 239; Burton IX 250. Chauvin V 212-14 No. 121; *ANE* 345-47 No. 260.□

K2287.2§, A Magi (Hindu, 'fire-worshipper', idolater, etc.) as villain. See: *DOTTI*; *GMC*.
al-'Amjad and al-'As¿ad: *Alf* II 121, 131; Burton 3, 34VII: 325. Chauvin V 208-10 No. 120[.1]; *ANE* 341-42 No. 61/pt. 2;

Hasan of Basrah: *Alf* III 306, 313; Burton VIII 15, 27. Chauvin VII 29-35 No. 212A; *ANE* 207-10 No. 230.□

K2287.3§, A Jew as villain. See: *DOTTI*; *GMC*.
Jânshâh: *Alf* III 47-48; Burton V 340. Chauvin VII 39-44 No. 153; *ANE* 238-41 No. 178;
Mercury ¿Alî: *Alf* III 240; Burton VII 197. Chauvin V 248-50 No. 147; *ANE* 301-3 No. 225.□

K2287.4§, A Christian as villain. See: *DOTTI*; *GMC*.
¿Alî Shâr and Zumurrud: *Alf* II 222; Burton IV 199ff. Chauvin V 89-91 No. 28; *ANE* 100-1 No. 82.□

K2288.1§, A European (*khawâgah*) as villain. See: *DOTTI*.
¿Alâ' al-Dîn Abû al-Shâmât: *Alf* II 176,-cf./(abduction); Burton IV 84-85. Chauvin V 43-49 No. 18; *ANE* 85-87 No. 63;
Nûr al-Dîn and Maryam: *Alf* IV 100; Burton VIII 310ff. Chauvin V 52-54 No. 271; *ANE* 98-99 No. 233.□

K2293, Treacherous old woman. See: *DOTTI*; *GMC*.
Portress Amînah: Bitten Cheek: *Alf* I 57; Burton I 174. Chauvin V 98-99 No. 33; *ANE* 326-27 No. 20;
Barber's Fifth Brother: Daydreams/Defeats Robbers: *Alf* I 120; Burton I 339-43. Chauvin V 161 No. 85; *ANE* 119-20 No. 33;
King ¿Umar al-Nu¿mân and Sons: *Alf* I 167,-ff./(*dâdah*/nurse), II 9; Burton II 88. Chauvin VI 112-24 No. 277; *ANE* 430-34 No. 39;
¿Azîz and ¿Azîzah: *Alf* I 283; Burton II 326. Chauvin V 144-45 No. 71; *ANE* 111-13 No. 41;
King ¿Umar al-Nu¿mân and Sons: *Alf* II 2,-(Sa¿dânah); Burton III 77. Chauvin VI 112-24 No. 277; *ANE* 430-34 No. 39;
Ni¿mah and Nu¿m: Stolen Wife Regained: *Alf* II 133; Burton IV 3. Chauvin VI 96-97 No. 263; *ANE* 314 No. 62;
¿Alâ' al-Dîn Abû al-Shâmât: *Alf* II 156; Burton IV 49. Chauvin V 43-49 No. 18; *ANE* 85-87 No. 63;
Wife's device to cheat: (Weeping Bitch as Bluff): *Alf* III 148; Burton VI 154. Chauvin VIII 45-46 No. 13; *ANE* 447-49 No. 193;
House with the Belvedere: *Alf* III 168-69; Burton VI 193-94. Chauvin VIII 57-58 No. 23; *ANE* 223 No. 203;
Jullanâr of the Sea: *Alf* III 269; Burton VII 305-6. Chauvin V 147-51 No. 73; *ANE* 248-51 No. 227.□

K2294.2§, ‡Treacherous host: imprisons guest (keeps guest as captive).
al-'Amjad and al-'As¿ad: *Alf* II 121; Burton III 327. Chauvin V 208-10 No. 120[.1]; *ANE* 341-42 No. 61/pt. 2.□

K2294.3§, Treacherous host: murders guest. See: *GMC*.
Jawdar and His Treacherous Brethren: *Alf* III 200-1,-cf./(poisons brother); Burton VI 255. Chauvin V 257-60 No. 154; *ANE* 244-45 No. 209;
¿Abdallah ibn Fâḍil: Treacherous Brothers: *Alf* IV 285,-(fratricide); Burton IX 342. Chauvin V 2-4 No. 2; *ANE* 63-65 No. 261.□

K2294.3.1§, ‡Messenger (envoy, ambassador) killed by host. See: *DOTTI*.
Nûr al-Dîn and Maryam: *Alf* IV 129; Burton IX 17. Chauvin V 52-54 No. 271; *ANE* 98-99 No. 233.□

K2296, Treacherous partner. See: *DOTTI*; *GMC*.
Bulûqiya/Ḥâsib/Queen of Vipers: *Alf* III 20; Burton V 300. Chauvin VII 54 No. 77; *ANE* 130-32 No. 177;
Abû Qîr and Abû Ṣîr: *Alf* IV 188ff.; Burton IX 142ff. Chauvin V 15-17 No. 10; *ANE* 75-77 No. 255.□

K2296.1, ‡Treacherous robber-partner. See: *DOTTI*.
Merchant from Sindah and Sharpers: *Alf* II 40; Burton III 158. Chauvin II 229 No. 154/17; *ANE* 297-98 No. 56.□

K2298, Treacherous counselor. See: *DOTTI*; *GMC*.
Abû Qîr and Abû Ṣîr: *Alf* IV 193; Burton IX 156. Chauvin V 15-17 No. 10; *ANE* 75-77 No. 255.□

K2299.1.1.1§, Treacherous magician abandons hero in treasure trove. See: *DOTTI*.
Bulûqiya/Ḥâsib/Queen of Vipers: *Alf* III 20,-cf./(partners); Burton V 301. Chauvin VII 54 No. 77; *ANE* 130-32 No. 177.□

K2299.1.2.1§, ‡Diviner (shaman) falsifies results of ritual.
¿Alâ' al-Dîn Abû al-Shâmât: *Alf* II 169,-(points to location of stolen goods); Burton IV 73. Chauvin V 43-49 No. 18; *ANE* 85-87 No. 63.□

K2299.2, Treacherous peoples (tribes [(nations)]).
Ghânim ibn Ayyûb: *Alf* I 147,-(*sûdân*); Burton II 48. Chauvin VI 14-16 No. 188; *ANE* 192-93 No. 36.□

K2299.3.1§, ‡Treacherous Bedouin. See: *DOTTI*.
Barber's Sixth Brother: Emasculated by Abductor: *Alf* I 123; Burton I 347-48. Chauvin V 163-64 No. 86; *ANE* 120 No. 34;
King ¿Umar al-Nu¿mân and Sons: *Alf* I 193,-ff.; Burton II 142. Chauvin VI 112-24 No. 277; *ANE* 430-34 No. 39;
Hammâd: Treacherous Bedouin: *Alf* II 16; Burton III 104-12. Chauvin VI 124 n. 1 No. 277; *ANE* 200 No. 43.□

K2299.6§, ‡Treacherous old man.
Devout Jewess and Wicked Elders: *Alf* II 286; Burton V 97. Chauvin VI 193-93 No. 362; *ANE* 169 No. 128.□

K2321.3§, ‡Dummy of predator (lion, wolf) set up to frighten owner into surrendering goods (money).
Shepherd and Rogue's Bluff: *Alf* IV 168-69; Burton IX 106. Chauvin II 223-24 No. 152/22; *ANE* 378 No. 253.□

K2351.5.0.2§, ‡Elephants frightened by defenders and driven back into attacker's camp to cause stampede.
Jânshâh: *Alf* III 61; Burton V 362. Chauvin VII 39-44 No. 153; *ANE* 238-41 No. 178.□

K2351.5.3§, ‡Adversary's horse frightened: it becomes unruly and brings about defeat of the rider. (N331.1.4§).
al-'Amjad and al-'As¿ad: *Alf* II 118,-cf./(executioner's horse runs away); Burton III 320. Chauvin V 208-10 No. 120[.1]; *ANE* 341-42 No. 61/pt. 2;
Mercury ¿Alî: *Alf* III 230; Burton VII 178. Chauvin V 248-50 No. 147; *ANE* 301-3 No. 225.□

K2357.10.1§, ‡Disguise as merchant to enter enemy's country (camp).
King ¿Umar al-Nu¿mân and Sons: *Alf* I 237; Burton II 235. Chauvin VI 112-24 No. 277; *ANE* 430-34 No. 39.□

K2360§, ‡Surprise attack ('treacherous' invasion). See: *DOTTI*.
First Qalandar: Brother-Sister Incest: *Alf* I 42; Burton I 111-12. Chauvin V 196-97 No. 115; *ANE* 337-38 No. 15.□

K2368, ‡Enemy deceived into overestimating opponents: retreat. [Bluff].
King Jalî¿âd and Shimâs: *Alf* IV 177,-(overawed); Burton IX 124. Chauvin VI 9 No. 184; *ANE* 237-38 No. 236.□

K2378.1.1§, ‡Game (of strategy) won through deliberately losing minor part.
Tawaddud: Slavegirl Sold and Regained: *Alf* III 7; Burton V 243. Chauvin VII 117-19 No. 387; *ANE* 408-10 No. 157.□

K2378.3, ‡Enemies deceived through shammed flight.
King ¿Umar al-Nu¿mân and Sons: *Alf* I 234; Burton II 232. Chauvin VI 112-24 No. 277; *ANE* 430-34 No. 39.□

K2378.6§, ‡Amazon maiden shams defeat when she sees how handsome her adversary (hero) is.
King ¿Umar al-Nu¿mân and Sons: *Alf* II 5,-(prediction); Burton III 82. Chauvin VI 112-24 No. 277; *ANE* 430-34 No. 39.□

K2400§, ‡Deception for deception (tit for tat): deceived person gets even in a like manner (same ruse, strategy, trick, etc.). See: *DOTTI*; *PSAE*.
Sweep and Noble Lady: Infidelity Repaid: *Alf* II 190; Burton IV 129. Chauvin VI 148 No. 306; *ANE* 403-4 No. 72;
Ridiculous Eye Salve: *Alf* II 287,-cf.; Burton V 99. Chauvin V 281 No. 165; *ANE* 236 No. 129;
Mercury ¿Alî: *Alf* III 236; Burton VII 187. Chauvin V 248-50 No. 147; *ANE* 301-3 No. 225.□

L. REVERSAL OF FORTUNE

L31, Youngest brother helps elder. See: *DOTTI.*
¿Abdallah ibn Fâḍil: Treacherous Brothers: *Alf* IV 271; Burton IX 312. Chauvin V 2-4 No. 2; *ANE* 63-65 No. 261.□

L41, ‡Younger brother given birthright of elder. See: *DOTTI*; *GMC.*
King ¿Umar al-Nu¿mân and Sons: *Alf* I 217; Burton II 191. Chauvin VI 112-24 No. 277; *ANE* 430-34 No. 39.□

L51, Favorite youngest daughter. See: *GMC.*
Three Apples: Hasty Uxoricide: *Alf* I 64; Burton I 193. Chauvin VI 144-45 No. 302; *ANE* 414-15 No. 21.□

L111.5.0.1§, ‡Bastard heroine.
King ¿Umar al-Nu¿mân and Sons: *Alf* I 208,-ff.; Burton II 174. Chauvin VI 112-24 No. 277; *ANE* 430-34 No. 39.□

L111.5.1.2§, ‡Girl born of brother-sister incest as heroine.
King ¿Umar al-Nu¿mân and Sons: *Alf* I 208; Burton II 174. Chauvin VI 112-24 No. 277; *ANE* 430-34 No. 39.□

L112.7.2§, ‡Scabby-headed (scald-head) person (*'aqra¿*) as hero. See: *DOTTI.*
Dalîla the Swindler: *Alf* III 213; Burton VII 145,-(mangy chap). Chauvin V 245-50 No. 147; *ANE* 163-64 No. 224.□

L114.1, Lazy hero. See: *DOTTI*; *GMC.*
Abû Muḥammad Lazybones: *Alf* II 206-16; Burton IV 162. Chauvin VI 64-67 No. 233; *ANE* 71-73 No. 78.□

L165, Lowly boy becomes king. See: *DOTTI.*
Island King/Pious Jewish Merchant: *Alf* III 17,-cf./(impoverished man); Burton V 293. Chauvin VI 161 No. 325; *ANE* 234 No. 174.□

L166§, ‡Powerless (lowly) boy made vizier. See: *DOTTI.*
al-'Amjad and al-'As¿ad: *Alf* II 127,-(fugitive prince); Burton III 339. Chauvin V 208-10 No. 120[.1]; *ANE* 341-42 No. 61/pt. 2.□

L181.1§, ‡Son born in answer to prayer proves a disappointment to parent(s). See: *DOTTI.*
King Jalî¿âd and Shimâs: *Alf* IV 134; Burton IX 35. Chauvin VI 9-11 No. 184; *ANE* 237-38 No. 236.□

L215.2§, ‡Unpromising animal (bird) chosen: proves magical. See: *DOTTI.*
Abû Muḥammad Lazybones: *Alf* II 208; Burton IV 167-68. Chauvin VI 64-67 No. 233; *ANE* 71-73 No. 78.□

L293§, ‡Formerly rich (powerful, pampered) person accepts work as menial (servant, waiter, doorkeeper, clerk, etc.). See: *DOTTI.*
Second Qalandar: Afrit's Wife: *Alf* I 43,-(firewood peddler); Burton I 115. Chauvin V 197-200 No. 116; *ANE* 338-39 No. 16;
Qamar al-Zamân and Budûr: *Alf* II 98,-(farm-hand/*murâbi¿*); Burton III 282. Chauvin V 204-12 No. 120; *ANE* 341-45 No. 61;
Man Who Never Laughs: *Alf* III 152; Burton VI 160. Chauvin VIII 47-48 No. 15; *ANE* 285-86 No. 195;
Jawdar and His Treacherous Brethren: *Alf* III 178,-(fisher); Burton VI 214. Chauvin V 257-60 No. 154; *ANE* 244-45 No. 209;
Abû Qîr and Abû Ṣîr: *Alf* IV 195,-(fisher); Burton IX 159. Chauvin V 15-17 No. 10; *ANE* 75-77 No. 255;
al-Rashîd and Omani Merchant: *Alf* IV 215; Burton IX 199. Chauvin VI 111-12 No. 276; *ANE* 201-2 No. 257;
Abû al-Ḥasan al-Khorâsânî (and Caliph's Favorite): *Alf* IV 230-31,-cf.; Burton IX 233. Chauvin V 218-20 No. 129; *ANE* 68-69 No. 259.□

L313§, ‡Few overcome numerous.
King ¿Umar al-Nu¿mân and Sons: *Alf* I 232,-(soldiers); Burton II 222. Chauvin VI 112-24 No. 277; *ANE* 430-34 No. 39.□

L400, Pride brought low.
Jeweler's Wife and Qamar al-Zamân: *Alf* IV 260; Burton IX 289. Chauvin V 212-14 No. 121; *ANE* 345-47 No. 260.□

L401§, Person (Pharaoh, Nimrod, etc.) sets self up as God: fails. See: *DOTTI*.
Wolf and Fox: *Alf* II 30,-cf./(wolf/allegorical); Burton III 133. Chauvin II 227 No. 6; *ANE* 450 No. 47.□

L405§, Rich (high) becomes poor (low). See: *DOTTI*; *GMC*. (Cf. L293§, L419.2, P501.3§).
Second Qalandar: Afrit's Wife: *Alf* I 42; Burton I 113. Chauvin V 197-200 No. 116; *ANE* 338-39 No. 16;
Nûr al-Dîn ¿Alî and Son: *Alf* I 69; Burton I 210-11. Chauvin VI 102-6 No. 270; *ANE* 317-19 No. 22;
King ¿Umar al-Nu¿mân and Sons: *Alf* I 188, 311-12; Burton II 133-34, III 55-56. Chauvin VI 112-24 No. 277; *ANE* 430-34 No. 39;
al-'Amjad and al-'As¿ad: *Alf* II 123,-(tailor's apprentice); Burton III 330. Chauvin V 208-10 No. 120[.1]; *ANE* 341-42 No. 61/pt. 2.□

L406§, ‡Hunter (predator) becomes hunted (prey). (Cf. K2173§).
Fisherman and Afrit: Ingratitude: *Alf* I 15-16,-cf./(afrit/man); Burton I 41-44. Chauvin VI 23-25 No. 195; *ANE* 183-84 No. 8;
Dalîla the Swindler: *Alf* III 225; Burton VII 168. Chauvin V 245-50 No. 147; *ANE* 163-64 No. 224.□

L408§, ‡Captor (jailer) falls in love with captive (prisoner)—captor humbled. (Cf. P310.5.2§, P311.1).
al-'Amjad and al-'As¿ad: *Alf* II 131; Burton III 345. Chauvin V 208-10 No. 120[.1]; *ANE* 341-42 No. 61/pt. 2.□

L413, Proud inscriptions sole remains [(relic)] of powerful king. See: *DOTTI*; *GMC*; *PSAE*. (Cf. V67.9.2§, V311.5§).
Jinn Imprisoned in Flasks: *Alf* III 125,-(poem); Burton VI 90,-(variant). Chauvin VII 113 No. 380=no/text; *ANE* 146 No. 180;
City of Brass: *Alf* III 130,-(poems); Burton VI 104. Chauvin V 32-35 No. 16; *ANE* 146-50 No. 180.□

L419.2, ‡King (prince) becomes beggar. See: *DOTTI*. (Cf. L405§).
First Qalandar: Brother-Sister Incest: *Alf* I 39-42,-(king's son); Burton I 104-13. Chauvin V 197-200 No. 116; *ANE* 338-39 No. 15.□

L428§, Only death puts an end to man's overweening ambition. See: *DOTTI*.
Birds, Beasts, and Carpenter: *Alf* II 25; Burton III 120. Chauvin II 225-26 No. 1; *ANE* 126 No. 44.□

L430, Arrogance repaid. See: *GMC*. (Cf. W166.3§).
Jullanâr of the Sea: *Alf* III 260,-(conceited king defeated); Burton VII 286. Chauvin V 147-51 No. 73; *ANE* 248-51 No. 227.□

L432.0.1§, ‡Impoverished husband begs from wife's paramour.
Jeweler's Wife and Qamar al-Zamân: *Alf* IV 260,-cf.; Burton IX 293-94. Chauvin V 212-14 No. 121; *ANE* 345-47 No. 260.□

L458§, Fortune of proud animal or bird (lion, eagle, falcon) reversed: humbled by lowly one. See: *GMC*. (Cf. U260.3§).
¿Alâ' al-Dîn Abû al-Shâmât: *Alf* II 169,-cf.; Burton IV 74. Chauvin V 43-49 No. 18; *ANE* 85-87 No. 63.□

L458.1§, ‡In old age, hawk (eagle, etc.) must feed on food left by creatures that were once his prey. (Cf. J761.5§).
Saker and Birds: *Alf* II 38-39; Burton III 155. Chauvin II 228 No. 13; *ANE* 357-58 No. 53.□

L485.1§, ‡Community site (city, town, tribal homestead, home, etc.) formerly alive is now lifeless (ruined, abandoned). (Cf. T44§).
Budûr and Jubayr ibn ¿Umayr: *Alf* II 239-40; Burton IV 239. Chauvin VII 93-94 No. 374; *ANE* 243-44 No. 83;
Ruined Baghdadi and His Slave-girl: *Alf* IV 131,-(poem); Burton IX 27. Chauvin V 152-53 No. 75; *ANE* 353 No. 235.□

L485.5§, ‡Tree formerly green and full of life (birds) is now dead (wood, tools, etc.).
Nûr al-Dîn and Maryam: *Alf* IV 85,-(poem); Burton VIII 281. Chauvin V 52-54 No. 271; *ANE* 98-99 No. 233.□

L490§, Lowly (poor) becomes high (rich). See: *DOTTI*.
Ensorcelled Prince/Husband: *Alf* I 31; Burton I 81. Chauvin VI 56-58 No. 222; *ANE* 176 No. 13;
Abû Qîr and Abû Ṣîr: *Alf* IV 187; Burton IX 144. Chauvin V 15-17 No. 10; *ANE* 75-77 No. 255.□

L490.1§, ‡Common person made ruler (king, queen). See: *DOTTI*. (Cf. H171.2, P11.1.1).
King ¿Umar al-Nu¿mân and Sons: *Alf* I 311,-(chamberlain becomes sultan); Burton III 55. Chauvin VI 112-24 No. 277; *ANE* 430-34 No. 39.□

L491§, Wealth leads to pride (vanity). See: *DOTTI*; *GMC*; *PSAE*. (Cf. U62.0.2§, W166§).
Angel of Death and Rich King: *Alf* III 9; Burton V 250. Chauvin VI 184-85 No. 350; *ANE* 104-5 No. 159.□

L501§, ‡Unhappy occasion (sadness) turns into happy one (joy).
Lover Who Feigned Himself a Thief: *Alf* II 206; Burton IV 159. Chauvin VII 134-35 No. 403; *ANE* 272 No. 76.□

L502§, ‡Feeling (sentiment, emotion) turns into its opposite.
Budûr and Jubayr ibn ¿Umayr: *Alf* II 240; Burton IV 240. Chauvin VII 93-94 No. 374; *ANE* 243-44 No. 83.□

L502.1§, ‡Hate turns into love (instantly).
Tailor's Story/Barber of Baghdad: *Alf* I 103; Burton I 302. Chauvin V 154-56 No. 78; *ANE* 405-6 No. 27.□

L502.2§, ‡Spurned person becomes loved and vice versa.
Budûr and Jubayr ibn ¿Umayr: *Alf* II 240; Burton IV 240. Chauvin VII 93-94 No. 374; *ANE* 243-44 No. 83.□

L505§, ‡Planned good deed preempted by hasty (foolish) act by intended recipient. (Cf. J675.0.1§, W196.2§).
Ḥammâd: Treacherous Bedouin: *Alf* II 20; Burton III 111. Chauvin VI 124 n. 1 No. 277; *ANE* 200 No. 43.□

L506§, ‡Happy occasion (joy) turns into an unhappy one (sadness). See: *DOTTI*. (Cf. Z77.6.1§).
Abû al-Ḥasan al-Khorâsânî (and Caliph's Favorite): *Alf* IV 237; Burton IX 245. Chauvin V 218-20 No. 129; *ANE* 68-69 No. 259.□

L506.0.2§, ‡'Joy unfulfilled' (happiness short-lived). (Cf. T44§).
Anîs al-Jalîs: *Alf* I 140,-cf./(poem/souring of love); Burton II 30,-(xxx/variant). Chauvin V 120-24 No. 58; *ANE* 316-17 No. 35;
¿Alâ' al-Dîn Abû al-Shâmât: *Alf* II 157,-(*farḥah mâ tammat*); Burton IV 52,-(,-(delight which is not fulfilled ...). Chauvin V 43-49 No. 18; *ANE* 85-87 No. 63.□

L506.1§, ‡Wedding celebration turns into sadness (funeral).
Dalîla the Swindler: *Alf* III 220; Burton VII 157. Chauvin V 245-50 No. 147; *ANE* 163-64 No. 224.□

M. ORDAINING THE FUTURE

M12, Irrevocable sentence carried out even when innocence is proved. See: *DOTTI.*
Reeve's Story: Why Maimed by Bride: *Alf* I 99,-(thumbs cut off); Burton I 287. Chauvin V 220-21 No. 305; *ANE* 351 No. 25.□

M100.1§, ‡Vow kept (covenant maintained) in spite of great odds. (Cf. W37.2.1§, W37.2.1§).
Ensorcelled Prince/Husband: *Alf* I 23-24,-(fish in frying pan); Burton I 63, 64. Chauvin VI 56-58 No. 222; *ANE* 176 No. 13;
Shipwrecked Woman and Her Child: *Alf* III 11; Burton V 259-61. Chauvin VI 160 No. 324; *ANE* 379 No. 164.□

M106.0.1§, ‡Oath honored (vow fulfilled) in spit of mental reservations—('merely in order not to violate oath').
Anîs al-Jalîs: *Alf* I 133,-(*'ibrâr al-yamîn*); Burton II 15. Chauvin V 120-24 No. 58; *ANE* 316-17 No. 35;
Sweep and Noble Lady: Infidelity Repaid: *Alf* II 190; Burton IV 129. Chauvin VI 148 No. 306; *ANE* 403-4 No. 72.□

M108.0.1§, ‡Treacherous violator of sacred oath. See: *DOTTI.* (Cf. M205, M209§, P520§, W37).
Ḥammâd: Treacherous Bedouin: *Alf* II 19; Burton III 111. Chauvin VI 124 n. 1 No. 277; *ANE* 200 No. 43;
Bulûqiya: *Alf* III 78,-(hero is); Burton V 390. Chauvin VII 54 No. 77; *ANE* 130-32 No. 177;
Jullanâr of the Sea: *Alf* III 265,-(treacherous queen); Burton VII 298. Chauvin V 147-51 No. 73; *ANE* 248-51 No. 227.□

M110.1.1§, ‡Swearing falsely (oath as a lie). (Cf. Q263).
King ¿Umar al-Nu¿mân and Sons: *Alf* II 8; Burton III 88. Chauvin VI 112-24 No. 277; *ANE* 430-34 No. 39;
Abû Qîr and Abû Ṣîr: *Alf* IV 192-93; Burton IX 154. Chauvin V 15-17 No. 10; *ANE* 75-77 No. 255.□

M113.1, Oath taken on sword. See: *DOTTI.*
¿Azîz and ¿Azîzah: *Alf* I 286,-(oath by sword); Burton II 332. Chauvin V 144-45 No. 71; *ANE* 111-13 No. 41.□

M114.1, Oath on sacred book. See: *GMC.*
¿Azîz and ¿Azîzah: *Alf* I 286,-cf.; Burton II 332. Chauvin V 144-45 No. 71; *ANE* 111-13 No. 41.□

M114.1.1, ‡Oath by Tora.
Masrûr and Zayn al-Mawâṣif: *Alf* IV 62,-(poem,/*tawrâh*); Burton VIII 226,-(Torah). Chauvin VI 82-84 No. 251; *ANE* 294-95 No. 232.□

M114.1.2§, ‡Oath by Bible (Evangel).
Copt Broker's Story: Lover's Sacrifices Repaid: *Alf* I 89,-(xxx/missing); Burton I 264. Chauvin VI 80 No. 249; *ANE* 313-14 No. 24;
Masrûr and Zayn al-Mawâṣif: *Alf* IV 62,-(poem); Burton VIII 226. Chauvin VI 82-84 No. 251; *ANE* 294-95 No. 232.□

M114.1.3§, ‡Oath (vow) taken on the Koran.
Portress Amînah: Bitten Cheek: *Alf* I 58; Burton I 178. Chauvin V 98-99 No. 33; *ANE* 326-27 No. 20;
¿Azîz and ¿Azîzah: *Alf* I 286,-(oath by *muṣḥaf*) and sword); Burton II 332. Chauvin V 144-45 No. 71; *ANE* 111-13 No. 41.□

M114.7.1§, ‡Oath by holy fire and light. (Cf. V1.6.3).
Jullanâr of the Sea: *Alf* III 267; Burton VII 302. Chauvin V 147-51 No. 73; *ANE* 248-51 No. 227;
Hasan of Basrah: *Alf* III 307; Burton VIII 18. Chauvin VII 29-35 No. 212A; *ANE* 207-10 No. 230.□

M115, Only one oath binding. It must be by so and so or else it is worthless.
¿Alâ' al-Dîn Abû al-Shâmât: *Alf* II 166,-(divorce); Burton IV 69. Chauvin V 43-49 No. 18; *ANE* 85-87 No. 63.□

M115.3§, ‡Oath so great it cannot be revoked nor made-up for by expiatory-deed (*kaffârah*). See: *DOTTI.* (Cf. V6§).

Sweep and Noble Lady: Infidelity Repaid: *Alf* II 190; Burton IV 129. Chauvin VI 148 No. 306; *ANE* 403-4 No. 72.□

M115.4§, ‡Beloved wife (woman) requires divorce-oath from her husband to ensure that her demands are met.
¿Alâ' al-Dîn Abû al-Shâmât: *Alf* II 166; Burton IV 69. Chauvin V 43-49 No. 18; *ANE* 85-87 No. 63.□

M116.4§, ‡Oath by sacred writing (or talisman). (Cf. D1266.1).
Eldest Lady's Story: Treacherous Sisters: *Alf* I 57,-(inscription on Solomon's Seal); Burton I 172. Chauvin V 4 No. 443; *ANE* 174-75 No. 19;
Qamar al-Zamân and Budûr: *Alf* II 71; Burton III 224. Chauvin V 204-12 No. 120; *ANE* 341-45 No. 61;
¿Alâ' al-Dîn Abû al-Shâmât: *Alf* II 180,-cf.; Burton IV 92. Chauvin V 43-49 No. 18; *ANE* 85-87 No. 63;
Sayf al-Mulûk: *Alf* III 289,-(inscription on Solomon's Seal); Burton VII 351. Chauvin VII 64-73 No. 348; *ANE* 362-64 No. 229;
¿Abdallah ibn Fâḍil: Treacherous Brothers: *Alf* IV 282; Burton IX 338. Chauvin V 2-4 No. 2; *ANE* 63-65 No. 261.□

M117.0.1§, *nadhr*/*'nadr'*: conditional vow: pledge to perform certain (good) act if prayer is answered (request is granted). See: *DOTTI*; *GMC*; *PSAE*. (Cf. M147§, M209§).
King ¿Umar al-Nu¿mân and Sons: *Alf* II 7; Burton III 87. Chauvin VI 112-24 No. 277; *ANE* 430-34 No. 39;
Qamar al-Zamân and Budûr: *Alf* II 103,-(poem/made by *Zamân*); Burton III 290. Chauvin V 204-12 No. 120; *ANE* 341-45 No. 61;
Tawaddud: Slavegirl Sold and Regained: *Alf* II 303-4; Burton V 189. Chauvin VII 117-19 No. 387; *ANE* 408-10 No. 157;
Nûr al-Dîn and Maryam: *Alf* IV 108,-cf./(to church); Burton VIII 324. Chauvin V 52-54 No. 271; *ANE* 98-99 No. 233.□

M117.2§, ‡Vow (threat) to commit certain act if certain condition is not met. (Cf. K1771, M170.1.1§, T311.2.2§).
Ma¿n Rewards a Bedouin for Gift: *Alf* II 182-83; Burton IV 98. Chauvin VI 78 No. 247; *ANE* 291 No. 66;
Serpent-charmer and Wife: *Alf* IV 146,-(*qatalnâ 'anfusanâ*); Burton IX 57,-("slay ourselves"). Chauvin II 220 No. 152/9; *ANE* 368 No. 244.□

M117.2.1§, ‡Vow to destroy goods if price is not fair (too low).
Ma¿n Rewards a Bedouin for Gift: *Alf* II 182-83; Burton IV 98. Chauvin VI 78 No. 247; *ANE* 291 No. 66.□

M119.0.1§, Swearing by God. See: *DOTTI*; *PSAE*.
Fisherman and Afrit: Ingratitude: *Alf* I 23; Burton I 62. Chauvin VI 26 No. 197; *ANE* 183-84 No. 8;
Ensorcelled Prince/Husband: *Alf* I 26,-(oath); Burton I 71. Chauvin VI 56-58 No. 222; *ANE* 176 No. 13;
Craft and Malice of Women/Frame: *Alf* III 177; Burton VI 212. Chauvin VIII 33-34 No. 1; *ANE* 160-61 No. 181.□

M119.0.1.2§, Swearing by one's own attributes: health, eyesight, etc.
King ¿Umar al-Nu¿mân and Sons: *Alf* I 194,-(own conical cap); Burton II 143,-(By the rights of my bonnet). Chauvin VI 112-24 No. 277; *ANE* 430-34 No. 39;
Dalîla the Swindler: *Alf* III 225,-(*wa ḥayât maqṣûṣî*); Burton VII 167,-(By the life of my browlock). Chauvin V 245-50 No. 147; *ANE* 163-64 No. 224.□

M119.0.1.3.1§, ‡Oath by one's own head.
King Sindbâd and Falcon: *Alf* I 19; Burton I 51. Chauvin V 289 No. 173; *ANE* 383 No. 10;
¿Alâ' al-Dîn Abû al-Shâmât: *Alf* II 166; Burton IV 69. Chauvin V 43-49 No. 18; *ANE* 85-87 No. 63;
Mock Caliph/¿Alî al-Jawharî: *Alf* II 195; Burton IV 139. Chauvin V 99-100 No. 174; *ANE* 304-5 No. 73;
Jawdar and His Treacherous Brethren: *Alf* III 201; Burton VI 256. Chauvin V 257-60 No. 154; *ANE* 244-45 No. 209.□

M119.0.1.3.2§, ‡Oath by one's own eye(s).

¿Azîz and ¿Azîzah: *Alf* I 278,-(coin/eye); Burton II 316. Chauvin V 144-45 No. 71; *ANE* 111-13 No. 41.□

M119.8, Oath taken by life of a person.
Qamar al-Zamân and Budûr: *Alf* II 108; Burton III 300,-(by people, great and small). Chauvin V 204-12 No. 120; *ANE* 341-45 No. 61;
Hasan of Basrah: *Alf* IV 11,-(queen); Burton VIII 57. Chauvin VII 29-35 No. 212A; *ANE* 207-10 No. 230.□

M119.8.2, Swearing by life of father [(or ancestors)]. See: *DOTTI*.
King and Vizier's Wife/Tracks of Lion: *Alf* III 140; Burton VI 131,-(honor of fathers and forefathers). Chauvin VIII 35 No. 2; *ANE* 261 No. 182;
Dalîla the Swindler: *Alf* III 225,-(head of grandfathers); Burton VII 167. Chauvin V 245-50 No. 147; *ANE* 163-64 No. 224.□

M119.8.2.1§, ‡Swearing by grave of ancestor(s).
Anîs al-Jalîs: *Alf* I 142, 145; Burton II 33. Chauvin V 120-24 No. 58; *ANE* 316-17 No. 35;
¿Alâ' al-Dîn Abû al-Shâmât: *Alf* II 164; Burton IV 64. Chauvin V 43-49 No. 18; *ANE* 85-87 No. 63;
Mock Caliph/¿Alî al-Jawharî: *Alf* II 195; Burton IV 139. Chauvin V 99-100 No. 174; *ANE* 304-5 No. 73.□

M119.8.3.2§, ‡Swearing by the milk suckled together during infancy (i.e., mother's or wet-nurse's). (Cf. M119.8.6.1.1§).
Sayf al-Mulûk: *Alf* III 295; Burton VII 365. Chauvin VII 64-73 No. 348; *ANE* 362-64 No. 229.□

M119.8.5§, ‡Swearing (pleading) 'by [value of] one's own life [for some one else]' (*bi-ḥayâtî-.../'wi-ḥayâtî-...'*). See: *DOTTI*. (Cf. M119.8.6§).
Porter and Ladies of Baghdad: *Alf* I 35; Burton I 93,-(missing). Chauvin V 251-52 No. 148; *ANE* 324-26 No. 14;
Anîs al-Jalîs: *Alf* I 138, 142; Burton II 26. Chauvin V 120-24 No. 58; *ANE* 316-17 No. 35;
¿Azîz and ¿Azîzah: *Alf* I 277, 286; Burton II 315. Chauvin V 144-45 No. 71; *ANE* 111-13 No. 41;
King ¿Umar al-Nu¿mân and Sons: *Alf* II 10; Burton III 94. Chauvin VI 112-24 No. 277; *ANE* 430-34 No. 39;
Birds, Beasts, and Carpenter: *Alf* II 25,-(young lion); Burton III 121,-(by my life). Chauvin II 225-26 No. 1; *ANE* 126 No. 44;
Qamar al-Zamân and Budûr: *Alf* II 110; Burton III 305. Chauvin V 204-12 No. 120; *ANE* 341-45 No. 61.□

M119.8.6§, ‡Swearing by love. (Cf. M119.8.5§).
King ¿Umar al-Nu¿mân and Sons: *Alf* I 193,-(poem); Burton II 140,-(By Love I swear). Chauvin VI 112-24 No. 277; *ANE* 430-34 No. 39.□

M119.8.6.1.1§, ‡Swearing by sanctity ('*ḥurmah*') of brother-sister love. (Cf. T415).
Hasan of Basrah: *Alf* III 318,-(*bi ḥurmat al-ḥubb* [which exists] between me and you); Burton VIII 37,-("by the honest love which is between us [??]). Chauvin VII 29-35 No. 212A; *ANE* 207-10 No. 230.□

M119.9§, Swearing by a prophet.
Craft and Malice of Women/Frame: *Alf* III 177; Burton VI 212. Chauvin VIII 33-34 No. 1; *ANE* 160-61 No. 181.□

M119.9.1.0.1§, ‡Oath by someone's own religion ("By your faith").
¿Alî Shâr and Zumurrud: *Alf* II 222,-(*wa ḥaqqu dînaka*); Burton IV 201,-("by the truth of thy religion"). Chauvin V 89-91 No. 28; *ANE* 100-1 No. 82;
Jullanâr of the Sea: *Alf* III 267; Burton VII 302,-("by whatso thou worshippest"). Chauvin V 147-51 No. 73; *ANE* 248-51 No. 227;
Sayf al-Mulûk: *Alf* III 298; Burton VII 369. Chauvin VII 64-73 No. 348; *ANE* 362-64 No. 229;
Nûr al-Dîn and Maryam: *Alf* IV 100; Burton VIII 310,-(by thy faith). Chauvin V 52-54 No. 271; *ANE* 98-99 No. 233.□

M119.9.3§, ‡Oath by Jesus (Christ, Messiah).
King ¿Umar al-Nu¿mân and Sons: *Alf* I 168,-ff.; Burton II 87,-(truth of the Messiah). Chauvin VI 112-24 No. 277; *ANE* 430-34 No. 39;
¿Alî Shâr and Zumurrud: *Alf* II 223; Burton IV 203,("the Messiah"). Chauvin V 89-91 No. 28; *ANE* 100-1 No. 82;

Nûr al-Dîn and Maryam: *Alf* IV 113-14, 129; Burton VIII 335, IX 17. Chauvin V 52-54 No. 271; *ANE* 98-99 No. 233.□

M119.9.3.1§, ‡Oath by 'The Virgin' (Mother of Christ).
¿Alî Shâr and Zumurrud: *Alf* II 223; Burton IV 203. Chauvin V 89-91 No. 28; *ANE* 100-1 No. 82.□

M119.9.5§, ‡Oath by Solomon.
Jânshâh: *Alf* III 65, 66; Burton V 368, 369. Chauvin VII 39-44 No. 153; *ANE* 238-41 No. 178.□

M124§, ‡Vow of cleanliness.
Reeve's Story: Why Maimed by Bride: *Alf* I 99; Burton I 287. Chauvin V 220-21 No. 305; *ANE* 351 No. 25.□

M131.1§, Vows of faithfulness exchanged between couple. See: *DOTTI*; *GMC*. (Cf. M135.3§).
Portress Amînah: Bitten Cheek: *Alf* I 58; Burton I 178. Chauvin V 98-99 No. 33; *ANE* 326-27 No. 20;
Mock Caliph/¿Alî al-Jawharî: *Alf* II 197,-(implicit); Burton IV 142. Chauvin V 99-100 No. 174; *ANE* 304-5 No. 73;
Sayf al-Mulûk: *Alf* III 298,-(covenant); Burton VII 369,-(covenant together). Chauvin VII 64-73 No. 348; *ANE* 362-64 No. 229.□

M131.1.1§, Vow to become unfaithful if spouse is unfaithful. See: *GMC*. (Cf. P187.1§).
Sweep and Noble Lady: Infidelity Repaid: *Alf* II 190; Burton IV 129. Chauvin VI 148 No. 306; *ANE* 403-4 No. 72.□

M131.3§, ‡Pledge of chastity written (embroidered) on girl's underwear (underpants). (Cf. K1872.8.3§).
Ghânim ibn Ayyûb: *Alf* I 153; Burton II 60. Chauvin VI 14 No. 188; *ANE* 192-93 No. 36.□

M131.4§, ‡Vow never to mate with the beloved in 'sin' (fornication).
Abû al-Ḥasan al-Khorâsânî (and Caliph's Favorite): *Alf* IV 235; Burton IX 239. Chauvin V 218-20 No. 129; *ANE* 68-69 No. 259.□

M135, ‡Vow never to remarry. See: *DOTTI*; *GMC*. (Cf. M255).
Shahriyâr and Shâhzamân: *Alf* I 5; Burton I 14. Chauvin V 188-89 No. 111; *ANE* 370-71 No. 1;
Husband and Parrot: *Alf* III 141,-(*'aqsama ... 'annahu lâ-yatazawwaj ... 'imra'h muddata ḥayâtih*); Burton I 53,-(xxx). Chauvin VI 139 No. 294; *ANE* 226 No. 11;
King's Son and Merchant's Wife: *Alf* III 156; Burton VI 169. Chauvin VIII 48-49 No. 16; *ANE* 263 No. 196.□

M135.3§, Spouse no-remarriage pact: each of husband and wife vows never to remarry if the other dies first. See: *DOTTI*; *GMC*. (Cf. M131.1§, M255).
¿Azîz and ¿Azîzah: *Alf* I 286,-cf.; Burton II 332. Chauvin V 144-45 No. 71; *ANE* 111-13 No. 41;
Sayf al-Mulûk: *Alf* III 298,-cf./(no love); Burton VII 369. Chauvin VII 64-73 No. 348; *ANE* 362-64 No. 229.□

M143§, ‡Wedding night vows and promises (made by bride or groom). (Cf. T160).
Dalîla the Swindler: *Alf* III 213; Burton VII 146. Chauvin V 245-50 No. 147; *ANE* 163-64 No. 224.□

M144.1§, ‡Husband vows (makes oath) not to take a second wife ("marry over", "to co-wife"). (Cf. J21.32, M255).
Dalîla the Swindler: *Alf* III 213; Burton VII 146. Chauvin V 245-50 No. 147; *ANE* 163-64 No. 224.□

M144.2§, ‡Husband breaks his vow not to take a second wife because first is barren. (Cf. T145.2).
Dalîla the Swindler: *Alf* III 213,-(intention); Burton VII 147. Chauvin V 245-50 No. 147; *ANE* 163-64 No. 224.□

M146.4.1§, Brother and brother arrange marriage of their unborn children (paternal-cousins) to each other. See: *DOTTI*; *GMC*.
Nûr al-Dîn ¿Alî and Son: *Alf* I 64; Burton I 196. Chauvin VI 102-6 No. 270; *ANE* 317-19 No. 22.□

M146.4.2§, ‡Brother and brother betroth their (adult) children.
¿Azîz and ¿Azîzah: *Alf* I 268; Burton II 299. Chauvin V 144-45 No. 71; *ANE* 111-13 No. 41.□

M147§, Conditional 'divorce-vow': oath that divorce will have occurred unless certain matter is brought to pass. See: *DOTTI*; *GMC*. (Cf. M117.0.1§, T196§, T283.1§).
¿Azîz and ¿Azîzah: *Alf* I 286; Burton II 332. Chauvin V 144-45 No. 71; *ANE* 111-13 No. 41;

¿Alâ' al-Dîn Abû al-Shâmât: *Alf* II 166, 167; Burton IV 69. Chauvin V 43-49 No. 18; *ANE* 85-87 No. 63;
Hârûn, Slave-girl and Judge Abû-Yûsuf: *Alf* II 202; Burton IV 153. Chauvin VII 114 No. 383; *ANE* 204 No. 75;
¿Alî Shâr and Zumurrud: *Alf* II 229; Burton IV 215,-(-(sugar rice)). Chauvin V 89-91 No. 28; *ANE* 100-1 No. 82;
Nûr al-Dîn and Maryam: *Alf* IV 83, 89, 101; Burton VIII 277, 287, 290. Chauvin V 52-54 No. 271; *ANE* 98-99 No. 233.□

M151.4.1§, ‡Vow not to take another person's food or drink until revenge is accomplished. (Cf. C240).
King ¿Umar al-Nu¿mân and Sons: *Alf* II 7; Burton III 87. Chauvin VI 112-24 No. 277; *ANE* 430-34 No. 39.□

M159§, ‡Oath (vow, pledge) of allegiance (to state, king, etc.). (Cf. P11.7§).
King ¿Umar al-Nu¿mân and Sons: *Alf* I 218,-(by army generals); Burton II 193,-(oath of fealty). Chauvin VI 112-24 No. 277; *ANE* 430-34 No. 39.□

M160.1§, ‡Vow (oath) to avenge murdered relative or friend.
King ¿Umar al-Nu¿mân and Sons: *Alf* I 186, 260,-(daughter); Burton II 129 279. Chauvin VI 112-24 No. 277; *ANE* 430-34 No. 39.□

M170.1.1§, ‡Vow (threat) to commit suicide if demand is not met. See: *DOTTI*. (Cf. M117.2§, T311.2.2§).
Nûr al-Dîn ¿Alî and Son: *Alf* I 76; Burton I 232. Chauvin VI 102-6 No. 270; *ANE* 317-19 No. 22;
Tâj al-Mulûk: *Alf* I 291; Burton III 10. Chauvin V 126-28 No. 60; *ANE* 406-8 No. 40;
¿Alâ' al-Dîn Abû al-Shâmât: *Alf* II 169,-cf./(kill you and kill my self, if you ...); Burton IV 74. Chauvin V 43-49 No. 18; *ANE* 85-87 No. 63;
Craft and Malice of Women/Frame: *Alf* III 150; Burton VI 150. Chauvin VIII 46-47 No. 14; *ANE* 196 No. 181;
Sayf al-Mulûk: *Alf* III 279,-(friendship); Burton VII 324-25. Chauvin VII 64-73 No. 348; *ANE* 362-64 No. 229;
Hasan of Basrah: *Alf* IV 14; Burton VIII 65. Chauvin VII 29-35 No. 212A; *ANE* 207-10 No. 230;
Serpent-charmer and Wife: *Alf* IV 146,-(*qatalnâ 'anfusanâ*); Burton IX 57,-("slay ourselves"). Chauvin II 220 No. 152/9; *ANE* 368 No. 244.□

M202, Fulfilling of bargain or promise. See: *DOTTI*; *GMC*.
Ishâq al-Mûṣilî and Merchant's Singer: *Alf* II 297,-(full month of service); Burton V 129-33. Chauvin VI 59 No. 225; *ANE* 233 No. 142.□

M202.9.1.1§, ‡"A free person's (noble) 'word' is a debt". See: *DOTTI*.
Ruined Baghdadi and His Slave-girl: *Alf* IV 133,-(Hashemite/implicit); Burton IX 32. Chauvin V 152-53 No. 75; *ANE* 353 No. 235.□

M203, King's promise irrevocable. See: *GMC*.
Ni¿mah and Nu¿m: Stolen Wife Regained: *Alf* II 144; Burton IV 22. Chauvin VI 96-97 No. 263; *ANE* 314 No. 62.□

M203.0.1§, ‡King's judgment irrevocable.
Qamar al-Zamân and Budûr: *Alf* II 68,-cf./(king as father); Burton III 219. Chauvin V 204-12 No. 120; *ANE* 341-45 No. 61;
Ni¿mah and Nu¿m: Stolen Wife Regained: *Alf* II 144,-(judgment against oneself); Burton IV 22. Chauvin VI 96-97 No. 263; *ANE* 314 No. 62.□

M205, Breaking of [(reneging on)] bargain or promise. See: *DOTTI*; *GMC*. (Cf. V6§).
Mouse and Cat: *Alf* IV 135,-(cat); Burton IX 38. Chauvin II 218 No. 152/2; *ANE* 305-6 No. 237;
King Jalî¿âd and Shimâs: *Alf* IV 164,-(by ruler); Burton IX 92-92. Chauvin VI 9 No. 184; *ANE* 237-38 No. 236.□

M205.6§, ‡Promise of safety made to an evil criminal broken. (Cf. J1675.9§).
King ¿Umar al-Nu¿mân and Sons: *Alf* II 16, 20-21; Burton III 103ff. Chauvin VI 112-24 No. 277; *ANE* 430-34 No. 39.□

M205.9.2§, ‡Woman as breaker of her word. (Cf. M205.9.7.1§).
Jullanâr of the Sea: *Alf* III 265-69,-(sorceress queen); Burton VII 298. Chauvin V 147-51 No. 73; *ANE* 248-51 No. 227.□

M205.9.7.1§, ‡Viper as breaker of her word (promise). (Cf. B3§, M205.9.2§).
Escaped Viper Ungrateful: *Alf* II 35; Burton III 145. Chauvin II 227 No. 9; *ANE* 450,/passim No. 47.□

M209§, Reminder of unfulfilled (forgotten) vow: recipient must execute own part of pledge (bargain). See: *DOTTI*; *GMC*. (Cf. M117.0.1§, Q559.12§).
Nûr al-Dîn and Maryam: *Alf* IV 108; Burton VIII 324. Chauvin V 52-54 No. 271; *ANE* 98-99 No. 233.□

M209.5§, ‡Certain word, act, or object reminds person of forgotten promise or vow. (Cf. J20§).
Anîs al-Jalîs: *Alf* I 144-45,-(singing); Burton II 42. Chauvin V 120-24 No. 58; *ANE* 316-17 No. 35.□

M223, ‡Blind promise (rash boon). Person grants wish before hearing it. See: *DOTTI*; *PSAE*. (Cf. J1675.9§, K2020§, M205.6§).
¿Alâ' al-Dîn Abû al-Shâmât: *Alf* II 166; Burton IV 68. Chauvin V 43-49 No. 18; *ANE* 85-87 No. 63;
Nûr al-Dîn and Maryam: *Alf* IV 104; Burton VIII 317. Chauvin V 52-54 No. 271; *ANE* 98-99 No. 233;
Abû al-Ḥasan al-Khorâsânî (and Caliph's Favorite): *Alf* IV 236; Burton IX 242-43. Chauvin V 218-20 No. 129; *ANE* 68-69 No. 259.□

M224§, ‡Blind promise of immunity from punishment. Person of authority (king, queen, father, etc.) grants request for safety for culprit before learning nature of offense. See: *DOTTI*. (Cf. J1675.9§, K2020§, M205.6§).
Barber's Third Brother: Exposes Blind Robbers: *Alf* I 115,-(to be given *'amân*); Burton I 331. Chauvin V 159-60 No. 83; *ANE* 118 No. 31.□

M224.1§, ‡Kerchief of safety (*maḥramat al-'amân*): cloth given to the accused indicating promise of immunity from punishment. See: *DOTTI*. (Cf. M302.7.2§).
Barber's Fifth Brother: Daydreams/Defeats Robbers: *Alf* I 121; Burton I 343. Chauvin V 161 No. 85; *ANE* 119-20 No. 33;
Mock Caliph/¿Alî al-Jawharî: *Alf* II 199; Burton IV 148,-("kerchief of immunity"). Chauvin V 99-100 No. 174; *ANE* 304-5 No. 73;
Jawdar and His Treacherous Brethren: *Alf* III 199,-(*thiyâb*); Burton VI 252,-(garment). Chauvin V 257-60 No. 154; *ANE* 244-45 No. 209;
Dalîla the Swindler: *Alf* III 226; Burton VII 169. Chauvin V 245-50 No. 147; *ANE* 163-64 No. 224.□

M241.5.3§, ‡Agreement that the employed (wage-earner) will support the unemployed. See: *DOTTI*.
Abû Qîr and Abû Ṣîr: *Alf* IV 184; Burton IX 138. Chauvin V 15-17 No. 10; *ANE* 75-77 No. 255.□

M246, Covenant of friendship. See: *DOTTI*.
Masrûr and Zayn al-Mawâṣif: *Alf* IV 57; Burton VIII 224. Chauvin VI 82-84 No. 251; *ANE* 294-95 No. 232.□

M250.1§, ‡Deathbed wish: dying person (father, mother, husband, wife, etc.) makes a wish. See: *DOTTI*. (Cf. J154, P527§).
Nûr al-Dîn ¿Alî and Son: *Alf* I 68,-(advice); Burton I 206,-(expanded/five "behests"). Chauvin VI 102-6 No. 270; *ANE* 317-19 No. 22;
Anîs al-Jalîs: *Alf* I 130; Burton II 8-10. Chauvin V 120-24 No. 58; *ANE* 316-17 No. 35;
¿Azîz and ¿Azîzah: *Alf* I 288,-(cousin-wife's); Burton III 5. Chauvin V 144-45 No. 71; *ANE* 111-13 No. 41;
King ¿Umar al-Nu¿mân and Sons: *Alf* I 311; Burton III 54. Chauvin VI 112-24 No. 277; *ANE* 430-34 No. 39;
¿Alî ibn Bakkâr: *Alf* II 63; Burton III 208. Chauvin V 153 No. 76; *ANE* 92-93 No. 60;
¿Alî Shâr and Zumurrud: *Alf* II 217,-cf./(advice); Burton IV 187. Chauvin V 89-91 No. 28; *ANE* 100-1 No. 82;
Tawaddud: Slavegirl Sold and Regained: *Alf* II 304,-cf./(creation of); Burton V 237. Chauvin VII 117-19 No. 387; *ANE* 408-10 No. 157;
Bulûqiya: *Alf* III 22,-cf.; Burton V 304. Chauvin VII 54 No. 77; *ANE* 130-32 No. 177;
Abû al-Ḥasan al-Khorâsânî (and Caliph's Favorite): *Alf* IV 231,-(father's instructions); Burton IX 233. Chauvin V 218-20 No. 129; *ANE* 68-69 No. 259;
Ma¿rûf the Cobbler: *Alf* IV 313,-(wife/mother); Burton X 47. Chauvin VI 81-82 No. 250; *ANE* 291-93 No. 262.□

M255, Deathbed promise concerning the second wife. See: *DOTTI*. (Cf. M135, M144.1§, V21.8§,on).
Anîs al-Jalîs: *Alf* I 129; Burton II 10. Chauvin V 120-24 No. 58; *ANE* 316-17 No. 35.□

M255.2§, ‡Son promises dying father not to take a second wife. (Cf. J21.32).
Anîs al-Jalîs: *Alf* I 129; Burton II 9. Chauvin V 120-24 No. 58; *ANE* 316-17 No. 35.□

M258, Promise to dying man sacred. See: *GMC*.
Devotee Prince: Ascetic's Death: *Alf* II 290-91; Burton V 113-16. Chauvin VI 193-94 No. 363; *ANE* 167-68 No. 134.□

M270§, ‡Freedom promised to slave (captive). (Cf. Q121.1).
Ruined Baghdadi and His Slave-girl: *Alf* IV 132, 133; Burton IX 29,31 . Chauvin V 152-53 No. 75; *ANE* 353 No. 235.□

M300.0.1§, Supernatural prophesying or proclaiming voice (*hâtif*). See: *DOTTI*; *GMC*. (Cf. F966).
Man Who Never Laughs: *Alf* III 155,-(*qâ'ilin yaqûl—wa huwa yasma¿u ṣawtah walâ yarâ shakhṣah wahuwa yunâdî* ...); Burton VI 166,-("he heard one speaking, albeit he saw no one, and saying ..."). Chauvin VIII 47-48 No. 15; *ANE* 285-86 No. 195.□

M300.0.2§, ‡Prophecy will take place only if certain condition exists.
Craft and Malice of Women/Frame: *Alf* III 139; Burton VI 124. Chauvin VIII 33-34 No. 1; *ANE* 160-61 No. 181.□

M301.11.1§, ‡al-Khiḍr as prophet (messenger of God). (Cf. N815.3§).
City of Brass: *Alf* III 137; Burton VI 119. Chauvin V 32-35 No. 16; *ANE* 146-50 No. 180;
¿Abdallah ibn Fâḍil: Treacherous Brothers: *Alf* IV 277; Burton IX 327. Chauvin V 2-4 No. 2; *ANE* 63-65 No. 261.□

M302.0.3§, *'istikhârah*: prophesying by asking God to indicate right choice (through: dream, opening Holy Book, rosary). See: *PSAE*. (Cf. M302.8).
Uns al-Wujûd and al-Ward: *Alf* II 271,-(by prayers); Burton V 37,-(prayer for right direction). Chauvin VI 127-29 No. 282; *ANE* 438 No. 104.□

M302.2, Man's fate written on his skull. See: *DOTTI*; *GMC*.
Birds, Beasts, and Carpenter: *Alf* II 22-25,-(xxx); Burton III 123 n. 1,-("That which is on our foreheads we must indeed fulfil"). Chauvin II 225-26 No. 1; *ANE* 126 No. 44.□

M302.4, Horoscope taken by means of stars. [Astrology]. See: *DOTTI*. (Cf. P481).
Tailor's Story/Barber of Baghdad: *Alf* I 105; Burton I 304-5. Chauvin V 154-56 No. 78; *ANE* 405-6 No. 27;
Bulûqiya/Ḥâsib/Queen of Vipers: *Alf* III 19; Burton V 299. Chauvin VII 54 No. 77; *ANE* 130-32 No. 177;
Jânshâh: *Alf* III 39,-(by astrologers); Burton V 329. Chauvin VII 39-44 No. 153; *ANE* 238-41 No. 178;
Craft and Malice of Women/Frame: *Alf* III 139; Burton VI 123-24. Chauvin VIII 33-34 No. 1; *ANE* 160-61 No. 181.□

M302.4.3§, ‡Sign of the Zodiac indicates (determines) future. See: *PSAE*. (Cf. M302.4.3§).
Tawaddud: Slavegirl Sold and Regained: *Alf* III 3; Burton V 234. Chauvin VII 117-19 No. 387; *ANE* 408-10 No. 157.□

M302.7.2§, ‡Dream interpreter declines to interpret dream. (Usually kin's dream). (Cf. M224.1§).
King Jalî¿âd and Shimâs: *Alf* IV 135,-(part of dream); Burton IX 34. Chauvin VI 9-11 No. 184; *ANE* 237-38 No. 236.□

M302.8, ‡ Prophesying from book. See: *DOTTI*. (Cf. J166, M363.5§).
Bulûqiya: *Alf* III 22, 76; Burton V 304, 387. Chauvin VII 54 No. 77; *ANE* 130-32 No. 177.□

M340, Unfavorable prophecies. See: *DOTTI*; *GMC*; *PSAE*.
Bulûqiya/Ḥâsib/Queen of Vipers: *Alf* III 19,-cf.; Burton V 299. Chauvin VII 54 No. 77; *ANE* 130-32 No. 177.□

M340.3, ‡Prophecy of general misfortune to newborn child.
King Jalî¿âd and Shimâs: *Alf* IV 134; Burton IX 35. Chauvin VI 9-11 No. 184; *ANE* 237-38 No. 236.□

M340.3.1§, ‡Prophecy: misfortune at outset of life (followed by relief).
Bulûqiya/Ḥâsib/Queen of Vipers: *Alf* III 19; Burton V 299. Chauvin VII 54 No. 77; *ANE* 130-32 No. 177;
Jânshâh: *Alf* III 40; Burton V 331. Chauvin VII 39-44 No. 153; *ANE* 238-41 No. 178;

Sayf al-Mulûk: *Alf* III 277/(xxx),-(absent); Burton VII 324-25. Chauvin VII 64-73 No. 348; *ANE* 362-64 No. 229.□

M341, Death prophesied. See: *DOTTI*; *GMC*; *PSAE*.
Craft and Malice of Women/Frame: *Alf* III 139; Burton VI 124. Chauvin VIII 33-34 No. 1; *ANE* 160-61 No. 181.□

M341.0.5§, Person knows time of own death. See: *DOTTI*; *GMC*. (Cf. V233.3.4§).
Devotee Prince: Ascetic's Death: *Alf* II 290; Burton V 113. Chauvin VI 193-94 No. 363; *ANE* 167-68 No. 134.□

M341.1.4, ‡Prophecy: death at certain age.
Craft and Malice of Women/Frame: *Alf* III 139; Burton VI 124. Chauvin VIII 33-34 No. 1; *ANE* 160-61 No. 181.□

M341.2.19, Prophecy: death at hands of certain person. See: *DOTTI*; *GMC*.
¿Alâ' al-Dîn Abû al-Shâmât: *Alf* II 178,-(captive); Burton IV 90. Chauvin V 43-49 No. 18; *ANE* 85-87 No. 63;
Sayf al-Mulûk: *Alf* III 288; Burton VII 350,-(son of a king of mankind). Chauvin VII 64-73 No. 348; *ANE* 362-64 No. 229.□

M363.5§, Coming of Prophet Mohammed (Islam) prophesied. (Cf. M302.8).
¿Alâ' al-Dîn Abû al-Shâmât: *Alf* II 178; Burton IV 80. Chauvin V 43-49 No. 18; *ANE* 85-87 No. 63;
Bulûqiya: *Alf* III 22; Burton V 304-5. Chauvin VII 54 No. 77; *ANE* 130-32 No. 177.□

M369.5, Prophecies concerning invasion and conquest. See: *GMC*.
City of Labtayt/Treasure of Tolède: *Alf* II 183; Burton IV 100. Chauvin VI 90-91 No. 254; *ANE* 265-66 No. 67.□

M369.5.3§, ‡Identity of future conqueror revealed in prophetic message (letter, portrait, etc.). (Cf. F789.4§).
City of Labtayt/Treasure of Tolède: *Alf* II 183; Burton IV 100. Chauvin VI 90-91 No. 254; *ANE* 265-66 No. 67.□

M369.7.2, ‡Prophecy about birth of heir. See: *DOTTI*. (Cf. P17.0.2.2§).
Bulûqiya/Ḥâsib/Queen of Vipers: *Alf* III 18,-cf.; Burton V 298-99. Chauvin VII 54 No. 77; *ANE* 130-32 No. 177;
Jânshâh: *Alf* III 39; Burton V 329. Chauvin VII 39-44 No. 153; *ANE* 238-41 No. 178.□

M369.7.2.1§, ‡Prophecy: son will be born and will succeed father.
Bulûqiya/Ḥâsib/Queen of Vipers: *Alf* III 19,-cf.; Burton V 299. Chauvin VII 54 No. 77; *ANE* 130-32 No. 177;
Jânshâh: *Alf* III 39; Burton V 329. Chauvin VII 39-44 No. 153; *ANE* 238-41 No. 178.□

M369.7.4§, ‡Prophecy: conception and birth of child will take place only with marriage (intercourse) with certain person. (Cf. T538.3§).
Jânshâh: *Alf* III 39,-(Ṭayghamûs); Burton V 329. Chauvin VII 39-44 No. 153; *ANE* 238-41 No. 178.□

M375.5§, ‡All persons (captives) from certain location massacred to avoid fulfillment of prophecy.
¿Alâ' al-Dîn Abû al-Shâmât: *Alf* II 176; Burton IV 86. Chauvin V 43-49 No. 18; *ANE* 85-87 No. 63.□

M391.0.1§, ‡Foretold prophecy fulfilled.
Butcher Wardân and Bear Lover: *Alf* II 252; Burton IV 296. Chauvin V 177-78 No. 101; *ANE* 442-43 No. 101.□

M439.1§, ‡Curse: blackened face (in public). (Cf. H244.1§, Z143.3.2§).
¿Azîz and ¿Azîzah: *Alf* I 277-78,-(xxx); Burton II 312,-(charcoal). Chauvin V 144-45 No. 71; *ANE* 111-13 No. 41.□

M400.1§, ‡Supplication (prayer that begs) for God's punishment (*da¿wah ¿alâ*).
Jawdar and His Treacherous Brethren: *Alf* III 178,-(mother curses sons); Burton VI 214. Chauvin V 257-60 No. 154; *ANE* 244-45 No. 209;
Jeweler's Wife and Qamar al-Zamân: *Alf* IV 261,-(by Baṣrah people); Burton IX 293. Chauvin V 212-14 No. 121; *ANE* 345-47 No. 260.□

M400.2§, ‡Covert curse: to invoke God as judge (advocate) of oneself against adversary's injustice (i.e., "God will justly punish you!"). (*ḥasbanah/iḥtisâb*). (Cf. A102.16, V90§).

Hasan of Basrah: *Alf* IV 41,-(*'iḥtisâb to ...*); Burton VIII 118,-(appeal to the Lord of the Heavens). Chauvin VII 29-35 No. 212A; *ANE* 207-10 No. 230.□

M401, Cursing match (flyting). See: *DOTTI*; *GMC*. (Cf. P427.7.4.3§).
Man from Yaman and Six Salve-girls: Flyting: *Alf* II 244-49,-cf.; Burton IV 245-60. Chauvin VI 151 No. 313; *ANE* 289-90 No. 84.□

M404, Unintentional curse or blessing takes effect. See: *DOTTI*; *GMC*.
Budûr and Jubayr ibn ¿Umayr: *Alf* II 239,-(love); Burton IV 238. Chauvin VII 93-94 No. 374; *ANE* 243-44 No. 83.□

M407.1§, ‡Casual (routine, matter of form) prayer for marriage to certain person takes effect. (Cf. N201, T68.9§).
Copt Broker's Story: Lover's Sacrifices Repaid: *Alf* I 91; Burton I 267. Chauvin VI 80 No. 249; *ANE* 313-14 No. 24.□

M411.0.2.1§, ‡Curse by woman—efficacious.
Portress Amînah: Bitten Cheek: *Alf* I 60,-(*'akhâfu ¿alyka min du¿â'ihâ*/fear for you from her...); Burton I 183,-(xxx/I fear lest her death be laid at thy door). Chauvin V 98-99 No. 33; *ANE* 326-27 No. 20.□

M411.19.1§, ‡Curse by fish (actually enchanted person).
Ensorcelled Prince/Husband: *Alf* I 30,-(at midnight/claim); Burton I 79. Chauvin VI 56-58 No. 222; *ANE* 176 No. 13.□

M411.25.1§, ‡Daughter curses her father. (Cf. P248.4§).
Qamar al-Zamân and Budûr: *Alf* II 79,-(*shaykh al-naḥas*/ill-omened/harbinger of misfortune); Burton III 240,-(the wretched old fellow). Chauvin V 204-12 No. 120; *ANE* 341-45 No. 61.□

M412, Time of giving curse.
Ensorcelled Prince/Husband: *Alf* I 30,-(at midnight); Burton I 79. Chauvin VI 56-58 No. 222; *ANE* 176 No. 13.□

M422, Curse transferred to another person or thing.
Budûr and Jubayr ibn ¿Umayr: *Alf* II 239; Burton IV 238. Chauvin VII 93-94 No. 374; *ANE* 243-44 No. 83.□

M422.1§, ‡Curse: "May what is afflicting me afflict you!".
Budûr and Jubayr ibn ¿Umayr: *Alf* II 239,-(love); Burton IV 238. Chauvin VII 93-94 No. 374; *ANE* 243-44 No. 83.□

M424§, ‡Curse removed when certain matter is brought to pass.
Ensorcelled Prince/Husband: *Alf* I 30; Burton I 80,-(spell). Chauvin VI 56-58 No. 222; *ANE* 176 No. 13.□

M440.1§, ‡Curse: absence of blessedness (*barakah*). (Cf. D1705§, D1752§).
Anûshirawân and Village Damsel: *Alf* II 285,-cf.; Burton V 87-88. Chauvin VI 26-27 No. 198; *ANE* 106 No. 121.□

M451.3.1§, ‡Curse that food turns into poison for eater.
Falcon and Partridge: *Alf* II 32,-(prey curses predator/falcon: "may He "...); Burton III 139,-(may Allah cause what thou eatest of my flesh to be a killing poison in thy maw!). Chauvin II 227 No. 7; *ANE* 180 No. 48;
Ma¿rûf the Cobbler: *Alf* IV 290; Burton X 4. Chauvin VI 81-82 No. 250; *ANE* 291-93 No. 262.□

M500§, ‡Supplication (prayer that begs) for God's (deity's) boon (*da¿wah li*). See: *DOTTI*.
Sweep and Noble Lady: Infidelity Repaid: *Alf* II 191; Burton IV 130. Chauvin VI 148 No. 306; *ANE* 403-4 No. 72;
Three Wishes: *Alf* III 162; Burton VI 180-81. Chauvin VIII 51-52 No. 19; *ANE* 419-20 No. 199;
Jawdar and His Treacherous Brethren: *Alf* III 178, 184,-(solicited by son); Burton VI 214. Chauvin V 257-60 No. 154; *ANE* 244-45 No. 209;
Ibrâhîm and Jamîlah: *Alf* IV 221,-(for gratuity given); Burton IX 213. Chauvin VI 52-53 No. 218; *ANE* 227-29 No. 258.□

M511.1.1§, ‡Supplication: blessed be the womb and the loins that brought person into being. (Cf. M440.1§, Q195).

Jeweler's Wife and Qamar al-Zamân: *Alf* IV 266; Burton IX 302. Chauvin V 212-14 No. 121; *ANE* 345-47 No. 260.□

M514§, ‡Supplication: forgiveness of sins (redemption).
Mock Caliph/¿Alî al-Jawharî: *Alf* II 200,-(*'istighfâr*); Burton IV 148. Chauvin V 99-100 No. 174; *ANE* 304-5 No. 73;
Qamar al-Zamân and Budûr: *Alf* II 110,-("*yamḥû bi faḍlihi ¿annâ ¿aẓîma al-dhunûb*"/ruse/pleading for sinful act); Burton III 305,-("absolve us of the excess of our heinous sins"). Chauvin V 204-12 No. 120; *ANE* 341-45 No. 61.□

N. CHANCE AND FATE

N1.7§, ‡Betting between supernatural beings (jinn, devils, etc.). See: *DOTTI.*
Qamar al-Zamân and Budûr: *Alf* II 76,-(jinn); Burton III 234-35. Chauvin V 204-12 No. 120; *ANE* 341-45 No. 61.□

N2.0.5§, ‡Wagers with uneven stakes (e.g., "If I win you pay me one, if you win I pay you two"). See: *DOTTI*; *PSAE.*
Masrûr and Zayn al-Mawâṣif: *Alf* IV 57-59; Burton VIII 216-18. Chauvin VI 82-84 No. 251; *ANE* 294-95 No. 232.□

N2.7, Love wagered in game.
Masrûr and Zayn al-Mawâṣif: *Alf* IV 57-59; Burton VIII 216-18. Chauvin VI 82-84 No. 251; *ANE* 294-95 No. 232.□

N2.8.1§, ‡Loser of wager (contest) is to disrobe publicly.
Tawaddud: Slavegirl Sold and Regained: *Alf* II 318, III 4-7; Burton V 205-44. Chauvin 7: 117-19 No. 387; *ANE* 408 No. 157.□

N8.1§, ‡Coquettishness of (enticements, seductive moves by) beloved causes man to lose game. (Cf. C105.1§, K92.4.1§, T26, T34.2, T59.1§).
King ¿Umar al-Nu¿mân and Sons: *Alf* I 172; Burton II 104. Chauvin VI 112-24 No. 277; *ANE* 430-34 No. 39;
Masrûr and Zayn al-Mawâṣif: *Alf* IV 57-59; Burton VIII 216-18. Chauvin VI 82-84 No. 251; *ANE* 294-95 No. 232.□

N9.1, ‡Gambler loses everything. See: *DOTTI.*
Sandal-wood Merchant and Sharpers: *Alf* III 174; Burton VI 203. Chauvin VIII 60-62 No. 26; *ANE* 359-60 No. 205;
Masrûr and Zayn al-Mawâṣif: *Alf* IV 57-59; Burton VIII 216-18. Chauvin VI 82-84 No. 251; *ANE* 294-95 No. 232.□

N74§, ‡Wager on who (whose) is the better (more powerful, beautiful, valuable, etc.). (Cf. H1596.0.2§, T2.3§).
Nûr al-Dîn ¿Alî and Son: *Alf* I 70,-cf.; Burton I 213-14. Chauvin VI 102-6 No. 270; *ANE* 317-19 No. 22;
Qamar al-Zamân and Budûr: *Alf* II 73-76; Burton III 225. Chauvin V 204-12 No. 120; *ANE* 341-45 No. 61.□

N91.1§, Purchase of fisherman's catch without knowledge of net's contents. See: *DOTTI.* (Cf. N100.1.2.2§).
Three Apples: Hasty Uxoricide: *Alf* I 61; Burton I 187. Chauvin VI 144-45 No. 302; *ANE* 414-15 No. 21.□

N100.1.1§, ‡Predestined livelihoods. See: *DOTTI.* (Cf. A661.0.1.1.4§).
King Jalî¿âd and Shimâs: *Alf* IV 139, 155; Burton IX 44, 76. Chauvin VI 9-11 No. 184; *ANE* 237-38 No. 236.□

N100.1.1.0.1§, ‡One creature's livelihood cannot be taken by another.
Spy, Fifth Maiden/¿Umar al-Nu¿mân: *Alf* I 224; Burton II 207. *ANE* 432 No. 39/passim.□

N100.1.1.1§, ‡Livelihoods are not earned according to a creature's actions—(they are preordained). (Cf. A604.5.2§, J1016§, J2068.3§, N190.0.1§).
Fisherman and Afrit: Ingratitude: *Alf* I 14,-(poem); Burton I 38. Chauvin VI 23-25 No. 195; *ANE* 183-84 No. 8.□

N100.1.1.2§, ‡'[Even if] you labor as savagely as a beast, other than your [predestined] livelihood you will not retain'.
King Jalî¿âd and Shimâs: *Alf* IV 155,-cf./(*'irtikâb al-mashaqqah*); Burton IX 76,-(incurring hardships and travail). Chauvin VI 9-11 No. 184; *ANE* 237-38 No. 236.□

N100.1.2.1§, ‡Fisherman casts net only limited number of times (e.g., once, twice, etc.). See: *DOTTI.*
Fisherman and Afrit: Ingratitude: *Alf* I 14,-(four); Burton I 38. Chauvin VI 23-25 No. 195; *ANE* 183-84 No. 8.□

N100.1.2.2§, ‡Fisherman casts net "on someone's luck": catch is indicative of that person's luck or fortune (*bakht* or *sa¿d*). (Cf. N91.1§).

Three Apples: Hasty Uxoricide: *Alf* I 61; Burton I 187. Chauvin VI 144-45 No. 302; *ANE* 414-15 No. 21;
Anîs al-Jalîs: *Alf* I 141; Burton II 31,-("cast in my name"). Chauvin V 120-24 No. 58; *ANE* 316-17 No. 35;
Sindbâd's Fifth Voyage: *Alf* III 111,-(dive); Burton VI 55. Chauvin VII 21-24 No. 373E; *ANE* 386 No. 179;
Landsman ¿Abdallah and Merman ¿Abdallah: *Alf* IV 198; Burton IX 165. Chauvin V 6-7 No. 3; *ANE* 65-66 No. 256.□

N100.1.4§, ‡Prey thought of as "God sent" ("fortune sent") one's way.
King ¿Umar al-Nu¿mân and Sons: *Alf* I 168,-cf.; Burton II 89. Chauvin VI 112-24 No. 277; *ANE* 430-34 No. 39;
Water-fowl and Tortoise: *Alf* II 28,-(bird's thought); Burton III 130. Chauvin II 226-27 No. 5; *ANE* 444 No. 46.□

N100.2§, ‡Predestined sinning (fornication, theft, killing, or the like). (Cf. A604.3§).
King ¿Umar al-Nu¿mân and Sons: *Alf* I 208,-(brother-sister incest); Burton II 175. Chauvin VI 112-24 No. 277; *ANE* 430-34 No. 39;
Qamar al-Zamân and Budûr: *Alf* II 110; Burton III 305. Chauvin V 204-12 No. 120; *ANE* 341-45 No. 61;
al-'Amjad and al-'As¿ad: *Alf* II 112-13,-(incestuous desire); Burton III 309. Chauvin V 208-10 No. 120[.1]; *ANE* 341-42 No. 61/pt.;
Sweep and Noble Lady: Infidelity Repaid: *Alf* II 190; Burton IV 129,-(Allah fore ordained to us). Chauvin VI 148 No. 306; *ANE* 403-4 No. 72;
Mock Caliph/¿Alî al-Jawharî: *Alf* II 200,-(sinning,/is "*mastûr*"); Burton IV 148,-(written in the Book of Destiny). Chauvin V 99-100 No. 174; *ANE* 304-5 No. 73;
Mercury ¿Alî: *Alf* III 232,-(fornication); Burton VII 182,-(decreed). Chauvin V 248-50 No. 147; *ANE* 301-3 No. 225.□

N101, Inexorable fate. [*qaḍâ'/qadar*]. See: *DOTTI*; *GMC*. (Cf. V318§).
Copt Broker's Story: Lover's Sacrifices Repaid: *Alf* I 89,-(poem); Burton I 275. Chauvin VI 80 No. 249; *ANE* 313-14 No. 24;
Sindbâd and Porter: *Alf* III 83; Burton VI 4. Chauvin VII 1 No. 373; *ANE* 383-85 No. 179/pt.;
Poisoning from Flying Kite: *Alf* III 173; Burton VI 201-2. Chauvin 8: 33-34 No. 1; *ANE* 160-61, No. 181/passim;
Hasan of Basrah: *Alf* III 305, 310,-(poem); Burton VIII 14,-(doom), 21. Chauvin VII 29-35 No. 212A; *ANE* 207-10 No. 230;
¿Abdallah ibn Fâḍil: Treacherous Brothers: *Alf* IV 269; Burton IX 309,-(decreed). Chauvin V 2-4 No. 2; *ANE* 63-65 No. 261.□

N101.0.1§, ‡'The pen has [already] run with His Judgment'.
Eldest Lady's Story: Treacherous Sisters: *Alf* I 54; Burton I 163,-("reed of Destiny"). Chauvin V 4 No. 443; *ANE* 174-75 No. 19;
Ghânim ibn Ayyûb: *Alf* I 157; Burton II 76. Chauvin VI 14 No. 188; *ANE* 192-93 No. 36;
King ¿Umar al-Nu¿mân and Sons: *Alf* I 192,-(poem,/*mâ khuṭṭa bi al-qalami*); Burton II 140,-(what the "Reed of Doom" wrote). Chauvin VI 112-24 No. 277; *ANE* 430-34 No. 39;
Sayf al-Mulûk: *Alf* III 284; Burton VII 342,-(the Pen runneth with that He decreeth). Chauvin VII 64-73 No. 348; *ANE* 362-64 No. 229;
Hasan of Basrah: *Alf* IV 45; Burton VIII 127. Chauvin VII 29-35 No. 212A; *ANE* 207-10 No. 230;
Nûr al-Dîn and Maryam: *Alf* IV 103; Burton VIII 313-14,-(Reed). Chauvin V 52-54 No. 271; *ANE* 98-99 No. 233.□

N101.0.1.1§, ‡'Destiny cannot be erased (altered, escaped)'. (Cf. A604.3§).
Dûban and King Yûnân: *Alf* I 20,-(poem); Burton I 56. Chauvin V 275-76 No. 156; *ANE* 459 No. 9;
First Qalandar: Brother-Sister Incest: *Alf* I 40,-(poem); Burton I 107. Chauvin V 196-97 No. 115; *ANE* 337-38 No. 15;
Ḥammâd: Treacherous Bedouin: *Alf* II 20,-(poem); Burton III 111. Chauvin VI 124 n. 1 No. 277; *ANE* 200 No. 43.□

N101.0.2§, ‡'What is written on the forehead will [inevitably] be witnessed by the eye'.
King ¿Umar al-Nu¿mân and Sons: *Alf* I 183; Burton II 124. Chauvin VI 112-24 No. 277; *ANE* 430-34 No. 39;

Sayf al-Mulûk: *Alf* III 284; Burton VII 342. Chauvin VII 64-73 No. 348; *ANE* 362-64 No. 229.□

N101.0.3§, ‡'Nothing shall befall us except what God has written for us'.
House with the Belvedere: *Alf* III 168; Burton VI 191. Chauvin VIII 57-58 No. 23; *ANE* 223 No. 203.□

N101.5§, 'At the time destined, sight is blinded' (i.e., at the fated moment vigil (alertness) will be unavailing. See: *DOTTI*; *GMC*.
Copt Broker's Story: Lover's Sacrifices Repaid: *Alf* I 94,-cf./(poem); Burton I 275. Chauvin VI 80 No. 249; *ANE* 313-14 No. 24;
Water-fowl and Tortoise: *Alf* II 29; Burton III 131. Chauvin II 226-27 No. 5; *ANE* 444 No. 46;
Sparrow as Peacock's Vizier: *Alf* II 41; Burton III 162. Chauvin II 230 No. 20; *ANE* 398 No. 59;
¿Alî Shâr and Zumurrud: *Alf* II 224,-(poem); Burton IV 204,("When Destiny descends she blinds our eyes"). Chauvin V 89-91 No. 28; *ANE* 100-1 No. 82;
Hungry Eagle Snared: *Alf* IV 152,-(*¿Uqâb kâsir*); Burton IX 70,-("Ossifrage"/bone-breaking). Chauvin II 127-128 No. 133,-cf.□

N101.5.1§, ‡'Caution does not prevent [(alter)] fate'. See: *DOTTI*. (Cf. A604.3.1§).
Birds, Beasts, and Carpenter: *Alf* II 26; Burton III 124. Chauvin II 225-26 No. 1; *ANE* 126 No. 44;
Water-fowl and Tortoise: *Alf* II 29,-(when life-span has elapsed); Burton III 131. Chauvin II 226-27 No. 5; *ANE* 444 No. 46;
Sparrow as Peacock's Vizier: *Alf* II 41; Burton III 162. Chauvin II 230 No. 20; *ANE* 398 No. 59;
¿Alâ' al-Dîn Abû al-Shâmât: *Alf* II 149; Burton IV 35. Chauvin V 43-49 No. 18; *ANE* 85-87 No. 63;
Bulûqiya: *Alf* III 75; Burton V 386,-(destiny doeth away with dexterity). Chauvin VII 54 No. 77; *ANE* 130-32 No. 177;
Hasan of Basrah: *Alf* III 310,-(poem); Burton VIII 21. Chauvin VII 29-35 No. 212A; *ANE* 207-10 No. 230;
Nûr al-Dîn and Maryam: *Alf* IV 102-3,-(poem); Burton VIII 314. Chauvin V 52-54 No. 271; *ANE* 98-99 No. 233.□

N101.5.1.1§, ‡What is not to be will not be; what will be will be ('*Que sera sera*, ...').
King ¿Umar al-Nu¿mân and Sons: *Alf* I 260,-(poem); Burton II 279. Chauvin VI 112-24 No. 277; *ANE* 430-34 No. 39.□

N107.2§, ‡Occurrence of a mishap indicates that another (usually greater) has been averted.
Portress Amînah: Bitten Cheek: *Alf* I 59; Burton I 180. Chauvin V 98-99 No. 33; *ANE* 326-27 No. 20.□

N107.2.2§, ‡'What is unknown [and could have happened] must have been greater [calamity].' ("*mâ khafiya kâna 'a¿ẓam*"). (Cf. V540.0.1§).
Portress Amînah: Bitten Cheek: *Alf* I 59; Burton I 180,-(averting worse). Chauvin V 98-99 No. 33; *ANE* 326-27 No. 20;
Mercury ¿Alî: *Alf* III 238; Burton VII 1 193,-("but for Allah's word, it had been worse"). Chauvin V 248-50 No. 147; *ANE* 301-3 No. 225.□

N117.1§, ‡Person's livelihood is found asleep or dead.
Fisherman and Afrit: Ingratitude: *Alf* I 14,-(poem); Burton I 39,-(breadless). Chauvin VI 23-25 No. 195; *ANE* 183-84 No. 8.□

N120.2§, ‡Name (word, statement, etc.) harbinger of evil. See: *DOTTI*. (Cf. C434.2§).
Budûr and Jubayr ibn ¿Umayr: *Alf* II 240; Burton IV 239. Chauvin VII 93-94 No. 374; *ANE* 243-44 No. 83.□

N122.1.3§, ‡Unlucky buildings. See: *DOTTI*.
House with the Belvedere: *Alf* III 167; Burton VI 190. Chauvin VIII 57-58 No. 23; *ANE* 223 No. 203.□

N122.1.3.1§, ‡House of misfortunes: whoever inhabits it suffers ill-fate. See: *DOTTI*.
House with the Belvedere: *Alf* III 167; Burton VI 190. Chauvin VIII 57-58 No. 23; *ANE* 223 No. 203.□

N125.7§, ‡First to come from certain direction chosen for task.
¿Alî Shâr and Zumurrud: *Alf* II 227; Burton IV 210,-(king). Chauvin V 89-91 No. 28; *ANE* 100-1 No. 82.□

N126.3.1§, ‡Man offered as prey so as to placate predator (lion, tiger) chosen by casting lots.

Mercury ¿Alî: *Alf* III 229; Burton VII 177. Chauvin V 248-50 No. 147; *ANE* 301-3 No. 225.□

N131.6.1§, ‡Person thought to bring bad luck exiled (ordered to leave town).
Second Qalandar: Afrit's Wife: *Alf* I 50,-(ill fate); Burton I 137. Chauvin V 197-200 No. 116; *ANE* 338-39 No. 16.□

N134.2§, Person with physical deformity brings bad luck (harbinger of evil). See: *GMC*.
Barber's Fourth Brother: Illusionary Experiences: *Alf* I 116,-cf.; Burton I 333. Chauvin V 160-61 No. 84; *ANE* 119 No. 32.□

N134.2.1§, One-eyed person brings bad luck. See: *DOTTI*; *GMC*. (Cf. J1289.21§).
Second Qalandar: Afrit's Wife: *Alf* I 50; Burton I 137. Chauvin V 197-200 No. 116; *ANE* 338-39 No. 16.□

N134.2.1.1.1§, ‡Person with bad left eye surely brings bad luck.
Barber's Fourth Brother: Illusionary Experiences: *Alf* I 116; Burton I 334. Chauvin V 160-61 No. 84; *ANE* 119 No. 32.□

N134.2.2§, ‡Ugly person brings bad luck.
Second Qalandar: Afrit's Wife: *Alf* I 50; Burton I 138. Chauvin V 197-200 No. 116; *ANE* 338-39 No. 16.□

N146, Man not fated to die cannot be killed. See: *DOTTI*; *GMC*.
King ¿Umar al-Nu¿mân and Sons: *Alf* II 10-11; Burton III 94,-("live man findeth no slayer, and though slain he shall not die"). Chauvin VI 112-24 No. 277; *ANE* 430-34 No. 39.□

N147§, ‡Predestined circumstances of death: time, place, agent, instrument, etc. of mortal's death preordained.
First Qalandar: Brother-Sister Incest: *Alf* I 40-41,-(poem); Burton I 107. Chauvin V 196-97 No. 115; *ANE* 337-38 No. 15;
Bulûqiya: *Alf* III 78; Burton V 390. Chauvin VII 54 No. 77; *ANE* 130-32 No. 177;
Sindbâd's Sixth Voyage: *Alf* III 114,-(poem); Burton VI 62. Chauvin VII 24-27 No. 373F; *ANE* 386 No. 179;
Ibrâhîm and Jamîlah: *Alf* IV 228,-(poem); Burton IX 226. Chauvin VI 52-53 No. 218; *ANE* 227-29 No. 258;
Ma¿rûf the Cobbler: *Alf* IV 316,-(poem), 317,-(poem); Burton X 51,-("decree of the Decreer and His written destiny"), 53. Chauvin VI 81-82 No. 250; *ANE* 291-93 No. 262.□

N147.2§, ‡Precautions taken to escape death at the hands of certain creature (agent) fail. See: *DOTTI*.
Bulûqiya: *Alf* III 78; Burton V 390. Chauvin VII 54 No. 77; *ANE* 130-32 No. 177.□

N170.0.1§, ‡Life (the world, fate, luck, etc.) is a revolving wheel: ups and downs. See: *DOTTI*.
King ¿Umar al-Nu¿mân and Sons: *Alf* I 194,-(poem); Burton II 143. Chauvin VI 112-24 No. 277; *ANE* 430-34 No. 39.□

N190§, ‡Fate's inexplicable inequalities (injustices). (Cf. J1016§, V318.3§, V540.0.1§).
Wolf and Fox: *Alf* II 33,-(poem/*dahr*/Time); Burton III 141,-(fortune/camel). Chauvin II 227 No. 6; *ANE* 450 No. 47.□

N190.0.1§, ‡Inexplicable inequality in possessions (wealth, power, etc.).
Fisherman and Afrit: Ingratitude: *Alf* I 14; Burton I 38. Chauvin VI 23-25 No. 195; *ANE* 183-84 No. 8;
Anîs al-Jalîs: *Alf* I 140-41,-(poem); Burton II 31,-(xxx). Chauvin V 120-24 No. 58; *ANE* 316-17 No. 35;
Sindbâd and Porter: *Alf* III 82,-(poem); Burton VI 2. Chauvin VII 1 No. 373; *ANE* 383-85 No. 179/pt.□

N190.0.1.1§, ‡'God grants whomsoever He pleases without limit'. See: *DOTTI*.
Anîs al-Jalîs: *Alf* I 140-41,-(poem/God grants and withholds); Burton II 30,-(xxx). Chauvin V 120-24 No. 58; *ANE* 316-17 No. 35;
Bulûqiya/Hâsib/Queen of Vipers: *Alf* III 18; Burton V 298,-(He favoureth whom He will without compt). Chauvin VII 54 No. 77; *ANE* 130-32 No. 177;
Sindbâd and Porter: *Alf* III 82; Burton VI 2. Chauvin VII 1 No. 373; *ANE* 383-85 No. 179/pt.;
Ma¿rûf the Cobbler: *Alf* IV 308-9,-cf./(poem); Burton X 35. Chauvin VI 81-82 No. 250; *ANE* 291-93 No. 262.□

N190.0.1.2§, ‡'God changes a situation to its opposite in a blink of an eye'.

King ¿Umar al-Nu¿mân and Sons: *Alf* II 13,-(implicit); Burton III 97-98. Chauvin VI 112-24 No. 277; *ANE* 430-34 No. 39;
¿Alâ' al-Dîn Abû al-Shâmât: *Alf* II 158,-cf./(poem); Burton IV 54. Chauvin V 43-49 No. 18; *ANE* 85-87 No. 63;
Abû Muhammad Lazybones: *Alf* II 213,-(poem); Burton IV 173. Chauvin VI 64-67 No. 233; *ANE* 71-73 No. 78;
Hasan of Basrah: *Alf* IV 17,-(poem); Burton VIII 70. Chauvin VII 29-35 No. 212A; *ANE* 207-10 No. 230.□

N191.1§, ‡"A wretch's [(criminal's, tyrant's, etc.)] span of life lasts".
¿Alâ' al-Dîn Abû al-Shâmât: *Alf* II 167; Burton IV 70. Chauvin V 43-49 No. 18; *ANE* 85-87 No. 63.□

N196.1§, ‡Person drowns trying to save another from drowning.
Fuller and His Son: Drowned: *Alf* III 141; Burton VI 134. Chauvin VIII 36 No. 4; *ANE* 189 No. 184.□

N201, ‡Wish for exalted husband realized. See: *DOTTI*; *GMC*. (Cf. P169.1.4§, P458.1§).
Copt Broker's Story: Lover's Sacrifices Repaid: *Alf* I 91,-cf.; Burton I 267. Chauvin VI 80 No. 249; *ANE* 313-14 No. 24.□

N206§, ‡Wish for change in physical characteristics realized. See: *DOTTI*.
Three Wishes: *Alf* III 162; Burton VI 181. Chauvin VIII 51-52 No. 19; *ANE* 419-20 No. 199.□

N207§, ‡Person (animal, bird) with certain qualities fated to perform task.
Butcher Wardân and Bear Lover: *Alf* II 252; Burton IV 296. Chauvin V 177-78 No. 101; *ANE* 442-43 No. 101.□

N207.1§, ‡Task can be performed only by person with certain social qualities (e.g., kinship ties, name, or the like). (Cf. X704§).
Jawdar and His Treacherous Brethren: *Alf* III 183,-(name); Burton VI 223. Chauvin V 257-60 No. 154; *ANE* 244-45 No. 209;
Hasan of Basrah: *Alf* III 308,-(name); Burton VIII 18. Chauvin VII 29-35 No. 212A; *ANE* 207-10 No. 230.□

N211.1, Lost ring found in fish. (Polycrates). See: *ANE*; *DOTTI*; *GMC*.
Abû Qîr and Abû Ṣîr: *Alf* IV 195; Burton IX 159. Chauvin V 15-17 No. 10; *ANE* 75-77 No. 255.□

N211.4§, ‡Lost goods (money) recovered by rightful owner.
Sindbâd's Third Voyage: *Alf* III 99; Burton VI 32. Chauvin VII 15-18 No. 373C; *ANE* 385-86 No. 179.□

N255, Escape from one misfortune into worse. See: *DOTTI*; *GMC*.
al-'Amjad and al-'As¿ad: *Alf* II 131,-cf./(from slaver into his daughter); Burton III 343. Chauvin V 208-10 No. 120[.1]; *ANE* 341-42 No. 61/pt. 2;
Jawdar and His Treacherous Brethren: *Alf* III 193,-(from slave labor to shipwreck); Burton VI 241. Chauvin V 257-60 No. 154; *ANE* 244-45 No. 209;
Sayf al-Mulûk: *Alf* III 293,-(from one demon to cannibal ogre); Burton VII 359. Chauvin VII 64-73 No. 348; *ANE* 362-64 No. 229;
Jackals and Wolf as Umpire: *Alf* IV 167,-cf./(from possible loss of part to one's own to losing all to wolf); Burton IX 103. Chauvin II 223 No. 152/21; *ANE* 235 No. 252.□

N255.7§, ‡Escape from predator of one kind only to be faced by another of more lethal type.
Sindbâd's Third Voyage: *Alf* III 97,-(from ogre to man-swallowing serpent/*thu¿bân*); Burton VI 27-28. Chauvin VII 15-18 No. 373C; *ANE* 385-86 No. 179;
Sindbâd's Seventh Voyage: *Alf* III 117,-(from whale to man-swallowing vipers); Burton VI 75. Chauvin VII 26-29 No. 373G; *ANE* 386-87 No. 179.□

N260.1§, ‡Childless person dies before birth of long awaited child.
Bulûqiya/Ḥâsib/Queen of Vipers: *Alf* III 19; Burton V 299. Chauvin VII 54 No. 77; *ANE* 130-32 No. 177.□

N260.2§, ‡Sudden death: apparently healthy person dies mysteriously.
¿Alâ' al-Dîn Abû al-Shâmât: *Alf* II 163,-(beloved wife); Burton IV 62. Chauvin V 43-49 No. 18; *ANE* 85-87 No. 63.□

N279.1§, ‡Crime solved because judge (ruler) knew real culprit. See: *DOTTI*. (Cf. W37.6§).

Jewish Doctor's Story: Sororicide: *Alf* I 102; Burton I 299. Chauvin VI 89 No. 253; *ANE* 242 No. 26.□

N301.1§, ‡Natural calamity befalls community (earthquake, flood, volcano, etc.). See: *DOTTI*.
King Jalî¿âd and Shimâs: *Alf* IV 139; Burton IX 44-45. Chauvin VI 9 No. 184; *ANE* 237-38 No. 236.□

N301.2.1§, ‡Shipwreck. Ship (ferry-boat) sinks: many drown, much is lost. See: *DOTTI*; *PSAE*. (Cf. F962.1.1§).
Third Qalandar: Magnetic Mountain: *Alf* I 51; Burton I 141. Chauvin V 200-3 No. 117; *ANE* 340-41 No. 18;
Qamar al-Zamân and Budûr: *Alf* II 88; Burton III 260,-(capsized). Chauvin V 204-12 No. 120; *ANE* 341-45 No. 61;
Island King/Pious Jewish Merchant: *Alf* III 16; Burton V 291. Chauvin VI 161 No. 325; *ANE* 234 No. 174;
Bulûqiya/Ḥâsib/Queen of Vipers: *Alf* III 18; Burton V 298. Chauvin VII 54 No. 77; *ANE* 130-32 No. 177;
Jawdar and His Treacherous Brethren: *Alf* III 193; Burton VI 242. Chauvin V 257-60 No. 154; *ANE* 244-45 No. 209;
Jullanâr of the Sea: *Alf* III 263; Burton VII 295. Chauvin V 147-51 No. 73; *ANE* 248-51 No. 227;
¿Abdallah ibn Fâḍil: Treacherous Brothers: *Alf* IV 271; Burton IX 314. Chauvin V 2-4 No. 2; *ANE* 63-65 No. 261.□

N310.0.1§, ‡Predestined separation (of families or lovers). (Cf. A604.3§, Z122.7§).
Qamar al-Zamân and Budûr: *Alf* II 103,-(poem); Burton III 290. Chauvin V 204-12 No. 120; *ANE* 341-45 No. 61.□

N317, Separation of family by shipwreck. See: *DOTTI*.
Island King/Pious Jewish Merchant: *Alf* III 16; Burton V 291. Chauvin VI 161 No. 325; *ANE* 234 No. 174;
Sayf al-Mulûk: *Alf* III 282,-cf.-(foster brothers); Burton VII 336-37. Chauvin VII 64-73 No. 348; *ANE* 362-64 No. 229.□

N318.2.1§, ‡Girl accidentally elopes with robber thinking he is her sweetheart. (Cf. R12.3.1§).
¿Alî Shâr and Zumurrud: *Alf* II 226; Burton IV 208. Chauvin V 89-91 No. 28; *ANE* 100-1 No. 82.□

N324.2§, ‡Transformed person unknowingly slaughtered (killed). See: *DOTTI*.
First Shaykh: Sorceress Wife: *Alf* I 10,-(wife as cow); Burton I 30. Chauvin VII 129-30 No. 396; *ANE* 376-77 No. 5.□

N325.4.1§, ‡Insane princess murders her maid(s).
al-Rashîd and Omani Merchant: *Alf* IV 217; Burton IX 203. Chauvin VI 111-12 No. 276; *ANE* 201-2 No. 257.□

N327§, ‡The seemingly murdered proves to be alive. (One person thinks mistakenly he had killed another). See: *DOTTI*. (Cf. E68, S123.1, W10.9.2§).
Hunchback's Tale: Resuscitated: *Alf* I 125; Burton I 351. Chauvin V 180-82 No. 105; *ANE* 224-25 No. 23.□

N331.1.4§, ‡Horse kills rider when it becomes unruly. (Cf. K2351.5.3§).
al-'Amjad and al-'As¿ad: *Alf* II 118,-cf./(executioner's horse runs away); Burton III 320. Chauvin V 208-10 No. 120[.1]; *ANE* 341-42 No. 61/pt. 2;
Mercury ¿Alî: *Alf* III 230; Burton VII 178. Chauvin V 248-50 No. 147; *ANE* 301-3 No. 225.□

N331.1.5§, ‡Object (rock, shoe, knife, etc.) thrown causes unintentional killing. See: *DOTTI*. (Cf. N337.8§).
Omar and Young Badawî: Returning to be Executed: *Alf* II 288; Burton V 102. Chauvin V 216 No. 125; *ANE* 429-30 No. 130.□

N331.1.5.1§, ‡Man throws object which accidentally kills a supernatural being (jinni, fairy, afrit, or the like). See: *DOTTI*. (Cf. N337).
Trader and Afrit: Accidental Fairy-cide: *Alf* I 8; Burton I 24. Chauvin VI 22-23 No. 194; *ANE* 419-20 No. 4.□

N332.3, Serpent carried by bird lets poison drop into milk and poisons drinkers. See: *GMC*.

Poisoning from Flying Kite: *Alf* III 173; Burton VI 202. Chauvin VIII 59-60 No. 25; *ANE* 383,/passim No. 181.□

N334.9§, ‡Accidental tragic consequences of game or joke—miscellaneous.
Birds, Beasts, and Carpenter: *Alf* II 25,-cf./(young lion strikes man in jest); Burton III 122. Chauvin II 225-26 No. 1; *ANE* 126 No. 44.□

N335.3.1§, ‡Eating certain part of animal causes death to eater. Organ (heart, liver, etc.) contained residuals of lethal substance (poison, arrowhead, pellets, etc.).
Wild Ass and Jackal: *Alf* IV 142,-(heart); Burton IX 49. Chauvin II 219 No. 152/6; *ANE* 449 No. 241.□

N335.9.1§, ‡Person killed (devoured) by land predator (lion, tiger, wolf, etc.). See: *DOTTI*.
Lovers of Banû ¿Udhrah and Lion: *Alf* III 209,-(lion); Burton VII 123. Chauvin V 116-17 No. 52; *ANE* 274 No. 218/[2].□

N335.9.2§, ‡Person killed (devoured) by water-animal (crocodile, hippopotamus, or the like).
Jânshâh: *Alf* III 73; Burton V 381. Chauvin VII 39-44 No. 153; *ANE* 238-41 No. 178.□

N337, Accidental death through misdirected weapon. See: *PSAE*.
Abû Qîr and Abû Ṣîr: *Alf* IV 195; Burton IX 159. Chauvin V 15-17 No. 10; *ANE* 75-77 No. 255.□

N337.4§, ‡Accidental death (killing) through ignorance of nature of object found (it proves to be a weapon). See: *DOTTI*.
Abû Qîr and Abû Ṣîr: *Alf* IV 195; Burton IX 159. Chauvin V 15-17 No. 10; *ANE* 75-77 No. 255.□

N337.8§, ‡Accidental death (killing) from misdirected blow. See: *DOTTI*. (Cf. N330.0.1§, N331.1.5.1§).
Trader and Afrit: Accidental Fairy-cide: *Alf* I 8,-cf.; Burton I 24. Chauvin VI 22-23 No. 194; *ANE* 419-20 No. 4.□

N337.8.1§, ‡Serious injury (or death) from pushing (slipping or the like) during quarrel. See: *DOTTI*.
¿Azîz and ¿Azîzah: *Alf* I 273; Burton II 307. Chauvin V 144-45 No. 71; *ANE* 111-13 No. 41.□

N338, Death as result of mistaken identity: wrong person killed. See: *DOTTI*.
Jewish qâḍî and His Devout Wife: *Alf* III 10,-(infant); Burton V 256. Chauvin VI 154-55 No. 321; *ANE* 242 No. 163.□

N339.12.0.1§, ‡Death from accidental choking on food (bone, fruit, seed, kernel, etc. stuck in throat). See: *DOTTI*. (Cf. K951).
Hunchback's Tale: Resuscitated: *Alf* I 85-87,-(seeming death); Burton I 255. Chauvin V 180-82 No. 105; *ANE* 224-25 No. 23.□

N340.0.1§, ‡Hasty killing or condemnation regretted. See: *DOTTI*.
al-'Amjad and al-'As¿ad: *Alf* II 121,-(condemning sons); Burton III 324. Chauvin V 208-10 No. 120[.1]; *ANE* 341-42 No. 61/pt. 2;
Stolen Necklace/Hasty Accusation: *Alf* III 164; Burton VI 182. Chauvin VIII 53 No. 20; *ANE* 398 No. 200;
King Jalî¿âd and Shimâs: *Alf* IV 171; Burton IX 112. Chauvin VI 9 No. 184; *ANE* 237-38 No. 236.□

N340.0.1.2§, ‡Hasty killing of community notables (elders) regretted; in time of national crisis they are needed for their wisdom and experience. (Cf. P500.3.1§).
King Jalî¿âd and Shimâs: *Alf* IV 171, 174-75; Burton IX 112, 117. Chauvin VI 9 No. 184; *ANE* 237-38 No. 236.□

N340.0.2§, ‡Hasty condemnation reprimanded. See: *DOTTI*.
Ibrâhîm and Jamîlah: *Alf* IV 228; Burton IX 228. Chauvin VI 52-53 No. 218; *ANE* 227-29 No. 258.□

N342.1.2§, ‡Virtuous woman (maiden) hastily condemned as adulteress (unchaste). See: *DOTTI*. (Cf. K2112).
King Dissuaded by Virtuous Wife: *Alf* II 294; Burton V 121-22. Chauvin VII 120-21 No. 391; *ANE* 260-61 No. 138.□

N342.2, Stumbling over bloody corpse brings accusation of murder. See: *ANE*; *DOTTI*; *GMC*.
Hunchback's Tale: Resuscitated: *Alf* I 87,-(seemingly dead); Burton I 257,-(stone dead). Chauvin V 180-82 No. 105; *ANE* 224-25 No. 23;
Ibrâhîm and Jamîlah: *Alf* IV 227; Burton IX 26. Chauvin VI 52-53 No. 218; *ANE* 227-29 No. 258.□

N342.8§, ‡Person hastily accused of murder. See: *DOTTI*.
Ibrâhîm and Jamîlah: *Alf* IV 227,-cf.; Burton IX 226. Chauvin VI 52-53 No. 218; *ANE* 227-29 No. 258.□

N344.2.1§, ‡Father condemns innocent son to death, believing him guilty of seeking to seduce father's wife (concubine). See: *DOTTI*. (Cf. J571.5, K2111, T92.9).
al-'Amjad and al-'As¿ad: *Alf* II 116; Burton III 315. Chauvin V 208-10 No. 120[.1]; *ANE* 341-42 No. 61/pt. 2.□

N347.6.1§, ‡Person falsely accused refuses conciliation (compensation).
Stolen Necklace/Hasty Accusation: *Alf* III 164; Burton VI 182-83. Chauvin VIII 53 No. 20; *ANE* 398 No. 200;
Lovers of Basra/Ḍamrah: *Alf* III 212,-cf./(handsome); Burton VII 135. Chauvin V 118 No. 54; *ANE* 273 No. 220.□

N347.7§, ‡Chaste person accidentally suspected of sexual crime (fornication). (Cf. T331).
Ghânim ibn Ayyûb: *Alf* I 158,-(*faḥasha bihâ*/fornicated with her); Burton II 68,-(slept with her). Chauvin VI 14 No. 188; *ANE* 192-93 No. 36.□

N348.0.1§, Female unjustly accused of sexual offense. See: *DOTTI*. (Cf. K2112.1).
Rake's Trick Against Chaste Wife: *Alf* III 142; Burton VI 135. Chauvin VIII 37 No. 5; *ANE* 350-1 No. 185.□

N348.1§, Husband suspects chaste wife of unfaithfulness upon seeing trace of male visitor ('tracks of lion'). See: *DOTTI*.
King Dissuaded by Virtuous Wife: *Alf* II 294; Burton V 121. Chauvin VII 120-21 No. 391; *ANE* 260-61 No. 138;
Rake's Trick Against Chaste Wife: *Alf* III 142,-cf.; Burton VI 135. Chauvin VIII 37 No. 5; *ANE* 350-1 No. 185.□

N349.4§, ‡Lover (spouse) offended through misunderstanding. See: *DOTTI*. (Cf. H1385.5).
Lovers of Basra/Ḍamrah: *Alf* III 211; Burton VII 132. Chauvin V 118 No. 54; *ANE* 273 No. 220.□

N349.4.1.1§, ‡Friendly kiss on cheek (homosocial) thought to be homoerotic. See: *DOTTI*. (Cf. K2113.5§, P610§, P180.8.3.1§).
Budûr and Jubayr ibn ¿Umayr: *Alf* II 237; Burton IV 234. Chauvin VII 93-94 No. 374; *ANE* 243-44 No. 83.□

N349.4.1.2§, ‡Rough homosocial play (involving physical contact) thought to be homoerotic.
Lovers of Basra/Ḍamrah: *Alf* III 211; Burton VII 132. Chauvin V 118 No. 54; *ANE* 273 No. 220.□

N349.4.1.2.1§, ‡Disheveled appearance (hair, robe, undergarment, or the like) during homosocial play thought to be due to homoerotic activity.
Lovers of Basra/Ḍamrah: *Alf* III 211; Burton VII 133. Chauvin V 118 No. 54; *ANE* 273 No. 220.□

N349.6§, ‡Animal's actions misunderstood—helpful animal condemned. See: *DOTTI*. (Cf. B772).
King Sindbâd and Falcon: *Alf* I 18; Burton I 51-52. Chauvin V 289 No. 173; *ANE* 383 No. 10;
Jullanâr of the Sea: *Alf* III 266,-(helpfulness mistaken for aggression); Burton VII 296. Chauvin V 147-51 No. 73; *ANE* 248-51 No. 227.□

N352, Bird carries off ring which lover has taken from sleeping mistress's finger. See: *ANE*; *DOTTI*.
Qamar al-Zamân and Budûr: *Alf* II 97; Burton III 279,-(from band of her petticoat-trousers). Chauvin V 204-12 No. 120; *ANE* 341-45 No. 61.□

N352.4§, ‡Bird steals jewels: person falsely accused of theft. See: *DOTTI*. (Cf. B778.5§).
Stolen Necklace/Hasty Accusation: *Alf* III 164; Burton VI 182. Chauvin VIII 53 No. 20; *ANE* 398 No. 200.□

N365.3, Unwitting brother-sister incest. See: *DOTTI*; *GMC*.
King ¿Umar al-Nu¿mân and Sons: *Alf* I 207; Burton II 172. Chauvin VI 112-24 No. 277; *ANE* 430-34 No. 39.□

N365.3.4§, ‡Man meets a girl of unknown genealogy and marries her; she proves to be his sister. (Cf. N734.1.1§, T53.0.3§, T415.5).
King ¿Umar al-Nu¿mân and Sons: *Alf* I 207; Burton II 172. Chauvin VI 112-24 No. 277; *ANE* 430-34 No. 39.□

N381, Drop of honey causes chain of accidents. [Bloody feud between villages ensues]. See: *DOTTI*; *GMC*.
Drop of Honey: *Alf* III 145; Burton VI 143. Chauvin VIII 41-42 No. 9; *ANE* 171-72 No. 189.□

N383.2, Man falls dead when he realizes that he has eaten bread from flour used for abscess plaster. See: *ANE*; *GMC*.
Miser and Cheap Loaves of Bread: *Alf* III 142; Burton VI 138. Chauvin VIII 38 No. 6; *ANE* 303-4 No. 186.□

N385.2§, ‡Disaster caused by failing (neglecting) to praise (thank) God. See: *DOTTI*. (Cf. Q223.2.1§, V90§).
Water-fowl and Tortoise: *Alf* II 26, 29,-(*tasbîḥ*); Burton III 124, 125,-("neglecting to say Subhan' Allah, glory to God"). Chauvin II 227 No. 6; *ANE* 450 No. 46.□

N385.6§, ‡Haphazard claim (lie) has unfortunate outcome: lie coincidentally corresponds to partial truth. (Cf. N680.3§).
Three Apples: Hasty Uxoricide: *Alf* I 63; Burton I 191. Chauvin VI 144-45 No. 302; *ANE* 414-15 No. 21.□

N390§, ‡Person gets lost or marooned. (Cf. F962.1.2§).
Prince and Ogress: *Alf* I 19; Burton I 54. Chauvin VI 26 No. 197; *ANE* 329 No. 12;
Bulûqiya: *Alf* III 23; Burton V 305. Chauvin VII 54 No. 77; *ANE* 130-32 No. 177;
King's Favorite Son and Ogress: *Alf* III 143; Burton VI 140. Chauvin VIII 40-41 No. 8B; *ANE* 264 No. 188.□

N390.1.1§, ‡Person a-traveling falls asleep and finds self in enemy's camp. (Cf. N711.10§).
Prince and Ogress: *Alf* I 19,-cf.; Burton I 54-55. Chauvin VI 26 No. 197; *ANE* 329 No. 12;
King ¿Umar al-Nu¿mân and Sons: *Alf* I 166; Burton II 85. Chauvin VI 112-24 No. 277; *ANE* 430-34 No. 39.□

N390.1.2§, ‡Person a-traveling finds self in dangerous territory (e.g., lion infested region, ogres' territory, or the like).
King's Favorite Son and Ogress: *Alf* III 144; Burton VI 140. Chauvin VIII 40-41 No. 8B; *ANE* 264 No. 188;
Lovers of Banû ¿Udhrah and Lion: *Alf* III 207; Burton VII 118. Chauvin V 106-7 No. 37, 116 No. 52; *ANE* 274 No. 218/[2].□

N390.2§, ‡Person separated from rest of travelers (caravan, ship, train, etc.) and is left behind. (Cf. R130).
Qamar al-Zamân and Budûr: *Alf* II 106,-(ship); Burton III 295. Chauvin V 204-12 No. 120; *ANE* 341-45 No. 61;
Bulûqiya: *Alf* III 23,-(ship); Burton V 305. Chauvin VII 54 No. 77; *ANE* 130-32 No. 177;
Sindbâd's Second Voyage: *Alf* III 88; Burton VI 15. Chauvin VII 9-14 No. 373B; *ANE* 385 No. 179;
Ruined Baghdadi and His Slave-girl: *Alf* IV 132; Burton IX 30. Chauvin V 152-53 No. 75; *ANE* 353 No. 235.□

N393.1§, ‡Parasite (sponger) sneaks into a party of seemingly important men, accompanied by guards, thinking that they are being escorted to feast. They prove to be prisoners to be executed. See: *DOTTI*. (Cf. K454§, U247.1§).
Barber's Tale of Himself: Joins Doomed Party: *Alf* I 109; Burton I 317. Chauvin V 156-57 No. 80; *ANE* 115-17 No. 28.□

N396.1§, ‡Captor(s) fall(s) asleep: captives escape. (Cf. D1960).
King ¿Umar al-Nu¿mân and Sons: *Alf* I 247; Burton II 256. Chauvin VI 112-24 No. 277; *ANE* 430-34 No. 39.□

N399.2, Man's inordinate laughter brings unfortunate results. See: *DOTTI*. (Cf. N457§).
Merchant's Curious Wife: *Alf* I 6; Burton I 20. Chauvin V 179-80 No. 104; *ANE* 298-99 No. 3.□

N411.3, Fortune from informing foreign king of use of saddle, bridle, and stirrups. See: *ANE*.
Sindbâd's Fourth Voyage: *Alf* III 101; Burton VI 39. Chauvin VII 18-20 No. 373D; *ANE* 386 No. 179.□

N411.5, ‡Sandalwood merchant sells his product at high price in land lacking sandalwood. See: *DOTTI*. (Cf. P210.1.2§).

Sindbâd's Seventh Voyage: *Alf* III 119; Burton VI 73-74. Chauvin VII 26-29 No. 373G; *ANE* 386-87 No. 179;
Sandal-wood Merchant and Sharpers: *Alf* III 174,-cf.; Burton VI 203. Chauvin VIII 60-62 No. 26; *ANE* 359-60 No. 205.□

N424§, ‡Warrior wishes he were confronting adversary; discovers that he is.
King ¿Umar al-Nu¿mân and Sons: *Alf* I 168-70,-(valiant maiden); Burton II 95-97. Chauvin VI 112-24 No. 277; *ANE* 430-34 No. 39.□

N430.3§, ‡Expert clerk (accountant, writer, etc.) needed abroad.
Second Qalandar: Afrit's Wife: *Alf* I 42; Burton I 115. Chauvin V 197-200 No. 116; *ANE* 338-39 No. 16.□

N443§, ‡Dangerous secret(s) learned.
¿Alî ibn Bakkâr: *Alf* II 51,-(about an affair); Burton III 184. Chauvin V 153 No. 76; *ANE* 92-93 No. 60.□

N443.1§, ‡Person's knowledge of secret puts his life in danger.
¿Alî ibn Bakkâr: *Alf* II 51; Burton III 184. Chauvin V 153 No. 76; *ANE* 92-93 No. 60.□

N445§, ‡Following clandestine traveler (usually on nocturnal trip) leads to learning secret. (Cf. U115).
¿Abdallah ibn Fâḍil: Treacherous Brothers: *Alf* IV 268; Burton IX 306. Chauvin V 2-4 No. 2; *ANE* 63-65 No. 261.□

N451, Secrets overheard from animal (demon) conversation. See: *DOTTI*. (Cf. B566.2§).
Merchant's Curious Wife: *Alf* I 6,-(animals); Burton I 22. Chauvin V 179-80 No. 104; *ANE* 298-99 No. 3.□

N455.2.9.1§, ‡Murder conspiracy overheard: victim-to-be warned.
King ¿Umar al-Nu¿mân and Sons: *Alf* II 10; Burton III 94. Chauvin VI 112-24 No. 277; *ANE* 430-34 No. 39.□

N455.6.1§, ‡King (husband) learns of wife's infidelity through overheard conversation between maids (servants). See: *DOTTI*. (Cf. N701§).
Ensorcelled Prince/Husband: *Alf* I 27; Burton I 70. Chauvin VI 56-58 No. 222; *ANE* 176 No. 13.
Ghânim ibn Ayyûb: *Alf* I 157,-cf./(crime against husband's favorite consort); Burton II 66. Chauvin VI 14 No. 188; *ANE* 192-93 No. 36.□

N455.9, ‡Location of sought object learned from overheard conversation. See: *DOTTI*.
Hasan of Basrah: *Alf* IV 8,-(plumage); Burton VIII 53. Chauvin VII 29-35 No. 212A; *ANE* 207-10 No. 230.□

N456, Enigmatical smile (laugh) reveals secret knowledge. See: *DOTTI*; *GMC*; *PSAE*.
Merchant's Curious Wife: *Alf* I 6,-cf.; Burton I 20. Chauvin V 179-80 No. 104; *ANE* 298-99 No. 3.□

N457§, Reason for smiling (laughing) without cause is demanded. See: *DOTTI*; *GMC*. (Cf. N399.2).
Merchant's Curious Wife: *Alf* I 6; Burton I 20. Chauvin V 179-80 No. 104; *ANE* 298-99 No. 3;
Hishâm and Arab Youth: *Alf* II 184-85; Burton IV 103. Chauvin V 288 No. 172; *ANE* 222-23 No. 68.□

N457.1§, ‡Reason for smiling (laughing) in face of death (execution) is demanded. See: *DOTTI*.
Hishâm and Arab Youth: *Alf* II 184-85; Burton IV 103. Chauvin V 288 No. 172; *ANE* 222-23 No. 68.□

N464.1§, ‡Secret discovered while lousing person. See: *DOTTI*.
Tâj al-Mulûk: *Alf* I 299,-(*fallî lî shûshanî*); Burton III 29,-(untwisting hair knot). Chauvin V 126-28 No. 60; *ANE* 406-8 No. 40.□

N474.1§, ‡Husband learns wife's secret when she talks in her sleep. (Cf. J1148§).
Masrûr and Zayn al-Mawâṣif: *Alf* IV 65; Burton VIII 232. Chauvin VI 82-84 No. 251; *ANE* 294-95 No. 232.□

N477§, ‡Sudden wealth invites suspicion (accusation). See: *DOTTI*. (Cf. K2127, W257§).
Jawdar and His Treacherous Brethren: *Alf* III 196; Burton VI 246. Chauvin V 257-60 No. 154; *ANE* 244-45 No. 209;
Landsman ¿Abdallah and Merman ¿Abdallah: *Alf* IV 201; Burton IX 173. Chauvin V 6-7 No. 3; *ANE* 65-66 No. 256.□

N482, Secret learned by torture. See: *GMC*. (Cf. J1141.1.19.1§).
¿Alâ' al-Dîn Abû al-Shâmât: *Alf* II 175; Burton IV 83. Chauvin V 43-49 No. 18; *ANE* 85-87 No. 63;
Bulûqiya: *Alf* III 77; Burton V 389,-(sore beating). Chauvin VII 54 No. 77; *ANE* 130-32 No. 177;
Jawdar and His Treacherous Brethren: *Alf* III 193,-(*¿adhâb*); Burton VI 241,-("put to question"). Chauvin V 257-60 No. 154; *ANE* 244-45 No. 209.□

N482.3§, Secret (truth) learned by threatening with torture (execution). (Cf. J1141.1.19.1.1§).
Qamar al-Zamân and Budûr: *Alf* II 107,-cf./(with death if owner of goods not brought); Burton III 298-99. Chauvin V 204-12 No. 120; *ANE* 341-45 No. 61;
Sayf al-Mulûk: *Alf* III 280; Burton VII 333. Chauvin VII 64-73 No. 348; *ANE* 362-64 No. 229;
Hasan of Basrah: *Alf* IV 14; Burton VIII 65. Chauvin VII 29-35 No. 212A; *ANE* 207-10 No. 230.□

N482.3.1§, Secret learned by threatening to have person (mother, daughter, etc.) dipped in boiling water. See: *DOTTI*; *GMC*.
Hasan of Basrah: *Alf* IV 14; Burton VIII 65. Chauvin VII 29-35 No. 212A; *ANE* 207-10 No. 230.□

N504.1§, ‡Finding wild honey as treasure.
Bulûqiya/Ḥâsib/Queen of Vipers: *Alf* III 19-20; Burton V 300. Chauvin VII 54 No. 77; *ANE* 130-32 No. 177;
Drop of Honey: *Alf* III 145,-cf.; Burton VI 143. Chauvin VIII 41-42 No. 9; *ANE* 171-72 No. 189.□

N504.2§, ‡Sunken (abandoned) ship as treasure.
Sindbâd's Sixth Voyage: *Alf* III 113; Burton VI 59. Chauvin VII 24-27 No. 373F; *ANE* 386 No. 179.□

N511, Treasure in ground. See: *DOTTI*; *GMC*.
Qamar al-Zamân and Budûr: *Alf* II 105; Burton III 294. Chauvin V 204-12 No. 120; *ANE* 341-45 No. 61.□

N512, ‡Treasure in underground chamber (cavern). See: *DOTTI*; *PSAE*. (Cf. N520§).
Qamar al-Zamân and Budûr: *Alf* II 105; Burton III 294. Chauvin V 204-12 No. 120; *ANE* 341-45 No. 61;
Butcher Wardân and Bear Lover: *Alf* II 252-53,-(al-Ḥâkim bi 'Amri-'Allâh); Burton IV 296. Chauvin V 177-78 No. 101; *ANE* 442-43 No. 101.□

N520§, ‡Treasure (riches) hidden in tomb (grave, cemetery). See: *DOTTI*; *PSAE*. (Cf. N512).
City of Brass: *Alf* III 132; Burton VI 113. Chauvin V 32-35 No. 16; *ANE* 146-50 No. 180;
¿Abdallah ibn Fâḍil: Treacherous Brothers: *Alf* IV 273,-cf.; Burton IX 323. Chauvin V 2-4 No. 2; *ANE* 63-65 No. 261.□

N527.3§, ‡Lost gem (diamond, ring, etc.) found in bird's stomach (gizzard).
Qamar al-Zamân and Budûr: *Alf* II 105; Burton III 294. Chauvin V 204-12 No. 120; *ANE* 341-45 No. 61.□

N531, Treasure discovered through a dream. See: *DOTTI*; *GMC*.
Third Qalandar: Magnetic Mountain: *Alf* I 52,-cf.; Burton I 142. Chauvin V 200-3 No. 117; *ANE* 340-41 No. 18.□

N531.7§, ‡Treasure discovered through supernatural voice (*hâtif*).
Island King/Pious Jewish Merchant: *Alf* III 16-17; Burton V 291. Chauvin VI 161 No. 325; *ANE* 234 No. 174.□

N534, Treasure discovered by accident. See: *DOTTI*; *GMC*.
Butcher Wardân and Bear Lover: *Alf* II 252; Burton IV 296. Chauvin V 177-78 No. 101; *ANE* 442-43 No. 101.□

N534.7.2§, ‡Man finds treasure while plowing field.
Ma¿rûf the Cobbler: *Alf* IV 304; Burton X 28. Chauvin VI 81-82 No. 250; *ANE* 291-93 No. 262.□

N538.2, Treasure from defeated giant. See: *DOTTI*; *GMC*.
Abû Muḥammad Lazybones: *Alf* II 216,-(afrit); Burton IV 178. Chauvin VI 64-67 No. 233; *ANE* 71-73 No. 78.□

N543, ‡Certain person to find treasure. See: *DOTTI*.
Jawdar and His Treacherous Brethren: *Alf* III 183,-(name); Burton VI 222-23. Chauvin V 257-60 No. 154; *ANE* 244-45 No. 209;

Hasan of Basrah: *Alf* III 308,-cf./(name); Burton VIII 18. Chauvin VII 29-35 No. 212A; *ANE* 207-10 No. 230.□

N543.4§, ‡Only one person can overcome treasure's protective measures (*raṣad*/incantations) and open it. (Cf. D731, N207§).
Jawdar and His Treacherous Brethren: *Alf* III 183,-cf.; Burton VI 222-23. Chauvin V 257-60 No. 154; *ANE* 244-45 No. 209;
Butcher Wardân and Bear Lover: *Alf* II 252; Burton IV 296. Chauvin V 177-78 No. 101; *ANE* 442-43 No. 101.□

N555, ‡Time favorable for unearthing treasure.
Jawdar and His Treacherous Brethren: *Alf* III 185,-(unspecified); Burton VI 227. Chauvin V 257-60 No. 154; *ANE* 244-45 No. 209.□

N581.3.1§, ‡Mechanical statue of armed human guards treasure. (Cf. D1620.1.2, E422.9.1.1§).
Third Qalandar: Magnetic Mountain: *Alf* I 51,-cf.; Burton I 141. Chauvin V 200-3 No. 117; *ANE* 340-41 No. 18;
City of Brass: *Alf* III 137; Burton VI 118. Chauvin V 32-35 No. 16; *ANE* 146-50 No. 180.□

N582, Serpent guards treasure. See: *DOTTI*; *GMC*; *PSAE*.
Jawdar and His Treacherous Brethren: *Alf* III 186,-("two snakes"); Burton VI 229,-("dragons"). Chauvin V 257-60 No. 154; *ANE* 244-45 No. 209.□

N582.1§, ‡Viper guards treasure. See: *DOTTI*; *PSAE*. (Cf. B3.2§).
Bulûqiya: *Alf* III 26-27; Burton V 312. Chauvin VII 54 No. 77; *ANE* 130-32 No. 177;
Sindbâd's Seventh Voyage: *Alf* III 117; Burton VI 69. Chauvin VII 26-29 No. 373G; *ANE* 386-87 No. 179.□

N610.1.0.2§, ‡Person attending call of nature observes (witnesses) crime committed (or planned).
Ma¿rûf the Cobbler: *Alf* IV 316,-(in *bayt al-râḥah*); Burton X 51,-(in "Chapel of Ease"). Chauvin VI 81-82 No. 250; *ANE* 291-93 No. 262.□

N610.3.1§, ‡Sex orgy (group sex) accidentally witnessed. (Cf. T402§).
Shahriyâr and Shâhzamân: *Alf* I 3; Burton I 6, 9. Chauvin V 188-91 No. 111; *ANE* 370-71 No. 1.□

N616§, ‡Confession to crime inadvertently made. (Cf. J1148§, J224.1§).
Ḥammâd: Treacherous Bedouin: *Alf* II 20; Burton III 104ff. Chauvin VI 124 n. 1 No. 277; *ANE* 200 No. 43.□

N616.1§, ‡Dispute (quarrel) over division of booty (bribe) betrays commission of crime.
Jawdar and His Treacherous Brethren: *Alf* III 193; Burton VI 241. Chauvin V 257-60 No. 154; *ANE* 244-45 No. 209.□

N619.2§, ‡Clue (evidence) to solving crime accidentally (unintentionally) discovered. See: *DOTTI*.
Three Apples: Hasty Uxoricide: *Alf* I 64; Burton I 193. Chauvin VI 144-45 No. 302; *ANE* 414-15 No. 21;
al-'Amjad and al-'As¿ad: *Alf* II 119-20; Burton III 323. Chauvin V 208-10 No. 120[.1]; *ANE* 341-42 No. 61/pt. 2;
Stolen Necklace/Hasty Accusation: *Alf* III 164; Burton VI 183. Chauvin VIII 53 No. 20; *ANE* 398 No. 200.□

N619.2.2§, ‡Physical evidence of crime accidentally found.
Three Apples: Hasty Uxoricide: *Alf* I 64,-(apple); Burton I 193. Chauvin VI 144-45 No. 302; *ANE* 414-15 No. 21.□

N619.2.2.1.1§, ‡Love letter by accuser accidentally found: it establishes innocence of accused. See: *DOTTI*.
al-'Amjad and al-'As¿ad: *Alf* II 119-20; Burton III 323. Chauvin V 208-10 No. 120[.1]; *ANE* 341-42 No. 61/pt. 2.□

N619.2.2.2§, ‡Person carrying (transporting) human corpse accidentally apprehended.
al-'Amjad and al-'As¿ad: *Alf* II 126; Burton III 337. Chauvin V 208-10 No. 120[.1]; *ANE* 341-42 No. 61/pt. 2.□

N636§, ‡Container(s) of ordinary goods purchased prove to be filled with gold (gems, or the like).
Qamar al-Zamân and Budûr: *Alf* II 107,-(olive-jars); Burton III 298. Chauvin V 204-12 No. 120; *ANE* 341-45 No. 61.□

N649.2§, ‡Concoction of harmful substances proves beneficial. (Cf. F959.9.0.1§).
Nûr al-Dîn and Maryam: *Alf* IV 117; Burton VIII 342. Chauvin V 52-54 No. 271; *ANE* 98-99 No. 233.□

N650, Life saved by accident.
King ¿Umar al-Nu¿mân and Sons: *Alf* II 10; Burton III 93-94. Chauvin VI 112-24 No. 277; *ANE* 430-34 No. 39.□

N659.6§, ‡Criminal's plan accidentally foiled. See: *DOTTI*; *PSAE*. (Cf. K1627.1§).
Ma¿rûf the Cobbler: *Alf* IV 316; Burton X 51. Chauvin VI 81-82 No. 250; *ANE* 291-93 No. 262.□

N659.6.1§, ‡Would-be killer's plan accidentally foiled (interrupted). See: *DOTTI*; *PSAE*.
King ¿Umar al-Nu¿mân and Sons: *Alf* II 10,-(mother walks in); Burton III 94. Chauvin VI 112-24 No. 277; *ANE* 430-34 No. 39;
al-'Amjad and al-'As¿ad: *Alf* II 118,-(executioner's horse runs away); Burton III 320. Chauvin V 208-10 No. 120[.1]; *ANE* 341-42 No. 61/pt. 2;
Ma¿rûf the Cobbler: *Alf* IV 316; Burton X 51. Chauvin VI 81-82 No. 250; *ANE* 291-93 No. 262.□

N660, ‡Accidental [extraordinary] escapes. (Cf. R177§).
Nûr al-Dîn and Maryam: *Alf* IV 108,-cf./(from execution); Burton VIII 324. Chauvin V 52-54 No. 271; *ANE* 98-99 No. 233.□

N660.1§, ‡Token from narrow escape from death. (Cf. F1068.1).
Sindbâd's First Voyage: *Alf* III 84; Burton VI 5. Chauvin VII 7-9 No. 373A; *ANE* 385 No. 179.□

N660.1.2§, ‡Missing flesh (organs) as token of narrow escape from drowning (being eaten by fish).
Sindbâd's First Voyage: *Alf* III 84; Burton VI 7. Chauvin VII 7-9 No. 373A; *ANE* 385 No. 179.□

N663§, ‡Prey escapes when predator is suddenly attacked by larger enemy. See: *DOTTI*. (Cf. K1626).
Mouse and Cat: *Alf* IV 136,-(mouse released by cat); Burton IX 38. Chauvin II 218 No. 152/2; *ANE* 305-6 No. 237;
Crow and Viper: *Alf* IV 141; Burton IX 46. Chauvin II 219 No. 152/5; *ANE* 162 No. 240.□

N680.3§, ‡Lucky liar: lie becomes truth by accident. See: *DOTTI*. (Cf. J679.5§, N385.6§, Q194§).
al-'Amjad and al-'As¿ad: *Alf* II 124,-(concerning house, servant/mamluk); Burton III 332-33. Chauvin V 208-10 No. 120[.1]; *ANE* 341-42 No. 61/pt. 2;
Ma¿rûf the Cobbler: *Alf* IV 308,-ff.; Burton X 34. Chauvin VI 81-82 No. 250; *ANE* 291-93 No. 262.□

N683.1§, ‡Female masking as man accidentally selected ruler (king, judge). See: *DOTTI*. (Cf. K1837.8, T315.2.6.1§).
Qamar al-Zamân and Budûr: *Alf* II 100,-cf./(groom and successor to king); Burton III 284. Chauvin V 204-12 No. 120; *ANE* 341-45 No. 61;
¿Alî Shâr and Zumurrud: *Alf* II 227; Burton IV 210,-(sultan). Chauvin V 89-91 No. 28; *ANE* 100-1 No. 82.□

N694.3§, Apparently dead man handed around. Revives—(bone in throat). See: *DOTTI*; *GMC*.
Hunchback's Tale: Resuscitated: *Alf* I 87; Burton I 255–352. Chauvin V 180-82 No. 105; *ANE* 224-25 No. 23.□

N701§, ‡Accidental discovery of infidelity: clandestine (sinful) lovers surprised together. See: *DOTTI*. (Cf. K1210.0.1§, K1551, N455.6.1§, N619§, T40§).
Ebony Horse: *Alf* II 256-57,-(unchastity); Burton V 9. Chauvin V 221-31 No. 130; *ANE* 172-74 No. 103;
Lady's Lovers as Pursuer and Fugitive: *Alf* III 143; Burton VI 138. Chauvin VIII 38-39 No. 7; *ANE* 267 No. 187.□

N701.1§, ‡Man returns home unexpectedly and finds wife (daughter) with paramour. See: *DOTTI*. (Cf. K1551, T40§).
Shahriyâr and Shâhzamân: *Alf* I 2; Burton I 4. Chauvin V 188-91 No. 111; *ANE* 370-71 No. 1.□

N701.2§, ‡Lover hidden in girl's (woman's) room accidentally discovered (by father, husband, etc.). See: *DOTTI*.
Tâj al-Mulûk: *Alf* I 303-4; Burton III 41. Chauvin V 126-28 No. 60; *ANE* 406-8 No. 40.□

N711.8§, ‡Lover sees beloved first while she is looking out of window. See: *DOTTI*. (Cf. T157, T16.3§).

¿Azîz and ¿Azîzah: *Alf* I 268; Burton II 300. Chauvin V 144-45 No. 71; *ANE* 111-13 No. 41.□

N711.9§, ‡Lover sees beloved first at marketplace (shop). See: *DOTTI*. (Cf. T31.4§).
¿Alî ibn Bakkâr: *Alf* II 41; Burton III 163. Chauvin V 153 No. 76; *ANE* 92-93 No. 60.□

N711.10§, ‡Hero sees maiden first in enemy's camp (land) and he is enamored. See: *DOTTI*. (Cf. T95.0.1).
King ¿Umar al-Nu¿mân and Sons: *Alf* I 166; Burton II 87. Chauvin VI 112-24 No. 277; *ANE* 430-34 No. 39.□

N722§, ‡Runaway machine carries youth to maiden (or vice versa) when it stops. (Cf. F414.1, P5.3.3§, T381.1.3§).
Ebony Horse: *Alf* II 256; Burton V 7. Chauvin V 221-31 No. 130; *ANE* 172-74 No. 103.□

N722.1§, ‡Youth testing flying machine (mechanical horse) lands on maiden's palace: they are enamored.
Ebony Horse: *Alf* II 255-56; Burton V 7. Chauvin V 221-31 No. 130; *ANE* 172-74 No. 103.□

N723.1§, ‡Drunken man lies down in basket he sees by the side of road: he is drawn up to female's apartment. (Cf. B582.2.1, K1343.1, P196.2§).
Isḥâq al-Mûṣilî and Khadîjah bint al-Ḥasan: *Alf* II 185; Burton IV 119. Chauvin V 241-42 No. 142; *ANE* 232 No. 71.□

N730, Accidental reunion of families. See: *DOTTI*; *GMC*.
King ¿Umar al-Nu¿mân and Sons: *Alf* II 21; Burton III 114. Chauvin VI 112-24 No. 277; *ANE* 430-34 No. 39;
Island King/Pious Jewish Merchant: *Alf* III 17-18; Burton V 293-94. Chauvin VI 161 No. 325; *ANE* 234 No. 174.□

N730.1.1§, ‡At reunion, brother and sister embrace and kiss each other. See: *DOTTI*. (Cf. T49.1.1§).
King ¿Umar al-Nu¿mân and Sons: *Alf* I 214; Burton II 186. Chauvin VI 112-24 No. 277; *ANE* 430-34 No. 39;
Ḥammâd: Treacherous Bedouin: *Alf* II 18-19,-(return from combat); Burton III 109. Chauvin VI 124 n. 1 No. 277; *ANE* 200 No. 43.□

N730.1.1.1§, ‡At reunion, brother and sister faint in each other's arms.
King ¿Umar al-Nu¿mân and Sons: *Alf* I 214; Burton II 186,-(fell down in fainting fit). Chauvin VI 112-24 No. 277; *ANE* 430-34 No. 39.□

N730.1.2§, ‡At reunion, lovers faint in each other's arms. See: *DOTTI*.
Uns al-Wujûd and al-Ward: *Alf* II 282-83; Burton V 61. Chauvin VI 127-29 No. 282; *ANE* 438 No. 104.□

N730.1.3§, ‡At reunion, brothers (half brothers, stepbrothers) embrace and kiss each other.
al-'Amjad and al-'As¿ad: *Alf* II 131; Burton III 347. Chauvin V 208-10 No. 120[.1]; *ANE* 341-42 No. 61/pt. 2;
Island King/Pious Jewish Merchant: *Alf* III 17,-cf.; Burton V 293. Chauvin VI 161 No. 325; *ANE* 234 No. 174.□

N730.3§, ‡At reunion, spouse's (husband's, wife's) expression of affection is restrained. (Cf. P210.0.3§, T202.3§).
King ¿Umar al-Nu¿mân and Sons: *Alf* I 215,-cf.; Burton II 188. Chauvin VI 112-24 No. 277; *ANE* 430-34 No. 39.□

N731, ‡Unexpected meeting of father and son.
Shahriyâr and Shahrzâd: *Alf* IV 317,-cf./(presented with his sons of whose birth he had no knowledge); Burton X 54. Chauvin V 190-91 No. 111/pt.; *ANE* 371 No. 1.□

N731.4, ‡At execution block condemned man discovered to be king's unknown son. See: *DOTTI*. (Cf. P230.9.2§, W37.5§).
Ibrâhîm and Jamîlah: *Alf* IV 228; Burton IX 227. Chauvin VI 52-53 No. 218; *ANE* 227-29 No. 258.□

N731.4.1§, ‡Condemned person(s) discovered to be king's close relative.
King ¿Umar al-Nu¿mân and Sons: *Alf* II 11; Burton III 99. Chauvin VI 112-24 No. 277; *ANE* 430-34 No. 39;
Ibrâhîm and Jamîlah: *Alf* IV 228; Burton IX 227. Chauvin VI 52-53 No. 218; *ANE* 227-29 No. 258.□

N733, Accidental meeting of brothers. See: *DOTTI*.
al-'Amjad and al-'As¿ad: *Alf* II 131,-cf.; Burton III 345. Chauvin V 208-10 No. 120[.1]; *ANE* 2 341-42 No. 61/pt.□

N733.3, Joseph and his brethren. Elder brothers unwittingly come to maltreated youngest in great need. See: *DOTTI*; *GMC*. (Cf. K2211.0.1).
Jawdar and His Treacherous Brethren: *Alf* III 195,-(simile/'proverbial usage'); Burton VI 244. Chauvin V 257-60 No. 154; *ANE* 244-45 No. 209.□

N734, Accidental meeting of brother and sister. See: *DOTTI*.
King ¿Umar al-Nu¿mân and Sons: *Alf* I 211-14; Burton II 179-87. Chauvin VI 112-24 No. 277; *ANE* 430-34 No. 39.□

N734.1.1§, ‡Man buys a slave-girl who proves to be his sister—she was abducted and sold into slavery. See: *DOTTI*. (Cf. N365.3.4§, T471.1).
King ¿Umar al-Nu¿mân and Sons: *Alf* I 199; Burton II 154. Chauvin VI 112-24 No. 277; *ANE* 430-34 No. 39.□

N734.3§, ‡Woman captive (prisoner) brought before king for punishment proves to be his sister. (Cf. R156).
King ¿Umar al-Nu¿mân and Sons: *Alf* II 11, 13,-(half sister); Burton III 97. Chauvin VI 112-24 No. 277; *ANE* 430-34 No. 39.□

N737, Accidental reunion of lovers. See: *DOTTI*.
Ghânim ibn Ayyûb: *Alf* I 159-60,-cf.; Burton II 72. Chauvin VI 14 No. 188; *ANE* 192-93 No. 36;
Ruined Baghdadi and His Slave-girl: *Alf* IV 130,-cf./(meeting); Burton IX 25. Chauvin V 152-53 No. 75; *ANE* 353 No. 235.□

N738.1.1§, ‡Captive proves to be victor's nephew. (He was about to be executed).
King ¿Umar al-Nu¿mân and Sons: *Alf* II 11,-(sister's son); Burton III 99. Chauvin VI 112-24 No. 277; *ANE* 430-34 No. 39.□

N741, ‡Unexpected meeting of husband and wife. See: *DOTTI*.
¿Alâ' al-Dîn Abû al-Shâmât: *Alf* II 177; Burton IV 88. Chauvin V 43-49 No. 18; *ANE* 85-87 No. 63;
¿Abdallah ibn Fâḍil: Treacherous Brothers: *Alf* IV 287; Burton IX 348. Chauvin V 2-4 No. 2; *ANE* 63-65 No. 261.□

N741.4, ‡Husband and wife reunited after long separation and tedious quest. See: *DOTTI*. (Cf. T96).
¿Alâ' al-Dîn Abû al-Shâmât: *Alf* II 177; Burton IV 88-89. Chauvin V 43-49 No. 18; *ANE* 85-87 No. 63;
Hasan of Basrah: *Alf* IV 37,-cf./(they meet), 54-55; Burton VIII 109, 144-45. Chauvin VII 29-35 No. 212A; *ANE* 207-10 No. 230.□

N747§, ‡Accidental meeting of victim (hero, heroine) and criminal (villain). See: *DOTTI*. (Cf. H11.1, Q550.0.1§).
King ¿Umar al-Nu¿mân and Sons: *Alf* II 15,-ff.,/(arrested as robber); Burton III 101. Chauvin VI 112-24 No. 277; *ANE* 430-34 No. 39.□

N748§, ‡Accidental meeting of separated friends, descendants of friends, or foster relatives.
Sayf al-Mulûk: *Alf* III 292,-(childhood friend); Burton VII 355. Chauvin VII 64-73 No. 348; *ANE* 362-64 No. 229;
Ma¿rûf the Cobbler: *Alf* IV 294,-(childhood friends); Burton X 9. Chauvin VI 81-82 No. 250; *ANE* 291-93 No. 262.□

N748.1§, ‡Accidental meeting of friend's son (daughter).
Budûr and Jubayr ibn ¿Umayr: *Alf* II 236,-(daughter); Burton IV 233. Chauvin VII 93-94 No. 374; *ANE* 243-44 No. 83;
al-Rashîd and Omani Merchant: *Alf* IV 215; Burton IX 201. Chauvin VI 111-12 No. 276; *ANE* 201-2 No. 257.□

N764.1§, ‡Unexpected meeting with self-banished man (in wilderness). (Cf. F567.4§).
Hammâd: Treacherous Bedouin: *Alf* II 16; Burton III 105. Chauvin VI 112-24 No. 277; *ANE* 430-34 No. 43;
Lovers of Banû ¿Udhrah and Lion: *Alf* III 207; Burton VII 118. Chauvin V 116-17 No. 52; *ANE* 274 No. 218/[2];

Ma¿rûf the Cobbler: *Alf* IV 294,-(in strange nation); Burton X 9. Chauvin VI 81-82 No. 250; *ANE* 291-93 No. 262.□

N765, ‡Meeting with robber band. See: *DOTTI*. (Cf. P475.1.0.1§).
Barber's Fifth Brother: Daydreams/Defeats Robbers: *Alf* I 120; Burton I 349. Chauvin V 161 No. 85; *ANE* 119-20 No. 33.□

N769.1§, ‡Person(s) given up for dead found alive. See: *DOTTI*; *PSAE*. (Cf. F989.26§, K1889.2).
¿Alî ibn Bakkâr: *Alf* II 59,-(reported as dead); Burton III 198. Chauvin V 153 No. 76; *ANE* 92-93 No. 60;
¿Alâ' al-Dîn Abû al-Shâmât: *Alf* II 177; Burton IV 88. Chauvin V 43-49 No. 18; *ANE* 85-87 No. 63;
Jewish qâḍî and His Devout Wife: *Alf* III 10; Burton V 256. Chauvin VI 154-55 No. 321; *ANE* 242 No. 163;
Shipwrecked Woman and Her Child: *Alf* III 12,-(infant); Burton V 260. Chauvin VI 160 No. 324; *ANE* 379 No. 164;
Sayf al-Mulûk: *Alf* III 292; Burton VII 355. Chauvin VII 64-73 No. 348; *ANE* 362-64 No. 229.□

N771.0.2§, ‡Person abandoned in cave (pit, well): adventures follow. See: *DOTTI*. (Cf. S146.2).
Bulûqiya/Ḥâsib/Queen of Vipers: *Alf* III 20; Burton V 301. Chauvin VII 54 No. 77; *ANE* 130-32 No. 177.□

N774, Adventures from pursuing enchanted animal (hind, boar, bird). See: *DOTTI*; *GMC*.
Jânshâh: *Alf* III 41,-(gazelle); Burton V 332. Chauvin VII 39-44 No. 153; *ANE* 238-41 No. 178;
King's Favorite Son and Ogress: *Alf* III 144,-cf.; Burton VI 140. Chauvin VIII 40-41 No. 8B; *ANE* 264 No. 188.□

N793.1§, ‡Mystic (spiritual) experience while in cave (in mountain). See: *DOTTI*. (Cf. F779.1§, Z186.8.2.2§).
Bulûqiya/Ḥâsib/Queen of Vipers: *Alf* III 20; Burton V 302ff. Chauvin VII 54 No. 77; *ANE* 130-32 No. 177;
Hasan of Basrah: *Alf* IV 38-39,-(treasure-trove); Burton VIII 113. Chauvin VII 29-35 No. 212A; *ANE* 207-10 No. 230.□

N794§, ‡Adventure from opening forbidden chamber (door). See: *DOTTI*. (Cf. C611).
Man Who Never Laughs: *Alf* III 155; Burton VI 162, 165-6. Chauvin VIII 47-48 No. 15; *ANE* 285-86 No. 195;
Hasan of Basrah: *Alf* III 314; Burton VIII 29. Chauvin VII 29-35 No. 212A; *ANE* 207-10 No. 230.□

N801.1§, ‡Helper loses his life. See: *DOTTI*; *GMC*. (Cf. V463).
Second Qalandar: Afrit's Wife: *Alf* I 49,-(demon/Afrit and disenchanter); Burton I 134-35. Chauvin V 197-200 No. 116; *ANE* 338-39 No. 16.□

N813, Helpful genie (spirit). See: *DOTTI*; *GMC*. (Cf. D1273.8§, N815.1.1§).
Nûr al-Dîn ¿Alî and Son: *Alf* I 70; Burton I 213. Chauvin VI 102-6 No. 270; *ANE* 317-19 No. 22;
Enchanted Spring: Change of Sex: *Alf* III 146-47,-(genie is royal prince); Burton VI 147. Chauvin VIII 43 No. 11; *ANE* 175-76 No. 191;
¿Abdallah ibn Fâḍil: Treacherous Brothers: *Alf* IV 279; Burton IX 331. Chauvin V 2-4 No. 2; *ANE* 63-65 No. 261;
Ma¿rûf the Cobbler: *Alf* IV 293; Burton X 60. Chauvin VI 81-82 No. 250; *ANE* 291-93 No. 262.□

N815.1.1§, ‡Fairy-woman (female-genie) as helper. See: *DOTTI*. (Cf. F302.0.3.3§, N813, T202.2.1§).
Second Shaykh: Treacherous Brothers: *Alf* I 11; Burton I 34. Chauvin V 6 No. 397; *ANE* 377-78 No. 6.□

N815.3§, al-Khiḍr as helper. See: *DOTTI*; *GMC*. (Cf. D1814.4§, M301.11.1§).
Abû Muḥammad Lazybones: *Alf* II 215,-(helper dressed in green/kills demon); Burton IV 175 n. 1. Chauvin VI 64-67 No. 233; *ANE* 71-73 No. 78;
Bulûqiya: *Alf* III 74; Burton V 384. Chauvin VII 54 No. 77; *ANE* 130-32 No. 177;
¿Abdallah ibn Fâḍil: Treacherous Brothers: *Alf* IV 287; Burton IX 348. Chauvin V 2-4 No. 2; *ANE* 63-65 No. 261.□

N823§, ‡Neighbors (friends) as helpers. See: *DOTTI*. (Cf. P305.1.2§).
Merchant's Curious Wife: *Alf* I 6; Burton I 21. Chauvin V 179-80 No. 104; *ANE* 298-99 No. 3.□

N825.2, Old man helper. See: *DOTTI*; *GMC*.
Tâj al-Mulûk: *Alf* I 290; Burton III 8. Chauvin V 126-28 No. 60; *ANE* 406-8 No. 40;

Hasan of Basrah: *Alf* IV 19; Burton VIII 71. Chauvin VII 29-35 No. 212A; *ANE* 207-10 No. 230;
Ruined Baghdadi and His Slave-girl: *Alf* IV 130,-(boatman); Burton IX 25. Chauvin V 152-53 No. 75; *ANE* 353 No. 235.□

N825.3, Old woman helper. See: *DOTTI*; *GMC*.
King ¿Umar al-Nu¿mân and Sons: *Alf* II 3; Burton III 78. Chauvin VI 112 No. 277; *ANE* 430-34 No. 39;
¿Alî Shâr and Zumurrud: *Alf* II 224,-(neighbor), 232-33,-(cares for sick hero); Burton IV 204-5, 222. Chauvin V 89-91 No. 28; *ANE* 100-1 No. 82;
Nûr al-Dîn and Maryam: *Alf* IV 108; Burton VIII 324. Chauvin V 52-54 No. 271; *ANE* 98-99 No. 233.□

N842.1, Cook as foster father. See: *DOTTI*; *GMC*.
Nûr al-Dîn ¿Alî and Son: *Alf* I 74; Burton I 226. Chauvin VI 102-6 No. 270; *ANE* 317-19 No. 22.□

N843, ‡Hermit as helper. See: *DOTTI*.
Uns al-Wujûd and al-Ward: *Alf* II 273, 275; Burton V 42, 45. Chauvin VI 127-29 No. 282; *ANE* 438 No. 104.□

N845, Magician as helper. See: *DOTTI*.
Jawdar and His Treacherous Brethren: *Alf* III 194; Burton VI 242. Chauvin V 257-60 No. 154; *ANE* 244-45 No. 209.□

N848, Saint (pious man) as helper. See: *DOTTI*. (Cf. V220.0.7§).
¿Alâ' al-Dîn Abû al-Shâmât: *Alf* II 154; Burton IV 46. Chauvin V 43-49 No. 18; *ANE* 85-87 No. 63.□

N851, Merchant as helper.
Ma¿rûf the Cobbler: *Alf* IV 290; Burton X 3. Chauvin VI 81-82 No. 250; *ANE* 291-93 No. 262.□

N854.3§, ‡Gardener as helper. See: *DOTTI*.
Qamar al-Zamân and Budûr: *Alf* II 98; Burton III 282. Chauvin V 204-12 No. 120; *ANE* 341-45 No. 61;
Ibrâhîm and Jamîlah: *Alf* IV 224; Burton IX 219. Chauvin VI 52 No. 218; *ANE* 227-29 No. 258.□

N862§, ‡Slave as helper. See: *DOTTI*. (Cf. K2251, N801.1§).
Ibn Sabâ'ik/Sayf al-Mulûk: *Alf* III 272,-(mameluke); Burton VII 313. Chauvin VII 65 No. 348/pt.; *ANE* 309-10 No. 228.□

N862.0.1§, ‡Slavegirl as helper.
Masrûr and Zayn al-Mawâṣif: *Alf* IV 61,-(helps mistress's lover); Burton VIII 216ff. Chauvin VI 82-84 No. 251; *ANE* 294-95 No. 232.□

N884.2§, Chivalrous (gallant) robber (thief). See: *DOTTI*; *GMC*. (Cf. N887§).
Mercury ¿Alî: *Alf* III 236; Burton VII 187. Chauvin V 248-50 No. 147; *ANE* 301-3 No. 225.□

N884.4§, Robber returns stolen goods. See: *DOTTI*.
¿Alî ibn Bakkâr: *Alf* II 59; Burton III 199. Chauvin V 153 No. 76; *ANE* 92-93 No. 60.□

N886, Blind man carries lame man. See: *ANE*; *DOTTI*; *GMC*.
Blind and Cripple Corporate: *Alf* IV 150; Burton IX 70. Chauvin II 221 No. 152/13; *ANE* 127 No. 247.□

N887§, Unlikely helpers. See: *DOTTI*. (Cf. B473.1§, F519.1.1§, N884.2§, R52.4§).
Sindbâd's Sixth Voyage: *Alf* III 114-15,-(natives); Burton VI 63-64. Chauvin VII 24-27 No. 373F; *ANE* 386 No. 179.□

N887.2.1§, ‡Wife (fiancee) helps her husband (fiance) reach his beloved. See: *DOTTI*. (Cf. T145.0.4.1§, W14.8§).
¿Azîz and ¿Azîzah: *Alf* I 271,-ff.; Burton II 273. Chauvin V 144-45 No. 71; *ANE* 111-13 No. 41.□

N887.5.1§, ‡Prostitute as helper.
Copt Broker's Story: Lover's Sacrifices Repaid: *Alf* I 94-95; Burton I 274-75. Chauvin VI 80 No. 249; *ANE* 313-14 No. 24.□

N887.5.1.1§, ‡Prostitute sacrifices herself for client who has shown her love. (Cf. V229.12).
Copt Broker's Story: Lover's Sacrifices Repaid: *Alf* I 94-95; Burton I 275-76. Chauvin VI 80 No. 249; *ANE* 313-14 No. 24.□

N888.1§, ‡Helper belonging to adversary religious persuasion. See: *DOTTI*.

Copt Broker's Story: Lover's Sacrifices Repaid: *Alf* I 94-95,-(partnership between Copt and Moslem); Burton I 277-78. Chauvin VI 80 No. 249; *ANE* 313-14 No. 24;

¿Alâ' al-Dîn Abû al-Shâmât: *Alf* II 177,-(European princess); Burton IV 88. Chauvin V 43-49 No. 18; *ANE* 85-87 No. 63;

Prior Becomes Moslem: al-Anbârî: *Alf* II 298,-(monk); Burton V 142. Chauvin V 237-38 No. 137; *ANE* 330-31 No. 147;

Nûr al-Dîn and Maryam: *Alf* IV 108; Burton VIII 324. Chauvin V 52-54 No. 271; *ANE* 98-99 No. 233.□

P2.2.1.1§, ‡No fisher would be corresponding with kings. (Cf. P335.3§).
Anîs al-Jalîs: *Alf* I 143; Burton II 39. Chauvin V 120-24 No. 58; *ANE* 316-17 No. 35.□

P2.2.1.2§, ‡No low rank person would be sitting down while addressing high rank. (Cf. P335.3§, Z179.1§).
Jawdar and His Treacherous Brethren: *Alf* III 198; Burton VI 249. Chauvin V 257-60 No. 154; *ANE* 244-45 No. 209.□

P2.2.1.3§, ‡No youth would feel free (at ease) in the company of elderly.
¿Alâ' al-Dîn Abû al-Shâmât: *Alf* II 151; Burton IV 38. Chauvin V 43-49 No. 18; *ANE* 85-87 No. 63.□

P2.2.1.3.1§, ‡Two simultaneous banquets held: one for beardless youths, the other for mature (bearded) men.
¿Alâ' al-Dîn Abû al-Shâmât: *Alf* II 151; Burton IV 38. Chauvin V 43-49 No. 18; *ANE* 85-87 No. 63.□

P2.3§, ‡Social expectations should be proportionate to the social status of the granting person. (Cf. J535§, W132§).
King ¿Umar al-Nu¿mân and Sons: *Alf* I 309; Burton III 50. Chauvin VI 112-24 No. 277; *ANE* 430-34 No. 39.□

P5§, ‡Indicators of social status ('status symbols'). See: *DOTTI*. (Cf. P13.9.3§, W164§).
Mock Caliph/¿Alî al-Jawharî: *Alf* II 191-200,-(general); Burton IV 130-34. Chauvin V 99-100 No. 174; *ANE* 304-5 No. 73;
Abû al-Ḥasan al-Khorâsânî (and Caliph's Favorite): *Alf* IV 229-30,-(house); Burton IX 229-32. Chauvin V 218-20 No. 129; *ANE* 68-69 No. 259.□

P5.2§, ‡Social connections (friends) as indicator of social status.
Jawdar and His Treacherous Brethren: *Alf* III 200; Burton VI 255. Chauvin V 257-60 No. 154; *ANE* 244-45 No. 209.□

P5.3§, ‡Possessions as indicators of social status. See: *DOTTI*.
Mock Caliph/¿Alî al-Jawharî: *Alf* II 191,-ff.; Burton IV 130-34. Chauvin V 99-100 No. 174; *ANE* 304-5 No. 73.□

P5.3.3§, ‡Means of transportation (airplane, automobile, carriage, horse, mule, etc.) as indicators of social status. See: *DOTTI*. (Cf. N722§).
Nuzhat al-Zamân Tested/¿Umar al-Nu¿mân: *Alf* I 201,-(barâzîn); Burton II 158,-(baggage beasts). Chauvin VI 116, n.1/passim No. 277; *ANE* 432,/passim No. 39.□

P5.3.3.1§, ‡Sedan carried by bearers indicates aristocracy of rider. (Cf. P96§).
Sweep and Noble Lady: Infidelity Repaid: *Alf* II 189; Burton IV 126. Chauvin VI 148 No. 306; *ANE* 403-4 No. 72.□

P5.3.4§—(formerly-P3.3.4§), ‡Owning own dwelling (house) as 'status symbol'.
al-'Amjad and al-'As¿ad: *Alf* II 124,-cf.; Burton III 333. Chauvin V 208-10 No. 120[.1]; *ANE* 341-42 No. 61/pt. 2.□

P5.3.4.3§, ‡Luxurious furnishings as indicator of social status.
Jawdar and His Treacherous Brethren: *Alf* III 199; Burton VI 252. Chauvin V 257-60 No. 154; *ANE* 244-45 No. 209.□

P5.3.5.1.1§, ‡Owning slaves of multi-racial, and multi-ethnic origins as 'status symbol'. (Cf. P170.0.2.1§).
Jawdar and His Treacherous Brethren: *Alf* III 196; Burton VI 246. Chauvin V 257-60 No. 154; *ANE* 244-45 No. 209.□

P5.3.6§, ‡Being surrounded by men of power (horsemen, fighters, guards, etc.) as status symbol.
Sweep and Noble Lady: Infidelity Repaid: *Alf* II 190; Burton IV 128. Chauvin VI 148 No. 306; *ANE* 403-4 No. 72;
Angel of Death and Proud King: *Alf* III 8,-(parade); Burton V 246,-(in state). Chauvin VI 183-84 No. 349/[pt. 1]; *ANE* 104 No. 158;
Lovers of Basra/Ḍamrah: *Alf* III 212; Burton VII 134. Chauvin V 118 No. 54; *ANE* 273 No. 220;

Mercury ¿Alî: *Alf* III 231,-(slaves); Burton VII 180. Chauvin V 248-50 No. 147; *ANE* 301-3 No. 225.□

P5.4.1§, ‡Formal (state) badge as indicator of social status. See: *PSAE*.
Abû al-Ḥasan al-Khorâsânî (and Caliph's Favorite): *Alf* IV 230,-cf.; Burton IX 232. Chauvin V 218-20 No. 129; *ANE* 68-69 No. 259.□

P5.6§, ‡Ability to speak foreign language as status symbol.
Ni¿mah and Nu¿m: Stolen Wife Regained: *Alf* II 138,-(Farsi); Burton IV 11. Chauvin VI 96-97 No. 263; *ANE* 314 No. 62.□

P5.7.0.1§, ‡Vagabonds live at the outskirts of city.
King ¿Umar al-Nu¿mân and Sons: *Alf* I 314,-(*ṣa¿âlîk*); Burton III 61. Chauvin VI 112-24 No. 277; *ANE* 430-34 No. 39;
¿Alî ibn Bakkâr: *Alf* II 58,-cf./(robbers); Burton III 197-98. Chauvin V 153 No. 76; *ANE* 92-93 No. 60.□

P7.1§, ‡Role strain (role conflict): effects of difficult choices between conflicting obligations. See: *DOTTI*. (Cf. P248§, W30§, W37.6§).
Anîs al-Jalîs: *Alf* I 129,-(father-vizier/mother-wife); Burton II 8. Chauvin V 120-24 No. 58; *ANE* 316-17 No. 35;
King ¿Umar al-Nu¿mân and Sons: *Alf* II 8-9,-(as wife/sister/paternal-aunt); Burton III 88-90. Chauvin VI 112-24 No. 277; *ANE* 430-34 No. 39.□

P9.1.1§, ‡Alumni of school (with sense of belonging among graduates of certain class, year, etc.).
Anîs al-Jalîs: *Alf* I 143; Burton II 37. Chauvin V 120-24 No. 58; *ANE* 316-17 No. 35.□

P10.0.1§, Hârûn ar-Rashîd: Caliph (sovereign). See: *DOTTI*; *GMC*.
First Qalandar: Brother-Sister Incest: *Alf* I 42; Burton I 112. Chauvin V 196-97 No. 115; *ANE* 337-38 No. 15;
Porter and Ladies of Baghdad: *Alf* I 60; Burton I 184. Chauvin V 251-52 No. 148; *ANE* 324-26 No. 14;
Hârûn, Slave-girl and Judge Abû-Yûsuf: *Alf* II 202; Burton IV 153. Chauvin VII 114 No. 383; *ANE* 204 No. 75;
Nûr al-Dîn and Maryam: *Alf* IV 126, 129; Burton IX 12, 17. Chauvin V 52-54 No. 271; *ANE* 98-99 No. 233;
Ibrâhîm and Jamîlah: *Alf* IV 228; Burton IX 228. Chauvin VI 52-53 No. 218; *ANE* 227-29 No. 258;
¿Abdallah ibn Fâḍil: Treacherous Brothers: *Alf* IV 268; Burton IX 310. Chauvin V 2-4 No. 2; *ANE* 63-65 No. 261.□

P11, ‡Choice of king. See: *DOTTI*. (Cf. B242, K815.8).
Crows and Hawk: *Alf* IV 144; Burton IX 53-54. Chauvin II 220 No. 152/8; *ANE* 162 No. 243.□

P11.1.1, King chosen by lot. See: *ANE*; *DOTTI*; *GMC*. (Cf. N683.1§).
¿Alî Shâr and Zumurrud: *Alf* II 227,-cf.; Burton IV 210. Chauvin V 89-91 No. 28; *ANE* 100-1 No. 82.□

P11.7§, ‡Ruler (king) chosen by mass pledge of allegiance (*bay¿ah*). (Cf. B236.0.2§, M159§, P506.0.2§).
Jawdar and His Treacherous Brethren: *Alf* III 200; Burton VI 255. Chauvin V 257-60 No. 154; *ANE* 244-45 No. 209;
Jullanâr of the Sea: *Alf* III 270; Burton VII 307,-(swearing fealty). Chauvin V 147-51 No. 73; *ANE* 248-51 No. 227;
Sayf al-Mulûk: *Alf* III 278-79; Burton VII 328. Chauvin VII 64-73 No. 348; *ANE* 362-64 No. 229;
King Jalî¿âd and Shimâs: *Alf* IV 161; Burton IX 87. Chauvin VI 9-11 No. 184; *ANE* 237-38 No. 236.□

P11.8§, ‡Dying (departing) king secures from courtiers (army generals) promise of allegiance (*¿ahd, mîthâq*) for his successor.
King ¿Umar al-Nu¿mân and Sons: *Alf* I 218,-(given to deceased king's son); Burton II 193,-(oath of fealty). Chauvin VI 112-24 No. 277; *ANE* 430-34 No. 39;
Jullanâr of the Sea: *Alf* III 254; Burton VII 276. Chauvin V 147-51 No. 73; *ANE* 248-51 No. 227;
King Jalî¿âd and Shimâs: *Alf* IV 160; Burton IX 87,-(an oath). Chauvin VI 9-11 No. 184; *ANE* 237-38 No. 236.□

P12.1, Hunting a madness of kings. (Cf. P806.7§, P807.3.1§).

Prince and Ogress: *Alf* I 19; Burton I 54. Chauvin VI 26 No. 197; *ANE* 329 No. 12;
Tâj al-Mulûk: *Alf* I 266; Burton II 293. Chauvin V 126-28 No. 60; *ANE* 406-8 No. 40;
King's Favorite Son and Ogress: *Alf* III 143; Burton VI 139-40. Chauvin VIII 40-41 No. 8B; *ANE* 264 No. 188.□

P12.2.0.1§, ‡Unjust (tyrannical) ruler uses fear to control subjects (troops). (Cf. P551, P788.2§).
Abû Qîr and Abû Ṣîr: *Alf* IV 195; Burton IX 159. Chauvin V 15-17 No. 10; *ANE* 75-77 No. 255.□

P12.2.1, Tyrannical king. See: *DOTTI*; *GMC*. (Cf. S485§, R230.0.1§).
Angel of Death and Jewish King: *Alf* III 9-10; Burton V 250. Chauvin VI 184-85 No. 351; *ANE* 104 No. 160;
Son of Unjust King: *Alf* IV 142; Burton IX 50. Chauvin II 219-20 No. 152/7; *ANE* 437 No. 242.□

P12.2.2§, Tyrannical viceroy (or minister). See: *GMC*.
Ni¿mah and Nu¿m: Stolen Wife Regained: *Alf* II 133; Burton IV 3. Chauvin VI 96-97 No. 263; *ANE* 314 No. 62.□

P12.2.2.1§, al-Ḥajjâj as tyrant. See: *DOTTI*; *GMC*.
Ni¿mah and Nu¿m: Stolen Wife Regained: *Alf* II 133, 144,-(kidnapper, liar); Burton IV 3, 22. Chauvin VI 96-97 No. 263; *ANE* 314 No. 62;
Hind bint al-Nu¿mân and al-Ḥajjâj: *Alf* III 201,-(implicit); Burton VII 96-99. Chauvin V 115-4 No. 50; *ANE* 221-22 No. 212.□

P12.6.0.1§, ‡Just king (ruler). See: *PSAE*. (Cf. P500.1.2§, W35.4.1§).
Jackals and Wolf as Umpire: *Alf* IV 167,-(lion); Burton IX 103-6. Chauvin II 223 No. 152/21; *ANE* 235 No. 252.□

P12.6.4.1§, ‡Officers vital to king's rule: judge, cook, scribe.
Spy, First Maiden/¿Umar al-Nu¿mân: *Alf* I 220; Burton II 199. *ANE* 432 No. 39/passim.□

P12.7.1§, ‡It is the ruler's responsibility to know the affairs (problems) of the subjects.
Nuzhat al-Zamân Tested/¿Umar al-Nu¿mân: *Alf* I 203; Burton II 163. Chauvin VI 116, n.1/passim No. 277; *ANE* 432,/passim No. 39.□

P12.11, ‡Uxorious king neglects duties. (Cf. T380.0.2.1§).
King Jalî¿âd and Shimâs: *Alf* IV 161, 164-65; Burton IX 90. Chauvin VI 9 No. 184; *ANE* 237-38 No. 236.□

P12.12.1§, ‡Impersonating (masking as) king is forbidden. (Cf. K1952.9.2§, P13.9.3§, P14.25.2.1§).
Abû al-Ḥasan al-Khorâsânî (and Caliph's Favorite): *Alf* IV 234,-cf./(no one dares); Burton IX 239. Chauvin V 218-20 No. 129; *ANE* 68-69 No. 259.□

P12.14.1§, ‡Modest ruler lives austerely. (Cf. W35.4.1§).
Nuzhat al-Zamân Tested/¿Umar al-Nu¿mân: *Alf* I 204; Burton II 165. Chauvin VI 116, n.1/passim No. 277; *ANE* 432,/passim No. 39.□

P12.15.5§, ‡Regal speech (conversation) of Kings.
Isḥâq al-Mûṣilî and Khadîjah bint al-Ḥasan: *Alf* II 186; Burton IV 121. Chauvin V 241-42 No. 142; *ANE* 232 No. 71.□

P12.15.5.1§, ‡Historical narratives and legends (*'akhbâr*) are habitual topics of conversations of kings (not merchants). (Cf. J169§).
Isḥâq al-Mûṣilî and Khadîjah bint al-Ḥasan: *Alf* II 186,-(*'akhbâr*); Burton IV 121,-(tales and adventures). Chauvin V 241-42 No. 142; *ANE* 232 No. 71.□

P13.5.2.1§, ‡Empowerment of ruler procedures: crowning, inaugurating ruler.
Anîs al-Jalîs: *Alf* I 143; Burton II 37-39. Chauvin V 120-24 No. 58; *ANE* 316-17 No. 35;
Sayf al-Mulûk: *Alf* III 278-79; Burton VII 328. Chauvin VII 64-73 No. 348; *ANE* 362-64 No. 229;
King Jalî¿âd and Shimâs: *Alf* IV 161; Burton IX 90. Chauvin VI 9-11 No. 184; *ANE* 237-38 No. 236.□

P13.5.2.2§, ‡Disempowerment of ruler procedures (dethroning, impeaching). (Cf. P16.3.5§).
Anîs al-Jalîs: *Alf* I 143; Burton II 37-39. Chauvin V 120-24 No. 58; *ANE* 316-17 No. 35.□

P13.9.3§, ‡Royal regalia (symbols of power). (Cf. P5§, P12.12.1§).
Angel of Death and Proud King: *Alf* III 8; Burton V 246. Chauvin VI 183-84 No. 349/[pt. 1]; *ANE* 104 No. 158;

Abû al-Ḥasan al-Khorâsânî (and Caliph's Favorite): *Alf* IV 230; Burton IX 232. Chauvin V 218-20 No. 129; *ANE* 68-69 No. 259.□

P13.9.3.1§, ‡King's crown. See: *DOTTI*; *PSAE*. (Cf. H1319.8.1§).
Abû Muḥammad Lazybones: *Alf* II 206; Burton IV 162. Chauvin VI 64-67 No. 233; *ANE* 71-73 No. 78.□

P13.9.3.1.1§, ‡Crown jewel(s). See: *DOTTI*. (Cf. H1319.8.1§).
Abû Muḥammad Lazybones: *Alf* II 206; Burton IV 162. Chauvin VI 64-67 No. 233; *ANE* 71-73 No. 78.□

P13.9.3.3.1§, ‡King's emblem (crown, name, seal, etc.) on royal property (palace, carriage, money, etc.). See: *DOTTI*. (Cf. Z134.3.0.1§).
Abû al-Ḥasan al-Khorâsânî (and Caliph's Favorite): *Alf* IV 230; Burton IX 232. Chauvin V 218-20 No. 129; *ANE* 68-69 No. 259;
¿Alâ' al-Dîn Abû al-Shâmât: *Alf* II 167,-(*khâtam al-mulk*); Burton IV 71,-(royal-signet). Chauvin V 43-49 No. 18; *ANE* 85-87 No. 63.□

P13.9.3.3.2§, ‡King's dagger (sword) of state.
King ¿Umar al-Nu¿mân and Sons: *Alf* I 218,-("namshah"); Burton II 193,-(dagger of state). Chauvin VI 112-24 No. 277; *ANE* 430-34 No. 39;
¿Alâ' al-Dîn Abû al-Shâmât: *Alf* II 167; Burton IV 71,-(dagger-sword). Chauvin V 43-49 No. 18; *ANE* 85-87 No. 63.□

P13.9.3.4§, ‡Ruler's procession (parade).
¿Alî ibn Bakkâr: *Alf* II 45,-(for domestic visit); Burton III 171. Chauvin V 153 No. 76; *ANE* 92-93 No. 60;
Abû al-Ḥasan al-Khorâsânî (and Caliph's Favorite): *Alf* IV 234; Burton IX 239. Chauvin V 218-20 No. 129; *ANE* 68-69 No. 259.□

P14.0.2§, ‡King (ruler, chief, etc.) as patron of sciences and discovery.
Ebony Horse: *Alf* II 256,-(implicit); Burton V 1,-("loved sciences and geometry"). Chauvin V 221-31 No. 130; *ANE* 172-74 No. 103.□

P14.12.0.1§, ‡Kings exchange presents (gifts). See: *DOTTI*.
King ¿Umar al-Nu¿mân and Sons: *Alf* I 164-65; Burton II 82. Chauvin VI 112-24 No. 277; *ANE* 430-34 No. 39;
Sindbâd's Sixth Voyage: *Alf* III 115; Burton VI 65-68. Chauvin VII 24-27 No. 373F; *ANE* 386 No. 179;
City of Brass: *Alf* III 138; Burton VI 121. Chauvin V 32-35 No. 16; *ANE* 146-50 No. 180.□

P14.15.1, ‡Old, wise counsellor of court. (Cf. J571.9.1§, P112§, T380.3.2§).
King ¿Umar al-Nu¿mân and Sons: *Alf* I 165,-(Dandân); Burton II 83. Chauvin VI 112-24 No. 277; *ANE* 430-34 No. 39.□

P14.15.2, ‡Court messenger. [(Envoy, ambassador, emissary)].
¿Abdallah ibn Fâḍil: Treacherous Brothers: *Alf* IV 266; Burton IX 304. Chauvin V 2-4 No. 2; *ANE* 63-65 No. 261.□

P14.15.2.2§, ‡Governor of district or province (in name of the sovereign).
Barber's Fifth Brother: Daydreams/Defeats Robbers: *Alf* I 121; Burton I 343. Chauvin V 161 No. 85; *ANE* 119-20 No. 33;
¿Abdallah ibn Fâḍil: Treacherous Brothers: *Alf* IV 266; Burton IX 304. Chauvin V 2-4 No. 2; *ANE* 63-65 No. 261.□

P14.15.3.1§, ‡Court singer (musician). See: *PSAE*.
Isḥâq al-Mûṣilî and Merchant's Singer: *Alf* II 297; Burton V 129. Chauvin VI 59 No. 225; *ANE* 233 No. 142.□

P14.15.4§, ‡Court joker (jester, fool). (Cf. P192.1).
Hunchback's Tale: Resuscitated: *Alf* I 88,-(hunchback); Burton I 261,-(jester). Chauvin VI 80 No. 249; *ANE* 313-14 No. 23.□

P14.15.5.1§, ‡Masrûr, Hârûn ar-Rashîd's court executioner. See: *DOTTI*.
Porter and Ladies of Baghdad: *Alf* I 35-36; Burton I 96. Chauvin V 251-52 No. 148; *ANE* 324-26 No. 14;

¿Alî ibn Bakkâr: *Alf* II 44,-(as messenger); Burton III 169. Chauvin V 153 No. 76; *ANE* 92-93 No. 60;
¿Alâ' al-Dîn Abû al-Shâmât: *Alf* II 158,-(with caliph and companions); Burton IV 54. Chauvin V 43-49 No. 18; *ANE* 85-87 No. 63;
Abû Muḥammad Lazybones: *Alf* II 206-7,-(as messenger); Burton IV 162. Chauvin VI 64-67 No. 233; *ANE* 71-73 No. 78;
Hasan of Basrah: *Alf* IV 10,-(as messenger); Burton VIII 56. Chauvin VII 29-35 No. 212A; *ANE* 207-10 No. 230.□

P14.19, King goes in disguise at night to observe his subjects. See: *DOTTI*; *GMC*. (Cf. K1812.17).
¿Alâ' al-Dîn Abû al-Shâmât: *Alf* II 158; Burton IV 54. Chauvin V 43-49 No. 18; *ANE* 85-87 No. 63;
Mock Caliph/¿Alî al-Jawharî: *Alf* II 191; Burton IV 130. Chauvin V 99-100 No. 174; *ANE* 304-5 No. 73.□

P14.19.1§, ‡King insists on learning secrets of his (appointed) official(s). (Cf. H1387§).
¿Abdallah ibn Fâḍil: Treacherous Brothers: *Alf* IV 268; Burton IX 308-9. Chauvin V 2-4 No. 2; *ANE* 63-65 No. 261.□

P14.25.0.1.1§, ‡Acts by monarch indicating end of official session (audience, assembly).
¿Alâ' al-Dîn Abû al-Shâmât: *Alf* II 163,-(*nafaḍa al-mindîl*); Burton IV 62,-(shaking the handkerchief). Chauvin V 43-49 No. 18; *ANE* 85-87 No. 63;
Ma¿rûf the Cobbler: *Alf* IV 313,-(*nafaḍa al-mindîl*); Burton X 47. Chauvin VI 81-82 No. 250; *ANE* 291-93 No. 262.□

P14.22.3§, ‡King keeps pigeons as pets (letter carriers) and pigeon-trainer (keeper) at his palace. See: *DOTTI*. (Cf. B291.1.0.1.1§, P14.15.2, P144.3§).
Dalîla the Swindler: *Alf* III 213; Burton VII 146. Chauvin V 245-50 No. 147; *ANE* 163-64 No. 224.□

P14.25.2§, ‡Protocol of courtier's interaction with sovereign (king).
King ¿Umar al-Nu¿mân and Sons: *Alf* I 218; Burton II 194. Chauvin VI 112-24 No. 277; *ANE* 430-34 No. 39.□

P14.25.2.1§, ‡Courtier must seek king's permission to travel. See: *PSAE*.
Ni¿mah and Nu¿m: Stolen Wife Regained: *Alf* II 144; Burton IV 23. Chauvin VI 96-97 No. 263; *ANE* 314 No. 62;
Sindbâd's First Voyage: *Alf* III 87; Burton VI 13. Chauvin VII 7-9 No. 373A; *ANE* 385 No. 179;
Hasan of Basrah: *Alf* IV 51,-(guest); Burton VIII 139. Chauvin VII 29-35 No. 212A; *ANE* 207-10 No. 230;
Nûr al-Dîn and Maryam: *Alf* IV 129,-(guest/protégé); Burton IX 17. Chauvin V 52-54 No. 271; *ANE* 98-99 No. 233;
Landsman ¿Abdallah and Merman ¿Abdallah: *Alf* IV 207,-cf./(foreigner); Burton IX 186. Chauvin V 6-7 No. 3; *ANE* 65-66 No. 256;
Jeweler's Wife and Qamar al-Zamân: *Alf* IV 261; Burton IX 293. Chauvin V 212-14 No. 121; *ANE* 345-47 No. 260.□

P14.26.1§, ‡King should aid friend (ally) who is being attacked.
King ¿Umar al-Nu¿mân and Sons: *Alf* I 165; Burton II 83-84. Chauvin VI 112-24 No. 277; *ANE* 430-34 No. 39.□

P16.1, King (prince) retires from world (becomes hermit, swineherd). See: *ANE*; *DOTTI*; *GMC*. (Cf. P426.2.1.2§, V462.0.1).
Devotee Prince: Ascetic's Death: *Alf* II 290,-(laborer); Burton V 112. Chauvin VI 193-94 No. 363; *ANE* 167-68 No. 134.□

P16.1.4, ‡Father abdicates in favor of son.
King ¿Umar al-Nu¿mân and Sons: *Alf* I 310,-(unfulfilled wish); Burton III 53. Chauvin VI 112-24 No. 277; *ANE* 430-34 No. 39;
Qamar al-Zamân and Budûr: *Alf* II 100,-cf./(son-in-law); Burton III 284. Chauvin V 204-12 No. 120; *ANE* 341-45 No. 61;
Craft and Malice of Women/Frame: *Alf* III 177,-(xxx); Burton VI 212. Chauvin VIII 33-34 No. 1; *ANE* 160-61 No. 181;
Sayf al-Mulûk: *Alf* III 278-79; Burton VII 326. Chauvin VII 64-73 No. 348; *ANE* 362-64 No. 229.□

P16.1.4.1§, ‡Patriarch (ruler) retires in favor of son (adopted son).
Ensorcelled Prince/Husband: *Alf* I 31; Burton I 81. Chauvin VI 56-58 No. 222; *ANE* 176 No. 13.□

P16.1.5§, ‡Ruler not expected to live long after abdication. (Cf. F1041.1.3, F1041.9.7.1§).
King ¿Umar al-Nu¿mân and Sons: *Alf* I 310; Burton III 53. Chauvin VI 112-24 No. 277; *ANE* 430-34 No. 39.□

P16.3.5§, King forced to abdicate or is dethroned. See: *DOTTI*. (Cf. P506§).
First Qalandar: Brother-Sister Incest: *Alf* I 40; Burton I 107. Chauvin V 196-97 No. 115; *ANE* 337-38 No. 15;
Abû al-Ḥasan al-Khorâsânî (and Caliph's Favorite): *Alf* IV 237,-cf.; Burton IX 245. Chauvin V 218-20 No. 129; *ANE* 68-69 No. 259.□

P16.3.6§, ‡Sovereign's viceroy ('sultan', 'king') dismissed (relieved, removed) from office.
Anîs al-Jalîs: *Alf* I 143; Burton II 37-39. Chauvin V 120-24 No. 58; *ANE* 316-17 No. 35.□

P17.0.2, Son succeeds father as king. See: *DOTTI*.
Ensorcelled Prince/Husband: *Alf* I 27; Burton I 69. Chauvin VI 56-58 No. 222; *ANE* 176 No. 13;
King ¿Umar al-Nu¿mân and Sons: *Alf* I 218; Burton II 191. Chauvin VI 112-24 No. 277; *ANE* 430-34 No. 39;
Qamar al-Zamân and Budûr: *Alf* II 65; Burton III 213. Chauvin V 204-12 No. 120; *ANE* 341-45 No. 61;
King Jalî¿âd and Shimâs: *Alf* IV 161; Burton IX 89. Chauvin VI 9-11 No. 184; *ANE* 237-38 No. 236.□

P17.0.2.0.1§, Eldest son succeeds father as king. (Cf. L41, P17.8, P30.2§).
King ¿Umar al-Nu¿mân and Sons: *Alf* I 162,-(intended); Burton II 77. Chauvin VI 112-24 No. 277; *ANE* 430-34 No. 39.□

P17.0.2.2§, ‡Birth of son (heir) sought in order to succeed father as king (chieftain, etc.). See: *DOTTI*. (Cf. M369.7.2, P233.0.2§, T145.2, T538.3§, T380.5.1§).
Qamar al-Zamân and Budûr: *Alf* II 65; Burton III 213. Chauvin V 204-12 No. 120; *ANE* 341-45 No. 61;
Craft and Malice of Women/Frame: *Alf* III 138; Burton VI 123. Chauvin VIII 33-34 No. 1; *ANE* 160-61 No. 181;
Jullanâr of the Sea: *Alf* III 248; Burton VII 265. Chauvin V 147-51 No. 73; *ANE* 248-51 No. 227.□

P17.0.2.3§, ‡Grandson succeeds his paternal grandfather (father's father) to the throne.
al-'Amjad and al-'As¿ad: *Alf* II 147; Burton IV 29. Chauvin V 208-10 No. 120[.1]; *ANE* 341-42 No. 61/pt. 2.□

P17.0.6§, ‡Son-in-law succeeds father-in-law as ruler (king, chief). See: *DOTTI*. (Cf. P261.1.1.2§, T68).
Qamar al-Zamân and Budûr: *Alf* II 100; Burton III 284. Chauvin V 204-12 No. 120; *ANE* 341-45 No. 61;
¿Alâ' al-Dîn Abû al-Shâmât: *Alf* II 162,-cf./(as head of guild); Burton IV 60-61. Chauvin V 43-49 No. 18; *ANE* 85-87 No. 63;
Sindbâd's Seventh Voyage: *Alf* III 119-20,-cf./(as market sheik); Burton VI 74. Chauvin VII 26-29 No. 373G; *ANE* 386-87 No. 179;
Jawdar and His Treacherous Brethren: *Alf* III 200; Burton VI 254. Chauvin V 257-60 No. 154; *ANE* 244-45 No. 209;
Landsman ¿Abdallah and Merman ¿Abdallah: *Alf* IV 202,-(promised); Burton IX 174. Chauvin V 6-7 No. 3; *ANE* 65-66 No. 256;
Ma¿rûf the Cobbler: *Alf* IV 313; Burton X 47. Chauvin VI 81-82 No. 250; *ANE* 291-93 No. 262.□

P17.15.2§, ‡Siblings in conflict over kingship. See: *DOTTI*.
King ¿Umar al-Nu¿mân and Sons: *Alf* I 199,-(passim); Burton II 154. Chauvin VI 112-24 No. 277; *ANE* 430-34 No. 39.□

P17.15.3.1§, ‡Wife (queen) murders her husband in (political) power conflict.
Ma¿rûf the Cobbler: *Alf* IV 315,-cf./(seeks to murder); Burton X 51. Chauvin VI 81-82 No. 250; *ANE* 291-93 No. 262.□

P17.3, Dying king names successor. See: *DOTTI*. (Cf. J154).
King Jalî¿âd and Shimâs: *Alf* IV 161; Burton IX 89. Chauvin VI 9-11 No. 184; *ANE* 237-38 No. 236.□

P17.4, Kingship rotates among brothers. See: *DOTTI*.
Nûr al-Dîn ¿Alî and Son: *Alf* I 64; Burton I 195. Chauvin VI 102-6 No. 270; *ANE* 317-19 No. 22;

King ¿Umar al-Nu¿mân and Sons: *Alf* II 14; Burton III 100. Chauvin VI 112-24 No. 277; *ANE* 430-34 No. 39;
al-'Amjad and al-'As¿ad: *Alf* II 112,-(*hukm*/rule: one day each); Burton III 309,-(judgement). Chauvin V 208-10 No. 120[.1]; *ANE* 341-42 No. 61/pt. 2.□

P17.8, Kingship given to younger brother. See: *DOTTI*; *GMC*. (Cf. L41, P17.0.2.0.1§).
King ¿Umar al-Nu¿mân and Sons: *Alf* I 217-18; Burton II 191. Chauvin VI 112-24 No. 277; *ANE* 430-34 No. 39.□

P17.15§, Conflict (war) over kingship. See: *DOTTI*; *GMC*; *PSAE*. (Cf. P506.5§, S73.1.1).
King ¿Umar al-Nu¿mân and Sons: *Alf* I 216; Burton II 191. Chauvin VI 112-24 No. 277; *ANE* 430-34 No. 39.□

P20.0.1§, Zubaydah: Caliph's wife (Hârûn ar-Rashîd). See: *DOTTI*; *GMC*.
Reeve's Story: Why Maimed by Bride: *Alf* I 98; Burton I 282. Chauvin V 220-21 No. 305; *ANE* 351 No. 25;
Ghânim ibn Ayyûb: *Alf* I 154; Burton II 61. Chauvin VI 14 No. 188; *ANE* 192-93 No. 36;
Mock Caliph/¿Alî al-Jawharî: *Alf* II 198; Burton IV 144. Chauvin V 99-100 No. 174; *ANE* 304-5 No. 73;
Hârûn and Zubaydah in Bath: *Alf* II 284; Burton V 76. Chauvin VI 142 No. 298; *ANE* 203-4 No. 111;
Hasan of Basrah: *Alf* IV 9; Burton VIII 55. Chauvin VII 29-35 No. 212A; *ANE* 207-10 No. 230.□

P20.5§, Queen as head of government. (Female as sovereign). See: *GMC*. (Cf. F112.4§, F112.4§).
al-'Amjad and al-'As¿ad: *Alf* II 127; Burton III 340. Chauvin V 208-10 No. 120[.1]; *ANE* 341-42 No. 61/pt. 2;
Man Who Never Laughs: *Alf* III 154; Burton VI 165. Chauvin VIII 47-48 No. 15; *ANE* 285-86 No. 195.□

P20.5.2§, ‡Female sovereign forbids husband (groom-to-be) from paying homage to her in demeaning manner (i.e., prostrating self, kissing ground, etc.). (Cf. C62.5.1.1§, P210.0.1§).
Man Who Never Laughs: *Alf* III 154; Burton VI 165. Chauvin VIII 47-48 No. 15; *ANE* 285-86 No. 195.□

P20.6§, ‡Government by women. See: *DOTTI*. (Cf. F112).
Man Who Never Laughs: *Alf* III 154; Burton VI 165. Chauvin VIII 47-48 No. 15; *ANE* 285-86 No. 195.□

P20.6.0.1§, ‡In state where women are the rulers men's roles are confined to manual civic labor.
Man Who Never Laughs: *Alf* III 154; Burton VI 165. Chauvin VIII 47-48 No. 15; *ANE* 285-86 No. 195.□

P21.3§, ‡Chieftainess intervenes to influence domestic dispute (marriage, etc.).
Sayf al-Mulûk: *Alf* III 299-300; Burton VIII 1. Chauvin VII 64-73 No. 348; *ANE* 362-64 No. 229.□

P29.7§, ‡Chieftainess as lesbian temptress. See: *DOTTI*. (Cf. K1397.6.1§, T462).
King ¿Umar al-Nu¿mân and Sons: *Alf* I 236,-(Roman); Burton II 234. Chauvin VI 112-24 No. 277; *ANE* 430-34 No. 39.□

P30.1.2§, ‡Royal son designated as governor (ruler, lord) of certain province or country.
King ¿Umar al-Nu¿mân and Sons: *Alf* I 187,-cf.; Burton II 131. Chauvin VI 112-24 No. 277; *ANE* 430-34 No. 39.□

P30.2§, ‡King's eldest son called crown-prince. (Cf. P17.0.2.0.1§).
King ¿Umar al-Nu¿mân and Sons: *Alf* I 162,-cf./(named as successor to kingship); Burton II 78,-(made heir to the kingdom), 99,-(Crown Prince). Chauvin VI 112-24 No. 277; *ANE* 430-34 No. 39.□

P30.2.1§, ‡King's son put in charge of army (military campaign).
King ¿Umar al-Nu¿mân and Sons: *Alf* I 165; Burton II 83. Chauvin VI 112-24 No. 277; *ANE* 430-34 No. 39.□

P31, Prince must learn a trade. See: *ANE*; *DOTTI*; *GMC*. (Cf. J1014§, P191.2§).
Anîs al-Jalîs: *Alf* I 141; Burton II 32. Chauvin V 120-24 No. 58; *ANE* 316-17 No. 35.□

P60.1§, ‡Character of gentlewoman (noble lady).
Ishâq al-Mûsilî and Khadîjah bint al-Hasan: *Alf* II 186; Burton IV 121-22. Chauvin V 241-42 No. 142; *ANE* 232 No. 71;

Mock Caliph/¿Alî al-Jawharî: *Alf* II 197; Burton IV 141. Chauvin V 99-100 No. 174; *ANE* 304-5 No. 73;
Uns al-Wujûd and al-Ward: *Alf* II 269; Burton V 32. Chauvin VI 127-29 No. 282; *ANE* 438 No. 104;
Tawaddud: Slavegirl Sold and Regained: *Alf* III 7-8,-(slave-girl); Burton V 245. Chauvin VII 117-19 No. 387; *ANE* 408-10 No. 157.□

P60.1.1§, ‡Diverse artistic skills of gentlewoman (poetry, music, singing, etc.).
Ni¿mah and Nu¿m: Stolen Wife Regained: *Alf* II 132-33; Burton IV 2-3. Chauvin VI 96-97 No. 263; *ANE* 314 No. 62;
Isḥâq al-Mûṣilî and Khadîjah bint al-Ḥasan: *Alf* II 186; Burton IV 121. Chauvin V 241-42 No. 142; *ANE* 232 No. 71.□

P60.1.2§, ‡Gentlewoman drinks (liquor).
Isḥâq al-Mûṣilî and Khadîjah bint al-Ḥasan: *Alf* II 186; Burton IV 121. Chauvin V 241-42 No. 142; *ANE* 232 No. 71;
Mock Caliph/¿Alî al-Jawharî: *Alf* II 197; Burton IV 142. Chauvin V 99-100 No. 174; *ANE* 304-5 No. 73;
Sayf al-Mulûk: *Alf* III 296,-(milk sisters); Burton VII 359. Chauvin VII 64-73 No. 348; *ANE* 362-64 No. 229.□

P60.1.3§, ‡Gentlewoman socializes with sophisticated men.
Isḥâq al-Mûṣilî and Khadîjah bint al-Ḥasan: *Alf* II 186; Burton IV 121. Chauvin V 241-42 No. 142; *ANE* 232 No. 71.□

P60.1.4§, ‡Gentlewoman observes sex mores (no physical contact, infidelity, or the like).
Isḥâq al-Mûṣilî and Khadîjah bint al-Ḥasan: *Alf* II 186; Burton IV 121. Chauvin V 241-42 No. 142; *ANE* 232 No. 71;
Mock Caliph/¿Alî al-Jawharî: *Alf* II 197; Burton IV 141. Chauvin V 99-100 No. 174; *ANE* 304-5 No. 73.□

P70§, Sherifs: descendants of Prophet Mohammed (*'ashrâf, sâdah*). See: *DOTTI*; *GMC*. (Cf. Z167.0.1§).
Ruined Baghdadi and His Slave-girl: *Alf* IV 130,-(Hâshimite man); Burton IX 24. Chauvin V 152-53 No. 75; *ANE* 353 No. 235.□

P71§, ‡Rights (privileges) of *'asharâf*.
Abû al-Ḥasan al-Khorâsânî (and Caliph's Favorite): *Alf* IV 230; Burton IX 231,-(noble). Chauvin V 218-20 No. 129; *ANE* 68-69 No. 259.□

P72§, ‡Restrictions on personal conduct in interacting with a *sharîf* (Hashemite). (Cf. C878.0.1§).
Ruined Baghdadi and His Slave-girl: *Alf* IV 130; Burton IX 26. Chauvin V 152-53 No. 75; *ANE* 353 No. 235.□

P91§, ‡Formal title (medal) bestowed by ruler (state). See: *DOTTI*; *PSAE*. (Cf. Q113.0.1, Q136.1.3§).
King ¿Umar al-Nu¿mân and Sons: *Alf* I 309; Burton III 50. Chauvin VI 112-24 No. 277; *ANE* 430-34 No. 39.□

P95§, ‡Jealousy (envy) among the royalty and nobility. (Cf. P152.1§, S123.1).
Ghânim ibn Ayyûb: *Alf* I 154; Burton II 61. Chauvin VI 14 No. 188; *ANE* 192-93 No. 36.□

P95.1§, ‡Sister (daughter) of vizier jealous of king's wife (daughter). (Some times vice versa). (Cf. T257.11.2§).
Mock Caliph/¿Alî al-Jawharî: *Alf* II 198,-(sister); Burton IV 145. Chauvin V 99-100 No. 174; *ANE* 304-5 No. 73.□

P96§, ‡Public facility (e.g., street, river, beach or the like) forbidden to public when in use by royalty. (Cf. C312.2.1).
Mock Caliph/¿Alî al-Jawharî: *Alf* II 191,-(river); Burton IV 130. Chauvin V 99-100 No. 174; *ANE* 304-5 No. 73.□

P96.1§, ‡Looking at royal (noble) person is forbidden (by law). (Cf. C312.2.1, P5.3.3.1§).
Sweep and Noble Lady: Infidelity Repaid: *Alf* II 188,-(by force); Burton IV 126. Chauvin VI 148 No. 306; *ANE* 403-4 No. 72.□

P96.2§, ‡Chieftainess of such rank that those who look at her are executed.

Jeweler's Wife and Qamar al-Zamân: *Alf* IV 242-43; Burton IX 256. Chauvin V 212-14 No. 121; *ANE* 345-47 No. 260.□

P110.0.1§, Ja¿far al-Barmakî: Hârûn ar-Rashîd's vizier. See: *DOTTI*; *GMC*.
Porter and Ladies of Baghdad: *Alf* I 35-36; Burton I 96. Chauvin V 251-52 No. 148; *ANE* 324-26 No. 14;
Three Apples: Hasty Uxoricide: *Alf* I 61; Burton I 186–94. Chauvin VI 144-45 No. 302; *ANE* 414-15 No. 21;
Mock Caliph/¿Alî al-Jawharî: *Alf* II 191, 198,-(sister of ...); Burton IV 130, 141. Chauvin V 99-100 No. 174; *ANE* 304-5 No. 73;
Hârûn, Slave-girl and Judge Abû-Yûsuf: *Alf* II 202; Burton IV 153. Chauvin VII 114 No. 383; *ANE* 204 No. 75;
Ridiculous Eye Salve: *Alf* II 287; Burton V 98-99. Chauvin V 281 No. 165; *ANE* 236 No. 129.□

P110.0.5§, ‡'Âṣif ibn Barkhiyâ, Solomon's vizier.
Fisherman and Afrit: Ingratitude: *Alf* I 15; Burton I 42, n. 2. Chauvin VI 23-25 No. 195; *ANE* 183-84 No. 8;
Jinn Imprisoned in Flasks: *Alf* III 129; Burton VI 98, 99. Chauvin VII 113 No. 380=no/text; *ANE* 146 No. 180;
Sayf al-Mulûk: *Alf* III 274; Burton VII 317. Chauvin VII 64-73 No. 348; *ANE* 362-64 No. 229;
Hasan of Basrah: *Alf* IV 48; Burton VIII 133. Chauvin VII 29-35 No. 212A; *ANE* 207-10 No. 230.□

P110.1§, ‡Female minister: she-vizier. See: *DOTTI*.
Man Who Never Laughs: *Alf* III 154; Burton VI 165. Chauvin VIII 47-48 No. 15; *ANE* 285-86 No. 195;
Landsman ¿Abdallah and Merman ¿Abdallah: *Alf* IV 202; Burton IX 175,-("Waziress"). Chauvin V 6-7 No. 3; *ANE* 65-66 No. 256.□

P110.1.1§, ‡Queen appoints woman as her she-vizier.
Landsman ¿Abdallah and Merman ¿Abdallah: *Alf* IV 202; Burton IX 175,-("Waziress"). Chauvin V 6-7 No. 3; *ANE* 65-66 No. 256.□

P110.1.3§, ‡Young boy (juvenile) appointed vizier. (Cf. J175.1§).
King Jalî¿âd and Shimâs: *Alf* IV 175; Burton IX 119-20. Chauvin VI 9 No. 184; *ANE* 237-38 No. 236.□

P112§, ‡Trusted vizier (royal minister). See: *DOTTI*; *PSAE*. (Cf. P14.15.1, P500.0.2.1§).
Anîs al-Jalîs: *Alf* I 125; Burton II 2. Chauvin V 120-24 No. 58; *ANE* 316-17 No. 35;
King ¿Umar al-Nu¿mân and Sons: *Alf* I 311,-(foundation of rule); Burton III 54. Chauvin VI 112-24 No. 277; *ANE* 430-34 No. 39.□

P112.1§, ‡Trusted vizier turns treacherous (evil). (Cf. K2298).
First Qalandar: Brother-Sister Incest: *Alf* I 40; Burton I 107. Chauvin V 196-97 No. 115; *ANE* 337-38 No. 15;
Ma¿rûf the Cobbler: *Alf* IV 298, 311; Burton X 16, 41. Chauvin VI 81-82 No. 250; *ANE* 291-93 No. 262.□

P112.1.1§, ‡Treacherous vizier usurps throne (government). See: *DOTTI*. (Cf. K2248).
First Qalandar: Brother-Sister Incest: *Alf* I 40; Burton I 107. Chauvin V 196-97 No. 115; *ANE* 337-38 No. 15;
Ma¿rûf the Cobbler: *Alf* IV 311; Burton X 43. Chauvin VI 81-82 No. 250; *ANE* 291-93 No. 262.□

P112.2.0.1§, ‡Unwise counsel by careless counselor (minister) proves disastrous.
King's Favorite Son and Ogress: *Alf* III 143; Burton VI 140. Chauvin VIII 40-41 No. 8B; *ANE* 264 No. 188.□

P112.3§, ‡Vizier as tale-teller. (Cf. P470§).
King ¿Umar al-Nu¿mân and Sons: *Alf* I 261; Burton II 283. Chauvin VI 112-24 No. 277; *ANE* 430-34 No. 39.□

P113§, ‡Rivaling ministers (ruler's advisors, counselors, etc.). See: *DOTTI*.
Anîs al-Jalîs: *Alf* I 125; Burton II 2. Chauvin V 120-24 No. 58; *ANE* 316-17 No. 35.□

P113.1§, ‡Good vizier and evil vizier as rivals.
Anîs al-Jalîs: *Alf* I 125; Burton II 2. Chauvin V 120-24 No. 58; *ANE* 316-17 No. 35.□

P140.0.2§, Influence peddling by 'power broker' ('*wâsṭah*'/*wâsiṭah*). See: *GMC*.

Sindbâd's First Voyage: *Alf* III 86; Burton VI 10. Chauvin VII 7-9 No. 373A; *ANE* 385 No. 179.□

P140.0.3§, Favor (pardon) won through intercession of person of influence. See: *DOTTI*; *PSAE*. (Cf. Q174.0.1§).
Three Apples: Hasty Uxoricide: *Alf* I 64,-(vizier's); Burton I 194. Chauvin VI 144-45 No. 302; *ANE* 414-15 No. 21;
Copt Broker's Story: Lover's Sacrifices Repaid: *Alf* I 94,-(victim of crime); Burton I 274. Chauvin VI 80 No. 249; *ANE* 313-14 No. 24;
Reeve's Story: Why Maimed by Bride: *Alf* I 98,-(marriage); Burton I 288. Chauvin V 220-21 No. 305; *ANE* 351 No. 25;
Ni¿mah and Nu¿m: Stolen Wife Regained: *Alf* II 144; Burton IV 21-23. Chauvin VI 96-97 No. 263; *ANE* 314 No. 62;
¿Alâ' al-Dîn Abû al-Shâmât: *Alf* II 166-67; Burton IV 70. Chauvin V 43-49 No. 18; *ANE* 85-87 No. 63;
Sweep and Noble Lady: Infidelity Repaid: *Alf* II 191; Burton IV 130. Chauvin VI 148 No. 306; *ANE* 403-4 No. 72;
Mock Caliph/¿Alî al-Jawharî: *Alf* II 198,-cf./(handmaids); Burton IV 145. Chauvin V 99-100 No. 174; *ANE* 304-5 No. 73;
Uns al-Wujûd and al-Ward: *Alf* II 282-83; Burton V 32–64. Chauvin VI 127-29 No. 282; *ANE* 438 No. 104;
Jânshâh: *Alf* III 72; Burton V 376. Chauvin VII 39-44 No. 153; *ANE* 238-41 No. 178;
Jawdar and His Treacherous Brethren: *Alf* III 195,-(mother's); Burton VI 245. Chauvin V 257-60 No. 154; *ANE* 244-45 No. 209;
Dalîla the Swindler: *Alf* III 225; Burton VII 167. Chauvin V 245-50 No. 147; *ANE* 163-64 No. 224.□

P144.1§, Tax-collector (*ṣarrâf, makkâs*, etc.). See: *GMC*.
¿Abdallah ibn Fâḍil: Treacherous Brothers: *Alf* IV 266-67,-cf.; Burton IX 304. Chauvin V 2-4 No. 2; *ANE* 63-65 No. 261.□

P144.2.1§, ‡Accountant. (Cf. H1574.5.1§).
Sindbâd's First Voyage: *Alf* III 86,-(at sea port); Burton VI 10. Chauvin VII 7-9 No. 373A; *ANE* 385 No. 179;
Ruined Baghdadi and His Slave-girl: *Alf* IV 133; Burton IX 30. Chauvin V 152-53 No. 75; *ANE* 353 No. 235;
al-Rashîd and Omani Merchant: *Alf* IV 215,-cf.; Burton IX 200. Chauvin VI 111-12 No. 276; *ANE* 201-2 No. 257.□

P144.3§, ‡Letter carrier (post-man, postal service). (Cf. P14.15.2, P14.22.3§).
Dalîla the Swindler: *Alf* III 213; Burton VII 146. Chauvin V 245-50 No. 147; *ANE* 163-64 No. 224.□

P148.1.1§, ‡Bully extorts tribute ('protection money', *'itâwah/ghafar*).
Dalîla the Swindler: *Alf* III 225,-(tribute offered by tavern owner); Burton VII 168. Chauvin V 245-50 No. 147; *ANE* 163-64 No. 224.□

P152§, Man so rich that others become jealous. (Cf. W195.4§).
Jawdar and His Treacherous Brethren: *Alf* III 196; Burton VI 246. Chauvin V 257-60 No. 154; *ANE* 244-45 No. 209.□

P152.1§, 'Abu-Muḥammad *al-Kaslân*'s wealth makes king jealous: (Abu-Muḥammad-the-lazy). See: *DOTTI*; *GMC*. (Cf. P95§).
Abû Muḥammad Lazybones: *Alf* II 206-7; Burton IV 162-63. Chauvin VI 64-67 No. 233; *ANE* 71-73 No. 78.□

P153§, Qârûn's wealth: incalculable. See: *GMC*. (Cf. Z93.3§).
Tawaddud: Slavegirl Sold and Regained: *Alf* II 318,-(formulaic/simile); Burton V 225. Chauvin VII 117-19 No. 387; *ANE* 408-10 No. 157.□

P156§, ‡Rich woman (maiden). See: *DOTTI*. (Cf. P761.2.2§).
Copt Broker's Story: Lover's Sacrifices Repaid: *Alf* I 91,-(heiress); Burton I 268. Chauvin VI 80 No. 249; *ANE* 313-14 No. 24;
Budûr and Jubayr ibn ¿Umayr: *Alf* II 235; Burton IV 233. Chauvin VII 93-94 No. 374; *ANE* 243-44 No. 83.□

P159.0.1.1§, ‡Source of the newly rich's wealth questioned (suspected). (Cf. K1966, K2127).
Hasan of Basrah: *Alf* IV 7; Burton VIII 51. Chauvin VII 29-35 No. 212A; *ANE* 207-10 No. 230;

Landsman ¿Abdallah and Merman ¿Abdallah: *Alf* IV 201; Burton IX 173. Chauvin V 6-7 No. 3; *ANE* 65-66 No. 256.□

P159.2§, ‡Rich man keeps a second residence for his own personal pleasure. (Cf. P431.5.1§, T49.3§, T450.5§).
al-'Amjad and al-'As¿ad: *Alf* II 124,-(for his *ḥaẓẓ*); Burton III 334. Chauvin V 208-10 No. 120[.1]; *ANE* 341-42 No. 61/pt. 2.□

P165§, Beggar-peddler (vendor).
Mercury ¿Alî: *Alf* III 227; Burton VII 172. Chauvin V 248-50 No. 147; *ANE* 301-3 No. 225.□

P165.1§, Street water-vendor. See: *GMC*. (Cf. P417.5§).
Mercury ¿Alî: *Alf* III 227; Burton VII 172. Chauvin V 248-50 No. 147; *ANE* 301-3 No. 225.□

P169.1§, ‡Poor social classes (professions).
Sindbâd and Porter: *Alf* III 81,-(porter); Burton VI 1. Chauvin VII 18 No. 373D; *ANE* 383-85 No. 179/pt.□

P169.1.2§, ‡Poor fisher. See: *DOTTI*. (Cf. P419§).
Fisherman and Afrit: Ingratitude: *Alf* I 14; Burton I 38. Chauvin VI 23-25 No. 195; *ANE* 183-84 No. 8;
Three Apples: Hasty Uxoricide: *Alf* I 61; Burton I 187. Chauvin VI 144-45 No. 302; *ANE* 414-15 No. 21;
Anîs al-Jalîs: *Alf* I 141; Burton II 31-32. Chauvin V 120-24 No. 58; *ANE* 316-17 No. 35.□

P169.1.6§, ‡Poor craftsman (cobbler, basket-maker, weaver, or the like).
Ma¿rûf the Cobbler: *Alf* IV 288; Burton X 1. Chauvin VI 81-82 No. 250; *ANE* 291-93 No. 262.□

P170.0.1, ‡Female slaves. (Cf. P268.0.1§).
Anîs al-Jalîs: *Alf* I 125; Burton II 2. Chauvin V 120-24 No. 58; *ANE* 316-17 No. 35.□

P170.0.1.1, Female salves as medium of exchange (unit of value—[monetary]). (Cf. P170.0.3.4§, F179§).
Jânshâh: *Alf* III 47, 64; Burton V 340. Chauvin VII 39-44 No. 153; *ANE* 238-41 No. 178;
Man of Upper Egypt and Frankish Wife: Alf IV 16?,-(text missing); Burton IX 22. Chauvin V 240 No. 140; *ANE*: No. 234.□

P170.0.2.1§, ‡Slave population (staff, crew) of multi-racial and multi-ethnic origins. (Cf. P5.3.5.1.1§, P551.0.3.2§).
Ebony Horse: *Alf* II 261; Burton V 21. Chauvin V 221-31 No. 130; *ANE* 172-74 No. 103;
Jawdar and His Treacherous Brethren: *Alf* III 196; Burton VI 246. Chauvin V 257-60 No. 154; *ANE* 244-45 No. 209.□

P170.0.3.1§, ‡Characteristic behavior (and physical traits) of eunuchs. (Cf. T479§).
Ghânim ibn Ayyûb: *Alf* I 147; Burton II 48. Chauvin VI 14-16 No. 188; *ANE* 192-93 No. 36.□

P170.0.3.4§, ‡Higher price for eunuch (as compared to male slave with genitalia). (Cf. P170.0.1.1, P180.8.1§).
Second Eunuch/Kâfûr's Half-lie: *Alf* I 150; Burton II 56. Chauvin V 278 No. 161; *ANE* 178-79 No. 38.□

P170.0.5§, ‡High cost of maintaining slaves (i.e., feeding, clothing, housing, and the like). (Cf. P180.8.1§).
¿Alâ' al-Dîn Abû al-Shâmât: *Alf* II 164; Burton IV 65. Chauvin V 43-49 No. 18; *ANE* 85-87 No. 63;
Abû Qîr and Abû Ṣîr: *Alf* IV 191; Burton IX 152. Chauvin V 15-17 No. 10; *ANE* 75-77 No. 255.□

P171.0.1§, Seal of slavery (humiliation). See: *DOTTI*; *GMC*.
Bahrâm and Datmâ: *Alf* III 164; Burton VI 185. Chauvin VIII 54-57 No. 22; *ANE* 114-15 No. 202.□

P171.3§, ‡Slave's name changed (by new owner).
Ni¿mah and Nu¿m: Stolen Wife Regained: *Alf* II 132; Burton IV 2. Chauvin VI 96-97 No. 263; *ANE* 314 No. 62.□

P173.0.1§, ‡Free person may not be sold as slave.
Dalîla the Swindler: *Alf* III 224; Burton VII 163. Chauvin V 245-50 No. 147; *ANE* 163-64 No. 224.□

P173.1, ‡Captive king's daughter as slave.
King ¿Umar al-Nu¿mân and Sons: *Alf* I 176,-ff.; Burton II 111. Chauvin VI 112-24 No. 277; *ANE* 430-34 No. 39.□

P173.3, ‡Captives from battle sold as slaves. See: *DOTTI*.
Nûr al-Dîn and Maryam: *Alf* IV 104; Burton VIII 316-17. Chauvin V 52-54 No. 271; *ANE* 98-99 No. 233;
Man of Upper Egypt and Frankish Wife: Alf IV 16?,-(text missing); Burton IX 21-22. Chauvin V 240 No. 140; *ANE*: No. 234.□

P173.3.1.1§, ‡Merman caught by human fisher becomes fisher's property (slave).
Landsman ¿Abdallah and Merman ¿Abdallah: *Alf* IV 200; Burton IX 170. Chauvin V 6-7 No. 3; *ANE* 65-66 No. 256.□

P173.6§, ‡Slaves acquired by abduction (kidnapping, raiding). (Cf. P173.3.1.1§, T194§).
Jawdar and His Treacherous Brethren: *Alf* III 196; Burton VI 246. Chauvin V 257-60 No. 154; *ANE* 244-45 No. 209;
Nûr al-Dîn and Maryam: *Alf* IV 103; Burton VIII 316. Chauvin V 52-54 No. 271; *ANE* 98-99 No. 233.□

P173.9.1§, ‡Slave purchased.
Anîs al-Jalîs: *Alf* I 125; Burton II 2. Chauvin V 120-24 No. 58; *ANE* 316-17 No. 35;
Page Feigns Knowing Bird Language: *Alf* III 157,-(boy); Burton VI 169. Chauvin VIII 49-50 No. 17; *ANE* 321-22 No. 197.□

P173.9.1.1§, ‡Slave with shortcoming(s) sold (purchased) 'As is'. See: *DOTTI*. (Cf. N801.1§, X901).
Second Eunuch/Kâfûr's Half-lie: *Alf* I 148; Burton II 51. Chauvin V 278 No. 161; *ANE* 178-79 No. 38.□

P173.9.2§, ‡Slave received or given as reward (grant, gift). See: *DOTTI*. (Cf. P180.3.1§).
King ¿Umar al-Nu¿mân and Sons: *Alf* I 163,-(Ṣafiyyah); Burton II 79,-(Sofiyah or Sophia). Chauvin VI 112-24 No. 277; *ANE* 430-34 No. 39;
¿Alâ' al-Dîn Abû al-Shâmât: *Alf* II 164; Burton IV 64. Chauvin V 43-49 No. 18; *ANE* 85-87 No. 63;
Hârûn, Slave-girl and Judge Abû-Yûsuf: *Alf* II 202-3; Burton IV 154. Chauvin VII 114 No. 383; *ANE* 204 No. 75;
Isḥâq al-Mûṣilî and Merchant's Singer: *Alf* II 296; Burton V 133. Chauvin VI 59 No. 225; *ANE* 233 No. 142;
Abû Qîr and Abû Ṣîr: *Alf* IV 191; Burton IX 147. Chauvin V 15-17 No. 10; *ANE* 75-77 No. 255.□

P173.9.5§, ‡Slave acquired as part of inheritance. (Cf. P761§, W14.8.2§).
Tawaddud: Slavegirl Sold and Regained: *Alf* II 304,-(slave-girl); Burton V 191. Chauvin VII 117-19 No. 387; *ANE* 408-10 No. 157.□

P174.0.1.1§, ‡Child (son) of slave-woman and free father becomes distinguished (i.e., savant, ruler, warrior, or the like).
¿Alî bin Ṭâhir and Mu'nis: *Alf* II 303; Burton V 164. Chauvin VI 154 No. 319; *ANE* 101 No. 153.□

P174.1§, ‡Slave and his possessions are owner's property.
Ghânim ibn Ayyûb: *Alf* I 162; Burton II 76. Chauvin VI 14 No. 188; *ANE* 192-93 No. 36.□

P174.2§, ‡Slave and owner's possessions (property). See: *DOTTI*.
Hârûn, Slave-girl and Judge Abû-Yûsuf: *Alf* II 202-3; Burton IV 154-55. Chauvin VII 114 No. 383; *ANE* 204 No. 75.□

P174.2.1§, ‡'Whatever belongs to the master is sinful for the slave [to enjoy without permission]'. (Cf. C792§).
Ghânim ibn Ayyûb: *Alf* I 155; Burton II 63. Chauvin VI 14 No. 188; *ANE* 192-93 No. 36.□

P174.2.2§, ‡Child acquired along with parent(s) as slaves. (Cf. P173.9.1§).
Ni¿mah and Nu¿m: Stolen Wife Regained: *Alf* II 132; Burton IV 1. Chauvin VI 96-97 No. 263; *ANE* 314 No. 62.□

P174.3§, ‡Slave's marital affairs.
Hârûn, Slave-girl and Judge Abû-Yûsuf: *Alf* II 202-3; Burton IV 154. Chauvin VII 114 No. 383; *ANE* 204 No. 75.□

P174.3.1§, ‡Owner has no legal right to force slave to divorce his wife. (Cf. P180.5§, P529.0.6.3§).
Hârûn, Slave-girl and Judge Abû-Yûsuf: *Alf* II 203; Burton IV 154. Chauvin VII 114 No. 383; *ANE* 204 No. 75.□

P178, Slaves freed. See: *DOTTI*; *GMC*. (Cf. J149.2.1§, V6§).

Qamar al-Zamân and Budûr: *Alf* II 80,-(*jinni*/won wager); Burton III 242-44. Chauvin V 204-12 No. 120; *ANE* 341-45 No. 61;
City of Brass: *Alf* III 136,-cf.; Burton VI 116,-("bondsmen and bondswomen"). Chauvin V 32-35 No. 16; *ANE* 146-50 No. 180.□

P178.0.2§, ‡Freed slaves ('*ma¿âtîq*') as social class (community).
Mercury ¿Alî: *Alf* III 238; Burton VII 194. Chauvin V 248-50 No. 147; *ANE* 301-3 No. 225.□

P178.0.1§, ‡Slave may not be 'freed' without ability to make a living independently. (Cf. P178.5.2§).
Second Eunuch/Kâfûr's Half-lie: *Alf* I 150; Burton II 55. Chauvin V 278 No. 161; *ANE* 178-79 No. 38.□

P178.2.2.1.1§, ‡Slave singing-woman (musician) freed in return for performing for master.
Ruined Baghdadi and His Slave-girl: *Alf* IV 133; Burton IX 32. Chauvin V 152-53 No. 75; *ANE* 353 No. 235.□

P178.3§, Freeing of slave(s) as expiatory-deed. See: *DOTTI*. (Cf. V6§).
King ¿Umar al-Nu¿mân and Sons: *Alf* I 199,-cf./(female slave); Burton II 154. Chauvin VI 112-24 No. 277; *ANE* 430-34 No. 39;
Nuzhat al-Zamân Tested/¿Umar al-Nu¿mân: *Alf* I 203-4,-cf.; Burton II 164. Chauvin VI 116, n.1/passim No. 277; *ANE* 432,/passim No. 39;
¿Alî ibn Bakkâr: *Alf* II 65,-(upon death of mistress/owner); Burton III 211. Chauvin V 153 No. 76; *ANE* 92-93 No. 60;
¿Alâ' al-Dîn Abû al-Shâmât: *Alf* II 166; Burton IV 67. Chauvin V 43-49 No. 18; *ANE* 85-87 No. 63;
City of Brass: *Alf* III 136,-cf./(queen's justice); Burton VI 116,-("bondsmen and bondswomen"). Chauvin V 32-35 No. 16; *ANE* 146-50 No. 180;
Masrûr and Zayn al-Mawâṣif: *Alf* IV 74; Burton VIII 248. Chauvin VI 82-84 No. 251; *ANE* 294-95 No. 232;
Landsman ¿Abdallah and Merman ¿Abdallah: *Alf* IV 200,-(captive merman); Burton IX 170. Chauvin V 6-7 No. 3; *ANE* 65-66 No. 256.□

P178.3.1.1§, ‡Slave-woman granted a wish by infatuated master: she asks to be freed. (Cf. W164.2.1.5§).
Abû al-Ḥasan al-Khorâsânî (and Caliph's Favorite): *Alf* IV 236; Burton IX 242-43. Chauvin V 218-20 No. 129; *ANE* 68-69 No. 259.□

P178.4§, ‡If abused, slave may demand to be sold.
Mercury ¿Alî: *Alf* III 244,-(slave-girl); Burton VII 203. Chauvin V 248-50 No. 147; *ANE* 301-3 No. 225;
Hasan of Basrah: *Alf* IV 9; Burton VIII 54. Chauvin VII 29-35 No. 212A; *ANE* 207-10 No. 230.□

P178.5§, ‡Slave may not be freed without his (her) consent.
Second Eunuch/Kâfûr's Half-lie: *Alf* I 150; Burton II 55. Chauvin V 278 No. 161; *ANE* 178-79 No. 38.□

P178.5.1§, ‡Slave refuses to be freed. See: *DOTTI*. (Cf. J684.6§).
Second Eunuch/Kâfûr's Half-lie: *Alf* I 148, 150; Burton II 55-54. Chauvin V 278 No. 161; *ANE* 178-79 No. 38;
Man of Upper Egypt and Frankish Wife: Alf IV 16?,-(text missing); Burton IX 23,-cf. Chauvin V 240 No. 140; *ANE*: No. 234.□

P178.5.2§, ‡Slave without profession (craft, skill, trade) that would permit making a living refuses to be freed. (Cf. J1014§, P31, P178.0.1§).
Second Eunuch/Kâfûr's Half-lie: *Alf* I 150; Burton II 55. Chauvin V 278 No. 161; *ANE* 178-79 No. 38.□

P178.9.1§, ‡Slave freed and taken as spouse. (Cf. T121.6.1§).
King ¿Umar al-Nu¿mân and Sons: *Alf* I 199; Burton II 154. Chauvin VI 112-24 No. 277; *ANE* 430-34 No. 39;
Man of Upper Egypt and Frankish Wife: Alf IV 16?,-(text missing); Burton IX 19-24. Chauvin V 240 No. 140; *ANE*: No. 234.□

P179.0.1§, ‡The ideal (perfect) slave. (Usually, a female). (Cf. P185.3.1§).
Anîs al-Jalîs: *Alf* I 127; Burton II 3-4. Chauvin V 120-24 No. 58; *ANE* 316-17 No. 35;
¿Alî Shâr and Zumurrud: *Alf* II 220; Burton IV 196. Chauvin V 89-91 No. 28; *ANE* 100-1 No. 82;

Man from Yaman and Six Salve-girls: Flyting: *Alf* II 249-50; Burton IV 259-60. Chauvin VI 151 No. 313; *ANE* 289-90 No. 84.□

P179.1.1§, ‡Slave-girl (woman) as scholar. See: *DOTTI*. (Cf. J155.0.1§).
King ¿Umar al-Nu¿mân and Sons: *Alf* I 198; Burton II 151. Chauvin VI 112-24 No. 277; *ANE* 430-34 No. 39.□

P179.1.1.1§, ‡Slave-girl with comprehensive knowledge of all arts and sciences: (Tawaddud: Slavegirl Sold and Regained, Nuzhat az-Zamân). See: *DOTTI*.
Anîs al-Jalîs: *Alf* I 127; Burton II 3-4. Chauvin V 120-24 No. 58; *ANE* 316-17 No. 35;
King ¿Umar al-Nu¿mân and Sons: *Alf* I 197-98, 200,-(enslaved princess); Burton II 151, 154ff. Chauvin VI 112-24 No. 277; *ANE* 430-34 No. 39.□

P179.1.2§, ‡Slave-girl as singer (musician-poetess). (Cf. P427.7.4.1§).
Ishâq al-Mûṣilî and Merchant's Singer: *Alf* II 296; Burton V 130-33. Chauvin VI 59 No. 225; *ANE* 233 No. 142.□

P179.1.3§, ‡Slave-girl as artisan (at craft, trade, vocation). (Cf. P209§, W40§).
Nûr al-Dîn and Maryam: *Alf* IV 101; Burton VIII 312. Chauvin V 52-54 No. 271; *ANE* 98-99 No. 233.□

P180.3§, ‡Joint ownership of slave. See: *DOTTI*.
Hârûn, Slave-girl and Judge Abû-Yûsuf: *Alf* II 202,-(half sold, half given as grant); Burton IV 154. Chauvin VII 114 No. 383; *ANE* 204 No. 75.□

P180.3.1§, ‡Man receives half ownership of slave-girl as grant. See: *DOTTI*. (Cf. P173.9.2§).
Hârûn, Slave-girl and Judge Abû-Yûsuf: *Alf* II 202; Burton IV 154. Chauvin VII 114 No. 383; *ANE* 204 No. 75.□

P180.4.1§, ‡Slave abused (mistreated). (Cf. S123.1).
al-Rashîd and Omani Merchant: *Alf* IV 215,-(beaten); Burton IX 199. Chauvin VI 111-12 No. 276; *ANE* 201-2 No. 257.□

P180.4.1.1§, ‡Slave beaten.
Tailor's Story/Barber of Baghdad: *Alf* I 107; Burton I 314. Chauvin V 154-56 No. 78; *ANE* 405-6 No. 27;
Second Eunuch/Kâfûr's Half-lie: *Alf* I 148; Burton II 51,-(broker). Chauvin V 278 No. 161; *ANE* 178-79 No. 38;
al-Rashîd and Omani Merchant: *Alf* IV 215; Burton IX 199. Chauvin VI 111-12 No. 276; *ANE* 201-2 No. 257.□

P180.4.1.1.1§, ‡Slave tortured.
Qamar al-Zamân and Budûr: *Alf* II 80,-(*khâdim*/servant); Burton III 242-44. Chauvin V 204-12 No. 120; *ANE* 341-45 No. 61.□

P180.4.2.1§, ‡Slave treated as if member of family (foster-child). See: *DOTTI*. (Cf. T405.3.3§).
Reeve's Story: Why Maimed by Bride: *Alf* I 98,-(slave-girl); Burton I 285. Chauvin V 220-21 No. 305; *ANE* 351 No. 25.□

P180.4.2.2§, ‡Free and slave raised together as foster ("sociological") siblings. See: *DOTTI*. (Cf. P274.2§).
First Eunuch: Bukhayt Deflowers Mistress: *Alf* I 148; Burton II 49. Chauvin V 277 No. 160; *ANE* 178 No. 37;
Ni¿mah and Nu¿m: Stolen Wife Regained: *Alf* II 132; Burton IV 2. Chauvin VI 96-97 No. 263; *ANE* 314 No. 62.□

P180.4.3§, ‡Privileged Slave(s). (Cf. P508.1§).
al-'Amjad and al-'As¿ad: *Alf* II 124; Burton III 333. Chauvin V 208-10 No. 120[.1]; *ANE* 341-42 No. 61/pt. 2.□

P180.4.3.1§, ‡Slave holds self superior to menial freeman. (Cf. P508.1§).
Nûr al-Dîn and Maryam: *Alf* IV 92,-(slave-girl); Burton VIII 294 n. 1,-(not "become a mere servant"/not "sully myself with menial service"). Chauvin V 52-54 No. 271; *ANE* 98-99 No. 233.□

P180.5§, Treatment of slave's children in relationship to master's. See: *DOTTI*; *GMC*. (Cf. P173.9.2§).

First Eunuch: Bukhayt Deflowers Mistress: *Alf* I 147; Burton II 49-50. Chauvin V 277 No. 160; *ANE* 178 No. 37.□

P180.8§, ‡Uxoriousness through slaves—(sexual liaison with slaves). See: *DOTTI*. (Cf. T380.0.1.1§).
King ¿Umar al-Nu¿mân and Sons: *Alf* I 168; Burton II 95. Chauvin VI 112-24 No. 277; *ANE* 430-34 No. 39.□

P180.8.0.1§, ‡Sexual relations between master and female-slaves discouraged (or condemned).
King ¿Umar al-Nu¿mân and Sons: *Alf* I 168; Burton II 95. Chauvin VI 112-24 No. 277; *ANE* 430-34 No. 39.□

P180.8.1§, ‡High price of slave-girls. (Cf. P170.0.3.4§, P170.0.5§, P529.0.2.3.1§, T52.0.1§, T52.0.6.1.2§, T450.0.2§).
Tawaddud: Slavegirl Sold and Regained: *Alf* III 8; Burton V 245. Chauvin VII 117-19 No. 387; *ANE* 408-10 No. 157.□

P180.8.1.1§, ‡Bride-wealth costs less than price of slave-girl.
Nûr al-Dîn and Maryam: *Alf* IV 101,-(less than half); Burton VIII 312. Chauvin V 52-54 No. 271; *ANE* 98-99 No. 233.□

P180.8.3.1§, ‡Lesbian liaison between mistress and female-slave condemned. (Cf. N349.4.1.1§, T462.4§).
Budûr and Jubayr ibn ¿Umayr: *Alf* II 237,-(suspected); Burton IV 234. Chauvin VII 93-94 No. 374; *ANE* 243-44 No. 83;
Lovers of Basra/Ḍamrah: *Alf* III 211,-cf.; Burton VII 132. Chauvin V 118 No. 54; *ANE* 273 No. 220.□

P180.8.5§, ‡At auction, slave-girl chooses her buyer (owner-to-be). See: *DOTTI*. (Cf. P774.3§).
¿Alî Shâr and Zumurrud: *Alf* II 217-18; Burton IV 192-97. Chauvin V 89-91 No. 28; *ANE* 100-1 No. 82;
Nûr al-Dîn and Maryam: *Alf* IV 92-93, 104,-cf./(promised); Burton VIII 294, 317. Chauvin V 52-54 No. 271; *ANE* 98-99 No. 233.□

P181.3.1§, ‡Eunuch as paternal figure for girl (young mistress)—as her *murabbî*/'male-governess'). (Cf. N862§, P170.0.3.1§, P181.3.1§, P272.5§).
Second Qalandar: Afrit's Wife: *Alf* I 48; Burton I 133. Chauvin V 197-200 No. 116; *ANE* 338-39 No. 16.□

P182§, Slave wooes his mistress. See: *DOTTI*.
First Eunuch: Bukhayt Deflowers Mistress: *Alf* I 148,-cf.; Burton II 50. Chauvin V 277 No. 160; *ANE* 178 No. 37;
King ¿Umar al-Nu¿mân and Sons: *Alf* I 184-85; Burton II 126. Chauvin VI 112-24 No. 277; *ANE* 430-34 No. 39.□

P185§, Faithful slave-woman. See: *GMC*. (Cf. P361.4.0.1§).
King ¿Umar al-Nu¿mân and Sons: *Alf* I 184; Burton II 128. Chauvin VI 112-24 No. 277; *ANE* 430-34 No. 39;
¿Alî ibn Bakkâr: *Alf* II 60, 65,-(slave-women/to deceased mistress); Burton III 201, 210-11. Chauvin V 153 No. 76; *ANE* 92-93 No. 60.□

P185.1§, Faithful slave-woman, faithless mistress (wife). See: *DOTTI*.
First Shaykh: Sorceress Wife: *Alf* I 10,-cf./(concubine); Burton I 27-31. Chauvin VII 129-30 No. 396; *ANE* 376-77 No. 5.□

P185.3.1§, ‡Beloved slave-girl asks impoverished master to sell her in order to pay creditors. See: *DOTTI*. (Cf. T292.3§, W13§).
Anîs al-Jalîs: *Alf* I 132; Burton II 14. Chauvin V 120-24 No. 58; *ANE* 316-17 No. 35;
Tawaddud: Slavegirl Sold and Regained: *Alf* II 305; Burton V 193. Chauvin VII 117-19 No. 387; *ANE* 408-10 No. 157;
Ruined Baghdadi and His Slave-girl: *Alf* IV 130; Burton IX 24. Chauvin V 152-53 No. 75; *ANE* 353 No. 235.□

P187§, Inherent rivalry between mistress and young female slave. (Cf. T257.2.3§).
Ghânim ibn Ayyûb: *Alf* I 154,-(Zubaydah-Qût al-Qulûb); Burton II 61. Chauvin VI 14-16 No. 188; *ANE* 192-93 No. 36.□

P187.1§, ‡Wife humiliated by husband's sexual liaison with slave-woman. (Cf. D661.6.1§, K1510.2, M131.1.1§, P268.2§, T234§, W164.5§).
Sweep and Noble Lady: Infidelity Repaid: *Alf* II 190; Burton IV 128. Chauvin VI 148 No. 306; *ANE* 403-4 No. 72;
Jullanâr of the Sea: *Alf* III 267,-cf./(mistress of slave); Burton VII 302. Chauvin V 147-51 No. 73; *ANE* 248-51 No. 227.□

P191.0.2.1§, ‡If wind were to blow, it would tear down a stranger's (foreigner's) palace [built on air (sand)]. (Cf. W22.3.1.1§).
Mercury ¿Alî: *Alf* III 228,-(poem); Burton VII 175. Chauvin V 248-50 No. 147; *ANE* 301-3 No. 225.□

P191.1.1§, Foreigners (strangers) are unconcerned about the seemliness of their social conduct. (Cf. U244§).
Ma¿rûf the Cobbler: *Alf* IV 294; Burton X 10. Chauvin VI 81-82 No. 250; *ANE* 291-93 No. 262.□

P191.1.3.1§, ‡"A stranger is blind [i.e., (ignorant])".
Budûr and Jubayr ibn ¿Umayr: *Alf* II 236,-cf./(excuse); Burton IV 232. Chauvin VII 93-94 No. 374; *ANE* 243-44 No. 83.□

P191.1.4§, ‡Parlance of foreigners (or professional groups).
¿Alî ibn Bakkâr: *Alf* II 59,-(of robbers/jargon); Burton III 200,-("barbarous jargon"). Chauvin V 153 No. 76; *ANE* 92-93 No. 60.□

P191.1.4.1§, ‡Parlance of foreigners ('*ruṭân*') not understood. See: *DOTTI*.
¿Alî ibn Bakkâr: *Alf* II 59; Burton III 200. Chauvin V 153 No. 76; *ANE* 92-93 No. 60;
Tawaddud: Slavegirl Sold and Regained: *Alf* III 7,-(by loser of game); Burton V 244,-(xxx). Chauvin VII 117-19 No. 387; *ANE* 408-10 No. 157;
Nûr al-Dîn and Maryam: *Alf* IV 123; Burton IX 4,-(slave's barbarous accents). Chauvin V 52-54 No. 271; *ANE* 98-99 No. 233;
Jeweler's Wife and Qamar al-Zamân: *Alf* IV 252; Burton IX 275,-(Levantines). Chauvin V 212-14 No. 121; *ANE* 345-47 No. 260.□

P191.1.5§, ‡Strangers are melancholy (sad, lonesome, homesick). (Cf. F569.3.1§, W22.3.1§).
Jullanâr of the Sea: *Alf* III 248,-(Jullanâr); Burton VII 266. Chauvin V 147-51 No. 73; *ANE* 248-51 No. 227.□

P191.1.5.1.1§, ‡Stranger weeps. (Cf. F1041.11.3§, F1051).
Qamar al-Zamân and Budûr: *Alf* II 104-5; Burton III 292. Chauvin V 204-12 No. 120; *ANE* 341-45 No. 61.□

P191.2§, ‡Foreigner (stranger) required to provide information on his social status and profession (craft, trade). (Usually at city gate). (Cf. P5.7.0.1§, P31, P522, P570.1.1.1§).
Ebony Horse: *Alf* II 263; Burton V 26. Chauvin V 221-31 No. 130; *ANE* 172-74 No. 103.□

P191.1.2§, Foreigners (strangers) should be gracious toward customs of host people (country).
Sindbâd's Fourth Voyage: *Alf* III 103-4,-cf./(local tradition applied to reluctant foreigner); Burton VI 39. Chauvin VII 18-20 No. 373D; *ANE* 386 No. 179.□

P191.3.1§, ‡Useful foreigner invited to settle in host country (and become citizen).
Sindbâd's Fourth Voyage: *Alf* III 103,-(*mustawṭin*); Burton VI 40. Chauvin VII 18-20 No. 373D; *ANE* 386 No. 179;
Abû Qîr and Abû Ṣîr: *Alf* IV 190; Burton IX 151. Chauvin V 15-17 No. 10; *ANE* 75-77 No. 255.□

P192.1, Professional fool [(jester)]. (Cf. P14.15.4§).
Hunchback's Tale: Resuscitated: *Alf* I 88; Burton I 261. Chauvin VI 80 No. 249; *ANE* 313-14 No. 23.□

P193.1§, Angry crowd (mob). See: *GMC*.
King Jalî¿âd and Shimâs: *Alf* IV 169; Burton IX 107. Chauvin VI 9 No. 184; *ANE* 237-38 No. 236.□

P193.3§, ‡Curious crowd of people.
Tailor's Story/Barber of Baghdad: *Alf* I 108; Burton I 314-15. Chauvin V 154-56 No. 78; *ANE* 405-6 No. 27;
Jeweler's Wife and Qamar al-Zamân: *Alf* IV 239; Burton IX 250. Chauvin V 212-14 No. 121; *ANE* 345-47 No. 260;
Ma¿rûf the Cobbler: *Alf* IV 293; Burton X 7. Chauvin VI 81-82 No. 250; *ANE* 291-93 No. 262.□

P193.3.1.1§, ‡Obnoxious children (hecklers). See: *DOTTI*.
¿Alî Shâr and Zumurrud: *Alf* II 224,-(heckle self-punishing man); Burton IV 204. Chauvin V 89-91 No. 28; *ANE* 100-1 No. 82;
Prior Becomes Moslem: al-Anbârî: *Alf* II 298; Burton V 143. Chauvin V 237-38 No. 137; *ANE* 330-31 No. 147;
Ma¿rûf the Cobbler: *Alf* IV 294; Burton X 8-9. Chauvin VI 81-82 No. 250; *ANE* 291-93 No. 262.□

P193.3.1.1.1§, ‡Obnoxious children injure person (by throwing stones or the like).
Prior Becomes Moslem: al-Anbârî: *Alf* II 298; Burton V 143. Chauvin V 237-38 No. 137; *ANE* 330-31 No. 147.□

P193.3.1.2§, ‡Obnoxious child as thief (pickpocket, thief's assistant). See: *DOTTI*.
Ma¿rûf the Cobbler: *Alf* IV 294; Burton X 8-9. Chauvin VI 81-82 No. 250; *ANE* 291-93 No. 262.□

P193.4§, ‡Sad (mourning, weeping, etc.) crowd. Usually helpless.
Three Apples: Hasty Uxoricide: *Alf* I 62; Burton I 189. Chauvin VI 144-45 No. 302; *ANE* 414-15 No. 21;
Anîs al-Jalîs: *Alf* I 144; Burton II 42. Chauvin V 120-24 No. 58; *ANE* 316-17 No. 35;
Lover Who Feigned Himself a Thief: *Alf* II 205; Burton IV 157. Chauvin VII 134-35 No. 403; *ANE* 272 No. 76.□

P195§, Drug-addicts, (*masaṭîl*: the 'stoned', the 'high').
¿Alâ' al-Dîn Abû al-Shâmât: *Alf* II 148; Burton IV 31. Chauvin V 43-49 No. 18; *ANE* 85-87 No. 63.□

P195.0.4.1§, ‡Disgraceful act(s) by drug addicts. (Cf. F1041.15.1§, J1913.4§, P196.1§, P780§, U283.1.3§).
King ¿Umar al-Nu¿mân and Sons: *Alf* I 188,-(passim); Burton II 134. Chauvin VI 112-24 No. 277; *ANE* 430-34 No. 39.□

P195.1§, *hashshâshîn* (hashish-smokers). See: *DOTTI*; *GMC*.
Hashish Eater's Dream: *Alf* II 9; Burton III 91. Chauvin VI 124 No. 278; *ANE* 216 No. 42;
Sweep and Noble Lady: Infidelity Repaid: *Alf* II 188; Burton IV 125,-("sweep"). Chauvin VI 148 No. 306; *ANE* 403-4 No. 72;
¿Alî Shâr and Zumurrud: *Alf* II 230; Burton IV 213,-(Hashish-eater). Chauvin V 89-91 No. 28; *ANE* 100-1 No. 82.□

P195.1.0.1§, ‡Hashish-smoking song or poem. (Cf. F950.0.2.1.1.1§).
Wolf and Fox: *Alf* II 33,-cf./(poem,/*ḥashîshah*/[double meaning ??]); Burton III 141,-(grass). Chauvin II 227 No. 6; *ANE* 450 No. 47.□

P195.1.3§, ‡Professionals (males) as consumers of narcotics. (Cf. F950.0.2.1.1.1§).
¿Alâ' al-Dîn Abû al-Shâmât: *Alf* II 148; Burton IV 31. Chauvin V 43-49 No. 18; *ANE* 85-87 No. 63.□

P196§, *khamorgiyyah, sukariyyîn* (drunkards). See: *GMC*.
Mock Caliph/¿Alî al-Jawharî: *Alf* II 193,-cf.; Burton IV 135. Chauvin V 99-100 No. 174; *ANE* 304-5 No. 73.□

P196.0.1§, ‡Poem or song of (liquor) drinking. (*khamriyyât*). (Cf. U283.1§).
Barber's Sixth Brother: Emasculated by Abductor: *Alf* I 123; Burton I 349. Chauvin V 163-64 No. 86; *ANE* 120 No. 34;
Nûr al-Dîn and Maryam: *Alf* IV 83; Burton VIII 277. Chauvin V 52-54 No. 271; *ANE* 98-99 No. 233.□

P196.1§, ‡Disgraceful act(s) by drunkards. (Cf. F1041.15.1§, J1326§, K1626.4§).
King ¿Umar al-Nu¿mân and Sons: *Alf* I 247,-cf.; Burton II 256. Chauvin VI 112-24 No. 277; *ANE* 430-34 No. 39;
Isḥâq al-Mûṣilî and Khadîjah bint al-Ḥasan: *Alf* II 185,-(sits in basket); Burton IV 120. Chauvin V 241-42 No. 142; *ANE* 232 No. 71;
Abû Qîr and Abû Ṣîr: *Alf* IV 182-83; Burton IX 134-35. Chauvin V 15-17 No. 10; *ANE* 75-77 No. 255.□

P196.1.2§, ‡Drunkard loses control over his social conduct. See: *PSAE*. (Cf. K332.3§).
Barber's Sixth Brother: Emasculated by Abductor: *Alf* I 123; Burton I 347. Chauvin V 163-64 No. 86; *ANE* 120 No. 34;

Lovers of Basra/Damrah: *Alf* III 211; Burton VII 132. Chauvin V 118 No. 54; *ANE* 273 No. 220; **Ruined Baghdadi and His Slave-girl**: *Alf* IV 132,-(gets marooned); Burton IX 30. Chauvin V 152-53 No. 75; *ANE* 353 No. 235.□

P196.1.2.1§, ‡Drunkard strikes parent(s).
Nûr al-Dîn and Maryam: *Alf* IV 89; Burton VIII 287. Chauvin V 52-54 No. 271; *ANE* 98-99 No. 233.□

P196.1.2.2§, ‡Drunkard commits rape (incest). See: *DOTTI*.
Anîs al-Jalîs: *Alf* I 128,-(slave-girl); Burton II 6. Chauvin V 120-24 No. 58; *ANE* 316-17 No. 35.□

P196.1.2.3§, ‡Drunkard commits murder. (Cf. K1626.4§).
al-'Amjad and al-'As¿ad: *Alf* II 125-26; Burton III 336-37. Chauvin V 208-10 No. 120[.1]; *ANE* 341-42 No. 61/pt. 2.□

P196.1.2.5§, ‡Drunkard fails at work (cannot fulfill terms of contracts). See: *DOTTI*; *PSAE*.
King ¿Umar al-Nu¿mân and Sons: *Alf* I 247; Burton II 255. Chauvin VI 112-24 No. 277; *ANE* 430-34 No. 39.□

P196.8.1§, ‡Drinking party (clique).
Barber's Sixth Brother: Emasculated by Abductor: *Alf* I 123; Burton I 347. Chauvin V 163-64 No. 86; *ANE* 120 No. 34;
Mock Caliph/¿Alî al-Jawharî: *Alf* II 193; Burton IV 134. Chauvin V 99-100 No. 174; *ANE* 304-5 No. 73.□

P196.8.1.1§, ‡Drinking (liquor) together establishes bond between drinking parties.
Hammâd: Treacherous Bedouin: *Alf* II 19; Burton III 110. Chauvin VI 124 n. 1 No. 277; *ANE* 200 No. 43.□

P196.8.2§, ‡Listening to song (music): an accompaniment of liquor-drinking. (Cf. F689.1§).
Anîs al-Jalîs: *Alf* I 140,-(poem); Burton II 30. Chauvin V 120-24 No. 58; *ANE* 316-17 No. 35;
Mock Caliph/¿Alî al-Jawharî: *Alf* II 193; Burton IV 135. Chauvin V 99-100 No. 174; *ANE* 304-5 No. 73.□

P196.8.2.1§, ‡"Liquor-drinking without listening may cause headaches (illness)". (Cf. F689.1.1§, P196.8.2.1§).
Budûr and Jubayr ibn ¿Umayr: *Alf* II 239,-cf./(listening avoided); Burton IV 237. Chauvin VII 93-94 No. 374; *ANE* 243-44 No. 83.□

P198§, *¿ilûq, khawalât* ('gays', 'faggots'). (Cf. Z179.1.3§).
Jawdar and His Treacherous Brethren: *Alf* III 198,-(simile); Burton VI 249. Chauvin V 257-60 No. 154; *ANE* 244-45 No. 209.□

P199.0.1§, ‡Song or poem concerning homosexuality. (Cf. F575.2, T463.3.1§).
Dispute Concerning Males and Females: *Alf* II 301-2; Burton V 156-58 161-63. Chauvin VI 153 No. 317; *ANE* 291 No. 151;
Jeweler's Wife and Qamar al-Zamân: *Alf* IV 239; Burton IX 250-51. Chauvin V 212-14 No. 121; *ANE* 345-47 No. 260.□

P200.0.1.3.1§, ‡Elder brother as head of family: younger siblings are in his charge. See: *DOTTI*.
Omar and Young Badawî: Returning to be Executed: *Alf* II 288; Burton V 102. Chauvin V 216 No. 125; *ANE* 429-30 No. 130.□

P200.4§, ‡Person lives alone, without family (no wife, no children, etc.). (Cf. P447§).
Tâj al-Mulûk: *Alf* I 261; Burton II 283-84. Chauvin V 126-28 No. 60; *ANE* 406-8 No. 40.□

P201.5§, ‡Reconciliation between hostile branches of family. (Cf. P310.5.1§).
King ¿Umar al-Nu¿mân and Sons: *Alf* II 21; Burton III 114. Chauvin VI 112-24 No. 277; *ANE* 430-34 No. 39;
Sayf al-Mulûk: *Alf* III 302,-(jinn nations); Burton VIII 5. Chauvin VII 64-73 No. 348; *ANE* 362-64 No. 229.□

P202.1.5.2§, ‡Wife blamed for husband's misconduct. See: *DOTTI*.
Water-carrier and Goldsmith's Wife: *Alf* II 286,-(implicit/conclusion); Burton V 90. Chauvin VI 192 No. 361; *ANE* 444 No. 122.□

P203.1§, ‡Family reunited in full (father, mother, and all children). See: *DOTTI*.

Hasan of Basrah: *Alf* IV 54,-(with mother); Burton VIII 154-55. Chauvin VII 29-35 No. 212A; *ANE* 207-10 No. 230;
Nûr al-Dîn and Maryam: *Alf* IV 129; Burton IX 18. Chauvin V 52-54 No. 271; *ANE* 98-99 No. 233.□

P203.6§, ‡Partial reuniting of family: only some members are included.
al-'Amjad and al-'As¿ad: *Alf* II 146-47; Burton IV 27-29. Chauvin V 208-10 No. 120[.1]; *ANE* 341-42 No. 61/pt. 2.□

P203.6.2§, ‡Reunion of mother and son. (Usually, son returns home to mother).
¿Azîz and ¿Azîzah: *Alf* I 307,-(as castrate); Burton III 46. Chauvin V 144-45 No. 71; *ANE* 111-13 No. 41;
Hasan of Basrah: *Alf* IV 54-55; Burton VIII 154-55. Chauvin VII 29-35 No. 212A; *ANE* 207-10 No. 230.□

P208.0.1§, ‡Document that designates a person's genealogy (ancestry). (Cf. Z167.0.1§).
Nûr al-Dîn ¿Alî and Son: *Alf* I 68; Burton I 207. Chauvin VI 102-6 No. 270; *ANE* 317-19 No. 22.□

P208.2§, ‡Matrilineal descent: child identified by mother's line. See: *DOTTI*; *PSAE*.
Jullanâr of the Sea: *Alf* III 270,-(son of queen Jullanâr-of-the-Sea); Burton VII 307. Chauvin V 147-51 No. 73; *ANE* 248-51 No. 227.□

P208.7.4§, ‡Children named according to omen.
¿Alâ' al-Dîn Abû al-Shâmât: *Alf* II 148; Burton IV 33. Chauvin V 43-49 No. 18; *ANE* 85-87 No. 63.□

P208.7.6§, ‡Children given humiliating (ugly) names (e.g., 'Floor-mop', 'Beggar', etc.)—as protection.
Barber's Third Brother: Exposes Blind Robbers: *Alf* I 114,-(Quffah, Soft-basket); Burton I 328,-(variant/Al-Fakik, the Gabbler). Chauvin V 159-60 No. 83; *ANE* 118 No. 31.□

P208.9.1§, ‡Good pedigree on both father's line of descent and mother's ('to be of *ḥasab* and *nasab*'). (Cf. H1381.3.1.5§).
Abû Muḥammad Lazybones: *Alf* II 211; Burton IV 171. Chauvin VI 64-67 No. 233; *ANE* 71-73 No. 78;
Jullanâr of the Sea: *Alf* III 255; Burton VII 279. Chauvin V 147-51 No. 73; *ANE* 248-51 No. 227.□

P209§, Working female as family provider. See: *GMC*.
Spy, Fourth Maiden/¿Umar al-Nu¿mân: *Alf* I 222; Burton II 204. *ANE* 432 No. 39/passim.□

P209.2§, Wife as provider. See: *DOTTI*.
Landsman ¿Abdallah and Merman ¿Abdallah: *Alf* IV 205; Burton IX 183. Chauvin V 6-7 No. 3; *ANE* 65-66 No. 256.□

P209.2.1§, ‡Mate (slave-girl, mistress, girlfriend) as provider.
Nûr al-Dîn and Maryam: *Alf* IV 97-98,-(slave-girl); Burton VIII 306. Chauvin V 52-54 No. 271; *ANE* 98-99 No. 233.□

P209.4§, Sister as provider. See: *DOTTI*; *GMC*.
Eldest Lady's Story: Treacherous Sisters: *Alf* I 53-54,-cf./(to sisters); Burton I 164. Chauvin V 4 No. 443; *ANE* 174-75 No. 19;
King ¿Umar al-Nu¿mân and Sons: *Alf* I 188; Burton II 133. Chauvin VI 112-24 No. 277; *ANE* 430-34 No. 39;
Spy, Fourth Maiden/¿Umar al-Nu¿mân: *Alf* I 222; Burton II 204. *ANE* 432 No. 39/passim.□

P210, Husband and wife. See: *DOTTI*.
Three Wishes: *Alf* III 162; Burton VI 180-81. Chauvin VIII 51-52 No. 19; *ANE* 419-20 No. 199.□

P210.0.1§, Husband as his wife's master. See: *DOTTI*; *GMC*.
Merchant's Curious Wife: *Alf* I 6,-cf.; Burton I 22-23. Chauvin V 179-80 No. 104; *ANE* 298-99 No. 3;
Ni¿mah and Nu¿m: Stolen Wife Regained: *Alf* II 134,-(*yâ sayyidî*); Burton IV 5,("O my lord"). Chauvin VI 96-97 No. 263; *ANE* 314 No. 62;
Jullanâr of the Sea: *Alf* III 251; Burton VII 273,-(her lord). Chauvin V 147-51 No. 73; *ANE* 248-51 No. 227;
Shahriyâr and Shahrzâd: *Alf* IV 317,-("*'anâ jariutuk*", etc.); Burton X 54-55,-("I am thine handmaid", etc.). Chauvin V 190-91 No. 111/pt.; *ANE* 371 No. 1.□

P210.0.1.1§, ‡Husband blames his wife for strangers's misconduct (life's common problems). (Cf. Z43.7.1§).
Jeweler's Wife and Qamar al-Zamân: *Alf* IV 238; Burton IX 249,-("abusing the boy's mother and cursing her"). Chauvin V 212-14 No. 121; *ANE* 345-47 No. 260.□

P210.0.2§, ‡Husband as his wife's disciplinarian. See: *DOTTI*. (Cf. T205.1§, W29.2§).
Merchant's Curious Wife: *Alf* I 6; Burton I 22-23. Chauvin V 179-80 No. 104; *ANE* 298-99 No. 3.□

P210.0.2.1§, ‡As maiden (virgin), a female is the charge of ('raised by') her father; as a wife, she is the charge of ('raised by') her husband. (Cf. P234).
Jeweler's Wife and Qamar al-Zamân: *Alf* IV 266,-(*ba¿lî*/husband); Burton IX 302,-(my lord and master). Chauvin V 212-14 No. 121; *ANE* 345-47 No. 260.□

P210.0.3§, ‡Husband and wife address each other formally. (Cf. N730.3§).
King ¿Umar al-Nu¿mân and Sons: *Alf* I 215; Burton II 188,-("Know, O Chamberlain, that thou ..."). Chauvin VI 112-24 No. 277; *ANE* 430-34 No. 39;
Shahriyâr and Shahrzâd: *Alf* IV 317,-("*janâb*"); Burton X 54,-("Thy Highnes"). Chauvin V 190-91 No. 111/pt.; *ANE* 371 No. 1.□

P210.0.5§, ‡Husband and wife in amicable relations. (Cf. T202.3§).
Hârûn and Arab Girl: *Alf* III 204; Burton VII 109-10. Chauvin VI 143 No. 300; *ANE* 202 No. 215;
Jullanâr of the Sea: *Alf* III 251,-(mer-woman); Burton VII 273. Chauvin V 147-51 No. 73; *ANE* 248-51 No. 227.□

P210.1§, ‡Wife's own property. (Cf. P529§, T101.1.1§).
Eldest Lady's Story: Treacherous Sisters: *Alf* I 53; Burton I 162. Chauvin V 4 No. 443; *ANE* 174-75 No. 19;
Copt Broker's Story: Lover's Sacrifices Repaid: *Alf* I 95; Burton I 277. Chauvin VI 80 No. 249; *ANE* 313-14 No. 24;
Abû al-Ḥasan al-Khorâsânî (and Caliph's Favorite): *Alf* IV 231,-(as mother); Burton IX 233. Chauvin V 218-20 No. 129; *ANE* 68-69 No. 259.□

P210.1.1§, ‡Wife offers to compensate her husband (for loss of goods) with her own money.
Anîs al-Jalîs: *Alf* I 128; Burton II 7. Chauvin V 120-24 No. 58; *ANE* 316-17 No. 35;
Ma¿rûf the Cobbler: *Alf* IV 302,-cf./(for investment); Burton X 24. Chauvin VI 81-82 No. 250; *ANE* 291-93 No. 262.□

P210.1.1.1§, ‡Wife (fiancée) wills all her property to husband (fiancé).
Copt Broker's Story: Lover's Sacrifices Repaid: *Alf* I 95; Burton I 276. Chauvin VI 80 No. 249; *ANE* 313-14 No. 24.□

P210.1.2§, ‡Woman's property that can be quickly converted into cash (e.g., gold jewelry, cooking copper-ware, etc.). (Cf. N411.5).
¿Alâ' al-Dîn Abû al-Shâmât: *Alf* II 157,-(gold jewelry); Burton IV 52. Chauvin V 43-49 No. 18; *ANE* 85-87 No. 63.□

P210.1.3§, ‡Mother (widow) helps son with her own money ("from my own father's money").
Abû al-Ḥasan al-Khorâsânî (and Caliph's Favorite): *Alf* IV 231; Burton IX 232. Chauvin V 218-20 No. 129; *ANE* 68-69 No. 259.□

P210.2.1§, ‡Wife knows her husband's secret(s).
Ma¿rûf the Cobbler: *Alf* IV 301; Burton X 22. Chauvin VI 81-82 No. 250; *ANE* 291-93 No. 262.□

P212.2§, ‡Wife sides with her husband's against her father. See: *DOTTI*.
Ma¿rûf the Cobbler: *Alf* IV 301,-(groom); Burton X 20. Chauvin VI 81-82 No. 250; *ANE* 291-93 No. 262.□

P212.2.1§, ‡Girl (wife, woman) sides with her beloved (husband) against her brother.
¿Alâ' al-Dîn Abû al-Shâmât: *Alf* II 180,-(European princess); Burton IV 92. Chauvin V 43-49 No. 18; *ANE* 85-87 No. 63.□

P212.3§, ‡Wife forgives culprit husband. See: *DOTTI*.
Ma¿rûf the Cobbler: *Alf* IV 301,-cf./(groom); Burton X 20. Chauvin VI 81-82 No. 250; *ANE* 291-93 No. 262.□

P213.3.1§, ‡Husband forgives adulterous wife. See: *DOTTI*. (Cf. K1501).

Masrûr and Zayn al-Mawâṣif: *Alf* IV 79,-(implicit); Burton VIII 262. Chauvin VI 82-84 No. 251; *ANE* 294-95 No. 232.□

P214.4§, ‡Wife avenges her husband. See: *DOTTI*.
Jawdar and His Treacherous Brethren: *Alf* III 200-1,-(brother); Burton VI 256. Chauvin V 257-60 No. 154; *ANE* 244-45 No. 209.□

P217.1§, ‡Woman (wife, daughter, sister) proves more responsible in keeping family assets. See: *DOTTI*.
Ma¿rûf the Cobbler: *Alf* IV 313; Burton X 46. Chauvin VI 81-82 No. 250; *ANE* 291-93 No. 262.□

P217.1.1§, ‡Woman entrusted with management of magic wishing ring. See: *DOTTI*.
al-Rashîd and Omani Merchant: *Alf* IV 215; Burton IX 199. Chauvin VI 111-12 No. 276; *ANE* 201-2 No. 257;
Ma¿rûf the Cobbler: *Alf* IV 313; Burton X 46. Chauvin VI 81-82 No. 250; *ANE* 291-93 No. 262.□

P218§, Good wife is the rarest thing in the world. See: *DOTTI*. (Cf. U253.1.2§).
Nûr al-Dîn ¿Alî and Son: *Alf* I 73,-cf./(poem); Burton I 223. Chauvin VI 102-6 No. 270; *ANE* 317-19 No. 22;
Qamar al-Zamân and Budûr: *Alf* II 76,-cf./(poem); Burton III 235. Chauvin V 204-12 No. 120; *ANE* 341-45 No. 61;
¿Alî Shâr and Zumurrud: *Alf* II 221,-cf./(poem); Burton IV 198. Chauvin V 89-91 No. 28; *ANE* 100-1 No. 82;
Jeweler's Wife and Qamar al-Zamân: *Alf* IV 266,-(implicit); Burton IX 303. Chauvin V 212-14 No. 121; *ANE* 345-47 No. 260.□

P220§, ‡Aging man's (husband's) fears (anxiety). See: *DOTTI*. (Cf. F547.3.7§, T367§).
¿Alâ' al-Dîn Abû al-Shâmât: *Alf* II 147; Burton IV 29. Chauvin V 43-49 No. 18; *ANE* 85-87 No. 63;
Dalîla the Swindler: *Alf* III 213; Burton VII 146-47. Chauvin V 245-50 No. 147; *ANE* 163-64 No. 224.□

P221§, ‡Wife's duties. (Cf. P529§, W29.2§).
Water-carrier and Goldsmith's Wife: *Alf* II 286; Burton V 90. Chauvin VI 192 No. 361; *ANE* 444 No. 122.□

P230.0.1§, Childlessness. See: *DOTTI*; *GMC*.
Tâj al-Mulûk: *Alf* I 261; Burton II 284. Chauvin V 126-28 No. 60; *ANE* 406-8 No. 40;
¿Alâ' al-Dîn Abû al-Shâmât: *Alf* II 147; Burton IV 29. Chauvin V 43-49 No. 18; *ANE* 85-87 No. 63.□

P230.0.1.1§, Misery of childlessness (person weeps). See: *DOTTI*; *GMC*; *PSAE*.
Qamar al-Zamân and Budûr: *Alf* II 65; Burton III 212-13. Chauvin V 204-12 No. 120; *ANE* 341-45 No. 61;
¿Alâ' al-Dîn Abû al-Shâmât: *Alf* II 147; Burton IV 29. Chauvin V 43-49 No. 18; *ANE* 85-87 No. 63;
Tawaddud: Slavegirl Sold and Regained: *Alf* II 303; Burton V 189. Chauvin VII 117-19 No. 387; *ANE* 408-10 No. 157;
Craft and Malice of Women/Frame: *Alf* III 138,-cf.; Burton VI 122. Chauvin VIII 33-34 No. 1; *ANE* 160-61 No. 181;
Dalîla the Swindler: *Alf* III 213; Burton VII 147. Chauvin V 245-50 No. 147; *ANE* 163-64 No. 224;
Jullanâr of the Sea: *Alf* III 247; Burton VII 264-65. Chauvin V 147-51 No. 73; *ANE* 248-51 No. 227;

Sayf al-Mulûk: *Alf* III 274-75; Burton VII 316. Chauvin VII 64-73 No. 348; *ANE* 362-64 No. 229;
King Jalî¿âd and Shimâs: *Alf* IV 134; Burton IX 33. Chauvin VI 9-11 No. 184; *ANE* 237-38 No. 236.□

P230.0.1.4§, ‡Each of childless husband and wife blames the other for childlessness (inability to reproduce). (Cf. Z103.2.1§).
Dalîla the Swindler: *Alf* III 213; Burton VII 147. Chauvin V 245-50 No. 147; *ANE* 163-64 No. 224.□

P230.0.2.1.1§, ‡'He who has begotten [children] will not have died [after his death]'.
Anîs al-Jalîs: *Alf* I 130; Burton II 11. Chauvin V 120-24 No. 58; *ANE* 316-17 No. 35;
Tawaddud: Slavegirl Sold and Regained: *Alf* II 304; Burton V 190. Chauvin VII 117-19 No. 387; *ANE* 408-10 No. 157;
Jullanâr of the Sea: *Alf* III 254; Burton VII 278. Chauvin V 147-51 No. 73; *ANE* 248-51 No. 227.□

P230.0.2.2.1§, ‡Importance of having a son (male child). See: *PSAE*. (Cf. P17.0.2.2§, P233.0.2§, S451.1.1§, T538.3§).
King ¿Umar al-Nu¿mân and Sons: *Alf* I 162; Burton II 78. Chauvin VI 112-24 No. 277; *ANE* 430-34 No. 39;
Bulûqiya/Ḥâsib/Queen of Vipers: *Alf* III 18; Burton V 298. Chauvin VII 54 No. 77; *ANE* 130-32 No. 177;
Jânshâh: *Alf* III 39; Burton V 329. Chauvin VII 39-44 No. 153; *ANE* 238-41 No. 178;
Fakir and Jar of Butter: *Alf* IV 137,-cf.; Burton IX 40-41. Chauvin II 218-19 No. 152/3; *ANE* 179-80 No. 238.□

P230.0.3§, Parent's fatigue: decreasing interest in children with passage of time (spiraling of troubles). See: *DOTTI*; *GMC*. (Cf. T189.3§, T503§).
Mercury ¿Alî: *Alf* III 228,-(debt and family/dependents); Burton VII 174. Chauvin V 248-50 No. 147; *ANE* 301-3 No. 225.□

P230.0.5§, "A mother draws in, a father drives out". See: *GMC*. (Cf. P231.3.5§).
Anîs al-Jalîs: *Alf* I 129,-(implicit); Burton II 8. Chauvin V 120-24 No. 58; *ANE* 316-17 No. 35.□

P230.0.6§, ‡The obedient child: heeds parent's instructions or advice.
Nûr al-Dîn and Maryam: *Alf* IV 90,-(son seeks father's permission); Burton VIII 265. Chauvin V 52-54 No. 271; *ANE* 98-99 No. 233;
Jeweler's Wife and Qamar al-Zamân: *Alf* IV 260; Burton IX 289. Chauvin V 212-14 No. 121; *ANE* 345-47 No. 260.□

P230.0.6.1§, ‡Parent consulted before task is undertaken or begun. (Cf. P231.3.5§).
Hasan of Basrah: *Alf* IV 8,-(mother); Burton VIII 52. Chauvin VII 29-35 No. 212A; *ANE* 207-10 No. 230.□

P230.9.1.1§, ‡Mother's advice ignored: disastrous results. See: *DOTTI*.
King ¿Umar al-Nu¿mân and Sons: *Alf* II 3; Burton III 78. Chauvin VI 112-24 No. 277; *ANE* 430-34 No. 39;
Hasan of Basrah: *Alf* III 303; Burton VIII 9. Chauvin VII 29-35 No. 212A; *ANE* 207-10 No. 230.□

P230.9.2§, ‡Man discovers that he has sired child(ren) of whom he had no knowledge. (Cf. N731.4, S11.9§, T641§).
Shahriyâr and Shahrzâd: *Alf* IV 317,-(three sons); Burton X 54. Chauvin V 190-91 No. 111/pt.; *ANE* 371 No. 1.□

P230.10.1§, Being motherless. See: *DOTTI*; *GMC*. (Cf. T604.0.2§).
Shahriyâr and Shahrzâd: *Alf* IV 317,-cf.; Burton X 54,-(become motherless). Chauvin V 190-91 No. 111/pt.; *ANE* 371 No. 1.□

P230.10.1.1§, 'The affairs of a motherless child would break one's heart'.
Shahriyâr and Shahrzâd: *Alf* IV 317,-cf.; Burton X 54,-cf. Chauvin V 190-91 No. 111/pt.; *ANE* 371 No. 1.□

P230.15§, ‡Parent(s) 'come(s) to' child (son, daughter) in vision. See: *DOTTI*. (Cf. E350§, T24.9.1.2.1§, V517§).
Nûr al-Dîn ¿Alî and Son: *Alf* I 69; Burton I 211. Chauvin VI 102-6 No. 270; *ANE* 317-19 No. 22;
Qamar al-Zamân and Budûr: *Alf* II 96; Burton III 277. Chauvin V 204-12 No. 120; *ANE* 341-45 No. 61;
Ḥâtim's Hospitality: *Alf* II 181-82; Burton IV 96. Chauvin VI 49 No. 215; *ANE* 216 No. 64.□

P231.0.1§, Mother of a son more valuable. See: *DOTTI*; *GMC*.
Shahriyâr and Shahrzâd: *Alf* IV 317,-(implicit); Burton X 54. Chauvin V 190-91 No. 111/pt.; *ANE* 371 No. 1.□

P231.3, Mother-love. See: *DOTTI*; *GMC*.
Anîs al-Jalîs: *Alf* I 129; Burton II 8. Chauvin V 120-24 No. 58; *ANE* 316-17 No. 35;
¿Azîz and ¿Azîzah: *Alf* I 307; Burton III 46-47. Chauvin V 144-45 No. 71; *ANE* 111-13 No. 41;
Jawdar and His Treacherous Brethren: *Alf* III 177-78,-(heart); Burton VI 215. Chauvin V 257-60 No. 154; *ANE* 244-45 No. 209;
Hasan of Basrah: *Alf* IV 14-15; Burton VIII 65. Chauvin VII 29-35 No. 212A; *ANE* 207-10 No. 230;
Nûr al-Dîn and Maryam: *Alf* IV 89; Burton VIII 288. Chauvin V 52-54 No. 271; *ANE* 98-99 No. 233.□

P231.3.0.2.1§, ‡Mother helps adult son with certain task.
Anîs al-Jalîs: *Alf* I 129,-(escape father's wrath); Burton II 32. Chauvin V 120-24 No. 58; *ANE* 316-17 No. 35;
¿Alâ' al-Dîn Abû al-Shâmât: *Alf* II 169,-cf./(acts as procuress); Burton IV 74. Chauvin V 43-49 No. 18; *ANE* 85-87 No. 63;
Jullanâr of the Sea: *Alf* III 269; Burton VII 306. Chauvin V 147-51 No. 73; *ANE* 248-51 No. 227.□

P231.3.0.2.2§, ‡Mother helps adult daughter with certain task.
Jullanâr of the Sea: *Alf* III 269; Burton VII 305-6. Chauvin V 147-51 No. 73; *ANE* 248-51 No. 227.□

P231.3.5§, Son confides in mother. See: *DOTTI*. (Cf. P230.0.5§, P230.0.6.1§).
Anîs al-Jalîs: *Alf* I 129; Burton II 8. Chauvin V 120-24 No. 58; *ANE* 316-17 No. 35;
King ¿Umar al-Nu¿mân and Sons: *Alf* II 3; Burton III 79. Chauvin VI 112-24 No. 277; *ANE* 430-34 No. 39;
¿Alâ' al-Dîn Abû al-Shâmât: *Alf* II 166; Burton IV 68. Chauvin V 43-49 No. 18; *ANE* 85-87 No. 63.□

P231.3.6§, ‡Mother protects guilty son (who had committed a crime). (Cf. R320.1§).
Anîs al-Jalîs: *Alf* I 129; Burton II 8. Chauvin V 120-24 No. 58; *ANE* 316-17 No. 35.□

P231.9§, ‡Mother in vision reproves son.
Hasan of Basrah: *Alf* IV 6, 9; Burton VIII 47-48. Chauvin VII 29-35 No. 212A; *ANE* 207-10 No. 230.□

P232.3§, ‡Mother and daughter in amicable relations. See: *DOTTI*.
Dalîla the Swindler: *Alf* III 213ff.,-(as swindlers); Burton VII 145ff. Chauvin V 245-50 No. 147; *ANE* 163-64 No. 224.□

P232.3.2§, ‡Daughter confides in her mother. See: *DOTTI*. (Cf. P231.3.5§).
Jewish Doctor's Story: Sororicide: *Alf* I 102; Burton I 299. Chauvin VI 89 No. 253; *ANE* 242 No. 26.□

P232.3.2.1§, ‡Daughter confesses murdering her sister to their mother. (Cf. U197.0.1§).
Jewish Doctor's Story: Sororicide: *Alf* I 102; Burton I 299. Chauvin VI 89 No. 253; *ANE* 242 No. 26.□

P233, Father and son. See: *DOTTI*; *GMC*.
Anîs al-Jalîs: *Alf* I 129; Burton II 8-10. Chauvin V 120-24 No. 58; *ANE* 316-17 No. 35.□

P233.0.1§, ‡Father-love for son. See: *DOTTI*; *PSAE*. (Cf. P233.0.2§).
Anîs al-Jalîs: *Alf* I 129; Burton II 8. Chauvin V 120-24 No. 58; *ANE* 316-17 No. 35;
Qamar al-Zamân and Budûr: *Alf* II 68-69, 103-4; Burton III 213, 290. Chauvin V 204-12 No. 120; *ANE* 341-45 No. 61;
King's Favorite Son and Ogress: *Alf* III 143; Burton VI 139. Chauvin VIII 40-41 No. 8B; *ANE* 264 No. 188;
House with the Belvedere: *Alf* III 166,-(passim); Burton VI 188. Chauvin VIII 57-58 No. 23; *ANE* 223 No. 203;
King Jalî¿âd and Shimâs: *Alf* IV 161; Burton IX 88. Chauvin VI 9-11 No. 184; *ANE* 237-38 No. 236.□

P233.0.2§, ‡Only sons, no daughters. See: *DOTTI*. (Cf. P230.0.2.2.1§).
Nuzhat al-Zamân Tested/¿Umar al-Nu¿mân: *Alf* I 206,-(twelve); Burton II 170. Chauvin VI 116, n.1/passim No. 277; *ANE* 432,/passim No. 39;
Landsman ¿Abdallah and Merman ¿Abdallah: *Alf* IV 202,-(nine); Burton IX 175. Chauvin V 6-7 No. 3; *ANE* 65-66 No. 256;
Shahriyâr and Shahrzâd: *Alf* IV 317,-(implicit); Burton X 54. Chauvin V 190-91 No. 111/pt.; *ANE* 371 No. 1.□

P233.6, Son avenges father. See: *DOTTI*; *GMC*.
¿Alâ' al-Dîn Abû al-Shâmât: *Alf* II 174,-(crime revealed); Burton IV 81. Chauvin V 43-49 No. 18; *ANE* 85-87 No. 63;
Ma¿rûf the Cobbler: *Alf* IV 316,-cf./(protects); Burton X 52. Chauvin VI 81-82 No. 250; *ANE* 291-93 No. 262.□

P233.10.1§, ‡Father in vision reproves son for neglecting duties. (Cf. E721.1.0.1§).

Qamar al-Zamân and Budûr: *Alf* II 96,-(*¿itâb*/reconciliatory reprimand); Burton III 277,-(reproach). Chauvin V 204-12 No. 120; *ANE* 341-45 No. 61.□

P234, Father and daughter. See: *DOTTI*; *GMC*.
King ¿Umar al-Nu¿mân and Sons: *Alf* I 185; Burton II 128-29. Chauvin VI 112-24 No. 277; *ANE* 430-34 No. 39;
Hârûn and Arab Girl: *Alf* III 204; Burton VII 110. Chauvin VI 143 No. 300; *ANE* 202 No. 215.□

P234.0.1§, Father of daughter(s) less powerful. See: *DOTTI*; *GMC*. (Cf. P261.1.1§, P261.2§).
Nûr al-Dîn ¿Alî and Son: *Alf* I 65; Burton I 196-97. Chauvin VI 102-6 No. 270; *ANE* 317-19 No. 22.□

P234.0.3.1§, ‡Three daughters. See: *DOTTI*. (Cf. P252.2, Z71.1.0.1.1§).
Ebony Horse: *Alf* II 254, 257; Burton V 1. Chauvin V 221-31 No. 130; *ANE* 172-74 No. 103.□

P234.0.3.2§, ‡Seven daughters. See: *DOTTI*.
Hasan of Basrah: *Alf* III 311,-(seven daughters/sisters); Burton VIII 24. Chauvin VII 29-35 No. 212A; *ANE* 207-10 No. 230.□

P234.0.4§, ‡One daughter, no sons. (Cf. T603.1§). See: *DOTTI*.
Uns al-Wujûd and al-Ward: *Alf* II 268,-(implicit); Burton V 32. Chauvin VI 127-29 No. 282; *ANE* 438 No. 104;
Ruined Baghdadi and His Slave-girl: *Alf* IV 133; Burton IX 30. Chauvin V 152-53 No. 75; *ANE* 353 No. 235;
Landsman ¿Abdallah and Merman ¿Abdallah: *Alf* IV 202; Burton IX 174. Chauvin V 6-7 No. 3; *ANE* 65-66 No. 256.□

P234.0.4.1§, ‡One daughter, many sons. See: *DOTTI*.
Nûr al-Dîn and Maryam: *Alf* IV 103; Burton VIII 316. Chauvin V 52-54 No. 271; *ANE* 98-99 No. 233.□

P234.2.1§, ‡Daughter(s) die(s) soon after father's death. (Cf. F1041.1.3).
Hârûn and Arab Girl: *Alf* III 204; Burton VII 110. Chauvin VI 143 No. 300; *ANE* 202 No. 215.□

P234.4§, ‡Daughter as her father's helper (adviser). See: *DOTTI*. (Cf. J1111.4.1§).
Shahriyâr and Shâhzamân: *Alf* I 5; Burton I 15. Chauvin V 188-89 No. 111; *ANE* 370-71 No. 1.□

P236, Undutiful children. See: *DOTTI*; *GMC*.
Jawdar and His Treacherous Brethren: *Alf* III 178, 189,-(reduce mother to begging); Burton VI 214, 234. Chauvin V 257-60 No. 154; *ANE* 244-45 No. 209.□

P236.10§, ‡Undutiful child strikes parent(s).
Nûr al-Dîn and Maryam: *Alf* IV 89; Burton VIII 287. Chauvin V 52-54 No. 271; *ANE* 98-99 No. 233.□

P243.0.2§, ‡Father-love for daughter. See: *DOTTI*. (Cf. P233.0.1§).
Qamar al-Zamân and Budûr: *Alf* II 86, 96; Burton III 255-56, 276. Chauvin V 204-12 No. 120; *ANE* 341-45 No. 61;
Ebony Horse: *Alf* II 256,-(had palace built for her); Burton V (xxx). Chauvin V 221-31 No. 130; *ANE* 172-74 No. 103;
Nûr al-Dîn and Maryam: *Alf* IV 103; Burton VIII 316. Chauvin V 52-54 No. 271; *ANE* 98-99 No. 233.□

P246.1§, ‡Father threatens to disown son. See: *DOTTI*.
Jeweler's Wife and Qamar al-Zamân: *Alf* IV 258; Burton IX 288,-("I am quit of thee ..."). Chauvin V 212-14 No. 121; *ANE* 345-47 No. 260.□

P248§, Generational gap. See: *DOTTI*; *GMC*.
Qamar al-Zamân and Budûr: *Alf* II 68; Burton III 218-19. Chauvin V 204-12 No. 120; *ANE* 341-45 No. 61.□

P248.1§, Son opposes his father's ways. See: *DOTTI*; *GMC*. (Cf. T131.1.2).
Qamar al-Zamân and Budûr: *Alf* II 68; Burton III 219. Chauvin V 204-12 No. 120; *ANE* 341-45 No. 61;
Devotee Prince: Ascetic's Death: *Alf* II 290; Burton V 111-12. Chauvin VI 193-94 No. 363; *ANE* 167-68 No. 134;
Bulûqiya: *Alf* III 22-23; Burton V 304-5. Chauvin VII 54 No. 77; *ANE* 130-32 No. 177;

Son of Unjust King: *Alf* IV 142; Burton IX 50. Chauvin II 219-20 No. 152/7; *ANE* 437 No. 242.□

P248.2§, Son opposes his mother's ways.
King ¿Umar al-Nu¿mân and Sons: *Alf* II 2; Burton III 76. Chauvin VI 112-24 No. 277; *ANE* 430-34 No. 39;
al-'Amjad and al-'As¿ad: *Alf* II 113-15,-cf.; Burton III 311-12. Chauvin V 208-10 No. 120[.1]; *ANE* 341-42 No. 61/pt. 2.□

P248.0.2§, ‡Rebellious youth: brash ways of the immature (*ṭaysh al-shabâb*). (Cf. J1450.1.1§).
Anîs al-Jalîs: *Alf* I 128,-cf.; Burton II 6-7. Chauvin V 120-24 No. 58; *ANE* 316-17 No. 35;
Ma¿rûf the Cobbler: *Alf* IV 294; Burton X 9. Chauvin VI 81-82 No. 250; *ANE* 291-93 No. 262.□

P248.4§, Daughter opposes her father's ways. See: *DOTTI*. (Cf. M411.25.1§).
Qamar al-Zamân and Budûr: *Alf* II 79; Burton III 240. Chauvin V 204-12 No. 120; *ANE* 341-45 No. 61;
¿Alâ' al-Dîn Abû al-Shâmât: *Alf* II 179; Burton IV 91. Chauvin V 43-49 No. 18; *ANE* 85-87 No. 63.□

P249.3§, ‡The rights of the aged (parents and the parent-like). See: *DOTTI*.
King Jalî¿âd and Shimâs: *Alf* IV 154-55; Burton IX 75. Chauvin VI 9-11 No. 184; *ANE* 237-38 No. 236.□

P250.0.1§, ‡Siblings undergo similar (identical) life experiences. See: *DOTTI*. (Cf. T685.1, Z97.7§).
Shahriyâr and Shâhzamân: *Alf* I 2; Burton I 4-06. Chauvin V 188-91 No. 111; *ANE* 370-71 No. 1.□

P250.0.2.0.1§, ‡Interreligious (interethnic) siblings—(half or foster brothers and sisters of different religious or ethnic groups—usually, Moslem and Christian, Arab and European/Frank, or the like). (Cf. V351.1§).
King ¿Umar al-Nu¿mân and Sons: *Alf* II 11-12; Burton III 95-97. Chauvin VI 112-24 No. 277; *ANE* 430-34 No. 39.□

P250.0.3§, ‡Full siblings: "from same loins (father)" and "from same womb (mother)". See: *PSAE*. (Cf. P283.0.1§).
Hasan of Basrah: *Alf* III 311,-(seven daughters/sisters); Burton VIII 24. Chauvin VII 29-35 No. 212A; *ANE* 207-10 No. 230;
¿Abdallah ibn Fâḍil: Treacherous Brothers: *Alf* IV 269; Burton IX 310. Chauvin V 2-4 No. 2; *ANE* 63-65 No. 261.□

P250.0.5.1§, ‡Inter-species milk-siblings—(jinn-*ince*). (Cf. F302.0.3§).
Sayf al-Mulûk: *Alf* III 288; Burton VII 349,-(sister by fosterage). Chauvin VII 64-73 No. 348; *ANE* 362-64 No. 229.□

P251.0.2§, Brothers in amicable relations. See: *DOTTI*; *GMC*.
al-'Amjad and al-'As¿ad: *Alf* II 121 121; Burton III 309, 325-26. Chauvin V 208-10 No. 120[.1]; *ANE* 341-42 No. 61/pt. 2.□

P251.0.2.2§, ‡Successful (rich) brother helps needy sibling(s). See: *DOTTI*. (Cf. L31).
¿Abdallah ibn Fâḍil: Treacherous Brothers: *Alf* IV 271; Burton IX 314. Chauvin V 2-4 No. 2; *ANE* 63-65 No. 261.□

P251.0.5§, Brother forgives his culprit brother(s). See: *DOTTI*; *GMC*. (Cf. P251.0.5§).
Second Shaykh: Treacherous Brothers: *Alf* I 12; Burton I 35,-(pardon). Chauvin V 6 No. 397; *ANE* 377-78 No. 6;
Jawdar and His Treacherous Brethren: *Alf* III 178, 191-92, 195; Burton VI 214-15, 238, 245. Chauvin V 257-60 No. 154; *ANE* 244-45 No. 209;
¿Abdallah ibn Fâḍil: Treacherous Brothers: *Alf* IV 271; Burton IX 312. Chauvin V 2-4 No. 2; *ANE* 63-65 No. 261.□

P251.3.1, Brothers strive to avenge each other. See: *DOTTI*; *GMC*.
al-'Amjad and al-'As¿ad: *Alf* II 112; Burton III 325-26. Chauvin V 208-10 No. 120[.1]; *ANE* 341-42 No. 61/pt. 2.□

P251.3.4§, ‡Reconciliation between hostile brothers. (Cf. P251.3.4§).
King ¿Umar al-Nu¿mân and Sons: *Alf* I 229; Burton II 217. Chauvin VI 112-24 No. 277; *ANE* 430-34 No. 39;
¿Abdallah ibn Fâḍil: Treacherous Brothers: *Alf* IV 284,-(of brothers); Burton IX 338. Chauvin V 2-4 No. 2; *ANE* 63-65 No. 261.□

P251.3.5§, ‡Competition in self-sacrifice between brothers: each offers to die first.
al-'Amjad and al-'As¿ad: *Alf* II 116-17; Burton III 316. Chauvin V 208-10 No. 120[.1]; *ANE* 2 341-42 No. 61./pt.□

P251.5, Two brothers. See: *DOTTI*; *PSAE*.
Shahriyâr and Shâhzamân: *Alf* I 2,-(foreword); Burton I 2. Chauvin V 188-91 No. 111; *ANE* 370-71 No. 1;
Nûr al-Dîn ¿Alî and Son: *Alf* I 64; Burton I 195. Chauvin VI 102-6 No. 270; *ANE* 317-19 No. 22;
Hasan of Basrah: *Alf* III 302,-(inconsequential); Burton VIII 7. Chauvin VII 29-35 No. 212A; *ANE* 207-10 No. 230.□

P251.5.3, Hostile brothers. [(Jealous brothers, in conflict)]. See: *DOTTI*; *GMC*. (Cf. P283.0.1§).
Second Shaykh: Treacherous Brothers: *Alf* I 11; Burton I 34-35. Chauvin V 6 No. 397; *ANE* 377-78 No. 6;
King ¿Umar al-Nu¿mân and Sons: *Alf* I 181,-cf.; Burton II 120. Chauvin VI 112-24 No. 277; *ANE* 430-34 No. 39.□

P251.6.1, Three brothers. See: *DOTTI*; *GMC*. (Cf. Z71.1.0.1.1§).
Second Shaykh: Treacherous Brothers: *Alf* I 11; Burton I 32-35. Chauvin V 6 No. 397; *ANE* 377-78 No. 6;
Jawdar and His Treacherous Brethren: *Alf* III 177,-(sons); Burton VI 213. Chauvin V 257-60 No. 154; *ANE* 244-45 No. 209;
¿Abdallah ibn Fâḍil: Treacherous Brothers: *Alf* IV 269; Burton IX 310. Chauvin V 2-4 No. 2; *ANE* 63-65 No. 261.□

P252.0.2§, Sisters in amicable relations. See: *DOTTI*.
Abû al-Ḥasan al-Khorâsânî (and Caliph's Favorite): *Alf* IV 234; Burton IX 239. Chauvin V 218-20 No. 129; *ANE* 68-69 No. 259.□

P252.0.3§, ‡Sister helps sister(s). See: *DOTTI*.
Second Shaykh: Treacherous Brothers: *Alf* I 13,-(jinn); Burton I 35. Chauvin V 6 No. 397; *ANE* 377-78 No. 6;
Jânshâh: *Alf* III 55; Burton V 351,-(eldest Princess). Chauvin VII 39-44 No. 153; *ANE* 238-41 No. 178;
Masrûr and Zayn al-Mawâṣif: *Alf* IV 68; Burton VIII 236. Chauvin VI 82-84 No. 251; *ANE* 294-95 No. 232;
Abû al-Ḥasan al-Khorâsânî (and Caliph's Favorite): *Alf* IV 234; Burton IX 239. Chauvin V 218-20 No. 129; *ANE* 68-69 No. 259.□

P252.0.3.1§, ‡Successful (rich) sister helps needy sibling(s). (Cf. L31).
Eldest Lady's Story: Treacherous Sisters: *Alf* I 54; Burton I 164. Chauvin V 4 No. 443; *ANE* 174-75 No. 19.□

P252.0.5§, Sister forgives her culprit sister(s). See: *DOTTI*; *GMC*.
Hasan of Basrah: *Alf* IV 50; Burton VIII 137. Chauvin VII 29-35 No. 212A; *ANE* 207-10 No. 230.□

P252.1, Two sisters. See: *DOTTI*.
Jewish Doctor's Story: Sororicide: *Alf* I 102,-(full-sisters); Burton I 299,-(sisters-german). Chauvin VI 89 No. 253; *ANE* 242 No. 26.□

P252.2, Three sisters. See: *DOTTI*. (Cf. P234.0.3.1§).
Eldest Lady's Story: Treacherous Sisters: *Alf* I 53; Burton I 162. Chauvin V 4 No. 443; *ANE* 174-75 No. 19;
Ebony Horse: *Alf* II 254-57; Burton V 1. Chauvin V 221-31 No. 130; *ANE* 172-74 No. 103;
Basra Girls in Poetry Contest: *Alf* III 205; Burton VII 110. Chauvin VI 144 No. 301; *ANE* 107-8 No. 216.□

P252.3, Seven sisters. See: *DOTTI*; *GMC*.
Hasan of Basrah: *Alf* III 311,-(seven daughters/sisters); Burton VIII 22. Chauvin VII 29-35 No. 212A; *ANE* 207-10 No. 230.□

P252.9.1§, ‡Sisters confusingly alike. Usually twin sisters. See: *DOTTI*. (Cf. P253.15§).
Hasan of Basrah: *Alf* IV 34; Burton VIII 103. Chauvin VII 29-35 No. 212A; *ANE* 207-10 No. 230.□

P253, Sister and brother. See: *DOTTI*.
Ghânim ibn Ayyûb: *Alf* I 146; Burton II 45. Chauvin VI 14-16 No. 188; *ANE* 192-93 No. 36;

King ¿Umar al-Nu¿mân and Sons: *Alf* I 188,-ff.; Burton II 132. Chauvin VI 112-24 No. 277; *ANE* 430-34 No. 39;
Jullanâr of the Sea: *Alf* III 249; Burton VII 269. Chauvin V 147-51 No. 73; *ANE* 248-51 No. 227.□

P253.0.1, Sister's son [(nephew) and mother's brother (*khâl*)]. See: *DOTTI*. (Cf. P297.2§).
Jullanâr of the Sea: *Alf* III 255; Burton VII 274. Chauvin V 147-51 No. 73; *ANE* 248-51 No. 227.□

P253.0.1.3§, ‡A sister's sacrifices (sufferings) for her brother's welfare. See: *DOTTI*.
King ¿Umar al-Nu¿mân and Sons: *Alf* I 188; Burton II 133-34. Chauvin VI 112-24 No. 277; *ANE* 430-34 No. 39.□

P253.0.2, ‡One sister and two brothers. See: *DOTTI*.
King ¿Umar al-Nu¿mân and Sons: *Alf* I 163, 181,-ff.; Burton II 80-81, 120. Chauvin VI 112-24 No. 277; *ANE* 430-34 No. 39.□

P253.2.4§, ‡Brother yearns for absent sister. See: *DOTTI*.
King ¿Umar al-Nu¿mân and Sons: *Alf* I 191-92,-(poem/"hawâ", 192, 210-14,-(poem); Burton II 137,-(love), 139-40, 178-87. Chauvin VI 112-24 No. 277; *ANE* 430-34 No. 39.□

P253.2.0.2§—(formerly-P253.0.2§), Sister yearns for absent brother. See: *GMC*.
Hasan of Basrah: *Alf* IV 9,-(no one else in her *fu'âd*/heart/poem); Burton VIII 64,-(mind). Chauvin VII 29-35 No. 212A; *ANE* 207-10 No. 230.□

P253.2.5§, Brother chooses (favors) sister over his own wife. See: *DOTTI*; *GMC*.
Ni¿mah and Nu¿m: Stolen Wife Regained: *Alf* II 136,-cf./(sister inspects brother's concubine); Burton IV 7. Chauvin VI 96-97 No. 263; *ANE* 314 No. 62.□

P253.2.6§, ‡Brother protects (defends) sister(s). See: *DOTTI*.
Hammâd: Treacherous Bedouin: *Alf* II 17-18; Burton III 106-13. Chauvin VI 124 n. 1 No. 277; *ANE* 200 No. 43.□

P253.6.1§, Sister is always consulted by her brother and her counsel sought. See: *DOTTI*; *GMC*. (Cf. J155.9.2§).
Ni¿mah and Nu¿m: Stolen Wife Regained: *Alf* II 136; Burton IV 7. Chauvin VI 96-97 No. 263; *ANE* 314 No. 62.□

P253.6.2§, ‡Trouble from ignoring sister's advice. See: *DOTTI*. (Cf. J1056§).
Hasan of Basrah: *Alf* III 314,-(foster sister); Burton VIII 28. Chauvin VII 29-35 No. 212A; *ANE* 207-10 No. 230.□

P253.6.5§, ‡Sister as the administrator (chieftainess) of her brother(s) home. See: *DOTTI*.
Ni¿mah and Nu¿m: Stolen Wife Regained: *Alf* II 136,-cf.; Burton IV 7. Chauvin VI 96-97 No. 263; *ANE* 314 No. 62.□

P253.9.4§, ‡Sister kills herself (commits suicide) because brother is dead. See: *DOTTI*.
Hammâd: Treacherous Bedouin: *Alf* II 20; Burton III 111. Chauvin VI 124 n. 1 No. 277; *ANE* 200 No. 43.□

P253.10, Great love of brothers for sister. See: *DOTTI*; *GMC*.
First Qalandar: Brother-Sister Incest: *Alf* I 42,-(since childhood); Burton I 110. Chauvin V 196-97 No. 115; *ANE* 337-38 No. 15.□

P253.10.0.1§, ‡Sister as brother's dearest relative. See: *DOTTI*. (Cf. P253.2.5§).
King ¿Umar al-Nu¿mân and Sons: *Alf* I 213,-(dearest *is* my sister); Burton II 185,-("dearest of all to me [...] my sister"). Chauvin VI 112-24 No. 277; *ANE* 430-34 No. 39.□

P253.10.1§, Sister as her brother's 'first love'. See: *DOTTI*; *GMC*. (Cf. P274.1, T42.2.1§).
King ¿Umar al-Nu¿mân and Sons: *Alf* I 210-14,-(poems); Burton II 178-87. Chauvin VI 112-24 No. 277; *ANE* 430-34 No. 39.□

P253.10.2§, Brothers compete for their sister's love (affection). See: *DOTTI*; *GMC*. (Cf. T92.5.0.1§).
King ¿Umar al-Nu¿mân and Sons: *Alf* I 207,-(implicit); Burton II 173. Chauvin VI 112-24 No. 277; *ANE* 430-34 No. 39.□

P253.15§, ‡Brother and sister who look alike. See: *DOTTI*. (Cf. F577.4.1§, P252.9.1§).
Ni¿mah and Nu¿m: Stolen Wife Regained: *Alf* II 139,-cf./(foster siblings); Burton IV 12,-("she favoureth thee in age and mien"). Chauvin VI 96-97 No. 263; *ANE* 314 No. 62;

Dispute Concerning Males and Females: *Alf* II 300; Burton V 155. Chauvin VI 153 No. 317; *ANE* 291 No. 151;
Jullanâr of the Sea: *Alf* III 250; Burton VII 270. Chauvin V 147-51 No. 73; *ANE* 248-51 No. 227;
Jeweler's Wife and Qamar al-Zamân: *Alf* IV 238,-cf./(sister "Kawkab" [i.e., Glimmering-star] and brother Qamar alike in beauty); Burton IX 247. Chauvin V 212-14 No. 121; *ANE* 345-47 No. 260.□

P254§, Brother and sister as partners. See: *DOTTI*. (Cf. P253.6.5§).
King ¿Umar al-Nu¿mân and Sons: *Alf* I 187,-ff.; Burton II 132. Chauvin VI 112-24 No. 277; *ANE* 430-34 No. 39.□

P254.0.1§, ‡Household composed of only brother and sister(s). They live alone in palace (house, cave, etc.). See: *DOTTI*. (Cf. P210, P605.5§, Z186.8§).
Ḥammâd: Treacherous Bedouin: *Alf* II 16; Burton III 105. Chauvin VI 124 n. 1 No. 277; *ANE* 200 No. 43;
Jeweler's Wife and Qamar al-Zamân: *Alf* IV 238,-cf./(seclude in palace, only parents and servant visit); Burton IX 247. Chauvin V 212-14 No. 121; *ANE* 345-47 No. 260.□

P254.2§, ‡Sister and brother worship together. (Cf. T317.3.1§)
King ¿Umar al-Nu¿mân and Sons: *Alf* I 187,-cf./(go on pilgrimage); Burton II 132. Chauvin VI 112-24 No. 277; *ANE* 430-34 No. 39.□

P257§, ‡Sister and brother quarrel (in conflict).
Jullanâr of the Sea: *Alf* III 249,-(temporary); Burton VII 269. Chauvin V 147-51 No. 73; *ANE* 248-51 No. 227.□

P260.2§, ‡In-laws as source of power—('*Abû-nasab*'). (Cf. T101.1.1§).
King ¿Umar al-Nu¿mân and Sons: *Alf* I 215,-(husband hopes for promotion); Burton II 188. Chauvin VI 112-24 No. 277; *ANE* 430-34 No. 39.□

P261.1§, ‡Father-in-law and son-in-law. See: *DOTTI*. (Cf. P265.3§, P293.6.4§, T101.1.1§).
Sindbâd's Seventh Voyage: *Alf* III 119; Burton VI 73. Chauvin VII 26-29 No. 373G; *ANE* 386-87 No. 179;
Landsman ¿Abdallah and Merman ¿Abdallah: *Alf* IV 202; Burton IX 175. Chauvin V 6-7 No. 3; *ANE* 65-66 No. 256;
Ma¿rûf the Cobbler: *Alf* IV 307, 311; Burton X 32. Chauvin VI 81-82 No. 250; *ANE* 291-93 No. 262.□

P261.1.1§, ‡Man fearful (distrustful) of daughter's husband (suitor). See: *DOTTI*. (Cf. P234.0.1§, T205.1§).
Tâj al-Mulûk: *Alf* I 306,-cf.; Burton III 42. Chauvin V 126-28 No. 60; *ANE* 406-8 No. 40.□

P261.1.1.2§, ‡Son-in-law and father-in-law (his wife's father) as rivals. (Cf. P17.0.6§).
¿Alâ' al-Dîn Abû al-Shâmât: *Alf* II 162,-(in heading guild); Burton IV 60-61. Chauvin V 43-49 No. 18; *ANE* 85-87 No. 63.□

P261.2§, ‡Father of only one daughter offers all his possessions to youth if he would marry his daughter. See: *DOTTI*. (Cf. P234.0.1§).
Sindbâd's Seventh Voyage: *Alf* III 119; Burton VI 74. Chauvin VII 26-29 No. 373G; *ANE* 386-87 No. 179.□

P264.3§, Kindly sister-in-law: aids her brother's wife. See: *DOTTI*; *GMC*. (Cf. P13.9.3§).
Hasan of Basrah: *Alf* IV 54,-cf./(foster-sister-in-law); Burton VIII 154. Chauvin VII 29-35 No. 212A; *ANE* 207-10 No. 230.□

P265.3§, ‡Helpful son(s)-in-law. See: *DOTTI*.
Sindbâd's Seventh Voyage: *Alf* III 119; Burton VI 74. Chauvin VII 26-29 No. 373G; *ANE* 386-87 No. 179.□

P264.6§, ‡Sister-in-law and her husband's brother (brother-in-law).
Jewish qâḍî and His Devout Wife: *Alf* III 10; Burton V 256. Chauvin VI 154-55 No. 321; *ANE* 242 No. 163.□

P268.2.2§, ‡Maidens agree to share one future husband—("One night forms and one night for you.").
Mercury ¿Alî: *Alf* III 244; Burton VII 203. Chauvin V 248-50 No. 147; *ANE* 301-3 No. 225.□

P268.0.1§, ‡Slave-women (of one man) as co-wives. (Cf. P170.0.1).

Man from Yaman and Six Salve-girls: Flyting: *Alf* II 245,-(*ḍurrah*/co-wife); Burton IV 248,-(co-concubine). Chauvin VI 151 No. 313; *ANE* 289-90 No. 84.□

P268.1§, Bad relations between co-wives (one *ḍurrah* and another). See: *DOTTI*.
First Shaykh: Sorceress Wife: *Alf* I 10; Burton I 28. Chauvin VII 129-30 No. 396; *ANE* 376-77 No. 5;
Ghânim ibn Ayyûb: *Alf* I 151,-cf./(wife and husband's beloved); Burton II 57. Chauvin VI 14-16 No. 188; *ANE* 192-93 No. 36;
Man from Yaman and Six Salve-girls: Flyting: *Alf* II 244-50,-cf./(slave-girls-in-man's-harem); Burton IV 245-60. Chauvin VI 151 No. 313; *ANE* 289-90 No. 84.□

P268.2§, Accommodation between co-wives. See: *DOTTI*; *GMC*. (Cf. P187.1§, W164.5§).
Qamar al-Zamân and Budûr: *Alf* II 112; Burton III 308. Chauvin V 204-12 No. 120; *ANE* 341-45 No. 61.□

P268.2.1§, ‡Absence of jealousy between (among) co-wives. See: *DOTTI*.
Qamar al-Zamân and Budûr: *Alf* II 112; Burton III 309. Chauvin V 204-12 No. 120; *ANE* 341-45 No. 61.□

P271.0.1§, ‡Foster parent (father, mother) is owed for rearing foster child.
¿Alâ' al-Dîn Abû al-Shâmât: *Alf* II 174; Burton IV 81. Chauvin V 43-49 No. 18; *ANE* 85-87 No. 63;
Hasan of Basrah: *Alf* IV 31; Burton VIII 99,-(fosterage and service). Chauvin VII 29-35 No. 212A; *ANE* 207-10 No. 230.□

P272.3.1§, Raped girl (mistress) as foster mother for her own child. See: *DOTTI*; *GMC*.
King ¿Umar al-Nu¿mân and Sons: *Alf* I 208,-cf./(accidental incest); Burton II 175. Chauvin VI 112-24 No. 277; *ANE* 430-34 No. 39.□

P272.5§, ‡Wet nurse (*murḍi¿ah*, '*dâdàh*', *murabbiyah*). See: *DOTTI*.
Portress Amînah: Bitten Cheek: *Alf* I 60,-(implicit/"raised you"); Burton I 183,-(right of "fosterage"). Chauvin V 98-99 No. 33; *ANE* 326-27 No. 20;
Tâj al-Mulûk: *Alf* I 297; Burton III 23. Chauvin V 126-28 No. 60; *ANE* 406-8 No. 40;
¿Alâ' al-Dîn Abû al-Shâmât: *Alf* II 149,-(raises infant); Burton IV 33. Chauvin V 43-49 No. 18; *ANE* 85-87 No. 63;
Sayf al-Mulûk: *Alf* III 277; Burton VII 324. Chauvin VII 64-73 No. 348; *ANE* 362-64 No. 229.□

P272.5.2§, ‡Governess (*qahramânah*)—oversees women's quarters. (Cf. P363.1.1§).
Reeve's Story: Why Maimed by Bride: *Alf* I 98; Burton I 282,(stewardess). Chauvin V 220-21 No. 305; *ANE* 351 No. 25;
Qamar al-Zamân and Budûr: *Alf* II 86; Burton III 255. Chauvin V 204-12 No. 120; *ANE* 341-45 No. 61;
Ni¿mah and Nu¿m: Stolen Wife Regained: *Alf* II 133; Burton IV 4,-(chamberwoman). Chauvin VI 96-97 No. 263; *ANE* 314 No. 62;
¿Alâ' al-Dîn Abû al-Shâmât: *Alf* II 156; Burton IV 49. Chauvin V 43-49 No. 18; *ANE* 85-87 No. 63;
Ibrâhîm and Jamîlah: *Alf* IV 225; Burton IX 221. Chauvin VI 52-53 No. 218; *ANE* 227-29 No. 258.□

P272.6.1§, ‡Old nurse provides information on true identity of family members. (Cf. P424.7§).
King ¿Umar al-Nu¿mân and Sons: *Alf* II 11; Burton III 95. Chauvin VI 112-24 No. 277; *ANE* 430-34 No. 39;
Jeweler's Wife and Qamar al-Zamân: *Alf* IV 244; Burton IX 258. Chauvin V 212-14 No. 121; *ANE* 345-47 No. 260.□

P274, Foster sister. See: *DOTTI*.
First Eunuch: Bukhayt Deflowers Mistress: *Alf* I 147-48,-cf./(slave/mistress); Burton II 49. Chauvin V 277 No. 160; *ANE* 178 No. 37;
Hasan of Basrah: *Alf* III 314; Burton VIII 28. Chauvin VII 29-35 No. 212A; *ANE* 207-10 No. 230.□

P274.1, Love between foster sister and foster brother. See: *DOTTI*; *GMC*. (Cf. P180.4.2.2§, P253.10.1§, T101.6§).
Ni¿mah and Nu¿m: Stolen Wife Regained: *Alf* II 132; Burton IV 2. Chauvin VI 96-97 No. 263; *ANE* 314 No. 62;
Hasan of Basrah: *Alf* III 318,-ff.; Burton VIII 38. Chauvin VII 29-35 No. 212A; *ANE* 207-10 No. 230.□

P274.2§, ‡Marriage (sexual liaison) between free and slave raised together as foster siblings. See: *DOTTI*. (Cf. P180.4.2.2§, P367.1§, T110.1§, T610.1.1§).
Ni¿mah and Nu¿m: Stolen Wife Regained: *Alf* II 143; Burton IV 21. Chauvin VI 96-97 No. 263; *ANE* 314 No. 62.□

P275.0.1§, ‡Youth (hero) adopted as foster son.
Ensorcelled Prince/Husband: *Alf* I 31; Burton I 81. Chauvin VI 56-58 No. 222; *ANE* 176 No. 13.□

P276§, Supernatural (jinni, afrit, dwarf) uncle (maternal or paternal).
Jullanâr of the Sea: *Alf* III 255,-cf.; Burton VII 274. Chauvin V 147-51 No. 73; *ANE* 248-51 No. 227.□

P282.3, Stepmother in love with stepson. See: *PSAE*.
al-'Amjad and al-'As¿ad: *Alf* II 113-14; Burton III 309. Chauvin V 208-10 No. 120[.1]; *ANE* 341-42 No. 61/pt. 2.□

P283.0.1§, ‡Half brother. (Cf. P250.0.3§).
al-'Amjad and al-'As¿ad: *Alf* II 112,-(from-father); Burton III 309. Chauvin V 208-10 No. 120[.1]; *ANE* 341-42 No. 61/pt. 2.□

P284.0.1§, ‡Half sister (from father or mother). See: *DOTTI*.
Eldest Lady's Story: Treacherous Sisters: *Alf* I 53-(from father); Burton I 162. Chauvin V 4 No. 443; *ANE* 174-75 No. 19;
Hasan of Basrah: *Alf* IV 36,-(from father); Burton VIII 107. Chauvin VII 29-35 No. 212A; *ANE* 207-10 No. 230.□

P292.2.1§, ‡Helpful (kind) father's mother (paternal grandmother).
Nûr al-Dîn ¿Alî and Son: *Alf* I 81; Burton I 235. Chauvin VI 102-6 No. 270; *ANE* 317-19 No. 22;
Sayf al-Mulûk: *Alf* III 299; Burton VII 370. Chauvin VII 64-73 No. 348; *ANE* 362-64 No. 229.□

P292.2.2§, ‡Helpful (kind) mother's mother (maternal grandmother).
Jullanâr of the Sea: *Alf* III 257, 269ff.; Burton VII 289, 306ff. Chauvin V 147-51 No. 73; *ANE* 248-51 No. 227.□

P293.1, Mother's brother as foster father. See: *DOTTI*; *GMC*. (Cf. P293.6.3§).
Omar and Young Badawî: Returning to be Executed: *Alf* II 289; Burton V 103. Chauvin V 216 No. 125; *ANE* 429-30 No. 130;
Jullanâr of the Sea: *Alf* III 254; Burton VII 278ff. Chauvin V 147-51 No. 73; *ANE* 248-51 No. 227.□

P293.6.1§, Father's brother (paternal-uncle) as helper. See: *DOTTI*; *GMC*. (Cf. P295.0.1.1§, R160.1§).
First Qalandar: Brother-Sister Incest: *Alf* I 41; Burton I 109. Chauvin V 196-97 No. 115; *ANE* 337-38 No. 15;
¿Alâ' al-Dîn Abû al-Shâmât: *Alf* II 157; Burton IV 52. Chauvin V 43-49 No. 18; *ANE* 85-87 No. 63.□

P293.6.2§, ‡Kind *¿amm* (father's brother, paternal-uncle).
Jewish Doctor's Story: Sororicide: *Alf* I 100,-(nine uncles); Burton I 289. Chauvin VI 89 No. 253; *ANE* 242 No. 26;
King ¿Umar al-Nu¿mân and Sons: *Alf* II 13; Burton III 98. Chauvin VI 112-24 No. 277; *ANE* 430-34 No. 39;
Hasan of Basrah: *Alf* IV 17-18,-(jinni); Burton VIII 71-72. Chauvin VII 29-35 No. 212A; *ANE* 207-10 No. 230.□

P293.6.3§, ‡Father's brother (paternal-uncle) as foster father. See: *DOTTI*. (Cf. P293.1).
First Qalandar: Brother-Sister Incest: *Alf* I 42; Burton I 111. Chauvin V 196-97 No. 115; *ANE* 337-38 No. 15.□

P293.6.4§, ‡Father's brother (paternal-uncle) as father-in-law. (Cf. P261.1§, P295.1.2§).
¿Alâ' al-Dîn Abû al-Shâmât: *Alf* II 157; Burton IV 52. Chauvin V 43-49 No. 18; *ANE* 85-87 No. 63.□

P293.7.3§, ‡'When flesh turns putrid [(is disgraced)], its [blood] relations become its only resort'. (Cf. T198§).
King ¿Umar al-Nu¿mân and Sons: *Alf* I 183; Burton II 124,-(when flesh stinketh). Chauvin VI 112-24 No. 277; *ANE* 430-34 No. 39.□

P294.0.1§, Paternal-aunt (*¿ammah*). See: *GMC*.
King ¿Umar al-Nu¿mân and Sons: *Alf* I 313-14, II 3,-(as mother); Burton III 59, 78. Chauvin VI 112-24 No. 277; *ANE* 430-34 No. 39.□

P294.0.1.2.1§, ‡Father's sister and her brother's son (nephew).
Nuzhat al-Zamân Tested/¿Umar al-Nu¿mân: *Alf* I 204-5,-(counsels nephew—the caliph); Burton II 166-67. Chauvin VI 116, n.1/passim No. 277; *ANE* 432,/passim No. 39;
King ¿Umar al-Nu¿mân and Sons: *Alf* II 7, 16; Burton II 86-87. Chauvin VI 112-24 No. 277; *ANE* 430-34 No. 39.□

P294.0.1.2.1.1§, ‡Father's sister (*¿ammah*) sides with her husband against her brother's son (nephew).
King ¿Umar al-Nu¿mân and Sons: *Alf* II 8-9; Burton III 88-90. Chauvin VI 112-24 No. 277; *ANE* 430-34 No. 39.□

P295.0.1.1§, ‡Paternal-cousin (*'ibn-¿amm*) helps his he-paternal-cousin. (Cf. P293.6.1§).
First Qalandar: Brother-Sister Incest: *Alf* I 39; Burton I 105. Chauvin V 196-97 No. 115; *ANE* 337-38 No. 15.□

P295.1§, Paternal-cousins (*'ibn-¿amm* and his *bint-¿amm*). See: *DOTTI*; *GMC*. (Cf. T380.2§).
Nûr al-Dîn ¿Alî and Son: *Alf* I 64ff.; Burton I 211ff. Chauvin VI 102-6 No. 270; *ANE* 317-19 No. 22;
King ¿Umar al-Nu¿mân and Sons: *Alf* I 312; Burton III 56-57. Chauvin VI 112-24 No. 277; *ANE* 430-34 No. 39;
Enchanted Spring: Change of Sex: *Alf* III 146; Burton VI 145. Chauvin VIII 43 No. 11; *ANE* 175-76 No. 191;
Lovers of Banû ¿Udhrah and Lion: *Alf* III 208; Burton VII 121. Chauvin V 116-17 No. 52; *ANE* 274 No. 218/[2];
Ibrâhîm and Jamîlah: *Alf* IV 220-27; Burton IX 211. Chauvin VI 52-53 No. 218; *ANE* 227-29 No. 258.□

P295.1.1.1§, ‡She-paternal-cousin (*bint-¿amm*) not secluded from her he-paternal-cousin (*'ibn-¿amm*). See: *DOTTI*. (Cf. K2211.4§, T380.2§, T416.8§).
¿Azîz and ¿Azîzah: *Alf* I 268; Burton II 299. Chauvin V 144-45 No. 71; *ANE* 111-13 No. 41;
King ¿Umar al-Nu¿mân and Sons: *Alf* I 310; Burton III 53. Chauvin VI 112-24 No. 277; *ANE* 430-34 No. 39.□

P295.1.2§, Marriage between *'ibn-¿amm* and his *bint-¿amm* (paternal-cousin). See: *DOTTI*; *GMC*. (Cf. P293.6.4§).
Merchant's Curious Wife: *Alf* I 6; Burton I 21. Chauvin V 179-80 No. 104; *ANE* 298-99 No. 3;
First Shaykh: Sorceress Wife: *Alf* I 8; Burton I 27. Chauvin VII 129-30 No. 396; *ANE* 376-77 No. 5;
Ensorcelled Prince/Husband: *Alf* I 27; Burton I 69. Chauvin VI 56-58 No. 222; *ANE* 176 No. 13;
Second Qalandar: Afrit's Wife: *Alf* I 45; Burton I 116. Chauvin V 197-200 No. 116; *ANE* 338-39 No. 16;
Three Apples: Hasty Uxoricide: *Alf* I 62; Burton I 190. Chauvin VI 144-45 No. 302; *ANE* 414-15 No. 21;
Nûr al-Dîn ¿Alî and Son: *Alf* I 70,-cf./(unwitting); Burton I 220. Chauvin VI 102-6 No. 270; *ANE* 317-19 No. 22;
¿Azîz and ¿Azîzah: *Alf* I 268; Burton II 299. Chauvin V 144-45 No. 71; *ANE* 111-13 No. 41;
Ni¿mah and Nu¿m: Stolen Wife Regained: *Alf* II 132; Burton IV 1. Chauvin VI 96-97 No. 263; *ANE* 314 No. 62;
Craft and Malice of Women/Frame: *Alf* III 138; Burton VI 122-23. Chauvin VIII 33-34 No. 1; *ANE* 160-61 No. 181.□

P295.1.3§, ‡Love (affection) between *'ibn-¿amm* and his *bint-¿amm*. See: *DOTTI*.
King ¿Umar al-Nu¿mân and Sons: *Alf* I 313,-(implicit); Burton III 60. Chauvin VI 112-24 No. 277; *ANE* 430-34 No. 39.□

P295.1.3.1§, ‡Love (affection) continues between *'ibn-¿amm* and his *bint-¿amm* after marriage to another. (Cf. T416.8§).
Lovers of Banû ¿Udhrah and Lion: *Alf* III 208,-(non-sexual); Burton VII 121-22. Chauvin V 116-17 No. 52; *ANE* 274 No. 218/[2].□

P297.2§, Sister's son (maternal-nephew). (Cf. P253.0.1).

Mercury ¿Alî: *Alf* III 245,-(of maternal aunt); Burton VII 206. Chauvin V 248-50 No. 147; *ANE* 301-3 No. 225.□

P297.2.1§, Bond between mother's brother (*khâl*) and sister's son. See: *DOTTI*; *GMC*. (Cf. R160.3.1§).
Jullanâr of the Sea: *Alf* III 255; Burton VII 278-79. Chauvin V 147-51 No. 73; *ANE* 248-51 No. 227.□

P302.0.1§, ‡'People are people only by the presence of other people—(*al-nâs bi al-nâs*)'. (Cf. J21.25.1§).
¿Alî ibn Bakkâr: *Alf* II 55,-(*al-nâs bi-al-nâs*); Burton III 191,-(men are still men). Chauvin V 153 No. 76; *ANE* 92-93 No. 60.□

P305.1§, ‡The rights of a neighbor.
Fox and Crow: *Alf* II 37; Burton III 150. Chauvin II 228 No. 11; *ANE* 188 No. 51.□

P305.1.1§, ‡Neighbor is almost a family member. See: *DOTTI*.
Spy, Fifth Maiden/¿Umar al-Nu¿mân: *Alf* I 224; Burton II 207. *ANE* 432 No. 39/passim;
Fox and Crow: *Alf* II 37; Burton III 150. Chauvin II 228 No. 11; *ANE* 188 No. 51.□

P305.1.1.1§, ‡'The Prophet recommended [caring for neighbors] as far as the seventh [house away]'. See: *DOTTI*. (Cf. P320.0.2.1.1§, W12.2.0.1§).
Fox and Crow: *Alf* II 37,-cf.; Burton III 150. Chauvin II 228 No. 11; *ANE* 188 No. 51.□

P305.1.2§, ‡Neighborly intervention (mediation). See: *DOTTI*. (Cf. N823§).
Merchant's Curious Wife: *Alf* I 6; Burton I 21. Chauvin V 179-80 No. 104; *ANE* 298-99 No. 3;
Rake's Trick Against Chaste Wife: *Alf* III 142; Burton VI 135-36. Chauvin VIII 37 No. 5; *ANE* 350-1 No. 185;
Ma¿rûf the Cobbler: *Alf* IV 290; Burton X 3-4. Chauvin VI 81-82 No. 250; *ANE* 291-93 No. 262.□

P305.1.3§, ‡The inquisitive (curious) neighbor. See: *DOTTI*.
Jawdar and His Treacherous Brethren: *Alf* III 193; Burton VI 241. Chauvin V 257-60 No. 154; *ANE* 244-45 No. 209.□

P305.3.1§, ‡Son of the neighborhood.
Jawdar and His Treacherous Brethren: *Alf* III 190,-(same lane); Burton VI 236,-(son of the/quarter). Chauvin V 257-60 No. 154; *ANE* 244-45 No. 209.□

P306§, ‡'Children of' ('sons-of', 'daughters-of') the same village or country (compatriots, co-villagers: '*baladiyyât*').
Ma¿rûf the Cobbler: *Alf* IV 296; Burton X 14,-(xxx). Chauvin VI 81-82 No. 250; *ANE* 291-93 No. 262.□

P310.0.1.1§, ‡'He who finds his beloved (ones) will forget his [mere] friend'.
¿Alâ' al-Dîn Abû al-Shâmât: *Alf* II 164; Burton IV 65. Chauvin V 43-49 No. 18; *ANE* 85-87 No. 63.□

P310.4.3§, ‡Father's friend as helper: he proves to be the true friend.
Nûr al-Dîn and Maryam: *Alf* IV 96-97,-(spice-vendor/merchant); Burton VIII 301-2,-("druggist"). Chauvin V 52-54 No. 271; *ANE* 98-99 No. 233;
al-Rashîd and Omani Merchant: *Alf* IV 215; Burton IX 201. Chauvin VI 111-12 No. 276; *ANE* 201-2 No. 257.□

P310.5.1§, ‡Enemies (combatants) turn true friends. See: *DOTTI*. (Cf. P201.5§).
King ¿Umar al-Nu¿mân and Sons: *Alf* II 21; Burton III 114. Chauvin VI 112-24 No. 277; *ANE* 430-34 No. 39.□

P310.5.2§, ‡Enemy heroine (princess) and hero (prince) become lovers. See: *DOTTI*. (Cf. L408§).
King ¿Umar al-Nu¿mân and Sons: *Alf* I 168,-ff.; Burton II 94. Chauvin VI 112-24 No. 277; *ANE* 430-34 No. 39.□

P311.0.2§, ‡Man and woman become sworn brethren. (Cf. F302.0.3§).
Masrûr and Zayn al-Mawâsif: *Alf* IV 57; Burton VIII 214. Chauvin VI 82-84 No. 251; *ANE* 294-95 No. 232.□

P311.1, Combatants become sworn brethren. See: *DOTTI*. (Cf. L408§).
Jawdar and His Treacherous Brethren: *Alf* III 199; Burton VI 252. Chauvin V 257-60 No. 154; *ANE* 244-45 No. 209.□

P311.4.1§, ‡Helpful friend born at the same time (day, hour, etc.) as hero.
Sayf al-Mulûk: *Alf* III 277; Burton VII 325. Chauvin VII 64-73 No. 348; *ANE* 362-64 No. 229.□

P311.5.1§, ‡Covenant of friendship: eating 'bread and salt' together. See: *DOTTI*. (Cf. P321, P351.1§).
King ¿Umar al-Nu¿mân and Sons: *Alf* I 170; Burton II 99. Chauvin VI 112-24 No. 277; *ANE* 430-34 No. 39;
¿Alî Shâr and Zumurrud: *Alf* II 222; Burton IV 200. Chauvin V 89-91 No. 28; *ANE* 100-1 No. 82;
Jawdar and His Treacherous Brethren: *Alf* III 194,-cf./(bread); Burton VI 243. Chauvin V 257-60 No. 154; *ANE* 244-45 No. 209;
Jullanâr of the Sea: *Alf* III 251; Burton VII 273. Chauvin V 147-51 No. 73; *ANE* 248-51 No. 227;
Masrûr and Zayn al-Mawâṣif: *Alf* IV 57; Burton VIII 224. Chauvin VI 82-84 No. 251; *ANE* 294-95 No. 232.□

P313.0.1§, ‡Milk-sisters.
Qamar al-Zamân and Budûr: *Alf* II 86-87; Burton III 256. Chauvin V 204-12 No. 120; *ANE* 341-45 No. 61;
Sayf al-Mulûk: *Alf* III 288,-(milk-sisters/jinn-human); Burton VII 349,-(sister by fosterage). Chauvin VII 64-73 No. 348; *ANE* 362-64 No. 229.□

P313.5§, Milk-brother and sister. See: *DOTTI*.
Qamar al-Zamân and Budûr: *Alf* II 86-87; Burton III 256,-(foster-brother). Chauvin V 204-12 No. 120; *ANE* 341-45 No. 61.□

P313.5.2§, ‡Affection (love) of milk-brother and sister for each other. (Cf. T405.3.3§).
Qamar al-Zamân and Budûr: *Alf* II 87ff.; Burton III 257ff. Chauvin V 204-12 No. 120; *ANE* 341-45 No. 61.□

P313.5.2.1§, ‡Milk-brother (-sister) as helper.
Qamar al-Zamân and Budûr: *Alf* II 87,-(helps sister); Burton III 256. Chauvin V 204-12 No. 120; *ANE* 341-45 No. 61.□

P318.1§, ‡End of friendship.
Landsman ¿Abdallah and Merman ¿Abdallah: *Alf* IV 207-8; Burton IX 187-88. Chauvin V 6-7 No. 3; *ANE* 65-66 No. 256.□

P319.0.1§, ‡True friend gives sincere advice. (Cf. J150.1§).
Spy, First Maiden/¿Umar al-Nu¿mân: *Alf* I 220; Burton II 197. *ANE* 432 No. 39/passim.□

P319.9§, ‡Friends suspend formalities (*kulfah/ḥishmah*) in dealing with each other. See: *DOTTI*.
Tailor's Story/Barber of Baghdad: *Alf* I 107; Burton I 312,-(ceremony). Chauvin V 154-56 No. 78; *ANE* 405-6 No. 27;
Page Feigns Knowing Bird Language: *Alf* III 157,-(seduction); Burton VI 171. Chauvin VIII 49-50 No. 17; *ANE* 321-22 No. 197.□

P320, Hospitality. Relation of host and guest. See: *DOTTI*; *GMC*. (Cf. W11, W12.2.2§).
Ḥâtim's Hospitality: *Alf* II 181; Burton IV 94-96. Chauvin VI 49 No. 215; *ANE* 216 No. 64.□

P320.0.1§, Hospitality for a certain required period (three, seven, forty days, or longer). (Cf. P320.0.1§).
Shahriyâr and Shâhzamân: *Alf* I 2,-(xxx); Burton I 3,-(three), 3 n. 1,-("Among Moslems it is Sunnat or practice of the Prophet"). Chauvin V 188-91 No. 111; *ANE* 370-71 No. 1;
Anîs al-Jalîs: *Alf* I 145,-(three days); Burton II 43. Chauvin V 120-24 No. 58; *ANE* 316-17 No. 35;
Isḥâq al-Mûṣilî and Khadîjah bint al-Ḥasan: *Alf* II 187,-(three); Burton IV 123. Chauvin V 241-42 No. 142; *ANE* 232 No. 71;
Lovers of Banû ¿Udhrah and Lion: *Alf* III 208,-(three days); Burton VII 124. Chauvin V 106-7 No. 37, 116 No. 52; *ANE* 274 No. 218/[2];
Hasan of Basrah: *Alf* III 314,-(three days), IV 51; Burton VIII 28, 139. Chauvin VII 29-35 No. 212A; *ANE* 207-10 No. 230;
al-Rashîd and Omani Merchant: *Alf* IV 215,-(three days); Burton IX 199. Chauvin VI 111-12 No. 276; *ANE* 201-2 No. 257;
¿Abdallah ibn Fâḍil: Treacherous Brothers: *Alf* IV 267; Burton IX 305. Chauvin V 2-4 No. 2; *ANE* 63-65 No. 261.□

P320.0.2§, ‡Hospitality to the stranger(s).
¿Alî ibn Bakkâr: *Alf* II 63,-(go to *wâlidatî*/my mother); Burton III 208,-("go to my parent"). Chauvin V 153 No. 76; *ANE* 92-93 No. 60;

Sindbâd's First Voyage: *Alf* III 88,-cf.; Burton VI 13. Chauvin VII 7-9 No. 373A; *ANE* 385 No. 179.□

P320.0.2.1.1§, ‡The Prophet recommended being hospitable to the stranger(s). (Cf. P305.1.1.1§).
King ¿Umar al-Nu¿mân and Sons: *Alf* I 189; Burton II 135. Chauvin VI 112-24 No. 277; *ANE* 430-34 No. 39;
Mouse and Cat: *Alf* IV 135,-cf.; Burton IX 35. Chauvin II 218 No. 152/2; *ANE* 305-6 No. 237.□

P320.0.5§, ‡Hospitality is an attitude (in the manner of how guest is received). See: *DOTTI*. (Cf. H486.6.1§, P324.0.1§).
Ma¿rûf the Cobbler: *Alf* IV 306-7; Burton X 31. Chauvin VI 81-82 No. 250; *ANE* 291-93 No. 262.□

P320.0.5.1§, ‡'An onion [offered as food of hospitality] from a gracious host is [equal to a roast] lamb'. (Cf. J708.8§, U84).
Ma¿rûf the Cobbler: *Alf* IV 306-7,-cf./(lentil); Burton X 31. Chauvin VI 81-82 No. 250; *ANE* 291-93 No. 262.□

P320.0.6.1§, ‡Guest must not violate sanctity of host's household (honor). See: *DOTTI*.
Budûr and Jubayr ibn ¿Umayr: *Alf* II 236; Burton IV 232. Chauvin VII 93-94 No. 374; *ANE* 243-44 No. 83.□

P320.0.6.2§, ‡Guest should not visit frequently (stay too long). (Cf. U86.0.1§).
Jeweler's Wife and Qamar al-Zamân: *Alf* IV 251; Burton IX 273. Chauvin V 212-14 No. 121; *ANE* 345-47 No. 260.□

P321, Salt of hospitality. Eating a man's salt creates mutual obligation. See: *GMC*.
Sindbâd and Porter: *Alf* III 83,-(implicit/become 'brothers'); Burton VI 4. Chauvin VII 1 No. 373; *ANE* 383-85 No. 179/pt.□

P321.3§, ‡Guest refuses food and drink to enforce demand. See: *DOTTI*. (Cf. K2025§, P790.2.3§).
Budûr and Jubayr ibn ¿Umayr: *Alf* II 238, 243; Burton IV 236, 244,-(monetary award). Chauvin VII 93-94 No. 374; *ANE* 243-44 No. 83.□

P322.0.1§, *'ijârah*: culprit, as guest or neighbor, is to be given refuge. See: *GMC*. (Cf. Q46).
Second Qalandar: Afrit's Wife: *Alf* I 47,-cf./(given to monkey); Burton I 127. Chauvin V 197-200 No. 116; *ANE* 338-39 No. 16;
Ni¿mah and Nu¿m: Stolen Wife Regained: *Alf* II 141; Burton IV 17. Chauvin VI 96-97 No. 263; *ANE* 314 No. 62;
Dalîla the Swindler: *Alf* III 223,-cf.; Burton VII 165. Chauvin V 245-50 No. 147; *ANE* 163-64 No. 224;
Sayf al-Mulûk: *Alf* III 301,-cf./(human given protection by jinn in-laws); Burton VIII 3. Chauvin VII 64-73 No. 348; *ANE* 362-64 No. 229.□

P322.2.1§, ‡Adversary (enemy) as guest in disguise. See: *DOTTI*.
King ¿Umar al-Nu¿mân and Sons: *Alf* I 168,-ff.; Burton II 94. Chauvin VI 112-24 No. 277; *ANE* 430-34 No. 39.□

P322.3, ‡Refugee entertained in holy place (church, monastery, etc.).
King ¿Umar al-Nu¿mân and Sons: *Alf* I 168,-ff.; Burton II 97. Chauvin VI 112-24 No. 277; *ANE* 430-34 No. 39.□

P322.4§, ‡Owner (host) helps uninvited guest in pretending to be the 'master of the house'. (Cf. K1816.13, K1952.8.1§).
al-'Amjad and al-'As¿ad: *Alf* II 124-25; Burton III 335. Chauvin V 208-10 No. 120[.1]; *ANE* 341-42 No. 61/pt. 2.□

P322.7§, ‡Animal given refuge (*'ijârah*) from pursuer. See: *DOTTI*. (Cf. V443.3§).
Second Qalandar: Afrit's Wife: *Alf* I 47; Burton I 127. Chauvin V 197-200 No. 116; *ANE* 338-39 No. 16;
Flea and She-mouse: *Alf* II 37; Burton III 152. Chauvin II 228 No. 12; *ANE* 186 No. 52.□

P324.0.1§, ‡Guest received with manifest signs of pleasure. See: *DOTTI*. (Cf. H486.6.1§, P320.0.5§).
Abû al-Ḥasan al-Khorâsânî (and Caliph's Favorite): *Alf* IV 229; Burton IX 230-31. Chauvin V 218-20 No. 129; *ANE* 68-69 No. 259.□

P324.0.2§, ‡Providing welcome (conversation, entertainment, 'greetings') is host's responsibility. See: *DOTTI*; *PSAE*. (Cf. W12).

Ishâq al-Mûṣilî and Khadîjah bint al-Ḥasan: *Alf* II 185,-(implicit); Burton IV 120. Chauvin V 241-42 No. 142; *ANE* 232 No. 71;
Abû al-Ḥasan al-Khorâsânî (and Caliph's Favorite): *Alf* IV 229; Burton IX 230. Chauvin V 218-20 No. 129; *ANE* 68-69 No. 259.□

P324.0.4.1§, ‡Man being evicted from earthly paradise (utopia) allowed to take some valuables (as parting present). (Cf. T52.0.8§, W37.8.1.1§).
Landsman ¿Abdallah and Merman ¿Abdallah: *Alf* IV 207-8; Burton IX 187-88. Chauvin V 6-7 No. 3; *ANE* 65-66 No. 256.□

P324.1, ‡Host treats guest with food and everything possible.
Abû al-Ḥasan al-Khorâsânî (and Caliph's Favorite): *Alf* IV 230; Burton IX 220-21. Chauvin V 218-20 No. 129; *ANE* 68-69 No. 259.□

P324.3, Guest's life inviolable. See: *GMC*.
King ¿Umar al-Nu¿mân and Sons: *Alf* I 173; Burton II 106. Chauvin VI 112-24 No. 277; *ANE* 430-34 No. 39.□

P324.3.1§, ‡Messenger's (envoy's, ambassador's) life inviolable. (Cf. P469.0.1§, S160.4, Q243.1.3.1§).
King ¿Umar al-Nu¿mân and Sons: *Alf* I 254; Burton II 268. Chauvin VI 112-24 No. 277; *ANE* 430-34 No. 39.□

P325.0.1§, Host surrenders his fiancée (sister) to his friend. See: *DOTTI*.
Anîs al-Jalîs: *Alf* I 142,-cf.-(beloved slave-girl); Burton II 34. Chauvin V 120-24 No. 58; *ANE* 316-17 No. 35;
Ghânim ibn Ayyûb: *Alf* I 162,-(favorite consort); Burton II 76. Chauvin VI 14 No. 188; *ANE* 192-93 No. 36.□

P327, Barmecide feast. [Host gives imaginary feast, guest repays (reciprocates) with a slap; host admires guest's daring and serves real banquet]. See: *ANE*; *DOTTI*. (Cf. X1§).
Barber's Sixth Brother: Emasculated by Abductor: *Alf* I 122-23; Burton I 344-48. Chauvin V 163-64 No. 86; *ANE* 120 No. 34.□

P335.1§, ‡Shabby hospitality (or inhospitality) betrays host's bad character. See: *DOTTI*. (Cf. H486.6.1§, W103§).
¿Alî Shâr and Zumurrud: *Alf* II 222; Burton IV 201. Chauvin V 89-91 No. 28; *ANE* 100-1 No. 82.□

P335.3§, ‡Host does not stand up for (notable) guest, nor invite him to be seated.
Jawdar and His Treacherous Brethren: *Alf* III 199,-(king slighted); Burton VI 252. Chauvin V 257-60 No. 154; *ANE* 244-45 No. 209.□

P339§, Excessive hospitality distrusted. See: *DOTTI*.
Qamar al-Zamân and Budûr: *Alf* II 108; Burton III 300. Chauvin V 204-12 No. 120; *ANE* 341-45 No. 61.□

P339.2§, ‡Too many unearned honors (awards) suspected of hiding dishonorable intentions. (Cf. P503.7§).
Qamar al-Zamân and Budûr: *Alf* II 108; Burton III 300-1. Chauvin V 204-12 No. 120; *ANE* 341-45 No. 61.□

P339.3§, ‡Excessive generosity (charity) distrusted. (Cf. W11.0.1§).
Ma¿rûf the Cobbler: *Alf* IV 308-9,-(poem); Burton X 36. Chauvin VI 81-82 No. 250; *ANE* 291-93 No. 262.□

P345.1§, ‡Corporal punishment (beating) by teacher is hard to accept at first, but leads to sweet (honey) ending.
Wolf and Fox: *Alf* II 30; Burton III 133. Chauvin II 227 No. 6; *ANE* 450 No. 47.□

P351.1§, ‡Covenant of brotherhood under God (*¿ahd Allâh*). (Cf. P311.5.1§).
Jawdar and His Treacherous Brethren: *Alf* III 183; Burton VI 223. Chauvin V 257-60 No. 154; *ANE* 244-45 No. 209.□

P351.2§, ‡Covenant of parentage under God (foster father-son, foster mother-daughter).
¿Alâ' al-Dîn Abû al-Shâmât: *Alf* II 164,-('in God's *¿ahd*'); Burton IV 62,-(son by covenant). Chauvin V 43-49 No. 18; *ANE* 85-87 No. 63.□

P360.0.1§, ‡Employer (boss) and employee. See: *DOTTI*.

Stolen Necklace/Hasty Accusation: *Alf* III 164; Burton VI 182-83. Chauvin VIII 53 No. 20; *ANE* 398 No. 200.□

P361, Faithful servant. See: *DOTTI*.
Jewish qâḍî and His Devout Wife: *Alf* III 10-11; Burton V 257. Chauvin VI 154-55 No. 321; *ANE* 242 No. 163.□

P361.4.0.1§, Faithful nurse (maid) protects master's children (wife). See: *DOTTI*. (Cf. P185.1§).
King ¿Umar al-Nu¿mân and Sons: *Alf* I 184; Burton II 128. Chauvin VI 112-24 No. 277; *ANE* 430-34 No. 39.□

P361.11.1.1§, ‡Mistress avenges her slave-girl (maidservant) who was maltreated (beaten) by master.
al-Rashîd and Omani Merchant: *Alf* IV 215; Burton IX 199ff. Chauvin VI 111-12 No. 276; *ANE* 201-2 No. 257.□

P363.1.1§, ‡Angry princess murders her nurse (governess).
Qamar al-Zamân and Budûr: *Alf* II 86; Burton III 255. Chauvin V 204-12 No. 120; *ANE* 341-45 No. 61.□

P365.5, ‡Slave corrupts mistress. (Cf. P367.1§).
King's Daughter and Ape: *Alf* II 253; Burton IV 297. Chauvin V 178 No. 102; *ANE* 262-63 No. 102.□

P367§, Faithless slave. See: *GMC*. (Cf. K2251, T471.5§).
King ¿Umar al-Nu¿mân and Sons: *Alf* I 183-85; Burton II 125-27. Chauvin VI 112-24 No. 277; *ANE* 430-34 No. 39.□

P367.1§, ‡Men-slaves corrupt (seduce) mistresses. See: *DOTTI*. (Cf. P274.2§, P365.5, P180.5§, T471.5§).
First Eunuch: Bukhayt Deflowers Mistress: *Alf* I 147-48; Burton II 50. Chauvin V 277 No. 160; *ANE* 178 No. 37;
Third Eunuch: Seduces Mistress and Son: *Alf* I 151,-(passim); Burton II 56/non-tale. Chauvin V 278 n. 1 No. [161B]; *ANE* 179,/passim No. 38.□

P368.1.1§, ‡Seducer bribes servant and gains access into mistress's home. (Cf. T452).
Rake's Trick Against Chaste Wife: *Alf* III 142; Burton VI 135. Chauvin VIII 37 No. 5; *ANE* 350-1 No. 185.□

P400.1.2§, ‡Master craftsman creates intricate (novel) work away from apprentices—usually at his home.
Jeweler's Wife and Qamar al-Zamân: *Alf* IV 246; Burton IX 263. Chauvin V 212-14 No. 121; *ANE* 345-47 No. 260.□

P402§, ‡Professional code of honor (rules of conduct for members of guild or profession; e.g., physicians, goldsmiths, clerics, water-carriers).
Water-carrier and Goldsmith's Wife: *Alf* II 286; Burton V 89-90. Chauvin VI 192 No. 361; *ANE* 444 No. 122.□

P426.0.2§, ‡Cleric as preacher (orator, *khaṭîb*).
Dispute Concerning Males and Females: *Alf* II 300,-(woman-preacher); Burton V 154. Chauvin VI 153 No. 317; *ANE* 291 No. 151.□

P406§, Head of a guild (*shâhbandar*, etc.). See: *DOTTI*.
¿Alâ' al-Dîn Abû al-Shâmât: *Alf* II 162,-(of merchants); Burton IV 60. Chauvin V 43-49 No. 18; *ANE* 85-87 No. 63;
Sindbâd's Seventh Voyage: *Alf* III 119-20,-(of merchants); Burton VI 74. Chauvin VII 26-29 No. 373G; *ANE* 386-87 No. 179;
Sandal-wood Merchant and Sharpers: *Alf* III 175,-(of thieves); Burton VI 204 n. 2. Chauvin VIII 60-62 No. 26; *ANE* 359-60 No. 205;
Nûr al-Dîn and Maryam: *Alf* IV 92-(*shaykh al-sûq* and its *muḥtasib*); Burton VIII 293,-(Syndic of the bazar and inspector thereof). Chauvin V 52-54 No. 271; *ANE* 98-99 No. 233.□

P406.2§, ‡Members of guild impeach (vote out) offending head of their guild.
¿Alâ' al-Dîn Abû al-Shâmât: *Alf* II 150,-(*¿azl min al-mashyakhah*); Burton IV 36-37,-(depose from the "Shaykh-ship"). Chauvin V 43-49 No. 18; *ANE* 85-87 No. 63.□

P407.1§, ‡Number of members of guild is fixed (i.e., forty, or the like).

Abû Qîr and Abû Ṣîr: *Alf* IV 186,-(forty); Burton IX 143. Chauvin V 15-17 No. 10; *ANE* 75-77 No. 255.□

P407.1.1§, ‡Membership in guild is hereditary (passes from father to son).
Abû Qîr and Abû Ṣîr: *Alf* IV 186; Burton IX 143. Chauvin V 15-17 No. 10; *ANE* 75-77 No. 255.□

P407.1.1.1§, ‡Stranger (outsider) refused membership in guild (not allowed to practice).
Abû Qîr and Abû Ṣîr: *Alf* IV 186; Burton IX 143. Chauvin V 15-17 No. 10; *ANE* 75-77 No. 255.□

P408.1§, ‡Ceremonial opening of market daily (affirmation of rank, prayers, etc.).
¿Alâ' al-Dîn Abû al-Shâmât: *Alf* II 150; Burton IV 36. Chauvin V 43-49 No. 18; *ANE* 85-87 No. 63.□

P408.3§, ‡Laboring (working) at night, selling by day. See: *DOTTI*.
Spy, Fourth Maiden/¿Umar al-Nu¿mân: *Alf* I 222; Burton II 204. *ANE* 432 No. 39/passim.□

P411.5§, ‡Gardener.
Wolf and Fox: *Alf* II 30-31,-(of vineyard); Burton III 134. Chauvin II 227 No. 6; *ANE* 450 No. 47;
Devout Jewess and Wicked Elders: *Alf* II 286; Burton V 97. Chauvin VI 193-93 No. 362; *ANE* 169 No. 128;
Man [Gardener] and His Wife: *Alf* IV 165; Burton IX 98. Chauvin II 223 No. 152/19; *ANE* 289 No. 250.□

P412, ‡Shepherd. See: *GMC*.
Hermit Tempted by Angel: *Alf* II 27; Burton III 126. Chauvin II 226 No. 3; *ANE* 221 No. 45/pt. 2.□

P413, Ferryman. See: *DOTTI*; *GMC*.
Mock Caliph/¿Alî al-Jawharî: *Alf* II 191,-cf./(boatman); Burton IV 130. Chauvin V 99-100 No. 174; *ANE* 304-5 No. 73.□

P413.0.1§, ‡Ferryman as helper.
Ibrâhîm and Jamîlah: *Alf* IV 223; Burton IX 216. Chauvin VI 52-53 No. 218; *ANE* 227-29 No. 258.□

P414, Hunter. See: *DOTTI*. (Cf. P806.7§).
Drop of Honey: *Alf* III 145; Burton VI 142. Chauvin VIII 41-42 No. 9; *ANE* 171-72 No. 189.□

P416.1§, ‡Full-time servant (maidservant). See: *DOTTI*.
Stolen Necklace/Hasty Accusation: *Alf* III 164; Burton VI 182. Chauvin VIII 53 No. 20; *ANE* 398 No. 200.□

P416.3.1§, ‡Doorkeeper as helper.
¿Alî ibn Bakkâr: *Alf* II 62; Burton III 206. Chauvin V 153 No. 76; *ANE* 92-93 No. 60;
Abû Qîr and Abû Ṣîr: *Alf* IV 188; Burton IX 145-(Concierge of the Khan). Chauvin V 15-17 No. 10; *ANE* 75-77 No. 255;
¿Abdallah ibn Fâḍil: Treacherous Brothers: *Alf* IV 287; Burton IX 347. Chauvin V 2-4 No. 2; *ANE* 63-65 No. 261.□

P416.3.4.1§, ‡Passage gained by appeasing or bribing doorkeeper.
Jawdar and His Treacherous Brethren: *Alf* III 197-98; Burton VI 249. Chauvin V 257-60 No. 154; *ANE* 244-45 No. 209;
Dalîla the Swindler: *Alf* III 214; Burton VII 148. Chauvin V 245-50 No. 147; *ANE* 163-64 No. 224.□

P417§, ‡Porter (carrier). See: *DOTTI*.
Porter and Ladies of Baghdad: *Alf* I 31; Burton I 82. Chauvin V 251-52 No. 148; *ANE* 324-26 No. 14;
Sindbâd and Porter: *Alf* III 81; Burton VI 1. Chauvin VII 1 No. 373; *ANE* 383-85 No. 179/pt.□

P417.1§, ‡Porter as lover. See: *DOTTI*; *GMC*.
Porter and Ladies of Baghdad: *Alf* I 31-35; Burton I 82-104. Chauvin V 251-52 No. 148; *ANE* 324-26 No. 14.□

P417.5§, Water-carrier (*saqqâ*, delivers water to homes. See: *DOTTI*; *GMC*. (Cf. P165.1§).
Water-carrier and Goldsmith's Wife: *Alf* II 285; Burton V 89. Chauvin VI 192 No. 361; *ANE* 444 No. 122.□

P418.2§—(formerly-P418§), Animal (donkey, mule, etc.) driver.

Copt Broker's Story: Lover's Sacrifices Repaid: *Alf* I 92-93,-cf.; Burton I 271, 272. Chauvin VI 80 No. 249; *ANE* 313-14 No. 24;
King ¿Umar al-Nu¿mân and Sons: *Alf* I 188; Burton II 134. Chauvin VI 112-24 No. 277; *ANE* 430-34 No. 39.□

P418.7§, ‡Travel-guide (caravan leader, navigator). See: *DOTTI*.
¿Alâ' al-Dîn Abû al-Shâmât: *Alf* II 154; Burton IV 43. Chauvin V 43-49 No. 18; *ANE* 85-87 No. 63;
Jinn Imprisoned in Flasks: *Alf* III 124; Burton VI 88. Chauvin VII 113 No. 380=no/text; *ANE* 146 No. 180;
Hasan of Basrah: *Alf* IV 52; Burton VIII 141. Chauvin VII 29-35 No. 212A; *ANE* 207-10 No. 230.□

P418.7.2§, ‡Travel-guide is indispensable (lives of travelers depend on him).
City of Brass: *Alf* III 132; Burton VI 108. Chauvin V 32-35 No. 16; *ANE* 146-50 No. 180.□

P419§, Fisher. See: *DOTTI*; *GMC*. (Cf. P806.7§).
Fisherman and Afrit: Ingratitude: *Alf* I 14,-(*al-ṣayyâd ma¿a al-¿ifrît*); Burton I 38. Chauvin VI 23-25 No. 195; *ANE* 183-84 No. 8;
Three Apples: Hasty Uxoricide: *Alf* I 61; Burton I 187. Chauvin VI 144-45 No. 302; *ANE* 414-15 No. 21;
Anîs al-Jalîs: *Alf* I 140-41; Burton II 31. Chauvin V 120-24 No. 58; *ANE* 316-17 No. 35;
Jawdar and His Treacherous Brethren: *Alf* III 179; Burton VI 215. Chauvin V 257-60 No. 154; *ANE* 244-45 No. 209;
Foolish Fisher: *Alf* IV 162; Burton IX 93. Chauvin II 222 No. 152/16; *ANE* 187 No. 248.□

P420.1§, ‡Proficiency in many fields of knowledge (sciences).
Bulûqiya: *Alf* III 80; Burton V 395-96. Chauvin VII 54 No. 77; *ANE* 130-32 No. 177.□

P421.0.1§, ‡Clever judge. See: *DOTTI*.
Hârûn, Slave-girl and Judge Abû-Yûsuf: *Alf* II 202; Burton IV 153-55. Chauvin VII 114 No. 383; *ANE* 204 No. 75.□

P421.0.3.1§, ‡Judge who becomes personally involved with litigant punished (rebuked). (Cf. J1192.5.1§).
Masrûr and Zayn al-Mawâṣif: *Alf* IV 77; Burton VIII 255. Chauvin VI 82-84 No. 251; *ANE* 294-95 No. 232.□

P423.0.2.1§, ‡"Children's teachers are lacking (deficient) in mind" (i.e., they are brainless). See: *DOTTI*. (Cf. W256.6.1§).
Schoolmaster Who Fell in Love by Report: Mourns: *Alf* II 292-93; Burton V 117. Chauvin VI 136 No. 287; *ANE* 367 No. 135.□

P424, Physician. See: *PSAE*. (Cf. J166, P424.10§).
Dûban and King Yûnân: *Alf* I 16,-(sage/philosopher/physician/herbalist); Burton I 45. Chauvin V 275-76 No. 156; *ANE* 459 No. 9;
Jewish Doctor's Story: Sororicide: *Alf* I 99; Burton I 288. Chauvin VI 89 No. 253; *ANE* 242 No. 26.□

P424.0.1§, ‡Physician as helper. (Cf. Q40.2§).
Ni¿mah and Nu¿m: Stolen Wife Regained: *Alf* II 137,-(helps hero find beloved); Burton IV 10. Chauvin VI 96-97 No. 263; *ANE* 314 No. 62.□

P424.2, Doctor who can cure can also poison. This reflection [(thought)] brings the doctor under king's suspicion. See: *ANE*; *DOTTI*; *GMC*. (Cf. W154.0.1§).
Dûban and King Yûnân: *Alf* I 21; Burton I 55. Chauvin V 275-76 No. 156; *ANE* 459 No. 9.□

P424.3.0.1§, ‡Unskilled physician(s). See: *DOTTI*. (Cf. P424.9§).
Ghânim ibn Ayyûb: *Alf* I 158-59,-(implicit); Burton II 70. Chauvin VI 14 No. 188; *ANE* 192-93 No. 36.□

P424.7§, Midwife (*dâyah, qâbilah*). See: *DOTTI*; *PSAE*. (Cf. P272.6.1§, P446.5§, T583).
¿Alâ' al-Dîn Abû al-Shâmât: *Alf* II 148; Burton IV 32. Chauvin V 43-49 No. 18; *ANE* 85-87 No. 63;
Jeweler's Wife and Qamar al-Zamân: *Alf* IV 245,-(as go-between); Burton IX 259. Chauvin V 212-14 No. 121; *ANE* 345-47 No. 260.□

P424.8§, ‡Attendant (trustee, sitter) to the invalid (the aged, a child. etc.). See: *DOTTI*.
Man Who Never Laughs: *Alf* III 152; Burton VI 160. Chauvin VIII 47-48 No. 15; *ANE* 285-86 No. 195.□

P424.9§, Barber as physician ('health-barber'). See: *DOTTI*; *GMC*.
Hunchback's Tale: Resuscitated: *Alf* I 125; Burton I 351. Chauvin V 180-82 No. 105; *ANE* 224-25 No. 23;
Dalîla the Swindler: *Alf* III 221; Burton VII 160. Chauvin V 245-50 No. 147; *ANE* 163-64 No. 224.□

P424.10§, Herbalist. (Cf. P424).
Ebony Horse: *Alf* II 261; Burton V 21. Chauvin V 221-31 No. 130; *ANE* 172-74 No. 103.□

P424.10.1§, Spice-vendor as herbalist (healer). See: *DOTTI*; *GMC*.
¿Alâ' al-Dîn Abû al-Shâmât: *Alf* II 148,-(*¿aṭṭâr*); Burton IV 30,-(druggist). Chauvin V 43-49 No. 18; *ANE* 85-87 No. 63.□

P425.0.1§, ‡Scribe as hero (sage). See: *PSAE*.
Second Qalandar: Afrit's Wife: *Alf* I 43; Burton I 113. Chauvin V 197-200 No. 116; *ANE* 338-39 No. 16.□

P425.2§, ‡Scribe writes in various styles. (Cf. F883.5§).
Second Qalandar: Afrit's Wife: *Alf* I 47,-cf.; Burton I 128. Chauvin V 197-200 No. 116; *ANE* 338-39 No. 16.□

P426.0.3§, Cleric (*¿arrîf, fi'î, muṭawwi¿, 'abûnâ*, father, etc.) as children's school-teacher. See: *DOTTI*; *GMC*. (Cf. T428§, X420§).
Schoolmaster Who Fell in Love by Report: Mourns: *Alf* II 292[]; Burton V 118. Chauvin VI 136 No. 287; *ANE* 367 No. 135;
Schoolmaster (Dominie) Castrates Self: *Alf* II 293; Burton V 118. Chauvin VI 137 No. 288; *ANE* 186 No. 136.□

P426.0.8§, ‡Immoral (corrupt) cleric (judge). See: *DOTTI*. (Cf. G11.9.0.1§).
Lady and Five Suitors Deceived: *Alf* III 158; Burton VI 173. Chauvin VIII 50-51 No. 18; *ANE* 266 No. 198;
Jeweler's Wife and Qamar al-Zamân: *Alf* IV 239,-(poem); Burton IX 25-51. Chauvin V 212-14 No. 121; *ANE* 345-47 No. 260.□

P426.2.1§, ‡Mystic (anchorite, ascetic, sufi, etc.). See: *DOTTI*. (Cf. P16.1).
Devotee Prince: Ascetic's Death: *Alf* II 289; Burton V 111. Chauvin VI 193-94 No. 363; *ANE* 167-68 No. 134.□

P426.2.1.1§, ‡Unreasonable mystic (sufi)—seems to speak nonsense. See: *DOTTI*. (Cf. J1742.6.1.3§).
Conversion of Princess by Khawwâṣ: *Alf* III 15,-(princess); Burton V 285. Chauvin V 239 No. 139; *ANE* 145 No. 171.□

P426.2.1.2§, ‡Person disappointed with social life becomes hermit (anchorite, ascetic, etc.). See: *DOTTI*. (Cf. M135, P16.1).
Stolen Necklace/Hasty Accusation: *Alf* III 164; Burton VI 183. Chauvin VIII 53 No. 20; *ANE* 398 No. 200.□

P426.2.3§, ‡Wanderer ('*sawwâḥ*'). (Usually due to mystical urges or disappointments especially in love). (Cf. J1077.2§).
Goldsmith and Cashmere Singer: *Alf* III 151; Burton VI 158. Chauvin VIII 46-47 No. 14; *ANE* 196 No. 194;
Son of Unjust King: *Alf* IV 142-3; Burton IX 50,-(pilgrim). Chauvin II 219-20 No. 152/7; *ANE* 437 No. 242;
Jeweler's Wife and Qamar al-Zamân: *Alf* IV 242,-(dervish); Burton IX 255. Chauvin V 212-14 No. 121; *ANE* 345-47 No. 260.□

P426.3.5§, ‡Helpful monk.
Prior Becomes Moslem: al-Anbârî: *Alf* II 298,-(hospitable); Burton V 141. Chauvin V 237-38 No. 137; *ANE* 330-31 No. 147.□

P426.4§, ‡Marriage-divorce cleric (*ma'dhûn*, judge).
¿Alâ' al-Dîn Abû al-Shâmât: *Alf* II 155; Burton IV 49. Chauvin V 43-49 No. 18; *ANE* 85-87 No. 63.□

P427, Druid (poet, learned man).
City of Brass: *Alf* III 132,-cf./(learned man); Burton VI 90,-(variant). Chauvin V 32-35 No. 16; *ANE* 146-50 No. 180.□

P427.5.0.1§, ‡Woman druid as physician.
King's Daughter and Ape: *Alf* II 253,-cf.; Burton IV 298. Chauvin V 178 No. 102; *ANE* 262-63 No. 102.□

P427.7.1, Extemporaneous composition by poets.
Dûban and King Yûnân: *Alf* I 22-23,-(*'anshada*); Burton I 60,-(improvise). Chauvin V 275-76 No. 156; *ANE* 459 No. 9;
Copt Broker's Story: Lover's Sacrifices Repaid: *Alf* I 89; Burton I 262,-(improvised). Chauvin VI 80 No. 249; *ANE* 313-14 No. 24;
Hârûn and Zubaydah in Bath: *Alf* II 284,-(poem); Burton V 76. Chauvin VI 142 No. 298; *ANE* 203-4 No. 111.□

P427.7.4, ‡Women poets. (Cf. Z87§).
Ma¿n Rewards Maidens for a Drink of Water: *Alf* II 182,-cf./(poems); Burton IV 97. Chauvin VI 78 No. 247; *ANE* 290 No. 65;
Hârûn and Arab Girl: *Alf* III 203-4; Burton VII 108-10. Chauvin VI 143 No. 300; *ANE* 202 No. 215;

Basra Girls in Poetry Contest: *Alf* III 205; Burton VII 110. Chauvin VI 144 No. 301; *ANE* 107-8 No. 216.□

P427.7.4.1§, ‡Slave-woman (slave-girl) as poetess. (Cf. P179.1.2§).
Man from Yaman and Six Salve-girls: Flyting: *Alf* II 244-50; Burton IV 245-60. Chauvin VI 151 No. 313; *ANE* 289-90 No. 84;
¿Alî bin Ṭâhir and Mu'nis: *Alf* II 303; Burton V 164. Chauvin VI 154 No. 319; *ANE* 101 No. 153.□

P427.7.4.3§, *raddâḥah, shalaq*: professional denigrator (satirist). Woman hired to publicly disgrace a person with vulgarities. (Cf. M401, Z87§, Z187§).
Man from Yaman and Six Salve-girls: Flyting: *Alf* II 244-49,-cf.; Burton IV 245-60. Chauvin VI 151 No. 313; *ANE* 289-90 No. 84.□

P428.0.1§, Singer(s). See: *GMC*.
Isḥâq al-Mûṣilî and Merchant's Singer: *Alf* II 294-7; Burton V 130. Chauvin VI 59 No. 225; *ANE* 233 No. 142.□

P428.9.1.1§, ‡Entertainer's-*nuqût*: monetary gift (gratuity) for a performance (by dancers, musicians, singers, etc.). See: *DOTTI*. (Cf. T136.4.0.1§).
Nûr al-Dîn ¿Alî and Son: *Alf* I 70,-(gold provided by jinni); Burton I 214-15. Chauvin VI 102-6 No. 270; *ANE* 317-19 No. 22;
Reeve's Story: Why Maimed by Bride: *Alf* I 98,-(with gold); Burton I 286,-(palms crossed with gold). Chauvin V 220-21 No. 305; *ANE* 351 No. 25;
Dalîla the Swindler: *Alf* III 220; Burton VII 159,-(largesse for). Chauvin V 245-50 No. 147; *ANE* 163-64 No. 224.□

P429.1, Astronomer. See: *DOTTI*. (Cf. P481).
Tawaddud: Slavegirl Sold and Regained: *Alf* II 319,-cf./(knowledge); Burton V 227. Chauvin VII 117-19 No. 387; *ANE* 408-10 No. 157.□

P430.1.1§, ‡Shopkeeper as source of news. (Tailor, grocer, carpenter, etc. provides helpful information on neighbors. (Cf. K1164§, P431.1).
Ibrâhîm and Jamîlah: *Alf* IV 222-23; Burton IX 214. Chauvin VI 52-53 No. 218; *ANE* 227-29 No. 258;
Abû al-Ḥasan al-Khorâsânî (and Caliph's Favorite): *Alf* IV 233; Burton IX 236. Chauvin V 218-20 No. 129; *ANE* 68-69 No. 259.□

P431, Merchant. (Cf. P715.1.1§).
Nûr al-Dîn ¿Alî and Son: *Alf* I 69; Burton I 211. Chauvin VI 102-6 No. 270; *ANE* 317-19 No. 22;
Ghânim ibn Ayyûb: *Alf* I 146; Burton II 45-76. Chauvin VI 14-16 No. 188; *ANE* 192-93 No. 36.□

P431.0.1§, ‡Woman (girl) merchant—businesswoman. See: *DOTTI*. (Cf. P761.2.2§).
Eldest Lady's Story: Treacherous Sisters: *Alf* I 53-54; Burton I 164. Chauvin V 4 No. 443; *ANE* 174-75 No. 19;
Copt Broker's Story: Lover's Sacrifices Repaid: *Alf* I 95,-(implicit, owner of real state and granary); Burton I 277. Chauvin VI 80 No. 249; *ANE* 313-14 No. 24.□

P431.0.3§, ‡Merchants cultivate (inspire) prosperity and disdain war (conflict).

King ¿Umar al-Nu¿mân and Sons: *Alf* I 237; Burton II 235. Chauvin VI 112-24 No. 277; *ANE* 430-34 No. 39.□

P431.0.4§, ‡'Do buying and selling; don't be a hireling'. (Cf. A1471.8.1§, J1014.1§).
¿Alâ' al-Dîn Abû al-Shâmât: *Alf* II 172; Burton IV 77,-(buy and sell, and repine not [??]). Chauvin V 43-49 No. 18; *ANE* 85-87 No. 63.□

P431.0.5§, Merchant's desire to conduct trade. See: *DOTTI*.
Jeweler's Wife and Qamar al-Zamân: *Alf* IV 244,-(youth's); Burton IX 257. Chauvin V 212-14 No. 121; *ANE* 345-47 No. 260.□

P431.1, Merchants as spreaders of news. (Cf. P430.1.1§, P469.3§).
King ¿Umar al-Nu¿mân and Sons: *Alf* I 320; Burton III 75. Chauvin VI 112-24 No. 277; *ANE* 430-34 No. 39;
Ebony Horse: *Alf* II 262-3; Burton V 25. Chauvin V 221-31 No. 130; *ANE* 172-74 No. 103.□

P431.1.1§, ‡Merchant reports his king's conduct (policies) to foreign ruler.
Sindbâd's Sixth Voyage: *Alf* III 115; Burton VI 67-68. Chauvin VII 24-27 No. 373F; *ANE* 386 No. 179.□

P431.2§, Merchant as trickster (cheat). See: *DOTTI*; *GMC*. (Cf. K2249.4).
Woman Who Made Husband Sift Dust: *Alf* III 145; Burton VI 143-44. Chauvin VIII 42 No. 10; *ANE* 452-53 No. 190;
Stolen Purse/Joint Depositors: *Alf* III 176; Burton VI 209. Chauvin VIII 63-64 No. 25; *ANE* 399 No. 207.□

P431.4§, ‡Merchant's possessions and activities.
¿Alâ' al-Dîn Abû al-Shâmât: *Alf* II 149; Burton IV 35. Chauvin V 43-49 No. 18; *ANE* 85-87 No. 63.□

P431.4.1§, ‡Rich merchant: merchant as wealthy (successful) man. See: *DOTTI*.
¿Alâ' al-Dîn Abû al-Shâmât: *Alf* II 149; Burton IV 35. Chauvin V 43-49 No. 18; *ANE* 85-87 No. 63;
Mock Caliph/¿Alî al-Jawharî: *Alf* II 196,-(*min al-'a¿yân*/of the notables); Burton IV 139-40. Chauvin V 99-100 No. 174; *ANE* 304-5 No. 73;
Hasan of Basrah: *Alf* IV 55; Burton VIII 155. Chauvin VII 29-35 No. 212A; *ANE* 207-10 No. 230;
Nûr al-Dîn and Maryam: *Alf* IV 80; Burton VIII 264. Chauvin V 52-54 No. 271; *ANE* 98-99 No. 233;
Abû al-Ḥasan al-Khorâsânî (and Caliph's Favorite): *Alf* IV 230; Burton IX 231-32. Chauvin V 218-20 No. 129; *ANE* 68-69 No. 259;
¿Abdallah ibn Fâḍil: Treacherous Brothers: *Alf* IV 269-70; Burton IX 311. Chauvin V 2-4 No. 2; *ANE* 63-65 No. 261.□

P431.4.2§, ‡Merchant so rich (successful) that all business transactions go through him.
¿Alâ' al-Dîn Abû al-Shâmât: *Alf* II 149; Burton IV 35. Chauvin V 43-49 No. 18; *ANE* 85-87 No. 63.□

P431.5.1§, ‡Traveling merchant has many 'homes' (wives): one in each city (country). (Cf. P159.2§).
¿Alâ' al-Dîn Abû al-Shâmât: *Alf* II 153; Burton IV 42. Chauvin V 43-49 No. 18; *ANE* 85-87 No. 63.□

P431.5.2§, ‡Traveling merchant's wife is always lonesome.
Lady and Five Suitors Deceived: *Alf* III 158,-(implicit); Burton VI 172. Chauvin VIII 50-51 No. 18; *ANE* 266 No. 198;
Masrûr and Zayn al-Mawâṣif: *Alf* IV 56,-ff.; Burton VIII 206. Chauvin VI 82-84 No. 251; *ANE* 294-95 No. 232.□

P431.5.2.1§, ‡Traveling merchant's wife becomes unfaithful. See: *DOTTI*; *PSAE*. (Cf. P529.0.6§).
Lady and Five Suitors Deceived: *Alf* III 158,-cf./(husband is a traveler); Burton VI 172. Chauvin VIII 50-51 No. 18; *ANE* 266 No. 198;
Masrûr and Zayn al-Mawâṣif: *Alf* IV 56,-ff.,-esp. 64; Burton VIII 210ff. Chauvin VI 82-84 No. 251; *ANE* 294-95 No. 232.□

P434§, Service broker: middleman, or middle-woman (*dallâlah*). See: *GMC*.
Portress Amînah: Bitten Cheek: *Alf* I 60,-(female,/passim); Burton I 183,-("procuratrix"). Chauvin V 98-99 No. 33; *ANE* 326-27 No. 20;

Copt Broker's Story: Lover's Sacrifices Repaid: *Alf* I 88; Burton I 262. Chauvin VI 80 No. 249; *ANE* 313-14 No. 24;
¿Alî Shâr and Zumurrud: *Alf* II 225,-cf./(helper); Burton IV 205. Chauvin V 89-91 No. 28; *ANE* 100-1 No. 82;
Hasan of Basrah: *Alf* IV 8,-(real estate); Burton VIII 52. Chauvin VII 29-35 No. 212A; *ANE* 207-10 No. 230.□

P434.1.0.1§, ‡Auctioneer in slaves (*nakhkhâs*).
Anîs al-Jalîs: *Alf* I 126-27; Burton II 2. Chauvin V 120-24 No. 58; *ANE* 316-17 No. 35;
Second Eunuch/Kâfûr's Half-lie: *Alf* I 148,-(*dallâl*); Burton II 51,-(broker). Chauvin V 278 No. 161; *ANE* 178-79 No. 38;
Man of Upper Egypt and Frankish Wife: Alf IV 16?,-(text missing); Burton IX 21-22,-(trading in captive slave-girls). Chauvin V 240 No. 140; *ANE*: No. 234;
Nûr al-Dîn and Maryam: *Alf* IV 92-96; Burton VIII 291-300. Chauvin V 52-54 No. 271; *ANE* 98-99 No. 233.□

P434.1.1§, ‡Auctioneer's fee. (Cf. P537.5§).
Nûr al-Dîn and Maryam: *Alf* IV 95,-(added to price of item); Burton VIII 300. Chauvin V 52-54 No. 271; *ANE* 98-99 No. 233.□

P434.1.1.1§, ‡Ten per cent is middleman's fee.
Copt Broker's Story: Lover's Sacrifices Repaid: *Alf* I 88; Burton I 263. Chauvin VI 80 No. 249; *ANE* 313-14 No. 24.□

P434.5§, *khâṭibah*: professional matchmaker (marriage broker). See: *DOTTI*; *GMC*.
Jeweler's Wife and Qamar al-Zamân: *Alf* IV 260; Burton IX 289. Chauvin V 212-14 No. 121; *ANE* 345-47 No. 260.□

P435.0.1§, ‡Money-exchanger (banker). (Cf. P447§).
Abû al-Ḥasan al-Khorâsânî (and Caliph's Favorite): *Alf* IV 231; Burton IX 232. Chauvin V 218-20 No. 129; *ANE* 68-69 No. 259.□

P440.1§, Artisan as trickster (cheat). See: *DOTTI*; *GMC*. (Cf. W111.2.10§).
Abû Qîr and Abû Ṣîr: *Alf* IV 186,-(dyers); Burton IX 125. Chauvin V 15-17 No. 10; *ANE* 75-77 No. 255.□

P441, Tailor. See: *DOTTI*; *GMC*.
Foolish Weaver: *Alf* II 40; Burton III 160. Chauvin II 229 No. 19; *ANE* 187 No. 58.□

P441.0.1§, ‡Tailor as helper.
Second Qalandar: Afrit's Wife: *Alf* I 43; Burton I 115. Chauvin V 197-200 No. 116; *ANE* 338-39 No. 16;
al-'Amjad and al-'As¿ad: *Alf* II 123,-(teaches hero); Burton III 331. Chauvin V 208-10 No. 120[.1]; *ANE* 341-42 No. 61/pt. 2;
Ibrâhîm and Jamîlah: *Alf* IV 222; Burton IX 215. Chauvin VI 52-53 No. 218; *ANE* 227-29 No. 258;
Abû al-Ḥasan al-Khorâsânî (and Caliph's Favorite): *Alf* IV 233; Burton IX 236. Chauvin V 218-20 No. 129; *ANE* 68-69 No. 259.□

P441.0.1.1§, ‡Hero (heroine) reaches forbidden island (river bank) by help of ferryman. (Cf. R43).
Ibrâhîm and Jamîlah: *Alf* IV 224; Burton IX 216. Chauvin VI 52-53 No. 218; *ANE* 227-29 No. 258.□

P446, Barber. See: *DOTTI*.
Abû Qîr and Abû Ṣîr: *Alf* IV 182; Burton IX 134ff. Chauvin V 15-17 No. 10; *ANE* 75-77 No. 255.□

P446.1, Barber as bungler of plans. See: *ANE*; *DOTTI*; *GMC*.
Tailor's Story/Barber of Baghdad: *Alf* I 103-9; Burton I 301-17. Chauvin V 154-56 No. 78; *ANE* 405-6 No. 27.□

P446.5§, Women's beautician (*ballânah, mâshṭah, ¿aggâfah*, etc.). See: *DOTTI*; *GMC*. (Cf. P424.7§).
King ¿Umar al-Nu¿mân and Sons: *Alf* I 198-99; Burton II 153,-(bath woman). Chauvin VI 112-24 No. 277; *ANE* 430-34 No. 39;
Abû Qîr and Abû Ṣîr: *Alf* IV 191; Burton IX 153. Chauvin V 15-17 No. 10; *ANE* 75-77 No. 255.□

P446.7§, Bathhouse (public) operator. See: *DOTTI*.
Bulûqiya: *Alf* III 76; Burton V 387,-(bathman). Chauvin VII 54 No. 77; *ANE* 130-32 No. 177;
Abû Qîr and Abû Ṣîr: *Alf* IV 189; Burton IX 149. Chauvin V 15-17 No. 10; *ANE* 75-77 No. 255.□

P447§, ‡Treasurer (bursar, *khâzindâr*, *ṣarrâf*, et.). (Cf. P760.2.1§).
Nuzhat al-Zamân Tested/¿Umar al-Nu¿mân: *Alf* I 203; Burton II 163. Chauvin VI 116, n.1/passim No. 277; *ANE* 432,/passim No. 39;
Budûr and Jubayr ibn ¿Umayr: *Alf* II 243,-(private); Burton IV 244. Chauvin VII 93-94 No. 374; *ANE* 243-44 No. 83;
Jawdar and His Treacherous Brethren: *Alf* III 196; Burton VI 246-47. Chauvin V 257-60 No. 154; *ANE* 244-45 No. 209.□

P447.0.2§, ‡Smith as helper. (Cf. K749.14§).
Masrûr and Zayn al-Mawâṣif: *Alf* IV 73-75; Burton VIII 245-49. Chauvin VI 82-84 No. 251; *ANE* 294-95 No. 232.□

P447.7, Goldsmith as lover. See: *DOTTI*; *GMC*.
Mock Caliph/¿Alî al-Jawharî: *Alf* II 196; Burton IV 140ff. Chauvin V 99-100 No. 174; *ANE* 304-5 No. 73;
Water-carrier and Goldsmith's Wife: *Alf* II 286; Burton V 89. Chauvin VI 192 No. 361; *ANE* 444 No. 122;
Goldsmith and Cashmere Singer: *Alf* III 150; Burton VI 156. Chauvin VIII 46-47 No. 14; *ANE* 196 No. 194.□

P447.7.0.1§, Jeweler (goldsmith). See: *DOTTI*. (Cf. F826.5§).
¿Alî ibn Bakkâr: *Alf* II 52,-(*Jawahirjiyy* as helper); Burton III 186. Chauvin V 153 No. 76; *ANE* 92-93 No. 60;
Mock Caliph/¿Alî al-Jawharî: *Alf* II 196; Burton IV 139. Chauvin V 99-100 No. 174; *ANE* 304-5 No. 73;
Water-carrier and Goldsmith's Wife: *Alf* II 285; Burton V 89. Chauvin VI 192 No. 361; *ANE* 444 No. 122;
Dalîla the Swindler: *Alf* III 220; Burton VII 158. Chauvin V 245-50 No. 147; *ANE* 163-64 No. 224;
Hasan of Basrah: *Alf* III 302; Burton VIII 7. Chauvin VII 29-35 No. 212A; *ANE* 207-10 No. 230.□

P448, Butcher. See: *PSAE*.
Barber's Fourth Brother: Illusionary Experiences: *Alf* I 116; Burton I 331–32. Chauvin V 160-61 No. 84; *ANE* 119 No. 32;
Lover Who Feigned Himself a Thief: *Alf* II 205; Burton IV 157. Chauvin VII 134-35 No. 403; *ANE* 272 No. 76;
Butcher Wardân and Bear Lover: *Alf* II 250; Burton IV 293. Chauvin V 177-78 No. 101; *ANE* 442-43 No. 101.□

P449.3.2.1§, ‡Passenger(s) invited to eat at ship-captain's table.
Abû Qîr and Abû Ṣîr: *Alf* IV 185; Burton IX 140. Chauvin V 15-17 No. 10; *ANE* 75-77 No. 255.□

P449.4.1§, ‡Diver seeking sea treasure (pearls, gold, or the like). (Cf. P488.1§).
Abû Muḥammad Lazybones: *Alf* II 208-9; Burton IV 167. Chauvin VI 64-67 No. 233; *ANE* 71-73 No. 78.□

P453.0.1§, Cobbler. See: *DOTTI*; *GMC*.
Ma¿rûf the Cobbler: *Alf* IV 288; Burton X 1. Chauvin VI 81-82 No. 250; *ANE* 291-93 No. 262.□

P456, Carpenter.
Birds, Beasts, and Carpenter: *Alf* II 24; Burton III 120. Chauvin II 225-26 No. 1; *ANE* 126 No. 44.□

P458.1§, ‡Firewood (underbrush) gatherer-vendor (*ḥaṭṭâb*). See: *DOTTI*.
Second Qalandar: Ạfrit's Wife: *Alf* I 43; Burton I 115. Chauvin V 197-200 No. 116; *ANE* 338-39 No. 16;
Bulûqiya/Ḥâsib/Queen of Vipers: *Alf* III 19; Burton V 299. Chauvin VII 54 No. 77; *ANE* 130-32 No. 177.□

P459.3§, Clothes dyer. See: *DOTTI*; *GMC*.
Abû Qîr and Abû Ṣîr: *Alf* IV 182; Burton IX 134ff. Chauvin V 15-17 No. 10; *ANE* 75-77 No. 255.□

P462.1.1§, ‡Robber (outlaw, master thief) employed as policeman (detective). See: *DOTTI*. (Cf. P194.9.1§, P475).
Dalîla the Swindler: *Alf* III 212-13; Burton VII 144. Chauvin V 245-50 No. 147; *ANE* 163-64 No. 224;
Mercury ¿Alî: *Alf* III 227; Burton VII 172. Chauvin V 248-50 No. 147; *ANE* 301-3 No. 225.□

P469.0.1§, ‡A news-bearer (envoy, messenger) is required only to convey the message. (Cf. P324.3.1§, Q243.1.3.1§).
King ¿Umar al-Nu¿mân and Sons: *Alf* I 254; Burton II 268. Chauvin VI 112-24 No. 277; *ANE* 430-34 No. 39.□

P469.1.1§, ‡Publication of news via media of mass communication (town-crier, tom-tom beater, radio, etc.). See: *DOTTI*. (Cf. P514§).
al-'Amjad and al-'As¿ad: *Alf* II 127, 131,-(criers/lost brother); Burton III 339, 347. Chauvin V 208-10 No. 120/[. 1]; *ANE* 341-42 No. 61/pt. 2;
¿Alâ' al-Dîn Abû al-Shâmât: *Alf* II 162, 171; Burton IV 61. Chauvin V 43-49 No. 18; *ANE* 85-87 No. 63;
Lover Who Feigned Himself a Thief: *Alf* II 204; Burton IV 156. Chauvin VII 134-35 No. 403; *ANE* 272 No. 76;
Man of Upper Egypt and Frankish Wife: Alf IV 16?,-(text missing); Burton IX 21,-(expiration of truce). Chauvin V 240 No. 140; *ANE*: No. 234;
¿Alî Shâr and Zumurrud: *Alf* II 228; Burton IV 212. Chauvin V 89-91 No. 28; *ANE* 100-1 No. 82.□

P469.1.1.1§, ‡Drum (tom-tom) beaten to declare newsworthy occurrence (event).
¿Alî Shâr and Zumurrud: *Alf* II 228; Burton IV 212,-(crier/proclaims). Chauvin V 89-91 No. 28; *ANE* 100-1 No. 82;
King Jalî¿âd and Shimâs: *Alf* IV 175,-(appointment of "second [highest] chair"/i.e., office); Burton IX 119. Chauvin VI 9 No. 184; *ANE* 237-38 No. 236.□

P469.2§, ‡Publication of certain event via musical procession—*zaffah* (for wedding, circumcision, pilgrimage, release from prison, or the like). (Cf. P965§).
Lover Who Feigned Himself a Thief: *Alf* II 205,-cf.; Burton IV 159. Chauvin VII 134-35 No. 403; *ANE* 272 No. 76.□

P469.3§, ‡Wanderer (traveler, stranger) as source of news. (Cf. P431.1).
Jânshâh: *Alf* III 59; Burton V 357. Chauvin VII 39-44 No. 153; *ANE* 238-41 No. 178;
Sayf al-Mulûk: *Alf* III 280; Burton VII 333. Chauvin VII 64-73 No. 348; *ANE* 362-64 No. 229.□

P469.4.1§, ‡Absent relative or friends found through advertising on mass-media (town crier, radio, etc.). (Cf. N730).
al-'Amjad and al-'As¿ad: *Alf* II 131; Burton III 347. Chauvin V 208-10 No. 120[.1]; *ANE* 2 341-42 No. 61/pt.□

P469.4.2§, ‡Reward promised publicly for information on missing person or object. (Cf. Q70§).
al-Rashîd and Omani Merchant: *Alf* IV 218,-(for his lovesick daughter); Burton IX 205. Chauvin VI 111-12 No. 276; *ANE* 201-2 No. 257.□

P470§, ‡Story-teller (narrator, tale-teller). (Cf. F956.7.6.2§, J163.5.3.1§, J170§, Z13.11.1§).
Shahriyâr and Shahrzâd: *Alf* I 7; Burton I 23. Chauvin V 188-89 No. 111; *ANE* 370-71 No. 1;
Kurd's Sack/¿Alî the Persian: *Alf* II 200; Burton IV 149. Chauvin V 279 No. 162; *ANE* 99-100 No. 74;
Ibn Sabâ'ik/Sayf al-Mulûk: *Alf* III 270; Burton VII 309. Chauvin VII 65 No. 348/pt.; *ANE* 309-10 No. 228.□

P470.0.1§, ‡Tale-teller needed (required)—so as to tell story. See: *DOTTI*; *PSAE*. (Cf. H1382.2, F956.7.6.3§).
Porter and Ladies of Baghdad: *Alf* I 35,-(*ḥikâyah aw nâdirah*/story or a rarity/anecdote); Burton I 95,-(story or rare adventure). Chauvin V 251-52 No. 148; *ANE* 324-26 No. 14;
Kurd's Sack/¿Alî the Persian: *Alf* II 200; Burton IV 149. Chauvin V 279 No. 162; *ANE* 99-100 No. 74;
Lovers of Banû ¿Udhrah and Lion: *Alf* III 206; Burton VII 117. Chauvin V 106-7 No. 37; *ANE* 274 No. 218/[2]/["Chauvin V 116 No. 52"];
Lovers of Basra/Ḍamrah: *Alf* III 210; Burton VII 130. Chauvin V 118 No. 54; *ANE* 273 No. 220;
Ibn Sabâ'ik/Sayf al-Mulûk: *Alf* III 271; Burton VII 309. Chauvin VII 65 No. 348/pt.; *ANE* 309-10 No. 228.□

P470.3§, ‡Adventurer (travelers) motivated by desire to learn stories (reports, news) of other peoples. (Cf. J1077.1§).
Sindbâd's Seventh Voyage: *Alf* III 116; Burton VI 69. Chauvin VII 24 No. 373F; *ANE* 386-87 No. 179.□

P475, Robber. See: *DOTTI*; *GMC*.
Merchant from Sindah and Sharpers: *Alf* II 39; Burton III 158. Chauvin II 229 No. 154/17; *ANE* 297-98 No. 56.□

P475.0.2§, ‡Robber of livestock. See: *DOTTI*. (Cf. H1229.5§, P559.1.3§).
King ¿Umar al-Nu¿mân and Sons: *Alf* II 3-6; Burton III 79-80. Chauvin VI 112-24 No. 277; *ANE* 430-34 No. 39.□

P475.0.2.3§, ‡Horse thief. See: *DOTTI*. (Cf. F989.17).
King ¿Umar al-Nu¿mân and Sons: *Alf* I 318; Burton III 72. Chauvin VI 112-24 No. 277; *ANE* 430-34 No. 39;
Nûr al-Dîn and Maryam: *Alf* IV 122; Burton IX 4. Chauvin V 52-54 No. 271; *ANE* 98-99 No. 233.□

P475.0.3§, ‡Pirate (robber on waterways). (Cf. R217.7§).
Nûr al-Dîn and Maryam: *Alf* IV 107; Burton VIII 323. Chauvin V 52-54 No. 271; *ANE* 98-99 No. 233.□

P475.0.3.1.1§, ‡Pirate (smuggler) throws person (cargo) overboard. (Cf. S142).
al-'Amjad and al-'As¿ad: *Alf* II 129-30; Burton III 343. Chauvin V 208-10 No. 120[.1]; *ANE* 341-42 No. 61/pt. 2.□

P475.1.0.1§, ‡Band of robbers. See: *DOTTI*. (Cf. N765).
Barber's Fifth Brother: Daydreams/Defeats Robbers: *Alf* I 120; Burton I 349–43. Chauvin V 161 No. 85; *ANE* 119-20 No. 33;
¿Alî ibn Bakkâr: *Alf* II 58; Burton III 196. Chauvin V 153 No. 76; *ANE* 92-93 No. 60.□

P475.1.1§, Forty robbers. See: *DOTTI*. (Cf. Z71.12).
¿Alî Shâr and Zumurrud: *Alf* II 226; Burton IV 208,-(sharpers). Chauvin V 89-91 No. 28; *ANE* 100-1 No. 82.□

P475.2, ‡Robbers defeated and killed. See: *DOTTI*.
Barber's Fifth Brother: Daydreams/Defeats Robbers: *Alf* I 120; Burton I 340–43. Chauvin V 161 No. 85; *ANE* 119-20 No. 33;
Mercury ¿Alî: *Alf* III 230; Burton VII 178. Chauvin V 248-50 No. 147; *ANE* 301-3 No. 225.□

P475.3§, ‡Honor among thieves. See: *DOTTI*. (Cf. N887§, U10.1.2§).
Nuzhat al-Zamân Tested/¿Umar al-Nu¿mân: *Alf* I 201; Burton II 159. Chauvin VI 116, n.1/passim No. 277; *ANE* 432,/passim No. 39.□

P479.1§, ‡Interpreter of dreams sought (to interpret vision).
King ¿Umar al-Nu¿mân and Sons: *Alf* II 11; Burton III 95. Chauvin VI 112-24 No. 277; *ANE* 430-34 No. 39;
Hasan of Basrah: *Alf* IV 39; Burton VIII 113-14. Chauvin VII 29-35 No. 212A; *ANE* 207-10 No. 230;
Masrûr and Zayn al-Mawâṣif: *Alf* IV 55; Burton VIII 205. Chauvin VI 82-84 No. 251; *ANE* 294-95 No. 232.□

P481, ‡Astrologer. See: *DOTTI*; *GMC*. (Cf. M302.4, P429.1).
Tawaddud: Slavegirl Sold and Regained: *Alf* II 319,-cf./(knowledge); Burton V 227,-("astronomer"). Chauvin VII 117-19 No. 387; *ANE* 408-10 No. 157.□

P483.3§, Snake-charmer (*ḥâwî*, *'Rifâ¿î'*). See: *DOTTI*; *GMC*.
Escaped Viper Ungrateful: *Alf* II 35; Burton III 145. Chauvin II 227 No. 9; *ANE* 450,/passim No. 47;
Mercury ¿Alî: *Alf* III 238; Burton VII 193. Chauvin V 248-50 No. 147; *ANE* 301-3 No. 225;
Serpent-charmer and Wife: *Alf* IV 145; Burton IX 56 n. 1,/"serpent-charmer". Chauvin II 220 No. 152/9; *ANE* 368 No. 244.□

P483.4§, ‡Acrobat. (Cf. F699.1).
Foolish Weaver: *Alf* II 40,-(imitated); Burton III 160. Chauvin II 229 No. 19; *ANE* 187 No. 58.□

P485, Philosopher. See: *DOTTI*.
Bulûqiya/Ḥâsib/Queen of Vipers: *Alf* III 18; Burton V 298. Chauvin VII 54 No. 77; *ANE* 130-32 No. 177.□

P485.5§, ‡Little demand in job market for the learned (with theoretical, abstract, or mere academic knowledge). (Cf. P770§, U69.1.1§, U86§, U248.6.1§).

Second Qalandar: Afrit's Wife: *Alf* I 43; Burton I 115. Chauvin V 197-200 No. 116; *ANE* 338-39 No. 16.□

P488.1§, ‡Open-pit miner. Seeking precious stones (metals) on mountain tops, valley floors, etc. See: *DOTTI*. (Cf. P449.4.1§).
Sindbâd's Second Voyage: *Alf* III 90-91; Burton VI 18-19. Chauvin VII 9-14 No. 373B; *ANE* 385 No. 179;
Hasan of Basrah: *Alf* III 310,-cf./(plant); Burton VIII 21. Chauvin VII 29-35 No. 212A; *ANE* 207-10 No. 230.□

P489.1.1§, ‡Garbage (manure) collector.
Sweep and Noble Lady: Infidelity Repaid: *Alf* II 188; Burton IV 125. Chauvin VI 148 No. 306; *ANE* 403-4 No. 72.□

P489.1.3§, ‡Stoker: furnace operator (in public facility).
King ¿Umar al-Nu¿mân and Sons: *Alf* I 188; Burton II 134. Chauvin VI 112-24 No. 277; *ANE* 430-34 No. 39.□

P500.0.1§, Types of rule (government): hereditary, election, selection, revolutionary-council, choice by lot (etc.). See: *DOTTI*.
Crows and Hawk: *Alf* IV 144; Burton IX 53-56. Chauvin II 220 No. 152/8; *ANE* 162 No. 243.□

P500.0.2.1§, ‡Regency (trusteeship): right to rule delegated temporarily to regent(s) or trustee(s). (Cf. P112§, P760.4.1§).
King ¿Umar al-Nu¿mân and Sons: *Alf* I 310; Burton III 53,-(guardian). Chauvin VI 112-24 No. 277; *ANE* 430-34 No. 39.□

P500.0.3§, ‡Principles (the craft) of governing: things a competent king (ruler) must do in order to succeed. (Cf. J154, J373§, P500.1§).
Nuzhat al-Zamân Tested/¿Umar al-Nu¿mân: *Alf* I 200-201; Burton II 156. Chauvin VI 116, n.1/passim No. 277; *ANE* 432,/passim No. 39;
Ni¿mah and Nu¿m: Stolen Wife Regained: *Alf* II 143-44,-(forgiveness); Burton IV 21. Chauvin VI 96-97 No. 263; *ANE* 314 No. 62;
King Jalî¿âd and Shimâs: *Alf* IV 161; Burton IX 89. Chauvin VI 9-11 No. 184; *ANE* 237-38 No. 236.□

P500.0.3.2§, ‡Deeds done by ruler to gain popularity—(e.g., reduce taxes, release prisoners, or the like). (Cf. P532.2§, P537.2§, Q117.1§).
Qamar al-Zamân and Budûr: *Alf* II 101, 112; Burton III 285. Chauvin V 204-12 No. 120; *ANE* 341-45 No. 61;
¿Alî Shâr and Zumurrud: *Alf* II 227; Burton IV 211. Chauvin V 89-91 No. 28; *ANE* 100-1 No. 82;
Jullanâr of the Sea: *Alf* III 255,-(help week against strong/poor against emir); Burton VII 279. Chauvin V 147-51 No. 73; *ANE* 248-51 No. 227.□

P500.1§, ‡Government under inherited right to rule subjects—(authoritarian, rights of kings). See: *DOTTI*. (Cf. J1809.3.2§, P11).
Sayf al-Mulûk: *Alf* III 278; Burton VII 327. Chauvin VII 64-73 No. 348; *ANE* 362-64 No. 229;
King Jalî¿âd and Shimâs: *Alf* IV 134,-ff.; Burton IX 33-35. Chauvin VI 9-11 No. 184; *ANE* 237-38 No. 236;
Hunter Rides Lion: Devoured: *Alf* IV 153; Burton IX 72. Chauvin II 222 No. 152/15.□

P500.1.0.1§, ‡A governmental (high) post is a term-assignment, not a perpetual designation (for occupant).
¿Alâ' al-Dîn Abû al-Shâmât: *Alf* II 162; Burton IV 61,-(offices are by investiture, not in perpetuity). Chauvin V 43-49 No. 18; *ANE* 85-87 No. 63.□

P500.1.2§, ‡King's injustice. See: *DOTTI*. (Cf. P12.6.0.1§).
Dûban and King Yûnân: *Alf* I 21; Burton I 58. Chauvin V 275-76 No. 156; *ANE* 459 No. 9;
Jawdar and His Treacherous Brethren: *Alf* III 193-94,-cf.; Burton VI 241-42. Chauvin V 257-60 No. 154; *ANE* 244-45 No. 209.□

P500.1.3§, ‡Tyrannical king views subjects as slaves (surfs).
Jullanâr of the Sea: *Alf* III 260,-(dogs); Burton VII 286. Chauvin V 147-51 No. 73; *ANE* 248-51 No. 227;
King Jalî¿âd and Shimâs: *Alf* IV 165; Burton IX 99. Chauvin VI 9 No. 184; *ANE* 237-38 No. 236.□

P500.2§, ‡Folly of ignoring wishes (opinion) of the majority. (Destructive to nation). (Cf. J21.57.1§).
King Jalî¿âd and Shimâs: *Alf* IV 161; Burton IX 89. Chauvin VI 9-11 No. 184; *ANE* 237-38 No. 236.□

P500.3.1§, ‡Absolute (despotic) ruler disposes of notables opposed to his conduct. (Cf. K811.1, N340.0.1.2§).
King Jalî¿âd and Shimâs: *Alf* IV 171; Burton IX 117. Chauvin VI 9 No. 184; *ANE* 237-38 No. 236.□

P501.2.2§, ‡Ruler (king, caliph, imam, emir) must be obeyed.
¿Abdallah ibn Fâḍil: Treacherous Brothers: *Alf* IV 283; Burton IX 339. Chauvin V 2-4 No. 2; *ANE* 63-65 No. 261.□

P501.3§, ‡Change in government (new ruler) brings about change in policy (practices). (Cf. L405§, L490§).
First Qalandar: Brother-Sister Incest: *Alf* I 40,-(rebellion); Burton I 107. Chauvin V 196-97 No. 115; *ANE* 337-38 No. 15.□

P501.3.1§, ‡New ruler mistreats supporter(s) of old.
First Qalandar: Brother-Sister Incest: *Alf* I 40; Burton I 107. Chauvin V 196-97 No. 115; *ANE* 337-38 No. 15.□

P502.3.1§, Assassination (political).
King ¿Umar al-Nu¿mân and Sons: *Alf* II 7; Burton II 86-87. Chauvin VI 112-24 No. 277; *ANE* 430-34 No. 39.□

P502.3.1.1§, Assassin. See: *GMC*.
¿Alâ' al-Dîn Abû al-Shâmât: *Alf* II 174,-(hired to kill caliph); Burton IV 81. Chauvin V 43-49 No. 18; *ANE* 85-87 No. 63.□

P503.0.1§, ‡Formal documents required for bureaucratic (formal) procedures. See: *DOTTI*; *PSAE*. (Cf. P522).
Anîs al-Jalîs: *Alf* I 143; Burton II 39. Chauvin V 120-24 No. 58; *ANE* 316-17 No. 35.□

P503.5.1§, ‡Favoritism toward relatives (nepotism).
Nuzhat al-Zamân Tested/¿Umar al-Nu¿mân: *Alf* I 204; Burton II 163-64. Chauvin VI 116, n.1/passim No. 277; *ANE* 432,/passim No. 39.□

P503.6§, ‡Hypocritical official (judge, governor, etc.). See: *DOTTI*.
Barber's Fifth Brother: Daydreams/Defeats Robbers: *Alf* I 121; Burton I 343. Chauvin V 161 No. 85; *ANE* 119-20 No. 33.□

P503.7§, ‡Bribery (*rashwah, 'burṭail'*). See: *DOTTI*. (Cf. K2096.6§, P339.2§).
Ghânim ibn Ayyûb: *Alf* I 157; Burton II 45-76. Chauvin VI 14 No. 188; *ANE* 192-93 No. 36;
¿Alî Shâr and Zumurrud: *Alf* II 221; Burton IV 198. Chauvin V 89-91 No. 28; *ANE* 100-1 No. 82;
Enchanted Spring: Change of Sex: *Alf* III 146,-(gift); Burton VI 147. Chauvin VIII 43 No. 11; *ANE* 175-76 No. 191;
Jeweler's Wife and Qamar al-Zamân: *Alf* IV 246; Burton IX 259. Chauvin V 212-14 No. 121; *ANE* 345-47 No. 260.□

P503.7.1§, ‡The power of bribery.
Tâj al-Mulûk: *Alf* I 299,-(gardener bribed); Burton III 30. Chauvin V 126-28 No. 60; *ANE* 406-8 No. 40;
Rake's Trick Against Chaste Wife: *Alf* III 142; Burton VI 135. Chauvin VIII 37 No. 5; *ANE* 350-1 No. 185.□

P503.7.2§, ‡Veiled bribery: exorbitant price (wages) paid for minor article (service). (Cf. J708.8§).
Ibrâhîm and Jamîlah: *Alf* IV 222; Burton IX 215. Chauvin VI 52-53 No. 218; *ANE* 227-29 No. 258;
Abû al-Ḥasan al-Khorâsânî (and Caliph's Favorite): *Alf* IV 233; Burton IX 237-38. Chauvin V 218-20 No. 129; *ANE* 68-69 No. 259.□

P503.7.2.1§, ‡Veiled bribe: tailor paid several gold coins as fee for sewing minor rip in garment. (Rip is induced by owner who needs information or help from tailor).
Ibrâhîm and Jamîlah: *Alf* IV 222; Burton IX 215. Chauvin VI 52-53 No. 218; *ANE* 227-29 No. 258;
Abû al-Ḥasan al-Khorâsânî (and Caliph's Favorite): *Alf* IV 233; Burton IX 237. Chauvin V 218-20 No. 129; *ANE* 68-69 No. 259.□

P505.1§, ‡Illegitimate order by ruler disobeyed. See: *DOTTI*. (Cf. P506.3§).

Nuzhat al-Zamân Tested/¿Umar al-Nu¿mân: *Alf* I 206,-cf./(counsel); Burton II 169. Chauvin VI 116, n.1/passim No. 277; *ANE* 432,/passim No. 39;
Ma¿rûf the Cobbler: *Alf* IV 311-12,-cf.; Burton X 44. Chauvin VI 81-82 No. 250; *ANE* 291-93 No. 262.□

P506§, Government seized by force (revolt, coup d'etat, etc.). See: *DOTTI*; *GMC*. (Cf. P16.3.5§).
First Qalandar: Brother-Sister Incest: *Alf* I 40; Burton I 107. Chauvin V 196-97 No. 115; *ANE* 337-38 No. 15;
Jawdar and His Treacherous Brethren: *Alf* III 201; Burton VI 256. Chauvin V 257-60 No. 154; *ANE* 244-45 No. 209;
Abû al-Hasan al-Khorâsânî (and Caliph's Favorite): *Alf* IV 237; Burton IX 245. Chauvin V 218-20 No. 129; *ANE* 68-69 No. 259.□

P506.0.2§, ‡Support (pledge of allegiance, backing, ballot, etc.) for new ruler secured by coercion (threat). (Cf. P11.7§).
Jawdar and His Treacherous Brethren: *Alf* III 201; Burton VI 256. Chauvin V 257-60 No. 154; *ANE* 244-45 No. 209.□

P506.3§, Rebellion against government. See: *DOTTI*; *GMC*; *PSAE*.
King Jalî¿âd and Shimâs: *Alf* IV 169; Burton IX 107. Chauvin VI 9 No. 184; *ANE* 237-38 No. 236.□

P507.0.2§, ‡Subjects must obey ruler (caliph, sultan, king).
King Jalî¿âd and Shimâs: *Alf* IV 154; Burton IX 73. Chauvin VI 9-11 No. 184; *ANE* 237-38 No. 236.□

P507.4.1.1.1§, ‡Solomon as prophet-king—(the first). See: *DOTTI*.
Jinn Imprisoned in Flasks: *Alf* III 122, 127; Burton VI 84, 97. Chauvin VII 113 No. 380=no/text; *ANE* 146 No. 180.□

P507.4.3.1§, ‡Nothing can match the long reach of a sacred government (Caliphate).
Hasan of Basrah: *Alf* IV 14,-cf.; Burton VIII 65. Chauvin VII 29-35 No. 212A; *ANE* 207-10 No. 230.□

P507.4.2§, ‡Caliph as "God's successor (representative, agent) on His Earth". (Cf. V294).
First Qalandar: Brother-Sister Incest: *Alf* I 42,-(*khalîfatu rabb al-¿Âlamîn*); Burton I 112,-("Viceregent of Allah upon earth"). Chauvin V 196-97 No. 115; *ANE* 337-38 No. 15;
Porter and Ladies of Baghdad: *Alf* I 60,-(*khalîfatu Allâh*); Burton I 184,-(Vicar of Allah). Chauvin V 251-52 No. 148; *ANE* 324-26 No. 14;
Nûr al-Dîn and Maryam: *Alf* IV 126, 124,-(*khalîfatu Allâh*); Burton IX 12, 15, 16-(Viceregent of Allah/vice). Chauvin V 52-54 No. 271; *ANE* 98-99 No. 233;
Ibrâhîm and Jamîlah: *Alf* IV 228,-(*khalîfatu Allâh*); Burton IX 228. Chauvin VI 52-53 No. 218; *ANE* 227-29 No. 258;
¿Abdallah ibn Fâdil: Treacherous Brothers: *Alf* IV 268/(xxx/missing),-(*"yâ khlîfah"*); Burton IX 310,-(Vicar of Allah). Chauvin V 2-4 No. 2; *ANE* 63-65 No. 261.□

P506.5§, ‡Sedition (*fitnah*): ideological camps resort to violence (war, conflict, riots) against each other. (Cf. P17.15§).
King ¿Umar al-Nu¿mân and Sons: *Alf* I 216, 6-7; Burton II 191, 85-86. Chauvin VI 112-24 No. 277; *ANE* 430-34 No. 39.□

P508.1§, ‡Mamelukes expected to rise to high ranks (become holders offices). (Cf. P180.4.3§).
Dalîla the Swindler: *Alf* III 222; Burton VII 162,-(become people of condition). Chauvin V 245-50 No. 147; *ANE* 163-64 No. 224.□

P509.3§, ‡Immunity of ruler (caliph, king, president, etc.) from personal responsibility for mistakes. Tendency of subjects (narrators) to view ruler as blameless (or as victim of bad advice). (Cf. Q171.0.1§).
King ¿Umar al-Nu¿mân and Sons: *Alf* I 183ff.,-(implicit); Burton II 124ff. Chauvin VI 112-24 No. 277; *ANE* 430-34 No. 39;
King Jalî¿âd and Shimâs: *Alf* IV 171-182,-(mass murder unpunished); Burton IX 108-34. Chauvin VI 9 No. 184; *ANE* 237-38 No. 236;
Shahriyâr and Shahrzâd: *Alf* IV 318,-(implicit); Burton X 54-55. Chauvin V 190-91 No. 111/pt.; *ANE* 371 No. 1.□

P509.3.1§, ‡Uxorious king neglects government, but only wives (concubines) blamed for poor affairs of state. (Cf. Q394).

King Jalî¿âd and Shimâs: *Alf* IV 182,-(consorts); Burton IX 133-34. Chauvin VI 9 No. 184; *ANE* 237-38 No. 236.□

P514§, ‡Publication of court's (king's) penalty (sentence). (Cf. P469.1.1§).
¿Alâ' al-Dîn Abû al-Shâmât: *Alf* II 171; Burton IV 75. Chauvin V 43-49 No. 18; *ANE* 85-87 No. 63.□

P514.1§, ‡Public execution of sentence (amputation, hanging, whipping, etc.). See: *DOTTI*. (Cf. P555.2.1.1).
Hunchback's Tale: Resuscitated: *Alf* I 87; Burton I 260. Chauvin V 180-82 No. 105; *ANE* 224-25 No. 23;
Anîs al-Jalîs: *Alf* I 144; Burton II 42. Chauvin V 120-24 No. 58; *ANE* 316-17 No. 35;
al-'Amjad and al-'As¿ad: *Alf* II 127; Burton III 338. Chauvin V 208-10 No. 120[.1]; *ANE* 341-42 No. 61/pt. 2.□

P518, Cities of refuge.
King ¿Umar al-Nu¿mân and Sons: *Alf* I 230,-(Constantinople); Burton II 218. Chauvin VI 112-24 No. 277; *ANE* 430-34 No. 39.□

P520§, Perjury at court of law. See: *DOTTI*; *GMC*. (Cf. J1192, M108.0.1§, Q263).
Devout Jewess and Wicked Elders: *Alf* II 286; Burton V 97. Chauvin VI 193-93 No. 362; *ANE* 169 No. 128;
Jewish qâḍî and His Devout Wife: *Alf* III 10; Burton V 256. Chauvin VI 154-55 No. 321; *ANE* 242 No. 163.□

P520.1§, Bribed witnesses. See: *DOTTI*; *GMC*. (Cf. J1158, K1266.1§).
¿Alâ' al-Dîn Abû al-Shâmât: *Alf* II 157; Burton IV 53. Chauvin VI 14 No. 188; *ANE* 192-93 No. 63.□

P520.2§, ‡Timid witness: denies having seen crime (accident, conflict, etc.). (Cf. J1158).
Jawdar and His Treacherous Brethren: *Alf* III 180; Burton VI 219. Chauvin V 257-60 No. 154; *ANE* 244-45 No. 209.□

P522.0.2§, ‡Religious laws: jurisprudence based on sacred dogma (sharia, *sharî¿ah*). See: *DOTTI*. (Cf. P505.1§, P522.0.3§).
Nuzhat al-Zamân Tested/¿Umar al-Nu¿mân: *Alf* I 206; Burton II 169. Chauvin VI 116, n.1/passim No. 277; *ANE* 432,/passim No. 39;
Hârûn, Slave-girl and Judge Abû-Yûsuf: *Alf* II 202; Burton IV 153-55. Chauvin VII 114 No. 383; *ANE* 204 No. 75.□

P522.0.2.1.1§, ‡Four judges (courts) for the Four Islamic Schools of Jurisprudence—(varying interpretations of sharia). See: *DOTTI*.
King ¿Umar al-Nu¿mân and Sons: *Alf* I 199, 216; Burton II 154, 191. Chauvin VI 112-24 No. 277; *ANE* 430-34 No. 39;
Masrûr and Zayn al-Mawâṣif: *Alf* IV 74; Burton VIII 248. Chauvin VI 82-84 No. 251; *ANE* 294-95 No. 232.□

P522.0.3§, ‡Legal devices that allow evading law. (Legal loopholes). See: *DOTTI*. (Cf. K1873§, P522.0.2§, P529§, P530§).
¿Alâ' al-Dîn Abû al-Shâmât: *Alf* II 155-57; Burton IV 48 n. 2,-(intermediary/*mustahill/mahillil*). Chauvin V 43-49 No. 18; *ANE* 85-87 No. 63;
Hârûn, Slave-girl and Judge Abû-Yûsuf: *Alf* II 202; Burton IV 153-55. Chauvin VII 114 No. 383; *ANE* 204 No. 75.□

P522.1, Lex talionis. One life for one life. See: *DOTTI*; *GMC*. (Cf. P535).
Trader and Afrit: Accidental Fairy-cide: *Alf* I 8; Burton I 24. Chauvin VI 22-23 No. 194; *ANE* 419-20 No. 4;
Omar and Young Badawî: Returning to be Executed: *Alf* II 288; Burton V 99-104. Chauvin V 216 No. 125; *ANE* 429-30 No. 130.□

P522.1.2.1§, ‡'An eye for an eye, a tooth for a tooth'.
First Qalandar: Brother-Sister Incest: *Alf* I 40,-cf./(maliciously applied); Burton I 107. Chauvin V 196-97 No. 115; *ANE* 337-38 No. 15.□

P522.1.4.4§, ‡Accidental wounding met with intentional (malicious) worse injury (or death).

First Qalandar: Brother-Sister Incest: *Alf* I 40; Burton I 107. Chauvin V 196-97 No. 115; *ANE* 337-38 No. 15.□

P522.2§, Vendetta: a life for a life, of equal (or higher) social rank. See: *DOTTI*; *GMC*; *PSAE*.
Drop of Honey: *Alf* III 145; Burton VI 143. Chauvin VIII 41-42 No. 9; *ANE* 171-72 No. 189;
Sayf al-Mulûk: *Alf* III 300,-(human's for jinni's); Burton VIII 2. Chauvin VII 64-73 No. 348; *ANE* 362-64 No. 229.□

P523.0.1.1§, ‡Person impoverished (bankrupted) by lawsuits. See: *DOTTI*.
Island King/Pious Jewish Merchant: *Alf* III 16,-cf./(false claims); Burton V 290. Chauvin VI 161 No. 325; *ANE* 234 No. 174;
Jawdar and His Treacherous Brethren: *Alf* III 178; Burton VI 214. Chauvin V 257-60 No. 154; *ANE* 244-45 No. 209;
Ma¿rûf the Cobbler: *Alf* IV 290-93,-(implicit); Burton X 4-5. Chauvin VI 81-82 No. 250; *ANE* 291-93 No. 262.□

P523.0.1.2§, ‡Fee for judge's (court's) emissary to be paid by the accused.
Ma¿rûf the Cobbler: *Alf* IV 291; Burton X 5,-(court runner). Chauvin VI 81-82 No. 250; *ANE* 291-93 No. 262.□

P523.2.1, Fool [(the insane)] not to be punished for his crime. See: *DOTTI*; *GMC*. (Cf. P526.3.1§, P526.0.5§).
Sweep and Noble Lady: Infidelity Repaid: *Alf* II 191; Burton IV 130. Chauvin VI 148 No. 306; *ANE* 403-4 No. 72.□

P524.5.1.1§, ‡Surety-giver condemned to death (execution) in lieu of surety-recipient. See: *DOTTI*. (Cf. R52.1§, W37.2.1§).
Omar and Young Badawî: Returning to be Executed: *Alf* II 288; Burton V 102-3. Chauvin V 216 No. 125; *ANE* 429-30 No. 130.□

P525.0.2§, Terms of contract (bargain) must be agreed upon in advance. See: *DOTTI*; *GMC*.
Abû Qîr and Abû Ṣîr: *Alf* IV 184; Burton IX 138. Chauvin V 15-17 No. 10; *ANE* 75-77 No. 255.□

P525.0.2.1§, ‡'Task begun under clear terms will be concluded with contentment'.
Budûr and Jubayr ibn ¿Umayr: *Alf* II 243; Burton IV 244. Chauvin VII 93-94 No. 374; *ANE* 243-44 No. 83;
Masrûr and Zayn al-Mawâṣif: *Alf* IV 57-58,-cf./(lack of contentment leads to regret); Burton VIII 218. Chauvin VI 82-84 No. 251; *ANE* 294-95 No. 232.□

P525.0.2.2.1§, ‡Worker's quitting time is (workday ends in) late afternoon.
Devotee Prince: Ascetic's Death: *Alf* II 290; Burton V 113. Chauvin VI 193-94 No. 363; *ANE* 167-68 No. 134.□

P525.0.2.3.1§, ‡'Entering a bathhouse [met with warm greetings] is unlike exiting it [sent off with the firm demand for paying as charged]'. See: *DOTTI*.
¿Azîz and ¿Azîzah: *Alf* I 268; Burton II 299. Chauvin V 144-45 No. 71; *ANE* 111-13 No. 41;
Hashish Eater's Dream: *Alf* II 10,-cf.; Burton III 93. Chauvin VI 124 No. 278; *ANE* 216 No. 42.□

P525.0.2.5.1§, ‡Agreements (on sale, betrothal, etc.) 'sealed' with reading passage from Holy Book. (Usually "The Opening/*al-Fâtiḥah*").
Jawdar and His Treacherous Brethren: *Alf* III 180; Burton VI 217. Chauvin V 257-60 No. 154; *ANE* 244-45 No. 209;
Abû Qîr and Abû Ṣîr: *Alf* IV 184; Burton IX 138. Chauvin V 15-17 No. 10; *ANE* 75-77 No. 255;
Landsman ¿Abdallah and Merman ¿Abdallah: *Alf* IV 200; Burton IX 170. Chauvin V 6-7 No. 3; *ANE* 65-66 No. 256.□

P525.3.2§, Vendetta-target: man marked for murder (death). See: *DOTTI*; *GMC*.
King ¿Umar al-Nu¿mân and Sons: *Alf* I 311,-(old woman); Burton III 54. Chauvin VI 112-24 No. 277; *ANE* 430-34 No. 39.□

P525.5§, ‡Blood inevitably will be avenged. See: *DOTTI*. (Cf. E451.9.1§).
King ¿Umar al-Nu¿mân and Sons: *Alf* I 186; Burton II 129. Chauvin VI 112-24 No. 277; *ANE* 430-34 No. 39.□

P525.5.1§, ‡Revenge accomplished after generation(s).
King ¿Umar al-Nu¿mân and Sons: *Alf* I 186,-(forty years), II 20-21; Burton II 129, III 103ff. Chauvin VI 112-24 No. 277; *ANE* 430-34 No. 39.□

P525.6§, ‡Respite from execution (death) granted for certain time (e.g., day, month, etc.). See: *DOTTI*. (Cf. R52.1§).
Trader and Afrit: Accidental Fairy-cide: *Alf* I 8,-(one year); Burton I 26. Chauvin VI 22-23 No. 194; *ANE* 419-20 No. 4;
Dûban and King Yûnân: *Alf* I 21,-(poem—line 3); Burton I 45-60. Chauvin V 275-76 No. 156; *ANE* 459 No. 9.□

P526.0.1§, ‡"Capital punishments are to be averted by doubts" (i.e., crime not proven beyond a reasonable doubt). (Cf. U10).
Lover Who Feigned Himself a Thief: *Alf* II 204; Burton IV 157. Chauvin VII 134-35 No. 403; *ANE* 272 No. 76.□

P526.0.2§, ‡'Accuser required to produce evidence (proof); denier (accused) required only to swear innocence.'. (Cf. J679.5§, M119.0.1§).
Spy, First Maiden/¿Umar al-Nu¿mân: *Alf* I 220; Burton II 198. Chauvin VI 116, n.1/passim No. 277; *ANE* 432,/passim No. 39.□

P526.0.2.2§, ‡Confession documented by witnesses.
Copt Broker's Story: Lover's Sacrifices Repaid: *Alf* I 89; Burton I 274. Chauvin VI 80 No. 249; *ANE* 313-14 No. 24.□

P526.0.3§, ‡Law must be applied equally to all. See: *DOTTI*.
Ni¿mah and Nu¿m: Stolen Wife Regained: *Alf* II 144; Burton IV 22-23. Chauvin VI 96-97 No. 263; *ANE* 314 No. 62.□

P526.0.4§, ‡Guilt by apathy, aiding, and/or abetting.
Craft and Malice of Women/Frame: *Alf* III 150,-cf.; Burton VI 150. Chauvin VIII 46-47 No. 14; *ANE* 196 No. 181.□

P526.0.5§, ‡Mitigating circumstances that lessen seriousness of crime. (Cf. P523.2.1).
Lover Who Feigned Himself a Thief: *Alf* II 205; Burton IV 157. Chauvin VII 134-35 No. 403; *ANE* 272 No. 76.□

P526.0.5.2.1§, ‡Mitigating circumstance: value of stolen item falls into category requiring lesser punishment (to be below *niṣâb*). (Cf. U25, U26§).
Lover Who Feigned Himself a Thief: *Alf* II 205; Burton IV 157,-(less than a quarter dinar). Chauvin VII 134-35 No. 403; *ANE* 272 No. 76.□

P526.3§, ‡Legal responsibility for consequences of one's own actions (inactions). See: *DOTTI*. (Cf. U169.3§, V5.0.1.1§).
Craft and Malice of Women/Frame: *Alf* III 150,-cf./(suicide/religious responsibility); Burton VI 150. Chauvin VIII 46-47 No. 14; *ANE* 196 No. 181;
Dalîla the Swindler: *Alf* III 218-19, 223,-(wali's); Burton VII 156, 163. Chauvin V 245-50 No. 147; *ANE* 163-64 No. 224.□

P526.3.1§, ‡Conditions that render a person not responsible for consequences of own actions (e.g., being a minor, insanity, drunkenness, etc.). See: *DOTTI*. (Cf. K332.3§, P523.2.1, P526.3§, P548.1§, T24.9.2.1.1§, V3.0.1.1§).
Second Qalandar: Afrit's Wife: *Alf* I 50,-(being ill-omened); Burton I 137. Chauvin V 197-200 No. 116; *ANE* 338-39 No. 16.□

P526.3.1.1§, ‡Predestined acts of fate (*"qaḍâ' wa qadar"*) render person not responsible for consequences of own actions. (Cf. W199.3.1§).
al-'Amjad and al-'As¿ad: *Alf* II 127,-(poem/thrown tied up in sea but commanded not to get wet); Burton III 341,-("God throws ..."). Chauvin V 208-10 No. 120[.1]; *ANE* 341-42 No. 61/pt. 2;
Poisoning from Flying Kite: *Alf* III 173-74; Burton VI 201-2. Chauvin 8: 33-34 No. 1; *ANE* 160-61, No. 181/passim .□

P526.4.1§, ‡'He who unlocks a door without [its] key is criminal'.
al-'Amjad and al-'As¿ad: *Alf* II 124,-cf.; Burton III 333. Chauvin V 208-10 No. 120[.1]; *ANE* 341-42 No. 61/pt. 2;
Mercury ¿Alî: *Alf* III 231; Burton VII 182. Chauvin V 248-50 No. 147; *ANE* 301-3 No. 225.□

P526.5§, Let the buyer beware: selling bad goods 'As is' is not cheating. See: *DOTTI*; *GMC*. (Cf. X901).

Second Eunuch/Kâfûr's Half-lie: *Alf* I 150; Burton II 51-56. Chauvin V 278 No. 161; *ANE* 178-79 No. 38.□

P527§, Legal will (testament) made before death—(legal preparations for death). See: *DOTTI*. (Cf. M250.1§, P761§, V67.9.2§).
Merchant's Curious Wife: *Alf* I 6; Burton I 21. Chauvin V 179-80 No. 104; *ANE* 298-99 No. 3;
Devotee Prince: Ascetic's Death: *Alf* II 290,-cf.; Burton V 113. Chauvin VI 193-94 No. 363; *ANE* 167-68 No. 134;
Jawdar and His Treacherous Brethren: *Alf* III 177-78; Burton VI 213. Chauvin V 257-60 No. 154; *ANE* 244-45 No. 209.□

P528§, ‡Euthanasia: mercy killing. Person (animal, demon, etc.) put to death so as to relieve his suffering. See: *DOTTI*. (Cf. C869.3§, J227.9.1§, W11.0.1§).
King Jalî¿âd and Shimâs: *Alf* IV 161,-(xxx); Burton IX 90, n. 1,-(comparative comment/absence os practice is "barbarity"). Chauvin VI 9-11 No. 184; *ANE* 237-38 No. 236.□

P529§, Legal aspects of marriage and divorce. See: *DOTTI*; *GMC*. (Cf. K1305§, P221§, P522.0.3§).
Hârûn, Slave-girl and Judge Abû-Yûsuf: *Alf* II 202; Burton IV 153-55. Chauvin VII 114 No. 383; *ANE* 204 No. 75;
Masrûr and Zayn al-Mawâṣif: *Alf* IV 79; Burton VIII 262. Chauvin VI 82-84 No. 251; *ANE* 294-95 No. 232.□

P529.0.1.2§, ‡Wife may be easily divorced and then restored. See: *DOTTI*. (Cf. U226.1§).
Spy, First Maiden/¿Umar al-Nu¿mân: *Alf* I 219-20; Burton II 197. Chauvin VI 116, n.1/passim No. 277; *ANE* 432,/passim No. 39.□

P529.0.1.4§, ‡Wife is to be 'retained with kindness (*ma¿rûf*), or released (divorced) with kindness'. See: *DOTTI*. (Cf. T199.3§, W14.0.2§).
Nuzhat al-Zamân Tested/¿Umar al-Nu¿mân: *Alf* I 202,-cf./(*ma¿rûf*); Burton II 159. Chauvin VI 116, n.1/passim No. 277; *ANE* 432,/passim No. 39;
Rake's Trick Against Chaste Wife: *Alf* III 142; Burton VI 136. Chauvin VIII 37 No. 5; *ANE* 350-1 No. 185.□

P529.0.2.2§, ‡Bride-to-be must give consent to her marriage. See: *DOTTI*. (Cf. T192).
Tâj al-Mulûk: *Alf* I 306; Burton III 44. Chauvin V 126-28 No. 60; *ANE* 406-8 No. 40;
Budûr and Jubayr ibn ¿Umayr: *Alf* II 243; Burton IV 244. Chauvin VII 93-94 No. 374; *ANE* 243-44 No. 83;
Hasan of Basrah: *Alf* IV 5; Burton VIII 46. Chauvin VII 29-35 No. 212A; *ANE* 207-10 No. 230.□

P529.0.2.2.2§, ‡Girl's consent to her marriage may not be secured except by kind means (*ma¿rûf*).
Mercury ¿Alî: *Alf* III 236, 240; Burton VII 189. Chauvin V 248-50 No. 147; *ANE* 301-3 No. 225.□

P529.0.2.2.3§, ‡Bride represented by deputy (e.g., father, uncle, etc.) in marriage ceremony.
¿Azîz and ¿Azîzah: *Alf* I 285; Burton II 331. Chauvin V 144-45 No. 71; *ANE* 111-13 No. 41.□

P529.0.2.2.4§, ‡Bride represents self in marriage ceremony. (Cf. T135.1).
¿Azîz and ¿Azîzah: *Alf* I 285,-cf./(selects/hires own representative); Burton II 331,-(deputed one). Chauvin V 144-45 No. 71; *ANE* 111-13 No. 41;
Mock Caliph/¿Alî al-Jawharî: *Alf* II 197,-cf.; Burton IV 142. Chauvin V 99-100 No. 174; *ANE* 304-5 No. 73.□

P529.0.2.3.1§, ‡*ṣadâq, 'mahr'* (marriage-present, bride-wealth, "bride-price," etc.). (Cf. P180.8.1§, T52.0.1§, T52.0.8§).
Nûr al-Dîn ¿Alî and Son: *Alf* I 65; Burton I 196-97. Chauvin VI 102-6 No. 270; *ANE* 317-19 No. 22;
¿Alâ' al-Dîn Abû al-Shâmât: *Alf* II 155; Burton IV 49. Chauvin V 43-49 No. 18; *ANE* 85-87 No. 63;
Landsman ¿Abdallah and Merman ¿Abdallah: *Alf* IV 202, 205; Burton IX 175, 183. Chauvin V 6-7 No. 3; *ANE* 65-66 No. 256.□

P529.0.4§, ‡Wife instructed to obey her husband, husband instructed to be gentle with wife. (Cf. J21.37.1§).
Ma¿rûf the Cobbler: *Alf* IV 290, 292; Burton X 4. Chauvin VI 81-82 No. 250; *ANE* 291-93 No. 262.□

P529.0.4.1§, ‡Wife (bride) is to obey husband (except in sin).

¿Abdallah ibn Fâḍil: Treacherous Brothers: *Alf* IV 277; Burton IX 327. Chauvin V 2-4 No. 2; *ANE* 63-65 No. 261.□

P529.0.4.1.2§, ‡Wife may not travel (leave house) without husband's permission (his approval is required). (Cf. K490.9.1§).
Ni¿mah and Nu¿m: Stolen Wife Regained: *Alf* II 134; Burton IV 6. Chauvin VI 96-97 No. 263; *ANE* 314 No. 62.□

P529.0.4.4§, ‡Husband is to attend to wife's sexual needs. (Cf. P529.0.6.1.1§, T185.3§).
¿Alâ' al-Dîn Abû al-Shâmât: *Alf* II 164-65,-(slave-woman's); Burton IV 65. Chauvin V 43-49 No. 18; *ANE* 85-87 No. 63.□

P529.0.6§, Husband's failure to honor legitimate marital obligations. (Cf. T315.2).
King and Vizier's Wife/Tracks of Lion: *Alf* III 140; Burton VI 131. Chauvin VIII 35 No. 2; *ANE* 261 No. 182.□

P529.0.6.1.1§, ‡Wife awarded divorce due to husband's continence (impotence). See: *DOTTI*. (Cf. P529.0.4.4§).
¿Alâ' al-Dîn Abû al-Shâmât: *Alf* II 165,-cf./(slave-woman as gift/retrieved); Burton IV 66. Chauvin V 43-49 No. 18; *ANE* 85-87 No. 63.□

P529.0.6.3§, ‡Divorced forced on couple who wish to remain wed illegal (illegitimate). (Cf. P174.3.1§, P529.4§, P530§, T197§).
¿Alâ' al-Dîn Abû al-Shâmât: *Alf* II 157,-cf./(attempted); Burton IV 52-53. Chauvin V 43-49 No. 18; *ANE* 85-87 No. 63.□

P529.0.8.1§, ‡Divorce by proxy.
Hind bint al-Nu¿mân and al-Ḥajjâj: *Alf* III 202; Burton VII 96. Chauvin V 115-4 No. 50; *ANE* 221-22 No. 212.□

P529.1§, Wife divorced without her knowledge (legal trick). (Cf. T197§).
Ruined Baghdadi and His Slave-girl: *Alf* IV 133; Burton IX 32. Chauvin V 152-53 No. 75; *ANE* 353 No. 235.□

P529.1.1§, Conversion to different religion to obtain divorce. See: *DOTTI*. (Cf. V333§).
Masrûr and Zayn al-Mawâṣif: *Alf* IV 74, 79,-cf.; Burton VIII 248, 262. Chauvin VI 82-84 No. 251; *ANE* 294-95 No. 232.□

P529.1.3§, ‡Marriage annulled (divorce imposed) because of spouse's different religion. See: *DOTTI*. (Cf. P529.1.1§, V84.0.1§).
Masrûr and Zayn al-Mawâṣif: *Alf* IV 76; Burton VIII 257. Chauvin VI 82-84 No. 251; *ANE* 294-95 No. 232.□

P529.2.1§, ‡Wife asks for divorce from her husband to enforce demand. See: *DOTTI*. (Cf. Q432.0.1§, T283).
Mercury ¿Alî: *Alf* III 241; Burton VII 200. Chauvin V 248-50 No. 147; *ANE* 301-3 No. 225.□

P529.2.1.1§, ‡Wife drives husband insane so as to induce him to divorce her. See: *DOTTI*. (Cf. K1874.2§).
Jeweler's Wife and Qamar al-Zamân: *Alf* IV 251; Burton IX 273ff. Chauvin V 212-14 No. 121; *ANE* 345-47 No. 260.□

P529.2.3§, ‡Wife (unintentionally) divorced because of 'divorce-vow' (divorce-oath) by husband. See: *DOTTI*. (Cf. M147§, T196§).
¿Alâ' al-Dîn Abû al-Shâmât: *Alf* II 155; Burton IV 47. Chauvin V 43-49 No. 18; *ANE* 85-87 No. 63;
Hârûn, Slave-girl and Judge Abû-Yûsuf: *Alf* II 202; Burton IV 153. Chauvin VII 114 No. 383; *ANE* 204 No. 75.□

P529.3§, Third divorce between man and same wife irrevocable. See: *DOTTI*; *GMC*.
Hârûn, Slave-girl and Judge Abû-Yûsuf: *Alf* II 202; Burton IV 153. Chauvin VII 114 No. 383; *ANE* 204 No. 75.□

P529.3.0.1§, ‡Triple (three-fold) divorce oath: one oath intended to be irrevocable. See: *DOTTI*. (Cf. P529.3§).
Qamar al-Zamân and Budûr: *Alf* II 104,-(poem/happiness 'divorced-thrice'); Burton III 292. Chauvin V 204-12 No. 120; *ANE* 341-45 No. 61;
Hârûn, Slave-girl and Judge Abû-Yûsuf: *Alf* II 202; Burton IV 153. Chauvin VII 114 No. 383; *ANE* 204 No. 75;

Bulûqiya: *Alf* III 76; Burton V 387. Chauvin VII 54 No. 77; *ANE* 130-32 No. 177;
Nûr al-Dîn and Maryam: *Alf* IV 91; Burton VIII 287, 290. Chauvin V 52-54 No. 271; *ANE* 98-99 No. 233.□

P529.4§, *muhallil*-marriage: legal device for reinstating thrice-divorced wife. See: *DOTTI*; *GMC*. (Cf. P529.0.6.3§, T53.7.1.0.1§).
¿Alâ' al-Dîn Abû al-Shâmât: *Alf* II 155; Burton IV 48. Chauvin V 43-49 No. 18; *ANE* 85-87 No. 63.□

P529.5§, *¿iddah*: required waiting period before a woman may remarry. See: *DOTTI*; *GMC*.
King ¿Umar al-Nu¿mân and Sons: *Alf* I 226,-(*'istibrâ'* for slave girls); Burton II 213,-(courses of being free from impurity [??]). Chauvin VI 112-24 No. 277; *ANE* 430-34 No. 39;
Qamar al-Zamân and Budûr: *Alf* II 104,-(poem); Burton III 292. Chauvin V 204-12 No. 120; *ANE* 341-45 No. 61;
Hârûn, Slave-girl and Judge Abû-Yûsuf: *Alf* II 202-3,-(*'istibrâ'*); Burton IV 154,-("prescribed period of purification"). Chauvin VII 114 No. 383; *ANE* 204 No. 75;
Jawdar and His Treacherous Brethren: *Alf* III 201; Burton VI 256,-(days of widowhood). Chauvin V 257-60 No. 154; *ANE* 244-45 No. 209;
Masrûr and Zayn al-Mawâṣif: *Alf* IV 79; Burton VIII 262,-(purification period). Chauvin VI 82-84 No. 251; *ANE* 294-95 No. 232;
Ma¿rûf the Cobbler: *Alf* IV 311; Burton X 43,-("period of widowhood"). Chauvin VI 81-82 No. 250; *ANE* 291-93 No. 262.□

P529.5.1§, ‡Woman's failure to observe required waiting period before remarrying (*¿iddah*) is sinful (illegitimate, fornication). (Cf. K1227.12§, Q241.4§).
Jawdar and His Treacherous Brethren: *Alf* III 201; Burton VI 256. Chauvin V 257-60 No. 154; *ANE* 244-45 No. 209;
Ma¿rûf the Cobbler: *Alf* IV 311; Burton X 44. Chauvin VI 81-82 No. 250; *ANE* 291-93 No. 262.□

P529.6.4§, ‡Nonsexual marriage for vanity (appearances). (Cf. K1351.4§).
Bahrâm and Datmâ: *Alf* III 165; Burton VI 186. Chauvin VIII 54-57 No. 22; *ANE* 114-15 No. 202.□

P529.6.4.1§, ‡Maiden marries an old man although he cannot perform (sexually): he marries her for vanity; she marries him for financial gain. (Cf. T52.0.1§, T101.3.2.2.1§).
Bahrâm and Datmâ: *Alf* III 166; Burton VI 186. Chauvin VIII 54-57 No. 22; *ANE* 114-15 No. 202.□

P530§, Legal *kafâ'ah*: marriage is to be between persons of equal social class (status compatibility required). See: *DOTTI*. (Cf. J700.1§, P522.0.3§, P529.0.6.3§).
Ebony Horse: *Alf* II 264,-cf./(non-*kafâ'ah*); Burton V 27. Chauvin V 221-31 No. 130; *ANE* 172-74 No. 103.□

P530.3§, ‡Marriage annulled (divorce imposed) because of husband's status as slave. See: *DOTTI*. (Cf. T131.12.1§).
Hârûn, Slave-girl and Judge Abû-Yûsuf: *Alf* II 202-3; Burton IV 155. Chauvin VII 114 No. 383; *ANE* 204 No. 75.□

P531.0.1§, ‡Taxation as primary source of government's (ruler's) income.
¿Abdallah ibn Fâḍil: Treacherous Brothers: *Alf* IV 266-67; Burton IX 304-6,-(tribute). Chauvin V 2-4 No. 2; *ANE* 63-65 No. 261.□

P532.1§, Heavy taxes. See: *DOTTI*; *GMC*; *PSAE*.
Son of Unjust King: *Alf* IV 142; Burton IX 50. Chauvin II 219-20 No. 152/7; *ANE* 437 No. 242;
Two Kings, Just and Unjust: *Alf* IV 149; Burton IX 65-67. Chauvin II 221 No. 152/12; *ANE* 422 No. 246.□

P532.2§, ‡Ruler increases (intends to increase) taxes. (Cf. P500.0.3.2§).
Anûshirawân and Village Damsel: *Alf* II 285; Burton V 88. Chauvin VI 26-27 No. 198; *ANE* 106 No. 121.□

P533.0.3§, ‡Law cleverly (evasively) interpreted or evaded (finding legal "loopholes"). See: *DOTTI*. (Cf. P421.0.1§).
Hârûn, Slave-girl and Judge Abû-Yûsuf: *Alf* II 202-3; Burton IV 153-55. Chauvin VII 114 No. 383; *ANE* 204 No. 75.□

P533.1, Hostages. See: *GMC*.

Two Kings, Just and Unjust: *Alf* IV 149; Burton IX 65-67. Chauvin II 221 No. 152/12; *ANE* 422 No. 246.□

P533.1.2§, ‡Merchants (travelers) as hostages.
Qamar al-Zamân and Budûr: *Alf* II 106; Burton III 298-99. Chauvin V 204-12 No. 120; *ANE* 341-45 No. 61.□

P534§, Forced labor. See: *DOTTI*; *GMC*. (Cf. R51.5§).
¿Alâ' al-Dîn Abû al-Shâmât: *Alf* II 177; Burton IV 86. Chauvin V 43-49 No. 18; *ANE* 85-87 No. 63;
Jawdar and His Treacherous Brethren: *Alf* III 193,-(aboard ship); Burton VI 242. Chauvin V 257-60 No. 154; *ANE* 244-45 No. 209;
Sayf al-Mulûk: *Alf* III 292; Burton VII 356. Chauvin VII 64-73 No. 348; *ANE* 362-64 No. 229.□

P535, Éric fines (imposed for personal injury, etc.).
Dispute Concerning Males and Females: *Alf* II 300,-(blood-price/passim); Burton V 156,-(blood money). Chauvin VI 153 No. 317; *ANE* 291 No. 151.□

P535.1§, Blood price: women (girls, maidens) given away in marriage as compensation for loss of life (involuntary manslaughter). See: *DOTTI*; *GMC*. (Cf. T142.4§).
Jeweler's Wife and Qamar al-Zamân: *Alf* IV 265,-cf.; Burton IX 301. Chauvin V 212-14 No. 121; *ANE* 345-47 No. 260.□

P535.5§, Blood price forgiven (or surrendered). See: *DOTTI*.
Trader and Afrit: Accidental Fairy-cide: *Alf* I 8,-(third); Burton I 27. Chauvin VI 22-23 No. 194; *ANE* 419-20 No. 4;
Three Apples: Hasty Uxoricide: *Alf* I 64; Burton I 194. Chauvin VI 144-45 No. 302; *ANE* 414-15 No. 21;
Omar and Young Badawî: Returning to be Executed: *Alf* II 288; Burton V 104. Chauvin V 216 No. 125; *ANE* 429-30 No. 130;
King Jalî¿âd and Shimâs: *Alf* IV 175,-(implicit/son forgives father's killer); Burton IX 119. Chauvin VI 9 No. 184; *ANE* 237-38 No. 236.□

P535.6§, ‡'Blood' (life) of a person condemned to death granted to another (to decide its fate). (Cf. J1181, M224§).
Hasan of Basrah: *Alf* IV 40; Burton VIII 117. Chauvin VII 29-35 No. 212A; *ANE* 207-10 No. 230.□

P535.9.0.1§, ‡Criminal's property confiscated and given to victim(s) of crime. (Cf. Q490§).
Ibrâhîm and Jamîlah: *Alf* IV 229; Burton IX 228. Chauvin VI 52-53 No. 218; *ANE* 227-29 No. 258.□

P535.9.2.1§, ‡Compensation for hand unjustly severed.
Jewish Doctor's Story: Sororicide: *Alf* I 102; Burton I 298. Chauvin VI 89 No. 253; *ANE* 242 No. 26.□

P535.9.3§, ‡Compensation for crime (or unjust official treatment) resulting in loss of portion of lifetime (wages, potential earnings, etc.). (Cf. Q102§).
Bulûqiya: *Alf* III 75; Burton V 386. Chauvin VII 54 No. 77; *ANE* 130-32 No. 177.□

P537, ‡Payment of stipend [(wages)]. See: *DOTTI*.
Dûban and King Yûnân: *Alf* I 18; Burton I 48. Chauvin V 289 No. 173; *ANE* 383 No. 9.□

P537.2§, ‡Ruler increases employees's stipends: wins their support. (Cf. P500.0.3.2§, Q111, Q111.8).
Qamar al-Zamân and Budûr: *Alf* II 101; Burton III 285. Chauvin V 204-12 No. 120; *ANE* 341-45 No. 61.□

P537.3§, ‡Position with steady stipend (salary) preferred.
Dalîla the Swindler: *Alf* III 213; Burton VII 146. Chauvin V 245-50 No. 147; *ANE* 163-64 No. 224.□

P538§, ‡Loss of stipend (wages). See: *DOTTI*. (Cf. P506.3§, P551, U25).
Dalîla the Swindler: *Alf* III 213; Burton VII 145. Chauvin V 245-50 No. 147; *ANE* 163-64 No. 224.□

P548.1§, ‡Legal aspects of being an adult. See: *DOTTI*. (Cf. C135§).
Qamar al-Zamân and Budûr: *Alf* II 108; Burton III 301. Chauvin V 204-12 No. 120; *ANE* 341-45 No. 61.□

P549.2§, ‡Crime against multiple parties.
Abû Qîr and Abû Ṣîr: *Alf* IV 197; Burton IX 163. Chauvin V 15-17 No. 10; *ANE* 75-77 No. 255.□

P549.2.1§, ‡One party forgives culprit, the other does not. (Cf. V441, W11.5.0.3§).
Abû Qîr and Abû Ṣîr: *Alf* IV 197; Burton IX 164-65. Chauvin V 15-17 No. 10; *ANE* 75-77 No. 255.□

P550.1.0.1§, ‡Warfare is men's alone—women do not know battle formation, strategy, etc.
King Jalî¿âd and Shimâs: *Alf* IV 171; Burton IX 112. Chauvin VI 9 No. 184; *ANE* 237-38 No. 236.□

P550.1.0.2§, ‡Lack of endurance in fight (battle). (Cf. P550.1.0.5.3.1§, Z62).
¿Alâ' al-Dîn Abû al-Shâmât: *Alf* II 180; Burton IV 93. Chauvin V 43-49 No. 18; *ANE* 85-87 No. 63.□

P550.1.0.5§, ‡Preparations (readiness) for war. See: *PSAE*. (Cf. P538§).
King ¿Umar al-Nu¿mân and Sons: *Alf* I 165; Burton II 85. Chauvin VI 112-24 No. 277; *ANE* 430-34 No. 39;
Jânshâh: *Alf* III 60; Burton V 359. Chauvin VII 39-44 No. 153; *ANE* 238-41 No. 178;
Sayf al-Mulûk: *Alf* III 281; Burton VII 335. Chauvin VII 64-73 No. 348; *ANE* 362-64 No. 229.□

P550.1.0.5.3.1§, ‡Troops refuse to fight. See: *PSAE*. (Cf. P550.1.0.2§).
King ¿Umar al-Nu¿mân and Sons: *Alf* II 6-7; Burton II 86. Chauvin VI 112-24 No. 277; *ANE* 430-34 No. 39.□

P550.1.1§, ‡Declaration of war. See: *PSAE*.
King Jalî¿âd and Shimâs: *Alf* IV 171,-cf.; Burton IX 111. Chauvin VI 9 No. 184; *ANE* 237-38 No. 236.□

P550.1.1.1§, ‡Drums of war (beaten).
King ¿Umar al-Nu¿mân and Sons: *Alf* I 165; Burton II 85. Chauvin VI 112-24 No. 277; *ANE* 430-34 No. 39.□

P550.1.1.2§, ‡Call to arms (*'istinfâr*). See: *PSAE*.
King ¿Umar al-Nu¿mân and Sons: *Alf* I 165, 229-31; Burton II 85, 217,-(summon the troops). Chauvin VI 112-24 No. 277; *ANE* 430-34 No. 39.□

P550.2§, ‡Peace for peace and war for war ('We befriend those who befriend us but fight those who wage war on us'). (Cf. P794.2.1§).
King ¿Umar al-Nu¿mân and Sons: *Alf* I 178; Burton II 116. Chauvin VI 112-24 No. 277; *ANE* 430-34 No. 39.□

P550.5§, ‡Preparation (education) of spies. (Cf. J675.0.1§).
King ¿Umar al-Nu¿mân and Sons: *Alf* I 184; Burton II 128. Chauvin VI 112-24 No. 277; *ANE* 430-34 No. 39.□

P551, Army. (Cf. P12.2.0.1§).
King ¿Umar al-Nu¿mân and Sons: *Alf* I 218,-cf./(in political process); Burton II 194. Chauvin VI 112-24 No. 277; *ANE* 430-34 No. 39.□

P551.0.3.2§, ‡Army of multi-ethnic groups: same state, several cultures. (Cf. P170.0.2.1§).
King ¿Umar al-Nu¿mân and Sons: *Alf* I 230,-ff.; Burton II 218. Chauvin VI 112-24 No. 277; *ANE* 430-34 No. 39.□

P551.0.3.3§, ‡Army of multi-national forces: several states contribute troops (a 'coalition').
King ¿Umar al-Nu¿mân and Sons: *Alf* I 230; Burton II 218. Chauvin VI 112-24 No. 277; *ANE* 430-34 No. 39.□

P551.10.4§, ‡Provider (*muqaddim*) of troops—(e.g., "Provider-of-forty").
Mercury ¿Alî: *Alf* III 227; Burton VII 172. Chauvin V 248-50 No. 147; *ANE* 301-3 No. 225.□

P551.5.1§, Army of women. See: *DOTTI*; *GMC*.
Man Who Never Laughs: *Alf* III 154; Burton VI 164. Chauvin VIII 47-48 No. 15; *ANE* 285-86 No. 195;
Hasan of Basrah: *Alf* IV 24,-cf.; Burton VIII 84. Chauvin VII 29-35 No. 212A; *ANE* 207-10 No. 230.□

P552, Battle formations. See: *PSAE*.
King ¿Umar al-Nu¿mân and Sons: *Alf* I 231,-ff., 252-53 ; Burton II 221-22, 267. Chauvin VI 112-24 No. 277; *ANE* 430-34 No. 39;
Qamar al-Zamân and Budûr: *Alf* II 103-4,-(army divided into six divisions); Burton III 290. Chauvin V 204-12 No. 120; *ANE* 341-45 No. 61;

Jinn Imprisoned in Flasks: *Alf* III 129,-(jinni's); Burton VI 99-100. Chauvin VII 113 No. 380=no/text; *ANE* 146 No. 180;
Hasan of Basrah: *Alf* IV 49; Burton VIII 136. Chauvin VII 29-35 No. 212A; *ANE* 207-10 No. 230.□

P553.3§, ‡Flying device (airplane, air-ship, 'wind-carpet') as weapons. Air force.
Ebony Horse: *Alf* II 258,-(flying horse as war machine); Burton V 13-15. Chauvin V 221-31 No. 130; *ANE* 172-74 No. 103;
Jinn Imprisoned in Flasks: *Alf* III 128; Burton VI 100. Chauvin VII 113 No. 380=no/text; *ANE* 146 No. 180.□

P553.9.1§, ‡'Virgin' weapon—unused.
Ma¿rûf the Cobbler: *Alf* IV 316; Burton X 52. Chauvin VI 81-82 No. 250; *ANE* 291-93 No. 262.□

P553.9.4§, ‡Golden weapons (armor, shield, sword, spear, or the like).
King ¿Umar al-Nu¿mân and Sons: *Alf* I 232; Burton II 224,-(hauberk). Chauvin VI 112-24 No. 277; *ANE* 430-34 No. 39;
Ma¿n Rewards Maidens for a Drink of Water: *Alf* II 182,-cf./(golden arrow); Burton IV 97. Chauvin VI 78 No. 247; *ANE* 290 No. 65.□

P555, Defeat in battle. (Cf. R75).
King ¿Umar al-Nu¿mân and Sons: *Alf* I 246; Burton II 253. Chauvin VI 112-24 No. 277; *ANE* 430-34 No. 39;
Jinn Imprisoned in Flasks: *Alf* III 129; Burton VI 100. Chauvin VII 113 No. 380=no/text; *ANE* 146 No. 180;
Jullanâr of the Sea: *Alf* III 259; Burton VII 287. Chauvin V 147-51 No. 73; *ANE* 248-51 No. 227;
Hasan of Basrah: *Alf* IV 50; Burton VIII 136. Chauvin VII 29-35 No. 212A; *ANE* 207-10 No. 230.□

P555.2.1.1, "Publication of slaying." Heads of slain enemies displayed. See: *GMC*; *PSAE*. (Cf. Q421.1).
Qamar al-Zamân and Budûr: *Alf* II 93; Burton III 256. Chauvin V 204-12 No. 120; *ANE* 341-45 No. 61.□

P556.7§, ‡Challenge to duel: weapon ready (open, drawn, unfolded, etc.). See: *PSAE*. (Cf. F690.1.1§, P677).
King ¿Umar al-Nu¿mân and Sons: *Alf* I 168; Burton II 89. Chauvin VI 112-24 No. 277; *ANE* 430-34 No. 39.□

P557.4, Customs concerning single combat.
King ¿Umar al-Nu¿mân and Sons: *Alf* I 174; Burton II 108. Chauvin VI 112-24 No. 277; *ANE* 430-34 No. 39.□

P557.5, ‡Warrior disgraced by slaying of those under his protection.
King ¿Umar al-Nu¿mân and Sons: *Alf* I 168,-cf.; Burton II 106,-(princess wants to avoid being disgraced). Chauvin VI 112-24 No. 277; *ANE* 430-34 No. 39.□

P557.8§, ‡Truce: respite from combat (duel).
Man of Upper Egypt and Frankish Wife: Alf IV 16?,-(text missing); Burton IX 21. Chauvin V 240 No. 140; *ANE*: No. 234.□

P557.8.1§, ‡Warring parties disengage at night.
King ¿Umar al-Nu¿mân and Sons: *Alf* I 255; Burton II 271. Chauvin VI 112-24 No. 277; *ANE* 430-34 No. 39.□

P558.3§, Battle-cry: sister's name. See: *DOTTI*; *GMC*.
Hammâd: Treacherous Bedouin: *Alf* II 19,-cf./(poem); Burton III 109. Chauvin VI 124 n. 1 No. 277; *ANE* 200 No. 43.□

P559.1§, ‡Spoils (booty) of war. (Cf. F1041.8.1.0.1§, P555, V357§).
King ¿Umar al-Nu¿mân and Sons: *Alf* II 6,-(raid); Burton II 85. Chauvin VI 112-24 No. 277; *ANE* 430-34 No. 39;
City of Labtayt/Treasure of Tolède: *Alf* II 184; Burton IV 100. Chauvin VI 90-91 No. 254; *ANE* 265-66 No. 67.□

P559.1.1.1§, ‡War booty presented to head of state of victorious army.
City of Labtayt/Treasure of Tolède: *Alf* II 184; Burton IV 101. Chauvin VI 90-91 No. 254; *ANE* 265-66 No. 67.□

P559.1.2.2§, ‡Slain (defeated) warrior's family as booty. See: *PSAE*.
Nûr al-Dîn and Maryam: *Alf* IV 103,-cf.; Burton VIII 316. Chauvin V 52-54 No. 271; *ANE* 98-99 No. 233.□

P559.1.3§, ‡War (raid) as means of acquiring wealth. (Cf. Cf. P475.0.2§, P563§, P761.2§).
King ¿Umar al-Nu¿mân and Sons: *Alf* II 3-6; Burton III 79-80. Chauvin VI 112-24 No. 277; *ANE* 430-34 No. 39.□

P563§, ‡Intertribal wars (raid and counter-raid). See: *DOTTI*. (Cf. P559.1.3§).
King ¿Umar al-Nu¿mân and Sons: *Alf* II 6,-cf./(raid); Burton II 84-85. Chauvin VI 112-24 No. 277; *ANE* 430-34 No. 39.□

P570§, ‡Fortifications of cities. See: *DOTTI*; *PSAE*. (Cf. F767).
Sayf al-Mulûk: *Alf* III 281; Burton VII 335. Chauvin VII 64-73 No. 348; *ANE* 362-64 No. 229.□

P570.1.1.1§, ‡City gate closed. See: *DOTTI*. (Cf. P191.2§).
Nûr al-Dîn ¿Alî and Son: *Alf* I 73,-(implicit); Burton I 224. Chauvin VI 102-6 No. 270; *ANE* 317-19 No. 22;
Ghânim ibn Ayyûb: *Alf* I 146; Burton II 47. Chauvin VI 14-16 No. 188; *ANE* 192-93 No. 36;
¿Alâ' al-Dîn Abû al-Shâmât: *Alf* II 154; Burton IV 43. Chauvin V 43-49 No. 18; *ANE* 85-87 No. 63;
Goldsmith and Cashmere Singer: *Alf* III 151; Burton VI 158. Chauvin VIII 46-47 No. 14; *ANE* 196 No. 194.□

P570.3.2§, ‡Access to city (castle) through water-tunnel or channel.
Abû Muhammad Lazybones: *Alf* II 216; Burton IV 176. Chauvin VI 64-67 No. 233; *ANE* 71-73 No. 78.□

P571§, ‡Siege: city (castle, troops, etc.) surrounded by enemy troops. See: *PSAE*.
King ¿Umar al-Nu¿mân and Sons: *Alf* I 244,-(passim); Burton II 249. Chauvin VI 112-24 No. 277; *ANE* 430-34 No. 39.□

P571.1§, ‡Siege lifted.
King ¿Umar al-Nu¿mân and Sons: *Alf* I 308; Burton III 48. Chauvin VI 112-24 No. 277; *ANE* 430-34 No. 39.□

P591.5.1§, ‡Hospitalization would ensure death for patient (due to poor care).
Ghânim ibn Ayyûb: *Alf* I 158-59; Burton II 70. Chauvin VI 14 No. 188; *ANE* 192-93 No. 36.□

P595§, ‡Homes for the poor (*tikiyyah*). (Cf. V401§).
¿Alâ' al-Dîn Abû al-Shâmât: *Alf* II 158,-(passim); Burton IV 55,(Convent). Chauvin V 43-49 No. 18; *ANE* 85-87 No. 63.□

P601.2.1§, ‡Custom observed because ancestors (forefathers) practiced it.
Sindbâd's Fourth Voyage: *Alf* III 102,-(burial alive); Burton VI 39. Chauvin VII 18-20 No. 373D; *ANE* 386 No. 179.□

P603.1§, ‡Storing provisions (rations) intended for consumption during extended period (season, year, etc.). See: *DOTTI*. (Cf. J711, P774.4.2§).
¿Azîz and ¿Azîzah: *Alf* I 286; Burton II 330. Chauvin V 144-45 No. 71; *ANE* 111-13 No. 41.□

P605.5§, Brother(s) and sister(s) share sleeping quarters. See: *DOTTI*; *GMC*. (Cf. P254.0.1§, T610.5.0.2§).
Hammâd: Treacherous Bedouin: *Alf* II 17,-ff./(implicit); Burton III 105. Chauvin VI 124 n. 1 No. 277; *ANE* 200 No. 43;
Ni¿mah and Nu¿m: Stolen Wife Regained: *Alf* II 132,-cf./(foster); Burton IV 2,-(reared one cradle). Chauvin VI 96-97 No. 263; *ANE* 314 No. 62;
Jeweler's Wife and Qamar al-Zamân: *Alf* IV 238,-cf./(secluded for fourteen years in a palace); Burton IX 247. Chauvin V 212-14 No. 121; *ANE* 345-47 No. 260.□

P605.5.1§, Sister and brother together asleep. See: *DOTTI*; *GMC*.
Ni¿mah and Nu¿m: Stolen Wife Regained: *Alf* II 132,-(adopted/foster), 143,-(slave-girl/jâriyah-foster sister); Burton IV 2, 21,-(reared in one bed). Chauvin VI 96-97 No. 263; *ANE* 314 No. 62.□

P605.9.1.1§, ‡Guest-room ('traveler's room', guest-house).
Hasan of Basrah: *Alf* IV 51,-(*dâr al-diyâfah*); Burton VIII 139,-(guest-house). Chauvin VII 29-35 No. 212A; *ANE* 207-10 No. 230.□

P610§, Homosociality: social relations between persons of the same sex. (Cf. J1768.2.1.1§, N349.4.1.1§, T311.8§, U284.3.3§).
Lovers of Basra/Ḍamrah: *Alf* III 211,-(girls' play); Burton VII 132. Chauvin V 118 No. 54; *ANE* 273 No. 220;
Abû Qîr and Abû Ṣîr: *Alf* IV 191,-(men/women's separate times); Burton IX 153. Chauvin V 15-17 No. 10; *ANE* 75-77 No. 255;
Jeweler's Wife and Qamar al-Zamân: *Alf* IV 252,-(husband and wife's lover); Burton IX 274. Chauvin V 212-14 No. 121; *ANE* 345-47 No. 260.□

P610.1.4.1§, ‡Men meet at neighborhood shop (usually owned by friend).
¿Alî ibn Bakkâr: *Alf* II 41; Burton III 163. Chauvin V 153 No. 76; *ANE* 92-93 No. 60.□

P610.1.2.1.1§, ‡*Bûẓah*-drinkers meet at *bûẓah*-house]. (Cf. F849.9.1§).
Mercury ¿Alî: *Alf* III 234; Burton VII 184,-(beer-ken). Chauvin V 248-50 No. 147; *ANE* 301-3 No. 225.□

P610.1.3§, ‡Men meet at bathhouse. See: *DOTTI*.
Tâj al-Mulûk: *Alf* I 293-94; Burton III 19. Chauvin V 126-28 No. 60; *ANE* 406-8 No. 40.□

P611, Women meet when bathing [in bathhouse]. See: *DOTTI*. (Cf. T380.1§).
Hasan of Basrah: *Alf* IV 9,-(at bathhouse); Burton VIII 54. Chauvin VII 29-35 No. 212A; *ANE* 207-10 No. 230.□

P611.2§, ‡Women's ways of greeting. (Cf. N349.4.1.1§).
Budûr and Jubayr ibn ¿Umayr: *Alf* II 237,-cf./(kissing cheek); Burton IV 234. Chauvin VII 93-94 No. 374; *ANE* 243-44 No. 83.□

P617, People weep when child is born. They sing and laugh at burial. See: *DOTTI*. (Cf. C898.1.1§).
Landsman ¿Abdallah and Merman ¿Abdallah: *Alf* IV 207,-cf.; Burton IX 187. Chauvin V 6-7 No. 3; *ANE* 65-66 No. 256.□

P617.1§, Singing and joy at a death. See: *DOTTI*; *GMC*. (Cf. V311.4.2§).
Angel of Death and Devout Man: *Alf* III 8-9,-cf./(pious man longs for death); Burton V 248. Chauvin VI 183-84 No. 349/[pt. 2]; *ANE* 104 No. 158/[pt. 2];
Landsman ¿Abdallah and Merman ¿Abdallah: *Alf* IV 207; Burton IX 187. Chauvin V 6-7 No. 3; *ANE* 65-66 No. 256.□

P630.2§, ‡A home may not be entered except by inhabitant's permission, and through (front) door.
Masrûr and Zayn al-Mawâṣif: *Alf* IV 56; Burton VIII 207. Chauvin VI 82-84 No. 251; *ANE* 294-95 No. 232.□

P632.6§, ‡Customs concerning seating in formal social gatherings. (Cf. P14.25.2§).
King ¿Umar al-Nu¿mân and Sons: *Alf* I 227,-(standing in royal court); Burton II 215. Chauvin VI 112-24 No. 277; *ANE* 430-34 No. 39;
¿Alâ' al-Dîn Abû al-Shâmât: *Alf* II 162,-(in royal court), 163,-(profession); Burton IV 61, 61-62. Chauvin V 43-49 No. 18; *ANE* 85-87 No. 63;
King Jalî¿âd and Shimâs: *Alf* IV 171,-(king's court); Burton IX 117. Chauvin VI 9 No. 184; *ANE* 237-38 No. 236;
al-Rashîd and Omani Merchant: *Alf* IV 209,-(rank); Burton IX 190. Chauvin VI 111-12 No. 276; *ANE* 201-2 No. 257.□

P634.0.1.2§, ‡Table manners and eating styles.
¿Alî Shâr and Zumurrud: *Alf* II 228-31; Burton IV 212-18. Chauvin V 89-91 No. 28; *ANE* 100-1 No. 82;
Tawaddud: Slavegirl Sold and Regained: *Alf* II 310; Burton V 206. Chauvin VII 117-19 No. 387; *ANE* 408-10 No. 157;
¿Abdallah ibn Fâḍil: Treacherous Brothers: *Alf* IV 282,-(*'akl al-ḥishmah*); Burton IX 337,-(as servants eat with their lords). Chauvin V 2-4 No. 2; *ANE* 63-65 No. 261.□

P634.0.1.4§, ‡(High)-table eating: sitting-up on chair at dining table.
Jawdar and His Treacherous Brethren: *Alf* III 201; Burton VI 256. Chauvin V 257-60 No. 154; *ANE* 244-45 No. 209.□

P634.0.3.7§, ‡Incense burnt after meal.
¿Alî ibn Bakkâr: *Alf* II 44; Burton III 168. Chauvin V 153 No. 76; *ANE* 92-93 No. 60.□

P634.0.8.2.1§, ‡Person refuses to drink with others (at tavern), and insists on drinking alone.

Mercury ¿Alî: *Alf* III 227; Burton VII 172. Chauvin V 248-50 No. 147; *ANE* 301-3 No. 225.□

P671, Woman veils self as expression of surprise. See: *GMC*.
¿Alâ' al-Dîn Abû al-Shâmât: *Alf* II 149; Burton IV 34. Chauvin V 43-49 No. 18; *ANE* 85-87 No. 63.□

P672, Pulling a man's beard as an insult. (Cf. Q497.2§).
Ma¿rûf the Cobbler: *Alf* IV 290; Burton X 3. Chauvin VI 81-82 No. 250; *ANE* 291-93 No. 262.□

P677, ‡Customs connected with dueling. See: *DOTTI*.
King ¿Umar al-Nu¿mân and Sons: *Alf* I 178,-cf., 233; Burton II 116-17. Chauvin VI 112-24 No. 277; *ANE* 430-34 No. 39.□

P677.4§, ‡Fair dueling: one against one. (Cf. F690.1.1§, W14.4.3.1§).
King ¿Umar al-Nu¿mân and Sons: *Alf* I 173-74, 254; Burton II 107. Chauvin VI 112-24 No. 277; *ANE* 430-34 No. 39.□

P678.1, Tearing garment as sign of grief. See: *GMC*.
Porter and Ladies of Baghdad: *Alf* I 37-038; Burton I 99. Chauvin V 251-52 No. 148; *ANE* 324-26 No. 14;
Tailor's Story/Barber of Baghdad: *Alf* I 107; Burton I 314. Chauvin V 154-56 No. 78; *ANE* 405-6 No. 27;
Hammâd: Treacherous Bedouin: *Alf* II 20; Burton III 111. Chauvin VI 124 n. 1 No. 277; *ANE* 200 No. 43;
Hasan of Basrah: *Alf* III 305; Burton VIII 14. Chauvin VII 29-35 No. 212A; *ANE* 207-10 No. 230.□

P681.0.1§, Mourning for a certain required period. See: *DOTTI*; *GMC*.
Ensorcelled Prince/Husband: *Alf* I 29,-(one year); Burton I 74. Chauvin VI 56-58 No. 222; *ANE* 176 No. 13;
Second Qalandar: Afrit's Wife: *Alf* I 50,-(seven days); Burton I 137,-(lamentations). Chauvin V 197-200 No. 116; *ANE* 338-39 No. 16.□

P681.0.5§, Mourning in silence. See: *GMC*.
Hârûn and Arab Girl: *Alf* III 204; Burton VII 110. Chauvin VI 143 No. 300; *ANE* 202 No. 215.□

P681.0.5.1§, ‡House of sorrows (*bayt al-'ahzân*): special quarters for grieving in solitude.
Ensorcelled Prince/Husband: *Alf* I 29; Burton I 74,-("House of Lamentations"/for females), n.1. Chauvin VI 56-58 No. 222; *ANE* 176 No. 13;
Qamar al-Zamân and Budûr: *Alf* II 104; Burton III 291,-(House of Lamentations). Chauvin V 204-12 No. 120; *ANE* 341-45 No. 61.□

P681.1.0.1§, Funeral procession. See: *DOTTI*; *GMC*.
Anîs al-Jalîs: *Alf* I 130; Burton II 10. Chauvin V 120-24 No. 58; *ANE* 316-17 No. 35;
Jawdar and His Treacherous Brethren: *Alf* III 201,-(humble); Burton VI 256. Chauvin V 257-60 No. 154; *ANE* 244-45 No. 209.□

P681.1.0.1.1§, ‡Social (and ritual) significances of funeral processions.
¿Alî ibn Bakkâr: *Alf* II 65; Burton III 211. Chauvin V 153 No. 76; *ANE* 92-93 No. 60.□

P681.1.0.1.1.1§, ‡Simple (austere) and lavish funeral processions. (Number and social class of mourners, quality of bier or coffin, etc.). See: *DOTTI*. (Cf. V61.0.4§, V68).
Nûr al-Dîn ¿Alî and Son: *Alf* I 68; Burton I 209. Chauvin VI 102-6 No. 270; *ANE* 317-19 No. 22;
¿Alî ibn Bakkâr: *Alf* II 65; Burton III 211. Chauvin V 153 No. 76; *ANE* 92-93 No. 60.□

P681.1.0.4§, ‡Condolences extended to family of deceased. See: *DOTTI*.
Second Qalandar: Afrit's Wife: *Alf* I 50; Burton I 138. Chauvin V 197-200 No. 116; *ANE* 338-39 No. 16;
¿Alî ibn Bakkâr: *Alf* II 64; Burton III 209. Chauvin V 153 No. 76; *ANE* 92-93 No. 60.□

P681.1.0.4.1§, ‡Public reception for mourners to extend their condolences (*ma¿zâ, ¿azâ*). Black (sugarless) coffee is served. (Cf. V65.6§).
Nûr al-Dîn ¿Alî and Son: *Alf* I 64; Burton I 195. Chauvin VI 102-6 No. 270-(ceremonial mourning); *ANE* 317-19 No. 22.□

P681.1.1.2§, Mourning: physical manifestations. See: *DOTTI*; *GMC*.
Ensorcelled Prince/Husband: *Alf* I 29; Burton I 74. Chauvin VI 56-58 No. 222; *ANE* 176 No. 13.□

P681.1.1.2.1§, Mourning: baring head (face) in public. See: *GMC*.

Second Eunuch/Kâfûr's Half-lie: *Alf* I 149; Burton II 51-52. Chauvin V 278 No. 161; *ANE* 178-79 No. 38.□

P681.1.1.2.1.1§, Mourning: tearing garment. See: *GMC*.
Qamar al-Zamân and Budûr: *Alf* II 104; Burton III 290. Chauvin V 204-12 No. 120; *ANE* 341-45 No. 61;
Ruined Baghdadi and His Slave-girl: *Alf* IV 133; Burton IX 31. Chauvin V 152-53 No. 75; *ANE* 353 No. 235.□

P681.1.1.2.2.1§, ‡Mourning: slapping own face (cheeks). (Cf. F956.7.7.2§).
Qamar al-Zamân and Budûr: *Alf* II 104; Burton III 290. Chauvin V 204-12 No. 120; *ANE* 341-45 No. 61.□

P681.1.1.2.3§, Mourning: rolling self in dust.
Second Eunuch/Kâfûr's Half-lie: *Alf* I 149; Burton II 51-52. Chauvin V 278 No. 161; *ANE* 178-79 No. 38.□

P681.1.1.2.3.1§, ‡Mourning: putting dust (dirt) on own head. See: *PSAE*.
Tailor's Story/Barber of Baghdad: *Alf* I 107; Burton I 314. Chauvin V 154-56 No. 78; *ANE* 405-6 No. 27;
Qamar al-Zamân and Budûr: *Alf* II 104,-(dust on head); Burton III 290. Chauvin V 204-12 No. 120; *ANE* 341-45 No. 61.□

P681.1.1.2.4§, Mourning: wearing only black (white) color clothes. (Cf. Z143.1).
Ensorcelled Prince/Husband: *Alf* I 29,-cf./(unspecified); Burton I 74. Chauvin VI 56-58 No. 222; *ANE* 176 No. 13;
Qamar al-Zamân and Budûr: *Alf* II 104,-(king orders all); Burton III 291. Chauvin V 204-12 No. 120; *ANE* 341-45 No. 61;
al-'Amjad and al-'As¿ad: *Alf* II 147; Burton IV 27-28. Chauvin V 208-10 No. 120[.1]; *ANE* 341-42 No. 61/pt. 2;
¿Alâ' al-Dîn Abû al-Shâmât: *Alf* II 163; Burton IV 63. Chauvin V 43-49 No. 18; *ANE* 85-87 No. 63;
Hârûn and Arab Girl: *Alf* III 204; Burton VII 110. Chauvin VI 143 No. 300; *ANE* 202 No. 215;
Ruined Baghdadi and His Slave-girl: *Alf* IV 133,-(black); Burton IX 31. Chauvin V 152-53 No. 75; *ANE* 353 No. 235.□

P681.1.1.2.7§, Mourning: abstinence from life's pleasures (non-essentials: e.g., fine foods, drinks, music, etc.).
King ¿Umar al-Nu¿mân and Sons: *Alf* I 315,-cf./(abstain from food and water); Burton III 63. Chauvin VI 112-24 No. 277; *ANE* 430-34 No. 39.□

P681.1.1.3.1§, Mourning: abstinence from sexual intercourse (erotic acts), communal activities, smiling, etc.
al-'Amjad and al-'As¿ad: *Alf* II 120; Burton III 324. Chauvin V 208-10 No. 120[.1]; *ANE* 341-42 No. 61/pt. 2;
Ruined Baghdadi and His Slave-girl: *Alf* IV 133,-cf.; Burton IX 24-32. Chauvin V 152-53 No. 75; *ANE* 353 No. 235.□

P681.1.1.4§, ‡Mourning: destruction of property (furniture broken, animal killed, etc.). See: *DOTTI*. (Cf. P681.1.1.2.1.1§).
Second Eunuch/Kâfûr's Half-lie: *Alf* I 149; Burton II 51-52. Chauvin V 278 No. 161; *ANE* 178-79 No. 38;
¿Alî ibn Bakkâr: *Alf* II 65; Burton III 211. Chauvin V 153 No. 76; *ANE* 92-93 No. 60;
Ruined Baghdadi and His Slave-girl: *Alf* IV 133,-(lute); Burton IX 31. Chauvin V 152-53 No. 75; *ANE* 353 No. 235.□

P681.1.1.5§, ‡Mourning: becoming averse to belongings (personal property) of the deceased (clothes, watch, room, bed, etc.).
¿Alî ibn Bakkâr: *Alf* II 65,-cf.; Burton III 211. Chauvin V 153 No. 76; *ANE* 92-93 No. 60;
Ruined Baghdadi and His Slave-girl: *Alf* IV 133; Burton IX 31. Chauvin V 152-53 No. 75; *ANE* 353 No. 235.□

P681.1.1.5.1§, ‡Mourning: belongings (personal property) of the deceased destroyed (or given away).
¿Alî ibn Bakkâr: *Alf* II 65,-(musical instruments); Burton III 211. Chauvin V 153 No. 76; *ANE* 92-93 No. 60.□

P682.0.4§, ‡Greeting back in response to a *salâm*-greeting (peace-greeting) is required (by sharia). (Cf. P790.2.2§).
Angel of Death and Proud King: *Alf* III 8; Burton V 246. Chauvin VI 183-84 No. 349/[pt. 1]; *ANE* 104 No. 158;
Nûr al-Dîn and Maryam: *Alf* IV 97; Burton VIII 302. Chauvin V 52-54 No. 271; *ANE* 98-99 No. 233.□

P682.4.1§, ‡Greeting according to social status: age, gender, rank, ethnic identity.
Conversion of Princess by Khawwâṣ: *Alf* III 15; Burton V 284-85. Chauvin V 239 No. 139; *ANE* 145 No. 171;
Jullanâr of the Sea: *Alf* III 247,-(failure to greet); Burton VII 266. Chauvin V 147-51 No. 73; *ANE* 248-51 No. 227.□

P682.4.2§, ‡Greeting according location and motion (one's physical position in relationship to another).
Nûr al-Dîn and Maryam: *Alf* IV 121,-(standing up-sitting down); Burton IX 2 n. 1. Chauvin V 52-54 No. 271; *ANE* 98-99 No. 233.□

P682.7§, ‡Forms of (non-verbal) greetings. See: *DOTTI*.
¿Azîz and ¿Azîzah: *Alf* I 268,-cf.; Burton II 300. Chauvin V 144-45 No. 71; *ANE* 111-13 No. 41.□

P682.7.3§, ‡Honoring guest by providing escort for arriving or departing. (Usually, for a certain distance). (Cf. P320.0.1§).
King ¿Umar al-Nu¿mân and Sons: *Alf* I 180, 229,-(arrival of brother); Burton II 119, 217. Chauvin VI 112-24 No. 277; *ANE* 430-34 No. 39;
Tâj al-Mulûk: *Alf* I 262, 264,-(three leagues/*farâsikh*), 307,-(three days); Burton II 286, 289, III 47. Chauvin V 126-28 No. 60; *ANE* 406-8 No. 40;
Sayf al-Mulûk: *Alf* III 286,-(by monkeys); Burton VII 346. Chauvin VII 64-73 No. 348; *ANE* 362-64 No. 229;
Hasan of Basrah: *Alf* IV 5,-(for three days); Burton VIII 46. Chauvin VII 29-35 No. 212A; *ANE* 207-10 No. 230.□

P710.0.2§, ‡Most powerful king (nation) and less powerful king (nation).
al-'Amjad and al-'As¿ad: *Alf* II 146,-cf./('heaviest army'); Burton IV 27. Chauvin V 208-10 No. 120[.1]; *ANE* 341-42 No. 61/pt. 2;
Hasan of Basrah: *Alf* III 319; Burton VIII 39. Chauvin VII 29-35 No. 212A; *ANE* 207-10 No. 230.□

P711.0.1§, ‡Intemperate patriotism (nationalistic extremism).
Ebony Horse: *Alf* II 263,-(Imperial-Persia); Burton V 26. Chauvin V 221-31 No. 130; *ANE* 172-74 No. 103.□

P712§, ‡Homesickness: yearning for homeland. See: *DOTTI*; *PSAE*.
Water-fowl and Tortoise: *Alf* II 28; Burton III 129. Chauvin II 226-27 No. 5; *ANE* 444 No. 46.□

P712.0.1§, ‡'Love for one's homeland is [part] of true faith'.
Jeweler's Wife and Qamar al-Zamân: *Alf* IV 265; Burton IX 301,-("mother-land"). Chauvin V 212-14 No. 121; *ANE* 345-47 No. 260.□

P715.1.1§, ‡Jew as merchant (businessman). (Cf. P431).
Nûr al-Dîn ¿Alî and Son: *Alf* I 69; Burton I 211. Chauvin VI 102-6 No. 270; *ANE* 317-19 No. 22.□

P715.9.2§, ‡Greco-Romans (al-Rûm/"Banû al-'Aṣfar/Children of the Yellow-One").
King ¿Umar al-Nu¿mân and Sons: *Alf* I 230; Burton II 220. Chauvin VI 112-24 No. 277; *ANE* 430-34 No. 39.□

P723.1.2.1§, ‡Farmer (peasant) as helper.
Jewish qâḍî and His Devout Wife: *Alf* III 10,-(forgive son's murder); Burton V 256. Chauvin VI 154-55 No. 321; *ANE* 242 No. 163;
Ma¿rûf the Cobbler: *Alf* IV 303-4; Burton X 27,-(plougher). Chauvin VI 81-82 No. 250; *ANE* 291-93 No. 262.□

P722.1§, ‡Gender as factor in population analyses. (Cf. B225.3§, F112).
Man Who Never Laughs: *Alf* III 154; Burton VI 165. Chauvin VIII 47-48 No. 15; *ANE* 285-86 No. 195;
Landsman ¿Abdallah and Merman ¿Abdallah: *Alf* IV 205; Burton IX 182. Chauvin V 6-7 No. 3; *ANE* 65-66 No. 256.□

P722.1.1§, ‡Community of only females (no men). (Cf. F112.2).

Landsman ¿Abdallah and Merman ¿Abdallah: *Alf* IV 205; Burton IX 182. Chauvin V 6-7 No. 3; *ANE* 65-66 No. 256.□

P722.2§, ‡Age as factor in population analyses.
Man Who Never Laughs: *Alf* III 152,-cf./(social group); Burton VI 161. Chauvin VIII 47-48 No. 15; *ANE* 285-86 No. 195.□

P722.3§, ‡Religion (religious denominations) as factor in population analyses. (Cf. A1650.2.1§, D692, V131.3§).
Ensorcelled Prince/Husband: *Alf* I 29; Burton I 77. Chauvin VI 56-58 No. 222; *ANE* 176 No. 13;
Landsman ¿Abdallah and Merman ¿Abdallah: *Alf* IV 205,-(monotheistic Moslems, *naṣârâ*/Nazarenes, Jews, and what not else); Burton IX 183,-("Moslems ..., Nazarenes, and what not else"). Chauvin V 6-7 No. 3; *ANE* 65-66 No. 256.□

P727.1§, ‡Characteristic behavior of Turks (Sarkassians, etc.). See: *DOTTI*. (Cf. W256.1§).
¿Alî Shâr and Zumurrud: *Alf* II 227,-(*¿âmmat al-'Atrâk*); Burton IV 211,-(common folk of the Turks). Chauvin V 89-91 No. 28; *ANE* 100-1 No. 82.□

P730.1.1§, ‡Nomadic tribe sought at usual camp site (homestead): not found. See: *DOTTI*. (Cf. T44.1§).
Lovers of Banû ¿Udhrah and Lion: *Alf* III 206; Burton VII 118. Chauvin V 116-17 No. 52; *ANE* 274 No. 218/[2].□

P731.0.1§, Bedouin behavior ('Arab'-ways) as 'The ideal'. See: *DOTTI*; *PSAE*.
Hishâm and Arab Youth: *Alf* II 184; Burton IV 101-3. Chauvin V 288 No. 172; *ANE* 222-23 No. 68.□

P731.0.3§, ‡Bedouin behavior as vile (anti-ideal). (Cf. W256.1§).
King ¿Umar al-Nu¿mân and Sons: *Alf* I 193,-ff.; Burton II 142. Chauvin VI 112-24 No. 277; *ANE* 430-34 No. 39;
Ḥammâd: Treacherous Bedouin: *Alf* II 20; Burton III 111. Chauvin VI 124 n. 1 No. 277; *ANE* 200 No. 43.□

P731.0.3.1§, ‡Bedouins (tribe) as raiders (bandits): they attack village, caravan, traveler, etc. to get booty. See: *DOTTI*.
Second Qalandar: Afrit's Wife: *Alf* I 43; Burton I 114. Chauvin V 197-200 No. 116; *ANE* 338-39 No. 16;
Barber's Sixth Brother: Emasculated by Abductor: *Alf* I 123; Burton I 347. Chauvin V 163-64 No. 86; *ANE* 120 No. 34;
King ¿Umar al-Nu¿mân and Sons: *Alf* II 14; Burton III 101. Chauvin VI 112-24 No. 277; *ANE* 430-34 No. 39;
¿Alâ' al-Dîn Abû al-Shâmât: *Alf* II 154; Burton IV 44. Chauvin V 43-49 No. 18; *ANE* 85-87 No. 63;
Mercury ¿Alî: *Alf* III 230; Burton VII 178. Chauvin V 248-50 No. 147; *ANE* 301-3 No. 225;
Jeweler's Wife and Qamar al-Zamân: *Alf* IV 244, 261; Burton IX 258, 293. Chauvin V 212-14 No. 121; *ANE* 345-47 No. 260;
Ma¿rûf the Cobbler: *Alf* IV 303,-(lie); Burton X 24,-(Arabs). Chauvin VI 81-82 No. 250; *ANE* 291-93 No. 262.□

P731.3.1§, ‡Nomad mocks (despises) sedentary (urban, rural) lifestyle (people). See: *PSAE*.
King ¿Umar al-Nu¿mân and Sons: *Alf* I 193-94; Burton II 142,-(city strumpet). Chauvin VI 112-24 No. 277; *ANE* 430-34 No. 39.□

P742.1§, ‡Elder sibling commands, younger obeys. (Cf. J155.9.2§, L41).
Shahriyâr and Shâhzamân: *Alf* I 2,-(brother/brother); Burton I 4. Chauvin V 188-91 No. 111; *ANE* 370-71 No. 1;
Nûr al-Dîn ¿Alî and Son: *Alf* I 64,-(brother/brother); Burton I 195. Chauvin VI 102-6 No. 270; *ANE* 317-19 No. 22.□

P750.0.1.0.1§, ‡Natural (prevailing) social order: high is high and low is low.
¿Alâ' al-Dîn Abû al-Shâmât: *Alf* II 169,-(lion-dog); Burton IV 74. Chauvin V 43-49 No. 18; *ANE* 85-87 No. 63.□

P751.1.1§, ‡Characteristic appearance of commoners (*al-¿awâm*, the lower social class).
¿Alî ibn Bakkâr: *Alf* II 61; Burton III 203,-(the common kind)1. Chauvin V 153 No. 76; *ANE* 92-93 No. 60.□

P750.0.1.1.1§, ‡The lowly may not aspire to acquire the noble's privileges (rights)'.
¿Alâ' al-Dîn Abû al-Shâmât: *Alf* II 169,-(dogs-lions); Burton IV 74. Chauvin V 43-49 No. 18; *ANE* 85-87 No. 63.□

P750.0.1.1.1.1§, ‡What is appropriate for the lion (master) is inappropriate for the dog (servant)'.
¿Alâ' al-Dîn Abû al-Shâmât: *Alf* II 165; Burton IV 65,-(what befitteth the lord befitteth not the thrall). Chauvin V 43-49 No. 18; *ANE* 85-87 No. 63.□

P750.0.3.1§, 'We all are children of Eve and Adam'.
Sindbâd and Porter: *Alf* III 82,-cf./(poem); Burton VI 2. Chauvin VII 1 No. 373; *ANE* 383-85 No. 179/pt.□

P751.3.0.1.1§, ‡Person (male) receiving western schooling addressed as "Effendi" (or by a similar title, e.g., "*bâsh-muhandis*"—'Master-engineer').
¿Alâ' al-Dîn Abû al-Shâmât: *Alf* II 157; Burton IV 53. Chauvin V 43-49 No. 18; *ANE* 85-87 No. 63.□

P752.1.1§, ‡'Folks follow (adopt) their kings's faith'. (Cf. V330.1§).
Nuzhat al-Zamân Tested/¿Umar al-Nu¿mân: *Alf* I 201,-(implicit); Burton II 157. Chauvin VI 116, n.1/passim No. 277; *ANE* 432,/passim No. 39.□

P752.2.1.1§, ‡Low rank brother demands that high rank brother honor him by paying him a visit.
Jawdar and His Treacherous Brethren: *Alf* III 200; Burton VI 255. Chauvin V 257-60 No. 154; *ANE* 244-45 No. 209;
¿Abdallah ibn Fâḍil: Treacherous Brothers: *Alf* IV 285; Burton IX 342. Chauvin V 2-4 No. 2; *ANE* 63-65 No. 261.□

P752.3.1§, ‡Guests of lower class not invited to home of (upper-class) 'host'. See: *DOTTI*.
Nûr al-Dîn and Maryam: *Alf* IV 102,-(*martabah*/social rank); Burton VIII 313,-(condition [!!]). Chauvin V 52-54 No. 271; *ANE* 98-99 No. 233.□

P752.5§, ‡Social class conflict (strife, struggle). See: *DOTTI*. (Cf. P152§, P795.0.4§).
Sindbâd and Porter: *Alf* III 81-83; Burton VI 1-3. Chauvin VII 1 No. 373; *ANE* 383-85 No. 179/pt.□

P753.0.1§, ‡Older person should "act his age". See: *DOTTI*. (Cf. J1848.3§, P249.3§).
Budûr and Jubayr ibn ¿Umayr: *Alf* II 236; Burton IV 232. Chauvin VII 93-94 No. 374; *ANE* 243-44 No. 83.□

P753.0.1.1§, ‡An elderly person rebuked for unseemly behavior (*"shayb-un wa ¿ayb-un"*/*'shâyib wi ¿âyib'*). See: *DOTTI*. (Cf. J126§).
¿Alâ' al-Dîn Abû al-Shâmât: *Alf* II 153; Burton IV 42-43. Chauvin V 43-49 No. 18; *ANE* 85-87 No. 63;
Budûr and Jubayr ibn ¿Umayr: *Alf* II 236; Burton IV 229. Chauvin VII 93-94 No. 374; *ANE* 243-44 No. 83.□

P753.1.1§, ‡Bearded men: notables. (Cf. J484.3§, U281.3.1§).
Bearded and Beardless Men as Lovers: *Alf* II 303,-cf.; Burton V 165. Chauvin V 112 No. 48; *ANE* 450 No. 154.□

P753.0.2§, ‡Social distance kept between members of age groups (men-boys, women-girls). (Cf. T380.1§).
¿Alâ' al-Dîn Abû al-Shâmât: *Alf* II 151,-(men-boys); Burton IV 38. Chauvin V 43-49 No. 18; *ANE* 85-87 No. 63.□

P753.0.2.1§, ‡Separate setting for juveniles (at eating, sleeping, etc.).
¿Alâ' al-Dîn Abû al-Shâmât: *Alf* II 151; Burton IV 38. Chauvin V 43-49 No. 18; *ANE* 85-87 No. 63.□

P760.0.2.1§, ‡'Properties of others are not unguarded'.
King ¿Umar al-Nu¿mân and Sons: *Alf* II 3,-(*sâ'ibah*); Burton III 78,-(like a scape-camel). Chauvin VI 112-24 No. 277; *ANE* 430-34 No. 39.□

P760.0.3§, ‡Wealth needs social power (governmental support).
Landsman ¿Abdallah and Merman ¿Abdallah: *Alf* IV 202; Burton IX 174. Chauvin V 6-7 No. 3; *ANE* 65-66 No. 256.□

P760.2.1§, ‡Public money (*al-mâl al-¿âm*, holdings of state treasury/"*bayt al-mâl*"). See: *DOTTI*. (Cf. P447§, W36.3§).

Nuzhat al-Zamân Tested/¿Umar al-Nu¿mân: *Alf* I 203, 206; Burton II 162, 170. Chauvin VI 116, n.1/passim No. 277; *ANE* 432,/passim No. 39.□

P760.2.1.2.2§, ‡Poor nation (king): treasury is empty.
Ma¿rûf the Cobbler: *Alf* IV 301; Burton X 21. Chauvin VI 81-82 No. 250; *ANE* 291-93 No. 262.□

P760.2.2.1§, ‡Hunting (fishing, etc.) on national reservation (king's park) forbidden. See: *DOTTI*. (Cf. U25.1§).
Anîs al-Jalîs: *Alf* I 140-41; Burton II 31. Chauvin V 120-24 No. 58; *ANE* 316-17 No. 35.□

P760.4§, Orphan's property. See: *DOTTI*.
Abû Muhammad Lazybones: *Alf* II 208; Burton IV 167. Chauvin VI 64-67 No. 233; *ANE* 71-73 No. 78.□

P760.4.1§, ‡Legal trustee (guardian) of orphan's property. See: *DOTTI*. (Cf. P500.0.2.1§).
Omar and Young Badawî: Returning to be Executed: *Alf* II 288; Burton V 102. Chauvin V 216 No. 125; *ANE* 429-30 No. 130.□

P760.5.2.1§, ‡Owner must mark property (be able to describe it).
Sindbâd's Third Voyage: *Alf* III 99; Burton VI 31-32. Chauvin VII 15-18 No. 373C; *ANE* 385-86 No. 179.□

P760.5.3.4.0.1.1§, ‡Ownership of a melody.
Ishâq al-Mûsilî and Merchant's Singer: *Alf* II 296; Burton V 130. Chauvin VI 59 No. 225; *ANE* 233 No. 142.□

P760.7.1§, ‡Cash preferred to real estate (live stock). See: *DOTTI*.
Abû Qîr and Abû Sîr: *Alf* IV 191; Burton IX 152. Chauvin V 15-17 No. 10; *ANE* 75-77 No. 255.□

P760.8.1.1§, ‡Attachment or garnishment of property. One party's possessions brought within the custody of the law in the interest of a second party, or immobilized when in possession of a third party). (Cf. P535.9.0.1§, Q490§, W38.1§).
Nûr al-Dîn ¿Alî and Son: *Alf* I 68; Burton I 209. Chauvin VI 102-6 No. 270; *ANE* 317-19 No. 22;
Abû Qîr and Abû Sîr: *Alf* IV 183,-cf.; Burton IX 137. Chauvin V 15-17 No. 10; *ANE* 75-77 No. 255.□

P760.9.1§, ‡Joint ownership (partnership). See: *DOTTI*. (Cf. K2296).
Qamar al-Zamân and Budûr: *Alf* II 106; Burton III 295. Chauvin V 204-12 No. 120; *ANE* 341-45 No. 61.□

P760.9.1.2§, ‡"Divider (*qassâm*)": legal umpire who divides shared property (inheritance) among disputants.
Jawdar and His Treacherous Brethren: *Alf* III 178; Burton VI 214. Chauvin V 257-60 No. 154; *ANE* 244-45 No. 209;
¿Abdallah ibn Fâdil: Treacherous Brothers: *Alf* IV 270; Burton IX 312, 314,-(departitor). Chauvin V 2-4 No. 2; *ANE* 63-65 No. 261.□

P760.9.1.3§, ‡Division of treasure trove between land owner and finder. (Cf. J1241).
Qamar al-Zamân and Budûr: *Alf* II 106; Burton III 295. Chauvin V 204-12 No. 120; *ANE* 341-45 No. 61.□

P761§, Inheritance. See: *DOTTI*; *PSAE*. (Cf. P173.9.5§, P527§, T52.0.8§).
Eldest Lady's Story: Treacherous Sisters: *Alf* I 53,-(from father); Burton I 162. Chauvin V 4 No. 443; *ANE* 174-75 No. 19;
Portress Amînah: Bitten Cheek: *Alf* I 57,-(from father); Burton I 174. Chauvin V 98-99 No. 33; *ANE* 326-27 No. 20.□

P761.0.2.1§, ‡A male inherits twice the share of a female. (Cf. P529§).
Dispute Concerning Males and Females: *Alf* II 300; Burton V 155-56. Chauvin VI 153 No. 317; *ANE* 291 No. 151.□

P761.0.4§, ‡When there is no heir, inheritance (estate) goes to state treasury. See: *DOTTI*.
Barber's Sixth Brother: Emasculated by Abductor: *Alf* I 123; Burton I 347. Chauvin V 163-64 No. 86; *ANE* 120 No. 34;
First Eunuch: Bukhayt Deflowers Mistress: *Alf* I 148,-(*bayt al-mâl*); Burton II 50,-(Royal Treasury/property of an intestate). Chauvin V 278 No. 161; *ANE* 178 No. 37;

¿Alâ' al-Dîn Abû al-Shâmât: *Alf* II 163,-(implicit); Burton IV 62. Chauvin V 43-49 No. 18; *ANE* 85-87 No. 63.□

P761.1§, Division of inheritance causes conflict. See: *DOTTI*; *GMC*.
Jawdar and His Treacherous Brethren: *Alf* III 177-78; Burton VI 213-14. Chauvin V 257-60 No. 154; *ANE* 244-45 No. 209;
Hasan of Basrah: *Alf* IV 42-43; Burton VIII 121. Chauvin VII 29-35 No. 212A; *ANE* 207-10 No. 230;
¿Abdallah ibn Fâḍil: Treacherous Brothers: *Alf* IV 270; Burton IX 312. Chauvin V 2-4 No. 2; *ANE* 63-65 No. 261.□

P761.1.1§, ‡Right of legitimate heir usurped—(usually by powerful relative). See: *DOTTI*.
King ¿Umar al-Nu¿mân and Sons: *Alf* I 311,-ff./(implicit/by regent); Burton III 55. Chauvin VI 112-24 No. 277; *ANE* 430-34 No. 39.□

P761.2§, ‡Inheritance as means of acquiring wealth. See: *DOTTI*. (Cf. P559.1.3§, W131.1).
¿Alâ' al-Dîn Abû al-Shâmât: *Alf* II 163,-cf./(estate of deceased bestowed); Burton IV 61-62. Chauvin V 43-49 No. 18; *ANE* 85-87 No. 63;
¿Alî Shâr and Zumurrud: *Alf* II 218; Burton IV 192. Chauvin V 89-91 No. 28; *ANE* 100-1 No. 82;
Budûr and Jubayr ibn ¿Umayr: *Alf* II 237,-(daughter inherits father's wealth); Burton IV 233. Chauvin VII 93-94 No. 374; *ANE* 243-44 No. 83;
Sindbâd's Seventh Voyage: *Alf* III 119,-(from father-in-law); Burton VI 74. Chauvin VII 26-29 No. 373G; *ANE* 386-87 No. 179.□

P761.2.1§, ‡Rich heir. See: *DOTTI*. (Cf. W131.1).
Mock Caliph/¿Alî al-Jawharî: *Alf* II 196; Burton IV 139-40148. Chauvin V 99-100 No. 174; *ANE* 304-5 No. 73;
Sindbâd's First Voyage: *Alf* III 83; Burton VI 4. Chauvin VII 7-9 No. 373A; *ANE* 385 No. 179;
Abû al-Ḥasan al-Khorâsânî (and Caliph's Favorite): *Alf* IV 230; Burton IX 233. Chauvin V 218-20 No. 129; *ANE* 68-69 No. 259.□

P761.2.2§, ‡Rich heiress. See: *DOTTI*. (Cf. P431.0.1§, T68).
Portress Amînah: Bitten Cheek: *Alf* I 57; Burton I 173. Chauvin V 98-99 No. 33; *ANE* 326-27 No. 20;
Copt Broker's Story: Lover's Sacrifices Repaid: *Alf* I 91; Burton I 267. Chauvin VI 80 No. 249; *ANE* 313-14 No. 24.□

P761.3.1§, ‡Heir repays inherited debt—(usually father's debt). See: *DOTTI*.
Reeve's Story: Why Maimed by Bride: *Alf* I 96; Burton I 279. Chauvin V 220-21 No. 305; *ANE* 351 No. 25;
¿Abdallah ibn Fâḍil: Treacherous Brothers: *Alf* IV 270,-cf.; Burton IX 311. Chauvin V 2-4 No. 2; *ANE* 63-65 No. 261.□

P761.4.1§, ‡Brothers insist on dividing inheritance and going separate ways.
Hasan of Basrah: *Alf* IV 42-43; Burton VIII 120-21. Chauvin VII 29-35 No. 212A; *ANE* 207-10 No. 230;
¿Abdallah ibn Fâḍil: Treacherous Brothers: *Alf* IV 270; Burton IX 312. Chauvin V 2-4 No. 2; *ANE* 63-65 No. 261.□

P763§, Ill-gotten (illicit) property (*mâl ḥarâm*). See: *DOTTI*; *GMC*.
Spy, Old Woman/¿Umar al-Nu¿mân: *Alf* I 225,-cf./(stipend/*mâl ḥalâl*); Burton II 209-10,-("lawful"). *ANE* 432 No. 39/passim.□

P767.1.1§, ‡Ruler (government) confiscates private property.
Abû Qîr and Abû Ṣîr: *Alf* IV 187,-(building to be destroyed and land site/seized); Burton IX 144. Chauvin V 15-17 No. 10; *ANE* 75-77 No. 255.□

P770§, ‡Markets: buying, selling, trading. See: *DOTTI*; *PSAE*.
Sandal-wood Merchant and Sharpers: *Alf* III 174; Burton VI 202-3. Chauvin VIII 60-62 No. 26; *ANE* 359-60 No. 205.□

P770.0.1§, ‡'Market's *shaikh*' (head of chamber of commerce, syndic). (Cf. P406§).
Copt Broker's Story: Lover's Sacrifices Repaid: *Alf* I 92,-(*naqîb*); Burton I 269,-(Syndic of travel). Chauvin VI 80 No. 249; *ANE* 313-14 No. 24;
Jewish Doctor's Story: Sororicide: *Alf* I 101; Burton I 296,-(Syndic of bazaar). Chauvin VI 89 No. 253; *ANE* 242 No. 26;

Ghânim ibn Ayyûb: *Alf* I 158-59; Burton II 70. Chauvin VI 14 No. 188; *ANE* 192-93 No. 36;
Tâj al-Mulûk: *Alf* I 292; Burton III 15,-(Overseer of the market). Chauvin V 126-28 No. 60; *ANE* 406-8 No. 40;
¿Alâ' al-Dîn Abû al-Shâmât: *Alf* II 147,-(*shâhbandar*); Burton IV 29,-(Consul). Chauvin V 43-49 No. 18; *ANE* 85-87 No. 63;
Landsman ¿Abdallah and Merman ¿Abdallah: *Alf* IV 201; Burton IX 173,-(syndic). Chauvin V 6-7 No. 3; *ANE* 65-66 No. 256.□

P770.0.1.1§, ‡Syndic (shaikh) of a certain profession or trade.
King ¿Umar al-Nu¿mân and Sons: *Alf* I 309,-(appointment as reward); Burton III 50. Chauvin VI 112-24 No. 277; *ANE* 430-34 No. 39.□

P770.0.2§, ‡Bill of sale (contract).
Nûr al-Dîn ¿Alî and Son: *Alf* I 69; Burton I 211. Chauvin VI 102-6 No. 270; *ANE* 317-19 No. 22.□

P771.1§, ‡Goods exchanged. See: *DOTTI*; *PSAE*. (Cf. J708.5§, T142§).
Sindbâd's Fifth Voyage: *Alf* III 111; Burton VI 57. Chauvin VII 21-24 No. 373E; *ANE* 386 No. 179.□

P771.1.3§, ‡Fruits (vegetables) exchanged for riches (precious stones). See: *DOTTI*.
Landsman ¿Abdallah and Merman ¿Abdallah: *Alf* IV 200; Burton IX 170. Chauvin V 6-7 No. 3; *ANE* 65-66 No. 256.□

P771.1.4.1§, ‡Bread for fisher's catch (fish).
Landsman ¿Abdallah and Merman ¿Abdallah: *Alf* IV 198; Burton IX 167. Chauvin V 6-7 No. 3; *ANE* 65-66 No. 256.□

P771.2.1§, ‡Marriage for service. (Cf. P771.3§).
Isḥâq al-Mûṣilî and Merchant's Singer: *Alf* II 297,-cf./(slave-girl); Burton V 132-33. Chauvin VI 59 No. 225; *ANE* 233 No. 142.□

P771.3§, ‡Goods for services. See: *DOTTI*. (Cf. P771.2.1§, T52.0.3§).
Sindbâd's Third Voyage: *Alf* III 97; Burton VI 29. Chauvin VII 15-18 No. 373C; *ANE* 385-86 No. 179.□

P771.3.1§, ‡Food for a service (e.g., ear of corn for a shave, an egg for knife sharpening, and the like). See: *DOTTI*; *PSAE*.
Abû Qîr and Abû Ṣîr: *Alf* IV 184-85; Burton IX 139. Chauvin V 15-17 No. 10; *ANE* 75-77 No. 255.□

P771.3.5§, ‡Hireling works for subsistence (food, lodging, etc.).
Jawdar and His Treacherous Brethren: *Alf* III 194; Burton VI 242. Chauvin V 257-60 No. 154; *ANE* 244-45 No. 209;
Ruined Baghdadi and His Slave-girl: *Alf* IV 133,-cf.; Burton IX 30. Chauvin V 152-53 No. 75; *ANE* 353 No. 235.□

P772.1§, ‡Merchant motivated by expectancy of profit.
Second Shaykh: Treacherous Brothers: *Alf* I 11; Burton I 32. Chauvin V 6 No. 397; *ANE* 377-78 No. 6;
Sindbâd's Fifth Voyage: *Alf* III 111; Burton VI 55. Chauvin VII 21-24 No. 373E; *ANE* 386 No. 179;

Abû al-Ḥasan al-Khorâsânî (and Caliph's Favorite): *Alf* IV 233; Burton IX 237. Chauvin V 218-20 No. 129; *ANE* 68-69 No. 259;
Ma¿rûf the Cobbler: *Alf* IV 309; Burton X 36. Chauvin VI 81-82 No. 250; *ANE* 291-93 No. 262.□

P772.1.1§, ‡Successful business: income surpasses expenditure.
Ruined Baghdadi and His Slave-girl: *Alf* IV 133; Burton IX 30. Chauvin V 152-53 No. 75; *ANE* 353 No. 235.□

P772.1.2§, ‡Merchant travels in search of profit (wealth). See: *DOTTI*. (Cf. P774.0.1§).
¿Alâ' al-Dîn Abû al-Shâmât: *Alf* II 151; Burton IV 39. Chauvin V 43-49 No. 18; *ANE* 85-87 No. 63;
Sindbâd and Porter: *Alf* III 83; Burton VI 4. Chauvin VII 7 No. 373; *ANE* 383-85 No. 179/pt.;
Nûr al-Dîn and Maryam: *Alf* IV 90; Burton VIII 264. Chauvin V 52-54 No. 271; *ANE* 98-99 No. 233;
Abû Qîr and Abû Ṣîr: *Alf* IV 184; Burton IX 138. Chauvin V 15-17 No. 10; *ANE* 75-77 No. 255.□

P772.4§, ‡Merchant's assistant (store hand) must get approval before selling costly items. (Cf. P431.4.1§).
¿Alâ' al-Dîn Abû al-Shâmât: *Alf* II 149; Burton IV 35. Chauvin V 43-49 No. 18; *ANE* 85-87 No. 63.□

P773§, ‡Publication of availability of goods or services (commercial advertisement). See: *DOTTI*.
Jânshâh: *Alf* III 47; Burton V 340. Chauvin VII 39-44 No. 153; *ANE* 238-41 No. 178;
Sindbâd's Seventh Voyage: *Alf* III 119,-(sandal wood); Burton VI 73. Chauvin VII 26-29 No. 373G; *ANE* 386-87 No. 179.□

P773.2§, ‡Advertisement: free services, reduced prices (or the like) at opening of new business. See: *DOTTI*.
Island King/Pious Jewish Merchant: *Alf* III 17; Burton V 291. Chauvin VI 161 No. 325; *ANE* 234 No. 174;
Abû Qîr and Abû Ṣîr: *Alf* IV 190; Burton IX 152. Chauvin V 15-17 No. 10; *ANE* 75-77 No. 255.□

P774.0.1§, ‡Goods or services marketed where they are unknown or scarce bring high prices (profit). (The capitalist ethic). (Cf. P772.1.2§, U86§, U249§).
Sindbâd and Porter: *Alf* III 83; Burton VI 4. Chauvin VII 1 No. 373; *ANE* 383-85 No. 179/pt.;
¿Abdallah ibn Fâḍil: Treacherous Brothers: *Alf* IV 271; Burton IX 313. Chauvin V 2-4 No. 2; *ANE* 63-65 No. 261.□

P774.0.2.1§, ‡'Figs (expensive) are for a few, sycamore fruits (cheap) are for many'. (Cf. U60.1§).
Qamar al-Zamân and Budûr: *Alf* II 109,-(poem); Burton III 302. Chauvin V 204-12 No. 120; *ANE* 341-45 No. 61.□

P774.1§, ‡Bargaining. See: *DOTTI*. (Cf. P431.2§).
King ¿Umar al-Nu¿mân and Sons: *Alf* I 194-97; Burton II 144-49. Chauvin VI 112-24 No. 277; *ANE* 430-34 No. 39.□

P774.1.2§, ‡Formulaic bargaining.
Ibrâhîm and Jamîlah: *Alf* IV 219,-cf.; Burton IX 207-8. Chauvin VI 52-53 No. 218; *ANE* 227-29 No. 258.□

P774.1.2.5§, ‡Seller: "How much would you pay?" Buyer: "'Only a father may name his child [(you cite your price)]'".
King ¿Umar al-Nu¿mân and Sons: *Alf* I 195; Burton II 146,-(none should name the son save his sire). Chauvin VI 112-24 No. 277; *ANE* 430-34 No. 39.□

P774.1.3§, ‡Price paid for an item viewed as whether one has emerged 'vanquished' or 'victor'. See: *DOTTI*.
Jeweler's Wife and Qamar al-Zamân: *Alf* IV 252,-(*ghâlib aw maghlûb?*); Burton IX 275,-("the worst or the best of the bargain"). Chauvin V 212-14 No. 121; *ANE* 345-47 No. 260.□

P774.2.0.1§, ‡High price drives away customer (buyer). (Cf. T52.0.2§).
Nûr al-Dîn ¿Alî and Son: *Alf* I 65,-cf./(*mahr*); Burton I 196. Chauvin VI 102-6 No. 270; *ANE* 317-19 No. 22.□

P774.2.0.2§, ‡Price-gouging: exorbitant price demanded for common commodity (e.g., food, clothing, fuel, etc.). See: *DOTTI*. (Cf. C787.3§).
¿Abdallah ibn Fâḍil: Treacherous Brothers: *Alf* IV 271,-(textile); Burton IX 313. Chauvin V 2-4 No. 2; *ANE* 63-65 No. 261.□

P774.2.1§, ‡Inflation: much money, few goods (thus, high prices). See: *DOTTI*. (Cf. P774.4.2§, U85§).
Jawdar and His Treacherous Brethren: *Alf* III 179; Burton VI 215. Chauvin V 257-60 No. 154; *ANE* 244-45 No. 209;
Landsman ¿Abdallah and Merman ¿Abdallah: *Alf* IV 198; Burton IX 166. Chauvin V 6-7 No. 3; *ANE* 65-66 No. 256.□

P774.2.1.1§, ‡Scarcity of goods causes merchant (baker, butcher, etc.) to ignore payers of cash (customers with money in hand).
Landsman ¿Abdallah and Merman ¿Abdallah: *Alf* IV 198; Burton IX 166. Chauvin V 6-7 No. 3; *ANE* 65-66 No. 256.□

P774.2.2§, ‡Government-subsidized prices. Ruler (king) pays portion of cost of necessities.

Abû Qîr and Abû Ṣîr: *Alf* IV 190,-(bathhouse); Burton IX 151. Chauvin V 15-17 No. 10; *ANE* 75-77 No. 255.□

P774.2.3.1§, ‡High wages for dangerous assignment (job). (Cf. J149§).
Jânshâh: *Alf* III 47, 64; Burton V 340. Chauvin VII 39-44 No. 153; *ANE* 238-41 No. 178.□

P774.2.5.1§, ‡High price for the unique ("collector's object").
¿Alî Shâr and Zumurrud: *Alf* II 220,-(had-made curtain/embroidery); Burton IV 196. Chauvin V 89-91 No. 28; *ANE* 100-1 No. 82;
Nûr al-Dîn and Maryam: *Alf* IV 97-98, 100,-(had-made girdle/cummerbund); Burton VIII 306, 310. Chauvin V 52-54 No. 271; *ANE* 98-99 No. 233.□

P774.2.5.2.2§, ‡Exorbitant (unbelievable) price for rare colt (horse). (Cf. B184.1.3.1§).
Sindbâd's First Voyage: *Alf* III 85; Burton VI 8,-(mint of money). Chauvin VII 7-9 No. 373A; *ANE* 385 No. 179.□

P774.3§, ‡Auction: selling to highest bidder. See: *DOTTI*. (Cf. P180.8.5§).
¿Alâ' al-Dîn Abû al-Shâmât: *Alf* II 165; Burton IV 67. Chauvin V 43-49 No. 18; *ANE* 85-87 No. 63;
Hasan of Basrah: *Alf* III 303; Burton VIII 10. Chauvin VII 29-35 No. 212A; *ANE* 207-10 No. 230.□

P774.3.1§, ‡Winner of bidding must honor his bid.
Nûr al-Dîn and Maryam: *Alf* IV 95,-(curse on reneger); Burton VIII 300. Chauvin V 52-54 No. 271; *ANE* 98-99 No. 233.□

P774.4§, ‡Low prices ('a bargain'). (Cf. M117.2.1§, W151.0.2§).
¿Alî Shâr and Zumurrud: *Alf* II 220; Burton IV 197. Chauvin V 89-91 No. 28; *ANE* 100-1 No. 82.□

P774.4.1§, ‡Sale of goods for less than market value signifies defect (problem).
Jewish Doctor's Story: Sororicide: *Alf* I 101; Burton I 296. Chauvin VI 89 No. 253; *ANE* 242 No. 26;
Thief and His Monkey: *Alf* II 40; Burton III 159. Chauvin II 229 No. 18; *ANE* 413 No. 57.□

P774.4.1.1§, ‡Article sold cheaply because stolen.
Jewish Doctor's Story: Sororicide: *Alf* I 101,-cf.; Burton I 296. Chauvin VI 89 No. 253; *ANE* 242 No. 26;
Thief and His Monkey: *Alf* II 40; Burton III 159. Chauvin II 229 No. 18; *ANE* 413 No. 57.□

P774.4.1.2§, ‡Article sold cheaply because useless (defective).
Thief and His Monkey: *Alf* II 40; Burton III 159. Chauvin II 229 No. 18; *ANE* 413 No. 57.□

P774.4.1.2.1§, ‡Bread sold cheaply because made from flour used for abscess plaster. (Cf. N383.2).
Miser and Cheap Loaves of Bread: *Alf* III 142; Burton VI 137. Chauvin VIII 38 No. 6; *ANE* 303-4 No. 186.□

P774.4.2§, ‡Low (depressed) prices because of abundant supplies (of goods, services). (Cf. P603.1§, P774.2.1§).
Nûr al-Dîn and Maryam: *Alf* IV 96,-(Frank slaves,/two hundred dinars); Burton VIII 302,-(one hundred dinars). Chauvin V 52-54 No. 271; *ANE* 98-99 No. 233.□

P774.4.1.3.1§, ‡Slave-girl sold cheaply because of her desire to be with certain master. (Cf. T52.0.6.1.2§).
¿Alî Shâr and Zumurrud: *Alf* II 220; Burton IV 197. Chauvin V 89-91 No. 28; *ANE* 100-1 No. 82.□

P774.4.1.2.5.1§, ‡Rent of house is very low because it is haunted (or the like). (Cf. N122.1.3.1§).
House with the Belvedere: *Alf* III 167; Burton VI 190. Chauvin VIII 57-58 No. 23; *ANE* 223 No. 203.□

P774.4.2.1§, ‡Supply and demand control prices.
Tawaddud: Slavegirl Sold and Regained: *Alf* III 2-3,-(implicit/seasonal produce); Burton V 231-32. Chauvin VII 117-19 No. 387; *ANE* 408-10 No. 157.□

P774.4.2.1.1§, ‡Price of produce dependent on season.
Tawaddud: Slavegirl Sold and Regained: *Alf* III 2-3; Burton V 231-32. Chauvin VII 117-19 No. 387; *ANE* 408-10 No. 157.□

P774.4.2.2§, ‡Merchant holds commodity out of market until price rises. (Cf. P.603.1§).
Sindbâd's Seventh Voyage: *Alf* III 119; Burton VI 73-74. Chauvin VII 26-29 No. 373G; *ANE* 386-87 No. 179.□

P774.4.3§, ‡Article sold cheaply because buyer is poor (needy). See: *DOTTI.*
Abû Qîr and Abû Ṣîr: *Alf* IV 190,-(bathing); Burton IX 150. Chauvin V 15-17 No. 10; *ANE* 75-77 No. 255;
al-Rashîd and Omani Merchant: *Alf* IV 215,-(jewels); Burton IX 201. Chauvin VI 111-12 No. 276; *ANE* 201-2 No. 257.□

P774.7§, ‡Goods should be examined ('present') before paying for them. (Cf. P526.5§).
Thief and His Monkey: *Alf* II 40; Burton III 159. Chauvin II 229 No. 18; *ANE* 413 No. 57.□

P774.7.1§, ‡Sales are final (no returning of merchandise allowed).
Jullanâr of the Sea: *Alf* III 269; Burton VII 305. Chauvin V 147-51 No. 73; *ANE* 248-51 No. 227.□

P774.8.2.1.1§, ‡Slave-girl (wife) sold subject to owner (husband) being able to withstand her absence. See: *DOTTI.*
Man from Yaman and Six Salve-girls: Flyting: *Alf* II 249,-cf.; Burton IV 250. Chauvin VI 151 No. 313; *ANE* 289-90 No. 84.□

P774.9.2§, ‡Unnamed prices. Goods or services offered without specifying price.
Abû Qîr and Abû Ṣîr: *Alf* IV 190; Burton IX 150. Chauvin V 15-17 No. 10; *ANE* 75-77 No. 255.□

P774.9.2.1§, ‡Buyer pays whatever he can afford.
Abû Qîr and Abû Ṣîr: *Alf* IV 190; Burton IX 150. Chauvin V 15-17 No. 10; *ANE* 75-77 No. 255.□

P775.0.1.1§, ‡Fish as medium of exchange (unit of value). See: *DOTTI.*
Landsman ¿Abdallah and Merman ¿Abdallah: *Alf* IV 205; Burton IX 183. Chauvin V 6-7 No. 3; *ANE* 65-66 No. 256.□

P775.2§, ‡Sharing, reciprocity, and voluntary redistribution of wealth. (Cf. J1514§, P320, V3.3§, V400).
Sindbâd's Second Voyage: *Alf* III 92; Burton VI 22,-("gave alms and largesse"). Chauvin VII 24 No. 373F; *ANE* 386 No. 179;
Sindbâd's Fourth Voyage: *Alf* III 106; Burton VI 47. Chauvin VII 24 No. 373F; *ANE* 386 No. 179;
Sindbâd's Sixth Voyage: *Alf* III 112; Burton VI 68. Chauvin VII 24-27 No. 373F; *ANE* 386 No. 179;

¿Abdallah ibn Fâḍil: Treacherous Brothers: *Alf* IV 271; Burton IX 314. Chauvin V 2-4 No. 2; *ANE* 63-65 No. 261.□

P775.2.0.3.1§, ‡Fineries as gift (e.g., cloth, garment, jewelry, or the like).
Hasan of Basrah: *Alf* IV 8,-(*tuḥaf*); Burton VIII 53,-(rarities). Chauvin VII 29-35 No. 212A; *ANE* 207-10 No. 230.□

P775.2.1.1§, ‡Gratuity given (demanded) at occurrence of happy event ("*ḥalâwah*/*ḥulwân* of" graduation, safe return, birth of child, etc.). (Cf. V400).
Tailor's Story/Barber of Baghdad: *Alf* I 104,-(*bishârah*); Burton I 306,-("gift of good news"). Chauvin V 154-56 No. 78; *ANE* 405-6 No. 27;
King ¿Umar al-Nu¿mân and Sons: *Alf* I 215; Burton II 188. Chauvin VI 112-24 No. 277; *ANE* 430-34 No. 39;
¿Alâ' al-Dîn Abû al-Shâmât: *Alf* II 162,-(*ḥalâwit al-salâmah*/musical performance/for being safe), 177; Burton IV 60,-(house-warming for thy deliverance), 88,-(thank-offering). Chauvin V 43-49 No. 18; *ANE* 85-87 No. 63;
Sindbâd's Second Voyage: *Alf* III 92; Burton VI 22. Chauvin VII 9-14 No. 373B; *ANE* 385 No. 179;
Sindbâd's Third Voyage: *Alf* III 99; Burton VI 34. Chauvin VII 15-18 No. 373C; *ANE* 385-86 No. 179;
Sindbâd's Fourth Voyage: *Alf* III 106; Burton VI 47. Chauvin VII 18-20 No. 373D; *ANE* 386 No. 179;
Sindbâd's Fifth Voyage: *Alf* III 112; Burton VI 57. Chauvin VII 21-24 No. 373E; *ANE* 386 No. 179;
Sindbâd's Sixth Voyage: *Alf* III 116; Burton VI 68. Chauvin VII 24-27 No. 373F; *ANE* 386 No. 179; **Nûr al-Dîn and Maryam**: *Alf* IV 109,-cf.; Burton VIII 325,-(douceur of thank-offering for deliverance). Chauvin V 52-54 No. 271; *ANE* 98-99 No. 233;
Ibrâhîm and Jamîlah: *Alf* IV 221,-(*ḥulwân*/tip for key to *khân*-room); Burton IX 212,-("key-money"). Chauvin VI 52-53 No. 218; *ANE* 227-29 No. 258.□

P775.2.1.2§, ‡Gratuity given (demanded) for delivering (being bearer of) good news (*bishârah*). (Cf. Q70§).

First Shaykh: Sorceress Wife: *Alf* I 10; Burton I 31. Chauvin VII 129-30 No. 396; *ANE* 376-77 No. 5;
Fisherman and Afrit: Ingratitude: *Alf* I 15; Burton I 41. Chauvin VI 23-25 No. 195; *ANE* 183-84 No. 8;
Jânshâh: *Alf* III 56; Burton V 354. Chauvin VII 39-44 No. 153; *ANE* 238-41 No. 178;
Hind bint al-Nu¿mân and al-Ḥajjâj: *Alf* III 202; Burton VII 97,-(reward for the glad tidings). Chauvin V 115-4 No. 50; *ANE* 221-22 No. 212.□

P775.2.2§, ‡Grant given for the purpose of advancing human knowledge (in the arts, sciences, personal improvement through education, etc.). (Cf. J149§, V401§, W11.0.1§).
Ibn Sabâ'ik/Sayf al-Mulûk: *Alf* III 271,-(story); Burton VII 309-10. Chauvin VII 65 No. 348/pt.; *ANE* 309-10 No. 228.□

P775.2.2.1§, ‡Grant for one full year ('Sabbatical') to produce unique work of art. (Cf. H1182).
Ibn Sabâ'ik/Sayf al-Mulûk: *Alf* III 271,-(story); Burton VII 309-10. Chauvin VII 65 No. 348/pt.; *ANE* 309-10 No. 228.□

P775.4§, ‡Necessity for investment: money that is not invested (added to) is inevitably exhausted. (Cf. J1014§, P31).
Abû al-Ḥasan al-Khorâsânî (and Caliph's Favorite): *Alf* IV 230-31,-(implicit); Burton IX 234. Chauvin V 218-20 No. 129; *ANE* 68-69 No. 259.□

P776§, ‡Credit (financial), banking, and trusteeship. (Cf. J1381.1§, J1385§, W38.1§).
Copt Broker's Story: Lover's Sacrifices Repaid: *Alf* I 88-89; Burton I 262. Chauvin VI 80 No. 249; *ANE* 313-14 No. 24.□

P776.0.1§, ‡Sale on credit: goods (services delivered, payment to be made later)—(lit.: '*shukuk*'/'doubt').
Copt Broker's Story: Lover's Sacrifices Repaid: *Alf* I 89-91; Burton I 266. Chauvin VI 80 No. 249; *ANE* 313-14 No. 24.□

P776.1.1§, ‡Person of good reputation given credit by merchants (bankers). See: *DOTTI*.
Jawdar and His Treacherous Brethren: *Alf* III 179; Burton VI 215. Chauvin V 257-60 No. 154; *ANE* 244-45 No. 209;
Landsman ¿Abdallah and Merman ¿Abdallah: *Alf* IV 198; Burton IX 166. Chauvin V 6-7 No. 3; *ANE* 65-66 No. 256;
Ma¿rûf the Cobbler: *Alf* IV 289-90; Burton X 2. Chauvin VI 81-82 No. 250; *ANE* 291-93 No. 262.□

P776.1.2.1§, ‡Beautiful woman given credit by merchant (banker). See: *DOTTI*. (Cf. F575.1.6.5.1§, K712.1§, K1226§).
Reeve's Story: Why Maimed by Bride: *Alf* I 97; Burton I 281. Chauvin V 220-21 No. 305; *ANE* 351 No. 25;
Abû al-Ḥasan al-Khorâsânî (and Caliph's Favorite): *Alf* IV 231-32; Burton IX 234. Chauvin V 218-20 No. 129; *ANE* 68-69 No. 259.□

P776.4§, ‡Living beyond one's means (on borrowed funds). See: *DOTTI*. (Cf. J1385§, K249.5§).
Nûr al-Dîn and Maryam: *Alf* IV 96-97,-(expensive slave-girl); Burton VIII 302. Chauvin V 52-54 No. 271; *ANE* 98-99 No. 233;
Ma¿rûf the Cobbler: *Alf* IV 296; Burton X 13-14. Chauvin VI 81-82 No. 250; *ANE* 291-93 No. 262.□

P776.5.1§, ‡Goods (tools) pawned so as to obtain cash (credit). See: *DOTTI*. (Cf. P777.2§).
Abû Qîr and Abû Ṣîr: *Alf* IV 183,-cf./(sold); Burton IX 134-35. Chauvin V 15-17 No. 10; *ANE* 75-77 No. 255;
Landsman ¿Abdallah and Merman ¿Abdallah: *Alf* IV 198; Burton IX 166. Chauvin V 6-7 No. 3; *ANE* 65-66 No. 256;
Ma¿rûf the Cobbler: *Alf* IV 291,-cf.; Burton X 5. Chauvin VI 81-82 No. 250; *ANE* 291-93 No. 262.□

P777§, ‡Raising a capital (for investment). See: *DOTTI*.
Sindbâd's First Voyage: *Alf* III 83; Burton VI 5. Chauvin VII 7-9 No. 373A; *ANE* 385 No. 179.□

P777.2§, ‡Selling (mortgaging) own property so as to raise capital. See: *DOTTI*. (Cf. P776.5.1§).
Sindbâd's First Voyage: *Alf* III 83-84; Burton VI 5. Chauvin VII 7-9 No. 373A; *ANE* 385 No. 179;
al-Rashîd and Omani Merchant: *Alf* IV 211; Burton IX 193. Chauvin VI 111-12 No. 276; *ANE* 201-2 No. 257.□

P778§, ‡Bankruptcy. See: *DOTTI*.
Dalîla the Swindler: *Alf* III 218; Burton VII 154. Chauvin V 245-50 No. 147; *ANE* 163-64 No. 224.□

P778.0.1§, ‡Publication (declaration) of bankruptcy.
Dalîla the Swindler: *Alf* III 218; Burton VII 154. Chauvin V 245-50 No. 147; *ANE* 163-64 No. 224.□

P778.1§, ‡Merchant loses all capital (goods) and becomes bankrupt. (Cf. N211.4§).
Sindbâd's Third Voyage: *Alf* III 98-99; Burton VI 30-31. Chauvin VII 15-18 No. 373C; *ANE* 385-86 No. 179;
¿Abdallah ibn Fâḍil: Treacherous Brothers: *Alf* IV 271; Burton IX 314. Chauvin V 2-4 No. 2; *ANE* 63-65 No. 261.□

P778.2§, ‡Legal seizure (impoundment) of remaining possessions of bankrupt person. See: *DOTTI*.
Abû Qîr and Abû Ṣîr: *Alf* IV 183; Burton IX 137. Chauvin V 15-17 No. 10; *ANE* 75-77 No. 255.□

P779.1.0.1§, ‡Transfer of technology (know-how): introducing an industry and accompaniments to country (region) where it is unknown.
Sindbâd's Fourth Voyage: *Alf* III 102; Burton VI 39. Chauvin VII 18-20 No. 373D; *ANE* 386 No. 179.□

P779.1.2§, ‡Imported fine weapons (sword, spear, etc.).
King ¿Umar al-Nu¿mân and Sons: *Alf* I 255,-(Indian sword); Burton II 269. Chauvin VI 112-24 No. 277; *ANE* 430-34 No. 39;
City of Brass: *Alf* III 134; Burton VI 113. Chauvin V 32-35 No. 16; *ANE* 146-50 No. 180.□

P779.1.3.1§, ‡Imported fine musical instruments.
King ¿Umar al-Nu¿mân and Sons: *Alf* I 171; Burton II 100. Chauvin VI 112-24 No. 277; *ANE* 430-34 No. 39;
¿Alâ' al-Dîn Abû al-Shâmât: *Alf* II 156,-(lute); Burton IV 50. Chauvin V 43-49 No. 18; *ANE* 85-87 No. 63;
Mock Caliph/¿Alî al-Jawharî: *Alf* II 193,-(lute); Burton IV 135,-(of Hindu make). Chauvin V 99-100 No. 174; *ANE* 304-5 No. 73;
Budûr and Jubayr ibn ¿Umayr: *Alf* II 238; Burton IV 237,-(Hindu lute). Chauvin VII 93-94 No. 374; *ANE* 243-44 No. 83;
Nûr al-Dîn and Maryam: *Alf* IV 85,-(lute/India); Burton VIII 281. Chauvin V 52-54 No. 271; *ANE* 98-99 No. 233.□

P779.1.5§, ‡Imported raw materials (wood, metal, etc.). See: *PSAE*.
¿Abdallah ibn Fâḍil: Treacherous Brothers: *Alf* IV 273,-(Chinese iron); Burton IX 318. Chauvin V 2-4 No. 2; *ANE* 63-65 No. 261.□

P779.2§, ‡Monopoly: commodity or service available through one source (agency) only. See: *DOTTI*.
¿Alâ' al-Dîn Abû al-Shâmât: *Alf* II 149,-(all cloth imports and exports must pass through his hands); Burton IV 35. Chauvin V 43-49 No. 18; *ANE* 85-87 No. 63;
Abû Qîr and Abû Ṣîr: *Alf* IV 186-87,-(clothes-dying); Burton IX 145. Chauvin V 15-17 No. 10; *ANE* 75-77 No. 255.□

P780§, Shameful (disgraceful) acts. See: *DOTTI*; *GMC*. (Cf. X52).
Dalîla the Swindler: *Alf* III 218-19,-(to be robbed in host's home); Burton VII 156. Chauvin V 245-50 No. 147; *ANE* 163-64 No. 224;
Abû Qîr and Abû Ṣîr: *Alf* IV 183,-(in trade); Burton IX 134-35. Chauvin V 15-17 No. 10; *ANE* 75-77 No. 255.□

P780.0.1§, ‡'No shame [should be experienced] in [pursuing] the licit (*lâ ¿ayba fî al-ḥalâl*'—e.g., marriage). See: *DOTTI*. (Cf. U300§).
Portress Amînah: Bitten Cheek: *Alf* I 58; Burton I 177. Chauvin V 98-99 No. 33; *ANE* 326-27 No. 20;
¿Azîz and ¿Azîzah: *Alf* I 285,-("*lâ ¿ayba* ..."/no shame); Burton II 331,-("There is no sin in a lawful put in"). Chauvin V 144-45 No. 71; *ANE* 111-13 No. 41.□

P780.0.1.1§, ‡No shame (blame) in exercising the unavoidable (the legitimate call of nature).
King ¿Umar al-Nu¿mân and Sons: *Alf* I 238,-(going to the *kanîf*); Burton II 236,-(going to the jakes). Chauvin VI 112-24 No. 277; *ANE* 430-34 No. 39.□

P783§, ‡Sorts of shameful (disgraceful) acts (*¿ayb*/'*¿aib*').

Man [Gardener] and His Wife: *Alf* IV 165; Burton IX 98. Chauvin II 223 No. 152/19; *ANE* 289 No. 250.□

P783.0.1§, ‡Person whose public behavior brings disgrace upon relatives—(*¿irrah*). (Cf. Z183.0.1§).
Ma¿rûf the Cobbler: *Alf* IV 288,-(*¿irrah*); Burton X 1. Chauvin VI 81-82 No. 250; *ANE* 291-93 No. 262.□

P783.1§, ‡Breaking wind in public: disgraceful. See: *DOTTI*.
Bull and Ass: *Alf* I 6; Burton I 20. Chauvin V 179-80 No. 104; *ANE* 129-30 No. 2;
Ridiculous Eye Salve: *Alf* II 287; Burton V 99. Chauvin V 281 No. 165; *ANE* 236 No. 129.□

P783.2§, ‡Public expression of erotic matters (love, sex): disgraceful. See: *DOTTI*. (Cf. T381.0.5.2§).
Uns al-Wujûd and al-Ward: *Alf* II 271; Burton V 37. Chauvin VI 127-29 No. 282; *ANE* 438 No. 104.□

P783.2.3§, ‡Baring body in public: disgraceful (shameful). See: *DOTTI*. (Cf. W44.3§).
Tailor's Story/Barber of Baghdad: *Alf* I 107,-(naked head/disheveled hair); Burton I 314 n. 1. Chauvin V 154-56 No. 78; *ANE* 405-6 No. 27;
Hasan of Basrah: *Alf* IV 3,-(*¿awrah*); Burton VIII 41. Chauvin VII 29-35 No. 212A; *ANE* 207-10 No. 230.□

P783.2.3.1§, ‡Exposing genitals in public: disgraceful (shameful). See: *DOTTI*. (Cf. C105.1§).
Hashish Eater's Dream: *Alf* II 10; Burton III 93. Chauvin VI 124 No. 278; *ANE* 216 No. 42.□

P783.3§, ‡Grooming self in public: disgraceful. (Cf. C106§).
Pretty Gray-haired Woman Retorts: *Alf* II 303; Burton V 163. Chauvin VI 153 No. 318; *ANE* 77-78 No. 152.□

P783.6§, ‡Atypical marriage: disgraceful (reproachable). (Cf. P529.4§).
¿Alâ' al-Dîn Abû al-Shâmât: *Alf* II 155,-(*muḥallil*); Burton IV 48. Chauvin V 43-49 No. 18; *ANE* 85-87 No. 63;
Ebony Horse: *Alf* II 257,-(secret); Burton V 11. Chauvin V 221-31 No. 130; *ANE* 172-74 No. 103.□

P788.1§, ‡Excessive shame (dishonor, disgrace: *¿âr, khizy*) from violation of mores. See: *DOTTI*. (Cf. T57.3§, W170§).
King ¿Umar al-Nu¿mân and Sons: *Alf* I 183, II 3,-cf./(*ma¿yarah*/reproach); Burton II 124, III 78. Chauvin VI 112-24 No. 277; *ANE* 430-34 No. 39;
al-'Amjad and al-'As¿ad: *Alf* II 113-14; Burton III 313. Chauvin V 208-10 No. 120[.1]; *ANE* 341-42 No. 61/pt. 2;
Tawaddud: Slavegirl Sold and Regained: *Alf* III 7; Burton V 242. Chauvin VII 117-19 No. 387; *ANE* 408-10 No. 157.□

P788.2§, ‡Social control by shaming (publicly) into compliance (conformity). See: *DOTTI*. (Cf. J2218.9.2§, P12.2.0.1§, W10.3.1.1§, W30§, W44§).
Tailor's Story/Barber of Baghdad: *Alf* I 108,-(judge shamed); Burton I 315. Chauvin V 154-56 No. 78; *ANE* 405-6 No. 27;
¿Alâ' al-Dîn Abû al-Shâmât: *Alf* II 151; Burton IV 39. Chauvin V 43-49 No. 18; *ANE* 85-87 No. 63;
Nûr al-Dîn and Maryam: *Alf* IV 100; Burton VIII 311. Chauvin V 52-54 No. 271; *ANE* 98-99 No. 233;
Jeweler's Wife and Qamar al-Zamân: *Alf* IV 239; Burton IX 249. Chauvin V 212-14 No. 121; *ANE* 345-47 No. 260.□

P788.2.1§, ‡Fear of public disgrace (*faḍîḥah*) obliges victim to be silent. See: *DOTTI*. (Cf. K1271.1, W14.5§, Z87§).
¿Alî ibn Bakkâr: *Alf* II 60; Burton III 200,-("scandal"). Chauvin V 153 No. 76; *ANE* 92-93 No. 60;
Mock Caliph/¿Alî al-Jawharî: *Alf* II 198; Burton IV 145. Chauvin V 99-100 No. 174; *ANE* 304-5 No. 73;
Devotee Prince: Ascetic's Death: *Alf* II 290; Burton V 112. Chauvin VI 193-94 No. 363; *ANE* 167-68 No. 134;
House with the Belvedere: *Alf* III 169; Burton VI 194. Chauvin VIII 57-58 No. 23; *ANE* 223 No. 203;
Man [Gardener] and His Wife: *Alf* IV 165,-cf.; Burton IX 98. Chauvin II 223 No. 152/19; *ANE* 289 No. 250;
Abû al-Ḥasan al-Khorâsânî (and Caliph's Favorite): *Alf* IV 231; Burton IX 233,-(dishonor). Chauvin V 218-20 No. 129; *ANE* 68-69 No. 259.□

P788.2.2§, ‡False accusation motivated by fear of public disgrace (*fadîhah*).
al-'Amjad and al-'As¿ad: *Alf* II 115-16; Burton III 314. Chauvin V 208-10 No. 120[.1]; *ANE* 341-42 No. 61/pt. 2;
Nûr al-Dîn and Maryam: *Alf* IV 108,-(implicit/concerning defloration); Burton VIII 324. Chauvin V 52-54 No. 271; *ANE* 98-99 No. 233;
Ma¿rûf the Cobbler: *Alf* IV 307, 308,-(actually true); Burton X 32. Chauvin VI 81-82 No. 250; *ANE* 291-93 No. 262.□

P790.0.1.1§, ‡Having a conversation (interesting social talk). (Cf. P324.0.2§, P610§).
¿Alâ' al-Dîn Abû al-Shâmât: *Alf* II 158,-(poem); Burton IV 54,-(converse to enjoy). Chauvin V 43-49 No. 18; *ANE* 85-87 No. 63;
Budûr and Jubayr ibn ¿Umayr: *Alf* II 235,-(with cup-companions, the witty, ...); Burton IV 229. Chauvin VII 93-94 No. 374; *ANE* 243-44 No. 83.□

P790.0.1.2§, ‡Invitation to have 'conversation'.
Ishâq al-Mûsilî and Khadîjah bint al-Hasan: *Alf* II 186; Burton IV 120. Chauvin V 241-42 No. 142; *ANE* 232 No. 71.□

P790.0.1.3§, ‡'Intimate conversations are trusts' (not to be revealed). (Cf. U197§).
Ishâq al-Mûsilî and Khadîjah bint al-Hasan: *Alf* II 186; Burton IV 121. Chauvin V 241-42 No. 142; *ANE* 232 No. 71.□

P790.1.2.1§, ‡Trellis (ululation) of joy (*'zaghrûtah'/zaghrûdah*). (Typically voiced by women at a joyous occasion such as a wedding, pilgrimage, winning at lawcourt, release from prison, etc.). See: *PSAE*.
King ¿Umar al-Nu¿mân and Sons: *Alf* I 163,-(birth); Burton II 80. Chauvin VI 112-24 No. 277; *ANE* 430-34 No. 39;
Qamar al-Zamân and Budûr: *Alf* II 103; Burton III 289. Chauvin V 204-12 No. 120; *ANE* 341-45 No. 61.□

P790.2.2§, ‡Refusal to respond to greeting as sign of anger. See: *DOTTI*. (Cf. P682.0.4§, Z141.1).
Nûr al-Dîn and Maryam: *Alf* IV 97,-(*shar¿î*-greeting); Burton VIII 302. Chauvin V 52-54 No. 271; *ANE* 98-99 No. 233;
Serpent-charmer and Wife: *Alf* IV 145; Burton IX 57. Chauvin II 220 No. 152/9; *ANE* 368 No. 244.□

P790.2.3§, ‡Refusal to accept food or drink as signs of anger (displeasure). See: *DOTTI*. (Cf. P321.3§, P529.2.1§, T24.6).
¿Alâ' al-Dîn Abû al-Shâmât: *Alf* II 147; Burton IV 30. Chauvin V 43-49 No. 18; *ANE* 85-87 No. 63.□

P790.3§, ‡Publication (signs) of grief (chagrin).
Ensorcelled Prince/Husband: *Alf* I 29; Burton I 74. Chauvin VI 56-58 No. 222; *ANE* 176 No. 13;
Sindbâd's Third Voyage: *Alf* III 92,-(by ship's captain); Burton VI 23. Chauvin VII 15-18 No. 373C; *ANE* 385-86 No. 179.□

P790.3.2§, ‡Slapping own face, tearing own clothes, etc. for grief. See: *DOTTI*.
Tailor's Story/Barber of Baghdad: *Alf* I 107,-(clothes torn, dust placed on head); Burton I 314. Chauvin V 154-56 No. 78; *ANE* 405-6 No. 27;
Barber's Fifth Brother: Daydreams/Defeats Robbers: *Alf* I 118; Burton I 338. Chauvin V 161 No. 85; *ANE* 119-20 No. 33;
Bulûqiya/Hâsib/Queen of Vipers: *Alf* III 20; Burton V 301. Chauvin VII 54 No. 77; *ANE* 130-32 No. 177.□

P791§, Cooperation: social interactional process. Joint activity in order to share a reward. See: *DOTTI*; *GMC*.
Blind and Cripple Corporate: *Alf* IV 150; Burton IX 69-70. Chauvin II 221 No. 152/13; *ANE* 127 No. 247.□

P793§, Rivalry: social interactional process. Recurrent conscious competition between the same parties. See: *GMC*. (Cf. W181).
Man from Yaman and Six Salve-girls: Flyting: *Alf* II 244-50; Burton IV 245-60. Chauvin VI 151 No. 313; *ANE* 289-90 No. 84.□

P794.2§, ‡Survival by eliminating rivals for scarce means of livelihood (resources). (Cf. J675.0.1§, K811.8.1§, U26§).

Wolf and Fox: *Alf* II 35,-cf./(fox-wolf); Burton III 146. Chauvin II 227 No. 6; *ANE* 450 No. 47.□

P794.2.1§, ‡Murder committed (war waged) to ensure one's own survival. (Cf. G78.1, P550.2§, Q171.0.1.1§, U26§).
Sindbâd's Fourth Voyage: *Alf* III 105; Burton VI 44. Chauvin VII 18-20 No. 373D; *ANE* 386 No. 179.□

P795§, Accommodation: social interactional process (detente). See: *DOTTI*; *GMC*. (Cf. J813§, V441, W11.5.0.3§).
Sindbâd and Porter: *Alf* III 122; Burton VI 77. Chauvin VII 26-29 No. 373G; *ANE* 386-87 No. 179.□

P795.0.1§, ‡Accommodation (reconciliation) preferred to open conflict. See: *DOTTI*.
Man from Yaman and Six Salve-girls: Flyting: *Alf* II 249,-cf.; Burton IV 259. Chauvin VI 151 No. 313; *ANE* 289-90 No. 84.□

P795.0.1.1§, ‡Reconciliatory-reprimand (*¿itâb*) among friends and lovers. (Complaining and seeking redress without offending). (Cf. T298).
Qamar al-Zamân and Budûr: *Alf* II 102,-(between wife and supposed husband); Burton III 287-88. Chauvin V 204-12 No. 120; *ANE* 341-45 No. 61;
Tâj al-Mulûk: *Alf* I 306,-(between king and son-in-law-to-be); Burton III 43. Chauvin V 126-28 No. 60; *ANE* 406-8 No. 40;
Abû Qîr and Abû Ṣîr: *Alf* IV 192-93; Burton IX 154. Chauvin V 15-17 No. 10; *ANE* 75-77 No. 255.□

P795.0.1.2§, ‡If reconciliation is accomplished, punishment is to be suspended.
¿Abdallah ibn Fâḍil: Treacherous Brothers: *Alf* IV 283; Burton IX 338. Chauvin V 2-4 No. 2; *ANE* 63-65 No. 261.□

P795.0.4§, ‡Accommodation among social classes (rich-poor, high-low, etc.). See: *DOTTI*. (Cf. P752.5§).
Sindbâd and Porter: *Alf* III 122; Burton VI 77. Chauvin VII 26-29 No. 373G; *ANE* 386-87 No. 179.□

P795.0.4.1§, ‡Accommodation through generosity (philanthropy, sharing of wealth). See: *DOTTI*. (Cf. W11).
Sindbâd and Porter: *Alf* III 122; Burton VI 77. Chauvin VII 26-29 No. 373G; *ANE* 386-87 No. 179.□

P796§, ‡Resolution of conflict (dispute) through a third party. See: *DOTTI*. (Cf. K452, T298.5§).
Jackals and Wolf as Umpire: *Alf* IV 167; Burton IX 103. Chauvin II 223 No. 152/21; *ANE* 235 No. 252;
¿Abdallah ibn Fâḍil: Treacherous Brothers: *Alf* IV 271; Burton IX 312. Chauvin V 2-4 No. 2; *ANE* 63-65 No. 261.□

P796.1§, ‡Arbitration (*taḥkîm*): arbitrator's (umpire's) judgment is binding (final). See: *DOTTI*.
King ¿Umar al-Nu¿mân and Sons: *Alf* I 216; Burton II 191. Chauvin VI 112-24 No. 277; *ANE* 430-34 No. 39.□

P796.6.1§, ‡Duel (with arms) to settle dispute.
King ¿Umar al-Nu¿mân and Sons: *Alf* I 254; Burton II 268. Chauvin VI 112-24 No. 277; *ANE* 430-34 No. 39.□

P798.1.0.5§, Triads revolving around brother and sister as unbalanced (Sethian syndrome). See: *DOTTI*; *GMC*.
Ghânim ibn Ayyûb: *Alf* I 146,-(brother-sister overrides daughter-father); Burton II 45. Chauvin VI 14-16 No. 188; *ANE* 192-93 No. 36;
Hammâd: Treacherous Bedouin: *Alf* II 17-18; Burton III 105-13. Chauvin VI 124 n. 1 No. 277; *ANE* 200 No. 43.□

P801.1§, ‡Polo ('ball an scepter', '*birjâs*'), played on horseback.
Dûban and King Yûnân: *Alf* I 17; Burton I 47. Chauvin V 275-76 No. 156; *ANE* 459 No. 9;
¿Alâ' al-Dîn Abû al-Shâmât: *Alf* II 174; Burton IV 81. Chauvin V 43-49 No. 18; *ANE* 85-87 No. 63.□

P801.2§, ‡Playing with a 'ball'. See: *DOTTI*.
Uns al-Wujûd and al-Ward: *Alf* II 269; Burton V 32,-(polo). Chauvin VI 127-29 No. 282; *ANE* 438 No. 104.□

P801.9.1.1§, ‡Women's wrestling (sports). (Cf. H1562.9).

King ¿Umar al-Nu¿mân and Sons: *Alf* I 166-67; Burton II 86-87. Chauvin VI 112-24 No. 277; *ANE* 430-34 No. 39.□

P801.9.1.1.1§, ‡Women's wrestling in the nude.
King ¿Umar al-Nu¿mân and Sons: *Alf* I 166-67; Burton II 87. Chauvin VI 112-24 No. 277; *ANE* 430-34 No. 39.□

P803.1§, ‡Chess, game of strategy. (Cf. F679.8, H509.3).
Hasan of Basrah: *Alf* III 310; Burton VIII 22. Chauvin VII 29-35 No. 212A; *ANE* 207-10 No. 230;
Masrûr and Zayn al-Mawâṣif: *Alf* IV 57-59; Burton VIII 216-18. Chauvin VI 82-84 No. 251; *ANE* 294-95 No. 232.□

P806.7§, ‡Hunting or fishing as hobby. (Cf. P12.1, P414, P419§).
Tâj al-Mulûk: *Alf* I 266; Burton II 293. Chauvin V 126-28 No. 60; *ANE* 406-8 No. 40;
King's Favorite Son and Ogress: *Alf* III 143; Burton VI 139-40. Chauvin VIII 40-41 No. 8B; *ANE* 264 No. 188.□

P806.7.1§, ‡Hunting with help of animals or birds (dogs, leopards, falcons, etc.). See: *DOTTI*; *PSAE*. (Cf. B455.2, F679.12.1§).
King Sindbâd and Falcon: *Alf* I 19,-(falcon); Burton I 51. Chauvin V 289 No. 173; *ANE* 383 No. 10;

Tâj al-Mulûk: *Alf* I 266; Burton II 293. Chauvin V 126-28 No. 60; *ANE* 406-8 No. 40.□

P807§, ‡Pastime and recreation (amusements, non-competitive play, etc.). See: *DOTTI*. (Cf. P791§).
King ¿Umar al-Nu¿mân and Sons: *Alf* I 260; Burton II 282. Chauvin VI 112-24 No. 277; *ANE* 430-34 No. 39.□

P807.1§, ‡Literature and other verbal expressive (artistic) activities as amusements.
Budûr and Jubayr ibn ¿Umayr: *Alf* II 235,-(by poets, the wise, ...); Burton IV 229. Chauvin VII 93-94 No. 374; *ANE* 243-44 No. 83.□

P807.1.0.1§, ‡Reading as a hobby.
Ibn Sabâ'ik/Sayf al-Mulûk: *Alf* III 273; Burton VII 312. Chauvin VII 65 No. 348/pt.; *ANE* 309-10 No. 228.□

P807.1.2§, ‡Listening to stories (tales) as hobby (for relaxation). See: *PSAE*. (Cf. F956.7.6.2§).
Shahriyâr and Shahrzâd: *Alf* I 7; Burton I 29. Chauvin V 188-89 No. 111; *ANE* 370-71 No. 1;
Porter and Ladies of Baghdad: *Alf* I 35; Burton I 95. Chauvin V 251-52 No. 148; *ANE* 324-26 No. 14;
Ibn Sabâ'ik/Sayf al-Mulûk: *Alf* III 272-73; Burton VII 313. Chauvin VII 65 No. 348/pt.; *ANE* 309-10 No. 228.□

P807.1.2.1§, ‡Tales told for entertainment at night time.
King ¿Umar al-Nu¿mân and Sons: *Alf* I 261; Burton II 283. Chauvin VI 112-24 No. 277; *ANE* 430-34 No. 39.□

P807.1.3§, ‡Listening to poetry as pastime. (Cf. H509.4.0.1§, P807.1.3§).
Basra Girls in Poetry Contest: *Alf* III 204; Burton VII 110. Chauvin VI 144 No. 301; *ANE* 107-8 No. 216.□

P807.1.4§, ‡Listening to music as recreation (pastime).
¿Alâ' al-Dîn Abû al-Shâmât: *Alf* II 158; Burton IV 54. Chauvin V 43-49 No. 18; *ANE* 85-87 No. 63.□

P807.3.1§, ‡Promenading as recreation.
¿Alâ' al-Dîn Abû al-Shâmât: *Alf* II 158; Burton IV 54. Chauvin V 43-49 No. 18; *ANE* 85-87 No. 63;
Budûr and Jubayr ibn ¿Umayr: *Alf* II 235,-(in garden); Burton IV 229. Chauvin VII 93-94 No. 374; *ANE* 243-44 No. 83;
Mercury ¿Alî: *Alf* III 227,-(in marketplaces); Burton VII 172. Chauvin V 248-50 No. 147; *ANE* 301-3 No. 225;
Masrûr and Zayn al-Mawâṣif: *Alf* IV 55; Burton VIII 205,-(in vergiers and flower-gardens). Chauvin VI 82-84 No. 251; *ANE* 294-95 No. 232.□

P807.3.2§, ‡Boating (sailing, rowing) as recreation. See: *PSAE*.
Budûr and Jubayr ibn ¿Umayr: *Alf* II 243; Burton IV 245. Chauvin VII 93-94 No. 374; *ANE* 243-44 No. 83.□

P807.8.2§, ‡Watching an erotic activity for amusement—usually by stealth. (Cf. Q243.9.1§).

Budûr and Jubayr ibn ¿Umayr: *Alf* II 235,-(suggested); Burton IV 229. Chauvin VII 93-94 No. 374; *ANE* 243-44 No. 83;
Ibrâhîm and Jamîlah: *Alf* IV 220-21; Burton IX 211. Chauvin VI 52-53 No. 218; *ANE* 227-29 No. 258.□

P961§, Celebration of a birth. See: *DOTTI*. (Cf. T583).
Tâj al-Mulûk: *Alf* I 265; Burton II 291. Chauvin V 126-28 No. 60; *ANE* 406-8 No. 40;
Sayf al-Mulûk: *Alf* III 277; Burton VII 324. Chauvin VII 64-73 No. 348; *ANE* 362-64 No. 229.□

P961.1§, Birth celebrated on seventh day (*subû¿*). See: *DOTTI*; *GMC*.
¿Alâ' al-Dîn Abû al-Shâmât: *Alf* II 148; Burton IV 32. Chauvin V 43-49 No. 18; *ANE* 85-87 No. 63.□

P965§, Celebration of a wedding. See: *GMC*. (Cf. P469.2§).
Qamar al-Zamân and Budûr: *Alf* II 96; Burton III 276. Chauvin V 204-12 No. 120; *ANE* 341-45 No. 61;
Lover Who Feigned Himself a Thief: *Alf* II 205; Burton IV 159. Chauvin VII 134-35 No. 403; *ANE* 272 No. 76;
Jullanâr of the Sea: *Alf* III 270; Burton VII 307. Chauvin V 147-51 No. 73; *ANE* 248-51 No. 227;
Jeweler's Wife and Qamar al-Zamân: *Alf* IV 260; Burton IX 289-90. Chauvin V 212-14 No. 121; *ANE* 345-47 No. 260;
Ma¿rûf the Cobbler: *Alf* IV 299-300; Burton X 18-19. Chauvin VI 81-82 No. 250; *ANE* 291-93 No. 262;
Shahriyâr and Shahrzâd: *Alf* IV 317-18,-cf.; Burton X 54. Chauvin V 190-91 No. 111/pt.; *ANE* 371 No. 1.□

P980§, Seasonal, secular, and national festivals. See: *GMC*.
Budûr and Jubayr ibn ¿Umayr: *Alf* II 243,-("Nawârîz"); Burton IV 244-45,-(New Year's day). Chauvin VII 93-94 No. 374; *ANE* 243-44 No. 83;
Lovers of Basra/Damrah: *Alf* III 210-12,-("Nawârîz"/passim); Burton VII 130,-(New Year's day). Chauvin V 118 No. 54; *ANE* 273 No. 220.□

P991.1§, Saint's day festival (*mawlid*, '*mûlid*'). See: *GMC*.
¿Alâ' al-Dîn Abû al-Shâmât: *Alf* II 152,-(al-Jîlânî's); Burton IV 41. Chauvin V 43-49 No. 18; *ANE* 85-87 No. 63.□

Q. REWARDS AND PUNISHMENTS

Q20.3§, ‡Thanking God rewarded (failure to do so punished). See: *DOTTI*. (Cf. V318.2§).
Spider Upbraids Wind: *Alf* IV 147,-cf./(she-spider rewarded); Burton IX 59-60. Chauvin II 220 No. 152/10; *ANE* 398 No. 245.□

Q20.3.1§, ‡Thanking God for an affliction rewarded.
Spider Upbraids Wind: *Alf* IV 147,-(she-spider rewarded/home restored); Burton IX 59-60. Chauvin II 220 No. 152/10; *ANE* 398 No. 245.□

Q22.1§, Placing one's faith in God alone rewarded. See: *DOTTI*; *GMC*.
Hishâm and Arab Youth: *Alf* II 184,-cf.; Burton IV 102. Chauvin V 288 No. 172; *ANE* 222-23 No. 68;
Fish and Crab: *Alf* IV 140,-cf.; Burton IX 44-45. Chauvin II 219 No. 152/4; *ANE* 185-86 No. 239.□

Q40, Kindness rewarded. See: *DOTTI*; *GMC*.
Flea and She-mouse: *Alf* II 35,-(giving protection); Burton III 154. Chauvin II 228 No. 12; *ANE* 186 No. 52;
Nûr al-Dîn and Maryam: *Alf* IV 104; Burton VIII 317. Chauvin V 52-54 No. 271; *ANE* 98-99 No. 233;
Landsman ¿Abdallah and Merman ¿Abdallah: *Alf* IV 200,-(baker's); Burton IX 171. Chauvin V 6-7 No. 3; *ANE* 65-66 No. 256.□

Q40.2§, ‡Kindness to the disabled (sick, wounded, etc.) rewarded. (Cf. Q57).
King ¿Umar al-Nu¿mân and Sons: *Alf* I 188,-ff.; Burton II 135. Chauvin VI 112-24 No. 277; *ANE* 430-34 No. 39.□

Q45, Hospitality rewarded. See: *DOTTI*; *GMC*.
Mouse and Cat: *Alf* IV 135; Burton IX 36. Chauvin II 218 No. 152/2; *ANE* 305-6 No. 237;
Ma¿rûf the Cobbler: *Alf* IV 317; Burton X 53. Chauvin VI 81-82 No. 250; *ANE* 291-93 No. 262.□

Q45.3.1§, ‡Dervish leaves money (under carpet or pillow) for hospitable host as reward. (Guest proves to be the ruler traveling incognito).
¿Alâ' al-Dîn Abû al-Shâmât: *Alf* II 158; Burton IV 55. Chauvin V 43-49 No. 18; *ANE* 85-87 No. 63.□

Q46, ‡Reward for protecting fugitive. (Cf. P322.0.1§, R201§).
Ni¿mah and Nu¿m: Stolen Wife Regained: *Alf* II 144,-(lover); Burton IV 23. Chauvin VI 96-97 No. 263; *ANE* 314 No. 62.□

Q48§, ‡Dutifulness toward parent(s) rewarded.
Island King/Pious Jewish Merchant: *Alf* III 16; Burton V 290-94. Chauvin VI 161 No. 325; *ANE* 234 No. 174.□

Q51, Kindness to animals rewarded. See: *DOTTI*. (Cf. V443.3§).
Abû Muhammad Lazybones: *Alf* II 208,-cf./(monkey/ape); Burton IV 167. Chauvin VI 64-67 No. 233; *ANE* 71-73 No. 78.□

Q56.4§, ‡Owner (ruler) rewards slave's love for previous master. See: *DOTTI*. (Cf. Q72.3§).
Tawaddud: Slavegirl Sold and Regained: *Alf* III 8; Burton V 245. Chauvin VII 117-19 No. 387; *ANE* 408-10 No. 157.□

Q56.6§, ‡Reward for lover's constancy and long-suffering.
Abû al-Hasan al-Khorâsânî (and Caliph's Favorite): *Alf* IV 235; Burton IX 245. Chauvin V 218-20 No. 129; *ANE* 68-69 No. 259.□

Q57, ‡Attendance on the sick rewarded. See: *DOTTI*. (Cf. Q40.2§, W10.9.1§).
King ¿Umar al-Nu¿mân and Sons: *Alf* I 309; Burton III 49-50. Chauvin VI 112-24 No. 277; *ANE* 430-34 No. 39;
Nûr al-Dîn and Maryam: *Alf* IV 104; Burton VIII 317. Chauvin V 52-54 No. 271; *ANE* 98-99 No. 233.□

Q64, Patience rewarded. See: *DOTTI*; *GMC*.
Crow and Viper: *Alf* IV 141; Burton IX 47. Chauvin II 219 No. 152/5; *ANE* 162 No. 240;
Spider Upbraids Wind: *Alf* IV 147; Burton IX 59-60. Chauvin II 220 No. 152/10; *ANE* 398 No. 245.□

Q68.1, Truth-speaking [(truthfulness)] rewarded. See: *DOTTI*; *GMC*.
Barber's Sixth Brother: Emasculated by Abductor: *Alf* I 123; Burton I 346-47. Chauvin V 163-64 No. 86; *ANE* 120 No. 34;
al-'Amjad and al-'As¿ad: *Alf* II 126-27; Burton III 339. Chauvin V 208-10 No. 120[.1]; *ANE* 341-42 No. 61/pt. 2;
Lover Who Feigned Himself a Thief: *Alf* II 205; Burton IV 159. Chauvin VII 134-35 No. 403; *ANE* 272 No. 76.□

Q69.0.1§, ‡Reward for telling story.
Tâj al-Mulûk: *Alf* I 308,-(praise); Burton III 47. Chauvin V 126-28 No. 60; *ANE* 406-8 No. 40;
Ridiculous Eye Salve: *Alf* II 287; Burton V 99. Chauvin V 281 No. 165; *ANE* 236 No. 129.□

Q69§, ‡Eloquence rewarded. See: *DOTTI*; *PSAE*.
Ghânim ibn Ayyûb: *Alf* I 162; Burton II 75. Chauvin VI 14 No. 188; *ANE* 192-93 No. 36;
Hârûn and Arab Girl: *Alf* III 204; Burton VII 109. Chauvin VI 143 No. 300; *ANE* 202 No. 215;
Masrûr and Zayn al-Mawâṣif: *Alf* IV 72,-(admired); Burton VIII 243. Chauvin VI 82-84 No. 251; *ANE* 294-95 No. 232.□

Q69.1§, ‡Mouth filled with jewels as reward for eloquence (story, wise-saying, etc.). See: *DOTTI*. (Cf. Q70§, Q92§, Q111.7).
Hishâm and Arab Youth: *Alf* II 185; Burton IV 103. Chauvin V 288 No. 172; *ANE* 222-23 No. 68.□

Q70§, ‡Being bearer of good news (tidings) rewarded. (Cf. P469.4.2§, P775.2.1.2§).
King ¿Umar al-Nu¿mân and Sons: *Alf* I 215; Burton II 188. Chauvin VI 112-24 No. 277; *ANE* 430-34 No. 39;
al-Rashîd and Omani Merchant: *Alf* IV 218; Burton IX 205. Chauvin VI 111-12 No. 276; *ANE* 201-2 No. 257.□

Q72, ‡Loyalty rewarded. See: *DOTTI*. (Cf. Q73.1§).
Jullanâr of the Sea: *Alf* III 269,-(grocer made king); Burton VII 307. Chauvin V 147-51 No. 73; *ANE* 248-51 No. 227.□

Q72.1, ‡Reward for loyalty to king. See: *DOTTI*.
¿Alâ' al-Dîn Abû al-Shâmât: *Alf* II 174; Burton IV 81. Chauvin V 43-49 No. 18; *ANE* 85-87 No. 63.□

Q72.3§, ‡Reward for loyalty to employer (master). See: *DOTTI*. (Cf. Q56.4§, W37.8.1.1§).
Ruined Baghdadi and His Slave-girl: *Alf* IV 133; Burton IX 29. Chauvin V 152-53 No. 75; *ANE* 353 No. 235.□

Q74§, ‡Gallantry (chivalry, courtliness) rewarded. (Cf. N884.2§, W14§).
Lover Who Feigned Himself a Thief: *Alf* II 205; Burton IV 158,159. Chauvin VII 134-35 No. 403; *ANE* 272 No. 76;
Isḥâq al-Mûṣilî and Merchant's Singer: *Alf* II 297,-(*murû'ah*); Burton V 133,-("right generous mind"). Chauvin VI 59 No. 225; *ANE* 233 No. 142.□

Q87, ‡Reward for preservation of chastity. See: *DOTTI*. (Cf. T331).
Hermit Tempted by Angel: *Alf* II 28,-(peaceful life); Burton III 127-28. Chauvin II 226 No. 3; *ANE* 221 No. 45/pt. 2;
Jewish Tray-maker and Temptress: *Alf* III 14; Burton V 268. Chauvin VI 187-88 No. 354; *ANE* 169 No. 166.□

Q87.4§, ‡Man rewarded for not taking advantage (not violating) vulnerable woman (drunk, fainted, etc.). See: *DOTTI*.
Ghânim ibn Ayyûb: *Alf* I 154,-cf.; Burton II 61. Chauvin VI 14 No. 188; *ANE* 192-93 No. 36;
Mercury ¿Alî: *Alf* III 236; Burton VII 187. Chauvin V 248-50 No. 147; *ANE* 301-3 No. 225.□

Q89.2§, ‡Jeweler rewarded for piercing gem (diamond).
Jeweler's Wife and Qamar al-Zamân: *Alf* IV 246; Burton IX 260. Chauvin V 212-14 No. 121; *ANE* 345-47 No. 260.□

Q91, ‡Reward for cleverness. (Cf. P251.6.1, P252.2, T92.0.2§).
Hârûn, Slave-girl and Judge Abû-Yûsuf: *Alf* II 204; Burton IV 155. Chauvin VII 114 No. 383; *ANE* 204 No. 75;
Anûshirawân and Village Damsel: *Alf* II 285; Burton V 88. Chauvin VI 26-27 No. 198; *ANE* 106 No. 121.□

Q91.3, King rewards poem. See: *DOTTI*.
Hishâm and Arab Youth: *Alf* II 185,-cf.; Burton IV 103. Chauvin V 288 No. 172; *ANE* 222-23 No. 68;
Hârûn and Zubaydah in Bath: *Alf* II 284,-(poem); Burton V 77. Chauvin VI 142 No. 298; *ANE* 203-4 No. 111.□

Q91.5§, ‡Poem as expression of gratitude for grant (reward) given.
Ma¿n Rewards Maidens for a Drink of Water: *Alf* II 182,-cf.; Burton IV 97. Chauvin VI 78 No. 247; *ANE* 290 No. 65.□

Q92§, Reward for unique story (life-experience). See: *DOTTI*; *GMC*. (Cf. P320).
Porter and Ladies of Baghdad: *Alf* I 38ff.; Burton I 107ff. Chauvin V 251-52 No. 148; *ANE* 324-26 No. 14;
Basra Girls in Poetry Contest: *Alf* III 205-6; Burton VII 113. Chauvin VI 144 No. 301; *ANE* 107-8 No. 216;
Ibn Sabâ'ik/Sayf al-Mulûk: *Alf* III 270; Burton VII 309. Chauvin VII 65 No. 348/pt.; *ANE* 309-10 No. 228.□

Q94, Reward for cure. See: *DOTTI*; *GMC*.
Bulûqiya: *Alf* III 80; Burton V 395. Chauvin VII 54 No. 77; *ANE* 130-32 No. 177;
Nûr al-Dîn and Maryam: *Alf* IV 117,-(curing horse); Burton VIII 342. Chauvin V 52-54 No. 271; *ANE* 98-99 No. 233.□

Q102§, ‡Compensation for lost property and rank—(reinstatement, restoration to previous station). See: *DOTTI*. (Cf. V233.3.5§).
Bulûqiya: *Alf* III 75,-cf.; Burton V 386. Chauvin VII 54 No. 77; *ANE* 130-32 No. 177.□

Q111, ‡Riches as reward. See: *DOTTI*.
¿Alâ' al-Dîn Abû al-Shâmât: *Alf* II 163; Burton IV 62. Chauvin V 43-49 No. 18; *ANE* 85-87 No. 63;
Hârûn, Slave-girl and Judge Abû-Yûsuf: *Alf* II 204,-(gold); Burton IV 155. Chauvin VII 114 No. 383; *ANE* 204 No. 75.□

Q111.2, ‡Riches as reward (for hospitality).
¿Alâ' al-Dîn Abû al-Shâmât: *Alf* II 160; Burton IV 56. Chauvin V 43-49 No. 18; *ANE* 85-87 No. 63;
Ma¿n Rewards Maidens for a Drink of Water: *Alf* II 182,-cf./(for drink of water); Burton IV 97. Chauvin VI 78 No. 247; *ANE* 290 No. 65.□

Q111.7, ‡Jewels as reward. See: *DOTTI*.
Hishâm and Arab Youth: *Alf* II 185; Burton IV 103. Chauvin V 288 No. 172; *ANE* 222-23 No. 68.□

Q111.8, ‡Large quantity of land as reward—[(*'iqṭâ¿*)]. See: *PSAE*.
Ibn Sabâ'ik/Sayf al-Mulûk: *Alf* III 270,-(for story); Burton VII 309. Chauvin VII 65 No. 348/pt.; *ANE* 309-10 No. 228.□

Q111.9§, ‡*'ib¿âdiyyah*: large quantity of land in remote area as lure for accepting exile to that area.
King ¿Umar al-Nu¿mân and Sons: *Alf* I 187,-cf./(to forget); Burton II 131. Chauvin VI 112-24 No. 277; *ANE* 430-34 No. 39.□

Q111.9.3§, ‡Other rewarding punishments: mixture of reward and punishment.
King ¿Umar al-Nu¿mân and Sons: *Alf* I 187; Burton II 132. Chauvin VI 112-24 No. 277; *ANE* 430-34 No. 39.□

Q112.3.1§, ‡Reward: becoming king's courtier (friend). See: *DOTTI*. (Cf. P427.7.4.3§).
Abû al-Ḥasan al-Khorâsânî (and Caliph's Favorite): *Alf* IV 237; Burton IX 246. Chauvin V 218-20 No. 129; *ANE* 68-69 No. 259.□

Q113.0.1, ‡High honors as reward. [Non-material reward]. (Cf. U69§).
al-'Amjad and al-'As¿ad: *Alf* II 126-27,-(vizier); Burton III 339. Chauvin V 208-10 No. 120[.1]; *ANE* 341-42 No. 61/pt. 2.□

Q113.0.1.1§, ‡High governmental office as reward—(e.g., vizier, counselor, etc.).
Ensorcelled Prince/Husband: *Alf* I 31; Burton I 81. Chauvin VI 56-58 No. 222; *ANE* 176 No. 13;
¿Alâ' al-Dîn Abû al-Shâmât: *Alf* II 162,-(*shâhbandar* of merchants); Burton IV 60,-(Provost of merchants). Chauvin V 43-49 No. 18; *ANE* 85-87 No. 63;
Ibn Sabâ'ik/Sayf al-Mulûk: *Alf* III 270,-(for story); Burton VII 309. Chauvin VII 65 No. 348/pt.; *ANE* 309-10 No. 228;

Ma¿rûf the Cobbler: *Alf* IV 317,-(*wazîr maymanah*); Burton X 53,-(Chief Counsellor). Chauvin VI 81-82 No. 250; *ANE* 291-93 No. 262.□

Q115.0.1§, ‡Person granted fulfilled wish(es) as reward. See: *DOTTI*.
Dalîla the Swindler: *Alf* III 226,-(stipend restored/"granted wish" missing); Burton VII 170-71. Chauvin V 245-50 No. 147; *ANE* 163-64 No. 224;
Jeweler's Wife and Qamar al-Zamân: *Alf* IV 245; Burton IX 260. Chauvin V 212-14 No. 121; *ANE* 345-47 No. 260;
Shahriyâr and Shahrzâd: *Alf* IV 317,-(Sheherezade); Burton X 54. Chauvin V 190-91 No. 111/pt.; *ANE* 371 No. 1.□

Q115.0.2§, ‡A person's need is met on his behalf as reward—(usually anonymously by king or the like). (Cf. W11.0.1§).
¿Alâ' al-Dîn Abû al-Shâmât: *Alf* II 160; Burton IV 56. Chauvin V 43-49 No. 18; *ANE* 85-87 No. 63.□

Q117§, ‡Debt (tax, tribute) forgiven or reduced as reward. See: *DOTTI*. (Cf. Q111).
King ¿Umar al-Nu¿mân and Sons: *Alf* I 199,-(ten percent customs/tax); Burton II 154,-(paying tithe on merchandise). Chauvin VI 112-24 No. 277; *ANE* 430-34 No. 39.□

Q117.1§, ‡Exemption from paying tax as reward. (Usually for a certain period).
King ¿Umar al-Nu¿mân and Sons: *Alf* I 197, 199; Burton II 150, 154. Chauvin VI 112-24 No. 277; *ANE* 430-34 No. 39;
Abû al-Hasan al-Khorâsânî (and Caliph's Favorite): *Alf* IV 237,-(for twenty years); Burton IX 246. Chauvin V 218-20 No. 129; *ANE* 68-69 No. 259.□

Q118§, ‡Marriage as reward. See: *DOTTI*. (Cf. P771.2.1§, Q432.0.1§).
Anûshirawân and Village Damsel: *Alf* II 285; Burton V 88. Chauvin VI 26-27 No. 198; *ANE* 106 No. 121;
Hârûn and Arab Girl: *Alf* III 204; Burton VII 109. Chauvin VI 143 No. 300; *ANE* 202 No. 215;
Ruined Baghdadi and His Slave-girl: *Alf* IV 133; Burton IX 29. Chauvin V 152-53 No. 75; *ANE* 353 No. 235;
Jeweler's Wife and Qamar al-Zamân: *Alf* IV 263; Burton IX 297. Chauvin V 212-14 No. 121; *ANE* 345-47 No. 260.□

Q121.1, ‡Slaves freed as reward. (Cf. M270§, P178).
¿Alî ibn Bakkâr: *Alf* II 62,-cf./(promised); Burton III 205. Chauvin V 153 No. 76; *ANE* 92-93 No. 60;
Ruined Baghdadi and His Slave-girl: *Alf* IV 133,-(woman-singer); Burton IX 32. Chauvin V 152-53 No. 75; *ANE* 353 No. 235.□

Q136§, ‡Non-material rewards. (Cf. Q113.0.1).
Tâj al-Mulûk: *Alf* I 308,-(praise); Burton III 47. Chauvin V 126-28 No. 60; *ANE* 406-8 No. 40;
Tawaddud: Slavegirl Sold and Regained: *Alf* III 8,-(to be restored to original master/owner); Burton V 245. Chauvin VII 117-19 No. 387; *ANE* 408-10 No. 157.□

Q136.1.3§, ‡Religious title as reward (e.g., "Crusader/*mujâhid*", "God's Sword", etc.). (Cf. P91§).
King ¿Umar al-Nu¿mân and Sons: *Alf* I 309; Burton III 50. Chauvin VI 112-24 No. 277; *ANE* 430-34 No. 39.□

Q137§, ‡To be made king's drinking companion (cup-companion, *nadîm*) as reward.
Anîs al-Jalîs: *Alf* I 145; Burton II 44. Chauvin V 120-24 No. 58; *ANE* 316-17 No. 35;
Tawaddud: Slavegirl Sold and Regained: *Alf* III 8; Burton V 245. Chauvin VII 117-19 No. 387; *ANE* 408-10 No. 157;
al-Rashîd and Omani Merchant: *Alf* IV 219; Burton IX 206. Chauvin VI 111-12 No. 276; *ANE* 201-2 No. 257;
Abû al-Hasan al-Khorâsânî (and Caliph's Favorite): *Alf* IV 237; Burton IX 246. Chauvin V 218-20 No. 129; *ANE* 68-69 No. 259.□

Q151.6, ‡Life spared as reward for hospitality. See: *DOTTI*.
Third Qalandar: Magnetic Mountain: *Alf* I 53; Burton I 162. Chauvin V 200-3 No. 117; *ANE* 340-41 No. 18.□

Q151.14§, ‡Life spared as reward for bizarre (but truthful) story. See: *DOTTI*.
Third Qalandar: Magnetic Mountain: *Alf* I 53; Burton I 161. Chauvin V 200-3 No. 117; *ANE* 340-41 No. 18.□

Q170.0.2§, ‡Forgiveness (redemption) of a person's past sins as divine reward.
Tawaddud: Slavegirl Sold and Regained: *Alf* II 312; Burton V 211. Chauvin VII 117-19 No. 387; *ANE* 408-10 No. 157.□

Q171.0.1§, Capital crime unpunished. See: *DOTTI*. (Cf. P140.0.3§, Q258.1§, V315.3§).
Three Apples: Hasty Uxoricide: *Alf* I 64,-cf./(lie that leads to murder); Burton I 194. Chauvin VI 144-45 No. 302; *ANE* 414-15 No. 21;
King Jalî¿âd and Shimâs: *Alf* IV 171ff.,-(massacring critics/notables); Burton IX 117ff. Chauvin VI 9 No. 184; *ANE* 237-38 No. 236.□

Q171.0.1.1§, Murder unpunished (forgiven). See: *DOTTI*; *GMC*.
Jewish Doctor's Story: Sororicide: *Alf* I 102; Burton I 294-95. Chauvin VI 89 No. 253; *ANE* 242 No. 26;
King ¿Umar al-Nu¿mân and Sons: *Alf* I 183,/(rape).; Burton II 124. Chauvin VI 112-24 No. 277; *ANE* 430-34 No. 39;
Qamar al-Zamân and Budûr: *Alf* II 86,-(princess murders nurse); Burton III 255. Chauvin V 204-12 No. 120; *ANE* 341-45 No. 61;
¿Alâ' al-Dîn Abû al-Shâmât: *Alf* II 171,-(highway murder); Burton IV 76. Chauvin V 43-49 No. 18; *ANE* 85-87 No. 63;
Sindbâd's Fourth Voyage: *Alf* III 105,-(implicit); Burton VI 44. Chauvin VII 18-20 No. 373D; *ANE* 386 No. 179;
Abû Qîr and Abû Ṣîr: *Alf* IV 195,-cf./(two men/accidentally killed); Burton IX 160. Chauvin V 15-17 No. 10; *ANE* 75-77 No. 255.□

Q171.2§, ‡Relief from distress (sins) on Judgment Day for act of charity.
¿Azîz and ¿Azîzah: *Alf* I 283; Burton II 327. Chauvin V 144-45 No. 71; *ANE* 111-13 No. 41.□

Q172, Reward: admission to heaven. See: *DOTTI*; *GMC*.
Mouse and Cat: *Alf* IV 135,-(for hospitality to strangers); Burton IX 36. Chauvin II 218 No. 152/2; *ANE* 305-6 No. 237.□

Q172.0.2, ‡Rewards in heaven.
Jewish Tray-maker and Temptress: *Alf* III 14; Burton V 268. Chauvin VI 187-88 No. 354; *ANE* 169 No. 166.□

Q172.0.3§, ‡Reward in the hereafter (Heaven) preferred to that in the here-and-now. See: *DOTTI*. (Cf. J3.2.4§, Q560.0.1§, W4.3§).
Nuzhat al-Zamân Tested/¿Umar al-Nu¿mân: *Alf* I 303, 206,-(caliph's); Burton II 170. Chauvin VI 116, n.1/passim No. 277; *ANE* 432,/passim No. 39;
Jewish Tray-maker and Temptress: *Alf* III 14; Burton V 268. Chauvin VI 187-88 No. 354; *ANE* 169 No. 166;
City of Brass: *Alf* III 131; Burton VI 105. Chauvin V 32-35 No. 16; *ANE* 146-50 No. 180.□

Q172.0.3.1§, ‡'The world (here-and-now) is the home for him who has no home [in the hereafter]'.
City of Brass: *Alf* III 131; Burton VI 105. Chauvin V 32-35 No. 16; *ANE* 146-50 No. 180.□

Q172.0.4§, Animal admitted to heaven. See: *DOTTI*; *GMC*. (Cf. E178.1.1§).
Tawaddud: Slavegirl Sold and Regained: *Alf* III 4; Burton V 235. Chauvin VII 117-19 No. 387; *ANE* 408-10 No. 157.□

Q172.4.1§, Palace in heaven (Paradise) assigned to person as reward. See: *DOTTI*.
Prior Becomes Moslem: al-Anbârî: *Alf* II 299,-cf./(pavilion); Burton V 143. Chauvin V 237-38 No. 137; *ANE* 330-31 No. 147.□

Q174.0.1§, *'ash-shafâ¿ah al-¿uẓmâ*: God grants person (prophet, saint) the boon of releasing souls from hell. See: *GMC*. (Cf. P140.0.2§).
Tawaddud: Slavegirl Sold and Regained: *Alf* III 6,-(three); Burton V 241. Chauvin VII 117-19 No. 387; *ANE* 408-10 No. 157.□

Q194§, ‡Reward: lie (benevolent) becomes truth. See: *DOTTI*.
Jewish Tray-maker and Temptress: *Alf* III 14,-(bread); Burton V 267-68. Chauvin VI 187-88 No. 354; *ANE* 169 No. 166.□

Q195, Blessings [as reward]. See: *DOTTI*.
Sindbâd's Third Voyage: *Alf* III 98,-(*du¿â' li*); Burton VI 29. Chauvin VII 15-18 No. 373C; *ANE* 385-86 No. 179.□

Q201.1§, ‡Husband who fails to punish his culprit wife is to be punished. See: *DOTTI*. (Cf. Q259.3§).
Jeweler's Wife and Qamar al-Zamân: *Alf* IV 265; Burton IX 300-1. Chauvin V 212-14 No. 121; *ANE* 345-47 No. 260.□

Q205§, Part of body involved in offense punished. See: *DOTTI*; *GMC*.
Nûr al-Dîn and Maryam: *Alf* IV 89,-(hand); Burton VIII 287. Chauvin V 52-54 No. 271; *ANE* 98-99 No. 233;
Ibrâhîm and Jamîlah: *Alf* IV 229; Burton IX 228. Chauvin VI 52-53 No. 218; *ANE* 227-29 No. 258.□

Q205.1§, ‡Limb (hand, foot, tongue, etc.) involved in offense cut off.
Ibrâhîm and Jamîlah: *Alf* IV 229; Burton IX 228. Chauvin VI 52-53 No. 218; *ANE* 227-29 No. 258.□

Q210.2§, ‡Attempted murder punished.
Ma¿rûf the Cobbler: *Alf* IV 316; Burton X 52. Chauvin VI 81-82 No. 250; *ANE* 291-93 No. 262.□

Q211.5.1§, ‡Hell as punishment for suicide.
Ruined Baghdadi and His Slave-girl: *Alf* IV 130; Burton IX 25. Chauvin V 152-53 No. 75; *ANE* 353 No. 235.□

Q212.6.1§, ‡Theft from place of worship punished.
Ma¿rûf the Cobbler: *Alf* IV 294,-(church/by Moslem children); Burton X 9. Chauvin VI 81-82 No. 250; *ANE* 291-93 No. 262.□

Q213, ‡Abduction punished.
Hammâd: Treacherous Bedouin: *Alf* II 20; Burton III 112. Chauvin VI 124 n. 1 No. 277; *ANE* 200 No. 43;
Ibrâhîm and Jamîlah: *Alf* IV 229; Burton IX 209. Chauvin VI 52-53 No. 218; *ANE* 227-29 No. 258.□

Q213.1§, ‡Kidnapping punished. (Cf. R10.3).
Hammâd: Treacherous Bedouin: *Alf* II 20; Burton III 111. Chauvin VI 124 n. 1 No. 277; *ANE* 200 No. 43.□

Q218§, ‡Political offenses (against the state) punished. See: *DOTTI*.
King Jalî¿âd and Shimâs: *Alf* IV 169-70; Burton IX 107-8. Chauvin VI 9 No. 184; *ANE* 237-38 No. 236.□

Q222.7§, ‡Punishment for violating sanctity of tomb (grave, cemetery). See: *DOTTI*; *PSAE*. (Cf. V67.9.2§).
Bulûqiya: *Alf* III 26; Burton V 312. Chauvin VII 54 No. 77; *ANE* 130-32 No. 177.□

Q223.1, Neglect to pray punished. See: *GMC*.
Water-fowl and Tortoise: *Alf* II 29; Burton III 131. Chauvin II 226-27 No. 5; *ANE* 444 No. 46.□

Q223.2.1§, ‡Neglect to praise (thank) God punished. (Cf. C3.1§, N385.2§).
Water-fowl and Tortoise: *Alf* II 29; Burton III 125. Chauvin II 227 No. 6; *ANE* 450 No. 46.□

Q225.5§, ‡Practice of nether magic (sorcery, witchcraft) punished as *kufr* (disbelief). See: *PSAE*. (Cf. G291, Q456.3§).
Goldsmith and Cashmere Singer: *Alf* III 150; Burton VI 156. Chauvin VIII 46-47 No. 14; *ANE* 196 No. 194.□

Q225.5.1§, ‡Alchemist is to be executed.
Hasan of Basrah: *Alf* III 303,-cf./(implicit); Burton VIII 11,-("magistrates will hear of us, and we shall lose our lives"). Chauvin VII 29-35 No. 212A; *ANE* 207-10 No. 230.□

Q232, Punishment for change of religious faith.
Nûr al-Dîn and Maryam: *Alf* IV 114,-(planned marriage); Burton VIII 337. Chauvin V 52-54 No. 271; *ANE* 98-99 No. 233.□

Q238.1§, ‡Punishment for drinking liquor.
Nûr al-Dîn and Maryam: *Alf* IV 89; Burton VIII 287. Chauvin V 52-54 No. 271; *ANE* 98-99 No. 233.□

Q241, Adultery punished. See: *DOTTI*; *GMC*. (Cf. Q499.2.1).

Landsman ¿Abdallah and Merman ¿Abdallah: *Alf* IV 205; Burton IX 183. Chauvin V 6-7 No. 3; *ANE* 65-66 No. 256.□

Q241.1, Desire to commit adultery punished. See: *DOTTI*; *GMC*. (Cf. D661.6.1§).
Water-carrier and Goldsmith's Wife: *Alf* II 285; Burton V 89-90. Chauvin VI 192 No. 361; *ANE* 444 No. 122.□

Q241.3§, Adultery observed: onlooker is outraged and punishes culprits. See: *DOTTI*.
Debauchee and Three Years Old Child: *Alf* III 176,-cf.; Burton VI 208. Chauvin VIII 62-63 No. 147; *ANE* 166-67 No. 206.□

Q241.4§, ‡Faithlessness in marriage punished. See: *DOTTI*.
Portress Amînah: Bitten Cheek: *Alf* I 59-60; Burton I 180-84. Chauvin V 98-99 No. 33; *ANE* 326-27 No. 20;
Sweep and Noble Lady: Infidelity Repaid: *Alf* II 190,-cf.; Burton IV 128. Chauvin VI 148 No. 306; *ANE* 403-4 No. 72;
Mock Caliph/¿Alî al-Jawharî: *Alf* II 198; Burton IV 146. Chauvin V 99-100 No. 174; *ANE* 304-5 No. 73.□

Q242, Incest punished. See: *DOTTI*; *GMC*.
First Qalandar: Brother-Sister Incest: *Alf* I 42; Burton I 109-10. Chauvin V 196-97 No. 115; *ANE* 337-38 No. 15;
King ¿Umar al-Nu¿mân and Sons: *Alf* I 207ff.,-cf./(unwitting incest unpunished); Burton II 172. Chauvin VI 112-24 No. 277; *ANE* 430-34 No. 39.□

Q243.1.3.1§, ‡Bearer of illicit (incestuous) love letter punished. (Cf. P324.3.1§, P469.0.1§).
al-'Amjad and al-'As¿ad: *Alf* II 113-14,-(incestuous); Burton III 311. Chauvin V 208-10 No. 120[.1]; *ANE* 341-42 No. 61/pt. 2.□

Q243.2, ‡Seduction punished.
Tâj al-Mulûk: *Alf* I 305,-(planned then abandoned); Burton III 42. Chauvin V 126-28 No. 60; *ANE* 406-8 No. 40.□

Q243.7§, Girl's (woman's) immodesty punished. See: *DOTTI*; *GMC*. (Cf. Q328.2§).
Pretty Gray-haired Woman Retorts: *Alf* II 302-3,-(rebuked); Burton V 163. Chauvin VI 153 No. 318; *ANE* 77-78 No. 152.□

Q243.9.1§, ‡Being a 'Peeping Tom' rebuked (punished). (Cf. P807.8.2§).
Budûr and Jubayr ibn ¿Umayr: *Alf* II 236; Burton IV 229. Chauvin VII 93-94 No. 374; *ANE* 243-44 No. 83.□

Q244, Punishment for ravisher. (Cf. Q258.1§).
Anîs al-Jalîs: *Alf* I 129,-(*naḥr*); Burton II 8,-(throat to be cut). Chauvin V 120-24 No. 58; *ANE* 316-17 No. 35.□

Q249§, ‡Punishment for failure (refusal) to consummate marriage. (Cf. T168.1§).
Qamar al-Zamân and Budûr: *Alf* II 102,-(promised by father of bride); Burton III 287. Chauvin V 204-12 No. 120; *ANE* 341-45 No. 61.□

Q253.1, Bestiality punished. See: *DOTTI*. (Cf. T465.9.3§).
Butcher Wardân and Bear Lover: *Alf* II 252; Burton IV 295. Chauvin V 177-78 No. 101; *ANE* 442-43 No. 101.□

Q258.1§, Rape unpunished. See: *GMC*.
King ¿Umar al-Nu¿mân and Sons: *Alf* I 183,-ff.; Burton II 124. Chauvin VI 112-24 No. 277; *ANE* 430-34 No. 39.□

Q259§, Killing for sexual honor.
Nûr al-Dîn and Maryam: *Alf* IV 108,-cf./(ritual killing/human sacrifice); Burton VIII 324. Chauvin V 52-54 No. 271; *ANE* 98-99 No. 233.□

Q259.3§, ‡Killing for sexual honor rewarded. (Cf. Q201.1§).
Three Apples: Hasty Uxoricide: *Alf* I 63,-(innocent wife); Burton I 191. Chauvin VI 144-45 No. 302; *ANE* 414-15 No. 21;
Butcher Wardân and Bear Lover: *Alf* II 252; Burton IV 295. Chauvin V 177-78 No. 101; *ANE* 442-43 No. 101;

Jeweler's Wife and Qamar al-Zamân: *Alf* IV 265; Burton IX 300. Chauvin V 212-14 No. 121; *ANE* 345-47 No. 260.□

Q261, Treachery punished. See: *DOTTI*; *GMC*.
Anîs al-Jalîs: *Alf* I 145; Burton II 44. Chauvin V 120-24 No. 58; *ANE* 316-17 No. 35;
Jackals and Wolf as Umpire: *Alf* IV 167; Burton IX 105. Chauvin II 223 No. 152/21; *ANE* 235 No. 252.□

Q263, Lying (perjury) punished. See: *DOTTI*. (Cf. M110.1.1§, P520§).
Jewish qâḍî and His Devout Wife: *Alf* III 10; Burton V 256. Chauvin VI 154-55 No. 321; *ANE* 242 No. 163.□

Q263.1, Death as punishment for perjury. See: *GMC*. (Cf. P520§).
Jullanâr of the Sea: *Alf* III 269,-cf./(lying); Burton VII 305. Chauvin V 147-51 No. 73; *ANE* 248-51 No. 227.□

Q264§, Repayment for good with evil (perfidy) punished. See: *DOTTI*; *GMC*. (Cf. W11.5.0.1§).
Fisherman and Afrit: Ingratitude: *Alf* I 15,-cf.; Burton I 44. Chauvin VI 23-25 No. 195; *ANE* 183-84 No. 8;
Mouse and Cat: *Alf* IV 135; Burton IX 37. Chauvin II 218 No. 152/2; *ANE* 305-6 No. 237;
Abû Qîr and Abû Ṣîr: *Alf* IV 189; Burton IX 148ff. Chauvin V 15-17 No. 10; *ANE* 75-77 No. 255;
Ma¿rûf the Cobbler: *Alf* IV 315-16,-(treacherous wife killed); Burton X 51. Chauvin VI 81-82 No. 250; *ANE* 291-93 No. 262.□

Q271.4.3§, ‡Beating as punishment for failure to pay for goods (services). See: *DOTTI*.
Hashish Eater's Dream: *Alf* II 10; Burton III 93. Chauvin VI 124 No. 278; *ANE* 216 No. 42.□

Q281, Ingratitude punished. See: *DOTTI*; *GMC*.
Dûban and King Yûnân: *Alf* I 22-23,-(with death); Burton I 60. Chauvin V 275-76 No. 156; *ANE* 459 No. 9.□

Q285.4, ‡Slave-driving punished.
Ḥammâd: Treacherous Bedouin: *Alf* II 20; Burton III 112. Chauvin VI 124 n. 1 No. 277; *ANE* 200 No. 43;
¿Alî Shâr and Zumurrud: *Alf* II 229-32,-(slavers); Burton IV 220-25. Chauvin V 89-91 No. 28; *ANE* 100-1 No. 82.□

Q296, ‡Injustice punished. See: *DOTTI*.
Jackals and Wolf as Umpire: *Alf* IV 167; Burton IX 105. Chauvin II 223 No. 152/21; *ANE* 235 No. 252.□

Q296.2§, ‡Unjust ruler reprimanded.
Nuzhat al-Zamân Tested/¿Umar al-Nu¿mân: *Alf* I 203; Burton II 163. Chauvin VI 116, n.1/passim No. 277; *ANE* 432,/passim No. 39.□

Q301, Jealousy punished.
Enchanted Spring: Change of Sex: *Alf* III 148,-cf.; Burton VI 149,-(father orders son's execution). Chauvin VIII 43 No. 11; *ANE* 175-76 No. 191.□

Q322.1§, ‡Failure to wash hands before (after) meal punished. See: *DOTTI*.
Reeve's Story: Why Maimed by Bride: *Alf* I 98; Burton I 286-87. Chauvin V 220-21 No. 305; *ANE* 351 No. 25.□

Q325.2§, ‡Disobedience to parents (father, mother) punished. See: *DOTTI*. (Cf. P248.1§).
Qamar al-Zamân and Budûr: *Alf* II 68; Burton III 219. Chauvin V 204-12 No. 120; *ANE* 341-45 No. 61.□

Q326, ‡Impudence [(insolence)] punished. See: *DOTTI*.
Hishâm and Arab Youth: *Alf* II 184; Burton IV 102. Chauvin V 288 No. 172; *ANE* 222-23 No. 68;
Nûr al-Dîn and Maryam: *Alf* IV 129; Burton IX 17. Chauvin V 52-54 No. 271; *ANE* 98-99 No. 233.□

Q328.2§, Woman baring her head in public punished. (Cf. Q243.7§).
Pretty Gray-haired Woman Retorts: *Alf* II 302-3,-(rebuked); Burton V 163. Chauvin VI 153 No. 318; *ANE* 77-78 No. 152.□

Q331.3§, ‡Conceit (arrogance) punished. See: *DOTTI*. (Cf. W166§).

King ¿Umar al-Nu¿mân and Sons: *Alf* I 241; Burton II 244,-(pride). Chauvin VI 112-24 No. 277; *ANE* 430-34 No. 39;
King Jalî¿âd and Shimâs: *Alf* IV 157; Burton IX 81. Chauvin VI 9-11 No. 184; *ANE* 237-38 No. 236.□

Q331.3.1§, ‡Rebuke (reprimand) for arrogance.
Tawaddud: Slavegirl Sold and Regained: *Alf* II 316; Burton V 221. Chauvin VII 117-19 No. 387; *ANE* 408-10 No. 157;
Angel of Death and Proud King: *Alf* III 8; Burton V 247. Chauvin VI 183-84 No. 349,[pt. 1]; *ANE* 104 No. 158.□

Q340.1§, ‡Meddling in prohibited (non-tabu) matters punished. (Cf. C411.1, J679.1§).
Porter and Ladies of Baghdad: *Alf* I 38; Burton I 107. Chauvin V 251-52 No. 148; *ANE* 324-26 No. 14.□

Q341, Curiosity punished. See: *DOTTI*; *GMC*.
Serpent-charmer and Wife: *Alf* IV 146,-cf.; Burton IX 57. Chauvin II 220 No. 152/9; *ANE* 368 No. 244.□

Q342, ‡Inquisitiveness punished.
Porter and Ladies of Baghdad: *Alf* I 35; Burton I 93. Chauvin V 251-52 No. 148; *ANE* 324-26 No. 14.□

Q382.1§, ‡Execution as punishment for failure to heal royal person (king, princess, etc.).
Qamar al-Zamân and Budûr: *Alf* II 86, 94; Burton III 256, 272. Chauvin V 204-12 No. 120; *ANE* 341-45 No. 61;
Conversion of Princess by Khawwâṣ: *Alf* III 15; Burton V 284. Chauvin V 239 No. 139; *ANE* 145 No. 171;
Sayf al-Mulûk: *Alf* III 280; Burton VII 332. Chauvin VII 64-73 No. 348; *ANE* 362-64 No. 229.□

Q394, Uxoriousness punished.
King Jalî¿âd and Shimâs: *Alf* IV 164,-cf., 179,-cf.; Burton IX 97, 127. Chauvin VI 9 No. 184; *ANE* 237-38 No. 236.□

Q402, Punishment of children for parents' offense. (Cf. S312.5§).
Landsman ¿Abdallah and Merman ¿Abdallah: *Alf* IV 205; Burton IX 183. Chauvin V 6-7 No. 3; *ANE* 65-66 No. 256.□

Q410.1.1§, ‡One wish granted before execution ('last wish'). See: *DOTTI*.
Anîs al-Jalîs: *Alf* I 144; Burton II 42. Chauvin V 120-24 No. 58; *ANE* 316-17 No. 35.□

Q410.1.2§, ‡Person to be executed is blindfolded.
Anîs al-Jalîs: *Alf* I 144; Burton II 42. Chauvin V 120-24 No. 58; *ANE* 316-17 No. 35;
Mock Caliph/¿Alî al-Jawharî: *Alf* II 198; Burton IV 145. Chauvin V 99-100 No. 174; *ANE* 304-5 No. 73.□

Q411.0.1.1, Adulterer killed [(death as punishment for adultery)]. See: *GMC*. (Cf. Q499.2.1).
Landsman ¿Abdallah and Merman ¿Abdallah: *Alf* IV 205,-(for men); Burton IX 183. Chauvin V 6-7 No. 3; *ANE* 65-66 No. 256.□

Q411.0.1.1.1§, ‡Husband kills adulteress wife. See: *DOTTI*. (Cf. Q241).
Husband and Parrot: *Alf* III 141; Burton I 54. Chauvin VI 139 No. 294; *ANE* 226 No. 11.□

Q411.0.2, Husband kills wife and paramour. See: *DOTTI*. (Cf. S60.0.1§).
Shahriyâr and Shâhzamân: *Alf* I 2; Burton I 4. Chauvin V 188-91 No. 111; *ANE* 370-71 No. 1.□

Q411.0.2.1§, ‡Husband kills adulteress wife and procuress (confederate, servant, etc.). See: *DOTTI*.
Jeweler's Wife and Qamar al-Zamân: *Alf* IV 265; Burton IX 300. Chauvin V 212-14 No. 121; *ANE* 345-47 No. 260.□

Q411.4, Death as punishment for treachery. See: *DOTTI*; *GMC*.
Anîs al-Jalîs: *Alf* I 145; Burton II 44. Chauvin V 120-24 No. 58; *ANE* 316-17 No. 35;
Hasan of Basrah: *Alf* III 313; Burton VIII 27. Chauvin VII 29-35 No. 212A; *ANE* 207-10 No. 230;
Ma¿rûf the Cobbler: *Alf* IV 313; Burton X 47. Chauvin VI 81-82 No. 250; *ANE* 291-93 No. 262.□

Q411.7, Death as punishment for ravisher. See: *GMC*.
Sayf al-Mulûk: *Alf* III 300,-(jinni); Burton VIII 2. Chauvin VII 64-73 No. 348; *ANE* 362-64 No. 229.□

Q413.0.1, ‡Threat of hanging.
¿Alî Shâr and Zumurrud: *Alf* II 228; Burton IV 212. Chauvin V 89-91 No. 28; *ANE* 100-1 No. 82.□

Q413.9.1.1§, ‡Hanging as punishment for disobeying ruler (king, caliph, etc.).
¿Alî Shâr and Zumurrud: *Alf* II 228; Burton IV 212. Chauvin V 89-91 No. 28; *ANE* 100-1 No. 82.□

Q415.0.1, ‡Punishment: being eaten by animals.
Shipwrecked Woman and Her Child: *Alf* III 12,-(sea beasts); Burton V 260. Chauvin VI 160 No. 324; *ANE* 379 No. 164.□

Q421, Punishment: beheading [(decapitation)]. See: *DOTTI*.
Barber's Tale of Himself: Joins Doomed Party: *Alf* I 110; Burton I 318. Chauvin V 156-57 No. 80; *ANE* 115-17 No. 28;
Anîs al-Jalîs: *Alf* I 145; Burton II 44. Chauvin V 120-24 No. 58; *ANE* 316-17 No. 35;
Hishâm and Arab Youth: *Alf* II 184,-(ordered); Burton IV 102. Chauvin V 288 No. 172; *ANE* 222-23 No. 68.□

Q421.1, Heads on stakes. Punishment by beheading and placing the heads on stakes. See: *DOTTI*; *GMC*. (Cf. H901.1, S139.2.2.1).
Qamar al-Zamân and Budûr: *Alf* II 86; Burton III 256. Chauvin V 204-12 No. 120; *ANE* 341-45 No. 61.□

Q422.3§, ‡Stoning to death (*rajm*) as punishment for adultery. See: *DOTTI*.
Devout Jewess and Wicked Elders: *Alf* II 286; Burton V 97. Chauvin VI 193-93 No. 362; *ANE* 169 No. 128;
Jewish qâḍî and His Devout Wife: *Alf* III 10; Burton V 256. Chauvin VI 154-55 No. 321; *ANE* 242 No. 163.□

Q431, Punishment: banishment (exile). See: *DOTTI*; *GMC*.
Barber's Fifth Brother: Daydreams/Defeats Robbers: *Alf* I 121; Burton I 343. Chauvin V 161 No. 85; *ANE* 119-20 No. 33;
Craft and Malice of Women/Frame: *Alf* III 177; Burton VI 212. Chauvin VIII 33-34 No. 1; *ANE* 160-61 No. 181.□

Q431.5.1, ‡Banishment for attempted seduction.
Barber's First Brother: Free Labor for Coquette: *Alf* I 112; Burton I 324. Chauvin V 157-58 No. 81; *ANE* 117 No. 29.□

Q431.8, ‡Banishment as punishment for adultery. (Cf. Q241).
Landsman ¿Abdallah and Merman ¿Abdallah: *Alf* IV 205,-(for females); Burton IX 183. Chauvin V 6-7 No. 3; *ANE* 65-66 No. 256.□

Q432.0.1§, Divorce as punishment. See: *DOTTI*; *GMC*. (Cf. P529.2.1§, Q118§, T196.7§, T283.1§).
King's Son and Merchant's Wife: *Alf* III 156; Burton VI 169. Chauvin VIII 48-49 No. 16; *ANE* 263 No. 196.□

Q432.0.1.1§, ‡Divorce threatened to enforce demand. (Cf. T283.1§).
Hunchback's Tale: Resuscitated: *Alf* I 124,-cf./(wife threatens husband); Burton I 349. Chauvin 5: 163-64 No. 86; *ANE* 120 No. 23;
Hârûn, Slave-girl and Judge Abû-Yûsuf: *Alf* II 202; Burton IV 153. Chauvin VII 114 No. 383; *ANE* 204 No. 75;
Bulûqiya: *Alf* III 76; Burton V 387. Chauvin VII 54 No. 77; *ANE* 130-32 No. 177;
Nûr al-Dîn and Maryam: *Alf* IV 91; Burton VIII 290. Chauvin V 52-54 No. 271; *ANE* 98-99 No. 233.□

Q433, Punishment: imprisonment.
Qamar al-Zamân and Budûr: *Alf* II 68; Burton III 220. Chauvin V 204-12 No. 120; *ANE* 341-45 No. 61.□

Q433.0.1§, ‡Imprisonment for life as punishment—('forever', 'for eternity').
¿Alâ' al-Dîn Abû al-Shâmât: *Alf* II 166; Burton IV 70. Chauvin V 43-49 No. 18; *ANE* 85-87 No. 63.□

Q433.1.2§, ‡Adulteress confined in isolated building. See: *DOTTI*.
Jeweler's Wife and Qamar al-Zamân: *Alf* IV 260; Burton IX 289. Chauvin V 212-14 No. 121; *ANE* 345-47 No. 260.□

Q433.7, ‡Imprisonment for treachery. See: *DOTTI*. (Cf. Q261, Q411.4).
Abû Muḥammad Lazybones: *Alf* II 216; Burton IV 178. Chauvin VI 64-67 No. 233; *ANE* 71-73 No. 78.□

Q433.7.1§, ‡Imprisonment for life for treacherous concubines.
King Jalî¿âd and Shimâs: *Alf* IV 182; Burton IX 134. Chauvin VI 9 No. 184; *ANE* 237-38 No. 236.□

Q434, ‡Punishment: fettering.
Masrûr and Zayn al-Mawâṣif: *Alf* IV 72-73; Burton VIII 245. Chauvin VI 82-84 No. 251; *ANE* 294-95 No. 232.□

Q437.2§, ‡Violators of mores (moral code) sold into slavery—(usually applied to females). (Cf. Q440.2§).
Jeweler's Wife and Qamar al-Zamân: *Alf* IV 260; Burton IX 289. Chauvin V 212-14 No. 121; *ANE* 345-47 No. 260.□

Q439§, Self-imposed (voluntary) exile as punishment. See: *DOTTI*; *GMC*.
King ¿Umar al-Nu¿mân and Sons: *Alf* I 187,-cf./(in order to forget); Burton II 132. Chauvin VI 112-24 No. 277; *ANE* 430-34 No. 39.□

Q440.2§, ‡Punishment: expulsion from tribe or nation (*khal¿*: 'extraction'). See: *DOTTI*. (Cf. Q437.2§).
Ibn Sabâ'ik/Sayf al-Mulûk: *Alf* III 271,-(for failure); Burton VII 309-10. Chauvin VII 65 No. 348/pt.; *ANE* 309-10 No. 228.□

Q442§, ‡Punishment: shunning (boycotting). See: *DOTTI*.
Ibn Sabâ'ik/Sayf al-Mulûk: *Alf* III 271,-(for failure); Burton VII 310,-(thou art not of us nor are we of thee). Chauvin VII 65 No. 348/pt.; *ANE* 309-10 No. 228.□

Q450.1, ‡Torture as punishment. See: *DOTTI*.
Stolen Necklace/Hasty Accusation: *Alf* III 164,-cf.; Burton VI 182-83. Chauvin VIII 53 No. 20; *ANE* 398 No. 200;
Hasan of Basrah: *Alf* IV 40; Burton VIII 116. Chauvin VII 29-35 No. 212A; *ANE* 207-10 No. 230.□

Q451, Mutilation as punishment. See: *DOTTI*.
Reeve's Story: Why Maimed by Bride: *Alf* I 99; Burton I 287. Chauvin V 220-21 No. 305; *ANE* 351 No. 25.□

Q451.0.2, ‡Threat to cut off hand or foot. (Cf. M147§).
Nûr al-Dîn and Maryam: *Alf* IV 89; Burton VIII 287. Chauvin V 52-54 No. 271; *ANE* 98-99 No. 233.□

Q451.1, Hands cut off as punishment. See: *DOTTI*; *GMC*. (Cf. Q205§).
Ibrâhîm and Jamîlah: *Alf* IV 229; Burton IX 228. Chauvin VI 52-53 No. 218; *ANE* 227-29 No. 258.□

Q451.1.1, Hands cut off as punishment for theft. See: *ANE*; *DOTTI*; *GMC*. (Cf. T39.1.4§).
Copt Broker's Story: Lover's Sacrifices Repaid: *Alf* I 94; Burton I 274. Chauvin VI 80 No. 249; *ANE* 313-14 No. 24;
Jewish Doctor's Story: Sororicide: *Alf* I 101; Burton I 297. Chauvin VI 89 No. 253; *ANE* 242 No. 26;
Lover Who Feigned Himself a Thief: *Alf* II 204; Burton IV 156. Chauvin VII 134-35 No. 403; *ANE* 272 No. 76.□

Q451.1.9.1§, ‡'Stuffing' as punishment: object forced into body orifice (anus). See: *DOTTI*. (Cf. T463.8§, Z197.3.4§).
Ma¿n Rewards a Bedouin for Gift: *Alf* II 182-83,-cf.; Burton IV 98. Chauvin VI 78 No. 247; *ANE* 291 No. 66.□

Q451.10, ‡Punishment: genitalia cut off. (Cf. S176).
Barber's Sixth Brother: Emasculated by Abductor: *Alf* I 123,-cf.; Burton I 348. Chauvin V 163-64 No. 86; *ANE* 120 No. 34.□

Q451.10.1, Punishment: castration. See: *DOTTI*; *GMC*.
First Eunuch: Bukhayt Deflowers Mistress: *Alf* I 148; Burton II 50. Chauvin V 277 No. 160; *ANE* 178 No. 37;

Second Eunuch/Kâfûr's Half-lie: *Alf* I 148; Burton II 55,-(gelding). Chauvin V 278 No. 161; *ANE* 178-79 No. 38;
Third Eunuch: Seduces Mistress and Son: *Alf* I 151,-(passim); Burton II 56/non-tale. Chauvin V No. [161B]; *ANE* 179,/passim No. 38.□

Q456.3§, ‡Burial alive in pit (well) as punishment for sorcery (witchcraft). See: *DOTTI*. (Cf. Q225.5§).
Goldsmith and Cashmere Singer: *Alf* III 150,-cf./(abandonment); Burton VI 157. Chauvin VIII 46-47 No. 14; *ANE* 196 No. 194.□

Q457.0.1§, ‡Flaying alive and then stuffing hide with straw as punishment.
¿Alî Shâr and Zumurrud: *Alf* II 229-31; Burton IV 215. Chauvin 5: 89-91 No. 28; *ANE* 100 No. 82.□

Q458.0.6, ‡Flogging as punishment for desire to commit adultery.
Portress Amînah: Bitten Cheek: *Alf* I 60,-cf.; Burton I 185. Chauvin V 98-99 No. 33; *ANE* 326-27 No. 20.□

Q458.0.6.1§, ‡Flogging as punishment for erotic indiscretions (minor sexual sins: kissing, hugging, etc.). See: *DOTTI*.
Portress Amînah: Bitten Cheek: *Alf* I 60; Burton I 185. Chauvin V 98-99 No. 33; *ANE* 326-27 No. 20;
Mock Caliph/¿Alî al-Jawharî: *Alf* II 199,-(act of jealousy); Burton IV 146. Chauvin V 99-100 No. 174; *ANE* 304-5 No. 73.□

Q458.1, Daily beatings as punishment. See: *ANE*; *DOTTI*; *GMC*. (Cf. D691, D2198.5§, S186.9.1§, T232.3.1§).
Eldest Lady's Story: Treacherous Sisters: *Alf* I 57; Burton I 172. Chauvin V 4 No. 443; *ANE* 174-75 No. 19;
¿Abdallah ibn Fâḍil: Treacherous Brothers: *Alf* IV 267-68; Burton IX 306. Chauvin V 2-4 No. 2; *ANE* 63-65 No. 261.□

Q458.3§, ‡Severe beating (flogging till fainting or "almost dead") as punishment. See: *DOTTI*. (Cf. F979.25.1.1§).
Merchant's Curious Wife: *Alf* I 6; Burton I 22. Chauvin V 179-80 No. 104; *ANE* 298-99 No. 3;
Portress Amînah: Bitten Cheek: *Alf* I 60; Burton I 183. Chauvin V 98-99 No. 33; *ANE* 326-27 No. 20;
Second Eunuch/Kâfûr's Half-lie: *Alf* I 148; Burton II 51. Chauvin V 278 No. 161; *ANE* 178-79 No. 38;
Hasan of Basrah: *Alf* IV 41-42; Burton VIII 119. Chauvin VII 29-35 No. 212A; *ANE* 207-10 No. 230.□

Q458.5§, ‡Beating with a whip (whipping, lashing) as punishment. See: *DOTTI*.
al-'Amjad and al-'As¿ad: *Alf* II 131,-cf./(torturing); Burton III 345,-(torturing). Chauvin V 208-10 No. 120[.1]; *ANE* 341-42 No. 61/pt. 2;
Hasan of Basrah: *Alf* III 307,-cf./(torturing), IV 41,-cf./(*with jarîd*); Burton VIII 16, 119,-(with palm-stick). Chauvin VII 29-35 No. 212A; *ANE* 207-10 No. 230.□

Q462, ‡Crucifixion as punishment. See: *DOTTI*.
King ¿Umar al-Nu¿mân and Sons: *Alf* II 21; Burton III 114. Chauvin VI 112-24 No. 277; *ANE* 430-34 No. 39;
Dalîla the Swindler: *Alf* III 223; Burton VII 164. Chauvin V 245-50 No. 147; *ANE* 163-64 No. 224;
Ibrâhîm and Jamîlah: *Alf* IV 229,-(for abduction); Burton IX 228. Chauvin VI 52-53 No. 218; *ANE* 227-29 No. 258;
¿Abdallah ibn Fâḍil: Treacherous Brothers: *Alf* IV 288; Burton IX 348-49. Chauvin V 2-4 No. 2; *ANE* 63-65 No. 261.□

Q462.0.1§, ‡Threatening with crucifixion (as punishment).
Nûr al-Dîn ¿Alî and Son: *Alf* I 82,-(threat/for poor cooking—under-peppered dish); Burton I 246. Chauvin VI 102-6 No. 270; *ANE* 317-19 No. 22;
Tâj al-Mulûk: *Alf* I 306,-(daughter threatens father); Burton III 44. Chauvin V 126-28 No. 60; *ANE* 406-8 No. 40.□

Q473, Punishment: disgraceful journey through streets. See: *GMC*.
Barber's Second Brother: Humiliated by Playgirl: *Alf* I 113; Burton I 328. Chauvin V 158 No. 82; *ANE* 117-18 No. 30;

King ¿Umar al-Nu¿mân and Sons: *Alf* II 21; Burton III 114. Chauvin VI 112-24 No. 277; *ANE* 430-34 No. 39;
Devout Jewess and Wicked Elders: *Alf* II 286,-(*faḍîḥah*); Burton V 97,-(cried name in public). Chauvin VI 193-93 No. 362; *ANE* 169 No. 128;
Masrûr and Zayn al-Mawâṣif: *Alf* IV 76; Burton VIII 257. Chauvin VI 82-84 No. 251; *ANE* 294-95 No. 232;
Abû Qîr and Abû Ṣîr: *Alf* IV 197; Burton IX 163. Chauvin V 15-17 No. 10; *ANE* 75-77 No. 255.□

Q473.5, Punishment: sending out of town on donkeys.
Barber's First Brother: Free Labor for Coquette: *Alf* I 112,-(camel); Burton I 324. Chauvin V 157-58 No. 81; *ANE* 117 No. 29;
King ¿Umar al-Nu¿mân and Sons: *Alf* II 21; Burton III 114. Chauvin VI 112-24 No. 277; *ANE* 430-34 No. 39.□

Q482, ‡Punishment: noble person must do menial service. See: *DOTTI*.
¿Alâ' al-Dîn Abû al-Shâmât: *Alf* II 170-71,-(kitchen maid); Burton IV 74. Chauvin V 43-49 No. 18; *ANE* 85-87 No. 63;
Hind bint al-Nu¿mân and al-Ḥajjâj: *Alf* III 202; Burton VII 98. Chauvin V 115-4 No. 50; *ANE* 221-22 No. 212.□

Q482.7§, ‡Punishment: nobleman must serve as servant (doorkeeper). See: *DOTTI*.
Hind bint al-Nu¿mân and al-Ḥajjâj: *Alf* III 202,-(camel-driver); Burton VII 98. Chauvin V 115-4 No. 50; *ANE* 221-22 No. 212.□

Q489.1§, ‡Husband withholds conjugal relations from wife as punishment.
King and Vizier's Wife/Tracks of Lion: *Alf* III 140; Burton VI 131. Chauvin VIII 35 No. 2; *ANE* 261 No. 182.□

Q490§, ‡Household (family) and property of ruler's enemy (criminal) confiscated, destroyed, or deemed available to the public (mob). (*'istibâḥah*). See: *DOTTI*. (Cf. P760.8.1.1§, R201§, S101.1§).
Anîs al-Jalîs: *Alf* I 135; Burton II 19. Chauvin V 120-24 No. 58; *ANE* 316-17 No. 35;
Ghânim ibn Ayyûb: *Alf* I 158; Burton II 68. Chauvin VI 14 No. 188; *ANE* 192-93 No. 36;
al-'Amjad and al-'As¿ad: *Alf* II 131; Burton III 347. Chauvin V 208-10 No. 120[.1]; *ANE* 341-42 No. 61/pt. 2.□

Q491, Indignity to corpse as punishment.
Three Apples: Hasty Uxoricide: *Alf* I 61,-cf./(cut up corpse); Burton I 187-88,-(corpse cut into nineteen pieces). Chauvin V 98-99 No. 33; *ANE* 326-27 No. 21.□

Q491.5, ‡Skull used as drinking cup.
Sayf al-Mulûk: *Alf* III 292,-cf./(ghoulish practice); Burton VII 358. Chauvin VII 64-73 No. 348; *ANE* 362-64 No. 229.□

Q491.6.2§, ‡Corpse of slain person thrown to carnivorous animals (dogs, wolves, etc.). See: *DOTTI*; *PSAE*.
Three Apples: Hasty Uxoricide: *Alf* I 60,-(to be cast into river); Burton I 187-88. Chauvin V 98-99 No. 33; *ANE* 326-27 No. 21;
Ḥammâd: Treacherous Bedouin: *Alf* II 20; Burton III 112. Chauvin VI 124 n. 1 No. 277; *ANE* 200 No. 43;
¿Alî Shâr and Zumurrud: *Alf* II 229-31,-cf.; Burton IV 215. Chauvin V 89-91 No. 28; *ANE* 100-1 No. 82.□

Q497.2§, ‡Beard plucked out as punishment. (Cf. P672).
Qamar al-Zamân and Budûr: *Alf* II 82,-cf.; Burton III 246. Chauvin V 204-12 No. 120; *ANE* 341-45 No. 61;
Masrûr and Zayn al-Mawâṣif: *Alf* IV 76; Burton VIII 252. Chauvin VI 82-84 No. 251; *ANE* 294-95 No. 232.□

Q494.4§, ‡Reprimand (censure, rebuke, censure, etc.) as punishment—usually, public.
¿Abdallah ibn Fâḍil: Treacherous Brothers: *Alf* IV 284; Burton IX 342,-(reproved). Chauvin V 2-4 No. 2; *ANE* 63-65 No. 261.□

Q499.2.1, Humiliating death as punishment for adultery. See: *GMC*. (Cf. Q411.0.1.1).
Second Qalandar: Afrit's Wife: *Alf* I 46; Burton I 122. Chauvin V 197-200 No. 116; *ANE* 338-39 No. 16.□

Q502, Wandering as punishment.
King ¿Umar al-Nu¿mân and Sons: *Alf* I 241; Burton II 244,-(love of travel). Chauvin VI 112-24 No. 277; *ANE* 430-34 No. 39.□

Q550.0.1§, 'Poetic justice'. See: *DOTTI*; *GMC*. (Cf. N747§, U10.0.1§, V301.1.0.1§).
Shipwrecked Woman and Her Child: *Alf* III 12,-(sea beasts); Burton V 260. Chauvin VI 160 No. 324; *ANE* 379 No. 164.□

Q550.2§, ‡Eternal punishment (forever).
Jinn Imprisoned in Flasks: *Alf* III 127; Burton VI 96,-(until the Day of Doom). Chauvin VII 113 No. 380=no/text; *ANE* 146 No. 180.□

Q550.0.3§, Murderer is himself (inevitably) murdered. See: *DOTTI*. (Cf. A194.2.1§).
Portress Amînah: Bitten Cheek: *Alf* I 60,-(xxx); Burton I 183,-("Whoso slayeth shall be slain"). Chauvin V 98-99 No. 33; *ANE* 326-27 No. 20;
Omar and Young Badawî: Returning to be Executed: *Alf* II 288,-cf./(*al-mar'u maqtûlun bi-mâ qatal*); Burton V 101,-(slain of that wherewith he slew). Chauvin V 216 No. 125; *ANE* 429-30 No. 130;
Shipwrecked Woman and Her Child: *Alf* III 12,-cf./(devoured by sea animal); Burton V 260. Chauvin VI 160 No. 324; *ANE* 379 No. 164.□

Q551.3.0.1.2§, ‡Eblis transformed from (mighty) hybrid form to worm (for disobeying own parent).
Bulûqiya: *Alf* III 33; Burton V 319. Chauvin VII 54 No. 77; *ANE* 130-32 No. 177.□

Q551.3.2.4.1§, ‡Punishment: transformation into mule. See: *DOTTI*. (Cf. D132.2.1§).
Third Shaykh: Transformation by Wife: *Alf* I 13,-(she-mule); Burton I 36. Chauvin VII 130 No. 398; *ANE* 378 No. 7.□

Q551.3.2.7, ‡Punishment: transformation to dog. See: *DOTTI*.
Second Shaykh: Treacherous Brothers: *Alf* I 11; Burton I 35. Chauvin V 6 No. 397; *ANE* 377-78 No. 6;
Eldest Lady's Story: Treacherous Sisters: *Alf* I 57,-(bitches); Burton I 172. Chauvin V 4 No. 443; *ANE* 174-75 No. 19;
¿Abdallah ibn Fâḍil: Treacherous Brothers: *Alf* IV 280; Burton IX 333. Chauvin V 2-4 No. 2; *ANE* 63-65 No. 261.□

Q551.3.4, Transformation into stone [(petrification)] as punishment. See: *DOTTI*; *GMC*. (Cf. D231, F768.1).
Abû Muḥammad Lazybones: *Alf* II 215,-(passim); Burton IV 175. Chauvin VI 64-67 No. 233; *ANE* 71-73 No. 78;
¿Abdallah ibn Fâḍil: Treacherous Brothers: *Alf* IV 277,-(*maskh*); Burton IX 327. Chauvin V 2-4 No. 2; *ANE* 63-65 No. 261.□

Q552.0.3§, ‡Nature ceases to be benevolent or bountiful as punishment—(weather, animals, plants, etc. stop giving). See: *DOTTI*. (Cf. U210.0.1§).
Anûshirawân and Village Damsel: *Alf* II 285; Burton V 88. Chauvin VI 26-27 No. 198; *ANE* 106 No. 121.□

Q552.1, Death by thunderbolt as punishment. See: *DOTTI*. (Cf. V220.0.7.1.1§).
Devout Jewess and Wicked Elders: *Alf* II 287,-(*ṣâ¿iqah*); Burton V 98,-("blasting leven-fire"). Chauvin VI 193-93 No. 362; *ANE* 169 No. 128.□

Q552.1.0.1§, ‡Death by shooting star as punishment. See: *DOTTI*. (Cf. A157.8.1§).
King's Favorite Son and Ogress: *Alf* III 144,-cf./(hand gesture); Burton VI 141. Chauvin VIII 40-41 No. 8B; *ANE* 264 No. 188.□

Q552.1.9§, ‡Incestuous person killed by thunderbolt (or is reduced to ashes, coal). See: *DOTTI*.
First Qalandar: Brother-Sister Incest: *Alf* I 42; Burton I 110. Chauvin V 196-97 No. 115; *ANE* 337-38 No. 15.□

Q552.3.3, ‡Drought as punishment. See: *DOTTI*.
King Jalî¿âd and Shimâs: *Alf* IV 173; Burton IX 116. Chauvin VI 9 No. 184; *ANE* 237-38 No. 236.□

Q552.13.2, ‡Destruction of property by fire from heaven as punishment. See: *DOTTI*.
Son of Unjust King: *Alf* IV 143; Burton IX 52. Chauvin II 219-20 No. 152/7; *ANE* 437 No. 242.□

Q555.6.1§, ‡Failure in mission as punishment for fornication while away from home (a-traveling).

Mercury ¿Alî: *Alf* III 231; Burton VII 181,-(whoredom in strangerhood). Chauvin V 248-50 No. 147; *ANE* 301-3 No. 225.□

Q559.12§, ‡Punishment for unfulfilled vow (promise) to God or saint. (Cf. M209§, V315.2.1§).
Sindbâd's Seventh Voyage: *Alf* III 117,-(*tawbah* from seafaring); Burton VI 70. Chauvin VII 26-29 No. 373G; *ANE* 386-87 No. 179.□

Q560.0.1§, ‡God's punishment may be in the here-and-now or in the hereafter (Hell).
Water-carrier and Goldsmith's Wife: *Alf* II 286,-(*qaṣâṣ*); Burton V 89-90. Chauvin VI 192 No. 361; *ANE* 444 No. 122.□

Q581, Villain nemesis. Person condemned to punishment he had suggested for others. See: *DOTTI*; *GMC*.
Anîs al-Jalîs: *Alf* I 144-45,-(beheading); Burton II 44. Chauvin V 120-24 No. 58; *ANE* 316-17 No. 35;
Abû Qîr and Abû Ṣîr: *Alf* IV 187,-(burning, drowning); Burton IX 164. Chauvin V 15-17 No. 10; *ANE* 75-77 No. 255.□

Q581.1, Unusual murder avenged in like manner. See: *DOTTI*.
Jawdar and His Treacherous Brethren: *Alf* III 201,-(poisoning); Burton VI 256. Chauvin V 257-60 No. 154; *ANE* 244-45 No. 209.□

Q584.1, Transformer transformed.
First Shaykh: Sorceress Wife: *Alf* I 10; Burton I 31. Chauvin VII 129-30 No. 396; *ANE* 376-77 No. 5.□

Q589.5§, ‡Killer animal killed (for revenge).
Lovers of Banû ¿Udhrah and Lion: *Alf* III 209; Burton VII 123. Chauvin V 116-17 No. 52; *ANE* 274 No. 218/[2].□

R. CAPTIVES AND FUGITIVES

R10.0.1§, ‡Person abducted (kidnapped) and held for ransom. See: *DOTTI*.
Barber's Sixth Brother: Emasculated by Abductor: *Alf* I 123; Burton I 347. Chauvin V 163-64 No. 86; *ANE* 120 No. 34.□

R10.1, Princess (maiden) abducted. See: *DOTTI*; *GMC*.
Ni¿mah and Nu¿m: Stolen Wife Regained: *Alf* II 143,-(beloved slave-girl); Burton IV 21. Chauvin VI 96-97 No. 263; *ANE* 314 No. 62.□

R10.1.1§, ‡Queen (royal consort) abducted. (Cf. K2058.2.3§).
King ¿Umar al-Nu¿mân and Sons: *Alf* I 227; Burton II 214. Chauvin VI 112-24 No. 277; *ANE* 430-34 No. 39.□

R10.3, Children abducted [(kidnaped)]. See: *DOTTI*; *GMC*.
Dalîla the Swindler: *Alf* III 220,-(by swindler); Burton VII 157. Chauvin V 245-50 No. 147; *ANE* 163-64 No. 224.□

R11.1, Princess (maiden) abducted by monster (ogre). See: *DOTTI*; *GMC*. (Cf. G302.7.2§, R16.3).
Jinni Keeps Mistress in Box: *Alf* I 4; Burton I 12. Chauvin V 188-89 No. 111; *ANE* 370 No. 1/pt.;
Abû Muhammad Lazybones: *Alf* II 212-13; Burton IV 172. Chauvin VI 64-67 No. 233; *ANE* 71-73 No. 78;
King's Son and Afrit's Mistress: *Alf* III 172; Burton VI 200. Chauvin VIII 59 No. 24; *ANE* 263-64 No. 204;
Sayf al-Mulûk: *Alf* III 287,-(jinni prince); Burton VII 348. Chauvin VII 64-73 No. 348; *ANE* 362-64 No. 229.□

R11.1.2§, ‡Princess (maiden) abducted by Afrit.
Second Qalandar: Afrit's Wife: *Alf* I 45; Burton I 116. Chauvin V 197-200 No. 116; *ANE* 338-39 No. 16.□

R11.1.3§, ‡Abduction by monster (afrit, jinni, etc.) serving human master (possessing magic object). See: *DOTTI*.
Jawdar and His Treacherous Brethren: *Alf* III 196; Burton VI 246. Chauvin V 257-60 No. 154; *ANE* 244-45 No. 209.□

R12, ‡Abduction by pirates. See: *DOTTI*.
¿Alâ' al-Dîn Abû al-Shâmât: *Alf* II 176; Burton IV 85. Chauvin V 43-49 No. 18; *ANE* 85-87 No. 63;
Nûr al-Dîn and Maryam: *Alf* IV 102, 107,-(holy warriors); Burton VIII 316. Chauvin V 52-54 No. 271; *ANE* 98-99 No. 233.□

R12.3.1§, ‡Princess (courtesan) on clandestine visit to lover abducted by robbers. See: *DOTTI*. (Cf. N318.2.1§).
¿Alî ibn Bakkâr: *Alf* II 58; Burton III 198. Chauvin V 153 No. 76; *ANE* 92-93 No. 60.□

R12.6§, ‡Abduction of person(s) for slavery. (Cf. F778.1§, K1817.4.0.1§).
Jawdar and His Treacherous Brethren: *Alf* III 195-96,-cf./(forced labor); Burton VI 244. Chauvin V 257-60 No. 154; *ANE* 244-45 No. 209.□

R12.6.1§, ‡Abduction of persons of different colors (from different lands) so as to furnish grand palace. (Cf. P173.6§).
Jawdar and His Treacherous Brethren: *Alf* III 195-96; Burton VI 246. Chauvin V 257-60 No. 154; *ANE* 244-45 No. 209.□

R12.6.2§, ‡Person(s) abducted and put to forced labor. (Cf. P534§, S73.0.3.2§).
Jawdar and His Treacherous Brethren: *Alf* III 191-93; Burton VI 239. Chauvin V 257-60 No. 154; *ANE* 244-45 No. 209.□

R16.3, ‡Woman abducted by (transformed) fairy. See: *DOTTI*. (Cf. F324, R11.1).
Second Qalandar: Afrit's Wife: *Alf* I 44,-(afrit); Burton I 116. Chauvin V 197-200 No. 116; *ANE* 338-39 No. 16;
King's Son and Afrit's Mistress: *Alf* III 172,-(afrit); Burton VI 200. Chauvin VIII 59 No. 24; *ANE* 263-64 No. 204;
Sayf al-Mulûk: *Alf* III 287,-(on wedding night); Burton VII 348. Chauvin VII 64-73 No. 348; *ANE* 362-64 No. 229.□

R18, Abduction by rejected suitor. See: *GMC*. (Cf. T194§).

Ebony Horse: *Alf* II 262; Burton V 20-21. Chauvin V 221-31 No. 130; *ANE* 172-74 No. 103; **Ibrâhîm and Jamîlah**: *Alf* IV 227; Burton IX 227. Chauvin VI 52-53 No. 218; *ANE* 227-29 No. 258.□

R22, ‡Abduction by giving soporific. See: *ANE*; *DOTTI*. (Cf. K1266.1§).
Ghânim ibn Ayyûb: *Alf* I 154; Burton II 56. Chauvin VI 14 No. 188; *ANE* 192-93 No. 36;
¿Alâ' al-Dîn Abû al-Shâmât: *Alf* II 176,-cf./(abduction); Burton IV 85. Chauvin V 43-49 No. 18; *ANE* 85-87 No. 63;
Hasan of Basrah: *Alf* III 305; Burton VIII 13. Chauvin VII 29-35 No. 212A; *ANE* 207-10 No. 230;
Ibrâhîm and Jamîlah: *Alf* IV 227; Burton IX 225. Chauvin VI 52-53 No. 218; *ANE* 227-29 No. 258.□

R22.1.1§, ‡Abduction by giving soporific and enclosing in chest. See: *DOTTI*. (Cf. K1342).
Hasan of Basrah: *Alf* III 305; Burton VIII 14. Chauvin VII 29-35 No. 212A; *ANE* 207-10 No. 230.□

R41.3, Captivity in dungeon. See: *DOTTI*; *GMC*. (Cf. K2294.2§).
al-'Amjad and al-'As¿ad: *Alf* II 121; Burton III 327. Chauvin V 208-10 No. 120[.1]; *ANE* 341-42 No. 61/pt. 2.□

R43, ‡Captivity on island. (Cf. P441.0.1.1§, S145).
Uns al-Wujûd and al-Ward: *Alf* II 272; Burton V 38. Chauvin VI 127-29 No. 282; *ANE* 438 No. 104.□

R44§, ‡Captivity in (exile to) remote corner of Earth—(e.g., Empty, Ruined, or Dark Quarter).
Ma¿rûf the Cobbler: *Alf* IV 312,-(maiden exiled); Burton X 45. Chauvin VI 81-82 No. 250; *ANE* 291-93 No. 262.□

R45, ‡Captivity in mound (cave, hollow hill). See: *DOTTI*. (Cf. F721.5.3§, T617).
King ¿Umar al-Nu¿mân and Sons: *Alf* I 247; Burton II 256. Chauvin VI 112-24 No. 277; *ANE* 430-34 No. 39.□

R51, Mistreatment of prisoners.
Sayf al-Mulûk: *Alf* III 292; Burton VII 356. Chauvin VII 64-73 No. 348; *ANE* 362-64 No. 229.□

R51.0.2§, ‡Prison as tomb (grave) for the living (prisoner is 'dead-but-alive')—fate more severe than death. (Cf. K512.6§, Z98§).
¿Alâ' al-Dîn Abû al-Shâmât: *Alf* II 166; Burton IV 68. Chauvin V 43-49 No. 18; *ANE* 85-87 No. 63.□

R51.4, Prisoners massacred.
¿Alâ' al-Dîn Abû al-Shâmât: *Alf* II 176,-(Moslems from Alexandria), 178; Burton IV 86. Chauvin V 43-49 No. 18; *ANE* 85-87 No. 63;
Nûr al-Dîn and Maryam: *Alf* IV 108; Burton VIII 324. Chauvin V 52-54 No. 271; *ANE* 98-99 No. 233.□

R51.5§, ‡Prisoners put to hard labor. (Cf. P534§).
¿Alâ' al-Dîn Abû al-Shâmât: *Alf* II 177; Burton IV 86-87. Chauvin V 43-49 No. 18; *ANE* 85-87 No. 63.□

R52.1§, ‡Captive (prisoner) given respite in order to fulfill obligations. See: *DOTTI*.
Trader and Afrit: Accidental Fairy-cide: *Alf* I 8; Burton I 25. Chauvin VI 22-23 No. 194; *ANE* 419-20 No. 4;
Omar and Young Badawî: Returning to be Executed: *Alf* II 288; Burton V 102. Chauvin V 216 No. 125; *ANE* 429-30 No. 130.□

R52.4§, ‡Falling in love with captive (prisoner). (Cf. N887§, T32.1, T91.6.4.1.3§, T404.4.2§).
Barber's Sixth Brother: Emasculated by Abductor: *Alf* I 123; Burton I 346. Chauvin V 163-64 No. 86; *ANE* 120 No. 34.□

R56.1§, ‡Men locked up in chest pollute one another (by urinating). See: *DOTTI*. (Cf. U11.1.3.1§).
Lady and Five Suitors Deceived: *Alf* III 160-61; Burton VI 178. Chauvin VIII 50-51 No. 18; *ANE* 266 No. 198.□

R61, Person sold into slavery. See: *DOTTI*. (Cf. Q437.2§, S73.0.3.2§).
Jawdar and His Treacherous Brethren: *Alf* III 191; Burton VI 238-39. Chauvin V 257-60 No. 154; *ANE* 244-45 No. 209.□

R75, Surrendering [military]. See: *GMC*. (Cf. P555).

First Qalandar: Brother-Sister Incest: *Alf* I 42; Burton I 112. Chauvin V 196-97 No. 115; *ANE* 337-38 No. 15.□

R77§, ‡Captive (prisoner, convict) ransomed or released: grateful for release.
Jewish qâḍî and His Devout Wife: *Alf* III 10-11; Burton V 258. Chauvin VI 154-55 No. 321; *ANE* 242 No. 163.□

R114.1§, ‡Captive ransoms self. (Cf. F341.2).
Two Kings, Just and Unjust: *Alf* IV 149,-cf.; Burton IX 66-67. Chauvin II 221 No. 152/12; *ANE* 422 No. 246.□

R121.7, ‡Lovers ransomed from prison.
Lady and Five Suitors Deceived: *Alf* III 158,-cf.; Burton VI 173. Chauvin VIII 50-51 No. 18; *ANE* 266 No. 198.□

R122.5.1§, ‡Storm lifts ship in the air thus saving it from attacking whale (monster).
Sindbâd's Seventh Voyage: *Alf* III 117; Burton VI 70. Chauvin VII 26-29 No. 373G; *ANE* 386-87 No. 179.□

R130, Rescue of abandoned or lost persons. (Cf. N390.2§).
Qamar al-Zamân and Budûr: *Alf* II 106; Burton III 296. Chauvin V 204-12 No. 120; *ANE* 341-45 No. 61.□

R134.1§, ‡Vanished wife (sweetheart) leaves instructions as to her whereabouts. See: *DOTTI*. (Cf. N737, T41.4§, T96).
Jânshâh: *Alf* III 58; Burton V 358. Chauvin VII 39-44 No. 153; *ANE* 238-41 No. 178.□

R138, Rescue from shipwreck. See: *DOTTI*.
Shipwrecked Woman and Her Child: *Alf* III 11; Burton V 260. Chauvin VI 160 No. 324; *ANE* 379 No. 164.□

R138.5§, ‡Sailor (traveler) left behind rescued by fellow sailors (travelers).
Qamar al-Zamân and Budûr: *Alf* II 106; Burton III 295-96. Chauvin V 204-12 No. 120; *ANE* 341-45 No. 61.□

R151, ‡Husband rescues wife. See: *DOTTI*.
Abû Muḥammad Lazybones: *Alf* II 216; Burton IV 177. Chauvin VI 64-67 No. 233; *ANE* 71-73 No. 78.□

R152, Wife rescues husband. See: *DOTTI*; *GMC*; *PSAE*. (Cf. J1112, K642.2.1§, T202.2.1§).
Tâj al-Mulûk: *Alf* I 299,-(birds); Burton III 31. Chauvin V 126-28 No. 60; *ANE* 406-8 No. 40;
Ma¿rûf the Cobbler: *Alf* IV 313; Burton X 45. Chauvin VI 81-82 No. 250; *ANE* 291-93 No. 262.□

R153.3.3.1§, Men relate bizarre experiences in order to free man captured by jinn. See: *DOTTI*; *GMC*.
Trader and Afrit: Accidental Fairy-cide: *Alf* I 8; Burton I 24-37. Chauvin VI 22-23 No. 194; *ANE* 419-20 No. 4.□

R154.3, ‡Daughter rescues father.
Ma¿rûf the Cobbler: *Alf* IV 313; Burton X 45. Chauvin VI 81-82 No. 250; *ANE* 291-93 No. 262.□

R155, Brothers rescue brothers. See: *DOTTI*.
Jawdar and His Treacherous Brethren: *Alf* III 195; Burton VI 244. Chauvin V 257-60 No. 154; *ANE* 244-45 No. 209.□

R156, Brother rescues sister(s). See: *DOTTI*; *GMC*. (Cf. N734.3§).
King ¿Umar al-Nu¿mân and Sons: *Alf* II 13; Burton III 96. Chauvin VI 112-24 No. 277; *ANE* 430-34 No. 39.□

R156.1, Brother kills man coming to seduce sister.
Ḥammâd: Treacherous Bedouin: *Alf* II 18,-cf./(marriage by force); Burton III 106-12. Chauvin VI 124 n. 1 No. 277; *ANE* 200 No. 43.□

R160.1§, Father's brother (paternal-uncle) as rescuer. (Cf. P293.6.1§).
Sayf al-Mulûk: *Alf* III 290-91; Burton VII 353-54. Chauvin VII 64-73 No. 348; *ANE* 362-64 No. 229.□

R160.3.1§, Mother's brother rescues sister's son. See: *DOTTI*.
Jullanâr of the Sea: *Alf* III 270; Burton VII 306-70. Chauvin V 147-51 No. 73; *ANE* 248-51 No. 227.□

R162, Rescue by captor's daughter (mother, wife). See: *DOTTI*; *GMC*. (Cf. T32.1, T404.4.2§).
al-'Amjad and al-'As¿ad: *Alf* II 131,-cf.; Burton III 347. Chauvin V 208-10 No. 120[.1]; *ANE* 341-42 No. 61/pt. 2;
¿Alâ' al-Dîn Abû al-Shâmât: *Alf* II 179; Burton IV 90ff. Chauvin V 43-49 No. 18; *ANE* 85-87 No. 63.□

R165.9.2§, ‡Rescue from prison by genie. See: *DOTTI*.
Jawdar and His Treacherous Brethren: *Alf* III 195; Burton VI 244. Chauvin V 257-60 No. 154; *ANE* 244-45 No. 209.□

R177§, ‡Execution postponed for a short while: condemned saved (miraculously or by unexpected development of events). See: *DOTTI*. (Cf. N660, V318.1§).
Porter and Ladies of Baghdad: *Alf* I 38; Burton I 103. Chauvin V 251-52 No. 148; *ANE* 324-26 No. 14;
Anîs al-Jalîs: *Alf* I 144; Burton II 42. Chauvin V 120-24 No. 58; *ANE* 316-17 No. 35;
King ¿Umar al-Nu¿mân and Sons: *Alf* I 247; Burton II 255. Chauvin VI 112-24 No. 277; *ANE* 430-34 No. 39;
Nûr al-Dîn and Maryam: *Alf* IV 108; Burton VIII 324. Chauvin V 52-54 No. 271; *ANE* 98-99 No. 233.□

R181, Demon enclosed in bottle released. See: *ANE*; *DOTTI*; *GMC*. (Cf. J1172.3.1.1§, K717).
Fisherman and Afrit: Ingratitude: *Alf* I 14; Burton I 40. Chauvin VI 23-25 No. 195; *ANE* 183-84 No. 8;
City of Brass: *Alf* III 138; Burton VI 121. Chauvin V 32-35 No. 16; *ANE* 146-50 No. 180.□

R185.3.2§, ‡Mortal hides from Angel of Death inside impenetrable enclosure (tower, strong-box, or the like).
Angel of Death and Rich King: *Alf* III 9,-cf./(sends messengers); Burton V 249. Chauvin VI 184-85 No. 350; *ANE* 104-5 No. 159.□

R190§, ‡Failure (inability) to rescue.
¿Alî Shâr and Zumurrud: *Alf* II 225; Burton IV 208-9. Chauvin V 89-91 No. 28; *ANE* 100-1 No. 82;
Nûr al-Dîn and Maryam: *Alf* IV 104; Burton VIII 316-17. Chauvin V 52-54 No. 271; *ANE* 98-99 No. 233;
Foolish Fisher: *Alf* IV 163,-(drowning fisher); Burton IX 93-94. Chauvin II 222 No. 152/16; *ANE* 187 No. 248;
Francolin and Tortoises: *Alf* IV 172; Burton IX 114. Chauvin II 224 No. 152/23; *ANE* 188 No. 254.□

R201§, ‡Reward promised for capturing fugitive, punishment for aiding him. (Cf. Q46, Q490§).
Anîs al-Jalîs: *Alf* I 135; Burton II 21. Chauvin V 120-24 No. 58; *ANE* 316-17 No. 35.□

R211.3.1§, ‡Escape (exit) through secret door. See: *DOTTI*.
Shahriyâr and Shâhzamân: *Alf* I 3; Burton I 9. Chauvin V 188-91 No. 111; *ANE* 370-71 No. 1;
Tâj al-Mulûk: *Alf* I 299,-(*bâb al-sirr*); Burton III 31,-(private door). Chauvin V 126-28 No. 60; *ANE* 406-8 No. 40;
Mock Caliph/¿Alî al-Jawharî: *Alf* II 192; Burton IV 132,-("secret postern"). Chauvin V 99-100 No. 174; *ANE* 304-5 No. 73;
Dalîla the Swindler: *Alf* III 222; Burton VII 162,-(private door). Chauvin V 245-50 No. 147; *ANE* 163-64 No. 224;
Hasan of Basrah: *Alf* IV 54,-cf./(entry); Burton VIII 144,-("private postern"). Chauvin VII 29-35 No. 212A; *ANE* 207-10 No. 230.□

R211.5.2.1§, ‡Fetters break (accidentally) and allow captive to escape. (Cf. N650).
King ¿Umar al-Nu¿mân and Sons: *Alf* I 247,-(broken due to ire); Burton II 255. Chauvin VI 112-24 No. 277; *ANE* 430-34 No. 39;
al-'Amjad and al-'As¿ad: *Alf* II 118; Burton III 321. Chauvin V 208-10 No. 120[.1]; *ANE* 341-42 No. 61/pt. 2.□

R212.3§, ‡Escape from grave (cave) by following wild animal (or animal's tracks).
Bulûqiya/Ḥâsib/Queen of Vipers: *Alf* III 20; Burton V 301. Chauvin VII 54 No. 77; *ANE* 130-32 No. 177;
Sindbâd's Fourth Voyage: *Alf* III 105; Burton VI 44-45. Chauvin VII 18-20 No. 373D; *ANE* 386 No. 179.□

R212.4§, ‡Escape from grave (cave) by following ray of light.
Bulûqiya/Ḥâsib/Queen of Vipers: *Alf* III 20; Burton V 301. Chauvin VII 54 No. 77; *ANE* 130-32 No. 177.□

R213.3§, ‡Abandoning own home (nest, den, etc.) to escape predator (intruder). (Cf. J838.1§).
Water-fowl and Tortoise: *Alf* II 28; Burton III 130,-(oppressor). Chauvin II 226-27 No. 5; *ANE* 444 No. 46;
Crow and Viper: *Alf* IV 141; Burton IX 46. Chauvin II 219 No. 152/5; *ANE* 162 No. 240.□

R213.4.1§, ‡Escape from home to avoid creditors. See: *DOTTI*. (Cf. K249.5§).
Island King/Pious Jewish Merchant: *Alf* III 16; Burton V 290. Chauvin VI 161 No. 325; *ANE* 234 No. 174;
Mercury ¿Alî: *Alf* III 228; Burton VII 175. Chauvin V 248-50 No. 147; *ANE* 301-3 No. 225;
Ma¿rûf the Cobbler: *Alf* IV 302; Burton X 24. Chauvin VI 81-82 No. 250; *ANE* 291-93 No. 262.□

R215, Escape from execution.
King ¿Umar al-Nu¿mân and Sons: *Alf* I 247; Burton II 256. Chauvin VI 112-24 No. 277; *ANE* 430-34 No. 39.□

R217.1§, ‡Escape from island on raft. See: *DOTTI*. (Cf. F671.3§).
Uns al-Wujûd and al-Ward: *Alf* II 275,-cf./(gourd/reaching island); Burton V 45. Chauvin VI 127-29 No. 282; *ANE* 438 No. 104;
Sindbâd's Third Voyage: *Alf* III 96; Burton VI 28. Chauvin VII 15-18 No. 373C; *ANE* 385-86 No. 179;
Sindbâd's Sixth Voyage: *Alf* III 114; Burton VI 62. Chauvin VII 24-27 No. 373F; *ANE* 386 No. 179;
Sindbâd's Seventh Voyage: *Alf* III 119; Burton VI 71-72. Chauvin VII 26-29 No. 373G; *ANE* 386-87 No. 179;
Sayf al-Mulûk: *Alf* III 285; Burton VII 342-43. Chauvin VII 64-73 No. 348; *ANE* 362-64 No. 229.□

R217.2§, ‡Passing ship (boat) rescues stranded person(s). See: *DOTTI*.
Second Qalandar: Afrit's Wife: *Alf* I 47,-cf./(boarding by stealth); Burton I 127. Chauvin V 197-200 No. 116; *ANE* 338-39 No. 16;
Qamar al-Zamân and Budûr: *Alf* II 105,-cf.; Burton III 296. Chauvin V 204-12 No. 120; *ANE* 341-45 No. 61;
Sindbâd's Third Voyage: *Alf* III 97; Burton VI 29. Chauvin VII 15-18 No. 373C; *ANE* 385-86 No. 179;
Sindbâd's Fourth Voyage: *Alf* III 106; Burton VI 47. Chauvin VII 18-20 No. 373D; *ANE* 386 No. 179;
Ruined Baghdadi and His Slave-girl: *Alf* IV 133; Burton IX 31. Chauvin V 152-53 No. 75; *ANE* 353 No. 235.□

R217.3§, ‡Escape to another land (country) by boarding ship at seaport. See: *DOTTI*.
Anîs al-Jalîs: *Alf* I 135,-cf./(the capital); Burton II 20. Chauvin V 120-24 No. 58; *ANE* 316-17 No. 35;
Nûr al-Dîn and Maryam: *Alf* IV 112; Burton VIII 332-33. Chauvin V 52-54 No. 271; *ANE* 98-99 No. 233.□

R217.7§, ‡Sea chase: escape and pursuit by means of ships. See: *DOTTI*. (Cf. P475.0.3§).
al-'Amjad and al-'As¿ad: *Alf* II 128-31; Burton III 343-34. Chauvin V 208-10 No. 120[.1]; *ANE* 341-42 No. 61/pt. 2;
Nûr al-Dîn and Maryam: *Alf* IV 113-14,-cf./; Burton VIII 335. Chauvin V 52-54 No. 271; *ANE* 98-99 No. 233.□

R219.5§, ‡Lovers flee to a different country (city).
Lady and Five Suitors Deceived: *Alf* III 160; Burton VI 178. Chauvin VIII 50-51 No. 18; *ANE* 266 No. 198.□

R225, Elopement. See: *DOTTI*; *GMC*. (Cf. T131.1.3.2§, T404.4.4§).
King ¿Umar al-Nu¿mân and Sons: *Alf* I 180; Burton II 119. Chauvin VI 112-24 No. 277; *ANE* 430-34 No. 39;
Jeweler's Wife and Qamar al-Zamân: *Alf* IV 257; Burton IX 285. Chauvin V 212-14 No. 121; *ANE* 345-47 No. 260.□

R225.0.1§, ‡Planned elopement foiled (fails). See: *DOTTI*.

Lovers of Banû ¿Udhrah and Lion: *Alf* III 209; Burton VII 122. Chauvin V 116-17 No. 52; *ANE* 274 No. 218/[2].□

R225.1, ‡Elopement on winged horse. See: *DOTTI*.
Ebony Horse: *Alf* II 260; Burton V 19-20. Chauvin V 221-31 No. 130; *ANE* 172-74 No. 103.□

R226§, Flight from home so as to escape wrath of patriarch (father, husband, master). See: *DOTTI*; *GMC*; *PSAE*.
Nûr al-Dîn and Maryam: *Alf* IV 89; Burton VIII 288. Chauvin V 52-54 No. 271; *ANE* 98-99 No. 233;
Ma¿rûf the Cobbler: *Alf* IV 292,-cf.; Burton X 6. Chauvin VI 81-82 No. 250; *ANE* 291-93 No. 262.□

R227.2, Flight from hated husband. See: *DOTTI*; *GMC*.
Masrûr and Zayn al-Mawâṣif: *Alf* IV 75; Burton VIII 250. Chauvin VI 82-84 No. 251; *ANE* 294-95 No. 232.□

R227.9.1.1§, ‡Husband flees from abusive wife. See: *DOTTI*.
Ma¿rûf the Cobbler: *Alf* IV 292-93; Burton X 6. Chauvin VI 81-82 No. 250; *ANE* 291-93 No. 262.□

R229§, ‡Flight of paramour: escape from girl's (woman's) home. See: *DOTTI*.
Lady's Lovers as Pursuer and Fugitive: *Alf* III 143; Burton VI 138-39. Chauvin VIII 38-39 No. 7; *ANE* 267 No. 187.□

R230.0.1§, ‡Flight from tyranny. (Cf. P12.2.1).
Son of Unjust King: *Alf* IV 142; Burton IX 50. Chauvin II 219-20 No. 152/7; *ANE* 437 No. 242.□

R264§, ‡Pursuit by a crowd of people.
Tailor's Story/Barber of Baghdad: *Alf* I 108; Burton I 316. Chauvin V 154-56 No. 78; *ANE* 405-6 No. 27.□

R273.1§, ‡Pursuer follows trail until the road parts into several; trail lost.
Qamar al-Zamân and Budûr: *Alf* II 104; Burton III 290. Chauvin V 204-12 No. 120; *ANE* 341-45 No. 61.□

R311, Tree refuge. See: *DOTTI*; *GMC*.
Jullanâr of the Sea: *Alf* III 259; Burton VII 287. Chauvin V 147-51 No. 73; *ANE* 248-51 No. 227.□

R315, Cave as refuge. See: *DOTTI*.
¿Alâ' al-Dîn Abû al-Shâmât: *Alf* II 180; Burton IV 93,-(cavern). Chauvin V 43-49 No. 18; *ANE* 85-87 No. 63.□

R315.3§, ‡Believers fall asleep for (seven) years in cave where they take refuge from heathen(s). See: *DOTTI*.
Hermit Tempted by Angel: *Alf* II 28,-(poem/simile); Burton III 128. Chauvin II 226 No. 3; *ANE* 221 No. 45/pt. 2.□

R319§, ‡Escape to graveyard (cemetery, tomb). See: *DOTTI*. (Cf. F946§).
First Qalandar: Brother-Sister Incest: *Alf* I 41-42; Burton I 105. Chauvin V 196-97 No. 115; *ANE* 337-38 No. 15.□

R319.1.2.1.1§, ‡Incestuous brother and sister live inside closed tomb so as to hide their illicit love. See: *DOTTI*. (Cf. T415).
First Qalandar: Brother-Sister Incest: *Alf* I 41-42; Burton I 105. Chauvin V 196-97 No. 115; *ANE* 337-38 No. 15.□

R320§, ‡Escape to relatives: fugitive seeks refuge at helpful relative or friend. (Cf. K2112.3).
Anîs al-Jalîs: *Alf* I 129,-(mother); Burton II 8. Chauvin V 120-24 No. 58; *ANE* 316-17 No. 35.□

R320.1§, ‡Mother hides (aids) her runaway child. (Cf. P231.3.6§).
Anîs al-Jalîs: *Alf* I 129; Burton II 8. Chauvin V 120-24 No. 58; *ANE* 316-17 No. 35.□

R325.0.1§, ‡Mosque as refuge.
Ghânim ibn Ayyûb: *Alf* I 158; Burton II 69. Chauvin VI 14 No. 188; *ANE* 192-93 No. 36;
¿Alî ibn Bakkâr: *Alf* II 63; Burton III 207-8. Chauvin V 153 No. 76; *ANE* 92-93 No. 60;
¿Alâ' al-Dîn Abû al-Shâmât: *Alf* II 154; Burton IV 46. Chauvin V 43-49 No. 18; *ANE* 85-87 No. 63.□

R341, ‡Escape by intervention of Providence. See: *DOTTI*. (Cf. V220.0.7.1.1§).

King ¿Umar al-Nu¿mân and Sons: *Alf* I 247,-cf./(fetters break due to *ḥikmah* known only to God); Burton II 256. Chauvin VI 112-24 No. 277; *ANE* 430-34 No. 39;
al-'Amjad and al-'As¿ad: *Alf* II 118,-cf.-(escape from execution); Burton III 320. Chauvin V 208-10 No. 120[.1]; *ANE* 2 341-42 No. 61/pt.;
¿Alâ' al-Dîn Abû al-Shâmât: *Alf* II 154,-(scorpion stings assailant), 176,-(old woman's request); Burton IV 46. Chauvin V 43-49 No. 18; *ANE* 85-87 No. 63.□

R347§, ‡Fate of the runaway (fugitive). See: *DOTTI.*
Nûr al-Dîn and Maryam: *Alf* IV 104,-cf./(war captive,/abducted); Burton VIII 316-17. Chauvin V 52-54 No. 271; *ANE* 98-99 No. 233.□

R347.2.1§, ‡Runaway forced to become prostitute (courtesan, dancer in tavern, etc.). See: *DOTTI.*
Jullanâr of the Sea: *Alf* III 249,-cf./(enslaved); Burton VII 269. Chauvin V 147-51 No. 73; *ANE* 248-51 No. 227.□

R347.3§, ‡Runaway becomes successful. See: *DOTTI*; *PSAE.*
Jullanâr of the Sea: *Alf* III 249,-cf./(mermaid marries king); Burton VII 286-69. Chauvin V 147-51 No. 73; *ANE* 248-51 No. 227;
Ma¿rûf the Cobbler: *Alf* IV 294; Burton X 9. Chauvin VI 81-82 No. 250; *ANE* 291-93 No. 262.□

R355, Eloping girl recaptured by parents. See: *DOTTI.*
Nûr al-Dîn and Maryam: *Alf* IV 114; Burton VIII 335. Chauvin V 52-54 No. 271; *ANE* 98-99 No. 233.□

S. UNNATURAL CRUELTY

S11.7§, ‡Father (ruler) hastily orders his son executed.
Craft and Malice of Women/Frame: *Alf* III 139; Burton VI 128. Chauvin VIII 33-34 No. 1; *ANE* 160-61 No. 181;
King's Son and Afrit's Mistress: *Alf* III 172; Burton VI 200. Chauvin VIII 59 No. 24; *ANE* 263-64 No. 204.□

S11.9§, Runaway father (deserts family). See: *DOTTI*; *GMC*. (Cf. P230.0.3§, P230.9.2§, S440§).
Ma¿rûf the Cobbler: *Alf* IV 292; Burton X 6. Chauvin VI 81-82 No. 250; *ANE* 291-93 No. 262.□

S21, Cruel son. See: *DOTTI*.
Jawdar and His Treacherous Brethren: *Alf* III 189,-(cruel to mother); Burton VI 234. Chauvin V 257-60 No. 154; *ANE* 244-45 No. 209.□

S22.1, Parricide to obtain kingship. See: *DOTTI*.
Abû al-Ḥasan al-Khorâsânî (and Caliph's Favorite): *Alf* IV 237; Burton IX 245. Chauvin V 218-20 No. 129; *ANE* 68-69 No. 259.□

S22.7.1§, ‡Daughter kills her father in order to be with beloved. (Cf. K2214.1.3§).
¿Alâ' al-Dîn Abû al-Shâmât: *Alf* II 179-80,-cf.; Burton IV 92. Chauvin V 43-49 No. 18; *ANE* 85-87 No. 63;
Mercury ¿Alî: *Alf* III 244; Burton VII 204. Chauvin V 248-50 No. 147; *ANE* 301-3 No. 225.□

S22.7.2§, ‡Daughter kills her father for being a disbeliever. (Cf. S73.1.7.2§).
Mercury ¿Alî: *Alf* III 244; Burton VII 204. Chauvin V 248-50 No. 147; *ANE* 301-3 No. 225.□

S25.2.1§, ‡Grandson kills his grandmother.
King ¿Umar al-Nu¿mân and Sons: *Alf* II 21,-(execution for treachery); Burton III 114. Chauvin VI 112-24 No. 277; *ANE* 430-34 No. 39.□

S31, Cruel stepmother. See: *DOTTI*; *GMC*. (Cf. K2218.3§).
Ma¿rûf the Cobbler: *Alf* IV 315; Burton X 49. Chauvin VI 81-82 No. 250; *ANE* 291-93 No. 262.□

S34, ‡Cruel stepsister(s). See: *DOTTI*.
Eldest Lady's Story: Treacherous Sisters: *Alf* I 56; Burton I 171. Chauvin V 4 No. 443; *ANE* 174-75 No. 19.□

S38.1§, ‡Stepson kills stepmother. See: *DOTTI*. (Cf. S24§).
Ma¿rûf the Cobbler: *Alf* IV 316; Burton X 52. Chauvin VI 81-82 No. 250; *ANE* 291-93 No. 262.□

S60.0.1§, Uxoricide (wife-killing). See: *DOTTI*; *GMC*. (Cf. Q411.0.2).
Shahriyâr and Shâhzamân: *Alf* I 5; Burton I 14. Chauvin V 188-89 No. 111; *ANE* 370-71 No. 1.□

S62.1.1§, Shahryâr (Sheheryar) kills a new wife (bride) every night so as to avenge self on women. See: *DOTTI*; *GMC*. (Cf. W255§, W256.6§, W28.5.1§).
Shahriyâr and Shâhzamân: *Alf* I 5; Burton I 14. Chauvin V 188-89 No. 111; *ANE* 370-71 No. 1.□

S62.5.1§, ‡Husband's infidelity (faithlessness) drives wife insane. (Cf. M131.1.1§).
Sweep and Noble Lady: Infidelity Repaid: *Alf* II 190,-cf.; Burton IV 128-29. Chauvin VI 148 No. 306; *ANE* 403-4 No. 72.□

S66.2§, ‡Abandoned (slighted) wife seeks to murder husband.
Ma¿rûf the Cobbler: *Alf* IV 316; Burton X 51. Chauvin VI 81-82 No. 250; *ANE* 291-93 No. 262.□

S71.2§, Cruel paternal-uncle (*¿amm*). See: *DOTTI*; *GMC*.
Lovers of Banû ¿Udhrah and Lion: *Alf* III 209; Burton VII 122. Chauvin V 116-17 No. 52; *ANE* 274 No. 218/[2].□

S72.1§, Cruel paternal-aunt (*¿ammah*). See: *DOTTI*; *GMC*.
King ¿Umar al-Nu¿mân and Sons: *Alf* II 9; Burton III 88-90. Chauvin VI 112-24 No. 277; *ANE* 430-34 No. 39.□

S73.0.1§, Sister cruel to her sister. See: *DOTTI*; *GMC*.
Hasan of Basrah: *Alf* IV 40-42,-(half sister); Burton VIII 116-18. Chauvin VII 29-35 No. 212A; *ANE* 207-10 No. 230.□

S73.0.3.1§, ‡News of birth of a brother kept from (jealous) elder brother. See: *DOTTI*. (Cf. S73.1.1, W183.1.1§).

King ¿Umar al-Nu¿mân and Sons: *Alf* I 163; Burton II 81. Chauvin VI 112-24 No. 277; *ANE* 430-34 No. 39.□

S73.0.3.2§, ‡Brother(s) sell(s) brother into slavery (forced labor). See: *DOTTI*.
Jawdar and His Treacherous Brethren: *Alf* III 191-93; Burton VI 238-39. Chauvin V 257-60 No. 154; *ANE* 244-45 No. 209.□

S73.1.1, Fratricide in order to gain control of kingship. See: *DOTTI*. (Cf. P17.15§).
King ¿Umar al-Nu¿mân and Sons: *Alf* I 163,-cf./(intended); Burton II 79. Chauvin VI 112-24 No. 277; *ANE* 430-34 No. 39;
Jawdar and His Treacherous Brethren: *Alf* III 200; Burton VI 255. Chauvin V 257-60 No. 154; *ANE* 244-45 No. 209.□

S73.1.2.0.1§, ‡Brother kills his brother.
Jawdar and His Treacherous Brethren: *Alf* III 201; Burton VI 256. Chauvin V 257-60 No. 154; *ANE* 244-45 No. 209.□

S73.1.2.1§, ‡Evil (elder) brother murders his good as well as evil brothers: he is jealous of the former and cannot trust the latter. (Cf. U304.5.3§).
Jawdar and His Treacherous Brethren: *Alf* III 201; Burton VI 256. Chauvin V 257-60 No. 154; *ANE* 244-45 No. 209.□

S73.1.3.1§, ‡Elder brother harbors intention of killing new sibling if a boy (brother).
King ¿Umar al-Nu¿mân and Sons: *Alf* I 163; Burton II 79. Chauvin VI 112-24 No. 277; *ANE* 430-34 No. 39.□

S73.1.4, Fratricide motivated by love-jealousy. See: *DOTTI*; *GMC*; *PSAE*.
Jawdar and His Treacherous Brethren: *Alf* III 201; Burton VI 256. Chauvin V 257-60 No. 154; *ANE* 244-45 No. 209;
¿Abdallah ibn Fâḍil: Treacherous Brothers: *Alf* IV 278,-(attempted); Burton IX 330. Chauvin V 2-4 No. 2; *ANE* 63-65 No. 261.□

S73.1.5§, ‡Sororicide motivated by love-jealousy: sister kills sister. See: *DOTTI*.
Eldest Lady's Story: Treacherous Sisters: *Alf* I 56,-(thrown into sea); Burton I 171. Chauvin V 4 No. 443; *ANE* 174-75 No. 19;
Jewish Doctor's Story: Sororicide: *Alf* I 101; Burton I 294-95. Chauvin VI 89 No. 253; *ANE* 242 No. 26.□

S73.1.7.2§, ‡Sister slays her brother in combat—(he is a disbeliever). See: *DOTTI*.
¿Alâ' al-Dîn Abû al-Shâmât: *Alf* II 180,-cf./(army defeated); Burton IV 93. Chauvin V 43-49 No. 18; *ANE* 85-87 No. 63;
Nûr al-Dîn and Maryam: *Alf* IV 125, 126; Burton IX 8, 10. Chauvin V 52-54 No. 271; *ANE* 98-99 No. 233.□

S75.1§, Cruel paternal-uncle's wife (*marat-¿amm*). See: *DOTTI*; *GMC*.
King ¿Umar al-Nu¿mân and Sons: *Alf* II 8; Burton III 88-90. Chauvin VI 112-24 No. 277; *ANE* 430-34 No. 39.□

S101§, Massacre: mass killing. See: *DOTTI*; *GMC*. (Cf. Z356.2§).
King Jalî¿âd and Shimâs: *Alf* IV 171,-(of notables); Burton IX 117. Chauvin VI 9 No. 184; *ANE* 237-38 No. 236.□

S101.1§, ‡Military atrocities (massacres, rapes, etc.). (Cf. Q490§).
Jânshâh: *Alf* III 60; Burton V 360,-(slaughtering the old). Chauvin VII 39-44 No. 153; *ANE* 238-41 No. 178.□

S103.2§, ‡Murder committed during robbery.
¿Alî ibn Bakkâr: *Alf* II 58; Burton III 196. Chauvin V 153 No. 76; *ANE* 92-93 No. 60.□

S105§, Rapist murders victim. See: *GMC*.
King ¿Umar al-Nu¿mân and Sons: *Alf* I 185; Burton II 129. Chauvin VI 112-24 No. 277; *ANE* 430-34 No. 39.□

S105.1§, ‡Murder committed during rape. (Helper, relative, or the like killed by rapist). (Cf. T471.0.4§, S103.2§).
Man [Gardener] and His Wife: *Alf* IV 165; Burton IX 99. Chauvin II 223 No. 152/19; *ANE* 289 No. 250.□

S110.0.2§, Suicide intended (attempted). See: *DOTTI*; *GMC*.
King ¿Umar al-Nu¿mân and Sons: *Alf* I 184,-(to escape seducer); Burton II 129. Chauvin VI 112-24 No. 277; *ANE* 430-34 No. 39;
Tâj al-Mulûk: *Alf* I 306; Burton III 44. Chauvin V 126-28 No. 60; *ANE* 406-8 No. 40;
Sayf al-Mulûk: *Alf* III 282,-(by drowning/due to grief over loss of friend); Burton VII 336-37. Chauvin VII 64-73 No. 348; *ANE* 362-64 No. 229;
Ruined Baghdadi and His Slave-girl: *Alf* IV 130,-(drowning); Burton IX 25. Chauvin V 152-53 No. 75; *ANE* 353 No. 235.□

S110.0.3§, ‡Suicide intended at hands of another—(by intentionally placing oneself where one must be killed).
Nûr al-Dîn and Maryam: *Alf* IV 117; Burton VIII 341. Chauvin V 52-54 No. 271; *ANE* 98-99 No. 233.□

S110.9.1§, ‡Attempted murder: unsuccessful attempt to murder person (intended victim escapes). See: *DOTTI*. (Cf. N659.6.1§, Q210.2§).
¿Abdallah ibn Fâḍil: Treacherous Brothers: *Alf* IV 278; Burton IX 330. Chauvin V 2-4 No. 2; *ANE* 63-65 No. 261;
Ma¿rûf the Cobbler: *Alf* IV 316; Burton X 52. Chauvin VI 81-82 No. 250; *ANE* 291-93 No. 262.□

S110.9.2.2.1§, ‡Husband wishes he had killed his wife.
Ma¿rûf the Cobbler: *Alf* IV 288,-(poem/ with poison); Burton X 1. Chauvin VI 81-82 No. 250; *ANE* 291-93 No. 262.□

S111, Murder by poisoning. See: *DOTTI*; *GMC*.
King ¿Umar al-Nu¿mân and Sons: *Alf* I 216; Burton II 191. Chauvin VI 112-24 No. 277; *ANE* 430-34 No. 39;
Jawdar and His Treacherous Brethren: *Alf* III 201; Burton VI 256. Chauvin V 257-60 No. 154; *ANE* 244-45 No. 209;
Merchant and Robbers: *Alf* IV 166; Burton IX 100-2. Chauvin II 223 No. 152/20; *ANE* 297 No. 251.□

S111.1.1§, ‡Murder with poisoned meal. See: *DOTTI*.
Jawdar and His Treacherous Brethren: *Alf* III 201; Burton VI 256. Chauvin V 257-60 No. 154; *ANE* 244-45 No. 209.□

S111.5, Murder with poisoned book. King wets finger to turn leaves and falls dead. See: *ANE*; *DOTTI*; *GMC*.
Dûban and King Yûnân: *Alf* I 22-23; Burton I 59. Chauvin V 275-76 No. 156; *ANE* 459 No. 9.□

S111.10§, ‡Murder by poisoned drink. (Cf. K1825.1.7§, Z111.9.2§).
Jawdar and His Treacherous Brethren: *Alf* III 201,-(in water); Burton VI 256. Chauvin V 257-60 No. 154; *ANE* 244-45 No. 209.□

S111.10.1§, ‡Murder by supposed blessed (holy) food or drink (elixir).
King ¿Umar al-Nu¿mân and Sons: *Alf* I 227; Burton II 214. Chauvin VI 112-24 No. 277; *ANE* 430-34 No. 39.□

S111.12.1§, ‡Murder by poisoned blade (knife, dagger, sword, etc.).
King ¿Umar al-Nu¿mân and Sons: *Alf* II 9,-cf./(planned); Burton III 90,-(tempered in water of death). Chauvin VI 112-24 No. 277; *ANE* 430-34 No. 39.□

S112.3.1§, ‡Killing (execution, murder) with molten metal (usually lead).
King ¿Umar al-Nu¿mân and Sons: *Alf* I 260,-(molten lead in vagina); Burton II 279. Chauvin VI 112-24 No. 277; *ANE* 430-34 No. 39.□

S113.2, ‡Murder by suffocation [(smothering)]. (Cf. K951).
Jeweler's Wife and Qamar al-Zamân: *Alf* IV 265; Burton IX 300. Chauvin V 212-14 No. 121; *ANE* 345-47 No. 260.□

S115.5.1§, ‡Suicide by falling on erect sword (dagger). See: *DOTTI*. (Cf. N337, Z197.3.1§).
Tâj al-Mulûk: *Alf* I 306,-(attempted); Burton III 44. Chauvin V 126-28 No. 60; *ANE* 406-8 No. 40;
Ḥammâd: Treacherous Bedouin: *Alf* II 20; Burton III 111. Chauvin VI 124 n. 1 No. 277; *ANE* 200 No. 43.□

S118.0.1§, Butcher as executioner. See: *DOTTI*; *GMC*.

Lover Who Feigned Himself a Thief: *Alf* II 205,-cf./(amputator); Burton IV 158. Chauvin VII 134-35 No. 403; *ANE* 272 No. 76;
Butcher Wardân and Bear Lover: *Alf* II 252,-cf.; Burton IV 295. Chauvin V 177-78 No. 101; *ANE* 442-43 No. 101.□

S118.3§, ‡Murder by cutting off head (decapitation).
Jewish Doctor's Story: Sororicide: *Alf* I 101; Burton I 295. Chauvin VI 89 No. 253; *ANE* 242 No. 26.□

S118.5§, Cut up corpse found (in chest, sack, etc.). See: *DOTTI*; *GMC*. (Cf. J1140.3§).
Three Apples: Hasty Uxoricide: *Alf* I 61; Burton I 187. Chauvin VI 144-45 No. 302; *ANE* 414-15 No. 21.□

S123, Burial alive. See: *DOTTI*; *GMC*.
First Qalandar: Brother-Sister Incest: *Alf* I 39-40,-cf.; Burton I 105-6. Chauvin V 196-97 No. 115; *ANE* 337-38 No. 15;
Masrûr and Zayn al-Mawâṣif: *Alf* IV 79; Burton VIII 262. Chauvin VI 82-84 No. 251; *ANE* 294-95 No. 232.□

S123.1, Burial alive of drugged person. See: *ANE*; *DOTTI*; *GMC*. (Cf. K1266.1§, P95§, S480§).
Ghânim ibn Ayyûb: *Alf* I 147, 151; Burton II 47, 57. Chauvin VI 14-16 No. 188; *ANE* 192-93 No. 36.□

S123.1.1§, ‡Burial alive of person in shock (dazed, stunned, etc.). (Cf. F1041.9.9.2§).
Masrûr and Zayn al-Mawâṣif: *Alf* IV 79,-(dazed); Burton VIII 262. Chauvin VI 82-84 No. 251; *ANE* 294-95 No. 232.□

S123.2, Burial of living husband or wife with dead spouse. See: *ANE*; *DOTTI*; *GMC*.
Sindbâd's Fourth Voyage: *Alf* III 103-4; Burton VI 41. Chauvin VII 18-20 No. 373D; *ANE* 386 No. 179.□

S132, ‡Murder by starvation. See: *DOTTI*.
King Jalî¿âd and Shimâs: *Alf* IV 182,-(execution); Burton IX 134. Chauvin VI 9 No. 184; *ANE* 237-38 No. 236.□

S133, Murder by beheading.
King ¿Umar al-Nu¿mân and Sons: *Alf* I 258; Burton II 275. Chauvin VI 112-24 No. 277; *ANE* 430-34 No. 39.□

S139.2.2.1, ‡Heads of slain enemies impaled upon stakes. (Cf. Q421.1).
King ¿Umar al-Nu¿mân and Sons: *Alf* II 6; Burton II 85. Chauvin VI 112-24 No. 277; *ANE* 430-34 No. 39.□

S142, Person thrown into water and abandoned. (Cf. P475.0.3.1.1§).
al-'Amjad and al-'As¿ad: *Alf* II 129-30; Burton III 344. Chauvin V 208-10 No. 120[.1]; *ANE* 341-42 No. 61/pt. 2.□

S142.1§, ‡Child (infant) thrown into water and abandoned.
Shipwrecked Woman and Her Child: *Alf* III 12; Burton V 260. Chauvin VI 160 No. 324; *ANE* 379 No. 164.□

S145, ‡Abandonment on an island. (Marooning). (Cf. R43).
Uns al-Wujûd and al-Ward: *Alf* II 272; Burton V 38. Chauvin VI 127-29 No. 282; *ANE* 438 No. 104.□

S146.1.3§, Wife abandons cruel husband in a well. See: *DOTTI*; *GMC*.
Masrûr and Zayn al-Mawâṣif: *Alf* IV 79,-cf.; Burton VIII 262. Chauvin VI 82-84 No. 251; *ANE* 294-95 No. 232.□

S146.2, ‡Abandonment in cave. See: *DOTTI*. (Cf. N771.0.2§).
Bulûqiya/Ḥâsib/Queen of Vipers: *Alf* III 20; Burton V 301. Chauvin VII 54 No. 77; *ANE* 130-32 No. 177.□

S147, Abandonment on mountain. See: *DOTTI*. (Cf. K2299.1.1.1§).
Second Qalandar: Afrit's Wife: *Alf* I 47; Burton I 127. Chauvin V 197-200 No. 116; *ANE* 338-39 No. 16;
Uns al-Wujûd and al-Ward: *Alf* II 280; Burton V 56. Chauvin VI 127-29 No. 282; *ANE* 438 No. 104;

Jânshâh: *Alf* III 49, 64-65; Burton V 342-43. Chauvin VII 39-44 No. 153; *ANE* 238-41 No. 178;
Hasan of Basrah: *Alf* III 310; Burton VIII 21. Chauvin VII 29-35 No. 212A; *ANE* 207-10 No. 230.□

S154§, ‡Abandonment on trash pile (dirt heap, manure heap, etc.). See: *DOTTI*.
King ¿Umar al-Nu¿mân and Sons: *Alf* I 188; Burton II 134. Chauvin VI 112-24 No. 277; *ANE* 430-34 No. 39.□

S160.4, Mutilation of envoys. See: *GMC*. (Cf. K2294.3.1§, P324.3.1§).
Jinn Imprisoned in Flasks: *Alf* III 128,-cf./(beating severely); Burton VI 98,-(grievous beating). Chauvin VII 113 No. 380=no/text; *ANE* 146 No. 180.□

S161, Mutilation: cutting off hands (arms). See: *ANE*; *DOTTI*; *GMC*. (Cf. F515.1.2§).
Reeve's Story: Why Maimed by Bride: *Alf* I 98-99; Burton I 287. Chauvin V 220-21 No. 305; *ANE* 351 No. 25.□

S166.5.1§, ‡Mutilation: lips cut off.
Barber's Sixth Brother: Emasculated by Abductor: *Alf* I 123; Burton I 347. Chauvin V 163-64 No. 86; *ANE* 120 No. 34.□

S176, Mutilation: sex organs cut off. See: *DOTTI*. (Cf. Q451.10).
¿Azîz and ¿Azîzah: *Alf* I 287; Burton III 2. Chauvin V 144-45 No. 71; *ANE* 111-13 No. 41.□

S176.1, Mutilation: emasculation. See: *DOTTI*; *GMC*.
Barber's Sixth Brother: Emasculated by Abductor: *Alf* I 123; Burton I 348. Chauvin V 163-64 No. 86; *ANE* 120 No. 34;
¿Azîz and ¿Azîzah: *Alf* I 287; Burton III 2. Chauvin V 144-45 No. 71; *ANE* 111-13 No. 41.□

S176.1.5§, ‡Master (mistress) emasculates slave.
Second Eunuch/Kâfûr's Half-lie: *Alf* I 148; Burton II 55. Chauvin V 278 No. 161; *ANE* 178-79 No. 38;
Third Eunuch: Seduces Mistress and Son: *Alf* I 151; Burton II 56/non-tale. Chauvin -5-278 n. 1 No. [161B]; *ANE* 179,/passim No. 38.□

S181.2§, ‡Torture by wounding and then placing salt in wounds.
Barber's Fifth Brother: Daydreams/Defeats Robbers: *Alf* I 120; Burton I 340. Chauvin V 161 No. 85; *ANE* 119-20 No. 33.□

S186, ‡Torturing by beating.
al-'Amjad and al-'As¿ad: *Alf* II 131; Burton III 345. Chauvin V 208-10 No. 120[.1]; *ANE* 341-42 No. 61/pt. 2;
Hasan of Basrah: *Alf* III 307; Burton VIII 16. Chauvin VII 29-35 No. 212A; *ANE* 207-10 No. 230.□

S186.1.2§, ‡Man dragged by his privates (testicles).
¿Azîz and ¿Azîzah: *Alf* I 287; Burton III 3. Chauvin V 144-45 No. 71; *ANE* 111-13 No. 41.□

S186.2.1§, ‡Woman struck on her vagina.
King ¿Umar al-Nu¿mân and Sons: *Alf* I 194,-cf./(threat); Burton II 143,-(tongue to be stuff up into coynte). Chauvin VI 112-24 No. 277; *ANE* 430-34 No. 39.□

S186.9.1§, ‡Marks (bruises, scars, etc.) on body tell-tale of cruel treatment (beating). (Cf. H614.5§, K2153.2§, Q458.1, T205.1§).
Porter and Ladies of Baghdad: *Alf* I 37; Burton I 99. Chauvin V 251-52 No. 148; *ANE* 324-26 No. 14;
Mock Caliph/¿Alî al-Jawharî: *Alf* II 195; Burton IV 137. Chauvin V 99-100 No. 174; *ANE* 304-5 No. 73;
Abû al-Ḥasan al-Khorâsânî (and Caliph's Favorite): *Alf* IV 231; Burton IX 234. Chauvin V 218-20 No. 129; *ANE* 68-69 No. 259.□

S188.1§, ‡Object stuffed (driven) into body orifice of victim (anus, vagina, mouth, etc.). See: *DOTTI*. (Cf. Z197.3.4§).
Ma¿n Rewards a Bedouin for Gift: *Alf* II 182-83; Burton IV 96. Chauvin VI 78 No. 247; *ANE* 291 No. 66.□

S189.1§, ‡Sick person abandoned.
King ¿Umar al-Nu¿mân and Sons: *Alf* I 188; Burton II 134. Chauvin VI 112-24 No. 277; *ANE* 430-34 No. 39;
Abû Qîr and Abû Ṣîr: *Alf* IV 188; Burton IX 142. Chauvin V 15-17 No. 10; *ANE* 75-77 No. 255.□

S210.1, ‡Child sold into slavery. See: *DOTTI*.
Page Feigns Knowing Bird Language: *Alf* III 156; Burton VI 169. Chauvin VIII 49-50 No. 17; *ANE* 321-22 No. 197.□

S260.1, Human sacrifice. See: *DOTTI*; *GMC*. (Cf. V12.1.1§).
Hasan of Basrah: *Alf* III 306; Burton VIII 15. Chauvin VII 29 No. 212A; *ANE* 207 No. 230;
Nûr al-Dîn and Maryam: *Alf* IV 114,-(pledged); Burton VIII 336. Chauvin V 52-54 No. 271; *ANE* 98-99 No. 233.□

S261, Foundation sacrifice. [Human]. See: *GMC*.
Nûr al-Dîn and Maryam: *Alf* IV 114,-(pledged); Burton VIII 335. Chauvin V 52-54 No. 271; *ANE* 98-99 No. 233.□

S262.3, ‡Sacrificial victim chosen by lot.
Mercury ¿Alî: *Alf* III 229,-cf.; Burton VII 177. Chauvin V 248-50 No. 147; *ANE* 301-3 No. 225.□

S270§, ‡Ritual purification through human sacrifice. (Cf. V12.1.1§).
Nûr al-Dîn and Maryam: *Alf* IV 108,-cf./(ritual killing/human sacrifice); Burton VIII 324. Chauvin V 52-54 No. 271; *ANE* 98-99 No. 233.□

S312.5§, ‡Illegitimate child punished. (Cf. Q402).
Landsman ¿Abdallah and Merman ¿Abdallah: *Alf* IV 205; Burton IX 183. Chauvin V 6-7 No. 3; *ANE* 65-66 No. 256.□

S322.0.3§, ‡Children abandoned to hide them from hostile relatives.
Uns al-Wujûd and al-Ward: *Alf* II 280; Burton V 56. Chauvin VI 127-29 No. 282; *ANE* 438 No. 104.□

S322.3.1, Jealous co-wife demands murder of woman's children. See: *DOTTI*; *GMC*.
First Shaykh: Sorceress Wife: *Alf* I 10,-cf.; Burton I 27-31. Chauvin VII 129-30 No. 396; *ANE* 376-77 No. 5.□

S440§, ‡Cast-off wife abandoned in foreign (faraway) land. See: *DOTTI*. (Cf. S11.9§).
Eldest Lady's Story: Treacherous Sisters: *Alf* I 53; Burton I 162. Chauvin V 4 No. 443; *ANE* 174-75 No. 19.□

S451.1.1§, Husband reinstates his outcast wife due to her giving birth to his child (son). See: *DOTTI*; *GMC*. (Cf. K2222.1§, P230.0.2.2.1§).
Shahriyâr and Shahrzâd: *Alf* IV 317-18,-cf.; Burton X 54. Chauvin V 190-91 No. 111/pt.; *ANE* 371 No. 1.□

S480§, ‡Cruelty to servants (slaves). See: *DOTTI*. (Cf. S123.1).
al-'Amjad and al-'As¿ad: *Alf* II 125; Burton III 336-37. Chauvin V 208-10 No. 120[.1]; *ANE* 341-42 No. 61/pt. 2.□

S481.1§, ‡Animal cruelly overworked (overburdened). See: *DOTTI*.
Bull and Ass: *Alf* I 6; Burton I 18-19. Chauvin V 179-80 No. 104; *ANE* 129-30 No. 2;
Birds, Beasts, and Carpenter: *Alf* II 22-24; Burton III 117-18. Chauvin II 225-26 No. 1; *ANE* 126 No. 44.□

S485§, King persecutes subjects. See: *DOTTI*. (Cf. P12.2.1).
Crows and Hawk: *Alf* IV 144; Burton IX 55. Chauvin II 220 No. 152/8; *ANE* 162 No. 243.□

T1.0.2§, ‡Fundamentals of pleasant coition (for the couple). (Cf. T59§).
Nuzhat al-Zamân Tested/¿Umar al-Nu¿mân: *Alf* I 202-3; Burton II 161-62. Chauvin VI 116, n.1/passim No. 277; *ANE* 432,/passim No. 39.□

T1.1§, ‡Nonsexual (*¿udhrî*, Platonic) love. See: *DOTTI*.
Lovers of Banû ¿Udhrah and Lion: *Alf* III 208; Burton VII 121. Chauvin V 116-17 No. 52; *ANE* 274 No. 218/[2].□

T1.3.1§, ‡Two lovers in one bed (the head of each resting on the other's arm) is the best scene in The Compassionate's creation. (Cf. A102.13, H659.13.1).
Nûr al-Dîn ¿Alî and Son: *Alf* I 73,-(poem); Burton I 223. Chauvin VI 102-6 No. 270; *ANE* 317-19 No. 22;
Qamar al-Zamân and Budûr: *Alf* II 76,-(poem); Burton III 235. Chauvin V 204-12 No. 120; *ANE* 341-45 No. 61;
¿Alî Shâr and Zumurrud: *Alf* II 221,-(poem); Burton IV 198. Chauvin V 89-91 No. 28; *ANE* 100-1 No. 82.□

T2.1§, ‡Women's lust (*shahwah*) is stronger than men's.
Qamar al-Zamân and Budûr: *Alf* II 79; Burton III 241. Chauvin V 204-12 No. 120; *ANE* 341-45 No. 61.□

T2.3§, ‡Intercourse with one person compared to that with another: physical attributes. See: *DOTTI*. (Cf. J81, N74§, T463.3§).
Jeweler's Wife and Qamar al-Zamân: *Alf* IV 265; Burton IX 301. Chauvin V 212-14 No. 121; *ANE* 345-47 No. 260.□

T5.1§, ‡Reasons causing lovers to be drawn to each other (e.g., beauty, age, kindness, courage, etc.).
Qamar al-Zamân and Budûr: *Alf* II 79; Burton III 241. Chauvin V 204-12 No. 120; *ANE* 341-45 No. 61;
Jeweler's Wife and Qamar al-Zamân: *Alf* IV 247; Burton IX 253. Chauvin V 212-14 No. 121; *ANE* 345-47 No. 260.□

T5.1.1§, ‡Lovers attracted to each other because of similarities in age.
Ghânim ibn Ayyûb: *Alf* I 153; Burton II 59. Chauvin VI 14 No. 188; *ANE* 192-93 No. 36.□

T5.1.3§, ‡Lovers attracted to each other because of similarities in beauty.
Nûr al-Dîn ¿Alî and Son: *Alf* I 66,-cf./(girl's father attracted by youth's beauty); Burton I 200. Chauvin VI 102-6 No. 270; *ANE* 317-19 No. 22;
Ghânim ibn Ayyûb: *Alf* I 153; Burton II 45-76. Chauvin VI 14 No. 188; *ANE* 192-93 No. 36.□

T5.1.3.1§, ‡Girl (woman) falls in love with man because of his beauty. See: *DOTTI*.
Qamar al-Zamân and Budûr: *Alf* II 108,-cf.; Burton III 300. Chauvin V 204-12 No. 120; *ANE* 341-45 No. 61;
al-'Amjad and al-'As¿ad: *Alf* II 112-13, 131; Burton III 309-10, 346. Chauvin V 208-10 No. 120[.1]; *ANE* 341-42 No. 61/pt. 2;
¿Alî Shâr and Zumurrud: *Alf* II 219; Burton IV 195. Chauvin V 89-91 No. 28; *ANE* 100-1 No. 82;
Jewish Tray-maker and Temptress: *Alf* III 13; Burton V 265. Chauvin VI 187-88 No. 354; *ANE* 169 No. 166;
Nûr al-Dîn and Maryam: *Alf* IV 99,-cf./(selects as master/owner); Burton VIII 299. Chauvin V 52-54 No. 271; *ANE* 98-99 No. 233;
Ibrâhîm and Jamîlah: *Alf* IV 226; Burton IX 222. Chauvin VI 52-53 No. 218; *ANE* 227-29 No. 258.□

T5.1.4§, ‡Girl attracted to man because of his chivalry (chastity). (Cf. A1557.3.1§, Q87.4§).
King ¿Umar al-Nu¿mân and Sons: *Alf* I 168ff.; Burton II 89. Chauvin VI 112-24 No. 277; *ANE* 430-34 No. 39;
Mercury ¿Alî: *Alf* III 236; Burton VII 189,-(chaste forbearance). Chauvin V 248-50 No. 147; *ANE* 301-3 No. 225;
Man of Upper Egypt and Frankish Wife: Alf IV 16?,-(text missing); Burton IX 22,-(slave-woman/new owner). Chauvin V 240 No. 140; *ANE*: No. 234.□

T9.0.1§, ‡Sexual frustration (deprivation). See: *DOTTI*. (Cf. T185.3§, T315.2.6§, U248.4§).

Qamar al-Zamân and Budûr: *Alf* II 101-2,-(ignored bride's); Burton III 287. Chauvin V 204-12 No. 120; *ANE* 341-45 No. 61;
al-Rashîd and Omani Merchant: *Alf* IV 213,-(poem,/female's); Burton IX 197. Chauvin VI 111-12 No. 276; *ANE* 201-2 No. 257.□

T9.1§, The power of sex: female's influence. See: *DOTTI*; *GMC*; *PSAE*. (Cf. K340.1§, T283).
Shahriyâr and Shâhzamân: *Alf* I 5,-(poem); Burton I 13. Chauvin V 188-89 No. 111; *ANE* 370-71 No. 1;
¿Alâ' al-Dîn Abû al-Shâmât: *Alf* II 166; Burton IV 69. Chauvin V 43-49 No. 18; *ANE* 85-87 No. 63;
Dalîla the Swindler: *Alf* III 225,-(successfully used on officers); Burton VII 167. Chauvin V 245-50 No. 147; *ANE* 163-64 No. 224;
King Jalî¿âd and Shimâs: *Alf* IV 161,-(immersion with a new group of women for a month at a time); Burton IX 90. Chauvin VI 9-11 No. 184; *ANE* 237-38 No. 236;
Masrûr and Zayn al-Mawâṣif: *Alf* IV 58,-(lover surrenders all property); Burton VIII 218-19. Chauvin VI 82-84 No. 251; *ANE* 294-95 No. 232;
Ma¿rûf the Cobbler: *Alf* IV 315-16,-(causes lowering guard protecting magic ring); Burton X 51. Chauvin VI 81-82 No. 250; *ANE* 291-93 No. 262.□

T9.1.1§, Scent of female used to coax male. See: *DOTTI*; *GMC*.
Sindbâd's First Voyage: *Alf* III 85,-(horses); Burton VI 8. Chauvin VII 7-9 No. 373A; *ANE* 385 No. 179.□

T9.2.0.1§, ‡Female lusting after a desirable male. (Cf. T474.0.2§).
Tâj al-Mulûk: *Alf* I 294,-(old woman—*rashahat fî sarâwîlihâ*); Burton III 21,-(sweated in her petticoat trousers). Chauvin V 126-28 No. 60; *ANE* 406-8 No. 40;
Tâj al-Mulûk: *Alf* I 303,-(*taḥarrakat ¿alayhâ al-shahwah*/sexual lust activated her); Burton III 37,-(overcome with love and longing). Chauvin V 126-28 No. 60; *ANE* 406-8 No. 40□

T11, ‡Falling in love with person never seen.
Schoolmaster Who Fell in Love by Report: Mourns: *Alf* II 292,-cf.; Burton V 117. Chauvin VI 136 No. 287; *ANE* 367 No. 135.□

T11.1, Love from mere mention or description. See: *DOTTI*; *GMC*.
Schoolmaster Who Fell in Love by Report: Mourns: *Alf* II 292[]; Burton V 117. Chauvin VI 136 No. 287; *ANE* 367 No. 135;
Jullanâr of the Sea: *Alf* III 257; Burton VII 290. Chauvin V 147-51 No. 73; *ANE* 248-51 No. 227;
Jeweler's Wife and Qamar al-Zamân: *Alf* IV 243; Burton IX 256. Chauvin V 212-14 No. 121; *ANE* 345-47 No. 260.□

T11.1.0.1§, ‡The ear may fall in love before the eye.
Ibrâhîm and Jamîlah: *Alf* IV 226,-(poem); Burton IX 222. Chauvin VI 52-53 No. 218; *ANE* 227-29 No. 258.□

T11.1.3§, ‡Husband's (merchant's) description of youth (client) causes wife to fall in love with youth.
Jeweler's Wife and Qamar al-Zamân: *Alf* IV 247; Burton IX 263. Chauvin V 212-14 No. 121; *ANE* 345-47 No. 260.□

T11.2, Love through sight of picture. See: *ANE*; *DOTTI*; *GMC*. (Cf. H1381.3.1.2.1).
Goldsmith and Cashmere Singer: *Alf* III 150; Burton VI 156. Chauvin VIII 46-47 No. 14; *ANE* 196 No. 194;
Sayf al-Mulûk: *Alf* III 279; Burton VII 330. Chauvin VII 64-73 No. 348; *ANE* 362-64 No. 229;
Ibrâhîm and Jamîlah: *Alf* IV 219; Burton IX 207. Chauvin VI 52-53 No. 218; *ANE* 227-29 No. 258.□

T11.4.5, ‡Love through finding lady's handkerchief.
¿Azîz and ¿Azîzah: *Alf* I 268; Burton II 300. Chauvin V 144-45 No. 71; *ANE* 111-13 No. 41.□

T11.9§, ‡Falling in love with thrilling music (melody, song, poem recitation).
¿Alâ' al-Dîn Abû al-Shâmât: *Alf* II 156; Burton IV 50. Chauvin V 43-49 No. 18; *ANE* 85-87 No. 63;
Isḥâq al-Mûṣilî and Merchant's Singer: *Alf* II 296; Burton V 130-31. Chauvin VI 59 No. 225; *ANE* 233 No. 142;
Masrûr and Zayn al-Mawâṣif: *Alf* IV 55; Burton VIII 206. Chauvin VI 82-84 No. 251; *ANE* 294-95 No. 232;
al-Rashîd and Omani Merchant: *Alf* IV 208-9; Burton IX 189. Chauvin VI 111-12 No. 276; *ANE* 201-2 No. 257.□

T15, ‡Love at first sight. See: *DOTTI*. (Cf. T16.3§, N711.8§).
Eldest Lady's Story: Treacherous Sisters: *Alf* I 55; Burton I 168. Chauvin V 4 No. 443; *ANE* 174-75 No. 19;
Nûr al-Dîn ¿Alî and Son: *Alf* I 74,-cf./(paternal); Burton I 226. Chauvin VI 102-6 No. 270; *ANE* 317-19 No. 22;
Copt Broker's Story: Lover's Sacrifices Repaid: *Alf* I 91; Burton I 267. Chauvin VI 80 No. 249; *ANE* 313-14 No. 24;
Reeve's Story: Why Maimed by Bride: *Alf* I 97; Burton I 280. Chauvin V 220-21 No. 305; *ANE* 351 No. 25;
Tailor's Story/Barber of Baghdad: *Alf* I 103; Burton I 302 303. Chauvin V 154-56 No. 78; *ANE* 405-6 No. 27;
Anîs al-Jalîs: *Alf* I 128; Burton II 6. Chauvin V 120-24 No. 58; *ANE* 316-17 No. 35;
¿Alî ibn Bakkâr: *Alf* II 41; Burton III 163. Chauvin V 153 No. 76; *ANE* 92-93 No. 60;
Ebony Horse: *Alf* II 256,-(princess in garden surrounded by mates); Burton V 8,-(variant/sleeping princess). Chauvin V 221-31 No. 130; *ANE* 172-74 No. 103;
Uns al-Wujûd and al-Ward: *Alf* II 269; Burton V 32. Chauvin VI 127-29 No. 282; *ANE* 438 No. 104;
Isḥâq al-Mûṣilî and Merchant's Singer: *Alf* II 295,-(for woman singer); Burton V 130. Chauvin VI 59 No. 225; *ANE* 233 No. 142;
Jawdar and His Treacherous Brethren: *Alf* III 200; Burton VI 253. Chauvin V 257-60 No. 154; *ANE* 244-45 No. 209.□

T16, ‡Man falls in love with a woman he sees bathing.
Jânshâh: *Alf* III 52, III 55,-cf.; Burton V 346. Chauvin VII 39-44 No. 153; *ANE* 238-41 No. 178;
Hasan of Basrah: *Alf* III 315; Burton VIII 31,-(birds, plunging into basin). Chauvin VII 29-35 No. 212A; *ANE* 207-10 No. 230.□

T16.1, Man falls in love by the sight of woman's white arms [(fingers)]. See: *DOTTI*; *GMC*.
Ni¿mah and Nu¿m: Stolen Wife Regained: *Alf* II 136,-(wrists); Burton IV 7. Chauvin VI 96-97 No. 263; *ANE* 314 No. 62.□

T16.0.3§, ‡Erotic experience from seeing a person bathing. See: *DOTTI*. (Cf. F779.1§).
Hârûn and Zubaydah in Bath: *Alf* II 284; Burton V 76. Chauvin VI 142 No. 298; *ANE* 203-4 No. 111□

T16.3§, ‡Man falls in love with girl upon seeing her face once (in garden field, meadow, window, etc.). See: *DOTTI*. (Cf. N711.8§, T15).
Tailor's Story/Barber of Baghdad: *Alf* I 103; Burton I 301-2. Chauvin V 154-56 No. 78; *ANE* 405-6 No. 27;
¿Azîz and ¿Azîzah: *Alf* I 268; Burton II 300. Chauvin V 144-45 No. 71; *ANE* 111-13 No. 41;
Tâj al-Mulûk: *Alf* I 290,-cf./(seeing embroidery by her); Burton III 8. Chauvin V 126-28 No. 60; *ANE* 406-8 No. 40;
Hammâd: Treacherous Bedouin: *Alf* II 16; Burton III 105. Chauvin VI 124 n. 1 No. 277; *ANE* 200 No. 43;
House with the Belvedere: *Alf* III 168; Burton VI 191. Chauvin VIII 57-58 No. 23; *ANE* 223 No. 203.□

T16.6§, ‡Passion (*hawâ*) aroused due to nakedness or body exposure caused by gust of wind (air: *hawâ'*). See: *DOTTI*. (Cf. T405.9.4§, Z55§, Z95§, Z97§).
Nûr al-Dîn ¿Alî and Son: *Alf* I 73,-(male's-body); Burton I 225-25. Chauvin VI 102-6 No. 270; *ANE* 317-19 No. 22;
King ¿Umar al-Nu¿mân and Sons: *Alf* I 182; Burton II 123. Chauvin VI 112-24 No. 277; *ANE* 430-34 No. 39;
Spy, Fifth Maiden/¿Umar al-Nu¿mân: *Alf* I 223,-cf./Moses becomes bashful; Burton II 206. *ANE* 432 No. 39/passim;
Qamar al-Zamân and Budûr: *Alf* II 97; Burton III 278. Chauvin V 204-12 No. 120; *ANE* 341-45 No. 61;
al-'Amjad and al-'As¿ad: *Alf* II 128,-cf.; Burton III 342. Chauvin V 208-10 No. 120[.1]; *ANE* 341-42 No. 61/pt. 2.□

T17.1§, Passion (love) through sight of handsome child (boy): "If the boy is that handsome, how more beautiful his mother must be!". (Cf. F575.3).

Jeweler's Wife and Qamar al-Zamân: *Alf* IV 242; Burton IX 254. Chauvin V 212-14 No. 121; *ANE* 345-47 No. 260.□

T22.2, Predestined wife. See: *DOTTI*; *GMC*.
¿Abdallah ibn Fâḍil: Treacherous Brothers: *Alf* IV 277; Burton IX 327. Chauvin V 2-4 No. 2; *ANE* 63-65 No. 261.□

T22.2.1§, Maiden found in deserted place is hero's predestined wife. See: *DOTTI*; *GMC*.
¿Abdallah ibn Fâḍil: Treacherous Brothers: *Alf* IV 277; Burton IX 327. Chauvin V 2-4 No. 2; *ANE* 63-65 No. 261.□

T22.3, Predestined husband. See: *DOTTI*.
¿Alâ' al-Dîn Abû al-Shâmât: *Alf* II 178; Burton IV 89. Chauvin V 43-49 No. 18; *ANE* 85-87 No. 63.□

T22.4, ‡Lovers fated to marry each other born at same time; identical prophecies for both. See: *DOTTI*.
Nûr al-Dîn ¿Alî and Son: *Alf* I 67; Burton I 203. Chauvin VI 102-6 No. 270; *ANE* 317-19 No. 22.□

T24.1, Love-sickness. See: *DOTTI*; *GMC*. (Cf. F1041.15.1§).
Tâj al-Mulûk: *Alf* I 267; Burton II 294-95. Chauvin V 126-28 No. 60; *ANE* 406-8 No. 40;
¿Alî ibn Bakkâr: *Alf* II 41-65; Burton III 163. Chauvin V 153 No. 76; *ANE* 92-93 No. 60;
Budûr and Jubayr ibn ¿Umayr: *Alf* II 240; Burton IV 240. Chauvin VII 93-94 No. 374; *ANE* 243-44 No. 83;
Ebony Horse: *Alf* II 259; Burton V 15. Chauvin V 221-31 No. 130; *ANE* 172-74 No. 103;
Lovers of Banû Ṭay'/Death from Love: *Alf* II 297; Burton V 137. Chauvin V 111 No. 45; *ANE* 273 No. 145;
Goldsmith and Cashmere Singer: *Alf* III 150; Burton VI 156. Chauvin VIII 46-47 No. 14; *ANE* 196 No. 194;
House with the Belvedere: *Alf* III 168; Burton VI 191. Chauvin VIII 57-58 No. 23; *ANE* 223 No. 203;
Lovers of Basra/Ḍamrah: *Alf* III 211; Burton VII 132. Chauvin V 118 No. 54; *ANE* 273 No. 220;
Sayf al-Mulûk: *Alf* III 280; Burton VII 333. Chauvin VII 64-73 No. 348; *ANE* 362-64 No. 229;
Hasan of Basrah: *Alf* III 318; Burton VIII 38. Chauvin VII 29-35 No. 212A; *ANE* 207-10 No. 230;
Ruined Baghdadi and His Slave-girl: *Alf* IV 130,-cf./(loss of beloved); Burton IX 25. Chauvin V 152-53 No. 75; *ANE* 353 No. 235;
al-Rashîd and Omani Merchant: *Alf* IV 217-18; Burton IX 204. Chauvin VI 111-12 No. 276; *ANE* 201-2 No. 257.□

T24.2.1, ‡Fainting away for love (or sexual desire). See: *DOTTI*. (Cf. F1041.17.3§, U248.4§).
¿Alâ' al-Dîn Abû al-Shâmât: *Alf* II 161,-(death from sexual desire); Burton IV 58. Chauvin V 43-49 No. 18; *ANE* 85-87 No. 63;
¿Alî ibn Bakkâr: *Alf* II 43, 50; Burton III 167, 172, 175. Chauvin V 153 No. 76; *ANE* 92-93 No. 60;
Ruined Baghdadi and His Slave-girl: *Alf* IV 131; Burton IX 27. Chauvin V 152-53 No. 75; *ANE* 353 No. 235.□

T24.2.3, ‡Fainting away from seeing an extraordinary beauty. See: *DOTTI*.
Jânshâh: *Alf* III 52; Burton V 347. Chauvin VII 39-44 No. 153; *ANE* 238-41 No. 178;
Sayf al-Mulûk: *Alf* III 297; Burton VII 368,-(fell down in a swoon). Chauvin VII 64-73 No. 348; *ANE* 362-64 No. 229;
Ibrâhîm and Jamîlah: *Alf* IV 225; Burton IX 221,-(fell into a swoon). Chauvin VI 52-53 No. 218; *ANE* 227-29 No. 258.□

T24.2.4§, ‡Fainting away from hearing love poem (song). (Cf. T75.3).
Budûr and Jubayr ibn ¿Umayr: *Alf* II 239; Burton IV 237. Chauvin VII 93-94 No. 374; *ANE* 243-44 No. 83.□

T24.3, Madness from love. See: *DOTTI*; *GMC*. (Cf. F1041.15.1§).
Qamar al-Zamân and Budûr: *Alf* II 86; Burton III 255. Chauvin V 204-12 No. 120; *ANE* 341-45 No. 61.□

T24.6, ‡Lover refuses food and drink.
Budûr and Jubayr ibn ¿Umayr: *Alf* II 240; Burton IV 240. Chauvin VII 93-94 No. 374; *ANE* 243-44 No. 83.□

T24.6.1§, ‡Person pines away from love.
Tâj al-Mulûk: *Alf* I 294; Burton III 21. Chauvin V 126-28 No. 60; *ANE* 406-8 No. 40;

Qamar al-Zamân and Budûr: *Alf* II 85; Burton III 254. Chauvin V 204-12 No. 120; *ANE* 341-45 No. 61;
Hasan of Basrah: *Alf* III 317-18; Burton VIII 33. Chauvin VII 29-35 No. 212A; *ANE* 207-10 No. 230. □

T24.6.1.1§, ‡Lover becomes 'as thin as a garment'.
Ghânim ibn Ayyûb: *Alf* I 160; Burton II 69,-(toothpick). Chauvin VI 14 No. 188; *ANE* 192-93 No. 36. □

T24.6.1.1.1§, ‡Lover so thin that had he (she) not spoken he could not have been seen.
King ¿Umar al-Nu¿mân and Sons: *Alf* I 198,-(poem); Burton II 152. Chauvin VI 112-24 No. 277; *ANE* 430-34 No. 39. □

T24.9.1§, ‡Lover sleepless. (Cf. J1080§).
Tâj al-Mulûk: *Alf* I 267; Burton II 295. Chauvin V 126-28 No. 60; *ANE* 406-8 No. 40;
¿Azîz and ¿Azîzah: *Alf* I 276, 286,-(for one year); Burton II 376,-(sleep is unlawful and to a lover undue), III 1. Chauvin V 144-45 No. 71; *ANE* 111-13 No. 41;
Hasan of Basrah: *Alf* III 314,-(poem); Burton VIII 28. Chauvin VII 29-35 No. 212A; *ANE* 207-10 No. 230;
Jeweler's Wife and Qamar al-Zamân: *Alf* IV 250; Burton IX 269. Chauvin V 212-14 No. 121; *ANE* 345-47 No. 260. □

T24.9.1.2§, ‡Lover hallucinates: sees image, hears voice or feels touch of absent beloved.
Lovers of Basra/Ḍamrah: *Alf* III 211; Burton VII 132. Chauvin V 118 No. 54; *ANE* 273 No. 220. □

T24.9.1.2.1§, ‡Lover falls asleep only in hope of being visited by the phantom (*ṭayf/khayâl*) of the beloved. (Cf. P230.15§).
King ¿Umar al-Nu¿mân and Sons: *Alf* II 2; Burton III 77. Chauvin VI 112-24 No. 277; *ANE* 430-34 No. 39;
Qamar al-Zamân and Budûr: *Alf* II 84,-cf./(poem: *ṭayf* cannot visit the sleepless); Burton III 252,-(fantom). Chauvin V 204-12 No. 120; *ANE* 341-45 No. 61. □

T24.9.2.1.1§, ‡Insane actions of poor man evicted from a woman's earthly paradise forgiven (excused). See: *DOTTI*. (Cf. F956.7.7.2§, P526.3.1§).
Sweep and Noble Lady: Infidelity Repaid: *Alf* II 191,-cf.; Burton IV 130. Chauvin VI 148 No. 306; *ANE* 403-4 No. 72. □

T24.9.4§, ‡Person will 'humiliate' self for love. (Cf. U248.0.3.2§, U248.4§).
King ¿Umar al-Nu¿mân and Sons: *Alf* II 2,-(*maṭâmi¿*/aspirations); Burton III 76. Chauvin VI 112-24 No. 277; *ANE* 430-34 No. 39;
Wolf and Fox: *Alf* II 31,-(poem); Burton III 135. Chauvin II 227 No. 6; *ANE* 450 No. 47. □

T24.9.5§, ‡Love-sickness is to be cured by attaining the beloved. (Cf. T81).
Ni¿mah and Nu¿m: Stolen Wife Regained: *Alf* II 138; Burton IV 10. Chauvin VI 96-97 No. 263; *ANE* 314 No. 62. □

T26, Attention distracted by sight of beloved.
Masrûr and Zayn al-Mawâṣif: *Alf* IV 57-59; Burton VIII 216-18. Chauvin VI 82-84 No. 251; *ANE* 294-95 No. 232. □

T26.3§, ‡Groom on way to own wedding distracted by sight of beautiful woman and misses ceremony. See: *DOTTI*. (Cf. N711.8§, T159§).
¿Azîz and ¿Azîzah: *Alf* I 268; Burton II 299. Chauvin V 144-45 No. 71; *ANE* 111-13 No. 41. □

T27.4§, Hero deflowers (marries) several maidens (seven, forty, etc.) all of whom are in 'love' with him. See: *DOTTI*; *GMC*.
Mercury ¿Alî: *Alf* III 246,-(one plus three); Burton VII 208. Chauvin V 248-50 No. 147; *ANE* 301-3 No. 225. □

T31.4§, ‡Falling in love (with friend's relative) while visiting friend. See: *DOTTI*. (Cf. N711.9§).
¿Alî ibn Bakkâr: *Alf* II 42,-cf.; Burton III 163. Chauvin V 153 No. 76; *ANE* 92-93 No. 60. □

T32.1, Lovers' meeting: hero in heroine's father's prison from which she helps him to escape. See: *DOTTI*. (Cf. R162).
Nûr al-Dîn and Maryam: *Alf* IV 108,-cf.; Burton VIII 325. Chauvin V 52-54 No. 271; *ANE* 98-99 No. 233. □

T33.1§, ‡Faithless woman transforms lovers (husbands) to animals (birds) and keeps them as pets. (Cf. D658.3.4§, G264, K2213.6, T232.3.1§).
Jullanâr of the Sea: *Alf* III 266; Burton VII 298. Chauvin V 147-51 No. 73; *ANE* 248-51 No. 227.□

T34.2, ‡Falling in love while playing game. (Cf. N8.1§).
Masrûr and Zayn al-Mawâṣif: *Alf* IV 57-59; Burton VIII 216-18. Chauvin VI 82-84 No. 251; *ANE* 294-95 No. 232.□

T35.0.1, Lover late at rendezvous; detained by incessant talker [(chatterer)]. See: *DOTTI*; *GMC*. (Cf. X252.3.3§).
Tailor's Story/Barber of Baghdad: *Alf* I 107; Burton I 313. Chauvin V 154-56 No. 78; *ANE* 405-6 No. 27.□

T35.0.2.1§, Lover falls asleep and misses rendezvous. (Cf. D1972). See: *DOTTI*; *GMC*.
¿Azîz and ¿Azîzah: *Alf* I 275-78; Burton II 312-15. Chauvin V 144-45 No. 71; *ANE* 111-13 No. 41;
¿Alî Shâr and Zumurrud: *Alf* II 225,-(rescuer); Burton IV 208-9. Chauvin V 89-91 No. 28; *ANE* 100-1 No. 82;
Ruined Baghdadi and His Slave-girl: *Alf* IV 132,-cf.; Burton IX 30. Chauvin V 152-53 No. 75; *ANE* 353 No. 235.□

T35.5, ‡Lover goes to see his beloved in her husband's (or her father's) house, defiant of the danger. See: *DOTTI*; *PSAE*.
¿Alî ibn Bakkâr: *Alf* II 44,-ff.; Burton III 169. Chauvin V 153 No. 76; *ANE* 92-93 No. 60.□

T35.9.1§, ‡Place of worship (church, mosque, temple, etc.) as lovers' rendezvous.
Nûr al-Dîn and Maryam: *Alf* IV 110,-(in church); Burton VIII 328. Chauvin V 52-54 No. 271; *ANE* 98-99 No. 233.□

T39§, ‡Beleaguered lovers. See: *DOTTI*. (Cf. K1210).
Tailor's Story/Barber of Baghdad: *Alf* I 103; Burton I 302ff. Chauvin V 154-56 No. 78; *ANE* 405-6 No. 27;
¿Alî ibn Bakkâr: *Alf* II 60; Burton III 200ff. Chauvin V 153 No. 76; *ANE* 92-93 No. 60.□

T39.1§, ‡Lover protects (defends) the beloved. See: *DOTTI*. (Cf. T39.1.4§).
Lover Who Feigned Himself a Thief: *Alf* II 204; Burton IV 158. Chauvin VII 134-35 No. 403; *ANE* 272 No. 76;
Ibrâhîm and Jamîlah: *Alf* IV 226-27,-(keeps rendezvous secret); Burton IX 223. Chauvin VI 52-53 No. 218; *ANE* 227-29 No. 258.□

T39.1.4§, ‡Girl (woman) confesses to sexual offense (unchastity, infidelity) so as to save her sweetheart from punishment for theft. (His hand was about to be cut off for entering her home secretly). (Cf. J229.17.1§, Q451.1.1, W14.8.4§, W37.5§).
Lover Who Feigned Himself a Thief: *Alf* II 205; Burton IV 158. Chauvin VII 134-35 No. 403; *ANE* 272 No. 76.□

T39.1.5§, ‡Lovers never betray each other's secrets. (Cf. W45.3§).
Budûr and Jubayr ibn ¿Umayr: *Alf* II 243; Burton IV 243. Chauvin VII 93-94 No. 374; *ANE* 243-44 No. 83.□

T39.1.2§, ‡Maiden throws herself on her beloved so as to protect him from execution. (Cf. Z66.5.0.1§).
Tâj al-Mulûk: *Alf* I 305; Burton III 41. Chauvin V 126-28 No. 60; *ANE* 406-8 No. 40.□

T40§, Lovers mentioned as brother and sister so as to escape detection. See: *DOTTI*; *GMC*.
Lady and Five Suitors Deceived: *Alf* III 158; Burton VI 173. Chauvin VIII 50-51 No. 18; *ANE* 266 No. 198.□

T41, Communication of lovers. See: *DOTTI*; *GMC*.
Masrûr and Zayn al-Mawâṣif: *Alf* IV 68,-(poem); Burton VIII 236. Chauvin VI 82-84 No. 251; *ANE* 294-95 No. 232.□

T41.4§, ‡Lovers exchange letters. See: *DOTTI*. (Cf. K1872.3.2§, R134.1§).
Tâj al-Mulûk: *Alf* I 296-98; Burton III 24-29. Chauvin V 126-28 No. 60; *ANE* 406-8 No. 40;
¿Alî ibn Bakkâr: *Alf* II 50ff.; Burton III 180ff. Chauvin V 153 No. 76; *ANE* 92-93 No. 60;
Budûr and Jubayr ibn ¿Umayr: *Alf* II 235-41; Burton IV 233. Chauvin VII 93-94 No. 374; *ANE* 243-44 No. 83;

Uns al-Wujûd and al-Ward: *Alf* II 270; Burton V 34. Chauvin VI 127-29 No. 282; *ANE* 438 No. 104;
King's Son and Merchant's Wife: *Alf* III 155-56; Burton VI 167-68. Chauvin VIII 48-49 No. 16; *ANE* 263 No. 196;
Lovers of Basra/Ḍamrah: *Alf* III 212,-cf.; Burton VII 134. Chauvin V 118 No. 54; *ANE* 273 No. 220.□

T41.4.1§, ‡Love letter contains token of love (lock of hair, perfume, or the like).
al-'Amjad and al-'As¿ad: *Alf* II 113-15; Burton III 311. Chauvin V 208-10 No. 120[.1]; *ANE* 341-42 No. 61/pt. 2.□

T41.7.1§, ‡Girl gives beloved money to pay for her bride-wealth (*mahr*). (Usually as "loan"). (Cf. P180.8.1.1§).
¿Alâ' al-Dîn Abû al-Shâmât: *Alf* II 157,-cf.; Burton IV 53. Chauvin V 43-49 No. 18; *ANE* 85-87 No. 63.□

T42.2.1§, – Lovers address each other as "Brother" and "Sister". (Cf. F302.0.3§, P253.10.1§).
Porter and Ladies of Baghdad: *Alf* I 35,-(xxx); Burton I 92-92,-("O my sister/s"). Chauvin V 251-52 No. 148; *ANE* 324-26 No. 14.□

T42.3§, Lover uses beggars's speech. See: *DOTTI*.
Reeve's Story: Why Maimed by Bride: *Alf* I 97,-cf./(*taṣaddaqî*); Burton I 280. Chauvin V 220-21 No. 305; *ANE* 351 No. 25;
¿Alî ibn Bakkâr: *Alf* II 43,-(poem); Burton III 166. Chauvin V 153 No. 76; *ANE* 92-93 No. 60.□

T42.3.1§, ‡Lover begs for erotic act (kiss, glance, regard, etc.) as alms-tax *zakâh*. (Cf. V3.3§, X598.1.2§).
Copt Broker's Story: Lover's Sacrifices Repaid: *Alf* I 91,-(glance,/*taṣaddaqî*); Burton I 267,-(favor me). Chauvin VI 80 No. 249; *ANE* 313-14 No. 24.□

T42.4.1§, ‡Expression of love (smile, kiss) will be reciprocated several folds (twofold, tenfold, hundredfold, etc.). (Cf. J1174.2, Z55.3§).
¿Alî ibn Bakkâr: *Alf* II 43,-(poem); Burton III 166. Chauvin V 153 No. 76; *ANE* 92-93 No. 60.□

T44§, ‡Bewailing separation from beloved. See: *DOTTI*. (Cf. H1385.5, L506.0.2§).
Anîs al-Jalîs: *Alf* I 140,-(poem), 142-43; Burton II 30,-(xxx), 34-35,-(variant). Chauvin V 120-24 No. 58; *ANE* 316-17 No. 35.□

T44.1§, ‡Lover wails (weeps) at home of departed beloved. (Cf. L485.1§).
Budûr and Jubayr ibn ¿Umayr: *Alf* II 240,-(poem); Burton IV 240. Chauvin VII 93-94 No. 374; *ANE* 243-44 No. 83;
Uns al-Wujûd and al-Ward: *Alf* II 280-81,-(poems); Burton V 57, 58. Chauvin VI 127-29 No. 282; *ANE* 438 No. 104;
Lovers of Banû ¿Udhrah and Lion: *Alf* III 207,-(poem); Burton VII 119. Chauvin V 116-17 No. 52; *ANE* 274 No. 218/[2].□

T49.1.1§, ‡Meeting of brother and sister described in terms of lovers's rendezvous. See: *DOTTI*. (Cf. T415).
King ¿Umar al-Nu¿mân and Sons: *Alf* I 191,-(poems), 210-215,-(poem); Burton II 137-39, Burton II 178-87. Chauvin VI 112-24 No. 277; *ANE* 430-34 No. 39.□

T49.2§, ‡Lovers break into seemingly empty house for rendezvous. See: *DOTTI*.
al-'Amjad and al-'As¿ad: *Alf* II 124; Burton III 333. Chauvin V 208-10 No. 120[.1]; *ANE* 341-42 No. 61/pt. 2.□

T49.3§, ‡Lovers rendezvous at friend's house (apartment). (Cf. P159.2§).
¿Alî ibn Bakkâr: *Alf* II 57; Burton III 194. Chauvin V 153 No. 76; *ANE* 92-93 No. 60.□

T50.1.2.1§, ‡Daughter(s) kept unwed by jealous father.
Hasan of Basrah: *Alf* III 311; Burton VIII 24. Chauvin VII 29-35 No. 212A; *ANE* 207-10 No. 230.□

T51, Wooing by emissary.
Tâj al-Mulûk: *Alf* I 262-64; Burton II 286-88. Chauvin V 126-28 No. 60; *ANE* 406-8 No. 40.□

T52.0.1§, Bride-wealth (*mahr*). See: *DOTTI*; *GMC*. (Cf. P180.8.1.1§, P529.0.2.3.1§, P529.6.4.1§).
Mock Caliph/¿Alî al-Jawharî: *Alf* II 197; Burton IV 142,-(marriage-settlement). Chauvin V 99-100 No. 174; *ANE* 304-5 No. 73;

Landsman ¿Abdallah and Merman ¿Abdallah: *Alf* IV 205,-(paid with fish); Burton IX 183. Chauvin V 6-7 No. 3; *ANE* 65-66 No. 256.□

T52.0.2§, Excessive (exaggerated) *mahr* demanded of suitor. See: *DOTTI*; *GMC*. (Cf. H301, T52.0.8§).
Abû Muḥammad Lazybones: *Alf* II 211; Burton IV 171. Chauvin VI 64-67 No. 233; *ANE* 71-73 No. 78;
Hind bint al-Nu¿mân and al-Ḥajjâj: *Alf* III 201; Burton VII 96. Chauvin V 115-4 No. 50; *ANE* 221-22 No. 212.□

T52.0.2.3§, ‡Failure (inability) to pay bride wealth (*mahr*) as obstacle for marriage. See: *DOTTI*.
Nûr al-Dîn ¿Alî and Son: *Alf* I 65; Burton I 196. Chauvin VI 102-6 No. 270; *ANE* 317-19 No. 22;
King ¿Umar al-Nu¿mân and Sons: *Alf* I 318, II 3,-(proper amount); Burton III 72, 78. Chauvin VI 112-24 No. 277; *ANE* 430-34 No. 39;
Ma¿rûf the Cobbler: *Alf* IV 299; Burton X 18. Chauvin VI 81-82 No. 250; *ANE* 291-93 No. 262.□

T52.0.2.3.1§, ‡Respite in payment of bride-wealth. (Cf. T52.0.6§).
Ma¿rûf the Cobbler: *Alf* IV 299; Burton X 18. Chauvin VI 81-82 No. 250; *ANE* 291-93 No. 262.□

T52.0.2.3.4§, ‡Suitor undergoes great difficulties seeking to acquire bride-wealth. (Cf. H1229.5§, T450.0.2.1.2§).
King ¿Umar al-Nu¿mân and Sons: *Alf* II 3ff.,-(raiding other tribes); Burton III 78ff. Chauvin VI 112-24 No. 277; *ANE* 430-34 No. 39.□

T52.0.3§, Bride acquired for labor (work) done for her father. See: *DOTTI*; *GMC*.
Spy, Fifth Maiden/¿Umar al-Nu¿mân: *Alf* I 223; Burton II 206. *ANE* 432 No. 39/passim.□

T52.0.6§, ‡Girl given to man in marriage as grant (*wahb*: without *mahr*). See: *DOTTI*. (Cf. T52.0.2.3.1§, T55, X598.1.2§).
Jeweler's Wife and Qamar al-Zamân: *Alf* IV 265; Burton IX 300. Chauvin V 212-14 No. 121; *ANE* 345-47 No. 260.□

T52.0.6.1§, ‡Woman marries herself to man (beloved) as grant (*wahb*: without *mahr*). See: *DOTTI*. (Cf. T55.0.1§, T404.2§).
Second Shaykh: Treacherous Brothers: *Alf* I 11; Burton I 34. Chauvin V 6 No. 397; *ANE* 377-78 No. 6;
Copt Broker's Story: Lover's Sacrifices Repaid: *Alf* I 95; Burton I 277. Chauvin VI 80 No. 249; *ANE* 313-14 No. 24;
¿Azîz and ¿Azîzah: *Alf* I 282; Burton II 331. Chauvin V 144-45 No. 71; *ANE* 111-13 No. 41.□

T52.0.6.1.1§, ‡Contrary to custom, girl pays *mahr* to beloved to marry her.
Mercury ¿Alî: *Alf* III 244; Burton VII 204. Chauvin V 248-50 No. 147; *ANE* 301-3 No. 225.□

T52.0.6.1.2§, ‡Slave-girl gives owner-to-be money with which to buy her. (She is infatuated with him, while he is impoverished and cannot afford the high price). (Cf. P180.8.1§, P774.4.1.3.1§).
¿Alî Shâr and Zumurrud: *Alf* II 220; Burton IV 197. Chauvin V 89-91 No. 28; *ANE* 100-1 No. 82;
Nûr al-Dîn and Maryam: *Alf* IV 95; Burton VIII 300-1. Chauvin V 52-54 No. 271; *ANE* 98-99 No. 233.□

T52.0.6.2§, ‡Parent (father) gives his daughter in marriage as grant (*wahb*: without *mahr*).
Jewish Doctor's Story: Sororicide: *Alf* I 102; Burton I 299. Chauvin VI 89 No. 253; *ANE* 242 No. 26.□

T52.0.8§, ‡End of marriage compensation (for wife)—(*mu'akhkhar ṣadâq*: deferred conditional portion of bride-wealth contracted at time of marriage). (Cf. P761§, T52.0.2.3.1§, W37.8.1.1§).
¿Azîz and ¿Azîzah: *Alf* I 285; Burton II 331,-(indebted). Chauvin V 144-45 No. 71; *ANE* 111-13 No. 41;
¿Alâ' al-Dîn Abû al-Shâmât: *Alf* II 155; Burton IV 49,(marriage-settlement). Chauvin V 43-49 No. 18; *ANE* 85-87 No. 63;
Hind bint al-Nu¿mân and al-Ḥajjâj: *Alf* III 201; Burton VII 96. Chauvin V 115-4 No. 50; *ANE* 221-22 No. 212.□

T52.0.8.0.1§, ‡Wife's share of deceased husband's property as end of marriage compensation.
Jawdar and His Treacherous Brethren: *Alf* III 177-78; Burton VI 213. Chauvin V 257-60 No. 154; *ANE* 244-45 No. 209.□

T52.3.1§, ‡Loads of gold (treasure) given as bride-wealth (*mahr*). See: *DOTTI*.

Jawdar and His Treacherous Brethren: *Alf* III 200; Burton VI 254,-(saddle bags full). Chauvin V 257-60 No. 154; *ANE* 244-45 No. 209;
Landsman ¿Abdallah and Merman ¿Abdallah: *Alf* IV 202,-(paid with fish); Burton IX 175,-(dowry). Chauvin V 6-7 No. 3; *ANE* 65-66 No. 256.□

T53.0.3§, ‡Inquiring about family of spouse-to-be (through friends, acquaintances, matchmakers, etc.). (Cf. N365.3.4§, T101.1.1§).
Reeve's Story: Why Maimed by Bride: *Alf* I 98; Burton I 285. Chauvin V 220-21 No. 305; *ANE* 351 No. 25.□

T53.0.4§, ‡Girls should not be too choosy in selecting groom. See: *DOTTI*. (Cf. P529.0.2.2§, T131).
¿Azîz and ¿Azîzah: *Alf* I 276,-cf.; Burton II 376. Chauvin V 144-45 No. 71; *ANE* 111-13 No. 41.□

T53.7.1.0.1§, ‡'Matchmake for your daughter, [but] don't matchmake for your son'. (Cf. P529.4§).
Jawdar and His Treacherous Brethren: *Alf* III 200,-cf./(implicit); Burton VI 255. Chauvin V 257-60 No. 154; *ANE* 244-45 No. 209;
Dalîla the Swindler: *Alf* III 215; Burton VII 150,-("Offer thy daughter in marriage ..."). Chauvin V 245-50 No. 147; *ANE* 163-64 No. 224.□

T53.7.1.1§, ‡Father as matchmaker. See: *DOTTI*.
Nûr al-Dîn ¿Alî and Son: *Alf* I 66,-(for daughter); Burton I 200. Chauvin VI 102-6 No. 270; *ANE* 317-19 No. 22;
Qamar al-Zamân and Budûr: *Alf* II 100,-(for daughter); Burton III 284. Chauvin V 204-12 No. 120; *ANE* 341-45 No. 61;
¿Alâ' al-Dîn Abû al-Shâmât: *Alf* II 155,-(for divorced daughter); Burton IV 48. Chauvin V 43-49 No. 18; *ANE* 85-87 No. 63;
Jawdar and His Treacherous Brethren: *Alf* III 200,-(bride's); Burton VI 253. Chauvin V 257-60 No. 154; *ANE* 244-45 No. 209;
Sindbâd's Seventh Voyage: *Alf* III 119; Burton VI 73. Chauvin VII 26-29 No. 373G; *ANE* 386-87 No. 179;
Ruined Baghdadi and His Slave-girl: *Alf* IV 133; Burton IX 30. Chauvin V 152-53 No. 75; *ANE* 353 No. 235;
al-Rashîd and Omani Merchant: *Alf* IV 218,-(for his lovesick daughter); Burton IX 204-5. Chauvin VI 111-12 No. 276; *ANE* 201-2 No. 257;
Ma¿rûf the Cobbler: *Alf* IV 298,-(for his daughter); Burton X 16. Chauvin VI 81-82 No. 250; *ANE* 291-93 No. 262.□

T53.7.2.1.0.1§, ‡Sister arranges for her brother and eligible girl (woman) to meet—(usually clandestinely). See: *DOTTI*. (Cf. T452).
Portress Amînah: Bitten Cheek: *Alf* I 57; Burton I 176-77. Chauvin V 98-99 No. 33; *ANE* 326-27 No. 20;
Hasan of Basrah: *Alf* III 319,-cf./(foster jinni sister); Burton VIII 39. Chauvin VII 29-35 No. 212A; *ANE* 207-10 No. 230.□

T53.7.2.3.2§, ‡Maternal-uncle as matchmaker.
Jullanâr of the Sea: *Alf* III 255; Burton VII 279. Chauvin V 147-51 No. 73; *ANE* 248-51 No. 227.□

T53.8§, ‡Servant (slave) as matchmaker. See: *DOTTI*.
Reeve's Story: Why Maimed by Bride: *Alf* I 97,-cf./(*khâdim*/go between); Burton I 282,-(eunuch). Chauvin V 220-21 No. 305; *ANE* 351 No. 25;
Masrûr and Zayn al-Mawâṣif: *Alf* IV 74,-cf./(to be rewarded for marrying mistress to lover); Burton VIII 249. Chauvin VI 82-84 No. 251; *ANE* 294-95 No. 232.□

T53.9.1§, ‡Ruler (king, caliph, emperor, etc.) as matchmaker. (Cf. T135.0.3.1§).
Porter and Ladies of Baghdad: *Alf* I 61,-(caliph); Burton I 185-86. Chauvin V 251-52 No. 148; *ANE* 324-26 No. 14;
Sindbâd's Fourth Voyage: *Alf* III 103,-(reward); Burton VI 40. Chauvin VII 18-20 No. 373D; *ANE* 386 No. 179.□

T55, Girl as wooer. Forthputting woman. See: *DOTTI*; *GMC*; *PSAE*. (Cf. T52.0.6.1§, T404§, W256.6.1.1§).
Porter and Ladies of Baghdad: *Alf* I 35,-cf.; Burton I 92-93. Chauvin V 251-52 No. 148; *ANE* 324-26 No. 14;
Copt Broker's Story: Lover's Sacrifices Repaid: *Alf* I 91-2; Burton I 269-71. Chauvin VI 80 No. 249; *ANE* 313-14 No. 24;

Barber's Sixth Brother: Emasculated by Abductor: *Alf* I 123; Burton I 346. Chauvin V 163-64 No. 86; *ANE* 120 No. 34;
¿Azîz and ¿Azîzah: *Alf* I 285; Burton II 330-32. Chauvin V 144-45 No. 71; *ANE* 111-13 No. 41;
¿Alî ibn Bakkâr: *Alf* II 42; Burton III 164. Chauvin V 153 No. 76; *ANE* 92-93 No. 60;
al-'Amjad and al-'As¿ad: *Alf* II 123; Burton III 327. Chauvin V 208-10 No. 120[.1]; *ANE* 341-42 No. 61/pt. 2;
Sweep and Noble Lady: Infidelity Repaid: *Alf* II 189-90; Burton IV 126-30. Chauvin VI 148 No. 306; *ANE* 403-4 No. 72;
Mock Caliph/¿Alî al-Jawharî: *Alf* II 197; Burton IV 140. Chauvin V 99-100 No. 174; *ANE* 304-5 No. 73;
Jewish Tray-maker and Temptress: *Alf* III 13,-cf.; Burton V 265. Chauvin VI 187-88 No. 354; *ANE* 169 No. 166;
Craft and Malice of Women/Frame: *Alf* III 139; Burton VI 124. Chauvin VIII 33-34 No. 1; *ANE* 160-61 No. 181;
Mercury ¿Alî: *Alf* III 231; Burton VII 181. Chauvin V 248-50 No. 147; *ANE* 301-3 No. 225.□

T55.0.1§, ‡Female (maiden, woman) as suitor: she proposes marriage to man. See: *DOTTI*.
¿Azîz and ¿Azîzah: *Alf* I 285; Burton II 330-32. Chauvin V 144-45 No. 71; *ANE* 111-13 No. 41.□

T55.5.2.1§, ‡Maiden moved by report that a youth is secretly love-sick (considering suicide) for her. (Cf. K1351).
Tailor's Story/Barber of Baghdad: *Alf* I 104; Burton I 306. Chauvin V 154-56 No. 78; *ANE* 405-6 No. 27.□

T55.6.3§, ‡Coquette: exhibitionist from vanity. (Cf. C105.1§, F565.5.1§, N8.1§, T404§).
¿Azîz and ¿Azîzah: *Alf* I 276,-cf.; Burton II 312. Chauvin V 144-45 No. 71; *ANE* 111-13 No. 41.□

T55.13§, ‡Wooing the naive man (boy).
¿Azîz and ¿Azîzah: *Alf* I 282; Burton II 331. Chauvin V 144-45 No. 71; *ANE* 111-13 No. 41.□

T55.14§, ‡Girl declares erotic intentions. (Cf. H607.3.1§).
¿Azîz and ¿Azîzah: *Alf* I 285; Burton II 331. Chauvin V 144-45 No. 71; *ANE* 111-13 No. 41.□

T56.8§, ‡Attracting by playing hard to get: coquette's strategy.
¿Azîz and ¿Azîzah: *Alf* I 276,-(*tata¿azzaz ¿lâ*); Burton II 312,-(making self inordinately dear and difficult to someone). Chauvin V 144-45 No. 71; *ANE* 111-13 No. 41.□

T57.3§, ‡Publication of love by man causes shame and disgrace to his beloved (her family). (Cf. P788.1§, T75.3).
King ¿Umar al-Nu¿mân and Sons: *Alf* I 313, II 3; Burton III 60,-(father heard of the verses), 78. Chauvin VI 112-24 No. 277; *ANE* 430-34 No. 39.□

T57.5§, ‡Declaration of love by girl shameful (act of immodesty). See: *DOTTI*. (Cf. Q243.7§, W44§, W170§).
King ¿Umar al-Nu¿mân and Sons: *Alf* II 3; Burton III 78. Chauvin VI 112-24 No. 277; *ANE* 430-34 No. 39;
Uns al-Wujûd and al-Ward: *Alf* II 271; Burton V 36-37. Chauvin VI 127-29 No. 282; *ANE* 438 No. 104.□

T57.5.1§, ‡Girl in love reproached as prostitute (whore). (Cf. K2112).
¿Alî Shâr and Zumurrud: *Alf* II 223; Burton IV 203,-("wanton minx and whore"). Chauvin V 89-91 No. 28; *ANE* 100-1 No. 82;
Hasan of Basrah: *Alf* IV 40, 41; Burton VIII 115, 118. Chauvin VII 29-35 No. 212A; *ANE* 207-10 No. 230.□

T57.5.2§, ‡Marriage due to love ('taken on love') as shameful (especially for female).
King ¿Umar al-Nu¿mân and Sons: *Alf* II 3; Burton III 78. Chauvin VI 112-24 No. 277; *ANE* 430-34 No. 39.□

T59§, ‡Accompaniments of coition.
¿Alî Shâr and Zumurrud: *Alf* II 234; Burton IV 226-27. Chauvin V 89-91 No. 28; *ANE* 100-1 No. 82.□

T59.0.1§, ‡Accompaniments of coition: behavioral manifestations. See: *DOTTI*. (Cf. T1.0.2§).
¿Azîz and ¿Azîzah: *Alf* I 285-86; Burton II 331. Chauvin V 144-45 No. 71; *ANE* 111-13 No. 41.□

T59.0.1.1.1§, ‡A female's characteristic reactions during sexual intercourse: racial and ethnic manifestations. (Cf. W256.1§).
¿Alî Shâr and Zumurrud: *Alf* II 234; Burton IV 227 n. 2,-(Abyssinian women). Chauvin V 89-91 No. 28; *ANE* 100-1 No. 82;
Nûr al-Dîn and Maryam: *Alf* IV 97; Burton VIII 304. Chauvin V 52-54 No. 271; *ANE* 98-99 No. 233.□

T59.0.1.2.1§, ‡Vocal manifestations (by female) of sexual enjoyment (*'ghang'*). See: *DOTTI*.
¿Azîz and ¿Azîzah: *Alf* I 285-86; Burton II 331. Chauvin V 144-45 No. 71; *ANE* 111-13 No. 41.□

T59.0.2.1§, ‡Male's inevitable shout (scream) at ejaculation (orgasm). (Cf. T160.0.4§).
Ma¿rûf the Cobbler: *Alf* IV 300; Burton X 21 n. 2,-("she cried the cry [of pain of defloration] that needs must be cried"). Chauvin VI 81-82 No. 250; *ANE* 291-93 No. 262.□

T59.0.3§, ‡Accompaniments of coition: accessories (food, drink, drug, music, lighting, etc.). See: *DOTTI*.
Copt Broker's Story: Lover's Sacrifices Repaid: *Alf* I 92,-(food); Burton I 270-71. Chauvin VI 80 No. 249; *ANE* 313-14 No. 24;
Jewish Doctor's Story: Sororicide: *Alf* I 100,-(food, liquor); Burton I 290. Chauvin VI 89 No. 253; *ANE* 242 No. 26.□

T59.1§, ‡Lovers' play (foreplay): embracing, kissing, necking, etc. (Cf. N8.1§).
Porter and Ladies of Baghdad: *Alf* I 33-35; Burton I 90. Chauvin V 251-52 No. 148; *ANE* 324-26 No. 14;
Copt Broker's Story: Lover's Sacrifices Repaid: *Alf* I 92; Burton I 270-71. Chauvin VI 80 No. 249; *ANE* 313-14 No. 24;
First Eunuch: Bukhayt Deflowers Mistress: *Alf* I 148; Burton II 49-50. Chauvin V 277 No. 160; *ANE* 178 No. 37;
Ghânim ibn Ayyûb: *Alf* I 153; Burton II 45-76. Chauvin VI 14 No. 188; *ANE* 192-93 No. 36;
¿Azîz and ¿Azîzah: *Alf* I 279; Burton II 318. Chauvin V 144-45 No. 71; *ANE* 111-13 No. 41;
Lady and Five Suitors Deceived: *Alf* III 159; Burton VI 175,-(jesting and toying). Chauvin VIII 50-51 No. 18; *ANE* 266 No. 198;
Sayf al-Mulûk: *Alf* III 287,-cf.; Burton VII 349. Chauvin VII 64-73 No. 348; *ANE* 362-64 No. 229;
al-Rashîd and Omani Merchant: *Alf* IV 213,-(poem); Burton IX 197. Chauvin VI 111-12 No. 276; *ANE* 201-2 No. 257;
Ma¿rûf the Cobbler: *Alf* IV 300; Burton X 21. Chauvin VI 81-82 No. 250; *ANE* 291-93 No. 262.□

T59.1.0.1§, ‡Lovers' kiss. See: *PSAE*.
¿Azîz and ¿Azîzah: *Alf* I 279; Burton II 318. Chauvin V 144-45 No. 71; *ANE* 111-13 No. 41.□

T59.1.1§, ‡Foreplay (conversing, kissing, etc.) before coition recommended. See: *DOTTI*.
Nuzhat al-Zamân Tested/¿Umar al-Nu¿mân: *Alf* I 202; Burton II 161. Chauvin VI 116, n.1/passim No. 277; *ANE* 432,/passim No. 39.□

T59.1.2§, ‡Foreplay alone does not satisfy sexual desire. See: *DOTTI*.
¿Alâ' al-Dîn Abû al-Shâmât: *Alf* II 155,-(poem); Burton IV 47. Chauvin V 43-49 No. 18; *ANE* 85-87 No. 63.□

T59.2§, ‡Non-penetration sexual intercourse. ('Brushing'). See: *DOTTI*. (Cf. Z197.3.4.0.2§).
al-Rashîd and Omani Merchant: *Alf* IV 213,-(poem); Burton IX 197. Chauvin VI 111-12 No. 276; *ANE* 201-2 No. 257.□

T59.2.1§, ‡Accidental defloration. See: *DOTTI*. (Cf. K1912).
First Eunuch: Bukhayt Deflowers Mistress: *Alf* I 147; Burton II 50. Chauvin V 277 No. 160; *ANE* 178 No. 37.□

T59.2.2§, ‡Sexual liaison that preserves the female's virginity.
Sayf al-Mulûk: *Alf* III 287; Burton VII 348. Chauvin VII 64-73 No. 348; *ANE* 362-64 No. 229.□

T59.2.3§, ‡Erotic advantage (hugging, kissing, touching) taken of sleeping person.
Qamar al-Zamân and Budûr: *Alf* II 79; Burton III 241. Chauvin V 204-12 No. 120; *ANE* 341-45 No. 61.□

T60§, ‡Sex games. Lovers pretend to be animals, objects, etc. See: *DOTTI*. (Cf. T283).
Porter and Ladies of Baghdad: *Alf* I 35; Burton I 93 n. 2,("orgie"[??], "debauchery is of the mind"). Chauvin V 251-52 No. 148; *ANE* 324-26 No. 14;

Qamar al-Zamân and Budûr: *Alf* II 110-11,-cf.; Burton III 304-6. Chauvin V 204-12 No. 120; *ANE* 341-45 No. 61.□

T60.0.1§, ‡Rough sex-game (or foreplay).
Barber's Second Brother: Humiliated by Playgirl: *Alf* I 113-14,-(lover-to-be slapped till fainting); Burton I 325. Chauvin V 158 No. 82; *ANE* 117-18 No. 30.□

T60.0.1.1§, ‡Injury from rough sex-game (or foreplay). (Cf. K2234§).
Porter and Ladies of Baghdad: *Alf* I 33-35,-cf./(slapping); Burton I 91. Chauvin V 251-52 No. 148; *ANE* 324-26 No. 14.□

T61.5.3, Unborn children promised in marriage to each other. See: *DOTTI*.
Nûr al-Dîn ¿Alî and Son: *Alf* I 64,-(plan unfulfilled); Burton I 196. Chauvin VI 102-6 No. 270; *ANE* 317-19 No. 22;
King ¿Umar al-Nu¿mân and Sons: *Alf* I 238; Burton II 238. Chauvin VI 112-24 No. 277; *ANE* 430-34 No. 39.□

T61.6.1§, Parents renege on betrothal promise. See: *DOTTI*; *GMC*.
King ¿Umar al-Nu¿mân and Sons: *Alf* II 8,-(fiancee's father); Burton III 88. Chauvin VI 112-24 No. 277; *ANE* 430-34 No. 39.□

T61.6.1.1§, ‡Father reneges on promise of giving own child (daughter, son) as prize. See: *DOTTI*.
Ebony Horse: *Alf* II 259; Burton V 17. Chauvin V 221-31 No. 130; *ANE* 172-74 No. 103.□

T63.2§, ‡Woman masking (disguised) as man selected as groom (husband). See: *DOTTI*. (Cf. T315.2.6.1§).
Qamar al-Zamân and Budûr: *Alf* II 98; Burton III 283. Chauvin V 204-12 No. 120; *ANE* 341-45 No. 61.□

T66.3§, ‡Lover's trusted companion (friend). See: *DOTTI*.
¿Alî ibn Bakkâr: *Alf* II 41ff.; Burton III 163. Chauvin V 153 No. 76; *ANE* 92-93 No. 60.□

T67.1, ‡Marriage to prince as reward for disenchanting him.
First Shaykh: Sorceress Wife: *Alf* I 10-11; Burton I 31. Chauvin VII 129-30 No. 396; *ANE* 376-77 No. 5.□

T67.4§, ‡Marriage to prince as reward for rescuing him (saving his life).
al-'Amjad and al-'As¿ad: *Alf* II 147; Burton IV 28. Chauvin V 208-10 No. 120[.1]; *ANE* 341-42 No. 61/pt. 2.□

T68, Princess offered as prize. See: *DOTTI*; *GMC*.
Ebony Horse: *Alf* II 254,-cf./(requested); Burton V 3. Chauvin V 221-31 No. 130; *ANE* 172-74 No. 103.□

T68.6§, ‡Princess offered as prize to man who can cure her. See: *DOTTI*.
Qamar al-Zamân and Budûr: *Alf* II 86; Burton III 256. Chauvin V 204-12 No. 120; *ANE* 341-45 No. 61.□

T68.9§, ‡Prayer (blessing) that marriage to certain person (maiden, youth) be another's reward (prize). See: *DOTTI*. (Cf. D1905.3, M407.1§, Q195).
Copt Broker's Story: Lover's Sacrifices Repaid: *Alf* I 91; Burton I 267. Chauvin VI 80 No. 249; *ANE* 313-14 No. 24.□

T69.2, Parents affiance children without their knowledge. See: *DOTTI*; *GMC*.
¿Azîz and ¿Azîzah: *Alf* I 268; Burton II 298-99. Chauvin V 144-45 No. 71; *ANE* 111-13 No. 41.□

T72, Woman won and then scorned. (Cf. J3.2.4§, T331).
Man of Upper Egypt and Frankish Wife: Alf IV 16?,-(text missing); Burton IX 20,-cf./(man refrains after paying fee). Chauvin V 240 No. 140; *ANE*: No. 234.□

T72.0.1§, Man loses battle of wits with (is humiliated by) girl (his paternal-cousin) then marries her for spite. See: *DOTTI*; *GMC*. (Cf. J1251.1, T289§).
Bahrâm and Datmâ: *Alf* III 164,-cf.; Burton VI 185. Chauvin VIII 54-57 No. 22; *ANE* 114-15 No. 202.□

T72.5§, Girl avenges being rejected as fiancée (wife).
Lovers of Basra/Damrah: *Alf* III 212; Burton VII 135. Chauvin V 118 No. 54; *ANE* 273 No. 220.□

T73§, ‡Man wins beloved and then seeks another 'love' (Solomon, ¿Antar, etc.). (Cf. W256.6.8.2§).

Sayf al-Mulûk: *Alf* III 298; Burton VII 369. Chauvin VII 64-73 No. 348; *ANE* 362-64 No. 229.□

T73.1§, ‡Beloved abandoned for the sake of another (new love).
Lovers of Basra/Ḍamrah: *Alf* III 212,-(*'istabdalnâ bihâ*); Burton VII 134,-(we have taken other in her stead). Chauvin V 118 No. 54; *ANE* 273 No. 220.□

T75.2.1, Rejected suitors' revenge. See: *DOTTI*; *GMC*.
¿Alî Shâr and Zumurrud: *Alf* II 222,-(buyer of slave-girl); Burton IV 201-2. Chauvin V 89-91 No. 28; *ANE* 100-1 No. 82;
Ebony Horse: *Alf* II 262; Burton V 20-21. Chauvin V 221-31 No. 130; *ANE* 172-74 No. 103;
Enchanted Spring: Change of Sex: *Alf* III 146; Burton VI 145. Chauvin VIII 43 No. 11; *ANE* 175-76 No. 191.□

T75.2.1.1§, ‡Rejected suitors casts forth successful one (or leaves him for dead).
Ibrâhîm and Jamîlah: *Alf* IV 227; Burton IX 225. Chauvin VI 52-53 No. 218; *ANE* 227-29 No. 258.□

T75.2.3§, ‡Refused suitor bewitches (seeks to bewitch) successful one. See: *DOTTI*.
Enchanted Spring: Change of Sex: *Alf* III 146; Burton VI 145. Chauvin VIII 43 No. 11; *ANE* 175-76 No. 191.□

T75.3, Unrequited love expressed in song (poem). See: *DOTTI*. (Cf. T57.3§).
King ¿Umar al-Nu¿mân and Sons: *Alf* I 211-14; Burton II 178-87. Chauvin VI 112-24 No. 277; *ANE* 430-34 No. 39;
Budûr and Jubayr ibn ¿Umayr: *Alf* II 238-39; Burton IV 237. Chauvin VII 93-94 No. 374; *ANE* 243-44 No. 83.□

T80.1.1§, ‡Beloved with heart of rock (ice, etc.).
Budûr and Jubayr ibn ¿Umayr: *Alf* II 243,-(poem); Burton IV 245. Chauvin VII 93-94 No. 374; *ANE* 243-44 No. 83.□

T80.2§, ‡Misery from unrequited love.
Ghânim ibn Ayyûb: *Alf* I 153-54; Burton II 62. Chauvin VI 14 No. 188; *ANE* 192-93 No. 36;
¿Azîz and ¿Azîzah: *Alf* I 282; Burton II 302-22. Chauvin V 144-45 No. 71; *ANE* 111-13 No. 41;
Budûr and Jubayr ibn ¿Umayr: *Alf* II 243,-(poem); Burton IV 244-45. Chauvin VII 93-94 No. 374; *ANE* 243-44 No. 83.□

T81, Death from love. See: *DOTTI*; *GMC*. (Cf. F1041.1.3, T24.9.5§, V462.2.3, V463.7.4§).
¿Alî ibn Bakkâr: *Alf* II 64, 65; Burton III 209, 211. Chauvin V 153 No. 76; *ANE* 92-93 No. 60;
Lovers of Banû ¿Udhrah and Lion: *Alf* III 209; Burton VII 123. Chauvin V 116-17 No. 52; *ANE* 274 No. 218/[2].□

T81.1.1§, ‡Lovers embrace each other and fall dead. (Cf. F1041.1.2.1).
Lovers of Banû Ṭay'/Death from Love: *Alf* II 297; Burton V 137. Chauvin V 111 No. 45; *ANE* 273 No. 145.□

T81.2, Death from unrequited love. See: *DOTTI*; *GMC*. (Cf. F1041.1.1).
¿Azîz and ¿Azîzah: *Alf* I 282; Burton II 322. Chauvin V 144-45 No. 71; *ANE* 111-13 No. 41;
¿Alâ' al-Dîn Abû al-Shâmât: *Alf* II 161,-cf./(death from sexual desire); Burton IV 58. Chauvin V 43-49 No. 18; *ANE* 85-87 No. 63;
Lovers of Banû Ṭay'/Death from Love: *Alf* II 297; Burton V 137. Chauvin V 111 No. 45; *ANE* 273 No. 145;
Masrûr and Zayn al-Mawâṣif: *Alf* IV 76-77,-cf./(sexual desire); Burton VIII 255. Chauvin VI 82-84 No. 251; *ANE* 294-95 No. 232.□

T81.3.1§, ‡Girl falls dead on lover's grave. See: *DOTTI*.
Prior Becomes Moslem: al-Anbârî: *Alf* II 299; Burton V 144. Chauvin V 237-38 No. 137; *ANE* 330-31 No. 147.□

T81.7, Woman dies on hearing of lover's or husband's death. See: *DOTTI*; *GMC*. (Cf. F1041.1.2).
¿Alî ibn Bakkâr: *Alf* II 65; Burton III 211. Chauvin V 153 No. 76; *ANE* 92-93 No. 60.□

T81.9.1.1§, ‡Girl wants to commit suicide because she thinks lover is dead.
Tâj al-Mulûk: *Alf* I 306; Burton III 44. Chauvin V 126-28 No. 60; *ANE* 406-8 No. 40;
Butcher Wardân and Bear Lover: *Alf* II 252,-cf./(to be killed as bear-lover); Burton IV 295. Chauvin V 177-78 No. 101; *ANE* 442-43 No. 101.□

T82.9.1§, ‡Lovesickness cured by love (fulfillment). (Cf. F950.4).
Jeweler's Wife and Qamar al-Zamân: *Alf* IV 264,-(*ḥabîbî wa ṭabîbî*/ my lover and my healer); Burton IX 299,-(my love and leach[!!]). Chauvin V 212-14 No. 121; *ANE* 345-47 No. 260;
Uns al-Wujûd and al-Ward: *Alf* II 269,-(*wiṣâl*); Burton V 34. Chauvin VI 127-29 No. 282; *ANE* 438 No. 104.□

T84, Lovers treacherously separated. See: *DOTTI*; *GMC*. (Cf. K1397.3§, T90.2§, T197§).
King ¿Umar al-Nu¿mân and Sons: *Alf* I 313,-cf./(at maturation); Burton III 56-57. Chauvin VI 112-24 No. 277; *ANE* 430-34 No. 39;
¿Alî Shâr and Zumurrud: *Alf* II 223; Burton IV 202-3. Chauvin V 89-91 No. 28; *ANE* 100-1 No. 82;
Uns al-Wujûd and al-Ward: *Alf* II 272; Burton V 37. Chauvin VI 127-29 No. 282; *ANE* 438 No. 104.□

T85.1, Woman thinking lover dead erects cenotaph and mourns before it. See: *DOTTI*; *GMC*.
Ensorcelled Prince/Husband: *Alf* I 29; Burton I 74. Chauvin VI 56-58 No. 222; *ANE* 176 No. 13.□

T86, Lovers buried in same grave. See: *ANE*; *DOTTI*; *GMC*.
Lovers of Banû ¿Udhrah and Lion: *Alf* III 210; Burton VII 124. Chauvin V 116-17 No. 52; *ANE* 274 No. 218/[2].□

T86.0.1§, ‡Lovers buried in side by side graves. See: *DOTTI*.
¿Alî ibn Bakkâr: *Alf* II 64-65,/implicit; Burton III 211. Chauvin V 153 No. 76; *ANE* 92-93 No. 60;
Jânshâh: *Alf* III 38,-cf.; Burton V 327. Chauvin VII 39-44 No. 153; *ANE* 238-41 No. 178.□

T86.0.1.1§, ‡Lover builds grave next to that of dead sweetheart and awaits own death.
Jânshâh: *Alf* III 38; Burton V 327. Chauvin VII 39-44 No. 153; *ANE* 238-41 No. 178.□

T86.6.1§, ‡Husband awaits own death at grave of his wife. See: *DOTTI*.
Jânshâh: *Alf* III 73; Burton V 381. Chauvin VII 39-44 No. 153; *ANE* 238-41 No. 178.□

T90.1§, ‡Enmity between lovers's families (tribes, nations) separates lovers (obstacle to marriage). See: *DOTTI*. (Cf. T84, T97, T197§).
Lovers of Banû Ṭay'/Death from Love: *Alf* II 297; Burton V 137-38. Chauvin V 111 No. 45; *ANE* 273 No. 145.□

T90.2§, ‡Lovers forcibly separated (literally). Pulled apart by relatives. (Cf. T84).
Lovers of Banû Ṭay'/Death from Love: *Alf* II 297; Burton V 137. Chauvin V 111 No. 45; *ANE* 273 No. 145.□

T91, Unequals in love. (Cf. J700.1§).
Sweep and Noble Lady: Infidelity Repaid: *Alf* II 190; Burton IV 126-30. Chauvin VI 148 No. 306; *ANE* 403-4 No. 72.□

T91.4.1, ‡Mature married woman in love with callow youth.
Jeweler's Wife and Qamar al-Zamân: *Alf* IV 249; Burton IX 268. Chauvin V 212-14 No. 121; *ANE* 345-47 No. 260.□

T91.6.4.1.3§, ‡Captor's daughter falls in love with captive man. (Cf. R52.4§).
al-'Amjad and al-'As¿ad: *Alf* II 131; Burton III 345. Chauvin V 208-10 No. 120[.1]; *ANE* 341-42 No. 61/pt. 2;
Mercury ¿Alî: *Alf* III 243; Burton VII 202. Chauvin V 248-50 No. 147; *ANE* 301-3 No. 225.□

T91.9§, Beautiful (handsome) and ugly (loathsome) in love. See: *DOTTI*; *GMC*.
Sweep and Noble Lady: Infidelity Repaid: *Alf* II 188,-cf.; Burton IV 125-30. Chauvin VI 148 No. 306; *ANE* 403-4 No. 72.□

T92.0.2§, ‡Selfishness of love: love does not allow for sharing the beloved (with others).
Budûr and Jubayr ibn ¿Umayr: *Alf* II 237,-(poem); Burton IV 234. Chauvin VII 93-94 No. 374; *ANE* 243-44 No. 83.□

T92.0.2.1§, ‡Lover abandons beloved upon discovering that a third party (lover) is involved.
Budûr and Jubayr ibn ¿Umayr: *Alf* II 237,-(poem); Burton IV 234. Chauvin VII 93-94 No. 374; *ANE* 243-44 No. 83;
Lovers of Basra/Ḍamrah: *Alf* III 212; Burton VII 132. Chauvin V 118 No. 54; *ANE* 273 No. 220.□

T92.1.1.1§, ‡Concubine of king loves (is loved by) younger man—(a commoner). See: *DOTTI*.
¿Alî ibn Bakkâr: *Alf* II 42; Burton III 163. Chauvin V 153 No. 76; *ANE* 92-93 No. 60.□

T92.4.3, ‡In darkness of night trickster instead of her chosen lover elopes with girl.
Nûr al-Dîn and Maryam: *Alf* IV 122; Burton IX 4. Chauvin V 52-54 No. 271; *ANE* 98-99 No. 233.□

T92.5.0.1§, Brothers as rivals in love. See: *DOTTI*; *GMC*.
King ¿Umar al-Nu¿mân and Sons: *Alf* I 207,-(implicit); Burton II 173. Chauvin VI 112-24 No. 277; *ANE* 430-34 No. 39.□

T92.9, Father and son as rivals in love. See: *DOTTI*; *GMC*. (Cf. W195.9.1§).
King ¿Umar al-Nu¿mân and Sons: *Alf* I 182; Burton II 120-21. Chauvin VI 112-24 No. 277; *ANE* 430-34 No. 39.□

T93.1, Disappointed lover becomes a wild man in the woods [(insane)]. (Cf. F567.4§, T24.3).
Lovers of Banû ¿Udhrah and Lion: *Alf* III 207; Burton VII 120. Chauvin V 116-17 No. 52; *ANE* 274 No. 218/[2].□

T92.9.3§, ‡Lustful father-in-law. He seduces (seeks to seduce) son's wife (fiancee).
King ¿Umar al-Nu¿mân and Sons: *Alf* I 181-82; Burton II 119-20. Chauvin VI 112-24 No. 277; *ANE* 430-34 No. 39.□

T92.9.3.1§, ‡Lecherous father-in-law rapes son's wife (fiancee). (Cf. K2218.2, T411, T471); Type: 931Z§.
King ¿Umar al-Nu¿mân and Sons: *Alf* I 182,-cf./(rapes son's wife-to-be); Burton II 123. Chauvin VI 112-24 No. 277; *ANE* 430-34 No. 39.□

T93.6§, ‡Disappointed lover becomes adventurer. (Cf. F950.0.2.1§).
King ¿Umar al-Nu¿mân and Sons: *Alf* I 187; Burton II 132. Chauvin VI 112-24 No. 277; *ANE* 430-34 No. 39.□

T95.0.1, Princess [(girl)] falls in love with father's enemy. See: *DOTTI*.
King ¿Umar al-Nu¿mân and Sons: *Alf* I 175; Burton II 110. Chauvin VI 112-24 No. 277; *ANE* 430-34 No. 39.□

T96, Lovers reunited after many adventure. See: *DOTTI*. (Cf. N741.4).
Ebony Horse: *Alf* II 267; Burton V 31. Chauvin V 221-31 No. 130; *ANE* 172-74 No. 103;
Ruined Baghdadi and His Slave-girl: *Alf* IV 133; Burton IX 32. Chauvin V 152-53 No. 75; *ANE* 353 No. 235;
al-Rashîd and Omani Merchant: *Alf* IV 218; Burton IX 206-7. Chauvin VI 111-12 No. 276; *ANE* 201-2 No. 257.□

T96.1§, ‡Lover united with beloved after long suffering (happy ending). See: *DOTTI*.
Ghânim ibn Ayyûb: *Alf* I 162; Burton II 76. Chauvin VI 14 No. 188; *ANE* 192-93 No. 36;
¿Alâ' al-Dîn Abû al-Shâmât: *Alf* II 181; Burton IV 94. Chauvin V 43-49 No. 18; *ANE* 85-87 No. 63;
Lover Who Feigned Himself a Thief: *Alf* II 205; Burton IV 159. Chauvin VII 134-35 No. 403; *ANE* 272 No. 76;
Budûr and Jubayr ibn ¿Umayr: *Alf* II 243; Burton IV 243-44. Chauvin VII 93-94 No. 374; *ANE* 243-44 No. 83;
Uns al-Wujûd and al-Ward: *Alf* II 282-83; Burton V 61–64. Chauvin VI 127-29 No. 282; *ANE* 438 No. 104;
Lovers of Basra/Damrah: *Alf* III 210-12,-cf./(handsome); Burton VII 130. Chauvin V 118 No. 54; *ANE* 273 No. 220;
Ibrâhîm and Jamîlah: *Alf* IV 229; Burton IX 228-29. Chauvin VI 52-53 No. 218; *ANE* 227-29 No. 258;
Abû al-Ḥasan al-Khorâsânî (and Caliph's Favorite): *Alf* IV 235; Burton IX 239-40. Chauvin V 218-20 No. 129; *ANE* 68-69 No. 259.□

T97, Father opposed to daughter's marriage. (Cf. T90.1§).
Hasan of Basrah: *Alf* IV 40; Burton VIII 113. Chauvin VII 29-35 No. 212A; *ANE* 207-10 No. 230.□

T98.5§, A parent's opposition (procrastination) causes child desiring marriage to express hostility. See: *DOTTI*; *GMC*.
Lovers of Banû ¿Udhrah and Lion: *Alf* III 208,-cf.; Burton VII 121. Chauvin V 116-17 No. 52; *ANE* 274 No. 218/[2].□

T100.0.2§, ‡Celibacy discouraged (inadvisable). See: *DOTTI*. (Cf. C160.0.1§).
Tâj al-Mulûk: *Alf* I 262,-(*lâ rahbâniyyah fî al-'Islâm*); Burton II 285,-(no monkery in Islam). Chauvin 5: 126-28 No. 60; *ANE* 406 No. 40;

Hasan of Basrah: *Alf* IV 50; Burton VIII 137. Chauvin VII 29-35 No. 212A; *ANE* 207-10 No. 230;
Masrûr and Zayn al-Mawâṣif: *Alf* IV 78; Burton VIII 257. Chauvin VI 82-84 No. 251; *ANE* 294-95 No. 232.□

T100.0.9.1§, ‡Marriage in order to enhance social (political, ethnic, religious, etc.) alliance. See: *DOTTI*. (Cf. T68, T145.2.1§).
Jawdar and His Treacherous Brethren: *Alf* III 200,-cf.; Burton VI 255. Chauvin V 257-60 No. 154; *ANE* 244-45 No. 209;
Landsman ¿Abdallah and Merman ¿Abdallah: *Alf* IV 202,-(economic/wealth); Burton IX 174. Chauvin V 6-7 No. 3; *ANE* 65-66 No. 256.□

T100.0.9.2§, ‡Marriage as treatment (cure) for unhappiness (immaturity). (Cf. F950.4).
Bulûqiya/Ḥâsib/Queen of Vipers: *Alf* III 19; Burton V 299. Chauvin VII 54 No. 77; *ANE* 130-32 No. 177;
al-Rashîd and Omani Merchant: *Alf* IV 218,-cf.; Burton IX 205-6. Chauvin VI 111-12 No. 276; *ANE* 201-2 No. 257.□

T100.0.9.3.1§, ‡Marriage arranged so as to be able to influence husband-to-be. (Cf. K1304§).
Jawdar and His Treacherous Brethren: *Alf* III 200; Burton VI 253. Chauvin V 257-60 No. 154; *ANE* 244-45 No. 209.□

T101.1.0.1§, ‡Bride chosen solely for her person.
Shahriyâr and Shahrzâd: *Alf* IV 317,-cf./(wife); Burton X 54. Chauvin V 190-91 No. 111/pt.; *ANE* 371 No. 1.□

T101.1.1§, Bride quality: family power (wealth, honor, status, etc.). See: *GMC*. (Cf. P260.2§).
Jeweler's Wife and Qamar al-Zamân: *Alf* IV 259; Burton IX 288. Chauvin V 212-14 No. 121; *ANE* 345-47 No. 260.□

T101.1.1.0.1§, ‡Bride quality: descent (ancestry, *'aṣl*).
Tâj al-Mulûk: *Alf* I 261; Burton II 284. Chauvin V 126-28 No. 60; *ANE* 406-8 No. 40.□

T101.1.2§, Bride quality: character (religiosity, patience, obedience). See: *DOTTI*.
Jeweler's Wife and Qamar al-Zamân: *Alf* IV 266; Burton IX 302. Chauvin V 212-14 No. 121; *ANE* 345-47 No. 260;
Shahriyâr and Shahrzâd: *Alf* IV 317; Burton X 54-55. Chauvin V 190-91 No. 111/pt.; *ANE* 371 No. 1.□

T101.1.2.0.2§, ‡Bride quality: virtue (conservatism). See: *DOTTI*. (Cf. W4§).
Shahriyâr and Shahrzâd: *Alf* IV 317; Burton X 54-55. Chauvin V 190-91 No. 111/pt.; *ANE* 371 No. 1.□

T101.1.3.1§, Bride quality: beauty. See: *DOTTI*.
Hârûn and Arab Girl: *Alf* III 204; Burton VII 108-10. Chauvin VI 143 No. 300; *ANE* 202 No. 215.□

T101.1.3.2.1§, ‡Bride quality: fertility. See: *DOTTI*. (Cf. T145.2).
Shahriyâr and Shahrzâd: *Alf* IV 317; Burton X 54-55. Chauvin V 190-91 No. 111/pt.; *ANE* 371 No. 1.□

T101.1.3.3§, Bride quality: strength, industriousness, housekeeping. See: *DOTTI*; *GMC*.
Nûr al-Dîn and Maryam: *Alf* IV 103,-cf.; Burton VIII 316. Chauvin V 52-54 No. 271; *ANE* 98-99 No. 233.□

T101.1.4.1§, ‡Bride quality: intelligence, insight (*fiṭnah*). See: *DOTTI*. (Cf. F575.0.2§).
Qamar al-Zamân and Budûr: *Alf* II 72; Burton III 226. Chauvin V 204-12 No. 120; *ANE* 341-45 No. 61;
Anûshirawân and Village Damsel: *Alf* II 285; Burton V 88. Chauvin VI 26-27 No. 198; *ANE* 106 No. 121;
Shahriyâr and Shahrzâd: *Alf* IV 317; Burton X 54. Chauvin V 190-91 No. 111/pt.; *ANE* 371 No. 1.□

T101.1.4.2§, ‡Bride quality: sophistication (knowledge of literature, arts, etc.).
Isḥâq al-Mûṣilî and Khadîjah bint al-Ḥasan: *Alf* II 188; Burton IV 124. Chauvin V 241-42 No. 142; *ANE* 232 No. 71;
Shahriyâr and Shahrzâd: *Alf* IV 317; Burton X 54. Chauvin V 190-91 No. 111/pt.; *ANE* 371 No. 1.□

T101.3.0.1.2§, ‡Father of bride-to-be declares accepting daughter's fiance without bride-wealth (literally or figuratively).
Jawdar and His Treacherous Brethren: *Alf* III 200; Burton VI 255. Chauvin V 257-60 No. 154; *ANE* 244-45 No. 209.□

T101.3.2.2.1§, ‡Rich suitor chosen as groom. (Cf. P529.6.4.1§).
Ma¿rûf the Cobbler: *Alf* IV 298,-(for own daughter); Burton X 16. Chauvin VI 81-82 No. 250; *ANE* 291-93 No. 262.□

T101.6§, ‡Milk (foster) brothers marry milk (foster) sisters. (Cf. P274.1, T121.6.2§).
Sayf al-Mulûk: *Alf* III 302,-(foster brothers-milk sisters); Burton VIII 6. Chauvin VII 64-73 No. 348; *ANE* 362-64 No. 229.□

T103§, ‡Promiscuous society (no-marriage life-style: sexual urges satisfied randomly). (Cf. F569.9§).
Landsman ¿Abdallah and Merman ¿Abdallah: *Alf* IV 205; Burton IX 183. Chauvin V 6-7 No. 3; *ANE* 65-66 No. 256.□

T108.1.1§, ‡Paternal-cousin as rejected suitor. See: *DOTTI*.
Enchanted Spring: Change of Sex: *Alf* III 146; Burton VI 145. Chauvin VIII 43 No. 11; *ANE* 175-76 No. 191;
Ibrâhîm and Jamîlah: *Alf* IV 227; Burton IX 225. Chauvin VI 52-53 No. 218; *ANE* 227-29 No. 258.□

T109.1§, Patrilocal residence: bride moves to home of groom's family. See: *DOTTI*; *GMC*.
Sindbâd's Seventh Voyage: *Alf* III 121,-(wife taken to husband's homeland); Burton VI 77. Chauvin VII 26-29 No. 373G; *ANE* 386-87 No. 179.□

T109.1.1.2.1§, ‡Husband has fun (recreation) with his sister(s), none with his wife.
Hasan of Basrah: *Alf* IV 8-9; Burton VIII 63-54. Chauvin VII 29-35 No. 212A; *ANE* 207-10 No. 230.□

T109.3§, Matrilocal residence: groom moves to home of bride's family. See: *DOTTI*; *GMC*.
Jewish Doctor's Story: Sororicide: *Alf* I 102; Burton I 299. Chauvin VI 89 No. 253; *ANE* 242 No. 26;
Sindbâd's Seventh Voyage: *Alf* III 119,-cf.; Burton VI 74. Chauvin VII 26-29 No. 373G; *ANE* 386-87 No. 179;
Ruined Baghdadi and His Slave-girl: *Alf* IV 133,-(implicit); Burton IX 30. Chauvin V 152-53 No. 75; *ANE* 353 No. 235.□

T109.6§, ‡Ambilocal residence: newlyweds reside alternately between groom's and bride's families.
Jânshâh: *Alf* III 71; Burton V 376. Chauvin VII 39-44 No. 153; *ANE* 238-41 No. 178;
Sayf al-Mulûk: *Alf* III 302; Burton VIII 6/. Chauvin VII 64-73 No. 348; *ANE* 362-64 No. 229.□

T110.1§, ‡Marriage of children. (Usually at first signs of sexual maturation). (Cf. T610.1.1§).
King ¿Umar al-Nu¿mân and Sons: *Alf* I 310,-(aged eight and twelve); Burton III 53-54. Chauvin VI 112-24 No. 277; *ANE* 430-34 No. 39;
Ni¿mah and Nu¿m: Stolen Wife Regained: *Alf* II 132,-(aged ten); Burton IV 2. Chauvin VI 96-97 No. 263; *ANE* 314 No. 62.□

T111.5.1§, ‡Marriage of human being and jinni (fairy). See: *DOTTI*. (Cf. F302).
Jânshâh: *Alf* III 71; Burton V 376. Chauvin VII 39-44 No. 153; *ANE* 238-41 No. 178.□

T111.5.1.2§, ‡Man marries jinni-woman. See: *DOTTI*.
Uns al-Wujûd and al-Ward: *Alf* II 280; Burton V 56. Chauvin VI 127-29 No. 282; *ANE* 438 No. 104;
Hasan of Basrah: *Alf* IV 5,-(in form of swan); Burton VIII 46. Chauvin VII 29-35 No. 212A; *ANE* 207-10 No. 230.□

T119.1§, ‡White husband, black wife. See: *DOTTI*. (Cf. T121.6.1§).
Mercury ¿Alî: *Alf* III 238; Burton VII 194. Chauvin V 248-50 No. 147; *ANE* 301-3 No. 225.□

T119.5§, ‡White wife, black husband.
Man of Upper Egypt and Frankish Wife: Alf IV 16?,-(text missing); Burton IX 19-24. Chauvin V 240 No. 140; *ANE*: No. 234□

T120§, ‡Interreligious marriages (love-affair): different denominations. See: *DOTTI*. (Cf. P529§, T131.8).

King ¿Umar al-Nu¿mân and Sons: *Alf* I 168,-ff.; Burton II 94. Chauvin VI 112-24 No. 277; *ANE* 430-34 No. 39;
Prior Becomes Moslem: al-Anbârî: *Alf* II 298,-cf.; Burton V 141. Chauvin V 237-38 No. 137; *ANE* 330-31 No. 147;
Masrûr and Zayn al-Mawâṣif: *Alf* IV 65, 79; Burton VIII 231, 262. Chauvin VI 82-84 No. 251; *ANE* 294-95 No. 232.□

T121.6.1§, Master (owner) marries slave-girl. See: *DOTTI*; *GMC*. (Cf. P178.9.1§).
King ¿Umar al-Nu¿mân and Sons: *Alf* I 199; Burton II 154. Chauvin VI 112-24 No. 277; *ANE* 430-34 No. 39;
¿Alâ' al-Dîn Abû al-Shâmât: *Alf* II 166; Burton IV 67. Chauvin V 43-49 No. 18; *ANE* 85-87 No. 63;
Man of Upper Egypt and Frankish Wife: Alf IV 16?,-(text missing); Burton IX 19-24. Chauvin V 240 No. 140; *ANE*: No. 234.□

T121.6.2§, ‡Youth marries slave-girl raised with him as foster-sister. See: *DOTTI*. (Cf. P274.1, T101.6§).
Ni¿mah and Nu¿m: Stolen Wife Regained: *Alf* II 132,-(child); Burton IV 2. Chauvin VI 96-97 No. 263; *ANE* 314 No. 62.□

T121.8, ‡King (rich man) weds common girl.
Eldest Lady's Story: Treacherous Sisters: *Alf* I 61,-(caliph marries *dallâlah*, son re-marries common girl); Burton I 186. Chauvin V 4 No. 443; *ANE* 174-75 No. 19.□

T121.9.1.1§, ‡Beautiful girl forced to marry ugly man. See: *DOTTI*. (Cf. T192).
Nûr al-Dîn and Maryam: *Alf* IV 114,-(planned marriage); Burton VIII 337. Chauvin V 52-54 No. 271; *ANE* 98-99 No. 233.□

T127.2§, ‡Husband and wife as contrasts: in temperament. See: *DOTTI*. (Cf. L114.1).
Ma¿rûf the Cobbler: *Alf* IV 288; Burton X 1. Chauvin VI 81-82 No. 250; *ANE* 291-93 No. 262.□

T127.3§, ‡Husband and wife as contrasts: in intelligence. See: *DOTTI*.
Three Wishes: *Alf* III 162; Burton VI 181. Chauvin VIII 51-52 No. 19; *ANE* 419-20 No. 199.□

T131, Marriage restrictions. See: *DOTTI*. (Cf. T90.1§).
Jullanâr of the Sea: *Alf* III 257,-(obstacles that may be raised to marriage); Burton VII 284. Chauvin V 147-51 No. 73; *ANE* 248-51 No. 227.□

T135.0.1§, ‡Marriage contract written (and signed). See: *PSAE*.
Portress Amînah: Bitten Cheek: *Alf* I 58-59; Burton I 180. Chauvin V 98-99 No. 33; *ANE* 326-27 No. 20;
Mock Caliph/¿Alî al-Jawharî: *Alf* II 197; Burton IV 142. Chauvin V 99-100 No. 174; *ANE* 304-5 No. 73.□

T131.1.1, Brother's consent to sister's marriage needed. See: *DOTTI*; *GMC*.
Ḥammâd: Treacherous Bedouin: *Alf* II 17; Burton III 105. Chauvin VI 124 n. 1 No. 277; *ANE* 200 No. 43.□

T131.1.2, Father's consent to son's (daughter's) marriage necessary. See: *DOTTI*; *GMC*.
Lover Who Feigned Himself a Thief: *Alf* II 205; Burton IV 159. Chauvin VII 134-35 No. 403; *ANE* 272 No. 76.□

T131.1.2.3, Father demands that son break all relations with his beloved. See: *DOTTI*.
Jeweler's Wife and Qamar al-Zamân: *Alf* IV 258-59; Burton IX 288. Chauvin V 212-14 No. 121; *ANE* 345-47 No. 260.□

T131.1.2.6§, ‡Child marries parent's choice.
Jeweler's Wife and Qamar al-Zamân: *Alf* IV 260; Burton IX 289. Chauvin V 212-14 No. 121; *ANE* 345-47 No. 260.□

T131.1.2.6.1§, ‡Son marries father's choice. See: *DOTTI*. (Cf. M146.4.1§).
Jeweler's Wife and Qamar al-Zamân: *Alf* IV 260; Burton IX 289. Chauvin V 212-14 No. 121; *ANE* 345-47 No. 260.□

T131.1.2.6.2§, ‡Daughter marries father's choice.
Jeweler's Wife and Qamar al-Zamân: *Alf* IV 260; Burton IX 297. Chauvin V 212-14 No. 121; *ANE* 345-47 No. 260.□

T131.1.3.2§, ‡Daughter chooses to be with her groom (lover) than with her own parents (who disapprove of marriage). (Cf. P529.0.2.2§, R225).
Ebony Horse: *Alf* II 260; Burton V 19. Chauvin V 221-31 No. 130; *ANE* 172-74 No. 103.□

T131.1.4§, Maternal-uncle's consent to nephew's (niece's) marriage necessary.
Mercury ¿Alî: *Alf* III 236,-(niece's); Burton VII 189,-(mother's brother). Chauvin V 248-50 No. 147; *ANE* 301-3 No. 225.□

T131.1.5.1§, Paternal-cousin's consent to marriage of his cousin (*bint-¿amm*) necessary. See: *DOTTI*.
Ishâq al-Mûṣilî and Khadîjah bint al-Ḥasan: *Alf* II 188; Burton IV 124. Chauvin V 241-42 No. 142; *ANE* 232 No. 71.□

T131.8, Different religion as obstacle for marriage. See: *GMC*.
¿Alâ' al-Dîn Abû al-Shâmât: *Alf* II 178,-(Moslem-Christian); Burton IV 89. Chauvin V 43-49 No. 18; *ANE* 85-87 No. 63;
Prior Becomes Moslem: al-Anbârî: *Alf* II 298; Burton V 141, . Chauvin V 237-38 No. 137; *ANE* 330-31 No. 147;
Mercury ¿Alî: *Alf* III 244; Burton VII 204. Chauvin V 248-50 No. 147; *ANE* 301-3 No. 225.□

T131.10.1§, A Moslem woman may marry only a Moslem man. See: *GMC*.
Mercury ¿Alî: *Alf* III 244,-cf./(slave-girl); Burton VII 203. Chauvin V 248-50 No. 147; *ANE* 301-3 No. 225;
Nûr al-Dîn and Maryam: *Alf* IV 129; Burton IX 17. Chauvin V 52-54 No. 271; *ANE* 98-99 No. 233.□

T131.11§, Lower social class as obstacle to marriage. See: *DOTTI*; *GMC*; *PSAE*.
¿Abdallah ibn Fâḍil: Treacherous Brothers: *Alf* IV 279,-(jinni's); Burton IX 331. Chauvin V 2-4 No. 2; *ANE* 63-65 No. 261.□

T131.12§, ‡Slave status as obstacle to marriage. See: *DOTTI*.
Hârûn, Slave-girl and Judge Abû-Yûsuf: *Alf* II 203; Burton IV 155. Chauvin VII 114 No. 383; *ANE* 204 No. 75.□

T131.12.1§, ‡Woman may not marry her slave. (Cf. P530.3§).
Hârûn, Slave-girl and Judge Abû-Yûsuf: *Alf* II 203; Burton IV 155. Chauvin VII 114 No. 383; *ANE* 204 No. 75.□

T131.12.4§, ‡Species as obstacle for marriage.
Jullanâr of the Sea: *Alf* III 250; Burton VII 271. Chauvin V 147-51 No. 73; *ANE* 248-51 No. 227;
Sayf al-Mulûk: *Alf* III 281; Burton VII 333. Chauvin VII 64-73 No. 348; *ANE* 362-64 No. 229.□

T131.12.4.1§, ‡Marriage between jinni (fairy) and Adamite opposed. (Cf. F300).
Uns al-Wujûd and al-Ward: *Alf* II 280; Burton V 56. Chauvin VI 127-29 No. 282; *ANE* 438 No. 104;
Hasan of Basrah: *Alf* IV 40; Burton VIII 116. Chauvin VII 29-35 No. 212A; *ANE* 207-10 No. 230.□

T131.13§, ‡Poverty as obstacle to marriage.
King ¿Umar al-Nu¿mân and Sons: *Alf* I 313; Burton III 60-61. Chauvin VI 112-24 No. 277; *ANE* 430-34 No. 39.□

T132, Preparation for wedding.
¿Azîz and ¿Azîzah: *Alf* I 268; Burton II 299. Chauvin V 144-45 No. 71; *ANE* 111-13 No. 41.□

T133.2, ‡Royal bride conducted by embassy to husband's kingdom. See: *DOTTI*. (Cf. T51).
Tâj al-Mulûk: *Alf* I 264; Burton II 289. Chauvin V 126-28 No. 60; *ANE* 406-8 No. 40.□

T135.0.2§, ‡Renewal of a wedding: procedures of marriage to same person repeated (usually under improved conditions). (Cf. V337§).
Tâj al-Mulûk: *Alf* I 308,-(wedding celebration); Burton III 47. Chauvin V 126-28 No. 60; *ANE* 406-8 No. 40;
Mock Caliph/¿Alî al-Jawharî: *Alf* II 199-200; Burton IV 148. Chauvin V 99-100 No. 174; *ANE* 304-5 No. 73;
Shahriyâr and Shahrzâd: *Alf* IV 317,-cf./(celebration); Burton X 55. Chauvin V 190-91 No. 111/pt.; *ANE* 371 No. 1.□

T135.0.3.1§, ‡Ruler (caliph, king, emperor, etc.) officiates marriage ceremony to honor couple. (Cf. T53.9.1§).

¿Alâ' al-Dîn Abû al-Shâmât: *Alf* II 181,-cf.; Burton IV 94. Chauvin V 43-49 No. 18; *ANE* 85-87 No. 63;
Mock Caliph/¿Alî al-Jawharî: *Alf* II 200; Burton IV 148. Chauvin V 99-100 No. 174; *ANE* 304-5 No. 73;
Ibrâhîm and Jamîlah: *Alf* IV 229; Burton IX 227-29. Chauvin VI 52-53 No. 218; *ANE* 227-29 No. 258;
¿Abdallah ibn Fâḍil: Treacherous Brothers: *Alf* IV 288; Burton IX 349. Chauvin V 2-4 No. 2; *ANE* 63-65 No. 261.□

T135.1, Marriage formula: "You are mine and I am yours".
Budûr and Jubayr ibn ¿Umayr: *Alf* II 243; Burton IV 244. Chauvin VII 93-94 No. 374; *ANE* 243-44 No. 83.□

T135.1.2§, Marriage formula: "I give in marriage the woman (girl) whom I represent". (Cf. P529.0.2.2.3§, T135.3).
¿Azîz and ¿Azîzah: *Alf* I 282; Burton II 331. Chauvin V 144-45 No. 71; *ANE* 111-13 No. 41.□

T135.3, Wedding by proxy [(surrogate)]. See: *DOTTI*; *GMC*.
Tâj al-Mulûk: *Alf* I 264; Burton II 289. Chauvin V 126-28 No. 60; *ANE* 406-8 No. 40.□

T135.8, Two or more weddings at one time as the end of a tale. (Cf. Z10.2.1§).
Ghânim ibn Ayyûb: *Alf* I 162; Burton II 76. Chauvin VI 14 No. 188; *ANE* 192-93 No. 36.□

T142§, Exchange marriage. See: *DOTTI*; *GMC*.
Ghânim ibn Ayyûb: *Alf* I 162; Burton II 76. Chauvin VI 14 No. 188; *ANE* 192-93 No. 36.□

T142.1.1§, ‡Other arrangements of exchange marriage involving brother and sister.
Ghânim ibn Ayyûb: *Alf* I 162,-(caliph and favorite concubine); Burton II 76. Chauvin VI 14 No. 188; *ANE* 192-93 No. 36.□

T136.0.1§, ‡Wedding celebration (festivity). (Cf. P965§).
Reeve's Story: Why Maimed by Bride: *Alf* I 98; Burton I 286. Chauvin V 220-21 No. 305; *ANE* 351 No. 25;
Ma¿rûf the Cobbler: *Alf* IV 299-300; Burton X 19. Chauvin VI 81-82 No. 250; *ANE* 291-93 No. 262.□

T136.1, ‡Wedding feast. (Cf. V65.6§).
Qamar al-Zamân and Budûr: *Alf* II 96; Burton III 276. Chauvin V 204-12 No. 120; *ANE* 341-45 No. 61.□

T136.4.0.1§, ‡Bride's *nuqûṭ*: gift (money) given to bride (to be reciprocated by her family). (Cf. J708.5§, P428.0.1§).
Reeve's Story: Why Maimed by Bride: *Alf* I 98,-cf./(with gold); Burton I 286,-(palms crossed with gold). Chauvin V 220-21 No. 305; *ANE* 351 No. 25;
Dalîla the Swindler: *Alf* III 220,-cf.; Burton VII 157. Chauvin V 245-50 No. 147; *ANE* 163-64 No. 224.□

T136.8.1§, ‡Bridal procession concludes wedding ceremonies.
Ma¿rûf the Cobbler: *Alf* IV 300; Burton X 19. Chauvin VI 81-82 No. 250; *ANE* 291-93 No. 262.□

T137.5, Bride (and party) fetched by groom and party after wedding. [*esh-shailah*]. See: *DOTTI*.
Tâj al-Mulûk: *Alf* I 264; Burton II 289-90. Chauvin V 126-28 No. 60; *ANE* 406-8 No. 40.□

T137.6.1§, ‡Groom leaves bride outside his home-country while he goes home to bring proper wedding party. (She is abducted or substituted). See: *DOTTI*. (Cf. T137.5).
Ebony Horse: *Alf* II 261; Burton V 20. Chauvin V 221-31 No. 130; *ANE* 172-74 No. 103.□

T142.4§, Compensation-bride (girl—usually sister of executed wife—given to wronged husband as restitution). See: *DOTTI*; *GMC*. (Cf. P535.1§).
Jewish Doctor's Story: Sororicide: *Alf* I 102; Burton I 299. Chauvin VI 89 No. 253; *ANE* 242 No. 26;
Jeweler's Wife and Qamar al-Zamân: *Alf* IV 263,-cf./(sister of offending adulterer); Burton IX 297. Chauvin V 212-14 No. 121; *ANE* 345-47 No. 260.□

T142.4.1§, ‡Husband of eloping adulteress kills her in paramour's home, he is rewarded with marriage to chaste sister of paramour (adultery-partner).

Jeweler's Wife and Qamar al-Zamân: *Alf* IV 265; Burton IX 300. Chauvin V 212-14 No. 121; *ANE* 345-47 No. 260.□

T144.0.1§, ‡Scarcity of true love.
Eldest Lady's Story: Treacherous Sisters: *Alf* I 54,-cf./(good men as husbands); Burton I 163. Chauvin V 4 No. 443; *ANE* 174-75 No. 19;
Nûr al-Dîn ¿Alî and Son: *Alf* I 73,-(poem); Burton I 223. Chauvin VI 102-6 No. 270; *ANE* 317-19 No. 22;
Qamar al-Zamân and Budûr: *Alf* II 76,-(poem); Burton III 235. Chauvin V 204-12 No. 120; *ANE* 341-45 No. 61;
¿Alî Shâr and Zumurrud: *Alf* II 221,-(poem); Burton IV 198. Chauvin V 89-91 No. 28; *ANE* 100-1 No. 82.□

T144.0.1.1§, ‡True love is for only one (and forsaking all others).
Nûr al-Dîn ¿Alî and Son: *Alf* I 73,-(poem); Burton I 223. Chauvin VI 102-6 No. 270; *ANE* 317-19 No. 22;
Qamar al-Zamân and Budûr: *Alf* II 76,-(poem); Burton III 235. Chauvin V 204-12 No. 120; *ANE* 341-45 No. 61;
¿Alî Shâr and Zumurrud: *Alf* II 221,-(poem); Burton IV 198. Chauvin V 89-91 No. 28; *ANE* 100-1 No. 82.□

T144.3.1§, ‡One wife divorced, another (new) acquired.
Ruined Baghdadi and His Slave-girl: *Alf* IV 133; Burton IX 32. Chauvin V 152-53 No. 75; *ANE* 353 No. 235.□

T145.0.4§, Happy polygynous marriage. See: *DOTTI*; *GMC*.
Qamar al-Zamân and Budûr: *Alf* II 112; Burton III 308. Chauvin V 204-12 No. 120; *ANE* 341-45 No. 61.□

T145.0.4.1§, ‡Wife (fertile) insists that her husband take additional wife (wives). See: *DOTTI*. (Cf. N887.2.1§).
Qamar al-Zamân and Budûr: *Alf* II 112,-cf.; Burton III 308. Chauvin V 204-12 No. 120; *ANE* 341-45 No. 61.□

T145.0.4.2§, ‡Sharing a husband by mutual agreement between women (a night for each).
¿Alâ' al-Dîn Abû al-Shâmât: *Alf* II 178; Burton IV 89. Chauvin V 43-49 No. 18; *ANE* 85-87 No. 63.□

T145.1.0.1§, Marriage to four women. See: *DOTTI*; *GMC*.
King ¿Umar al-Nu¿mân and Sons: *Alf* I 162-63; Burton II 78. Chauvin VI 112-24 No. 277; *ANE* 430-34 No. 39;
Mercury ¿Alî: *Alf* III 246; Burton VII 208. Chauvin V 248-50 No. 147; *ANE* 301-3 No. 225.□

T145.1.0.2§, ‡Marriage to two women. See: *DOTTI*.
Qamar al-Zamân and Budûr: *Alf* II 112; Burton III 308. Chauvin V 204-12 No. 120; *ANE* 341-45 No. 61;
¿Alâ' al-Dîn Abû al-Shâmât: *Alf* II 181; Burton IV 94. Chauvin V 43-49 No. 18; *ANE* 85-87 No. 63.□

T145.2, Second wife taken because first is barren. See: *DOTTI*; *GMC*. (Cf. M144.2§, T380.5.1§).
First Shaykh: Sorceress Wife: *Alf* I 8-9,-(concubine); Burton I 27. Chauvin VII 129-30 No. 396; *ANE* 376-77 No. 5.□

T145.2.1§, Additional wife (wives) taken because of 'compelling' commitments (indebtedness, gratitude, family alliance, etc.). See: *DOTTI*; *GMC*. (Cf. T100.0.9.1§).
Qamar al-Zamân and Budûr: *Alf* II 112; Burton III 308. Chauvin V 204-12 No. 120; *ANE* 341-45 No. 61;
Landsman ¿Abdallah and Merman ¿Abdallah: *Alf* IV 202,-(economic/wealth); Burton IX 174. Chauvin V 6-7 No. 3; *ANE* 65-66 No. 256.□

T145.10.3§, Polygynist's wife is to use love philtre (charm). See: *GMC*.
Dalîla the Swindler: *Alf* III 213; Burton VII 147. Chauvin V 245-50 No. 147; *ANE* 163-64 No. 224.□

T159§, ‡Failure to attend own wedding: ceremony spoiled. See: *DOTTI*. (Cf. T26.3§).
¿Azîz and ¿Azîzah: *Alf* I 270; Burton II 303. Chauvin V 144-45 No. 71; *ANE* 111-13 No. 41.□

T160, Consummation of marriage. (Cf. M143§).

Tâj al-Mulûk: *Alf* I 265; Burton II 290,-(Allah filled his heart with her love [??]). Chauvin V 126-28 No. 60; *ANE* 406-8 No. 40;
Qamar al-Zamân and Budûr: *Alf* II 96; Burton III 276. Chauvin V 204-12 No. 120; *ANE* 341-45 No. 61;
Jânshâh: *Alf* III 71; Burton V 376. Chauvin VII 39-44 No. 153; *ANE* 238-41 No. 178.□

T160.0.1§, Defloration. See: *GMC*.
Tâj al-Mulûk: *Alf* I 307, 308,-(*dakhala ¿alâ*); Burton III 47. Chauvin V 126-28 No. 60; *ANE* 406-8 No. 40;
Qamar al-Zamân and Budûr: *Alf* II 96,-(attain his desire); Burton III 276. Chauvin V 204-12 No. 120; *ANE* 341-45 No. 61;
Man Who Never Laughs: *Alf* III 155,-(*'azâla bakâratahâ*); Burton VI 165,-(he did away her hymen). Chauvin VIII 47-48 No. 15; *ANE* 285-86 No. 195;
Jullanâr of the Sea: *Alf* III 248,-(of mermaid); Burton VII 266. Chauvin V 147-51 No. 73; *ANE* 248-51 No. 227.□

T160.0.2§, Traumatic (cruel) defloration. See: *DOTTI*; *GMC*. (Cf. T59.0.2.1§, T289§).
King ¿Umar al-Nu¿mân and Sons: *Alf* I 182-83,-(victim drugged); Burton II 123. Chauvin VI 112-24 No. 277; *ANE* 430-34 No. 39;
Bahrâm and Datmâ: *Alf* III 166; Burton VI 187. Chauvin VIII 54-57 No. 22; *ANE* 114-15 No. 202.□

T160.0.2.3§, ‡Defloration in presence of others.
Anîs al-Jalîs: *Alf* I 128; Burton II 6. Chauvin V 120-24 No. 58; *ANE* 316-17 No. 35.□

T160.0.2.3.1.1§, ‡Groom 'deflowers' bride in front of her sister—(Sheherezade deflowered). (Cf. J126§, C119.5§).
Shahriyâr and Shahrzâd: *Alf* I 7; Burton I 24. Chauvin V 188-89 No. 111; *ANE* 370-71 No. 1.□

T160.0.3§, Publication of defloration: blood displayed. See: *DOTTI*; *GMC*.
Qamar al-Zamân and Budûr: *Alf* II 103,-(self-publication); Burton III 289. Chauvin V 204-12 No. 120; *ANE* 341-45 No. 61;
First Eunuch: Bukhayt Deflowers Mistress: *Alf* I 148; Burton II 50 n. 1. Chauvin V 277 No. 160; *ANE* 178 No. 37.□

T160.0.4§, ‡Traumatic happenings at first coition (consummation of marriage). See: *DOTTI*. (Cf. H175.7§, J10.1.1.2§, T59.0.2.1§).
Reeve's Story: Why Maimed by Bride: *Alf* I 98-99; Burton I 286-87. Chauvin V 220-21 No. 305; *ANE* 351 No. 25;
Ma¿rûf the Cobbler: *Alf* IV 300,-cf.; Burton X 21 n. 2,-("she cried the cry [of pain of defloration] that needs must be cried"). Chauvin VI 81-82 No. 250; *ANE* 291-93 No. 262.□

T160.1§, ‡Prayer (religious ritual) precedes consummation of marriage. See: *DOTTI*. (Cf. C3.1§).
Qamar al-Zamân and Budûr: *Alf* II 101; Burton III 285. Chauvin V 204-12 No. 120; *ANE* 341-45 No. 61.□

T163§, ‡Happy consummation of marriage, (gratifying for the couple). (Cf. J10.1.1.2§).
Portress Amînah: Bitten Cheek: *Alf* I 58-59; Burton I 180. Chauvin V 98-99 No. 33; *ANE* 326-27 No. 20;
Mock Caliph/¿Alî al-Jawharî: *Alf* II 197; Burton IV 143. Chauvin V 99-100 No. 174; *ANE* 304-5 No. 73.□

T164§, ‡Obstacles to consummation of marriage: consummation postponed.
Nûr al-Dîn and Maryam: *Alf* IV 114,-(building fortified palace/castle); Burton VIII 337. Chauvin V 52-54 No. 271; *ANE* 98-99 No. 233.□

T167§, Signs of exercise of coition. See: *DOTTI*.
Rake's Trick Against Chaste Wife: *Alf* III 141; Burton VI 135. Chauvin VIII 37 No. 5; *ANE* 350-1 No. 185.□

T167.1.1§, ‡Bathing together indicates exercise of coition.
Budûr and Jubayr ibn ¿Umayr: *Alf* II 243,-(getting out of bath together); Burton IV 244. Chauvin VII 93-94 No. 374; *ANE* 243-44 No. 83;
Uns al-Wujûd and al-Ward: *Alf* II 282-83; Burton V 64. Chauvin VI 127-29 No. 282; *ANE* 438 No. 104.□

T167.1.2§, ‡Going to bathhouse indicates exercise of coition.

Rake's Trick Against Chaste Wife: *Alf* III 142; Burton VI 135 n. 1. Chauvin VIII 37 No. 5; *ANE* 350-1 No. 185.□

T168.1§, ‡Groom's failure to consummate marriage (deflower bride) as offense. See: *DOTTI*. (Cf. Q249§, T315.2).
Qamar al-Zamân and Budûr: *Alf* II 102; Burton III 288. Chauvin V 204-12 No. 120; *ANE* 341-45 No. 61.□

T182.1§, Excessive sexual intercourse causes sickness (blindness).
Tawaddud: Slavegirl Sold and Regained: *Alf* II 318; Burton V 225. Chauvin VII 117-19 No. 387; *ANE* 408-10 No. 157;
King Jalî¿âd and Shimâs: *Alf* IV 164-65; Burton IX 97-98. Chauvin VI 9 No. 184; *ANE* 237-38 No. 236.□

T182.1.4§, ‡Worms in vagina from abnormal sexual intercourse (e.g., bestiality, interracial, etc.).
King's Daughter and Ape: *Alf* II 253; Burton IV 298. Chauvin V 178 No. 102; *ANE* 262-63 No. 102.□

T185.3§, ‡Complaint about unsatisfactory coition (sex, love-life, etc.)—in general. See: *DOTTI*. (Cf. H597.1§, P529.0.4.4§, T9.0.1§, T339§).
Qamar al-Zamân and Budûr: *Alf* II 102; Burton III 287-88. Chauvin V 204-12 No. 120; *ANE* 341-45 No. 61.□

T187§, Coition posture. See: *GMC*.
Nuzhat al-Zamân Tested/¿Umar al-Nu¿mân: *Alf* I 202; Burton II 161. Chauvin VI 116, n.1/passim No. 277; *ANE* 432,/passim No. 39.□

T187.0.1§, ‡Female's 'correct' coition posture: laying on back, legs raised upwards (with man on top). See: *DOTTI*.
Nuzhat al-Zamân Tested/¿Umar al-Nu¿mân: *Alf* I 202; Burton II 161. Chauvin VI 116, n.1/passim No. 277; *ANE* 432,/passim No. 39;
Qamar al-Zamân and Budûr: *Alf* II 109,-(poem/implicit); Burton III 304. Chauvin V 204-12 No. 120; *ANE* 341-45 No. 61.□

T187.0.2§, ‡Female's coition posture compared to supplication posture (pleading with God); (i.e., being on her back with legs raised toward heaven). (Cf. U318.1§, Z106§, Z179.4§).
Qamar al-Zamân and Budûr: *Alf* II 109,-(poem); Burton III 304. Chauvin V 204-12 No. 120; *ANE* 341-45 No. 61.□

T188§, Practices believed to ensure birth of sons (male offspring). See: *DOTTI*; *GMC*; *PSAE*.
Sayf al-Mulûk: *Alf* III 275; Burton VII 321. Chauvin VII 64-73 No. 348; *ANE* 362-64 No. 229.□

T188.1§, ‡Eating flesh of (male) snake or serpent ensures birth of sons. (Cf. D1347.7§).
Sayf al-Mulûk: *Alf* III 275; Burton VII 322-23. Chauvin VII 64-73 No. 348; *ANE* 362-64 No. 229.□

T189.3§, ‡Child interrupts adults' (parents's) sexual intercourse. See: *DOTTI*. (Cf. C119.5§, H659.13.1, J126§, P230.0.3§).
Debauchee and Three Years Old Child: *Alf* III 176; Burton VI 208. Chauvin VIII 62-63 No. 147; *ANE* 166-67 No. 206.□

T192, Marriage by force [(coercion)]. See: *DOTTI*; *GMC*. (Cf. T121.9.1.1§).
Hasan of Basrah: *Alf* IV 2,-cf./(human-jinn); Burton VIII 40. Chauvin VII 29-35 No. 212A; *ANE* 207-10 No. 230;
Goldsmith and Cashmere Singer: *Alf* III 151,-cf./(treachery); Burton VI 157-58. Chauvin VIII 46-47 No. 14; *ANE* 196 No. 194.□

T192.1.3§, ‡Girl married to a man for whom she has no affection (love). See: *DOTTI*.
¿Alâ' al-Dîn Abû al-Shâmât: *Alf* II 155; Burton IV 48. Chauvin V 43-49 No. 18; *ANE* 85-87 No. 63;
Lovers of Banû ¿Udhrah and Lion: *Alf* III 208; Burton VII 121. Chauvin V 116-17 No. 52; *ANE* 274 No. 218/[2].□

T192.3§, ‡Marriage due to girl's (premarital) pregnancy. See: *DOTTI*.
First Eunuch: Bukhayt Deflowers Mistress: *Alf* I 147-48; Burton II 50. Chauvin V 277 No. 160; *ANE* 178 No. 37.□

T194§, Marriage by abduction (or raid). See: *DOTTI*; *GMC*. (Cf. P173.6§, R18, T192).

Second Qalandar: Afrit's Wife: *Alf* I 45,-cf.; Burton I 117. Chauvin V 197-200 No. 116; *ANE* 338-39 No. 16.□

T194.1§, ‡Suitor (raider): "Either you give me your sister (daughter) in marriage or I kill you.
Hammâd: Treacherous Bedouin: *Alf* II 17; Burton III 105. Chauvin VI 124 n. 1 No. 277; *ANE* 200 No. 43.□

T196§, Wife divorced because of a trifle. See: *DOTTI*; *GMC*. (Cf. M147§).
House with the Belvedere: *Alf* III 169,-(suspicion); Burton VI 194. Chauvin VIII 57-58 No. 23; *ANE* 223 No. 203.□

T196.7§, ‡Wife divorced for minor (erotic) indiscretion. See: *DOTTI*. (Cf. Q458.0.6.1§, U230.0.2§).
Portress Amînah: Bitten Cheek: *Alf* I 60; Burton I 185. Chauvin V 98-99 No. 33; *ANE* 326-27 No. 20.□

T197§, Wife's relatives (father, brother, etc.) force her divorce from husband without her consent. See: *DOTTI*. (Cf. P529.0.6.3§, P529.1§, T84, T90.1§).
¿Alâ' al-Dîn Abû al-Shâmât: *Alf* II 157,-(attempted); Burton IV 53. Chauvin V 43-49 No. 18; *ANE* 85-87 No. 63;
Ruined Baghdadi and His Slave-girl: *Alf* IV 133,-(father/implicit); Burton IX 32. Chauvin V 152-53 No. 75; *ANE* 353 No. 235.□

T197.3.1§, ‡Brother invites (coaxes) his married sister to leave her husband.
Jullanâr of the Sea: *Alf* III 250; Burton VII 271. Chauvin V 147-51 No. 73; *ANE* 248-51 No. 227.□

T198§, Return to parents' (father's) home after end of marital relations (divorce, or death of spouse). See: *DOTTI*; *GMC*.
Portress Amînah: Bitten Cheek: *Alf* I 60; Burton I 183. Chauvin V 98-99 No. 33; *ANE* 326-27 No. 20;
Jeweler's Wife and Qamar al-Zamân: *Alf* IV 266; Burton IX 302. Chauvin V 212-14 No. 121; *ANE* 345-47 No. 260.□

T198.3.1§, ‡Angered wife (*ghaḍbânah*): leaving husband's home for own family's (father's, brother's, etc.). (Cf. H420.1§, W14.5§, W29.2§).
King ¿Umar al-Nu¿mân and Sons: *Alf* II 11; Burton III 94. Chauvin VI 112-24 No. 277; *ANE* 430-34 No. 39.□

T199.3§, ‡First wife kept by husband (as less favored co-wife, or as deserted wife).
Ma¿rûf the Cobbler: *Alf* IV 315-16; Burton X 49-50. Chauvin VI 81-82 No. 250; *ANE* 291-93 No. 262.□

T199.3.1§, ‡First wife not divorced out of kindness to her. See: *DOTTI*. (Cf. P529.0.1.4§, T198§, W10).
Ma¿rûf the Cobbler: *Alf* IV 315-16; Burton X 49-50. Chauvin VI 81-82 No. 250; *ANE* 291-93 No. 262.□

T202.1.2§, ‡Trouble for couple (wife and husband) who are two of a kind. (Cf. T298).
Abû al-Ḥasan al-Khorâsânî (and Caliph's Favorite): *Alf* IV 235; Burton IX 242. Chauvin V 218-20 No. 129; *ANE* 68-69 No. 259.□

T202.1.2.1§, ‡Difficult reconciliation between the beautiful and the powerful: prevented by pride of beauty, and by pride of power (office, kingship, etc.). (Cf. W164§).
Abû al-Ḥasan al-Khorâsânî (and Caliph's Favorite): *Alf* IV 235; Burton IX 242. Chauvin V 218-20 No. 129; *ANE* 68-69 No. 259.□

T202.2§, ‡Happy cross-species marriage or sexual liaison (supernatural wife, husband, lover, etc.). See: *DOTTI*.
Hasan of Basrah: *Alf* IV 54-55; Burton VIII 155. Chauvin VII 29-35 No. 212A; *ANE* 207-10 No. 230.□

T202.2.1§, ‡Supernatural wife (lover) affectionate toward her human husband. See: *DOTTI*. (Cf. N815.1.1§).
Second Shaykh: Treacherous Brothers: *Alf* I 11; Burton I 34-35. Chauvin V 6 No. 397; *ANE* 377-78 No. 6.□

T202.3§, ‡Affectionate couple. (Cf. P210.0.5§).

¿Alâ' al-Dîn Abû al-Shâmât: *Alf* II 147,-(*ma¿ahu zawjah yuḥibbuhâ wa tuḥibbuh*/with him is a wife whom he loved and she loved him); Burton IV 29,-(owned a wife[!!] whom he loved and who loved him). Chauvin V 43-49 No. 18; *ANE* 85-87 No. 63;
Ma¿rûf the Cobbler: *Alf* IV 301,-(second wife); Burton X 20-21. Chauvin VI 81-82 No. 250; *ANE* 291-93 No. 262.□

T205.1§, Wife-beating. See: *DOTTI*; *GMC*. (Cf. P210.0.2§, P261.1.1§, S186.9.1§).
Merchant's Curious Wife: *Alf* I 6; Burton I 22. Chauvin V 179-80 No. 104; *ANE* 298-99 No. 3.□

T206§, ‡Husband impoverishes his wife: wastes her property. (Cf. P210.1§).
Eldest Lady's Story: Treacherous Sisters: *Alf* I 53-54; Burton I 162. Chauvin V 4 No. 443; *ANE* 174-75 No. 19.□

T210.1, Faithful wife. See: *DOTTI*.
Jewish qâḍî and His Devout Wife: *Alf* III 10; Burton V 256. Chauvin VI 154-55 No. 321; *ANE* 242 No. 163;
King and Vizier's Wife/Tracks of Lion: *Alf* III 140; Burton VI 131. Chauvin VIII 35 No. 2; *ANE* 261 No. 182;
Ma¿rûf the Cobbler: *Alf* IV 302, 311,-ff./(second wife); Burton X 24, 43. Chauvin VI 81-82 No. 250; *ANE* 291-93 No. 262.□

T210.1.1§, ‡Wife keeps husband's secret(s). See: *DOTTI*. (Cf. J155.4).
Ma¿rûf the Cobbler: *Alf* IV 303-4; Burton X 24. Chauvin VI 81-82 No. 250; *ANE* 291-93 No. 262.□

T211.10.1§, Faithful widow refuses to remarry. See: *DOTTI*; *GMC*.
Jeweler's Wife and Qamar al-Zamân: *Alf* IV 266; Burton IX 303. Chauvin V 212-14 No. 121; *ANE* 345-47 No. 260.□

T230.4§, ‡Faithless paternal-cousin-wife. See: *DOTTI*.
Ensorcelled Prince/Husband: *Alf* I 27; Burton I 69-82. Chauvin VI 56-58 No. 222; *ANE* 176 No. 13.□

T232.2, Adulteress chooses loathly paramour.
Sweep and Noble Lady: Infidelity Repaid: *Alf* II 190; Burton IV 129. Chauvin VI 148 No. 306; *ANE* 403-4 No. 72.□

T232.3.1§, Adulteress transforms her husband into an ass (dog) to avenge slaying of loathly paramour. See: *DOTTI*; *GMC*. (Cf. D691, T33.1§).
Third Shaykh: Transformation by Wife: *Alf* I 13,-(dog); Burton I 36. Chauvin VII 130 No. 398; *ANE* 378 No. 7.□

T232.4, Woman enamored of repulsive and abusive lover. See: *DOTTI*. (Cf. T480.1§).
Ensorcelled Prince/Husband: *Alf* I 28; Burton I 71. Chauvin VI 56-58 No. 222; *ANE* 176 No. 13.□

T234§, ‡Wronged wife chooses loathly paramour to spite her faithless husband. See: *DOTTI*. (Cf. K1510.2, K2400§, P187.1§).
Sweep and Noble Lady: Infidelity Repaid: *Alf* II 190; Burton IV 129. Chauvin VI 148 No. 306; *ANE* 403-4 No. 72.□

T251, The shrewish wife. See: *DOTTI*.
Ma¿rûf the Cobbler: *Alf* IV 288; Burton X 1. Chauvin VI 81-82 No. 250; *ANE* 291-93 No. 262.□

T252, The overbearing wife. See: *DOTTI*.
Ma¿rûf the Cobbler: *Alf* IV 288; Burton X 1. Chauvin VI 81-82 No. 250; *ANE* 291-93 No. 262.□

T252.2, Cock shows browbeaten husband how to rule wife. See: *DOTTI*.
Merchant's Curious Wife: *Alf* I 6; Burton I 21. Chauvin V 179-80 No. 104; *ANE* 298-99 No. 3.□

T252.9.4§, ‡Men who obey women's whimsical (irrational) urges must share the blame for the misdeed.
King Jalî¿âd and Shimâs: *Alf* IV 182; Burton IX 134. Chauvin VI 9 No. 184; *ANE* 237-38 No. 236.□

T253.1, ‡Nagging wife drives husband to prepare for suicide. See: *DOTTI*. (Cf. T255.8§).
Merchant's Curious Wife: *Alf* I 6; Burton I 21-22. Chauvin V 179-80 No. 104; *ANE* 298-99 No. 3.□

T255.8§, ‡The obstinate wife: refuses to heed sound advice. See: *DOTTI*. (Cf. T253.1).
Merchant's Curious Wife: *Alf* I 6; Burton I 21. Chauvin V 179-80 No. 104; *ANE* 298-99 No. 3.□

T257.0.2§, Insane (absurd, irrational) acts due to excessive jealousy. See: *DOTTI*; *GMC*. (Cf. P95.1§).

¿Azîz and ¿Azîzah: *Alf* I 287; Burton III 2-3. Chauvin V 144-45 No. 71; *ANE* 111-13 No. 41; **Mock Caliph/¿Alî al-Jawharî**: *Alf* II 198; Burton IV 145. Chauvin V 99-100 No. 174; *ANE* 304-5 No. 73.□

T257.1, ‡Woman [(wife)] jealous of a fair maid in her house. See: *DOTTI*.
Ghânim ibn Ayyûb: *Alf* I 154; Burton II 61. Chauvin VI 14-16 No. 188; *ANE* 192-93 No. 36.□

T257.2.3§, ‡Jealous wife (mistress) murders (seeks to murder) her rival. See: *DOTTI*. (Cf. P187§, S123.1).
Ghânim ibn Ayyûb: *Alf* I 154; Burton II 61. Chauvin VI 14-16 No. 188; *ANE* 192-93 No. 36.□

T257.9.0.1§, ‡Jealous man (husband) keeps wife locked up. (Cf. J674.4§, T380.2.1§).
Second Qalandar: Afrit's Wife: *Alf* I 45,-(jinni); Burton I 116. Chauvin V 197-200 No. 116; *ANE* 338-39 No. 16;
King's Son and Merchant's Wife: *Alf* III 155-56; Burton VI 167. Chauvin VIII 48-49 No. 16; *ANE* 263 No. 196;
King's Son and Afrit's Mistress: *Alf* III 172,-(afrit); Burton VI 199. Chauvin VIII 59 No. 24; *ANE* 263-64 No. 204.□

T257.9.0.2§, ‡Jealous husband tortures wife. See: *DOTTI*.
Second Qalandar: Afrit's Wife: *Alf* I 45; Burton I 119. Chauvin V 197-200 No. 116; *ANE* 338-39 No. 16.□

T257.11.1§, ‡Jealous wife keeps husband locked in house. See: *DOTTI*.
¿Azîz and ¿Azîzah: *Alf* I 286; Burton II 332. Chauvin V 144-45 No. 71; *ANE* 111-13 No. 41.□

T257.11.2§, ‡Jealous wife punishes husband severely for mere association with another woman. (Husband beaten, mutilated, or the like). (Cf. P95.1§, T257.0.2§).
¿Azîz and ¿Azîzah: *Alf* I 287; Burton III 2. Chauvin V 144-45 No. 71; *ANE* 111-13 No. 41;
Mock Caliph/¿Alî al-Jawharî: *Alf* II 198; Burton IV 145. Chauvin V 99-100 No. 174; *ANE* 304-5 No. 73.□

T258.2, Wife insists upon knowing husband's secret. See: *DOTTI*; *GMC*.
Merchant's Curious Wife: *Alf* I 6; Burton I 20. Chauvin V 179-80 No. 104; *ANE* 298-99 No. 3;
Serpent-charmer and Wife: *Alf* IV 145; Burton IX 57. Chauvin II 220 No. 152/9; *ANE* 368 No. 244;
Ma¿rûf the Cobbler: *Alf* IV 301; Burton X 22. Chauvin VI 81-82 No. 250; *ANE* 291-93 No. 262.□

T271.3§, ‡Man who lost his sex organ (eunuch) twitted for being 'without' a member. See: *DOTTI*. (Cf. F547.3.1.2.1§, T479.1§).
Three Wishes: *Alf* III 162; Burton VI 181. Chauvin VIII 51-52 No. 19; *ANE* 419-20 No. 199.□

T271.5§, Virgin wife, after years of marriage. See: *GMC*.
Sayf al-Mulûk: *Alf* III 287,-(to jinni prince); Burton VII 349. Chauvin VII 64-73 No. 348; *ANE* 362-64 No. 229.□

T276§, The intelligent (clever) wife. See: *DOTTI*.
King Dissuaded by Virtuous Wife: *Alf* II 294; Burton V 121. Chauvin VII 120-21 No. 391; *ANE* 260-61 No. 138.□

T277.2§, ‡Wife steals from her husband. See: *DOTTI*; *PSAE*. (Cf. K1874.2.1§, W131.4§).
Ma¿rûf the Cobbler: *Alf* IV 316,-cf./(magic ring); Burton X 52. Chauvin VI 81-82 No. 250; *ANE* 291-93 No. 262.□

T277.2.1§, ‡Husband ruined by his wife's theft; he is left with nothing.
Jeweler's Wife and Qamar al-Zamân: *Alf* IV 261; Burton IX 292. Chauvin V 212-14 No. 121; *ANE* 345-47 No. 260.□

T283, Wife withholds [sexual] intercourse from husband to enforce demand. See: *DOTTI*; *GMC*. (Cf. P529.2.1§, T9.1§).
¿Alâ' al-Dîn Abû al-Shâmât: *Alf* II 166; Burton IV 69. Chauvin V 43-49 No. 18; *ANE* 85-87 No. 63.□

T283.1§, ‡Wife threatens to leave husband to enforce demand. (Cf. M147§, Q432.0.1.1§).
Hunchback's Tale: Resuscitated: *Alf* I 124; Burton I 349. Chauvin 5: 163-64 No. 86; *ANE* 120 No. 23.□

T289§, ‡Marital rape: husband has sex with his wife by forces. (Cf. T72.0.1§, T160.0.2§, T471).
Bahrâm and Datmâ: *Alf* III 166; Burton VI 187. Chauvin VIII 54-57 No. 22; *ANE* 114-15 No. 202.□

T290§, ‡Conjugal pleasures are to be had in private. (Cf. C119.5§).
Man [Gardener] and His Wife: *Alf* IV 165; Burton IX 98. Chauvin II 223 No. 152/19; *ANE* 289 No. 250.□

T292.3§, ‡Slave-girl (beloved) unwillingly sold (given away) by master (owner). See: *DOTTI*. (Cf. P185.3.1§).
Anîs al-Jalîs: *Alf* I 142; Burton II 34-35. Chauvin V 120-24 No. 58; *ANE* 316-17 No. 35;
Man from Yaman and Six Salve-girls: Flyting: *Alf* II 249; Burton IV 249-50. Chauvin VI 151 No. 313; *ANE* 289-90 No. 84;
Nûr al-Dîn and Maryam: *Alf* IV 101,-(sold); Burton VIII 312-13. Chauvin V 52-54 No. 271; *ANE* 98-99 No. 233;
Ruined Baghdadi and His Slave-girl: *Alf* IV 130; Burton IX 24. Chauvin V 152-53 No. 75; *ANE* 353 No. 235.□

T298, Reconciliation of separated couple. See: *DOTTI*. (Cf. T202.1.2§).
Reeve's Story: Why Maimed by Bride: *Alf* I 99; Burton I 287. Chauvin V 220-21 No. 305; *ANE* 351 No. 25;
Ma¿rûf the Cobbler: *Alf* IV 313-14; Burton X 49. Chauvin VI 81-82 No. 250; *ANE* 291-93 No. 262.□

T298.0.1.1§, ‡Husband seeks to reconcile his unhappy wife. See: *DOTTI*. (Cf. T198§).
Sweep and Noble Lady: Infidelity Repaid: *Alf* II 190; Burton IV 128. Chauvin VI 148 No. 306; *ANE* 403-4 No. 72;
Jullanâr of the Sea: *Alf* III 248,-cf.; Burton VII 267. Chauvin V 147-51 No. 73; *ANE* 248-51 No. 227.□

T298.0.2§, ‡Divorced wife reinstated (by husband). See: *DOTTI*.
Portress Amînah: Bitten Cheek: *Alf* I 61; Burton I 186. Chauvin V 98-99 No. 33; *ANE* 326-27 No. 20;
House with the Belvedere: *Alf* III 172; Burton VI 199. Chauvin VIII 57-58 No. 23; *ANE* 223 No. 203.□

T298.2§, ‡Wrongly (hastily) condemned spouse accepts reconciliation. See: *DOTTI*.
King and Vizier's Wife/Tracks of Lion: *Alf* III 140; Burton VI 131. Chauvin VIII 35 No. 2; *ANE* 261 No. 182;
House with the Belvedere: *Alf* III 172; Burton VI 199. Chauvin VIII 57-58 No. 23; *ANE* 223 No. 203.□

T298.5§, ‡Reconciliation of estranged couple through mediator. See: *DOTTI*. (Cf. P796§, W14.5§).
Portress Amînah: Bitten Cheek: *Alf* I 61; Burton I 186. Chauvin V 98-99 No. 33; *ANE* 326-27 No. 20;
Rake's Trick Against Chaste Wife: *Alf* III 142; Burton VI 136. Chauvin VIII 37 No. 5; *ANE* 350-1 No. 185;
Lovers of Basra/Ḍamrah: *Alf* III 212,-(fails); Burton VII 132-34. Chauvin V 118 No. 54; *ANE* 273 No. 220;
Ma¿rûf the Cobbler: *Alf* IV 290; Burton X 1. Chauvin VI 81-82 No. 250; *ANE* 291-93 No. 262.□

T300.0.1§, ‡Preservation of sexual honor (*¿irḍ/'¿arḍ'*) is most important. See: *DOTTI*.
Tawaddud: Slavegirl Sold and Regained: *Alf* III 7,-(implicit); Burton V 242. Chauvin VII 117-19 No. 387; *ANE* 408-10 No. 157;
¿Abdallah ibn Fâḍil: Treacherous Brothers: *Alf* IV 279; Burton IX 331. Chauvin V 2-4 No. 2; *ANE* 63-65 No. 261.□

T300.0.1.1.2§, ‡'Only blood (killing) would cleanse defiled (damaged) sexual honor'.
Nûr al-Dîn and Maryam: *Alf* IV 108,-cf./(ritual killing/human sacrifice); Burton VIII 324. Chauvin V 52-54 No. 271; *ANE* 98-99 No. 233.□

T306§, Wife's nakedness or exposure. See: *DOTTI*; *GMC*; *PSAE*. (Cf. C106.1§).
Hârûn and Zubaydah in Bath: *Alf* II 284; Burton V 76. Chauvin VI 142 No. 298; *ANE* 203-4 No. 111.□

T311, Woman averse to marriage. See: *DOTTI*. (Cf. F1040.7.1§).
Portress Amînah: Bitten Cheek: *Alf* I 60,-cf.; Burton I 183. Chauvin V 98-99 No. 33; *ANE* 326-27 No. 20;

Ibrâhîm and Jamîlah: *Alf* IV 220; Burton IX 211. Chauvin VI 52-53 No. 218; *ANE* 227-29 No. 258.□

T311.0.1, Woman's aversion to marriage motivated through a dream. See: *ANE*; *DOTTI*; *GMC*. (Cf. T339§).
Tâj al-Mulûk: *Alf* I 299; Burton III 31. Chauvin V 126-28 No. 60; *ANE* 406-8 No. 40.□

T311.0.2§, Husband (wife) overcomes aversion to conjugal relations through vision (dream) in which a sacred person instructs resumption of coition. See: *DOTTI*; *GMC*.
King Dissuaded by Virtuous Wife: *Alf* II 294; Burton V 122. Chauvin VII 120-21 No. 391; *ANE* 260-61 No. 138.□

T311.2.2§, ‡Girl threatens to kill herself (and husband-to-be) if forced to marry. (Cf. M170.1.1§).
Tâj al-Mulûk: *Alf* I 291; Burton III 10. Chauvin V 126-28 No. 60; *ANE* 406-8 No. 40.□

T311.8§, ‡Aversion to (dislike of) members of the opposite sex. (Cf. P610§).
Tailor's Story/Barber of Baghdad: *Alf* I 103; Burton I 301. Chauvin V 154-56 No. 78; *ANE* 405-6 No. 27.□

T311.8.1§, ‡Man averse to women (misogynist).
Tailor's Story/Barber of Baghdad: *Alf* I 103; Burton I 301. Chauvin V 154-56 No. 78; *ANE* 405-6 No. 27;
Qamar al-Zamân and Budûr: *Alf* II 66; Burton III 214. Chauvin V 204-12 No. 120; *ANE* 341-45 No. 61.□

T311.8.2§, ‡Woman (girl, maiden) averse to men (misandrist).
Ibrâhîm and Jamîlah: *Alf* IV 220; Burton IX 211. Chauvin VI 52-53 No. 218; *ANE* 227-29 No. 258.□

T311.8.2.1§, ‡Chieftainess (maiden) averse to marriage (conjugal relations) lives in a community (colony) of only females.
Ibrâhîm and Jamîlah: *Alf* IV 222; Burton IX 215. Chauvin VI 52-53 No. 218; *ANE* 227-29 No. 258.□

T315.2, The continent husband. See: *DOTTI*; *GMC*. (Cf. P529.0.4.4§, P529.0.6§, T168.1§).
King Dissuaded by Virtuous Wife: *Alf* II 294; Burton V 122. Chauvin VII 120-21 No. 391; *ANE* 260-61 No. 138.□

T315.2.6§, ‡The (seemingly) continent man reveals secret of his abstinence—(usually to his disappointed wife). (Cf. T9.0.1§).
Qamar al-Zamân and Budûr: *Alf* II 103,-(woman); Burton III 288. Chauvin V 204-12 No. 120; *ANE* 341-45 No. 61;
¿Alâ' al-Dîn Abû al-Shâmât: *Alf* II 165; Burton IV 65. Chauvin V 43-49 No. 18; *ANE* 85-87 No. 63.□

T315.2.6.1§, ‡Continent husband's secret: "I am a woman like you!" "I have no organ," or the like. See: *DOTTI*. (Cf. N683.1§, T63.2§).
Qamar al-Zamân and Budûr: *Alf* II 103; Burton III 288. Chauvin V 204-12 No. 120; *ANE* 341-45 No. 61.□

T315.2.6.2§, ‡Continent man's secret: "I am in love with someone else".
¿Alâ' al-Dîn Abû al-Shâmât: *Alf* II 165,-(implicit); Burton IV 66. Chauvin V 43-49 No. 18; *ANE* 85-87 No. 63.□

T316§, Widow with children is expected to remain chaste and unwed (celibate) for the rest of her life. See: *DOTTI*.
Jullanâr of the Sea: *Alf* III 255,-(implicit); Burton VII 279. Chauvin V 147-51 No. 73; *ANE* 248-51 No. 227;
Jeweler's Wife and Qamar al-Zamân: *Alf* IV 266,-(implicit); Burton IX 303. Chauvin V 212-14 No. 121; *ANE* 345-47 No. 260.□

T317.2, Repression of lust through prayer. (Cf. K490.2.2§).
Hermit Tempted by Angel: *Alf* II 27; Burton III 126. Chauvin II 226 No. 3; *ANE* 221 No. 45/pt. 2;
Qamar al-Zamân and Budûr: *Alf* II 101,-cf.; Burton III 285. Chauvin V 204-12 No. 120; *ANE* 341-45 No. 61;
Jeweler's Wife and Qamar al-Zamân: *Alf* IV 241; Burton IX 254. Chauvin V 212-14 No. 121; *ANE* 345-47 No. 260.□

T0317.3§, ‡Image of chaste lover (sweetheart, relative, etc.). (Cf. P254.2§).
King ¿Umar al-Nu¿mân and Sons: *Alf* I 187,-cf./(brother finds sister *qâ'imah tuṣallî*); Burton II 132,-("standing at prayer"). Chauvin VI 112-24 No. 277; *ANE* 430-34 No. 39.□

T317.3.1§, ‡Chaste lover (sweetheart) reading the holy book.
Eldest Lady's Story: Treacherous Sisters: *Alf* I 55,-(young man); Burton I 168. Chauvin V 4 No. 443; *ANE* 174-75 No. 19;
¿Abdallah ibn Fâḍil: Treacherous Brothers: *Alf* IV 274,-(maiden); Burton IX 320. Chauvin V 2-4 No. 2; *ANE* 63-65 No. 261.□

T320, Escape from undesired lover. See: *DOTTI*.
King ¿Umar al-Nu¿mân and Sons: *Alf* I 184-85; Burton II 128-29. Chauvin VI 112-24 No. 277; *ANE* 430-34 No. 39.□

T320.1, Oft-proved fidelity. Repeated attempts to seduce innocent woman. She escapes them all. See: *DOTTI*; *GMC*.
Jewish qâḍî and His Devout Wife: *Alf* III 10; Burton V 256-59. Chauvin VI 154-55 No. 321; *ANE* 242 No. 163.□

T320.1.2§, ‡Virtue preserved—(woman's or man's). See: *DOTTI*. (Cf. K2120§, T331).
Ghânim ibn Ayyûb: *Alf* I 153,-cf.; Burton II 60. Chauvin VI 14 No. 188; *ANE* 192-93 No. 36;
King ¿Umar al-Nu¿mân and Sons: *Alf* I 185,-(seducer rejected); Burton II 128-29. Chauvin VI 112-24 No. 277; *ANE* 430-34 No. 39;
Isḥâq al-Mûṣilî and Khadîjah bint al-Ḥasan: *Alf* II 186,-cf.; Burton IV 121-22. Chauvin V 241-42 No. 142; *ANE* 232 No. 71;
Shipwrecked Woman and Her Child: *Alf* III 12,-(cruel seducer); Burton V 260. Chauvin VI 160 No. 324; *ANE* 379 No. 164;
Jawdar and His Treacherous Brethren: *Alf* III 201,-(sinful/unlawful marriage prevented); Burton VI 256. Chauvin V 257-60 No. 154; *ANE* 244-45 No. 209.□

T323, Escape from undesired lover by strategy. See: *DOTTI*; *GMC*.
Nûr al-Dîn and Maryam: *Alf* IV 121-22; Burton IX 2. Chauvin V 52-54 No. 271; *ANE* 98-99 No. 233;
Jawdar and His Treacherous Brethren: *Alf* III 201,-(lover put off); Burton VI 256. Chauvin V 257-60 No. 154; *ANE* 244-45 No. 209.□

T326.5§, ‡Suicide to preserve chastity.
¿Abdallah ibn Fâḍil: Treacherous Brothers: *Alf* IV 287; Burton IX 348. Chauvin V 2-4 No. 2; *ANE* 63-65 No. 261.□

T329§, Clitoridectomy (excision of girls): so as to ensure future chastity. See: *GMC*. (Cf. V82.2§).
King ¿Umar al-Nu¿mân and Sons: *Alf* I 236,-(xxx); Burton II 234 n. 2,-(physiological-comparative). Chauvin VI 112-24 No. 277; *ANE* 430-34 No. 39.□

T330.1§, ‡Dervish (cleric) tempted. (Cf. H1579.1.1§, T463).
Jeweler's Wife and Qamar al-Zamân: *Alf* IV 240-42,-(by boy,/unsuccessfully); Burton IX 252-53. Chauvin V 212-14 No. 121; *ANE* 345-47 No. 260.□

T331, Man unsuccessfully tempted by a woman. [Chaste man]. See: *DOTTI*; *GMC*. (Cf. K1683.3§, N347.7§, T72).
al-'Amjad and al-'As¿ad: *Alf* II 113-14; Burton III 311. Chauvin V 208-10 No. 120[.1]; *ANE* 341-42 No. 61/pt. 2;
Jewish Tray-maker and Temptress: *Alf* III 13; Burton V 265. Chauvin VI 187-88 No. 354; *ANE* 169 No. 166;
Sayf al-Mulûk: *Alf* III 284; Burton VII 341. Chauvin VII 64-73 No. 348; *ANE* 362-64 No. 229.□

T331.8.1§, ‡Youth in love with unattainable maiden refuses her offer of sexual liaison—(offer made to get rid of him). (Cf. F1041.8.2.1§).
Prior Becomes Moslem: al-Anbârî: *Alf* II 298; Burton V 142. Chauvin V 237-38 No. 137; *ANE* 330-31 No. 147.□

T332, Man tempted by fiend [(devil)] in woman's shape. (Or woman by fiend in man's shape). See: *ANE*; *GMC*; *PSAE*.
Hermit Tempted by Angel: *Alf* II 27,-cf./(angel); Burton III 126. Chauvin II 226 No. 3; *ANE* 221 No. 45/pt. 2.□

T332.3§, ‡Man tempted by angel in woman's shape.
Hermit Tempted by Angel: *Alf* II 27; Burton III 126. Chauvin II 226 No. 3; *ANE* 221 No. 45/pt. 2.□

T334.3§, ‡Chaste person prefers reunion with the beloved in heaven.
Prior Becomes Moslem: al-Anbârî: *Alf* II 298; Burton V 143. Chauvin V 237-38 No. 137; *ANE* 330-31 No. 147.□

T339§, Husband averse to conjugal relations. See: *DOTTI*; *GMC*. (Cf. T311.0.1).
Nûr al-Dîn and Maryam: *Alf* IV 121; Burton IX 2. Chauvin V 52-54 No. 271; *ANE* 98-99 No. 233.□

T339.1§, ‡Man's aversion to sex motivated through woman's pledge (religious). See: *DOTTI*.
Ghânim ibn Ayyûb: *Alf* I 154-55,-(caliph's favorite); Burton II 62,-(awe of-the-Caliph). Chauvin VI 14 No. 188; *ANE* 192-93 No. 36.□

T339.2§, ‡Aversion to conjugal relations motivated by suspicion of faithlessness. See: *DOTTI*. (Cf. P529.0.6§, T283).
King and Vizier's Wife/Tracks of Lion: *Alf* III 140; Burton VI 131. Chauvin VIII 35 No. 2; *ANE* 261 No. 182.□

T350, Chaste sleeping together. See: *DOTTI*.
Ghânim ibn Ayyûb: *Alf* I 154-55,-cf.; Burton II 59-60. Chauvin VI 14 No. 188; *ANE* 192-93 No. 36.□

T351, Sword of chastity. See: *DOTTI*; *GMC*.
Sayf al-Mulûk: *Alf* III 289; Burton VII 352. Chauvin VII 64-73 No. 348; *ANE* 362-64 No. 229.□

T366.1§, ‡Female 'too wide'. (Cf. F547.5.2.1§, Z186.9§).
Qamar al-Zamân and Budûr: *Alf* II 109,-(wider than,/poem); Burton III 304. Chauvin V 204-12 No. 120; *ANE* 341-45 No. 61.□

T367§, ‡Impotence (the impotent man). (Cf. P220§, T469§, U260.3§).
Nûr al-Dîn and Maryam: *Alf* IV 92, 104; Burton VIII 293, 317. Chauvin V 52-54 No. 271; *ANE* 98-99 No. 233.□

T367.2.1§, ‡Women disregard men with gray hair (beard). (Cf. P220§).
Jeweler's Wife and Qamar al-Zamân: *Alf* IV 255-56,-(poem); Burton IX 282. Chauvin V 212-14 No. 121; *ANE* 345-47 No. 260.□

T367.2.1.1§, ‡Girl ridicules impotent (old) man. (Cf. J445.2.1.1.1§, F547.3.7§).
Nûr al-Dîn and Maryam: *Alf* IV 92,-(poem); Burton VIII 293. Chauvin V 52-54 No. 271; *ANE* 98-99 No. 233.□

T380.0.1.1§, ‡Royal harem (with hundreds of women). (Cf. P180.8§, T469.2§).
Abû al-Hasan al-Khorâsânî (and Caliph's Favorite): *Alf* IV 233; Burton IX 238. Chauvin V 218-20 No. 129; *ANE* 68-69 No. 259.□

T380.0.2.1§, ‡Excessive association with members of opposite sex inadvisable. (Cf. P12.1.1, T469§).
King Jalî¿âd and Shimâs: *Alf* IV 164-65; Burton IX 97. Chauvin VI 9 No. 184; *ANE* 237-38 No. 236.□

T380.0.2.1.1§, ‡Man (king) must limit time he spends with females (wife, concubine, etc.).
King Jalî¿âd and Shimâs: *Alf* IV 164; Burton IX 97. Chauvin VI 9 No. 184; *ANE* 237-38 No. 236.□

T380.0.2.3§, ‡Men will always try to seduce women, it is a woman's responsibility to refuse (remain chaste). (Cf. T380.5§, W256.6.8.1§).
Jeweler's Wife and Qamar al-Zamân: *Alf* IV 263; Burton IX 297. Chauvin V 212-14 No. 121; *ANE* 345-47 No. 260.□

T380.1§, ‡Social distance kept between persons of opposite sexes. See: *DOTTI*. (Cf. P753.0.2§, P611).
¿Alâ' al-Dîn Abû al-Shâmât: *Alf* II 149; Burton IV 34. Chauvin V 43-49 No. 18; *ANE* 85-87 No. 63.□

T380.2§, Girl secluded (veiled) at puberty. See: *DOTTI*; *GMC*.
King ¿Umar al-Nu¿mân and Sons: *Alf* I 313; Burton III 60. Chauvin VI 112-24 No. 277; *ANE* 430-34 No. 39.□

T380.2.0.1§, ‡Pubescent female speaks (to male) from behind barrier (veil, curtain).
Dispute Concerning Males and Females: *Alf* II 300; Burton V 155. Chauvin VI 153 No. 317; *ANE* 291 No. 151.□

T380.2.0.2§, ‡Female singer performs (for male audience) from behind curtain.
Isḥâq al-Mûṣilî and Merchant's Singer: *Alf* II 297; Burton V 133. Chauvin VI 59 No. 225; *ANE* 233 No. 142;
Ruined Baghdadi and His Slave-girl: *Alf* IV 132; Burton IX 27, 28. Chauvin V 152-53 No. 75; *ANE* 353 No. 235.□

T380.2.0.3§, ‡Women's time: period reserved for females only in public facilities (e.g., bathhouse, beach, etc.).
Abû Qîr and Abû Ṣîr: *Alf* IV 191; Burton IX 153. Chauvin V 15-17 No. 10; *ANE* 75-77 No. 255.□

T380.2.1§, ‡Intemperance in maintaining modesty (female seclusion). (Cf. H62.1.5.1§, T257.9.0.1§, U284.3§).
Qamar al-Zamân and Budûr: *Alf* II 78-79,-(poem); Burton III 239. Chauvin V 204-12 No. 120; *ANE* 341-45 No. 61.□

T380.2.1.1.1§, ‡Female (girl, virgin, maiden, etc.) secludes (veils) self from male animal (usually: ass, horse, lion). See: *DOTTI*.
First Shaykh: Sorceress Wife: *Alf* I 10; Burton I 30. Chauvin VII 129-30 No. 396; *ANE* 376-77 No. 5;
Third Shaykh: Transformation by Wife: *Alf* I 13; Burton I 36. Chauvin VII 130 No. 398; *ANE* 378 No. 7;
Second Qalandar: Afrit's Wife: *Alf* I 48; Burton I 133. Chauvin V 197-200 No. 116; *ANE* 338-39 No. 16;
Jullanâr of the Sea: *Alf* III 262; Burton VII 293. Chauvin V 147-51 No. 73; *ANE* 248-51 No. 227.□

T380.2.4§, ‡Females in whom men would have no sexual interest are exempt from observing modesty code in male's presence. (E.g., extremely old or sick woman).
Pretty Gray-haired Woman Retorts: *Alf* II 303,-cf.; Burton V 163-64. Chauvin VI 153 No. 318; *ANE* 77-78 No. 152.□

T380.3.1§, Certain (non-threatening) males are viewed as unworthy of woman's modesty (e.g., slave, singer).
Second Qalandar: Afrit's Wife: *Alf* I 48; Burton I 133. Chauvin V 197-200 No. 116; *ANE* 338-39 No. 16;
Water-carrier and Goldsmith's Wife: *Alf* II 286,-cf./(water-carrier); Burton V 89. Chauvin VI 192 No. 361; *ANE* 444 No. 122.□

T380.3.2§, ‡Trusted males allowed in women's quarters: e.g., cleric, instructor, teacher, healer-shaman, (and the like). See: *DOTTI*; *PSAE*. (Cf. P14.15.1).
Water-carrier and Goldsmith's Wife: *Alf* II 286,-(water-carrier); Burton V 89. Chauvin VI 192 No. 361; *ANE* 444 No. 122.□

T380.4.1§, ‡Milk-sister secluded from her milk-brother.
Qamar al-Zamân and Budûr: *Alf* II 87; Burton III 257. Chauvin V 204-12 No. 120; *ANE* 341-45 No. 61.□

T380.5§, A male's privileges. See: *GMC*. (Cf. T380.0.2.3§).
al-'Amjad and al-'As¿ad: *Alf* II 124,-(thus, lovers to meet in man's place); Burton III 332,-("'Men shall have the pre-eminence above women, ...'"). Chauvin V 208-10 No. 120[.1]; *ANE* 341-42 No. 61/pt. 2;
¿Alâ' al-Dîn Abû al-Shâmât: *Alf* II 157; Burton IV 52. Chauvin V 43-49 No. 18; *ANE* 85-87 No. 63;
Dispute Concerning Males and Females: *Alf* II 300-2; Burton V 154-63. Chauvin VI 153 No. 317; *ANE* 291 No. 151.□

T380.5.1§, ‡A boy (son) is preferred to a girl (daughter). See: *DOTTI*. (Cf. P17.0.2.2§, P234.0.1§, T145.2).
Nûr al-Dîn ¿Alî and Son: *Alf* I 65; Burton I 196,-(masculine worthier than feminine). Chauvin VI 102-6 No. 270; *ANE* 317-19 No. 22;
King ¿Umar al-Nu¿mân and Sons: *Alf* I 163; Burton II 81. Chauvin VI 112-24 No. 277; *ANE* 430-34 No. 39;
¿Alâ' al-Dîn Abû al-Shâmât: *Alf* II 157,-(paternal nephew favored at expense of own daughter); Burton IV 52. Chauvin V 43-49 No. 18; *ANE* 85-87 No. 63.□

T380.6.1§, ‡A man's chivalrous acts toward woman. (Cf. T331).
Spy, Fifth Maiden/¿Umar al-Nu¿mân: *Alf* I 223; Burton II 206. *ANE* 432 No. 39/passim;

Mercury ¿Alî: *Alf* III 236; Burton VII 187. Chauvin V 248-50 No. 147; *ANE* 301-3 No. 225.□

T380.6.1.1.1§, ‡Gentleman avoids gazing at (watching, scrutinizing) woman's body. (Cf. A1557.3.1§, T481.0.2§).
Spy, Fifth Maiden/¿Umar al-Nu¿mân: *Alf* I 223; Burton II 206. *ANE* 432 No. 39/passim.□

T380.6.1.2§, ‡Chivalrous man does not take advantage of woman when she is helpless (unconscious, drunk, drugged or the like). (Cf. K1381.3§).
Ebony Horse: *Alf* II 256,-(implicit); Burton V 9. Chauvin V 221-31 No. 130; *ANE* 172-74 No. 103;
Mercury ¿Alî: *Alf* III 236; Burton VII 187. Chauvin V 248-50 No. 147; *ANE* 301-3 No. 225.□

T380.7§, ‡The unveiled female—(practicing *sufûr*). (Cf. C106§).
al-'Amjad and al-'As¿ad: *Alf* II 123; Burton III 327. Chauvin V 208-10 No. 120[.1],-(poem); *ANE* 341-42 No. 61;
Pretty Gray-haired Woman Retorts: *Alf* II 302-3,-(rebuked); Burton V 163. Chauvin VI 153 No. 318; *ANE* 77-78 No. 152;
Dalîla the Swindler: *Alf* III 225,-(seduction); Burton VII 167. Chauvin V 245-50 No. 147; *ANE* 163-64 No. 224.□

T381.0.2.1§, ‡Wife imprisoned in underground palace (chamber) to preserve chastity. See: *DOTTI*. (Cf. F721.5.3§).
Second Qalandar: Afrit's Wife: *Alf* I 43; Burton I 117. Chauvin V 197-200 No. 116; *ANE* 338-39 No. 16.□

T381.0.5§, ‡Virgin(s) exiled to earthly paradise (palace) to prevent knowledge of men. See: *DOTTI*.
Hasan of Basrah: *Alf* III 311,-(seven); Burton VIII 23. Chauvin VII 29-35 No. 212A; *ANE* 207-10 No. 230.□

T381.0.5.2§, ‡Virgin exiled (imprisoned) for falling in (declaring) love. See: *DOTTI*. (Cf. T57.5§).
Uns al-Wujûd and al-Ward: *Alf* II 271-72; Burton V 37. Chauvin VI 127-29 No. 282; *ANE* 438 No. 104.□

T381.1.3§, ‡Guarded maiden first seen by hero when he accidentally wanders into her quarters. See: *DOTTI*. (Cf. N722§).
Ebony Horse: *Alf* II 256; Burton V 8-9. Chauvin V 221-31 No. 130; *ANE* 172-74 No. 103.□

T382, Attempt to keep wife chaste by carrying her in box. See: *DOTTI*; *GMC*.
Jinni Keeps Mistress in Box: *Alf* I 4,-(jinni/giant); Burton I 12-13. Chauvin V 188-89 No. 111; *ANE* 370 No. 1/pt.;
King's Son and Afrit's Mistress: *Alf* III 172,-(afrit); Burton VI 199. Chauvin VIII 59 No. 24; *ANE* 263-64 No. 204.□

T402§, ‡Group sexual intercourse ('pagan', 'sex orgy'). (Cf. C119.5§, T290§).
Shahriyâr and Shâhzamân: *Alf* I 3; Burton I 9. Chauvin V 188-91 No. 111; *ANE* 370-71 No. 1.□

T403§, 'Womanizer', 'play-boy' (*zîr-nisâ*): habitual seducer of women. See: *DOTTI*; *GMC*.
Anîs al-Jalîs: *Alf* I 127,-(young boy); Burton II 5. Chauvin V 120-24 No. 58; *ANE* 316-17 No. 35;
Masrûr and Zayn al-Mawâṣif: *Alf* IV 55,-(*yatalhhâ bi hawâ al-nisâ'*); Burton VIII 205. Chauvin VI 82-84 No. 251; *ANE* 294-95 No. 232.□

T404§, 'Play-girl': immodest woman as seducer of men. See: *DOTTI*; *GMC*. (Cf. T55, T455.8.1§).
Porter and Ladies of Baghdad: *Alf* I 33-35; Burton I 90-93. Chauvin V 251-52 No. 148; *ANE* 324-26 No. 14;
Barber's First Brother: Free Labor for Coquette: *Alf* I 111,-(woman and husband); Burton I 320–24. Chauvin V 157-58 No. 81; *ANE* 117 No. 29;
Barber's Second Brother: Humiliated by Playgirl: *Alf* I 113-14; Burton I 325–28. Chauvin V 158 No. 82; *ANE* 117-18 No. 30.□

T404.2§, ‡Woman pays man for sexual intercourse with her. (Cf. T52.0.6.1§, T55, T404§, T450.4.1.1§).
Sweep and Noble Lady: Infidelity Repaid: *Alf* II 190; Burton IV 128. Chauvin VI 148 No. 306; *ANE* 403-4 No. 72.□

T404.3§, ‡Promiscuous female. See: *DOTTI*. (Cf. T454.1§).
Jewish Doctor's Story: Sororicide: *Alf* I 100; Burton I 292. Chauvin VI 89 No. 253; *ANE* 242 No. 26;

Jullanâr of the Sea: *Alf* III 265-66,-(queen); Burton VII 299. Chauvin V 147-51 No. 73; *ANE* 248-51 No. 227.□

T404.3.1§, ‡Girl accepts first invitation (from a stranger) to sexual intimacy (intercourse).
Jewish Doctor's Story: Sororicide: *Alf* I 100; Burton I 292. Chauvin VI 89 No. 253; *ANE* 242 No. 26.□

T404.4§, ‡Temptress seeks to seduce man. (Cf. K2111).
Barber's First Brother: Free Labor for Coquette: *Alf* I 111,-cf.; Burton I 319–24. Chauvin V 157-58 No. 81; *ANE* 117 No. 29;
Barber's Sixth Brother: Emasculated by Abductor: *Alf* I 123; Burton I 347. Chauvin V 163-64 No. 86; *ANE* 120 No. 34;
¿Azîz and ¿Azîzah: *Alf* I 285,-cf.; Burton II 331. Chauvin V 144-45 No. 71; *ANE* 111-13 No. 41;
al-'Amjad and al-'As¿ad: *Alf* II 116,-(stepmother); Burton III 314. Chauvin V 208-10 No. 120[.1]; *ANE* 341-42 No. 61/pt. 2;
King's Son and Afrit's Mistress: *Alf* III 172-73; Burton VI 200. Chauvin VIII 59 No. 24; *ANE* 263-64 No. 204.□

T404.4.2§, ‡Captor's wife (daughter) seeks to seduce captive (prisoner). (Cf. R52.4§, R162).
Barber's Sixth Brother: Emasculated by Abductor: *Alf* I 123; Burton I 347. Chauvin V 163-64 No. 86; *ANE* 120 No. 34;
Sayf al-Mulûk: *Alf* III 284; Burton VII 341. Chauvin VII 64-73 No. 348; *ANE* 362-64 No. 229.□

T404.4.4§, ‡Unchaste wife elopes with her husband's guest (friend). (Cf. R225).
Jeweler's Wife and Qamar al-Zamân: *Alf* IV 257; Burton IX 285. Chauvin V 212-14 No. 121; *ANE* 345-47 No. 260.□

T405.2§, Mother's nakedness or exposure. See: *DOTTI*. (Cf. C119.5§, D1767.1.1.1.1§).
Debauchee and Three Years Old Child: *Alf* III 176; Burton VI 208. Chauvin VIII 62-63 No. 147; *ANE* 166-67 No. 206;
Jawdar and His Treacherous Brethren: *Alf* III 186; Burton VI 229. Chauvin V 257-60 No. 154; *ANE* 244-45 No. 209.□

T405.3.3§, ‡Nakedness or exposure of those who are brother-sister-like. See: *DOTTI*. (Cf. P313.5.2§, P180.4.2.1§).
First Eunuch: Bukhayt Deflowers Mistress: *Alf* I 147; Burton II 49. Chauvin V 277 No. 160; *ANE* 178 No. 37;
Hasan of Basrah: *Alf* III 310,-(foster-sister changes clothes brother); Burton VIII 23. Chauvin VII 29-35 No. 212A; *ANE* 207-10 No. 230.□

T405.9.4§, ‡Exposure (of privates) caused by gust of wind (lifting up tail of dress, robe, shirt, gown, etc.). See: *DOTTI*.
Nûr al-Dîn ¿Alî and Son: *Alf* I 73; Burton I 224. Chauvin VI 102-6 No. 270; *ANE* 317-19 No. 22.□

T409.1§, ‡Trophy of seduction (ring, garment, etc.): lover (seducer, rapist) keeps reminders of sexual conquests. See: *DOTTI*. (Cf. T403§, T404§, T468§, T469§).
Jinni Keeps Mistress in Box: *Alf* I 4,-(rings); Burton I 12. Chauvin V 188-89 No. 111; *ANE* 370 No. 1/pt.;
King's Son and Afrit's Mistress: *Alf* III 172-73,-(rings); Burton VI 200. Chauvin VIII 59 No. 24; *ANE* 263-64 No. 204.□

T409.2.1§, ‡Bathhouse as stage for illicit sexual relations. See: *DOTTI*.
Tâj al-Mulûk: *Alf* I 293,-cf./(youth bathes sodomist); Burton III 17-18. Chauvin V 126-28 No. 60; *ANE* 406-8 No. 40.□

T409.3.1§, ‡Stepmother's incestuous desire for stepson masked as maternal affection (love). See: *DOTTI*; *PSAE*. (Cf. P282.3, T418).
al-'Amjad and al-'As¿ad: *Alf* II 112-13; Burton III 309. Chauvin V 208-10 No. 120[.1]; *ANE* 341-42 No. 61/pt. 2.□

T411.3§, ‡Lecherous father-in-law. (Cf. K2218.2, T92.9.3.1§).
King ¿Umar al-Nu¿mân and Sons: *Alf* I 182,-cf./(rapes son's wife-to-be); Burton II 123. Chauvin VI 112-24 No. 277; *ANE* 430-34 No. 39.□

T415, Brother-sister incest. See: *ANE*; *DOTTI*; *GMC*. (Cf. M119.8.6.1.1§).

First Qalandar: Brother-Sister Incest: *Alf* I 42; Burton I 104-13. Chauvin V 196-97 No. 115; *ANE* 337-38 No. 15;
King ¿Umar al-Nu¿mân and Sons: *Alf* I 207; Burton II 172. Chauvin VI 112-24 No. 277; *ANE* 430-34 No. 39.□

T415.0.1§, ‡Brother and sister guilty of incest forgiven. See: *DOTTI*.
King ¿Umar al-Nu¿mân and Sons: *Alf* I 215,-(implicit); Burton II 188. Chauvin VI 112-24 No. 277; *ANE* 430-34 No. 39.□

T415.5, Brother-sister marriage. See: *DOTTI*; *GMC*; *PSAE*. (Cf. N365.3.4§).
King ¿Umar al-Nu¿mân and Sons: *Alf* I 207; Burton II 172. Chauvin VI 112-24 No. 277; *ANE* 430-34 No. 39.□

T416§, Paternal-cousin (*bint-¿amm*) as substitute for sister. See: *DOTTI*; *GMC*.
Nûr al-Dîn ¿Alî and Son: *Alf* I 70,-cf./(*'akhawân* or *'awlâd ¿amm*); Burton I 214,-("like brother and sister or at least [paternal] cousins"). Chauvin VI 102-6 No. 270; *ANE* 317-19 No. 22.□

T416.8§, Adultery (sexual liaison) between *'ibn-¿amm* and his *bint-¿amm* (paternal-cousins). See: *DOTTI*; *GMC*. (Cf. P295.1.3.1§).
Nûr al-Dîn ¿Alî and Son: *Alf* I 70,-(arranged by fairies); Burton I 220. Chauvin VI 102-6 No. 270; *ANE* 317-19 No. 22.□

T418, Lustful stepmother. See: *DOTTI*. (Cf. K2111.5.1§, T409.3.1§).
al-'Amjad and al-'As¿ad: *Alf* II 113-14; Burton III 309. Chauvin V 208-10 No. 120[.1]; *ANE* 341-42 No. 61/pt. 2.□

T425, Brother-in-law seduces (seeks to seduce) sister-in-law. [Lecherous brother-in-law]. See: *DOTTI*; *GMC*. (Cf. K2211.1).
Jewish qâḍî and His Devout Wife: *Alf* III 10; Burton V 256. Chauvin VI 154-55 No. 321; *ANE* 242 No. 163.□

T425.3§, Brother wants to marry widow of his deceased brother. (Cf. W195.9.2§).
Jawdar and His Treacherous Brethren: *Alf* III 201; Burton VI 256. Chauvin V 257-60 No. 154; *ANE* 244-45 No. 209.□

T428§, Lecherous (lustful) clergyman (judge, dervish, holy man, etc.): seeks to seduce girl left in his trust. See: *DOTTI*; *GMC*. (Cf. K2285.1.1§, P426.0.8§).
Lady and Five Suitors Deceived: *Alf* III 158-59,-cf.; Burton VI 173. Chauvin VIII 50-51 No. 18; *ANE* 266 No. 198.□

T450.0.1§, ‡Prostitute (whore, etc.). See: *DOTTI*. (Cf. R347.2.1§).
¿Alî Shâr and Zumurrud: *Alf* II 218,-(*al-nisâ' al-zawânî*); Burton IV 190,-(whoreson fellows). Chauvin V 89-91 No. 28; *ANE* 100-1 No. 82.□

T450.0.2§, ‡High price for sexual pleasure (illicit love). (Cf. P180.8.1§, T459.1§).
Copt Broker's Story: Lover's Sacrifices Repaid: *Alf* I 93; Burton I 269-73. Chauvin VI 80 No. 249; *ANE* 313-14 No. 24;
Hashish Eater's Dream: *Alf* II 9; Burton III 91. Chauvin VI 124 No. 278; *ANE* 216 No. 42;
Masrûr and Zayn al-Mawâṣif: *Alf* IV 58; Burton VIII 218-19. Chauvin VI 82-84 No. 251; *ANE* 294-95 No. 232.□

T450.0.2.1§, ‡Illicit sexual pleasure: a costly addiction. (Cf. F1041.15.1§).
Copt Broker's Story: Lover's Sacrifices Repaid: *Alf* I 93; Burton I 272. Chauvin VI 80 No. 249; *ANE* 313-14 No. 24;
al-Rashîd and Omani Merchant: *Alf* IV 215; Burton IX 199. Chauvin VI 111-12 No. 276; *ANE* 201-2 No. 257.□

T450.0.2.1.1§, ‡Rich man (heir) bankrupted by sexual addiction.
Copt Broker's Story: Lover's Sacrifices Repaid: *Alf* I 93; Burton I 272. Chauvin VI 80 No. 249; *ANE* 313-14 No. 24;
¿Alî Shâr and Zumurrud: *Alf* II 218; Burton IV 190. Chauvin V 89-91 No. 28; *ANE* 100-1 No. 82.□

T450.0.2.1.2§, ‡Stealing to pay for sexual pleasure (love). (Cf. T52.0.2.3.4§, T469§).
Copt Broker's Story: Lover's Sacrifices Repaid: *Alf* I 93; Burton I 273. Chauvin VI 80 No. 249; *ANE* 313-14 No. 24.□

T450.0.2.1.3§, ‡Lover surrenders all his properties to beloved (prostitute) in hope of receiving sexual favor. See: *PSAE* [113 No. 7]. (Cf. T9.1§).
Masrûr and Zayn al-Mawâṣif: *Alf* IV 58; Burton VIII 218-19. Chauvin VI 82-84 No. 251; *ANE* 294-95 No. 232.□

T450.4.1.1§, ‡Prostitute refunds all payments made by favorite lover.
Copt Broker's Story: Lover's Sacrifices Repaid: *Alf* I 95; Burton I 276. Chauvin VI 80 No. 249; *ANE* 313-14 No. 24;
Masrûr and Zayn al-Mawâṣif: *Alf* IV 62,-cf./(rich woman/became lover); Burton VIII 227. Chauvin VI 82-84 No. 251; *ANE* 294-95 No. 232;
Man of Upper Egypt and Frankish Wife: Alf IV 16?,-(text missing); Burton IX 20,-cf./(inadvertently). Chauvin V 240 No. 140; *ANE*: No. 234.□

T450.4.2§, ‡Female escort pays her favorite client so that he can afford her fee. (Cf. T455.8.1§).
al-Rashîd and Omani Merchant: *Alf* IV 215; Burton IX 199. Chauvin VI 111-12 No. 276; *ANE* 201-2 No. 257.□

T450.5§, ‡Site for illicit sexual encounter negotiated: "Your place or mine?". (Cf. P159.2§).
al-'Amjad and al-'As¿ad: *Alf* II 124; Burton III 332. Chauvin V 208-10 No. 120[.1]; *ANE* 2 341-42 No. 61/pt.;
Mercury ¿Alî: *Alf* III 231; Burton VII 181. Chauvin V 248-50 No. 147; *ANE* 301-3 No. 225.□

T450.7.1§, ‡Prostitute becomes ascetic (nun, hermit, etc.).
Copt Broker's Story: Lover's Sacrifices Repaid: *Alf* I 95; Burton I 277. Chauvin VI 80 No. 249; *ANE* 313-14 No. 24.□

T452, Bawds. Professional go-betweens. See: *DOTTI*; *GMC*. (Cf. P368.1.1§, T53.7.2.1.0.1§).
House with the Belvedere: *Alf* III 168-89,-(old woman); Burton VI 193-94. Chauvin VIII 57-58 No. 23; *ANE* 223 No. 203.□

T452.0.1.1§, ‡Procuress's substitute client: one client lost, another found.
Wife's device to cheat: (Weeping Bitch as Bluff): *Alf* III 149; Burton VI 154. Chauvin VIII 45-46 No. 13; *ANE* 447-49 No. 193.□

T452.1, Mother as procuress of bedmate for her son. See: *GMC*.
¿Alâ' al-Dîn Abû al-Shâmât: *Alf* II 169; Burton IV 74. Chauvin V 43-49 No. 18; *ANE* 85-87 No. 63.□

T452.2§, Old woman as procuress. See: *DOTTI*; *GMC*. (Cf. K2131.6§).
Portress Amînah: Bitten Cheek: *Alf* I 57-60; Burton I 174. Chauvin V 98-99 No. 33; *ANE* 326-27 No. 20;
Tailor's Story/Barber of Baghdad: *Alf* I 103,-(go-between); Burton I 302. Chauvin V 154-56 No. 78; *ANE* 405-6 No. 27;
¿Azîz and ¿Azîzah: *Alf* I 283,-cf.; Burton II 326. Chauvin V 144-45 No. 71; *ANE* 111-13 No. 41;
Tâj al-Mulûk: *Alf* I 299,-(*fî al-ḥarâm*/"in sin"); Burton III 29,-(unite two lovers, though in defiance of right and law). Chauvin V 126-28 No. 60; *ANE* 406-8 No. 40;
Ni¿mah and Nu¿m: Stolen Wife Regained: *Alf* II 133,-cf.; Burton IV 3. Chauvin VI 96-97 No. 263; *ANE* 314 No. 62;
Wife's device to cheat: (Weeping Bitch as Bluff): *Alf* III 148; Burton VI 152. Chauvin VIII 45-46 No. 13; *ANE* 447-49 No. 193;
House with the Belvedere: *Alf* III 170; Burton VI 195-96. Chauvin VIII 57-58 No. 23; *ANE* 223 No. 203;
Man of Upper Egypt and Frankish Wife: Alf IV 16?,-(text missing); Burton IX 20. Chauvin V 240 No. 140; *ANE*: No. 234;
Jeweler's Wife and Qamar al-Zamân: *Alf* IV 246; Burton IX 261. Chauvin V 212-14 No. 121; *ANE* 345-47 No. 260.□

T453.3.1§, ‡Wife learns her husband's secret through arousing his love (lust).
Ma¿rûf the Cobbler: *Alf* IV 301; Burton X 22. Chauvin VI 81-82 No. 250; *ANE* 291-93 No. 262.□

T454.1§, ‡'Chaste' woman succumbs to sexual lure. See: *DOTTI*. (Cf. K1351, K2021.1, T404.3§, T455.6).
Portress Amînah: Bitten Cheek: *Alf* I 59; Burton I 179. Chauvin V 98-99 No. 33; *ANE* 326-27 No. 20;

House with the Belvedere: *Alf* III 170-71; Burton VI 195-96. Chauvin VIII 57-58 No. 23; *ANE* 223 No. 203.□

T454.1.1§, ‡Woman succumbs to seduction for a trifle (little pay, food). See: *DOTTI*. (Cf. T454.1§).
Woman Who Made Husband Sift Dust: *Alf* III 145; Burton VI 143. Chauvin VIII 42 No. 10; *ANE* 452-53 No. 190.□

T455.1, ‡Woman sells [(sexual)] favors to obtain a jewel.
Bahrâm and Datmâ: *Alf* III 166; Burton VI 186. Chauvin VIII 54-57 No. 22; *ANE* 114-15 No. 202.□

T455.3.2§, ‡Woman allows shopkeeper a kiss for new cloth (merchandise). See: *DOTTI*.
Portress Amînah: Bitten Cheek: *Alf* I 58-59; Burton I 179. Chauvin V 98-99 No. 33; *ANE* 326-27 No. 20;
Woman Who Made Husband Sift Dust: *Alf* III 145,-(sexual liaison/unspecified); Burton VI 143,-("he won his will with her"). Chauvin VIII 42 No. 10; *ANE* 452-53 No. 190.□

T455.3.3§, ‡Woman promises sexual favors in order to rescue her beloved. (Cf. K1386.1§).
Lady and Five Suitors Deceived: *Alf* III 158-59; Burton VI 173. Chauvin VIII 50-51 No. 18; *ANE* 266 No. 198.□

T455.6, Woman sells [(sexual)] favors for large sums of money (property). See: *DOTTI*; *GMC*; *PSAE*.
Copt Broker's Story: Lover's Sacrifices Repaid: *Alf* I 93; Burton I 269, 272. Chauvin VI 80 No. 249; *ANE* 313-14 No. 24.□

T455.8.1§, ‡Female companionship for a fee (pay). (Escort service). (Cf. T450.4.2§).
al-Rashîd and Omani Merchant: *Alf* IV 212, 215; Burton IX 194. Chauvin VI 111-12 No. 276; *ANE* 201-2 No. 257.□

T455.8.1.1§, ‡Female companionship service managed (owned) by father of its top girl. (Cf. K1501, T404§, T452).
al-Rashîd and Omani Merchant: *Alf* IV 215; Burton IX 196, 199. Chauvin VI 111-12 No. 276; *ANE* 201-2 No. 257.□

T459.1§, ‡Lover (customer) impoverished by payments (gifts) to prostitute(s). (Cf. T450.0.2§).
Copt Broker's Story: Lover's Sacrifices Repaid: *Alf* I 93; Burton I 272. Chauvin VI 80 No. 249; *ANE* 313-14 No. 24;
Hashish Eater's Dream: *Alf* II 9,-cf.; Burton III 91. Chauvin VI 124 No. 278; *ANE* 216 No. 42;
Masrûr and Zayn al-Mawâṣif: *Alf* IV 57-59; Burton VIII 216-18. Chauvin VI 82-84 No. 251; *ANE* 294-95 No. 232.□

T461.0.1§, ‡Erotic fetishism. See: *DOTTI*. (Cf. Z141.4.1§).
Sayf al-Mulûk: *Alf* III 280,-(woman's cape/picture); Burton VII 333. Chauvin VII 64-73 No. 348; *ANE* 362-64 No. 229.□

T462, Lesbian love. See: *DOTTI*; *GMC*. (Cf. P29.7§).
King ¿Umar al-Nu¿mân and Sons: *Alf* I 236; Burton II 234,-(tribadism). Chauvin VI 112-24 No. 277; *ANE* 430-34 No. 39;
Lovers of Basra/Ḍamrah: *Alf* III 211,-(suspected); Burton VII 133. Chauvin V 118 No. 54; *ANE* 273 No. 220.□

T462.4§, ‡Male-woman (*"marah-ḍakar"/'imra'ah dhakar*): 'dike'—(lesbian seducer).
King ¿Umar al-Nu¿mân and Sons: *Alf* I 236; Burton II 234. Chauvin VI 112-24 No. 277; *ANE* 430-34 No. 39.□

T462.4.1§, ‡Woman seeks to seduce girl (woman).
King ¿Umar al-Nu¿mân and Sons: *Alf* I 236; Burton II 234. Chauvin VI 112-24 No. 277; *ANE* 430-34 No. 39.□

T462.5§, ‡'Straight' girl submits (succumbs) to lesbian seduction.
King ¿Umar al-Nu¿mân and Sons: *Alf* I 236,-(through blackmail); Burton II 234. Chauvin VI 112-24 No. 277; *ANE* 430-34 No. 39.□

T463, Homosexual love (male). See: *DOTTI*; *GMC*. (Cf. P610§, J1768.2.1.1§, U284.3.3§).
al-'Amjad and al-'As¿ad: *Alf* II 124,-(passim); Burton III 334. Chauvin V 208-10 No. 120[.1]; *ANE* 341-42 No. 61/pt. 2;
¿Alâ' al-Dîn Abû al-Shâmât: *Alf* II 153-54; Burton IV 42. Chauvin V 43-49 No. 18; *ANE* 85-87 No. 63;

Mercury ¿Alî: *Alf* III 229,-cf./(unfulfilled attraction); Burton VII 177. Chauvin V 248-50 No. 147; *ANE* 301-3 No. 225.□

T463.0.1§, Pseudo-homosexual (male) attraction: man falls in love with another man who turns out to be a woman in disguise. See: *DOTTI*.
Qamar al-Zamân and Budûr: *Alf* II 100,cf./(female masking as male/every one who looked—*yabillu sarâwîlah*); Burton III 284,-(bepissed their bag-trousers). Chauvin V 204-12 No. 120; *ANE* 341-45 No. 61;
Man Who Never Laughs: *Alf* III 154,-cf./(implicit); Burton VI 165. Chauvin VIII 47-48 No. 15; *ANE* 285-86 No. 195.□

T463.3§, ‡Relative pleasures of homoeroticism (homosexual love). See: *DOTTI*. (Cf. U284.3§).
Jeweler's Wife and Qamar al-Zamân: *Alf* IV 239,-(poem); Burton IX 250-51. Chauvin V 212-14 No. 121; *ANE* 345-47 No. 260.□

T463.3.1§, ‡Homoerotic description of boy's (man's) beauty. See: *DOTTI*. (Cf. P199.0.1§, U284.3§).
Nûr al-Dîn ¿Alî and Son: *Alf* I 67,-(poem); Burton I 203. Chauvin VI 102-6 No. 270; *ANE* 317-19 No. 22;
Anîs al-Jalîs: *Alf* I 126-27,-(poem: creation of beautiful eyes); Burton II 4-5. Chauvin V 120-24 No. 58; *ANE* 316-17 No. 35;
Tâj al-Mulûk: *Alf* I 266,-(poem), 292-94; Burton II 292, III 16-19. Chauvin V 126-28 No. 60; *ANE* 406-8 No. 40;
Qamar al-Zamân and Budûr: *Alf* II 67,-(poem), 78-79,-(poem); Burton III 218, 239. Chauvin V 204-12 No. 120; *ANE* 341-45 No. 61;
Dispute Concerning Males and Females: *Alf* II 300, 301,-(poem); Burton V 154-163, 156. Chauvin VI 153 No. 317; *ANE* 291 No. 151;
Jeweler's Wife and Qamar al-Zamân: *Alf* IV 239,-(poem), 246-47; Burton IX 250-51, 263. Chauvin V 212-14 No. 121; *ANE* 345-47 No. 260.□

T463.5§, ‡Man seeks to seduce boy (youth). See: *DOTTI*. (Cf. T463, T472§).
Tâj al-Mulûk: *Alf* I 293-94; Burton III 19-20. Chauvin V 126-28 No. 60; *ANE* 406-8 No. 40;
¿Alâ' al-Dîn Abû al-Shâmât: *Alf* II 153,-(kiss), 155,-(kiss); Burton IV 42-43, 47. Chauvin V 43-49 No. 18; *ANE* 85-87 No. 63;
Mercury ¿Alî: *Alf* III 229; Burton VII 177. Chauvin V 248-50 No. 147; *ANE* 301-3 No. 225.□

T463.5.1§, ‡Boy (child) seduced by man. See: *DOTTI*.
Third Eunuch: Seduces Mistress and Son: *Alf* I 151,-(passim); Burton II 56/non-tale. Chauvin V 278 n. 1 No. [161B]; *ANE* 179,/passim No. 38.□

T463.7§, ‡Pseudo-homosexual submission: 'straight' man (husband) submits to homosexual lure. Seducer proves to be woman (his wife) masking as man. See: *DOTTI*.
Qamar al-Zamân and Budûr: *Alf* II 109; Burton III 304-5. Chauvin V 204-12 No. 120; *ANE* 341-45 No. 61;
¿Alî Shâr and Zumurrud: *Alf* II 234; Burton IV 226-27. Chauvin V 89-91 No. 28; *ANE* 100-1 No. 82.□

T463.8§, ‡Anal intercourse (sodomy). See: *DOTTI*. (Cf. J1288.3§, Q451.1.9.1§, U284.2.1§).
Qamar al-Zamân and Budûr: *Alf* II 109,-(poem); Burton III 302. Chauvin V 204-12 No. 120; *ANE* 341-45 No. 61;
Pretty Gray-haired Woman Retorts: *Alf* II 303,-(poem); Burton V 164,-("raked"). Chauvin VI 153 No. 318; *ANE* 77-78 No. 152.□

T463.9.1§, ‡Sodomist does not distinguish between male and female.
Tâj al-Mulûk: *Alf* I 292; Burton III 16. Chauvin V 126-28 No. 60; *ANE* 406-8 No. 40;
Dalîla the Swindler: *Alf* III 215; Burton VII 151. Chauvin V 245-50 No. 147; *ANE* 163-64 No. 224;
Jeweler's Wife and Qamar al-Zamân: *Alf* IV 239; Burton IX 250. Chauvin V 212-14 No. 121; *ANE* 345-47 No. 260.□

T464.2§, ‡Boy tempts man (sexually). (Cf. H1579.1.1§).
Jeweler's Wife and Qamar al-Zamân: *Alf* IV 240; Burton IX 252. Chauvin V 212-14 No. 121; *ANE* 345-47 No. 260.□

T465.9.1§, ‡Sexual intercourse with monkey (ape). See: *DOTTI*.
King's Daughter and Ape: *Alf* II 253; Burton IV 297. Chauvin V 178 No. 102; *ANE* 262-63 No. 102.□

T465.9.3§, ‡Sexual intercourse with bear. (Cf. Q253.1).
Butcher Wardân and Bear Lover: *Alf* II 251; Burton IV 294. Chauvin V 177-78 No. 101; *ANE* 442-43 No. 101.□

T466.3§, ‡Violation of modesty of female corpse punished. See: *DOTTI*.
City of Brass: *Alf* III 136,-(with death); Burton VI 118. Chauvin V 32-35 No. 16; *ANE* 146-50 No. 180.□

T467, The amorous bite.
Jeweler's Wife and Qamar al-Zamân: *Alf* IV 249; Burton IX 268. Chauvin V 212-14 No. 121; *ANE* 345-47 No. 260.□

T467.3§, ‡Honey (liquor, nectar) from biting lip (of the beloved). (Cf. T59.1.0.1§, Z62).
Tâj al-Mulûk: *Alf* I 262,-(poem); Burton II 285. Chauvin V 126-28 No. 60; *ANE* 406-8 No. 40.□

T467.3.1§, ‡Moist kiss that yields honey, liquor, or nectar. (Sweet saliva, mouth moisture/*rîq*). (Cf. T59.1.0.1§).
Copt Broker's Story: Lover's Sacrifices Repaid: *Alf* I 92,-(tongue), 128; Burton I 270. Chauvin VI 80 No. 249; *ANE* 313-14 No. 24;
King ¿Umar al-Nu¿mân and Sons: *Alf* I 214,-(poem); Burton II 186,-(sipping lips red bright). Chauvin VI 112-24 No. 277; *ANE* 430-34 No. 39;
Tâj al-Mulûk: *Alf* I 268; Burton II 296. Chauvin V 126-28 No. 60; *ANE* 406-8 No. 40;
King ¿Umar al-Nu¿mân and Sons: *Alf* I 312,-(poem); Burton III 57. Chauvin VI 112-24 No. 277; *ANE* 430-34 No. 39;
Qamar al-Zamân and Budûr: *Alf* II 66, 67,-(poem/male's), 90,-(poem); Burton III 215, 263. Chauvin V 204-12 No. 120; *ANE* 341-45 No. 61;
¿Alî Shâr and Zumurrud: *Alf* II 220,-(poem/male's/homoerotic); Burton IV 195. Chauvin V 89-91 No. 28; *ANE* 100-1 No. 82;
Dispute Concerning Males and Females: *Alf* II 301,-(lip like *al-râḥ*); Burton V 159. Chauvin VI 153 No. 317; *ANE* 291 No. 151;
Jullanâr of the Sea: *Alf* III 248; Burton VII 266. Chauvin V 147-51 No. 73; *ANE* 248-51 No. 227;
Nûr al-Dîn and Maryam: *Alf* IV 93,-(sweeter than sugar); Burton VIII 298. Chauvin V 52-54 No. 271; *ANE* 98-99 No. 233;
al-Rashîd and Omani Merchant: *Alf* IV 213,-(poem/spittle would render sea sweet); Burton IX 196. Chauvin VI 111-12 No. 276; *ANE* 201-2 No. 257;
¿Abdallah ibn Fâḍil: Treacherous Brothers: *Alf* IV 275,-(poem/spittle would render sea sweeter than honey); Burton IX 321,-(crache in Ocean's face ...). Chauvin V 2-4 No. 2; *ANE* 63-65 No. 261;
Ma¿rûf the Cobbler: *Alf* IV 300; Burton X 21. Chauvin VI 81-82 No. 250; *ANE* 291-93 No. 262.□

T467.3.2§, ‡Lovers sip their drink from each other's mouths.
Masrûr and Zayn al-Mawâṣif: *Alf* IV 67,-(wine); Burton VIII 233. Chauvin VI 82-84 No. 251; *ANE* 294-95 No. 232.□

T468§, Nymphomania: a woman's abnormal and insatiable desire (uncontrollable appetite) for sex. See: *DOTTI*.
King ¿Umar al-Nu¿mân and Sons: *Alf* I 236; Burton II 234. Chauvin VI 112-24 No. 277; *ANE* 430-34 No. 39;
¿Azîz and ¿Azîzah: *Alf* I 285; Burton II 331. Chauvin V 144-45 No. 71; *ANE* 111-13 No. 41;
Butcher Wardân and Bear Lover: *Alf* II 252; Burton IV 294. Chauvin V 177-78 No. 101; *ANE* 442-43 No. 101;
King's Daughter and Ape: *Alf* II 253; Burton IV 297. Chauvin V 178 No. 102; *ANE* 262-63 No. 102;
Jullanâr of the Sea: *Alf* III 264-66; Burton VII 296. Chauvin V 147-51 No. 73; *ANE* 248-51 No. 227.□

T469§, Satyriasis: a man's abnormal and insatiable desire (appetite) for sex. See: *DOTTI*; *GMC*. (Cf. F575.1.6.2.2§, T380.0.2.1§, T450.0.2.1.1§, T610.5.0.1.1§).
Porter and Ladies of Baghdad: *Alf* I 35,-cf./(mule's); Burton I 93. Chauvin V 251-52 No. 148; *ANE* 324-26 No. 14;
King Jalî¿âd and Shimâs: *Alf* IV 161, 164-65; Burton IX 90, 97. Chauvin VI 9-11 No. 184; *ANE* 237-38 No. 236.□

T469.0.1§, ‡*al-fuḥûlah*: male's capacity to procreate (ejaculate, impregnate). (Cf. T469.2§).

King ¿Umar al-Nu¿mân and Sons: *Alf* I 168; Burton II 95. Chauvin VI 112-24 No. 277; *ANE* 430-34 No. 39;
¿Alâ' al-Dîn Abû al-Shâmât: *Alf* II 157,-(four times); Burton IV 52 n. 2. Chauvin V 43-49 No. 18; *ANE* 85-87 No. 63;
Abû al-Hasan al-Khorâsânî (and Caliph's Favorite): *Alf* IV 233; Burton IX 238,-(every night). Chauvin V 218-20 No. 129; *ANE* 68-69 No. 259.□

T469.1§, ‡Male with access to many females (as concubines, wives). (Uxoriousness). See: *DOTTI*.
King ¿Umar al-Nu¿mân and Sons: *Alf* I 162-63; Burton II 78. Chauvin VI 112-24 No. 277; *ANE* 430-34 No. 39.□

T469.1.1§, ‡Access to "more females than Solomon had (as wives, concubines)". I.e., hundreds, thousands. See: *DOTTI*. (Cf. V210.0.6§, Z62).
King Jalî¿âd and Shimâs: *Alf* IV 161; Burton IX 90. Chauvin VI 9-11 No. 184; *ANE* 237-38 No. 236.□

T469.2§, ‡Sexual intercourse with a different woman daily the year round. (Cf. F781.2.2§, T380.0.1.1§, T469.0.1§, Z72.6).
King ¿Umar al-Nu¿mân and Sons: *Alf* I 168; Burton II 95. Chauvin VI 112-24 No. 277; *ANE* 430-34 No. 39;
Abû al-Hasan al-Khorâsânî (and Caliph's Favorite): *Alf* IV 233,-cf.; Burton IX 238,-(every night). Chauvin V 218-20 No. 129; *ANE* 68-69 No. 259.□

T471, Rape. See: *DOTTI*. (Cf. T289§).
Bahrâm and Datmâ: *Alf* III 164; Burton VI 187. Chauvin VIII 54-57 No. 22; *ANE* 114-15 No. 202;
Man [Gardener] and His Wife: *Alf* IV 165; Burton IX 99. Chauvin II 223 No. 152/19; *ANE* 289 No. 250.□

T471.0.4§, ‡Rapist threatens victim with weapon (knife, gun, etc.). (Cf. S105§, K1381.1§, K2234.2§).
King ¿Umar al-Nu¿mân and Sons: *Alf* I 184-85; Burton II 129. Chauvin VI 112-24 No. 277; *ANE* 430-34 No. 39.□

T471.0.5§, Compassionate treatment of rape victim. See: *DOTTI*; *GMC*.
King ¿Umar al-Nu¿mân and Sons: *Alf* I 185; Burton II 129. Chauvin VI 112-24 No. 277; *ANE* 430-34 No. 39.□

T471.0.8.1§, ‡Rape victim accepts her ravisher as husband. See: *DOTTI*.
Bahrâm and Datmâ: *Alf* III 166; Burton VI 188. Chauvin VIII 54-57 No. 22; *ANE* 114-15 No. 202.□

T471.5§, Slave (servant) rapes his mistress. See: *DOTTI*; *GMC*. (Cf. K2251, P367§).
King ¿Umar al-Nu¿mân and Sons: *Alf* I 184,-cf./(attempts); Burton II 129. Chauvin VI 112-24 No. 277; *ANE* 430-34 No. 39.□

T472§, Sodomy-rape (man, boy). See: *DOTTI*.
Third Eunuch: Seduces Mistress and Son: *Alf* I 151,-(passim); Burton II 56/non-tale. Chauvin V 278 n. 1 No. [161B]; *ANE* 179,/passim No. 38.□

T472.0.1§, Pedophilia. An adult's abnormal sexual desire for children. See: *GMC*. (Cf. H1579.1§).
¿Alâ' al-Dîn Abû al-Shâmât: *Alf* II 151; Burton IV 38. Chauvin V 43-49 No. 18; *ANE* 85-87 No. 63.□

T474.0.1§, ‡Nocturnal emission (*'ihtilâm*, involuntary emission, 'wet dream'). See: *DOTTI*. (Cf. C60.1.2§).
¿Alâ' al-Dîn Abû al-Shâmât: *Alf* II 165; Burton IV 67,-(nocturnal-pollution). Chauvin V 43-49 No. 18; *ANE* 85-87 No. 63;
Mercury ¿Alî: *Alf* III 233; Burton VII 183. Chauvin V 248-50 No. 147; *ANE* 301-3 No. 225.□

T474.0.2§, ‡Emission (ejaculation) from lusting after (seeing) a sexually desirable person. (Cf. F575, F575.2, F1041.8.1, T9.2.0.1§, T481.0.2.1§).
Tâj al-Mulûk: *Alf* I 294,-(old woman—*rashahat fî sarâwîlihâ*); Burton III 21,-(sweated in her petticoat trousers). Chauvin V 126-28 No. 60; *ANE* 406-8 No. 40;
Qamar al-Zamân and Budûr: *Alf* II 100,-cf./(every one who looked—*yabillu sarâwîlah*); Burton III 284,-(bepissed their bag-trousers). Chauvin V 204-12 No. 120; *ANE* 341-45 No. 61.□

T479§, ‡Eunuch's sexual activities. See: *DOTTI*; *PSAE*. (Cf. P170.0.3.1§, T315.2.6.1§).
First Eunuch: Bukhayt Deflowers Mistress: *Alf* I 148,-(continued); Burton II 50. Chauvin V 277 No. 160; *ANE* 178 No. 37.□

T479.1§, ‡Eunuch as lover (husband). (Cf. T271.3§).
Uns al-Wujûd and al-Ward: *Alf* II 270,-(passim); Burton V 46 n. 1,-(eunuch's sexual life). Chauvin VI 127-29 No. 282; *ANE* 438 No. 104.□

T479.2§, ‡Eunuch's sexual liaison with mistress. See: *DOTTI*. (Cf. T59.1§).
First Eunuch: Bukhayt Deflowers Mistress: *Alf* I 148; Burton II 50. Chauvin V 277 No. 160; *ANE* 178 No. 37.□

T480.1§, Loathsome paramour: black slave. See: *DOTTI*; *GMC*. (Cf. T232.4).
Shahriyâr and Shâhzamân: *Alf* I 2-3; Burton I 4-05. Chauvin V 188-91 No. 111; *ANE* 370-71 No. 1;
Third Shaykh: Transformation by Wife: *Alf* I 13; Burton I 36. Chauvin VII 130 No. 398; *ANE* 378 No. 7;
King's Daughter and Ape: *Alf* II 253; Burton IV 297. Chauvin V 178 No. 102; *ANE* 262-63 No. 102.□

T480.2§, ‡Loathsome paramour: most filthy (lowest of the low) man. See: *DOTTI*. (Cf. F1012.1.5§).
Sweep and Noble Lady: Infidelity Repaid: *Alf* II 188; Burton IV 125-26. Chauvin VI 148 No. 306; *ANE* 403-4 No. 72.□

T481.0.1§, ‡Adulterous desire (desire to commit fornication). See: *DOTTI*. (Cf. V301.1§).
Water-carrier and Goldsmith's Wife: *Alf* II 286; Burton V 90. Chauvin VI 192 No. 361; *ANE* 444 No. 122.□

T481.0.2§, ‡Lustful regard—('fornication-with-eye'). See: *DOTTI*. (Cf. H808.1§, J2203.1§).
Second Qalandar: Afrit's Wife: *Alf* I 46; Burton I 122,-("advowtry"). Chauvin V 197-200 No. 116; *ANE* 338-39 No. 16;
Jullanâr of the Sea: *Alf* III 266,-cf./('reach out with eye'); Burton VII 301,-(cast eyes upon). Chauvin V 147-51 No. 73; *ANE* 248-51 No. 227.□

T481.0.2.1§, ‡Accusation: fornication committed with the eye. See: *DOTTI*. (Cf. T474.0.2§, V301.1§).
Second Qalandar: Afrit's Wife: *Alf* I 46; Burton I 122. Chauvin V 197-200 No. 116; *ANE* 338-39 No. 16.□

T481.1, ‡Adulteress roughly treated by her lover. See: *DOTTI*. (Cf. T480.1§).
Ensorcelled Prince/Husband: *Alf* I 28; Burton I 72. Chauvin VI 56-58 No. 222; *ANE* 176 No. 13.□

T483§, ‡Woman with multiple sex partners (lovers, paramour, etc.). See: *DOTTI*. (Cf. T468§).
Lady's Lovers as Pursuer and Fugitive: *Alf* III 143; Burton VI 138. Chauvin VIII 38-39 No. 7; *ANE* 267 No. 187.□

T501.1§, ‡Procreation as religious duty. (Cf. T100.0.2§).
Tâj al-Mulûk: *Alf* I 261; Burton II 284. Chauvin V 126-28 No. 60; *ANE* 406-8 No. 40;
Hasan of Basrah: *Alf* IV 50,-(implicit); Burton VIII 137. Chauvin VII 29-35 No. 212A; *ANE* 207-10 No. 230.□

T501.2§, ‡Being fruitful (having many children) as the purpose of marriage. (Cf. P230.0.1.1§).
Tâj al-Mulûk: *Alf* I 261; Burton II 284. Chauvin V 126-28 No. 60; *ANE* 406-8 No. 40.□

T502.1§, ‡Conception begins with ejaculation from man's (father's) loins into woman's (mother's) womb.
Jeweler's Wife and Qamar al-Zamân: *Alf* IV 266,-cf./(implicit); Burton IX 303. Chauvin V 212-14 No. 121; *ANE* 345-47 No. 260.□

T502.1.1§, ‡Offspring from the same male (*¿aṣab, ṣulb*/muscle, agnates).
Reeve's Story: Why Maimed by Bride: *Alf* I 98,-(*ṣulb*); Burton I 285. Chauvin V 220-21 No. 305; *ANE* 351 No. 25;
King ¿Umar al-Nu¿mân and Sons: *Alf* II 11; Burton III 95,-(of same flesh and blood). Chauvin VI 112-24 No. 277; *ANE* 430-34 No. 39.□

T503§, ‡Too many children. See: *DOTTI*. (Cf. P230.0.3§).
Landsman ¿Abdallah and Merman ¿Abdallah: *Alf* IV 198,-(ten); Burton IX 165. Chauvin V 6-7 No. 3; *ANE* 65-66 No. 256;
Anîs al-Jalîs: *Alf* I 141,-('*¿ailah*'/dependents); Burton II 32. Chauvin V 120-24 No. 58; *ANE* 316-17 No. 35.□

T503.1§, ‡Complaint about too many children (dependents). See: *DOTTI*.

Three Apples: Hasty Uxoricide: *Alf* I 61; Burton I 187. Chauvin VI 144-45 No. 302; *ANE* 414-15 No. 21.□

T511.2, ‡Conception from eating plant.
¿Alâ' al-Dîn Abû al-Shâmât: *Alf* II 148,-cf./(hashish, opium ... "male-gum" ...); Burton IV 32. Chauvin V 43-49 No. 18; *ANE* 85-87 No. 63.□

T511.7.4.1§, ‡Conception from eating snake (serpent).
Sayf al-Mulûk: *Alf* III 275; Burton VII 321. Chauvin VII 64-73 No. 348; *ANE* 362-64 No. 229.□

T538.3§, ‡Aged man sires a child. (Cf. M369.7.4§, P17.0.2.2§, P230.0.2.2.1§).
Jânshâh: *Alf* III 40,-(Ṭayghamûs); Burton V 331. Chauvin VII 39-44 No. 153; *ANE* 238-41 No. 178.□

T548.1, Child born in answer to prayer. [('*ṭulbah*')]. See: *DOTTI*; *GMC*; *PSAE*.
Tawaddud: Slavegirl Sold and Regained: *Alf* II 303-4; Burton V 189. Chauvin VII 117-19 No. 387; *ANE* 408-10 No. 157;
Bulûqiya/Ḥâsib/Queen of Vipers: *Alf* III 18-19; Burton V 298. Chauvin VII 54 No. 77; *ANE* 130-32 No. 177;
Craft and Malice of Women/Frame: *Alf* III 138-39; Burton VI 123. Chauvin VIII 33-34 No. 1; *ANE* 160-61 No. 181.□

T570.0.2§, ‡Immediate conception (pregnancy from first intercourse).
Nûr al-Dîn ¿Alî and Son: *Alf* I 72; Burton I 223. Chauvin VI 102-6 No. 270; *ANE* 317-19 No. 22;
King ¿Umar al-Nu¿mân and Sons: *Alf* I 183; Burton II 124. Chauvin VI 112-24 No. 277; *ANE* 430-34 No. 39.□

T570.1§, Pregnant woman's wish (craving). See: *DOTTI*; *GMC*. (Cf. J1343.0.2§).
Qamar al-Zamân and Budûr: *Alf* II 106,-cf./(olives); Burton III 297-98. Chauvin V 204-12 No. 120; *ANE* 341-45 No. 61;
Mercury ¿Alî: *Alf* III 237; Burton VII 191. Chauvin V 248-50 No. 147; *ANE* 301-3 No. 225.□

T579.8.5§, ‡Signs of pregnancy: no menstruation (for three consecutive months).
¿Alâ' al-Dîn Abû al-Shâmât: *Alf* II 148,-(absence of menstruation); Burton IV 32,-(no blood). Chauvin V 43-49 No. 18; *ANE* 85-87 No. 63.□

T581.2.0.2§, ‡Child born of drowning woman abandoned.
Shipwrecked Woman and Her Child: *Alf* III 12; Burton V 259. Chauvin VI 160 No. 324; *ANE* 379 No. 164.□

T583, Accompaniments of childbirth. (Cf. P424.7§, P961§).
Tâj al-Mulûk: *Alf* I 265; Burton II 290-91. Chauvin V 126-28 No. 60; *ANE* 406-8 No. 40;
Jullanâr of the Sea: *Alf* III 249; Burton VII 268-69. Chauvin V 147-51 No. 73; *ANE* 248-51 No. 227.□

T583.0.1.1§, ‡Birth stool posture—(crouching position for childbirth). See: *PSAE*.
King ¿Umar al-Nu¿mân and Sons: *Alf* I 163, 208; Burton II 80, 174. Chauvin VI 112-24 No. 277; *ANE* 430-34 No. 39;
Tâj al-Mulûk: *Alf* I 265; Burton II 290,-(stool of delivery). Chauvin V 126-28 No. 60; *ANE* 406-8 No. 40.□

T583.0.1.2§, ‡Labor-pains (pangs of labor, '*ṭalq*'/*makhâḍ*).
King ¿Umar al-Nu¿mân and Sons: *Alf* I 208; Burton II 174. Chauvin VI 112-24 No. 277; *ANE* 430-34 No. 39;
Tâj al-Mulûk: *Alf* I 265; Burton II 290,-(stool of delivery). Chauvin V 126-28 No. 60; *ANE* 406-8 No. 40.□

T585, Precocious infant.
Nûr al-Dîn ¿Alî and Son: *Alf* I 76; Burton I 231. Chauvin VI 102-6 No. 270; *ANE* 317-19 No. 22.□

T585.1.1§, ‡Extraordinarily large newborn (looks much older than real age).
¿Alâ' al-Dîn Abû al-Shâmât: *Alf* II 148; Burton IV 33. Chauvin V 43-49 No. 18; *ANE* 85-87 No. 63.□

T587.0.1§, Twin brother and sister. See: *DOTTI*. (See: T685).
King ¿Umar al-Nu¿mân and Sons: *Alf* I 163; Burton II 80-81. Chauvin VI 112-24 No. 277; *ANE* 430-34 No. 39.□

T591.1, Magic remedies for barrenness or impotence. See: *GMC*.

Dalîla the Swindler: *Alf* III 213; Burton VII 147. Chauvin V 245-50 No. 147; *ANE* 163-64 No. 224.□

T591.5§, Pregnancy induced by abnormal means (magic, philtre, potion, etc.). See: *DOTTI*; *GMC*.
¿Alâ' al-Dîn Abû al-Shâmât: *Alf* II 148,-cf./(hashish, opium ... "male-gum" ...); Burton IV 32. Chauvin V 43-49 No. 18; *ANE* 85-87 No. 63;
Sayf al-Mulûk: *Alf* III 275,-(supernatural snake/serpent); Burton VII 322. Chauvin VII 64-73 No. 348; *ANE* 362-64 No. 229.□

T591.5.1.1§, ‡'*ṣûfah*': inseminating agent placed on ball of wool (cotton or the like) and 'worn' by woman (i.e., placed in vagina as love-philtre). Typically, it contains human semen.
Dalîla the Swindler: *Alf* III 213,-(*daqq al-ṣûf*/pounding wool); Burton VII 147,-("beating wool"). Chauvin V 245-50 No. 147; *ANE* 163-64 No. 224.□

T593.0.1§, ‡Failure to publicize (celebrate) birth of child causes problems. (Cf. T641§).
¿Alâ' al-Dîn Abû al-Shâmât: *Alf* II 150; Burton IV 36. Chauvin V 43-49 No. 18; *ANE* 85-87 No. 63;
Shahriyâr and Shahrzâd: *Alf* IV 317,-cf./(father unaware of birth of three sons); Burton X 54. Chauvin V 190-91 No. 111/pt.; *ANE* 371 No. 1.□

T596.1.1.1§, ‡Father names child.
King ¿Umar al-Nu¿mân and Sons: *Alf* I 208,-(daughter); Burton II 174. Chauvin VI 112-24 No. 277; *ANE* 430-34 No. 39;
¿Alâ' al-Dîn Abû al-Shâmât: *Alf* II 148,-(male); Burton IV 33. Chauvin V 43-49 No. 18; *ANE* 85-87 No. 63.□

T596.1.1.1.1§, ‡Father names baby boy.
¿Alâ' al-Dîn Abû al-Shâmât: *Alf* II 148; Burton IV 33. Chauvin V 43-49 No. 18; *ANE* 85-87 No. 63.□

T596.1.1.2.1§, ‡Mother names baby girl.
¿Alâ' al-Dîn Abû al-Shâmât: *Alf* II 148; Burton IV 33. Chauvin V 43-49 No. 18; *ANE* 85-87 No. 63.□

T596.5§, ‡Naming of newborn on seventh day of birth (*subû¿*). (Cf. P961.1§).
King ¿Umar al-Nu¿mân and Sons: *Alf* I 208; Burton II 174. Chauvin VI 112-24 No. 277; *ANE* 430-34 No. 39;
¿Alâ' al-Dîn Abû al-Shâmât: *Alf* II 148; Burton IV 33. Chauvin V 43-49 No. 18; *ANE* 85-87 No. 63.□

T603.1§, ‡Pampered son(s). See: *DOTTI*.
Jewish Doctor's Story: Sororicide: *Alf* I 100,-(and paternal nephew); Burton I 289. Chauvin VI 89 No. 253; *ANE* 242 No. 26;
¿Azîz and ¿Azîzah: *Alf* I 268,-(the only child); Burton II 299. Chauvin V 144-45 No. 71; *ANE* 111-13 No. 41;
¿Alâ' al-Dîn Abû al-Shâmât: *Alf* II 149; Burton IV 34-36. Chauvin V 43-49 No. 18; *ANE* 85-87 No. 63;
King's Favorite Son and Ogress: *Alf* III 143,-cf./(favorite); Burton VI 139. Chauvin VIII 40-41 No. 8B; *ANE* 264 No. 188.□

T604.0.2§, ‡No one can care for child like its (biological) mother. (Cf. P230.10.1§).
Shahriyâr and Shahrzâd: *Alf* IV 317; Burton X 54,-("will find none among women to rear them as they should be reared"). Chauvin V 190-91 No. 111/pt.; *ANE* 371 No. 1.□

T604.1§, ‡Mother protects infant (child). See: *DOTTI*.
Wolf and Fox: *Alf* II 31,-cf./(mother is to help her son the wolf); Burton III 136. Chauvin II 227 No. 6; *ANE* 450 No. 47.□

T604.3§, ‡Mother instructs (teaches) child (infant). See: *DOTTI*.
Nûr al-Dîn ¿Alî and Son: *Alf* I 81-82,-(teaches son how to cook); Burton I 244. Chauvin VI 102-6 No. 270; *ANE* 317-19 No. 22.□

T604.7§, ‡Mother weans child.
¿Alâ' al-Dîn Abû al-Shâmât: *Alf* II 149, 172,-(at age two); Burton IV 33, 78. Chauvin V 43-49 No. 18; *ANE* 85-87 No. 63;
Bulûqiya/Ḥâsib/Queen of Vipers: *Alf* III 19,-(passim); Burton V 299. Chauvin VII 54 No. 77; *ANE* 130-32 No. 177.□

T605.0.1.1§, ‡Wet nurse (as surrogate mother). (Cf. P272.5§).

¿Alâ' al-Dîn Abû al-Shâmât: *Alf* II 149,-(raises infant); Burton IV 33. Chauvin V 43-49 No. 18; *ANE* 85-87 No. 63.□

T610.1§, ‡Maturation (sexual). See: *DOTTI*.
King ¿Umar al-Nu¿mân and Sons: *Alf* I 312; Burton III 56-57. Chauvin VI 112-24 No. 277; *ANE* 430-34 No. 39.□

T610.1.1§, ‡Sexual awakening: becoming aware of own sexuality (adolescence, puberty). See: *DOTTI*. (Cf. P274.2§, T110.1§).
First Eunuch: Bukhayt Deflowers Mistress: *Alf* I 147; Burton II 49-50. Chauvin V 277 No. 160; *ANE* 178 No. 37;
King ¿Umar al-Nu¿mân and Sons: *Alf* I 312-13,-(of 'paternal cousins'); Burton III 56-57. Chauvin VI 112-24 No. 277; *ANE* 430-34 No. 39;
Ni¿mah and Nu¿m: Stolen Wife Regained: *Alf* II 132; Burton IV 2. Chauvin VI 96-97 No. 263; *ANE* 314 No. 62.□

T610.2.1§, ‡Girl's puberty.
First Eunuch: Bukhayt Deflowers Mistress: *Alf* I 147,-cf.; Burton II 49-50. Chauvin V 277 No. 160; *ANE* 178 No. 37.□

T610.2.4§, ‡Boy's puberty.
¿Alâ' al-Dîn Abû al-Shâmât: *Alf* II 165; Burton IV 67. Chauvin V 43-49 No. 18; *ANE* 85-87 No. 63;
Jeweler's Wife and Qamar al-Zamân: *Alf* IV 240-42; Burton IX 252-54. Chauvin V 212-14 No. 121; *ANE* 345-47 No. 260.□

T610.2.4.1§, ‡Boy's first ejaculation.
First Eunuch: Bukhayt Deflowers Mistress: *Alf* I 147,-(intercourse); Burton II 50. Chauvin V 277 No. 160; *ANE* 178 No. 37;
¿Alâ' al-Dîn Abû al-Shâmât: *Alf* II 165; Burton IV 67. Chauvin V 43-49 No. 18; *ANE* 85-87 No. 63.□

T610.5§, ‡Reaching puberty: behavioral indicators. (Cf. T9.0.1§).
Ni¿mah and Nu¿m: Stolen Wife Regained: *Alf* II 132; Burton IV 2. Chauvin VI 96-97 No. 263; *ANE* 314 No. 62.□

T610.5.0.1§, ‡Uncontrollable first sexual encounter.
First Eunuch: Bukhayt Deflowers Mistress: *Alf* I 148; Burton II 50. Chauvin V 277 No. 160; *ANE* 178 No. 37.□

T610.5.0.1.1§, ‡Multiple orgasms at first sexual encounter (wedding night). (Cf. T469§).
Nûr al-Dîn ¿Alî and Son: *Alf* I 72,-(fifteen); Burton I 223,-(fifteen assaults). Chauvin VI 102-6 No. 270; *ANE* 317-19 No. 22.□

T610.5.0.2§, ‡Incestuous tendency during childhood. (Cf. P605.5§).
First Qalandar: Brother-Sister Incest: *Alf* I 42; Burton I 110. Chauvin V 196-97 No. 115; *ANE* 337-38 No. 15;
Ni¿mah and Nu¿m: Stolen Wife Regained: *Alf* II 132,-(if not my sister, the I take her for wife); Burton IV 2. Chauvin VI 96-97 No. 263; *ANE* 314 No. 62.□

T615, Supernatural growth [of infant]. See: *DOTTI*; *GMC*.
Nûr al-Dîn ¿Alî and Son: *Alf* I 76; Burton I 231. Chauvin VI 102-6 No. 270; *ANE* 317-19 No. 22.□

T615.6§, ‡Precocious child beats playmates (pupils at school).
Nûr al-Dîn ¿Alî and Son: *Alf* I 76; Burton I 231,-("bully his schoolfellows and abuse them and bash them and thrash them [...]"). Chauvin VI 102-6 No. 270; *ANE* 317-19 No. 22.□

T617, Boy reared in ignorance of the world. See: *DOTTI*; *PSAE*. (Cf. R45).
Ibrâhîm and Jamîlah: *Alf* IV 219; Burton IX 207. Chauvin VI 52-53 No. 218; *ANE* 227-29 No. 258.□

T641§, ‡Paternity (legitimacy) of child questioned. See: *DOTTI*. (Cf. P230.9.2§).
¿Alâ' al-Dîn Abû al-Shâmât: *Alf* II 150; Burton IV 36. Chauvin V 43-49 No. 18; *ANE* 85-87 No. 63.□

T645.0.2§, ‡One's own ring exchanged with that of sleeping person (maiden, youth).

Qamar al-Zamân and Budûr: *Alf* II 78; Burton III 238. Chauvin V 204-12 No. 120; *ANE* 341-45 No. 61.□

T670.1§, ‡Childless couple adopt child. See: *DOTTI*.
Nûr al-Dîn ¿Alî and Son: *Alf* I 74,-cf./(childless man adopts youth); Burton I 226. Chauvin VI 102-6 No. 270; *ANE* 317-19 No. 22.□

T682, Hero a posthumous son. See: *GMC*.
Bulûqiya/Ḥâsib/Queen of Vipers: *Alf* III 19; Burton V 299. Chauvin VII 54 No. 77; *ANE* 130-32 No. 177.□

T685, Twins. See: *DOTTI*. (See: T587.0.1§).
King ¿Umar al-Nu¿mân and Sons: *Alf* I 163; Burton II 80-81. Chauvin VI 112-24 No. 277; *ANE* 430-34 No. 39.□

T0685.1, Twin adventurers. (Cf. P250.0.1§).
King ¿Umar al-Nu¿mân and Sons: *Alf* I 187ff.; Burton II 132ff. Chauvin VI 112-24 No. 277; *ANE* 430-34 No. 39.□

U5.1§, Successor falls short. (Cf. J816.5§).
Nuzhat al-Zamân Tested/¿Umar al-Nu¿mân: *Alf* I 203; Burton II 162. Chauvin VI 116, n.1/passim No. 277; *ANE* 432,/passim No. 39.□

U6.1§, Pious descendant, impious parents. See: *GMC*.
Devotee Prince: Ascetic's Death: *Alf* II 291,-(son and father/piety-wise); Burton V 115,-(son/sire). Chauvin VI 193-94 No. 363; *ANE* 167-68 No. 134;
Son of Unjust King: *Alf* IV 142; Burton IX 50. Chauvin II 219-20 No. 152/7; *ANE* 437 No. 242.□

U10, Justice and injustice. See: *DOTTI*; *GMC*.
Two Kings, Just and Unjust: *Alf* IV 149; Burton IX 65-67. Chauvin II 221 No. 152/12; *ANE* 422 No. 246.□

U10.0.1§, ‡'What you do (deal) to others will be done (dealt) back to you'. See: *DOTTI*. (Cf. K2400§, Q550.0.1§, U213§).
Ensorcelled Prince/Husband: *Alf* I 24,-cf./(poem/fishes'); Burton I 63. Chauvin VI 56-58 No. 222; *ANE* 176 No. 13;
Mouse and Cat: *Alf* IV 136; Burton IX 38. Chauvin II 218 No. 152/2; *ANE* 305-6 No. 237;
Jeweler's Wife and Qamar al-Zamân: *Alf* IV 262-63,-(poem); Burton IX 294. Chauvin V 212-14 No. 121; *ANE* 345-47 No. 260.□

U10.1§, ‡Justice is required in all situations.
Spy, First Maiden/¿Umar al-Nu¿mân: *Alf* I 220; Burton II 198. *ANE* 432 No. 39/passim.□

U10.1.1§, ‡Equality under the law guarantees that the powerful not aspire to favors and that the week not despair of receiving justice.
Spy, First Maiden/¿Umar al-Nu¿mân: *Alf* I 220,-(as dispensed by judge); Burton II 198. *ANE* 432 No. 39/passim.□

U10.1.2§, ‡Justice (honor) among a band of thieves, who are unjust to the public, is necessary for their cohesion. (Cf. Z98§).
Nuzhat al-Zamân Tested/¿Umar al-Nu¿mân: *Alf* I 202; Burton II 159. Chauvin VI 116, n.1/passim No. 277; *ANE* 432,/passim No. 39.□

U10.2§, ‡An accomplice to crime is guilty of that crime.
Boy and thieves: Guilty Accomplice: *Alf* IV 164; Burton IX 96. Chauvin II 222-23 No. 152/17; *ANE* 128 No. 249.□

U10.3.1§, ‡Human nature (the unconscious mind, the *nafs*, etc.) urges wickedness (injustice, aggression, etc.). (Cf. U249§, W35).
Sindbâd's Third Voyage: *Alf* III 92, 100; Burton VI 23,-("heart"). Chauvin VII 15-18 No. 373C; *ANE* 385-86 No. 179;
Sindbâd's Fourth Voyage: *Alf* III 100; Burton VI 34. Chauvin VII 18-20 No. 373D; *ANE* 386 No. 179.□

U10.3.1.1§, ‡Injustice lurks (is latent) in human psyche (*nafs*), powerfulness evokes it, powerlessness (personal weakness) suppresses it. (Cf. W181.0.1§).
Dûban and King Yûnân: *Alf* I 18,-(*ẓulm*/injustice); Burton I 49,-(oppression). Chauvin V 289 No. 173; *ANE* 383 No. 9.□

U10.4.1§, ‡Injustice ignored (not punished) because the truly just are gone (not to be found).
Nuzhat al-Zamân Tested/¿Umar al-Nu¿mân: *Alf* I 203; Burton II 162. Chauvin VI 116, n.1/passim No. 277; *ANE* 432,/passim No. 39.□

U10.5.2§, ‡Victim of sexual coercion (rape, abuse) becomes sexual predator (rapist). See: *DOTTI*.
Jinni Keeps Mistress in Box: *Alf* I 3,-(female); Burton I 11. Chauvin V 188-89 No. 111; *ANE* 370 No. 1/pt.;
King's Son and Afrit's Mistress: *Alf* III 172,-(female); Burton VI 200. Chauvin VIII 59 No. 24; *ANE* 263-64 No. 204.□

U11.1.3.1§, ‡Dignitaries (clerics), locked up in chest by woman they sought to seduce, concerned about becoming ritually polluted (defiled) by one another in the crowded quarters. See: *DOTTI*. (Cf. C60§, R56.1§).

Lady and Five Suitors Deceived: *Alf* III 160-61; Burton VI 178. Chauvin VIII 50-51 No. 18; *ANE* 266 No. 198.□

U20§, Opposites are ever present side by side: good-evil (honesty-fraud, truth-falsehood). See: *DOTTI*; *GMC*. (Cf. A1100.2§, F810.1.1§, U103§).
Tawaddud: Slavegirl Sold and Regained: *Alf* III 3,-cf.; Burton V 234,-(contraries). Chauvin VII 117-19 No. 387; *ANE* 408-10 No. 157.□

U24.3§, ‡'[Knowledge of having done] evil is sufficient [punishment] for its doer'. (Cf. W11.5.0.1§).
Second Shaykh: Treacherous Brothers: *Alf* I 13; Burton I 35,-(proverb). Chauvin V 6 No. 397; *ANE* 377-78 No. 6;
Fisherman and Afrit: Ingratitude: *Alf* I 23; Burton I 61. Chauvin VI 26 No. 197; *ANE* 183-84 No. 8;
Nûr al-Dîn and Maryam: *Alf* IV 110,-(poem/*nadâmâh*/rue); Burton VIII 323,-(xxx). Chauvin V 52-54 No. 271; *ANE* 98-99 No. 233.□

U25, Theft to avoid starvation forgiven. See: *DOTTI*; *GMC*. (Cf. V310.6§, W14.1.2§).
Dalîla the Swindler: *Alf* III 225,-cf.; Burton VII 170-71. Chauvin V 245-50 No. 147; *ANE* 163-64 No. 224.□

U25.1§, ‡Illegal acquisition of food from protected areas (by hunting, fishing, fruit-picking, etc.) to avoid starvation forgiven.
Anîs al-Jalîs: *Alf* I 140-41,-(fishing); Burton II 31. Chauvin V 120-24 No. 58; *ANE* 316-17 No. 35.□

U26§, ‡Murder to avoid starvation (or in self-defense) unpunished. See: *DOTTI*. (Cf. N337.8§, P535.1§, P794.2.1§).
Sindbâd's Fourth Voyage: *Alf* III 105; Burton VI 44. Chauvin VII 18-20 No. 373D; *ANE* 386 No. 179.□

U29.1.1§, ‡'Injustice (tyranny) will inevitably be vanished'.
Jawdar and His Treacherous Brethren: *Alf* III 178,-(poem); Burton VI 214. Chauvin V 257-60 No. 154; *ANE* 244-45 No. 209.□

U44.1§, ‡'Like fish: the large eat the small.'. (Cf. G99§).
Landsman ¿Abdallah and Merman ¿Abdallah: *Alf* IV 204; Burton IX 179. Chauvin V 6-7 No. 3; *ANE* 65-66 No. 256.□

U60.0.2§, ‡Poverty: described.
Copt Broker's Story: Lover's Sacrifices Repaid: *Alf* I 93,-(poem); Burton I 272. Chauvin VI 80 No. 249; *ANE* 313-14 No. 24.□

U60.0.2.1§, ‡The poor are avoided. See: *DOTTI*.
Anîs al-Jalîs: *Alf* I 130; Burton II 11. Chauvin V 120-24 No. 58; *ANE* 316-17 No. 35;
King ¿Umar al-Nu¿mân and Sons: *Alf* I 311,-(implicit); Burton III 55-56. Chauvin VI 112-24 No. 277; *ANE* 430-34 No. 39.□

U60.0.4§, ‡Poverty (being penniless) is humiliating.
Anîs al-Jalîs: *Alf* I 130,-(poem); Burton II 11. Chauvin V 120-24 No. 58; *ANE* 316-17 No. 35.□

U60.1§, ‡The poor are numerous, the rich are few. (Cf. P774.0.2.1§).
Qamar al-Zamân and Budûr: *Alf* II 109,-(poem); Burton III 302. Chauvin V 204-12 No. 120; *ANE* 341-45 No. 61.□

U60.2§, ‡Lifestyle of the poor (laborers) and that of the rich (aristocrats) contrasted. See: *DOTTI*. (Cf. F569.9§, P169.1§).
Anîs al-Jalîs: *Alf* I 140-41,-(poem,/fisherman-consumer/rich-poor); Burton II 31,-(xxx). Chauvin V 120-24 No. 58; *ANE* 316-17 No. 35;
Foolish Weaver: *Alf* II 40; Burton III 160. Chauvin II 229 No. 19; *ANE* 187 No. 58.□

U61.0.2§, ‡Luck (dice, Time) does not give to the needy. (Cf. Z122.7§).
Mercury ¿Alî: *Alf* III 227,-cf./(implicit); Burton VII 174. Chauvin V 248-50 No. 147; *ANE* 301-3 No. 225.□

U61.0.2.2§, ‡'A poor man does not become rich; if he did, he would die'.
Mercury ¿Alî: *Alf* III 227; Burton VII 174,-(is never satisfied). Chauvin V 248-50 No. 147; *ANE* 301-3 No. 225.□

U62.0.2§, ‡Poverty leads to insolence (bad manners). (Cf. L491§).

Anîs al-Jalîs: *Alf* I 141,/(breaking law); Burton II 32. Chauvin V 120-24 No. 58; *ANE* 316-17 No. 35;
Sindbâd and Porter: *Alf* III 83; Burton VI 4. Chauvin VII 1 No. 373; *ANE* 383-85 No. 179/pt.□

U64.2§, ‡Forgetfulness due to immersion in (preoccupation with) concerns of life (afflictions, problems). (Cf. G303.9.4.5.4§, U263§).
Anîs al-Jalîs: *Alf* I 144; Burton II 42-42. Chauvin V 120-24 No. 58; *ANE* 316-17 No. 35;
Sayf al-Mulûk: *Alf* III 292,-(faithful friend); Burton VII 355. Chauvin VII 64-73 No. 348; *ANE* 362-64 No. 229.□

U64.2.1§, ‡Spouse (sweetheart) forgotten due to groom's immersion in (preoccupation with) other matters.
Anîs al-Jalîs: *Alf* I 144,-cf./(master-slave girl); Burton II 42-43. Chauvin V 120-24 No. 58; *ANE* 316-17 No. 35.□

U66, Every man has his price. [Behavior potential]. See: *DOTTI*. (Cf. K712§, U249§).
Ma¿rûf the Cobbler: *Alf* IV 315-16,-cf./(sexual pleasure outweighs safety); Burton X 51. Chauvin VI 81-82 No. 250; *ANE* 291-93 No. 262.□

U66.0.1§, ‡Bid raised for a commodity (service) until reluctant provider accepts. (Cf. P774.1§). See: *DOTTI*.
Nûr al-Dîn and Maryam: *Alf* IV 100; Burton VIII 311. Chauvin V 52-54 No. 271; *ANE* 98-99 No. 233.□

U69§, ‡Money (gold) is all powerful. See: *DOTTI*.
Anîs al-Jalîs: *Alf* I 130,-(poem); Burton II 11. Chauvin V 120-24 No. 58; *ANE* 316-17 No. 35;
Abû Muḥammad Lazybones: *Alf* II 211,-(-poem); Burton IV 171. Chauvin VI 64-67 No. 233; *ANE* 71-73 No. 78;
¿Alî Shâr and Zumurrud: *Alf* II 217,-(man's worth is his possessiones); Burton IV 188-89. Chauvin V 89-91 No. 28; *ANE* 100-1 No. 82.□

U69.1.1§, ‡Quest for only wealth (money) causes decline in other worthy aspects of life (wisdom, fine arts, etc.). (Cf. P485.5§).
Second Qalandar: Afrit's Wife: *Alf* I 43; Burton I 115. Chauvin V 197-200 No. 116; *ANE* 338-39 No. 16.□

U69.3§, ‡Money is a homeland when one is away from his homeland. (Cf. H767.4§).
al-Rashîd and Omani Merchant: *Alf* IV 215,-(poem); Burton IX 199.-(money). Chauvin VI 111-12 No. 276; *ANE* 201-2 No. 257.□

U69.3.1§, ‡Being poor in own homeland is like being away from home (a stranger).
al-Rashîd and Omani Merchant: *Alf* IV 215,-(poem); Burton IX 199,-("Lack of good"). Chauvin VI 111-12 No. 276; *ANE* 201-2 No. 257.□

U84, Price of an object depends on where it is on sale. See: *DOTTI*.
Nûr al-Dîn ¿Alî and Son: *Alf* I 65,-(poem); Burton I 196. Chauvin VI 102-6 No. 270; *ANE* 317-19 No. 22;
Nûr al-Dîn and Maryam: *Alf* IV 97-98; Burton VIII 306. Chauvin V 52-54 No. 271; *ANE* 98-99 No. 233;
Abû Qîr and Abû Ṣîr: *Alf* IV 186,-(service/dying/cheaper in own country); Burton IX 142. Chauvin V 15-17 No. 10; *ANE* 75-77 No. 255.□

U85§, Demand (need) renders the valueless valuable.
Nûr al-Dîn and Maryam: *Alf* IV 97-98,-(cheap thread becomes valuable belt); Burton VIII 306. Chauvin V 52-54 No. 271; *ANE* 98-99 No. 233.□

U86§, ‡Scarcity renders the common valuable, abundance renders the valuable common (mundane). See: *DOTTI*. (Cf. B266.2§, P774.0.1§).
Nûr al-Dîn ¿Alî and Son: *Alf* I 65,-(poem); Burton I 196. Chauvin VI 102-6 No. 270; *ANE* 317-19 No. 22.□

U86.0.1§, ‡'To visit sparingly is to be loved increasingly' (i.e., 'Absence makes the heart grow fonder'). (Cf. P320.0.6.2§).
Jeweler's Wife and Qamar al-Zamân: *Alf* IV 251,-cf.; Burton IX 273,-(visits grow over frequent). Chauvin V 212-14 No. 121; *ANE* 345-47 No. 260.□

U86.1§, ‡In its homeland a valuable herb (incense) is only a weed—(because of plentitude). See: *PSAE*.

Nûr al-Dîn ¿Alî and Son: *Alf* I 65,-(poem); Burton I 196. Chauvin VI 102-6 No. 270; *ANE* 317-19 No. 22.□

U87.1.3§, Clothes make the man. See: *DOTTI*.
Foolish Weaver: *Alf* II 40,-cf.; Burton III 160. Chauvin II 229 No. 19; *ANE* 187 No. 58;
Illiterate Schoolmaster: *Alf* II 293; Burton V 120,-(he "greatened histurban "). Chauvin VI 137 No. 289; *ANE* 231 No. 137.□

U86.2§, ‡In the land of precious stones a gem is merely a pebble—(because of plentitude).
Landsman ¿Abdallah and Merman ¿Abdallah: *Alf* IV 205; Burton IX 183,-("stones without worth"). Chauvin V 6-7 No. 3; *ANE* 65-66 No. 256.□

U87.2§, Window-dressing sells.
Foolish Weaver: *Alf* II 40; Burton III 160. Chauvin II 229 No. 19; *ANE* 187 No. 58;
Thief and His Monkey: *Alf* II 40; Burton III 159. Chauvin II 229 No. 18; *ANE* 413 No. 57.□

U87.3.1§, ‡'Life (business) is pretence (fib) and ruse (strategy)'. See: *DOTTI*. (Cf. P431.2§, P773§, P776.1.1§).
Ma¿rûf the Cobbler: *Alf* IV 294; Burton X 10,-("The world is show and trickery"). Chauvin VI 81-82 No. 250; *ANE* 291-93 No. 262.□

U87.3.2§, ‡Fine craftsman finds no work because he is poor (lives in shabby surroundings).
Abû Qîr and Abû Ṣîr: *Alf* IV 184,-(claim); Burton IX 138. Chauvin V 15-17 No. 10; *ANE* 75-77 No. 255.□

U101§, ‡Hedonism: seeking pleasure as the main goal in life.
King Jalî¿âd and Shimâs: *Alf* IV 157, 158; Burton IX 80,-(inclination of the soul to lusts), 82. Chauvin VI 9-11 No. 184; *ANE* 237-38 No. 236.□

U101.0.2§, ‡Greatest pleasures are those of the flesh: eating flesh, riding flesh (horse), flesh entering into flesh (sexual intercourse). (Cf. H659.13.1, J1413§, W31.1.3§, Z192.1.1§).
Man from Yaman and Six Salve-girls: Flyting: *Alf* II 247; Burton IV 254. Chauvin VI 151 No. 313; *ANE* 289-90 No. 84;
Tawaddud: Slavegirl Sold and Regained: *Alf* III 7,-cf./(riddle/eating); Burton V 242. Chauvin VII 117-19 No. 387; *ANE* 408-10 No. 157.□

U101.1§, ‡Not thinking of the consequences of pleasure-seeking leads to hedonistic living (sinful indulgence). (Cf. J3.2.4§).
King Jalî¿âd and Shimâs: *Alf* IV 159; Burton IX 85-86. Chauvin VI 9-11 No. 184; *ANE* 237-38 No. 236.□

U102.1§, ‡'The psyche (self) is ever an instigator of the-sinful [(*al-sû'*, wicked inclinations)]'. (Cf. A65§, A1384.3§, W181.0.1§, W251§).
Sindbâd's Second Voyage: *Alf* III 92; Burton VI 23,-("human heart is naturally prone to evil"). Chauvin VII 24 No. 373F; *ANE* 386 No. 179;
Hasan of Basrah: *Alf* III 315,-(*al-nafsu 'ammartun be-'al-sû'*); Burton VIII 31,(soul to evil prompting). Chauvin VII 29-35 No. 212A; *ANE* 207-10 No. 230.□

U103§, ‡Contrasts are drawn to each other ('Opposites attract'). See: *DOTTI*. (Cf. A1100.2§, F579.1.1§, U20§, U129.5§).
King ¿Umar al-Nu¿mân and Sons: *Alf* I 171,-(Western and Eastern/'Ibrîzah and Sharrakân); Burton II 100. Chauvin VI 112-24 No. 277; *ANE* 430-34 No. 39.□

U103.0.1§, ‡The beauty of an entity (object) is brought out by its opposite.
Ni¿mah and Nu¿m: Stolen Wife Regained: *Alf* II 143,-(verse); Burton IV 20,-(contraries). Chauvin VI 96-97 No. 263; *ANE* 314 No. 62.□

U110, Appearances deceive. See: *DOTTI*; *GMC*. (Cf. J1809.5§).
Thief and His Monkey: *Alf* II 40; Burton III 159. Chauvin II 229 No. 18; *ANE* 413 No. 57;
Schoolmaster Who Fell in Love by Report: Mourns: *Alf* II 292; Burton V 117. Chauvin VI 136 No. 287; *ANE* 367 No. 135;
Illiterate Schoolmaster: *Alf* II 293,-(large turban); Burton V 120. Chauvin VI 137 No. 289; *ANE* 231 No. 137.□

U110.3.1§, ‡'Not every round thing is a nut, [nor] elongated thing a banana, [nor] ...'.
Anîs al-Jalîs: *Alf* I 132,-cf.; Burton II 15. Chauvin V 120-24 No. 58; *ANE* 316-17 No. 35.□

U110.3.3.4.1§, ‡'A viper (snake) shows smooth exterior but hides deadly venom'.
Escaped Viper Ungrateful: *Alf* II 35,-(poem); Burton III 145. Chauvin II 227 No. 9; *ANE* 450,/passim No. 47.□

U111.2.1§, ‡'Not whomsoever wore a turban is a judge (cleric), nor whosoever rode a horse is a horseman'.
Illiterate Schoolmaster: *Alf* II 293,-cf./(large turban); Burton V 120. Chauvin VI 137 No. 289; *ANE* 231 No. 137.□

U115, The skeleton in the closet. An apparently happy man lets another see the actual misery of his existence. See: *DOTTI*; *GMC*. (Cf. H1387§, N445§).
¿Abdallah ibn Fâḍil: Treacherous Brothers: *Alf* IV 268; Burton IX 308. Chauvin V 2-4 No. 2; *ANE* 63-65 No. 261.□

U119.8.3§, ‡Large army does not guarantee victory. (Cf. U119.8.3§).
King ¿Umar al-Nu¿mân and Sons: *Alf* I 232; Burton II 222. Chauvin VI 112-24 No. 277; *ANE* 430-34 No. 39.□

U121.0.2§, Like mother, like daughter.
Jewish Doctor's Story: Sororicide: *Alf* I 102,-(implicit); Burton I 299 n. 1. Chauvin VI 89 No. 253; *ANE* 242 No. 26.□

U121.0.3§, Like father, like son. See: *DOTTI*.
King Jalî¿âd and Shimâs: *Alf* IV 175,-(implicit/Shimâs and son); Burton IX 119ff. Chauvin VI 9 No. 184; *ANE* 237-38 No. 236.□

U129.5§, ‡Likeness attracts. (Cf. P610§, U103§, W30§, W30.5§).
Tâj al-Mulûk: *Alf* I 267; Burton II 296. Chauvin V 126-28 No. 60; *ANE* 406-8 No. 40.□

U129.5.2§, ‡Physical peculiarity (handicap) unites. See: *DOTTI*.
Third Qalandar: Magnetic Mountain: *Alf* I 53,-(being one-eyed); Burton I 152. Chauvin V 200-3 No. 117; *ANE* 340-41 No. 18;
Tâj al-Mulûk: *Alf* I 267,-cf./(emotional/misery); Burton II 296. Chauvin V 126-28 No. 60; *ANE* 406-8 No. 40.□

U135, Longing for accustomed food and living. See: *DOTTI*. (Cf. J1343.0.2§).
Qamar al-Zamân and Budûr: *Alf* II 106,-cf./(olives); Burton III 297-98. Chauvin V 204-12 No. 120; *ANE* 341-45 No. 61.□

U135.0.1§, ‡Deeds betray ancestry (origins). See: *DOTTI*. (Cf. H5§, H1381.3.1.5§).
Fisherman and Afrit: Ingratitude: *Alf* I 23,-(*radî' al-'aṣl*/of bad ancestry); Burton I 61,-("evil-doer" [??]). Chauvin VI 26 No. 197; *ANE* 183-84 No. 8;
Anîs al-Jalîs: *Alf* I 145,-(*'aṣl*/ancestry); Burton II 44,-("mother's milk"). Chauvin V 120-24 No. 58; *ANE* 316-17 No. 35.□

U138.3.1§, ‡'A betrayer may not be trusted [again]'. (Cf. J21.30.1§, W154.29§).
Jeweler's Wife and Qamar al-Zamân: *Alf* IV 259; Burton IX 288. Chauvin V 212-14 No. 121; *ANE* 345-47 No. 260.□

U145§, Greatness receives no recognition among one's own.
Nûr al-Dîn ¿Alî and Son: *Alf* I 65,-(poem); Burton I 196. Chauvin VI 102-6 No. 270; *ANE* 317-19 No. 22.□

U149.2.1.1§, ‡'Afflictions for some people are benefits for others'.
¿Abdallah ibn Fâḍil: Treacherous Brothers: *Alf* IV 285; Burton IX 342,-("misfortune"/"fortuneth"). Chauvin V 2-4 No. 2; *ANE* 63-65 No. 261.□

U160, Misfortune with oneself to blame the hardest. See: *DOTTI*.
Third Qalandar: Magnetic Mountain: *Alf* I 51; Burton I 140,-(xxx). Chauvin V 200-3 No. 117; *ANE* 340-41 No. 18;
Foolish Fisher: *Alf* IV 163; Burton IX 93-94. Chauvin II 222 No. 152/16; *ANE* 187 No. 248;
Francolin and Tortoises: *Alf* IV 172,-(prey blames self); Burton IX 114-15. Chauvin II 224 No. 152/23; *ANE* 188 No. 254.□

U163§, Lampooned by his own student, shot by his own apprentice. See: *GMC*.
Ma¿rûf the Cobbler: *Alf* IV 297,-cf.; Burton X 14. Chauvin VI 81-82 No. 250; *ANE* 291-93 No. 262.□

U163.1§, ‡Master teaches apprentice a skill (tactic, trick), apprentice uses the newly acquired skill against the master.
Ma¿rûf the Cobbler: *Alf* IV 297,-(getting credit when penniless); Burton X 14. Chauvin VI 81-82 No. 250; *ANE* 291-93 No. 262.□

U169.1.1§, ‡"*mishsh*'s worms are 'from it and in it' (i.e., inbred)".
¿Alâ' al-Dîn Abû al-Shâmât: *Alf* II 168,-(vinegar's); Burton IV 72,-(vinegar worm). Chauvin V 43-49 No. 18; *ANE* 85-87 No. 63.□

U169.3§, ‡You reap what you sow, 'Time' (fate) not to be blamed. (Cf. A604.3§, P526.3§, U210.0.1§, Z122.7.1§).
Dûban and King Yûnân: *Alf* I 22-23,-(poem); Burton I 60. Chauvin V 275-76 No. 156; *ANE* 459 No. 9.□

U169.5.1§, ‡Rape victim blames self.
King ¿Umar al-Nu¿mân and Sons: *Alf* I 183,-(*'anâ al-jâniyah ¿alâ nafsî*); Burton II 124,-(I who sinned against my own self [??]). Chauvin VI 112-24 No. 277; *ANE* 430-34 No. 39.□

U180.0.1§, Truth told (confession) while drunk. See: *DOTTI*. (Cf. K332.3§, K1165).
Hammâd: Treacherous Bedouin: *Alf* II 19,-(identity revealed); Burton III 110. Chauvin VI 124 n. 1 No. 277; *ANE* 200 No. 43;
¿Alâ' al-Dîn Abû al-Shâmât: *Alf* II 173,-(crime revealed); Burton IV 79-80. Chauvin V 43-49 No. 18; *ANE* 85-87 No. 63;
Ishâq al-Mûsilî and Khadîjah bint al-Hasan: *Alf* II 188,-cf.; Burton IV 124. Chauvin V 241-42 No. 142; *ANE* 232 No. 71;
Mercury ¿Alî: *Alf* III 234; Burton VII 185. Chauvin V 248-50 No. 147; *ANE* 301-3 No. 225;
Jullanâr of the Sea: *Alf* III 267; Burton VII 302. Chauvin V 147-51 No. 73; *ANE* 248-51 No. 227;
Ma¿rûf the Cobbler: *Alf* IV 309-10; Burton X 37. Chauvin VI 81-82 No. 250; *ANE* 291-93 No. 262.□

U192.0.1§, ‡Truth is savior. (Cf. J751.1).
Nuzhat al-Zamân Tested/¿Umar al-Nu¿mân: *Alf* I 202,-(poem); Burton II 160. Chauvin VI 112-124 No. 277; *ANE* 432,/passim No. 39;
King Jalî¿âd and Shimâs: *Alf* IV 161; Burton IX 89. Chauvin VI 9-11 No. 184; *ANE* 237-38 No. 236;
Abû Qîr and Abû Sîr: *Alf* IV 196; Burton IX 162. Chauvin V 15-17 No. 10; *ANE* 75-77 No. 255;
¿Abdallah ibn Fâdil: Treacherous Brothers: *Alf* IV 269; Burton IX 310,-(Ark of safety). Chauvin V 2-4 No. 2; *ANE* 63-65 No. 261;
Ma¿rûf the Cobbler: *Alf* IV 302,-(poem); Burton X 23. Chauvin VI 81-82 No. 250; *ANE* 291-93 No. 262.□

U192.4§, ‡Adviser (truth speaker) disliked (mistreated).
Dûban and King Yûnân: *Alf* I 21,-(poem/"my advice"); Burton I 58,-("my kindness"). Chauvin V 275-76 No. 156; *ANE* 459 No. 9.□

U193.1§, ‡'Tidy (neat) lies more effective than untidy (scattered) truths'—former more believable. See: *DOTTI*. (Cf. J21.13).
Ma¿rûf the Cobbler: *Alf* IV 294-95; Burton X 10-11. Chauvin VI 81-82 No. 250; *ANE* 291-93 No. 262.□

U197§, ‡Secrets: unshared 'truths'. See: *DOTTI*. (Cf. P790.0.1.3§, W45.3§).
King ¿Umar al-Nu¿mân and Sons: *Alf* II 3,-cf./(betrayed); Burton III 78. Chauvin VI 112-24 No. 277; *ANE* 430-34 No. 39.□

U197.0.1§, ‡Grave secret should not be shared even with one's own clothes (organs).
¿Alî ibn Bakkâr: *Alf* II 51,-cf.; Burton III 184. Chauvin V 153 No. 76; *ANE* 92-93 No. 60.□

U197.1.1§, ‡"If a secret becomes known by another (more than one), it has [in reality] spread".
Porter and Ladies of Baghdad: *Alf* I 33,-(poem); Burton I 87. Chauvin V 251-52 No. 148; *ANE* 324-26 No. 14.□

U210.0.1§, Just subjects, just ruler; unjust subjects, unjust ruler. See: *DOTTI*; *GMC*. (Cf. P500.1.2§, W35).
Dûban and King Yûnân: *Alf* I 22-23,-cf./(poem); Burton I 60. Chauvin V 275-76 No. 156; *ANE* 459 No. 9;

Nuzhat al-Zamân Tested/¿Umar al-Nu¿mân: *Alf* I 205,-('head' and 'body'); Burton II 168. Chauvin VI 116, n.1/passim No. 277; *ANE* 432,/passim No. 39.□

U213§, Life is: 'Blow for blow' (tit for tat). See: *DOTTI*; *GMC*. (Cf. K2400§, U10.0.1§).
Water-carrier and Goldsmith's Wife: *Alf* II 286; Burton V 90. Chauvin VI 192 No. 361; *ANE* 444 No. 122.□

U226.1§, ‡Friendship (amity, love, 'hearts'), like glass, cannot be mended if broken. See: *DOTTI*. (Cf. P529.0.1.2§).
Spy, First Maiden/¿Umar al-Nu¿mân: *Alf* I 220; Burton II 197. *ANE* 432 No. 39/passim;
Ma¿rûf the Cobbler: *Alf* IV 315,-(poem); Burton X 50. Chauvin VI 81-82 No. 250; *ANE* 291-93 No. 262.□

U230.0.2§, Cardinal sins (*kabâ'ir*), and minor sins (*ṣaghâ'ir*). See: *GMC*. (Cf. J2202.1§, T196.7§, V6.0.1§).
Spy, Fifth Maiden/¿Umar al-Nu¿mân: *Alf* I 223; Burton II 205,-(sins great and small). *ANE* 432 No. 39/passim.□

U230.0.3§, ‡Sinning is preordained (predestined). (Cf. J1391.12§, N101.0.1§).
Man Who Never Laughs: *Alf* III 153,-cf./(breaking tabu); Burton VI 162. Chauvin VIII 47-48 No. 15; *ANE* 285-86 No. 195.□

U230.0.3.1§, ‡Sinner merely 'fulfills' the preordained (predestined).
Mercury ¿Alî: *Alf* III 233,-(implicit); Burton VII 182. Chauvin V 248-50 No. 147; *ANE* 301-3 No. 225.□

U230.0.5.1§, ‡God sets the unjust (tyrant) against sinner as punishment. See: *DOTTI*. (Cf. J21.55.5§).
¿Alî Shâr and Zumurrud: *Alf* II 217; Burton IV 189. Chauvin V 89-91 No. 28; *ANE* 100-1 No. 82.□

U233§, ‡Virtuous (innocent) person successfully tempted. See: *DOTTI*. (Cf. T331, W131).
Mercury ¿Alî: *Alf* III 233,-cf.; Burton VII 182-83. Chauvin V 248-50 No. 147; *ANE* 301-3 No. 225;
Nûr al-Dîn and Maryam: *Alf* IV 83; Burton VIII 278. Chauvin V 52-54 No. 271; *ANE* 98-99 No. 233.□

U233.1§, ‡Non-drinker succumbs to group pressure (temptation) and drinks (liquor). (Cf. K289.9.3.1§).
Anîs al-Jalîs: *Alf* I 137,-(old gardener/host); Burton II 25-26. Chauvin V 120-24 No. 58; *ANE* 316-17 No. 35;
Nûr al-Dîn and Maryam: *Alf* IV 83; Burton VIII 278. Chauvin V 52-54 No. 271; *ANE* 98-99 No. 233.□

U235.0.1§, ‡'Lying brings forth (generates) hate and enmity'. See: *DOTTI*. (Cf. X901).
King ¿Umar al-Nu¿mân and Sons: *Alf* I 170; Burton II 99. Chauvin VI 112-24 No. 277; *ANE* 430-34 No. 39.□

U239.1.1§, ‡One lie calls for another.
Ma¿rûf the Cobbler: *Alf* IV 297; Burton X 15. Chauvin VI 81-82 No. 250; *ANE* 291-93 No. 262.□

U244§, ‡Anonymity encourages irresponsibility (recklessness). (Cf. P191.1.1§).
Ma¿rûf the Cobbler: *Alf* IV 294; Burton X 10. Chauvin VI 81-82 No. 250; *ANE* 291-93 No. 262.□

U244.1§, ‡"Where you are unknown, you may do as you please".
Ma¿rûf the Cobbler: *Alf* IV 294; Burton X 10,-("the land where none wotteth thee, there do whatso liketh thee"); . Chauvin 6: 81-82 No. 250; *ANE* 291 No. 262.□

U245§, Empathy: one person (animal) experiences pain or pleasure, another also feels its effects. "Vicarious instigation". See: *DOTTI*; *GMC*. (Cf. F789.4.1§, F956.7.6.2§, J170.5§).
Landsman ¿Abdallah and Merman ¿Abdallah: *Alf* IV 202-3,-(baker experiences fear upon hearing that fisher is punished); Burton IX 176. Chauvin V 6-7 No. 3; *ANE* 65-66 No. 256.□

U245.0.1§, ‡Contagiousness of mood(s). See: *DOTTI*. (Cf. J451).
Hunchback's Tale: Resuscitated: *Alf* I 88,-(happy hunchback); Burton I 261. Chauvin VI 80 No. 249; *ANE* 313-14 No. 23.□

U245.0.1.1§, ‡'He who is a neighbor of the happy (fortunate) will become likewise happy, and he who is a neighbor of [an unhappy] blacksmith will get burned with his fire [(gloom)]'.
¿Alî Shâr and Zumurrud: *Alf* II 217; Burton IV 187. Chauvin V 89-91 No. 28; *ANE* 100-1 No. 82.□

U245.0.1.1.1§, ‡Contagious weeping: it causes all to weep as well. (Cf. F1051).

First Qalandar: Brother-Sister Incest: *Alf* I 41; Burton I 108. Chauvin V 196-97 No. 115; *ANE* 337-38 No. 15;
Nûr al-Dîn ¿Alî and Son: *Alf* I 77,-(weeping/father-son); Burton I 233. Chauvin VI 102-6 No. 270; *ANE* 317-19 No. 22;
King ¿Umar al-Nu¿mân and Sons: *Alf* I 196,-(weeping/merchant-enslaved maiden), 238; Burton II 148, 241. Chauvin VI 112-24 No. 277; *ANE* 430-34 No. 39;
Tâj al-Mulûk: *Alf* I 292,-(weeping/friends); Burton III 13. Chauvin V 126-28 No. 60; *ANE* 406-8 No. 40;
King ¿Umar al-Nu¿mân and Sons: *Alf* II 11,-(at sister's weeping); Burton III 97-98. Chauvin VI 112-24 No. 277; *ANE* 430-34 No. 39;
Wolf and Fox: *Alf* II 31,-(fox's); Burton III 135. Chauvin II 227 No. 6; *ANE* 450 No. 47;
¿Alî ibn Bakkâr: *Alf* II 51, 55, 105; Burton III 183, 193, 293. Chauvin V 153 No. 76; *ANE* 92-93 No. 60;
Qamar al-Zamân and Budûr: *Alf* II 104,-(weeping/soldiers-king); Burton III 290. Chauvin V 204-12 No. 120; *ANE* 341-45 No. 61;
Bulûqiya: *Alf* III 38,-(vipers weep for hero), 78; Burton V 328, 390. Chauvin VII 39-44 No. 153; *ANE* 238-41 No. 177;
Hasan of Basrah: *Alf* III 318,-(foster sister weeps); Burton VIII 37. Chauvin VII 29-35 No. 212A; *ANE* 207-10 No. 230;
al-Rashîd and Omani Merchant: *Alf* IV 210,-(weeping along with singer); Burton IX 192. Chauvin VI 111-12 No. 276; *ANE* 201-2 No. 257.□

U246§, Empathetic punishments. See: *DOTTI*.
¿Alî Shâr and Zumurrud: *Alf* II 229,-(guests at banquet); Burton IV 215. Chauvin V 89-91 No. 28; *ANE* 100-1 No. 82.□

U246.1§, 'The onion vendor was beaten: the garlic vendor cried'.
Landsman ¿Abdallah and Merman ¿Abdallah: *Alf* IV 202-03,-cf./(principle: baker experiences fear upon hearing that fisher is punished); Burton IX 176. Chauvin V 6-7 No. 3; *ANE* 65-66 No. 256.□

U247§, Empathetic rewards. See: *GMC*.
Dalîla the Swindler: *Alf* III 212,-cf.; Burton VII 145. Chauvin V 245-50 No. 147; *ANE* 163-64 No. 224.□

U247.1§, Pleasure felt from another's happy experience (a distant relative's or an acquaintance's). (Cf. N393.1§).
King ¿Umar al-Nu¿mân and Sons: *Alf* II 8,-(praising); Burton III 89-(folk ape one another). Chauvin VI 112-24 No. 277; *ANE* 430-34 No. 39.□

U248.0.2§, ‡"It" taken to mean what listener has in mind. See: *DOTTI*. (Cf. J1820, K1073.1§, Z95.0.1§).
Stolen Purse/Joint Depositors: *Alf* III 177,-cf./(comb-purse); Burton VI 209. Chauvin VIII 63-64 No. 25; *ANE* 399 No. 207.□

U248.0.3§, ‡Wants affect perception (cognitions). See: *DOTTI*.
King ¿Umar al-Nu¿mân and Sons: *Alf* I 169; Burton II 96. Chauvin VI 112-24 No. 277; *ANE* 430-34 No. 39.□

U248.0.3.2§, ‡Aspirations (*maṭâmi¿*/strong wants) lead to risk-taking (dangers to one's safety). (Cf. T24.9.4§).
King ¿Umar al-Nu¿mân and Sons: *Alf* II 2,-(*maṭâmi¿*/aspirations); Burton III 77,-(Idle desires abase men's necks). Chauvin VI 112-24 No. 277; *ANE* 430-34 No. 39;
Wolf and Fox: *Alf* II 31,-(poem); Burton III 135,-(greed). Chauvin II 227 No. 6; *ANE* 450 No. 47.□

U248.1§, Hunger affects perception. See: *DOTTI*; *GMC*. (Cf. J716§).
Escaped Viper Ungrateful: *Alf* II 35; Burton III 145. Chauvin II 227 No. 9; *ANE* 450,/passim No. 47;
Crow and Viper: *Alf* IV 141; Burton IX 46. Chauvin II 219 No. 152/5; *ANE* 162 No. 240;
Hungry Eagle Snared: *Alf* IV 152,-(*¿Uqâb kâsir*); Burton IX 70,-("Ossifrage"/bone-breaking). Chauvin II 127-128 No. 133,-cf.;
Hyunter Rides Lion: *Alf* IV 153; Burton IX 72. Chauvin II 222 No. 152/15.□

U248.4§, ‡Sexual desire (love) affects perception. (Cf. F657.2§, T9.0.1§, T24.2.1, T24.9.4§, U248.0.3§, W255.2.1§).

King ¿Umar al-Nu¿mân and Sons: *Alf* I 169,-(maiden's beauty); Burton II 96. Chauvin VI 112-24 No. 277; *ANE* 430-34 No. 39;
Budûr and Jubayr ibn ¿Umayr: *Alf* II 239,-(poem); Burton IV 239. Chauvin VII 93-94 No. 374; *ANE* 243-44 No. 83.□

U248.6.1§, ‡Scribe's mental set (imagination, phantasy). (Cf. P425.2§, Z70.6§).
Porter and Ladies of Baghdad: *Alf* I 32,-(*sijill/kitâb*); Burton I 84,-(variant/rolls of a piece of brocade). Chauvin V 251-52 No. 148; *ANE* 324-26 No. 14;
Second Qalandar: Afrit's Wife: *Alf* I 46,-(fonts/script); Burton I 128. Chauvin V 197-200 No. 116; *ANE* 338-39 No. 16.□

U248.6.1.1§, ‡Man of letters views others as either poetry-makers or prose-makers.
Anîs al-Jalîs: *Alf* I 142,-cf./(poetry praised); Burton II 35,-(verses are pearls on string). Chauvin VII 93-94 No. 374; *ANE* 243-44 No. 35;
Budûr and Jubayr ibn ¿Umayr: *Alf* II 236,-(*al-nâẓim wa al-nâthir*/"rhymer and proser"); Burton IV 231,-("proser and rhymer"). Chauvin VII 93-94 No. 374; *ANE* 243-44 No. 83.□

U249§, Behavior potential: expected effort (trouble) required for performing task, and self-interest, determine whether task will be undertaken. See: *DOTTI*; *GMC*. (Cf. P774.0.1§, U66).
Ma¿rûf the Cobbler: *Alf* IV 315-16,-(sexual pleasure outweighs safety); Burton X 51. Chauvin VI 81-82 No. 250; *ANE* 291-93 No. 262.□

U249.0.1§, ‡Motivation: no action (behavior) without reason (stimulus). (Cf. U311.0.1§).
¿Alî ibn Bakkâr: *Alf* II 54-55,-cf./(*shahwât*); Burton III 191-92. Chauvin V 153 No. 76; *ANE* 92-93 No. 60.□

U249.0.8§, ‡'If cause [of the bizarre] becomes known, bewilderment [over it] would cease'. See: *DOTTI*. (Cf. H1319.7§).
Man Who Never Laughs: *Alf* III 155,-(reason for wailing/implicit); Burton VI 166. Chauvin VIII 47-48 No. 15; *ANE* 285-86 No. 195.□

U249.1§, ‡'Rewards are earned in proportion to expended labor'. See: *DOTTI*. (Cf. J1016§).
Nûr al-Dîn ¿Alî and Son: *Alf* I 65,-cf./(poem); Burton I 197-98. Chauvin VI 102-6 No. 270; *ANE* 317-19 No. 22.□

U249.1.3§, ‡'He who seeks high honors (high rank) must stay up nights [at work]'. (Cf. J285.0.1.1§, W113.2§).
Sindbâd's First Voyage: *Alf* III 83,-(poem); Burton VI 5. Chauvin VII 7-9 No. 373A; *ANE* 385 No. 179.□

U249.1.4§, ‡'He who does not endanger himself on quest does not attain his goal' (i.e, 'Nothing ventured, nothing gained').
Uns al-Wujûd and al-Ward: *Alf* II 275; Burton V 45-46. Chauvin VI 127-29 No. 282; *ANE* 438 No. 104.□

U250.0.1§, Death is inevitable. See: *DOTTI*; *GMC*. (Cf. N260.2§, Z42.1.1§, Z111.9.1§).
Anîs al-Jalîs: *Alf* I 129-30; Burton II 9. Chauvin V 120-24 No. 58; *ANE* 316-17 No. 35;
King ¿Umar al-Nu¿mân and Sons: *Alf* I 192,-(poem/implicit); Burton II 139. Chauvin VI 112-24 No. 277; *ANE* 430-34 No. 39;
¿Alâ' al-Dîn Abû al-Shâmât: *Alf* II 163,-(poem); Burton IV 63. Chauvin V 43-49 No. 18; *ANE* 85-87 No. 63;
Tawaddud: Slavegirl Sold and Regained: *Alf* III 6,-cf./(undeniable truth,/riddle); Burton V 242. Chauvin VII 117-19 No. 387; *ANE* 408-10 No. 157;
Angel of Death and Rich King: *Alf* III 9; Burton V 250. Chauvin VI 184-85 No. 350; *ANE* 104-5 No. 159;
Jinn Imprisoned in Flasks: *Alf* III 126,-(poem); Burton VI 91,-(variant). Chauvin VII 113 No. 380=no/text; *ANE* 146 No. 180;
City of Brass: *Alf* III 130-31,-(poem); Burton VI 104. Chauvin V 32-35 No. 16; *ANE* 146-50 No. 180.□

U253.1.1.1§, ‡'A living dog is better than a dead lion'.
Sindbâd's First Voyage: *Alf* III 83; Burton VI 5. Chauvin VII 7-9 No. 373A; *ANE* 385 No. 179.□

U253.1.2§, ‡One's own life is the most valuable (irreplaceable). (Cf. J234.2§, P218§).
Anîs al-Jalîs: *Alf* I 135,-(poem); Burton II 19. Chauvin V 120-24 No. 58; *ANE* 316-17 No. 35;

Sindbâd's Sixth Voyage: *Alf* III 114,-(poem); Burton VI 62. Chauvin VII 24-27 No. 373F; *ANE* 386 No. 179.□

U253.1.2.1.1§, ‡When one is alive (healthy) any loss of wealth, power, etc. can be recovered.
Hind bint al-Nu¿mân and al-Ḥajjâj: *Alf* III 203,-(poem); Burton VII 99. Chauvin V 115-4 No. 50; *ANE* 221-22 No. 212;
¿Abdallah ibn Fâḍil: Treacherous Brothers: *Alf* IV 272,-("like fingernail clippings"/poem); Burton IX 314. Chauvin V 2-4 No. 2; *ANE* 63-65 No. 261.□

U253.5.1§, ‡'The day of [one's own] death is preferable to the day of birth'.
Sindbâd's First Voyage: *Alf* III 83; Burton VI 5. Chauvin VII 7-9 No. 373A; *ANE* 385 No. 179.□

U253.5.2§, ‡'The tomb is preferable to a palace'. (Cf. V68).
Sindbâd's First Voyage: *Alf* III 83; Burton VI 5,-("want"). Chauvin VII 7-9 No. 373A; *ANE* 385 No. 179.□

U253.5.3.1§, ‡'A dead person has no friends'.
King ¿Umar al-Nu¿mân and Sons: *Alf* I 311; Burton III 55. Chauvin VI 112-24 No. 277; *ANE* 430-34 No. 39.□

U260.1§, ‡Things change (with time).
¿Alâ' al-Dîn Abû al-Shâmât: *Alf* II 152; Burton IV 41. Chauvin V 43-49 No. 18; *ANE* 85-87 No. 63.□

U260.1.1§, ‡'Every era has its own state-of-affairs, and its own men (leaders)'.
¿Alâ' al-Dîn Abû al-Shâmât: *Alf* II 152; Burton IV 41. Chauvin V 43-49 No. 18; *ANE* 85-87 No. 63.□

U260.2§, ‡The past will never return. See: *DOTTI*.
Man Who Never Laughs: *Alf* III 155; Burton VI 166. Chauvin VIII 47-48 No. 15; *ANE* 285-86 No. 195.□

U260.3§, ‡Effects of aging are irreversible. (Cf. L458§, T367§).
Pretty Gray-haired Woman Retorts: *Alf* II 303,-(poem); Burton V 164. Chauvin VI 153 No. 318; *ANE* 77-78 No. 152.□

U262, Suffering healed by time.
Sindbâd's Fifth Voyage: *Alf* III 106; Burton VI 48. Chauvin VII 21-24 No. 373E; *ANE* 386 No. 179;

Sindbâd's Sixth Voyage: *Alf* III 112; Burton VI 58. Chauvin VII 24-27 No. 373F; *ANE* 386 No. 179.□

U262.1§, ‡'Grief, like happiness, is never everlasting.
Shahriyâr and Shâhzamân: *Alf* I 5,-(poem); Burton I 15. Chauvin V 188-89 No. 111; *ANE* 370-71 No. 1.□

U263§, ‡Memory diminished by time. Forgetting (what had been learned) due to passage of time. See: *DOTTI*. (Cf. U64.2§).
Sindbâd's Fifth Voyage: *Alf* III 106,-cf.; Burton VI 48. Chauvin VII 21-24 No. 373E; *ANE* 386 No. 179.□

U274§, ‡Casualness (carelessness) brings about mistakes.
Man Who Had a Milk-camel: Loses Both: *Alf* IV 164; Burton IX 97. Chauvin VI 9 No. 184.□

U275§, A professional's own: it shows no benefit from his expertness. (Cf. J1062).
Sick Man Tries to Heal Another: *Alf* II 32; Burton III 140. Chauvin II 227 No. 8.□

U275.2§, ‡Needle dresses people while she herself is naked.
Tawaddud: Slavegirl Sold and Regained: *Alf* III 6,-(poem,/riddle); Burton V 240-41. Chauvin VII 117-19 No. 387; *ANE* 408-10 No. 157.□

U281§, Merits and demerits of physical attributes. See: *DOTTI*.
Budûr and Jubayr ibn ¿Umayr: *Alf* II 243,-(poem); Burton IV 245,-(water soft frame heart rock-hard). Chauvin VII 93-94 No. 374; *ANE* 243-44 No. 83.□

U281.1§, Merits and demerits of color (black, white). See: *DOTTI*; *GMC*. (Cf. Z142, Z143.5§).
Man from Yaman and Six Salve-girls: Flyting: *Alf* II 245-47,-(poem); Burton IV 248. Chauvin VI 151 No. 313; *ANE* 289-90 No. 84.□

U281.3.1§, ‡Merits and demerits of being bearded and being beardless. (Cf. J484.2§, K1590.1.1.1§).
Dispute Concerning Males and Females: *Alf* II 302,-(poem/beard mars beauty of face); Burton V 161 n. 4,-(black ink on white paper). Chauvin VI 153 No. 317; *ANE* 291 No. 151;
Bearded and Beardless Men as Lovers: *Alf* II 303; Burton V 165. Chauvin V 112 No. 48; *ANE* 450 No. 154.□

U281.4.1§, ‡Bigger is better.
Man from Yaman and Six Salve-girls: Flyting: *Alf* II 245; Burton IV 247. Chauvin VI 151 No. 313; *ANE* 289-90 No. 84.□

U281.4.3.1§, ‡Thinness (slenderness) is beautiful.
Man from Yaman and Six Salve-girls: Flyting: *Alf* II 247; Burton IV 254. Chauvin VI 151 No. 313; *ANE* 289-90 No. 84.□

U283.1§, ‡Merits and demerits of liquor.
Tawaddud: Slavegirl Sold and Regained: *Alf* II 317; Burton V 224. Chauvin VII 117-19 No. 387; *ANE* 408-10 No. 157.□

U283.1.1§, ‡Merits of liquor.
Nûr al-Dîn and Maryam: *Alf* IV 83; Burton VIII 277. Chauvin V 52-54 No. 271; *ANE* 98-99 No. 233;
Ma¿rûf the Cobbler: *Alf* IV 310; Burton X 38. Chauvin VI 81-82 No. 250; *ANE* 291-93 No. 262.□

U283.1.1.1§, ‡Liquor causes pleasure (enjoyment, joy). (Cf. F950.0.1.4§).
Sindbâd's Fifth Voyage: *Alf* III 108; Burton VI 52. Chauvin VII 21-24 No. 373E; *ANE* 386 No. 179.□

U283.1.1.2§, ‡Liquor causes courage (makes person courageous).
Sindbâd's Fifth Voyage: *Alf* III 108; Burton VI 52. Chauvin VII 21-24 No. 373E; *ANE* 386 No. 179.□

U283.1.1.3§, ‡Liquor improves health (helps digestion).
Tawaddud: Slavegirl Sold and Regained: *Alf* II 317; Burton V 224. Chauvin VII 117-19 No. 387; *ANE* 408-10 No. 157;
Sindbâd's Fifth Voyage: *Alf* III 108; Burton VI 52. Chauvin VII 21-24 No. 373E; *ANE* 386 No. 179.□

U283.1.3§, ‡Demerits (evils) of liquor.
¿Alî Shâr and Zumurrud: *Alf* II 217-18; Burton IV 189. Chauvin V 89-91 No. 28; *ANE* 100-1 No. 82.□

U284.1.1§, ‡'Had it not been for sin, redemption (forgiveness) would not have existed'. (Cf. V21.7§, V441).
Jawdar and His Treacherous Brethren: *Alf* III 199; Burton VI 252. Chauvin V 257-60 No. 154; *ANE* 244-45 No. 209;
Hasan of Basrah: *Alf* III 307; Burton VIII 18,-("but for sin, there were no pardon"). Chauvin VII 29-35 No. 212A; *ANE* 207-10 No. 230.□

U284.2.1§, ‡Hand used in cleaning privates preferred (by paramour, hopeful seducer). (Cf. C548.1§, T463.8§).
Sweep and Noble Lady: Infidelity Repaid: *Alf* II 190,-(poem); Burton IV 129. Chauvin VI 148 No. 306; *ANE* 403-4 No. 72.□

U284.3§, ‡Merits and demerits of homoerotic love (male: sodomy). See: *DOTTI*. (Cf. T463.3§, U281.2§).
Qamar al-Zamân and Budûr: *Alf* II 78-79,-(poem); Burton III 239. Chauvin V 204-12 No. 120; *ANE* 341-45 No. 61;
Dispute Concerning Males and Females: *Alf* II 300-2; Burton V 155-63. Chauvin VI 153 No. 317; *ANE* 291 No. 151.□

U284.3.1§, ‡ ‡To a male, another male (boy) is always available (but a female is not). (Cf. T380.2.1§).
Qamar al-Zamân and Budûr: *Alf* II 78-79,-(poem); Burton III 239. Chauvin V 204-12 No. 120; *ANE* 341-45 No. 61.□

U284.3.3§, ‡For a male, another male is more physically animated (rough). (Cf. P610§, T60.0.1§, T463).

Tâj al-Mulûk: *Alf* I 292,-(*yamîlu 'ilâ al-humûsah*); Burton III 16,-(inclining to the sour rather than the sweet). Chauvin V 126-28 No. 60; *ANE* 406-8 No. 40.□

U287.1.1§, ‡Merits and demerits of hair-coloring.
Pretty Gray-haired Woman Retorts: *Alf* II 303,-(poem); Burton V 163-64. Chauvin VI 153 No. 318; *ANE* 77-78 No. 152.□

U290§, ‡Merits and demerits of travel. (Cf. J1077§).
¿Alâ' al-Dîn Abû al-Shâmât: *Alf* II 151; Burton IV 39. Chauvin V 43-49 No. 18; *ANE* 85-87 No. 63.□

U300§, Relativity of perception: "adaptation level" (judgment depends on circumstances, objects of comparison, frame of reference, or context). See: *DOTTI*; *GMC*. (Cf. P191.1.3.1§).
Landsman ¿Abdallah and Merman ¿Abdallah: *Alf* IV 206-7,-(tailless human among tailed species); Burton IX 185-86. Chauvin V 6-7 No. 3; *ANE* 65-66 No. 256.□

U303.1.2§, ‡In the country of the tailed race, a tailless human is an oddity (ridiculed). See: *DOTTI*. (Cf. W30.1§).
Landsman ¿Abdallah and Merman ¿Abdallah: *Alf* IV 206; Burton IX 185-86. Chauvin V 6-7 No. 3; *ANE* 65-66 No. 256.□

U303.3§, ‡Distance is relative.
Ensorcelled Prince/Husband: *Alf* I 31,-cf./(traversing enchanted/disenchanted kingdom); Burton I 80. Chauvin VI 56-58 No. 222; *ANE* 176 No. 13.□

U304§, Relativity of perceiving quality. See: *DOTTI*; *GMC*.
Mercury ¿Alî: *Alf* III 227,-(important and unimportant persons); Burton VII 173. Chauvin V 248-50 No. 147; *ANE* 301-3 No. 225.□

U304.0.3§, ‡When there is no choice, the least will satisfy, but when there are choices the better will be desired.
Jawdar and His Treacherous Brethren: *Alf* III 190,-(food); Burton VI 235. Chauvin V 257-60 No. 154; *ANE* 244-45 No. 209.□

U304.4§, ‡Relativity of perceiving stature (size, importance, or the like).
Mercury ¿Alî: *Alf* III 227; Burton VII 173,-("'Little folk are one thing and great folk another'"). Chauvin V 248-50 No. 147; *ANE* 301-3 No. 225.□

U304.5.3§, ‡One who is capable of committing treachery (an immorality) for 'your sake' is capable of the same for another's. (Cf. S73.1.2.1§, U138.3.1§).
Jeweler's Wife and Qamar al-Zamân: *Alf* IV 258-59; Burton IX 288. Chauvin V 212-14 No. 121; *ANE* 345-47 No. 260.□

U305.1§, ‡Gradual increments: gives sense of 'moderate' total. See: *DOTTI*.
Jeweler's Wife and Qamar al-Zamân: *Alf* IV 247-48,-cf./(incremental gratuities); Burton IX 254-55. Chauvin V 212-14 No. 121; *ANE* 345-47 No. 260.□

U305.2.1.1§, ‡Insect bites (stings) become less irritating when frequent.
Anîs al-Jalîs: *Alf* I 141; Burton II 32. Chauvin V 120-24 No. 58; *ANE* 316-17 No. 35.□

U310.0.1§, Freedom (liberty) above all. See: *DOTTI*; *GMC*.
Man Who Had a Milk-camel: Loses Both: *Alf* IV 164; Burton IX 97,-("milch-camel"). Chauvin VI 9 No. 184.□

U310.1.1§, ‡Hunger as overpowering need (drive, motivation). (Cf. J716§).
Fox and Crow: *Alf* II 37,-(starved fox eats own young); Burton III 150. Chauvin II 228 No. 154.11, VI 10, No. 184.11; *ANE* 188 No. 51;
¿Alî Shâr and Zumurrud: *Alf* II 221,-(food, followed by sexual gratification); Burton IV 197. Chauvin V 89-91 No. 28; *ANE* 100-1 No. 82;
Sindbâd's Sixth Voyage: *Alf* III 115; Burton VI 64. Chauvin VII 24-27 No. 373F; *ANE* 386 No. 179.□

U310.1.1.2§, ‡Hunger must satisfied before attending secondary needs (e.g., entertainment, socializing, or the like). (Cf. J716§, U248.1§).
Barber's Sixth Brother: Emasculated by Abductor: *Alf* I 122,-(hunger-entertainment); Burton I 344. Chauvin V 163-64 No. 86; *ANE* 120 No. 34;
¿Alî Shâr and Zumurrud: *Alf* II 221; Burton IV 197. Chauvin V 89-91 No. 28; *ANE* 100-1 No. 82;

Sindbâd's Sixth Voyage: *Alf* III 115,-(food first); Burton VI 64. Chauvin VII 24-27 No. 373F; *ANE* 386 No. 179.□

U311.0.1§, ‡Biological drives (*al-gharâ'iz*) motivate everyone. (They are universal). (Cf. U249.0.1§).
¿Alî ibn Bakkâr: *Alf* II 54,-("'souls' are uniform in *shahwât*/desires"); Burton III 191,-(souls are active in their lusts). Chauvin V 153 No. 76; *ANE* 92-93 No. 60;
King Jalî¿âd and Shimâs: *Alf* IV 160,-(food, drink, sex, death); Burton IX 87. Chauvin VI 9-11 No. 184; *ANE* 237-38 No. 236.□

U311.0.2§, ‡Content person: fed, "watered", sheltered, and safe.
Sindbâd's Sixth Voyage: *Alf* III 115; Burton VI 64. Chauvin VII 24-27 No. 373F; *ANE* 386 No. 179.□

U311.4.1.1§, ‡Sleep as one of life's pleasures (lusts).
King Jalî¿âd and Shimâs: *Alf* IV 160; Burton IX 87. Chauvin VI 9-11 No. 184; *ANE* 237-38 No. 236.□

U315.0.1§, ‡Aesthetic (artistic) wants can be as powerful as physical needs.
¿Alâ' al-Dîn Abû al-Shâmât: *Alf* II 158,-(music/food); Burton IV 54. Chauvin V 43-49 No. 18; *ANE* 85-87 No. 63.□

U315.0.1.1§, ‡Listening to music (song) is food for the soul.
¿Alâ' al-Dîn Abû al-Shâmât: *Alf* II 158,-(*qût al-arwâḥ*); Burton IV 54,-(viands for souls). Chauvin V 43-49 No. 18; *ANE* 85-87 No. 63.□

U315.1.1§, ‡Togetherness in social gathering more important than food (drink).
¿Alâ' al-Dîn Abû al-Shâmât: *Alf* II 158,-(poem/one liner); Burton IV 54,-(eating joyeth only cattle-kind). Chauvin V 43-49 No. 18; *ANE* 85-87 No. 63.□

U318§, ‡Fusion of wants (needs): two or more needs (drives) addressed together (e.g., sex and religiosity, food and control, etc.).
¿Alî Shâr and Zumurrud: *Alf* II 234; Burton IV 227. Chauvin V 89-91 No. 28; *ANE* 100-1 No. 82;
Jeweler's Wife and Qamar al-Zamân: *Alf* IV 252,-(ablution-sexual intercourse); Burton IX 275. Chauvin V 212-14 No. 121; *ANE* 345-47 No. 260.□

U315.2§, ‡Productivity wants (household duties, making a living) can be as powerful as physical needs.
Nûr al-Dîn and Maryam: *Alf* IV 97,-(for the girl: labor first, sex second); Burton VIII 302-3. Chauvin V 52-54 No. 271; *ANE* 98-99 No. 233.□

U318.1§, ‡Sexual needs and religious needs fused.
King ¿Umar al-Nu¿mân and Sons: *Alf* I 225,-(implicit); Burton II 212. Chauvin VI 112-24 No. 277; *ANE* 430-34 No. 39;
¿Azîz and ¿Azîzah: *Alf* I 279,-(*ṭawâf*); Burton II 318. Chauvin V 144-45 No. 71; *ANE* 111-13 No. 41;
Qamar al-Zamân and Budûr: *Alf* II 109; Burton III 304. Chauvin V 204-12 No. 120; *ANE* 341-45 No. 61;
¿Alî Shâr and Zumurrud: *Alf* II 234; Burton IV 227. Chauvin V 89-91 No. 28; *ANE* 100-1 No. 82.□

U318.1.1§, ‡Sexual intercourse (coition) expressed in terms of performance of religious duties (praying, kneeling, circumambulation, etc.). (Cf. T187.0.2§, X598.1.2§, Z106§, Z138.5.0.1§, Z186.6§, Z186.7§, Z186.8.0.1§).
¿Azîz and ¿Azîzah: *Alf* I 279,-(*ṭawâf*); Burton II 318. Chauvin V 144-45 No. 71; *ANE* 111-13 No. 41;
Qamar al-Zamân and Budûr: *Alf* II 110; Burton III 305. Chauvin V 204-12 No. 120; *ANE* 341-45 No. 61;
¿Alî Shâr and Zumurrud: *Alf* II 234,-(her *miḥrab, sujûd-qiyâm, tasbîḥ-ghanj*/prayer leader-prayer niche, prostration-standing up erect, ...); Burton IV 227. Chauvin V 89-91 No. 28; *ANE* 100-1 No. 82.□

V. RELIGION AND RELIGIOUS SERVICES

V1.1.2.2§, ‡Person worshipped (venerated)—deified human. (Cf. A573.1§).
Sayf al-Mulûk: *Alf* III 286,-cf./(by monkeys); Burton VII 346. Chauvin VII 64-73 No. 348; *ANE* 362-64 No. 229;
King Jalî¿âd and Shimâs: *Alf* IV 155,-cf./(courtiers prostrate themselves before lad); Burton IX 76. Chauvin VI 9-11 No. 184; *ANE* 237-38 No. 236.□

V1.1.3.1§, ‡Spiritually advantageous death. See: *PSAE*. (Cf. V58.1.1.1§, V233.3.4§, Z111.9.4§).
Angel of Death and Devout Man: *Alf* III 8-9; Burton V 248. Chauvin VI 183-84 No. 349/[pt. 2]; *ANE* 104 No. 158/[pt. 2].□

V1.2.5§, ‡Demon (devil, jinni, afrit, etc.) enters into idol and animates it. (Cf. F415).
Jinn Imprisoned in Flasks: *Alf* III 127; Burton VI 98. Chauvin VII 113 No. 380; *ANE* 146 No. 180.□

V1.2.5.1§, ‡Demon inside idol gives instructions (commands).
Jinn Imprisoned in Flasks: *Alf* III 127; Burton VI 97. Chauvin VII 113 No. 380; *ANE* 146 No. 180.□

V1.4.2, Worship of the sun. See: *GMC*.
Sayf al-Mulûk: *Alf* III 274; Burton VII 314. Chauvin VII 64-73 No. 348; *ANE* 362-64 No. 229.□

V1.4.4, Worship of the stars [(planets)]. See: *DOTTI*; *GMC*.
Eldest Lady's Story: Treacherous Sisters: *Alf* I 55; Burton I 169. Chauvin V 4 No. 443; *ANE* 174-75 No. 19.□

V1.6.3, Worship of fire.
al-'Amjad and al-'As¿ad: *Alf* II 121; Burton III 326. Chauvin V 208-10 No. 120[.1]; *ANE* 341-42 No. 61/pt. 2;
Jullanâr of the Sea: *Alf* III 267; Burton VII 301-2. Chauvin V 147-51 No. 73; *ANE* 248-51 No. 227;
Sayf al-Mulûk: *Alf* III 274; Burton VII 314. Chauvin VII 64-73 No. 348; *ANE* 362-64 No. 229;
Hasan of Basrah: *Alf* III 307; Burton VIII 16-17. Chauvin VII 29-35 No. 212A; *ANE* 207-10 No. 230.□

V1.11, Worship of idols.
¿Abdallah ibn Fâḍil: Treacherous Brothers: *Alf* IV 276; Burton IX 324-25. Chauvin V 2-4 No. 2; *ANE* 63-65 No. 261.□

V1.11.5§, ‡Worship of precious stone idol.
Jinn Imprisoned in Flasks: *Alf* III 127,-(red agate); Burton VI 97. Chauvin VII 113 No. 380=no/text; *ANE* 146 No. 180.□

V1.11.8.1.1§, ‡Idol in eagle form.
Abû Muḥammad Lazybones: *Alf* II 216,-(talisman/¿*Uqâb*); Burton IV 177,-(vulture). Chauvin VI 64-67 No. 233; *ANE* 71-73 No. 78.□

V1.11.9.1§, ‡Material from which idol is made indicates owner's social status (class, rank).
¿Abdallah ibn Fâḍil: Treacherous Brothers: *Alf* IV 276; Burton IX 325. Chauvin V 2-4 No. 2; *ANE* 63-65 No. 261.□

V3§, Required religious services ('pillars,' corners, *'arkân, furûḍ*) and fundamental beliefs. See: *GMC*. (Cf. V4.3§, Z152.6.4§).
Tawaddud: Slavegirl Sold and Regained: *Alf* II 306; Burton V 196. Chauvin VII 117-19 No. 387; *ANE* 408-10 No. 157.□

V3.0.1.1§, ‡Required punishment for sin not assigned (registered, administered) to minors (pre-adolescents).
Qamar al-Zamân and Budûr: *Alf* II 108; Burton III 301. Chauvin V 204-12 No. 120; *ANE* 341-45 No. 61.□

V3.0.2§, ‡Missed required religious service is to be performed at later time (as make-up). (Cf. V6§).
¿Alî ibn Bakkâr: *Alf* II 47,-(prayers); Burton III 174. Chauvin V 153 No. 76; *ANE* 92-93 No. 60.□

V3.1§, ‡Required declaration of faith (*shahâdah*, "Testimony").
Ensorcelled Prince: *Alf* I 30-31; Burton I 79. Chauvin VI 56-58 No. 222; *ANE* 176 No. 13.□

V3.2.1§, ‡Merits of prayers.
Tawaddud: Slavegirl Sold and Regained: *Alf* II 306,-(ten); Burton V 197. Chauvin VII 117-19 No. 387; *ANE* 408-10 No. 157.□

V3.3§, ‡Required alms-tax (*zakâh*, given out yearly—compare: tithe). (Cf. P775.2§, T42.3.1§, V400).
Tawaddud: Slavegirl Sold and Regained: *Alf* II 308; Burton V 201. Chauvin VII 117-19 No. 387; *ANE* 408-10 No. 157.□

V4.3§, ‡*al-sunnah*: the preferred way for Moslems, as set by the Prophet. (Cf. V3§).
Dispute Concerning Males and Females: *Alf* II 300,-(blood-price); Burton V 156,-(blood money). Chauvin VI 153 No. 317; *ANE* 291 No. 151;
Tawaddud: Slavegirl Sold and Regained: *Alf* II 306-10; Burton V 195-210,-(sunnah/tradition). Chauvin VII 117-19 No. 387; *ANE* 408-10 No. 157;
Hasan of Basrah: *Alf* IV 4,-(marriage); Burton VIII 43. Chauvin VII 29-35 No. 212A; *ANE* 207-10 No. 230.□

V4.4§, ‡Extra religious exercise (prayers, fasting, etc.) undertaken for extra religious credit. (Cf. V6§).
King ¿Umar al-Nu¿mân and Sons: *Alf* I 225-26,-cf./(for beautiful damsels); Burton II 211. Chauvin VI 112-24 No. 277; *ANE* 430-34 No. 39.□

V4.4.2§, ‡Voluntary acts of kindness earn extra religious credit—(e.g., partaking in funeral, kindness to animal and the like). (Cf. Q40, Q51).
Ghânim ibn Ayyûb: *Alf* I 146,-(*'ajr*); Burton II 46,-("win the meed of good deeds"). Chauvin VI 14-16 No. 188; *ANE* 192-93 No. 36.□

V4.5.5§, ‡Cleansing self of effects of coition (by bathing) as intercessor. (Cf. V96.3§).
Nuzhat al-Zamân Tested/¿Umar al-Nu¿mân: *Alf* I 202,-(*kaffârah*); Burton II 161. Chauvin VI 116, n.1/passim No. 277; *ANE* 432,/passim No. 39.□

V4.5.6§, ‡Pilgrimage and *¿umrah* as intercessor(s). (Cf. V85.0.1.1.1§).
Landsman ¿Abdallah and Merman ¿Abdallah: *Alf* IV 203,-cf.; Burton IX 178. Chauvin V 6-7 No. 3; *ANE* 65-66 No. 256.□

V4.5.17§, ‡*tashahhud* (uttering the testimony that 'There is no god but God') as intercessor.
Ensorcelled Prince/Husband: *Alf* I 31,-cf.; Burton I 79. Chauvin VI 56-58 No. 222; *ANE* 176 No. 13.□

V5, Negligence in religious exercise. See: *GMC*.
Hermit and Pigeons: *Alf* II 27,-(prayers); Burton III 126. Chauvin II 226 No. 2; *ANE* 221 No. 45/pt. 1;
Water-fowl and Tortoise: *Alf* II 26, 29,-(prayers/*tasbîḥ*); Burton III 124, 125, 131. Chauvin II 226-27 No. 5; *ANE* 444 No. 46.□

V5.0.1.1§, ‡'The sin [for this misdeed (injustice)] would be around one's neck' (or 'on your head'). (Cf. K2173§, P526.3§).
Craft and Malice of Women/Frame: *Alf* III 150; Burton VI 155. Chauvin VIII 46-47 No. 14,-cf.; *ANE* 196 No. 181.□

V6§, Expiatory-deed (*kaffârah*): negligence in religious exercise made-up for by additional good deeds. See: *GMC*. (Cf. M115.3§, M205, P178.3§, V3.0.2§, V315).
Anîs al-Jalîs: *Alf* I 133; Burton II 15. Chauvin V 120-24 No. 58; *ANE* 316-17 No. 35;
Nuzhat al-Zamân Tested/¿Umar al-Nu¿mân: *Alf* I 202; Burton II 161. Chauvin VI 116, n.1/passim No. 277; *ANE* 432,/passim No. 39;
King ¿Umar al-Nu¿mân and Sons: *Alf* I 214,-(poem/*Zamân*'s broken oath); Burton II 186,-("Time, expiate thy sin"). Chauvin VI 112-24 No. 277; *ANE* 430-34 No. 39;
Spy, Fifth Maiden/¿Umar al-Nu¿mân: *Alf* I 223; Burton II 205-07. *ANE* 432 No. 39/passim;
Tawaddud: Slavegirl Sold and Regained: *Alf* III 5,-(recommended); Burton V 237,-(penance). Chauvin VII 117-19 No. 387; *ANE* 408-10 No. 157;
Masrûr and Zayn al-Mawâṣif: *Alf* IV 74; Burton VIII 248. Chauvin VI 82-84 No. 251; *ANE* 294-95 No. 232.□

V6.0.1§, ‡Minor good-deeds erase cardinal misdeeds (sins).
Spy, Fifth Maiden/¿Umar al-Nu¿mân: *Alf* I 223,-cf./(variations); Burton II 205. *ANE* 432 No. 39/passim.□

V7§, Religious exercise (fasting, pilgrimage, prayers, etc.) performed by proxy (surrogate). See: *GMC*. (Cf. V65.8§).
¿Abdallah ibn Fâḍil: Treacherous Brothers: *Alf* IV 270,-cf.; Burton IX 311. Chauvin V 2-4 No. 2; *ANE* 63-65 No. 261.□

V8.9.2§, ‡Religious 'esprit de corps': all members of the faith as one corpse (body, family, nation, etc.). (Cf. P305.1.1.1§, U245§, W12.2.0.1§).
Fox and Crow: *Alf* II 37; Burton III 150. Chauvin II 228 No. 11; *ANE* 188 No. 51.□

V8.9.2.0.1§, ‡Communal (group, *jamâ¿ah*) exercising of religious service favored—(e.g., prayers, pilgrimage). See: *DOTTI*. (Cf. V4.3§).
Devotee Prince: Ascetic's Death: *Alf* II 290; Burton V 112,-(with congregation). Chauvin VI 193-94 No. 363; *ANE* 167-68 No. 134.□

V9§, Religious faith conquers adversity (sickness, despair, poverty, etc.). See: *DOTTI*. (Cf. F950).
King Jalî¿âd and Shimâs: *Alf* IV 139; Burton IX 44. Chauvin VI 9 No. 184; *ANE* 237-38 No. 236.□

V11.9.2§, ‡Sacrifice to fire (fire-god). (Cf. V11.9.2§).
al-'Amjad and al-'As¿ad: *Alf* II 122; Burton III 327. Chauvin V 208-10 No. 120[.1]; *ANE* 341-42 No. 61/pt. 2.□

V12.1.1§, ‡Human as (religious) sacrifice. See: *DOTTI*. (Cf. S260.1, S270§, V544§).
Nûr al-Dîn and Maryam: *Alf* IV 108,-cf./(ritual killing); Burton VIII 324. Chauvin V 52-54 No. 271; *ANE* 98-99 No. 233.□

V21, Confession brings forgiveness of sin. See: *GMC*. (Cf. A102.14.3§, J224.1§, V315.1).
Wolf and Fox: *Alf* II 30,-(implicit); Burton III 132. Chauvin II 227 No. 6; *ANE* 450 No. 47.□

V21.7§, ‡Redemption (by God) dependent on forgiveness by victim. See: *DOTTI*. (Cf. U284.1.1§).
Water-carrier and Goldsmith's Wife: *Alf* II 286,-cf.; Burton V 90. Chauvin VI 192 No. 361; *ANE* 444 No. 122.□

V28.0.1§, ‡*tashahhud* (uttering the testimony: "No god but God, and Mohammed is His Messenger"): dying Moslem's last rite. (Cf. V3.1§).
Second Qalandar: Afrit's Wife: *Alf* I 49-50; Burton I 136. Chauvin V 197-200 No. 116; *ANE* 338-39 No. 16;
Anîs al-Jalîs: *Alf* I 130; Burton II 10. Chauvin V 120-24 No. 58; *ANE* 316-17 No. 35;
King ¿Umar al-Nu¿mân and Sons: *Alf* I 319; Burton III 74. Chauvin VI 112-24 No. 277; *ANE* 430-34 No. 39;
¿Alî Shâr and Zumurrud: *Alf* II 218; Burton IV 190,-(pronouncing the profession of the Faith"). Chauvin V 89-91 No. 28; *ANE* 100-1 No. 82;
Uns al-Wujûd and al-Ward: *Alf* II 272; Burton V 37. Chauvin VI 127-9 No. 282; *ANE* 438 No. 104;
Bulûqiya: *Alf* III 22; Burton V 304. Chauvin VII 54 No. 77; *ANE* 130-32 No. 177.□

V28.1.1§, ‡Person about to be executed is asked to state the *shahâdah*. See: *DOTTI*.
Portress Amînah: Bitten Cheek: *Alf* I 59; Burton I 181,-("profession of Faith"). Chauvin V 98-99 No. 33; *ANE* 326-27 No. 20.□

V52.8, ‡Prayer brings death to enemy. See: *DOTTI*.
Devout Jewess and Wicked Elders: *Alf* II 286; Burton V 98. Chauvin VI 193-93 No. 362; *ANE* 169 No. 128;
Son of Unjust King: *Alf* IV 143; Burton IX 52. Chauvin II 219-20 No. 152/7; *ANE* 437 No. 242.□

V52.8.1§, ‡Prayer kills predator (ogre, wolf, etc.). See: *DOTTI*. (Cf. V59.3.1§).
Falcon and Partridge: *Alf* II 32,-(meat becomes poison); Burton III 139. Chauvin II 227 No. 7; *ANE* 180 No. 48;
King's Favorite Son and Ogress: *Alf* III 144; Burton VI 142. Chauvin VIII 40-41 No. 8B; *ANE* 264 No. 188.□

V57.4§, ‡Thanksgiving prayer (acknowledges man's gratitude to God for His gifts). (Cf. C3.1§, C119.4§, N385.2§).
Nuzhat al-Zamân Tested/¿Umar al-Nu¿mân: *Alf* I 202,-(after coition); Burton II 161. Chauvin VI 116, n.1/passim No. 277; *ANE* 432,/passim No. 39.□

V58.1.1.1§, ‡Dying while praying is desirable. (Cf. V1.1.3.1§).
Angel of Death and Devout Man: *Alf* III 8-9; Burton V 248. Chauvin VI 183-84 No. 349/[pt. 2]; *ANE* 104 No. 158/[pt. 2].□

V58.4.1§, Ablution before prayer. See: *DOTTI*; *GMC*. (Cf. C60§).
Spy, Old Woman/¿Umar al-Nu¿mân: *Alf* I 224,-cf.; Burton II 205-07. *ANE* 432 No. 39/passim.□

V59.0.1§, ‡Prayers answered especially when gates of sky (heavens) are open. (Cf. D1761.3.1§).

Ibrâhîm and Jamîlah: *Alf* IV 225,-(passim); Burton IX 221. Chauvin VI 52-53 No. 218; *ANE* 227-29 No. 258.□

V59.3§, ‡Escape (deliverance) from danger as answer to prayer.
Prince and Ogress: *Alf* I 20; Burton I 55. Chauvin V 275-76 No. 156; *ANE* 459 No. 12;
Shipwrecked Woman and Her Child: *Alf* III 12; Burton V 260. Chauvin VI 160 No. 324; *ANE* 379 No. 164.□

V59.3.1§, ‡Prayer causes predator (ogre, wolf, etc.) to spare life of would-be prey (victim). See: *DOTTI*. (Cf. V52.8.1§).
Prince and Ogress: *Alf* I 20; Burton I 55. Chauvin V 275-76 No. 156; *ANE* 459 No. 9;
Mouse and Cat: *Alf* IV 135,-cf./(pleading by God); Burton IX 35-36. Chauvin II 218 No. 152/2; *ANE* 305-6 No. 237.□

V59.4§, ‡Series of answered prayers—one fulfilled prayer calls for the fulfillment of another. See: *DOTTI*.
Three Wishes: *Alf* III 162; Burton VI 180-81. Chauvin VIII 51-52 No. 19; *ANE* 419-20 No. 199.□

V60.0.1.1§, ‡Speedy burial required.
Tawaddud: Slavegirl Sold and Regained: *Alf* II 304,-(implicit); Burton V 190. Chauvin VII 117-19 No. 387; *ANE* 408-10 No. 157.□

V60.0.1.2§, ‡'Bestowing dignity upon the deceased (corpse) is by burying him (it)'. See: *DOTTI*.
¿Alâ' al-Dîn Abû al-Shâmât: *Alf* II 163; Burton IV 62. Chauvin V 43-49 No. 18; *ANE* 85-87 No. 63.□

V61.0.3§, A family's burial-yard (*hoash*) in cemetery. See: *GMC*.
Ghânim ibn Ayyûb: *Alf* I 146-47; Burton II 47,-(Santon's tomb). Chauvin VI 14-16 No. 188; *ANE* 192-93 No. 36.□

V61.0.3.1§, Necropolis. (Cf. F768.2.1§).
Devotee Prince: Ascetic's Death: *Alf* II 290,-(woman lives in cemetery); Burton V 113. Chauvin VI 193-94 No. 363; *ANE* 167-68 No. 134.□

V61.0.4§, ‡Corpse encased in coffin (casket.
Sindbâd's Fourth Voyage: *Alf* III 103; Burton VI 41. Chauvin VII 18-20 No. 373D; *ANE* 386 No. 179.□

V61.0.7.1§, ‡Burial inside the house of the deceased. See: *DOTTI*.
Hasan of Basrah: *Alf* IV 6; Burton VIII 48. Chauvin VII 29-35 No. 212A; *ANE* 207-10 No. 230.□

V61.8.2.1§, ‡Burial into earth returns man (Adamite) to place of origin (from where he had come—'ashes to ashes, dust to dust'). (Cf. Z111.9.3§).
¿Alî Shâr and Zumurrud: *Alf* II 218,-ff./(poem); Burton IV 190. Chauvin V 89-91 No. 28; *ANE* 100-1 No. 82;
Tawaddud: Slavegirl Sold and Regained: *Alf* III 5,-cf./(begin-end); Burton V 237. Chauvin VII 117-19 No. 387; *ANE* 408-10 No. 157.□

V65.0.1§, Commemoration of death on fortieth-day (*'arba¿în*). See: *GMC*.
¿Abdallah ibn Fâdil: Treacherous Brothers: *Alf* IV 270,-cf.; Burton IX 311. Chauvin V 2-4 No. 2; *ANE* 63-65 No. 261.□

V65.6§, Funeral feast. See: *DOTTI*; *GMC*. (Cf. J1347.2.5§, P681.1.0.4.1§, T136.1, V65.8.2§).
Ghânim ibn Ayyûb: *Alf* I 146; Burton II 47. Chauvin VI 14-16 No. 188; *ANE* 192-93 No. 36;
¿Abdallah ibn Fâdil: Treacherous Brothers: *Alf* IV 270; Burton IX 311. Chauvin V 2-4 No. 2; *ANE* 63-65 No. 261.□

V65.7§, Visiting the dead. See: *DOTTI*; *GMC*. (Cf. V311.5§).
Nûr al-Dîn ¿Alî and Son: *Alf* I 69; Burton I 210. Chauvin VI 102-6 No. 270; *ANE* 317-19 No. 22;
¿Azîz and ¿Azîzah: *Alf* I 282; Burton II 324-25. Chauvin V 144-45 No. 71; *ANE* 111-13 No. 41;
¿Alî ibn Bakkâr: *Alf* II 65; Burton III 211. Chauvin V 153 No. 76; *ANE* 92-93 No. 60.□

V65.8§, ‡Deeds done (at grave-side) on behalf of the deceased—('mercy-soliciting' deeds). See: *DOTTI*. (Cf. X420§).
Copt Broker's Story: Lover's Sacrifices Repaid: *Alf* I 95; Burton I 277. Chauvin VI 80 No. 249; *ANE* 313-14 No. 24.□

V65.8.1§, ‡Holy text recited 'over the soul of deceased'. See: *DOTTI*. (Cf. V7§).

Copt Broker's Story: Lover's Sacrifices Repaid: *Alf* I 95; Burton I 277,-(pious perfection of the Koran ...). Chauvin VI 80 No. 249; *ANE* 313-14 No. 24;
Ghânim ibn Ayyûb: *Alf* I 146, 156,-(*khatmât*); Burton II 47, 66,-(perfections). Chauvin VI 14-16 No. 188; *ANE* 192-93 No. 36;
¿Azîz and ¿Azîzah: *Alf* I 281,-(*khatmah*); Burton II 322. Chauvin V 144-45 No. 71; *ANE* 111-13 No. 41.□

V65.8.2§, ‡Food given to the needy 'over the soul of deceased' ('mercy-crackers,' or the like). See: *DOTTI*. (Cf. V65.6§).
Copt Broker's Story: Lover's Sacrifices Repaid: *Alf* I 95; Burton I 277. Chauvin VI 80 No. 249; *ANE* 313-14 No. 24;
Ḥâtim's Hospitality: *Alf* II 181; Burton IV 95. Chauvin VI 49 No. 215; *ANE* 216 No. 64;
¿Abdallah ibn Fâḍil: Treacherous Brothers: *Alf* IV 270,-cf.; Burton IX 311. Chauvin V 2-4 No. 2; *ANE* 63-65 No. 261.□

V65.8.3§, ‡Money given to the poor 'over the soul of deceased'. See: *DOTTI*.
Copt Broker's Story: Lover's Sacrifices Repaid: *Alf* I 95; Burton I 277. Chauvin VI 80 No. 249; *ANE* 313-14 No. 24;
Ghânim ibn Ayyûb: *Alf* I 159,-cf.; Burton II 72,-(by "princess of beneficent ladies"). Chauvin VI 14 No. 188; *ANE* 192-93 No. 36;
¿Azîz and ¿Azîzah: *Alf* I 282; Burton II 324. Chauvin V 144-45 No. 71; *ANE* 111-13 No. 41.□

V67, Accompaniments of burial [(i.e., things buried with corpse)].
Ghânim ibn Ayyûb: *Alf* I 146,-cf.; Burton II 46. Chauvin VI 14-16 No. 188; *ANE* 192-93 No. 36.□

V67.3.1.2§, ‡Corpse of dead (mummy) adorned with much jewelry. (Cf. F827.9.4.1§).
City of Brass: *Alf* III 136; Burton VI 117-18. Chauvin V 32-35 No. 16; *ANE* 146-50 No. 180.□

V67.9.2§, ‡Tomb has instructions to would-be robber(s). (Cf. L413, P527§, Q222.7§).
City of Brass: *Alf* III 136-37; Burton VI 118. Chauvin V 32-35 No. 16; *ANE* 146-50 No. 180.□

V67.9.2.1§, ‡Tomb robber may take treasure but may not violate owner's (corpse's) modesty, so states a tome inscription.
City of Brass: *Alf* III 136-37; Burton VI 118. Chauvin V 32-35 No. 16; *ANE* 146-50 No. 180.□

V68, Preparations for burial. See: *DOTTI*; *PSAE*. (Cf. P681.1.0.1.1.1§).
Anîs al-Jalîs: *Alf* I 130,-(poem); Burton II 10,-(variant). Chauvin V 120-24 No. 58; *ANE* 316-17 No. 35.□

V68.2.1§, ‡Mouth and rectum of dead stuffed with cotton.
¿Alî Shâr and Zumurrud: *Alf* II 219,-(poem/passim); Burton IV 193. Chauvin V 89-91 No. 28; *ANE* 100-1 No. 82;
Nûr al-Dîn and Maryam: *Alf* IV 93,-(rhetorical); Burton VIII 284. Chauvin V 52-54 No. 271; *ANE* 98-99 No. 233.□

V68.7§, ‡Corpse of female prepared for burial by female (undertaker's assistant). See: *DOTTI*.
Prior Becomes Moslem: al-Anbârî: *Alf* II 299; Burton V 144. Chauvin V 237-38 No. 137; *ANE* 330-31 No. 147.□

V76§, *¿îd*: Moslem bairam(s). See: *DOTTI*; *GMC*. (Cf. V544§).
Mercury ¿Alî: *Alf* III 239,-cf./(*¿îd*); Burton VII 196. Chauvin V 248-50 No. 147; *ANE* 301-3 No. 225.□

V82.1§, Circumcision of a male. See: *DOTTI*; *GMC*.
¿Alâ' al-Dîn Abû al-Shâmât: *Alf* II 149; Burton IV 34. Chauvin V 43-49 No. 18; *ANE* 85-87 No. 63.□

V82.0.1§, ‡Circumcision is required for cleanliness (of male or female).
Tawaddud: Slavegirl Sold and Regained: *Alf* II 311; Burton V 209 n. 3. Chauvin VII 117-19 No. 387; *ANE* 408-10 No. 157.□

V82.2§, Clitoridectomy: female excision (circumcision) as religious ritual. See: *DOTTI*. (Cf. T329§).
King ¿Umar al-Nu¿mân and Sons: *Alf* I 236,-(xxx); Burton II 234 n. 2,-cf./(physiological-comparative). Chauvin VI 112-24 No. 277; *ANE* 430-34 No. 39.□

V84.0.1§, ‡*takfîr*: person judged as having become a disbeliever. (Cf. P529.1.3§).

Ma¿rûf the Cobbler: *Alf* IV 313; Burton X 44,-(Munkar and eke Nakir). Chauvin VI 81-82 No. 250; *ANE* 291-93 No. 262.□

V85.0.1.1.1§, ‡Visit to Prophet's Tomb (in Medina). (Cf. V113.0.3§).
Landsman ¿Abdallah and Merman ¿Abdallah: *Alf* IV 203; Burton IX 178. Chauvin V 6-7 No. 3; *ANE* 65-66 No. 256.□

V85.0.1.1.1.1§, ‡Visiting Prophet's Tomb obliges him to intercede (in the hereafter) in behalf of the visitor. (Cf. J708.5§, Q174.0.1§, V4.5.6§, V521.1.1§).
Landsman ¿Abdallah and Merman ¿Abdallah: *Alf* IV 203; Burton IX 178. Chauvin V 6-7 No. 3; *ANE* 65-66 No. 256.□

V85.0.1.3§, ‡*'taqdîs'*: pilgrimage to al-Quds (Jerusalem) by Moslems or Christians. (Cf. V535).
King ¿Umar al-Nu¿mân and Sons: *Alf* I 187; Burton II 132-33. Chauvin VI 112-24 No. 277; *ANE* 430-34 No. 39.□

V85.1.0.1§, ‡*al-mahmal*: ceremonial sending of drapes ("veil") for the Black Stone (in Mecca). (Cf. V135.0.1.1§).
King ¿Umar al-Nu¿mân and Sons: *Alf* I 187; Burton II 131. Chauvin VI 112-24 No. 277; *ANE* 430-34 No. 39.□

V85.3§, ‡Pilgrimage rituals (sacrifice, circumambulation, stoning Satan, etc.). See: *DOTTI*.
Jawdar and His Treacherous Brethren: *Alf* III 194,-(circumambulation); Burton VI 242. Chauvin V 257-60 No. 154; *ANE* 244-45 No. 209.□

V85.5§, ‡Happenings (to pilgrim) during journey to (from) holy land. See: *DOTTI*. (Cf. P731.0.3.1§).
King ¿Umar al-Nu¿mân and Sons: *Alf* I 187,-ff.; Burton II 133-34. Chauvin VI 112-24 No. 277; *ANE* 430-34 No. 39;
Shipwrecked Woman and Her Child: *Alf* III 11,-(female); Burton V 259. Chauvin VI 160 No. 324; *ANE* 379 No. 164.□

V85.5.2§, ‡Burial in holy land.
Conversion of Princess by Khawwâs: *Alf* III 15,-(Mecca); Burton V 286. Chauvin V 239 No. 139; *ANE* 145 No. 171;
City of Brass: *Alf* III 138,-(Jerusalem); Burton VI 121. Chauvin V 32-35 No. 16; *ANE* 146-50 No. 180.□

V85.5.3§, ‡Unexpected encounters during pilgrimage. (Cf. V225).
Sweep and Noble Lady: Infidelity Repaid: *Alf* II 188; Burton IV 125. Chauvin VI 148 No. 306; *ANE* 403-4 No. 72;
Jawdar and His Treacherous Brethren: *Alf* III 194; Burton VI 242. Chauvin V 257-60 No. 154; *ANE* 244-45 No. 209.□

V90§, Miraculous effects of invoking God's attributes (*basmalah, hasbanah, hawqalah*, etc.). See: *DOTTI*. (Cf. D1273.3, D2071.1.4.0.2§, M400.2§, V316, Z13.9.1§).
First Qalandar: Brother-Sister Incest: *Alf* I 41,-cf./(protection); Burton I 109. Chauvin V 196-97 No. 115; *ANE* 337-38 No. 15;
King ¿Umar al-Nu¿mân and Sons: *Alf* I 166,-(*hawqalah*), II 14; Burton II 86, 101,-(xxx). Chauvin VI 112-24 No. 277; *ANE* 430-34 No. 39;
Qamar al-Zamân and Budûr: *Alf* II 81,-(*'ism-Allâh hawalayk*); Burton III 246,-(Allah's name encompass thee about). Chauvin V 204-12 No. 120; *ANE* 341-45 No. 61;
¿Alî Shâr and Zumurrud: *Alf* II 224,-(*hasbanah*), 232,-(*'innâ li-Allâh* ...); Burton IV 203, 221. Chauvin V 89-91 No. 28; *ANE* 100-1 No. 82;
City of Brass: *Alf* III 132; Burton VI 109. Chauvin V 32-35 No. 16; *ANE* 146-50 No. 180;
Ma¿rûf the Cobbler: *Alf* IV 291,-(husband *yahtasib* against wife); Burton X 5,-("calling on Allah for aid against"). Chauvin VI 81-82 No. 250; *ANE* 291-93 No. 262.□

V90.0.1§, ‡Miraculous power of uttering (mentioning) God's name. See: *DOTTI*.
¿Alâ' al-Dîn Abû al-Shâmât: *Alf* II 180,-(trees spring up); Burton IV 92. Chauvin V 43-49 No. 18; *ANE* 85-87 No. 63.□

V96.3§, Bathing after sexual intercourse is required. See: *GMC*. (Cf. C60.1§).
Nuzhat al-Zamân Tested/¿Umar al-Nu¿mân: *Alf* I 202; Burton II 161. Chauvin VI 116, n.1/passim No. 277; *ANE* 432,/passim No. 39;
Nûr al-Dîn and Maryam: *Alf* IV 97; Burton VIII 305. Chauvin V 52-54 No. 271; *ANE* 98-99 No. 233.□

V96.3.1§, ‡Bathing is required after autoerotic ejaculation (due to dream, masturbation, excitement, etc.). (Cf. C1.1.1§).
Mercury ¿Alî: *Alf* III 233; Burton VII 183. Chauvin V 248-50 No. 147; *ANE* 301-3 No. 225.□

V113.0.2, Vow to visit shrine.
Nûr al-Dîn and Maryam: *Alf* IV 103,-(monastery); Burton VIII 316. Chauvin V 52-54 No. 271; *ANE* 98-99 No. 233.□

V113.0.3§, ‡Tomb as shrine. (Cf. V61.0.1§).
Sindbâd's Seventh Voyage: *Alf* III 117,-(Solomon's); Burton VI 69. Chauvin VII 26-29 No. 373G; *ANE* 386-87 No. 179.□

V113.6§, ‡Evil doer enshrined (as saint).
Abû Qîr and Abû Ṣîr: *Alf* IV 197; Burton IX 165. Chauvin V 15-17 No. 10; *ANE* 75-77 No. 255.□

V152.1§, ‡Sacred sword.
King ¿Umar al-Nu¿mân and Sons: *Alf* I 312,-(poem/¿Alî's/simile/passim); Burton III 57. Chauvin VI 112-24 No. 277; *ANE* 430-34 No. 39.□

V152.1.1§, ‡Imam ¿Alî's sword. (Dhu-l-Fiqâr).
King ¿Umar al-Nu¿mân and Sons: *Alf* I 312,-(poem/passim); Burton III 57. Chauvin VI 112-24 No. 277; *ANE* 430-34 No. 39.□

V126, ‡Image of saint speaks. See: *GMC*. (Cf. V220.0.6§).
King ¿Umar al-Nu¿mân and Sons: *Alf* I 238; Burton II 237. Chauvin VI 112-24 No. 277; *ANE* 430-34 No. 39.□

V131.3§, Color of robe or head-wear (turban) marks members of religious group (denomination, sect, brotherhood). See: *DOTTI*; *GMC*. (Cf. D170.1§, D692, P722.3§).
Abû al-Ḥasan al-Khorâsânî (and Caliph's Favorite): *Alf* IV 230,-cf.; Burton IX 229-32. Chauvin V 218-20 No. 129; *ANE* 68-69 No. 259.□

V135.0.1.1§, ‡Sacred drapes. (Cf. V85.1.0.1§).
Sweep and Noble Lady: Infidelity Repaid: *Alf* II 188; Burton IV 125. Chauvin VI 148 No. 306; *ANE* 403-4 No. 72.□

V210, Religious founders. [Messengers of God]. See: *DOTTI*.
Tawaddud: Slavegirl Sold and Regained: *Alf* II 311,-(passim); Burton V 210. Chauvin VII 117-19 No. 387; *ANE* 408-10 No. 157.□

V210.0.2§, ‡Miracles manifested (by God) at hands of His Messengers (and Prophets). (*mu¿jizât/mu¿jizah*). See: *DOTTI*. (Cf. V220.0.6§).
Devout Jewess and Wicked Elders: *Alf* II 287,-(Daniel); Burton V 98. Chauvin VI 193-93 No. 362; *ANE* 169 No. 128.□

V210.0.6§, Polygyny among the prophets. See: *DOTTI*; *GMC*. (Cf. W29.3.1§).
King Jalî¿âd and Shimâs: *Alf* IV 161; Burton IX 90. Chauvin VI 9-11 No. 184; *ANE* 237-38 No. 236.□

V213§, Abraham as prophet (founder): God's bosom-friend. See: *DOTTI*; *GMC*.
King ¿Umar al-Nu¿mân and Sons: *Alf* I 187,-(passim/*al-Khalîl*); Burton II 132. Chauvin VI 112-24 No. 277; *ANE* 430-34 No. 39.□

V214§, Moses as prophet (founder). See: *DOTTI*; *GMC*.
Spy, Fifth Maiden/¿Umar al-Nu¿mân: *Alf* I 223; Burton II 205-6. *ANE* 432 No. 39/passim.□

V215§, Mohammed as prophet (founder). (Cf. A5.5.1§, H1258.1§).
Nuzhat al-Zamân Tested/¿Umar al-Nu¿mân: *Alf* I 204; Burton II 166-67,-("a blessing to some and a bane to others"). Chauvin VI 116, n.1/passim No. 277; *ANE* 432,/passim No. 39.□

V218.1§, ‡Torturing as means of bringing about religious conversion.
al-'Amjad and al-'As¿ad: *Alf* II 131; Burton III 345. Chauvin V 208-10 No. 120[.1]; *ANE* 341-42 No. 61/pt. 2;
¿Alî Shâr and Zumurrud: *Alf* II 223; Burton IV 203. Chauvin V 89-91 No. 28; *ANE* 100-1 No. 82;
Hasan of Basrah: *Alf* III 307; Burton VIII 17. Chauvin VII 29-35 No. 212A; *ANE* 207-10 No. 230.□

V218.2§, ‡Secret believer(s) in the true faith. (Cf. Z358§).

Eldest Lady's Story: Treacherous Sisters: *Alf* I 55-56; Burton I 169. Chauvin V 4 No. 443; *ANE* 174-75 No. 19.□

V219.1§, ‡Pleading to prophet (messenger of God) for help. (Cf. V220.0.7§).
¿Alî Shâr and Zumurrud: *Alf* II 224,-(Mohammed); Burton IV 203,-(calling for succour). Chauvin V 89-91 No. 28; *ANE* 100-1 No. 82.□

V220.0.1.1§, *quṭb* (arch-saint): supreme-saint.
Bulûqiya: *Alf* III 74,-(passim/*'aqṭâb*); Burton V 384, n. 1,-("princes of the faith"). Chauvin VII 54 No. 77; *ANE* 130-32 No. 177.□

V220.0.4§, Woman saint (*shaikhah/waliyyah/qiddîsah*, 'saintess').
Prior Becomes Moslem: al-Anbârî: *Alf* II 299,-("*waliyyah*"); Burton V 144,-("saintess"). Chauvin V 237-38 No. 137; *ANE* 330-31 No. 147.□

V220.0.6§, Miracle-like manifestation by saint (*karâmah*). See: *DOTTI*; *GMC*. (Cf. H257, H1573.2.1, V126).
King ¿Umar al-Nu¿mân and Sons: *Alf* I 238,-ff.; Burton II 237. Chauvin VI 112-24 No. 277; *ANE* 430-34 No. 39;
Devotee Prince: Ascetic's Death: *Alf* II 290,-cf./(bird obeys saintly youth); Burton V 111-12. Chauvin VI 193-94 No. 363; *ANE* 167-68 No. 134.□

V220.0.6.1§, ‡Saint's (hermit's) *barakah* (blessedness). (Cf. D1705§, D1713).
King ¿Umar al-Nu¿mân and Sons: *Alf* I 256; Burton II 272. Chauvin VI 112-24 No. 277; *ANE* 430-34 No. 39;
Dalîla the Swindler: *Alf* III 217; Burton VII 150. Chauvin V 245-50 No. 147; *ANE* 163-64 No. 224.□

V220.0.7§, Pleading to a saint for help. See: *DOTTI*; *GMC*. (Cf. N848).
¿Alâ' al-Dîn Abû al-Shâmât: *Alf* II 154,-(*sayyidah* Nafîsah); Burton IV 46. Chauvin V 43-49 No. 18; *ANE* 85-87 No. 63.□

V220.0.7.1.1§, ‡Pleading to saint for help brings about providential relief. (Cf. R341).
¿Alâ' al-Dîn Abû al-Shâmât: *Alf* II 154; Burton IV 46. Chauvin 5: 43-49 No. 18; *ANE* 85 No. 63;
Ma¿rûf the Cobbler: *Alf* IV 300,-(*Ya 'abâ al-lithâmayn* [i.e., al-Sayyid al-Badawî]); Burton X 20,-(sire of the chin-veils twain). Chauvin 6: 81-82 No. 250; *ANE* 291 No. 262.□

V220.0.7.1.1.1§, ‡Intended victim appeals to saint for help: attacker suffers instant calamity (stung by scorpion, killed by thunderbolt or the like). (Cf. Q552.1).
¿Alâ' al-Dîn Abû al-Shâmât: *Alf* II 154; Burton IV 46. Chauvin V 43-49 No. 18; *ANE* 85-87 No. 63.□

V220.0.14§, ‡Congregating places for saints.
Bulûqiya: *Alf* III 74; Burton V 384. Chauvin VII 54 No. 77; *ANE* 130-32 No. 177.□

V220.0.15.3.1§, ‡Holy man's staff blossoms and yields any desired food when driven into ground. (Moses' cane). (Cf. D1472.2.12§).
Jânshâh: *Alf* III 67,-cf./(magician's staff); Burton V 371. Chauvin VII 39-44 No. 153; *ANE* 238-41 No. 178.□

V221, Miraculous healing by saints. See: *DOTTI*; *GMC*. (Cf. H413.7§, V9§).
Conversion of Princess by Khawwâṣ: *Alf* III 15,-(spiritual); Burton V 284-85. Chauvin V 239 No. 139; *ANE* 145 No. 171;
Dalîla the Swindler: *Alf* III 214,-(swindler's claim); Burton VII 149. Chauvin V 245-50 No. 147; *ANE* 163-64 No. 224.□

V222.12.3§, ‡Holy man plants a seed that becomes fruit-bearing tree instantly. (Cf. F971.1.2§, V210.0.2§).
¿Abdallah ibn Fâḍil: Treacherous Brothers: *Alf* IV 277; Burton IX 327. Chauvin V 2-4 No. 2; *ANE* 63-65 No. 261.□

V223.0.1.0.2§, ‡Spirituality gives clairvoyance.
King Jalî¿âd and Shimâs: *Alf* IV 174; Burton IX 117,-("spiritual virtue"/"darkest secrets"). Chauvin VI 9 No. 184; *ANE* 237-38 No. 236.□

V223.5.0.1§, Saint knows all systems of communication (languages of animals, of jinn, of objects, etc.). See: *GMC*. (Cf. B216.1§, K1969.5.1§).

City of Brass: *Alf* III 132,-cf./(all tongues and scripts); Burton VI 90,-(variant). Chauvin V 32-35 No. 16; *ANE* 146-50 No. 180.□

V223.10§, Holy men (saints, prophets) as workmen (craftsmen, tradesmen). See: *GMC*.
Devotee Prince: Ascetic's Death: *Alf* II 290,-(mason); Burton V 112. Chauvin VI 193-94 No. 363; *ANE* 167-68 No. 134.□

V225, Saint in several places at once. [*min 'ahl-al-khuṭwah, min al-'abdâl*]. See: *DOTTI*; *GMC*. (Cf. D2122.5, V85.5.3§).
King ¿Umar al-Nu¿mân and Sons: *Alf* I 241,-(*'abdâl*); Burton II 244,-(ecstatics). Chauvin VI 112-24 No. 277; *ANE* 430-34 No. 39;
Bulûqiya: *Alf* III 74; Burton V 384. Chauvin VII 54 No. 77; *ANE* 130-32 No. 177.□

V228.5.1§, Saint walks upon water. See: *DOTTI*; *GMC*.
King ¿Umar al-Nu¿mân and Sons: *Alf* I 241; Burton II 244. Chauvin VI 112-24 No. 277; *ANE* 430-34 No. 39.□

V229.8.3§, ‡Saint's (holy man's) shadow causes supernatural concealment (invisibility). (Cf. D1983.3.1§, D1981.2).
King ¿Umar al-Nu¿mân and Sons: *Alf* I 245; Burton II 251. Chauvin VI 112-24 No. 277; *ANE* 430-34 No. 39.□

V229.12, Sinful beauty is converted and spends the end of her life doing penance (Mary Magdalene, Mary of Egypt, [Fâṭimah Bint-Birrî], and Thais). (Cf. J167.3§, N887.5.1.1§).
Copt Broker's Story: Lover's Sacrifices Repaid: *Alf* I 95; Burton I 277. Chauvin VI 80 No. 249; *ANE* 313-14 No. 24.□

V229.29§, ‡Saint can fly in the air ('flying-saint'). (Cf. F231.3.1§).
King ¿Umar al-Nu¿mân and Sons: *Alf* I 249,-(*min al-'awliyâ' al-ṭayyârah*); Burton II 260. Chauvin VI 112-24 No. 277; *ANE* 430-34 No. 39.□

V231.1, Angel in bird shape. See: *DOTTI*; *GMC*.
Bulûqiya: *Alf* III 35; Burton V 323. Chauvin VII 54 No. 77; *ANE* 130-32 No. 177.□

V231.6, Angel in the form of an old man. See: *DOTTI*; *GMC*.
Angel of Death and Proud King: *Alf* III 8; Burton V 247. Chauvin VI 183-84 No. 349/[pt. 1]; *ANE* 104 No. 158.□

V231.7.1§, ‡Angel with lion-face.
Bulûqiya: *Alf* III 37; Burton V 325. Chauvin VII 54 No. 77; *ANE* 130-32 No. 177.□

V231.7.2§, ‡Angel with face of bull (ox).
Bulûqiya: *Alf* III 35, 37; Burton V 323. Chauvin VII 54 No. 77; *ANE* 130-32 No. 177.□

V231.9.1§, ‡Angel in human form (shape)—general. See: *DOTTI*. (Cf. G303.3.1, V233.0.1.4§).
Hermit Tempted by Angel: *Alf* II 27; Burton III 126. Chauvin II 226 No. 3; *ANE* 221 No. 45/pt. 2;
Angel of Death and Rich King: *Alf* III 9; Burton V 249. Chauvin VI 184-85 No. 350; *ANE* 104-5 No. 159;
Bulûqiya: *Alf* III 35; Burton V 323. Chauvin VII 54 No. 77; *ANE* 130-32 No. 177.□

V232, Angel as helper. See: *DOTTI*; *GMC*. (Cf. A494.0.1.1§, F499.9.1§).
Jewish Tray-maker and Temptress: *Alf* III 13; Burton V 267. Chauvin VI 187-88 No. 354; *ANE* 169 No. 166;
Bulûqiya: *Alf* III 28,-(Gabriel [!!]); Burton V 312. Chauvin VII 54 No. 77; *ANE* 130-32 No. 177.□

V232.2.1§, ‡Mortal falling (jumping) from great height carried safely to ground by angel. See: *DOTTI*.
Jewish Tray-maker and Temptress: *Alf* III 13; Burton V 267. Chauvin VI 187-88 No. 354; *ANE* 169 No. 166.□

V233, Angel of death. See: *ANE*; *DOTTI*; *GMC*.
Angel of Death and Proud King: *Alf* III 8; Burton V 247. Chauvin VI 183-84 No. 349/[pt. 1]; *ANE* 104 No. 158.□

V233.0.1.4§, ‡Angel of death in human form. See: *DOTTI*. (Cf. V231.9.1§).
Angel of Death and Rich King: *Alf* III 9; Burton V 248-50. Chauvin VI 184-85 No. 350; *ANE* 104-5 No. 159.□

V233.3.1§, ‡Mortal asks Angel of Death (Azrael) for respite. See: *DOTTI*.

Angel of Death and Proud King: *Alf* III 8; Burton V 248. Chauvin VI 183-84 No. 349.[pt. 1]; *ANE* 104 No. 158;
Angel of Death and Jewish King: *Alf* III 9-10; Burton V 251. Chauvin VI 184-85 No. 351; *ANE* 104 No. 160.□

V233.3.1.1§, ‡Request for respite from death denied. (Cf. V233.3.3§).
Angel of Death and Proud King: *Alf* III 8; Burton V 247. Chauvin VI 183-84 No. 349/[pt. 1]; *ANE* 104 No. 158;
Angel of Death and Jewish King: *Alf* III 9; Burton V 251. Chauvin VI 184-85 No. 351; *ANE* 104 No. 160.□

V233.3.3§, ‡Angel of Death (Azrael) offers pious mortal (saint, prophet) respite. (Cf. V233.3.1.1§).
Angel of Death and Devout Man: *Alf* III 8; Burton V 247. Chauvin VI 183-84 No. 349/[pt. 2]; *ANE* 104 No. 158/[pt. 2].□

V233.3.4§, ‡Angel of Death gives mortal choice as to how (when) to die. (Cf. M341.0.5§, V1.1.3.1§).
Angel of Death and Devout Man: *Alf* III 8-9; Burton V 248. Chauvin VI 183-84 No. 349/[pt. 2]; *ANE* 104 No. 158/[pt. 2].□

V233.3.5§, ‡Mortal destined to die offers a substitute to Angel of Death. (Offer rejected).
Angel of Death and Rich King: *Alf* III 9; Burton V 249. Chauvin VI 184-85 No. 350; *ANE* 104-5 No. 159.□

V235, Mortal visited by angel.
Hermit Tempted by Angel: *Alf* II 27,-cf.; Burton III 126. Chauvin II 226 No. 3; *ANE* 221 No. 45/pt. 2.□

V236.5§, Hârût and Mârût as fallen angels. See: *DOTTI*; *GMC*.
Man from Yaman and Six Salve-girls: Flyting: *Alf* II 249,-cf./(poem/simile/Hârût as master magician); Burton IV 258. Chauvin VI 151 No. 313; *ANE* 289-90 No. 84.□

V247.0.1§, ‡Archangels are the chiefs of angels (*al-ru'asâ'*). (Cf. A661.0.1.3.1§, A671.1.1§, A1093.1§).
Bulûqiya: *Alf* III 38,-(four on mission); Burton V 327. Chauvin V 120-24 No. 58; *ANE* 130-32 No. 177.□

V294, ‡The Pope. (Cf. P507.4.2§).
King ¿Umar al-Nu¿mân and Sons: *Alf* I 232; Burton II 222-24. Chauvin VI 112-24 No. 277; *ANE* 430-34 No. 39.□

V298§, ‡The pious (as quasi-sacred persons). (Cf. W4§).
Spy, Fourth Maiden/¿Umar al-Nu¿mân: *Alf* I 222; Burton II 203. *ANE* 432 No. 39/passim;
Jewish qâḍî and His Devout Wife: *Alf* III 10; Burton V 256. Chauvin VI 154-55 No. 321; *ANE* 242 No. 163.□

V298.2§, ‡Pious couple. (Cf. W4§).
Jewish Tray-maker and Temptress: *Alf* III 13-14; Burton V 264-69. Chauvin VI 187-88 No. 354; *ANE* 169 No. 166.□

V298.2.1§, ‡Pious man (husband).
Devotee Prince: Ascetic's Death: *Alf* II 289,-(youth); Burton V 111. Chauvin VI 193-94 No. 363; *ANE* 167-68 No. 134.□

V298.2.2§, ‡Pious woman (wife).
King ¿Umar al-Nu¿mân and Sons: *Alf* I 163,-(concubine, *kânat ¿alâ ṣalâh*); Burton II 280,-("During her pregnancy she was instant in prayer" [??]). Chauvin VI 112-24 No. 277; *ANE* 430-34 No. 39;
Devout Jewess and Wicked Elders: *Alf* II 286; Burton V 97. Chauvin VI 193-93 No. 362; *ANE* 169 No. 128;
Stolen Necklace/Hasty Accusation: *Alf* III 164,-(woman-servant); Burton VI 182-83. Chauvin VIII 53 No. 20; *ANE* 398 No. 200.□

V301.1§, ‡"Deeds are [judged] according to intent (*niyyât*)". See: *DOTTI*. (Cf. C827§, T481.0.1§, U213§, V315.2§, W4.1§).
Ghânim ibn Ayyûb: *Alf* I 157,-(blessedness of intent); Burton II 76. Chauvin VI 14 No. 188; *ANE* 192-93 No. 36;
Spy, Second Maiden/¿Umar al-Nu¿mân: *Alf* I 220-21; Burton II 199,-(works). *ANE* 432 No. 39/passim;

King's Favorite Son and Ogress: *Alf* III 143-44,-(treacherous intent/fin); Burton VI 141. Chauvin VIII 40-41 No. 8B; *ANE* 264 No. 188.□

V301.1.0.1§, ‡Sincerity of intent rewarded (miraculously), insincerity punished. (Cf. Q550.0.1§).
Spy, Fifth Maiden/¿Umar al-Nu¿mân: *Alf* I 223,-(*tashîh al-damâ'ir*); Burton II 205,-(making sound the secret thoughts). *ANE* 432 No. 39/passim;
al-'Amjad and al-'As¿ad: *Alf* II 119,-(*khulûs al-niyyah*); Burton III 321,-(purity of intentions). Chauvin V 208-10 No. 120[.1]; *ANE* 341-42 No. 61/pt. 2;
Hasan of Basrah: *Alf* IV 26,-(*sidqu niyyatik*); Burton VIII 88,-(truth of thine intent). Chauvin 7: 29 No. 212A; *ANE* 207 No. 230.□

V310.1§, ‡Religious universe (all of God's creation, animate and inanimate, worship). (Cf. A6.1§).
Birds, Beasts, and Carpenter: *Alf* II 26; Burton III 125. Chauvin II 225-26 No. 1; *ANE* 126 No. 44.□

V310.6§, ‡'Necessities legitimize (justify) commission of the sinful'. (Cf. G78.1, K1873§, U25, U26§).
Anîs al-Jalîs: *Alf* I 130,-cf.; Burton II 14,-("Need hath its own law"). Chauvin V 120-24 No. 58; *ANE* 316-17 No. 35;
King ¿Umar al-Nu¿mân and Sons: *Alf* I 237; Burton II 236,-(in need evil becometh good deed). Chauvin VI 112-24 No. 277; *ANE* 430-34 No. 39.□

V311.3, Given choice between life and heaven, person chooses latter. See: *DOTTI*.
Jewish Tray-maker and Temptress: *Alf* III 14,-cf./(worldly or afterlife reward); Burton V 268-69. Chauvin VI 187-88 No. 354; *ANE* 169 No. 166.□

V311.3.0.1§, ‡Seek the hereafter, life in the here-and-now is fleeting. (Futility of worldly life: death nullifies all). (Cf. Z42.1.1§).
King ¿Umar al-Nu¿mân and Sons: *Alf* I 192,-(poem/life is like traveler's resting station); Burton II 139. Chauvin VI 112-24 No. 277; *ANE* 430-34 No. 39;
City of Brass: *Alf* III 136; Burton VI 117. Chauvin V 32-35 No. 16; *ANE* 146-50 No. 180;
Two Kings, Just and Unjust: *Alf* IV 149,-cf.; Burton IX 65-67. Chauvin II 221 No. 152/12; *ANE* 422 No. 246.□

V311.4§, ‡Death heralds beginning of eternal life. (Cf. Z10.2.5.1§).
City of Brass: *Alf* III 135; Burton VI 116. Chauvin V 32-35 No. 16; *ANE* 146-50 No. 180.□

V311.4.1§, ‡Life (here-and-now) is only a preparation for the afterlife. (Cf. Z91.0.1§).
Nûr al-Dîn ¿Alî and Son: *Alf* I 68; Burton I 206. Chauvin VI 102-6 No. 270; *ANE* 317-19 No. 22;
King ¿Umar al-Nu¿mân and Sons: *Alf* I 192,-(poem,/life is transitory); Burton II 139,-(like a wanderer's place of rest). Chauvin VI 112-24 No. 277; *ANE* 430-34 No. 39.□

V311.4.2§, ‡For the pious, death is a joyous event (for it signals that meeting God is approaching). (Cf. P617.1§).
Angel of Death and Devout Man: *Alf* III 8-9; Burton V 248. Chauvin VI 183-84 No. 349/[pt. 2]; *ANE* 104 No. 158/[pt. 2].□

V311.5§, Visiting graveyards—as reminder of death and the life to come—is recommended. See: *DOTTI*; *GMC*; *PSAE*. (Cf. L413, V65.7§).
Spy, Second Maiden/¿Umar al-Nu¿mân: *Alf* I 221,-cf.; Burton II 200. *ANE* 432 No. 39/passim;
Devotee Prince: Ascetic's Death: *Alf* II 289; Burton V 111. Chauvin VI 193-94 No. 363; *ANE* 167-68 No. 134.□

V315, Belief in the atonement. See: *GMC*. (Cf. V6§).
Sindbâd's Seventh Voyage: *Alf* III 117,-(*tawbah* from sea-voyaging); Burton VI 70,-("renouncement"). Chauvin VII 26-29 No. 373G; *ANE* 386-87 No. 179.□

V315.0.1§, ‡Repentance (*al-tawbah*) was created to countervail sinning. (Cf. A604.3.1§, U20§).
King Jalî¿âd and Shimâs: *Alf* IV 157; Burton IX 80,-(penitence). Chauvin VI 9-11 No. 184; *ANE* 237-38 No. 236.□

V315.1, Power of repentance. See: *DOTTI*; *GMC*. (Cf. V337§).
Qamar al-Zamân and Budûr: *Alf* II 110,-(poem); Burton III 305. Chauvin V 204-12 No. 120; *ANE* 341-45 No. 61;
Jewish qâdî and His Devout Wife: *Alf* III 10; Burton V 257, 258. Chauvin VI 154-55 No. 321; *ANE* 242 No. 163.□

V315.1.0.1§, ‡Demon repents (atones). (Cf. R181).
City of Brass: *Alf* III 138; Burton VI 121. Chauvin V 32-35 No. 16; *ANE* 146-50 No. 180.□

V315.2§, ‡Repentance intended. See: *DOTTI*. (Cf. V301.1§).
Qamar al-Zamân and Budûr: *Alf* II 110,-(hypocritical); Burton III 305. Chauvin V 204-12 No. 120; *ANE* 341-45 No. 61;
Sindbâd's Seventh Voyage: *Alf* III 117, 121,-(from distant travel); Burton VI 70, 75. Chauvin VII 26-29 No. 373G; *ANE* 386-87 No. 179.□

V315.2.1§, ‡Penitent forswears sinful activity (occupation). (Cf. Q559.12§).
Merchant's Curious Wife: *Alf* I 6,-cf./(curiosity); Burton I 22. Chauvin V 179-80 No. 104; *ANE* 298-99 No. 3;
Ruined Baghdadi and His Slave-girl: *Alf* IV 133,-(singing); Burton IX 32. Chauvin V 152-53 No. 75; *ANE* 353 No. 235;
Abû al-Ḥasan al-Khorâsânî (and Caliph's Favorite): *Alf* IV 236,-(singing); Burton IX 245. Chauvin V 218-20 No. 129; *ANE* 68-69 No. 259;
Shahriyâr and Shahrzâd: *Alf* IV 317,cf.; Burton X 54-55. Chauvin V 190-91 No. 111/pt.; *ANE* 371 No. 1.□

V315.2.2§, ‡Observance of religious services (e.g. pilgrimage, alms-giving, etc.) accompanies repentance and foreswearing sinful activity. (Cf. V532).
Abû al-Ḥasan al-Khorâsânî (and Caliph's Favorite): *Alf* IV 237,-(pilgrimage); Burton IX 245. Chauvin V 218-20 No. 129; *ANE* 68-69 No. 259.□

V315.3§, Sincere repentance obliterates sins and brings redemption (forgiveness). See: *DOTTI*; *GMC*. (Cf. A102.14.3§, Q171.0.1§, V445§).
Debauchee and Three Years Old Child: *Alf* III 176,-cf.; Burton VI 208. Chauvin VIII 62-63 No. 147; *ANE* 166-67 No. 206;
King Jalî¿âd and Shimâs: *Alf* IV 174; Burton IX 118. Chauvin VI 9 No. 184; *ANE* 237-38 No. 236.□

V316, Efficacy of prayer. See: *GMC*. (Cf. M500§).
Prince and Ogress: *Alf* I 20; Burton I 55. Chauvin VI 26 No. 197; *ANE* 329 No. 12;
King's Favorite Son and Ogress: *Alf* III 143; Burton VI 142. Chauvin VIII 40-41 No. 8B; *ANE* 264 No. 188.□

V318§, Fatalism. Belief in predestination, not free-will. See: *DOTTI*; *GMC*. (Cf. N101).
Bulûqiya: *Alf* III 75; Burton V 386. Chauvin VII 54 No. 77; *ANE* 130-32 No. 177;
Poisoning from Flying Kite: *Alf* III 173-74; Burton VI 202. Chauvin VIII 59-60 No. 25; *ANE* 383,/passim No. 181;
King Jalî¿âd and Shimâs: *Alf* IV 155; Burton IX 76. Chauvin VI 9-11 No. 184; *ANE* 237-38 No. 236.□

V318.0.1.2§, ‡Debate as to whether "man is compelled (*musayyar*) or freewilled (*mukhayyr*)".
King Jalî¿âd and Shimâs: *Alf* IV 158; Burton IX 85. Chauvin VI 9-11 No. 184; *ANE* 237-38 No. 236.□

V318.1§, ‡Submission to fate (God's prejudgment: *qaḍâ', qadar*) a mark of true faith. See: *DOTTI*; *PSAE*. (Cf. C61.5§, N190§).
Dûban and King Yûnân: *Alf* I 20,-(poem); Burton I 56. Chauvin V 275-76 No. 156; *ANE* 459 No. 9;
Poisoning from Flying Kite: *Alf* III 173-74; Burton VI 201-2. Chauvin 8: 33-34 No. 1; *ANE* 160-61 No. 181/passim;
Fish and Crab: *Alf* IV 140,-(recommended); Burton IX 45. Chauvin II 219 No. 152/4; *ANE* 185-86 No. 239;
Landsman ¿Abdallah and Merman ¿Abdallah: *Alf* IV 200,-(by merman); Burton IX 170. Chauvin V 6-7 No. 3; *ANE* 65-66 No. 256;
¿Abdallah ibn Fâḍil: Treacherous Brothers: *Alf* IV 269,-cf.; Burton IX 309. Chauvin V 2-4 No. 2; *ANE* 63-65 No. 261.□

V318.1.2.1§, ‡"What God wills becomes; what He does not will does not become".
Qamar al-Zamân and Budûr: *Alf* II 78,-(sexual desire); Burton III 237. Chauvin V 204-12 No. 120; *ANE* 341-45 No. 61.□

V318.1.2.2§, ‡God casts urges (drives, motivation) upon creatures to cause them to act in a certain manner (i.e., falling in love, experiencing sexual desire, etc.).
Tâj al-Mulûk: *Alf* I 264,-(love); Burton II 289-90. Chauvin V 126-28 No. 60; *ANE* 406-8 No. 40;
Qamar al-Zamân and Budûr: *Alf* II 77-78; Burton III 237,-(Allah awoke in him the desire of coition). Chauvin V 204-12 No. 120; *ANE* 341-45 No. 61;

¿Alâ' al-Dîn Abû al-Shâmât: *Alf* II 173,-(love for child); Burton IV 78,-(inclining heart). Chauvin V 43-49 No. 18; *ANE* 85-87 No. 63;
Francolin and Tortoises: *Alf* IV 172,-(upon tortoises); Burton IX 113,-(made him lovely in their eyes). Chauvin II 224 No. 152/23; *ANE* 188 No. 254.□

V318.2§, ‡"Only God is to be thanked for an affliction (*makrûh*: a disliked matter, seeming harm)". See: *DOTTI*. (Cf: Q20.3§).
Spider Upbraids Wind: *Alf* IV 147,-cf./(she-spider/loss of home); Burton IX 59-60. Chauvin II 220 No. 152/10; *ANE* 398 No. 245.□

V318.3§, ‡The seemingly illogical (inexplicable) occurs "for wisdom known [only] to God". (Cf. J164, N190§, V540.0.1§).
King ¿Umar al-Nu¿mân and Sons: *Alf* I 247,-(guards fall asleep); Burton II 256. Chauvin VI 112-24 No. 277; *ANE* 430-34 No. 39;
Sindbâd and Porter: *Alf* III 82; Burton VI 2. Chauvin VII 1 No. 373; *ANE* 383-85 No. 179/pt.□

V318.4§, ‡Questioning God's seemingly inequitable allotment of assets (wealth, beauty, health, etc.) forbidden (mark of lack of faith). (Cf. C61.5§).
Ma¿rûf the Cobbler: *Alf* IV 308-9,-(poem); Burton X 35. Chauvin VI 81-82 No. 250; *ANE* 291-93 No. 262.□

V329§, ‡Heretics, heathens (idolators), and disbelievers—miscellaneous.
Nûr al-Dîn and Maryam: *Alf* IV 128; Burton IX 15. Chauvin V 52-54 No. 271; *ANE* 98-99 No. 233.□

V329.1.1§, ‡Heathen (idolator) refuses to accept God's true religion (Judaism, Christianity, Islam) in spite of knowing "it is the truth". See: *DOTTI*. (Cf. V330.0.1§).
Jinn Imprisoned in Flasks: *Alf* III 127; Burton VI 97. Chauvin VII 113 No. 380=no/text; *ANE* 146 No. 180;
¿Abdallah ibn Fâḍil: Treacherous Brothers: *Alf* IV 277; Burton IX 326. Chauvin V 2-4 No. 2; *ANE* 63-65 No. 261.□

V329.2§, ‡Heresy: deifying a human being—(*'aṣnamah*). (Cf. P507.4.2§).
Wolf and Fox: *Alf* II 30,-(fox deifies wolf); Burton III 133. Chauvin II 227 No. 6; *ANE* 450 No. 47.□

V329.3§, ‡Heresy: rejecting fundamental tenet(s) of faith. (*râfiḍî*). (Cf. K1872.6§).
¿Alâ' al-Dîn Abû al-Shâmât: *Alf* II 172, 174; Burton IV 78,-(Rejecter, a [Shiite]). Chauvin V 43-49 No. 18; *ANE* 85-87 No. 63;
King Jalî¿âd and Shimâs: *Alf* IV 156; Burton IX 79,-("misbelief"). Chauvin VI 9-11 No. 184; *ANE* 237-38 No. 236.□

V330.0.1§, ‡Invitation to convert to the true religion (addressed to heathen or disbeliever). (Cf. V329.1.1§).
Jinn Imprisoned in Flasks: *Alf* III 127,-(Solomon's); Burton VI 97. Chauvin VII 113 No. 380=no/text; *ANE* 146 No. 180;
¿Abdallah ibn Fâḍil: Treacherous Brothers: *Alf* IV 277; Burton IX 324, 326. Chauvin V 2-4 No. 2; *ANE* 63-65 No. 261.□

V330.1§, ‡Reasons for converting from one faith to another (other than belief in its 'correctness'). (Cf. P752.1.1§).
Prior Becomes Moslem: al-Anbârî: *Alf* II 299; Burton V 141. Chauvin V 237-38 No. 137; *ANE* 330-31 No. 147.□

V333§, Conversion to Islam. See: *DOTTI*; *GMC*. (Cf. P529.1.1§).
King ¿Umar al-Nu¿mân and Sons: *Alf* II 21,-(by all); Burton III 114. Chauvin VI 112-24 No. 277; *ANE* 430-34 No. 39;
al-'Amjad and al-'As¿ad: *Alf* II 131-32; Burton III 346. Chauvin V 208-10 No. 120[.1]; *ANE* 341-42 No. 61/pt. 2;
¿Alâ' al-Dîn Abû al-Shâmât: *Alf* II 178; Burton IV 89. Chauvin V 43-49 No. 18; *ANE* 85-87 No. 63;
Conversion of Princess by Khawwâṣ: *Alf* III 15; Burton V 285. Chauvin V 239 No. 139; *ANE* 145 No. 171;
Mercury ¿Alî: *Alf* III 246; Burton VII 207. Chauvin V 248-50 No. 147; *ANE* 301-3 No. 225;
Masrûr and Zayn al-Mawâṣif: *Alf* IV 79; Burton VIII 262. Chauvin VI 82-84 No. 251; *ANE* 294-95 No. 232;

Nûr al-Dîn and Maryam: *Alf* IV 104, 128; Burton VIII 317. Chauvin V 52-54 No. 271; *ANE* 98-99 No. 233;
Man of Upper Egypt and Frankish Wife: Alf IV 16?,-(text missing); Burton IX 22. Chauvin V 240 No. 140; *ANE*: No. 234;
¿Abdallah ibn Fâḍil: Treacherous Brothers: *Alf* IV 277; Burton IX 327. Chauvin V 2-4 No. 2; *ANE* 63-65 No. 261.□

V333.1§, ‡Conversion to Islam through miracle. See: *DOTTI*.
Prior Becomes Moslem: al-Anbârî: *Alf* II 298; Burton V 144. Chauvin V 237-38 No. 137; *ANE* 330-31 No. 147;
Sayf al-Mulûk: *Alf* III 276,-cf.; Burton VII 321. Chauvin VII 64-73 No. 348; *ANE* 362-64 No. 229.□

V334.1§, ‡Moslem jinni (fairy). See: *DOTTI*.
Second Shaykh: Treacherous Brothers: *Alf* I 12; Burton I 35. Chauvin V 6 No. 397; *ANE* 377-78 No. 6;
Porter and Ladies of Baghdad: *Alf* I 60,-(caliph marries *dallâlah*); Burton I 185. Chauvin V 251-52 No. 148; *ANE* 324-26 No. 14;
Nûr al-Dîn ¿Alî and Son: *Alf* I 69,-(*al-jinn al-mu'minîn*); Burton I 211,-(jinn who were of the true believers). Chauvin VI 102-6 No. 270; *ANE* 317-19 No. 22;
Qamar al-Zamân and Budûr: *Alf* II 71; Burton III 224,-(of the true-believing Jinn). Chauvin V 204-12 No. 120; *ANE* 341-45 No. 61;
Abû Muḥammad Lazybones: *Alf* II 212-13,-(in viper form); Burton IV 173,-(serpent). Chauvin VI 64-67 No. 233; *ANE* 71-73 No. 78;
Sayf al-Mulûk: *Alf* III 279,-(king of ...); Burton VII 331. Chauvin VII 64-73 No. 348; *ANE* 362-64 No. 229;
Hasan of Basrah: *Alf* IV 49,-(afrit); Burton VIII 134. Chauvin VII 29-35 No. 212A; *ANE* 207-10 No. 230.□

V337§, ‡Renewal of one's faith. (Usually as confirmation or being 'born-again' in that faith). (Cf. T135.0.2§, V315.1).
¿Alâ' al-Dîn Abû al-Shâmât: *Alf* II 178; Burton IV 90. Chauvin V 43-49 No. 18; *ANE* 85-87 No. 63;
Mercury ¿Alî: *Alf* III 246; Burton VII 207-8. Chauvin V 248-50 No. 147; *ANE* 301-3 No. 225.□

V339.1§, ‡Pretended conversion to a faith while secretly believing in another. (Religious hypocrites). See: *DOTTI*. (Cf. K2010).
¿Alâ' al-Dîn Abû al-Shâmât: *Alf* II 151,-(Magi); Burton IV 38. Chauvin V 43-49 No. 18; *ANE* 85-87 No. 63.□

V351, Duel (debate) to prove which religion is better. See: *DOTTI*.
King ¿Umar al-Nu¿mân and Sons: *Alf* I 168; Burton II 94-95. Chauvin VI 112-24 No. 277; *ANE* 430-34 No. 39.□

V351.1§, ‡Interreligious rivalries. See: *DOTTI*.
Ma¿rûf the Cobbler: *Alf* IV 294,-cf./(Copt-Moslem/children); Burton X 9. Chauvin VI 81-82 No. 250; *ANE* 291-93 No. 262.□

V357§, ‡Holy war (crusade, jihâd-*muqaddas*, etc.). See: *DOTTI*. (Cf. K2360§, P559.1§).
King ¿Umar al-Nu¿mân and Sons: *Alf* I 164,-ff.; Burton II 82. Chauvin VI 112-24 No. 277; *ANE* 430-34 No. 39;
Tâj al-Mulûk: *Alf* I 304; Burton III 39. Chauvin V 126-28 No. 60; *ANE* 406-8 No. 40;
Bulûqiya: *Alf* III 32; Burton V 317. Chauvin VII 54 No. 77; *ANE* 130-32 No. 177;
Jinn Imprisoned in Flasks: *Alf* III 127-28; Burton VI 97-98. Chauvin VII 113 No. 380=no/text; *ANE* 146 No. 180;
Man of Upper Egypt and Frankish Wife: Alf IV 16?,-(text missing); Burton IX 19. Chauvin V 240 No. 140; *ANE*: No. 234.□

V357.2§, ‡Jinn (fairies) wage holy war.
Bulûqiya: *Alf* III 32; Burton V 317,-(war upon the unbelieving Jann). Chauvin VII 54 No. 77; *ANE* 130-32 No. 177.□

V371§, Moslem traditions about *al-kitâbiyyîn* ("People-of-the-Book": Jews and Christians). See: *DOTTI*; *GMC*.
King ¿Umar al-Nu¿mân and Sons: *Alf* I 168; Burton II 95. Chauvin VI 112-24 No. 277; *ANE* 430-34 No. 39;

Nûr al-Dîn and Maryam: *Alf* IV 128; Burton IX 15. Chauvin V 52-54 No. 271; *ANE* 98-99 No. 233.□

V372§, Christian traditions about Moslems.
King ¿Umar al-Nu¿mân and Sons: *Alf* I 168, 186,-cf.; Burton II 95. Chauvin VI 112-24 No. 277; *ANE* 430-34 No. 39.□

V381.0.2.2§, ‡Believer destroys idol to prove to its worshippers (idolator) that it can neither help nor harm.
¿Abdallah ibn Fâḍil: Treacherous Brothers: *Alf* IV 277; Burton IX 324. Chauvin V 2-4 No. 2; *ANE* 63-65 No. 261.□

V381.0.3§, ‡Idol humiliated (i.e., by slapping, spitting, etc.).
¿Abdallah ibn Fâḍil: Treacherous Brothers: *Alf* IV 277,-(slapped on neck); Burton IX 326. Chauvin V 2-4 No. 2; *ANE* 63-65 No. 261.□
V384.0.1§, ‡Interpretation by the overt (literal, *al-ẓâhir, Ẓâhirite*) and interpretation by the covert (veiled, *al-bâṭin, Bâṭinite*). (Cf. H580, Z95.0.1§).
Anîs al-Jalîs: Alf I 140,-(passim); Burton II 29 n. 2. Chauvin V 120-24 No. 58; ANE 316-17 No. 35.□

V384.1.3§, ‡Extreme religious interpretations concerning angels (and similar supernatural beings). (Cf. F499.9.1§).
Dispute Concerning Males and Females: *Alf* II 302,-(nymphs of Paradise); Burton V 160. Chauvin VI 153 No. 317; *ANE* 291 No. 151.□

V400, Charity.
¿Alî Shâr and Zumurrud: *Alf* II 235,-(*taṣaddaqa wa whaba*/gave charity and awarded grants); Burton IV 228. Chauvin V 89-91 No. 28; *ANE* 100-1 No. 82;
Sindbâd's Second Voyage: *Alf* III 92,-(*taṣaddaqa wa whaba*); Burton VI 22,-(gave alms and largesse and bestowed curious gifts and made presents). Chauvin VII 9-14 No. 373B; *ANE* 385 No. 179;
Sindbâd's Third Voyage: *Alf* III 99; Burton VI 34. Chauvin VII 15-18 No. 373C; *ANE* 385-86 No. 179;
Sindbâd's Fourth Voyage: *Alf* III 106; Burton VI 47. Chauvin VII 18-20 No. 373D; *ANE* 386 No. 179;
Sindbâd's Fifth Voyage: *Alf* III 112; Burton VI 57. Chauvin VII 21-24 No. 373E; *ANE* 386 No. 179;

Sindbâd's Sixth Voyage: *Alf* III 116; Burton VI 68. Chauvin VII 24-27 No. 373F; *ANE* 386 No. 179.□

V401§, ‡Charitable endowment (*waqf/'awqâf*): property whose income is to be used for maintaining philanthropic institution (e.g., school, hospital, orphanage, shrine, etc.). (Cf. P775.2.2§, W11).
Jawdar and His Treacherous Brethren: *Alf* III 200-1; Burton VI 254. Chauvin V 257-60 No. 154; *ANE* 244-45 No. 209;
Abû Qîr and Abû Ṣîr: *Alf* IV 197; Burton IX 164. Chauvin V 15-17 No. 10; *ANE* 75-77 No. 255.□

V441, Forgiveness [as religious virtue]. See: *DOTTI*; *GMC*. (Cf. P549.2.1§, P795§, U284.1.1§).
Spy, Old Woman/¿Umar al-Nu¿mân: *Alf* I 225; Burton II 210,-(as excuse). *ANE* 432 No. 39/passim;

Wolf and Fox: *Alf* II 31-32; Burton III 136. Chauvin II 227 No. 6; *ANE* 450 No. 47;
Omar and Young Badawî: Returning to be Executed: *Alf* II 289; Burton V 104. Chauvin V 216 No. 125; *ANE* 429-30 No. 130.□

V441.0.1§, ‡God forgives all except partnerism (polytheism, *shirk*) and causing harm to people (fellow man). (Cf. A102.14.3§).
Spy, Second Maiden/¿Umar al-Nu¿mân: *Alf* I 221,-(poem); Burton II 202. *ANE* 432 No. 39/passim.□

V441.0.2§, ‡'He who forgives a creature of his kind receives forgiveness from the Creator'.
Mouse and Cat: *Alf* IV 135-36; Burton IX 36. Chauvin II 218 No. 152/2; *ANE* 305-6 No. 237.□

V443.3§, Compassion toward animals recommended. See: *DOTTI*; *GMC*. (Cf. P322.7§, Q51).
Landsman ¿Abdallah and Merman ¿Abdallah: *Alf* IV 200; Burton IX 170. Chauvin V 6-7 No. 3; *ANE* 65-66 No. 256.□

V443.3.2§, ‡Sparing life of nursing animal (with young). See: *DOTTI*. (Cf. W14§).

King ¿Umar al-Nu¿mân and Sons: *Alf* II 7,-(to nursing gazelle); Burton III 87. Chauvin VI 112-24 No. 277; *ANE* 430-34 No. 39.□

V445§, Forgiveness (redemption) as divine. (Cf. V315.3§).
Qamar al-Zamân and Budûr: *Alf* II 109; Burton III 304. Chauvin V 204-12 No. 120; *ANE* 341-45 No. 61.□

V461.5.1§, (*khulwah*): cloistered meditation. See: *GMC*. (Cf. V462.8.9§).
Anîs al-Jalîs: *Alf* I 139; Burton II 29. Chauvin V 120-24 No. 58; *ANE* 316-17 No. 35.□

V462, Asceticism [(*taṣawwuf, zuhd*)]. See: *GMC*.
Spy, Second Maiden/¿Umar al-Nu¿mân: *Alf* I 221,-(general); Burton II 201,-(anecdotes of devotees). *ANE* 432 No. 39/passim;
Spy, Third Maiden/¿Umar al-Nu¿mân: *Alf* I 222; Burton II 202. *ANE* 432 No. 39/passim.□

V462.0.1, Kingship renounced to become an ascetic. (Cf. P16.1).
Devotee Prince: Ascetic's Death: *Alf* II 290; Burton V 111. Chauvin VI 193-94 No. 363; *ANE* 167-68 No. 134.□

V462.2.3, Death from ascetic devotions. See: *GMC*. (Cf. T81).
Copt Broker's Story: Lover's Sacrifices Repaid: *Alf* I 95; Burton I 277. Chauvin VI 80 No. 249; *ANE* 313-14 No. 24;
Devotee Prince: Ascetic's Death: *Alf* II 290; Burton V 112. Chauvin VI 193-94 No. 363; *ANE* 167-68 No. 134;
Conversion of Princess by Khawwâṣ: *Alf* III 15-6; Burton V 286. Chauvin V 239 No. 139; *ANE* 145 No. 171.□

V462.2.3.1§, ‡Ascetic dies (faints) from awesomeness of holy thought (passage, image, etc.). (Cf. Z63.7.1§).
Spy, Fourth Maiden/¿Umar al-Nu¿mân: *Alf* I 223,-(gallbladder ruptures/"*'infaṭarat*"); Burton II 205,-(gall bladder bursts). *ANE* 432 No. 39/passim.□

V462.3.1§, ‡Weeping by the pious as worship. (Cf. F1051).
Spy, Third Maiden/¿Umar al-Nu¿mân: *Alf* I 222; Burton II 202. *ANE* 432 No. 39/passim.□

V462.7, Ascetic cleric never smiles. See: *DOTTI*.
Man Who Never Laughs: *Alf* III 152,-cf.; Burton VI 166. Chauvin VIII 47-48 No. 15; *ANE* 285-86 No. 195.□

V462.8.9§, ‡Accompaniments of sufi ascetic worship (*khulwah*). (Cf. V461.5.1§).
Anîs al-Jalîs: *Alf* I 139; Burton II 29. Chauvin V 120-24 No. 58; *ANE* 316-17 No. 35.□

V462.8.9.1§, ‡Marvelous occurrences during ascetic (sufi) worship—(*tagallî/julwât*).
Anîs al-Jalîs: *Alf* I 139; Burton II 29. Chauvin V 120-24 No. 58; *ANE* 316-17 No. 35.□

V463, Religious martyrdom. See: *GMC*. (Cf. N801.1§).
King ¿Umar al-Nu¿mân and Sons: *Alf* I 240; Burton II 242-43. Chauvin VI 112-24 No. 277; *ANE* 430-34 No. 39.□

V463.0.1§, ‡Martyrs are alive (in heavens).
King ¿Umar al-Nu¿mân and Sons: *Alf* I 240,-(*mujâhidîn/'aḥyâ'un ghayru 'amwâtin*); Burton II 242 n. 1,-(the slain live again without suffering death). Chauvin VI 112-24 No. 277; *ANE* 430-34 No. 39.□

V463.7.1§, ‡Martyrdom: giving own life for a religious cause ('for the sake of God').
King ¿Umar al-Nu¿mân and Sons: *Alf* I 240; Burton II 242. Chauvin VI 112-24 No. 277; *ANE* 430-34 No. 39.□

V463.7.3§, ‡Martyrdom: being unjustly killed (executed).
Eldest Lady's Story: Treacherous Sisters: *Alf* I 56,-(drowning); Burton I 171. Chauvin V 4 No. 443; *ANE* 174-75 No. 19.□

V463.7.4§, ‡Martyrdom: dying from (for) love. (Cf. T81, W13§).
¿Azîz and ¿Azîzah: *Alf* I 282,-(poem), 286,-(xxx); Burton II 325-30 n. 1,-("her youth was lost on Allah's way"). Chauvin V 144-45 No. 71; *ANE* 111-13 No. 41.□

V463.7.5§, ‡Martyrdom: dying accidental, unnatural (violent) death (e.g., drowning, burning, etc.). See: *DOTTI*; *PSAE*.

Eldest Lady's Story: Treacherous Sisters: *Alf* I 56,-(drowning); Burton I 171. Chauvin V 4 No. 443; *ANE* 174-75 No. 19;
Sindbâd's Third Voyage: *Alf* III 96,-(drowning); Burton VI 26. Chauvin VII 15-18 No. 373C; *ANE* 385-86 No. 179;
¿Abdallah ibn Fâḍil: Treacherous Brothers: *Alf* IV 284; Burton IX 340. Chauvin V 2-4 No. 2; *ANE* 63-65 No. 261.□

V465.1.1, ‡Incontinent monk (priest).
Masrûr and Zayn al-Mawâṣif: *Alf* IV 77,-(monk); Burton VIII 256. Chauvin VI 82-84 No. 251; *ANE* 294-95 No. 232.□

V469.1.1§, ‡Luke as the falsifier of the Evangel.
King ¿Umar al-Nu¿mân and Sons: *Alf* I 234,-(*muḥarrif al-'injîl*); Burton II 226. Chauvin VI 112-24 No. 277; *ANE* 430-34 No. 39.□

V510.0.1§, ‡Visions of God's domain.
Bulûqiya: *Alf* III 79; Burton V 393,-(seven Heavens and all that therein). Chauvin VII 54 No. 77; *ANE* 130-32 No. 177;
Three Wishes: *Alf* III 162; Burton VI 181. Chauvin VIII 51-52 No. 19; *ANE* 419-20 No. 199.□

V511.1.3§, ‡Visions of rewards in heaven (paradise). See: *DOTTI*.
Prior Becomes Moslem: al-Anbârî: *Alf* II 299; Burton V 143. Chauvin V 237-38 No. 137; *ANE* 330-31 No. 147.□

V514, Non-religious visions. See: *GMC*.
Tâj al-Mulûk: *Alf* I 299; Burton III 31. Chauvin V 126-28 No. 60; *ANE* 406-8 No. 40;
Hasan of Basrah: *Alf* IV 39; Burton VIII 113-14. Chauvin VII 29-35 No. 212A; *ANE* 207-10 No. 230;
Masrûr and Zayn al-Mawâṣif: *Alf* IV 55; Burton VIII 205. Chauvin VI 82-84 No. 251; *ANE* 294-95 No. 232;
King Jalî¿âd and Shimâs: *Alf* IV 135; Burton IX 34. Chauvin VI 9-11 No. 184; *ANE* 237-38 No. 236.□

V515, Allegorical visions.
Tâj al-Mulûk: *Alf* I 299; Burton III 31. Chauvin V 126-28 No. 60; *ANE* 406-8 No. 40.□

V515.1, Allegorical visions—religious. See: *DOTTI*; *GMC*.
Prior Becomes Moslem: al-Anbârî: *Alf* II 299,-(paradise); Burton V 143. Chauvin V 237-38 No. 137; *ANE* 330-31 No. 147.□

V515.1.1, ‡Vision of chairs (thrones) in heaven. Chairs of gold, silver, crystal (glass) assigned to saints according to merit. See: *DOTTI*.
Jewish Tray-maker and Temptress: *Alf* III 14; Burton V 268. Chauvin VI 187-88 No. 354; *ANE* 169 No. 166.□

V515.2, Allegorical visions—political. See: *DOTTI*; *GMC*.
King ¿Umar al-Nu¿mân and Sons: *Alf* II 11; Burton III 95. Chauvin VI 112-24 No. 277; *ANE* 430-34 No. 39.□

V517§, Instructive sleeper's-vision or dream (*ru'yah, manâm*). See: *DOTTI*; *GMC*; *PSAE*. (Cf. G302.9.6, J157).
Third Qalandar: Magnetic Mountain: *Alf* I 52; Burton I 142. Chauvin V 200-3 No. 117; *ANE* 340-41 No. 18;
Nûr al-Dîn ¿Alî and Son: *Alf* I 69; Burton I 210. Chauvin VI 102-6 No. 270; *ANE* 317-19 No. 22;
Tâj al-Mulûk: *Alf* I 299; Burton III 31. Chauvin V 126-28 No. 60; *ANE* 406-8 No. 40;
Hermit Tempted by Angel: *Alf* II 27; Burton III 127. Chauvin II 226 No. 3; *ANE* 221 No. 45/pt. 2;
Ḥâtim's Hospitality: *Alf* II 181; Burton IV 96. Chauvin VI 49 No. 215; *ANE* 216 No. 64;
Mercury ¿Alî: *Alf* III 243; Burton VII 203. Chauvin V 248-50 No. 147; *ANE* 301-3 No. 225;
Hasan of Basrah: *Alf* IV 38-39; Burton VIII 113. Chauvin VII 29-35 No. 212A; *ANE* 207-10 No. 230.□

V521.1.1§, Prophet Mohammed as the Intercessor (*ash-shafî¿*).
Shipwrecked Woman and Her Child: *Alf* III 12,-(poem); Burton V 261. Chauvin VI 160 No. 324; *ANE* 379 No. 164;
Landsman ¿Abdallah and Merman ¿Abdallah: *Alf* IV 203; Burton IX 178. Chauvin V 6-7 No. 3; *ANE* 65-66 No. 256.□

V532, Pilgrimage to Mecca. See: *DOTTI*; *GMC*. (Cf. V315.2.2§).
Jawdar and His Treacherous Brethren: *Alf* III 194,-(circumambulation); Burton VI 242. Chauvin V 257-60 No. 154; *ANE* 244-45 No. 209;
Abû al-Ḥasan al-Khorâsânî (and Caliph's Favorite): *Alf* IV 237,-(passim); Burton IX 245. Chauvin V 218-20 No. 129; *ANE* 68-69 No. 259.□

V535, ‡Pilgrimage to Jerusalem. See: *DOTTI*. (Cf. V85.0.1.3§).
King ¿Umar al-Nu¿mân and Sons: *Alf* I 187; Burton II 132. Chauvin VI 112-24 No. 277; *ANE* 430-34 No. 39;
Jewish qâḍî and His Devout Wife: *Alf* III 10; Burton V 256. Chauvin VI 154-55 No. 321; *ANE* 242 No. 163.□

V540.0.1§, ‡Providence (God's wisdom) is behind seemingly apparent injustice (i.e., 'The Lord moves in mysterious ways'). See: *DOTTI*. (Cf. N190§, V318.3§).
Shipwrecked Woman and Her Child: *Alf* III 12,-(poem/*lutf khafiyy*); Burton V 261. Chauvin VI 160 No. 324; *ANE* 379 No. 164;
Spider Upbraids Wind: *Alf* IV 147; Burton IX 59-60. Chauvin II 220 No. 152/10; *ANE* 398 No. 245.□

V540.1§, ‡New lifespan willed ('written') by God for mortal (creature).
Sindbâd's First Voyage: *Alf* III 87; Burton VI 12. Chauvin VII 7-9 No. 373A; *ANE* 385 No. 179.□

V544§, God furnishes substitute (ram) for human sacrifice. See: *GMC*. (Cf. V12.1.1§, V76§).
¿Alâ' al-Dîn Abû al-Shâmât: *Alf* II 171,-(passim); Burton IV 75. Chauvin V 43-49 No. 18; *ANE* 85-87 No. 63.□

V546§, ‡Person about to be swallowed by monster is saved by a natural phenomenon (storm, earthquake, etc.). (Cf. N255).
Sindbâd's Seventh Voyage: *Alf* III 117; Burton VI 70. Chauvin VII 26-29 No. 373G; *ANE* 386-87 No. 179.□

W. TRAITS OF CHARACTER

W3§, *'ibn-ḥalâl* ('of legitimate birth', i.e., of good character, noble). See: *DOTTI*; *GMC*. (Cf. W103§, W251§).
Jawdar and His Treacherous Brethren: *Alf* III 194; Burton VI 243,("the ingenuous"). Chauvin V 257-60 No. 154; *ANE* 244-45 No. 209;
Abû Qîr and Abû Ṣîr: *Alf* IV 196; Burton IX 162,-("flower of the well-born"). Chauvin V 15-17 No. 10; *ANE* 75-77 No. 255.□

W3.0.1§, ‡Conduct (behavior, traits) of person of noble character. See: *DOTTI*. (Cf. W11.5.0.3.1§).
Jawdar and His Treacherous Brethren: *Alf* III 194; Burton VI 243. Chauvin V 257-60 No. 154; *ANE* 244-45 No. 209;
Abû Qîr and Abû Ṣîr: *Alf* IV 196; Burton IX 162. Chauvin V 15-17 No. 10; *ANE* 75-77 No. 255.□

W4§, ‡Religiosity (piety): most favorable trait of character. See: *DOTTI*. (Cf. H69§, K2058.2§, V298§).
Nuzhat al-Zamân Tested/¿Umar al-Nu¿mân: *Alf* I 204,-(poem,/fear of God/*taqwâ Allâh*); Burton II 166,-(most pious). Chauvin VI 112-124 No. 277; *ANE* 432,/passim No. 39;
Spy, Third Maiden/¿Umar al-Nu¿mân: *Alf* I 222; Burton II 202. *ANE* 432 No. 39/passim;
Devout Jewess and Wicked Elders: *Alf* II 286; Burton V 97-98. Chauvin VI 193-93 No. 362; *ANE* 169 No. 128;
Jewish Tray-maker and Temptress: *Alf* III 13; Burton V 264-69. Chauvin VI 187-88 No. 354; *ANE* 169 No. 166.□

W4.1§, ‡Being motivated solely by consideration of God's commandments (i.e., doing or avoiding 'for God's sake'—not for secular consideration). See: *DOTTI*. (Cf. V301.1§, V400, W11).
Nûr al-Dîn ¿Alî and Son: *Alf* I 70,-(afrit/jinni helps hero); Burton I 214. Chauvin VI 102-6 No. 270; *ANE* 317-19 No. 22;
Spy, Second Maiden/¿Umar al-Nu¿mân: *Alf* I 221,-(Israelites); Burton II 201-2. *ANE* 432 No. 39/passim;
Tawaddud: Slavegirl Sold and Regained: *Alf* II 313-14,(*al-khalîl*); Burton V 216,-(detached from the world in the love of Allah ...). Chauvin VII 117-19 No. 387; *ANE* 408-10 No. 157;
Man of Upper Egypt and Frankish Wife: Alf IV 16?,-(text missing); Burton IX 20-21. Chauvin V 240 No. 140; *ANE*: No. 234;
Abû Qîr and Abû Ṣîr: *Alf* IV 188,-(porter); Burton IX 146. Chauvin V 15-17 No. 10; *ANE* 75-77 No. 255.□

W4.2§, ‡Creature (animal, plant, inanimate object, etc.) that praises or worships favored.
Hermit and Pigeons: *Alf* II 27; Burton III 126. Chauvin II 226 No. 2; *ANE* 221 No. 45/pt. 1.□

W4.2.1§, ‡Hermit (anchorite, monk, saint) prefers dove (pigeon) for company. (Its cooing is worship). (Cf. H887.2§).
Hermit and Pigeons: *Alf* II 27; Burton III 126. Chauvin II 226 No. 2; *ANE* 221 No. 45/pt. 1.□

W4.3§, ‡Pious (just) person motivated by thought of standing before (answering to) God at Judgment Day. See: *DOTTI*. (Cf. J3.2.4§, V3.9.2.3§, V298§).
Nuzhat al-Zamân Tested/¿Umar al-Nu¿mân: *Alf* I 203, 206; Burton II 162,-(Resurrection Day), 170. Chauvin VI 116, n.1/passim No. 277; *ANE* 432,/passim No. 39.□

W10, Kindness. (Cf. J1514§).
¿Alî ibn Bakkâr: *Alf* II 41,-cf.; Burton III 163. Chauvin V 153 No. 76; *ANE* 92-93 No. 60.□

W10.3§, ‡Person so kind that he does not turn down any request (i.e., cause disappointment, or injured pride). (Cf. W164.2§).
Ma¿rûf the Cobbler: *Alf* IV 296; Burton X 12. Chauvin VI 81-82 No. 250; *ANE* 291-93 No. 262.□

W10.3.1.1§, ‡'The Prophet accepted a gift, [so should you]!'. (Cf. P788.2§).
¿Alâ' al-Dîn Abû al-Shâmât: *Alf* II 162; Burton IV 60. Chauvin V 43-49 No. 18; *ANE* 85-87 No. 63.□

W10.3.2§, ‡Gift accepted (in principle), and instantly 'presented' back to giver.
King ¿Umar al-Nu¿mân and Sons: *Alf* II 2; Burton III 76,-(steed). Chauvin VI 112-24 No. 277; *ANE* 430-34 No. 39;
Sayf al-Mulûk: *Alf* III 291; Burton VII 355. Chauvin VII 64-73 No. 348; *ANE* 362-64 No. 229;

Nûr al-Dîn and Maryam: *Alf* IV 89; Burton VIII 286. Chauvin V 52-54 No. 271; *ANE* 98-99 No. 233.□

W10.9.1§, ‡Kindness: nursing the sick. See: *DOTTI*. (Cf. Q57).
Ghânim ibn Ayyûb: *Alf* I 158-59; Burton II 69. Chauvin VI 14 No. 188; *ANE* 192-93 No. 36;
King ¿Umar al-Nu¿mân and Sons: *Alf* I 189-90; Burton II 135-37. Chauvin VI 112-24 No. 277; *ANE* 430-34 No. 39;
Nûr al-Dîn and Maryam: *Alf* IV 104; Burton VIII 317. Chauvin V 52-54 No. 271; *ANE* 98-99 No. 233;
Abû Qîr and Abû Ṣîr: *Alf* IV 188; Burton IX 146. Chauvin V 15-17 No. 10; *ANE* 75-77 No. 255.□

W10.9.2§, ‡Person seemingly dead (fatally wounded) is nursed back to health. See: *DOTTI*. (Cf. E68, N327§).
Ensorcelled Prince/Husband: *Alf* I 29,-cf.; Burton I 74. Chauvin VI 56-58 No. 222; *ANE* 176 No. 13;
Ghânim ibn Ayyûb: *Alf* I 151; Burton II 57. Chauvin VI 14 No. 188; *ANE* 192-93 No. 36;
King ¿Umar al-Nu¿mân and Sons: *Alf* I 189; Burton II 135-37. Chauvin VI 112-24 No. 277; *ANE* 430-34 No. 39.□

W10.9.4§, ‡Pity felt for the afflicted: act of kindness follows. See: *DOTTI*.
Abû Muḥammad Lazybones: *Alf* II 208; Burton IV 167. Chauvin VI 64-67 No. 233; *ANE* 71-73 No. 78.□

W10.9.4.1§, ‡Lady sees a man grieving over loss of all his belongings: she gives him money out of pity.
Barber's Fifth Brother: Daydreams/Defeats Robbers: *Alf* I 118; Burton I 339. Chauvin V 161 No. 85; *ANE* 119-20 No. 33.□

W10.9.5.1.6.1§, ‡Animal spared cruel treatment by own kind.
Abû Muḥammad Lazybones: *Alf* II 208; Burton IV 167. Chauvin VI 64-67 No. 233; *ANE* 71-73 No. 78.□

W11, Generosity [and philanthropy]. See: *DOTTI*; *GMC*. (Cf. J708.5§, P320, P775.2.2§, P795.0.4.1§).
Nuzhat al-Zamân Tested/¿Umar al-Nu¿mân: *Alf* I 202,-(poem); Burton II 159-60. Chauvin VI 112-124 No. 277; *ANE* 432,/passim No. 39;
Tawaddud: Slavegirl Sold and Regained: *Alf* III 8,-(Abbasids); Burton V 245. Chauvin VII 117-19 No. 387; *ANE* 408-10 No. 157.□

W11.0.1§, Philanthropy: giving without expectations of repayment. See: *DOTTI*. (Cf. P339.3§, W14.0.2§).
Sindbâd's Second Voyage: *Alf* III 92,-(*taṣaddaqa wa whaba*); Burton VI 22,-(gave alms and largesse and bestowed curious gifts and made presents). Chauvin VII 9-14 No. 373B; *ANE* 385 No. 179;
Sindbâd's Third Voyage: *Alf* III 99; Burton VI 34. Chauvin VII 15-18 No. 373C; *ANE* 385-86 No. 179;
Sindbâd's Fourth Voyage: *Alf* III 106; Burton VI 47. Chauvin VII 18-20 No. 373D; *ANE* 386 No. 179;
Sindbâd's Fifth Voyage: *Alf* III 112; Burton VI 57. Chauvin VII 21-24 No. 373E; *ANE* 386 No. 179;

Sindbâd's Sixth Voyage: *Alf* III 116; Burton VI 68. Chauvin VII 24-27 No. 373F; *ANE* 386 No. 179.□

W11.5, Generosity toward enemy. (Cf. J26, K2059.9.2§, W14§, Q264§, W12.6§).
Jânshâh: *Alf* III 72,-(aggressor king captured and forgiven); Burton V 376. Chauvin VII 39-44 No. 153; *ANE* 238-41 No. 178.□

W11.5.0.1§, ‡Enemy's evil deeds met (repaid) with good ones. See: *DOTTI*. (Cf. Q264§, W154.0.1§, V441).
Ghânim ibn Ayyûb: *Alf* I 159; Burton II 71. Chauvin VI 14 No. 188; *ANE* 192-93 No. 36;
Ḥammâd: Treacherous Bedouin: *Alf* II 19; Burton III 110. Chauvin VI 124 n. 1 No. 277; *ANE* 200 No. 43;
Ma¿n Rewards a Bedouin for Gift: *Alf* II 182-83,-cf.; Burton IV 99. Chauvin VI 78 No. 247; *ANE* 291 No. 66.□

W11.5.0.3§, ‡Forgiveness as personal virtue. See: *DOTTI*. (Cf. P549.2.1§, P795§, V441).

Anîs al-Jalîs: *Alf* I 129,-(implicit/father-forgives son); Burton II 9. Chauvin V 120-24 No. 58; *ANE* 316-17 No. 35;
Nuzhat al-Zamân Tested/¿Umar al-Nu¿mân: *Alf* I 202,-(poem); Burton II 160,-(mercy). Chauvin VI 112-124 No. 277; *ANE* 432,/passim No. 39;
Wolf and Fox: *Alf* II 30,-(poem); Burton III 136. Chauvin II 227 No. 6; *ANE* 450 No. 47;
Omar and Young Badawî: Returning to be Executed: *Alf* II 289; Burton V 104. Chauvin V 216 No. 125; *ANE* 429-30 No. 130;
Jewish qâḍî and His Devout Wife: *Alf* III 11; Burton V 258. Chauvin VI 154-55 No. 321; *ANE* 242 No. 163;
Stolen Necklace/Hasty Accusation: *Alf* III 164; Burton VI 183. Chauvin VIII 53 No. 20; *ANE* 398 No. 200. □

W11.5.0.3.0.1§, ‡'Forgiving is [to forego punishment] when capable [to punish]'.
Wolf and Fox: *Alf* II 31-32; Burton III 136. Chauvin II 227 No. 6; *ANE* 450 No. 47;
Ni¿mah and Nu¿m: Stolen Wife Regained: *Alf* II 143; Burton IV 21. Chauvin VI 96-97 No. 263; *ANE* 314 No. 62;
Tawaddud: Slavegirl Sold and Regained: *Alf* II 309; Burton V 207,-(mercy). Chauvin VII 117-19 No. 387; *ANE* 408-10 No. 157. □

W11.5.0.3.1§, ‡'Forgiveness is a trait of the noble'. See: *DOTTI*. (Cf. W3§).
Wolf and Fox: *Alf* II 30; Burton III 136,-(forgiveness). Chauvin II 227 No. 6; *ANE* 450 No. 47;
King Jalî¿âd and Shimâs: *Alf* IV 176; Burton IX 120,-(clemency). Chauvin VI 9 No. 184; *ANE* 237-38 No. 236. □

W11.5.0.3.3§, ‡'A vile forgives not even when able [to pardon]'. (Cf. W103§).
Abû Qîr and Abû Ṣîr: *Alf* IV 187,-(competitors); Burton IX 145. Chauvin V 15-17 No. 10; *ANE* 75-77 No. 255. □

W11.5.1.2§, ‡Victim pardons (forgives) oppressor. See: *DOTTI*. (Cf. P212.3§).
Water-carrier and Goldsmith's Wife: *Alf* II 286,-(attempted seduction); Burton V 90. Chauvin VI 192 No. 361; *ANE* 444 No. 122. □

W11.7.3§, ‡Impoverished nobleman unwillingly sells beloved slave-girl; buyer takes notice of their love and gives her back (as gift). See: *DOTTI*. (Cf. P185.3.1§, Q56.4§).
Tawaddud: Slavegirl Sold and Regained: *Alf* II 305,-cf.; Burton V 193. Chauvin VII 117-19 No. 387; *ANE* 408-10 No. 157. □

W11.17.1§, ‡Generous gambler: gives winnings back to loser.
Masrûr and Zayn al-Mawâṣif: *Alf* IV 57-59; Burton VIII 216-18. Chauvin VI 82-84 No. 251; *ANE* 294-95 No. 232. □

W12, Hospitality as a virtue. See: *DOTTI*; *GMC*.
Ma¿rûf the Cobbler: *Alf* IV 304; Burton X 27. Chauvin VI 81-82 No. 250; *ANE* 291-93 No. 262. □

W12.2.0.1§, ‡'The Prophet recommended [hospitality to] the stranger'. (Cf. P305.1.1.1§, P320).
Anîs al-Jalîs: *Alf* I 136; Burton II 23. Chauvin V 120-24 No. 58; *ANE* 316-17 No. 35;
Fox and Crow: *Alf* II 37,-cf.; Burton III 150. Chauvin II 228 No. 11; *ANE* 188 No. 51. □

W12.2.2§, ‡Hospitable person cannot eat except with guests (strangers). (Cf. P320).
Sindbâd's First Voyage: *Alf* III 88,-cf.; Burton VI 13-14. Chauvin VII 7-9 No. 373A; *ANE* 385 No. 179;
Abû al-Ḥasan al-Khorâsânî (and Caliph's Favorite): *Alf* IV 229; Burton IX 229-30. Chauvin V 218-20 No. 129; *ANE* 68-69 No. 259. □

W12.5.1§, ‡Interreligious hospitality: hospitality to member(s) of opposing religion (usually during time of open conflict).
Copt Broker's Story: Lover's Sacrifices Repaid: *Alf* I 89,-cf.; Burton I 264. Chauvin VI 80 No. 249; *ANE* 313-14 No. 24;
Prior Becomes Moslem: al-Anbârî: *Alf* II 298; Burton V 141. Chauvin V 237-38 No. 137; *ANE* 330-31 No. 147. □

W12.5.1.1§, ‡Christian hospitable to Moslem in frontier town (or vice versa).
Prior Becomes Moslem: al-Anbârî: *Alf* II 298; Burton V 141. Chauvin V 237-38 No. 137; *ANE* 330-31 No. 147. □

W12.6§, ‡Hospitality to enemy (adversary). (Cf. W11.5).

Jeweler's Wife and Qamar al-Zamân: *Alf* IV 260,-(betrayed husband); Burton IX 294. Chauvin V 212-14 No. 121; *ANE* 345-47 No. 260.□

W13§, Self-abnegation (altruism, self-denial, selflessness). See: *DOTTI*; *GMC*. (Cf. V463.7.4§).
Spy, Old Woman/¿Umar al-Nu¿mân: *Alf* I 224-25,-(Imam al-Shâfi¿î); Burton II 207-8. *ANE* 432 No. 39/passim.□

W14§, *shahâmah, nakhwah, murû'ah* (gallantry, chivalry, courtliness, graciousness). See: *DOTTI*. (Cf. J1847.5§, W11.5).
Barber's Tale of Himself: Joins Doomed Party: *Alf* I 110,-(*murû'ah*); Burton I 318. Chauvin V 156-57 No. 80; *ANE* 115-17 No. 28;
Lover Who Feigned Himself a Thief: *Alf* II 205; Burton IV 155-59. Chauvin VII 134-35 No. 403; *ANE* 272 No. 76.□

W14.0.1§, ‡Kindness as *murû'ah* (chivalry, etc.). See: *DOTTI*. (Cf. V443.3.2§).
Spy, Fifth Maiden/¿Umar al-Nu¿mân: *Alf* I 223,-(Moses helps shepherdess); Burton II 206. *ANE* 432 No. 39/passim;
King ¿Umar al-Nu¿mân and Sons: *Alf* II 7,-(to nursing gazelle); Burton III 87. Chauvin VI 112-24 No. 277; *ANE* 430-34 No. 39.□

W14.0.2§, ‡Helpfulness (without expectation of reward). (*ma¿rûf*). See: *DOTTI*. (Cf. J708.8§, W11.0.1§).
First Qalandar: Brother-Sister Incest: *Alf* I 39; Burton I 104. Chauvin V 196-97 No. 115; *ANE* 337-38 No. 15;
Abû Qîr and Abû Ṣîr: *Alf* IV 188; Burton IX 145. Chauvin V 15-17 No. 10; *ANE* 75-77 No. 255.□

W14.0.3§, ‡Protection given to fugitive who asks for it (*'istijârah/'ijârah*). (Protector imperils self).
Second Qalandar: Afrit's Wife: *Alf* I 47,-(monkey); Burton I 127. Chauvin V 197-200 No. 116; *ANE* 338-39 No. 16;
¿Alâ' al-Dîn Abû al-Shâmât: *Alf* II 175; Burton IV 83. Chauvin V 43-49 No. 18; *ANE* 85-87 No. 63;
Hasan of Basrah: *Alf* IV 24; Burton VIII 84. Chauvin VII 29-35 No. 212A; *ANE* 207-10 No. 230.□

W14.1.2§, ‡Pity-evoking thief granted the loot by owner. (Cf. U25).
Copt Broker's Story: Lover's Sacrifices Repaid: *Alf* I 94; Burton I 274. Chauvin VI 80 No. 249; *ANE* 313-14 No. 24.□

W14.4.1§, ‡Chivalry: refusal to fight a woman. See: *DOTTI*.
King ¿Umar al-Nu¿mân and Sons: *Alf* II 5,-(*¿âr* to kill); Burton III 82. Chauvin VI 112-24 No. 277; *ANE* 430-34 No. 39.□

W14.4.3.1§, ‡Christian heroine (warrior-maiden) refuses to duel with a lone Moslem hero who challenged her at her own home (camp).
King ¿Umar al-Nu¿mân and Sons: *Alf* I 168; Burton II 94. Chauvin VI 112-24 No. 277; *ANE* 430-34 No. 39.□

W14.5§, Husband instructs adulteress wife to go to her parents' home, to demand divorce, and to reject his offers of reconciliation. See: *GMC*. (Cf. P788.2.1§).
House with the Belvedere: *Alf* III 169,-cf./(wife innocent); Burton VI 194. Chauvin VIII 57-58 No. 23; *ANE* 223 No. 203.□

W14.6.1§, ‡Lover caught while on clandestine visit to his beloved claims to be a thief in order to protect her reputation (honor). (Cf. J224.2§, Q451.1.1, T40§).
Lover Who Feigned Himself a Thief: *Alf* II 204; Burton IV 158. Chauvin VII 134-35 No. 403; *ANE* 272 No. 76.□

W14.8§, ‡Right to a woman (girl) surrendered or claimed as an act of gallantry. See: *DOTTI*.
Anîs al-Jalîs: *Alf* I 142; Burton II 35. Chauvin V 120-24 No. 58; *ANE* 316-17 No. 35;
Man from Yaman and Six Salve-girls: Flyting: *Alf* II 250; Burton IV 260. Chauvin VI 151 No. 313; *ANE* 289-90 No. 84;
Tawaddud: Slavegirl Sold and Regained: *Alf* III 8; Burton V 245. Chauvin VII 117-19 No. 387; *ANE* 408-10 No. 157;
Ruined Baghdadi and His Slave-girl: *Alf* IV 132; Burton IX 24-32. Chauvin V 152-53 No. 75; *ANE* 353 No. 235.□

W14.8.2§, ‡New owner surrenders purchased slave-girl to previous owner. (Cf. P173.9.5§).

Man from Yaman and Six Salve-girls: Flyting: *Alf* II 250; Burton IV 260. Chauvin VI 151 No. 313; *ANE* 289-90 No. 84.□

W14.8.4§, ‡Trespasses by woman (maiden) and her lover forgiven so that they may be united. (Cf. T39.1.4§).
Lover Who Feigned Himself a Thief: *Alf* II 205; Burton IV 158-59. Chauvin VII 134-35 No. 403; *ANE* 272 No. 76;
Abû al-Ḥasan al-Khorâsânî (and Caliph's Favorite): *Alf* IV 237; Burton IX 244. Chauvin V 218-20 No. 129; *ANE* 68-69 No. 259.□

W17§, ‡Cheerfulness (pleasantness). Being of bright and smiling face, friendly, sociable, etc. (Cf. F580§).
¿Alî ibn Bakkâr: *Alf* II 41; Burton III 163. Chauvin V 153 No. 76; *ANE* 92-93 No. 60;
Sindbâd and Porter: *Alf* III 83; Burton VI 3. Chauvin VII 1 No. 373; *ANE* 383-85 No. 179/pt.□

W22.3.1§, ‡Aversion to estrangement from homeland (*ghurbah*, strangerhood, exile-like). (Cf. P191.1.5§).
Water-fowl and Tortoise: *Alf* II 28-29,-(*waḥshah*); Burton III 129. Chauvin II 226-27 No. 5; *ANE* 444 No. 46;
Qamar al-Zamân and Budûr: *Alf* II 98; Burton III 282. Chauvin V 204-12 No. 120; *ANE* 341-45 No. 61;
Devotee Prince: Ascetic's Death: *Alf* II 292,-(poem); Burton V 116. Chauvin VI 193-94 No. 363; *ANE* 167-68 No. 134;
Bulûqiya: *Alf* III 74; Burton V 384. Chauvin VII 54 No. 77; *ANE* 130-32 No. 177;
Sindbâd's First Voyage: *Alf* III 86; Burton VI 10. Chauvin VII 7-9 No. 373A; *ANE* 385 No. 179.□

W22.3.1.1§, ‡Living as a stranger in foreign land is like building palaces on wind (castles on sand). (Cf. P712§, P191.0.2.1§).
Mercury ¿Alî: *Alf* III 228,-(poem); Burton VII 175. Chauvin V 248-50 No. 147; *ANE* 301-3 No. 225.□

W22.3.3.3§, ‡Never left home, neither to condole nor to congratulate.
Dalîla the Swindler: *Alf* III 214; Burton VII 149. Chauvin V 248-50 No. 147; *ANE* 163-64 No. 224.□

W25.0.1.1§, ‡Equanimity recommended.
Nuzhat al-Zamân Tested/¿Umar al-Nu¿mân: *Alf* I 202,-(poem); Burton II 160,-(ruth and mildness). Chauvin VI 112-124 No. 277; *ANE* 432,/passim No. 39;
Jawdar and His Treacherous Brethren: *Alf* III 195,-(*ḥalîm*); Burton VI 248,-("merciful"). Chauvin V 257-60 No. 154; *ANE* 244-45 No. 209.□

W26, Patience. See: *DOTTI*; *GMC*. (Cf. Z95.1§).
Ensorcelled Prince/Husband: *Alf* I 29,-(poem); Burton I 74. Chauvin VI 56-58 No. 222; *ANE* 176 No. 13;
Spider Upbraids Wind: *Alf* IV 147,-(spider's); Burton IX 59. Chauvin II 220 No. 152/10; *ANE* 398 No. 245.□

W26.0.1.2§, ‡'Patience is good' [i.e., (recommended)]. See: *DOTTI*. (Cf. J850§).
Second Qalandar: Afrit's Wife: *Alf* I 50,-(poem); Burton I 138. Chauvin V 197-200 No. 116; *ANE* 338-39 No. 16;
King ¿Umar al-Nu¿mân and Sons: *Alf* I 314,-(recommended); Burton III 61. Chauvin VI 112-24 No. 277; *ANE* 430-34 No. 39;
¿Alâ' al-Dîn Abû al-Shâmât: *Alf* II 158,-(poem); Burton IV 54. Chauvin V 43-49 No. 18; *ANE* 85-87 No. 63;
Masrûr and Zayn al-Mawâṣif: *Alf* IV 72; Burton VIII 243. Chauvin VI 82-84 No. 251; *ANE* 294-95 No. 232.□

W26.0.2.1.1§, ‡Don't live on borrowed funds: live on earnings (profits from investments).
Ma¿rûf the Cobbler: *Alf* IV 296; Burton X 14. Chauvin VI 81-82 No. 250; *ANE* 291-93 No. 262.□

W26.1§, Job's patience. See: *DOTTI*; *GMC*.
¿Azîz and ¿Azîzah: *Alf* I 277; Burton II 315. Chauvin V 144-45 No. 71; *ANE* 111-13 No. 41.□

W27, Gratitude. See: *DOTTI*; *GMC*. (Cf. J708.8§).
Ensorcelled Prince/Husband: *Alf* I 29,-(poem); Burton I 75. Chauvin VI 56-58 No. 222; *ANE* 176 No. 13;

King ¿Umar al-Nu¿mân and Sons: *Alf* I 312,-(to impoverished relatives); Burton III 56. Chauvin VI 112-24 No. 277; *ANE* 430-34 No. 39;
Jewish qâḍî and His Devout Wife: *Alf* III 11; Burton V 257. Chauvin VI 154-55 No. 321; *ANE* 242 No. 163.□

W27.3§, ‡Gratitude for employment (earning a livelihood: 'bread and salt').
Jawdar and His Treacherous Brethren: *Alf* III 194,-(twenty dinars); Burton VI 243. Chauvin V 257-60 No. 154; *ANE* 244-45 No. 209.□

W28.5.1§, ‡Maiden offers to sacrifice herself for womankind. (Sheherezade). See: *DOTTI*. (Cf. S62.1.1§, Z66.5.0.1§).
Shahriyâr and Shâhzamân: *Alf* I 5,-(*fidâ'*); Burton I 15. Chauvin V 188-89 No. 111; *ANE* 370-71 No. 1.□

W28.5.3§, ‡One sweetheart offers to sacrifice self for the other. (Cf. Z66.5§).
Basra Girls in Poetry Contest: *Alf* III 205-6; Burton VII 113. Chauvin VI 144 No. 301; *ANE* 107-8 No. 216.□

W29§, Constancy. (Cf. W27).
¿Azîz and ¿Azîzah: *Alf* I 281; Burton II 323. Chauvin V 144-45 No. 71; *ANE* 111-13 No. 41;
Wolf and Fox: *Alf* II 34; Burton III 143,-(faith). Chauvin II 227 No. 6; *ANE* 450 No. 47.□

W29.0.1§, ‡'Constancy (*wafâ'*) is commendable, treachery (*ghadr*) is deplorable'.
¿Azîz and ¿Azîzah: *Alf* I 281; Burton II 323. Chauvin V 144-45 No. 71; *ANE* 111-13 No. 41;
King ¿Umar al-Nu¿mân and Sons: *Alf* II 8,-(*ghadr*/even to foreigners/strangers); Burton III 89. Chauvin VI 112-24 No. 277; *ANE* 430-34 No. 39;
Wolf and Fox: *Alf* II 34; Burton III 143,-(faith). Chauvin II 227 No. 6; *ANE* 450 No. 47.□

W29.2§, ‡ ‡The good wife (woman): no divorce, no remarriage, no desertion due to vanity (*baṭar*), no disagreement with husband, no quitting of husband's home to parents's due to unhappiness (*gaḍbânah*). See: *DOTTI*. (Cf. P210.0.2§, P221§, T198.3.1§, W116.0.1§).
Jeweler's Wife and Qamar al-Zamân: *Alf* IV 265; Burton IX 302. Chauvin V 212-14 No. 121; *ANE* 345-47 No. 260.□

W29.3.1§, ‡Human males (men) are lacking in constancy (when compared to jinn women, female-jinn). See: *DOTTI*. (Cf. V210.0.6§, W256.6.8.1§).
Sayf al-Mulûk: *Alf* III 297-98; Burton VII 368-69. Chauvin VII 64-73 No. 348; *ANE* 362-64 No. 229.□

W30§, Conformity. See: *DOTTI*; *GMC*. (Cf. P788.2§).
Nûr al-Dîn and Maryam: *Alf* IV 100; Burton VIII 311. Chauvin V 52-54 No. 271; *ANE* 98-99 No. 233.□

W30.1§, ‡The need to be like the others in own social group. See: *DOTTI*. (Cf. P788.2§, U303.1.2§, P788.2§).
Landsman ¿Abdallah and Merman ¿Abdallah: *Alf* IV 206; Burton IX 185-86. Chauvin V 6-7 No. 3; *ANE* 65-66 No. 256.□

W30.5§, Misery loves miserable company. See: *DOTTI*; *GMC*. (Cf. H1314§, J886§).
Shahriyâr and Shâhzamân: *Alf* I 3,-(two brothers); Burton I 9. Chauvin V 188-91 No. 111; *ANE* 370-71 No. 1;
Portress Amînah: Bitten Cheek: *Alf* I 60,-(afflicted women); Burton I 187. Chauvin V 98-99 No. 33; *ANE* 326-27 No. 20;
Tâj al-Mulûk: *Alf* I 267; Burton II 296. Chauvin V 126-28 No. 60; *ANE* 406-8 No. 40.□

W30.5.2§, ‡A clique of sorrowers bewail their misfortune: a number of persons (small group) united by regret for having lost. See: *DOTTI*.
Lady and Five Suitors Deceived: *Alf* III 162; Burton VI 179. Chauvin VIII 50-51 No. 18; *ANE* 266 No. 198.□

W30.5.2.1§, ‡A clique of men expelled from earthly paradise (utopia) bewail their eviction. See: *DOTTI*.
Third Qalandar: Magnetic Mountain: *Alf* I 53; Burton I 161. Chauvin V 200-3 No. 117; *ANE* 340-41 No. 18;
Man Who Never Laughs: *Alf* III 155,-(eleven); Burton VI 160. Chauvin VIII 47-48 No. 15; *ANE* 285-86 No. 195.□

W30.5.2.3§, ‡A group of men beguiled into shameful (ridiculous) exposure laugh together at one another. (Cf. X52).
Lady and Five Suitors Deceived: *Alf* III 162; Burton VI 179. Chauvin VIII 50-51 No. 18; *ANE* 266 No. 198.□

W31.1.3§, ‡Obedient wife as 'the joy of the heart'. (Cf. U101.0.2§).
Tawaddud: Slavegirl Sold and Regained: *Alf* III 7,-cf./(riddle); Burton V 242. Chauvin VII 117-19 No. 387; *ANE* 408-10 No. 157.□

W32.2§, Brave (courageous) man preferred. See: *DOTTI*; *GMC*.
King ¿Umar al-Nu¿mân and Sons: *Alf* I 174-75,-cf./(invincible enemy); Burton II 109. Chauvin VI 112-24 No. 277; *ANE* 430-34 No. 39.□

W35, Justice. See: *DOTTI*; *GMC*. (Cf. U10.3.1§).
Three Apples: Hasty Uxoricide: *Alf* I 61; Burton I 188. Chauvin VI 144-45 No. 302; *ANE* 414-15 No. 21.□

W35.4.1§, ‡'Justice of ¿Umar (Omar [Ibn al-Khaṭṭâb])'. See: *DOTTI*. (Cf. P12.14.1§, Z121.5§).
Nuzhat al-Zamân Tested/¿Umar al-Nu¿mân: *Alf* I 203; Burton II 163-64. Chauvin VI 116, n.1/passim No. 277; *ANE* 432,/passim No. 39;
Omar and Young Badawî: Returning to be Executed: *Alf* II 287-88; Burton V 99-104. Chauvin V 216 No. 125; *ANE* 429-30 No. 130.□

W36§, ‡Reverse nepotism: harsher (less fair) treatment for self and relatives (friends). See: *DOTTI*. (Cf. J708.8§, W13§).
Nuzhat al-Zamân Tested/¿Umar al-Nu¿mân: *Alf* I 206; Burton II 170. Chauvin VI 116, n.1/passim No. 277; *ANE* 432,/passim No. 39.□

W36.3§, ‡Ruler confiscates a small coin (penny/*dirham*) his son had illegally taken from public treasury. (Cf. P760.2.1§).
Nuzhat al-Zamân Tested/¿Umar al-Nu¿mân: *Alf* I 203; Burton II 162. Chauvin VI 116, n.1/passim No. 277; *ANE* 432,/passim No. 39.□

W37, Conscientiousness. See: *DOTTI*. (Cf. W37.5.2§).
Three Apples: Hasty Uxoricide: *Alf* I 61,-(in seeking justice); Burton I 188. Chauvin VI 144-45 No. 302; *ANE* 414-15 No. 21;
King ¿Umar al-Nu¿mân and Sons: *Alf* I 191,-(stoker's); Burton II 139. Chauvin VI 112-24 No. 277; *ANE* 430-34 No. 39.□

W37.2.1§, Man keeps promise to return to be executed by king: forgiven. See: *DOTTI*; *GMC*. (Cf. M100.1§).
Trader and Afrit: Accidental Fairy-cide: *Alf* I 8,-cf.; Burton I 25. Chauvin VI 22-23 No. 194; *ANE* 419-20 No. 4;
Omar and Young Badawî: Returning to be Executed: *Alf* II 288; Burton V 103. Chauvin V 216 No. 125; *ANE* 429-30 No. 130.□

W37.5§, ‡Culprit (criminal) confesses upon seeing innocent person convicted of his crime. See: *DOTTI*. (Cf. J1141.4, J1148§, K1627.1§, N731.4, T39.1.4§, U10, W35).
al-'Amjad and al-'As¿ad: *Alf* II 127; Burton III 338. Chauvin V 208-10 No. 120[.1]; *ANE* 341-42 No. 61/pt. 2.□

W37.5.1§, ‡At the execution (hanging, crucifixion), a Moslem, a Christian, and a Jew each declares that he is the culprit upon seeing the other about to be unjustly executed for it. See: *DOTTI*.
Hunchback's Tale: Resuscitated: *Alf* I 87; Burton I 260. Chauvin V 180-82 No. 105; *ANE* 224-25 No. 23.□

W37.5.2§, ‡At the unjust execution of officer (vizier) for failing to solve crime, onlooker confesses. See: *DOTTI*. (Cf. P251.3.5§).
Three Apples: Hasty Uxoricide: *Alf* I 62; Burton I 189. Chauvin VI 144-45 No. 302; *ANE* 414-15 No. 21.□

W37.6§, ‡Betraying secret (breaking promise of confidentiality) in order to prevent greater injustice. See: *DOTTI*. (Cf. N279.1§, P7.1§).
Jewish Doctor's Story: Sororicide: *Alf* I 102,-(implicit); Burton I 299. Chauvin VI 89 No. 253; *ANE* 242 No. 26.□

W37.8§, ‡*dhimmah*: economic, political, governmental, conscientiousness and honesty. (Cf. V371§).

Three Apples: Hasty Uxoricide: *Alf* I 61,-(caliph's); Burton I 188,-(responsibility on the Day of Doom). Chauvin VI 144-45 No. 302; *ANE* 414-15 No. 21;
¿Azîz and ¿Azîzah: *Alf* I 285,-(bride's debt to groom); Burton II 331. Chauvin V 144-45 No. 71; *ANE* 111-13 No. 41;
Jawdar and His Treacherous Brethren: *Alf* III 194; Burton VI 243. Chauvin V 257-60 No. 154; *ANE* 244-45 No. 209.□

W37.8.0.1§, ‡Acquitting someone's conscience of responsibility (*'ibrâ' al-dhimmah*).
Jeweler's Wife and Qamar al-Zamân: *Alf* IV 257; Burton IX 285. Chauvin V 212-14 No. 121; *ANE* 345-47 No. 260.□

W37.8.1.1§, ‡End of employment gift (given to hireling). (Cf. Q72.3§, P324.0.4.1§, T52.0.8§).
Jawdar and His Treacherous Brethren: *Alf* III 194; Burton VI 243. Chauvin V 257-60 No. 154; *ANE* 244-45 No. 209.□

W38.1§, Property rights protected. See: *DOTTI*. (Cf. P760.8.1.1§).
Copt Broker's Story: Lover's Sacrifices Repaid: *Alf* I 88-89; Burton I 263-64. Chauvin VI 80 No. 249; *ANE* 313-14 No. 24;
Abû Muḥammad Lazybones: *Alf* II 208; Burton IV 167-68. Chauvin VI 64-67 No. 233; *ANE* 71-73 No. 78.□

W38.2§, ‡Orphan's property protected (hidden, put in trust, etc.) until he becomes of age. See: *DOTTI*. (Cf. P776§, V401§).
Omar and Young Badawî: Returning to be Executed: *Alf* II 288; Burton V 102. Chauvin V 216 No. 125; *ANE* 429-30 No. 130.□

W38.3§, ‡Unguarded (unattended) property protected. See: *DOTTI*.
Sindbâd's First Voyage: *Alf* III 87; Burton VI 11-12. Chauvin VII 7-9 No. 373A; *ANE* 385 No. 179.□

W39.1.1§, ‡A person of noble character (*ḥûrr, 'aṣîl, nabîl,* etc.) readily believes kind talk (the seemingly truthful).
Ma¿rûf the Cobbler: *Alf* IV 294-95; Burton X 10. Chauvin VI 81-82 No. 250; *ANE* 291-93 No. 262.□

W39.1.2§, ‡A person of noble character is easily deceived by kind talk.
Anîs al-Jalîs: *Alf* I 145,-(poem); Burton II 44. Chauvin V 120-24 No. 58; *ANE* 316-17 No. 35.□

W40§, ‡Self-reliance as trait of character. See: *DOTTI*.
Sindbâd's Sixth Voyage: *Alf* III 114; Burton VI 62. Chauvin VII 24-27 No. 373F; *ANE* 386 No. 179.□

W40.0.1§, ‡'Nothing scratches one's skin except [(i.e., as effectively as)] one's own fingernail'.
Masrûr and Zayn al-Mawâṣif: *Alf* IV 77; Burton VIII 256. Chauvin VI 82-84 No. 251; *ANE* 294-95 No. 232.□

W40.0.2§, ‡Don't send an emissary (a proxy) on grave assignment—(do it yourself).
Sindbâd's Sixth Voyage: *Alf* III 114,-(poem); Burton VI 62. Chauvin VII 24-27 No. 373F; *ANE* 386 No. 179.□

W40.2§, ‡Lion powerful because of attending to own needs.
First Qalandar: Brother-Sister Incest: *Alf* I 41,-(poem); Burton I 109. Chauvin V 196-97 No. 115; *ANE* 337-38 No. 15.□

W41§, ‡Resolve (determination, willpower, endurance, 'grit').
Jinni Keeps Mistress in Box: *Alf* I 4; Burton I 12. Chauvin V 188-89 No. 111; *ANE* 370 No. 1/pt.;
King's Son and Afrit's Mistress: *Alf* III 172; Burton VI 199. Chauvin VIII 59 No. 24; *ANE* 263-64 No. 204.□

W42§, ‡Contentment: satisfaction with one's lot in life (*riḍâ*). (Cf. W151).
Crow and Viper: *Alf* IV 141; Burton IX 47. Chauvin II 219 No. 152/5; *ANE* 162 No. 240.□

W42.1§, ‡One should be content with own lot in life (kismet).
Wild Ass and Jackal: *Alf* IV 142; Burton IX 48-50. Chauvin II 219 No. 152/6; *ANE* 449 No. 241.□

W44§, ‡Proper bashfulness (*ḥayâ'/khafar, kusûf/khajal*). A person's modesty (social sensitiveness, shyness, or decency). See: *DOTTI*. (Cf. P788.2§, P610§, P788.2§, W170§, Z94.5.1§).

Tailor's Story/Barber of Baghdad: *Alf* I 107,-cf./(*ḥishmah*); Burton I 312. Chauvin V 154-56 No. 78; *ANE* 405-6 No. 27;
Ghânim ibn Ayyûb: *Alf* I 146,-(*ḥayâ'*); Burton II 46. Chauvin VI 14-16 No. 188; *ANE* 192-93 No. 36;
Hârûn and Zubaydah in Bath: *Alf* II 284; Burton V 76. Chauvin VI 142 No. 298; *ANE* 203-4 No. 111;
Sayf al-Mulûk: *Alf* III 294-95,-(between sisters prevents telling truth/love); Burton VII 364. Chauvin VII 64-73 No. 348; *ANE* 362-64 No. 229.□

W44.0.1§, ‡"[Proper] bashfulness is [an aspect] of godliness (*'îmân*)".
Nuzhat al-Zamân Tested/¿Umar al-Nu¿mân: *Alf* I 201,-(*'îmân/ḥayâ'*); Burton II 159,-(faith/modesty). Chauvin VI 116, n.1/passim No. 277; *ANE* 432,/passim No. 39;
¿Alâ' al-Dîn Abû al-Shâmât: *Alf* II 149; Burton IV 34,-(modesty is a point of the Faith). Chauvin V 43-49 No. 18; *ANE* 85-87 No. 63.□

W44.3§, ‡Bashfulness at nakedness or body exposure. (Cf. A1557.3.1§, P783.2.3§).
Hârûn and Zubaydah in Bath: *Alf* II 284; Burton V 76. Chauvin VI 142 No. 298; *ANE* 203-4 No. 111;
Jânshâh: *Alf* III 55; Burton V 350. Chauvin VII 39-44 No. 153; *ANE* 238-41 No. 178;
Hasan of Basrah: *Alf* IV 3; Burton VIII 41. Chauvin VII 29-35 No. 212A; *ANE* 207-10 No. 230.□

W45.3§, ‡Person of honor keeps secret. (Cf. T39.1.5§, U197§).
Porter and Ladies of Baghdad: *Alf* I 33,-(poem); Burton I 87. Chauvin V 251-52 No. 148; *ANE* 324-26 No. 14.□

W45.3.1§, ‡"A noble person's heart (chest) is a secret's grave".
Qamar al-Zamân and Budûr: *Alf* II 103,-(*'aḥrâr*); Burton III 289. Chauvin V 204-12 No. 120; *ANE* 341-45 No. 61.□

W47§, ‡Eloquence. See: *DOTTI*; *PSAE*. (Cf. H507).
King ¿Umar al-Nu¿mân and Sons: *Alf* I 171,-(*balâghah*); Burton II 102,-(sweet speech). Chauvin VI 112-24 No. 277; *ANE* 430-34 No. 39;
Tâj al-Mulûk: *Alf* I 264; Burton II 287. Chauvin V 126-28 No. 60; *ANE* 406-8 No. 40;
¿Alî bin Ṭâhir and Mu'nis: *Alf* II 303; Burton V 164. Chauvin VI 154 No. 319; *ANE* 101 No. 153;
Hârûn and Arab Girl: *Alf* III 203; Burton VII 108. Chauvin VI 143 No. 300; *ANE* 202 No. 215.□

W47.1.3§, ‡"A person dies from his misstatement ('tongue-slip'), but does not die from his misdeed ('foot-slip'). See: *DOTTI*.
Qamar al-Zamân and Budûr: *Alf* II 69,-(poem); Burton III 221. Chauvin V 204-12 No. 120; *ANE* 341-45 No. 61.□

W47.1.3.1§, ‡"A human being's affliction comes from the tongue".
¿Abdallah ibn Fâḍil: Treacherous Brothers: *Alf* IV 269; Burton IX 309. Chauvin V 2-4 No. 2; *ANE* 63-65 No. 261.□

W49.1§, ‡Grooming (toiletry) recommended. See: *DOTTI*. (Cf. V4.5.5§).
Nuzhat al-Zamân Tested/¿Umar al-Nu¿mân: *Alf* I 202; Burton II 160. Chauvin VI 116, n.1/passim No. 277; *ANE* 432,/passim No. 39.□

W50§, ‡Humility as trait of character. See: *PSAE*. (Cf. W13§, W166§, Z13.11.1§).
Spy, Old Woman/¿Umar al-Nu¿mân: *Alf* I 224-25,-(Imam al-Shâfi¿î's/implicit); Burton II 207-8. *ANE* 432 No. 39/passim.□

W103§, *'ibn-ḥarâm* ('bastard', 'of illegitimate birth', i.e., of bad character, vile). See: *DOTTI*; *GMC*. (Cf. W3§, W251§).
Nûr al-Dîn ¿Alî and Son: *Alf* I 79,-(person suspected to be); Burton I 231. Chauvin VI 102-6 No. 270; *ANE* 317-19 No. 22;
Anîs al-Jalîs: *Alf* I 130; Burton II 13,-(whoreson). Chauvin V 120-24 No. 58; *ANE* 316-17 No. 35;
Second Eunuch/Kâfûr's Half-lie: *Alf* I 150; Burton II 55. Chauvin V 278 No. 161; *ANE* 178-79 No. 38;
¿Alî Shâr and Zumurrud: *Alf* II 222; Burton IV 201. Chauvin V 89-91 No. 28; *ANE* 100-1 No. 82.□

W111.1.1.6§, ‡Man (boy) too lazy to move out of burning sun into shade. See: *DOTTI*.
Abû Muḥammad Lazybones: *Alf* II 207-8; Burton IV 166. Chauvin VI 64-67 No. 233; *ANE* 71-73 No. 78.□

W111.1.7§, ‡Man too lazy to speak. See: *DOTTI*.
Barber's Tale of Himself: Joins Doomed Party: *Alf* I 110,-cf.; Burton I 317–18. Chauvin V 156-57 No. 80; *ANE* 115-17 No. 28.□

W111.2.10§, Procrastinating craftsmen (hirelings, workers): "Tomorrow!". See: *DOTTI*; *GMC*; *PSAE*. (Cf. K2250.2§).
Abû Qîr and Abû Ṣîr: *Alf* IV 183; Burton IX 135. Chauvin V 15-17 No. 10; *ANE* 75-77 No. 255.□

W112.1.1§, ‡'A dog follows the person (owner) who keeps it hungry'. (Cf. J405.1.1§, W40§).
Nuzhat al-Zamân Tested/¿Umar al-Nu¿mân: *Alf* I 201; Burton II 158. Chauvin VI 116, n.1/passim No. 277; *ANE* 432,/passim No. 39.□

W113§, Lack of ambition. See: *DOTTI*; *GMC*. (Cf. J532§).
King ¿Umar al-Nu¿mân and Sons: *Alf* I 309; Burton III 50. Chauvin VI 112-24 No. 277; *ANE* 430-34 No. 39.□

W113.2§, ‡'He who looks upward tires himself'. (Cf. J285.0.1.1§).
Saker and Birds: *Alf* II 39; Burton III 155. Chauvin II 228 No. 13; *ANE* 357-58 No. 53.□

W115.0.1§, ‡Remarkably dirty person. See: *DOTTI*.
Anîs al-Jalîs: *Alf* I 141,-(fisher); Burton II 31-32. Chauvin V 120-24 No. 58; *ANE* 316-17 No. 35;
Sweep and Noble Lady: Infidelity Repaid: *Alf* II 189; Burton IV 125-26. Chauvin VI 148 No. 306; *ANE* 403-4 No. 72.□

W115.5.1§, ‡Garment so full of lice (fleas) it moves.
Anîs al-Jalîs: *Alf* I 141; Burton II 31. Chauvin V 120-24 No. 58; *ANE* 316-17 No. 35.□

W116.0.1§, ‡Vain dissatisfaction with one's 'good enough' share of God's boon (*baṭar*).
Wolf and Fox: *Alf* II 30,-(fatal); Burton III 133,-("insolence" [??]). Chauvin II 227 No. 6; *ANE* 450 No. 47.□

W116.7, Use of strange language to show one's high education [(*taḥadhluq*)]. See: *DOTTI*; *GMC*; *PSAE*.
Birds, Beasts, and Carpenter: *Alf* II 23,-(*hayhât, hayhât*—see Mot. Z61.0.1§, below); Burton III 115. Chauvin II 225-26 No. 1; *ANE* 126 No. 44;
Dispute Concerning Males and Females: *Alf* II 301,-(*ḥaṣḥaṣah*); Burton V 159,-(manifest). Chauvin VI 153 No. 317; *ANE* 291 No. 151;
Tawaddud: Slavegirl Sold and Regained: *Alf* II 304,-(*suqiṭa fî yadayhi*/lit.); Burton V 191,-(bit his hands in bitter penitence). Chauvin VII 117-19 No. 387; *ANE* 408-10 No. 157;
City of Brass: *Alf* III 135,-(*al-Sarmadiyy*); Burton VI 115. Chauvin V 32-35 No. 16; *ANE* 146-50 No. 180.□

W121.3.1§, ‡Coward's excuse: "I am horseman (knight) of only play and jest!". (Cf. J2631.1§, W166.2§).
King ¿Umar al-Nu¿mân and Sons: *Alf* II 4; Burton III 80,-(sport and jest). Chauvin VI 112-24 No. 277; *ANE* 430-34 No. 39.□

W121.7.1§, ‡Cowardly man flees: saves self but abandons wife (daughter). See: *DOTTI*. (Cf. W154.2.4.1§).
Tâj al-Mulûk: *Alf* I 299,-(birds); Burton III 31. Chauvin V 126-28 No. 60; *ANE* 406-8 No. 40.□

W121.7.2§, ‡Man whose wife (fiancee, daughter) has been abducted ridiculed as coward when he does not give chase.
Nûr al-Dîn and Maryam: *Alf* IV 115; Burton VIII 338. Chauvin V 52-54 No. 271; *ANE* 98-99 No. 233.□

W122.1§, ‡'As restlessness as a bean on fire'.
¿Azîz and ¿Azîzah: *Alf* I 287; Burton III 2. Chauvin V 144-45 No. 71; *ANE* 111-13 No. 41.□

W123.2§, ‡Farmer cannot decide whether to sow or not; regrets indecision at harvest time (dies of sorrow). See: *DOTTI*. (Cf. J1071).
Lazy Sower (Farmer): *Alf* II 39,-(*zâri¿*); Burton III 156,-("husbandman"). Chauvin II 229 No. 16.□

W125, Gluttony. See: *DOTTI*; *GMC*. (Cf. F632.0.1§).
Abû Qîr and Abû Ṣîr: *Alf* IV 185; Burton IX 141. Chauvin V 15-17 No. 10; *ANE* 75-77 No. 255.□

W129.1§, ‡Person who doubts a prediction (belief, claim, etc.) fails to see that he is living proof of its validity. See: *DOTTI*.

Tailor's Story/Barber of Baghdad: *Alf* I 108,-(by barber); Burton I 317. Chauvin V 154-56 No. 78; *ANE* 405-6 No. 27.□

W130.0.1.1§, ‡A *fâgir* (a sociopath, person who feels no remorse, has no conscience). (Cf. L401§, N191.1§, S101§).
Wolf and Fox: *Alf* II 34; Burton III 143. Chauvin II 227 No. 6; *ANE* 450 No. 47.□

W131, Profligacy. See: *GMC*.
Anîs al-Jalîs: *Alf* I 130; Burton II 11. Chauvin V 120-24 No. 58; *ANE* 316-17 No. 35.□

W131.1, Profligate [(heir)] wastes entire fortune before beginning his own adventures. See: *ANE*; *DOTTI*; *GMC*. (Cf. P761.2.1§).
¿Alî Shâr and Zumurrud: *Alf* II 218; Burton IV 190-91. Chauvin V 89-91 No. 28; *ANE* 100-1 No. 82;
Tawaddud: Slavegirl Sold and Regained: *Alf* II 304; Burton V 181. Chauvin VII 117-19 No. 387; *ANE* 408-10 No. 157;
Sindbâd's First Voyage: *Alf* III 83; Burton VI 4. Chauvin VII 7-9 No. 373A; *ANE* 385 No. 179;
Man Who Never Laughs: *Alf* III 152; Burton VI 160. Chauvin VIII 47-48 No. 15; *ANE* 285-86 No. 195;
Ruined Baghdadi and His Slave-girl: *Alf* IV 129; Burton IX 24. Chauvin V 152-53 No. 75; *ANE* 353 No. 235;
al-Rashîd and Omani Merchant: *Alf* IV 215,-cf.; Burton IX 199. Chauvin VI 111-12 No. 276; *ANE* 201-2 No. 257;
Abû al-Hasan al-Khorâsânî (and Caliph's Favorite): *Alf* IV 230-31; Burton IX 233. Chauvin V 218-20 No. 129; *ANE* 68-69 No. 259.□

W132§, ‡Lack of 'sense of proportionality,' in action or reaction. See: *DOTTI*. (Cf. P2.3§).
Reeve's Story: Why Maimed by Bride: *Alf* I 98-99,-(severe punishment/minor offense); Burton I 287. Chauvin V 220-21 No. 305; *ANE* 351 No. 25.□

W132.1.2.2.1§, ‡Finger chopped off in order to steal ring.
Jawdar and His Treacherous Brethren: *Alf* III 201; Burton VI 256. Chauvin V 257-60 No. 154; *ANE* 244-45 No. 209.□

W132.3§, ‡Excessive (cruel) punishment for trivial error. See: *DOTTI*.
Reeve's Story: Why Maimed by Bride: *Alf* I 99; Burton I 287. Chauvin V 220-21 No. 305; *ANE* 351 No. 25.□

W132.3.1§, ‡Hand (finger) cut off because unwashed (dirty, smelly, etc.).
Reeve's Story: Why Maimed by Bride: *Alf* I 98-99; Burton I 287. Chauvin V 220-21 No. 305; *ANE* 351 No. 25.□

W137.0.1§, ‡Curiosity (inquisitiveness) brings troubles upon the curious. See: *DOTTI*. (Cf. Q341, Q342).
Spy, First Maiden/¿Umar al-Nu¿mân: *Alf* I 219; Burton II 196,-(impertinence). *ANE* 432 No. 39/passim;
Serpent-charmer and Wife: *Alf* IV 145; Burton IX 57. Chauvin II 220 No. 152/9; *ANE* 368 No. 244.□

W151, Greed. See: *DOTTI*; *GMC*.
She-mouse and Ichneumon: *Alf* II 35-6; Burton III 148. Chauvin II 228 No. 10; *ANE* 306 No. 49;
Escaped Viper Ungrateful: *Alf* II 35,-cf.; Burton III 145. Chauvin II 227 No. 9; *ANE* 450,/passim No. 47;
¿Alî Shâr and Zumurrud: *Alf* II 222,-(hero's); Burton IV 201. Chauvin V 89-91 No. 28; *ANE* 100-1 No. 82;
¿Abdallah ibn Fâdil: Treacherous Brothers: *Alf* IV 278; Burton IX 329. Chauvin V 2-4 No. 2; *ANE* 63-65 No. 261.□

W151.0.2§, Greed makes fraud possible. See: *DOTTI*.
King ¿Umar al-Nu¿mân and Sons: *Alf* I 225,-(implicit); Burton II 212. Chauvin VI 112-24 No. 277; *ANE* 430-34 No. 39;
Thief and His Monkey: *Alf* II 40; Burton III 159. Chauvin II 229 No. 18; *ANE* 413 No. 57;
¿Alî Shâr and Zumurrud: *Alf* II 222,-(implicit); Burton IV 201. Chauvin V 89-91 No. 28; *ANE* 100-1 No. 82.□

W151.0.2.1.1§, ‡'The imposter ruins the greedy's home' (i.e., bankrupts greedy).

Ma¿rûf the Cobbler: *Alf* IV 298; Burton X 16,-(impostor-covetous). Chauvin VI 81-82 No. 250; *ANE* 291-93 No. 262.□

W151.0.3§, Greed corrodes gains. See: *DOTTI*; *GMC*. (Cf. J514).
Flea and She-mouse: *Alf* II 37; Burton III 151-54. Chauvin II 228 No. 12; *ANE* 186 No. 52;
Jawdar and His Treacherous Brethren: *Alf* III 181; Burton VI 219. Chauvin V 257-60 No. 154; *ANE* 244-45 No. 209.□

W151.0.3.1§, ‡Merchant (adventurer) facing mortal danger blames greed for his misfortune. (Cf. J1063.0.1§).
Sindbâd's Seventh Voyage: *Alf* III 117; Burton VI 70. Chauvin VII 26-29 No. 373G; *ANE* 386-87 No. 179.□

W151.0.4§, ‡Greed leads to cruelty (hardheartedness). See: *DOTTI*.
Jawdar and His Treacherous Brethren: *Alf* III 195; Burton VI 244,-("covetise"). Chauvin V 257-60 No. 154; *ANE* 244-45 No. 209.□

W151.0.5.1§, ‡'Nothing kills an Adamite as greed'.
Tawaddud: Slavegirl Sold and Regained: *Alf* III 7; Burton V 244. Chauvin VII 117-19 No. 387; *ANE* 408-10 No. 157.□

W151.0.6§, ‡Greedy is despised.
City of Brass: *Alf* III 136; Burton VI 118. Chauvin V 32-35 No. 16; *ANE* 146-50 No. 180.□

W151.9.3§, ‡Greedy (ambitious) person pursues large game (animal, fish) without regard to safety: loses his life. (Cf. J716.1§).
Foolish Fisher: *Alf* IV 163; Burton IX 93-94. Chauvin II 222 No. 152/16; *ANE* 187 No. 248.□

W151.9.4§, ‡Greedy grant recipient. Wants more of the gratuity (gift, alms, tip, etc.) given him.
Mercury ¿Alî: *Alf* III 227; Burton VII 173. Chauvin V 248-50 No. 147; *ANE* 301-3 No. 225.□

W153, Miserliness. See: *DOTTI*; *GMC*.
Miser and Cheap Loaves of Bread: *Alf* III 142; Burton VI 137. Chauvin VIII 38 No. 6; *ANE* 303-4 No. 186.□

W154.0.1§, Perfidy: repayment of good deeds with evil ones. See: *DOTTI*; *GMC*. (Cf. J1514.2§, P424.2, W11.5.0.1§, W154.29§).
Fisherman and Afrit: Ingratitude: *Alf* I 15; Burton I 43. Chauvin VI 23-25 No. 195; *ANE* 183-84 No. 8;
Dûban and King Yûnân: *Alf* I 21; Burton I 58. Chauvin V 275-76 No. 156; *ANE* 459 No. 9;
¿Azîz and ¿Azîzah: *Alf* I 289,-(to *bint-¿amm*); Burton III 7,-(nought but ill for nought but good). Chauvin V 144-45 No. 71; *ANE* 111-13 No. 41;
Birds, Beasts, and Carpenter: *Alf* II 24; Burton III 120. Chauvin II 225-26 No. 1; *ANE* 126 No. 44;
Wolf and Fox: *Alf* II 34,-(*ghadr*); Burton III 143,-(faithlessness). Chauvin II 227 No. 6; *ANE* 450 No. 47;
Escaped Viper Ungrateful: *Alf* II 35; Burton III 145. Chauvin II 227 No. 9; *ANE* 450,/passim No. 47;
Bulûqiya: *Alf* III 78; Burton V 390-91. Chauvin VII 54 No. 77; *ANE* 130-32 No. 177;
Jawdar and His Treacherous Brethren: *Alf* III 201; Burton VI 256. Chauvin V 257-60 No. 154; *ANE* 244-45 No. 209;
¿Abdallah ibn Fâḍil: Treacherous Brothers: *Alf* IV 285; Burton IX 342. Chauvin V 2-4 No. 2; *ANE* 63-65 No. 261.□

W154.0.2§, ‡Betrayal of 'bread and salt' (covenant of friendship). See: *DOTTI*.
Hasan of Basrah: *Alf* III 306, 313; Burton VIII 16. Chauvin VII 29-35 No. 212A; *ANE* 207-10 No. 230.□

W154.2.3§, ‡Cat ungrateful for rescue by mouse. See: *DOTTI*.
Mouse and Cat: *Alf* IV 135-36; Burton IX 37-8. Chauvin II 218 No. 152/2; *ANE* 305-6 No. 237.□

W154.2.4.1§, ‡Female bird (pigeon) releases her mate from net; he flees when she is caught. (Cf. W121.7.1§).
Tâj al-Mulûk: *Alf* I 299; Burton III 31. Chauvin V 126-28 No. 60; *ANE* 406-8 No. 40.□

W154.3.4.1§, ‡Healed patient ungrateful: killed by physician (healer). See: *DOTTI*.
Dûban and King Yûnân: *Alf* I 21; Burton I 57. Chauvin V 275-76 No. 156; *ANE* 459 No. 9.□

W154.5.1.5§, Crocodile wants to eat his rescuer. See: *DOTTI*; *GMC*.
Dûban and King Yûnân: *Alf* I 21,-(passim/abandoned); Burton I 58. Chauvin V 275-76 No. 156; *ANE* 459 No. 9.□

W154.29§, Ingratitude due to nature. See: *DOTTI*. (Cf. W256.9.1.1.1§).
Escaped Viper Ungrateful: *Alf* II 35; Burton III 145. Chauvin II 227 No. 9; *ANE* 450,/passim No. 47;
Bulûqiya: *Alf* III 34,-(Adamite); Burton V 322. Chauvin VII 54 No. 77; *ANE* 130-32 No. 177;
Mouse and Cat: *Alf* IV 135-36,-(cat's); Burton IX 37-38. Chauvin II 218 No. 152/2; *ANE* 305-6 No. 237.□

W154.29.0.1§, ‡'Adamites (mankind) as ungrateful by nature'. (Cf. A185.9.1§).
Birds, Beasts, and Carpenter: *Alf* II 24; Burton III 120. Chauvin II 225-26 No. 1; *ANE* 126 No. 44;
Bulûqiya: *Alf* III 34-35,-cf./(breakers of promises); Burton V 322. Chauvin VII 54 No. 77; *ANE* 130-32 No. 177.□

W154.29.3§, ‡Hyena ("'Um-¿Âmir") kills man who had given her refuge. See: *DOTTI*.
Fisherman and Afrit: Ingratitude: *Alf* I 15,-(poem/simile); Burton I 43. Chauvin VI 23-25 No. 195; *ANE* 183-84 No. 8.□

W155, Hardness of heart. See: *DOTTI*; *GMC*. (Cf. Z152.6.1.1§).
King ¿Umar al-Nu¿mân and Sons: *Alf* I 241; Burton II 244. Chauvin VI 112-24 No. 277; *ANE* 430-34 No. 39;
Hasan of Basrah: *Alf* IV 41,-(of sister toward sister); Burton VIII 119. Chauvin VII 29-35 No. 212A; *ANE* 207-10 No. 230.□

W155.0.2§, ‡Hardheartedness from fullness (of stomach). (Cf. F1041.9.8§, U248.1§).
Spy, Old Woman/¿Umar al-Nu¿mân: *Alf* I 224; Burton II 208. *ANE* 432 No. 39/passim.□

W155.1, Hardhearted horse allows ass to be overburdened until it is crushed. Horse must then assume the load. See: *DOTTI*. (Cf. K1678§).
Bull and Ass: *Alf* I 6,-cf./(bull); Burton I 18. Chauvin V 179-80 No. 104; *ANE* 129-30 No. 2.□

W157, Dishonesty. See: *DOTTI*.
¿Alî Shâr and Zumurrud: *Alf* II 222,-(hero's); Burton IV 201. Chauvin V 89-91 No. 28; *ANE* 100-1 No. 82;
Abû Qîr and Abû Ṣîr: *Alf* IV 183; Burton IX 134-35. Chauvin V 15-17 No. 10; *ANE* 75-77 No. 255.□

W160.1§, ‡Eating from market (at restaurant) reduces one's moral worth. See: *DOTTI*.
Nûr al-Dîn ¿Alî and Son: *Alf* I 80-81; Burton I 235,-("common cook-shop"). Chauvin VI 102-6 No. 270; *ANE* 317-19 No. 22.□

W160.1.1§, ‡Servant punished for taking young master to restaurant (to eat): practice teaches bad habit(s).
Nûr al-Dîn ¿Alî and Son: *Alf* I 81; Burton I 235. Chauvin VI 102-6 No. 270; *ANE* 317-19 No. 22.□

W164§, Pride (self-esteem, self-respect). See: *GMC*. (Cf. T202.1.2.1§, W166§).
Hishâm and Arab Youth: *Alf* II 184; Burton IV 101-3. Chauvin V 288 No. 172; *ANE* 222-23 No. 68.□

W164.1.5§, Publication of one's own physical attributes. See: *DOTTI*; *GMC*.
Man from Yaman and Six Salve-girls: Flyting: *Alf* II 244-48; Burton IV 245-59. Chauvin VI 151 No. 313; *ANE* 289-90 No. 84.□

W164.1.8§, Publication of one's own character and personality attributes. See: *DOTTI*; *GMC*.
Man from Yaman and Six Salve-girls: Flyting: *Alf* II 244-49; Burton IV 245-60. Chauvin VI 151 No. 313; *ANE* 289-90 No. 84.□

W164.2§, Injured pride. See: *DOTTI*; *GMC*. (Cf. K1210, T72.0.1§).
Sweep and Noble Lady: Infidelity Repaid: *Alf* II 190; Burton IV 129. Chauvin VI 148 No. 306; *ANE* 403-4 No. 72;
Hind bint al-Nu¿mân and al-Ḥajjâj: *Alf* III 202,-(divorce—reason unknown); Burton VII 97. Chauvin V 115-4 No. 50; *ANE* 221-22 No. 212;
Abû al-Ḥasan al-Khorâsânî (and Caliph's Favorite): *Alf* IV 236-37; Burton IX 242. Chauvin V 218-20 No. 129; *ANE* 68-69 No. 259.□

W164.2.1.5§, ‡Pride of noble person (king, princess, etc.) injured when beloved prefers a commoner. (Cf. P178.3.1.1§).
Abû al-Ḥasan al-Khorâsânî (and Caliph's Favorite): *Alf* IV 237; Burton IX 242. Chauvin V 218-20 No. 129; *ANE* 68-69 No. 259.□

W164.2.3§, ‡Woman's femininity injured (by man). See: *DOTTI*.
Bahrâm and Datmâ: *Alf* III 164; Burton VI 187. Chauvin VIII 54-57 No. 22; *ANE* 114-15 No. 202.□

W164.2.3.1§, ‡Woman (girl) slighted by man avenges self. See: *DOTTI*.
Lovers of Basra/Ḍamrah: *Alf* III 212; Burton VII 134. Chauvin V 118 No. 54; *ANE* 273 No. 220.□

W164.5§, Wife too proud to accept husband's marriage to another. See: *DOTTI*; *GMC*. (Cf. P187.1§, P268.2§).
Sweep and Noble Lady: Infidelity Repaid: *Alf* II 190,-cf.; Burton IV 129. Chauvin VI 148 No. 306; *ANE* 403-4 No. 72.□

W166§, Arrogance (conceit). See: *DOTTI*; *GMC*. (Cf. H649.1§, L491§, W164§, W50§).
King ¿Umar al-Nu¿mân and Sons: *Alf* I 241-42,-(*kibr*); Burton II 244. Chauvin VI 112-24 No. 277; *ANE* 430-34 No. 39;
Hishâm and Arab Youth: *Alf* II 184,-(causes loss of prey); Burton IV 103. Chauvin V 288 No. 172; *ANE* 222-23 No. 68;
Tawaddud: Slavegirl Sold and Regained: *Alf* II 316; Burton V 221. Chauvin VII 117-19 No. 387; *ANE* 408-10 No. 157;
Angel of Death and Proud King: *Alf* III 8; Burton V 247. Chauvin VI 183-84 No. 349/[pt. 1]; *ANE* 104 No. 158;
King Jalî¿âd and Shimâs: *Alf* IV 157; Burton IX 81. Chauvin VI 9-11 No. 184; *ANE* 237-38 No. 236.□

W166.0.1§, ‡Arrogance as false pride: sense of inferiority coupled with ignorance.
Barber's Fifth Brother: Daydreams/Defeats Robbers: *Alf* I 118, 120; Burton I 338–39, 340 n. 1,-(Gold makes bold). Chauvin V 161 No. 85; *ANE* 119-20 No. 33.□

W166.1§, ‡Self-praise.
Barber's Tale of Himself: Joins Doomed Party: *Alf* I 110; Burton I 318ff. Chauvin V 156-57 No. 80; *ANE* 115-17 No. 28;
Ebony Horse: *Alf* II 257; Burton V 12. Chauvin V 221-31 No. 130; *ANE* 172-74 No. 103.□

W166.2§, ‡Bragging: false self-aggrandizement (boasting). See: *DOTTI*. (Cf. C549§, W121.3.1§).
Barber's Tale of Himself: Joins Doomed Party: *Alf* I 110,-(silence/wisdom); Burton I 318ff. Chauvin V 156-57 No. 80; *ANE* 115-17 No. 28.□

W166.3§, ‡Haughtiness brings failure (punishment). (Cf. L430).
King ¿Umar al-Nu¿mân and Sons: *Alf* I 232,-(arrogance of power/numbers); Burton II 222,-(over confidence in own numbers). Chauvin VI 112-24 No. 277; *ANE* 430-34 No. 39;
Jawdar and His Treacherous Brethren: *Alf* III 197-98; Burton VI 248,-(pride). Chauvin V 257-60 No. 154; *ANE* 244-45 No. 209.□

W170§, ‡Shamelessness: person feels no shame. See: *DOTTI*. (Cf. P780§, W44§, W155, Z94.5.1§).
Abû Qîr and Abû Ṣîr: *Alf* IV 182; Burton IX 134. Chauvin V 15-17 No. 10; *ANE* 75-77 No. 255.□

W170.1§, ‡Lack of bashfulness (*qillat ḥayâ'*). See: *DOTTI*. (Cf. W44§, W187, Z94.5.1.3§).
Budûr and Jubayr ibn ¿Umayr: *Alf* II 236; Burton IV 231. Chauvin VII 93-94 No. 374; *ANE* 243-44 No. 83;
Pretty Gray-haired Woman Retorts: *Alf* II 303; Burton V 163. Chauvin VI 153 No. 318; *ANE* 77-78 No. 152;
Hasan of Basrah: *Alf* IV 41; Burton VIII 119,-(brazenfacedness). Chauvin VII 29-35 No. 212A; *ANE* 207-10 No. 230;
Ma¿rûf the Cobbler: *Alf* IV 288; Burton X 1,-(scanty of shame). Chauvin VI 81-82 No. 250; *ANE* 291-93 No. 262.□

W170.1.1§, ‡Shameless public stare (posture) where submissiveness (bashfulness) is required (*¿ain qawayyah*).
Hasan of Basrah: *Alf* IV 41; Burton VIII 119,-(brazenfacedness). Chauvin VII 29-35 No. 212A; *ANE* 207-10 No. 230.□

W171, Two-facedness. See: *DOTTI*. (Cf. W171).

King ¿Umar al-Nu¿mân and Sons: *Alf* II 8,-(King Sâsân's); Burton III 88. Chauvin VI 112-24 No. 277; *ANE* 430-34 No. 39.□

W171.3§, ‡Being a flatterer (*mitayyibâtî, massâh-gûkh*). See: *DOTTI*. (Cf. J814).
King ¿Umar al-Nu¿mân and Sons: *Alf* II 8,-(poem); Burton III 89. Chauvin VI 112-24 No. 277; *ANE* 430-34 No. 39.□

W172.5§, Self-pity. See: *DOTTI*. (Cf. J227.9.1§).
Dalîla the Swindler: *Alf* III 213; Burton VII 147. Chauvin V 248-50 No. 147; *ANE* 163-64 No. 224.□

W172.5.1§, Publication of self-pity. See: *GMC*.
Second Qalandar: Afrit's Wife: *Alf* I 50,-(poem); Burton I 138. Chauvin V 197-200 No. 116; *ANE* 338-39 No. 16;
Lover Who Feigned Himself a Thief: *Alf* II 204,-(poem); Burton IV 155. Chauvin VII 134-35 No. 403; *ANE* 272 No. 76;
Budûr and Jubayr ibn ¿Umayr: *Alf* II 236,-(poem); Burton IV 230-31. Chauvin VII 93-94 No. 374; *ANE* 243-44 No. 83;
Sindbâd and Porter: *Alf* III 82,-(poem); Burton VI 2. Chauvin VII 1 No. 373; *ANE* 383-85 No. 179/pt.;
Sindbâd's Sixth Voyage: *Alf* III 114; Burton VI 59. Chauvin VII 24-27 No. 373F; *ANE* 386 No. 179.□

W172.5.1.1§, ‡Self-pity song (poem): *mawwâl 'ahmar* ('red-*mawwâl*'), *ghurbah*-song ('song of strangerhood', being a stranger')—i.e., 'the blues'. See: *DOTTI*. (Cf. Z141.1).
King ¿Umar al-Nu¿mân and Sons: *Alf* I 192; Burton II 140. Chauvin VI 112-24 No. 277; *ANE* 430-34 No. 39;
Devotee Prince: Ascetic's Death: *Alf* II 292,-(poem); Burton V 116. Chauvin VI 193-94 No. 363; *ANE* 167-68 No. 134;
Sindbâd and Porter: *Alf* III 82,-(poem); Burton VI 2. Chauvin VII 1 No. 373; *ANE* 383-85 No. 179/pt.□

W173.1§, Perfect said to be defective. See: *DOTTI*.
¿Alâ' al-Dîn Abû al-Shâmât: *Alf* II 156,-cf.; Burton IV 49. Chauvin V 43-49 No. 18; *ANE* 85-87 No. 63.□

W174.1§, Perfection is God's alone.
Jullanâr of the Sea: *Alf* III 248; Burton VII 267. Chauvin V 147-51 No. 73; *ANE* 248-51 No. 227.□

W177§, ‡The character of the newly-rich (newly-powerful). (Cf. L490§,-L499§).
Ma¿rûf the Cobbler: *Alf* IV 296-97; Burton X 13-15. Chauvin VI 81-82 No. 250; *ANE* 291-93 No. 262.□

W180.0.1.1§, ‡Person denounced as narcissistic.
Qamar al-Zamân and Budûr: *Alf* II 102,-(*mu¿jab bi-nafsih*); Burton III 288,-(proud of himself). Chauvin V 204-12 No. 120; *ANE* 341-45 No. 61.□

W180.1§, ‡"If I cannot have it (him, her, etc.), no one else will!" Useful thing (object, person, etc.) destroyed so that others may not benefit from it.
¿Azîz and ¿Azîzah: *Alf* I 287,-cf.; Burton III 2,-(not live either for me or for her [??]). Chauvin V 144-45 No. 71; *ANE* 111-13 No. 41.□

W180.1.1§, ‡Jealous person destroys (seeks to destroy) inconstant paramour. See: *DOTTI*. (Cf. K871.3.2§).
¿Azîz and ¿Azîzah: *Alf* I 287,-("mutilé"); Burton III 2. Chauvin V 144-45 No. 71; *ANE* 111-13 No. 41.□

W181, Jealousy. See: *DOTTI*; *GMC*; *PSAE*. (Cf. P793§, W195).
Dûban and King Yûnân: *Alf* I 18; Burton I 49. Chauvin V 275-76 No. 156; *ANE* 459 No. 9;
Abû Qîr and Abû Sîr: *Alf* IV 193; Burton IX 156. Chauvin V 15-17 No. 10; *ANE* 75-77 No. 255.□

W181.0.1§, ‡'Nobody is jealousy-free (envy-free)'. (Cf. U102.1§).
Dûban and King Yûnân: *Alf* I 18; Burton I 49. Chauvin V 289 No. 173; *ANE* 383 No. 9.□

W183§, ‡*Shamâtah*: Pleasure (rejoicing) at another's misfortune. (Cf. U245§, W195, X1§).
¿Alî Shâr and Zumurrud: *Alf* II 230; Burton IV 217,-(people exulted over his mishap). Chauvin V 89-91 No. 28; *ANE* 100-1 No. 82;

Lovers of Basra/Ḍamrah: *Alf* III 212; Burton VII 135,-("she prostrated herself in gratitude to Allah and exultation over Zamrah's defeat" [??]). Chauvin V 118 No. 54; *ANE* 273 No. 220.□

W183.1.1§, ‡Brother pleased with news of disappearance of his sibling(s). (Cf. S73.0.3.1§, S73.1.1).
King ¿Umar al-Nu¿mân and Sons: *Alf* I 207; Burton II 174,-(joy). Chauvin VI 112-24 No. 277; *ANE* 430-34 No. 39.□

W185, Violence of temper. See: *DOTTI*.
Jullanâr of the Sea: *Alf* III 256,-(no one is more *'aḥmaq*); Burton VII 281,-(violent tempered). Chauvin V 147-51 No. 73; *ANE* 248-51 No. 227;
Abû Qîr and Abû Ṣîr: *Alf* IV 183; Burton IX 136,-(wrath). Chauvin V 15-17 No. 10; *ANE* 75-77 No. 255.□

W187, Insolence. See: *DOTTI*. (Cf. W170.1§, Z88§, Z94.5.1§).
Hishâm and Arab Youth: *Alf* II 184-85; Burton IV 101-3. Chauvin V 288 No. 172; *ANE* 222-23 No. 68;
Ebony Horse: *Alf* II 257,-(in addressing-king); Burton V 12. Chauvin V 221-31 No. 130; *ANE* 172-74 No. 103;
Sayf al-Mulûk: *Alf* III 290-91,-(of ship's captain); Burton VII 354. Chauvin VII 64-73 No. 348; *ANE* 362-64 No. 229.□

W187.1§, ‡Lack of good manners (*qillat 'adab*).
Jewish Doctor's Story: Sororicide: *Alf* I 99; Burton I 288. Chauvin VI 89 No. 253; *ANE* 242 No. 26;
Jawdar and His Treacherous Brethren: *Alf* III 197-98; Burton VI 249. Chauvin V 257-60 No. 154; *ANE* 244-45 No. 209;
Jullanâr of the Sea: *Alf* III 247; Burton VII 266. Chauvin V 147-51 No. 73; *ANE* 248-51 No. 227;
Nûr al-Dîn and Maryam: *Alf* IV 92; Burton VIII 293,-(wanting in self-respect [??]). Chauvin V 52-54 No. 271; *ANE* 98-99 No. 233;
Jeweler's Wife and Qamar al-Zamân: *Alf* IV 248,-cf./(*¿adîm al-dhawq*); Burton IX 266,-(lack tact). Chauvin V 212-14 No. 121; *ANE* 345-47 No. 260.□

W187.1.1§, ‡Bad character (*sû' al-khuluq*) is incurable.
Tawaddud: Slavegirl Sold and Regained: *Alf* III 7,-(riddling question); Burton V 242,-(ill-nature). Chauvin VII 117-19 No. 387; *ANE* 408-10 No. 157.□

W195, Envy. See: *DOTTI*; *GMC*; *PSAE*. (Cf. W181).
Bull and Ass: *Alf* I 6,-(implicit); Burton I 16. Chauvin V 179-80 No. 104; *ANE* 129-30 No. 2;
Enchanted Spring: Change of Sex: *Alf* III 148; Burton VI 149. Chauvin VIII 43 No. 11; *ANE* 175-76 No. 191.□

W195.0.1§, ‡"Everyone that has been blessed (endowed) with an asset is envied".
Abû Qîr and Abû Ṣîr: *Alf* IV 194; Burton IX 158,-(prospered). Chauvin V 15-17 No. 10; *ANE* 75-77 No. 255.□

W195.3§, Being loved (favored) within family envied. See: *DOTTI*; *GMC*.
King ¿Umar al-Nu¿mân and Sons: *Alf* I 186-87,-(siblings); Burton II 130. Chauvin VI 112-24 No. 277; *ANE* 430-34 No. 39;
Jawdar and His Treacherous Brethren: *Alf* III 177, 193; Burton VI 213-14. Chauvin V 257-60 No. 154; *ANE* 244-45 No. 209.□

W195.4§, Wealth (material possessions) envied. See: *DOTTI*; *PSAE*. (Cf. P152§).
Second Shaykh: Treacherous Brothers: *Alf* I 11; Burton I 34,-(jealous). Chauvin V 6 No. 397; *ANE* 377-78 No. 6;
Abû Muḥammad Lazybones: *Alf* II 206-7; Burton IV 1162-63. Chauvin VI 64-67 No. 233; *ANE* 71-73 No. 78;
Sindbâd and Porter: *Alf* III 81; Burton VI 2. Chauvin VII 1 No. 373; *ANE* 383-85 No. 179/pt.;
Ibn Sabâ'ik/Sayf al-Mulûk: *Alf* III 271,-(king's grant); Burton VII 309. Chauvin VII 65 No. 348/pt.; *ANE* 309-10 No. 228;
¿Abdallah ibn Fâḍil: Treacherous Brothers: *Alf* IV 285; Burton IX 342. Chauvin V 2-4 No. 2; *ANE* 63-65 No. 261.□

W195.4.1.3§, ‡Native envies foreigner's wealth (estates).
Dalîla the Swindler: *Alf* III 212; Burton VII 145. Chauvin V 248-50 No. 147; *ANE* 163-64 No. 224.□

W195.6§, Social status (influence, authority) envied. See: *DOTTI*; *PSAE*.

Bull and Ass: *Alf* I 6,-cf./(value to owner); Burton I 16. Chauvin V 179-80 No. 104; *ANE* 129-30 No. 2;
al-'Amjad and al-'As¿ad: *Alf* II 112,-(amity between privileged brothers); Burton III 309. Chauvin V 208-10 No. 120[.1]; *ANE* 341-42 No. 61/pt. 2;
Dalîla the Swindler: *Alf* III 213; Burton VII 146. Chauvin V 248-50 No. 147; *ANE* 163-64 No. 224;
¿Abdallah ibn Fâḍil: Treacherous Brothers: *Alf* IV 285; Burton IX 342. Chauvin V 2-4 No. 2; *ANE* 63-65 No. 261.□

W195.7§, Success in craft envied. See: *DOTTI*.
Dalîla the Swindler: *Alf* III 220,-(making sale); Burton VII 158. Chauvin V 248-50 No. 147; *ANE* 163-64 No. 224.□

W195.8§, Offspring (having children) envied. See: *DOTTI*; *GMC*.
King ¿Umar al-Nu¿mân and Sons: *Alf* I 163,-(birth of children); Burton II 81. Chauvin VI 112-24 No. 277; *ANE* 430-34 No. 39.□

W195.9§, Beauty of one's spouse (lover) envied. See: *DOTTI*; *GMC*.
Second Shaykh: Treacherous Brothers: *Alf* I 11; Burton I 34. Chauvin V 6 No. 397; *ANE* 377-78 No. 6.□

W195.9.1§, Father envies son's beautiful wife (wives). See: *DOTTI*; *GMC*. (Cf. T92.9).
King ¿Umar al-Nu¿mân and Sons: *Alf* I 180,-(wife-to-be); Burton II 119-20. Chauvin VI 112-24 No. 277; *ANE* 430-34 No. 39.□

W195.9.2§, Brother envies brother's beautiful wife (wives). See: *DOTTI*; *GMC*.
Jewish qâḍî and His Devout Wife: *Alf* III 10,-(desires her); Burton V 256. Chauvin VI 154-55 No. 321; *ANE* 242 No. 163;
¿Abdallah ibn Fâḍil: Treacherous Brothers: *Alf* IV 278; Burton IX 329. Chauvin V 2-4 No. 2; *ANE* 63-65 No. 261.□

W195.9.3§, Sister envies sister's handsome husband (suitor, lover). See: *DOTTI*.
Eldest Lady's Story: Treacherous Sisters: *Alf* I 56; Burton I 171. Chauvin V 4 No. 443; *ANE* 174-75 No. 19.□

W196.2§, ‡Had the impatient not acted in haste, his request would have been granted. (Cf. L505§).
Ḥammâd: Treacherous Bedouin: *Alf* II 20,-(marriage); Burton III 111. Chauvin VI 124 n. 1 No. 277; *ANE* 200 No. 43.□

W197§, Being a nag. See: *DOTTI*.
¿Alî ibn Bakkâr: *Alf* II 53,-(*'ilḥâḥ*); Burton III 186,-(press question). Chauvin V 153 No. 76; *ANE* 92-93 No. 60;
King Jalî¿âd and Shimâs: *Alf* IV 161,-cf./(don't nag); Burton IX 89. Chauvin VI 9-11 No. 184; *ANE* 237-38 No. 236.□

W198.0.1§, ‡Tyranny brings about destruction (to tyrant and subjects).
Wolf and Fox: *Alf* II 30,-(" *'iftirâ'*"); Burton III 132. Chauvin II 227 No. 6; *ANE* 450 No. 47.□

W198.1§, ‡Characteristic behavior of the tyrant (the unjust).
Wolf and Fox: *Alf* II 30,-(wolf's); Burton III 132-33. Chauvin II 227 No. 6; *ANE* 450 No. 47.□

W198.2.2§, ‡'Tyrant's death is a relief [from God]'.
Wolf and Fox: *Alf* II 34,-cf.; Burton III 143,-(the wicked). Chauvin II 227 No. 6; *ANE* 450 No. 47.□

W198.3.2§, ‡Looking upon a tyrant's face is a sin.
Spy, Third Maiden/¿Umar al-Nu¿mân: *Alf* I 222; Burton II 202. *ANE* 432 No. 39/passim.□

W199.3.1§, ‡Blaming the higher (supernatural) powers for one's own misdeeds. (Cf. A604.3§, J1063.0.1§, N101, P526.3.1.1§).
¿Abdallah ibn Fâḍil: Treacherous Brothers: *Alf* IV 271; Burton IX 311. Chauvin V 2-4 No. 2; *ANE* 63-65 No. 261.□

W199.3.1.1§, ‡Misfortune attributed to "God's Will", good fortune to oneself.
King Jalî¿âd and Shimâs: *Alf* IV 159; Burton IX 85. Chauvin VI 9-11 No. 184; *ANE* 237-38 No. 236.□

W199.3.2.1§, ‡Treacherous changeableness of fortune (life, 'the world').
King ¿Umar al-Nu¿mân and Sons: *Alf* I 192,-(poem); Burton II 139. Chauvin VI 112-24 No. 277; *ANE* 430-34 No. 39.□

W199.3.3§, ‡Blaming "The other"—('people/society,' 'adversaries/enemies,' 'blamers,' 'censurers', 'the envious', etc.). (Cf. J1360§, K2059.9.2§).
Ma¿n Rewards a Bedouin for Gift: *Alf* II 183,-(person as bad omen); Burton IV 99. Chauvin VI 78 No. 248; *ANE* 291 No. 66.□

W199.3.3.1§, ‡Blaming the Evil Eye for misfortune (misdeed). (Cf. D2071).
¿Abdallah ibn Fâḍil: Treacherous Brothers: *Alf* IV 271; Burton IX 314. Chauvin V 2-4 No. 2; *ANE* 63-65 No. 261.□

W199.3.4.1§, ‡"The Devil made me do it".
Ḥammâd: Treacherous Bedouin: *Alf* II 20; Burton III 111. Chauvin VI 124 n. 1 No. 277; *ANE* 200 No. 43.□

W199.9.1§, ‡Self-deception: liar believes his lie and behaves accordingly. See: *DOTTI*. (Cf. J953, X902).
Ma¿rûf the Cobbler: *Alf* IV 296,-(*ḥamlah*/caravan of goods); Burton X 14. Chauvin VI 81-82 No. 250; *ANE* 291-93 No. 262.□

W199.9.2§, ‡Self-deceiver tries to persuade his partner in fabricating a lie that their lie is the truth. See: *DOTTI*.
Ma¿rûf the Cobbler: *Alf* IV 296; Burton X 14. Chauvin VI 81-82 No. 250; *ANE* 291-93 No. 262.□

W201.1.1.1.1.1§, ‡Indicator of manliness: slighting women's opinion. (Cf. J21.37).
Man [Gardener] and His Wife: *Alf* IV 165,-(passim); Burton IX 98. Chauvin II 223 No. 152/19; *ANE* 289 No. 250.□

W202.1.2.3.1§, ‡Indicator of female: manner of walking (taking short steps, shaking hips, etc.).
Ni¿mah and Nu¿m: Stolen Wife Regained: *Alf* II 140; Burton IV 16. Chauvin VI 96-97 No. 263; *ANE* 314 No. 62.□

W203.4§, ‡Excessive experiencing of shame (public). See: *DOTTI*.
Jeweler's Wife and Qamar al-Zamân: *Alf* IV 239,-(*khajal*); Burton IX 249,-(ashamed and confounded). Chauvin V 212-14 No. 121; *ANE* 345-47 No. 260.□

W205.0.1§, ‡Authoritarian person pride.
Qamar al-Zamân and Budûr: *Alf* II 68; Burton III 219. Chauvin V 204-12 No. 120; *ANE* 341-45 No. 61.□

W206§, Authoritarian person's (father's) 'love'. See: *DOTTI*; *GMC*.
Qamar al-Zamân and Budûr: *Alf* II 68; Burton III 213. Chauvin V 204-12 No. 120; *ANE* 341-45 No. 61.□

W209.1§, ‡Lonesome person seeks companionship. See: *DOTTI*.
Barber's Sixth Brother: Emasculated by Abductor: *Alf* I 124,-(wife); Burton I 349. Chauvin V 163-64 No. 86; *ANE* 120 No. 34.□

W210§, Daydreaming. See: *DOTTI*; *GMC*. (Cf. F1046§, J2060).
Barber's Fifth Brother: Daydreams/Defeats Robbers: *Alf* I 117-18; Burton I 335–37. Chauvin V 161 No. 85; *ANE* 119-20 No. 33;
Fakir and Jar of Butter: *Alf* IV 137; Burton IX 40-41. Chauvin II 218-19 No. 152/3; *ANE* 179-80 No. 238.□

W211, Active imagination [(unrealistic thinking)]. See: *DOTTI*.
Barber's Fifth Brother: Daydreams/Defeats Robbers: *Alf* I 118; Burton I 335–37. Chauvin V 161 No. 85; *ANE* 119-20 No. 33;
Fakir and Jar of Butter: *Alf* IV 138-38; Burton IX 40-41. Chauvin II 218-19 No. 152/3; *ANE* 179-80 No. 238.□

W217§, ‡Resourcefulness. See: *DOTTI*. (Cf. Q91).
Sayf al-Mulûk: *Alf* III 285,-(escaping on raft); Burton VII 342. Chauvin VII 64-73 No. 348; *ANE* 362-64 No. 229.□

W217.3§, ‡When a female is resolved to do something it will be done, regardless of obstacles. (Cf. W256.6§).
Shahriyâr and Shâhzamân: *Alf* I 5; Burton I 13. Chauvin V 188-89 No. 111; *ANE* 370-71 No. 1;
Hasan of Basrah: *Alf* IV 9; Burton VIII 54. Chauvin VII 29-35 No. 212A; *ANE* 207-10 No. 230.□

W250.1§, ‡Basic types of personality reckoned according to the elements.

Tawaddud: Slavegirl Sold and Regained: *Alf* III 3-4; Burton V 234,-("humors"). Chauvin VII 117-19 No. 387; *ANE* 408-10 No. 157.□

W250.1.1§, · ▬ Personality type: *hawâ'î* ('aerial', whimsical, impressionable).
Tawaddud: Slavegirl Sold and Regained: *Alf* III 3-4; Burton V 234,-("humors"). Chauvin VII 117-19 No. 387; *ANE* 408-10 No. 157.□

W250.1.2§, · ▬ Personality type: *turâbî* ('earth-prone', melancholic, passive).
Tawaddud: Slavegirl Sold and Regained: *Alf* III 3-4; Burton V 234,-("humors"). Chauvin VII 117-19 No. 387; *ANE* 408-10 No. 157.□

W250.1.3§, · ▬ Personality type: *nârî* ('fiery', explosive-aggressive).
Tawaddud: Slavegirl Sold and Regained: *Alf* III 3-4; Burton V 234,-("humors"). Chauvin VII 117-19 No. 387; *ANE* 408-10 No. 157.□

W250.1.4§, ‡Personality type: *mâ'î* (aquatic, 'watery').
Tawaddud: Slavegirl Sold and Regained: *Alf* III 4; Burton V 234,-(Aquarius). Chauvin VII 117-19 No. 387; *ANE* 408-10 No. 157.□

W250.5§, ‡Types of women—(three). See: *DOTTI*.
Nuzhat al-Zamân Tested/¿Umar al-Nu¿mân: *Alf* I 201-2; Burton II 159. Chauvin VI 116, n.1/passim No. 277; *ANE* 432,/passim No. 39.□

W250.5.1§, ‡Female-type: believer (pious)—aids to husband. (Cf. J482.4§).
Nuzhat al-Zamân Tested/¿Umar al-Nu¿mân: *Alf* I 201-2,-(*¿alâ al-Dahr*); Burton II 159,-(against fate). Chauvin VI 116, n.1/passim No. 277; *ANE* 432,/passim No. 39.□

W250.5.2§, ‡Female-type: for procreation only.
Nuzhat al-Zamân Tested/¿Umar al-Nu¿mân: *Alf* I 201; Burton II 159. Chauvin VI 116, n.1/passim No. 277; *ANE* 432,/passim No. 39.□

W250.5.3§, ‡Female-type: God's affliction—a shackle around man's neck.
Nuzhat al-Zamân Tested/¿Umar al-Nu¿mân: *Alf* I 201-2,(*ghill*); Burton II 159,-(shackle). Chauvin VI 116, n.1/passim No. 277; *ANE* 432,/passim No. 39.□

W250.6§, ‡Types of men—(three).
Nuzhat al-Zamân Tested/¿Umar al-Nu¿mân: *Alf* I 202; Burton II 159. Chauvin VI 116, n.1/passim No. 277; *ANE* 432,/passim No. 39.□

W250.6.1§, ‡Male-type: wise—of sound judgement.
Nuzhat al-Zamân Tested/¿Umar al-Nu¿mân: *Alf* I 202; Burton II 159. Chauvin VI 116, n.1/passim No. 277; *ANE* 432,/passim No. 39.□

W250.6.2§, ‡Male-type: wiser—seeks counsel in what he knows not. (Cf. J21.57§).
Nuzhat al-Zamân Tested/¿Umar al-Nu¿mân: *Alf* I 202; Burton II 159. Chauvin VI 116, n.1/passim No. 277; *ANE* 432,/passim No. 39.□

W250.6.3§, ‡Male-type: rudderless (*ḥâ'ir*)—knows not, obey's no adviser.
Nuzhat al-Zamân Tested/¿Umar al-Nu¿mân: *Alf* I 202; Burton II 159. Chauvin VI 116, n.1/passim No. 277; *ANE* 432,/passim No. 39.□

W251§, Beliefs (theories) about composition of character (personality). See: *GMC*. (Cf. W3§, W103§).
¿Alî Shâr and Zumurrud: *Alf* II 222,-(bastard); Burton IV 201,-("son of a whore"). Chauvin V 89-91 No. 28; *ANE* 100-1 No. 82.□

W251.1§, Physiognomy (*firâsah*): the judging of character. See: *DOTTI*; *GMC*.
Tâj al-Mulûk: *Alf* I 296,-(passim); Burton III 23,-(sagacity). Chauvin V 126-28 No. 60; *ANE* 406-8 No. 40;
Nûr al-Dîn and Maryam: *Alf* IV 109,-(passim); Burton VIII 326. Chauvin V 52-54 No. 271; *ANE* 98-99 No. 233.□

W251.2.3§, Parentage as basis for judging character.
Jeweler's Wife and Qamar al-Zamân: *Alf* IV 266,-(loins/womb); Burton IX 302,-(father/womb). Chauvin V 212-14 No. 121; *ANE* 345-47 No. 260.□

W251.2.3.2.0.1§, ‡Mother as vessel (or as earth for a plant). (Cf. Z187§).
Tâj al-Mulûk: *Alf* I 261; Burton II 284. Chauvin V 126-28 No. 60; *ANE* 406-8 No. 40.□

W252§, One becomes what one is instructed he is—("looking-glass self"). See: *DOTTI*. (Cf. K2059.9.2§).
Ma¿rûf the Cobbler: *Alf* IV 296-97,-(imposter merchant); Burton X 14-15. Chauvin VI 81-82 No. 250; *ANE* 291-93 No. 262.□

W254§, ‡Residence of certain human attributes and feelings (emotions/sentiments) within organs of the body.
Tawaddud: Slavegirl Sold and Regained: *Alf* II 315; Burton V 218. Chauvin VII 117-19 No. 387; *ANE* 408-10 No. 157.□

W254.0.3§, ‡Spleen as seat of laughter.
Tawaddud: Slavegirl Sold and Regained: *Alf* II 315; Burton V 220. Chauvin VII 117-19 No. 387; *ANE* 408-10 No. 157.□

W254.0.4§, ‡Kidneys as seat of slyness (wiliness, deception).
Tawaddud: Slavegirl Sold and Regained: *Alf* II 315; Burton V 220,-(craft). Chauvin VII 117-19 No. 387; *ANE* 408-10 No. 157.□

W254.2§, ‡Empathy in sorrow (pity, compassion) resides in liver (also in eye, soul, or heart—especially woman's). See: *DOTTI*. (Cf. U245§).
First Shaykh: Sorceress Wife: *Alf* I 10,-(*"hashâshat kabidî"*); Burton I 30,-(core of heart). Chauvin VII 129-30 No. 396; *ANE* 376-77 No. 5;
¿Alî ibn Bakkâr: *Alf* II 61,-('fire in liver'/acute anxiety); Burton III 204,(xxx). Chauvin V 153 No. 76; *ANE* 92-93 No. 60;
Qamar al-Zamân and Budûr: *Alf* II 96,-(*fa-yâ-kabidî, ...*/passim/poem); Burton III 277,-(heart). Chauvin V 204-12 No. 120; *ANE* 341-45 No. 61;
Tawaddud: Slavegirl Sold and Regained: *Alf* II 315; Burton V 220,-("pity"). Chauvin VII 117-19 No. 387; *ANE* 408-10 No. 157;
Hasan of Basrah: *Alf* IV 6,-(*kabid*/liver); Burton VIII 49,-(heart). Chauvin VII 29-35 No. 212A; *ANE* 207-10 No. 230;
Masrûr and Zayn al-Mawâṣif: *Alf* IV 55,-(*kabid ḥazîn*/saddened liver); Burton VIII 205,-(sorrowful heart). Chauvin VI 82-84 No. 251; *ANE* 294-95 No. 232.□

W255§, Halo effect perception: exaggerated generalization of a trait of character. (Cf. S62.1.1§, X901).
¿Alî ibn Bakkâr: *Alf* II 64; Burton III 210. Chauvin V 153 No. 76; *ANE* 92-93 No. 60;
Ma¿rûf the Cobbler: *Alf* IV 295,-(two persons from Egypt); Burton X 12. Chauvin VI 81-82 No. 250; *ANE* 291-93 No. 262.□

W255.1.1§, ‡'Eye-of-hate': magnifies demerits and reduces merits—(*¿ayn al-bughḍ*).
Ma¿rûf the Cobbler: *Alf* IV 303,-cf., 315; Burton X 26,-(eye of disparagement). Chauvin VI 81-82 No. 250; *ANE* 291-93 No. 262.□

W255.2.1§, ‡'Eye-of-love': magnifies merits and reduces demerits—(*¿ayn al-riḍâ*)—eye-of-contentment. See: *DOTTI*. (Cf. U248.4§).
¿Alî ibn Bakkâr: *Alf* II 64,-(lover/caliph); Burton III 210,-("saw all her actions in a favourable light"). Chauvin V 153 No. 76; *ANE* 92-93 No. 60.□

W256.1§, Stereotyping: ethnic and national traits. See: *DOTTI*; *GMC*; *PSAE*. (Cf. F610.0.7§, W256.1§).
¿Alî Shâr and Zumurrud: *Alf* II 227,-(Turks); Burton IV 211. Chauvin V 89-91 No. 28; *ANE* 100-1 No. 82;
Hasan of Basrah: *Alf* III 303,-(*'a¿âjim*/Persians); Burton VIII 9. Chauvin VII 29-35 No. 212A; *ANE* 207-10 No. 230.□

W256.1.1§, ‡Ethnic (national) slur.
King ¿Umar al-Nu¿mân and Sons: *Alf* II 5,-(*'a¿âjim*'s dog); Burton III 83,-(Persian dog). Chauvin VI 112-24 No. 277; *ANE* 430-34 No. 39;
Hasan of Basrah: *Alf* III 305,-(Arabs' dog); Burton VIII 13. Chauvin VII 29-35 No. 212A; *ANE* 207-10 No. 230.□

W256.2§, Stereotyping: social class. See: *DOTTI*.
Ishâq al-Mûṣilî and Khadîjah bint al-Ḥasan: *Alf* II 185,-(commoners/*sûqah*); Burton IV 120,-(trade folk). Chauvin V 241-42 No. 142; *ANE* 232 No. 71.□

W256.3§, Stereotyping: profession (occupation). See: *GMC*.

Jeweler's Wife and Qamar al-Zamân: *Alf* IV 239,-(dervishes); Burton IX 251,-("All Dervishes are lewd fellows"). Chauvin V 212-14 No. 121; *ANE* 345-47 No. 260.□

W256.5§, Stereotyping: racial traits. See: *DOTTI*. (Cf. Z143.4§).
Ghânim ibn Ayyûb: *Alf* I 147; Burton II 48. Chauvin VI 14-16 No. 188; *ANE* 192-93 No. 36.□

W256.5.1§, ‡Stereotyping: treacherous race.
Ghânim ibn Ayyûb: *Alf* I 147,-(*al-Sudân*); Burton II 48,-(blackamoors). Chauvin VI 14-16 No. 188; *ANE* 192-93 No. 36.□

W256.6§, Stereotyping: gender (sex) traits. See: *DOTTI*; *PSAE*. (Cf. S62.1.1§, Z190§).
Qamar al-Zamân and Budûr: *Alf* II 66,-(poem/women); Burton III 216. Chauvin V 204-12 No. 120; *ANE* 341-45 No. 61;
Jeweler's Wife and Qamar al-Zamân: *Alf* IV 256,-(poem/women); Burton IX 282. Chauvin V 212-14 No. 121; *ANE* 345-47 No. 260.□

W256.6.1§, 'Women are lacking in mind and religion'. See: *DOTTI*; *GMC*. (Cf. A1331.3§, J21.37, J1701.0.1§, P423.0.2.1§).
Second Qalandar: Afrit's Wife: *Alf* I 46; Burton I 122. Chauvin V 197-200 No. 116; *ANE* 338-39 No. 16;
al-'Amjad and al-'As¿ad: *Alf* II 113; Burton III 311,-(imperfect in reason and religion). Chauvin V 208-10 No. 120[.1]; *ANE* 341-42 No. 61/pt. 2;
Landsman ¿Abdallah and Merman ¿Abdallah: *Alf* IV 207,-cf./(youngsters and this woman lack mind); Burton IX 186,-("lack wit"). Chauvin V 6-7 No. 3; *ANE* 65-66 No. 256;
Jeweler's Wife and Qamar al-Zamân: *Alf* IV 264; Burton IX 298. Chauvin V 212-14 No. 121; *ANE* 345-47 No. 260.□

W256.6.1.1§, ‡Stereotyping: women surrender instantly to sexual temptation. See: *PSAE*. (Cf. T55).
King ¿Umar al-Nu¿mân and Sons: *Alf* II 5,-cf./(weaken before male's beauty); Burton III 82. Chauvin VI 112-24 No. 277; *ANE* 430-34 No. 39.□

W256.6.1.1.1§, ‡Stereotyping: women are sex-crazed (nymphomaniacs).
King's Daughter and Ape: *Alf* II 253,-(Arabic title: *dâ' ghalabt al-shahwah ¿alâ al-nisâ'*); Burton IV 297. Chauvin V 178 No. 102; *ANE* 262-63 No. 102.□

W256.6.1.1.1.1§, ‡Stereotyping: woman's mood is dependent on her vagina.
Shahriyâr and Shâhzamân: *Alf* I 5,-(poem); Burton I 13,-(parts). Chauvin V 188-89 No. 111; *ANE* 370-71 No. 1.□

W256.6.2.1§, ‡"Truly their wiles are great!": A statement about women made by a courtier in Pharaoh's (Potiphar's) court.
Craft and Malice of Women/Frame: *Alf* III 138, 158,-(tale title); Burton VI 122, 172,-(malice). Chauvin VIII 33-34 No. 1; *ANE* 160-61 No. 181;
Husband and Parrot: *Alf* III 141; Burton I (xxx). Chauvin VI 139 No. 294; *ANE* 226 No. 11.□

W256.6.2.3§, ‡Women are obstinate (persistent). (Cf. W217.3§).
Shahriyâr and Shâhzamân: *Alf* I 5; Burton I 13. Chauvin V 188-89 No. 111; *ANE* 370-71 No. 1.□

W256.6.2.4§, ‡Women are meddlers (curious, inquisitive). See: *DOTTI*.
Serpent-charmer and Wife: *Alf* IV 145; Burton IX 56-58. Chauvin II 220 No. 152/9; *ANE* 368 No. 244.□

W256.6.2.5§, ‡Women are treacherous. (Cf. W256.6.8.1.2§).
Hermit Tempted by Angel: *Alf* II 27; Burton III 127. Chauvin II 226 No. 3; *ANE* 221 No. 45/pt. 2;
Lady's Lovers as Pursuer and Fugitive: *Alf* III 143; Burton VI 138-39. Chauvin VIII 38-39 No. 7; *ANE* 267 No. 187.□

W256.6.3.1§, ‡Women's character: 'crooked [like a] rib'. (Cf. A1371.5§).
Nuzhat al-Zamân Tested/¿Umar al-Nu¿mân: *Alf* I 202; Burton II 161. Chauvin VI 116, n.1/passim No. 277; *ANE* 432,/passim No. 39.□

W256.6.3.2§, ‡Women are satans.
al-'Amjad and al-'As¿ad: *Alf* II 117,-(poem); Burton III 318. Chauvin V 208-10 No. 120[.1]; *ANE* 341-42 No. 61/pt. 2.□

W256.6.3.2.1§, ‡Women, like Satan, are the source of all troubles (disasters). See: *DOTTI*. (Cf. A1331.3§, Z94.5.2.1§).

Shahriyâr and Shâhzamân: *Alf* I 5,-(poem); Burton I 13. Chauvin V 188-89 No. 111; *ANE* 370-71 No. 1;
al-'Amjad and al-'As¿ad: *Alf* II 117,-(poem/'in worldly life and religion'); Burton III 318. Chauvin V 208-10 No. 120[.1]; *ANE* 341-42 No. 61/pt. 2;
King Jalî¿âd and Shimâs: *Alf* IV 173, 182; Burton IX 115. Chauvin VI 9 No. 184; *ANE* 237-38 No. 236.□

W256.6.3.2.2§, ‡Wise (good) man pays no attention to women. (Cf. J21.37.1§).
Nuzhat al-Zamân Tested/¿Umar al-Nu¿mân: *Alf* I 201; Burton II 159. Chauvin VI 116, n.1/passim No. 277; *ANE* 432,/passim No. 39.□

W256.6.8§, ‡Males stereotyped: all males (human or beast) are alike.
Tâj al-Mulûk: *Alf* I 299-300; Burton III 31. Chauvin V 126-28 No. 60; *ANE* 406-8 No. 40;
Sayf al-Mulûk: *Alf* III 297,-cf.; Burton VII 368. Chauvin VII 64-73 No. 348; *ANE* 362-64 No. 229.□

W256.6.8.1§, ‡Men cannot resist temptation. See: *DOTTI*. (Cf. T73§, T380.0.2.3§).
Jeweler's Wife and Qamar al-Zamân: *Alf* IV 263; Burton IX 297. Chauvin V 212-14 No. 121; *ANE* 345-47 No. 260.□

W256.6.8.1.2§, ‡Men are treacherous. (Cf. W256.6.2.5§).
Rake's Trick Against Chaste Wife: *Alf* III 141; Burton VI 135, 136. Chauvin VIII 37 No. 5; *ANE* 350-1 No. 185;
Bahrâm and Datmâ: *Alf* III 166,-cf.; Burton VI 188. Chauvin VIII 54-57 No. 22; *ANE* 114-15 No. 202.□

W256.6.8.2§, ‡'Men hold no goodness for women' (i.e., there is no lasting benefit for a woman in a man).
Tâj al-Mulûk: *Alf* I 299-300,-("*al-rijâlu jamî¿uhum mâ ¿indahum khayrun li-al-nisa'*"); Burton III 31,-("and men in general lack grace and goodness to women"). Chauvin V 126-28 No. 60; *ANE* 406-8 No. 40;
Sayf al-Mulûk: *Alf* III 298; Burton VII 368,-(no true love in men). Chauvin VII 64-73 No. 348; *ANE* 362-64 No. 229.□

W256.6.8.3.1§, ‡Men believe that a female is prone to fornication (when away from home).
Hasan of Basrah: *Alf* IV 9,-(*fâḥishah*); Burton VIII 54. Chauvin VII 29-35 No. 212A; *ANE* 207-10 No. 230.□

W256.7.2§, ‡Stereotyping: foolishness (callowness, inexperience) of the young. (Cf. J1450.1.1§).
Stolen Purse/Joint Depositors: *Alf* III 177; Burton VI 210. Chauvin VIII 63-64 No. 25; *ANE* 399 No. 207;
Boy and thieves: Guilty Accomplice: *Alf* IV 163,-cf.; Burton IX 95. Chauvin II 222-23 No. 152/17; *ANE* 128 No. 249.□

W256.8.3.1§, ‡Persons with long beards are fools (short on brains). (Cf. H49.2.1§).
Nûr al-Dîn and Maryam: *Alf* IV 94; Burton VIII 298. Chauvin V 52-54 No. 271; *ANE* 98-99 No. 233.□

W256.9.1§, ‡Stereotyping kind (species).
Birds, Beasts, and Carpenter: *Alf* II 22,-(Adamites); Burton III 115. Chauvin II 225-26 No. 1; *ANE* 126 No. 44.□

W256.9.1.1§, ‡Stereotyping: mankind (Adamites).
Birds, Beasts, and Carpenter: *Alf* II 22,-(poem/hypocrites); Burton III 115. Chauvin II 225-26 No. 1; *ANE* 126 No. 44;
Sayf al-Mulûk: *Alf* III 297-98,-(*al-'ince laysa lahum mawaddah*/human-beings have no [ability for] affection); Burton VII 368,-(there is no true love in men). Chauvin VII 64-73 No. 348; *ANE* 362-64 No. 229.□

W256.9.1.1.1§, ‡Stereotyping: Adamites are treacherous (cruel, etc.). See: *DOTTI*. (Cf. W154.29§).
Bulûqiya: *Alf* III 34; Burton V 322. Chauvin VII 54 No. 77; *ANE* 130-32 No. 177;
Sayf al-Mulûk: *Alf* III 297-98; Burton VII 368-69. Chauvin VII 64-73 No. 348; *ANE* 362-64 No. 229.□

W256.9.1.1.2§, ‡Stereotyping: Adamites are silly (fickle).
Hasan of Basrah: *Alf* IV 4,-("*¿uqûl banî Âdam khafîfah*/Adamites are light-brained"); Burton VIII 45,-("sons of Adam are light of wits"). Chauvin VII 29-35 No. 212A; *ANE* 207-10 No. 230.□

W257§, Surprise at finding a positive where only the negative is presumed.
Isḥâq al-Mûṣilî and Khadîjah bint al-Ḥasan: *Alf* II 185,-(sophistication among *al-sûqah*); Burton IV 120,-(such culture among the trade folk). Chauvin V 241-42 No. 142; *ANE* 232 No. 71;
Schoolmaster Who Fell in Love by Report: Mourns: *Alf* II 292; Burton V 117. Chauvin VI 136 No. 287; *ANE* 367 No. 135;
Schoolmaster (Dominie) Castrates Self: *Alf* II 293,-(neatly dressed, seemingly sane); Burton V 118-19. Chauvin VI 137 No. 288; *ANE* 186 No. 136.□

X. HUMOR

X1§, ‡Practical joke (joker): amusement derived from discomfiting others. (Cf. P327, W183§, X901).
Nûr al-Dîn ¿Alî and Son: *Alf* I 82-84,-cf./(by wife on husband); Burton I 246-47. Chauvin VI 102-6 No. 270; *ANE* 317-19 No. 22;
Barber's Sixth Brother: Emasculated by Abductor: *Alf* I 122-23; Burton I 343-48. Chauvin V 163-64 No. 86; *ANE* 120 No. 34.□

X52, Ridiculous nakedness or exposure. See: *DOTTI*; *GMC*; *PSAE*. (Cf. K1226§, P780§).
Barber's Second Brother: Humiliated by Playgirl: *Alf* I 113; Burton I 328. Chauvin V 158 No. 82; *ANE* 117-18 No. 30.□

X120.0.1§, ‡Humor of blindness.
Barber's Third Brother: Exposes Blind Robbers: *Alf* I 114-5; Burton I 329. Chauvin V 159-60 No. 83; *ANE* 118 No. 31.□

X143, ‡Humor of lameness. See: *DOTTI*.
Tailor's Story/Barber of Baghdad: *Alf* I 103; Burton I 300-1. Chauvin V 154-56 No. 78; *ANE* 405-6 No. 27.□

X144§, ‡Humor of being hunchbacked (hunchbackedness). See: *DOTTI*. (Cf. C867.2.3§, F519.1§, F576.2§).
Hunchback's Tale: Resuscitated: *Alf* I 85; Burton I 255. Chauvin V 180-82 No. 105; *ANE* 224-25 No. 23.□

X150§, ‡Humor on thinness. (Cf. U281.4.3.1§).
Man from Yaman and Six Salve-girls: Flyting: *Alf* II 247,-(poem); Burton IV 254. Chauvin VI 151 No. 313; *ANE* 289-90 No. 84.□

X150.1§, ‡Intercourse with thin woman not satisfying. (Cf. Z84.2.2.1.2§).
Man from Yaman and Six Salve-girls: Flyting: *Alf* II 247,-(poem); Burton IV 254. Chauvin VI 151 No. 313; *ANE* 289-90 No. 84.□

X150.1.1§, ‡Callous (scar) from sexual intercourse with thin woman.
Man from Yaman and Six Salve-girls: Flyting: *Alf* II 248; Burton IV 254. Chauvin VI 151 No. 313; *ANE* 289-90 No. 84.□

X151, Humor of fatness. See: *GMC*. (Cf. J1410).
Man from Yaman and Six Salve-girls: Flyting: *Alf* II 248; Burton IV 252-48. Chauvin VI 151 No. 313; *ANE* 289-90 No. 84.□

X151.4.1§, ‡Person so fat that own hands cannot reach own privates.
Man from Yaman and Six Salve-girls: Flyting: *Alf* II 248; Burton IV 252. Chauvin VI 151 No. 313; *ANE* 289-90 No. 84.□

X252.3.2§, Barber's insensitiveness (*talâmah, burûd*) and inquisitiveness (meddling, curiosity). See: *DOTTI*; *GMC*.
Tailor's Story/Barber of Baghdad: *Alf* I 103-9; Burton I 301-17. Chauvin V 154-56 No. 78; *ANE* 405-6 No. 27.□

X252.3.3§, Barber's talkativeness (chatter). See: *DOTTI*. (Cf. J1215§, T35.0.1).
Tailor's Story/Barber of Baghdad: *Alf* I 103-9; Burton I 301-17. Chauvin V 154-56 No. 78; *ANE* 405-6 No. 27.□

X252.3.3.1§, ‡Barber as know-all expert. See: *DOTTI*. (Cf. J1215§).
Tailor's Story/Barber of Baghdad: *Alf* I 103-9; Burton I 301-17. Chauvin V 154-56 No. 78; *ANE* 405-6 No. 27.□

X350, Jokes on teachers. See: *DOTTI*.
Schoolmaster Who Fell in Love by Report: Mourns: *Alf* II 292[]; Burton V 117-18. Chauvin VI 136 No. 287; *ANE* 367 No. 135;
Schoolmaster (Dominie) Castrates Self: *Alf* II 293; Burton V 119. Chauvin VI 137 No. 288; *ANE* 186 No. 136.□

X372.4, ‡Foolish doctor performs useless operation. (Cf. K1073.1§).
Dalîla the Swindler: *Alf* III 221; Burton VII 161. Chauvin V 245-50 No. 147; *ANE* 163-64 No. 224.□

X420§, Jokes on performers of grave-side rituals (*'fu'ahâ'*/lower clerics: *fuqahâ*). See: *DOTTI*; *GMC*. (Cf. P120).
Illiterate Schoolmaster: *Alf* II 293,-(*mujâwir*); Burton V 119,-(menials of mosque). Chauvin VI 137 No. 289; *ANE* 231 No. 137.□

X420.2.1§, ‡Song or poem (usually in hymn-style) concerning love of rich foods (meat, sweet delicacy). (Cf. F849.1.1§, J1343, W125).
Second Qalandar: Afrit's Wife: *Alf* I 48,-(variant); Burton I 131,-(variant). Chauvin V 197-200 No. 116; *ANE* 338-39 No. 16.□

X579§, ‡Humor of ridiculous (miserly, deceptive) prices and payments.
Ridiculous Eye Salve: *Alf* II 287; Burton V 98-99. Chauvin V 281 No. 165; *ANE* 236 No. 129.□

X598.1.2§, Erotic act (kissing, embracing, etc.) as alms. See: *GMC*. (Cf. T42.3§).
Reeve's Story: Why Maimed by Bride: *Alf* I 97,-(*zawrah*/visit); Burton I 280,-(favour). Chauvin V 220-21 No. 305; *ANE* 351 No. 25;
¿Alî bin Ṭâhir and Mu'nis: *Alf* II 303,-cf./(*'iḥsân* to lover); Burton V 164,-(grant favors to lover). Chauvin VI 154 No. 319; *ANE* 101 No. 153.□

X704§, ‡Humor concerning sex organ (size, color, consistency, etc.). (Cf. F547.5.2.1§, Z105§).
Qamar al-Zamân and Budûr: *Alf* II 109,-cf./(poem: wider than king's conquered lands); Burton III 304. Chauvin V 204-12 No. 120; *ANE* 341-45 No. 61;
Three Wishes: *Alf* III 162,-(elongated-squash); Burton VI 181. Chauvin VIII 51-52 No. 19; *ANE* 419-20 No. 199;
Nûr al-Dîn and Maryam: *Alf* IV 92,-(wax); Burton VIII 293. Chauvin V 52-54 No. 271; *ANE* 98-99 No. 233.□

X840§, Humor concerning hallucinatory conceptualization (mental images, abstractions) induced by drug. See: *DOTTI*; *GMC*.
Hashish Eater's Dream: *Alf* II 10; Burton III 91-93. Chauvin VI 124 No. 278; *ANE* 216 No. 42.□

X901, One lie a year. [Man is believed because of his general truthfulness]. See: *ANE*; *DOTTI*; *GMC*. (Cf. P173.9.1.1§, U235.0.1§, ‡W255§, X1§).
Second Eunuch/Kâfûr's Half-lie: *Alf* I 148; Burton II 51. Chauvin V 278 No. 161; *ANE* 178-79 No. 38.□

X901.1§, ‡Half a lie twice a year: disastrous results from less potent lie. See: *DOTTI*.
Second Eunuch/Kâfûr's Half-lie: *Alf* I 148; Burton II 54. Chauvin V 278 No. 161; *ANE* 178-79 No. 38.□

X902, Liar comes to believe his own lie [due to repetition]. See: *DOTTI*. (Cf. W199.9.1§).
Ma¿rûf the Cobbler: *Alf* IV 296,-cf.; Burton X 14. Chauvin VI 81-82 No. 250; *ANE* 291-93 No. 262.□

X905.3.1§, ‡Claims of ownership of purse (box) supported by descriptions of fantastic contents: farms, villages, cities, schools, peoples, normal and deviant social groups, etc. See: *DOTTI*.
Kurd's Sack/¿Alî the Persian: *Alf* II 201-2; Burton IV 150-52. Chauvin V 279 No. 162; *ANE* 99-100 No. 74.□

X1505.2§, Land where all are cheaters. See: *DOTTI*.
Sandal-wood Merchant and Sharpers: *Alf* III 175; Burton VI 202-7. Chauvin VIII 60-62 No. 26; *ANE* 359-60 No. 205.□

X1727.2§, ‡Beard likened to animal's tail. (Cf. H49.2.1§).
Nûr al-Dîn and Maryam: *Alf* IV 94; Burton VIII 298. Chauvin V 52-54 No. 271; *ANE* 98-99 No. 233.□

Z. MISCELLANEOUS GROUPS OF MOTIFS AND SYMBOLISM

Z1.0.1§, ‡*'inshâ*-style literary composition: constituted mainly from copied (memorized) famous quotations. See: *PSAE*. (Cf. W47§, Z61.0.1§).
Alf laylah wa laylah: *Alf* I 1-4 316,-(entire work); Burton I-X: all. Chauvin V 1ff./(stylistic features not treated);
Ma¿rûf the Cobbler: *Alf* IV 310,-(garden); Burton X 38. Chauvin VI 81-82 No. 250; *ANE* 291-93 No. 262.□

Z1.1§, ‡Holy passages (from scripture) as formulas (usually in non-holy contexts, e.g., "The Lord says '....'," "The Holy Book states," or the like). See: *DOTTI*.
Tâj al-Mulûk: *Alf* I 294,-(*mâ'in mahîn*); Burton III 16,-(vile water). Chauvin V 126-28 No. 60; *ANE* 406 No. 40;
¿Alâ' al-Dîn Abû al-Shâmât: *Alf* II 172,-(*nisyan mansiyyan*); Burton IV 78,-("forgotten as though he never had been). Chauvin V 43-49 No. 18; *ANE* 85-87 No. 63;
Lover Who Feigned Himself a Thief: *Alf* II 204,-(*wamâ Allâhu bi-ẓallâmin* ...); Burton IV 156,-("God is not unjust towards mankind."). Chauvin VII 134-35 No. 403; *ANE* 272 No. 76;
Tawaddud: Slavegirl Sold and Regained: *Alf* II 304,-(*suqiṭa fî yadayhi*); Burton V 191 n. 1. Chauvin VII 117-19 No. 387; *ANE* 408-10 No. 157;
Tawaddud: Slavegirl Sold and Regained: *Alf* II 305,-(*kawkabun durriyy*).; Burton V 194,-(sparkling star). Chauvin VII 117-19 No. 387; *ANE* 408-10 No. 157;
Ma¿rûf the Cobbler: *Alf* IV 305,-(*Irama dhât al-¿imâd* ...); Burton X 29. Chauvin VI 81-82 No. 250; *ANE* 291-93 No. 262;
Nûr al-Dîn and Maryam: *Alf* IV 128,-cf./(quote: "*wa lan yaj¿alâ Allâhu li al-kâfirîna, ...*"); Burton IX 16,-("'Allah will by no means make a way for the Infidels ..."). Chauvin V 52-54 No. 271; *ANE* 98-99 No. 233.□

Z1.1.1§, ‡Scriptural (scripture-like) formulas: (e.g., *yâ 'ayyuhâ* ... ('O ye who ...') *'inna 'Allâha* ... (Verily, The Lord ...), etc. See: *PSAE*.
Anîs al-Jalîs: *Alf* I 138,-(*ja¿ala li kulli shay'in sababâ*); Burton II 26. Chauvin V 120-24 No. 58; *ANE* 316-17 No. 35;
Mock Caliph/¿Alî al-Jawharî: *Alf* II 200,-(*kâna dhâlika fî al-kitâbi masṭûran*"); Burton IV 148,-(this was written in the Book of Destiny). Chauvin V 99-100 No. 174; *ANE* 304-5 No. 73;
Sindbâd and Porter: *Alf* III 82,-("*tughnî man tashâ' wa tufqiru man tashâ'* ..."); Burton VI 2,-("whom Thou wilt Thou makest poor and whom Thou wilt Thou makest rich! ..."). Chauvin VII 1 No. 373; *ANE* 383-85 No. 179/pt.;
Ruined Baghdadi and His Slave-girl: *Alf* IV 130,-(*'inna dhâlika l-¿aẓîm*); Burton IX 24-32. Chauvin V 152-53 No. 75; *ANE* 353 No. 235;
¿Abdallah ibn Fâḍil: Treacherous Brothers: *Alf* IV 276,-(idol worship/raising of sky); Burton IX 325. Chauvin V 2-4 No. 2; *ANE* 63-65 No. 261.□

Z10.0.2§, ‡Formula: affirmation of religious truth (e.g., 'Oneness of God', sacredness of prophet, etc.). (Cf. Z10.2.5§).
Sayf al-Mulûk: *Alf* III 302; Burton VIII 6. Chauvin VII 64-73 No. 348; *ANE* 362-64 No. 229;
Hasan of Basrah: *Alf* IV 55,-(*lahu al-mulku wa al-malakût*); Burton VIII 155,-("hath dominion over the Seen and the Unseen"). Chauvin VII 29-35 No. 212A; *ANE* 207-10 No. 230;
Nûr al-Dîn and Maryam: *Alf* IV 129; Burton IX 18. Chauvin V 52-54 No. 271; *ANE* 98-99 No. 233;
Ruined Baghdadi and His Slave-girl: *Alf* IV 133; Burton IX 32. Chauvin V 152-53 No. 75; *ANE* 353 No. 235.□

Z10.2.1§, ‡Happy end formula. See: *DOTTI*. (Cf. T135.8).
Budûr and Jubayr ibn ¿Umayr: *Alf* II 243; Burton IV 245. Chauvin VII 93-94 No. 374; *ANE* 243-44 No. 83.□

Z10.2.1.1§, ‡Happy procreation end formula.
¿Alî Shâr and Zumurrud: *Alf* II 235,-(begot children by her); Burton IV 228. Chauvin V 89-91 No. 28; *ANE* 100-1 No. 82.□

Z10.2.1.2§, ‡Misery to the adversary ('censurers,' 'envious') as happy formula.
Mock Caliph/¿Alî al-Jawharî: *Alf* II 200,-(*'ikmâd al-ḥasûd*); Burton IV 148,-(to their enviers mortification and misery). Chauvin V 99-100 No. 174; *ANE* 304-5 No. 73.□

Z10.2.5§, ‡Glorification of God formulas. (Cf. Z10.0.2§).

Uns al-Wujûd and al-Ward: *Alf* II 284; Burton V 64. Chauvin VI 127-29 No. 282; *ANE* 438 No. 104;
Nûr al-Dîn and Maryam: *Alf* IV 129; Burton IX 18. Chauvin V 52-54 No. 271; *ANE* 98-99 No. 233;
Ruined Baghdadi and His Slave-girl: *Alf* IV 133; Burton IX 32. Chauvin V 152-53 No. 75; *ANE* 353 No. 235;
Abû Qîr and Abû Ṣîr: *Alf* IV 197,-(*al-Bâqî ¿lâ al-dawâm* ...); Burton IX 165,-(Him who endureth for ever ...). Chauvin V 15-17 No. 10; *ANE* 75-77 No. 255;
Landsman ¿Abdallah and Merman ¿Abdallah: *Alf* IV 208; Burton IX 188. Chauvin V 6-7 No. 3; *ANE* 65-66 No. 256;
al-Rashîd and Omani Merchant: *Alf* IV 219; Burton IX 207. Chauvin VI 111-12 No. 276; *ANE* 201-2 No. 257;
Ibrâhîm and Jamîlah: *Alf* IV 229; Burton IX 209. Chauvin VI 52-53 No. 218; *ANE* 227-29 No. 258;
Abû al-Ḥasan al-Khorâsânî (and Caliph's Favorite): *Alf* IV 237; Burton IX 246. Chauvin V 218-20 No. 129; *ANE* 68-69 No. 259;
Jeweler's Wife and Qamar al-Zamân: *Alf* IV 266; Burton IX 304. Chauvin V 212-14 No. 121; *ANE* 345-47 No. 260;
¿Abdallah ibn Fâḍil: Treacherous Brothers: *Alf* IV 288; Burton IX 349. Chauvin V 2-4 No. 2; *ANE* 63-65 No. 261;
Ma¿rûf the Cobbler: *Alf* IV 317; Burton X 53. Chauvin VI 81-82 No. 250; *ANE* 291-93 No. 262;
Shahriyâr and Shahrzâd: *Alf* IV 318; Burton X 54-55. Chauvin V 190-91 No. 111/pt.; *ANE* 371 No. 1.□

Z10.2.5.1§, ‡'The Death-giver to nations and the Resurrector of corpses' (i.e., God). (Cf. V311.4§).
King Jalî¿âd and Shimâs: *Alf* IV 182; Burton IX 134,-("causeth peoples to pass away, and quickeneth the bones that rot in decay"). Chauvin VI 9 No. 184; *ANE* 237-38 No. 236.□

Z10.5.1§, ‡Plain repetition.
King Jalî¿âd and Shimâs: *Alf* IV 169,-("yahjîmû ¿alayh ..."); Burton IX 107. Chauvin VI 9 No. 184; *ANE* 237-38 No. 236.□

Z10.5.2§, ‡Repetition: speech and action.
Jawdar and His Treacherous Brethren: *Alf* III 187,-(commands-actions); Burton VI 230. Chauvin V 257-60 No. 154; *ANE* 244-45 No. 209.□

Z10.8.1§, ‡Emphasis: character addressed by full name, each component separately (e.g., "O you Zayd, O you Son of ¿Amr!", "Yâ Sindibâd, yâ Baḥarî!," etc.). (Cf. Z13.5.2§).
Sindbâd's Seventh Voyage: *Alf* III 117; Burton VI 70. Chauvin VII 26-29 No. 373G; *ANE* 386-87 No. 179.□

Z13.5.2§, ‡Tale character (speaker) instructs self (unusually reprimandingly and emphatically). (Cf. Z10.8.1§).
Sindbâd's Seventh Voyage: *Alf* III 117,-("I said to myself: 'Yâ Sindbâd, yâ Baḥarî, you have ...!'"); Burton VI 70. Chauvin VII 26-29 No. 373G; *ANE* 386-87 No. 179.□

Z13.7§, Tale-teller addresses question along with answer to listener. See: *GMC*.
Hârûn, Slave-girl and Judge Abû-Yûsuf: *Alf* II 204,-(*'ayyuhâ al-muta'addib*/you, who are seeking to learn morals); Burton IV 155 n. 1,-(writer addresses polite reader). Chauvin VII 114 No. 383; *ANE* 204 No. 75.□

Z13.9.1§, ‡Speaker wards off evil effects of own speech (words). (Cf. C434§, V90§).
Ma¿rûf the Cobbler: *Alf* IV 290,-(*'aba¿ad*); Burton X 4. Chauvin VI 81-82 No. 250; *ANE* 291-93 No. 262.□

Z13.11.1§, ‡Uncertainty about accuracy of truthful report: "And God knows best", "And God is Omniscient" (or the like). (Cf. P470§, W50§).
Ni¿mah and Nu¿m: Stolen Wife Regained: *Alf* II 132,-(*'Allâhu 'a¿lam*); Burton III 348,-("but Allah alone is All knowing"). Chauvin VI 96-97 No. 263; *ANE* 314 No. 62;
al-'Amjad and al-'As¿ad: *Alf* II 147; Burton IV 29. Chauvin V 208-10 No. 120[.1]; *ANE* 2 341-42 No. 61/pt.;
Jânshâh: *Alf* III 40,-(of prophecy); Burton V 331. Chauvin VII 39-44 No. 153; *ANE* 238-41 No. 178;
Bulûqiya: *Alf* III 81; Burton V 396. Chauvin VII 54 No. 77; *ANE* 130-32 No. 177;
Stolen Purse/Joint Depositors: *Alf* III 177; Burton VI 209. Chauvin VIII 63-64 No. 25; *ANE* 399 No. 207;
Mercury ¿Alî: *Alf* III 246-47; Burton VII 209. Chauvin V 248-50 No. 147; *ANE* 301-3 No. 225.□

Z16, Tales ending with a question: [(dilemma tales)]. See: *DOTTI*; *GMC*.
King's Son and Afrit's Mistress: *Alf* III 173,-cf./(responsibility for killing); Burton VI 200. Chauvin VIII 59 No. 24; *ANE* 263-64 No. 204.□

Z19.2, Tales filled with contradictions. See: *DOTTI*; *GMC*.
Kurd's Sack/¿Alî the Persian: *Alf* II 201-2; Burton IV 149-52. Chauvin V 279 No. 162; *ANE* 99-100 No. 74.□

Z19.3§, Etiological tales: 'That-is-why'-tales. See: *DOTTI*.
Water-carrier and Goldsmith's Wife: *Alf* II 286,-(of proverb); Burton V 89-90. Chauvin VI 192 No. 361; *ANE* 444 No. 122.□

Z40.3§, ‡Utility cycle of animal (bird): one use when young, another when mature, another when less vigorous, finally discarded or killed and organs processed into goods. See: *DOTTI*.
Birds, Beasts, and Carpenter: *Alf* II 23-24; Burton III 119. Chauvin II 225-26 No. 1; *ANE* 126 No. 44.□

Z40.3.1§, ‡Utility cycle of horse: broken when young and spirited, saddled and ridden for speed when vigorous, harnessed to mill (wheel) when slows, slaughtered and organs processed into utensils when old.
Birds, Beasts, and Carpenter: *Alf* II 23-24; Burton III 119. Chauvin II 225-26 No. 1; *ANE* 126 No. 44.□

Z42.1.1§, Death is the strongest. See: *DOTTI*; *GMC*. (Cf. U250.0.1§, V311.3.0.1§, Z111.9.1§).
Birds, Beasts, and Carpenter: *Alf* II 24,-cf./(than Adamites); Burton III 120. Chauvin II 225-26 No. 1; *ANE* 126 No. 44.□

Z43.7.1§, ‡Pecking order: chain of aggressive actions and displaced reactions, started against the weak and ending with the weakest. See: *DOTTI*. (Cf. P210.0.1.1§, Z194.3.1.1§).
¿Azîz and ¿Azîzah: *Alf* I 273,-(female cousin kicked); Burton II 307. Chauvin V 144-45 No. 71; *ANE* 111-13 No. 41;
Jeweler's Wife and Qamar al-Zamân: *Alf* IV 238,-cf./(father/husband blames mother/wife of his son); Burton IX 249. Chauvin V 212-14 No. 121; *ANE* 345-47 No. 260.□

Z49.13.1§, ‡Chain of killings: drop of honey falls on bird, cat kills bird, dog kills cat, cat's owner kills dog, dog's owner kills cat's owner, bloody feud between villages ensues. See: *DOTTI*.
Drop of Honey: *Alf* III 145; Burton VI 143. Chauvin VIII 41-42 No. 9; *ANE* 171-72 No. 189.□

Z51, ‡Chains involving contradictions or extremes. See: *DOTTI*.
Kurd's Sack/¿Alî the Persian: *Alf* II 201-2; Burton IV 150-52. Chauvin V 279 No. 162; *ANE* 99-100 No. 74.□

Z55§, ‡Process ascends (escalated) to its natural or logical climax (conclusion). See: *DOTTI*.
Barber's Third Brother: Exposes Blind Robbers: *Alf* I 114-5; Burton I 328–331. Chauvin V 159-60 No. 83; *ANE* 118 No. 31.□

Z55.1§, ‡Biological process carried to its climax. See: *DOTTI*.
Porter and Ladies of Baghdad: *Alf* I 35,-cf.; Burton I 92. Chauvin V 251-52 No. 148; *ANE* 324-26 No. 14.□

Z55.3§, ‡Social (interactional) process carried to its climax. See: *DOTTI*. (Cf. T42.4.1§).
Fisherman and Afrit: Ingratitude: *Alf* I 15,-cf./(afrit's ascending rewards); Burton I 42. Chauvin VI 23-25 No. 195; *ANE* 183-84 No. 8.□

Z61.0.1§, ‡'*hayhât! hayhât*!' (Never!). (Literary usage). (Cf. Z1.0.1§).
Birds, Beasts, and Carpenter: *Alf* II 23; Burton III 120,-(naught ...). Chauvin II 225-26 No. 1; *ANE* 126 No. 44;
Angel of Death and Jewish King: *Alf* III 10; Burton V 251,-(Naught ...). Chauvin VI 184-85 No. 351; *ANE* 104 No. 160;
Bulûqiya: *Alf* III 26; Burton V 310,-(Far, far is it from your power). Chauvin VII 54 No. 77; *ANE* 130-32 No. 177;
Man Who Never Laughs: *Alf* III 155; Burton VI 166. Chauvin VIII 47-48 No. 15; *ANE* 285-86 No. 195;
Mercury ¿Alî: *Alf* III 232; Burton VII 184. Chauvin V 248-50 No. 147; *ANE* 301-3 No. 225;
Sayf al-Mulûk: *Alf* III 298,-(poem); Burton VII 39,-(Far be it). Chauvin VII 64-73 No. 348; *ANE* 362-64 No. 229.□

Z62, Proverbial simile. See: *DOTTI*; *GMC*. (Cf. F827.9.4.1§, P550.1.0.2§, Z117.6.2§, Z179.1.2.2.1§, Z193.3.1.1.1§).
Tâj al-Mulûk: *Alf* I 290,-(*ka-'ishtiyâq al-ẓam'an 'ilâ al-mâ'*); Burton III 9,-(as one athirst longeth for water). Chauvin V 126-28 No. 60; *ANE* 406-8 No. 40;
Tâj al-Mulûk: *Alf* I 292,-(angel-like/beauty of young man); Burton III 15. Chauvin V 126-28 No. 60; *ANE* 406-8 No. 40;
Qamar al-Zamân and Budûr: *Alf* II 109,-(wider than,/poem); Burton III 304. Chauvin V 204-12 No. 120; *ANE* 341-45 No. 61;
¿Alâ' al-Dîn Abû al-Shâmât: *Alf* II 180,-(endurance in battle); Burton IV 93,-("as the stake in bran"). Chauvin V 43-49 No. 18; *ANE* 85-87 No. 63;
¿Alî Shâr and Zumurrud: *Alf* II 226,-(beard—quills), 234,-(hot bath—vagina); Burton IV 208. Chauvin V 89-91 No. 28; *ANE* 100-1 No. 82;
Man from Yaman and Six Salve-girls: Flyting: *Alf* II 249,-(simile/'rust of [un-tinned] copper'/[*ginzâr*/poison]); Burton IV 259,-(rust of brass pot). Chauvin VI 151 No. 313; *ANE* 289-90 No. 84;
Sindbâd's Fifth Voyage: *Alf* III 107,-(garden-paradise); Burton VI 50. Chauvin VII 21-24 No. 373E; *ANE* 386 No. 179;
Sindbâd's Seventh Voyage: *Alf* III 118,-("*ka-al-farkh al-dâyikh*/like a dizzy/giddy chick"); Burton VI 71,-("giddy as a chick"). Chauvin VII 26-29 No. 373G; *ANE* 386-87 No. 179;
Jawdar and His Treacherous Brethren: *Alf* III 184,-(moon-like/maiden); Burton VI 226. Chauvin V 257-60 No. 154; *ANE* 244-45 No. 209;
Dalîla the Swindler: *Alf* III 215,-(saw); Burton VII 151. Chauvin V 245-50 No. 147; *ANE* 163-64 No. 224;
Nûr al-Dîn and Maryam: *Alf* IV 93,-(old man: "like a falling wall or an afrit incinerated by star"); Burton VIII 294,(like a wall ready to fall,/like Ifrit smitten down of a fire-ball). Chauvin V 52-54 No. 271; *ANE* 98-99 No. 233;
Man Who Had a Milk-camel: Loses Both: *Alf* IV 164,-cf./(like she-camel's owner); Burton IX 97. Chauvin VI 9 No. 184.□

Z62.5.1§, ‡Celestial beauty (to be like moon, sun, star, dawn, etc.). See: *DOTTI*. (Cf. F574, F575).
Eldest Lady's Story: Treacherous Sisters: *Alf* I 55,-(poem); Burton I 167. Chauvin V 4 No. 443; *ANE* 174-75 No. 19;
Anîs al-Jalîs: *Alf* I 126-27,-(poem); Burton II 3. Chauvin V 120-24 No. 58; *ANE* 316-17 No. 35;
King ¿Umar al-Nu¿mân and Sons: *Alf* I 170,-(full moon surrounded by stars); Burton II 99. Chauvin VI 112-24 No. 277; *ANE* 430-34 No. 39;
Tâj al-Mulûk: *Alf* I 290,-(*qamar*/moon); Burton III 9. Chauvin V 126-28 No. 60; *ANE* 406-8 No. 40;
¿Alî ibn Bakkâr: *Alf* II 54,-(sun); Burton III 191. Chauvin V 153 No. 76; *ANE* 92-93 No. 60;
Ebony Horse: *Alf* II 254,-cf./(full moon); Burton V 2-3. Chauvin V 221-31 No. 130; *ANE* 172-74 No. 103;
Isḥâq al-Mûṣilî and Khadîjah bint al-Ḥasan: *Alf* II 185; Burton IV 120. Chauvin V 241-42 No. 142; *ANE* 232 No. 71;
Budûr and Jubayr ibn ¿Umayr: *Alf* II 235,-(full moon of the fourteenth); Burton IV 231. Chauvin VII 93-94 No. 374; *ANE* 243-44 No. 83;
Uns al-Wujûd and al-Ward: *Alf* II 278; Burton V 54. Chauvin VI 127-29 No. 282; *ANE* 438 No. 104.□

Z62.5.1.2§, ‡'As beautiful as (more beautiful than) the sun'. See: *DOTTI*.
Jinni Keeps Mistress in Box: *Alf* I 3,-(poem); Burton I 11. Chauvin V 188-89 No. 111; *ANE* 370 No. 1/pt.□

Z62.5.1.5.1§, ‡[As beautiful as] 'a houri' (nymph of paradise). (Cf. F499.2).
Nûr al-Dîn ¿Alî and Son: *Alf* I 69,-(male); Burton I 217. Chauvin VI 102-6 No. 270; *ANE* 317-19 No. 22;
Qamar al-Zamân and Budûr: *Alf* II 95; Burton III 273. Chauvin V 204-12 No. 120; *ANE* 341-45 No. 61;
Ni¿mah and Nu¿m: Stolen Wife Regained: *Alf* II 140,-(male); Burton IV 15. Chauvin VI 96-97 No. 263; *ANE* 314 No. 62;
¿Alî Shâr and Zumurrud: *Alf* II 220,-(poem); Burton IV 195. Chauvin V 89-91 No. 28; *ANE* 100-1 No. 82;
Dispute Concerning Males and Females: *Alf* II 302,-(supernatural male/*wildân*); Burton V 160. Chauvin VI 153 No. 317; *ANE* 291 No. 151;

Hasan of Basrah: *Alf* IV 16,-(poem); Burton VIII 66. Chauvin VII 29-35 No. 212A; *ANE* 207-10 No. 230.□

Z62.5.5.1§, ‡Crystal-like body organs (semi-transparent).
Nûr al-Dîn ¿Alî and Son: *Alf* I 73; Burton I 224. Chauvin VI 102-6 No. 270; *ANE* 317-19 No. 22.□

Z62.6.1§, ‡'As smooth as silk'.
Nûr al-Dîn and Maryam: *Alf* IV 97,-(smoother than); Burton VIII 303,-(softer). Chauvin V 52-54 No. 271; *ANE* 98-99 No. 233.□

Z62.6.4§, ‡As soft as dough. (Cf. F575.1.5.12.1§).
Masrûr and Zayn al-Mawâṣif: *Alf* IV 57; Burton VIII 217,-(paste). Chauvin VI 82-84 No. 251; *ANE* 294-95 No. 232.□

Z62.9.1.1§, ‡The 'compared to' (*mushabbah bihi*) is superior to what is being 'compared'. (Cf. Z119.3.1§).
Dispute Concerning Males and Females: *Alf* II 302; Burton V 160. Chauvin VI 153 No. 317; *ANE* 291 No. 151.□

Z63.1.2§—(formerly-Z63.2§), 'Eblis's hope in [admission to] paradise'. See: *GMC*.
Jeweler's Wife and Qamar al-Zamân: *Alf* IV 264; Burton IX 300. Chauvin V 212-14 No. 121; *ANE* 345-47 No. 260.□

Z63.3.1.1§, ‡External indicators signifying humiliation: to be subjected to sexual aggression.
Porter and Ladies of Baghdad: *Alf* I 34-35,-cf.; Burton I 92. Chauvin V 251-52 No. 148; *ANE* 324-26 No. 14.□

Z63.3.3§, ‡Personal manifestations signifying (as indicators of) failure (humiliation, submission).
Jeweler's Wife and Qamar al-Zamân: *Alf* IV 260,-(gen.—like "*maqâṭî¿* of pilgrims/abandoned and left to die); Burton IX 290,-(an offcast of the pilgrims). Chauvin V 212-14 No. 121; *ANE* 345-47 No. 260.□

Z63.3.3.1§, ‡To be 'slapped on the nape (back) of neck'—humiliation. See: *DOTTI*.
Porter and Ladies of Baghdad: *Alf* I 35; Burton I 92. Chauvin V 251-52 No. 148; *ANE* 324-26 No. 14;
Barber's Second Brother: Humiliated by Playgirl: *Alf* I 113; Burton I 325-26. Chauvin V 158 No. 82; *ANE* 117-18 No. 30;
Barber's Sixth Brother: Emasculated by Abductor: *Alf* I 123; Burton I 346. Chauvin V 163-64 No. 86; *ANE* 120 No. 34;
Hashish Eater's Dream: *Alf* II 10; Burton III 93. Chauvin VI 124 No. 278; *ANE* 216 No. 42;
Abû Qîr and Abû Ṣîr: *Alf* IV 197; Burton IX 163. Chauvin V 15-17 No. 10; *ANE* 75-77 No. 255.□

Z63.3.3.1.4§, ‡To be beaten with shoe (slipper, clog, etc.). (Cf. Z179.2.3.1§).
First Qalandar: Brother-Sister Incest: *Alf* I 42; Burton I 110-11. Chauvin V 196-97 No. 115; *ANE* 337-38 No. 15;
Tâj al-Mulûk: *Alf* I 299; Burton III 30. Chauvin V 126-28 No. 60; *ANE* 406-8 No. 40;
Wife's device to cheat: (Weeping Bitch as Bluff): *Alf* III 149; Burton VI 155. Chauvin VIII 45-46 No. 13; *ANE* 447-49 No. 193;
Masrûr and Zayn al-Mawâṣif: *Alf* IV 76; Burton VIII 257. Chauvin VI 82-84 No. 251; *ANE* 294-95 No. 232.□

Z63.3.3.1.5§, ‡To bite earth ('biting the dust')—humiliation, defeat.
Hasan of Basrah: *Alf* III 306,-(*¿aḍḍa al-'arḍ bi-'asnânih*); Burton VIII 16,-("biting the deck with his fore-teeth"). Chauvin VII 29-35 No. 212A; *ANE* 207-10 No. 230.□

Z63.5.1§, 'Eve is fertile', 'A womb brings forth': formulas signifying futility of conceit. See: *DOTTI*; *GMC*.
Mercury ¿Alî: *Alf* III 227; Burton VII 174. Chauvin V 248-50 No. 147; *ANE* 301-3 No. 225.□

Z63.7.1§, ‡Exasperation: 'one's gallbladder (*marârah*) bursts'. (Cf. V462.2.3).
Tailor's Story/Barber of Baghdad: *Alf* I 106; Burton I 306. Chauvin V 154-56 No. 78; *ANE* 405-6 No. 27;
Spy, Fourth Maiden/¿Umar al-Nu¿mân: *Alf* I 223,-cf.; Burton II 205. *ANE* 432 No. 39/passim;
King ¿Umar al-Nu¿mân and Sons: *Alf* I 234; Burton II 228. Chauvin VI 112-24 No. 277; *ANE* 430-34 No. 39;
¿Azîz and ¿Azîzah: *Alf* I 281; Burton II 322 n. 1. Chauvin V 144-45 No. 71; *ANE* 111-13 No. 41;

Sindbâd's Fourth Voyage: *Alf* III 104; Burton VI 42,-("gall-bladder"). Chauvin VII 18-20 No. 373D; *ANE* 386 No. 179;
Hasan of Basrah: *Alf* III 316,-(poem); Burton VIII 32,-(heart). Chauvin VII 29-35 No. 212A; *ANE* 207-10 No. 230;
Ma¿rûf the Cobbler: *Alf* IV 308; Burton X 34. Chauvin VI 81-82 No. 250; *ANE* 291-93 No. 262.□

Z63.7.3§, ‡Futility: striking at cold iron (to reshape it).
Nûr al-Dîn ¿Alî and Son: *Alf* I 73,-(poem); Burton I 223. Chauvin VI 102-6 No. 270; *ANE* 317-19 No. 22;
Qamar al-Zamân and Budûr: *Alf* II 76,-(poem); Burton III 235. Chauvin V 204-12 No. 120; *ANE* 341-45 No. 61;
¿Alî Shâr and Zumurrud: *Alf* II 221,-(poem); Burton IV 198. Chauvin V 89-91 No. 28; *ANE* 100-1 No. 82.□

Z63.8.2.3.1§, ‡Stark difference: 'This is honey, this is vinegar!'
Sindbâd and Porter: *Alf* III 82,-(poem); Burton VI 2. Chauvin VII 1 No. 373; *ANE* 383-85 No. 179/pt.□

Z63.9§, ‡Formulas signifying evident absence of differences (and presence of uniformity, similarity).
Sindbâd and Porter: *Alf* III 82,-(*nutfah*); Burton VI 2. Chauvin VII 1 No. 373; *ANE* 383-85 No. 179/pt.□

Z63.9.1§, ‡'The clay is from the [same earth-] clay, and the dough-turn (*lattah*) is from the dough [in the kneading tray]'. (Cf. P750.0.3.1§).
Sindbâd and Porter: *Alf* III 82,-(poem/*nutfah*); Burton VI 2,-(little drop of sperm). Chauvin VII 1 No. 373; *ANE* 383-85 No. 179/pt.□

Z63.10.2.1§, ‡'Go: with no expulsion [intended]'.
Nûr al-Dîn ¿Alî and Son: *Alf* I 71; Burton I 220,-(get up and go). Chauvin VI 102-6 No. 270; *ANE* 317-19 No. 22.□

Z63.10.2.2§, ‡'Show us the width of [the back of] your shoulders'.
Porter and Ladies of Baghdad: *Alf* I 35; Burton I 93. Chauvin V 251-52 No. 148; *ANE* 324-26 No. 14.□

Z65.1.2§, ‡Snow-white.
Qamar al-Zamân and Budûr: *Alf* II 97; Burton III 278. Chauvin V 204-12 No. 120; *ANE* 341-45 No. 61.□

Z65.3.1.1§, ‡'A milk-[white] day' (i.e., as white and pure as milk: an auspicious time).
Mock Caliph/¿Alî al-Jawharî: *Alf* II 196; Burton IV 140. Chauvin V 99-100 No. 174; *ANE* 304-5 No. 73.□

Z65.4§, White cheese (butter) is softest: female. See: *DOTTI*. (Cf. F575.1.5.12.1§).
Qamar al-Zamân and Budûr: *Alf* II 110; Burton III 306. Chauvin V 204-12 No. 120; *ANE* 341-45 No. 61.□

Z66.1§, To be 'in (on) one's eyes'—endearment. See: *DOTTI*; *GMC*. (Cf. F1035.6.2.1§).
Ghânim ibn Ayyûb: *Alf* I 153; Burton II 45-76. Chauvin VI 14 No. 188; *ANE* 192-93 No. 36;
¿Alî ibn Bakkâr: *Alf* II 57; Burton III 195. Chauvin V 153 No. 76; *ANE* 92-93 No. 60;
Sindbâd's Sixth Voyage: *Alf* III 115; Burton VI 66. Chauvin VII 24-27 No. 373F; *ANE* 386 No. 179;

Lady and Five Suitors Deceived: *Alf* III 159; Burton VI 176. Chauvin VIII 50-51 No. 18; *ANE* 266 No. 198;
Jawdar and His Treacherous Brethren: *Alf* III 179; Burton VI 215. Chauvin V 257-60 No. 154; *ANE* 244-45 No. 209.□

Z66.2§, ‡To be dearer than one's self.
Basra Girls in Poetry Contest: *Alf* III 205; Burton VII 113. Chauvin VI 144 No. 301; *ANE* 107-8 No. 216.□

Z66.2.2.1§, ‡To be done "out of one's own eyes". See: *DOTTI*. (Cf. Z67.1§).
Jewish Doctor's Story: Sororicide: *Alf* I 101; Burton I 294. Chauvin VI 89 No. 253; *ANE* 242 No. 26;
Jawdar and His Treacherous Brethren: *Alf* III 184; Burton VI 226. Chauvin V 257-60 No. 154; *ANE* 244-45 No. 209.□

Z66.5§, ‡Dear relative(s) as would-be ransom (sacrifice). (Cf. W28.5.3§).
Nuzhat al-Zamân Tested/¿Umar al-Nu¿mân: *Alf* I 205,-(by father and mother); Burton II 169,-("Thou art to me as my father and my mother"). Chauvin VI 116, n.1/passim No. 277; *ANE* 432,/passim No. 39;
Basra Girls in Poetry Contest: *Alf* III 205, 6; Burton VII 113. Chauvin VI 144 No. 301; *ANE* 107-8 No. 216.□

Z66.5.0.1§, ‡Oneself as would-be ransom (sacrifice). (Cf. T39.1.2§, W28.5.1§).
Shahriyâr and Shâhzamân: *Alf* I 5,-cf./(Shahrzâd); Burton I 15. Chauvin V 188-89 No. 111; *ANE* 370-71 No. 1;
Ghânim ibn Ayyûb: *Alf* I 149; Burton II 53. Chauvin VI 14-16 No. 188; *ANE* 192-93 No. 36;
Basra Girls in Poetry Contest: *Alf* III 205, 6; Burton VII 113. Chauvin VI 144 No. 301; *ANE* 107-8 No. 216;
Hasan of Basrah: *Alf* III 318,-(hero's jinni sister); Burton VIII 37. Chauvin VII 29-35 No. 212A; *ANE* 207-10 No. 230.□

Z66.5.3.1§, ‡Woman's own husband as would-be ransom (sacrifice). See: *DOTTI*.
Jeweler's Wife and Qamar al-Zamân: *Alf* IV 256; Burton IX 284,-("sacrifice my husband to thee"). Chauvin V 212-14 No. 121; *ANE* 345-47 No. 260.□

Z66.6.1§, ‡Endearment: to be kissed between the eyes.
Tâj al-Mulûk: *Alf* I 265; Burton II 290. Chauvin V 126-28 No. 60; *ANE* 406-8 No. 40;
King ¿Umar al-Nu¿mân and Sons: *Alf* I 320; Burton III 76. Chauvin VI 112-24 No. 277; *ANE* 430-34 No. 39;
Hammâd: Treacherous Bedouin: *Alf* II 18, 19; Burton III 107, 109. Chauvin VI 124 n. 1 No. 277; *ANE* 200 No. 43;
Hammâd: Treacherous Bedouin: *Alf* II 18, 19; Burton III 107, 109. Chauvin VI 124 n. 1 No. 277; *ANE* 200 No. 43;
Water-fowl and Tortoise: *Alf* II 29,-(animals); Burton III 131. Chauvin II 226-27 No. 5; *ANE* 444 No. 46;
Qamar al-Zamân and Budûr: *Alf* II 71,-(fairy/human), 73; Burton III 224, 228. Chauvin V 204-12 No. 120; *ANE* 341-45 No. 61;
Lover Who Feigned Himself a Thief: *Alf* II 205; Burton IV 158. Chauvin VII 134-35 No. 403; *ANE* 272 No. 76;
Ebony Horse: *Alf* II 259; Burton V 15. Chauvin V 221-31 No. 130; *ANE* 172-74 No. 103;
Jânshâh: *Alf* III 55; Burton V 351. Chauvin VII 39-44 No. 153; *ANE* 238-41 No. 178;
Stolen Purse/Joint Depositors: *Alf* III 177; Burton VI 211. Chauvin VIII 63-64 No. 25; *ANE* 399 No. 207;
Mercury ¿Alî: *Alf* III 230; Burton VII 178. Chauvin V 248-50 No. 147; *ANE* 301-3 No. 225;
Jullanâr of the Sea: *Alf* III 249; Burton VII 269. Chauvin V 147-51 No. 73; *ANE* 248-51 No. 227;
Hasan of Basrah: *Alf* IV 4, 46; Burton VIII 43, 129. Chauvin VII 29-35 No. 212A; *ANE* 207-10 No. 230;
Nûr al-Dîn and Maryam: *Alf* IV 89, 103; Burton VIII 286, 315. Chauvin V 52-54 No. 271; *ANE* 98-99 No. 233;
Jeweler's Wife and Qamar al-Zamân: *Alf* IV 241,-(seductive/homosexual/test), 260; Burton IX 254, 289. Chauvin V 212-14 No. 121; *ANE* 345-47 No. 260.□

Z67.0.2§, ‡Aggrandizement: to be addressed indirectly via one's 'presence' (*hadrah*), 'highness' (*rif¿ah*), or the like. See: *DOTTI*.
Abû al-Hasan al-Khorâsânî (and Caliph's Favorite): *Alf* IV 230,-cf./(*janâb-ikum*); Burton IX 231,-("your honours"). Chauvin V 218-20 No. 129; *ANE* 68-69 No. 259;
Shahriyâr and Shahrzâd: *Alf* IV 317,-(*janâb-ik*); Burton X 54,-("Thy Highness"). Chauvin V 190-91 No. 111/pt.; *ANE* 371 No. 1.□

Z67.1§, To be 'on top of one's head'—aggrandizement. See: *DOTTI*; *GMC*. (Cf. Z66.2.2.1§).
Jewish Doctor's Story: Sororicide: *Alf* I 101; Burton I 294. Chauvin VI 89 No. 253; *ANE* 242 No. 26;
¿Alî ibn Bakkâr: *Alf* II 42, 57; Burton III 164. Chauvin V 153 No. 76; *ANE* 92-93 No. 60;
Sindbâd's Sixth Voyage: *Alf* III 115; Burton VI 66. Chauvin VII 24-27 No. 373F; *ANE* 386 No. 179;

Lady and Five Suitors Deceived: *Alf* III 159; Burton VI 176. Chauvin VIII 50-51 No. 18; *ANE* 266 No. 198;

Jawdar and His Treacherous Brethren: *Alf* III 179, 184; Burton VI 216. Chauvin V 257-60 No. 154; *ANE* 244-45 No. 209.□

Z67.5§, ‡Esteem: to be addressed as respected relative (with social distance kept).
¿Alî Shâr and Zumurrud: *Alf* II 226; Burton IV 209. Chauvin V 89-91 No. 28; *ANE* 100-1 No. 82.□

Z67.5.2§, ‡Esteem: woman addressed as "*khâlah* (maternal-aunt)".
Tailor's Story/Barber of Baghdad: *Alf* I 104,-(*bishârah*); Burton I 303,-("naunty mine"). Chauvin V 154-56 No. 78; *ANE* 405-6 No. 27;
¿Azîz and ¿Azîzah: *Alf* I 283; Burton II 326,-("old naunty"). Chauvin V 144-45 No. 71; *ANE* 111-13 No. 41;
¿Alî Shâr and Zumurrud: *Alf* II 226; Burton IV 209,-("O my aunt"). Chauvin V 89-91 No. 28; *ANE* 100-1 No. 82.□

Z67.7.1§, ‡Weightiness: "To be engraven with needles on eye-corners of mankind (*'âmâq al-bashar*)" (Cf. J170.2§).
Trader and Afrit: Accidental Fairy-cide: *Alf* I 8; Burton I 26. Chauvin VI 22-23 No. 194; *ANE* 419-20 No. 4;
Ensorcelled Prince/Husband: *Alf* I 27; Burton I 69. Chauvin VI 56-58 No. 222; *ANE* 176 No. 13;
Porter and Ladies of Baghdad: *Alf* I 39; Burton I 104. Chauvin V 251-52 No. 148; *ANE* 324-26 No. 14;
Second Qalandar: Afrit's Wife: *Alf* I 42; Burton I 113. Chauvin V 197-200 No. 116; *ANE* 338-39 No. 16;
Eldest Lady's Story: Treacherous Sisters: *Alf* I 53; Burton I 162. Chauvin V 4 No. 443; *ANE* 174-75 No. 19;
al-'Amjad and al-'As¿ad: *Alf* II 127; Burton III 339. Chauvin V 208-10 No. 120[.1]; *ANE* 2 341-42 No. 61/pt.;
Mock Caliph/¿Alî al-Jawharî: *Alf* II 195; Burton IV 139. Chauvin V 99-100 No. 174; *ANE* 304-5 No. 73;
Abû Muḥammad Lazybones: *Alf* II 207; Burton IV 165. Chauvin VI 64-67 No. 233; *ANE* 71-73 No. 78.□

Z69.4.1§, ‡"Spitting on" (spitting in, or at)—disgust. See: *DOTTI*.
First Qalandar: Brother-Sister Incest: *Alf* I 41; Burton I 110. Chauvin V 196-97 No. 115; *ANE* 337-38 No. 15;
Qamar al-Zamân and Budûr: *Alf* II 73; Burton III 229. Chauvin V 204-12 No. 120; *ANE* 341-45 No. 61;
Ma¿rûf the Cobbler: *Alf* IV 311; Burton X 43. Chauvin VI 81-82 No. 250; *ANE* 291-93 No. 262.□

Z70.5.3§, ‡'Summer-time cloud': inconsequential—(where it never rains during summer).
Sindbâd's Second Voyage: *Alf* III 89,-cf.; Burton VI 16. Chauvin VII 9-14 No. 373B; *ANE* 385 No. 179.□

Z70.6§, ‡To be like (as useless as) suspended grammatical rule (e.g., *tanwîn al-'iḍâfah*, unvoiced/silent letter). (Cf. U248.6.1§, Z119.3.2§).
Jeweler's Wife and Qamar al-Zamân: *Alf* IV 251; Burton IX 272. Chauvin V 212-14 No. 121; *ANE* 345-47 No. 260.□

Z71.1, Formulistic number: three. See: *DOTTI*.
Shahriyâr and Shahrzâd: *Alf* IV 317; Burton X 54-56. Chauvin V 190-91 No. 111/pt.; *ANE* 371 No. 1.□

Z71.1.0.1.1§, ‡Three sons. (Cf. P234.0.3.1§, P251.6.1).
Jawdar and His Treacherous Brethren: *Alf* III 177-78; Burton VI 213. Chauvin V 257-60 No. 154; *ANE* 244-45 No. 209;
Shahriyâr and Shahrzâd: *Alf* IV 317; Burton X 54-56. Chauvin V 190-91 No. 111/pt.; *ANE* 371 No. 1.□

Z71.5, Formulistic number: seven. See: *DOTTI*; *GMC*.
Jinni Keeps Mistress in Box: *Alf* I 3,-(padlocks, keys); Burton I 10. Chauvin V 188-89 No. 111; *ANE* 370 No. 1/pt.;
Porter and Ladies of Baghdad: *Alf* I 38,-(slaves/executioners); Burton I 107. Chauvin V 251-52 No. 148; *ANE* 324-26 No. 14;
Qamar al-Zamân and Budûr: *Alf* II 96,-(days); Burton III 276. Chauvin V 204-12 No. 120; *ANE* 341-45 No. 61;

Sindbâd and Porter: *Alf* III 83,-(voyages); Burton VI 4. Chauvin VII 1 No. 373; *ANE* 383-85 No. 179/pt.;
Man Who Never Laughs: *Alf* III 154,-(happy years); Burton VI 165. Chauvin VIII 47-48 No. 15; *ANE* 285-86 No. 195;
Hasan of Basrah: *Alf* IV 18; Burton VIII 73. Chauvin VII 29-35 No. 212A; *ANE* 207-10 No. 230;
Boy and thieves: Guilty Accomplice: *Alf* IV 163,-(thieves); Burton IX 95. Chauvin II 222-23 No. 152/17; *ANE* 128 No. 249.□

Z71.5.0.1, Formulistic numbers: sevenfold (e.g., 49, 70, 70,000, 7,777).
Hasan of Basrah: *Alf* IV 46,-(seven-sevens); Burton VIII 132. Chauvin VII 29-35 No. 212A; *ANE* 207-10 No. 230;
Budûr and Jubayr ibn ¿Umayr: *Alf* II 234; Burton IV 230. Chauvin VII 93-94 No. 374; *ANE* 243-44 No. 83.□

Z71.5.0.1.1.1§, ‡Moon of the 'fourteenth [day of lunar month]': (full). (Cf. Z159.3.2§).
Jinni Keeps Mistress in Box: *Alf* I 3; Burton I 11. Chauvin V 188-89 No. 111; *ANE* 370 No. 1/pt.;
Jullanâr of the Sea: *Alf* III 265; Burton VII 298. Chauvin V 147-51 No. 73; *ANE* 248-51 No. 227.□

Z71.5.0.1.2§, ‡Fourteen portions (two sevens). See: *DOTTI*.
Hasan of Basrah: *Alf* IV 17,-(*hilâl*/crescent); Burton VIII 70,-(moon). Chauvin VII 29-35 No. 212A; *ANE* 207-10 No. 230.□

Z71.5.6.17§, ‡Seven mighty creatures (animals). (Cf. B15.7.18§).
Tawaddud: Slavegirl Sold and Regained: *Alf* III 7,-(locust/viper's tail); Burton V 242,-(beasts). Chauvin VII 117-19 No. 387; *ANE* 408-10 No. 157.□

Z71.5.9§, Seven lean years. See: *DOTTI*; *GMC*.
City of Brass: *Alf* III 136,-cf./(drought); Burton VI 116. Chauvin V 32-35 No. 16; *ANE* 146-50 No. 180.□

Z71.5.13§, ‡Seven hazards (ordeals, tribulation, etc.). See: *DOTTI*. (Cf. A671.0.5.1§, E422.9.2.1§).
Jawdar and His Treacherous Brethren: *Alf* III 186; Burton VI 229-30. Chauvin V 257-60 No. 154; *ANE* 244-45 No. 209.□

Z71.5.13.1§, ‡Seven gates (chambers) of danger.
Jawdar and His Treacherous Brethren: *Alf* III 186; Burton VI 229. Chauvin V 257-60 No. 154; *ANE* 244-45 No. 209.□

Z71.5.2, ‡Journey beyond seven seas. See: *DOTTI*.
Bulûqiya: *Alf* III 24; Burton V 307. Chauvin VII 54 No. 77; *ANE* 130-32 No. 177.□

Z71.5.2.0.1§, Seven seas surround the earth. (Cf. A872.1).
Bulûqiya: *Alf* III 24,-(passim); Burton V 307. Chauvin VII 54 No. 77; *ANE* 130-32 No. 177.□

Z71.5.2.4§, ‡Seven regions of earth—(*'aqṭâr, 'aqâlîm*).
City of Labtayt/Treasure of Tolède: *Alf* II 184,-(*al-'aqâlîm al-sab¿ah*); Burton IV 101,-(seven climates of the world). Chauvin VI 90-91 No. 254; *ANE* 265-66 No. 67.□

Z71.5.2.5§, ‡Series (combinations) of seven topographical features of earth (seven mountains, seven valleys, seven seas, etc.). (Cf. A874§).
Hasan of Basrah: *Alf* IV 18; Burton VIII 73. Chauvin VII 29-35 No. 212A; *ANE* 207-10 No. 230.□

Z71.5.5.0.1§, ‡Seven voyages (journeys).
Sindbâd and Porter: *Alf* III 81-122; Burton VI 4ff. Chauvin VII 1 No. 373; *ANE* 383-85 No. 179/pt.□

Z71.8, ‡Formulistic number twelve. (Cf. Z72.8§).
Nuzhat al-Zamân Tested/¿Umar al-Nu¿mân: *Alf* I 206,-(sons/pennies/*dirhams*); Burton II 171. Chauvin VI 116, n.1/passim No. 277; *ANE* 432,/passim No. 39.□

Z71.8.6.1§, ‡Twenty-four carats/karats: completeness (perfection: as in full acre, pure gold). (Cf. W174.1§).
Jullanâr of the Sea: *Alf* III 260; Burton VII 289. Chauvin V 147-51 No. 73; *ANE* 248-51 No. 227.□

Z71.12, Formulistic number: forty. See: *DOTTI*; *GMC*.
Qamar al-Zamân and Budûr: *Alf* II 86,-(heads); Burton III 256. Chauvin V 204-12 No. 120; *ANE* 341-45 No. 61;

Jawdar and His Treacherous Brethren: *Alf* III 191,-(sorts of dishes), 192,-(dinars); Burton VI 226 237. Chauvin V 257-60 No. 154; *ANE* 244-45 No. 209;
Mercury ¿Alî: *Alf* III 227,-(xxx); Burton VII 171,-(slaves, dogs, dresses, carrying pigeons). Chauvin V 248-50 No. 147; *ANE* 301-3 No. 225;
Jullanâr of the Sea: *Alf* III 264,-(days); Burton VII 296. Chauvin V 147-51 No. 73; *ANE* 248-51 No. 227;
Abû Qîr and Abû Ṣîr: *Alf* IV 186,-(dyers); Burton IX 143. Chauvin V 15-17 No. 10; *ANE* 75-77 No. 255.□

Z71.12.2§, ‡Forty persons (maidens, slaves, etc.). See: *DOTTI*.
Prior Becomes Moslem: al-Anbârî: *Alf* II 299,-(monks); Burton V 141, 144. Chauvin V 237-38 No. 137; *ANE* 330-31 No. 147;
Mercury ¿Alî: *Alf* III 227,-("*tâbi¿*"/follower); Burton VII 172,-("men"/lads). Chauvin V 248-50 No. 147; *ANE* 301-3 No. 225;
Masrûr and Zayn al-Mawâṣif: *Alf* IV 77,-(monks); Burton VIII 256. Chauvin VI 82-84 No. 251; *ANE* 294-95 No. 232.□

Z71.12.2.1§, ‡Forty maidens (slave-girls, etc.). See: *DOTTI*.
Jawdar and His Treacherous Brethren: *Alf* III 195,-(slaves); Burton VI 246. Chauvin V 257-60 No. 154; *ANE* 244-45 No. 209.□

Z71.16.18§, ‡Formalistic number: one thousand.
Shahriyâr and Shâhzamân: *Alf* I 5,-(books); Burton I 15. Chauvin V 188-89 No. 111; *ANE* 370-71 No. 1.□

Z71.16.18.1§, ‡Formalistic number: a thousand thousands (i.e., one million).
Ma¿rûf the Cobbler: *Alf* IV 304; Burton X 28. Chauvin VI 81-82 No. 250; *ANE* 291-93 No. 262.□

Z72.6, ‡Three hundred and sixty-five [(sixty-six)]. (Cf. F781.2.2§, T469.2§).
King ¿Umar al-Nu¿mân and Sons: *Alf* I 168; Burton II 78. Chauvin VI 112-24 No. 277; *ANE* 430-34 No. 39.□

Z72.8§, ‡Twelve things (objects, persons, animals, etc.)—one for each month. (Cf. F771.15.2§, Z71.8).
King ¿Umar al-Nu¿mân and Sons: *Alf* I 168; Burton II 78. Chauvin VI 112-24 No. 277; *ANE* 430-34 No. 39.□

Z77.1§, ‡'To fill out the eye [(of someone)]' (i.e., be appealing, impressive). (Cf. Z186.9.2§).
Ibrâhîm and Jamîlah: *Alf* IV 226,-(male filling out female's eye: *mâ mala'tu ¿aynî min dhakarin ghayrak*); Burton IX 222, n. 2,-("no male hath ever filled mine eyes ..."). Chauvin VI 52-53 No. 218; *ANE* 227-29 No. 258.□

Z77.6.1§, ‡Failed joy.
¿Alâ' al-Dîn Abû al-Shâmât: *Alf* II 157; Burton IV 52. Chauvin V 43-49 No. 18; *ANE* 85-87 No. 63.□

Z77.6.1.1§, ‡'O you, joy-incomplete: the crow took you and flew away'. (Cf. L506§).
¿Alâ' al-Dîn Abû al-Shâmât: *Alf* II 157; Burton IV 52. Chauvin V 43-49 No. 18; *ANE* 85-87 No. 63.□

Z84.0.1§, ‡Person labeled: "Bastard!" ("Child of fornication!"). (Cf. H1381.2.2.1.1).
King ¿Umar al-Nu¿mân and Sons: *Alf* II 4; Burton III 81,-(sons of whores). Chauvin VI 112-24 No. 277; *ANE* 430-34 No. 39;
Qamar al-Zamân and Budûr: *Alf* II 68,-(father/son); Burton III 219. Chauvin V 204-12 No. 120; *ANE* 341-45 No. 61.□

Z84.1.1.1§, ‡Insult: mention of mother's privates (vagina, buttocks). See: *DOTTI*.
Ma¿n Rewards a Bedouin for Gift: *Alf* II 182-83,-cf./(*ḥirr 'ummih*/his mother's vagina); Burton IV 98,-(harem/honor). Chauvin VI 78 No. 247; *ANE* 291 No. 66.□

Z84.2.2.1.1§, ‡Insult: needle-like (in thinness).
Man from Yaman and Six Salve-girls: Flyting: *Alf* II 247,-cf.; Burton IV 254. Chauvin VI 151 No. 313; *ANE* 289-90 No. 84.□

Z84.2.2.1.2§, ‡Insult: woman with "sparrow's-legs" "stick-legs, poker-like, or the like).
Man from Yaman and Six Salve-girls: Flyting: *Alf* II 247; Burton IV 254. Chauvin VI 151 No. 313; *ANE* 289-90 No. 84.□

Z84.2.2.2§, ‡Insult: fatness. (Cf. J1413§, Z84.2.2.2§).
Man from Yaman and Six Salve-girls: Flyting: *Alf* II 248; Burton IV 254. Chauvin VI 151 No. 313; *ANE* 289-90 No. 84.□

Z84.4.1§, Insult: homosexuality. See: *GMC*. (Cf. K2113.5§).
Anîs al-Jalîs: *Alf* I 143,-(*¿ilq*/satan); Burton II 39,-(gallows-bird"). Chauvin V 120-24 No. 58; *ANE* 316-17 No. 35;
Jawdar and His Treacherous Brethren: *Alf* III 198,-(simile/*¿ilûq*); Burton VI 249,-("gallows bird"). Chauvin V 257-60 No. 154; *ANE* 244-45 No. 209;
Jullanâr of the Sea: *Alf* III 260, 268, 269,-(*¿ilq la'îm*); Burton VII 287,-(miserable gallows bird). Chauvin V 147-51 No. 73; *ANE* 248-51 No. 227;
Hasan of Basrah: *Alf* III 305,-(*¿ilq*); Burton VIII 13,-(gallows-carrion [??]). Chauvin VII 29-35 No. 212A; *ANE* 207-10 No. 230.□

Z84.4.1.1§, ‡Insult: lesbian. (Cf. T462).
Hasan of Basrah: *Alf* IV 46,-(*musâḥiqah*); Burton VIII 130,-("tribade/Musáhikah," "[also] applied to masturbators of the gender feminine" n. 2). Chauvin VII 29-35 No. 212A; *ANE* 207-10 No. 230.□

Z84.4.5.2§, ‡Insult: whore (*'sharmûṭah/qaḥbah'/¿âhirah*). See: *DOTTI*.
Hasan of Basrah: *Alf* IV 46; Burton VIII 130. Chauvin VII 29-35 No. 212A; *ANE* 207-10 No. 230.□

Z84.4.6§, ‡Insult: pimp. See: *DOTTI*.
Tailor's Story/Barber of Baghdad: *Alf* I 109,-(*qawwâd*); Burton I 316. Chauvin V 154-56 No. 78; *ANE* 405-6 No. 27;
House with the Belvedere: *Alf* III 171,-cf./(your pimping); Burton VI 196,-(going between). Chauvin VIII 57-58 No. 23; *ANE* 223 No. 203;
Ma¿rûf the Cobbler: *Alf* IV 290; Burton X 3. Chauvin VI 81-82 No. 250; *ANE* 291-93 No. 262.□

Z84.5.1§, ‡Insult: being a 'jinx' (harbinger of evil, *mash'ûm/manḥûs*, etc.). See: *DOTTI*.
Second Qalandar: Afrit's Wife: *Alf* I 50,-cf.; Burton I 138. Chauvin V 197-200 No. 116; *ANE* 338-39 No. 16;
Debauchee and Three Years Old Child: *Alf* III 176; Burton VI 208. Chauvin VIII 62-63 No. 147; *ANE* 166-67 No. 206.□

Z87§, *radḥ, tashlîq, taghgîr*: women's formulistic insults (poetic vulgarities, often obscene). (Cf. P788.2.1§).
Man from Yaman and Six Salve-girls: Flyting: *Alf* II 245-49; Burton IV 245-60. Chauvin VI 151 No. 313; *ANE* 289-90 No. 84.□

Z87.1§, Women's duel with formulistic insults (*radḥ, tashlîq*). See: *DOTTI*. (Cf. P427.7.4.3§).
Man from Yaman and Six Salve-girls: Flyting: *Alf* II 244-49; Burton IV 245-60. Chauvin VI 151 No. 313; *ANE* 289-90 No. 84.□

Z88§, ‡Sarcasm. See: *DOTTI*; *PSAE*. (Cf. Q331.3.1§, W187).
Fisherman and Afrit: Ingratitude: *Alf* I 15,-(*mawt=bishârah*); Burton I 41,-(death=good tidings). Chauvin VI 23-25 No. 195; *ANE* 183-84 No. 8;
Anîs al-Jalîs: *Alf* I 139,-(sinful behavior=saint's *karâmât*); Burton II 28. Chauvin V 120-24 No. 58; *ANE* 316-17 No. 35;
Qamar al-Zamân and Budûr: *Alf* II 82,-(*bishârah*/son became insane); Burton III 247. Chauvin V 204-12 No. 120; *ANE* 341-45 No. 61;
Budûr and Jubayr ibn ¿Umayr: *Alf* II 242; Burton IV 243,-(do folk write with their feet). Chauvin VII 93-94 No. 374; *ANE* 243-44 No. 83;
Ebony Horse: *Alf* II 263,-(Imperial/"*kisrawiyy*"); Burton V 26. Chauvin V 221-31 No. 130; *ANE* 172-74 No. 103.□

Z91.0.1§, Other formulas of other-world (hereafter). (Cf. V311.4.1§).
Nûr al-Dîn ¿Alî and Son: *Alf* I 68; Burton I 206. Chauvin VI 102-6 No. 270; *ANE* 317-19 No. 22.□

Z93.3§, ‡Incalculable: defies consumption. (Cf. P153§).
Tawaddud: Slavegirl Sold and Regained: *Alf* II 318,-(simile/Korah's wealth); Burton V 225. Chauvin VII 117-19 No. 387; *ANE* 408-10 No. 157.□

Z93.3.1§, ‡Incalculable: 'Fires cannot devour it [all]'.
Jeweler's Wife and Qamar al-Zamân: *Alf* IV 245; Burton IX 261. Chauvin V 212-14 No. 121; *ANE* 345-47 No. 260;
Ma¿rûf the Cobbler: *Alf* IV 295; Burton X 12. Chauvin VI 81-82 No. 250; *ANE* 291-93 No. 262.□

Z93.2.4§, ‡Innumerable: 'Like locusts'.
Hasan of Basrah: *Alf* IV 24; Burton VIII 84. Chauvin VII 29-35 No. 212A; *ANE* 207-10 No. 230.□

Z94§, ‡Formulas for traits of character (personality, mood, etc.). (Cf. Z94.2.2.1§).
¿Azîz and ¿Azîzah: *Alf* I 276; Burton II 312. Chauvin V 144-45 No. 71; *ANE* 111-13 No. 41.□

Z94.2.2§, ‡Symbolism: balanced and imbalanced persons.
¿Azîz and ¿Azîzah: *Alf* I 276; Burton II 312. Chauvin V 144-45 No. 71; *ANE* 111-13 No. 41.□

Z94.2.2.1§, ‡Symbolism: salted and unsalted character—(balanced and imbalanced persons). (Cf. Z94§).
¿Azîz and ¿Azîzah: *Alf* I 276; Burton II 312. Chauvin V 144-45 No. 71; *ANE* 111-13 No. 41.□

Z94.3.2§, ‡Pride: to be with mended countenance (*magbûr el-khâṭir*).
Ma¿rûf the Cobbler: *Alf* IV 290; Burton X 3,-(heart at ease). Chauvin VI 81-82 No. 250; *ANE* 291-93 No. 262.□

Z94.5.1§, ‡Formulas for imperviousness (insensitiveness, shamelessness). See: *DOTTI*. (Cf. W155).
Abû Qîr and Abû Ṣîr: *Alf* IV 182; Burton IX 134. Chauvin V 15-17 No. 10; *ANE* 75-77 No. 255.□

Z94.5.1.1§, ‡"Cheek (face) carved out of mosque's (church's, temple's) threshhold" (i.e., trodden stone, insensitive). See: *DOTTI*.
Abû Qîr and Abû Ṣîr: *Alf* IV 182; Burton IX 134. Chauvin V 15-17 No. 10; *ANE* 75-77 No. 255.□

Z94.5.1.3§, ‡Rude stare. (Cf. D2071).
Hasan of Basrah: *Alf* IV 41; Burton VIII 119,-(brazenfacedness). Chauvin VII 29-35 No. 212A; *ANE* 207-10 No. 230.□

Z94.5.2.1§, ‡Troublemaker labeled: afrit, jinni, devil, satan, Eblis, etc. See: *DOTTI*. (Cf. F200.9.1§).
Jeweler's Wife and Qamar al-Zamân: *Alf* IV 256,-(poem,/women-"satans"); Burton IX 282. Chauvin V 212-14 No. 121; *ANE* 345-47 No. 260.□

Z94.5.6.1§, ‡Greedy hoarder labeled "ogre" (*ghûl*), "whale" (*ḥût*), or the like. (Cf. F632.0.1.1§).
Jawdar and His Treacherous Brethren: *Alf* III 180; Burton VI 218. Chauvin V 257-60 No. 154; *ANE* 244-45 No. 209;
Abû Qîr and Abû Ṣîr: *Alf* IV 185; Burton IX 140. Chauvin V 15-17 No. 10; *ANE* 75-77 No. 255.□

Z95§, Puns (homophony). See: *GMC*; *PSAE*. (Cf. Z97§).
Qamar al-Zamân and Budûr: *Alf* II 95,-(*siwâka-siwâka*=toothpick-only you/*'arâka-'arâka*=caper tree-I see you/poem); Burton III 275,-(toothstick-'Siwak'/caper-tree-'Arak'). Chauvin V 204-12 No. 120; *ANE* 341-45 No. 61;
Dalîla the Swindler: *Alf* III 215,-(*kîs, kuss, kisâ'*); Burton VII 151,-("coin, clothing, and coynte."). Chauvin V 245-50 No. 147; *ANE* 163-64 No. 224.□

Z95.0.1§, ‡Double-meaning: word or phrase that denotes more than one meaning. See: *DOTTI*; *PSAE*. (Cf. H845.1.1§, K362.10, U248.0.2§, V384.0.1§).
Ma¿n Rewards a Bedouin for Gift: *Alf* II 182-83,-(*ḥirr 'ummih*/mother's vagina); Burton IV 98,-99-(harem/honor). Chauvin VI 78 No. 247; *ANE* 291 No. 66;
Jawdar and His Treacherous Brethren: *Alf* III 196,-(*khaliyyah/khiliyyât*); Burton VI 246,-("pun" n. 1). Chauvin V 257-60 No. 154; *ANE* 244-45 No. 209;
Jeweler's Wife and Qamar al-Zamân: *Alf* IV 250,-(*genitive preposition/ḥarf jarr*/lit.: letter that does the dragging), 260,-(khaliyyah-khiliyyât/poem); Burton IX 272. Chauvin V 212-14 No. 121; *ANE* 345-47 No. 260.□

Z95.1§, ‡Homophony: "*ṣabr*" ([sweet] patience)—"*ṣabr*" ([bitter] aloe). See: *DOTTI*. (Cf. J850§, W26).
Sayf al-Mulûk: *Alf* III 283,-(poem); Burton VII 337-38. Chauvin VII 64-73 No. 348; *ANE* 362-64 No. 229.□

Z97§, ‡Alliteration (simple, plain). See: *DOTTI*. (Cf. T16.6§, Z95§).
Second Qalandar: Afrit's Wife: *Alf* I 50,-(poem/line 4—*sarâ'ir/sirr/sarîrah*); Burton I 138. Chauvin V 197-200 No. 116; *ANE* 338-39 No. 16;
Dalîla the Swindler: *Alf* III 215,-(*kîs, kuss, kisâ'*—/purse, 'puss', clothing); Burton VII 151,-("coin, clothing, and coynte"). Chauvin V 245-50 No. 147; *ANE* 163-64 No. 224;
Jeweler's Wife and Qamar al-Zamân: *Alf* IV 239,-(Zaynab-Zayd, i.e.,female-male/poem); Burton IX 249. Chauvin V 212-14 No. 121; *ANE* 345-47 No. 260.□

Z97.7§, ‡Lovers's (or brother-sister's) alliterative names mirroring each other (e.g., gods Nun-Nanoid, gods Amon-Agminate, Ḥamad-Ḥamdah, Sâmî-Sâmyah, etc.). "Phonetic bifurcation". (Cf. P250.0.1§).
¿Azîz and ¿Azîzah: *Alf* I 268-90; Burton II 2298ff. Chauvin V 144-45 No. 71; *ANE* 111-13 No. 41; **Ni¿mah and Nu¿m: Stolen Wife Regained**: *Alf* II 132-47; Burton IV 1-29. Chauvin VI 96-97 No. 263; *ANE* 314 No. 62.□

Z98§, Contradictions (oxymoron). See: *DOTTI*; *GMC*. (Cf. U10.1.2§).
Kurd's Sack/¿Alî the Persian: *Alf* II 201-2; Burton IV 150-52. Chauvin V 279 No. 162; *ANE* 99-100 No. 74.□

Z98.1§, ‡Rhetorical (poetic) oxymoron. See: *DOTTI*.
King ¿Umar al-Nu¿mân and Sons: *Alf* I 214,-(poem/pleasure-attack); Burton II 187. Chauvin VI 112-24 No. 277; *ANE* 430-34 No. 39;
Qamar al-Zamân and Budûr: *Alf* II 72,-(poem/stand-sit), 109,-(poem/raised downward); Burton III 226, 304. Chauvin V 204-12 No. 120; *ANE* 341-45 No. 61;
Ma¿n Rewards Maidens for a Drink of Water: *Alf* II 182,-(poems/life-death); Burton IV 97. Chauvin VI 78 No. 247; *ANE* 290 No. 65;
Jânshâh: *Alf* III 57,-(poem/pleasure-attack); Burton V 355,-(stress of joy). Chauvin VII 39-44 No. 153; *ANE* 238-41 No. 178.□

Z100.1, Names of giants (Fomorians) with sinister significance.
¿Alâ' al-Dîn Abû al-Shâmât: *Alf* II 154,-cf./("... Abû-Nâb"); Burton IV 44. Chauvin V 43-49 No. 18; *ANE* 85-87 No. 63.□

Z100.2§, ‡Awe-evoking names of powerful jinn. (Cf. F252.1.0.1.1§—(formerly-F252.1.0.1§)).
Sayf al-Mulûk: *Alf* III 279,-(Shammâkh ibn Sharûkh); Burton VII 331,-(Shahyal bin Sharukh). Chauvin VII 64-73 No. 348; *ANE* 362-64 No. 229.□

Z100.2.1§, ‡Awe-evoking name of jinni: Ra¿d-Qâṣif (Roaring-Thunder).
Jawdar and His Treacherous Brethren: *Alf* III 182; Burton VI 221-22. Chauvin V 257-60 No. 154; *ANE* 244-45 No. 209.□

Z100.2.3§, ‡Awe-evoking name of jinni king: Ṣakhr (Rock).
Bulûqiya: *Alf* III 32; Burton V 316. Chauvin VII 54 No. 77; *ANE* 130-32 No. 177.□

Z103.1.1§, ‡Rock (stone, bad earth): barrenness (sterility). See: *DOTTI*.
¿Alâ' al-Dîn Abû al-Shâmât: *Alf* II 148; Burton IV 30. Chauvin V 43-49 No. 18; *ANE* 85-87 No. 63.□

Z103.1.2§, ‡Unfertilized ('clear') "male's egg": sterility. (Cf. B754.4.4§).
¿Alâ' al-Dîn Abû al-Shâmât: *Alf* II 148; Burton IV 30,-(thin seed). Chauvin V 43-49 No. 18; *ANE* 85-87 No. 63;
Dalîla the Swindler: *Alf* III 213; Burton VII 147,-(weak and watery sperm). Chauvin V 245-50 No. 147; *ANE* 163-64 No. 224.□

Z103.1.2.1§, ‡Fertilized ('clouded') "male's egg": fertility.
¿Alâ' al-Dîn Abû al-Shâmât: *Alf* II 148; Burton IV 30,-(thick seed). Chauvin V 43-49 No. 18; *ANE* 85-87 No. 63.□

Z103.2.1§, ‡He-mule: sterility. See: *DOTTI*. (Cf. Z193.1§).
Dalîla the Swindler: *Alf* III 213; Burton VII 147. Chauvin V 245-50 No. 147; *ANE* 163-64 No. 224.□

Z105§, ‡Shape (form, color) symbolism: association based on similarities of visually perceived properties of object. See: *DOTTI*. (Cf. X1727.2§, Z141, Z186.7.2§, Z192.0.1.4.1§).
Nûr al-Dîn ¿Alî and Son: *Alf* I 73,-(*surrah muḥaqqaqah*/cupped navel); Burton I 224n. 5,-(xxx/"with something below it" [??]). Chauvin VI 102-6 No. 270; *ANE* 317-19 No. 22;
King ¿Umar al-Nu¿mân and Sons: *Alf* I 170; Burton II 98. Chauvin VI 112-24 No. 277; *ANE* 430-34 No. 39;
Hashish Eater's Dream: *Alf* II 10,-(the cut watermelon); Burton III 92, 93. Chauvin VI 124 No. 278; *ANE* 216 No. 42;
Qamar al-Zamân and Budûr: *Alf* II 72,-(poem); Burton III 226. Chauvin V 204-12 No. 120; *ANE* 341-45 No. 61;
Budûr and Jubayr ibn ¿Umayr: *Alf* II 242,-("L" embraces "A"); Burton IV 243. Chauvin VII 93-94 No. 374; *ANE* 243-44 No. 83;
Tawaddud: Slavegirl Sold and Regained: *Alf* II 304,-(poem/gardens of Eden); Burton V 192,-(garths of Eden). Chauvin VII 117-19 No. 387; *ANE* 408-10 No. 157;

Hasan of Basrah: *Alf* III 316,-(¿*Uqâb*/poem/vulva); Burton VIII 33,-(hummock great of span). Chauvin VII 29-35 No. 212A; *ANE* 207-10 No. 230;
Tawaddud: Slavegirl Sold and Regained: *Alf* II 304,-(poem/narcissus flower); Burton V 190. Chauvin VII 117-19 No. 387; *ANE* 408-10 No. 157;
Tawaddud: Slavegirl Sold and Regained: *Alf* II 318-19,-(button/button-hole); Burton V 227. Chauvin VII 117-19 No. 387; *ANE* 408-10 No. 157;
Three Wishes: *Alf* III 162,-(elongated-squash); Burton VI 181. Chauvin VIII 51-52 No. 19; *ANE* 419-20 No. 199;
Nûr al-Dîn and Maryam: *Alf* IV 92,-(wax); Burton VIII 293. Chauvin V 52-54 No. 271; *ANE* 98-99 No. 233;
Nûr al-Dîn and Maryam: *Alf* IV 97; Burton VIII 304,-("pearl unthridden"). Chauvin V 52-54 No. 271; *ANE* 98-99 No. 233.□

Z105.1.0.1§, ‡Symbolism: center (centrality)—chieftainship, power, etc.
Hârûn and Arab Girl: *Alf* III 204; Burton VII 109,-(middle in dwelling/highest in tentpoles). Chauvin VI 143 No. 300; *ANE* 202 No. 215.□

Z106§, ‡Action (movement) symbolism: association based on motion similarities. See: *DOTTI*. (Cf. J80, U318.1.1§, Z170.0.1§, Z186.1.2§, Z197.3.4.0.2§).
Porter and Ladies of Baghdad: *Alf* I 35,-(mule's); Burton I 92. Chauvin V 251-52 No. 148; *ANE* 324-26 No. 14;
¿Azîz and ¿Azîzah: *Alf* I 279; Burton II 318. Chauvin V 144-45 No. 71; *ANE* 111-13 No. 41.□

Z107§, ‡Consistency (texture) symbolism: association based on sensation (touch) similarities.
Bearded and Beardless Men as Lovers: *Alf* II 303; Burton V 165,-(cucumber's fuzz). Chauvin V 112 No. 48; *ANE* 450 No. 154;
Hasan of Basrah: *Alf* III 316,-(rabbit with ears cropped/*maqṭûsh*); Burton VIII 33. Chauvin VII 29-35 No. 212A; *ANE* 207-10 No. 230;
Nûr al-Dîn and Maryam: *Alf* IV 91, 97,-(softer than a sheep's tail); Burton VIII 291, 303. Chauvin V 52-54 No. 271; *ANE* 98-99 No. 233.□

Z111.9.1§, ‡'The destroyer of pleasures and disperser of throngs'—(death). (Cf. U250.0.1§, Z42.1.1§).
Nûr al-Dîn ¿Alî and Son: *Alf* I 84; Burton I 254. Chauvin VI 102-6 No. 270; *ANE* 317-19 No. 22;
King ¿Umar al-Nu¿mân and Sons: *Alf* II 21,-(defeater); Burton III 114. Chauvin VI 112-24 No. 277; *ANE* 430-34 No. 39;
Ni¿mah and Nu¿m: Stolen Wife Regained: *Alf* II 144; Burton IV 23. Chauvin VI 96-97 No. 263; *ANE* 314 No. 62;
al-'Amjad and al-'As¿ad: *Alf* II 147,-(defeater); Burton IV 29. Chauvin V 208-10 No. 120[.1]; *ANE* 341-42 No. 61/pt. 2;
¿Alâ' al-Dîn Abû al-Shâmât: *Alf* II 181,-(defeater); Burton IV 94. Chauvin V 43-49 No. 18; *ANE* 85-87 No. 63;
Mock Caliph/¿Alî al-Jawharî: *Alf* II 200; Burton IV 148. Chauvin V 99-100 No. 174; *ANE* 304-5 No. 73;
¿Alî Shâr and Zumurrud: *Alf* II 235; Burton IV 228. Chauvin V 89-91 No. 28; *ANE* 100-1 No. 82;
Man from Yaman and Six Salve-girls: Flyting: *Alf* II 250,-(defeater); Burton IV 260. Chauvin VI 151 No. 313; *ANE* 289-90 No. 84;
King's Daughter and Ape: *Alf* II 254,-(defeater); Burton IV 299. Chauvin V 178 No. 102; *ANE* 262-63 No. 102;
Ebony Horse: *Alf* II 267,-(defeater); Burton V 32. Chauvin V 221-31 No. 130; *ANE* 172-74 No. 103;
Uns al-Wujûd and al-Ward: *Alf* II 284,-(defeater); Burton V 64. Chauvin VI 127-29 No. 282; *ANE* 438 No. 104;
Angel of Death and Jewish King: *Alf* III 10,-(Angel describes self); Burton V 251. Chauvin VI 184-85 No. 351; *ANE* 104 No. 160;
Bulûqiya: *Alf* III 81,-(defeater); Burton V 396. Chauvin VII 54 No. 77; *ANE* 130-32 No. 177;
Mercury ¿Alî: *Alf* III 246-47,-(defeater); Burton VII 209. Chauvin V 248-50 No. 147; *ANE* 301-3 No. 225;
Jullanâr of the Sea: *Alf* III 270; Burton VII 307. Chauvin V 147-51 No. 73; *ANE* 248-51 No. 227;
Sayf al-Mulûk: *Alf* III 302; Burton VIII 6. Chauvin VII 64-73 No. 348; *ANE* 362-64 No. 229;
Hasan of Basrah: *Alf* IV 55; Burton VIII 155. Chauvin VII 29-35 No. 212A; *ANE* 207-10 No. 230;
Masrûr and Zayn al-Mawâṣif: *Alf* IV 80; Burton VIII 263. Chauvin VI 82-84 No. 251; *ANE* 294-95 No. 232;

Nûr al-Dîn and Maryam: *Alf* IV 129,-("defeater"); Burton IX 18. Chauvin V 52-54 No. 271; *ANE* 98-99 No. 233;
Landsman ¿Abdallah and Merman ¿Abdallah: *Alf* IV 208,-("defeater"); Burton IX 188. Chauvin V 6-7 No. 3; *ANE* 65-66 No. 256;
¿Abdallah ibn Fâdil: Treacherous Brothers: *Alf* IV 288,-("defeater"); Burton IX 349. Chauvin V 2-4 No. 2; *ANE* 63-65 No. 261;
Ma¿rûf the Cobbler: *Alf* IV 317,-("defeater"); Burton X 53. Chauvin VI 81-82 No. 250; *ANE* 291-93 No. 262;
Shahriyâr and Shahrzâd: *Alf* IV 318,-("defeater"); Burton X 55. Chauvin V 190-91 No. 111/pt.; *ANE* 371 No. 1.□

Z111.9.1.1§, ‡'The demolisher of palaces and filler of graves'—(death).
Sindbâd and Porter: *Alf* III 122; Burton VI 77. Chauvin VII 26-29 No. 373G; *ANE* 386-87 No. 179;
Abû al-Hasan al-Khorâsânî (and Caliph's Favorite): *Alf* IV 237,-cf.; Burton IX 246. Chauvin V 218-20 No. 129; *ANE* 68-69 No. 259.□

Z111.9.2§, ‡To be dealt the cup (drink) of death. (Cf. S111.10§).
Sindbâd and Porter: *Alf* III 122; Burton VI 77. Chauvin VII 26-29 No. 373G; *ANE* 386-87 No. 179.□

Z111.9.3§, ‡Returning to earth whence man (one) came—death. (Cf. A1241.5.2§, V61.8.2.1§).
Tawaddud: Slavegirl Sold and Regained: *Alf* III 5,-(also, poem); Burton V 237. Chauvin VII 117-19 No. 387; *ANE* 408-10 No. 157.□

Z111.9.4§, ‡God retrieves His Breath (Deposit)—death. (Cf. C898.1.1§, C898.1.1§, V1.1.3.1§).
Landsman ¿Abdallah and Merman ¿Abdallah: *Alf* IV 207-8; Burton IX 187. Chauvin V 6-7 No. 3; *ANE* 65-66 No. 256.□

Z113.1§, Life (the world) personified as a beautiful young woman. See: *GMC*.
Dispute Concerning Males and Females: *Alf* II 302,-(*al-dunyâ ¿ibârh ¿an al-nisâ'*); Burton V 160,-("world meaneth woman"). Chauvin VI 153 No. 317; *ANE* 291 No. 151.□

Z115, ‡Wind personified. See: *DOTTI*.
Spider Upbraids Wind: *Alf* IV 147; Burton IX 59. Chauvin II 220 No. 152/10; *ANE* 398 No. 245.□

Z117.6§, ‡Musical instrument personified.
¿Alâ' al-Dîn Abû al-Shâmât: *Alf* II 162,-(lute); Burton IV 60. Chauvin V 43-49 No. 18; *ANE* 85-87 No. 63;
Tawaddud: Slavegirl Sold and Regained: *Alf* III 7,-(mother-child); Burton V 245. Chauvin VII 117-19 No. 387; *ANE* 408-10 No. 157;
Nûr al-Dîn and Maryam: *Alf* IV 85,-(poem—lute); Burton VIII 281. Chauvin V 52-54 No. 271; *ANE* 98-99 No. 233;
al-Rashîd and Omani Merchant: *Alf* IV 210,-(lute/baby); Burton IX 191. Chauvin VI 111-12 No. 276; *ANE* 201-2 No. 257.□

Z117.6.1§, ‡"Musical instrument speaks".
¿Alâ' al-Dîn Abû al-Shâmât: *Alf* II 162; Burton IV 60. Chauvin V 43-49 No. 18; *ANE* 85-87 No. 63.□

Z117.6.2§, ‡Musician's (singer's) love for musical instrument: "mother and her child". (Cf. F679.9.1§, Z62).
Mock Caliph/¿Alî al-Jawharî: *Alf* II 193,-(lute); Burton IV 135. Chauvin V 99-100 No. 174; *ANE* 304-5 No. 73;
Tawaddud: Slavegirl Sold and Regained: *Alf* III 7-8; Burton V 245. Chauvin VII 117-19 No. 387; *ANE* 408-10 No. 157;
al-Rashîd and Omani Merchant: *Alf* IV 210,-(lute); Burton IX 191,-(mother over babe). Chauvin VI 111-12 No. 276; *ANE* 201-2 No. 257.□

Z119.0.2§, ‡Word believed to have capacity (power) to create. (Blasphemous belief). (Cf. A611.0.1.1§, V329§).
King Jalî¿âd and Shimâs: *Alf* IV 156; Burton IX 79,-("Word hath inherent and positive power"). Chauvin VI 9-11 No. 184; *ANE* 237-38 No. 236.□

Z119.1.1.1§, ‡Lover hugs beloved like a certain letter conjoins with another (e.g., in Arabic script: the *'Alif* (A) and the *Lâm* (L); in Latin script: the bar—symbolizing a male—in the letters A, E, t).
Budûr and Jubayr ibn ¿Umayr: *Alf* II 242,-("L" embraces "A"); Burton IV 243. Chauvin VII 93-94 No. 374; *ANE* 243-44 No. 83.□

Z119.3§, ‡Grammar personified.
Jeweler's Wife and Qamar al-Zamân: *Alf* IV 251; Burton IX 272. Chauvin V 212-14 No. 121; *ANE* 345-47 No. 260.□

Z119.3.1§, ‡The *fâ¿il* ('doer,' active subject of a verbal clause) is superior to the *maf¿ûl* ('done to', object, passive participle). (Cf. P198§, Z62.9.1.1§, Z106§).
Dispute Concerning Males and Females: *Alf* II 300; Burton V 156 n. 1. Chauvin VI 153 No. 317; *ANE* 291 No. 151.□

Z119.3.2§, ‡Rules of grammar as symbols of erotic actions. See: *DOTTI*.
Jeweler's Wife and Qamar al-Zamân: *Alf* IV 251,-(*ṣilah*/syndetic relative clause, *'idâfah*/genitive construction, nunnation, etc.); Burton IX 272. Chauvin V 212-14 No. 121; *ANE* 345-47 No. 260.□

Z119.6§, ‡Eloquence personified.
Dûban and King Yûnân: *Alf* I 17,-(poem-line1); Burton I 47. Chauvin V 275-76 No. 156; *ANE* 459 No. 9.□

Z120.4.2.1§, ‡Fire speaks to person (warns, instructs, or the like).
Jewish Tray-maker and Temptress: *Alf* III 14; Burton V 267-68. Chauvin VI 187-88 No. 354; *ANE* 169 No. 166.□

Z121.5§, ‡Justice personified. See: *DOTTI*.
Omar and Young Badawî: Returning to be Executed: *Alf* II 288,-(as ¿Umar ibn al-Khaṭṭâb); Burton V 99-104. Chauvin V 216 No. 125; *ANE* 429-30 No. 130.□

Z122, Time personified. (Cf. K2059.9.2§, W199.3.3§).
Dûban and King Yûnân: *Alf* I 17,-(poem—line 3); Burton I 47. Chauvin V 275-76 No. 156; *ANE* 459 No. 9;
Second Qalandar: Afrit's Wife: *Alf* I 45,—(*zamân*/treachery/poem); Burton I 118,-(rule of life). Chauvin V 197-200 No. 116; *ANE* 338-39 No. 16;
Anîs al-Jalîs: *Alf* I 140,-(*dahr*/poem); Burton II 30,-(xxx). Chauvin V 120-24 No. 58; *ANE* 316-17 No. 35;
¿Alâ' al-Dîn Abû al-Shâmât: *Alf* II 158,-(poem); Burton IV 54. Chauvin V 43-49 No. 18; *ANE* 85-87 No. 63.□

Z122.6§, ‡Dawn (morning, daytime) personified.
Nûr al-Dîn and Maryam: *Alf* IV 83,(poem/*hatafa al-fajru*/dawn 'yelled'), 110,-(*fajr*/kohl in dawn's eyes); Burton VIII 276,-(Dawn heralds ...), Burton VIII 328,-("Kohl in Morning's Eyes"). Chauvin V 52-54 No. 271; *ANE* 98-99 No. 233.□

Z122.7§, Temporal forces (quasi powers of fate) personified: 'Time' (*ed-Dahr, ez-Zamân/zamàn, el-'Ayyâm*). See: *DOTTI*; *GMC*. (Cf. A102.6.1.1§, C494.1§, J482.4§, W199.3.3§).
Dûban and King Yûnân: *Alf* I 20,-(*dahr*/poem); Burton I 56. Chauvin V 275-76 No. 156; *ANE* 459 No. 9;
King ¿Umar al-Nu¿mân and Sons: *Alf* I 194, 214,-(poem), 214, -(poem,/must perform *kaffârah*); Burton II 143. Chauvin VI 112-24 No. 277; *ANE* 430-34 No. 39;
Qamar al-Zamân and Budûr: *Alf* II 103,-(poem/*Zamân* makes *nadhr*); Burton III 290,-(Fortune had sworn). Chauvin V 204-12 No. 120; *ANE* 341-45 No. 61;
Abû al-Ḥasan al-Khorâsânî (and Caliph's Favorite): *Alf* IV 235,-(*dahr*/poem); Burton IX 242. Chauvin V 218-20 No. 129; *ANE* 68-69 No. 259.□

Z122.7.1§, ‡Temporal forces ('Time') responsible for man's misfortune (troubles). (Cf. K2059.9.2§).
Dûban and King Yûnân: *Alf* I 23,-(poem); Burton I 60. Chauvin V 275-76 No. 156; *ANE* 459 No. 9;
Jeweler's Wife and Qamar al-Zamân: *Alf* IV 262,-(poem/*dahr*); Burton IX 295,-(The world). Chauvin V 212-14 No. 121; *ANE* 345-47 No. 260.□

Z122.9.1.2§, ‡Nights (days, years) are pregnant with events by Time (fate) and give birth to the wondrous.
¿Alâ' al-Dîn Abû al-Shâmât: *Alf* II 158,-(poem); Burton IV 54. Chauvin V 43-49 No. 18; *ANE* 85-87 No. 63.□

Z125.9.1§, ‡Hospitality (generosity) personified (as Ḥâtim aṭ-Ṭâ'î, or the like). See: *DOTTI*.
Ḥâtim's Hospitality: *Alf* II 181,-(Ḥâtim); Burton IV 95-96. Chauvin VI 49 No. 215; *ANE* 216 No. 64;

Ma¿n Rewards a Bedouin for Gift: *Alf* II 182-83,-(Ma¿n); Burton IV 97-99. Chauvin VI 78 No. 247; *ANE* 291 No. 66;
Ma¿n Rewards Maidens for a Drink of Water: *Alf* II 182; Burton IV 97. Chauvin VI 78 No. 247; *ANE* 290 No. 65.□

Z134, Fortune personified. See: *DOTTI*; *GMC*.
Nûr al-Dîn and Maryam: *Alf* IV 96,-(*sa¿âdah*/poem); Burton VIII 301,-("Boon Fortune"). Chauvin V 52-54 No. 271; *ANE* 98-99 No. 233.□

Z134.3.0.1§, ‡Symbolism of coins (monetary bills of different denominations). (Cf. P13.9.3.3.1§).
Hind bint al-Nu¿mân and al-Ḥajjâj: *Alf* III 203; Burton VII 99. Chauvin V 115-4 No. 50; *ANE* 221-22 No. 212.□

Z137.1§, ‡'The tongue of someone's condition (situation)'.
Dûban and King Yûnân: *Alf* I 22-23,-(poem/*lisân al-ḥâl*); Burton I 60,-(tongue of things). Chauvin V 275-76 No. 156; *ANE* 459 No. 9;
¿Alî Shâr and Zumurrud: *Alf* II 232,-(poem); Burton IV 220,-(case's tongue). Chauvin V 89-91 No. 28; *ANE* 100-1 No. 82;
Uns al-Wujûd and al-Ward: *Alf* II 272,-(poem); Burton V 38. Chauvin VI 127-29 No. 282; *ANE* 438 No. 104;
Nûr al-Dîn and Maryam: *Alf* IV 85,-(poem), 93; Burton VIII 281,-(tongue of the case), 295. Chauvin V 52-54 No. 271; *ANE* 98-99 No. 233;
Abû al-Ḥasan al-Khorâsânî (and Caliph's Favorite): *Alf* IV 229,-(house/tongue of praise); Burton IX 229. Chauvin V 218-20 No. 129; *ANE* 68-69 No. 259.□

Z138.5§, ‡Sex organ personified. See: *DOTTI*.
Porter and Ladies of Baghdad: *Alf* I 35; Burton I 91-93. Chauvin V 251-52 No. 148; *ANE* 324-26 No. 14.□

Z138.5.0.1§, ‡Sex organ given name (e.g., "Sheik/Revered So-and-so, Abu-So-and-so"—typically male-name). (Cf. U318.1.1§, Z183.5.1§).
Qamar al-Zamân and Budûr: *Alf* II 72,-(*barkat al-shaykh 'alladhî baynahumâ*/the blessedness of the ...); Burton III 227,-(xxx). Chauvin 5: 204 No. 120; *ANE* 341-45 No. 61;
¿Alâ' al-Dîn Abû al-Shâmât: *Alf* II 157,-(*Shaykh* Dhakariyyâ Abu-el-¿Urûq); Burton IV 50,-("Shaykh Zachary of shaggery, O father of veins"). Chauvin 5: 43-49 No. 18; *ANE* 85 No. 63;
Ma¿rûf the Cobbler: *Alf* IV 300,-(*Ya 'abâ al-lithâmayn* [i.e., al-Sayyid al-Badawî]); Burton X 20,-(sire of the chin-veils twain/"kissing or breaking" [n. 1: questionable/??]). Chauvin 6: 81-82 No. 250; *ANE* 291 No. 262.□

Z138.5.2§, ‡Vagina personified.
Qamar al-Zamân and Budûr: *Alf* II 72,-(*shaykh*); Burton III 227,-(xxx). Chauvin V 204-12 No. 120; *ANE* 341-45 No. 61.□

Z139.3, ‡Wine personified. (Cf. P196.0.1§).
Isḥâq al-Mûṣilî and Khadîjah bint al-Ḥasan: *Alf* II 185,-cf./(made me do it); Burton IV 120,-(led me to). Chauvin V 241-42 No. 142; *ANE* 232 No. 71.□

Z139.9.3.2§, ‡Water jug (jar, bottle, inkwell, etc.)—female, vagina, womb, (or body orifice). See: *DOTTI*.
Dispute Concerning Males and Females: *Alf* II 302,-(inkwell/implicit); Burton V 161. Chauvin VI 153 No. 317; *ANE* 291 No. 151;
Hind bint al-Nu¿mân and al-Ḥajjâj: *Alf* III 202-3,-(plate/cup); Burton VII 98,-(vessel). Chauvin V 115-4 No. 50; *ANE* 221-22 No. 212;
Nûr al-Dîn and Maryam: *Alf* IV 97,-(bottle); Burton VIII 304. Chauvin V 52-54 No. 271; *ANE* 98-99 No. 233.□

Z139.9.4§, ‡Dry container (box, chest, trunk, bag, pocket, etc.)—anal or vaginal orifice. See: *DOTTI*.
¿Alâ' al-Dîn Abû al-Shâmât: *Alf* II 157,-(*ḥoqq* lid/right size); Burton IV 52 n. 2,-(box-cover). Chauvin V 43-49 No. 18; *ANE* 85-87 No. 63;
Dalîla the Swindler: *Alf* III 215,-(*kîs, kuss*, ...—/purse, 'puss', .../[word association]); Burton VII 151. Chauvin V 245-50 No. 147; *ANE* 163-64 No. 224.□

Z139.9.5.1§, ‡Belt (worn around waist) personified—strength, support, power.
King ¿Umar al-Nu¿mân and Sons: *Alf* II 11; Burton III 95. Chauvin VI 112-24 No. 277; *ANE* 430-34 No. 39.□

Z140.0.1§, ‡Symbolism of color combinations.
Hammâd: Treacherous Bedouin: *Alf* II 17,-(raven-snow/black-white); Burton III 105. Chauvin VI 124 n. 1 No. 277; *ANE* 200 No. 43;
Basra Girls in Poetry Contest: *Alf* III 206,-(red/yellow); Burton VII 113,-(rosy/saffron). Chauvin VI 144 No. 301; *ANE* 107-8 No. 216;
Lovers of Basra/Damrah: *Alf* III 210,-(whiteness of body/redness of dress); Burton VII 130. Chauvin V 118 No. 54; *ANE* 273 No. 220.□

Z141, ‡Symbolic color: red.
Ensorcelled Prince/Husband: *Alf* I 29; Burton I 77. Chauvin VI 56-58 No. 222; *ANE* 176 No. 13.□

Z141.1, Red garment to show anger of king. See: *GMC*. (Cf. W172.5.1.1§).
¿Alâ' al-Dîn Abû al-Shâmât: *Alf* II 168; Burton IV 72,-(scarlet). Chauvin V 43-49 No. 18; *ANE* 85-87 No. 63.□

Z141.4.1§, ‡Man experiences penis-erection from touching watermelon (uncut): thus he realizes that it is ripe (red inside). See: *DOTTI*. (Cf. T461.0.1§, Z141.4.1§).
Hashish Eater's Dream: *Alf* II 10,-cf.; Burton III 93. Chauvin VI 124 No. 278; *ANE* 216 No. 42.□

Z142, Symbolic color: white. See: *GMC*.
Ensorcelled Prince/Husband: *Alf* I 29; Burton I 77. Chauvin VI 56-58 No. 222; *ANE* 176 No. 13.□

Z142.6§, ‡White as symbol of peacefulness (passivity).
Jawdar and His Treacherous Brethren: *Alf* III 198,-(white suit); Burton VI 250. Chauvin V 257-60 No. 154; *ANE* 244-45 No. 209.□

Z143, Symbolic color: black.
¿Azîz and ¿Azîzah: *Alf* I 274; Burton II 309. Chauvin V 144-45 No. 71; *ANE* 111-13 No. 41.□

Z143.1, Black as symbol of grief [(mourning)]. (Cf. P681.1.1.2.4§).
al-'Amjad and al-'As¿ad: *Alf* II 146; Burton IV 28. Chauvin V 208-10 No. 120[.1]; *ANE* 2 341-42 No. 61/pt.□

Z143.3.2§, ‡'Black face': inauspicious person. (Cf. H244.1§, M439.1§).
Reeve's Story: Why Maimed by Bride: *Alf* I 99; Burton I 287. Chauvin V 220-21 No. 305; *ANE* 351 No. 25;
Tailor's Story/Barber of Baghdad: *Alf* I 103,-(xxx); Burton I 301. Chauvin V 154-56 No. 78; *ANE* 405-6 No. 27;
Man from Yaman and Six Salve-girls: Flyting: *Alf* II 246; Burton IV 250. Chauvin VI 151 No. 313; *ANE* 289-90 No. 84.□

Z143.4§, ‡Blackness as symbol of (physical) strength. (Cf. W256.5§).
Jullanâr of the Sea: *Alf* III 266,-(copulating bird); Burton VII 298. Chauvin V 147-51 No. 73; *ANE* 248-51 No. 227.□

Z143.5§, ‡Black is beautiful. (Cf. U281.1§).
Man from Yaman and Six Salve-girls: Flyting: *Alf* II 245; Burton IV 247-48. Chauvin VI 151 No. 313; *ANE* 289-90 No. 84.□

Z144, Symbolic color: blue. See: *GMC*.
Ensorcelled Prince/Husband: *Alf* I 29; Burton I 77. Chauvin VI 56-58 No. 222; *ANE* 176 No. 13.□

Z148.0.1§—(formerly-Z147.0.1§), Symbolic color: yellow.
Ensorcelled Prince/Husband: *Alf* I 29; Burton I 77. Chauvin VI 56-58 No. 222; *ANE* 176 No. 13.□

Z148.1§, ‡Yellow as pleasant color.
Man from Yaman and Six Salve-girls: Flyting: *Alf* II 248,-(blonde); Burton IV 248, 256. Chauvin VI 151 No. 313; *ANE* 289-90 No. 84.□

Z148.1.1§, ‡Blond is beautiful.
Man from Yaman and Six Salve-girls: Flyting: *Alf* II 248; Burton IV 256. Chauvin VI 151 No. 313; *ANE* 289-90 No. 84.□

Z152.6.1.1§, ‡Rock (stone): hardness of heart. (Cf. W155).
Jânshâh: *Alf* III 52,-(poems); Burton V 346. Chauvin VII 39-44 No. 153; *ANE* 238-41 No. 178.□

Z152.6.4§, ‡Corner(s) of a building (*rukn,/'arkân*): strength. See: *PSAE*. (Cf. V3§, Z186.7.2§, Z186.8§, Z199.2.1§).

Ma¿rûf the Cobbler: *Alf* IV 300; Burton X 21. Chauvin VI 81-82 No. 250; *ANE* 291-93 No. 262.□

Z152.6.6§, ‡Precious stone symbolism (pearl, gem, etc.)—beloved female.
Hasan of Basrah: *Alf* IV 39,-(seven gems-seven sisters); Burton VIII 113. Chauvin VII 29-35 No. 212A; *ANE* 207-10 No. 230.□

Z152.9.1§, ‡Mercury: elusiveness, evasiveness.
Mercury ¿Alî: *Alf* III 227; Burton VII 172. Chauvin V 248-50 No. 147; *ANE* 301-3 No. 225.□

Z159.2.4§, ‡Symbolism: sun—a beauty. See: *DOTTI*. (Cf. F574).
Jinni Keeps Mistress in Box: *Alf* I 3,-(poem); Burton I 11. Chauvin V 188-89 No. 111; *ANE* 370 No. 1/pt.;
Hammâd: Treacherous Bedouin: *Alf* II 18,-(sun behind cloud); Burton III 108. Chauvin VI 124 n. 1 No. 277; *ANE* 200 No. 43;
¿Alî ibn Bakkâr: *Alf* II 42,-(poem); Burton III 163. Chauvin V 153 No. 76; *ANE* 92-93 No. 60;
¿Abdallah ibn Fâḍil: Treacherous Brothers: *Alf* IV 274,-(shining sun in the heart of clear sky); Burton IX 320. Chauvin V 2-4 No. 2; *ANE* 63-65 No. 261.□

Z159.3.2§, ‡Symbolism: moon—beauty. See: *DOTTI*. (Cf. Z71.5.0.1.1.1§).
Jinni Keeps Mistress in Box: *Alf* I 3,-(moon of 14); Burton I 10, 11. Chauvin V 188-89 No. 111; *ANE* 370 No. 1/pt.;
Jewish Doctor's Story: Sororicide: *Alf* I 101; Burton I 292. Chauvin VI 89 No. 253; *ANE* 242 No. 26;
Sweep and Noble Lady: Infidelity Repaid: *Alf* II 190,-(male); Burton IV 128,-(rising moon). Chauvin VI 148 No. 306; *ANE* 403-4 No. 72;
Lover Who Feigned Himself a Thief: *Alf* II 205; Burton IV 158. Chauvin VII 134-35 No. 403; *ANE* 272 No. 76;
Basra Girls in Poetry Contest: *Alf* III 206,-(simile/red-yellow); Burton VII 113,-(rosy-saffron). Chauvin VI 144 No. 301; *ANE* 107-8 No. 216;
Hasan of Basrah: *Alf* IV 5; Burton VIII 46. Chauvin VII 29-35 No. 212A; *ANE* 207-10 No. 230;
Masrûr and Zayn al-Mawâṣif: *Alf* IV 55; Burton VIII 206. Chauvin VI 82-84 No. 251; *ANE* 294-95 No. 232.□

Z159.4.2§, ‡Symbolism: star—beauty.
Porter and Ladies of Baghdad: *Alf* I 32,-(*kawâkib*); Burton I 86. Chauvin V 251-52 No. 148; *ANE* 324-26 No. 14.□

Z165.0.1§, ‡Symbolism: prickly softness of fuzz on fruit or vegetable (e.g., peach fuzz, 'chick's down')—pubescent human body hair. (Cf. Z107§).
Bearded and Beardless Men as Lovers: *Alf* II 303; Burton V 165. Chauvin V 112 No. 48; *ANE* 450 No. 154;
Tawaddud: Slavegirl Sold and Regained: *Alf* II 304,-(poem); Burton V 190. Chauvin VII 117-19 No. 387; *ANE* 408-10 No. 157.□

Z166.1§, A certain fruit (apple, pomegranate, orange, watermelon, etc.) as symbol of female's physical attributes. See: *DOTTI*; *GMC*.
Hashish Eater's Dream: *Alf* II 10,-(watermelon); Burton III 93. Chauvin VI 124 No. 278; *ANE* 216 No. 42.□

Z166.1.1§, Symbolism: pomegranate (apple, orange)—breast. See: *DOTTI*; *GMC*.
King ¿Umar al-Nu¿mân and Sons: *Alf* I 170; Burton II 98. Chauvin VI 112-24 No. 277; *ANE* 430-34 No. 39;
Ibrâhîm and Jamîlah: *Alf* IV 225; Burton IX 221. Chauvin VI 52-53 No. 218; *ANE* 227-29 No. 258.□

Z166.3.1.1§, ‡Cucumber, banana, carrot, radish, etc.—penis. See: *DOTTI*. (Cf. F547.3.1.2.1§).
Ma¿n Rewards a Bedouin for Gift: *Alf* II 182-83,-cf./(*qaththâ'*/curled cucumber); Burton IV 98-99. Chauvin VI 78 No. 247; *ANE* 291 No. 66;
Three Wishes: *Alf* III 162,-(*zirr*/elongated squash); Burton VI 181. Chauvin VIII 51-52 No. 19; *ANE* 419-20 No. 199.□

Z166.4§, Symbolism: fruit (vegetable)—taste, texture, color, and form.
¿Azîz and ¿Azîzah: *Alf* I 277; Burton II 314. Chauvin V 144-45 No. 71; *ANE* 111-13 No. 41.□

Z166.4.1§, Fruit symbolism: positive qualities.

Nûr al-Dîn and Maryam: *Alf* IV 80-83; Burton VIII 266-73. Chauvin V 52-54 No. 271; *ANE* 98-99 No. 233.□

Z166.4.3§, Fruit (vegetable) symbolism: negative qualities.
Man from Yaman and Six Salve-girls: Flyting: *Alf* II 249,-(simile, molokhiyyah-plant of Bâb al-Lûq/Cairo district); Burton IV 259,-(mallow ...). Chauvin VI 151 No. 313; *ANE* 289-90 No. 84.□

Z167.0.1§, Family-tree (genealogy). (Cf. P208.0.1§, P70§).
Nûr al-Dîn ¿Alî and Son: *Alf* I 68; Burton I 207. Chauvin VI 102-6 No. 270; *ANE* 317-19 No. 22.□

Z167.0.2§, Symbolism: tree trunk—patriarch.
King Jalî¿âd and Shimâs: *Alf* IV 134-35; Burton IX 34,-(root). Chauvin VI 9-11 No. 184; *ANE* 237-38 No. 236.□

Z167.0.2.1§, Symbolism: tree limbs (boughs, branches)—children. See: *GMC*.
King Jalî¿âd and Shimâs: *Alf* IV 134; Burton IX 33. Chauvin VI 9-11 No. 184; *ANE* 237-38 No. 236.□

Z167.2.2.1§, Symbolism: carob tree—decay. See: *GMC*.
¿Azîz and ¿Azîzah: *Alf* I 277,-cf.; Burton II 314. Chauvin V 144-45 No. 71; *ANE* 111-13 No. 41;
Qamar al-Zamân and Budûr: *Alf* II 105,-cf.; Burton III 294. Chauvin V 204-12 No. 120; *ANE* 341-45 No. 61.□

Z167.5§, ‡Symbolism: tree trunk—male. See: *DOTTI*.
King Jalî¿âd and Shimâs: *Alf* IV 135; Burton IX 34,-(son). Chauvin VI 9-11 No. 184; *ANE* 237-38 No. 236.□

Z168.1§, Symbolism: garden (field)—a female. See: *DOTTI*. (Cf. Z186.2.0.1§, Z198.1.2§).
King ¿Umar al-Nu¿mân and Sons: *Alf* I 214,-(poem); Burton II 186. Chauvin VI 112-24 No. 277; *ANE* 430-34 No. 39;
¿Azîz and ¿Azîzah: *Alf* I 273-74; Burton II 309. Chauvin V 144-45 No. 71; *ANE* 111-13 No. 41;
King Dissuaded by Virtuous Wife: *Alf* II 294,-(earth for planting); Burton V 122,-(field). Chauvin VII 120-21 No. 391; *ANE* 260-61 No. 138;
King and Vizier's Wife/Tracks of Lion: *Alf* III 140; Burton VI 131. Chauvin VIII 35 No. 2; *ANE* 261 No. 182;
Hasan of Basrah: *Alf* III 315; Burton VIII 28. Chauvin VII 29-35 No. 212A; *ANE* 207-10 No. 230;
Masrûr and Zayn al-Mawâṣif: *Alf* IV 55, 70,-(dream of rendezvous and embrace in *rawḍah*/garden); Burton VIII 205-6, 242,-(xxx). Chauvin VI 82-84 No. 251; *ANE* 294-95 No. 232.□

Z168.2§, ‡That which is below woman's navel (pocket): "'gardens'"—vagina.
Tawaddud: Slavegirl Sold and Regained: *Alf* II 304,-(gardens of Eden/poem); Burton V 192,-(garths of Eden). Chauvin VII 117-19 No. 387; *ANE* 408-10 No. 157.□

Z169§, ‡Flower symbolism. See: *DOTTI*. (Cf. Z175.1).
Nûr al-Dîn and Maryam: *Alf* IV 80-83; Burton VIII 266-73. Chauvin V 52-54 No. 271; *ANE* 98-99 No. 233.□

Z170.0.1§, ‡Symbolism: eating (swallowing, chewing)—sexual activity. See: *DOTTI*. (Cf. Z106§).
Porter and Ladies of Baghdad: *Alf* I 35,-(mule eating flowers, sesame); Burton I 92. Chauvin V 251-52 No. 148; *ANE* 324-26 No. 14;
Dalîla the Swindler: *Alf* III 215; Burton VII 151,-(figs and pomegranates). Chauvin 5: 245-50 No. 147; *ANE* 163 No. 224.□

Z170.7.1§, ‡Foods with elongated form—e.g., sausage,/hot-dog, '*ṣubâ¿*-of-...', e.g., 'finger-of-*kuftah* (stick-of-ground-meat), 'finger-of-stuffed-[grape-leaves]', or the like: penis. See: *DOTTI*. (Cf. Z166.3.1.1§).
Three Wishes: *Alf* III 162,-(*zirr*/ elongated-squash); Burton VI 181. Chauvin VIII 51-52 No. 19; *ANE* 419-20 No. 199.□

Z175, Sign language. Message delivered by means of the fingers, etc. See: *DOTTI*; *GMC*.
¿Azîz and ¿Azîzah: *Alf* I 270, 272; Burton II 300. Chauvin V 144-45 No. 71; *ANE* 111-13 No. 41.□

Z175.1, Language of flowers: [symbolic]. See: *DOTTI*. (Cf. D1610.3.0.1§).
Nûr al-Dîn and Maryam: *Alf* IV 80-83; Burton VIII 266-73. Chauvin V 52-54 No. 271; *ANE* 98-99 No. 233.□

Z178.9.1§, ‡Chess-playing symbolically interpreted. (Cf. F679.8).

Masrûr and Zayn al-Mawâṣif: *Alf* IV 57-59; Burton VIII 216-18. Chauvin VI 82-84 No. 251; *ANE* 294-95 No. 232.□

Z179.1§, ‡Ascendance-descendance (social): act allegorically interpreted. (Cf. P2.2.1.2§).
Shahriyâr and Shahrzâd: *Alf* IV 317,-(kissing foot, ground, child, etc.); Burton X 54-55. Chauvin V 190-91 No. 111/pt.; *ANE* 371 No. 1.□

Z179.1.2.1§, ‡Male laid on his stomach—submission.
¿Alî Shâr and Zumurrud: *Alf* II 234; Burton IV 226-27. Chauvin V 89-91 No. 28; *ANE* 100-1 No. 82.□

Z179.1.2.1.1§, ‡Submission: kneeling. See: *DOTTI*. (Cf. K1289.1§).
King Jalî¿âd and Shimâs: *Alf* IV 134,-(*sujûd li*/prostrating self before), 155; Burton IX 34, 76,-(prostrating themselves). Chauvin VI 9-11 No. 184; *ANE* 237-38 No. 236.□

Z179.1.2.1.1.1§, ‡Submission: kissing ground (before a certain person). See: *DOTTI*; *PSAE*. (Cf. Z179.2.1§).
Shahriyâr and Shahrzâd: *Alf* I 7,-(xxx); Burton I 24. Chauvin V 190 No. 111/pt.; *ANE* 371 No. 1;
Hunchback's Tale: Resuscitated: *Alf* I 88; Burton I 255–352. Chauvin V 180-82 No. 105; *ANE* 224-25 No. 23;
Barber's Fifth Brother: Daydreams/Defeats Robbers: *Alf* I 118; Burton I 337. Chauvin V 161 No. 85; *ANE* 119-20 No. 33;
Ghânim ibn Ayyûb: *Alf* I 157; Burton II 76, 68. Chauvin VI 14 No. 188; *ANE* 192-93 No. 36;
King ¿Umar al-Nu¿mân and Sons: *Alf* I 164-65,-ff., 224,-(nine times), 228; Burton II 82. Chauvin VI 112-24 No. 277; *ANE* 430-34 No. 39;
Tâj al-Mulûk: *Alf* I 264,-cf./(king kisses ground before emissary—gratitude); Burton II 288. Chauvin V 126-28 No. 60; *ANE* 406-8 No. 40;
Qamar al-Zamân and Budûr: *Alf* II 107; Burton III 298. Chauvin V 204-12 No. 120; *ANE* 341-45 No. 61;
¿Alâ' al-Dîn Abû al-Shâmât: *Alf* II 162, 163; Burton IV 60. Chauvin V 43-49 No. 18; *ANE* 85-87 No. 63;
Abû Muḥammad Lazybones: *Alf* II 206,-("the lad/*ghulâm* kissed ..."); Burton IV 162,-("Lady Zubaydah kisseth the earth before thee"). Chauvin VI 64-67 No. 233; *ANE* 71-73 No. 78;
Sindbâd and Porter: *Alf* III 82; Burton VI 3. Chauvin VII 1 No. 373; *ANE* 383-85 No. 179/pt.;
Mercury ¿Alî: *Alf* III 245; Burton VII 207. Chauvin V 248-50 No. 147; *ANE* 301-3 No. 225;
Jullanâr of the Sea: *Alf* III 254,-(to sister's husband); Burton VII 276. Chauvin V 147-51 No. 73; *ANE* 248-51 No. 227;
Sayf al-Mulûk: *Alf* III 286,-cf./(by monkeys); Burton VII 346. Chauvin VII 64-73 No. 348; *ANE* 362-64 No. 229;
Hasan of Basrah: *Alf* IV 5; Burton VIII 46. Chauvin VII 29-35 No. 212A; *ANE* 207-10 No. 230;
Ibrâhîm and Jamîlah: *Alf* IV 225 ; Burton IX 220, 222. Chauvin VI 52-53 No. 218; *ANE* 227-29 No. 258;
Ma¿rûf the Cobbler: *Alf* IV 301; Burton X 21. Chauvin VI 81-82 No. 250; *ANE* 291-93 No. 262;
Shahriyâr and Shahrzâd: *Alf* IV 317; Burton X 55. Chauvin V 190-91 No. 111/pt.; *ANE* 371 No. 1.□

Z179.1.2.2.1§, ‡Female laid on her back with legs raised upward (toward heaven): submission to higher power (praying, supplication). (Cf. Z62).
Qamar al-Zamân and Budûr: *Alf* II 109,-(poem); Burton III 304. Chauvin V 204-12 No. 120; *ANE* 341-45 No. 61.□

Z179.1.3§, ‡Body posture indicates sexual orientation. (Cf. P198§).
Jawdar and His Treacherous Brethren: *Alf* III 198; Burton VI 249. Chauvin V 257-60 No. 154; *ANE* 244-45 No. 209.□

Z179.2§, ‡Kissing allegorically interpreted. See: *PSAE*.
Shahriyâr and Shahrzâd: *Alf* IV 317; Burton X 54-55. Chauvin V 190-91 No. 111/pt.; *ANE* 371 No. 1.□

Z179.2.1§, ‡Hand kissed: respect (appeasement, reverence). See: *DOTTI*. (Cf. Z179.1.2.1.1.1§).
Trader and Afrit: Accidental Fairy-cide: *Alf* I 8; Burton I 27. Chauvin VI 22-23 No. 194; *ANE* 419-20 No. 4;
Anîs al-Jalîs: *Alf* I 129, 136; Burton II 9. Chauvin V 120-24 No. 58; *ANE* 316-17 No. 35;
¿Alâ' al-Dîn Abû al-Shâmât: *Alf* II 157; Burton IV 53. Chauvin V 43-49 No. 18; *ANE* 85-87 No. 63;

Sweep and Noble Lady: Infidelity Repaid: *Alf* II 190; Burton IV 128. Chauvin VI 148 No. 306; *ANE* 403-4 No. 72;
Bulûqiya: *Alf* III 74; Burton V 384,-(feet kissed/variant). Chauvin VII 54 No. 77; *ANE* 130-32 No. 177;
Wife's device to cheat: (Weeping Bitch as Bluff): *Alf* III 149-50; Burton VI 155. Chauvin VIII 45-46 No. 13; *ANE* 447-49 No. 193;
Jawdar and His Treacherous Brethren: *Alf* III 196; Burton VI 246. Chauvin V 257-60 No. 154; *ANE* 244-45 No. 209;
Dalîla the Swindler: *Alf* III 214; Burton VII 148. Chauvin V 245-50 No. 147; *ANE* 163-64 No. 224;
Abû Qîr and Abû Ṣîr: *Alf* IV 195; Burton IX 158. Chauvin V 15-17 No. 10; *ANE* 75-77 No. 255;
Jeweler's Wife and Qamar al-Zamân: *Alf* IV 259,-(drawing); Burton IX (xxx). Chauvin V 212-14 No. 121; *ANE* 345-47 No. 260.□

Z179.2.3§, ‡Foot kissed: servility, paying homage, pleading of desperation.
Merchant's Curious Wife: *Alf* I 6,-(husband's); Burton I 23. Chauvin V 179-80 No. 104; *ANE* 298-99 No. 3;
Anîs al-Jalîs: *Alf* I 141, 145; Burton II 31, 42. Chauvin V 120-24 No. 58; *ANE* 316-17 No. 35;
Ghânim ibn Ayyûb: *Alf* I 153,-cf./(leg and foot—erotic); Burton II 60. Chauvin VI 14 No. 188; *ANE* 192-93 No. 36;
Bulûqiya: *Alf* III 76; Burton V 387. Chauvin VII 54 No. 77; *ANE* 130-32 No. 177;
Wife's device to cheat: (Weeping Bitch as Bluff): *Alf* III 149; Burton VI 155. Chauvin VIII 45-46 No. 13; *ANE* 447-49 No. 193;
Hasan of Basrah: *Alf* IV 4,-(affection), 54,-(jinn daughter in law's); Burton VIII 43, 154. Chauvin VII 29-35 No. 212A; *ANE* 207-10 No. 230;
Shahriyâr and Shahrzâd: *Alf* IV 317; Burton X 54. Chauvin V 190-91 No. 111/pt.; *ANE* 371 No. 1.□

Z179.2.3.1§, ‡Shoe (sandals) kissed: pleading of desperation. (Cf. Z63.3.3.1.4§).
Sayf al-Mulûk: *Alf* III 299; Burton VII 373,-(sandals). Chauvin VII 64-73 No. 348; *ANE* 362-64 No. 229.□

Z179.4§, ‡Directions and motions (east—west, in—out, up—down, etc.) allegorically interpreted. See: *DOTTI*. (Cf. T187.0.2§).
Qamar al-Zamân and Budûr: *Alf* II 109,-(poem/up-down); Burton III 304. Chauvin V 204-12 No. 120; *ANE* 341-45 No. 61.□

Z179.2.5§, ‡Head kissed: endearment, reconciliation.
Barber's Fifth Brother: Daydreams/Defeats Robbers: *Alf* I 118; Burton I 337. Chauvin V 161 No. 85; *ANE* 119-20 No. 33;
Hasan of Basrah: *Alf* IV 4; Burton VIII 43. Chauvin VII 29-35 No. 212A; *ANE* 207-10 No. 230.□

Z183.0.1§, Meaning of a name. See: *DOTTI*; *GMC*; *PSAE*. (Cf. A102.0.1.1§, A1241.0.1§).
King ¿Umar al-Nu¿mân and Sons: *Alf* I 163,-(Ṣafiyyah); Burton II 79 n. 1,-("Sofiyah or Sophia"). Chauvin VI 112-24 No. 277; *ANE* 430-34 No. 39;
Ebony Horse: *Alf* II 264,-(Persian "Ḥarjah"); Burton V 27,-(Harjah/"There is no such name", n. 1). Chauvin V 221-31 No. 130; *ANE* 172-74 No. 103;
Uns al-Wujûd and al-Ward: *Alf* II 269, 280,-(al-Ward); Burton V 32. Chauvin VI 127-29 No. 282; *ANE* 438 No. 104;
Tawaddud: Slavegirl Sold and Regained: *Alf* II 314,-(Adam); Burton V 218. Chauvin VII 117-19 No. 387; *ANE* 408-10 No. 157;
Jânshâh: *Alf* III 68,-("Qal¿at Jawhar"/Jewels' Fortress); Burton V 373. Chauvin VII 39-44 No. 153; *ANE* 238-41 No. 178;
City of Brass: *Alf* III 132,-(City of Brass); Burton VI 101. Chauvin V 32-35 No. 16; *ANE* 146-50 No. 180;
Mercury ¿Alî: *Alf* III 227,-(mercury—metal); Burton VII 172,-(quicksilver). Chauvin V 248-50 No. 147; *ANE* 301-3 No. 225;
Jullanâr of the Sea: *Alf* III 264,-(Lâb); Burton VII 295. Chauvin V 147-51 No. 73; *ANE* 248-51 No. 227;
Landsman ¿Abdallah and Merman ¿Abdallah: *Alf* IV 203,-(¿Abd-Allâh); Burton IX 177,-(servants of Allah). Chauvin V 6-7 No. 3; *ANE* 65-66 No. 256;
Ma¿rûf the Cobbler: *Alf* IV 288,-(*¿irrah*); Burton X 1. Chauvin VI 81-82 No. 250; *ANE* 291-93 No. 262.□

Z183.0.1.1§, Beautiful and ugly names. See: *DOTTI*; *GMC*.
¿Alâ' al-Dîn Abû al-Shâmât: *Alf* II 165,-(Ḥabẓlam Baẓâẓâ); Burton IV 67. Chauvin V 43-49 No. 18; *ANE* 85-87 No. 63.□

Z183.0.1.3.1§, ‡Name that fits the name-bearer—e.g., girl named Jamîlah (Beautiful) is actually 'beautiful', a man named Ghûl (Ogre) is actually 'ogre-like'.
Masrûr and Zayn al-Mawâṣif: *Alf* IV 74; Burton VIII 248. Chauvin VI 82-84 No. 251; *ANE* 294-95 No. 232.□

Z183.2.1.1§, ‡Child named "Predestined: Thus-it-Became" ("Quḍiya-fa-kân"), "What-was-has-Been" ("Kâna-mâ-kân"). See: *DOTTI*. (Cf. A611.0.1.1§).
King ¿Umar al-Nu¿mân and Sons: *Alf* I 208; Burton II 175. Chauvin VI 112-24 No. 277; *ANE* 430-34 No. 39.□

Z183.5.1§, "Father-of-..." (*'Abu-...*/"*Bu-...*"). See: *GMC*. (Cf. Z138.5.0.1§).
¿Alâ' al-Dîn Abû al-Shâmât: *Alf* II 157,-(Abu-el-¿Urûq); Burton IV 51. Chauvin V 43-49 No. 18; *ANE* 85-87 No. 63.□

Z183.7§, ‡Personal names formed from one of God's names (deus-nymics)—e.g., ¿Abd-Allâh, ¿Abd-al-Karîm, 'Amatu-Allâh etc.
Landsman ¿Abdallah and Merman ¿Abdallah: *Alf* IV 200; Burton IX 177. Chauvin V 6-7 No. 3; *ANE* 65-66 No. 256;
¿Abdallah ibn Fâḍil: Treacherous Brothers: *Alf* IV 288; Burton IX 349. Chauvin V 2-4 No. 2; *ANE* 63-65 No. 261.□

Z183.9.2§, ‡Names given a game's play-pieces (e.g., chess' king, queen, knight, elephant, dog, pawn, etc.). See: *PSAE*. (Cf. Z178.9.1§).
King ¿Umar al-Nu¿mân and Sons: *Alf* I 172,-(poem); Burton II 104. Chauvin VI 112-24 No. 277; *ANE* 430-34 No. 39;
Tawaddud: Slavegirl Sold and Regained: *Alf* III 7; Burton V 243. Chauvin VII 117-19 No. 387; *ANE* 408-10 No. 157;
Masrûr and Zayn al-Mawâṣif: *Alf* IV 57-59; Burton VIII 216-18. Chauvin VI 82-84 No. 251; *ANE* 294-95 No. 232.□

Z186.0.1§, Symbolism: erotic—general.
Hârûn and Zubaydah in Bath: *Alf* II 284,-(poem,/water/pitcher); Burton V 76. Chauvin VI 142 No. 298; *ANE* 203-4 No. 111.□

Z186.1.1§, Symbolism: sewing implements—sex organs. See: *GMC*.
Tawaddud: Slavegirl Sold and Regained: *Alf* II 318-19; Burton V 227. Chauvin VII 117-19 No. 387; *ANE* 408-10 No. 157.□

Z186.1.2§, ‡Symbolism: button going into button hole—sexual intercourse. (Cf. Z106§).
Shahriyâr and Shâhzamân: *Alf* I 3,-(xxx); Burton I 6,-(as a button loop clasps a button). Chauvin V 188-91 No. 111; *ANE* 370-71 No. 1;
Tawaddud: Slavegirl Sold and Regained: *Alf* II 318-19; Burton V 227. Chauvin VII 117-19 No. 387; *ANE* 408-10 No. 157.□

Z186.2.0.1§, Symbolism: water going through field (irrigation canal)—sexual intercourse. See: *DOTTI*; *GMC*. (Cf. Z168.1§).
King ¿Umar al-Nu¿mân and Sons: *Alf* I 214,-(poem); Burton II 186. Chauvin VI 112-24 No. 277; *ANE* 430-34 No. 39;
King and Vizier's Wife/Tracks of Lion: *Alf* III 140; Burton VI 131. Chauvin VIII 35 No. 2; *ANE* 261 No. 182.□

Z186.2.1§, Symbolism: diving into watermelon after cutting it with knife—sexual intercourse. See: *DOTTI*; *GMC*. (Cf. Z141.4.1§).
Hashish Eater's Dream: *Alf* II 10,-cf.; Burton III 92, 93. Chauvin VI 124 No. 278; *ANE* 216 No. 42.□

Z186.3.1§, Symbolism: mouse entering hole (crack)—sexual intercourse. See: *DOTTI*. (Cf. Z186.7§).
Porter and Ladies of Baghdad: *Alf* I 35,-cf./(mule entering lodge/"*khân* Abî Manṣûr"); Burton I 92. Chauvin V 251-52 No. 148; *ANE* 324-26 No. 14.□

Z186.4§, Symbolism: firing off cannon (gun)—sexual intercourse. See: *DOTTI*.
Nûr al-Dîn ¿Alî and Son: *Alf* I 72; Burton I 223. Chauvin VI 102-6 No. 270; *ANE* 317-19 No. 22;

Ma¿rûf the Cobbler: *Alf* IV 300; Burton X 20-21. Chauvin VI 81-82 No. 250; *ANE* 291-93 No. 262.□

Z186.4.0.1§, ‡Symbolism: firing on fortress (citadel)—ejaculation, orgasm (sexual intercourse). (Cf. Z186.8§).
Nûr al-Dîn ¿Alî and Son: *Alf* I 72; Burton I 223. Chauvin VI 102-6 No. 270; *ANE* 317-19 No. 22;
Ma¿rûf the Cobbler: *Alf* IV 300; Burton X 21. Chauvin VI 81-82 No. 250; *ANE* 291-93 No. 262.□

Z186.6§, Symbolism: buttocks—dome (shrine). See: *GMC*. (Cf. F575.1.5.1§).
Hasan of Basrah: *Alf* III 315,-(vagina)-cf.; Burton VIII 31. Chauvin VII 29-35 No. 212A; *ANE* 207-10 No. 230.□

Z186.6.2§, ‡Symbolism: buttocks—sand dunes (hill). (Cf. F575.1.5.1.2§).
Qamar al-Zamân and Budûr: *Alf* II 72,-(poem); Burton III 226. Chauvin V 204-12 No. 120; *ANE* 341-45 No. 61.□

Z186.7§, Symbolism: vagina—saint's shrine—('*shaikh* So-and-so'). See: *GMC*. (Cf. Z186.3.1§).
¿Azîz and ¿Azîzah: *Alf* I 279,-(*ṭawâf*); Burton II 318. Chauvin V 144-45 No. 71; *ANE* 111-13 No. 41;
Qamar al-Zamân and Budûr: *Alf* II 72, 110; Burton III 227, 305. Chauvin V 204-12 No. 120; *ANE* 341-45 No. 61;
¿Alâ' al-Dîn Abû al-Shâmât: *Alf* II 157,-(*Shaikh* Zakariyyâ); Burton IV 51. Chauvin V 43-49 No. 18; *ANE* 85-87 No. 63;
Hasan of Basrah: *Alf* III 315; Burton VIII 31-31. Chauvin VII 29-35 No. 212A; *ANE* 207-10 No. 230.□

Z186.7.1§, ‡Symbolism: circumambulation (*ṭawâf*) of shrine—foreplay (or sexual intercourse). (Cf. U318.1.1§, Z106§).
¿Azîz and ¿Azîzah: *Alf* I 279,-cf.; Burton II 318. Chauvin V 144-45 No. 71; *ANE* 111-13 No. 41.□

Z186.7.2§, ‡Symbolism: prayer niche (*miḥrâb*) or pulpit—vagina. (Cf. Z152.6.4§).
Qamar al-Zamân and Budûr: *Alf* II 110-11,-(poem); Burton III 306. Chauvin V 204-12 No. 120; *ANE* 341-45 No. 61;
¿Alî Shâr and Zumurrud: *Alf* II 234; Burton IV 227. Chauvin V 89-91 No. 28; *ANE* 100-1 No. 82.□

Z186.8§, ‡Symbolism: building (palace, house, inn, etc.)—female. See: *DOTTI*. (Cf. Z152.6.4§, Z186.4.0.1§, Z187§).
Porter and Ladies of Baghdad: *Alf* I 35,-(*khân*); Burton I 92. Chauvin V 251-52 No. 148; *ANE* 324-26 No. 14;
Nûr al-Dîn ¿Alî and Son: *Alf* I 72,-(citadel); Burton I 223. Chauvin VI 102-6 No. 270; *ANE* 317-19 No. 22;
Hasan of Basrah: *Alf* III 315, 316,-(with house-top and corners); Burton VIII 28, 29. Chauvin VII 29-35 No. 212A; *ANE* 207-10 No. 230.□

Z186.8.0.1§, ‡Symbolism: sexual intercourse expressed in terms of traveling (voyage) from one site to another. See: *DOTTI*. (Cf. U318.1.1§).
¿Alâ' al-Dîn Abû al-Shâmât: *Alf* II 157; Burton IV 51. Chauvin V 43-49 No. 18; *ANE* 85-87 No. 63.□

Z186.8.1§, ‡Door (gate, entrance, corridor, lane) to building (house)—vagina. See: *DOTTI*.
Porter and Ladies of Baghdad: *Alf* I 34-35; Burton I 94. Chauvin V 251-52 No. 148; *ANE* 324-26 No. 14;
¿Alâ' al-Dîn Abû al-Shâmât: *Alf* II 157; Burton IV 51. Chauvin V 43-49 No. 18; *ANE* 85-87 No. 63;
¿Alî Shâr and Zumurrud: *Alf* II 234; Burton IV 227. Chauvin V 89-91 No. 28; *ANE* 100-1 No. 82;
Man Who Never Laughs: *Alf* III 153,-cf./(*dahlîz ḍayyiq*); Burton VI 163,-(narrow passage). Chauvin VIII 47-48 No. 15; *ANE* 285-86 No. 195.□

Z186.8.1.1§, ‡Erotic experience from opening forbidden chamber (door). See: *DOTTI*. (Cf. N794§).
Jânshâh: *Alf* III 50; Burton V 345. Chauvin VII 39-44 No. 153; *ANE* 238-41 No. 178;
Man Who Never Laughs: *Alf* III 153, 155; Burton VI 163. Chauvin VIII 47-48 No. 15; *ANE* 285-86 No. 195;
House with the Belvedere: *Alf* III 168,-cf./(unused/covered with spider-web); Burton VI 191. Chauvin VIII 57-58 No. 23; *ANE* 223 No. 203;
Hasan of Basrah: *Alf* III 315; Burton VIII 29. Chauvin VII 29-35 No. 212A; *ANE* 207-10 No. 230.□

Z186.8.2.2§, ‡Symbolism: cave, lion's den, pit—vagina. (Cf. N793.1§).

¿Alâ' al-Dîn Abû al-Shâmât: *Alf* II 169,-(implicit); Burton IV 74. Chauvin V 43-49 No. 18; *ANE* 85-87 No. 63.□

Z186.8.3§, ‡Women are like an inn (bathhouse), one man goes in another comes out. (Cf. F779.1§).
Qamar al-Zamân and Budûr: *Alf* II 66,-(poem); Burton III 216. Chauvin V 204-12 No. 120; *ANE* 341-45 No. 61.□

Z186.9§, Symbolism: ring—body orifice. (Cf. H1580.1.3.1§).
¿Azîz and ¿Azîzah: *Alf* I 278,-(coin/eye).-cf.; Burton II 316. Chauvin V 144-45 No. 71; *ANE* 111-13 No. 41;
Qamar al-Zamân and Budûr: *Alf* II 108,-cf./(poem/*dînâr*); Burton III 301,-(gold piece). Chauvin V 204-12 No. 120; *ANE* 341-45 No. 61.□

Z186.9.1§, Symbolism: ring—mouth (small). See: *GMC*. (Cf. F544.0.7.1§).
Porter and Ladies of Baghdad: *Alf* I 32; Burton I 84,-(her mouth was the ring of Sulayman). Chauvin 5: 251 No. 148; *ANE* 324 No. 14;
Hasan of Basrah: *Alf* III 316,-(*ka-khâtam Sulaymân*/mouth like Solomon's ring), IV 29,-(*famm ka-khâtam ¿aqîq*); Burton VIII 31,(mouth magical as Solomon'a seal), Burton VIII 93,-(mouth like seal of cornelian). Chauvin VII 29-35 No. 212A; *ANE* 207-10 No. 230□

Z186.9.2§, Symbolism: 'eye'—vagina, anus. (Cf. Z77.1§).
Ibrâhîm and Jamîlah: *Alf* IV 226,-cf./(implicit/fill eye); Burton IX 222. Chauvin VI 52-53 No. 218; *ANE* 227-29 No. 258.□

Z186.9.2.4§, ‡Symbolism: 'mouth'—vagina.
King ¿Umar al-Nu¿mân and Sons: *Alf* I 194,-cf./(word association); Burton II 143,-(tongue to be stuff up into coynte). Chauvin VI 112-24 No. 277; *ANE* 430-34 No. 39;
al-Rashîd and Omani Merchant: *Alf* IV 213,-(poem/word association); Burton IX 197,("toothstick"). Chauvin VI 111-12 No. 276; *ANE* 201-2 No. 257.□

Z187.1§, ‡Symbolism: luminous houseboat (ship)—life's pleasures (love of life). See: *DOTTI*. (Cf. Z113.1§).
Man Who Never Laughs: *Alf* III 154,-cf./(golden barque); Burton VI 163. Chauvin VIII 47-48 No. 15; *ANE* 285-86 No. 195.□

Z187§, ‡Symbolism: vessel (boat, ship, etc.)—female. (Cf. W251.2.3.2.0.1§, Z186.8§).
Man Who Never Laughs: *Alf* III 153-54,-(golden barque); Burton VI 163. Chauvin VIII 47-48 No. 15; *ANE* 285-86 No. 195.□

Z187.1.1§, ‡Sexually abused woman likened to 'sunken ship'.
¿Alî Shâr and Zumurrud: *Alf* II 226; Burton IV 209,-("water-logged ship"). Chauvin V 89-91 No. 28; *ANE* 100-1 No. 82.□

Z189§, Symbolism concerning virginity and defloration. See: *DOTTI*; *GMC*.
¿Azîz and ¿Azîzah: *Alf* I 286,-(poem); Burton II 331. Chauvin V 144-45 No. 71; *ANE* 111-13 No. 41;
Hasan of Basrah: *Alf* III 315-16,-(poem: tight like my livelihood); Burton VIII 32. Chauvin VII 29-35 No. 212A; *ANE* 207-10 No. 230.□

Z189.1.2§, Symbolism: unpierced and pierced gem (pearl)—virgin and non-virgin. See: *DOTTI*. (Cf. Z192.1.1§).
Nûr al-Dîn ¿Alî and Son: *Alf* I 72; Burton I 223. Chauvin VI 102-6 No. 270; *ANE* 317-19 No. 22;
¿Alâ' al-Dîn Abû al-Shâmât: *Alf* II 181; Burton IV 94. Chauvin V 43-49 No. 18; *ANE* 85-87 No. 63;
Mock Caliph/¿Alî al-Jawharî: *Alf* II 197; Burton IV 144. Chauvin V 99-100 No. 174; *ANE* 304-5 No. 73;
Mercury ¿Alî: *Alf* III 246; Burton VII 208. Chauvin V 248-50 No. 147; *ANE* 301-3 No. 225;
Nûr al-Dîn and Maryam: *Alf* IV 97; Burton VIII 304,-("pearl unthridden"). Chauvin V 52-54 No. 271; *ANE* 98-99 No. 233.□

Z189.2.1§, Symbolism: 'With God's seal'—virgin. See: *DOTTI*; *GMC*.
Sayf al-Mulûk: *Alf* III 287,-cf./(in the condition in which God created me); Burton VII 349,-(as Allah Almighty created me). Chauvin VII 64-73 No. 348; *ANE* 362-64 No. 229.□

Z189.2.2§, ‡Symbolism: "breaking seal"—deflower.
Shahriyâr and Shahrzâd: *Alf* I 7,-cf./("*'azâlâ bakâratahâ*/removed her virginity"); Burton I 24. Chauvin V 188-89 No. 111; *ANE* 370-71 No. 1;

Man Who Never Laughs: *Alf* III 155,-cf./(" *'azâlâ bakâratahâ*/removed her virginity"); Burton VI 165-66. Chauvin VIII 47-48 No. 15; *ANE* 285-86 No. 195;
Hasan of Basrah: *Alf* IV 5,-(*fadda khitmahâ*); Burton VIII 46,-(pierced the forge). Chauvin VII 29-35 No. 212A; *ANE* 207-10 No. 230.□

Z189.2.2.1§, ‡Symbolism: "breaking seal of bottle"—be first to enjoy contents.
Tawaddud: Slavegirl Sold and Regained: *Alf* II 304; Burton V 191. Chauvin VII 117-19 No. 387; *ANE* 408-10 No. 157.□

Z189.3.1§, ‡Symbolism: "take/remove face (crust)"—deflower.
Shahriyâr and Shahrzâd: *Alf* I 7,-cf./(*'akhadha bakâratahâ*); Burton I 24,-(did away with his bride's maidenhead). Chauvin V 188-89 No. 111; *ANE* 370-71 No. 1;
King ¿Umar al-Nu¿mân and Sons: *Alf* I 207,-(*'akhadha wajhahâ*); Burton II 172. Chauvin VI 112-24 No. 277; *ANE* 430-34 No. 39.□

Z190§, Animal symbolism: a certain animal (bird) as symbol of human attributes. See: *DOTTI*.
Tâj al-Mulûk: *Alf* I 299; Burton III 31. Chauvin V 126-28 No. 60; *ANE* 406-8 No. 40.□

Z191.3.1§, ‡Dove (pigeon)—female's physical attributes.
Jânshâh: *Alf* III 50; Burton V 345. Chauvin VII 39-44 No. 153; *ANE* 238-41 No. 178;
Masrûr and Zayn al-Mawâṣif: *Alf* IV 55; Burton VIII 205. Chauvin VI 82-84 No. 251; *ANE* 294-95 No. 232.□

Z191.4.1§, ‡Mourning dove—female's physical attributes. See: *DOTTI*.
Jânshâh: *Alf* III 50-51; Burton V 345-46. Chauvin VII 39-44 No. 153; *ANE* 238-41 No. 178;
Masrûr and Zayn al-Mawâṣif: *Alf* IV 55; Burton VIII 205. Chauvin VI 82-84 No. 251; *ANE* 294-95 No. 232.□

Z192.0.1.1§, ‡Rabbit (bunny)—female's genitalia. (Cf. Z107§).
Hasan of Basrah: *Alf* III 316,-(with ears cropped/*maqṭûsh*); Burton VIII 33,-(hare with ears back). Chauvin VII 29-35 No. 212A; *ANE* 207-10 No. 230.□

Z192.0.1.4.1§, ‡Shape of *al-¿Uqâb* (Phoenix-like eagle—usually female)—female's genitalia. (Z105§).
Hasan of Basrah: *Alf* III 316,-(*¿Uqâb*/female-eagle/poem); Burton VIII 33,-(hummock great of span). Chauvin VII 29-35 No. 212A; *ANE* 207-10 No. 230.□

Z192.0.2.1§, ‡Sheep's tail (fat)—female's buttocks. (Cf. Z107§).
Nûr al-Dîn and Maryam: *Alf* IV 91, 97,-(softer than a '*liyyah*' [i.e., *'ilyah*]); Burton VIII 291, 303. Chauvin V 52-54 No. 271; *ANE* 98-99 No. 233.□

Z192.0.1.4§, ‡Bird's down—female's genitalia.
Hasan of Basrah: *Alf* III 316,-(*¿Uqâb*/poem); Burton VIII 33,-(hummock great of span). Chauvin VII 29-35 No. 212A; *ANE* 207-10 No. 230.□

Z192.1.1§, ‡Mare (filly)—female with sex-appeal (fertile). See: *DOTTI*. (Cf. U101.0.2§).
Nûr al-Dîn ¿Alî and Son: *Alf* I 72; Burton I 223. Chauvin VI 102-6 No. 270; *ANE* 317-19 No. 22;
Mock Caliph/¿Alî al-Jawharî: *Alf* II 197; Burton IV 144. Chauvin V 99-100 No. 174; *ANE* 304-5 No. 73;
Hind bint al-Nu¿mân and al-Ḥajjâj: *Alf* III 201,-(poem); Burton VII 97. Chauvin V 115-4 No. 50; *ANE* 221-22 No. 212;
Mercury ¿Alî: *Alf* III 246; Burton VII 208. Chauvin V 248-50 No. 147; *ANE* 301-3 No. 225.□

Z192.1.1.1§, ‡Unridden filly—a virgin. (Usually occurs in conjunction with Mot. Z189.1.2§). See: *DOTTI*. (Cf. Z189.1.2§).
Nûr al-Dîn ¿Alî and Son: *Alf* I 72; Burton I 223. Chauvin VI 102-6 No. 270; *ANE* 317-19 No. 22;
Nûr al-Dîn and Maryam: *Alf* IV 97,-(unridden *maṭiyyah*/riding animal); Burton VIII 304,-("filly ... unridden"). Chauvin V 52-54 No. 271; *ANE* 98-99 No. 233.□

Z192.2.1§, ‡Symbolism: viper—treacherous female. See: *DOTTI*. (Cf. B3§, B225.3§, Z194.2.4§).
House with the Belvedere: *Alf* III 167,-(*¿ajûz shamṭâ' ka ḥayyah raqṭâ'*); Burton VI 190,-("grizzled crone, as she were a snake speckled white and black"). Chauvin VIII 57-58 No. 23; *ANE* 223 No. 203;

Hasan of Basrah: *Alf* IV 15,-(simile/*ytalawwâ ka al-'af¿â*), 25,-(simile); Burton VIII 66,-(writhing like a scotched snake [??]), 86,-(pied snake). Chauvin VII 29-35 No. 212A; *ANE* 207-10 No. 230;
Ma¿rûf the Cobbler: *Alf* IV 315,-(simile); Burton X 49,-(snake). Chauvin VI 81-82 No. 250; *ANE* 291-93 No. 262.□

Z193.1§, Domestic animal—male's physical attributes. See: *DOTTI*; *GMC*.
Porter and Ladies of Baghdad: *Alf* I 35,-cf./(mule); Burton I 93. Chauvin V 251-52 No. 148; *ANE* 324-26 No. 14.□

Z193.3.1.1.1§, ‡Cock's job (duty): 'eat, drink, and f... (copulate)'. (Cf. Z62).
¿Azîz and ¿Azîzah: *Alf* I 285,-(you "... *tankaḥ*"); Burton II 331,-("eat and drink and tread"). Chauvin V 144-45 No. 71; *ANE* 111-13 No. 41.□

Z194.1.1§, ‡Camel symbolism.
Dalîla the Swindler: *Alf* III 213-14; Burton VII 167,-(Camel-shoulder). Chauvin V 245-50 No. 147; *ANE* 163-64 No. 224.□

Z194.1.3.1§, ‡He-mule—worthless (stupid) male.
Hind bint al-Nu¿mân and al-Ḥajjâj: *Alf* III 201,-(poem); Burton VII 97. Chauvin V 115-4 No. 50; *ANE* 221-22 No. 212.□

Z194.1.3.2.1§, ‡He-mule—sexual stamina. (Cf. F547.3.0.1§).
Porter and Ladies of Baghdad: *Alf* I 35,-cf./(mule entering lodge/*khân*); Burton I 92. Chauvin V 251-52 No. 148; *ANE* 324-26 No. 14.□

Z194.2.1.2§, ‡Lion—power (chieftainship, kingship). See: *DOTTI*. (Cf. B240.4, J814).
¿Alâ' al-Dîn Abû al-Shâmât: *Alf* II 169; Burton IV 74. Chauvin V 43-49 No. 18; *ANE* 85-87 No. 63;
King Dissuaded by Virtuous Wife: *Alf* II 294; Burton V 121. Chauvin VII 120-21 No. 391; *ANE* 260-61 No. 138.□

Z194.2.4§, ‡Serpent, male-snake (*ḥanash*, *thu¿bân*)—treacherous (evil) male. (Cf. Z192.2.1§).
King ¿Umar al-Nu¿mân and Sons: *Alf* II 7,-(simile/*yatalawwâ ka al-thu¿bân*); Burton III 87,-(squirming like a snake). Chauvin VI 112-24 No. 277; *ANE* 430-34 No. 39;
Dalîla the Swindler: *Alf* III 213,-(can wile *al-thu¿bân*/male snake out of his den); Burton VII 145,-("could wile the very dragon out of his den"). Chauvin V 248-50 No. 147; *ANE* 163-64 No. 224.□

Z194.3.1.1§, ‡Cock: ruler of hens. See: *DOTTI*. (Cf. Z43.7.1§).
Merchant's Curious Wife: *Alf* I 6; Burton I 21. Chauvin V 179-80 No. 104; *ANE* 298-99 No. 3.□

Z194.9.5§, ‡Bird snatching precious object and flying away with it—loss of dear person or asset.
Hasan of Basrah: *Alf* IV 39; Burton VIII 113. Chauvin VII 29-35 No. 212A; *ANE* 207-10 No. 230;
Masrûr and Zayn al-Mawâṣif: *Alf* IV 55; Burton VIII 205. Chauvin VI 82-84 No. 251; *ANE* 294-95 No. 232.□

Z197.3.1§, ‡Knife, sword, dagger, saw, etc.—penis (male). See: *DOTTI*. (Cf. S115.5.1§, Z197.3.1§).
Dalîla the Swindler: *Alf* III 215; Burton VII 151. Chauvin V 245-50 No. 147; *ANE* 163-64 No. 224.□

Z197.3.1.0.1§, ‡Cutting (chopping, sawing, etc.)—sexual intercourse.
Dalîla the Swindler: *Alf* III 215,-(*qalâqsî*'s knife); Burton VII 151,-(colocasia seller's knife). Chauvin 5: 245-50 No. 147; *ANE* 163 No. 224.□

Z197.3.1.0.3§, ‡Blade going into or out of sheath—sexual intercourse.
King ¿Umar al-Nu¿mân and Sons: *Alf* II 3,-cf./(poem/line 3); Burton III 78. Chauvin VI 112-24 No. 277; *ANE* 430-34 No. 39.□

Z197.3.4§, ‡Spear, peg, wedge, screw-driver, pen, key, needle, plough, etc.—penis. See: *DOTTI*. (Cf. Q451.1.9.1§).
First Eunuch: Bukhayt Deflowers Mistress: *Alf* I 148,-(penis/key); Burton II 49. Chauvin V 277 No. 160; *ANE* 178 No. 37;
Dispute Concerning Males and Females: *Alf* II 302,-(pen); Burton V 151,-(reed). Chauvin VI 153 No. 317; *ANE* 291 No. 151;
Nûr al-Dîn and Maryam: *Alf* IV 97,-(spear); Burton VIII 304. Chauvin V 52-54 No. 271; *ANE* 98-99 No. 233.□

Z197.3.4.0.1§, ‡Piercing (stabbing, puncturing, etc.)—sexual intercourse (penetration). See: *DOTTI*.
Qamar al-Zamân and Budûr: *Alf* II 109,-(poem: stab with penis); Burton III 302,-(Thrust boldly). Chauvin V 204-12 No. 120; *ANE* 341-45 No. 61.□

Z197.3.4.0.2§, ‡'Brushing [with brush]'—non-penetration sexual intercourse. (Cf. T59.2§, Z106§).
al-Rashîd and Omani Merchant: *Alf* IV 213,-cf./(poem/*siwâk*); Burton IX 197,("toothstick"). Chauvin VI 111-12 No. 276; *ANE* 201-2 No. 257.□

Z198.1.2§, ‡Planting (seeding, sowing)—sexual intercourse (impregnation). See: *DOTTI*. (Cf. Z168.1§).
King Dissuaded by Virtuous Wife: *Alf* II 294; Burton V 121-22. Chauvin VII 120-21 No. 391; *ANE* 260-61 No. 138.□

Z199.2.1§, ‡Symbolic number four: power (stability). See: *PSAE*. (Cf. Z152.6.4§).
Porter and Ladies of Baghdad: *Alf* I 33,-(women's fortune/mirth complete only when foursome); Burton I 86, 87. Chauvin V 251-52 No. 148; *ANE* 324-26 No. 14;
Hasan of Basrah: *Alf* III 315,-(palace on four pedestals); Burton VIII 28. Chauvin VII 29-35 No. 212A; *ANE* 207-10 No. 230.□

Z201.1§, ‡Story told by tale-character(s) as an account of own personal experience—"I"-tale, "We"-tale. See: *DOTTI*. (Cf. J169.0.1§).
First Shaykh: Sorceress Wife: *Alf* I 8-9; Burton I 27-31. Chauvin VII 129-30 No. 396; *ANE* 376-77 No. 5;
Second Shaykh: Treacherous Brothers: *Alf* I 11; Burton I 32-35. Chauvin V 6 No. 397; *ANE* 377-78 No. 6;
Third Shaykh: Transformation by Wife: *Alf* I 13; Burton I 36-37. Chauvin VII 130 No. 398; *ANE* 378 No. 7;
Ensorcelled Prince/Husband: *Alf* I 27; Burton I 69-82. Chauvin VI 56-58 No. 222; *ANE* 176 No. 13;
First Qalandar: Brother-Sister Incest: *Alf* I 39; Burton I 104-13. Chauvin V 196-97 No. 115; *ANE* 337-38 No. 15;
Second Qalandar: Afrit's Wife: *Alf* I 42; Burton I 113-39. Chauvin V 197-200 No. 116; *ANE* 338-39 No. 16;
Third Qalandar: Magnetic Mountain: *Alf* I 51; Burton I 141ff. Chauvin V 200-3 No. 117; *ANE* 340-41 No. 18;
Eldest Lady's Story: Treacherous Sisters: *Alf* I 53; Burton I 162-73. Chauvin V 4 No. 443; *ANE* 174-75 No. 19;
Portress Amînah: Bitten Cheek: *Alf* I 57; Burton I 173-84. Chauvin V 98-99 No. 33; *ANE* 326-27 No. 20;
Reeve's Story: Why Maimed by Bride: *Alf* I 96; Burton I 278-88. Chauvin V 220-21 No. 305; *ANE* 351 No. 25;
Tailor's Story/Barber of Baghdad: *Alf* I 103-9; Burton I 300-17. Chauvin V 154-56 No. 78; *ANE* 405-6 No. 27;
First Eunuch: Bukhayt Deflowers Mistress: *Alf* I 147; Burton II 49-50. Chauvin V 277 No. 160; *ANE* 178 No. 37;
¿Azîz and ¿Azîzah: *Alf* I 268ff.; Burton II 298ff. Chauvin V 144-45 No. 71; *ANE* 111-13 No. 41;
Ḥammâd: Treacherous Bedouin: *Alf* II 16; Burton III 104. Chauvin VI 124 n. 1 No. 277; *ANE* 200 No. 43;
Sweep and Noble Lady: Infidelity Repaid: *Alf* II 188-90; Burton IV 125-29. Chauvin VI 148 No. 306; *ANE* 403-4 No. 72;
Mock Caliph/¿Alî al-Jawharî: *Alf* II 195ff.; Burton IV 139ff. Chauvin V 99-100 No. 174; *ANE* 304-5 No. 73;
Kurd's Sack/¿Alî the Persian: *Alf* II 201-2; Burton IV 150-52. Chauvin V 279 No. 162; *ANE* 99-100 No. 74;
Butcher Wardân and Bear Lover: *Alf* II 250-53; Burton IV 293-97. Chauvin V 177-78 No. 101; *ANE* 442-43 No. 101;
Sindbâd and Porter: *Alf* III 83; Burton VI 4ff. Chauvin VII 1 No. 373; *ANE* 383-85 No. 179/pt.;
Lovers of Banû 'Udhra and Lion: *Alf* III 206; Burton VII 118. Chauvin V 116-17 No. 52; *ANE* 274 No. 218/[2];
Lovers of Basra/Ḍamrah: *Alf* III 210-12; Burton VII 130. Chauvin V 118 No. 54; *ANE* 273 No. 220;
Abû al-Ḥasan al-Khorâsânî (and Caliph's Favorite): *Alf* IV 230-37; Burton IX 232ff. Chauvin V 218-20 No. 129; *ANE* 68-69 No. 259;
Man of Upper Egypt and Frankish Wife: Alf IV 16?,-(text missing); Burton IX 19-24. Chauvin V 240 No. 140; *ANE*: No. 234□

Z203§, Heroes of *siyar* (Abu-Zaid, ¿Antar, el-Baṭṭâl, Sayf, ez-Ẓâhir, ez-Zîr, etc.). (Cf. J169§).
King ¿Umar al-Nu¿mân and Sons: *Alf* I 162-261, 290-320, II 1-21; Burton II 77-283, III 93-114. Chauvin VI 112-24 No. 277; *ANE* 430-34 No. 39.□

Z292.0.1.1§, ‡Tragic ending of a story (tale): all die. See: *DOTTI*. (Cf. Z10.2.1§).
¿Alî ibn Bakkâr: *Alf* II 65; Burton III 211-12. Chauvin V 153 No. 76; *ANE* 92-93 No. 60;

Jânshâh: *Alf* III 73; Burton V 381. Chauvin VII 39-44 No. 153; *ANE* 238-41 No. 178;
Man Who Never Laughs: *Alf* III 155; Burton VI 166. Chauvin VIII 47-48 No. 15; *ANE* 285-86 No. 195;
Jawdar and His Treacherous Brethren: *Alf* III 201; Burton VI 256. Chauvin V 257-60 No. 154; *ANE* 244-45 No. 209.□

Z301.1§, ‡The one thing lacking. See: *DOTTI.*
Abû Qîr and Abû Ṣîr: *Alf* IV 193,-(hair-remover); Burton IX 155. Chauvin V 15-17 No. 10; *ANE* 75-77 No. 255.□

Z356, Unique survivor. Only one person left from destruction of his community. See: *DOTTI.* (Cf. K437.6§, Z358§).
Eldest Lady's Story: Treacherous Sisters: *Alf* I 56; Burton I 171. Chauvin V 4 No. 443; *ANE* 174-75 No. 19;
¿Abdallah ibn Fâḍil: Treacherous Brothers: *Alf* IV 277,-(petrification); Burton IX 327. Chauvin V 2-4 No. 2; *ANE* 63-65 No. 261.□

Z356.2§, ‡Sole survivor of massacre (mass killing). (Cf. S101§).
Nûr al-Dîn and Maryam: *Alf* IV 108; Burton VIII 324. Chauvin V 52-54 No. 271; *ANE* 98-99 No. 233.□

Z356.3§, ‡Sole survivor of tragic accident (calamity: shipwreck, fire, earthquake, etc.). See: *DOTTI*; *PSAE.*
Sindbâd's Third Voyage: *Alf* III 96,-cf./(one of three); Burton VI 28-29. Chauvin VII 15-18 No. 373C; *ANE* 385-86 No. 179;
Sindbâd's Fifth Voyage: *Alf* III 107,-(attack by roc), 111,-(drowning); Burton VI 49, 55. Chauvin VII 21-24 No. 373E; *ANE* 386 No. 179;
Sayf al-Mulûk: *Alf* III 285; Burton VII 343. Chauvin VII 64-73 No. 348; *ANE* 362-64 No. 229;
Jawdar and His Treacherous Brethren: *Alf* III 193,-(shipwreck); Burton VI 242. Chauvin V 257-60 No. 154; *ANE* 244-45 No. 209;
Jullanâr of the Sea: *Alf* III 263; Burton VII 295. Chauvin V 147-51 No. 73; *ANE* 248-51 No. 227.□

Z358§, ‡Unique exception from disbelief: only one person in a community of disbelievers adheres to the true faith. (Cf. Z356§, V218.2§).
Eldest Lady's Story: Treacherous Sisters: *Alf* I 55-56,-(old woman); Burton I 168-69. Chauvin V 4 No. 443; *ANE* 174-75 No. 19;
¿Alâ' al-Dîn Abû al-Shâmât: *Alf* II 178; Burton IV 89. Chauvin V 43-49 No. 18; *ANE* 85-87 No. 63;
¿Abdallah ibn Fâḍil: Treacherous Brothers: *Alf* IV 277; Burton IX 327. Chauvin V 2-4 No. 2; *ANE* 63-65 No. 261.□

Other References to Motifs

Titles of Tales

According to Burton's Translation (Nos. 1-169)[93]

Shaded titles indicate tales (texts) not present in the Arabic edition treated in the present index.

A plus sign (+) indicates a title of a *Nights* story added by the present writer to Burton's list of tales.

Remarks on Burton's transliterations:

No under-dotted letters are used.

Long vowels are not regularly indicated in tale texts: e.g., "O Hammad, I am 'Abbád bin Tamím bin Sa'labáh"/"*yâ Ḥammâd, 'anâ ¿Âbid bin Tamîm bin Tha¿labah*" (Burton Vol. 3, p. 110/*Alf* Vol. 2 p. 19). However, occasionally, a long vowel is indicated by an accent (e.g., 'Abbád bin Tamím ...), mostly in explanatory notes.

': Is used for the Arabic *hamzah*, *¿ayn*, or as an English apostrophe. I.e., respectively, "'Ayyub" for 'Ayyûb (Vol. 2, p. 45, *Alf*, Vol.1, p. 246), "Al-Nu'uman" for Al-Nu¿mân or "Ja'afar" for Ja¿far, and Shaykh's, Merchant's, etc. For clarity, the letter ¿ was substituted for Burton's "'" where relevant.

K/k: Is used for Q/q (the Arabic *qâf*, indicated by a "q" or by an under-dotted q; e.g., "Kamar" for Qamar/Moon; Kut al-Kulub for Qût al-Qulûb).

Z/z: Is used for Ḍ/ḍ (the Arabic *ḍâd*, indicated by an under-dotted "d"; e.g., "kazi" for *qâḍî*/judge).

No. BURTON'S TALE TITLE	page	*ANE* No.	*Alf lylah*:vol., pp.
Vol. I			
[0] Story of King Shahryar and his brother	2	1	*A*:1 2-5, *A*:4 317-18
+*0-1*. [Jinni Keeps Mistress in Box]	10	1	*A*:1 5
a. Tale of the Bull and the Ass	16	2	*A*:1 5-6
+*a1*. [Merchant's Curious Wife]	20	3	*A*:1 6-7
+*0a*. [Shahriyâr and Shahrzâd]	23	1	*A*:1 7ff.
1. Tale of the Trader and the Jinni	24	4	*A*:1 8-14
a. The First Shaykh's Story	27	5	*A*:1 9-11
b. The Second Shaykh's Story	32	6	*A*:1 11-13
c. The Third Shaykh's Story	36	7	*A*:1 13-14
2. The Fisherman and the Jinni	38	8	*A*:1 14-16
a. Tale of the Wazir and the Sage Duban	45	9	*A*:1 16-18, 21-23
ab. Story of King Sindibad [Sindbad] and his Falcon	50	10	*A*:1 18-19
ac. Tale of the Husband and the Parrot	52	11	*A*:3 140-41
ad. Tale of the Prince and the Ogress	54	12	*A*:1 19-20
b. Tale of the Ensorcelled Prince	69	13	*A*:1 23-31
3. The Porter and the Three Ladies of Baghdad	82	14	*A*:1 31-9, 61
a. The First Kalandar's Tale	104	15	*A*:1 39-42
b. The Second Kalandar's Tale	113	16	*A*:1 42-51
ba. Tale of the Envier and the Envied	123	17	
c. The Third Kalandar's Tale	139	18	*A*:1 51-53
d. The Eldest Lady's Tale	162	19	*A*:1 53-57
e. Tale of the Portress	173	20	*A*:1 57-61
Conclusion of the Story of the Porter and three Ladies	184	14	*A*:1 61
4. Tale of the Three Apples	186	21	*A*:1 61-64
5. Tale of Nur Al-Din and his Son Badr Al-Din Hasan	195	22	*A*:1 64-84
6. The Hunchback's Tale	225	23	*A*:1 85-88
a. The Nazarene [Copt] Broker's Story	262	24	*A*:1 88-96
b. The Reeve's Tale	278	25	*A*:1 96-099
c. Tale of the Jewish Doctor	288	26	*A*:1 99-102
d. Tale of the Tailor	300	27	*A*:1 102-9

[93] "Comparative Table of the Tales in the Principal Editions of the Thousand and One Nights." (Burton, Vol. 10, pp. 515-23). It should be noted that the numbering of tales in the first four volumes (1-4) is incongruent with the numbers given in the inclusive and final Table cited in part here: numbering was discontinued in volumes 5-10; only units within a major story were indicated by italicized letters (e.g., *a*, *b*, *c*, *aa*, etc.).

No. BURTON'S TALE TITLES	p.	*ANE* No.	*Alf lylah*:v. pp.
e. The Barber's Tale of Himself	317	28	*A*:1: 109-10, 125
ea. The Barber's Tale of his First Brother	319	29	*A*:1 110-12
eb. The Barber's Tale of his Second Brother	324	30	*A*:1 112-14
ec. The Barber's Tale of his Third Brother	328	31	*A*:1 114-15
ed. The Barber's Tale of his Fourth Brother	331	32	*A*:1 115-17
ee. The Barber's Tale of his Fifth Brother	335	33	*A*:1 117-21
ef. The Barber's Tale of his Sixth Brother	343	34	*A*:1 121-25
The End of the Tailor's Tale	348	27	*A*:1 125
Vol. II			
7. Nur Al-Din Ali and the Damsel Anis Al-Jalis	1	35	*A*:1 125-45
8. Tale of Ghanim Bin Ayyub, the Distraught, the Thrall o' Love	45	36	*A*:1 146-62
a. Tale of the First Eunuch, Bukhayt	49	37	*A*:1 147-48
b. Tale of the Second Eunuch, Kafur	51	38	*A*:1 148-51
+*c*. [Third Eunuch: Seduces Mistress and Son]	56	38	*A*:1 151-(passim)
9. Tale of King Omar Bin Al-Nu¿uman, and his sons Sharrkan and Zau Al-Makan	77	39	*A*:1 162-61, 290-320, *A*:2 1-21
+*9.1a*. [Nuzhat al-Zamân Tested/¿Umar al-Nu¿mân]	156	39	*A*:1 200-7
+*9.1b1*. [Spy, First Maiden/¿Umar al-Nu¿mân]	196	39	*A*:1 219-20
+*9.1b2*. [Spy, Second Maiden/¿Umar al-Nu¿mân]	199	39	*A*:1 220-22
+*9.1b3*. [Spy, Third Maiden/¿Umar al-Nu¿mân]	202	39	*A*:1 222
+*9.1b4*. [Spy, Fourth Maiden/¿Umar al-Nu¿mân]	203	39	*A*:1 222-23
+*9.1b5*. [Spy, Fifth Maiden/¿Umar al-Nu¿mân]	205	39	*A*:1 223-24
+*9.1b6*. [Spy, Old Woman/¿Umar al-Nu¿mân]	207	39	*A*:1 224-25
a. Tale of Taj Al-Muluk and the Princess Dunya	283	40	*A*:1 261-68, 290-308
aa. Tale of Aziz and Azizah	298	41	*A*:1 268-90
Vol. III			
aa. Continuation of the Tale of Aziz and Azizah	1	41	
ab. Conclusion of the Tale of King Omar Bin Al-Nu¿uman ...	48	39	*A*:2 1-21
b. Tale of the Hashish-Eater	91	42	*A*:2 9-10
c. Tale of Hammad the Badawi	104	43	*A*:2 16-20
10. The Birds and Beasts and the Carpenter	114	44	*A*:2 29-32
11. The Hermits	125	45	*A*:2 27-28
+*11a*. [Hermit and Pigeons]	126	45/1	*A*:2 27
+*11b*. [Hermit Tempted by Angel]	126	45/2	*A*:2 27-28
12. The Water-fowl and the Tortoise	129	46	*A*:2 28-29
13. The Wolf and the Fox	132	47	*A*:2 29-35
a. Tale of the Falcon and the Partridge	138	48	*A*:2 32
+*b*. [Sick Man Tries to Heal Another]	140	0	*A*:2 32
+*c*. [Escaped Viper Ungrateful]	145	47	*A*:2 35
14. The Mouse and the Ichneumon	147	49	*A*:2 35-36
15. The Cat and the Crow	149	50	*A*:2 36-37
16. The Fox and the Crow	150	51	*A*:2 37
a. The Flea and the Mouse	151	52	*A*:2 37-38
b. The Saker and the Birds	154	53	*A*:2 38-39
c. The Sparrow and the Eagle	155	0	
+*d*. [Lazy Sower (Farmer, "husbandman")]	156	0	*A*:2 39
17. The Hedgehog and the Wood Pigeons	156	55	*A*:2 39
a. The Merchant and the Two Sharpers	158	56	*A*:2 39-40
18. The Thief and his Monkey	159	57	*A*:2 40
a. The Foolish Weaver	150	58	*A*:2 40
19. The Sparrow and the Peacock	161	59	*A*:2 40-41
20. Ali Bin Bakkar and Shams Al-Nahar	162	60	*A*:2 41-65
21. Tale of Kamar Al-Zaman	212	61	*A*:2 65-112, 146-47
+*1a*. [al-'Amjad and al-'As¿ad]	309	61	*A*:2 112-32, 144-47
Vol. IV			
Tale of Kamar Al-Zaman (continued)		61	
a. Ni¿amah [Ni¿mah] bin Al-Rabia and Naomi [Nu¿m] his Slave-girl	1	62	*A*:2 132-44
b. Conclusion of the Tale of Kamar Al-Zaman	23	61	*A*:2 146-47
22. Ala Al-Din Abu Al-Shamat	29	63	*A*:2 147-81
23. Hatim of the Tribe of Tayy	94	64	*A*:2 181-82
24. Ma¿an the son of Zaidah and the three Girls	96	65	*A*:2 182
25. Ma¿an son of Zaidah and the Badawi	97	66	*A*:2 182-83
26. The City of Labtayt	99	67	*A*:2 183-84
27. The Caliph Hisham and the Arab Youth	101	68	*A*:2 184-85
28. Ibrahim bin Al-Mahdi and the Barber-Surgeon	103	69	
29. The City of Many-columned Iram and Abdullah son of Abi Kalabah	113	70	

No.	BURTON'S TALE TITLES	p.	*ANE* No.	*Alf lylah*:v. pp.
30.	Isaac of Mosul	119	71	*A*:2 185-88
31.	The Sweep and the Noble Lady	125	72	*A*:2 188-91
32.	The Mock Caliph	130	73	*A*:2 191-200
33.	Ali the Persian	149	74	*A*:2 200-2
34.	Harun Al-Rashid and the Slave-Girl and the Imam Abu Yusuf	153	75	*A*:2 202-4
35.	The Lover who feigned himself a Thief	155	76	*A*:2 204-6
36.	Ja¿afar the Barmecide and the Bean-Seller	159	77	
37.	Abu Mohammed hight Lazybones	162	78	*A*:2 206-16
38.	Generous dealing of Yahya bin Khalid the Barmecide with Mansur	179	79	
39.	Generous Dealing of Yahya son of Khalid with a man who forged a letter in his name	181	80	
40.	Caliph Al-Maamun and the Strange Scholar	185	81	
41.	Ali Shar and Zumurrud	187	82	*A*:2 217-35
42.	The Loves of Jubayr Bin Umayr and the Lady Budur	228	83	*A*:2 235-43
43.	The Man of Al-Yaman and his six Slave-Girls	245	84	*A*:2 243-50
44.	Harun Al-Rashid and the Damsel and Abu Nowas	261	85	
45.	The Man who stole the dish of gold whereon the dog ate	265	86	
46.	The Sharper of Alexandria and the Chief of Police	269	87	
47.	Al-Malik Al-Nasir and the three Chiefs of Police	271	88	
	a. Story of the Chief of the new Cairo Police	271	89	
	b. Story of the Chief of the Bulak Police	273	90	
	[c]. Story of the Chief of the Old Cairo Police	274	88	
48.	The Thief and the Shroff	275	92	
49.	The Chief of the Kus Police and the Sharper	276	93	
50.	Ibrahim bin al-Mahdi and the Merchant's Sister	278	94	
51.	The Woman whose hands were cut off for alms-giving	281	95	
52.	The devout Israelite	283	96	
53.	Abu Hassan Al-Ziyadi and the Khorasan Man	285	97	
54.	The Poor Man and his Friend in Need	288	98	
55.	The Ruined Man who became rich again through a dream	289	99	
56.	Caliph Al-Mutawakkil and his Concubine Mahbubah	291	100	
57.	Wardan the Butcher's Adventure with the Lady and the Bear	293	101	*A*:2 250-53
58.	The King's Daughter and the Ape	297	102	*A*:2 253-54
	Vol. V			
59.	The Ebony Horse	1	103	*A*:2 254-67
60.	Uns Al-Wujud and the Wazir's Daughter Rose-in-Hood	32	104	*A*:2 267-84
61.	Abu Nowas with the Three Boys and the Caliph Harun Al-Rashid	64	105	
62.	Abdullah bin Ma¿amar with the Man of Bassorah and his Slave-Girl	69	106	
63.	The Lovers of the Banu Ozrah	70	218	*A*:3 206-10
64.	The Wazir of Al-Yaman and his young Brother	71	108	
65.	The Loves of the Boy and Girl at School	73	109	
66.	Al-Mutalammis and his Wife Umaymah	74	110	
67.	Harun Al-Rashid and Zubaydah in the Bath	75	111	*A*:2 284-85
68.	Harun Al-Rashid and the Three Poets	77	112	
69.	Mus¿ab bin Al-Zubayr and Ayishah his Wife	79	113	
70.	Abu Al-Aswad and his Slave-Girl	80	114	
71.	Harun Al-Rashid and the two Slave-Girls	81	115	
72.	Harun Al-Rashid and the Three Slave-Girls	81	116	
73.	The Miller and his Wife	82	117	
74.	The Simpleton and the Sharper	83	118	
75.	The Kazi Abu Yusuf with Harun Al-Rashid and Queen Zubaydah	85	75	*A*:2 202-4
76.	The Caliph Al-Hakim and the Merchant	86	120	
77.	King Kisra Anushirwan and the Village Damsel	87	121	*A*:2 285
78.	The Water-carrier and the Goldsmith's Wife	89	122	*A*:2 285-86
79.	Khusrau and Shirin and the Fisherman	91	123	
80.	Yahya bin Khalid and the Poor Man	92	124	
81.	Mohammed al-Amin and the Slave-Girl	93	125	
82.	The Sons of Yahya bin Khalid and Said bin Salim	94	126	
83.	The Woman's Trick against her Husband	96	127	
84.	The Devout Woman and the Two Wicked Elders	97	128	*A*:2 286-87
85.	Ja¿afar the Barmecide and the old Badawi [(Ridiculous Eye Salve)]	98	129	*A*:2 287
86.	Omar bin Al-Khattab and the Young Badawi	99	130	*A*:2 287-89
87.	Al-Maamun and the Pyramids of Eygpt	105	131	
88.	The Thief and the Merchant	107	132	
89.	Masrur the Eunuch and Ibn Al-Karibi	109	133	
90.	The Devotee Prince	111	134	*A*:2 289-92
91.	The Schoolmaster who fell in Love by Report	117	135	*A*:2 292-93

No.	BURTON'S TALE TITLES	p.	*ANE* No.	*Alf lylah*:v. pp.
92.	The Foolish Dominie	118	136	*A*:2 293
93.	The Illiterate who set up for a Schoolmaster	119	137	*A*:2 293-94
94.	The King and the Virtuous Wife	121	138	*A*:2 294
95.	Abd Al Rahman the Maghribi's story of the Rukh	122	139	
96.	Adi bin Zayd and the Princess Hind	124	140	
97.	Di¿ibil Al-Khuza¿i with the Lady and Muslim bin Al-Walid	127	141	
98.	Isaac of Mosul and the Merchant	129	142	*A*:2 294-97
99.	The Three Unfortunate Lovers	133	143	
100.	How Abu Hasan brake Wind	135	144	
101.	The Lovers of the Banu Tayy	137	145	*A*:2: 297
102.	The Mad Lover	138	146	
103.	The Prior who became a Moslem	141	147	*A*:2 297-300
104.	*The Loves of Abu Isa and Kurrat Al-Ayn/[¿Ayn]*	*145*	*148*	
105.	*Al-Amin and his Uncle Ibrahim bin Al-Mahdi*	*152*	*149*	
106.	*Al-Fath bin Khakan and Al-Mutawakkil*	*153*	*150*	
107.	The Man's dispute with Learned Woman concerning the relative excellence of male and female	154	151	*A*:2 300-2
108.	Abu Suwayd and the pretty Old Woman	163	152	*A*:2 302-3
109.	Ali bin Tahir and the girl Muunis	164	153	*A*:2 303
110.	The Woman who had a Boy, and the other who had a Man to lover	165	154	*A*:2 303
111.	Ali the Cairene and the Haunted House in Baghdad	166	155	
112.	The Pilgrim Man and the Old Woman	186	156	
113.	Abu Al-Husn and his Slave-girl Tawaddud	189	157	*A*:2 303-19, *A*:3 2-8
114.	The Angel of Death with the Proud King and the Devout Man	246	158	*A*:3 8
	+*a*. [Angel of Death and Devout Man]	247	158	*A*:3 8-9
115.	The Angel of Death and the Rich King	248	159	*A*:3 9-10
116.	The Angel of Death and the King of the Children of Israel	250	160	*A*:3 9-10
117.	Iskandar zu Al-Karnayn and a certain Tribe of Poor Folk	252	161	
118.	The Righteousness of King Anushirwan	254	162	
119.	The Jewish Kazi and his Pious Wife	256	163	*A*:3 10-11
120.	The Shipwrecked Woman and her Child	259	164	*A*:3 11-13
121.	The Pious Black Slave	261	165	
122.	The Devout Tray-maker and his Wife	264	166	*A*:3 13-14
123.	Al-Hajjaj bin Yusuf and the Pious Man	269	167	
124.	The Blacksmith who could Handle Fire Without Hurt	261	168	
125.	The Devotee to whom Allah gave a Cloud for Service and the Devout King	274	169	
126.	The Moslem Champion and the Christian Damsel	277	170	
127.	The Christian King's Daughter and the Moslem	283	171	
128.	The Prophet and the Justice of Providence	286	172	
129.	The Ferryman of the Nile and the Hermit	288	173	
130.	The Island King and the Pious Israelite	290	174	*A*:3 16-17
131.	*Abu Al-Hasan and Abu Ja¿afar the Leper*	*294*	*175*	
132.	The Queen of the Serpents	298	177	*A*:3 18-81
	a. The Adventure of Bulukiya	304	177	*A*:3 22-23, 73-81
	b. The Story of Janshah	329	178	*A*:3 38-73
	Vol. VI			
133.	Sindbad the Seaman and Sindbad the Landsman	1		179*A*:3 81-83
	a. The First Voyage of Sindbad the Seaman	4		179*A*:3 83-88
	b. The Second Voyage of Sindbad the Seaman	14	179	*A*:3 88-92
	c. The Third Voyage of Sindbad the Seaman	22	179	*A*:3 92-100
	d. The Fourth Voyage of Sindbad the Seaman	34	179	*A*:3 100-6
	e. The Fifth Voyage of Sindbad the Seaman	48	179	*A*:3 106-12
	f. The Sixth Voyage of Sindbad the Seaman	58	179	*A*:3 112-16
	ff. The Sixth Voyage of Sindbad the Seaman	00	0	
	g. The Seventh Voyage of Sindbad the Seaman	68	179	*A*:3 116-22
	gg. The Seventh Voyage of Sindbad [...] [(Elephants' Cemetery)]	78	179	
+133-1.	[Jinn Imprisoned in Flasks (Cucurbites)]	83	180	*A*:3 122-29
134.	The City of Brass	83	180	*A*:3 129-38
135.	The Craft and Malice of Women:	122	181	*A*:3 138-39
	a. The King and his Wazir's Wife	129	182	*A*:3 139-40
	b. The Confectioner, his Wife and the Parrot	132	11	*A*:3 140-41
	c. The Fuller and his Son	134	184	*A*:3 141
	d. The Rake's Trick against the Chaste Wife	135	185	*A*:3 141-42
	e. The Miser and the Loaves of Bread	137	186	*A*:3 142-43
	f. The Lady and her two Lovers	138	188	*A*:3 143-44
	g. The King's Son and the Ogress	139	188	*A*:3 143-44

No. BURTON'S TALE TITLES	p.	*ANE* No.	*Alf lylah*:v. pp.
h. The Drop of Honey	142	189	*A*:3 145
i. The Woman who made her husband sift dust	143	190	*A*:3 145
j. The Enchanted Spring	145	191	*A*:3 146-48
k. The Wazir's Son and the Hammam-keeper's Wife	150	192	
l. The Wife's device to cheat her Husband	152	193	*A*:3 148-49
m. The Goldsmith and the Cashmere Singing-girl	156	194	*A*:3 150-51
n. The Man who never laughed during the rest of his days	160	195	*A*:3 152-55
o. The King's Son and the Merchant's Wife	167	196	*A*:3 155-56
p. The Page who feigned to know the Speech of Birds	169	197	*A*:3 156-57
q. The Lady and her five Suitors	172	198	*A*:3 158-62
r. The Three Wishes, or the Man who longed to see the Night of Power	180	199	*A*:3 162
s. The Stolen Necklace	182	200	*A*:3 163-64
t. The Two Pigeons	183	201	
u. Prince Behram and the Princess Al-Datma	184	202	*A*:3 164-66
v. The House with the Belvedere	188	203	*A*:3 166-72
w. The King's Son and the Ifrit's Mistress	199	204	*A*:3 172-73
+*w1*. [Poisoning from Flying Kite]	201	181	*A*:3 173-74
x. The Sandal-wood Merchant and the Sharpers	202	205	*A*:3 174-76
y. The Debauchee and the Three-year-old Child	208	206	*A*:3 176
z. The Stolen Purse	209	207	*A*:3 176-77
aa. The Fox and the Folk	211	208	
136. Judar and his Brethren	213	209	*A*:3 177-201
137. The History of Gharib and his Brother Ajib	257	210	
Vol. VII			
The History of Gharib and His Brother Ajib (continued)	257	210	
138. Otbah and Rayya	91	211	
139. Hind, daughter of Al-Nu¿man and Al-Hajjaj	96	212	*A*:3 201-3
140. Khuzaymah bin Bishr and Ekrimah al-Fayyaz	*99*	*213*	
141. Yunus the Scribe and the Caliph Walid bin Sahl	*104*	*214*	
142. Harun Al-Rashid and the Arab Girl	108	215	*A*:3 203-4
143. Al-Asma¿i and the three girls of Bassorah	110	216	*A*:3 204-6
144. Ibrahim of Mosul and the Devil	113	221	
145. The Lovers of the Banu Uzrah	117	218	*A*:3 206-10
146. The Badawi and his Wife	124	219	
147. The Lovers of Bassorah	130	220	*A*:3 210-12
148. Ishak of Mosul and his Mistress and the Devil	*136*	*221*	
149. The Lovers of Al-Medinah	*139*	*222*	
150. Al-Malik Al-Nasir and his Wazir	*142*	*223*	
151. The Rogueries of Dalilah the Crafty and her Daughter Zaynab the Coney-Catcher	144	224	*A*:3 212-27
a. The Adventures of Mercury Ali of Cairo	172	225	*A*:3 227-47
152. Ardashir and Hayat Al-Nufus	209	226	
153. Julnar the Sea-born and her son King Badr Basim of Persia	264	227	*A*:3 247-70
154. King Mohammed bin Sabaik and the Merchant Hasan	308	228	*A*:3 270-73
a. Story of Prince Sayf Al-Muluk and the Princess Badi¿a[t] Al-Jamal	314	229	*A*:3 274-302
Vol. VIII			
154. King Mohammed Bin Sabaik and the Merchant Hasan (continued)	1		228
a. Story of Prince Sayf Al-Muluk [...] (continued)			229
155. Hasan of Bassorah	7		230*A*:3 302-19, *A*:4 2-55
156. Khalifah the Fisherman of Baghdad	145	231	
a. The same from the Breslau Edition	184	0	
157. Masrur and Zayn Al-Mawassif	205	232	*A*:4 55-80
158. Ali Nur Al-Din and Miriam the Girdle-Girl	264	233	*A*:4 80-129
Vol. IX			
Ali Nur Al-Din and Miriam the Girdle-Girl (continued)	1		233
159. The Man of Upper Egypt and his Frankish Wife	10	234	*A*:4 161/missing[94]
160. The Ruined Man of Baghdad and his Slave-Girl	24	235	*A*:4 129-34
161. King Jali¿ad of Hind and his Wazir Shimas, followed by the history of King Wird Khan, son of King Jali¿ad, with his Women and Wazirs	32	236	*A*:4 134-82
a. The Mouse and the Cat	35	237	*A*:4 135-37
b. The Fakir and his Jar of Butter	40	238	*A*:4 137-39
c. The Fishes and the Crab	43	239	*A*:4 139-41
d. The Crow and the Serpent	46	240	*A*:4 141
e. The Wild Ass and the jackal	48	241	*A*:4 141-42

[94] For details, see: Introduction, p. 2 n. 9.

No. BURTON'S TALE TITLES	p.	*ANE* No.	*Alf lylah*:v. pp.
f. The Unjust King and the Pilgrim Prince	50	242	*A*:4 142-44
g. The Crows and the Hawk	53	243	*A*:4 144-45
h. The Serpent-Charmer and his Wife	56	244	*A*:4 145-46
i. The Spider and the Wind	59	245	*A*:4 146-47
j. The Two Kings	65	246	*A*:4 149-50
k. The Blind Man and the Cripple	67	247	*A*:4 150-52
+*k-1*. [Hungry Eagle Snared]	69	0	*A*:4 152
+*k-2*. [Hunter Rides Lion: Devoured]	72	0	*A*:4 153
l. The Foolish Fisherman	93	248	*A*:4 162-63
m. The Boy and the Thieves	95	249	*A*:4 163-65
+*m-1*. [The Man who had a Milch-camel]	97	0	*A*:4 164
n. The Man [(Gardner)] and his Wife	98	250	*A*:4 165
o. The Merchant and the Robbers	100	251	*A*:4 166
p. The Jackals and the Wolf	103	252	*A*:4 167-68
q. The Shepherd and the Rogue	106	253	*A*:4 168-69
r. The Francolin and the Tortoises	113	254	*A*:4 172-73
Conclusion of the history of King Wird Khan	115	236	
162. Abu Kir the Dyer and Abu Sir the Barber	134	255	*A*:4 182-97
163. Abdullah the Fisherman and Abdullah the Merman	165	256	*A*:4 198-208
164. Harun Al-Rashid and Abu Hasan, the Merchant of Oman	188	257	*A*:4 208-19
165. Ibrahim and Jamilah	207	258	*A*:4 219-29
166. Abu Al-Hasan of Khorasan	229	259	*A*:4 229-37
167. Kamar Al-Zaman and the Jeweller's Wife	246	260	*A*:4 237-66
168. Abdullah bin Fazil and his Brothers	304	261	*A*:4 266-88
Vol. X			
169. Ma¿aruf the Cobbler and his wife Fatimah	1		262*A*:4 288-317
0a. Conclusion [of *Alf laylah wa laylah*]	54	1	*A*:4 317-18

Alphabetical Index of Motifs

Note: A number of entries that are part of motifs may not appear in the *Nights* under the word used as the heading of the entry. Examples are: Bata, *¿aggâfah*, Susanna, al-Zîr, etc. However, the themes these words represent are relevant to the text treated. For example, Bata, of the ancient Egyptian tale of "The Two Brothers", does not appear in the *Nights* but it represents the theme of "Innocent (chaste) man slandered as seducer...": Mot. K2120§; the title "*¿aggâfah*" does not appear in the *Nights*, but it stands for "Women's beautician ...": Mot. P446.5§.

REGISTER OF TALE-TYPES

0004, *Carrying the Sham-Sick Trickster*. [Fox feigns illness and rides on dupe's back]. (See: *DOTTI*; *GMC*/MAP).
Sindbâd's Fifth Voyage,-cf./demon-human: *Alf* III 106-12; Burton VI 48-58; *ANE* No. 179,/5□

0006, *Animal Captor Persuaded to Talk* and release victim from his mouth. (See: *DOTTI*; *GMC*/MAP).
Hishâm and Arab Youth,-cf.,: *Alf* II 184-85; Burton IV 101-3; *ANE* No. 68□

0030, *The Fox Tricks the Wolf into Falling into a Pit*. Race. (See: *DOTTI*; *GMC*/MAP).
Wolf and Fox: *Alf* II 29-32; Burton III 132-46; *ANE* No. 47□

0031, *The Fox Climbs from the Pit on the Wolf's Back*. (See: *DOTTI*; *GMC*/MAP).
Wolf and Fox: *Alf* II 29-32; Burton III 132-46; *ANE* No. 47□

0035§, *Trickster Leads Dupe into Trap by Flattery*. (See: *DOTTI*; *GMC*/MAP).
Wolf and Fox: *Alf* II 29-32; Burton III 132-46; *ANE* No. 47;
She-mouse and Ichneumon,-cf.,: *Alf* II 35; Burton III 147-48; *ANE* No. 49□

0051***, *Fox as Umpire to Divide Cheese*. [Eats it all under pretence of making uneven halves even: remainder is his fee]. (See: *DOTTI*; *GMC*/MAP).
Jackals and Wolf as Umpire,-cf./gen. theme,: *Alf* IV 167-68; Burton IX 103-6; *ANE* No. 252□

0109§, *Triumph of the Weak*. Weak emerges victorious over strong.. (See: *DOTTI*).
Mouse and Cat: *Alf* IV 135-37; Burton IX 35-39; *ANE* No. 237□

0155, *The Ungrateful Serpent Returned to Captivity*. [Usually by clever umpire]. (See: *DOTTI*; *GMC*/MAP).
Wolf and Fox,-cf./intro.: *Alf* II 29-32; Burton III 132-46; *ANE* No. 47□

0157, *Learning to Fear Men*. [Painful lesson for powerful predator (lion, tiger, etc.)]. (See: *DOTTI*; *GMC*/MAP).
Birds, Beasts, and Carpenter,-cf./pt.,: *Alf* II 21-27; Burton III 114-25; *ANE* No. 44□

0178C§, *The Thirsty King Kills his Faithful Falcon*. Regrets his hasty act. (Cf. 756K§) (See: *DOTTI*; *GMC*/MAP; ATU 170C).
King Sindbâd and Falcon: *Alf* I 18-19; Burton I 50-52; *ANE* No. 10□

0207A, *Ass Induces Overworked Bullock to Feign Sickness*. Ass must do bullock's work [...]. (See: *DOTTI*; *GMC*/MAP).
Bull and Ass: *Alf* I 5-6; Burton I 16-19; *ANE* No. 2□

0208*, *Duck Persuades Cock to Cut off his Crest and Spurs*. (See: *DOTTI*; *GMC*/MAP).
Francolin and Tortoises,-cf.,: *Alf* IV 172-73; Burton IX 113-15; *ANE* No. 254□

0221, *The Election of Bird-king*. [One] (Wren) wins by cleverness. (See: *DOTTI*).
Crows and Hawk,-cf.,: *Alf* IV 144--45; Burton IX 53-56; *ANE* No. 243□

0223, *The Bird and the Jackal as Friends*. [By feigning illness, confederates help each other steal food (or play tricks on others). (See: *DOTTI*; *GMC*/MAP).
Cat and Crow: *Alf* II 36-37; Burton III 149-50; *ANE* No. 50;
Flea and She-mouse,-cf.,: *Alf* II 35-38; Burton III 151-54; *ANE* No. 52□

0224A§, *Polygynist Bird (Animal) Must Lie and Flatter Constantly*. Trouble for Crow with two wives: kite and Owl). (See: *DOTTI*; *GMC*/MAP).
Cat and Crow,-cf.,: *Alf* II 36-37; Burton III 149-50; *ANE* No. 50□

0227, *Geese Ask for Respite for Prayer*. [They fly away]. (See: *DOTTI*; *GMC*/MAP).
Jewish Tray-maker and Temptress-cf./theme,: *Alf* III 13-14; Burton V 264-69; *ANE* No. 166□

0246A§, *Bird's (Animals's) Talkativeness (Inquisitiveness) Brings about its Capture*. (See: *DOTTI*; *GMC*/MAP).
Sparrow as Peacock's Vizier,-cf.,: *Alf* II 40-41; Burton III 161-62; *ANE* No. 59□

0276**, *The Flea, the Louse, and the Bug*. Flea by jumping about betrays others to man, who kills them. (See: *DOTTI*; *GMC*/MAP).
Flea and She-mouse: *Alf* II 35-38; Burton III 151-54; *ANE* No. 52□

0302, *The Ogre's (Devil's) Heart in the Egg*. [Demon with external soul killed]. (See: *DOTTI*; *GMC*/MAP).
Ibn Sabâ'ik/Sayf al-Mulûk: *Alf* III 270-73; Burton VII 308-73; *ANE* No. 228□

0303,:-I, *The Twins or Blood-Brothers*. (See: *DOTTI*; *GMC*/MAP).
Ibn Sabâ'ik/Sayf al-Mulûk: *Alf* III 270-73; Burton VII 308-73; *ANE* No. 228□

0303B§, *Six Jealous Brothers Against their Youngest: to whom Does the Extra Bride Belong?* (See: *DOTTI*; *GMC*/MAP; cf. 551A§).
¿Abdallah ibn Fâḍel: Treacherous Brothers,-cf./psych./pattern: *Alf* IV 266-88; Burton IX 304-49; *ANE* No. 261□

0311D§, *A Woman is Rescued from Magician (Ogre, Witch) by a Relative Other than her Father or Brother*(e.g., rescued by her husband, paternal-cousin, fiancé, etc.). (See: *DOTTI*; *GMC*/MAP).
Abû Muḥammad Lazybones: *Alf* II 206-16; Burton IV 162-78; *ANE* No. 78□

0322*, *Magnetic Mountain Pulls Everything to it*. Rescue by help of giant bird. Princess won. (See: *DOTTI*; *GMC*/MAP).
Third Qalandar: Magnetic Mountain: *Alf* I 51-53; Burton I 139-61; *ANE* No. 18□

0325,:IV(b), ·Transformation combat= =*The Magician and his Pupil* (See: *DOTTI*; *GMC*/MAP).
Jullanâr of the Sea: *Alf* III 247-70; Burton VII 264-308; *ANE* No. 227□

0327, *The Children and the Ogre*. (See: *DOTTI*; *GMC*/MAP).
Prince and Ogress,-cf.,: *Alf* I 19-20; Burton I 54-55; *ANE* No. 12;
King's Favorite Son and Ogress,-cf.,: *Alf* III 143-44; Burton VI 139-42; *ANE* No. 188□

0331, *The Spirit in the Bottle*. [Jinni released, then tricked back into captivity]. (See: *DOTTI*; *GMC*/MAP).
Fisherman and Afrit: Ingratitude: *Alf* I 14-16; Burton I 38-82; *ANE* No. 8□

0332, *Godfather Death*. [Attempts to deceive Death (Azrael) prove futile]. (See: *DOTTI*; *GMC*/MAP).
Angel of Death and Proud King,-cf./theme,: *Alf* III 8-9; Burton V 246-48; *ANE* No. 158;
Angel of Death and Proud King,-cf./antithetical,-(332,-X): *Alf* III 8-9; Burton V 246-48; *ANE* No. 158;
Angel of Death and Jewish King,-cf./theme,: *Alf* III 9-10; Burton V 250-52; *ANE* No. 160□

0400, *The Man on a Quest for his Lost Wife*. [Supernatural (fairy) wife departs for own homeland]. (See: *DOTTI*; *GMC*/MAP).
Jânshâh: *Alf* III 58ff.; Burton V 357ff.; *ANE* No. 178;
al-Ḥasan al-Baṣrî: *Alf* IV 12ff.; Burton VIII Burton VIII 61ff.; *ANE* No. 230□

0434B§, *Bird Steals Bride's Jewel (Necklace, Scarf, etc.) thus Causing Separation of Couple*. (See: *DOTTI*; *GMC*/MAP).
Qamar al-Zamân and Budûr: *Alf* II 97ff.; Burton III 279ff.; *ANE* No. 61□

0449,—(formerly-449*), *The Tsar's Dog (Sidi Numan)*. [Dog saves master from faithless wife and her loathsome paramour]. (See: *DOTTI*; *GMC*/MAP).
Third Shaykh: Transformation by Wife,-cf.,: *Alf* I 13-14; Burton I 36-37; *ANE* No. 7;
Ensorcelled Prince: *Alf* I 23-31; Burton I:69-82; *ANE* No. 13□

0462A1§, *Co-wife Transforms her Rival into an Animal (Bird) and Demands its Slaughter*. (See: *DOTTI*).
First Shaykh: Sorceress Wife: *Alf* I 9-11; Burton I 27-31; *ANE* No. 5□

0462A2§, *Woman (Wife) Buries Alive her Rival for Man (Husband)*. (See: *DOTTI*).
Ghânim ibn Ayyûb: *Alf* I 147, 151; Burton II 47, 57; *ANE* No. 36□

0465A*,/1512§, ‡*The Fickle Wife [of the Conscript] and the General*. [They elope]. (See: Type: 1512§).
Masrûr and Zayn al-Mawâṣif,-cf./psych.-pattern,: *Alf* IV 55-80; Burton VIII 205-63; *ANE* No. 232□

0470C§, *Man in Utopian Otherworld Cannot Resist Interfering: He is Expelled*. ("It Serves me Right!"). (See: *DOTTI*; *GMC*/MAP).
Man Who Never Laughs: *Alf* III 152-55; Burton VI 160-67; *ANE* No. 195□

0470C1§, *Man Punished For Entering Forbidden Chamber and Riding Flying Horse*. (See: *DOTTI*).

Third Qalandar: Magnetic Mountain: *Alf* I 51-53; Burton I 139-61; *ANE* No. 18□

0470F§, *Utopian Otherworld where Death is a Joyous Occasion*. (Mourner expelled: "¿Abdullâh-of-the-land and ¿Abdullâh-of-the-sea"). (See: *DOTTI*; *GMC*/MAP).
Landsman ¿Abdallah and Merman ¿Abdallah: *Alf* IV 198-208; Burton IX 165-88; *ANE* No. 256□

0472§, *Eccentric Occurrences Witnessed by Chieftain (King and Vizier) in Marketplace Reveal Life Experiences*. (See: *DOTTI*; *GMC*/MAP; cf. 516Z§).
Abû al-Ḥasan al-Khorâsânî (and Caliph's Favorite),-cf.,/(Mot. H591.4.4.1§, T96) *Alf* IV 229-37; Burton IX 229-46; *ANE* No. 259□

0516A1§, *The Body Talk by the Princess*, interpreted for the love-sick husband (by his wife, fiancee). (See: *DOTTI*).
¿Azîz and ¿Azîzah: *Alf* I 268-90; Burton II 298-333, III 1-8; *ANE* No. 41□

0516E§, *Villain Abducts Heroine; her Sweetheart Pursues and Rescues her*. (See: *DOTTI*; *GMC*/MAP).
¿Alî Shâr and Zumurrud: *Alf* II 217-35; Burton IV:187-28; *ANE* No. 82;
Ebony Horse: *Alf* II 254-67; Burton V 1–32; *ANE* No. 103;
Uns al-Wujûd and al-Ward,-cf.,: *Alf* II 267-84; Burton V 32–64; *ANE* No. 104;
Nûr al-Dîn and Maryam,-cf.,: *Alf* IV 80-129; Burton VIII 264-349, IX 1-18; *ANE* No. 233;
Ibrâhîm and Jamîlah,-cf./parents exile daughter: *Alf* IV 219-29; Burton IX 207-29; *ANE* No. 258□

0516Z§, *‡Lovers Reunited After Trouble (Adventures)--Miscellaneous*. (Cf. 472§).
Abû al-Ḥasan al-Khorâsânî (and Caliph's Favorite),-cf.,/(Mot. H591.4.4.1§, T96) *Alf* IV 229-37; Burton IX 229-46; *ANE* No. 259□

0518, *Devils (Giants) Fight over Magic Object*. [Umpire steals it]. (See: *DOTTI*; *GMC*/MAP).
al-Ḥasan al-Basrî,-Mot./(F359.3.1§) *Alf* III 302-19, IV 2-55 (esp. p. 43); Burton VIII 7-145 (esp. p. 122); *ANE* No. 230□

0519, *The Strong Woman as Bride (Brunhilde)*. The helper in the suitor test. (See: *DOTTI*; *GMC*/MAP).
Bahrâm and Datmâ,-cf.,: *Alf* III 164-66; Burton VI 184-88; *ANE* No. 202□

0519A§, *Adversaries (Combatants) Become Lovers* Hero encounters a valiant warrior who proves to be a maiden masking as man. (See: *DOTTI*; *GMC*/MAP).
Dalîla the Swindler,-cf.,: *Alf* III 236; Burton VII 187; *ANE* No. 224;
Mercury ¿Alî: *Alf* III 246; Burton VII 172-209; *ANE* No. 225□

0520A§, *Blind and Lame (Cripple) Abandoned: they Overcome Adversity*. (See: *DOTTI*; *GMC*/MAP).
Blind and Cripple Corporate: *Alf* IV 150-52; Burton IX:67-69; *ANE* No. 247□

0551A§, *Only One Brother is Successful in Seeking Riches (Wealth)*. Other brothers are jealous. (See: *DOTTI*; cf. 303B§).
Second Shaykh: Treacherous Brothers: *Alf* I 11-13; Burton I 32-35; *ANE* No. 6;
¿Abdallah ibn Fâḍel: Treacherous Brothers: *Alf* IV 266-88; Burton IX 304-49; *ANE* No. 261□

0551B§, *Only One Sister is Successful on Quest (Seeking Riches)*. Other sisters are jealous. (See: *DOTTI*).
Eldest Lady's Story: Treacherous Sisters: *Alf* I 53-57; Burton I 162-73; *ANE* No. 19□

0555, *The Fisher and his Wife*. [Wishes granted: wasted (used foolishly)]. (See: *DOTTI*; *GMC*/MAP).
Night of al-Qadr: *Alf* III 162; Burton VI 180-81; *ANE* No. 199□

0560, *The Magic Ring*. [Lost, but recovered by grateful cat, dog, and mouse]. (See: *DOTTI*; *GMC*/MAP).
Ma¿rûf the Cobbler,-cf./intro.,: *Alf* IV 288-317; Burton I0 1-53; *ANE* No. 262□

0561, *Aladdin*. [Magic wishing lamp (ring) from treasure trove stolen and subsequently recovered by means of another magic object]. (See: *DOTTI*; *GMC*/MAP).
Jawdar and His Treacherous Brethren,-cf.,: *Alf* III 177-201; Burton VI 213-57; *ANE* No. 209□

0563, *The Magic Providing Purse and "Out, Boy, Out of the Sack!"*. [[Magic objects usurped, recovered via another object]. (See: *DOTTI*; *GMC*/MAP).
Jawdar and His Treacherous Brethren,-cf.,: *Alf* III 193; Burton VI 241; *ANE* No. 209□

0565A§, *Jinni-helper Turns Against Master: Demon Monkey and Lazy Boy*. (Muḥammad al-kaslân). (See: *DOTTI*; *GMC*/MAP).
Abû Muḥammad Lazybones: *Alf* II 206-16; Burton IV 162-78; *ANE* No. 78□

0567A, *The Magic Bird-Heart and the Separated Brothers*. [Faithless mother, faithful servant-woman]. (See: *DOTTI*; *GMC*/MAP).
al-'Amjad and al-'As¿ad,-cf./pt./III-V,: *Alf* I 12-32, 146-47; Burton III 309-48, IV 23-29; *ANE* No. 61□

0575, ‡*The Prince's Wings*. [Youth flies with artificial wings to princess in tower].
Ebony Horse,-cf., (after: ATU/*ANE*): *Alf* II 254-67; Burton V 1–32; *ANE* No. 103□

0612B§, *Person Entombed Alive with Dead Relative (Wife, Sister, Husband, etc.) Escapes from Grave*: Hangs on to (or, fastens his teeth on) an animal. (See: *DOTTI*; *GMC*/MAP).
Sindbâd's Fourth Voyage: *Alf* III 102ff.; Burton VI 39ff.; *ANE* No. 179,/4 □

0613A1§,/980* *The Vile Dyer Seeks to Eliminate the Noble Barber*. (Abu-Qîr and Abu-Ṣîr).
Abû Qîr and Abû Ṣîr: *Alf* IV 182-97; Burton IX 134-65; *ANE* No. 255□

0620A§, *Benevolent (Hospitable) Lies and Malevolent (Miserly) Ones Become Truths*. (See: *DOTTI*; *GMC*/MAP).
Jewish Tray-maker and Temptress,-cf.,: *Alf* III 13-14; Burton V 264-69; *ANE* No. 166□

0670, *The Animal Language*. Man learns from animals (birds) how to control his wife. (See: *DOTTI*; *GMC*/MAP).
Merchant's Curious Wife: *Alf* I 5-6; Burton I 19-23; *ANE* No. 3□

0681, *King in the Bath; Years of Experience in a Moment*. (See: *DOTTI*; *GMC*/MAP).
Hashish Eater's Dream,-cf./psych.-pattern,: *Alf* II 9-10; Burton III 91-93; *ANE* No. 42□

0705B§, *"I Have Begotten Children from my Loins, and from my Womb!": Khurâfah's Experience*. (See: *DOTTI*; *GMC*/MAP).
Enchanted Spring: Change of Sex,-cf./(only-Mot. D12) *Alf* III 146-48; Burton VI 145-50; *ANE* No. 191□

0712, *Crescentia [the Faith-healer]*. The slandered and banished wife is reinstated through her miraculous healing powers. (See: *DOTTI*; *GMC*/MAP).
Jewish qâḍî and His Devout Wife: *Alf* III 10-11; Burton V 256-59; *ANE* No. 163□

0726B§, *Peculiar Personal Appearance Reveals Life Experiences*. (Adventures by shabby-looking (deformed) guests told to hostess). (See: *DOTTI*).
Reeve's Story: Why Maimed by Bride: *Alf* I 96-099; Burton I:278–288; *ANE* No. 25□

0736A, *The Ring of Polycrates*. [Thrown (lost) in river, found in fish]. (See: *DOTTI*; *GMC*/MAP).
Abû Qîr and Abû Ṣîr: *Alf* IV 182-97; Burton IX 134-65; *ANE* No. 255□

0750D2§, *Ingratitude (Perfidy) Paid Back Posthumously*. Dead man's revenge. (See: *DOTTI*).
Dûban and King Yûnân: *Alf* I 16-23; Burton I 45-60; *ANE* No. 9□

0750J§, *Job Rewarded for his Patience (Faith)*. Miraculously healed. (See: *DOTTI*; *GMC*/MAP).
Spider Upbraids Wind,-cf./pattern,: *Alf* IV 146-47; Burton IX 59-60; *ANE* No. 245□

0756K§, *Host Hastily Kills his only Animal in Order to Feed his Guests*. (Ḥâtim aṭ-Ṭâ'î's hospitality). (Cf. 178C§). (See: *DOTTI*).
Ḥâtim's Hospitality,-cf.,: *Alf* II 181-82; Burton IV 94-96; *ANE* No. 64□

0759C, *The Widow's Meal*. [Wind's seemingly cruel action vindicated]. (See: *DOTTI*; *GMC*/MAP).
Spider Upbraids Wind,-cf.,: *Alf* IV 146-47; Burton IX 59-60; *ANE* No. 245□

0763, *The Treasure Finders who Murder one Another*. (See: *DOTTI*; *GMC*/MAP).
Merchant from Sindah and Sharpers: *Alf* II 39-40; Burton III 158; *ANE* No. 56□

0779, *Miscellaneous Divine Rewards and Punishments*. (See: *DOTTI*; *GMC*/MAP).
Conversion of Princess by Khawwâṣ,-cf./gen.,: *Alf* III 14-16; Burton V 283-86; *ANE* No. 171;
Son of Unjust King,-cf./gen.,: *Alf* IV 142-44; Burton IX 50-53; *ANE* No. 242□

0779D§, *Nature Changes According to How People Treat One Another*. (See: *DOTTI*; *GMC*/MAP).
Nuzhat al-Zamân Tested/¿Umar al-Nu¿mân,-cf.,/non-tale/(Mot. U210.0.1§) *Alf* I 205; BRT2 168; *ANE* No. 39;

Anûshirawân and Village Damsel: *Alf* II 285; Burton V 87-88; *ANE* No. 121□

0779F§, *Life is: 'A Blow for a Blow'*. (See: *DOTTI*; *GMC*/MAP).
Water-carrier and Goldsmith's Wife: *Alf* II 285-86; Burton V 89-90; *ANE* No. 122□

0779J3§, *Hard-hearted Ruler Won over (Converted): Man Keeps Promise to Return to be Executed*. (See: *DOTTI*; *GMC*/MAP).
Trader and Afrit: Accidental Killing: *Alf* I 8-14; Burton I 24-37; *ANE* No. 4;
Young Badawî Returns to be Executed,-cf.,: *Alf* II 287-89; Burton V 99-104; *ANE* No. 130□

0779J4§, *Conversion from One Religion to Another through Miracle*. Other occurrences. (See: *DOTTI*).
Prior Becomes Moslem: al-Anbârî: *Alf* II 298-300; Burton V 141-45; *ANE* No. 147□

0802C*, *The Rooms in Heaven*. [Palace in Paradise for the true believer]. (See: *DOTTI*; *GMC*/MAP).
Prior Becomes Moslem: al-Anbârî: *Alf* II 298-300; Burton V 141-45; *ANE* No. 147;
Jewish Tray-maker and Temptress: *Alf* III 13-14; Burton V 264-69; *ANE* No. 166□

0817*, *Devil Leaves at Mention of God's Name*. (See: *DOTTI*; *GMC*/MAP).
King's Favorite Son and Ogress,-cf.,/(ogress): *Alf* III 143-44; Burton VI 139-42; *ANE* No. 188□

0832, *The Disappointed Fisher*. [Murders son to get his predestined share of livelihood (a fish), but share disappears with son's death]. (See: *DOTTI*; *ANE* 432 No. 39/passim).
Spy, Fifth Maiden/¿Umar al-Nu¿mân,-cf.,/non-tale/(Mot. N100.1.1.0.1§) *Alf* I 224; Burton II 207; *ANE* No. 39□

0837A§, *The Evil Counsel (Remedy): Applied to Counselor*. (Villain nemesis). (See: *DOTTI*; *GMC*/MAP).
Anîs al-Jalîs,-cf.,: *Alf* I 125-45; Burton II 1-44; *ANE* No. 35□

0855B§, *Interim (Substitute) Groom Proves to be the Better Man*. Husband for a night is kept. (See: *DOTTI*).
¿Alâ' al-Dîn Abû al-Shâmât: *Alf* II 155ff.; Burton IV 48ff.; *ANE* No. 63;
Hârûn, Slave-girl and Judge Abû-Yûsuf,-cf./theme,: *Alf* II 202-4; Burton IV 153-55; *ANE* No. 75□

0859D, *"All of These are Mine,"* says wooer as he strokes his whiskers. (See: *DOTTI*; *GMC*/MAP).
Bahrâm and Datmâ,-cf./(Mot. K830.1.1§) *Alf* III 164-66; Burton VI 184-88; *ANE* No. 202□

0859F§, *Runaway Husband Transported by Jinni, Pretends to Wealth, and Wins Princess*. (Ma¿rûf the Cobbler). (See: *DOTTI*; *GMC*/MAP, ATU 859).
Ma¿rûf the Cobbler: *Alf* IV 288-317; Burton I0 1-53; *ANE* No. 262□

0861, *Sleeping at the Rendezvous*. [Clandestine lover captured by girl's family]. (See: *DOTTI*; *GMC*/MAP).
¿Azîz and ¿Azîzah: *Alf* I 275-79; Burton II 311-15; *ANE* No. 41□

0871B§, *Spirits Transport Young Man to Sleeping Girl*. (See: *DOTTI*; *GMC*/MAP).
Nûr al-Dîn ¿Alî and Son: *Alf* I 72-84; Burton I 214–254; *ANE* No. 22;
Qamar al-Zamân and Budûr: *Alf* II 71ff.; Burton III 224ff.; *ANE* No. 61□

0873, *The King Discovers his Unknown Son*. [Token found at son's execution]. (See: *DOTTI*; *GMC*/MAP).
Nûr al-Dîn ¿Alî and Son,-cf./(Mot. H175.7§) *Alf* I 81-84; Burton I 244; *ANE* No. 22□

0875, *The Clever Peasant Girl*. [She solves riddles, performs impossible tasks, marries king, and chooses him as dearest possession]. (See: *DOTTI*; *GMC*/MAP).
Tawaddud-cf.,/gen.,: *Alf* II 305ff.; Burton V 244ff.; *ANE* No. 157□

0876, *The Clever Maiden and the Suitors*. Answers and understands enigmatic questions. (See: *DOTTI*).
Nuzhat al-Zamân Tested/¿Umar al-Nu¿mân,-cf./theme,: *Alf* I 200-6; BRT2 156-171; *ANE* No. 39;

Hârûn and Arab Girl,-cf./theme,: *Alf* III 203-4; Burton VII 108-10; *ANE* No. 215□

0881, *Oft-proved Fidelity*. [Woman successfully resists a series of cruel attempts to violate her]. (See: *DOTTI*; *GMC*/MAP).
Jewish qâḍî and His Devout Wife: *Alf* III 10-11; Burton V 256-59; *ANE* No. 163;
Shipwrecked Woman and Her Child: *Alf* III 11-13; Burton V 259-61; *ANE* No. 164□

0883§,/(=ATU/883/883A) *Innocent Slandered (Suspected) Female.* (General). (See: *DOTTI*; *GMC*/MAP).
Three Apples: Hasty Murder: *Alf* I 61-64; Burton I 186–194; *ANE* No. 21;
Virtuous Jewess and Wicked Elders: *Alf* II 286-87; Burton V 97-98; *ANE* No. 128;
Budûr and Jubayr ibn ¿Umayr,-cf.,: *Alf* II 234-43; Burton IV:228-45; *ANE* No. 83;
Goldsmith and Cashmere Singer: *Alf* III 150-52; Burton VI 156-59; *ANE* No. 194□

0883E§, *The Innocent Slandered Wife: Falsified Evidence.* (Usually by her mother-in-law, sister-in-law). (See: *DOTTI*; *GMC*/MAP).
Rake's Trick Against Chaste Wife: *Alf* III 141-42; Burton VI 135-36; *ANE* No. 185□

0883F§,/981B*, *Innocent Wife Suspected: "Tracks of the Lion (King, Chief, her Father-in-law, etc.)".* (See: *DOTTI*; *GMC*/MAP).
King Dissuaded by Virtuous Wife: *Alf* II 294; Burton V 121-22; *ANE* No. 138;
King and Vizier's Wife/Tracks of Lion: *Alf* III 139-40; Burton VI 129-32; *ANE* No. 182□

0884A, *The Girl Disguised as Man is Wooed by the Queen.* (See: *DOTTI*; *GMC*/MAP).
Qamar al-Zamân and Budûr,: *Alf* II 100-112; Burton III 283, IV 23-29; *ANE* No. 61□

0884B*, *Girl Dressed as a Man Deceives the King.* (See: *DOTTI*; *GMC*/MAP).
¿Alî Shâr and Zumurrud: *Alf* II 217-35; Burton IV:187-28; *ANE* No. 82□

0885**, *The Foster Children.* ['Brother and sister' fall in (incestuous) love with each other. They learn that one was adopted: they get married]. (See: *DOTTI*; *GMC*/MAP).
Ni¿mah and Nu¿m: Wife Lost and Regained: *Alf* II 132-47; Burton IV 1-23; *ANE* No. 62□

0895B§, *Host Surrenders his Wife (Sister) to Guest.* Guest fell in love with her unaware of her identity. (See: *DOTTI*; *GMC*/MAP).
Anîs al-Jalîs,-cf.: *Alf* I 125-45; Burton II 1-44; *ANE* No. 35□

0891B*, *The King's Glove.* [Left on bed of innocent wife of courtier makes her suspect of infidelity]. (See: See 883F§).
King Dissuaded by Virtuous Wife: *Alf* II 294; Burton V 121-22; *ANE* No. 138;
King and Vizier's Wife/Tracks of Lion: *Alf* III 139-40; Burton VI 129-32; *ANE* No. 182;
Rake's Trick Against Chaste Wife: *Alf* III 141-42; Burton VI 135-36; *ANE* No. 185□

0895B1§, *Husband Divorces his Chaste Wife so that she may be Reunited with her First Love.* (Khaḍrah). (See: *DOTTI*; *GMC*/MAP).
Tawaddud: *Alf* II 303-19, *Alf* III 2-8; Burton V 189-245; *ANE* No. 157□

0910, *Precepts Bought or Given Prove Correct.* [General]. (See: *DOTTI*).
¿Alî Shâr and Zumurrud,-cf.,: *Alf* II 217-35; Burton IV:187-28; *ANE* No. 82□

0910M§, ‡*Glory (Success, Profit) is Achieved in Proportion to Hard Work and Risk-taking.*
Sindbâd and Porter: *Alf* III 81-83; Burton VI 1-4; *ANE* No. 179□

0910Z§, *Story Bought or Given Proves Valuable (True).* (See: *DOTTI*).
Sindbâd and Porter: *Alf* III 81-83; Burton VI 1-4; *ANE* No. 179□

0912§, *"Do not Make an Oath." Dying Father's Counsel.* (See: *DOTTI*; *GMC*/MAP).
Island King/Pious Jewish Merchant: *Alf* III 16-18; Burton V 290-94; *ANE* No. 174□

0916A§, *Evil Vizier (Concubine) Incites the King Against the King's Son (Brother).* (See: *DOTTI*; *GMC*/MAP).
Craft and Malice of Women/Frame: *Alf* III 138-39; Burton VI 122-212; *ANE* No. 181;
King Jalî¿âd and Shimâs: *Alf* IV 134-84; Burton IX 32-134; *ANE* No. 236□

0917§, *Innocent (Chaste) Man Slandered as Seducer (Rapist): Subsequently Vindicated.* (Batu/Baîtî and Anubis's wife, Joseph and Pharaoh's wife, etc.). (See: *DOTTI*).
al-'Amjad and al-'As¿ad: *Alf* I 12-32, 146-47; Burton III 309-48, IV 23-29; *ANE* No. 61□

0918§, *Wise (Learned) Judicial Decisions.* Legal defenses based on knowledge of the law. (See: *DOTTI*).
Hârûn, Slave-girl and Judge Abû-Yûsuf: *Alf* II 202-4; Burton IV 153-55; *ANE* No. 75□

0919§, *Exemplary Justice.* Stories about ideal application (by king, judge, etc.) of law. (See: *DOTTI*).
Nuzhat al-Zamân Tested/¿Umar al-Nu¿mân,-cf./(Mot. K1039§) *Alf* I 203; Burton II 164; *ANE* No. 39□

0920G§, *Deeds Betray Ancestry (Origins)*. (See: *DOTTI*; *GMC*/MAP).
Anîs al-Jalîs: *Alf* I 145; Burton II 44; *ANE* No. 35□

0926C, *Cases Solved in a Manner Worthy of Solomon*. (See: *DOTTI*; *GMC*/MAP).
Virtuous Jewess and Wicked Elders: *Alf* II 286-87; Burton V 97-98; *ANE* No. 128□

0926K1§, ‡*Accusation of Theft Proves to Be Unjust*: missing article (coin, jewel, food) stolen by another (usually by animal or bird).
Stolen Necklace/Hasty Accusation: *Alf* III 163-64; Burton VI 182-83; *ANE* No. 200□

0926K§, *Examination of Physical Evidence Leads to Culprit (Criminal)*. (See: *DOTTI*; *GMC*/MAP).
Three Apples: Hasty Murder,-cf.,: *Alf* I 61-64; Burton I 186–194; *ANE* No. 21;
Jewish Doctor's Story: Sororicide,-cf.,: *Alf* I 99-102; Burton I 288–300; *ANE* No. 26□

0926M§, *Mysterious Crime (Murder) Solved through Induced Confession*--(from culprit, confederate, witness). (See: *DOTTI*).
Jewish Doctor's Story: Sororicide,-cf.,: *Alf* I 99-102; Burton I 288–300; *ANE* No. 26□

0927C§, *Execution Forestalled by Fate (or Cleverness)*. (See: *DOTTI*; *GMC*/MAP).
Barber's Tale of Himself: Joins Doomed Party,-cf.,: *Alf* I 109-10; Burton I 317–19; *ANE* No. 28□

0931Z§, ‡*Girl (woman) Raped by Paternal Figure* (father-in-law, guardian, teacher, grandparent or the like). (See: 674B§,).
¿Umar al-Nu¿mân and Sons: *Alf* I 182-83; Burton II 123; *ANE* No. 39□

0932§,/0933, *Brother-sister Incest: the Sethian Complex (Syndrome)*. (Cf. 938*) (See: *DOTTI*; *GMC*/MAP).
First Qalandar: Brother-Sister Incest: *Alf* I 39-42; Burton I 104-13; *ANE* No. 15;
¿Umar al-Nu¿mân and Sons: *Alf* I 207; Burton II 172; *ANE* No. 39□

0934N§, ‡"*Caution Does not Alter Destiny (the Preordained)*"--various narratives.
Birds, Beasts, and Carpenter: *Alf* II 21-27; Burton III 114-25; *ANE* No. 44;
Water-fowl and Tortoise: *Alf* II 26-29; Burton III 129-32; *ANE* No. 46;
Sparrow as Peacock's Vizier: *Alf* II 40-41; Burton III 161-62; *ANE* No. 59□

0936*, *The Golden Mountain*. [Treacherous magician (merchant) has youth carried by bird to mountain top and abandons him]. (See: *DOTTI*; *GMC*/MAP).
Jânshâh: *Alf* III 49, 64-65; Burton V 342-43; *ANE* No. 178;
al-Ḥasan al-Baṣrî: *Alf* III 310; Burton VIII 21; *ANE* No. 230□

0936A§, *Voyages (Adventures) of an Entrepreneur*. (Sindbâd the Sailor). (Focus). (See: *DOTTI*; *GMC*/MAP).
Sindbâd's First Voyage: *Alf* III 83-88; Burton VI 4-14; *ANE* No. 179,/1;
Sindbâd's Second Voyage: *Alf* III 88-92,Burton VI 14-22; *ANE* No. 179,/2;
Sindbâd's Third Voyage: *Alf* III 92-100; Burton VI 22-34; *ANE* No. 179,/3;
Sindbâd's Fourth Voyage: *Alf* III 100-6; Burton VI 34-48; *ANE* No. 179,/4;
Sindbâd's Fifth Voyage: *Alf* III 106-12; Burton VI 48-58; *ANE* No. 179,/5;
Sindbâd's Sixth Voyage: *Alf* III 112-16; Burton VI 58-68; *ANE* No. 179,/6;
Sindbâd's Seventh Voyage: *Alf* III 116-22; Burton VI 68-77; *ANE* No. 179,/7□

0938, *Placidas (Eustacius)*. [Loses all in mishaps, then regains all]. (See: *DOTTI*; *GMC*/MAP).
¿Alâ' al-Dîn Abû al-Shâmât,-cf.,: *Alf* II 147-81; Burton IV 29-94; *ANE* No. 63;
Island King/Pious Jewish Merchant,-cf.,: *Alf* III 16-18; Burton V 290-94; *ANE* No. 174□

0938*, *Master Discovers that Slave Girl he wants to Marry Is a Near Relative*. (See: 932§-933§).
¿Umar al-Nu¿mân and Sons: *Alf* I 208; Burton II 174; *ANE* No. 39□

0938C§, *Wife Unwittingly Sold, and Restored with Help from Grateful Friend*. (See: *DOTTI*; *GMC*/MAP) .
Anîs al-Jalîs,-cf.,: *Alf* I 142; Burton II 34-35; *ANE* No. 35;
Nûr al-Dîn and Maryam,-cf.,: *Alf* IV 101; Burton VIII 312-13; *ANE* No. 233;
Ruined Baghdadi and His Slave-girl,-cf.,: *Alf* IV 130; Burton IX 24; *ANE* No. 235□

0953A§, *Captive in Jinn-land is Ransomed by Telling Stories*: ("Khurâfah's Report"). (See: *DOTTI*; *GMC*/MAP).
Trader and Afrit: Accidental Killing,-cf.,: *Alf* I 8-14; Burton I 24-37; *ANE* No. 4;
Enchanted Spring: Change of Sex,-cf./theme: *Alf* III 146-48; Burton VI 145-50; *ANE* No. 191□

0956A, *At the Robber's House*. [Man avenges himself on murderous robbers and takes their treasure]. (See: *DOTTI* .
Barber's Fifth Brother: Daydreams/Defeats Robbers,-cf.,: *Alf* I 117-21; Burton I 335–343; *ANE* No. 33□

0970, *The Twining Branches*. Two branches grow from the grave of unfortunate lovers [...]. (See: *DOTTI*; *GMC*/MAP).
Jânshâh,-cf.,: *Alf* III 38-73; Burton V 329-81; *ANE* No. 178□

0971§, *Despairing Lover Commits Suicide or Becomes Insane*. (See: *DOTTI*; *GMC*/MAP).
¿Alî ibn Bakkâr: *Alf* II 41-65; Burton III 162-212; *ANE* No. 60;
Lovers of Banû 'Udhra and Lion: *Alf* III 206-10; Burton VII 110-13; *ANE* No. 218□

0971A§, *Insanity and Death from Unrequited Love*. (Qays and Lylâ). (See: *DOTTI*; *GMC*/MAP).
Lovers of Banû Ṭay'/Death from Love: *Alf* II 297; Burton V 137-38; *ANE* No. 145;
Prior Becomes Moslem: al-Anbârî: *Alf* II 298-300; Burton V 141-45; *ANE* No. 147□

0971C§, *Insanity (Death) from Death of Beloved Sibling (Brother, Sister)*. (The Khansâ' Syndrome). (See: *DOTTI*).
Ḥammâd: Treacherous Bedouin: *Alf* II 16-20; Burton III 104-11; *ANE* No. 43□

0978, *The Youth in the Land of the Cheaters*. (See: *DOTTI*; *GMC*/MAP).
Sandal-wood Merchant and Sharpers: *Alf* III 174-76; Burton VI 202-7; *ANE* No. 205□

0980*,/613A1§, *The Painter and the Architect*. [The vile dyer and the noble barber (Abu-Qîr and Abu-Ṣîr)]. (See: *DOTTI*; *GMC*/MAP).
Abû Qîr and Abû Ṣîr: *Alf* IV 182-97; Burton IX 134-65; *ANE* No. 255□

0983, *The Dishes of the Same Flavor*. Man thus shown that one woman is like another [...]. (See: *DOTTI*; *GMC*/MAP).
King and Vizier's Wife/Tracks of Lion: *Alf* III 139-40; Burton VI 129-32; *ANE* No. 182□

0990, *The Seemingly Dead Revives*. [Host suspects that he has killed his guest (who choked on food) and places the 'corpse' in the street where one passersby after another suspects that he himself has caused the death]. (See: *DOTTI*; *GMC*/MAP).
The Hunchback: *Alf* I 85-88; Burton I 255–352; *ANE* No. 23□

0992A, *The Adulteress's Penance*. [Humiliating treatment by husband]. (See: *DOTTI*; *GMC*/MAP).
Portress Amînah: Bitten Cheek,-cf.,: *Alf* I 57-61; Burton I 173-84; *ANE* No. 20□

0993§, *Faithlessness (Adultery, Attempted Seduction) Revealed and Punished*. (See: *DOTTI*; *GMC*/MAP).
Shahriyâr and Shâhzamân: *Alf* I 2-5; Burton I 24, X 54-62; *ANE* No. 1;
Second Qalandar: Afrit's Wife,-cf.,: *Alf* I 42-51; Burton I 113-39; *ANE* No. 16;
Jeweler's Wife and Qamar al-Zamân: *Alf* IV 260-65; Burton IX 289-302; *ANE* No. 260□

1137, *The Ogre Blinded (Polyphemus)*. (See: *DOTTI*; *GMC*/MAP).
Sindbâd's Third Voyage: *Alf* III 96-100; Burton VI 27; *ANE* No. 179,/3 □

1139A§, *The Ogre Induced to Carry Adversary*. (See: *DOTTI*).
Sindbâd's Fifth Voyage,-cf.,: *Alf* III 106-12; Burton VI 48-58; *ANE* No. 179,/5 □

1174, *Making a Rope of Sand*. [Task]. (See: *DOTTI*; *GMC*/MAP).
Sandal-wood Merchant and Sharpers,-cf./motif: *Alf* III 174-76; Burton VI 202-7; *ANE* No. 205□

1217§, *Indecision: Trying to Find the Perfect Solution (or Article)--(Regretted)*. (See: *DOTTI*).
Hedgehog and Wood-pigeons: *Alf* II 39; Burton III 156-58; *ANE* No. 55□·

122Z, *Other Tricks to Escape from Captor*. (See: *DOTTI*; *GMC*/MAP).
Hishâm and Arab Youth,-cf.,-(poem/Arabic): *Alf* II 184-85; Burton IV 101-3; *ANE* No. 68□

1233A§, *Meddler Tries to Save Friend from Presumed Peril: Causes him Much Harm*. (The Barber of Baghdad). (See: *DOTTI*).
Tailor's Story/Barber of Baghdad: *Alf* I 107-9; Burton I 314–16; *ANE* No. 27□

1305D§, *Treasuring Gold Alone Proves Ruinous*: (Food production neglected). (See: *DOTTI*).
Jinn Imprisoned in Flasks,-cf.,: *Alf* III 122-29; Burton VI 83-122; *ANE* No. 180□

1331E*§, *Illiterate Teacher (Sheik, etc.) Reads a Letter for a Woman*: Comic Results. (See: *DOTTI*; *GMC*/MAP; ATU 1331).
Illiterate Schoolmaster: *Alf* II 293-94; Burton V 119-21; *ANE* No. 137□

1340§, *Talkativeness Brings about Misfortune (Punishment): Silence would have Spared*. (See: *DOTTI*; *GMC*/MAP; ATU 1341A).
Barber's Tale of Himself: Joins Doomed Party,-cf.,: *Alf* I 109-10; Burton I 317–19; *ANE* No. 28□

1351E§, *Doctor Duped into Performing Surgery on Healthy Unsuspecting Victim* (e.g., circumcision, teeth-pulling, branding, etc.). (See: *DOTTI*).
Dalîla the Swindler: *Alf* III 221; Burton VII 161; *ANE* No. 224□

1353A§, *Old Woman as Trouble Maker: the Marked Cloth in Chaste Wife's Room*. (See: *DOTTI*; *GMC*/MAP; ATU 1378).
House with the Belvedere: *Alf* III 166-72; Burton VI 188-99; *ANE* No. 203□

1358B, *Husband Carries off Box Containing Hidden Paramour*. (See: *DOTTI*; *GMC*/MAP).
King's Son and Merchant's Wife,-cf.,: *Alf* III 155-56; Burton VI 167-69; *ANE* No. 196□

1359D§, *Wife and Paramour Outwit Husband*. (See: *DOTTI*; *GMC*/MAP).
Woman Who Made Husband Sift Dust,-cf.,: *Alf* III 145; Burton VI 143-44; *ANE* No. 190;
King's Son and Merchant's Wife,-cf.,: *Alf* III 155-56; Burton VI 167-69; *ANE* No. 196;
Page Feigns Knowing Bird Language: *Alf* III 156-57; Burton VI 169-72; *ANE* No. 197;
Jeweler's Wife and Qamar al-Zamân: *Alf* IV 237-66; Burton IX 246-304; *ANE* No. 260□

1366§, *Groom Traumatized by his Maniac Bride*. (Insane wife terrorizes husband). (See: *DOTTI*).
Reeve's Story: Why Maimed by Bride: *Alf* I 96-099; Burton I:278–288; *ANE* No. 25□

1378, *The Marked Coat in the Wife's Room*. [False token of woman's infidelity]. (See: *DOTTI*; *GMC*/MAP).
House with the Belvedere: *Alf* III 166-72; Burton VI 188-99; *ANE* No. 203□

1388C§, *Attempts to Gain Hospitality from a Miser: Futile*. (See: *DOTTI*; *GMC*/MAP; ATU 1704).
Barber's Sixth Brother: Emasculated by Abductor,-cf./(Mot. P327) *Alf* I 121-25; Burton I 343-48; *ANE* No. 34□

1419D, *The Lovers as Pursuer and Fugitive*. [Paramour thus escapes]. (See: *DOTTI*; *GMC*/MAP).
Lady's Lovers as Pursuer and Fugitive: *Alf* III 143; Burton VI 138-39; *ANE* No. 187□

1419E, *Underground Passage to Paramour's House* (Inclusa) [Woman visits her lover]. (See: *DOTTI*; *GMC*/MAP).
Jeweler's Wife and Qamar al-Zamân: *Alf* IV 252; Burton IX 274; *ANE* No. 260□

1419M§, *Chaste Wife Teaches Distrustful (Suspicious, Jealous) Husband Lesson in Trust*. (See: *DOTTI*; *GMC*/MAP).
Weeping Bitch: Chaste Wife Bluffed, cf./(Mot. K1514.4.1.1§) *Alf* III 148-49; Burton VI 152-56; *ANE* No. 193□

1420A, *The Broken (Removed) Article*. [Paramour's explanation to cuckolded husband]. (See: *DOTTI*).
Goldsmith and Cashmere Singer,-cf.,: *Alf* III 150-52; Burton VI 156-59; *ANE* No. 194;
Jeweler's Wife and Qamar al-Zamân: *Alf* IV 252-55; Burton IX 275-79; *ANE* No. 260□

1422, *Parrot Unable to Tell Husband Details of Wife's Infidelity*. [Thus husband hoodwinked]. (See: *DOTTI*; *GMC*/MAP).
Husband and Parrot: *Alf* III 140-41; Burton I:52-54; *ANE* No. 11□

1424B§, *Seduction by Other Tricks*. Sexual intercourse under pretence of strengthening, increasing eyesight, (or the like). (See: *DOTTI*; *GMC*/MAP).
Page Feigns Knowing Bird Language: *Alf* III 156-57; Burton VI 169-72; *ANE* No. 197□

1425B§, *Seduction: Putting the Bird (or Animal) in its Natural Habitat*. (See: *DOTTI*; *GMC*/MAP).
Porter and Ladies of Baghdad: *Alf* I 35; Burton I:092; *ANE* No. 14□

1426, *The Wife Kept in a Box*. [She, nonetheless, commits adultery (is unfaithful)]. (See: *DOTTI*; *GMC*/MAP).
Jinni Keeps Mistress in Box: *Alf* I 5; Burton I 10-13; *ANE* No. 1-1;
Second Qalandar: Afrit's Wife,-cf.,: *Alf* I 42-51; Burton I 113-39; *ANE* No. 16;
King's Son and Afrit's Mistress: *Alf* III 172-73; Burton VI 199-202; *ANE* No. 204□

1426*, *Man with Unfaithful Wife Comforted.* [... He sees another cuckolded]. (See: *DOTTI*; *GMC*/MAP).
Jinni Keeps Mistress in Box: *Alf* I 5; Burton I 10-13; *ANE* No. 1-1□

1426A§, *Cuckolded Husband Kills a New Bride each Night* so as to avenge self on women. (Shehryâr). (See: *DOTTI*; *GMC*/MAP; ATU 875B*).
Shahriyâr and Shâhzamân: *Alf* I 5; Burton I 14; *ANE* No. 1□

1430B§, *Foolish Plans for the Unsold Milk (Honey, Eggs, etc.).* (See: *DOTTI*; *GMC*/MAP).
Barber's Fifth Brother: Daydreams/Defeats Robbers: *Alf* I 117-21; Burton I 335–343; *ANE* No. 33;
Foolish Weaver,-cf.,: *Alf* II 40; Burton III 159-60; *ANE* No. 58;
Fakir and Jar of Butter: *Alf* IV 137-39; Burton IX 40-43; *ANE* No. 238□

1469§, *Foolish Person Tricked into a Humiliating (Disgraceful) Position.* (See: *DOTTI*; *GMC*/MAP).
Barber's Second Brother: Humiliated by Playgirl: *Alf* I 113-14; Burton I:324–28; *ANE* No. 30□

1504§, *Wife of Philanderer Gets Revenge by Having an Affair Herself.* Usually with a loathly paramour so as to further spite her faithless husband. (See: *DOTTI*).
Sweep and Noble Lady: Infidelity Repaid: *Alf* II 188-91; Burton IV 125-30; *ANE* No. 72□

1511, *The Faithless Queen.* [Wife prefers loathsome paramour]. (See: *DOTTI*; *GMC*/MAP).
Ensorcelled Prince: *Alf* I 23-31; Burton I:69-82; *ANE* No. 13□

1512§,/465A*, □*Faithless Wife Elopes with her Paramour (Husband's Fried).* (Usually, husband pursues fleeing lovers). (Cf. 465A*).
Masrûr and Zayn al-Mawâṣif: *Alf* IV 55-80; Burton VIII 205-63; *ANE* No. 232□

1515, *The Weeping Bitch.* [Said to be transformed woman who rejected lover: trick to frighten virtuous woman]. (See: *DOTTI*; *GMC*/MAP).
Weeping Bitch: Chaste Wife Bluffed: *Alf* III 148-49; Burton VI 152-56; *ANE* No. 193□

1525, *The Master Thief.* (See: *DOTTI*; *GMC*/MAP).
Merchant and Robbers,-cf.,: *Alf* IV 166; Burton IX 100-2; *ANE* No. 251□

1525A, *Theft of Dog, Horse, Sheet or ring.* [Series of thefts committed as result of boasting]. (See: *DOTTI*; *GMC*/MAP).
Mercury ¿Alî: *Alf* III 237-40; Burton VII 190-97; *ANE* No. 225□

1525J2, *Thief Sent into Well by Trickster.* [Thief's clothes stolen as he supposedly tries to help trickster recover lost object]. (See: *DOTTI*; *GMC*/MAP).
Mercury ¿Alî: *Alf* III 233; Burton VII 183; *ANE* No. 225□

1525W§, *Leaving Infant (Corpse, Hireling) with Merchant as Security*. Supposed buyer does not return with merchandise. (See: *DOTTI*; *GMC*/MAP; ATU 1525Z*).
Dalîla the Swindler: *Alf* III 220; Burton VII 157; *ANE* No. 224□

1526, *The Beggar and the Robbers.* [Beggar dressed up as getleman: goods received on his credit (or an infant is used as surety)]. (See: *DOTTI*; *GMC*/MAP).
Dalîla the Swindler,-cf.,: *Alf* III 220; Burton VII 157; *ANE* No. 224□

1526D§, *Other Tricks by Parasites (Spongers) to Win a Free Supper (Meal).* (*ṭufayyliyyîn*'s ruses). (See: *DOTTI*; *GMC*/MAP).
Barber's Tale of Himself: Joins Doomed Party,-(Mot. N393.1§) *Alf* I 109-10; Burton I 317–19; *ANE* No. 28□

1535, *The Rich and the Poor Peasant.* (Unibos). [Series of tricks by trickster, and disastrous imitations by gullible rival(s)]. (See: *DOTTI*; *GMC*/MAP).
Dalîla the Swindler,-cf./pt./Va/(Mot. K842) '*Alf* III 224; Burton VII 164; *ANE* No. 224□

1538A§, *Female Master Thief.* Woman (girl) performs series of tricks (to avenge injustice to husband (father), or to fulfill a pledge). (See: *DOTTI*; *GMC*/MAP; ATU 1525Z*).
Dalîla the Swindler: *Alf* III 212-27; Burton VII 144-71; *ANE* No. 224□

1542**, *The Maiden's Honor.* [...] The tailor promises to sew up her "honor" (virginity). (See: *DOTTI*; *GMC*/MAP).
First Eunuch: Bukhayt Deflowers Mistress,-cf./(Mot. K1912.1§) *Alf* I 147-49; Burton II 49-50; *ANE* No. 37□

1543C1§, *Erotic Dream Interrupted*. (See: *DOTTI*).
Hashish Eater's Dream: *Alf* II 9-10; Burton III: 91-93; *ANE* No. 42□

1560, *Make-believe Eating; Make-believe Work*. (See: *DOTTI*).
Barber's Sixth Brother: Emasculated by Abductor,-cf./(Mot. P327) *Alf* I 121-25; Burton I 343-48; *ANE* No. 34□

1562F§, *Getting Stuck in Food Container due to Greed (Gluttony)*. (See: *DOTTI*; ATU 1294A).
Foolish Fisher/psych.-pattern/Mot./(W151.9.3§) *Alf* IV 162-63; Burton IX 93-95; *ANE* No. 248□

1572J1§, *Interrupted Sexual Intercourse*--(Miscellaneous circumstances). (See: *DOTTI*).
Debauchee and Three Years Old Child: *Alf* III 176; Burton VI 208-9; *ANE* No. 206□

1591, *The Three Joint Depositors*. [Money deposited by all three, must be withdrawn by all three]. (See: *DOTTI*; *GMC*/MAP).
Stolen Purse/Joint Depositors: *Alf* III 176-77; Burton VI 209-11; *ANE* No. 207□

1645D§, *Perilous Journey in Search of Treasure Trove*. (See: *DOTTI*; *GMC*/MAP).
Treasure of Tolède/Labtayt,-cf.,: *Alf* II 183-84; Burton IV 99-101; *ANE* No. 67;
Jinn Imprisoned in Flasks: *Alf* III 122-29; Burton VI 83-122; *ANE* No. 180;
¿Abdallah ibn Fâḍel: Treacherous Brothers,-cf.,: *Alf* IV 266-88; Burton IX 304-49; *ANE* No. 261□

1651C§, *Fortune in Distant Trade*.
Sindbâd's First Voyage,/gen.,: *Alf* III 83-88; Burton VI 4-14; *ANE* No. 179,/1;
Sindbâd's Third Voyage: *Alf* III 92-100; Burton VI 22-34; *ANE* No. 179,/3;
Sindbâd's Fourth Voyage: *Alf* III 100-6; Burton VI 34-48; *ANE* No. 179,/4;
Sindbâd's Seventh Voyage: *Alf* III 116-22; Burton VI 68-77; *ANE* No. 179,/7□

1681*, *Foolish Man Builds Aircastles*. (See: *DOTTI*; *GMC*/MAP).
Fakir and Jar of Butter: *Alf* IV 137-39; Burton IX 40-43; *ANE* No. 238□

1730, *The Entrapped Suitors*. (Lai l'épervier). [Would-be seducers hidden, chased away]. (See: *DOTTI*; *GMC*/MAP).
Lady and Five Suitors Deceived,-cf.,: *Alf* III 158-62; Burton VI 172-79; *ANE* No. 198□

1730C§, *Chaste Woman and her Husband Humiliate the Importunate Seducer (Paramour)*. (See: *DOTTI*; *GMC*/MAP).
Barber's First Brother: Free Labor for Coquette: *Alf* I 111-12; Burton I 319–24; *ANE* No. 29□

1862, *Jokes on Doctors (Physicians)*. (See: *DOTTI*).
Ridiculous Eye Salve,-cf.,: *Alf* II 287; Burton V 98-99; *ANE* No. 129□

1871A§, *Beggar is Asked to Come Upstairs then Turned down*. (See: *DOTTI*; *GMC*/MAP).
Barber's Third Brother: Exposes Blind Robbers: *Alf* I 114-15; Burton I 328–331; *ANE* No. 31□

1873§, *Jokes (Anecdotes) on School-teachers*. (See: *DOTTI*).
Schoolmaster in Mourning: *Alf* II 292-93; Burton V 117-18; *ANE* No. 135;
Schoolmaster Mutilates Self: *Alf* II 293; Burton V 118-19; *ANE* No. 136□

1874E§, *Shameless Violator(s) of Sex Mores*. (See: *DOTTI*).
Debauchee and Three Years Old Child: *Alf* III 176; Burton VI 208-9; *ANE* No. 206□

1889H, □*Submarine Otherworld*. Marine counterpart to land. (See: *DOTTI*; *GMC*/MAP).
Jullanâr of the Sea: *Alf* III 247-70; Burton VII 264-308; *ANE* No. 227;
Landsman ¿Abdallah and Merman ¿Abdallah: *Alf* IV 198-208; Burton IX 165-88; *ANE* No. 256□

1931A§, *The News from Home: Ascending Calamities*. (See: *DOTTI*; *GMC*/MAP; ATU 1931).
Second Eunuch/Kâfûr's Half-lie: *Alf* I 148-51; Burton II 51-56; *ANE* No. 38□

2036, *Drop of Honey Causes Chain of Accidents*. [Bloody feud between villages ensues]. (See: *DOTTI*; *GMC*/MAP).
Drop of Honey: *Alf* III 145; Burton VI 142-43; *ANE* No. 189□

2335, *Tales Filled with Contradictions*. (See: *DOTTI*; *GMC*/MAP).
Kurd's Sack/¿Alî the Persian: *Alf* II 200-2; Burton IV 149-52; *ANE* No. 74;
Ridiculous Eye Salve,-cf.,: *Alf* II 287; Burton V 98-99; *ANE* No. 129□

2412§, *Unclassified Formula Tales*. (See: *DOTTI*; *GMC*/MAP).
Kurd's Sack/¿Alî the Persian: *Alf* II 200-2; Burton IV 149-52; *ANE* No. 74□

Other References to Tale-types

APPENDIX

Titles of Tales Nos. 170-262 in Burton's Translation

On basis of his extensive examination of the various manuscripts and published editions bearing the title of *'Alf laylah wa laylah*, Burton designated forty-five texts (tales) as alien to the anthology and remarcks:

> All tales which there is good reason to believe do not belong to the genuine Nights are marked with an asterisk.[95]

No. Title

170· Asleep and Awake
a. Story of the Lackpenny and the Cook
171· The Caliph Omar ben Abdulaziz and the Poets
172· El Hejjaj and the Three Young Men
173· Haroun Er Reshid and the Woman of the Barmecides
174· The Ten Viziers, or the History of King Azadbekht and his Son
a. Of the uselessness of endeavor against persistent ill-fortune
aa. Story of the Unlucky Merchant [Merchant Who Lost His Luck]
b. Of looking to the issues of affairs
bb. Story of the Merchant and his Sons
c. Of the advantages of Patience
cc. Story of Abou Sabir
d. Of the ill effects of Precipitation
dd. Story of Prince Bihzad
e. Of the issues of good and evil actions
ee. Story of King Dabdin and his Viziers
f. Of Trust in God
ff. Story of King Bekhtzeman
g. Of Clemency
gg. Story of King Bihkerd
h. Of Envy and Malice
hh. Story of Ilan Shah and Abou Temam
i. Of Destiny, or that which is written on the Forehead
ii. Story of King Ibrahim and his Son
j. Of the appointed Term, which if it be advanced, may not be deferred, and if it be deferred, may not be advanced
jj. Story of King Suleiman Shah and his Sons
k. Of the speedy Relief of God
kk. Story of the Prisoner, and how God gave him relief
175· Jaafer Ben Zehya and Abdulmelik Ben Salih the Abbaside
176· Er Reshid and the Barmecides
177· Ibn Es-Semmak and Er-Reshid
178· El Mamoun and Zubeideh
179· En Numan and the Arab of the Benou Tai
180· Firouz and his Wife

---

[95]Burton, Vol. 10, p. 514. See also note 9, p. 2, above.

In their *Arabian Nights Encyclopedia*, Marzolph et al. include a previously untreated anthology designated as the "Reinhardt manuscript" (Aboubakr Chraïbi, ed., *Contes nouveaux des 1001 Nuits: Étude du manuscrit Reinhardt*. Paris, 1996). The texts from that work are assigned the numbers 519-551. Only one tale (no. 543) is found also in another European-oriented anthology; the rest are unique to Reinhardt's edition. (For an evaluation of the contents, see *ANE*, Vol. 1, p. 20; also see Vol. 2, pp. 745-82.

181· King Shah Bekht and his Vizier Er Rehwan
- *a*. Story of the Man of Khorassan his son and his governor
- *b*. Story of the Singer and the Druggist
- *c*. Story of the King who knew the quintessence of things
- *d*. Story of the Rich Man who gave his fair Daughter in Marriage to the Poor Old Man
- *e*. Story of the Rich Man and his Wasteful Son
- *f*. The King's Son who fell in love with the Picture
- *g*. Story of the Fuller and his Wife
- *h*. Story of the Old Woman, the Merchant, and the King
- *i*. Story of the credulous Husband
- *j*. Story of the Unjust King and the Tither
  - *jj*. Story of David and Solomon
- *k*. Story of the Thief and the Woman
- *l*. Story of the Three Men and our Lord Jesus
  - *ll*. The Disciple's Story
- *m*. Story of the Dethroned King whose kingdom and good were restored to him
- *n*. Story of the Man whose caution was the cause of his Death
- *o*. Story of the Man who was lavish of his house and his victual to one whom he knew not
- *p*. Story of the Idiot and the Sharper
- *q*. Story of Khelbes and his Wife and the Learned Man
- *r*. Story of the Pious Woman accused of lewdness
- *s*. Story of the Journeyman and the Girl
- *t*. Story of the Weaver who became a Physician by his Wife's commandment
- *u*. Story of the Two Sharpers who cheated each his fellow
- *v*. Story of the Sharpers with the Moneychanger and the Ass
- *w*. Story of the Sharper and the Merchants
  - *wa*. Story of the Hawk and the Locust
- *x*. Story of the King and his Chamberlain's Wife
  - *xa*. Story of the Old Woman and the Draper's Wife
- *y*. Story of the Foul-favoured Man and his Fair Wife
- *z*. Story of the King who lost Kingdom and Wife and Wealth, and God restored them to him
- *aa*. Story of Selim and Selma [his sister]
- *bb*. Story of the King of Hind and his Vizier

182· El Melik Ez Zahir Rukneddin Bibers El Bunducdari, and the Sixteen Officers of Police
- *a*. The First Officer's Story
- *b*. The Second Officer's Story
- *c*. The Third Officer's Story
- *d*. The Fourth Officer's Story
- *e*. The Fifth Officer's Story
- *f*. The Sixth Officer's Story
- *g*. The Seventh Officer's Story
- *h*. The Eighth Officer's Story
  - *ha*. The Thief's Story
- *i*. The Ninth Officer's Story
- *j*. The Tenth Officer's Story
- *k*. The Eleventh Officer's Story
- *l*. The Twelfth Officer's Story
- *m*. The Thirteenth Officer's Story
- *n*. The Fourteenth Officer's Story
  - *na*. A Merry Jest of a Thief
  - *nb*. Story of the Old Sharper
- *o*. The Fifteenth Officer's Story
- *p*. The Sixteenth Officer's Story

183· Abdallah Ben Nafi, and the King's Son of Cashgbar

a. Story of the Damsel Tuhfet El Culoub and Khalif Haroun Er Reshid
184· Women's Craft
185· Noureddin Ali of Damascus and the Damsel Sitt El Milah
186· El Abbas and the King's Daughter of Baghdad
187· The Two Kings and the Vizier's daughters
188· The Favourite and her Lover
189· The Merchant of Cairo and the Favourite of the Khalif El Mamoun El Hakim bi Amrillah
190· Conclusion
*191· History of Prince Zeyn Alasnam
*192· History of Codadad and his Brothers
**a*. History of the Princess of Deryabar
*193· Story of Aladdin, or the Wonderful Lamp
*194· Adventures of the Caliph Harun Al-Rashid
**a*. Story of the Blind Man, Baba Abdallah
**b*. Story of Sidi Numan
**c*. Story of Cogia Hassan Alhabbal
*195· Story of Ali Baba and the Forty Thieves
*196· Story of Ali Cogia, a Merchant of Baghdad
*197· Story of Prince Ahmed and the Fairy Peri Banou
*198· Story of the Sisters who envied their younger sister
199· (Anecdote of Jaafar the Barmecide = No. 39)
200· The Adventures of Ali and Zaher of Damascus
201· The Adventures of the Fisherman, Judar of Cairo, and his meeting with the Moor Mahmood and the Sultan Beibars
202· The Physician and the young man of Mosul
203· Story of the Sultan of Yemen and his three sons
204· Story of the Three Sharpers and the Sultan
a. Adventures of the Abdicated Sultan
b. History of Mahummud, Sultan of Cairo
c. Story of the First Lunatic
d. (Story of the Second Lunatic = No.184)
e. Story of the Sage and his Pupil
f. Night adventure of the Sultan
g. Story of the first foolish man
h. Story of the broken-backed Schoolmaster
i. Story of the wry-mouthed Schoolmaster
j. The Sultan's second visit to the Sisters
k. Story of the Sisters and the Sultana, their mother
205· Story of the Avaricious Cauzee and his wife
206· Story of the Bang-Eater and the Cauzee
a. Story of the Bang-Eater and his wife
b. Continuation of the Fisherman, or Bang-Eater's Adventures
207· The Sultan and the Traveller Mhamood Al Hyjemmee
a. The Koord Robber (= No.33)
b. Story of the Husbandman
c. Story of the Three Princes and Enchanting Bird
d. Story of a Sultan of Yemen and his three Sons
e. Story of the first Sharper in the Cave
f. Story of the second Sharper
g. Story of the third Sharper
h. History of the Sultan of Hind
208· Story of the Fisherman's Son
209· Story of Abou Neeut and Abou Neeuteen
210· Story of the Prince of Sind, and Fatima, daughter of Amir Bin Naomaun
211· Story of the Lovers of Syria, or the Heroine
212· Story of Hyjauje, the tyrannical Governor of Confeh, and the young Syed

213· Story of the Sultan Haieshe
214· Story told by a Fisherman
215· The Adventures of Mazin of Khorassaun
216· Adventure of Haroon Al Rusheed
a. Story of the Sultan of Bussorah
b. Nocturnal adventures of Haroon Al Rusheed
e. Story related by Munjaub
d. Story of the Sultan, the Dirveshe and the Barber's Son
e. Story of the Bedouin's Wife
f. Story of the Wife and her two Gallants
217· Adventures of Aleefa, daughter of Mherejaun, Sultan of Hind, and Eusuff, son of Sohul, Sultan of Sind
218· Adventures of the three Princes, [S]ons of the Sultan of China
219· Story of the Gallant Officer
220· Story of another officer
221· Story of the Idiot and his Asses
222· Story of the Lady of Cairo and the Three Debauchees
223· Story of the Good Vizier unjustly imprisoned
224· Story of the Prying Barber and the young man of Cairo
225· Story of the Lady of Cairo and her four Gallants
a. The Cauzee's Story
b. The Syrian
c. The Caim-makaum's Wife
d. Story told by the Fourth Gallant
226· Story of a Hump-backed Porter
227· The Aged Porter of Cairo and the Artful Female Thief
228· Mhassun and his tried friend Mouseh
229· Mahummud Julbee, son to an Ameer of Cairo
230· The Farmer's Wife
231· The Artful Wife
232· The Cauzee's Wife
233· Story of the Merchant, his Daughter, and the Prince of Eerauk
234· The Two Orphans
235· Story of another Farmer's Wife
236· Story of the Son who attempted his Father's Wives
237· The Two Wits of Cairo and Syria
238· Ibrahim and Mouseh
239· The Viziers Ahmed and Mahummud
240· The Son addicted to Theft
241· Adventures of the Cauzee, his Wife, &c.
a. The Sultan's Story of Himself
242· Story of Shaykh Nukheet the Fisherman, who became favourite to a Sultan
a. Story of the King of Andalusia
243· Story of Teilone, Sultan of Egypt
244· Story of the Retired Man and his Servant
245· The Merchant's Daughter who married the Emperor of China
*246· New Adventures of the Caliph Harun Al-Rashid
*247· The Physician and the young Purveyor of Bagdad
*248· The Wise Heycar
*249· Attaf the Generous
*250· Prince Habib and Dorrat-al-Gawas
*251· The Forty Wazirs
**a*. Story of Shaykh Shahabeddin
**b*. Story of the Gardener, his Son, and the Ass
**c*. The Sultan Mahmoud and his Wazir
**d*. Story of the Brahman Padmanaba and the young Fyquai
**e*. Story of Sultan Akshid

P500.2§, ‡Folly of ignoring wishes (opinion) of the majority. (Destructive to nation). (Cf. J21.57.1§).
King Jalî¿âd and Shimâs: *Alf* IV 161; Burton IX 89. Chauvin VI 9-11 No. 184; *ANE* 237-38 No. 236.□

P500.3.1§, ‡Absolute (despotic) ruler disposes of notables opposed to his conduct. (Cf. K811.1, N340.0.1.2§).
King Jalî¿âd and Shimâs: *Alf* IV 171; Burton IX 117. Chauvin VI 9 No. 184; *ANE* 237-38 No. 236.□

P501.2.2§, ‡Ruler (king, caliph, imam, emir) must be obeyed.
¿Abdallah ibn Fâḍil: Treacherous Brothers: *Alf* IV 283; Burton IX 339. Chauvin V 2-4 No. 2; *ANE* 63-65 No. 261.□

P501.3§, ‡Change in government (new ruler) brings about change in policy (practices). (Cf. L405§, L490§).
First Qalandar: Brother-Sister Incest: *Alf* I 40,-(rebellion); Burton I 107. Chauvin V 196-97 No. 115; *ANE* 337-38 No. 15.□

P501.3.1§, ‡New ruler mistreats supporter(s) of old.
First Qalandar: Brother-Sister Incest: *Alf* I 40; Burton I 107. Chauvin V 196-97 No. 115; *ANE* 337-38 No. 15.□

P502.3.1§, Assassination (political).
King ¿Umar al-Nu¿mân and Sons: *Alf* II 7; Burton II 86-87. Chauvin VI 112-24 No. 277; *ANE* 430-34 No. 39.□

P502.3.1.1§, Assassin. See: *GMC*.
¿Alâ' al-Dîn Abû al-Shâmât: *Alf* II 174,-(hired to kill caliph); Burton IV 81. Chauvin V 43-49 No. 18; *ANE* 85-87 No. 63.□

P503.0.1§, ‡Formal documents required for bureaucratic (formal) procedures. See: *DOTTI*; *PSAE*. (Cf. P522).
Anîs al-Jalîs: *Alf* I 143; Burton II 39. Chauvin V 120-24 No. 58; *ANE* 316-17 No. 35.□

P503.5.1§, ‡Favoritism toward relatives (nepotism).
Nuzhat al-Zamân Tested/¿Umar al-Nu¿mân: *Alf* I 204; Burton II 163-64. Chauvin VI 116, n.1/passim No. 277; *ANE* 432,/passim No. 39.□

P503.6§, ‡Hypocritical official (judge, governor, etc.). See: *DOTTI*.
Barber's Fifth Brother: Daydreams/Defeats Robbers: *Alf* I 121; Burton I 343. Chauvin V 161 No. 85; *ANE* 119-20 No. 33.□

P503.7§, ‡Bribery (*rashwah, 'burṭail'*). See: *DOTTI*. (Cf. K2096.6§, P339.2§).
Ghânim ibn Ayyûb: *Alf* I 157; Burton II 45-76. Chauvin VI 14 No. 188; *ANE* 192-93 No. 36;
¿Alî Shâr and Zumurrud: *Alf* II 221; Burton IV 198. Chauvin V 89-91 No. 28; *ANE* 100-1 No. 82;
Enchanted Spring: Change of Sex: *Alf* III 146,-(gift); Burton VI 147. Chauvin VIII 43 No. 11; *ANE* 175-76 No. 191;
Jeweler's Wife and Qamar al-Zamân: *Alf* IV 246; Burton IX 259. Chauvin V 212-14 No. 121; *ANE* 345-47 No. 260.□

P503.7.1§, ‡The power of bribery.
Tâj al-Mulûk: *Alf* I 299,-(gardener bribed); Burton III 30. Chauvin V 126-28 No. 60; *ANE* 406-8 No. 40;
Rake's Trick Against Chaste Wife: *Alf* III 142; Burton VI 135. Chauvin VIII 37 No. 5; *ANE* 350-1 No. 185.□

P503.7.2§, ‡Veiled bribery: exorbitant price (wages) paid for minor article (service). (Cf. J708.8§).
Ibrâhîm and Jamîlah: *Alf* IV 222; Burton IX 215. Chauvin VI 52-53 No. 218; *ANE* 227-29 No. 258;
Abû al-Ḥasan al-Khorâsânî (and Caliph's Favorite): *Alf* IV 233; Burton IX 237-38. Chauvin V 218-20 No. 129; *ANE* 68-69 No. 259.□

P503.7.2.1§, ‡Veiled bribe: tailor paid several gold coins as fee for sewing minor rip in garment. (Rip is induced by owner who needs information or help from tailor).
Ibrâhîm and Jamîlah: *Alf* IV 222; Burton IX 215. Chauvin VI 52-53 No. 218; *ANE* 227-29 No. 258;
Abû al-Ḥasan al-Khorâsânî (and Caliph's Favorite): *Alf* IV 233; Burton IX 237. Chauvin V 218-20 No. 129; *ANE* 68-69 No. 259.□

P505.1§, ‡Illegitimate order by ruler disobeyed. See: *DOTTI*. (Cf. P506.3§).

Supplementary General Index